The Big Book of
SHOW BUSINESS AWARDS

DAVID SHEWARD

BILLBOARD BOOKS
An imprint of Watson-Guptll Publications/New York

To my parents,
John and Marjorie Sheward,
for their love and encouragement
and for letting me stay up late
to watch all those award shows.

Senior Editor: Bob Nirkind
Edited by: Lester Strong
Book design: Bob Fillie, Graphiti Graphics
Cover design: Daniel Pelavin
Production Manager: Hector Campbell
All photos courtesy of Photo Fest

First published 1997 by Billboard Books,
an imprint of Watson-Guptill Publications,
a division of Billboard Productions, Inc.,
at 1515 Broadway, New York, NY 10036

Library of Congress Cataloging-in-Publication Data
David Sheward, 1959-
    The big book of show business awards / David Sheward.
    p.   cm.
    ISBN 0-8230-7630-X
    1. Performing arts—United States—Awards. I. Title.
    PN2270.A93S54 1997
    791.079173—dc21   97-15655
                      CIP

Manufactured in the United States of America

First printing, 1997

1 2 3 4 5 6 7 8 9 / 99 98 97

CONTENTS

INTRODUCTION *1*

PART ONE *Film* *3*

PART TWO *Music* *203*

PART THREE *Television* *299*

PART FOUR *Theater* *453*

APPENDIX *592*
BIBLIOGRAPHY *595*
INDEX *596*

ACKNOWLEDGMENTS

Thanks to the following individuals and organizations for their contributions to this project: Paul Lukas, formerly of Watson-Guptill, who first gave the book the go-ahead; Bob Nirkind, Amy Borrell, and Lester Strong, who picked up the ball and ran with it; Ron and Howard Mandelbaum of Photofest; the entire staff of *Back Stage* for their support and encouragement during the writing of this book; the staff of the Lincoln Center Library for the Performing Arts; Ross Wetzsteon of the *Village Voice* and Obie founder Jerry Tallmer for information on the Obie Awards; my fellow Drama Desk member Sam Norkin for the history of the DD Awards; The Shefrin Company for information on the American Music Awards; the National Academy of Cable Programming for a record of the Cable ACE winners; the Country Music Association for updates on its awards; Ken Detelich for his advice and suggestions; and, of course, my best friend and partner in life, Jerry Katz, for everything.

INTRODUCTION

A streaker upstaging David Niven at the Oscars . . . Frank Sinatra being cut off in the middle of a mawkish speech at the Grammys . . . Julie Andrews refusing her Tony nomination after her fellow *Victor/Victoria* cast members were "egregiously overlooked" . . . Goldie Hawn at the Oscars and later Suzanne Pleshette at the Emmys, both crying "Oh my God, it's George C. Scott."

These fabulous flubs and memorable mishaps are what make award shows such captivating spectacles. Once a year we get to see our favorite stars, usually well rehearsed and perfectly composed, sweating over reading the names of nominees and struggling with awkward jokes provided to them on the teleprompter. In short—we find out they're human.

That's the basic appeal of these gorgeous monsters and that's why we'll sit through hours of tedious acceptance speeches and cheesey production numbers. Maybe someone will slip up, trip off the stage, or say what they really think about their fellow toilers in the show-biz vineyards. That's why I used to beg my parents to let me stay up late on Oscar (or any other award show) night. It's also the reason for this book. There is no one volume which covers the foibles and follies of *all* the major award ceremonies between two covers. Here you'll find a complete list of winners and nominees in the major categories for the Oscars, Grammys, Emmys,

and Tonys—as well as for several other groups that award prizes—along with inside information on the maneuvering and manipulations that go on behind the scenes in the attempt to win those prizes and to put on the awards shows.

In addition to being a reference source and argument settler, *The Big Book of Show Business Awards* also provides an opportunity for comparison. If you think Tom Cruise or Eddie Murphy was gypped out of an Oscar, you'll find that they did win accolades from the National Board of Review and the National Film Critics Society.

There are four sections, each devoted to a different medium (Film, Music, Television, and Theater). Within each section, the awards for that medium are listed chronologically beginning with the first presentation of the oldest type of award.

I strove to include as many major prizes as possible, not only the well-known ones but also the critics' awards such as those bestowed by the New York Film Critics Circle, the Drama Desk, and the *Village Voice* with its Obies. In between the nominees and winners, I've sandwiched tidbits of juicy gossip and amusing anecdotes.

The appendix contains cross-referenced award facts such who has won the most of which prizes and which performers are quadruple and triple winners.

So, let's open up the envelope and see who gets the awards. . . .

Charles "Buddy" Rogers
and Clara Bow in *Wings*,
the first film to win
the Best Picture Oscar.

PART 1

Film

FOR GEORGE C. SCOTT the ceremony was a "meat parade." Marlene Dietrich called it "one of the greatest frauds of the century." Marion Davies felt these awards were a "cruel joke hatched up by a cruel town." Frank Capra enthused that they were "the most wonderful thing that has ever been thought of for advertising" while Federico Fellini called it "the supreme prize."

The object of such contradictory quotes is the biggest award of them all, the Oscar. Bestowed annually by the Academy of Motion Picture Arts and Sciences, the little golden man is the most coveted honor in filmdom. An Oscar can add millions to a film's box office take as well as launch a new career or boost a sagging one.

But the movie industry and the public at large have always had a love-hate relationship with Oscar. Filmmakers claim to hate the crass campaigning for the prize, but that doesn't prevent studios and potential nominees from taking out expensive "For Your Consideration" ads in trade publications like *Variety* and *The Hollywood Reporter*. The picture with the biggest box-office receipts and content appealing to the lowest common denominator is often the Oscar champ, claim the cynics. Yet every year, the Oscarcast is among the highest-rated TV programs.

There are several other honors for cinematic achievements, most presented without the three-ring circus atmosphere which distinguishes the Oscars. The National Board of Review started out as an industry watchdog in 1909, screening films before their general release and offering opinions on the morality of each feature—sort of an early rating system. The Board began making an annual list of the top films and later conferred honors for best acting, directing, and writing.

The New York Film Critics Circle originated in 1935 with the goal of presenting awards objectively without Hollywood politics (but during its first 30 years, the Circle agreed with the Academy more often than not).

In 1966, the National Society of Film Critics was formed to combat what it called the New York group's "middle-brow" tastes. The Society's membership overlapped the Circle's but also included many critics for national publications. 1975 saw the birth of the Los Angeles Film Critics Association to represent the views of writers from the film capital. The Hollywood Foreign Press Association is another group of film journalists to hand out prizes. Its Golden Globe Awards were at first called a cheap imitation of the Oscars, but they have grown in prestige since their 1944 inception.

While the reviewers' prizes are regarded by film purists as the more worthy since they are free of sentimentality and electioneering from the studios, when it comes to that honored spot on the mantle, for many moviemakers Oscar is still the winner.

ACADEMY AWARDS (OSCARS)

PRODUCTION
The Last Command
The Racket
Seventh Heaven
The Way of All Flesh
Wings

ARTISTIC QUALITY OF PRODUCTION
Chang
The Crowd
Sunrise

All the official lists of Academy Award winners cite *Wings*, Paramount's World War I buddy film, as the first best Picture. Actually there were two winners. *Wings* won for best Production, officially defined as "the most outstanding motion picture considering all elements that contribute to a picture's greatness." But there was a second category, Artistic Quality of Production, given for "the most artistic, unique, and/or original motion picture without reference to cost or magnitude."

The Central Board of Judges, who picked the winners, wanted to give the "Artistic" award to *The Crowd*, a realistic study of one man's battle against urban despair. But Louis B. Mayer, head of MGM, argued that giving such a "depressing" picture the award would send the wrong message and kept the judges up all night until they switched allegiance to *Sunrise*, a weepy melodrama.

The Jazz Singer, the first film to employ a limited use of sound, was judged ineligible. The Academy thought it would be unfair to allow it to compete with silent pictures, so they gave its studio Warner Brothers a special award.

ACTOR
Richard Barthelmess (*The Noose* and *The Patent Leather Kid*)
Charles Chaplin (*The Circus*)
Emil Jannings (*The Last Command* and *The Way of All Flesh*)

The advent of talking pictures spelled the end of Emil Jannings' American screen career. The German actor had a poor command of the English language and decided to return to his native country rather than face possible humiliation. He was scheduled to leave in a matter of weeks when he learned of his status as the first best Actor winner. Instead of waiting for the awards banquet, he sent a telegram requesting the award be presented to him before his departure, "I therefore ask you to kindly hand me now already the statuette award to me." The only ceremony for Jannings was a brief photo session taken with the award by the Paramount publicity department.

In both of his Oscar-winning films, Jannings played a powerful figure brought to misery by unkind circumstances. His own life paralleled his performances. After returning to the fatherland, the actor became head of Hitler's anti-British film unit under the command of Propaganda Minister Joseph Goebbels. Once World War II ended, Jannings was blacklisted by the Allied countries and died in obscurity in 1950.

ACTRESS
Louise Dresser (*A Ship Comes In*)
Janet Gaynor (*Seventh Heaven, Street Angel,* and *Sunrise*)
Gloria Swanson (*Sadie Thompson*)

DIRECTOR
Frank Borzage (*Seventh Heaven*)
Herbert Brenon (*Sorrell and Son*)
King Vidor (*The Crowd*)

COMEDY DIRECTION
Charles Chaplin (*The Circus*)
Lewis Milestone (*Two Arabian Knights*)
Ted Wilde (*Speedy*)

ORIGINAL WRITING
Anthony Coldeway (*Glorious Betsy*)
Alfred Cohn (*The Jazz Singer*)
Benjamin Glazer (*Seventh Heaven*)

ADAPTED WRITING
Lajos Biro (*The Last Command*)
Ben Hecht (*Underworld*)
Rupert Hughes (*The Patent Leather Kid*)

TITLE WRITING

Gerald Duffy (*The Private Life of Helen of Troy*)
Joseph Farnham (*The Fair Co-ed*)
Joseph Farnham (*Laugh, Clown, Laugh*)
Joseph Farnham (*Telling the World*)
George Marion, Jr. (*Oh, Kay!*)

This category vanished with the silents and was eliminated the following year.

OTHER AWARDS

Cinematography: Charles Rosher, Karl Struss (*Sunrise*); Interior Decoration: William Cameron Menzies (*The Dove* and *The Tempest*); Engineering Effects: Roy Pomeroy (*Wings*).

SPECIAL AWARDS

Warner Brothers for producing *The Jazz Singer*; Charles Chaplin for writing, directing, producing, and acting in *The Circus*.

The official version of the origin of the Academy of Motion Picture Arts and Sciences is one of pure and pristine motives. The Academy was founded to improve the moral tone of movies in light of criticism from the church and the threat of censorship from the government. But the true story is somewhat more down-to-earth.

In 1926, MGM mogul Louis B. Mayer wanted to build a house by the beach. He contracted his own studio's carpenters to build it. When he found out the costs would be prohibitively expensive due to the standard contract the workers had wrested from the studio, it sent shivers down the producer's spine. Not only because he would have to use outside labor, but for fear of the implications. If his own craftsmen were unionized, how long would it be before the actors, writers, and directors followed suit? The omnipotent power of the producer and the studios over talent would crumble.

To prevent this nightmare, Mayer decided to create an organization run by studio management to handle all labor negotiations. The high-toned Academy was the result, with an annual awards ceremony as an afterthought to lend the whole operation a patina of class.

Cedric Gibbons, Mayer's art director, sketched the golden athletic figure plunging a sword into the center of a reel of film which became the award. The reel contained five slots meant to represent the Academy's five original branches: producers, direc-

The crowd at the first presentation of the Academy Awards on May 16, 1929, at the Roosevelt Hotel in Hollywood.

tors, writers, actors, and technicians. The nickname Oscar would not come about until a few years later. For now they were simply called Academy Awards of Merit.

The initial nominating system was three-layered and elitist. Each member would cast a nominating vote for their branch for any film released from August 1, 1927, to July 31, 1928. Then a Board of Judges from each of the five branches would meet to select the nominees. Finally, a Board of Central Judges, comprised of one member from each branch, picked the winners. So Hollywood's top prize was chosen by five people. Guess who was chairman of this board of judges? Louis B. Mayer, of course.

The winners were announced on February 18, 1929, after the Central Board of Judges met. The first Academy Awards were held on May 16, 1929, at the Hollywood Roosevelt Hotel. Academy President and host Douglas Fairbanks, Sr., handed out all the statuettes in five minutes. (Losing nominees were given "Honorable Mention" certificates.) The bulk of the evening was taken up with speeches on the intentions of the spanking new Academy and all the wonderful services it was going to provide for the film community. Al Jolson, star of *The Jazz Singer* which received a "special" consolation prize, concluded the festivities with a swipe at the fledgling accolade: "I notice they gave *The Jazz Singer* a statuette. But they didn't give me one. I could use one; they look heavy and I need another paperweight."

ACADEMY AWARDS (OSCARS)

PICTURE
Alibi
Broadway Melody
Hollywood Revue
In Old Arizona
The Patriot

The best Production and Artistic Quality of Production categories were combined into one: best Picture. *Broadway Melody*, the 1928–29 winner, was one of the first all-talking, all-singing musicals. It even had a brief Technicolor sequence.

ACTOR
George Bancroft (*Thunderbolt*)
Warner Baxter (*In Old Arizona*)
Chester Morris (*Alibi*)
Paul Muni (*The Valiant*)
Lewis Stone (*The Patriot*)

ACTRESS
Ruth Chatterton (*Madame X*)
Betty Compson (*The Barker*)
Jeanne Eagels (*The Letter*)
Bessie Love (*Broadway Melody*)
Mary Pickford (*Coquette*)

Known as "America's sweetheart," Mary Pickford made the uneasy transition from silents to sound with *Coquette*, an adaptation of a Helen Hayes stage vehicle about a Southern flirt. The film actress's performance received mixed notices. Pickford, the only actress among the Academy's founders and wife of its first president Douglas Fairbanks, Sr., was the first to actively electioneer for an Academy Award. By inviting all five of the Central Board of Judges to her home, Pickfair, for tea she gave birth to Oscar campaigning. Dissent over Oscar picks was also born with her win.

Columnists complained Pickford triumphed because of her status as an Academy founder and that Ruth Chatterton or Jeanne Eagels, both veterans of the stage and more skilled at using their voices, should have taken home the prize. Due to these gripes and the fact that most of the 1928–29 winners were Academy members, the voting system was changed the following year to eliminate complaints of favoritism.

DIRECTOR
Lionel Barrymore (*Madame X*)
Harry Beaumont (*Broadway Melody*)
Irving Cummings (*In Old Arizona*)
Frank Lloyd (*The Divine Lady, Weary River,* and *Drag*)
Ernst Lubitsch (*The Patriot*)

WRITING
Tom Barry (*In Old Arizona*)
Tom Barry (*The Valiant*)
Elliott Clawson (*The Leatherneck*)
Hans Kraly (*The Patriot*)

(Left to right) Mary Doran, Anita Page, Bessie Love, and Charles King sing *The Broadway Melody*, Oscar's best Picture of 1928–29 and the first of a series of similarly titled MGM musicals.

Josephine Lovett (*Our Dancing Daughters*)
Bess Meredyth (*Wonder of Women*)

OTHER AWARDS
Cinematography: Clyde DeVinna (*White Shadows in the South Seas*); Interior Decoration: Cedric Gibbons (*The Bridge of San Luis Rey*).

After one year of existence, the Academy Awards were beginning to take on prestige. This was mainly through the powerful influence of newspaper magnate William Randolph Hearst. Hoping for a little gold statuette for his mistress, actress Marion Davies, Hearst urged his top gossip columnist Louella Parsons to push the awards in her column.

She did, and when Louella spoke, Hollywood and the nation listened.

To heighten suspense, winners would not be announced until the night of the banquet and there would be no Honorable Mention certificates for the losers.

The dinner was held on April 30, 1930, at the Coconut Grove of the Los Angeles Ambassador Hotel and hosted by the Academy's new president William C. DeMille (brother of Cecil B.). For the first time the presentation was broadcast live on a local radio station.

Also for the first and so far only time, no movie won more than one Oscar.

Mary Pickford with her Oscar. By inviting the Academy judges to her home for tea, she became the first performer to campaign for the award.

1929-30

ACADEMY AWARDS (OSCARS)

PICTURE
All Quiet on the Western Front
The Big House
Disraeli
The Divorcee
The Love Parade

"I hear there's talk that the motion picture we honor tonight may win a Nobel Peace Prize," declared Louis B. Mayer upon presenting Universal's Carl Laemmle with the Best Picture Award for that studio's anti-war drama *All Quiet on the Western Front*. Mayer's Nobel prediction did not come true.

ACTOR
George Arliss (*Disraeli*)
George Arliss (*The Green Goddess*)
Wallace Beery (*The Big House*)
Maurice Chevalier (*The Love Parade*)
Maurice Chevalier (*The Big Pond*)

Ronald Coleman (*Bulldog Drummond*)
Ronald Coleman (*Condemned*)
Lawrence Tibbet (*The Rogue Song*)

Nominees were previously eligible to win for more than one film. For example, Janet Gaynor was named the first Best Actress for three films (*Seventh Heaven, Street Angel,* and *Sunrise*). This year, the rules changed and everybody got separate nominations. George Arliss won for his portrayal of Queen Victoria's Prime Minister *Disraeli*, but lost for *The Green Goddess*.

ACTRESS
Nancy Carroll (*The Devil's Holiday*)
Ruth Chatterton (*Sarah and Son*)
Greta Garbo (*Anna Christie*)
Greta Garbo (*Romance*)
Norma Shearer (*The Divorcee*)
Norma Shearer (*Their Own Desire*)
Gloria Swanson (*The Trespasser*)

For the second consecutive year, there were complaints about Oscar's choice for Best Actress. Norma Shearer was the wife of MGM head of production Irving Thalberg. There were rumors that MGM employees, a sizable block of Academy voters, had been sent a memo to vote for her if they knew what was good for them. Greta Garbo and Gloria Swanson had been mentioned as likely winners for their stronger performances. Nonnominee Joan Crawford snippily commented, "What do you expect? She sleeps with the boss."

Keeping things in the family, Shearer's brother Douglas also won for his sound recording of *The Big House*.

DIRECTOR
Clarence Brown (*Anna Christie*)
Clarence Brown (*Romance*)
Robert Z. Leonard (*The Divorcee*)
Ernst Lubitsch (*The Love Parade*)
Lewis Milestone (*All Quiet on the Western Front*)
King Vidor (*Hallelujah*)

WRITING
George Abbott, Maxwell Anderson, Dell Andrews
    (*All Quiet on the Western Front*)
Howard Estabrook (*Street of Chance*)

Julian Josephson (*Disraeli*)
Frances Marion (*The Big House*)
John Meehan (*The Divorcee*)

OTHER AWARDS
Cinematography: Joseph T. Rucker, Willard Van Der Veer (*With Byrd at the South Pole*); Interior Decoration: Herman Rosse (*King of Jazz*); Sound Recording: Douglas Shearer (*The Big House*).

In the wake of Mary Pickford's Oscar for a weak performance in *Coquette*, Academy members were now allowed to vote directly for nominees without going through a Board of Judges. The winners would also be chosen by the entire membership rather than a five-member panel. The awards were held on November 5, 1930, at the Ambassador Hotel, just seven months after the previous ceremony. This was an attempt to bring the presentation closer to the period of eligibilty for nomination (August of one year to July of the next).

One of the Academy's founders, actor Conrad Nagel, hosted, substituting for Academy president William C. DeMille who was on vacation. The awards were not yet a mandatory social event.

NATIONAL BOARD OF REVIEW

BEST AMERICAN FILMS
All Quiet on the Western Front, Holiday, Laughter, The Man from Blankelys, Men without Women, Morocco, Outward Bound, Romance, The Street of Chance, Tol'able David.

BEST FOREIGN FILMS
High Treason (Germany), *Old and New* (USSR), *Soil* (USSR), *Storm Over Asia* (USSR), *Zwei Herzen im 3/4 Takt* (Germany).

The National Board of Review had previously passed judgment on the moral content of movies and offered recommendations to the public in the form of lists, such as "Pictures Boys Want and Grown-Ups Endorse" and "Monthly List of Selected Pictures." This year it began making public its list of best films.

1930-31

ACADEMY AWARDS (OSCARS)

PICTURE
Cimarron
East Lynne
The Front Page
Skippy
Trader Horn

RKO's *Cimarron*, based on Edna Ferber's novel about the settling of Oklahoma, was the first Western to win best Picture and until *Dances with Wolves* (1990) and *Unforgiven* (1992) it was the only one.

ACTOR
Lionel Barrymore (*A Free Soul*)
Jackie Cooper (*Skippy*)
Richard Dix (*Cimarron*)
Frederic March (*The Royal Family of Broadway*)
Adolphe Menjou (*The Front Page*)

Lionel Barrymore had been nominated in 1928–29 for best Director for *Madame X*. His *A Free Soul* nod made him the first person to have been nominated in two different categories. When sibling Ethel won best Supporting Actress for 1944's *None But the Lonely Heart*, they became the only brother and sister to win acting Oscars.

Ten-year-old Jackie Cooper, who remains the youngest best Actor nominee ever, fell asleep on best Actress nominee Marie Dressler's arm halfway through the ceremony.

ACTRESS
Marlene Dietrich (*Morocco*)
Marie Dressler (*Min and Bill*)
Irene Dunne (*Cimarron*)
Ann Harding (*Holiday*)
Norma Shearer (*A Free Soul*)

A stunned Marie Dressler eased the sleeping Jackie Cooper off her arm, and slowly made it to the stage to accept her award. "Like an old Model T Ford, I had to be cranked up," she quipped. The sixty-two-year-old actress had won for her frumpish, waterfront hotel-owner in *Min and Bill*, triumphing over such glamour gals as Marlene Dietrich and Norma Shearer.

DIRECTOR
Clarence Brown (*A Free Soul*)
Lewis Milestone (*The Front Page*)
Wesley Ruggles (*Cimarron*)
Norman Taurog (*Skippy*)
Josef von Sternberg (*Morocco*)

Taurog, the victim of a recent accident, hobbled to the stage on crutches, to accept his award for directing *Skippy*, which starred his nephew, nominee Jackie Cooper.

ORIGINAL SCREENPLAY
John Bright, Kubec Glasmon (*The Public Enemy*)
Rowland Brown (*Doorway to Hell*)
Harry D'Abbadie D'Arrast, Douglas Doty,
    Donald Ogden Stewart (*Laughter*)
Lucien Hubbard, Joseph Jackson (*Smart Money*)
John Monk Saunders (*The Dawn Patrol*)

ADAPTED SCREENPLAY
Howard Estabrook (*Cimarron*)
Francis Faragoh, Robert N. Lee (*Little Caesar*)
Horace Jackson (*Holiday*)
Joseph L. Mankewicz, Sam Mintz (*Skippy*)
Seton Miller, Fred Niblo, Jr.
    (*The Criminal Code*)

OTHER AWARDS
Cinematography: Floyd Crosby (*Tabu*); Interior Decoration: Max Ree (*Cimarron*); Sound Recording: Paramount Studio Sound Department.

By 1931, the Oscars had become prestigous enough to merit the attendance of U.S. Vice President Charles Curtis. One of the speakers, J. N. Heiskell, the president of the American Newspaper Publishers Association, took the opportunity to skewer the Hoover administration over the Depression and Prohibition.

NATIONAL BOARD OF REVIEW

BEST AMERICAN FILMS
Cimarron, City Lights, City Streets, Dishonored,

The Front Page, The Guardsman, Quick Millions, Rango, Surrender, Tabu.

BEST FOREIGN FILMS
Die Dreigroschenoper (Germany), *Das Lied vom Leben* (Germany), *Le Million* (France), *Sous les Toits de Paris* (France), *Vier von der Infanterie* (Germany).

ACADEMY AWARDS (OSCARS)

PICTURE
Arrowsmith
Bad Girl
The Champ
Five Star Hotel
Grand Hotel
One Hour with You
Shanghai Express
Smiling Lieutenant

Grand Hotel was the first Hollywood picture to boast an all-star cast. Irving Thalberg, MGM's head of production, came up with the idea. Since one star could carry a picture to box office glory, why not cram every star on the lot into a big, expensive vehicle? Wallace Beery, John and Lionel Barrymore, Greta Garbo, Joan Crawford, and Lewis Stone were the guests whose lives and loves intersected at a busy Berlin hotel. While the film itself won an Oscar for Louis B. Mayer, its two brightest stars were frozen out of the nominations.

Although he turned in two of the year's best performances (in *Grand Hotel* and *A Bill of Divorcement*), John Barrymore was snubbed by the Academy. His brother Lionel and sister Ethel would both win Oscars, but John, regarded as the most dynamic talent of the three, would never even receive a nomination. Many insiders saw Barrymore's Oscar snub as punishment by powerful and jealous producers for the actor's drinking, womanizing, and refusal to partake in the Hollywood roundelay of tame house parties.

Like her co-star, Greta Garbo was not nominated despite her career-defining performance in which she uttered the immortal line "I want to be alone." The reclusive diva shared with her character a desire for solitude and many credit her refusal to play the movieland social game as the reason for her Oscar-less status. The New York Film Critics Circle, unconcerned with studio politics or who attended which soiree, would later name her best Actress twice.

ACTOR (TIE)
Wallace Beery (*The Champ*)
Alfred Lunt (*The Guardsman*)
Frederic March (*Dr. Jekyll and Mr. Hyde*)

Frederic March had been announced as the winner for his dual portrayal of *Dr. Jekyll and Mr. Hyde*, but it was discovered that Wallace Beery had lost by only one vote. By Academy rules, a difference of less than three votes was counted as a tie. As Louis B. Mayer was making his acceptance speech for *Grand Hotel*'s best Picture win, another statuette was sent for. After Mayer's lengthy oration, host Conrad Nagel informed the audience of the tie and Beery was hastily called to the podium. March had an infamous witticism based on the fact that both he and Beery had just adopted children: "It seems a little odd that we were both given awards for the best male performance of the year."

ACTRESS
Marie Dressler (*Emma*)
Lynn Fontanne (*The Guardsman*)
Helen Hayes (*The Sin of Madelon Claudet*)

The First Lady of the American Theater, Helen Hayes, did not have an equally stellar screen career. She was in Hollywood to be with her husband, screenwriter Charles MacArthur, and succumbed to the pressure of Irving Thalberg who insisted she make a picture. Her first effort was a creaky soap opera about an unmarried mother. She was worried Louis B. Mayer would halt production, the film was so bad. Thanks to rewrites by her husband, *The Sin of Madelon Claudet* passed muster. Respect for her status as a stage star garnered her an Oscar. She did make a few other films including *Arrowsmith*, *A Farewell to Arms,* and *Anastasia* and later won a second Academy Award for *Airport*. But she is chiefly remembered for her theater work.

When faced with another melodramatic script to produce, Thalberg was later quoted as saying, "Let's face it. We win Academy Awards with crap like *Madelon Claudet*."

DIRECTOR
Frank Borzage (*Bad Girl*)
King Vidor (*The Champ*)
Josef von Sternberg (*Shanghai Express*)

ORIGINAL SCREENPLAY
Lucien Hubbard (*Star Witness*)
Grover Jones, William Slavens McNutt
    (*Lady and Gent*)
Frances Marion (*The Champ*)
Adela Rogers St. John (*What Price Hollywood*)

ADAPTED SCREENPLAY
Edwin Burke (*Bad Girl*)
Percy Heath, Samuel Hoffenstein (*Dr. Jekyll and
    Mr. Hyde*)
Sidney Howard (*Arrowsmith*)

OTHER AWARDS
Cinematography: Lee Garmes (*Shanghai Express*);
Interior Decoration: Gordon Wiles (*Transatlantic*);
Sound Recording: Paramount Studio Sound
Department; Comedy Short Subject: *The Music
Box*; Novelty Short Subject: *Wrestling Swordfish*;
Animated Short Subject: *Flowers and Trees*.

SPECIAL AWARD
Walt Disney for the creation of Mickey Mouse.

Short subjects joined the ranks of Academy Award honorees this year. This was in recognition of their clout at the box office. Features were routinely accompanied by newsreels and short films, both animated and live-action, which were often as popular as the main attraction itself. The Academy appointed a special committee to choose the first Short Subject nominees. It consisted of Walt Disney, Mack Sennett, Laurel and Hardy, and Leon Schlesinger, producer of Warner Brothers' *Looney Tunes*. Not surprisingly, each of the judges was nominated.

On awards night at the Fiesta Room of the Ambassador Hotel, Disney screened a special cartoon featuring animated caricatures of all the nominees. The cartoonist received the first two of his record 32 Oscars, one for creating Mickey Mouse and another for the short *Flowers and Trees*. The ceremony was hosted by new Academy president, actor Conrad Nagel.

NATIONAL BOARD OF REVIEW

BEST AMERICAN FILMS
I Am a Fugitive from a Chain Gang, As You Desire Me, A Bill of Divorcement, A Farewell to Arms, Madame Racketeer, Payment Deferred, Scarface, Tarzan the Ape Man, Trouble in Paradise, Two Seconds.

BEST FOREIGN FILMS
A Nous La Liberte (France), *Der Andere* (Germany), *The Battle of Gallipolli* (UK), *Golden Mountains* (USSR), *Kameradschaft* (Germany), *Mädchen in Uniform* (Germany), *Der Raub der Mona Lisa* (Germany), *Reserved for Ladies* (UK), *Road to Life* (USSR), *Zwei Menschen* (Germany).

1932-33

ACADEMY AWARDS (OSCARS)

PICTURE
Cavalcade
A Farewell to Arms
42nd Street
I Am a Fugitive from a Chain Gang
Lady for a Day
Little Women
The Private Life of Henry VIII
She Done Him Wrong
Smilin' Thru
State Fair

While Noel Coward's *Calvacade* told the sweeping story of a British family from the end of Queen Victoria's reign through 1932, it was filmed in Hollywood by Fox Studios. The Academy was impressed by the huge scope and in keeping with its affection for "big stories" (like last year's *Grand Hotel*) voted it Best Picture.

ACTOR

Leslie Howard (*Berkeley Square*)
Charles Laughton (*The Private Life of Henry VIII*)
Paul Muni (*I Am a Fugitive from a Chain Gang*)

ACTRESS

Katharine Hepburn (*Morning Glory*)
May Robson (*Lady for a Day*)
Diana Wynyard (*Calvalcade*)

Charles Laughton and Katharine Hepburn were unpopular winners, both Hollywood outsiders. Hepburn was an East Coast stage actress who was perceived as aloof by the movieland community and Laughton a British star in a British-made film. Paul Muni and May Robson were thought to be shoe-ins. In close voting, the Academy proved the awards weren't always a popularity contest. Neither of the winners showed at the ceremony.

DIRECTOR

Frank Capra (*Lady for a Day*)
George Cukor (*Little Women*)
Frank Lloyd (*Calvalcade*)

After Will Rogers opened the envelope containing the name of the winner for Best Director, one of the most embarassing moments in Oscar history occurred. The humorist, who was acting as host for the evening, declared "Come and get it, Frank." Frank Capra left his table and started to make his way to the stage. Then a spotlight picked out another man pushing towards the winner's circle—Frank Lloyd, the real victor. Capra later stated the return to his table was the "longest, saddest, most shattering walk in my life." The following year, Capra would get the trophy he missed (it would be for *It Happened One Night*) and become the Academy's president.

ORIGINAL SCREENPLAY

Robert Lord (*One Way Passage*)
Frances Marion (*The Prizefighter and the Lady*)
Charles MacArthur (*Rasputin and the Empress*)

ADAPTED SCREENPLAY

Paul Green, Sonya Levien (*State Fair*)
Victor Heerman, **Sarah Y. Mason** (*Little Women*)
Robert Riskin (*Lady for a Day*)

OTHER AWARDS

Cinematography: Charles Bryant Lang, Jr. (*Calvalcade*); Interior Decoration: William S. Darling (*Cavalcade*); Sound Recording: Harold C. Lewis (*A Farewell to Arms*); Assistant Director: Charles Barton, Paramount, Scott Beal, Universal, Charles Dorian, MGM, Fred Fox, United Artists, Gordon Hollinghead, Warner Brothers, Dewey Starkey, RKO Radio, William Tummel, Fox; Comedy Short Subject: *So This Is Harris*; Novelty Short Subject: *Krakatoa*; Animated Short Subject: *The Three Little Pigs*.

When Walt Disney won his third Academy Award—for *The Three Little Pigs*—he became the first to call the statuette Oscar in an acceptance speech. Previously, Oscar had been employed as a derogatory epithet, but Disney's usage was with respect and the monicker became official.

There are several versions of the origin of the nickname. Bette Davis claimed she bestowed it when she won in 1936 (for 1935's *Dangerous*) and noticed the figure's backside resembled that of her then husband Harmon Oscar Nelson. Margaret Herrick, the Academy's librarian, is said to have remarked on her first day of work in 1931 that the statuette looked like her Uncle Oscar. Columnist Sidney Skolsky stated he was the first to use the name in his report on the 1932–33 awards. Wishing to debunk the snobbery of the prizes, he stated he used "Oscar" since that was a name employed in a popular vaudeville sketch.

Since Disney's speech was made on March 16, 1934, two years before Davis won and two days before Skolsky wrote his column, the Herrick story has the prior claim.

While the awards now had a name, they were quickly losing the bulk of the voters. Academy members were leaving the organization in droves, performers to the newly formed Screen Actors Guild and scribes to the Screen Writers Guild. The defections were in protest over an Academy-proposed temporary fifty percent pay-cut for all personnel due to the Depression and a salary cap for actors, writers, and directors, but not studio executives.

The Academy would eventually recover its membership, but not its status as a labor negotiator.

Charles Laughton in *The Private Life of Henry VIII* (1933 best Actor Oscar).

NATIONAL BOARD OF REVIEW

BEST AMERICAN PICTURES
Topaze, Berkeley Square, Cavalcade, Little Women, Mama Loves Papa, The Pied Piper, She Done Him Wrong, State Fair, Three-Cornered Moon, Zoo in Budapest.

BEST FOREIGN FILMS
Hertha's Erwachen (Germany), *Ivan* (USSR), *M* (Germany), *Morgenroth* (Germany), *Niemandsland* (Germany), *Poil de Carotte* (France), *The Private Life of Henry VIII* (UK), *Quatorze Juliet* (France), *Rome Express* (UK), *La Sang d'un Poete* (France).

ACADEMY AWARDS (OSCARS)

PICTURE
The Barretts of Wimpole Street
Cleopatra
Flirtation Walk
The Gay Divorcee
Here Comes the Navy
The House of Rothschild
Imitation of Life
It Happened One Night
One Night of Love
The Thin Man
Viva Villa
The White Parade

Humiliated at last year's ceremony, Frank Capra more than made up for the hurt with a clean sweep of the 1934 Oscars. His romantic comedy, *It Happened One Night*, was the first picture to win all five top awards: Picture, Actor (Clark Gable as an earthy reporter), Actress (Claudette Colbert as the spoiled heiress he wins), Director (Capra), and Screenplay (adapted by Robert Riskin from a *Cosmopolitan* magazine story). This record would hold until 1975's *One Flew over the Cuckoo's Nest* and 1991's *The Silence of the Lambs*.

ACTOR
Clark Gable (*It Happened One Night*)
Frank Morgan (*Affairs of Cellini*)
William Powell (*The Thin Man*)

ACTRESS
Claudette Colbert (*It Happened One Night*)
Grace Moore (*One Night of Love*)
Norma Shearer (*The Barretts of Wimpole Street*)

There was such an uproar when Bette Davis was not nominated for her blistering portrayal of the amoral, Cockney tramp Mildred in *Of Human Bondage* that Academy president Howard Estabrook announced write-in votes would be accepted. Davis claimed her boss, Jack Warner of Warner Brothers, urged his employees not to vote for her because she had made *Bondage* while on loan to RKO.

When Davis stated she would attend the ceremony, all three of the official nominees thought she would be an easy winner and declined to show up. Despite the write-in campaign, Davis still lost to Colbert. An Academy press agent was dispatched to the Los Angeles train station where the new Best Actress was set to board the express for New York. "But I'll miss my train," she told the nervous publicist. He persuaded the conductor to hold the train, got the star in a cab, and raced to the Biltmore Hotel. Little Shirley Temple, standing on a chair, presented Colbert, in coat and traveling clothes, with the Oscar. The winner made a brief speech, posed for pictures with Temple, and ran off to catch her train.

DIRECTOR
Frank Capra (*It Happened One Night*)
Victor Schertzinger (*One Night of Love*)
W. S. Van Dyke (*The Thin Man*)

ORIGINAL SCREENPLAY
Arthur Caesar (*Manhattan Melodrama*)
Mauri Grashin (*Hide-Out*)
Norman Krasna (*The Richest Girl in the World*)

ADAPTED SCREENPLAY
Frances Goodrich, Albert Hackett (*The Thin Man*)
Ben Hecht (*Viva Villa*)
Robert Riskin (*It Happened One Night*)

OTHER AWARDS

Musical Score: Columbia Studio Music Department, Louis Silvers, head, thematic music by Victor Schertzinger and Gus Kahn (*One Night of Love*); Song: "The Continental" from *The Gay Divorcee*, music by Con Conrad, lyrics by Herb Magidson; Cinematography: Victor Milner (*Cleopatra*); Interior Decoration: Cedric Gibbons, Frederic Hope (*The Merry Widow*); Film Editing: Conrad Nervig (*Eskimo*); Sound Recording: Paul Neal (*One Night of Love*); Assistant Director: John Waters (*Viva Villa*).

Comedy Short Subject: *La Cucaracha*; Novelty Short Subject: *City of Wax*; Animated Short Subject: *The Tortoise and the Hare*.

SPECIAL AWARD

Shirley Temple (miniature statuette).

The eligibilty period for Oscars was switched from August–July to January–December, making the time of the nominees' releases closer to the awards which were now regularly presented in the late spring.

Awards for film editing and musical scoring were added. For the first four years of the scoring award the prize went to the head of the winning studio's music department rather than to the actual composer.

After presenting Colbert with the Best Actress award, six-year-old Shirley Temple was given a special Oscar by the evening's host humorist Irving S. Cobb. The youngster attempted to grab the prize from Cobb's hands before he finished his speech.

NATIONAL BOARD OF REVIEW

BEST AMERICAN FILMS

It Happened One Night, The Count of Monte Cristo, Crime without Passion, Eskimo, The First World War, The Lost Patrol, Lot in Sodom (short), No Greater Glory, The Thin Man, Viva Villa.

BEST FOREIGN FILMS

Man of Aran (UK), *The Blue Light* (Germany), *Catherine the Great* (UK), *The Constant Nymph* (UK), *Madame Bovary* (France).

1935

ACADEMY AWARDS (OSCARS)

PICTURE

Alice Adams
Broadway Melody of 1936
Captain Blood
David Copperfield
The Informer
Les Miserables
Lives of a Bengal Lancer
A Midsummer Night's Dream
Mutiny on the Bounty
Naughty Marietta
Ruggles of Red Gap
Top Hat

ACTOR

Clark Gable (*Mutiny on the Bounty*)
Charles Laughton (*Mutiny on the Bounty*)
Victor McLaglen (*The Informer*)
Franchot Tone (*Mutiny on the Bounty*)

ACTRESS

Elisabeth Bergner (*Escape Me Never*)
Claudette Colbert (*Private Worlds*)
Bette Davis (*Dangerous*)
Katharine Hepburn (*Alice Adams*)
Miriam Hopkins (*Becky Sharp*)
Merle Oberon (*The Dark Angel*)

To make up for her *Of Human Bondage* loss the previous year, Bette Davis was given her first of two Oscars, for *Dangerous*—a performance she felt was inferior to Katharine Hepburn's in *Alice Adams*. This began the Oscar Consolation Prize trend of rewarding an artist not for the work nominated but for earlier, overlooked efforts.

DIRECTOR

John Ford (*The Informer*)
Henry Hathaway (*Lives of a Bengal Lancer*)
Frank Lloyd (*Mutiny on the Bounty*)

ORIGINAL STORY

Moss Hart (*Broadway Melody of 1936*)

Don Hartman, Stephen Avery (*The Gay Deception*)
Ben Hecht, Charles MacArthur (*The Scoundrel*)

SCREENPLAY

Achmed Abdullah, John L. Balderston, Grover Jones, William Slavens McNutt, Waldemar Young (*Lives of a Bengal Lancer*)
Jules Furthman, Talbot Jennings, Carey Wilson (*Mutiny on the Bounty*)
Dudley Nichols (*The Informer*)

OTHER AWARDS

Musical Score: RKO Radio Studio Music Department., Max Steiner head, score by Max Steiner (*The Informer*); Song: "Lullaby of Broadway" from *Gold Diggers of 1935*, music by Harry Warren, lyrics by Al Dubin; Cinematography: Hal Mohr (*A Midsummer Night's Dream*); Interior Decoration: Richard Day (*The Dark Angel*); Film Editing: Ralph Dawson (*A Midsummer Night's Dream*); Sound Recording: Douglas Shearer (*Naughty Marietta*); Assistant Director: Clem Beauchamp, Paul Wing (*Lives of a Bengal Lancer*); Dance Direction: David Gould for "I've Got a Feeling You're Fooling" number from *Broadway Melody of 1936* and "Straw Hat" number from *Folies Bergere*.

Comedy Short Subject: *How to Sleep*; Novelty Short Subject: *Wings over Mt. Everest*; Animated Short Subject: *Three Orphan Kittens*.

SPECIAL AWARD

D. W. Griffith.

Following the lead of the actors and the writers, the directors left the Academy to form their own union. Not only did they desert, but the new directors' group and all the other guilds were urging their members to boycott the awards ceremony to show their displeasure with the Academy's studio-favored labor practices. Academy membership dropped from 600 to 40. Newly elected president Frank Capra had inherited a diminished and nearly bankrupt organization.

Determined to keep the awards going, Capra and the Academy Board paid for the Oscar dinner out of their own pockets. In order to insure the integrity of the voting, Capra hired the accounting firm of Price Waterhouse and continued the practice of write-in ballots (as a result Hal Mohr became the only write-in Oscar winner in history, triumphing in the Cinematography category for *A Midsummer Night's Dream*).

To counter the threat of a boycott, the new president made the ceremony into a tribute to D. W. Griffith, the silent film pioneer now neglected by Hollywood. The presence of the great director might cause the young filmmakers to forget their political arguments with the Academy and show up to pay their respects. While many nominees stayed away and Adapted Screenplay winner Dudley Nichols refused his award, Capra counted the evening a success with most of the winners present. But a majority of the new union cardholders were no-shows. Invitations were extended to such lower-level studios employees as secretaries and clerks in order to fill the seats.

MGM took out the first trade ads for Oscars for its adaptation of Eugene O'Neill's *Ah, Wilderness!*. No nominations resulted.

NATIONAL BOARD OF REVIEW

BEST AMERICAN FILMS

The Informer, Alice Adams, Anna Karenina, David Copperfield, The Gilded Lily, Les Miserables, The Lives of a Bengal Lancer, Mutiny on the Bounty, Ruggles of Red Gap, Who Killed Cock Robin?

BEST FOREIGN FILMS

Chapayev (USSR), *Crime and Punishment* (France), *Le Dernier Milliardaire* (France), *The Man Who Knew Too Much* (UK), *Marie Chapdelaine* (France), *La Maternelle* (France), *The New Gulliver* (USSR), *Peasants* (USSR), *Thunder in the East* (France), *The Youth of Maxim* (USSR).

NEW YORK FILM CRITICS CIRCLE

In order to award excellence in the cinema without the Hollywood hoopla and politicking which marked the Oscars, a group of New York City-based movie reviewers banded together to form the New York Film Critics Circle. A few years after its debut, the Circle elected Bosley Crowther of *The New York Times* as its president. Until 1968 when he retired from the *Times* and the Circle, Crowther's tastes dominated the organization's choices. He enjoyed large-sized Hollywood epics based on plays and novels as well as liberal treatment of social themes like those explored in *Gentlemen's Agreement, On the Waterfront,* and *All the King's Men.* During his tenure, the Circle agreed with the Academy on best Picture eighteen out of twenty-eight times.

The first NYFCC dinner was broadcast over NBC's radio network. Both acting winners were absent. Their awards were collected by the consuls-general of their respective native lands: Britain (Charles Laughton) and Sweden (Greta Garbo). So the evening would not be a total loss, Victor McLaglen, Margot Grahame, and Preston Foster performed a scene from the best film *The Informer,* via hook-up from Hollywood.

Picture: *The Informer*; Actor: Charles Laughton (*Mutiny on the Bounty* and *Ruggles of Red Gap*); Actress: Greta Garbo (*Anna Karenina*); Director: John Ford (*The Informer*).

ACADEMY AWARDS (OSCARS)

PICTURE
Anthony Adverse
Dodsworth
The Great Ziegfeld
Libeled Lady
Mr. Deeds Goes to Town
Romeo and Juliet
San Francisco
The Story of Louis Pasteur
A Tale of Two Cities
Three Smart Girls

In a bit of political manuevering, MGM took the best Picture Oscar for *The Great Ziegfeld,* a grandiose, not entirely truthful, musical biography of Broadway showman Florenz Ziegfeld. Metro and Warner Brothers had the largest blocks of Academy voters. Louis B. Mayer of Metro made a deal with Jack Warner. If Warners would back

Ziegfeld for the top picture award, Metro would get behind WB contract player Paul Muni for best Actor.

ACTOR
Gary Cooper (*Mr. Deeds Goes to Town*)
Walter Huston (*Dodsworth*)
Paul Muni (*The Story of Louis Pasteur*)
William Powell (*My Man Godfrey*)
Spencer Tracy (*San Francisco*)

Presenter Victor MacLaglen went on longer than winner Paul Muni, who later said, "Victor talked so long . . . I thought I was presenting the award to him."

ACTRESS
Irene Dunne (*Theodora Goes Wild*)
Gladys George (*Valiant Is the Word for Carrie*)
Carole Lombard (*My Man Godfrey*)
Luise Rainer (*The Great Ziegfeld*)
Norma Shearer (*Romeo and Juliet*)

The 1936 best Actress race was one of the tightest ever. Norma Shearer had the sympathy vote since her husband Irving Thalberg had just died of pneumonia. MGM was putting its considerable muscle behind Luise Rainer. But Rainer was expected to win the following year for the just-released *The Good Earth,* and Shearer already had an Oscar. Carole Lombard expected to reap the benefits of a split vote and emerge the victor.

The Oscar voting had ended at 5 p.m. on the night of the awards. Members of the press, under strict orders not to release the information until after the ceremony, were given the results at 8 p.m. Somehow the identity of the winners was leaked and MGM publicity men were sent to grab the absent Rainer and get her on stage in time for her category.

Just as Claudette Colbert had been yanked off a train to pick up her Oscar two years before, Rainer and her new husband playwright Clifford Odets rushed to the Biltmore Hotel, arriving at 10:30 p.m. just before the ceremony commenced.

SUPPORTING ACTOR
Mischa Auer (*My Man Godfrey*)
Walter Brennan (*Come and Get It*)

Stuart Erwin (*Pigskin Parade*)
Basil Rathbone (*Romeo and Juliet*)
Akim Tamiroff (*The General Died at Dawn*)

In order to win back the support of the defecting actors, the number of acting nominees was increased from three to five and two new categories were added—best Supporting Actor and best Supporting Actress. These winners were given plaques for the first few years rather than statuettes. The Screen Actors Guild responded to these overtures by dropping its boycott of the awards.

SUPPORTING ACTRESS
Beulah Bondi (*The Gorgeous Hussy*)
Alice Brady (*My Man Godfrey*)
Bonita Granville (*These Three*)
Maria Ouspenskaya (*Dodsworth*)
Gale Sondergaard (*Anthony Adverse*)

Gale Sondergaard was the first Oscar recipient to win for her first picture.

DIRECTOR
Frank Capra (*Mr. Deeds Goes to Town*)
Gregory La Cava (*My Man Godfrey*)
Robert Z. Leonard (*The Great Ziegfeld*)
W. S. Van Dyke (*San Francisco*)
William Wyler (*Dodsworth*)

ORIGINAL STORY
Pierre Collings, Sheridan Gibney (*The Story of Louis Pasteur*)
Adele Commandini (*Three Smart Girls*)
Robert Hopkins (*San Francisco*)
Norman Krasna (*Fury*)
William Anthony McGuire (*The Great Ziegfeld*)

SCREENPLAY
Pierre Collings, Sheridan Gibney (*The Story of Louis Pasteur*)
Frances Goodrich, Albert Hackett (*After the Thin Man*)
Eric Hatch, Morris Ryskind (*My Man Godfrey*)
Sidney Howard (*Dodsworth*)
Robert Riskin (*Mr. Deeds Goes to Town*)

OTHER AWARDS
Score: Warner Bros. Music Department, Leo Forbstein, head, score by Erich Wolfgang Korngold (*Anthony Adverse*); Song: "The Way You Look Tonight" from *Swing Time*, music by Jerome Kern, lyrics by Dorothy Fields; Cinematography: Gaetano Gaudio (*Anthony Adverse*); Interior Decoration: Richard Day (*Dodsworth*); Film Editing: Ralph Dawson (*Anthony Adverse*); Sound Recording: Douglas Shearer (*San Francisco*); Dance Direction: Seymour Felix ("A Pretty Girl Is Like a Melody" number from *The Great Ziegfeld*); Assistant Director: Jack Sullivan (*Charge of the Light Brigade*).

Short Subjects: One-Reel: *Bored of Education*; Two-Reel: *The Public Pays*; Color: *Give Me Liberty*; Animated: *Country Cousin*.

SPECIAL AWARDS
The March of Time newsreels; W. Howard Greene and Harold Rosson for the color cinematography of *The Garden of Allah*.

To recapture the film community's interest in the Oscar, Academy president Frank Capra forced his board of directors to vote the organization out of all labor dealings between talent and management. He also liberalized the nominating procedures. Nominations would now be made by a committee of fifty Academy members, representing all five of the Academy branches.

Academy finances were still in sorry shape. Capra had to charge $5 for members and $10 for guests to attend the awards banquet. Ringside seats went for $25 a pop.

Capra also announced the inception of the Irving Thalberg Memorial Award for distinguised work by a producer, in honor of the late MGM head of production.

NATIONAL BOARD OF REVIEW

BEST AMERICAN FILMS
Mr. Deeds Goes to Town, The Story of Louis Pasteur, Modern Times, Fury, Winterset, The Devil Is a Sissy, Ceiling Zero, Romeo and Juliet, The Prisoner of Zenda, Green Pastures.

BEST FOREIGN FILMS
Carnival in Flanders (*La Kermesse Heroique*)

(France), *The New Earth* (The Netherlands), *Rembrandt* (UK), *The Ghost Goes West* (UK), *Nine Days a Queen* (UK), *We Are from Kronstadt* (USSR), *Son of Mongolia* (USSR), *The Yellow Cruise* (France), *Les Miserables* (France), *The Secret Agent* (UK).

NEW YORK FILM CRITICS CIRCLE

Picture: *Mr. Deeds Goes to Town*; Actor: Walter Huston (*Dodsworth*); Actress: Luise Rainer (*The Great Ziegfeld*); Director: Rouben Mamoulian (*The Gay Desperado*); Foreign Film: *Carnival in Flanders* (*La Kermesse Heroique*).

ACADEMY AWARDS (OSCARS)

PICTURE
The Awful Truth
Captains Courageous
Dead End
The Good Earth
In Old Chicago
The Life of Emile Zola
Lost Horizon
100 Men and a Girl
Stage Door
A Star Is Born

ACTOR
Charles Boyer (*Conquest*)
Fredric March (*A Star Is Born*)
Robert Montgomery (*Night Must Fall*)
Paul Muni (*The Life of Emile Zola*)
Spencer Tracy (*Captains Courageous*)

Spencer Tracy hated the curly wig and Portugese accent he adopted for *Captains Courageous* and felt the unnominated Lionel Barrymore was a better best Actor choice for his work in the same film. In a hospital bed recovering from a hernia operation, Tracy was not at the ceremony. The ubiquitous Louis B. Mayer, the actor's boss at MGM, accepted the award with the statement, "Tracy is a fine actor, but he is most important because he understands why it is necessary to take orders from the front office." When he heard Mayer's speech, Tracy commented, "Was that a compliment or a threat?"

ACTRESS
Irene Dunne (*The Awful Truth*)
Greta Garbo (*Camille*)
Janet Gaynor (*A Star Is Born*)
Luise Rainer (*The Good Earth*)
Barbara Stanwyck (*Stella Dallas*)

Luise Rainer demonstrated her versatility with her back-to-back Oscar performances. In 1936, she was the glamourous entertainer Anna Held, wife of *The Great Ziegfeld*. The following year, she offered an equally convincing performance as the Chinese peasant O-Lan, the long-suffering heroine of the MGM adaptation of Pearl Buck's *The Good Earth*.

Same as last year, Rainer elected not to attend, thinking Greta Garbo would triumph for *Camille*. Once again, summoned by Metro publicists from her home, she and husband Clifford Odets raced to the ceremony.

After her consecutive double victory, the first in Oscar history, Rainer's star waned. Unwilling to play in the mediocre scripts she was assigned by MGM and faced with a crumbling marriage to Odets, she left Hollywood and later married a London publisher. Her virtual disappearance from the spotlight after such a brilliant start gave rise to the legend of the Oscar curse—all those who won the little golden man too quickly were supposedly doomed to equally quick obscurity.

SUPPORTING ACTOR
Ralph Bellamy (*The Awful Truth*)
Thomas Mitchell (*The Hurricane*)
Joseph Schildkraut (*The Life of Emile Zola*)
H. B. Warner (*Lost Horizon*)
Roland Young (*Topper*)

SUPPORTING ACTRESS
Alice Brady (*In Old Chicago*)
Andrea Leeds (*Stage Door*)
Anne Shirley (*Stella Dallas*)
Claire Trevor (*Dead End*)
Dame May Whitty (*Night Must Fall*)

Winner Alice Brady was home on Oscar night with a broken ankle. In one of the earliest instances of award show gate-crashing, an unknown man accepted her statuette and left the Biltmore Hotel and was never heard from again. Brady was given another Oscar at an informal ceremony a few days later.

DIRECTOR
William Dieterle (*The Life of Emile Zola*)
Sidney Franklin (*The Good Earth*)
Gregory La Cava (*Stage Door*)
Leo McCarey (*The Awful Truth*)
William Wellman (*A Star Is Born*)

Preferring another film of his, *Make Way for Tomorrow*, McCarey said, "Thanks, but you gave it to me for the wrong picture."

ORIGINAL STORY
Niven Busch (*In Old Chicago*)
Heinz Herald, Geza Herczeg (*The Life of Emile Zola*)
Hans Kraly (*100 Men and a Girl*)
Robert Lord (*Black Legion*)
William A. Wellman, Robert Carson (*A Star Is Born*)

SCREENPLAY
Alan Campbell, Robert Carson, Dorothy Parker (*A Star Is Born*)
Marc Connolly, John Lee Mahin, Dale Van Every (*Captains Courageous*)
Vina Delmar (*The Awful Truth*)
Heinz Herald, Geza Herczeg, Norman Reilly Raine (*The Life of Emile Zola*)
Morris Ryskind, Anthony Veiller (*Stage Door*)

OTHER AWARDS
Musical Score: Universal Studio Music Department, Charles Previn, head (*100 Men and a Girl*); Song: "Sweet Leilani" from *Waikiki Wedding*, music and lyrics by Harry Owens; Cinematography: Karl Freund (*The Good Earth*); Interior Decoration: Stephen Gooson (*Lost Horizon*); Film Editing: Gene Havlick, Gene Milford (*Lost Horizon*); Sound Recording: Thomas Moulton (*The Hurricane*); Assistant Director: Robert Webb (*In Old Chicago*); Dance Direction: Hermes Pan ("Fun House" number from *Damsel in Distress*).

SHORT SUBJECTS
One-Reel: *Private Life of the Gannetts*; Two-Reel: *Torture Money*; Color: *Penny Wisdom*; Animated: *The Old Mill*.

SPECIAL AWARDS
Mack Sennett; ventriloquist/comedian Edgar Bergen (wooden statuette); The Museum of Modern Art Film Library; W. Howard Greene for the color cinematography of *A Star Is Born*; Darryl F. Zanuck (Irving Thalberg Award).

Frank Capra continued to build membership in the Academy. To encourage joining, he eliminated the fifty-member nominating committee. Academy members now voted directly for nominees. He even allowed members of the new unions representing actors, directors, and writers to vote for the awards whether they belonged to the Academy or not. The Screen Extras Guild was permitted to vote on the winners for best Picture, Song, and the acting awards. A new charter officially removed the Academy from all labor disputes, and screenwriter Dudley Nichols finally accepted the Oscar he had refused two years earlier.

A flash flood delayed the awards ceremony by a week. Like winners Spencer Tracy and Alice Brady, the announced host George Jessel was laid up. The comedian had the flu and was replaced by comedian Bob "Bazooka" Burns.

NATIONAL BOARD OF REVIEW

In additional to listing its choices for top films, this year the Board began cited outstanding acting.

BEST AMERICAN FILMS
Night Must Fall, The Life of Emile Zola, Black Legion, Camille, Make Way for Tomorrow, The Good Earth, They Won't Forget, Captains Courageous, A Star Is Born, Stage Door.

BEST FOREIGN FILMS
The Eternal Mask (Austria/Switzerland), *The Lower Depths* (France), *Baltic Deputy* (USSR), *Mayerling* (France), *The Spanish Earth* (Spain), *Golgotha* (France), *Elephant Boy* (UK), *Rembrandt* (UK), *Janosik* (Czechoslovakia), *The Wedding of Palo* (Greenland/Denmark).

BEST ACTING (listed alphabetically)
Harry Baur (*The Golem*), Humphrey Bogart (*Black Legion*), Charles Boyer (*Conquest*), Nikolai Cherkassov (*Baltic Deputy*), Danielle Darrieux (*Mayerling*), Greta Garbo (*Camille*), Robert Montgomery (*Night Must Fall*), Maria Ouspenskaya (*Conquest*), Luise Rainer (*The Good Earth*), Joseph Schildkraut (*The Life of Emile Zola*), Mathias Wieman (*The Eternal Mask*), Dame May Whitty (*Night Must Fall*).

NEW YORK FILM CRITICS CIRCLE

Picture: *The Life of Emile Zola*; Actor: Paul Muni (*The Life of Emile Zola*); Actress: Greta Garbo (*Camille*); Director: Gregory La Cava (*Stage Door*); Foreign Film: *Mayerling*.

ACADEMY AWARDS (OSCARS)

PICTURE
The Adventures of Robin Hood
Alexander's Ragtime Band
Boys Town
The Citadel
Four Daughters
Grand Illusion
Jezebel
Pygmalion
Test Pilot
You Can't Take It with You

Frank Capra was now king of the Oscars. After having been humiliated at the 1932–33 awards by Will Rogers' slip of the Franks, he became the Academy's president, saved it from extinction, and won two of the statuettes (for *It Happened One Night* and *Mr. Deeds Goes to Town*). In 1938, not only did he win a third (for his adaptation of the George S. Kaufman-Moss Hart Broadway hit *You Can't Take It with You*), but he was also elected president of the young Directors Guild. He proved as great a champion for his new organization as he had for the Academy. When the producers balked at recognizing the Guild as the sole bargaining

agent for the directors, Capra resigned as head of the Academy and threatened a boycott of the awards—just as he had been threatened three years earlier. By the night of the banquet the producers backed down.

Oscar trivia: Jean Renoir's *Grand Illusion*, the French anti-war classic, was the first foreign-language film to be nominated for best Picture.

Snow White and the Seven Dwarfs was the biggest grossing picture of the year. The Academy didn't want to nominate a cartoon for best Picture, so they gave its producer Walt Disney a special Oscar—along with seven miniatures. The prejudice against feature-length animation held until 1991 when another Disney picture, *Beauty and the Beast*, received a best Picture nomination.

ACTOR
Charles Boyer (*Algiers*)
James Cagney (*Angels with Dirty Faces*)
Robert Donat (*The Citadel*)
Leslie Howard (*Pygmalion*)
Spencer Tracy (*Boys Town*)

Repeating Luise Rainer's consecutive Oscar wins, Spencer Tracy became the first leading actor to win twice in a row. This feat was not repeated until Tom Hanks triumphed for *Philadelphia* (1993) and *Forest Gump* (1994). Tracy's second Oscar was for playing Father Flanagan, the real-life priest who founded Boys Town, a home for wayward juveniles. When he received his second Oscar, he found it was inscribed to Dick Tracy. When the award was returned to be corrected, an MGM publicist announced Tracy was planning to have it inscribed to Father Flanagan and donate it to the real Boys Town. The actor informed the publicist he wanted to keep the award. To save face, the Academy dispatched two Oscars, one for Tracy, another for Boys Town.

ACTRESS
Fay Bainter (*White Banners*)
Bette Davis (*Jezebel*)
Wendy Hiller (*Pygmalion*)
Norma Shearer (*Marie Antoinette*)
Margaret Sullavan (*Three Comrades*)

Bette Davis got her second Oscar as the temper-

Spencer Tracy and Bette Davis with their 1938 Oscars. It was the second win for both.

mental Southern flirt in *Jezebel*, a role she had to battle her boss Jack Warner to get. After the win, she was not satisfied with the scripts he was presenting her and she was placed on suspension.

Ironically, next year's winner would also be playing a Southern belle, Vivien Leigh in a little something called *Gone with the Wind*.

SUPPORTING ACTOR
Walter Brennan (*Kentucky*)
John Garfield (*Four Daughters*)
Gene Lockhart (*Algiers*)
Robert Morley (*Marie Antoinette*)
Basil Rathbone (*If I Were King*)

Warner Brothers promoted leading man John Garfield as a supporting actor, not wanting him to compete with another WB star James Cagney. Neither won.

The Supporting Actor victor Walter Brennan was another double Oscar winner that year. Two years later he would take a third. The grizzled character man would keep the record for most acting Oscars until Katharine Hepburn tied him in 1968 and then surpassed him in 1981.

SUPPORTING ACTRESS
Fay Bainter (*Jezebel*)
Beulah Bondi (*Of Human Hearts*)
Billie Burke (*Merrily We Live*)
Spring Byington (*You Can't Take It with You*)
Miliza Korjus (*The Great Waltz*)

Bainter was the first performer to be nominated in two categories in the same year. Later double nominees include Barry Fitzgerald, Teresa Wright, Jessica Lange, Sigourney Weaver, Al Pacino, Emma Thompson, and Holly Hunter.

DIRECTOR
Frank Capra (*You Can't Take It with You*)
Michael Curtiz (*Angels with Dirty Faces*)
Michael Curtiz (*Four Daughters*)
Norman Taurog (*Boys Town*)
King Vidor (*The Citadel*)

ORIGINAL STORY
Irving Berlin (*Alexander's Ragtime Band*)
Rowland Brown (*Angels with Dirty Faces*)
Marcella Burke, Frederick Kohner
   (*Mad about Music*)
Eleanore Griffin, Dore Schary (*Boys Town*)
John Howard Lawson (*Blockade*)
Frank Wead (*Test Pilot*)

SCREENPLAY
Lenore Coffee, Julius J. Epstein
   (*Four Daughters*)
Ian Dalrymple, Elizabeth Hill, Frank Wead
   (*The Citadel*)
John Meehan, Dore Schary (*Boys Town*)
Robert Riskin (*You Can't Take It with You*)
George Bernard Shaw; adaptation by **Ian
   Dalrymple, Cecil Lewis**, and **W. P. Lipscomb**
   (*Pygmalion*)

The curmudgeonly and brilliant playwright George Bernard Shaw was indignant that he should even be nominated or presented with an award, feeling his work and standing as the world's greatest living dramatist should speak for itself. "It's an insult for them to offer me any honor, as if they never heard of me before—and it's very likely they never have," he fumed. His bluster to the contrary, the Academy sent the persnickety Shaw his Oscar and Mary Pickford stated she saw it prominently placed in the author's home when she visited.

OTHER AWARDS
Original Score: Erich Wolfgang Korngold (*The Adventures of Robin Hood*); Score: Alfred Newman (*Alexander's Ragtime Band*); Song: "Thanks for the Memory" from *The Big Broadcast of 1938*, music by Ralph Raigner, lyrics by Leo Robin; Cinematography: Joseph Ruttenberg (*The Great Waltz*); Interior Decoration: Carl J. Weyl (*The Adventures of Robin Hood*); Film Editing: Ralph Dawson (*The Adventures of Robin Hood*); Sound Recording: Thomas Moulton (*The Cowboy and the Lady*).

SHORT SUBJECTS
One-Reel: *That Mothers Might Live*; Two-Reel: *Declaration of Independence*; Animated: *Ferdinand the Bull*.

SPECIAL AWARDS
Deanna Durbin and Mickey Rooney (outstanding juvenile players); Harry M. Warner for producing a series of historical short subjects; Walt Disney for *Snow White and the Seven Dwarfs* (one statuette and seven miniature statuettes); Oliver Marsh and Allen Davey for the color cinematography of *Sweethearts*; visual and sound effects crew of *Spawn of the North*; J. Arthur Ball for contributions to the advancement of color photography in films; Hal B. Wallis (Irving Thalberg Award).

Comedian Bob Hope made the first of his many Oscar appearances. He presented the Best Short Subject awards and his theme song "Thanks for the Memory" won for Best Song. The Screen Extras Guild did not get to vote on that one. The previous year's winner "Sweet Leilani" was seen as a grave mistake since it won over the evergreen classic "They Can't Take That Away from Me" by George and Ira Gershwin. The Academy blamed the extras for the oversight and eliminated them from participating in the best Song ballot. But they were still permitted to vote for best Picture and the acting categories.

Radio was excluded from the dinner. At least that was the plan. Local broadcaster George Fisher, who had rigged the public address system for the evening, also planted a mike in the sound booth at the back of the banquet room and began airing the program over Los Angeles station KNX. Near the top of the ceremony, the bootleg broadcast was discovered and security men smashed through the door of the booth with axes, ending the illegal feed.

NATIONAL BOARD OF REVIEW

BEST AMERICAN FILMS
The Citadel, Snow White and the Seven Dwarfs, The Beachcomber, To the Victor, Sing You Sinners, The Edge of the World, Of Human Hearts, Jezebel, South Riding, Three Comrades.

BEST FOREIGN FILMS
Grand Illusion (France), *Un Carnet de Bal* (France), *Generals without Buttons* (France), *Peter the First* (USSR).

BEST ACTING (ALPHABETICALLY)
Lew Ayres (*Holiday*), Pierre Blanchar, Harry Baur, Louis Jouvet, and Raimu (*Un Carnet de Bal*), James Cagney (*Angels with Dirty Faces*), Joseph Calleia (*Algiers*), Chico (*The Adventures of Chico*), Robert Donat (*The Citadel*), Will Fyffe (*To the Victor*), Pierre Fresnay, Jean Gabin, Dita Parlo, and Erich von Stroheim (*Grand Illusion*), John Garfield (*Four Daughters*), Wendy Hiller (*Pygmalion*), Charles Laughton and Elsa Lanchester (*The Beachcomber*), Robert Morley (*Marie Antoinette*), Ralph Richardson (*South Riding* and *The Citadel*), Margaret Sullavan (*Three Comrades*), Spencer Tracy (*Boys Town*).

NEW YORK FILM CRITICS CIRCLE

Picture: *The Citadel*; Actor: James Cagney (*Angels with Dirty Faces*); Actress: Margaret Sullavan (*Three Comrades*); Director: Alfred Hitchcock (*The Lady Vanishes*); Foreign Film: *Grand Illusion*; Special Award: *Snow White and the Seven Dwarfs*.

1939

ACADEMY AWARDS (OSCARS)

PICTURE
Dark Victory
Gone with the Wind
Goodbye, Mr. Chips
Love Affair
Mr. Smith Goes to Washington
Ninotchka
Of Mice and Men
Stagecoach
The Wizard of Oz
Wuthering Heights

Nineteen thirty-nine is remembered as the zenith of the Hollywood studio system and Oscar's greatest year to date. Each of the ten nominated best Pictures is today regarded as a classic.

Gone with the Wind, David O. Selznick's larger-than-life filmization of Margaret Mitchell's Civil War saga, received a record thirteen nominations. Its winning score card was also one for the record books, taking home a total of eight—with two special awards thrown in (the Thalberg award for Selznick and an honorary Oscar to William Cameron Menzies for his color photography). This feat would remain unsurpassed until *All about Eve* (1950) collected fourteen nominations, and *Gigi* (1958) grabbed nine statuettes. *Ben-Hur* defeated *Gigi* by winning eleven Oscars the following year, a record which still stands as the most won.

ACTOR
Robert Donat (*Goodbye, Mr. Chips*)
Clark Gable (*Gone with the Wind*)
Laurence Olivier (*Wuthering Heights*)
Mickey Rooney (*Babes in Arms*)
James Stewart (*Mr. Smith Goes to Washington*)

When Clark Gable lost to Robert Donat, he sulked to his wife Carole Lombard, who attempted to cheer him up. "Don't be blue," she is reported to have said. "I just know we'll bring one home next year."

"No," Gable replied, "This was my last chance."

"Not you, you self-centered bastard," Lombard retorted. "I mean me!"

ACTRESS
Bette Davis (*Dark Victory*)
Irene Dunne (*Love Affair*)
Greta Garbo (*Ninotchka*)
Greer Garson (*Goodbye, Mr. Chips*)
Vivien Leigh (*Gone with the Wind*)

The battle for best Actress was between last year's winner Bette Davis for her nobly dying heroine in Warners' weepy *Dark Victory* and British import Vivien Leigh as the immortal Scarlett O'Hara. Leigh's win from the New York Film Critics Circle was thought to give her the edge in the Oscar race.

SUPPORTING ACTOR
Brian Aherne (*Juarez*)
Harry Carey (*Mr. Smith Goes to Washington*)
Brian Donlevy (*Beau Geste*)
Thomas Mitchell (*Stagecoach*)
Claude Rains (*Mr. Smith Goes to Washington*)

Mitchell also appeared in two other top films of the year, *Gone with the Wind* and *Mr. Smith Goes to Washington*.

SUPPORTING ACTRESS
Olivia de Havilland (*Gone with the Wind*)
Geraldine Fitzgerald (*Wuthering Heights*)
Hattie MacDaniel (*Gone with the Wind*)
Edna May Oliver (*Drums along the Mohawk*)
Maria Ouspenskaya (*Love Affair*)

Not only was Hattie MacDaniel the first black person to win an Oscar, she was also the first to attend the awards dinner as a guest rather than as a servant.

DIRECTOR
Frank Capra (*Mr. Smith Goes to Washington*)
Victor Fleming (*Gone with the Wind*)
John Ford (*Stagecoach*)
Sam Wood (*Goodbye, Mr. Chips*)
William Wyler (*Wuthering Heights*)

ORIGINAL STORY
Mildred Cram, Leo McCarey (*Love Affair*)
Lewis R. Foster (*Mr. Smith Goes to Washington*)

Felix Jackson (*Bachelor Mother*)
Melchior Lengyel (*Ninotchka*)
Lamar Trotti (*Young Mr. Lincoln*)

SCREENPLAY
Charles Brackett, Walter Reisch, Billy Wilder (*Ninotchka*)
Sidney Buchanan (*Mr. Smith Goes to Washington*)
Ben Hecht, Charles MacArthur (*Wuthering Heights*)
Sidney Howard (*Gone with the Wind*)
Eric Maschwitz, R.C. Sherriff, Claudine West (*Goodbye, Mr. Chips*)

Sidney Howard was the first posthumous Oscar winner, having been run over by a tractor on his Massachusettes farm shortly before the ceremony. Though he received sole credit for the script of *Gone with the Wind*, David Selznick actually had a dozen scribes working on it.

OTHER AWARDS
Score: Richard Hageman, Frank Harling, John Leipold, Leo Shuken (*Stagecoach*); Original Score: Herbert Stothart (*The Wizard of Oz*); Song: "Over the Rainbow" from *The Wizard of Oz*, music by Harold Arlen, lyrics by E. Y. Harburg; Cinematography: color—Ernest Haller, Ray Rennahan (*Gone with the Wind*), black and white—Gregg Toland (*Wuthering Heights*); Interior Decoration: Lyle Wheeler (*Gone with the Wind*); Film Editing: Hal C. Kern, James E. Newcom (*Gone with the Wind*); Sound Recording: Bernard B. Brown (*When Tomorrow Comes*); Special Effects: E. H. Hansen (photographic), Fred Sersen (sound) (*The Rains Came*).

SHORT SUBJECTS
One-Reel: *Busy Little Bears*; Two-Reel: *Sons of Liberty*; Animated: *The Ugly Duckling*.

SPECIAL AWARDS
Douglas Fairbanks, Sr.; The Motion Picture Relief Fund; Judy Garland (outstanding juvenile performance); William Cameron Menzies for the color photography of *Gone with the Wind*; The Technicolor Company; David O. Selznick (Irving Thalberg Award).

Vivien Leigh and Hattie McDaniel took lead and supporting actress Oscars for *Gone with the Wind* (1939). McDaniel was the first African-American to win.

Though he was no longer Academy president, Frank Capra continued to be a strong influence on the Oscars. He began the evening by introducing his successor Walter Wanger and was at work behind the scenes as director of a short subject on Oscar night Warner Brothers was filming.

After making a hit as a presenter the year before, Bob Hope hosted for the first time. "What a wonderful thing, this benefit for David Selznick," he quipped.

As per usual, the winners' names were released to the press before the dinner began at 8:30 p.m. with the provision they not be printed until after the banquet. The *Los Angeles Times* broke its word and published the results in its 8:45 p.m. edition. Those arriving late were able to pick up the paper and see if they had won or not. This led to the practise of those infamous sealed envelopes so no one but Price Waterhouse would know who would get to take Oscar home until the envelopes were opened at the ceremony.

NATIONAL BOARD OF REVIEW

BEST AMERICAN FILMS
Confessions of a Nazi Spy, Wuthering Heights, Stagecoach, Ninotchka, Young Mr. Lincoln, Crisis, Goodbye, Mr. Chips, Mr. Smith Goes to Washington, The Roaring Twenties, U-Boat 29.

BEST FOREIGN FILMS
Port of Shadows (France), *Harvest* (France), *Alexander Nevsky* (USSR), *The End of a Day* (France), *Robert Koch* (Germany).

BEST ACTING (ALPHABETICALLY)
James Cagney (*The Roaring Twenties*), Bette Davis (*Dark Victory* and *The Old Maid*), Geraldine Fitzgerald (*Dark Victory* and *Wuthering Heights*), Henry Fonda (*Young Mr. Lincoln*), Jean Gabin (*Port of Shadows*), Greta Garbo (*Ninotchka*), Francis Lederer and Paul Lukas (*Confessions of a Nazi Spy*), Thomas Mitchell (*Stagecoach*), Laurence

Olivier (*Wuthering Heights*), Flora Robson (*We Are Not Alone*), Michel Simon (*Port of Shadows* and *The End of a Day*).

NEW YORK FILM CRITICS CIRCLE

Picture: *Wuthering Heights*; Actor: James Stewart (*Mr. Smith Goes to Washington*); Actress: Vivien Leigh (*Gone with the Wind*); Director: John Ford (*Stagecoach*); Foreign Film: *Harvest* (France).

The Critics Circle split the wealth between its five favorite films, giving one award to each. The group was evenly divided between *Gone with the Wind* and *Mr. Smith Goes to Washington* for Best Picture. After 13 long ballots with neither picture obtaining the necessary two-thirds majority, they compromised and gave the prize to *Wuthering Heights*.

The presentation was broadcast over a national hook-up on NBC radio. New York Mayor Fiorello LaGuardia hosted. From Hollywood, Laurence Olivier and Merle Oberon performed a scene from *Wuthering Heights* and James Stewart did a monologue from *Mr. Smith*. His Honor got into trouble when he forgot to mention *Harvest*, the winner of the best foreign-film award. Anare R. Heymann, president of the French Film Center, telegraphed his protests over the accidental slight and refused to accept the award.

1940

ACADEMY AWARDS (OSCARS)

PICTURE
All This, and Heaven, Too
Foreign Correspondent
The Grapes of Wrath
The Great Dictator
Kitty Foyle
The Letter
The Long Voyage Home
Our Town
The Philadelphia Story
Rebecca

To ensure a repeat of his *Gone with the Wind* triumph of the year before, producer David O.

Selznick staged an elaborate Hollywood premiere for his *Rebecca*. He got another bushel of nominations (eleven) but the adaptation of Daphne du Maurier's suspense novel received only one award—best Picture. Among the losers was the film's director Alfred Hitchcock. The rotund British master of the macabre would be nominated a total of five times without a single win.

ACTOR
Charles Chaplin (*The Great Dictator*)
Henry Fonda (*The Grapes of Wrath*)
Raymond Massey (*Abe Lincoln in Illinois*)
Laurence Olivier (*Rebecca*)
James Stewart (*The Philadelphia Story*)

James Stewart's Oscar for *The Philadelphia Story*, in which he supported Katharine Hepburn and Cary Grant, was seen as a consolation prize for not winning for the previous year's *Mr. Smith Goes to Washington*. Stewart sent his Oscar to his father's Pennsylvania hardware store where it was displayed in a case formerly occupied by kitchen knives.

ACTRESS
Bette Davis (*The Letter*)
Joan Fontaine (*Rebecca*)
Katharine Hepburn (*The Philadelphia Story*)
Ginger Rogers (*Kitty Foyle*)
Martha Scott (*Our Town*)

Long thought of as only a song and dance woman, Ginger Rogers pleasantly surprised Hollywood as *Kitty Foyle*, a shopgirl who achieves success and a troubled love life. She acquired the role only after Katharine Hepburn turned it down.

SUPPORTING ACTOR
Albert Basserman (*Foreign Correspondent*)
Walter Brennan (*The Westerner*)
William Gargan (*They Knew What They Wanted*)
Jack Oakie (*The Great Dictator*)
James Stephenson (*The Letter*)

Walter Brennan's win over the more heavily favored Jack Oakie—for his caricature of Mussolini in Charlie Chaplin's *The Great Dictator*—was said to be due to the block voting of the extras. The thrice-Oscared Brennan had risen from their ranks and the background players were fiercely loyal to their own.

SUPPORTING ACTRESS
Judith Anderson (*Rebecca*)
Jane Darwell (*The Grapes of Wrath*)
Ruth Hussey (*The Philadelphia Story*)
Barbara O'Neil (*All This, and Heaven, Too*)
Marjorie Rambeau (*Primose Path*)

Jane Darwell told the press after winning, "Awards are nice, but I'd rather have a job." She stated she hadn't been before the cameras in seven months. Twentieth Century-Fox, which had Darwell under contract, took her to task for revealing her light workload, but studio head Darryl F. Zanuck did offer her a co-starring role the day after the awards.

DIRECTOR
George Cukor (*The Philadelphia Story*)
John Ford (*The Grapes of Wrath*)
Alfred Hitchcock (*Rebecca*)
Sam Wood (*Kitty Foyle*)
William Wyler (*The Letter*)

ORIGINAL STORY
Hugo Butler, Dore Schary (*Edison the Man*)
Benjamin Glazer, **John S. Toldy** (*Arise, My Love*)
Stuart N. Lake (*The Westerner*)
Leo McCarey, Bella Spewack, Samuel Spewack
   (*My Favorite Wife*)
Walter Reisch (*Comrade X*)

ORIGINAL SCREENPLAY
Charles Bennett, Joan Harrison (*Foreign
   Correspondent*)
Norman Burnside, Heinz Herald, John Huston
   (*Dr. Ehrlich's Magic Bullet*)
Charles Chaplin (*The Great Dictator*)
Ben Hecht (*Angels Over Broadway*)
Preston Sturges (*The Great McGinty*)

SCREENPLAY
Nunnally Johnson (*The Grapes of Wrath*)
Dudley Nichols (*The Long Voyage Home*)
Robert E. Sherwood, Joan Harrison (*Rebecca*)
Donald Ogden Stewart (*The Philadelphia Story*)
Dalton Trumbo (*Kitty Foyle*)

In contrast to the usual effusive thanks which mark acceptance speeches, Donald Ogden Stewart refreshingly admitted, "I am entirely and solely responsible for the success of *The Philadelphia Story*."

OTHER AWARDS
Score: Alfred Newman (*Tin Pan Alley*); Original Score: Leigh Harline, Paul J. Smith, Ned Washington (*Pinocchio*); Song: "When You Wish Upon a Star" from *Pinocchio*, music by Leigh Harline, lyrics by Ned Washington; Cinematography: color—George Perinal (*The Thief of Bagdad*), black and white—George Barnes (*Rebecca*); Interior Decoration: color—Vincent Korda (*The Thief of Bagdad*), black and white—Cedric Gibbons, Paul Groesse (*Pride and Prejudice*); Film Editing: Anne Bauchens (*North West Mounted Police*); Sound Recording: Douglas Shearer (*Strike Up the Band*); Special Effects: Lawrence Butler (photographic), Jack Whitney (sound) (*The Thief of Bagdad*).

SHORT SUBJECTS
One-Reel: *Quicker 'N a Wink*; Two-Reel: *Teddy, the Rough Rider*; Animated: *Milky Way*.

SPECIAL AWARDS
Bob Hope; Col. Nathan Levinson for services to the industry.

Bob Hope emceed again and received an honorary award for his humanitarian work. President Franklin D. Roosevelt was invited to speak, but the war in Europe necessitated his staying in Washington. Instead, he spoke to the audience at Hollywood's biggest night via radio in an address which was also broadcast to the country. Oscar attendees didn't hear some of FDR's remarks since they were being directed on how to look as they were listening while a Fox MovieTone newsreel crew filmed the event. Fox's Darryl F. Zanuck made sure only employees of his studio were shown in the footage.

NATIONAL BOARD OF REVIEW

BEST AMERICAN FILMS
The Grapes of Wrath, The Great Dictator, Of Mice and Men, Our Town, Fantasia, The Long Voyage

Dorothy Commingore and *wunderkind* Orson Welles in *Citizen Kane* (1941). Although hailed by critics and regarded today as the best film ever made, *Kane* was virtually shut out of the Oscar winners' circle.

Home, Foreign Correspondent, The Biscuit Eater, Gone with the Wind, Rebecca.

BEST FOREIGN FILM
The Baker's Wife (France).

BEST ACTING (ALPHABETICALLY)
Jane Bryan (*We Are Not Alone*), Charles Chaplin (*The Great Dictator*), Jane Darwell (*The Grapes of Wrath*), Betty Field (*Of Mice and Men*), Henry Fonda (*The Grapes of Wrath* and *Return of Frank James*), Joan Fontaine (*Rebecca*), Greer Garson (*Pride and Prejudice*), William Holden (*Our Town*), Vivien Leigh (*Gone with the Wind* and *Waterloo Bridge*), Thomas Mitchell (*The Long*

Voyage Home), Raimu (*The Baker's Wife*), Ralph Richardson (*The Fugitive*), Ginger Rogers (*The Primrose Path*), George Sanders (*Rebecca*), Martha Scott (*Our Town*), James Stewart (*The Shop around the Corner*), Conrad Veidt (*Escape*).

BEST DOCUMENTARY
The Fight for Life.

NEW YORK FILM CRITICS CIRCLE

Picture: *The Grapes of Wrath*; Actor: Charles Chaplin (*The Great Dictator*); Actress: Katharine Hepburn (*The Philadelphia Story*); Director: John Ford (*The Grapes of Wrath* and *The Long Voyage*

Home); Foreign Film: *The Baker's Wife*; Special Award: Walt Disney (*Fantasia*).

Scandal faced the New York critics when reviewer Lee Mortimer of the *Mirror* revealed that Circle president Bosley Crowther of the *Times* had pressured the group to bestow the best Actor honor on Charlie Chaplin for *The Great Dictator*. Crowther argued that the comedian would make a great draw for the ceremony's radio broadcast. Mortimer also stated Hepburn won only after the critic from the *World-Telegram* browbeat his fellow scribblers into voting for her. Chaplin subsequently refused the Gotham scribes' award.

1941

ACADEMY AWARDS (OSCARS)

PICTURE
Blossoms in the Dust
Citizen Kane
Here Comes Mr. Jordan
Hold Back the Dawn
How Green Was My Valley
The Little Foxes
The Maltese Falcon
One Foot in Heaven
Sergeant York
Suspicion

Twenty-five-year-old Orson Welles took Hollywood by storm with his debut film *Citizen Kane*, a brilliant biopic based on the life of newspaper magnate William Randolph Hearst. The actor-writer-director-producer became the first person to receive four nominations for one picture. The record was not matched until 1978 when Warren Beatty was nominated for wearing the same four hats for *Heaven Can Wait*.

Kane is still listed on critics' polls as one of the best pictures ever made. But audiences and the movieland community weren't so enthuiastic about it in 1941. Powerful gossip columnist Louella Parsons lambasted the film, calling it a "hatchet job" on her publisher Hearst. The Hearst newspaper chain refused to run anything on pictures made by RKO, the studio behind *Kane*, and threatened not to take advertisements from theater chains booking the film. It became unpopular to praise *Kane* in Hollywood. The film's single Oscar win—for Herman J. Mankiewicz and Welles' screenplay—was greeted with boos from a clique of Parsons partisans. Under these circumstances, it was no surprise the best Picture Oscar did not go to *Kane* but to *How Green Was My Valley*, John Ford's sentimental tale of a Welsh mining family.

ACTOR
Gary Cooper (*Sergeant York*)
Cary Grant (*Penny Serenade*)
Walter Huston (*All That Money Can Buy*)
Robert Montgomery (*Here Comes Mr. Jordan*)
Orson Welles (*Citizen Kane*)

ACTRESS
Bette Davis (*The Little Foxes*)
Olivia de Havilland (*Hold Back the Dawn*)
Joan Fontaine (*Suspicion*)
Greer Garson (*Blossoms in the Dust*)
Barbara Stanwyck (*Ball of Fire*)

De Havilland and Fontaine were the first sisters to be nominated in the same category. Many felt Fontaine's win as the shy heroine of *Suspicion* was a consolation for her losing the previous year for a similar role in another Hitchcock film *Rebecca*. The elder sister de Havilland was greatly disappointed, having lost a previous Oscar bid in 1939 for *Gone with the Wind* to Hattie McDaniel for the same film. She would get her revenge by taking Oscar home in 1946 and 1949.

SUPPORTING ACTOR
Walter Brennan (*Sergeant York*)
Charles Coburn (*The Devil and Miss Smith*)
Donald Crisp (*How Green Was My Valley*)
James Gleason (*Here Comes Mr. Jordan*)
Sydney Greenstreet (*The Maltese Falcon*)

SUPPORTING ACTRESS
Sara Allgood (*How Green Was My Walley*)
Mary Astor (*The Great Lie*)
Patricia Collinge (*The Little Foxes*)
Teresa Wright (*The Little Foxes*)
Margaret Wycherly (*Sergeant York*)

DIRECTOR

John Ford (*How Green Was My Valley*)
Alexander Hall (*Here Comes Mr. Jordan*)
Howard Hawks (*Sergeant York*)
Orson Welles (*Citizen Kane*)
William Wyler (*The Little Foxes*)

ORIGINAL STORY

Richard Connell, Robert Presnell (*Meet John Doe*)
Monckton Hoffe (*The Lady Eve*)
Thomas Monroe, Billy Wilder (*Ball of Fire*)
Harry Segall (*Here Comes Mr. Jordan*)
Gordon Wellesley (*Night Train*)

ORIGINAL SCREENPLAY

Harry Chandlee, Abem Finkel, John Huston,
   Howard Koch (*Sergeant York*)
Paul Jarrico (*Tom, Dick, and Harry*)
Norman Krasna (*The Devil and Miss Jones*)
Herman J. Mankiewicz, Orson Welles
   (*Citizen Kane*)
Karl Tunberg, Darrell Ware (*Tall, Dark, and
   Handsome*)

SCREENPLAY

Charles Brackett, Billy Wilder (*Hold Back the
   Dawn*)
Sidney Buchanan, Seton I. Miller (*Here Comes
   Mr. Jordan*)
Philip Dunne (*How Green Was My Valley*)
Lillian Hellman (*The Little Foxes*)
John Huston (*The Maltese Falcon*)

OTHER AWARDS

Score of a Dramatic Picture: Bernard Herrmann
(*All That Money Can Buy*); Score of a Musical
Picture: Frank Churchill, Oliver Wallace (*Dumbo*);
Song: "The Last Time I Saw Paris" from *Lady Be
Good*, music by Jerome Kern, lyrics by Oscar
Hammerstein II; Cinematography: color—Ernest
Palmer, Ray Rennahan (*Blood and Sand*), black
and white—Arthur Miller (*How Green Was My
Valley*); Interior Decoration: color—Cedric
Gibbons, Urie McCleary, Edwin B. Willis
(*Blossoms in the Dust*), black and white—Richard
Day, Nathan Juran, Thomas Little (*How Green
Was My Valley*); Film Editing: William Holmes
(*Sergeant York*); Sound Recording: Jack Whitney,

General Service (*That Hamilton Woman*); Special
Effects: Farciot Edouart, Gordon Jennings
(photographic), Louis Mesenkop (sound) (*I
Wanted Wings*). Documentary: *Churchill's Island*;
One-Reel Short Subject: *Of Pups and Puzzles*;
Two-Reel Short Subject: *Main Street on the March*;
Animated Short Subject: *Lend a Paw*.

SPECIAL AWARDS

Rey Scott for producing *Kukan*; The British
Ministry of Information for its documentary
Target for Tonight; Leopold Stokowski for *Fantasia*;
Walt Disney, William Garity, John N.A. Hawkins,
and the RCA Manufacturing Co. for the sound in
Fantasia; Walt Disney (Irving Thalberg Award).

War came to Hollywood and the film community
was determined to do its bit. But not too much.
Newly appointed Academy president Bette Davis
had some pretty radical ideas for the 1941 Oscars.
She suggested the usual banquet be canceled, the
ceremony be held in a theater instead of a hotel,
the paying public be admitted, and the proceeds be
donated to British War Relief. Furthermore, the
attendees should forgo the usual glamourous evening wear. Because of the Japanese attack on Pearl
Harbor and fears of a similar raid on Los Angeles,
the dazzling searchlights illuminating the skylight
on Oscar night would have to be eliminated.

   The Academy balked at most of Davis's propos-
als. The ceremony would still be held at the
Biltmore Hotel, but referred to as a "dinner" rather
than a "banquet." There would be music, but no
dancing. Formal wear would be frowned upon.
Ladies were requested not to wear corsages but to
donate the money to the Red Cross. Davis resigned
the presidency in protest despite Darryl F. Zanuck's
threat that if she did she'd "never work in this town
again." The previous president Walter Wanger
resumed his office and Davis returned to a more
familiar position with the Academy, that of a nominee. She received her fifth Oscar nomination for
The Little Foxes.

   Bob Hope hosted again and presented a joke
Oscar-in-drag to Jack Benny for his gender-cross-
ing role in *Charlie's Aunt*. Portions of the awards
ceremony were broadcast nationwide on CBS
radio. Speakers included Presidental candidate
Wendell Willkie and Chinese ambassador Dr. Hu

Shih. Presenter Cecil B. De Mille committed the faux pas of the evening by referring to Dr. Shih as "the Jap—I mean, Chinese, ambassador."

NATIONAL BOARD OF REVIEW

BEST AMERICAN FILMS
Citizen Kane, How Green Was My Valley, The Little Foxes, The Stars Look Down, Dumbo, High Sierra, Here Comes Mr. Jordan, Tom, Dick, and Harry, The Road to Zanzibar, The Lady Eve.

BEST FOREIGN FILM
Pepe le Moko (France).

BEST DOCUMENTARIES
Target for Tonight, The Forgotten Village, Ku Kan, The Land.

BEST ACTING (alphabetically)
Sara Allgood (*How Green Was My Valley*), Mary Astor (*The Great Lie* and *The Maltese Falcon*), Ingrid Bergman (*Rage in Heaven*), Humphrey Bogart (*High Sierra* and *The Maltese Falcon*), Gary Cooper (*Sergeant York*), Donald Crisp (*How Green Was My Valley*), Bing Crosby (*The Road to Zanzibar* and *The Birth of the Blues*), George Coulouris (*Citizen Kane*), Patricia Collinge and Bette Davis (*The Little Foxes*), Isobel Elsom (*Ladies in Retirement*), Joan Fontaine (*Suspicion*), Greta Garbo (*Two-Faced Woman*), James Gleason (*Meet John Doe* and *Here Comes Mr. Jordan*), Walter Huston (*All That Money Can Buy*), Ida Lupino (*High Sierra* and *Ladies in Retirement*), Roddy McDowall (*How Green Was My Valley*), Robert Montgomery (*Rage in Heaven* and *Here Comes Mr. Jordan*), Ginger Rogers (*Tom, Dick, and Harry*), James Stephenson (*The Letter* and *Shining Victory*), Orson Welles (*Citizen Kane*).

NEW YORK FILM CRITICS CIRCLE

Picture: *Citizen Kane*; Actor: Gary Cooper (*Sergeant York*); Actress: Joan Fontaine (*Suspicion*); Director: John Ford (*How Green Was My Valley*).

Because of World War II, almost no foreign films were reaching American theaters and the critics suspended that category. They also revised their rules. To prevent the fourteen rounds of balloting of 1939, the Circle voted a maximum of six ballots. A two-thirds majority was necessary to win. If one was not reached after five ballots, a simple majority on the sixth and last ballot would decided the winner. The new rules came into play when voting for Best Picture went to five ballots. On the last go-around *Citizen Kane* defeated Hollywood's choice *How Green Was My Valley* by ten votes to seven.

ACADEMY AWARDS (OSCARS)

PICTURE
The Invaders
Kings Row
The Magnificent Ambersons
Mrs. Miniver
The Pied Piper
The Pride of the Yankees
Random Harvest
The Talk of the Town
Wake Island
Yankee Doodle Dandy

Reflecting Hollywood's preoccupation with World War II, 1942's big winner was *Mrs. Miniver*, William Wyler's melodrama detailing the struggles of a typical British family during the blitz. This hymn to the fortitude of our cousins across the sea was filmed on an MGM backlot.

Orson Welles was snubbed for a second year when his *The Magnificent Ambersons* was shut out of the winners' circle. Judging the film a flop, RKO had cut it drastically and released it on the bottom half of a double bill with a Lupe Velez vehicle called *Mexican Spitfire Sees a Ghost*. Despite this awful treatment, *Ambersons* did get a best Picture nomination and Agnes Moorehead's memorable performance as the pathetic Aunt Fanny was in the running for best Supporting Actress.

ACTOR
James Cagney (*Yankee Doodle Dandy*)
Ronald Coleman (*Random Harvest*)

1942 Oscar winners Van Heflin (in uniform), Greer Garson, James Cagney, and Teresa Wright.

Gary Cooper (*The Pride of the Yankees*)
Walter Pidgeon (*Mrs. Miniver*)
Monty Woolley (*The Pied Piper*)

Eschewing machine guns for tap shoes, James Cagney won his only Oscar by forgoing his usual role of a gangster to play song-and-dance man George M. Cohan in *Yankee Doodle Dandy*. He quoted Cohen's famous curtain line in his speech, "My mother thanks you, my father thanks you, my sister thanks you, and I thank you."

ACTRESS
Bette Davis (*Now, Voyager*)
Greer Garson (*Mrs. Miniver*)
Katharine Hepburn (*Woman of the Year*)
Rosalind Russell (*My Sister Eileen*)
Teresa Wright (*The Pride of the Yankees*)

Greer Garson gave the longest Oscar acceptance speech on record for her portrayal of the valiant British housewife Mrs. Miniver. "Her acceptance speech is longer than her part," quipped an audience member. The length of her oration has grown in Oscar folklore to an entire hour, but the actual timing was five and a half minutes.

SUPPORTING ACTOR
William Bendix (*Wake Island*)
Van Heflin (*Johnny Eager*)
Walter Huston (*Yankee Doodle Dandy*)
Frank Morgan (*Tortilla Flat*)
Henry Travers (*Mrs. Miniver*)

SUPPORTING ACTRESS
Gladys Cooper (*Now, Voyager*)
Agnes Moorehead (*The Magnificent Ambersons*)
Susan Peters (*Random Harvest*)
Dame May Whitty (*Mrs. Miniver*)
Teresa Wright (*Mrs. Miniver*)

DIRECTOR
Michael Curtiz (*Yankee Doodle Dandy*)
John Farrow (*Wake Island*)
Mervyn LeRoy (*Random Harvest*)
Sam Wood (*Kings Row*)
William Wyler (*Mrs. Miniver*)

ORIGINAL STORY
Irving Berlin (*Holiday Inn*)
Robert Buckner (*Yankee Doodle Dandy*)
Paul Gallico (*The Pride of the Yankees*)

Sidney Harmon (*The Talk of the Town*)
Emeric Pressburger (*The Invaders*)

ORIGINAL SCREENPLAY
W. R. Burnett, Frank Butler (*Wake Island*)
Frank Butler, Don Hartman (*The Road to Morocco*)
Michael Kanin, Ring Lardner, Jr. (*Woman of the Year*)
George Oppenheimer (*The War against Mrs. Hadley*)
Michael Powell, Emeric Pressburger (*One of Our Aircraft Is Missing*)

SCREENPLAY
Rodney Ackland, Emeric Pressburger (*The Invaders*)
Sidney Buchman, Irwin Shaw (*The Talk of the Town*)
George Froeschel, James Hilton, Claudine West, Arthur Wimperis (*Mrs. Miniver*)
George Froeschel, Claudine West, Arthur Wimperis (*Random Harvest*)
Herman J. Mankiewicz, Jo Swerling (*The Pride of the Yankees*)

OTHER AWARDS
Score of a Dramatic or Comedy Picture: Max Steiner (*Now, Voyager*); Score of a Musical Picture: Ray Heindorf, Heinz Roemheld (*Yankee Doodle Dandy*); Song: "White Christmas" from *Holiday Inn*, music and lyrics by Irving Berlin; Cinematography: color—Leon Shamrey (*The Black Swan*), black and white—Joseph Ruttenberg (*Mrs. Miniver*); Interior Decoration: color—Richard Day, Joseph Wright, Thomas Little (*My Gal Sal*), black and white—Richard Day, Joseph Wright, Thomas Little (*This Above All*); Film Editing: Daniel Mandell (*Mrs. Miniver*); Sound Recording: Nathan Levinson (*Yankee Doodle Dandy*); Special Effects: Farcoit Edouart, Gordon Jennings, William L. Pereira (photographic), Louis Mesernkop (sound) (*Reap the Wild Wind*).

Irving Berlin became the second person to present himself with an Oscar when he announced the winner of the Best Song—his own "White Christmas." (Walt Disney was the first self-presenter.)

Documentary (four awards):*Battle of Midway, Kokoda Front Line, Moscow Strikes Back*, and *Prelude to War*; One-Reel Short Subject: *Speaking to Animals and Their Families*; Two-Reel Short Subject: *Beyond the Line of Duty*; Animated Short Subject: *Der Fuehrer's Face*.

SPECIAL AWARDS
Charles Boyer; Noel Coward for *In Which We Serve*; MGM for its *Andy Hardy* series; Sidney Franklin (Irving Thalberg Award).

As World War II raged on, Hollywood continued to contribute to the fight. Film stars like James Stewart, Clark Gable, Tyrone Power, and Alan Ladd were enlisting. Bette Davis and John Garfield started the Hollywood Canteen to entertain servicemen and servicewomen. The Oscar was now made of plaster so the precious metals previously used could go toward building arms. The documentary category swelled to twenty-five nominees and four winners to include war features from every Allied country and every branch of the military.

Despite their patriotic fervor, the Oscars came under fire. Although Bob Hope did his best in his now perennial position as emcee, the ceremony was rated boring. "Probably no big event ever attracted more tiresome speakers voicing greater dullness and long-winded speeches, consuming, with the awards, the better part of three hours," complained *The Hollywood Reporter*. There was a crush of tables and chairs with barely any room on the dance floor. Academy founder and the second Best Actress winner Mary Pickford resigned from the organization because she and her husband Buddy Rogers had been given a seat at the back of the auditorium "in Arizona." Academy president Walter Wanger concluded the evening by promising next year's awards would be presented in a different format.

NATIONAL BOARD OF REVIEW

BEST ENGLISH-LANGUAGE FILMS
In Which We Serve, One of Our Aircraft Is Missing, Mrs. Miniver, Journey for Margaret, Wake Island, The Male Animal, The Major and the Minor, Sullivan's Travels, The Moon and Sixpence, The Pied Piper.

BEST DOCUMENTARY
Moscow Strikes Back.

BEST ACTING (alphabetically)
Ernest Anderson (*In This Our Life*), Florence Bates (*The Moon and Sixpence*), James Cagney (*Yankee Doodle Dandy*), Jack Carson (*The Male Animal*), Charles Coburn (*H.M. Pulham, Esq.*, *In This Our Life*, and *Kings Row*), Greer Garson (*Mrs. Miniver* and *Random Harvest*), Sidney Greenstreet (*Across the Pacific*), William Holden (*The Remarkable Andrew*), Tim Holt (*The Magnificent Ambersons*), Glynis Johns (*The Invaders*), Gene Kelly (*For Me and My Girl*), Diana Lynn (*The Major and the Minor*), Ida Lupino (*Moontide*), Bernard Miles and John Mills (*In Which We Serve*), Agnes Moorehead (*The Magnificent Ambersons*), Hattie McDaniel (*In This Our Life*), Thomas Mitchell (*Moontide*), Margaret O'Brien (*Journey for Margaret*), Susan Peters (*Random Harvest*), Edward G. Robinson (*Tales of Manhattan*), Ginger Rogers (*Roxie Hart* and *The Major and the Minor*), George Sanders (*The Moon and Sixpence*), Ann Sheridan (*Kings Row*), William Severn (*Journey for Margaret*), Rudy Vallee (*The Palm Beach Story*), Anton Walbrook (*The Invaders*), Googie Withers (*One of Our Aircraft Is Missing*), Monty Woolley (*The Pied Piper*), Teresa Wright (*Mrs. Miniver*), and Robert Young (*H.M. Pulham, Esq.*, *Joe Smith, American*, and *Journey for Margaret*).

NEW YORK FILM CRITICS CIRCLE

Picture: *In Which We Serve*; Actor: James Cagney (*Yankee Doodle Dandy*); Actress: Agnes Moorehead (*The Magnificent Ambersons*); Director: John Farrow (*Wake Island*).

Noel Coward's English-made naval drama *In Which We Serve* was shut out of the Oscars when the Academy shifted its cut-off date from January 12 to December 31. *Serve* had no Hollywood backing and couldn't afford to switch its January premiere. Coward, who wrote, co-directed, and starred in the film, was given a special Oscar as compensation. The New York Critics still considered it the best film of 1942. It was in official Oscar competition in 1943.

1943

ACADEMY AWARDS (OSCARS)

PICTURE
Casablanca
For Whom the Bell Tolls
Heaven Can Wait
The Human Comedy
In Which We Serve
Madame Curie
The More the Merrier
The Ox-Bow Incident
The Song of Bernadette
Watch on the Rhine

Regarded as a timeless classic today, Warner Brothers' *Casablanca* was not the Oscar front-runner for best Picture of 1943. The smart money was on Fox's soulful *The Song of Bernadette*, a two-hour-and-forty-five-minute religious epic. Studio head Darryl F. Zanuck campaigned heavily for *Bernadette*, taking out a three-page ad spread in the trades, with the first page reading "The Story of a Masterpiece." But the campaign backfired. *Bernadette* was in a limited release at higher ticket prices to give it the prestigious air of a special event. Extras, a powerful voting block, couldn't afford the higher admission and opted for the less pretenious—and cheaper—*Casablanca*.

ACTOR
Humphrey Bogart (*Casablanca*)
Gary Cooper (*For Whom the Bell Tolls*)
Paul Lukas (*Watch on the Rhine*)
Walter Pidgeon (*Madame Curie*)
Mickey Rooney (*The Human Comedy*)

ACTRESS
Jean Arthur (*The More the Merrier*)
Ingrid Bergman (*For Whom the Bell Tolls*)
Joan Fontaine (*The Constant Nymph*)
Greer Garson (*Madame Curie*)
Jennifer Jones (*The Song of Bernadette*)

After winning for her performance as the saintly peasant girl who sees a vision of the Virgin Mary, Jennifer Jones apologized to her friend Ingrid

(Left to right) **Paul Henreid, Ingrid Bergman, Claude Rains, and Humphrey Bogart** in the immortal *Casablanca*, winner of best Picture, Director, and Adapted Screenplay Oscars for 1943.

Bergman backstage. "You should have won," she told her fellow nominee. Ironically, thirty-one years later, Bergman would apologize for winning her third Oscar to loser Valentina Cortese, citing the French actress's performance in *Day for Night* as superior to her own brief cameo in *Murder on the Orient Express*.

SUPPORTING ACTOR
Charles Bickford (*The Song of Bernadette*)
Charles Coburn (*The More the Merrier*)
J. Carroll Naish (*Sahara*)
Claude Rains (*Casablanca*)
Akim Tamiroff (*For Whom the Bell Tolls*)

Supporting actors and actresses received statuettes rather than plaques beginning this year.

SUPPORTING ACTRESS
Gladys Cooper (*The Song of Bernadette*)
Paulette Goddard (*So Proudly We Hail*)
Katina Paxinou (*For Whom the Bell Tolls*)
Anne Revere (*The Song of Bernadette*)
Lucille Watson (*Watch on the Rhine*)

Greek actress Katina Paxinou brought the chill of war into the Oscar proceedings when she thanked her colleagues at the Royal Theatre in Athens. "I hope they are still alive," she said, "but I doubt it." Appropriately she was Oscared for playing a freedom fighter in the screen version of Ernest Hemingway's novel of the Spanish Civil War, *For Whom the Bell Tolls*.

DIRECTOR
Clarence Brown (*The Human Comedy*)
Michael Curtiz (*Casablanca*)
Henry King (*The Song of Bernadette*)
Ernst Lubitsch (*Heaven Can Wait*)
George Stevens (*The More the Merrier*)

ORIGINAL STORY
Steve Fisher (*Destination Tokyo*)
Guy Gilpatric (*Action in the North Atlantic*)
Gordon McDonnell (*Shadow of a Doubt*)
Frank Ross, Robert Russell (*The More the Merrier*)
William Saroyan (*The Human Comedy*)

ORIGINAL SCREENPLAY
Noel Coward (*In Which We Serve*)
Lillian Hellman (*The North Star*)
Norman Krasna (*Princess O'Rourke*)
Dudley Nichols (*Air Force*)
Allan Scott (*So Proudly We Hail*)

SCREENPLAY
**Julius J. Epstein, Philip G. Epstein,
   Howard Koch** (*Casablanca*)
Richard Flournoy, Lewis R. Foster, Frank Ross,
   Robert Russell (*The More the Merrier*)
Lillian Hellman, Dashiell Hammett
   (*Watch on the Rhine*)
Nunally Johnson (*Holy Matrimony*)
George Seaton (*The Song of Bernadette*)

OTHER AWARDS
Score of a Dramatic or Comedy Picture: Alfred
Newman (*The Song of Bernadette*); Score of a
Musical Picture: Ray Heindorf (*This Is the Army*);
Song: "You'll Never Know" from *Hello, Frisco,
Hello*, music by Harry Warren, lyrics by Mack
Gordon; Cinematography: color—Hal Mohr,
W. Howard Greene (*The Phantom of the Opera*),
black and white—Arthur Miller (*The Song of
Bernadette*); Interior Decoration: color—Alexander
Golitzen, John B. Goodman, Russell A. Gausman,
Ira S. Webb (*The Phantom of the Opera*), black and
white—James Basevi, William Darling, Thomas
Little (*The Song of Bernadette*); Film Editing:
George Amy (*Air Force*); Sound Recording:
Stephen Dunn (*This Land Is Mine*); Special
Effects: Fred Sersen (photographic), Roger
Herman (sound) (*Crash Dive*).
   Documentary: *Desert Victory*; Documentary
Short Subject: *December 7th*; One-Reel Short
Subject: *Amphibious Fighters*; Two-Reel Short
Subject: *Heavenly Music*; Animated Short Subject:
Yankee Doodle Mouse.

SPECIAL AWARDS
George Pal for the Puppetoons series; Hal B.
Wallis (Irving Thalberg Award).

The war continued to predominate the Oscars.
Most of the winning films dealt with the topic—
Casablanca with its wartime romance between the
cynical Humphrey Bogart and the idealistic Ingrid
Bergman, and *Watch on the Rhine* with Paul Lukas
as a noble anti-Nazi bringing his struggle into an
American home.
   In keeping with the trend of the last few years,
the ceremony itself was making more concessions
to the global situation. Academy president Walter
Wanger stole Bette Davis's idea and moved the
awards from a hotel banquet hall to a theater,
Grauman's Chinese with the famous footprints. A
limited number of passes were given to servicemen
who watched the proceedings from ten tiers of
bleachers on the Grauman's stage.
   In order to avoid the lengthy speeches of the
previous year's show, Wanger hired Kay Kyser and
his orchestra to put on a USO-style variety show
instead of the usual roster of boring speakers. This
marked the beginning of the transformation of the
Oscars from an insiders' intimate dinner to the
entertainment extravaganza it is today. The latter
half of the show was broadcast on national radio.
Jack Benny acted as host since Bob Hope had a
bad cold. The Screen Directors' Guild threatened
a boycott of the awards because their category had
been placed early in the evening, prior to the
broadcast. The matter was resolved when complete
radio coverage for the entire ceremony was negotiated for the 1944 awards and Mark Sandrich, the
Guild's president, was chosen to produce the show.

NATIONAL BOARD OF REVIEW

BEST ENGLISH-LANGUAGE FILMS
*The Ox-Bow Incident, Watch on the Rhine, Air
Force, Holy Matrimony, The Hard Way, Casablanca,
Lassie Come Home, Bataan, The Moon Is Down,
Next of Kin.*

BEST FOREIGN-LANGUAGE FILMS
None cited this year.

BEST ACTORS

Paul Lukas (*Watch on the Rhine*), Henry Morgan (*The Ox-Bow Incident* and *Happy Land*), Cedric Hardwicke (*The Moon Is Down* and *The Cross of Lorraine*).

BEST ACTRESSES

Gracie Fields (*Holy Matrimony*), Katina Paxinou (*For Whom the Bell Tolls*), Teresa Wright (*Shadow of a Doubt*).

BEST DIRECTORS

Michael Curtiz (*Casablanca* and *This Is the Army*), Tay Garnett (*Bataan* and *The Cross of Lorraine*), William A. Wellman (*The Ox-Bow Incident*).

NEW YORK FILM CRITICS CIRCLE

Picture: *Watch on the Rhine*; Actor: Paul Lukas (*Watch on the Rhine*); Actress: Ida Lupino (*The Hard Way*); Director: George Stevens (*The More the Merrier*).

HOLLYWOOD FOREIGN PRESS ASSOCIATION GOLDEN GLOBE AWARDS

The Hollywood Foreign Press Association, established in 1940, was composed of reporters covering the film community for publications abroad. They began presenting their Golden Globe Awards this year. In later years, they would expand the number of categories and, unlike the Oscar, give separate prizes for Drama and Comedy or Musical performances.

Best Picture (Drama): *The Song of Bernadette*; Actor: Paul Lukas (*Watch on the Rhine*); Actress: Jennifer Jones (*The Song of Bernadette*).

1944

ACADEMY AWARDS (OSCARS)

PICTURE
Double Indemnity
Gaslight
Going My Way

Since You Went Away
Wilson

Overcrowded for many years, the best Picture category was given strict orders to go on a diet and slimmed down from ten to five nominees. The top candidates for the first five-picture race were *Going My Way*, a simple, warmhearted comedy about a Catholic priest, and *Wilson*, an overblown biopic of our twenty-sixth President. Each film had ten nominations apiece. *Wilson* took the lion's share of technical awards, but *Going My Way* grabbed the major prizes—for Picture, Actor, Supporting Actor, Director, and Screenplay. Fox's Darryl Zanuck was given the Irving Thalberg Award as a consolation prize, but was embittered that his pet prestige project had lost the big one.

ACTOR
Charles Boyer (*Gaslight*)
Bing Crosby (*Going My Way*)
Barry Fitzgerald (*Going My Way*)
Cary Grant (*None But the Lonely Heart*)
Alexander Knox (*Wilson*)

Bing Crosby did not expect to win and was spending the afternoon on the golf course. He agreed to attend the ceremony only after studio publicity men got his mother to call him and shame him into going. When he did win, the singer joked that his triumph would provide crony Bob Hope with plenty of material for the latter's radio show. Oscar host Hope sneaked up behind the winner during his speech and began making faces to the delight of the audience. After Crosby exited, Hope started in right away, stating giving an Oscar to Crosby was like listening to Samuel Goldwyn deliver a talk at Oxford.

ACTRESS
Ingrid Bergman (*Gaslight*)
Claudette Colbert (*Since You Went Away*)
Bette Davis (*Mr. Skeffington*)
Greer Garson (*Mrs. Parkington*)
Barbara Stanwyck (*Double Indemnity*)

Ingrid Bergman's first Oscar was for her Victorian housewife terrorized by husband Charles Boyer in *Gaslight*. Many felt she was being rewarded for losing the previous year in *For Whom the Bell Tolls*. At the time of her win, she was filming *The Bells of St. Mary's*, a sequel to *Going My Way* with Crosby, Fitzgerald, and director-writer Leo McCarey. "I'm afraid if I didn't have an Oscar too, they wouldn't speak to me," she joked.

SUPPORTING ACTOR
Hume Cronyn (*The Seventh Cross*)
Barry Fitzgerald (*Going My Way*)
Claude Rains (*Mr. Skeffington*)
Clifton Webb (*Laura*)
Monty Woolley (*Since You Went Away*)

Barry Fitzgerald holds a unique place in Oscar history as the only person to be nominated in both the leading and supporting categories for the same performance. His lovable old Irish priest in *Going My Way* received enough votes in both areas to put him in the top five. The Academy changed the rules so that a similar double nomination could not occur again. Now studios specify for which category they wish an actor or actress to be considered.

A few weeks after acquiring the statuette, Fitzgerald accidentally decapitated it while practicing his golf swing. The awards were still made of plaster then. The Academy replaced the headless award, so technically Fitzgerald got two Oscars to go with his two nominations.

SUPPORTING ACTRESS
Ethel Barrymore (*None But the Lonely Heart*)
Jennifer Jones (*Since You Went Away*)
Angela Lansbury (*Gaslight*)
Aline MacMahon (*Dragon Seed*)
Agnes Moorehead (*Mrs. Parkington*)

Ethel Barrymore joined her brother Lionel in the Oscar winner's circle, making them the first and so far only brother and sister to take home acting Oscars. Sisters Olivia de Havilland and Joan Fontaine are the only pair of same-sex siblings to be similarly honored.

DIRECTOR
Alfred Hitchcock (*Lifeboat*)
Henry King (*Wilson*)
Leo McCarey (*Going My Way*)
Otto Preminger (*Laura*)
Billy Wilder (*Double Indemnity*)

ORIGINAL STORY
David Boehm, Chandler Srague (*A Guy Named Joe*)
Edward Doherty, Jules Shermer (*The Sullivans*)
Leo McCarey (*Going My Way*)
Alfred Neumann, Joseph Thann (*None Shall Escape*)
John Steinbeck (*Lifeboat*)

ORIGINAL SCREENPLAY
Jerome Cady (*A Wing and a Prayer*)
Richard Connell, Gladys Lehman (*Two Girls and a Sailor*)
Preston Sturges (*Hail the Conquering Hero*)
Preston Sturges (*The Miracle of Morgan's Creek*)
Lamar Trotti (*Wilson*)

SCREENPLAY
John L. Balderston, Walter Reisch, John Van Druten (*Gaslight*)
Irving Brecher, Fred F. Finkelhoffe (*Meet Me in St. Louis*)
Frank Butler, Frank Cavett (*Going My Way*)
Raymond Chandler, Billy Wilder (*Double Indemnity*)
Jay Dratler, Samuel Hoffenstein, Betty Reinheart (*Laura*)

OTHER AWARDS
Score of a Dramatic or Comedy Picture: Max Steiner (*Since You Went Away*); Score of a Musical Picture: Carmen Dragon, Morris Stoloff (*Cover Girl*); Song: "Swinging on a Star" from *Going My Way*, music by James Van Heusen, lyrics by Johnny Burke; Cinematography: color—Leon Shamroy (*Wilson*), black and white—Joseph LaShelle (*Laura*); Art Direction: color—Wiard Ihnen, Thomas Little (*Wilson*), black and white—Cedric Gibbons, William Ferrari, Edwin B. Willis, Paul Huldschinsky (*Gaslight*); Film Editing: Barbara McLean (*Wilson*); Sound Recording: Twentieth Century-Fox Studio Sound Department (*Wilson*); Special Effects: A. Arnold Gillespie, Donald Jahraus, Warren Newcombe (photographic), Douglas Shearer (sound) (*Thirty Seconds over Tokyo*).

Documentary: *The Fighting Lady*; Documentary Short Subject: *With the Marines at Tarawa*; One-Reel Short Subject: *Who's Who in Animal Land*;

Two-Reel Short Subject: *I Won't Play*; Animated Short Subject: *Mouse Trouble*.

SPECIAL AWARDS

Margaret O'Brien (outstanding juvenile performance); Bob Hope; Darryl F. Zanuck (Irving Thalberg Award).

Mark Sandrich, who was scheduled to produce the 1944 Oscars, had several ideas for improving them. As each nominee's name was read, a brief clip of his or her performance would be shown on a giant screen. Unfortunately, Sandrich died of a heart attack a few days before the big night. The evening was co-hosted by John Cromwell, director of the nominated *Since You Went Away*, and Oscar's most loyal host Bob Hope. Once again the event took place at Grauman's Chinese Theatre, but this time the entire ceremony was broadcast on radio. The ABC network carried the show, the first to be heard by the general public in its entirety.

NATIONAL BOARD OF REVIEW

BEST ENGLISH-LANGUAGE FILMS
None But the Lonely Heart, Going My Way, The Miracle of Morgan's Creek, Hail the Conquering Hero, The Song of Bernadette, Wilson, Meet Me in St. Louis, Thirty Seconds over Tokyo, Thunder Rock, Lifeboat.

BEST FOREIGN FILMS
None cited.

BEST DOCUMENTARIES
The Memphis Belle, Attack! The Battle for New Britain, With the Marines at Tarawa, Battle for the Marianas, Tunisian Victory.

BEST ACTING (alphabetically)
Ethel Barrymore (*None But the Lonely Heart*), Ingrid Bergman (*Gaslight*), Eddie Bracken (*Hail the Conquering Hero*), Humphrey Bogart (*To Have and Have Not*), Bing Crosby (*Going My Way*), June Duprez (*None But the Lonely Heart*), Barry Fitzgerald (*Going My Way*), Betty Hutton (*The Miracle of Morgan's Creek*), Margaret O'Brien (*Meet Me in St. Louis*), Franklin Pangborn (*Hail the Conquering Hero*).

NEW YORK FILM CRITICS CIRCLE

Picture: *Going My Way*; Actor: Barry Fitzgerald (*Going My Way*); Actress: Tallulah Bankhead (*Lifeboat*); Director: Leo McCarey (*Going My Way*).

While the Circle's choice of *Going My Way* predicted the film's later Oscar triumphs, the tempestuous Tallulah Bankhead failed to receive even an Oscar nomination for her sharp-tongued reporter in Alfred Hitchcock's *Lifeboat*. "Did I get an Academy Oscar? No! The people who vote in that free-for-all don't know on which side their crepes Suzettes are buttered," she acidly commented in her memoirs.

HOLLYWOOD FOREIGN PRESS ASSOCIATION GOLDEN GLOBE AWARDS

Picture: *Going My Way*; Actor: Alexander Knox (*Wilson*); Actress: Ingrid Bergman (*Gaslight*); Supporting Actor: Barry Fitzgerald (*Going My Way*); Supporting Actress: Agnes Moorehead (*Mrs. Parkington*).

Because of the war, the recipients of the Golden Globe Awards received their citations by the mail. There was no ceremony.

1945

ACADEMY AWARDS (OSCARS)

PICTURE
Anchors Aweigh
The Bells of St. Mary's
The Lost Weekend
Mildred Pierce
Spellbound

ACTOR
Bing Crosby (*The Bells of St. Mary's*)
Gene Kelly (*Anchors Aweigh*)
Ray Milland (*The Lost Weekend*)
Gregory Peck (*The Keys of the Kingdom*)
Cornel Wilde (*A Song to Remember*)

"It's Four Roses against Old Granddad" was how host Bob Hope summarized the main race in the

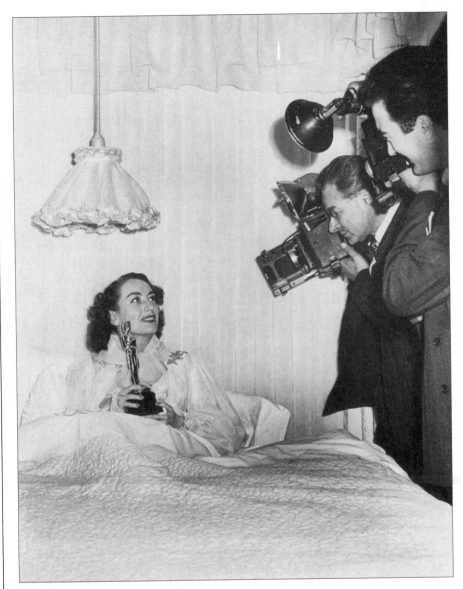

Joan Crawford managed to overcome her "case of the flu" to pose for photographers with her brand-new 1945 Oscar.

best Actor category. He was referring to Ray Milland's realistic portrait of an alcoholic in *The Lost Weekend* and Bing Crosby's reprise of a good-hearted priest in *The Bells of St. Marys'*, a sequel to last year's best Picture *Going My Way*. When Milland won, he was so stunned, he didn't even speak but merely smiled and bowed after receiving the award from Ingrid Bergman.

ACTRESS

Ingrid Bergman (*The Bells of St. Mary's*)
Joan Crawford (*Mildred Pierce*)

Greer Garson (*The Valley of Decision*)
Jennifer Jones (*Love Letters*)
Gene Tierney (*Leave Her to Heaven*)

Joan Crawford wanted an Oscar—bad! And she stopped at nothing to get one. Determined to ride her comeback role—the long-suffering mother in *Mildred Pierce*— Crawford became the first Oscar nominee to employ a publicist (Henry Rogers) in launching a campaign to win the award. Rogers planted items in all the columns and spread the word that Crawford's performance was her best ever, even before she finished filming it.

On the big night itself, Crawford demurred attending, claiming she had a bad cold. What she actually had was a bad case of stage fright. Photographers were stationed at the Crawford manse and were ready when the shoulder-padded star won the golden guy. *Pierce*'s director Michael Curtiz accepted the award for his leading lady and brought it to her bedside, accompanied by flashing bulbs. Every front page featured blow-ups of Joan, looking remarkably well for a sick lady, sitting up in bed with her new acquisition.

SUPPORTING ACTOR

Michael Chekhov (*Spellbound*)
John Dall (*The Corn Is Green*)
James Dunn (*A Tree Grows in Brooklyn*)
Robert Mitchum (*The Story of G.I. Joe*)
J. Carroll Naish (*A Medal for Benny*)

SUPPORTING ACTRESS

Eve Arden (*Mildred Pierce*)
Ann Blythe (*Mildred Pierce*)
Angela Lansbury (*The Picture of Dorian Gray*)
Joan Lorring (*The Corn Is Green*)
Anne Revere (*National Velvet*)

Like Gale Sondergaard, the first winner in this category, and Lee Grant, a Supporting Actress winner in 1976, Anne Revere would later become a victim of blacklisting in the 1950s because of suspected leftist leanings.

DIRECTOR

Clarence Brown (*National Velvet*)
Alfred Hitchcock (*Spellbound*)
Leo McCarey (*The Bells of St. Mary's*)
Jean Renoir (*The Southerner*)
Billy Wilder (*The Lost Weekend*)

ORIGINAL STORY

Alvah Bessie (*Objective, Burma*)
Charles G. Booth (*The House on 92nd Street*)
Laszlo Gorog, Thomas Monroe (*The Affairs of Susan*)
Ernst Marischka (*A Song to Remember*)
John Steinbeck, Jack Wagner (*A Medal for Bennie*)

ORIGINAL SCREENPLAY

Myles Connolly (*Music for Millions*)
Milton Holmes (*Salty O'Rourke*)
Harry Kurnitz (*What Next, Corporal Hargrove?*)
Richard Schweizer (*Marie-Louise*)
Philip Yordan (*Dillinger*)

SCREENPLAY

Leopold Atlas, Guy Endore, Philip Stevenson (*The Story of G.I. Joe*)
Charles Brackett, Billy Wilder (*The Lost Weekend*)
Frank Davis, Tess Slesinger (*A Tree Grows in Brooklyn*)
Ranald MacDougall (*Mildred Pierce*)
Albert Maltz (*Pride of the Marines*)

OTHER AWARDS

Score of a Dramatic or Comedy Picture: Mikos Rozsa (*Spellbound*); Score of a Musical Picture: Georgie Stoll (*Anchors Aweigh*); Song: "It Might as Well Be Spring" from *State Fair*, music by Richard Rodgers, lyrics by Oscar Hammerstein, II; Cinematography: color—Leon Shamroy (*Leave Her to Heaven*), black and white—Harry Stradling (*The Picture of Dorian Gray*); Interior Decoration: color—Hans Dreier, Ernst Fegte, Sam Comer (*Frenchman's Creek*), black and white—A. Roland Fields (*Blood on the Sun*); Film Editing: Robert J. Kern (*National Velvet*); Sound Recording: Stephen Dunn (*The Bells of St. Marys*); Special Effects: John Fulton (photgraphic), A. W. Johns (*Wonder Man*).

Documentary: *The True Glory*; Documentary Short Subject: *Hitler Lives?*; One-Reel Short Subject: *Stairway to Light*; Two-Reel Short Subject: *Star in the Night*; Animated Short Subject: *Quiet Please*.

SPECIAL AWARDS

Walter Wanger, for six years of service as president of the Academy; Peggy Ann Garner (outstanding juvenile performance); *The House I Live In*, RKO short subject; Republic Studio for building a new musical recording studio.

Oscar was restored from plaster to bronze as the war ended and the boys returned home. The film community celebrated by having Hollywood war vets like Caesar Romero, John Huston, and writers Robert Riskin, Sy Bartlett, and Peter Viertel relate war stories during the 1945 Oscar ceremony at Grauman's Chinese Theatre.

Former winner James Stewart co-hosted with Bob Hope, who was presented with a joke Oscar by the Academy's new president Jean Hersholt. Unlike the previous year, ABC covered only the major awards in its radio broadcast. For the first time excerpts from the nominated best Songs were sung by the likes of Frank Sinatra, Dick Haymes, Dinah Shore, and Kathryn Grayson. Nominee Bing Crosby was to have also vocalized two nominees from films he had appeared in that year, but at the last minute he failed to show up.

NATIONAL BOARD OF REVIEW

Picture: *The True Glory*; Actor: Ray Milland (*The Lost Weekend*); Actress: Joan Crawford (*Mildred Pierce*); Director: Jean Renoir (*The Southerner*).

TEN BEST FILMS

The True Glory, The Lost Weekend, The Southerner, The Story of G.I. Joe, The Last Chance, Colonel Blimp, A Tree Grows in Brooklyn, The Fighting Lady, The Way Ahead, The Clock.

The Board began an anti-Hollywood streak by naming a documentary *The True Glory* as Best Picture. In the next four years, the NRB would choose foreign films as the best.

NEW YORK FILM CRITICS CIRCLE

Picture: *The Lost Weekend*; Actor: Ray Milland (*The Lost Weekend*); Actress: Ingrid Bergman (*The Bells of St. Mary's* and *Spellbound*); Director: Billy Wilder (*The Lost Weekend*); Special Awards: Documentaries *The True Glory* and *The Fighting Lady*.

HOLLYWOOD FOREIGN PRESS ASSOCIATION GOLDEN GLOBE AWARDS

Picture: *The Lost Weekend*; Actor: Ray Milland (*The Lost Weekend*); Actress: Ingrid Bergman (*The Bells of St. Mary's*); Supporting Actor: J. Carroll Naish (*A Medal for Benny*); Supporting Actress: Angela Lansbury (*The Picture of Dorian Gray*); Film Promoting International Understanding: *The House I Live In*.

1946

ACADEMY AWARDS (OSCARS)

PICTURE

The Best Years of Our Lives
Henry V
It's a Wonderful Life
The Razor's Edge
The Yearling

Hollywood reflected the problems of returning World War II vets in MGM's *The Best Years of Our Lives*, the top Oscar winner of 1946 with six awards. The film caused a rift between director William Wyler and producer Samuel Goldwyn, with Wyler claiming Goldwyn denied him proper on-screen credit and later suing the producer for cheating him out of his share of the profits.

ACTOR

Frederic March (*The Best Years of Our Lives*)
Laurence Olivier (*Henry V*)
Larry Parks (*The Jolson Story*)
Gregory Peck (*The Yearling*)
James Stewart (*It's a Wonderful Life*)

ACTRESS

Olivia de Havilland (*To Each His Own*)
Celia Johnson (*Brief Encounter*)
Jennifer Jones (*Duel in the Sun*)
Rosalind Russell (*Sister Kenny*)
Jane Wyman (*The Yearling*)

Impressed with the results of 1945's best Actress derby, Olivia de Havilland hired publicist Henry Rogers who guided Joan Crawford to her *Mildred Pierce* win. De Havilland had appeared in two vehicles in 1946 and didn't want to split the vote by promoting both. She had to choose between Universal's *The Dark Mirror*, a murder mystery in which she played contrasting twins, and Paramount's *To Each His Own*, a sentimental soap opera wherein de Havilland gives up her illegitimate child to be raised by another woman. She went with the latter since her role was more sympathetic.

After winning, the actress publicly snubbed her

sister Joan Fontaine who was at the ceremony to present the best Actor award.

SUPPORTING ACTOR
Charles Coburn (*The Green Years*)
William Demarest (*The Jolson Story*)
Claude Rains (*Notorious*)
Harold Russell (*The Best Years of Our Lives*)
Clifton Webb (*The Razor's Edge*)

Harold Russell, a veteran who had lost both of his hands in the war, was the most popular winner of 1946, garnering a best Supporting Actor prize as well as a special award for "bringing hope and courage to his fellow veterans through his appearance in *The Best Years of Our Lives*." The audience at the Shrine Auditorium gave him the longest sustained ovation of the evening. The nonprofessional stated he had no plans to continue acting and did not make another film until 1980's *Inside Moves*.

SUPPORTING ACTRESS
Ethel Barrymore (*The Spiral Staircase*)
Anne Baxter (*The Razor's Edge*)
Lillian Gish (*Duel in the Sun*)
Flora Robson (*Saratoga Trunk*)
Gale Sondergaard (*Anna and the King of Siam*)

DIRECTOR
Clarence Brown (*The Yearling*)
Frank Capra (*It's a Wonderful Life*)
David Lean (*Brief Encounter*)
Robert Siodmak (*The Killers*)
William Wyler (*The Best Years of Our Lives*)

ORIGINAL STORY
Charles Brackett (*To Each His Own*)
Clemence Dane (*Vacation from Marriage*)
Jack Patrick (*The Strange Loves of Martha Ivers*)
Vladimir Pozner (*The Dark Mirror*)
Victor Trivas (*The Stranger*)

ORIGINAL SCREENPLAY
Muriel and **Sydney Box** (*The Seventh Veil*)
Raymond Chandler (*The Blue Dahlia*)
Ben Hecht (*Notorious*)
Norman Panama, Melvin Frank (*The Road to Utopia*)

Jacques Prevent (*Children of Paradise*)

SCREENPLAY
Sergio Amidei, Federico Fellini (*Open City*)
Sally Benson, Talbot Jennings (*Anna and the King of Siam*)
Anthony Havelock-Allan, David Lean, Ronald Neame (*Brief Encounter*)
Robert E. Sherwood (*The Best Years of Our Lives*)
Anthony Veiller (*The Killers*)

OTHER AWARDS
Score of a Dramatic or Comedy Picture: Hugo Friedhofer (*The Best Years of Our Lives*); Score of a Musical Picture: Morris Stoloff (*The Jolson Story*); Song: "On the Atchinson, Topeka, and Santa Fe" from *The Harvey Girls*, music by Harry Warren, lyrics by Johnny Mercer; Cinematography: color—Charles Rosher, Leonard Smith, Arthur Arling (*The Yearling*), black and white—Arthur Miller (*The Best Years of Our Lives*); Interior Decoration: color—Cedric Gibbons, Paul Groesse, Edwin B. Willis (*The Yearling*), black and white—Lyle Wheeler, William Darling, Thomas Little, Frank E. Hughes (*Anna and the King of Siam*); Film Editing: Daniel Mandell (*The Best Years of Our Lives*); Sound Recording: John Livadry (*The Jolson Story*); Special Effects: Thomas Howard (*Blithe Spirit*).

Documentary Short Subject: *Seeds of Destiny* (no award for Documentary Feature); One-Reel Short Subject: *Facing Your Danger*; Two-Reel Short Subject: *A Boy and His Dog*; Animated Short Subject: *The Cat Concerto*.

SPECIAL AWARDS
Laurence Olivier for producing, directing, and acting in *Henry V*; Harold Russell; Ernst Lubitsch; Claude Jarman, Jr. (outstanding juvenile performance).

With World War II over, Hollywood was facing competition from the overseas market. Foreign films were beginning to show up on American screens again and audiences were liking them. The British won two of the screenwriting awards and entries from France (*Children of Paradise*) and Italy (*Open City*) were also in the running. Another English production, David Lean's film version of

Noel Coward's ghostly comedy *Blithe Spirit*, took the Special Effects accolade. Laurence Olivier was presented with a special award for his adaptation of Shakespeare's *Henry V*, an English import which was also nominated for Best Picture and Best Actor.

The ceremony had moved from Grauman's Chinese to the much larger Shrine Auditorium. Jack Benny was the host. The evening began with a compilation of clips from previous Oscar-winning films. In keeping with Murphy's Law, everything that could go wrong with the segment did. The projectionist inserted the film incorrectly and it was shown upside down and backwards on the ceiling rather than on the giant screen provided. As the disaster unreeled, Ronald Reagan, then president of the Screen Actors Guild, went blithely on delivering his onstage narration as if nothing were amiss.

NATIONAL BOARD OF REVIEW

Picture: *Henry V*; Actor: Laurence Olivier (*Henry V*); Actress: Anna Magnani (*Open City*); Director: William Wyler (*The Best Years of Our Lives*).

TEN BEST FILMS
(including foreign films)
Henry V, Open City (also cited as best foreign-language film), *The Best Years of Our Lives, Brief Encounter, A Walk in the Sun, It Happened at the Inn, My Darling Clementine, The Diary of a Chambermaid, The Killers, Anna and the King of Siam.*

NEW YORK FILM CRITICS CIRCLE

Picture: *The Best Years of Our Lives*; Actor: Laurence Olivier (*Henry V*); Actress: Celia Johnson (*Brief Encounter*); Director: William Wyler (*The Best Years of Our Lives*); Foreign Film: *Open City*.

Both the National Board of Review and the New York Film Critics recognized the growing European influence by voting their acting awards to Brits Laurence Olivier and Celia Johnson and Italian Anna Magnani. The Board gave its Best Picture Award to *Henry V*.

HOLLYWOOD FOREIGN PRESS ASSOCIATION GOLDEN GLOBE AWARDS

Picture (Drama): *The Best Years of Our Lives*; Actor: Gregory Peck (*The Yearling*); Actress: Rosalind Russell (*Sister Kenny*); Supporting Actor: Clifton Webb (*The Razor's Edge*; Supporting Actress: Anne Baxter (*The Razor's Edge*); Director: Frank Capra (*It's a Wonderful Life*); Film Promoting International Understanding: *The Last Chance* (Switzerland); Award for Best Nonprofessional Acting: Harold Russell (*The Best Years of Our Lives*).

CANNES FILM FESTIVAL

Grand Prix (shared among 11 films): *The Red Earth* (Denmark), *The Lost Weekend* (USA), *La Symphonie Pastorale* (France), *Brief Encounter* (Britain), *Neecha Nagar* (India), *Open City* (Italy), *Maria Candelaria* (Mexico), *The Prize* (Sweden), *The Last Chance* (Switzerland), *Men without Wings* (Czechoslovakia), *The Turning Point* (USSR).

Actor: Ray Milland (*The Lost Weekend*); Actress: Michele Morgan (*La Symphonie Pastorale*); Director: Rene Clement (*La Bataille du Rail*) (France); Special Jury Prize: *La Bataille du Rail*); Prize for Peace: *The Last Chance*; Animation Award: *Make Mine Music* (USA).

Delayed by the war—it was set to premiere in 1939—the Cannes Film Festival held its first beglittered fortnight in 1946. A star-filled marketplace on the French Riveria, Cannes screens up to 600 movies from around the world in two hectic weeks every year. It is considered the most important festival in Europe. Awards are presented for the best of the pictures shown. From 1946 to 1954 the top prize was called the Grand Prix, but was changed in 1955 to the Golden Palm.

1947

ACADEMY AWARDS (OSCARS)

PICTURE
The Bishop's Wife
Crossfire

Gentlemen's Agreement
Great Expectations
Miracle on 34th Street

Darryl F. Zanuck was finally rewarded with an Oscar after his bitter disappointment at losing for *Wilson*. His win was for another "message picture," *Gentlemen's Agreement*, based on Laura Z. Hobson's novel about anti-Semitism.

Crossfire, another nominee for best Picture, also dealt with religious prejudice. Its off-screen story was equally controversial. Producer Adrian Scott and writer-director Edward Dmytryk had refused to testify before the House Un-American Activities Committee after the picture was completed. They were subsequently fired from RKO and blacklisted in the industry, but received Oscar nominations anyway.

ACTOR
Ronald Coleman (*A Double Life*)
John Garfield (*Body and Soul*)
Gregory Peck (*Gentlemen's Agreement*)
William Powell (*Life with Father*)
Michael Redgrave (*Mourning Becomes Electra*)

ACTRESS
Joan Crawford (*Possessed*)
Susan Hayward (*Smash Up—The Story of a Woman*)
Dorothy McGuire (*Gentlemen's Agreement*)
Rosalind Russell (*Mourning Becomes Electra*)
Loretta Young (*The Farmer's Daughter*)

The third time was not a charm for publicist Henry Rogers. After launching successful best Actress campaigns for Joan Crawford and Olivia de

Frederic March presents the 1947 best Actress Oscar to dark horse winner Loretta Young. Rosalind Russell was the odds-on favorite.

Havilland, Rogers was hired by Rosalind Russell to snare an Oscar for her performance in RKO's slow-moving film adpatation of Eugene O'Neill's stage tragedy *Mourning Becomes Electra*. Vegas oddmakers and a poll of Academy voters published by *Variety* put Russell on top. But when the envelope was opened and the winner was announced, an audible gasp came from the audience. The name on the card was Loretta Young for her turn as a housemaid-turned-politician in *The Farmer's Daughter*. Russell's defeat was blamed on Dore Schary, head of production at RKO, who refused to promote *Electra* because it was made before his tenure at the studio began. He pushed *Daughter* since he brought the project with him from his former professional home, the Selznick studio.

SUPPORTING ACTOR
Charles Bickford (*The Farmer's Daughter*)
Thomas Gomez (*Ride the Pink Horse*)
Edmund Gwenn (*Miracle on 34th Street*)
Robert Ryan (*Crossfire*)
Richard Widmark (*Kiss of Death*)

"There really is a Santa Claus," enthused Edmund Gwenn upon accepting his Oscar for playing Kris Kringle, or a reasonable facsimile, in the holiday classic *Miracle on 34th Street*.

SUPPORTING ACTRESS
Ethel Barrymore (*The Paradine Case*)
Gloria Grahame (*Crossfire*)
Celeste Holm (*Gentlemen's Agreement*)
Marjorie Main (*The Egg and I*)
Anne Revere (*Gentlemen's Agreement*)

DIRECTOR
George Cukor (*A Double Life*)
Edward Dmytryk (*Crossfire*)
Elia Kazan (*Gentlemen's Agreement*)
Henry Koster (*The Bishop's Wife*)
David Lean (*Great Expectations*)

ORIGINAL STORY
Georges Chaperot, Rene Wheeler (*A Cage of Nightingales*)
Valentine Davies (*Miracle on 34th Street*)
Herbert Clyde Lewis, Frederick Stephani (*It Happened on Fifth Avenue*)

Eleazar Lipsky (*Kiss of Death*)
Dorothy Parker, Frank Cavert (*Smash Up—The Story of a Woman*)

ORIGINAL SCREENPLAY
Sergio Amidei, Adolfo Franci, C. G. Viola, Cesare Zavattini (*Shoeshine*)
Charles Chaplin (*Monsieur Verdoux*)
Ruth Gordon, Garson Kanin (*A Double Life*)
Abraham Polonsky (*Body and Soul*)
Sidney Sheldon (*The Bachelor and the Bobby-Soxer*)

SCREENPLAY
Moss Hart (*Gentlemen's Agreement*)
David Lean, Ronald Neame, Anthony Havelock-Allen (*Great Expectations*)
Richard Murphy (*Boomerang*)
John Paxton (*Crossfire*)
George Seaton (*Miracle on 34th Street*)

OTHER AWARDS
Score of a Dramatic or Comedy Picture: Miklos Rozsa (*A Double Life*); Score of a Musical Picture: Alfred Newman (*Mother Wore Tights*); Song: "Zip-A-Dee-Doo-Dah" from *Song of the South*, music by Allie Wrubel, lyrics by Ray Gilbert; Cinematography: color—Jack Cadriff (*Black Narcissus*), black and white—Guy Green (*Great Expectations*); Art Direction: color—Alfred Junge (*Black Narcissus*), black and white—John Bryan, Wilfred Shingleton (*Great Expectations*); Film Editing: Francis Lyon, Robert Parrish (*Body and Soul*); Sound Recording: Goldwyn Sound Department (*The Bishop's Wife*); Special Effects: A. Arnold Gillespie, Warren Newcombe (photographic), Douglas Shearer, Michael Steinore (sound) (*Green Dolphin Street*).

Documentary: *Design for Death*; Documentary Short Subject: *First Steps*; One-Reel Short Subject: *Goodbye Miss Turlock*; Two-Reel Short Subject: *Climbing the Matterhorn*; Animated Short Subject: *Tweetie Pie*.

Note: Interior Decoration was officially changed to Art Direction.

After winning the Animated Short Subject category four years in a row, Tom and Jerry finally lost to another cartoon pair, Sylvester and Tweetie.

SPECIAL AWARDS

James Baskette for his portayal of Uncle Remus in *Song of the South*; *Bill and Coo*, live-action short subject; *Shoeshine*; Col. William N. Elig, Albert E. Smith, Thomas Armat, and George K. Spoor, film pioneers.

Oscar celebrated his twentieth anniversary at the Shrine Auditorium with a giant cake bedecked with statuettes rather than candles. ABC again carried the ceremony to a national audience, this time from beginning to end. The unlikely pair of musical-juvenile-turned-film-noir-detective Dick Powell and character actress Agnes Moorehead served as hosts.

The British continued their invasion of the film community by sweeping both the Cinematography and Art Direction awards—*Black Narcissus* for color and *Great Expectations* for black and white. Jean Simmons, the ingenue of *Expectations*, had been called upon to accept for any absent British winner. She wound up heading for the stage four times and greatly charmed the audience. Among those enchanted was Cecil B. DeMille, who offered her a part in his upcoming epic *Samson and Delilah*. She turned him down, claiming a prior commitment: playing Ophelia in Laurence Olivier's cinematic *Hamlet*, a film which would continue the English encroachment on the Oscars. The Academy acknowledged another foreign inter-loper by bestowing a special award on the acclaimed Italian feature *Shoeshine*. Academy president Jean Hersholt suggested it was time for a Foreign-Language Film Oscar. Honorary Oscars would go to such films until 1956, when best Foreign-Language Film would become a regular category.

NATIONAL BOARD OF REVIEW

Picture: *Monsieur Verdoux*; Actor: Michael Redgrave (*Mourning Becomes Electra*); Actress: Celia Johnson (*This Happy Breed*); Director: Elia Kazan (*Gentlemen's Agreement* and *Boomerang*).

TEN BEST FILMS

Monsieur Verdoux, Great Expectations, Shoeshine (Italy), *Crossfire, Boomerang, Odd Man Out, Gentlemen's Agreement, To Live in Peace* (Italy), *It's a Wonderful Life, The Overlanders.*

NEW YORK FILM CRITICS AWARDS

Picture: *Gentlemen's Agreement*; Actor: William Powell (*Life with Father* and *The Senator Was Indiscreet*); Actress: Deborah Kerr (*Black Narcissus* and *The Adventuress*); Director: Elia Kazan (*Gentlemen's Agreement* and *Boomerang*); Foreign Film: *To Live in Peace.*

HOLLYWOOD FOREIGN PRESS ASSOCIATION GOLDEN GLOBE AWARDS

Picture (Drama): *Gentlemen's Agreement*; Actor: Ronald Coleman (*A Double Life*); Actress: Rosalind Russell (*Mourning Becomes Electra*); Supporting Actor: Edmund Gwenn (*Miracle on 34th Street*); Supporting Actress: Celeste Holm (*Gentlemen's Agreement*); Most Promising Newcomer (Male): Richard Widmark (*Kiss of Death*); Most Promising Newcomer (Female): Lois Maxwell (*That Hagen Girl*); Director: Elia Kazan (*Gentlemen's Agreement*); Screenplay: George Seaton (*Miracle on 34th Street*); Score: Max Steiner (*Life with Father*); Cinematography: Jack Cadriff (*Black Narcissus*).

SPECIAL AWARDS

Dean Stockwell (outstanding juvenile perform-ance); the Hindustani version of Walt Disney's *Bambi* for furthering the influence of the screen.

CANNES FILM FESTIVAL

Grand Prix Award (shared by five films): *Antoine et Antoinette* (France), *Les Maudits* (France), *Crossfire* (USA), *Ziegfeld Follies* (USA), *Dumbo* (USA).

No acting awards were presented.

ACADEMY AWARDS (OSCARS)

PICTURE
Hamlet
Johnny Belinda
The Red Shoes
The Snake Pit

Treasure of Sierra Madre

Many Hollywood studio executives felt there was something rotten in the state of Tinseltown when the Oscar for best Picture went to Laurence Olivier's screen version of *Hamlet*. Olivier also won Best Actor for his self-directed portrayal of Shakespeare's Melancholy Dane. He's the only performer to direct himself to an Oscar. The British-produced drama was the first non-American film to take the top prize and several Yankee moguls were outraged that a foreigner was taking their top prize.

ACTOR
Lew Ayres (*Johnny Belinda*)
Montgomery Clift (*The Search*)
Dan Dailey (*When My Baby Smiles at Me*)
Laurence Olivier (*Hamlet*)
Clifton Webb (*Sitting Pretty*)

ACTRESS
Ingrid Bergman (*Joan of Arc*)
Olivia de Havilland (*The Snake Pit*)
Irene Dunne (*I Remember Mama*)
Barbara Stanwyck (*Sorry, Wrong Number*)
Jane Wyman (*Johnny Belinda*)

Although Olivia de Havilland won the best Actress prize from the New York Film Critics and the National Board of Review for playing an inmate of an insane asylum in *The Snake Pit*, Oscar night was a disappointment for her. She lost to Jane Wyman's deaf-mute victim in *Johnny Belinda*. De Havilland blamed the loss on the conniving of her sister Joan Fontaine, who mounted a major campaign for the top actress accolade for her performance in *Letter from an Unknown Woman*. Fontaine failed to receive a nomination, but de Havilland believed her sibling had sabotaged her chance for a *Snake Pit* win.

Aside from Wyman's bravura performance, another factor in her favor was sympathy votes because of her recent loss of a baby and her divorce from Ronald Reagan.

De Havilland also couldn't have been too happy to see her former lover John Huston's double triumph for writing and directing *Treasure of Sierra Madre*. Their affair had ended badly. Huston later reported he believed de Havilland's husband

Marcus Goodrich was carrying a gun on Oscar night and intended to shoot him if given the slightest provocation.

SUPPORTING ACTOR
Charles Bickford (*Johnny Belinda*)
Jose Ferrer (*Joan of Arc*)
Oscar Homolka (*I Remember Mama*)
Walter Huston (*Treasure of Sierra Madre*)
Cecil Kellaway (*The Luck of the Irish*)

John Huston won for directing and writing *Treasure of Sierra Madre*, while his father Walter was named Best Supporting Actor. Huston had also directed Claire Trevor to a Supporting Actress Oscar for *Key Largo*. In 1985, Huston's daughter Anjelica would win a Supporting Actress Oscar for *Prizzi's Honor*, making the Huston clan the only three-generational Oscar family.

SUPPORTING ACTRESS
Barbara Bel Geddes (*I Remember Mama*)
Ellen Corby (*I Remember Mama*)
Agnes Moorehead (*Johnny Belinda*)
Jean Simmons (*Hamlet*)
Claire Trevor (*Key Largo*)

DIRECTOR
John Huston (*Treasure of Sierra Madre*)
Anatole Litvak (*The Snake Pit*)
Jean Negulesco (*Johnny Belinda*)
Laurence Olivier (*Hamlet*)
Fred Zinnemann (*The Search*)

MOTION PICTURE STORY
Borden Chase (*Red River*)
Frances and Robert Flaherty (*The Louisiana Story*)
Emeric Pressburger (*The Red Shoes*)
Richard Schweizer, **David Wechsler** (*The Search*)
Borden Chase (*The Naked City*)

SCREENPLAY
Charles Brackett, Billy Wilder, Richard L. Breen
 (*A Foreign Affair*)
John Huston (*Treasure of Sierra Madre*)
Frank Partos, Millen Brand (*The Snake Pit*)
Richard Schweizer, David Wechsler (*The Search*)
Irmgard Von Cube, Allen Vincent
 (*Johnny Belinda*)

Hamlet, starring and directed by Laurence Olivier (seated), was the first British film to win the Academy Award for best Picture, in 1948. Eileen Herlie played Gertrude and Basil Sydney played Claudius.

OTHER AWARDS

Scoring of a Dramatic or Comedy Picture: Brian Easdale (*The Red Shoes*); Scoring of a Musical Picture: Johnny Green and Roger Edens (*Easter Parade*); Original Song: "Buttons and Bows" from *The Paleface*, music and lyrics by Jay Livingston and Ray Evans; Cinematography color—Joseph Valentine, William V. Skall, Winton Hoch (*Joan of Arc*), black and white—William Daniels (*The Naked City*): Art Direction: color—Hein Heckroth, Arthur Lawson (*The Red Shoes*), black and white—Roger K. Furse, Carmen Dillon (*Hamlet*); Costume Design: color—Dorothy Jeakins and Karinska (*Joan of Arc*), black and white—Roger K. Furse (*Hamlet*); Film Editing: Paul Weatherwax (*The Naked City*); Sound Recording: 20th Century Sound Department (*The Snake Pit*); Special Effects: Paul Eagler, J. McMillan Johnson, Russell Shearman, Clarence Slifer (visual), Charles Freeman, James G. Stewart (audible) (*Portrait of Jennie*).

Documentary: *The Secret Land*; Documentary Short Subject: *Toward Independence*; One-Reel Short Subject: *Symphony of a City*; Two-Reel Short Subject: *Seal Island*; Animated Short Subject: *The Little Orphan*.

Note: The costume design category was added and the writing awards were reduced from three (Original Story, Original Screenplay, and Screenplay) to two (Motion Picture Story and Screenplay).

SPECIAL AWARDS

Monsiuer Vincent (France) (outstanding foreign-language film); Ivan Jandl (outstanding juvenile actor); theatre owner Sid Grauman; producer Adolph Zukor; Walter Wanger for producing *Joan of Arc*.

The Olivier double win didn't soothe the rancorous relations between the studios and the Academy. Because of a recent anti-trust Supreme Court ruling, the Big Five studios—MGM, Warners, Fox, Paramount, and RKO—were ordered to divest themselves of their chain of movie theaters. As a result, the Big Five had to tighten their belts and withdrew economic support of the Oscar ceremonies.

Academy president Jean Hersholt opened the Oscar radio broadcast by blasting the studios but without specifically citing their financial pullout. Hersholt concluded by announcing he was resigning to be replaced by writer-producer Charles Brackett immediately after the show. Once the news of the withdrawal was announced, it appeared as if it were sour grapes for losing to the British. The studios were eventually shamed into rebacking the awards by the industry press.

Another loser at the festivities was producer and former Academy president Walter Wanger, whose overblown *Joan of Arc* starring Ingrid Bergman won for Cinematography and Costumes but lost in the major categories. Although Wanger received a consolation "special" Oscar, the production failed to return its initial cost and bankrupted the producer. His career took another nosedive two years later when, in a fit of jealousy, he shot the agent of his wife Joan Bennett.

NATIONAL BOARD OF REVIEW

Picture: *Paisan* (Italy); Actor: Walter Huston (*Treasure of Sierra Madre*); Actress: Olivia de Havilland (*The Snake Pit*); Director: Roberto Rossellini (*Paisan*).

TEN BEST FILMS

Paisan, Day of Wrath (Denmark), *The Search, Treasure of Sierra Madre, Louisiana Story, Hamlet, The Snake Pit, Johnny Belinda, Joan of Arc, The Red Shoes.*

NEW YORK FILM CRITICS AWARDS

Picture: *Treasure of Sierra Madre*; Actor: Laurence Olivier (*Hamlet*); Actress: Olivia de Havilland (*The Snake Pit*); Director: John Huston (*Treasure of Sierra Madre*); Foreign Film: *Paisan.*

HOLLYWOOD FOREIGN PRESS ASSOCIATION GOLDEN GLOBES AWARDS

Picture (Drama) (tie): *Treasure of Sierra Madre, Johnny Belinda*; Actor: Laurence Olivier (*Hamlet*); Actress: Jane Wyman (*Johnny Belinda*); Supporting Actor: Walter Huston (*Treasure of Sierra Madre*); Supporting Actress: Ellen Corby (*I Remember Mama*); Director: John Huston (*Treasure of Sierra Madre*); Screenplay: Richard Schweizer (*The Search*); Cinematography: Gabriel Figueroa (*The Pearl*); Music: Brian Easdale (*The Red Shoes*).

SPECIAL AWARDS

Ivan Jandl (*The Search*) (outstanding juvenile actor); Film Promoting International Understanding: *The Search.*

CANNES FILM FESTIVAL

Because of a lack of funds, the festival was canceled for 1948.

1949

ACADEMY AWARDS (OSCARS)

PICTURE

All the King's Men
Battleground
The Heiress
A Letter to Three Wives
12 O'Clock High

Columbia studio head Harry Cohn refused to launch an Oscar campaign for *All the Kings' Men*, Robert Rossen's adaptation of Robert Penn Warren's Pulitzer-Prize winning novel about a Southern despot based on Louisiana governor Huey Long. Cohn felt it would be a waste of his money and Rossen had to beg the mogul to release the film in Los Angeles before Christmas in order qualify for Oscar consideration. Rossen paid for *King*'s trade ads out of his own pocket and garnered seven Oscar nominations for the film. Despite Cohn's negligence, *King* took three major awards: Picture, Actor (Broderick Crawford as the Huey Long clone), and Supporting Actress (Mercedes McCambridge in her film debut as his tough secretary).

ACTOR
Broderick Crawford (*All the King's Men*)
Kirk Douglas (*Champion*)
Gregory Peck (*12 O'Clock High*)
Richard Todd (*The Hasty Heart*)
John Wayne (*The Sands of Iwo Jima*)

The son of actress Helen Broderick, Broderick Crawford had toiled in dozens of B-films before playing the role of a lifetime—corrupt, self-centered politician Willy Stark in *All the King's Men*. His Oscar would not lead to starring roles in movies, but he did continue as a reliable character man in TV series like *Highway Patrol*.

ACTRESS
Jeanne Crain (*Pinky*)
Olivia de Havilland (*The Heiress*)
Susan Hayward (*My Foolish Heart*)
Deborah Kerr (*Edward My Son*)
Loretta Young (*Come to the Stable*)

While *The Heiress* was not a box-office hit, it did garner rave reviews for its star Olivia de Havilland as the title character, a plain, naive spinster who is transformed into an avenging schemer by the cruelty of her father (Ralph Richardson) and a feckless fortune hunter (Montgomery Clift). De Havilland also won the Best Actress accolades from the New York Film Critics Circle and the Hollywood Foreign Press Association and was an easy favorite for a second Oscar.

Cherry Jones would win a 1994–95 Tony Award in the same role for the Broadway revival of the stage version.

SUPPORTING ACTOR
John Ireland (*All the King's Men*)

Dean Jagger (*12 O'Clock High*)
Arthur Kennedy (*Champion*)
Ralph Richardson (*The Heiress*)
James Whitmore (*Battleground*)

SUPPORTING ACTRESS
Ethel Barrymore (*Pinky*)
Celeste Holm (*Come to the Stable*)
Elsa Lancaster (*Come to the Stable*)
Mercedes McCambridge (*All the King's Men*)
Ethel Waters (*Pinky*)

DIRECTOR
Joseph L. Mankiewicz (*A Letter to Three Wives*)
Carol Reed (*The Fallen Idol*)
Robert Rossen (*All the King's Men*)
William A. Wellman (*Battleground*)
William Wyler (*The Heiress*)

MOTION PICTURE STORY
Harry Brown (*The Sands of Iwo Jima*)
Virginia Kellog (*White Heat*)
Clare Booth Luce (*Come to the Stable*)
Douglas Morrow (*The Stratton Story*)
Shirley W. Smith, Valentine Davis (*It Happens Every Spring*)

SCREENPLAY
Carl Foreman (*Champion*)
Graham Green (*The Fallen Idol*)
Joseph L. Mankiewicz (*A Letter to Three Wives*)
Robert Rossen (*All the King's Men*)
Cesare Zavattini *The Bicycle Thief*)

STORY AND SCREENPLAY
Sidney Buchman (*Jolson Sings Again*)
T. E. B. Clarke (*Passport to Pimlico*)
Alfred Hayes, Federico Fellini, Sergio Amidei, Marcello Pagliero, Roberto Rosselini (*Paisan*)
Helen Levitt, Janice Loeb, Sidney Meyers (*The Quiet One*)
Robert Pirosh (*Battleground*)

The writing division was split back into three from last year's two. The new categories were Motion Picture Story, Screenplay, and Story and Screenplay.

OTHER AWARDS

Score of a Dramatic or Comedy Picture: Aaron Copland (*The Heiress*); Score of a Musical Picture: Roger Edens, Lennie Hayton (*On the Town*); Song: "Baby, It's Cold Outside" from *Neptune's Daughter*, music and lyrics by Frank Loesser; Cinematography: color—Winton Hoch (*She Wore a Yellow Ribbon*), black and white—Paul C. Vogel (*Battleground*); Art Direction: color—Cedric Gibbons, Paul Groesse, Edwin B. Willis, Jack D. Moore (*Little Women*), black and white—John Meehan, Harry Horner, Emile Kuri (*The Heiress*); Costume Design: color—Leah Rhodes, Travilla and Marjorie Best (*The Adventures of Don Juan*), black and white—Edith Head, Gloria Steele (*The Heiress*); Film Editing: Harry Gerstad (*Champion*); Sound Recording: Twentieth Century-Fox Sound Department (*12 O'Clock High*); Special Effects: *Mighty Joe Young*.

Costume designer Edith Head won the first of her eight Oscars for the second of her thirty-five nominations.

Documentary: *Daybreak in Udi*; Documentary Short Subject (tie): *A Chance to Live* and *So Much for So Little*; One-Reel Short Subject: *Aquatic House Party*; Two-Reel Short Subject: *Van Gogh*; Animated Short Subject: *For Scent-imental Reasons*.

SPECIAL AWARDS

The Bicycle Thief (Italy) (outstanding foreign-language film); Bobby Driscoll (outstanding juvenile performance); Fred Astaire; Cecil B. DeMille; Jean Hersholt.

After removing financial backing for the 1948 Oscars, the studios renewed their commitment to supporting the awards. The 1949 ceremony was held at the Pantages Theatre, where it would take place for the next ten years. Former Academy president Jean Hersholt was given an honorary Oscar for forcing the studios into re-upping the Oscar night bankroll.

Eve Arden and Ronald Reagan provided commentary for radio audiences while Paul Douglas, a rough-hewn character actor who starred as one of the husbands in the Oscar-winning *A Letter to Three Wives*, served as host.

One of the evening's highlights was Red

Skelton's flubbing a line from nominated best Song "Baby, It's Cold Outside," which he had sung in the Esther Williams aquatic vehicle *Neptune's Daughter*. There were some sour grapes over "Baby" winning because songwriter Frank Loesser and his wife Lynn had performed it at parties for many years before it appeared in the film. (Oscar rules state a song must be written especially for a picture to be nominated.) The Academy ruled the song was never performed professionally prior to its on-screen debut, and therefore Loesser kept his Oscar.

NATIONAL BOARD OF REVIEW

Picture: *The Bicycle Thief*; Actor: Ralph Richardson (*The Heiress* and *The Fallen Idol*); Actress: No choice; Director: Vittorio De Sica (*The Bicycle Thief*).

TEN BEST FILMS

The Bicycle Thief (Italy), *The Quiet One*, *Intruder in the Dust*, *The Heiress*, *Devil in the Flesh* (France), *Quartet* (Britain), *Germany, Year Zero* (France/Italy), *Home of the Brave*, *A Letter to Three Wives*, *The Fallen Idol* (Britain).

NEW YORK FILM CRITICS CIRCLE

Picture: *All the King's Men*; Actor: Broderick Crawford (*All the King's Men*); Actress: Olivia de Havilland (*The Heiress*); Director: Carol Reed (*The Fallen Idol*); Foreign-Language Film: *The Bicycle Thief*.

HOLLYWOOD FOREIGN PRESS ASSSOCIATION GOLDEN GLOVE AWARDS

Picture (Drama): *All the King's Men*; Actor: Broderick Crawford (*All the King's Men*); Actress: Olivia de Havilland (*The Heiress*); Supporting Actor: James Whitmore (*Battleground*); Supporting Actress and Most Promising Newcomer (Female): Mercedes McCambridge (*All the King's Men*); Most Promising Newcomer (Male): Richard Todd (*The Hasty Heart*); Director: Robert Rossen (*All the King's Men*); Screenplay: Robert Pirosh (*Battleground*); Score: Johnny Green (*The Inspector General*); Cinematography: color—Walt Disney

Studios (*Ichabod and Mr. Toad*), black and white—Frank Planer (*Champion*); Foreign-Language Film: *The Bicycle Thief*; Film Promoting International Understanding: *The Hasty Heart*.

CANNES FILM FESTIVAL

Grand Prix: *The Third Man* (Britain); Actor: Edward G. Robinson (*House of Strangers*) (USA); Actress: Isa Miranda (*The Walls of Malapaga*) (France/Italy); Director: Rene Clement (*The Walls of Malapaga*).

ACADEMY AWARDS (OSCARS)

PICTURE
All about Eve
Born Yesterday
Father of the Bride
King Solomon's Mines
Sunset Boulevard

All about Eve has a permanent place in Oscar history books with fourteen nominations, the most for any film. It's unlikely that another film will match this record since *Eve* had two actresses in the running for both the leading and supporting categories, and got nods for Art Direction, Cinematography, and Costume Design—in black and white. Because of the lack of grey-toned films these days, the Academy no longer distinguishes between black-and-white and color. With a narrower field of categories, few contemporary films get nominations in the double digits.

Based on a short story by Mary Orr, *Eve* is an astonishingly witty comedy about an aging Broadway star (Bette Davis in a comeback role intended for an ailing Claudette Colbert) pursued by a clever, young newcomer (Anne Baxter) out to take over her career. A Broadway musical version of the story, entitled *Applause*, would win the 1969–70 Tony for best Musical. Baxter would take over the Davis role late in the run of the show.

Also in the running for 1950 Oscars was another show-biz tale of an over-the-hill diva, *Sunset*

Boulevard with Gloria Swanson as the divinely mad former silent-star Norma Desmond. *Sunset* was also musicalized and won a best Musical Tony in 1994–95.

ACTOR
Louis Calhern (*The Magnificent Yankee*)
Jose Ferrer (*Cyrano de Bergerac*)
William Holden (*Sunset Boulevard*)
James Stewart (*Harvey*)
Spencer Tracy (*Father of the Bride*)

ACTRESS
Anne Baxter (*All about Eve*)
Bette Davis (*All about Eve*)
Judy Holliday (*Born Yesterday*)
Eleanor Parker (*Caged*)
Gloria Swanson (*Sunset Boulevard*)

Once again Harry Cohn had little faith in an eventual Oscar winner. He bought the play *Born Yesterday* for Columbia as a vehicle for Rita Hayworth. The star demurred, stating she was quitting the profession to become the full-time wife to Egytian playboy Aly Kahn. George Cukor, the director of the project, lobbied for Judy Holliday, the originator of the role of the dumb-like-a-fox chorus girl on Broadway, to take over for Hayworth. Cohn felt she didn't have enough marquee value and axed the idea. Cukor then cast Holliday in a striking supporting role in *Adam's Rib*, a vehicle for Katharine Hepburn and Spencer Tracy with a screenplay by Ruth Gordon and Garson Kanin (author of *Born Yesterday*). Holliday was praised by the critics, got to repeat her stage role in *Yesterday*, and won the Oscar. Industry experts speculated she was helped by the fact that both Bette Davis and Anne Baxter were nominated for *All about Eve* and split the vote.

SUPPORTING ACTOR
Jeff Chandler (*Broken Arrow*)
Edmund Gwenn (*Mister 880*)
Sam Jaffe (*The Asphalt Jungle*)
George Sanders (*All about Eve*)
Erich von Stroheim (*Sunset Boulevard*)

SUPPORTING ACTRESS
Hope Emerson (*Caged*)

All About Eve (1950) holds the record for most Oscar nominations with fourteen. Anne Baxter (far left) and Bette Davis (second from left) were both nominated as best Actress and canceled each other out. George Sanders (far right) won the Supporting Actor prize. The young actress in the middle is the then-unknown Marilyn Monroe.

Celeste Holm (*All About Eve*)
Josephine Hull (*Harvey*)
Nancy Olson (*Sunset Boulevard*)
Thelma Ritter (*All about Eve*)

DIRECTOR
George Cukor (*Born Yesterday*)
John Huston (*The Asphalt Jungle*)
Joseph L. Mankiewicz (*All about Eve*)
Carol Reed (*The Third Man*)
Billy Wilder (*Sunset Boulevard*)

Joseph L. Mankiewicz is the only Oscar recipient to win two years in a row for both writing and directing. He added a pair of golden guys for *All about Eve* to the duo he garnered for the previous year's *A Letter to Three Wives*.

MOTION PICTURE STORY
Edna and **Edward Anhalt** (*Panic in the Streets*)
William Bowers, Andre de Toth (*The Gunfighter*)

Giuseppe De Santis, Carlo Lizzani (*Bitter Rice*)
Sy Gomberg (*When Willie Comes Marching Home*)
Leonard Spigelgass (*Mystery Street*)

SCREENPLAY
Michael Blankfort (*Broken Arrow*)
Frances Goodrich, Albert Hackett (*Father of the Bride*)
Ben Maddow, John Huston (*The Asphalt Jungle*)
Albert Mannheimer (*Born Yesterday*)
Joseph L. Mankiewicz (*All about Eve*)

STORY AND SCREENPLAY
Charles Brackett, Billy Wilder, D. M. Marshman, Jr. (*Sunset Boulevard*)
Carl Foreman (*The Men*)
Ruth Gordon, Garson Kanin (*Adam's Rib*)
Virginia Kellogg, Bernard C. Schoenfeld (*Caged*)
Joseph L. Mankiewicz, Lesser Samuels (*No Way Out*)

Each writing category featured a husband-and-wife team: Edna and Edward Anhalt, Frances Goodrich and Albert Hackett, Ruth Gordon and Garson Kanin. Only the Anhalts won.

OTHER AWARDS

Score of a Dramatic or Comedy Picture: Franz Waxman (*Sunset Boulevard*); Score of a Musical Picture: Adolph Deutsch, Roger Edens (*Annie Get Your Gun*); Song: "Mona Lisa" from *Captain Carey, USA*, music and lyrics by Ray Evans and Jay Livingston; Cinematography: color—Robert Surtees (*King Solomon's Mines*), black and white—Robert Krasker (*The Third Man*); Art Direction: color—Hans Dreier, Walter Tyler, Sam Comer, Ray Moyer (*Samson and Delilah*), black and white—Hans Dreier, John Meehan, Sam Comer, Ray Moyer (*Sunset Boulevard*); Costume Design: color—Edith Head, Dorothy Jenkins, Elois Jenssen, Gile Steele, Gwen Wakeling (*Samson and Delilah*), black and white—Edith Head, Charles LeMaire (*All about Eve*); Film Editing: Ralph E. Winters, Conrad A. Nervig (*King Solomon's Mines*); Sound Recording: Twentieth Century-Fox Sound Department (*All about Eve*).

Documentary: *The Titan: Story of Michelangelo*; Documentary Short Subject: *Why Korea?*; One-Reel Short Subject: *Granddad of Races*; Two-Reel Short Subject: *In Beaver Valley*; Animated Short Subject: *Gerald McBoing-Boing*.

SPECIAL AWARDS

George Murphy; Louis B. Mayer; *The Walls of Malapago* (France/Italy) (outstanding foreign-language film); Darryl F. Zanuck (Irving Thalberg Award).

Oscar officially recognized the East Coast affiliations of some movie stars this year. Nominees Jose Ferrer and Gloria Swanson were starring on Broadway in a revival of *Twentieth Century*, the Ben Hecht-Charles MacArthur satire on Hollywood. Since they could not leave their show, Ferrer announced he was hosting a birthday party for Swanson on Oscar night at New York's La Zambra restaurant. Fellow nominees and Gothamites Judy Holliday, Celeste Holm (*All about Eve*), and Sam Jaffe (*The Asphalt Jungle*) as well as Los Angelino George Cukor would also attend. With so many potential winners in the Big

Apple, the Academy arranged a radio hook-up to the Manhattan eatery. When Ferrer won, his acceptance speech was carried over the airwaves to the Pantages Theatre for the official Oscar ceremony. Photographers urged Holliday and Swanson to playfully grapple with a prop Oscar. They reluctantly complied. A few moments later when Holliday won, the radio connection had failed and only those at La Zambra heard her speech.

Meanwhile, back in L.A., Fred Astaire made an elegant master of ceremonies and Marilyn Monroe made her only Oscar appearance by presenting the Sound Award. Moments before her entrance, she burst into tears because her dress was torn. Some quick mending and she was on. Handsome leading man John Lund (*To Each His Own, A Foreign Affair*) hid his good looks when he provided radio commentary. Television had not yet invaded Tinseltown or the Oscars.

But another menace was creeping into Hollywood. Red-baiting and Communist witch-hunting had made deep inroads in the film community. Both winners of the leading acting Oscars had come under the bright glare of suspicion for ultra-leftist sympathies. Judy Holliday was one of 151 performers named in the publication *Red Channels* as having Communists leanings. She was invesitaged by the FBI and given a "clean" bill of political health. Jose Ferrer was subpoened by the House Un-American Activities Committee soon after being nominated. He responded by taking out trade ads stating he had never been a Communist or a sympathizer. Neither star suffered any permanent damage to their careers, but many others would not be so lucky.

NATIONAL BOARD OF REVIEW

Picture: *Sunset Boulevard*; Actor: Alec Guinness (*Kind Hearts and Coronets*); Actress: Gloria Swanson (*Sunset Boulevard*); Director: John Huston (*The Asphalt Jungle*); Foreign-Language Film: *The Titan* (Italy).

TEN BEST FILMS (AMERICAN)

Sunset Boulevard, All about Eve, The Asphalt Jungle, The Men, Edge of Doom, 12 O'Clock High, Panic in the Streets, Cyrano de Bergerac, No Way Out, Stage Fright.

e Titan (Italy), *Whisky Galore* (Britain), *The*
bird Man (Britain), *Kind Hearts and Coronets*
Britain), *Paris 1900* (France).

NEW YORK FILM CRITICS CIRCLE

Picture: *All about Eve*; Actor: Gregory Peck (*12
O'Clock High*); Actress: Bette Davis (*All about Eve*);
Director: Joseph L. Mankiewicz (*All about Eve*);
Foreign-Language Film: *The Ways of Love* (France/
Italy).

The Film Critics awards were presented in a private
ceremony rather than the announced public one at
Radio City Music Hall. The reason for the switch?
Fear of picketing by the Catholic Church. The subject of the protest? *The Miracle*, one of three short
films which made up *The Ways of Love*, an anthology movie chosen by the Circle as best foreign
work. Cardinal Spellman had declared *The Miracle*
blasphemous. The picture's director Roberto
Rossellini would again encounter censure from
America several years later when he embarked on
an affair with the married film star Ingrid
Bergman.

HOLLYWOOD FOREIGN PRESS ASSOCIATION GOLDEN GLOBE AWARDS

Picture (Drama): *Sunset Boulevard*; Actor (Drama):
Jose Ferrer (*Cyrano de Bergerac*); Actress (Drama):
Gloria Swanson (*Sunset Boulevard*); Actor
(Comedy or Musical): Fred Astaire (*Three Little
Words*); Actress (Comedy or Musical): Judy
Holliday (*Born Yesterday*); Supporting Actor:
Edmund Gwenn (*Mister 880*); Supporting
Actress: Josephine Hull (*Harvey*); Most Promising
Newcomer: Gene Nelson (*Tea for Two*); Director:
Billy Wilder (*Sunset Boulevard*); Screenplay: Joseph
Mankiewicz (*All about Eve*); Musical Score: Franz
Waxman (*Sunset Boulevard*); Cinematography:
color—Robert Surtees (*King Solomon's Mines*),
black and white—Frank Planer (*Cyrano de
Bergerac*); Film Promoting International
Understanding: *Broken Arrow*; World Film Favorite
(Male): Gregory Peck; World Film Favorite
(Female): Jane Wyman.

CANNES FILM FESTIVAL

Due to a lack of funds, the Cannes Festival was not
held this year.

1951

ACADEMY AWARDS (OSCARS)

PICTURE
An American in Paris
Decision before Dawn
A Place in the Sun
Quo Vadis
A Streetcar Named Desire

An American in Paris, MGM's lavish musical featuring inventive choreography from Gene Kelly
and a pastiche score of songs by the Gershwin
brothers, was the unexpected best Picture Oscar
winner. It beat out more heavily favored dramas—
A Place in the Sun (the National Board of Review's
choice) and *A Streetcar Named Desire* (the New
York Film Critics' pick for best picture).

Several critics blasted the Academy for giving its
top prize to a "frivolous" musical and many
claimed MGM's large block of votes was responsible for the win. *The Hollywood Reporter* called the
griping "hogwash. The best picture ALWAYS wins
and it's made no difference whether that best was
from the largest or the smallest studio."

ACTOR
Humphrey Bogart (*The African Queen*)
Marlon Brando (*A Streetcar Named Desire*)
Montgomery Clift (*A Place in the Sun*)
Arthur Kennedy (*Bright Victory*)
Frederic March (*Death of a Salesman*)

Humphrey Bogart had always publicly scoffed at
awards, stating the only way to tell who was best
was to have all the nominees play Hamlet and then
pick the winner. Privately, he hired a press agent to
launch a campaign to remind voters about his
long, and so far Oscarless, career. Bogie went to the
awards expecting Marlon Brando to win for his
earthy, animalistic Stanley Kowalski in *A Streetcar
Named Desire*. But the iconoclastic Brando had not

participated in any Oscar publicity and Bogart took home the coveted statuette.

ACTRESS
Katharine Hepburn (*The African Queen*)
Vivien Leigh (*A Streetcar Named Desire*)
Eleanor Parker (*Detective Story*)
Shelley Winters (*A Place in the Sun*)
Jane Wyman (*The Blue Veil*)

A Streetcar Named Desire, based on Tennessee Williams' award-winning play, was the first film to win three acting awards. Of the winners only one was present at the ceremony. Both Vivien Leigh, who played the faded Southern belle Blanche DuBois, and Kim Hunter, who played her more practical sister Stella, were in New York—Leigh on Broadway with her husband Laurence Olivier and Hunter at home in Greenwich Village playing cards with her husband and friends. Both heard the results over the radio. Greer Garson accepted for Leigh and Bette Davis did the same for Hunter. Karl Malden (Blanche's suitor Mitch) was on hand in Hollywood to pick up his Oscar.

SUPPORTING ACTOR
Leo Genn (*Quo Vadis*)
Karl Malden (*A Streetcar Named Desire*)
Kevin McCarthy (*Death of a Salesman*)
Peter Ustinov (*Quo Vadis*)
Gig Young (*Come Fill the Cup*)

SUPPORTING ACTRESS
Joan Blondell (*The Blue Veil*)
Mildred Dunnock (*Death of a Salesman*)
Lee Grant (*Detective Story*)
Kim Hunter (*A Streetcar Named Desire*)
Thelma Ritter (*The Mating Season*)

DIRECTOR
John Huston (*The African Queen*)
Elia Kazan (*A Streetcar Named Desire*)
Vincente Minnelli (*An American in Paris*)
George Stevens (*A Place in the Sun*)
William Wyler (*Detective Story*)

MOTION PICTURE STORY
Budd Boetticher, Ray Nazarro (*The Bullfighter and the Lady*)

Paul Dehn, James Bernard (*Seven Days to Noon*)
Alfred Hayes, Stewart Stern (*Teresa*)
Oscar Millard (*The Frogmen*)
Robert Riskin, Liam O'Brian (*Here Comes the Groom*)

SCREENPLAY
James Agee, John Huston (*The African Queen*)
Jacques Natanson, Max Ophuls (*La Ronde*)
Michael Wilson, Harry Brown (*A Place in the Sun*)
Tennessee Williams (*A Streetcar Named Desire*)
Philip Yordan, Robert Wyler (*Detective Story*)

STORY AND SCREENPLAY
Philip Dunn (*David and Bathsheba*)
Clarence Greene, Russell Rouse (*The Well*)
Alan Jay Lerner (*An American in Paris*)
Robert Pirosh (*Go for Broke!*)
Billy Wilder, Lesser Samuels, Walter Newman (*The Big Carnival*)

OTHER AWARDS
Score of a Dramatic or Comedy Picture: Franz Waxman (*A Place in the Sun*); Score of a Musical Picture: Johnny Green, Saul Chaplin (*An American in Paris*); Song: "In the Cool, Cool, Cool of the Evening" from *Here Comes the Groom*, music by Hoagy Carmichael, lyrics by Johnny Mercer; Cinematography: color—Alfred Gilks, John Alton (*An American in Paris*), black and white—William C. Mellor (*A Place in the Sun*); Art Direction: color—Cedric Gibbons, Preston Ames, Edwin B. Willis, Keogh Gleason (*An American in Paris*), black and white—Richard Day, George James Hopkins (*A Streetcar Named Desire*); Costume Design: color—Orry-Kelly, Walter Plunkett, Irene Sharaff (*An American in Paris*), black and white—Edith Head (*A Place in the Sun*); Film Editing: William Hornbeck (*A Place in the Sun*); Sound Recording: Douglas Shearer (*The Great Caruso*); Special Effects: *When Worlds Collide*.

Documentary: *Kon-Tiki*; Documentary Short Subject: *Benjy*; One-Reel Short Subject: *World of Kids*; Two-Reel Short Subject: *Nature's Half-Acre*; Animated Short Subject: *Two Mousketeers*.

SPECIAL AWARDS

Gene Kelly; *Rashomon* (Japan) (outstanding foreign-language film); Arthur Freed (Irving Thalberg Award).

Host Danny Kaye requested winners to keep their acceptance speeches short. "In the past, various subtleties have been used," he joked in his opening monologue written for him by his wife Sylvia Fine, "trapdoors, disappearing microphones, an ex-blocker from Penn State. To no avail…the Academy asks that your speech be no longer than the movie itself."

Academy president Charles Brackett opened the ceremony by claiming that movies had met the challenge of the new medium television with serious, adult films like *A Place in the Sun* and *A Streetcar Named Desire*. By the next year, the large and small screens would be making an unlikely alliance when the Oscars would be telecast for the first time.

NATIONAL BOARD OF REVIEW

Picture: *A Place in the Sun*; Actor: Richard Basehart (*Fourteen Hours*); Actress: Jan Sterling (*The Big Carnival*); Director: Akira Kurosawa (*Rashomon*); Screenplay: T. E. B. Clark (*The Lavendar Hill Mob*); Foreign Film: *Rashomon*.

BEST AMERICAN FILMS

A Place in the Sun, Red Badge of Courage, An American in Paris, Death of a Salesman, Detective Story, A Streetcar Named Desire, Decision before Dawn, Strangers on a Train, Quo Vadis, Fourteen Hours.

BEST FOREIGN FILMS

Rashomon (Japan), *The River* (India), *Miracle in Milan* (Italy), *Kon-Tiki* (Norway/Sweden), *The Browning Version* (Britain).

NEW YORK FILM CRITICS CIRCLE

Picture: *A Streetcar Named Desire*; Actor: Arthur Kennedy (*Bright Victory*); Actress: Vivien Leigh (*A Streetcar Named Desire*); Director: Elia Kazan (*A Streetcar Named Desire*); Foreign Film: *Miracle in Milan*.

Excerpts from the Critics Circle ceremony were broadcast on Ed Sullivan's *Toast of the Town* TV show.

HOLLYWOOD FOREIGN PRESS ASSOCIATION GOLDEN GLOBE AWARDS

Picture (Drama): *A Place in the Sun*; Picture (Comedy or Musical): *An American in Paris*; Actor (Drama): Frederic March (*Death of a Salesman*); Actress (Drama): Jane Wyman (*The Blue Veil*); Actor (Comedy/Musical): Danny Kaye (*On the Riviera*); Actress (Comedy/Musical): June Allyson (*Too Young to Kiss*); Supporting Actor: Peter Ustinov (*Quo Vadis*); Supporting Actress: Kim Hunter (*A Streetcar Named Desire*); Most Promising Newcomer (Male): Kevin McCarthy (*Death of a Salesman*); Most Promising Newcomer (Female): Pier Angeli (*Teresa*); Director: Laslo Benedek (*Death of a Salesman*); Screenplay: Robert Buckner (*Bright Victory*); Musical Score: Victor Young (*September Affair*); Cinematography: color—Robert Surtees, William V. Skall (*Quo Vadis*), black and white—Frank Planer (*Death of a Salesman*); Film Promoting International Understanding: *The Day the Earth Stood Still*.

SPECIAL AWARD

Cecil B. DeMille (Cecil B. DeMille Award).

CANNES FILM FESTIVAL

Grand Prix (tie): *Miracle in Milan* and *Miss Julie* (Sweden); Actor: Michael Redgrave (*The Browning Version*); Actress: Bette Davis (*All about Eve*); Director: Luis Bunuel (*Los Olvidados*) (Mexico); Special Jury Prizes: *All about Eve* and *The Browning Version*.

1952

ACADEMY AWARDS (OSCARS)

PICTURE

The Greatest Show on Earth
High Noon

Ivanhoe
Moulin Rogue
The Quiet Man

For the second year in a row, the best Picture Oscar went to a splashy, "entertainment-for-its-own sake" crowd-pleaser over a deeper drama. Cecil B. DeMille's melodramatic circus epic *The Greatest Show on Earth* defeated *High Noon*, perhaps the best Western ever made. *Noon* incisively tells the story of a nonconformist sherriff (Gary Cooper) deserted by the cowardly townspeople he has sworn to protect when a trio of desperados come gunning for him. The real-life story of the picture's screenwriter Carl Foreman soon paralleled his script when he was subpoenaed to testify before the House Un-American Activities Committee. The author refused and rabid anti-Communist gossip columnist Hedda Hopper mounted a successful campaign to blacklist him. Thus, *Show* beat out *Noon*. Foreman, unemployable in Hollywood, moved to England and staged a comeback with *The Bridge on the River Kwai* (1957), which did receive a best Picture Oscar.

ACTOR
Marlon Brando (*Viva Zapata!*)
Gary Cooper (*High Noon*)
Kirk Douglas (*The Bad and the Beautiful*)
Jose Ferrer (*Moulin Rouge*)
Alec Guinness (*The Lavender Hill Mob*)

Ironically, the absent Gary Cooper's award was accepted by John Wayne, one of the Hollywood right-wingers who publicly blasted Foreman for his anti-HUAC stand. Wayne even went so far as to joke that he wished he had gotten the lead in *High Noon* instead of Cooper. But would the Duke have worked with an accused Communist sympathizer?

ACTRESS
Shirley Booth (*Come Back, Little Sheba*)
Joan Crawford (*Sudden Fear*)
Bette Davis (*The Star*)
Julie Harris (*The Member of the Wedding*)
Susan Hayward (*With a Song in My Heart*)

Shirley Booth tripped on her way up the stairs of New York's Century Theatre to accept her Oscar. The actress was then appearing on Broadway in

The Time of the Cuckoo and attended the Oscar East Coast ceremony. Her winning performance was for the slatternly housewife in William Inge's *Come Back, Little Sheba*, a Tony-winning role she created on Broadway. After the ceremony, she spoke to reporters and stated she felt it wasn't fair that she won because "there is all the difference in the world playing a character more than a thousand times, as I did, and getting your lines on the set in the morning and having to face the camera with them in the afternoon."

Booth was the first of many Oscar winners who originated their roles on stage and received Tony Awards for them, including Yul Brynner (*The King and I*), Anne Bancroft (*The Miracle Worker*), Rex Harrison (*My Fair Lady*), Jack Albertson (*The Subject Was Roses*), Paul Scofield (*A Man for All Seasons*), and Joel Grey (*Cabaret*).

SUPPORTING ACTOR
Richard Burton (*My Cousin Rachel*)
Arthur Hunnicutt (*The Big Sky*)
Victor McLaglen (*The Quiet Man*)
Jack Palance (*Sudden Fear*)
Anthony Quinn (*Viva Zapata!*)

Anthony Quinn was in Mexico filming a Western with his fellow winner Gary Cooper. The award was accepted by his wife—the daughter of another Oscar recipient Cecil B. DeMille. Quinn was a surprise winner for his performance as the dissolute brother of Marlon Brando's Emiliano Zapata. *Variety* had predicted the prize would go to a new young leading man from Wales named Richard Burton.

SUPPORTING ACTRESS
Gloria Grahame (*The Bad and the Beautiful*)
Jean Hagen (*Singin' in the Rain*)
Colette Marchand (*Moulin Rouge*)
Terry Moore (*Come Back, Little Sheba*)
Thelma Ritter (*With a Song in My Heart*)

DIRECTOR
Cecil B. DeMille (*The Greatest Show on Earth*)
John Ford (*The Quiet Man*)
John Huston (*Moulin Rouge*)
Joseph L. Mankiewicz (*Five Fingers*)
Fred Zinnemann (*High Noon*)

MOTION PICTURE STORY

Edna and Edward Anhalt (*The Sniper*)
Frederic M. Frank, **Theodore St. John**,
    Frank Cavett (*The Greatest Show on Earth*)
Martin Goldsmith, Jack Leonard
    (*The Narrow Margin*)
Leo McCarey (*My Son John*)
Guy Tropser (*The Pride of St. Louis*)

SCREENPLAY

Carl Foreman (*High Noon*)
Roger MacDougall, John Dighton, Alexander
    Mackendrick (*The Man in the White Suit*)
Frank S. Nugent (*The Quiet Man*)
Charles Schnee (*The Bad and the Beautiful*)
Michael Wilson (*Five Fingers*)

STORY AND SCREENPLAY

Sydney Boehm (*The Atomic City*)
T. E. B. Clarke (*The Lavender Hill Mob*)
Ruth Gordon, Garson Kanin (*Pat and Mike*)
Terrence Rattigan (*Breaking the Sound Barrier*)
John Steinbeck (*Viva Zapata!*)

OTHER AWARDS

Score of a Dramatic or Comedy Picture: Dimitri
Tiomkin (*High Noon*); Score of a Musical Picture:
Alfred Newman (*With a Song in My Heart*); Song:
"High Noon (Do Not Forsake Me, Oh My
Darlin')" from *High Noon*, music by Dimitri
Tiomkin, lyrics by Ned Washington; Cinema-
tography: color—Winton C. Hoch, Archie Short
(*The Quiet Man*), black and white—Robert
Surtees (*The Bad and the Beautiful*); Art
Direction: color—Paul Sheriff, Marcel Vertes
(*Moulin Rouge*), black and white—Cedric
Gibbons, Edward Carfagno, Edwin B. Willis,
Keogh Gleason (*The Bad and the Beautiful*);
Costume Design: color—Marcel Vertes (*Moulin
Rouge*), black and white—Helen Rose (*The Bad
and the Beautiful*); Film Editing: Elmo Williams,
Harry Gerstad (*High Noon*); Sound Recording:
London Film Sound Department (*Breaking the
Sound Barrier*); Special Effects: *Plymouth
Adventure*.

Documentary: *The Sea around Us*;
Documentary Short Subject: *Neighbors*; One-Reel
Short Subject: *Light in the Window*; Two-Reel

Short Subject: *Water Birds*; Animated Short
Subject: *Johann Mouse*.

SPECIAL AWARDS

Cinematographer George Alfred Mitchell;
producer Jospeh M. Schenck; Merion C. Cooper
for innovations and contributions to the motion
picture industry; Bob Hope; Harold Lloyd;
Forbidden Games (France) (outstanding foreign-
language film); Cecil B. DeMille (Irving Thalberg
Award).

Long regarded as an enemy, television finally got
together with the movies on March 19, 1953,
when the 1952 Oscars were presented over the
video airwaves for the first time. It was a shotgun
marriage made of necessity. Four major studios—
Columbia, Republic, Universal-International, and
Warner Brothers—announced they were no longer
backing the Oscars. Before Academy president
Charles Brackett could wring his hands too much,
RCA bought the rights to broadcast the ceremony
over its network NBC.

Bob Hope had not hosted the show since 1946
because he had defected to TV. He was invited
back to emcee the Hollywood event at the Pantages
Theatre. Former Academy president Conrad Nagel
performed similar duties at the Century Theatre in
New York where nominees with East Coast commitments could attend. Via transcontinental hook-
up, TV audiences were switched back and forth
from Los Angeles to the Big Apple. As it turned
out there were only two winners in Gotham—best
Actress Shirley Booth and Boris Vermont, producer
of the winning One-Reel Short Subject.

Entertainment included the staples we have all
come to know and dread: performances of the
nominated songs, stale topical jokes, and a parade
of previous winners including the second best
Actress Mary Pickford who presented the best
Picture Oscar to her former stage co-star Cecil B.
DeMille.

Bosley Crowther of *The New York Times* admitted the first Oscar telecast was "as neat and successful a maneuver of a publicity stunt as has happened
in years," but called the program "pedestrian and
conventional." But the ratings were spectacular.
The show drew the highest TV audience ever. As
producers had feared, the box office take for that

night had dropped, but the free publicity for all the nominated pictures was judged worth the loss. Oscar and the "idiot box" were now eternally joined.

NATIONAL BOARD OF REVIEW

Picture: *The Quiet Man*; Actor: Ralph Richardson (*Breaking the Sound Barrier*); Actress: Shirley Booth (*Come Back, Little Sheba*); Director: David Lean (*Breaking the Sound Barrier*); Foreign Film: *Breaking the Sound Barrier* (Britain).

BEST AMERICAN FILMS
The Quiet Man, High Noon, Limelight, Five Fingers, The Snows of Kilimanjaro, The Thief, The Bad and the Beautiful, Singin' in the Rain, Above and Beyond, My Son John.

BEST FOREIGN FILMS
Breaking the Sound Barrier (Britain), *The Man in the White Suit* (Britain), *Forbidden Games* (France), *Beauty and the Devil* (Italy/France), *Where No Vultures Fly* (Britain).

NEW YORK FILM CRITICS CIRCLE

Picture: *High Noon*; Actor: Ralph Richardson (*Breaking the Sound Barrier*); Actress: Shirley Booth (*Come Back, Little Sheba*); Director: Fred Zinnemann (*High Noon*); Foreign-Language Film: *Forbidden Games.*

HOLLYWOOD FOREIGN PRESS ASSOCIATION GOLDEN GLOBE AWARDS

Picture (Drama): *The Greatest Show on Earth*; Picture (Comedy or Musical): *With a Song in My Heart*; Actor (Drama): Gary Cooper (*High Noon*); Actress (Drama): Shirley Booth (*Come Back, Little Sheba*); Actor (Comedy/Musical): Donald O'Connor (*Singin' in the Rain*); Actress (Comedy/Musical): Susan Hayward (*With a Song in My Heart*); Supporting Actor: Millard Mitchell (*My Six Convicts*); Supporting Actress: Katy Jurado (*High Noon*); Most Promising Newcomer (Male): Richard Burton (*My Cousin Rachel*); Most Promising Newcomer (Female): Colette Marchand (*Moulin Rouge*); Director: Cecil B. DeMille (*The Greatest Show on Earth*); Screenplay: Michael Wilson (*Five Fingers*); Musical Score: Dimitri Tiomkin (*High Noon*); Cinematography: color— George Barnes, J. Peverell Marley (*The Greatest Show on Earth*), black and white—Floyd Crosby (*High Noon*); Film Promoting International Understanding: *Anything Can Happen*; World Film Favorite (Male): John Wayne; World Film Favorite (Female): Susan Hayward.

SPECIAL AWARDS

Walt Disney (Cecil B. DeMille Award); Brandon de Wilde (*The Member of the Wedding*), Francis Kee Teller (*Navajo*) (outstanding juvenile actors).

CANNES FILM FESTIVAL

Grand Prix (tie): *Two Pennyworth of Hope* (Italy) and *Othello* (Morocco); Actor: Marlon Brando (*Viva Zapata!*); Actress: Lee Grant (*Detective Story*); Director: Christian-Jaque (*Fanfan La Tulipe*) (France); Special Jury Prize: *Nous Sommes Tous des Assassins* (France).

ACADEMY AWARDS (OSCARS)

PICTURE
From Here to Eternity
Julius Caesar
The Robe
Roman Holiday
Shane

Columbia's *From Here to Eternity*, based on James Jones' best-selling novel of life on a pre-Pearl Harbor Army base in Hawaii, tied *Gone with the Wind*'s record of eight Oscars and thirteen nominations.

ACTOR
Marlon Brando (*Julius Caesar*)
Richard Burton (*The Robe*)
Montgomery Clift (*From Here to Eternity*)
William Holden (*Stalag 17*)
Burt Lancaster (*From Here to Eternity*)

ACTRESS
Leslie Caron (*Lili*)
Ava Gardner (*Mogambo*)
Audrey Hepburn (*Roman Holiday*)
Deborah Kerr (*From Here to Eternity*)
Maggie McNamara (*The Moon Is Blue*)

Like Shirley Booth the year before, Audrey Hepburn received her Oscar for her first film while performing on Broadway. After finishing the evening performance as a water sprite in *Ondine*, Hepburn was rushed by police escort to the Century Theatre. The play had started ten minutes early and the intermission was cut by five minutes in order to get Hepburn to the New York Oscar site. She removed her stage make-up and wig in the car.

SUPPORTING ACTOR
Eddie Albert (*Roman Holiday*)
Brandon de Wilde (*Shane*)
Jack Palance (*Shane*)
Frank Sinatra (*From Here to Eternity*)
Robert Strauss (*Stalag 17*)

Oh, what a little Oscar can do. The career of crooner Frank Sinatra was in the doldrums with slumping record sales and few acting offers. When Eli Wallach dropped out of a supporting role in *From Here to Eternity*, the singer practically begged Columbia's Harry Cohn for the role. It was only after Sinatra's wife Ava Gardner personally wrote to Cohn that the mogul agreed to cast Frankie—for the low salary of $8,000. But the gamble more than paid off. The singer-actor got to show off his rarely seen dramatic abilities and the Supporting Actor award revitalized his career.

SUPPORTING ACTRESS
Grace Kelly (*Mogambo*)
Geraldine Page (*Hondo*)
Marjorie Rambeau (*Torch Song*)
Donna Reed (*From Here to Eternity*)
Thelma Ritter (*Pickup on South Street*)

Donna Reed used her Oscar to get out of a confining contract with Columbia. With the exception of *From Here to Eternity*, she was dissatisfied with the roles the studio was assigning her. She would later quit films altogether to become the embodiment of the suburban housewife in her TV series *The Donna Reed Show*, quite a stretch from the prostitute she played in *Eternity*.

DIRECTOR
George Stevens (*Shane*)
Charles Walters (*Lili*)
Billy Wilder (*Stalag 17*)
William Wyler (*Roman Holiday*)
Fred Zinnemann (*From Here to Eternity*)

MOTION PICTURE STORY
Ray Ashley, Morris Engel, Ruth Orkin
   (*Little Fugitive*)
Alec Coppel (*The Captain's Paradise*)
Ian McLellan Hunter (*Roman Holiday*)
Louis L'Amour (*Hondo*) (ineligible)
Beirne Lay, Jr. (*Above and Beyond*)

Western author Louis L'Amour disqualified himself from the Motion Picture Story category by revealing to the Academy that his work was not original but based on a short story he had previously published in *Collier's* magazine.

In another complication, the winner Ian McLellan Hunter was absent from the ceremony. Conservative gossip columnist Mike Connolly angrily reported he was in Mexico dodging a subpoena from the Commie-hunters on the House Un-American Activities Committee. Years later, it would be revealed Hunter was a front for another blacklisted writer, Dalton Trumbo.

SCREENPLAY
Eric Ambler (*The Cruel Sea*)
Helen Deutsch (*Lili*)
A. B. Guthrie, Jr. (*Shane*)
Ian McLellan Hunter, John Dighton
   (*Roman Holiday*)
Daniel Taradash (*From Here to Eternity*)

STORY AND SCREENPLAY
Charles Brackett, Walter Reisch, Richard Breen
   (*Titanic*)
Betty Comden, Adolph Green (*The Band Wagon*)
Millard Kaufman (*Take the High Ground*)
Richard Murphy (*The Desert Rats*)
Sam Rolfe, Harold Jack Bloom (*The Naked Spur*)

OTHER AWARDS

Score of a Dramatic or Comedy Picture: Bronislau Kaper (*Lili*); Score of a Musical Picture: Alfred Newman (*Call Me Madame*); Song: "Secret Love" from *Calamity Jane*, music by Sammy Fain, lyrics by Paul Francis Webster; Cinematography: color—Loyal Griggs (*Shane*), black and white—Burnett Guffey (*From Here to Eternity*); Art Direction: color—Lyle Wheeler, George W. Davis, Walter M. Scott, Paul S. Fox (*The Robe*), black and white—Cedric Gibbons, Edward Carfagno, Edwin B. Willis, Hugh Hunt (*Julius Caesar*); Costume Design: color—Charles LeMaire, Emile Santiago (*The Robe*), black and white—Edith Head (*Roman Holiday*); Film Editing: William Lyon (*From Here to Eternity*); Sound Recording: Columbia Sound Department, John P. Livadary, sound director (*From Here to Eternity*); Special Effects: *War of the Worlds*.

Documentary: *The Living Desert*; Documentary Short Subject: *The Alaskan Eskimo*; One-Reel Short Subject: *The Merry Wives of Windsor Overture*; Two-Reel Short Subject: *Bear Country*; Animated Short Subject: *Toot, Whistle, Plunk, and Boom*.

Walt Disney added another four Oscars to his previous collection of eighteen. "This may be my year to retire," he joked upon receiving his fourth statuette of the evening.

SPECIAL AWARDS

Pete Smith for his series of short subjects; Twentieth Century-Fox for introducing CinemaScope; Joseph I. Breen for his management of the Motion Picture Code; Bell and Howell Company for pioneering and basic achievements in the motion picture industry; George Stevens (Irving Thalberg Award).

For his second year on television, Oscar once again split the broadcast between Hollywood and New York (Audrey Hepburn was the sole New York winner). Because the program was being sponsored by Oldsmobile, Crysler spokesman Bob Hope was forced to bow out as host. Donald O'Connor was his replacement for the West Coast and Frederic March emceed from New York. The prepared patter did not go over well. ("On with the reading of the will," quipped O'Connor when a joke fell flat.)

The technological highlight of the evening was a split-screen effect in which the two hosts appeared to be talking to each other. In addition, there were remotes from Mexico and Philadelphia where the previous year's winners Gary Cooper and Shirley Booth made presentations for the new best Actress and best Actor. A new element was added to the program—live commercials for Oldsmobiles starring former Oscar host Paul Douglas, new TV star Betty White, and a gaggle of dancers.

Sounding like reviews of future Oscarcasts, *Life* magazine grumbled, "The production numbers were tired, the humor strained, and the commercials far too long."

NATIONAL BOARD OF REVIEW

Picture: *Julius Caesar*; Actor: James Mason (*Face to Face, The Desert Rats, The Man Between,* and *Julius Caesar*); Actress: Jean Simmons (*Young Bess, The Robe,* and *The Actress*); Director: George Stevens (*Shane*); Foreign Film: *A Queen Is Crowned* (Britain).

BEST AMERICAN FILMS

Julius Caesar, Shane, From Here to Eternity, Martin Luther, Lili, Roman Holiday, Stalag 17, The Little Fugitive, Mogambo, The Robe.

BEST FOREIGN FILMS

A Queen Is Crowned (Britain), *Moulin Rouge* (Britain), *The Little World of Don Camillo* (France/Italy), *Strange Decpetion* (Italy), *Conquest of Everest* (Britain).

NEW YORK FILM CRITICS CIRCLE

Picture: *From Here to Eternity*; Actor: Burt Lancaster (*From Here to Eternity*); Actress: Audrey Hepburn (*Roman Holiday*); Director: Fred Zinnemann (*From Here to Eternity*); Foreign-Language Film: *Justice Is Done* (France).

HOLLYWOOD FOREIGN PRESS ASSOCIATION GOLDEN GLOBE AWARDS

Picture (Drama): *The Robe*; Actor (Drama): Spencer Tracy (*The Actress*); Actress (Drama): Audrey Hepburn (*Roman Holiday*); Actor (Comedy or Musical): David Niven (*The Moon Is Blue*); Actress (Comedy or Musical): Ethel Merman (*Call Me Madam*); Supporting Actor: Frank Sinatra (*From Here to Eternity*); Supporting Actress: Grace Kelly (*Mogambo*); Most Promising Newcomers (Male): Hugh O'Brian, Steve Forrest, Richard Egan; Most Promising Newcomers (Female): Pat Crowley, Bella Darvi, Barbara Rush; Director: Fred Zinnemann (*From Here to Eternity*); Screenplay: Helen Deutsch (*Lili*); Film Promoting International Understanding: *Little Boy Lost*; Western Star: Guy Madison; Documentary of Historical Interest: *A Queen Is Crowned*; World Film Favorite (Male) (tie): Robert Taylor, Alan Ladd; World Film Favorite (Female): Marilyn Monroe.

SPECIAL AWARDS
Walt Disney (*The Living Desert*); producer Jack Cummings; Darryl F. Zanuck (Cecil B. DeMille Award).

CANNES FILM FESTIVAL

Grand Prix: *The Wages of Fear* (France/Italy); Actor: Charles Vanel (*The Wages of Fear*); Actress: Shirley Booth (*Come Back, Little Sheba*); Special Award: Walt Disney.

ACADEMY AWARDS (OSCARS)

PICTURE
The Caine Mutiny
The Country Girl
On the Waterfront
Seven Brides for Seven Brothers
Three Coins in the Fountain

Bucking the trend toward Technicolor, wide-screen epics, Oscar continued to honor regular-sized, black and white dramas. *On the Waterfront*, an independent film shot for the low budget of $800,000 on location in Hoboken, New Jersey, won eight Oscars, tying the record set by *Gone with the Wind* and the previous year's *From Here to Eternity*.

Many saw the film as an attempt by director Elia Kazan and screenwriter Budd Schulberg to justify their friendly testimony before the House Un-American Activities Committee. *Waterfront's* hero Terry Malloy (Marlon Brando) cooperates with a panel investigating corruption in his longshoreman's union. Kazan and Schulberg named former colleagues as members of the Communist Party.

ACTOR
Humphrey Bogart (*The Caine Muntiny*)
Marlon Brando (*On the Waterfront*)
Bing Crosby (*The Country Girl*)
James Mason (*A Star Is Born*)
Dan O'Herlihy (*The Adventures of Robinson Crusoe*)

A cooperative Marlon Brando accepted his Oscar from Bette Davis. Her head shaved for the role of Queen Elizabeth I, Davis sported a bizarre skull cap. Backstage, Brando was friendly with the press and joked around with emcee Bob Hope. Eighteen years later, the iconoclastic Method actor would be anything but hospitable to Hollywood, refusing his second Oscar.

ACTRESS
Dorothy Dandridge (*Carmen Jones*)
Judy Garland (*A Star Is Born*)
Audrey Hepburn (*Sabrina*)
Grace Kelly (*The Country Girl*)
Jane Wyman (*Magnificent Obsession*)

"The greatest robbery since Brinks" was how Groucho Marx described Grace Kelly's surprise upset over Judy Garland. The glamorous Kelly won for her work as the drab wife of an alcoholic Bing Crosby in the screen adaptation of Clifford Odets' play *The Country Girl*. Judy Garland was starring in a lavish musical version of *A Star Is Born*, the old Janet Gaynor vehicle. The film was a comeback for the star after she was booted out of MGM when she proved unable to complete *Annie Get Your Gun*.

Two days before the ceremony, Garland gave birth to her son Joey Luft. Still hospitalized, she was unable to attend the awards. But the awards came to her. A camera crew quickly set up outside of her sickroom with Lauren Bacall standing by

Bette Davis presented Marlon Brando with his 1954 Oscar for *On the Waterfront*. Davis's odd skullcap was used to conceal her bald head, which she had shaved for the role of Elizabeth I in *The Virgin Queen*.

with a prop Oscar should the actress-singer win. When Kelly's name was read by William Holden, the crew packed up and left without a word.

Kelly's win should not have been that surprising. She had appeared in three other films that year—*Dial M for Murder, Rear Window,* and *Green Fire*. While a critical smash, *A Star Is Born* was a box-office disappointment and Warner Brothers refused to mount an Oscar campaign. In addition, Garland had a reputation of being difficult and wasting time on the set.

Two years later, Kelly left the film world to marry Prince Rainier of Monaco. Garland went back to concerts and personal appearances, not making another film for six years.

SUPPORTING ACTOR

Lee J. Cobb (*On the Waterfront*)
Karl Malden (*On the Waterfront*)
Edmond O'Brien (*The Barefoot Contessa*)
Rod Steiger (*On the Waterfront*)
Tom Tully (*The Caine Mutiny*)

SUPPORTING ACTRESS

Nina Foch (*Executive Suite*)
Katy Jurado (*Broken Arrow*)
Eva Marie Saint (*On the Waterfront*)
Jan Sterling (*The High and the Mighty*)
Claire Trevor (*The High and the Mighty*)

In order to avoid the battle between Kelly and

Garland, Eva Marie Saint, the leading lady of *On the Waterfront*, was promoted as a supporting actress. When she won, she was eight months pregnant. "I may have the baby right here," she laughed as she accepted the award from Frank Sinatra.

DIRECTOR
Alfred Hitchcock (*Rear Window*)
Elia Kazan (*On the Waterfront*)
George Seaton (*The Country Girl*)
William Wellman (*The High and the Mighty*)
Billy Wilder (*Sabrina*)

MOTION PICTURE STORY
François Boyer (*Forbidden Games*)
Jed Harris, Tom Reed (*Night People*)
Ettore Margadonna (*Bread, Love, and Dreams*)
Lamara Trotti (*There's No Business Like Show Business*)
Philip Yordan (*Broken Lance*)

SCREENPLAY
Albert Hackett, Frances Goodrich, Dorothy Kingsley (*Seven Brides for Seven Brothers*)
John Michael Hayes (*Rear Window*)
Stanley Roberts (*The Caine Mutiny*)
George Seaton (*The Country Girl*)
Billy Wilder, Samuel Taylor, Ernest Lehman (*Sabrina*)

STORY AND SCREENPLAY
Valentine Davis, Oscar Brodney (*The Glenn Miller Story*)
Joseph L. Mankiewicz (*The Barefoot Contessa*)
Norman Panama, Melvin Frank (*Knock on Wood*)
William Rose (*Genevieve*)
Budd Schulberg (*On the Waterfront*)

OTHER AWARDS
Scoring of a Dramatic or Musical Picture: Dimitri Tiomkin (*The High and the Mighty*); Score of a Musical Picture: Adolph Deutsch, Saul Chaplin (*Seven Brides for Seven Brothers*); Song: "Three Coins in the Fountain" from *Three Coins in the Fountain*, music by Jule Styne, lyrics by Sammy Cahn; Cinematography: color—Milton Krasner (*Three Coins in the Fountain*), black and white—Boris Kaufman (*On the Waterfront*); Art Direction: color—John Meehan, Emile Kuri (*20,000 Leagues under the Sea*), black and white—Richard Day (*On the Waterfront*); Costume Design: color—Sanzo Wada (*Gate of Hell*), black and white—Edith Head (*Sabrina*); Film Editing: Gene Milford (*On the Waterfront*); Sound Recording: Universal-International Sound Department (*The Glenn Miller Story*); Special Effects: *20,000 Leagues under the Sea*.

Documentary: *The Vanishing Prairie*; Documentary Short Subject: *Thursday's Children*; One-Reel Short Subject: *The Mechanical Age*; Two-Reel Short Subject: *A Time Out of War*; Animated Short Subject: *When Magoo Flew*.

SPECIAL AWARDS
Greta Garbo; Danny Kaye; Jon Whiteley and Vincent Winter (outstanding juvenile performances); *Gate of Hell* (Japan) (outstanding foreign-language film).

The first two Oscar shows had done so well in the ratings that NBC decided to telecast the announcements of the nominees. Jack Webb, the monotone-voiced Sargeant Joe Friday of TV's *Dragnet*, hosted the affair. Potential nominees gathered at various Hollywood hotspots including Romanoff's, Ciro's, the Coconut Grove, and NBC's Burbank Studio made up to look like a nightclub. Stars like Humphrey Bogart, Donna Reed, and Irene Dunne co-hosted with columnists Louella Parsons and Sheilah Graham and *Photoplay* editor Ann Higgenbothen.

As it turned out, many of the nominees weren't even present and those that were had little more to do than smile at the camera and hug the nearest person. The show was choatic and confused. "At the program's close," *The New York Times* reported, "Mr. Bogart, purposely killing time, enlivened matters by trying to chisel drinks from Romanoff." Despite universally negative reviews, the program was a hit with TV viewers and returned the following year.

As for the Oscar show itself, Bob Hope returned as host despite the fact that Oldsmobile was still the offical sponsor. Long commercials for the automobile punctuated the broadcast (Hope joked his clothes had gone out of style during one of them). Four-time Oscar nominee Thelma Ritter was the host for the New York end of the broadcast where Eva Marie Saint accepted her Oscar.

After the best Picture went to *On the Waterfront*, Hope told the television audience, "Get an Oldsmobile and drive to the movies. Good night from Oldsmobile." This meant the portion of the show Oldsmobile had paid for was over and there were still special awards to be presented. But most of those in the Pantages Theatre thought it meant the whole affair had concluded and got up to leave. They had to be stopped at the door and sent back to their seats. Many stations also thought the curtain had been wrung down and went to local programming.

NATIONAL BOARD OF REVIEW

Picture: *On the Waterfront*; Actor: Bing Crosby (*The Country Girl*); Actress: Grace Kelly (*The Country Girl, Dial M for Murder,* and *Rear Window*); Supporting Actor: John Williams (*Sabrina* and *Dial M for Murder*); Supporting Actress: Nina Foch (*Executive Suite*); Director: Renato Castellani (*Romeo and Juliet*); Foreign Film: *Romeo and Juliet* (Britain/Italy).

BEST AMERICAN FILMS
On the Waterfront, Seven Brides for Seven Brothers, The Country Girl, A Star Is Born, Executive Suite, The Vanishing Prairie, Sabrina, 20,000 Leagues under the Sea, The Unconquered, Beat the Devil.

BEST FOREIGN FILMS
Romeo and Juliet (Britain/Italy), *The Heart of the Matter* (Britain), *Gate of Hell* (Japan), *Diary of a Country Priest* (France), *The Little Kidnappers* (Britain), *Genevieve* (Britain), *Beauties of the Night* (France/Italy), *Mr. Hulot's Holiday* (France), *The Detective* (Britain), *Bread, Love, and Dreams* (Italy).

SPECIAL AWARDS
Michael Kidd for the choreography of *Seven Brides for Seven Brothers*; Machiyo Kyo for the modernization of Japanese acting in *Gate of Hell* and *Ugetsu*; *Hansel and Gretel* for its new methods of puppet animation.

NEW YORK FILM CRITICS CIRCLE

Picture: *On the Waterfront*; Actor: Marlon Brando (*On the Waterfront*); Actress: Grace Kelly (*The Country Girl, Rear Window,* and *Dial M for Murder*); Director: Elia Kazan (*On the Waterfront*); Foreign-Language Film: *Gate of Hell* (Japan).

HOLLYWOOD FOREIGN PRESS ASSOCIATION GOLDEN GLOBE AWARDS

Picture (Drama): *On the Waterfront*; Picture (Comedy or Musical): *Carmen Jones*; Actor (Drama): Marlon Brando (*On the Waterfront*); Actress (Drama): Grace Kelly (*The Country Girl*); Actor (Comedy or Musical): James Mason (*A Star Is Born*); Actress (Comedy or Musical): Judy Garland (*A Star Is Born*); Supporting Actor: Edmond O'Brien (*The Barefoot Contessa*); Supporting Actress: Jan Sterling (*The High and the Mighty*); Most Promising Newcomers (Male): Joe Adams, George Nader, Jeff Richards; Most Promsing Newcomers (Female): Shirley MacLaine, Kim Novak, Karen Sharpe; Director: Elia Kazan (*On the Waterfront*); Screenplay: Billy Wilder, Samuel Taylor, Ernest Lehman (*Sabrina*); Foreign Films: (four awards) *Genevieve* (England), *No Way Back* (Germany), *Twenty-Four Eyes* (Japan), *La Mujer de las Camelias* (Argentina); Cinematography: color—Joseph Ruttenberg (*Brigadoon*), black and white—Boris Kaufman (*On the Waterfront*); Film Promoting International Understanding: *Broken Lance*; World Film Favorite (Male): Gregory Peck; World Film Favorite (Female): Audrey Hepburn.

SPECIAL AWARDS
Jean Hersholt (Cecil B. DeMille Award); John Ford (Pioneer Award); Dr. Herbert Kalmus (Pioneer Award for Color); Dimitri Tiomkin for musical contribution; *Anywhere in Our Time* (special award for experimental film).

CANNES FILM FESTIVAL

Grand Prix: *Gate of Hell* (Japan); Special Jury Prize: Rene Clement (*Knave of Hearts*) (United Kingdom); International Prize: *The Last Bridge* (Austria), Maria Schell for performance in *The Last Bridge*; National Recognition Awards: *The Living*

Desert, Avant le Deluge (France), *Two Acres of Land* (India), *Neapolitan Carousel* (Italy), *Chronicle of Poor Lovers* (Italy), *Five Boys from Barska Street* (Poland), *The Great Adventure* (Sweden), *The Great Warrior, Skanderberg* (USSR); Special Recognition Award: *From Here to Eternity*.

ACADEMY AWARDS (OSCARS)

PICTURE
Love Is a Many-Splendored Thing
Marty
Mister Roberts
Picnic
The Rose Tattoo

The movies were becoming deeper in debt to TV. Not only were the video Oscarcasts providing the greatest publicity, but the 1955 best Picture Oscar went to a film based on a TV play. *Marty*, Paddy Chayefsky's simple story of a homely butcher and a plain schoolteacher, was a direct hit when it appeared on *Philco TV Playhouse* in 1953 with Rod Steiger and Nancy Marchand in the leads. Not expecting a film version to make money, actor Burt Lancaster and producer Harold Hecht bought the rights figuring they could make up the loss as a tax write-off. But *Marty* struck a chord with audiences and began to take off. The film's low budget allowed for a tremendous profit. The producers actually spent more on the film's Oscar campaign in the trades than on the production itself. Subsequent hit films based on TV plays included *Patterns, Twelve Angry Men, Requiem for a Heavyweight, The Miracle Worker, Days of Wine and Roses,* and *Judgement at Nuremberg.*

Marty was also the last of the small-scale, black-and-white Oscar best Pictures of the 1950s. Splashy, large-scale, color films *Around the World in 80 Days, The Bridge on the River Kwai, Gigi,* and *Ben-Hur* followed.

ACTOR
Ernest Borgnine (*Marty*)
James Cagney (*Love Me or Leave Me*)
James Dean (*East of Eden*)
Frank Sinatra (*The Man with the Golden Arm*)
Spencer Tracy (*Bad Day at Black Rock*)

Like Broderick Crawford before him, Ernest Borgnine was a little-recognized character actor who shot to Oscar glory, was cast in few leading film roles, and subsequently found his greatest recognition on television. (Borgnine achieved his household-name status through the World War II sitcom *McHale's Navy.*) He landed the title role in *Marty* when Rod Steiger who played it on TV was unavailable.

ACTRESS
Susan Hayward (*I'll Cry Tomorrow*)
Katharine Hepburn (*Summertime*)
Jennifer Jones (*Love Is a Many-Splendored Thing*)
Anna Magnani (*The Rose Tattoo*)
Eleanor Parker (*Interrupted Melody*)

Italian actress Anna Magnani was not present at the Pantages Theatre to accept the accolade for her fiery widow in *The Rose Tattoo*, a role Tennessee Williams had written especially for her. Maureen Stapleton played it on stage because Magnani was not confident enough in her English. She was proficient in her new language by the time the film was made.

The Magnani Oscar was accepted by her co-star Marisa Pavan. The winner was asleep in Rome. She was informed of the triumph by a reporter who disturbed her slumber by telephoning. Her immediate reaction to winning an Oscar: "If you are kidding, I will get up right away and kill you wherever you are."

SUPPORTING ACTOR
Arthur Kennedy (*Trial*)
Jack Lemmon (*Mister Roberts*)
Joe Mantell (*Marty*)
Sal Mineo (*Rebel without a Cause*)
Arthur O'Connell (*Picnic*)

SUPPORTING ACTRESS
Betsy Blair (*Marty*)
Jo Van Fleet (*East of Eden*)
Peggy Lee (*Pete Kelly's Blues*)
Marisa Pavan (*The Rose Tattoo*)
Natalie Wood (*Rebel without a Cause*)

DIRECTOR
Elia Kazan (*East of Eden*)
David Lean (*Summertime*)
Joshua Logan (*Picnic*)
Delbert Mann (*Marty*)
John Sturges (*Bad Day at Black Rock*)

MOTION PICTURE STORY
Joe Connelly, Bob Mosher (*The Private War of Major Benson*)
Daniel Fuchs (*Love Me or Leave Me*)
Jean Marsan, Henry Troyat, Jacques Perret, Henri Verneuil, Raoul Ploquin (*The Sheep Has Five Legs*)
Beirne Lay, Jr. (*Strategic Air Command*)
Nicholas Ray (*Rebel without a Cause*)

SCREENPLAY
Richard Brooks (*Blackboard Jungle*)
Paddy Chayefsky (*Marty*)
Daniel Fuchs, Isobel Lennart (*Love Me or Leave Me*)
Millard Kaufman (*Bad Day at Black Rock*)
Paul Osborn (*East of Eden*)

STORY AND SCREENPLAY
Betty Comden, Adolph Green (*It's Always Fair Weather*)
William Ludwig, Sonya Levien (*Interrupted Melody*)
Melville Shavelson, Jack Rose (*The Seven Little Foys*)
Milton Sperling, Emmet Lavery (*The Court-Martial of Billy Mitchell*)
Jacques Tati, Henri Marquet (*Mr. Hulot's Holiday*)

OTHER AWARDS
Score of a Dramatic or Comedy Picture: Alfred Newman (*Love Is a Many-Splendored Thing*); Score of a Musical Picture: Robert Russell Bennett, Jay Blackton, Adolph Deutsch (*Oklahoma!*); Song: "Love Is a Many-Splendored Thing" from *Love Is a Many-Splendored Thing*, music by Sammy Fain, lyrics by Paul Francis Webster; Cinematography: color—Robert Burks (*To Catch a Thief*), black and white—James Wong Howe (*The Rose Tattoo*); Art Direction: color—William Flannery, Jo Mielziner, Robert Priestley (*Picnic*), black and white—Hal Pereira, Tambi Larsen, Sam Comer, Arthur Krams (*The Rose Tattoo*); Costume Design: color—Charles LeMaire (*Love Is a Many-Splendored Thing*), black and white—Helen Rose (*I'll Cry Tomorrow*); Film Editing: Charles Nelson, William A. Lyon (*Picnic*); Sound Recording: Fred Haynes, Todd-AO Sound Department (*Oklahoma!*); Special Effects: *The Bridges at Toko-Ri*.

Documentary: *Helen Keller in Her Story*; Documentary Short Subject: *Men against the Arctic*; One-Reel Short Subject: *Survival City*; Two-Reel Short Subject: *The Face of Lincoln*; Animated Short Subject: *Speedy Gonzales*.

SPECIAL AWARD
Samurai, The Legend of Musashi (Japan) (oustanding foreign-language film).

Once again Oldsmobile footed the bill for the Oscar TV presentation on NBC. Chrysler must have put its foot down because Bob Hope was not permitted to host. His substitute was another screen comedian Jerry Lewis whose biggest laughs were gotten out of sight of the TV audience. While four long-winded Oldsmobile commercials of two minutes and fifteen seconds each were presented, Lewis drew howls from the audience in the Pantages Theatre by yawning, fighting drooping eyelids, and pretending to nod off from boredom. Claudette Colbert, Oscar winner for *It Happened One Night*, and director/writer Joseph L. Mankiewicz were hosts from the New York segment where *Marty* author Paddy Chayefsky was the only winner.

The nominations were again publicized with a video show of their own. Frederic March emceed from an NBC studio. Only six nominees were present who were asked to sign their names on a blackboard as if they were on *What's My Line?* The nomination-announcement show drew nasty notices from critics but huge ratings from a star-hungry public. Despite the numbers, the Academy scrapped the idea and the nominations were henceforth read at a news conference.

NATIONAL BOARD OF REVIEW
Picture: *Marty*; Actor: Ernest Borgnine (*Marty*); Actress: Anna Magnani (*The Rose Tattoo*);

Supporting Actor: Charles Bickford (*Not as a Stranger*); Supporting Actress: Marjorie Rambeau (*A Man Called Peter* and *The View from Pompey's Head*); Director: William Wyler (*The Desperate Hours*); Foreign Film: *The Prisoner* (Britain).

BEST AMERICAN FILMS
Marty, East of Eden, Mister Roberts, Bad Day at Black Rock, Summertime, The Rose Tattoo, A Man Called Peter, Not as a Stranger, Picnic, The African Lion.

BEST FOREIGN FILMS
The Prisoner (Britain), *The Great Adventure* (Sweden), *The Divided Heart* (Britain), *Les Diaboliques* (France), *The End of the Affair* (Britain).

NEW YORK FILM CRITICS CIRCLE

Picture: *Marty*; Actor: Ernest Borgnine (*Marty*); Actress: Anna Magnani (*The Rose Tattoo*); Director: David Lean (*Summertime*); Foreign-Language Film (tie): *Les Diaboliques* (France) and *Umberto D* (Italy).

This was the first tie for the foreign-language award in the Circle's history.

HOLLYWOOD FOREIGN PRESS ASSOCIATION GOLDEN GLOBE AWARDS

Picture (Drama): *East of Eden*; Picture (Comedy or Musical): *Guys and Dolls*; Actor (Drama): Ernest Borgnine (*Marty*); Actress (Drama): Anna Magnani (*The Rose Tattoo*); Actor (Comedy or Musical): Tom Ewell (*The Seven-Year Itch*); Actress (Comedy or Musical): Jean Simmons (*Guys and Dolls*); Supporting Actor: Arthur Kennedy (*The Trial*); Supporting Actress: Marisa Pavan (*The Rose Tattoo*); Most Promising Newcomers (Male): Ray Danton, Russ Tamblyn; Most Promising Newcomers (Female): Anita Ekberg, Virginia Shaw, Dana Wynter; Director: Joshua Logan (*Picnic*); Foreign Film (five winners): *Ordet* (Denmark), *Stella* (Greece), *Eyes of Children* (Japan), *Sons, Mothers, and a General* (Germany) *Dangerous Curves* (Brazil); Outdoor Drama: *Wichita*; Film Promoting International Understanding: *Love Is a Many-Splendored Thing*; Cecil B. DeMille Award:

Jack Warner; Hollywood Citizenship Award: Esther Williams; Posthumous Award for Best Dramatic Actor: James Dean; World Film Favorite (Male): Marlon Brando; World Film Favorite (Female): Grace Kelly.

CANNES FILM FESTIVAL

Golden Palm: *Marty*; Actor (tie): Ernest Borgnine (*Marty*) and Spencer Tracy (*Bad Day at Black Rock*); Actress: Betsy Blair (*Marty*); Director (tie): Jules Dassin (*Rififi*) (France) and Serge Vasiliev (*Heroes of Shipka*) (Bulgaria); Special Jury Prize: *The Lost Continent* (Italy).

Not only was *Marty* the first American film to win the Golden Palm, it was also the first to win both the top prize at Cannes and the best Picture Oscar.

ACADEMY AWARDS (OSCARS)

PICTURE
Around the World in 80 Days
Friendly Persuasion
Giant
The King and I
The Ten Commandments

After three years of black and white, normal-size best Pictures, Oscar went for a Technicolor, wide-screen, three-hour extravanganza: Mike Todd's *Around the World in 80 Days*. The flamboyant producer had conquered Broadway and was doing the same to Hollywood with his first picture. The epic featured dozens of exotic locales, cameos from every big name in the business from Noel Coward and Marlene Dietrich to Frank Sinatra and Red Skelton, and was presented on a reserved-seating, limited-screen basis. When Janet Gaynor announced the multi-million dollar adaptation of the Jules Verne classic had won the top Oscar, Todd kissed his wife Elizabeth Taylor, bounded down the aisle and then slowed his pace to a dignified walk by the time he got to he podium. Todd's rocket ride was short-lived. He died in a plane crash a year later.

(From left) Robert Newton, Cantinflas, Shirley MacLaine, and David Niven in *Around the World in 80 Days*, winner of the 1956 best Picture Award from the Oscars, National Board of Review, New York Film Critics Circle, and Hollywood Foreign Press Association.

ACTOR

Yul Brynner (*The King and I*)
James Dean (*Giant*)
Kirk Douglas (*Lust for Life*)
Rock Hudson (*Giant*)
Laurence Olivier (*Richard III*)

When he played the implacable Siamese monarch in the Broadway version of Rodgers and Hammerstein's musical *The King and I*, Yul Brynner was given supporting-player billing below the title. The real star was Gertrude Lawrence as the governess who tames the king. He received a "featured actor" Tony Award. During the course of the run, he was elevated to star status and for the movie was unquestionably the leading man. The fact that the bald sex symbol was also in two other high-profile pictures the same year—*Anastasia* and

The Ten Commandments—helped his Oscar chances.

ACTRESS

Carroll Baker (*Baby Doll*)
Ingrid Bergman (*Anastasia*)
Katharine Hepburn (*The Rainmaker*)
Nancy Kelly (*The Bad Seed*)
Deborah Kerr (*The King and I*)

Ingrid Bergman's *Anastasia* Oscar was a "Welcome Back" from Hollywood in the form of a statuette. The Swedish star had the left the film colony (and her husband and family) in 1949 for a love affair with the Italian director Roberto Rossellini and a continued career in Europe. She bore Rossellini's child without benefit of a marriage certificate. For this, Bergman was castigated in the American press and condemned in Congress. When they were preparing the film of the stage play *Anastasia*, a drama of an amnesiac who may or may not be the daughter of the murdered Tsar of Russia, Darryl Zanuck of Fox felt it was time for Bergman to return to American movies and cast her in the title role.

Anastasia was shot in Paris, where Bergman was residing on Academy Awards night. (She was playing in a French translation of Robert Anderson's Broadway hit *Tea and Sympathy*.) The star was in a bathtub in her hotel room when her son played a radio rebroadcast of the Oscar ceremony. Cary Grant accepted the award for his *Notorious* co-star and began his speech "Dear Ingrid, wherever you are."

"I'm in the bathtub," she replied.

SUPPORTING ACTOR
Don Murray (*Bus Stop*)
Anthony Perkins (*Friendly Persuasion*)
Anthony Quinn (*Lust for Life*)
Mickey Rooney (*The Bold and the Brave*)
Robert Stack (*Written on the Wind*)

Anthony Quinn was once again an upset winner. Just as he had beaten favorite Richard Burton in 1952, he triumphed over Robert Stack, the victor in *Variety*'s straw poll of Oscar voters. Quinn also starred in 1956's *La Strada*, the first competitive winner of the Foreign-Language Film Oscar.

SUPPORTING ACTRESS
Mildred Dunnock (*Baby Doll*)
Eileen Heckart (*The Bad Seed*)
Mercedes McCambridge (*Giant*)
Patty McCormick (*The Bad Seed*)
Dorothy Malone (***Written on the Wind***)

DIRECTOR
Michael Anderson (*Around the World in 80 Days*)
Walter Lang (*The King and I*)
George Stevens (*Giant*)
King Vidor (*War and Peace*)
William Wyler (*Friendly Persuasion*)

MOTION PICTURE STORY
Edward Bernds, Elwood Ullman (*High Society*)
   (withdrawn from final ballot)

Leo Katcher (*The Eddie Duchin Story*)
Robert Rich (*The Brave One*)
Jean-Paul Sartre (*The Proud and the Beautiful*)
Cesare Zavattini (*Umberto D*)

The 1956 writing nominations were a tangled mess. In the Motion Picture Story category, meant for original ideas for screenplays, the Academy committed one of its most embarrassing errors ever. The nomination of *High Society* was called into question since the screenplay was a musical version of *The Philadelphia Story*. Then it turned out that Edward Bernds and Elwood Ullman had not written the story for the musical *High Society*, but for another picture with the same name: a Bowery Boys comedy. The authors graciously withdrew from consideration.

   To further complicate matters, the winner of the award, Robert Rich, was actually a *nom de plume* for blacklistee Dalton Trumbo. This after the Academy passed a rule change which forbade awards to go to Communists or those who refused to testify before Congress about their political affiliations—the very reason for Trumbo's ouster from the industry.

   Amid all this confusion, the fact that French existentialist philosopher Jean-Paul Sartre was nominated was a mere sidelight.

ADAPTED SCREENPLAY
Norman Corwin (*Lust for Life*)
Fred Guiol, Ivan Moffat (*Giant*)
James Poe, **John Farrow**, **S. J. Perelman**
   (*Around the World in 80 Days*)
Tennessee Williams (*Baby Doll*)
(*Friendly Persuasion*) (writer Michael Wilson
   ineligible for nomination under Academy
   by-laws)

The controversy continued into the Adapted Screenplay division. Michael Wilson (*Friendly Persuasion*) was the first victim of the new anti-Commie Academy rule. He had refused to testify before the House Un-American Activities Committee and was therefore ineligible for an Oscar.

   There was also a dispute between the three authors of the *Around the World in 80 Days* script. Producer Mike Todd wanted the sole credit to go to humorist S. J. Perelman. James Poe and John

Farrow (the original director of the picture before Todd fired him) protested to the Writers Guild and forced the flamboyant producer to add their names to the credits. Poe accepted for himself and Farrow in Hollywood while Hermione Gingold picked up Perelman's award in New York. Gingold's dry reading of the absent humorist's remarks were the hit of the Oscarcast. She stated the only reason Perelman agreed to work on the film was the expressed understanding that it would never be shown.

ORIGINAL SCREENPLAY

Federico Fellini, Tullio Pinelli (*La Strada*)
Albert Lamorisse (*The Red Balloon*)
Robert Lewin (*The Bold and the Brave*)
William Rose (*The Lady Killers*)
Andrew L. Stone (*Julie*)

To cap the writing controversies and conundrums, the winner of the original screenplay prize—France's *The Red Balloon*—contained no dialogue.

FOREIGN-LANGUAGE FILM

The Captain of Kopenick (Germany)
Gervaise (France)
Harp of Burma (Japan)
La Strada (Italy)
Qivitoq (Denmark)

OTHER AWARDS

Score of a Dramatic or Comedy Picture: Victor Young (*Around the World in 80 Days*); Score of a Musical Picture: Alfred Newman, Ken Darby (*The King and I*); Original Song: "Whatever Will Be, Will Be (Que Sera, Sera)" from *The Man Who Knew Too Much*, music and lyrics by Jay Livingston, Ray Evans; Cinematography: color—Lionel Lindon (*Around the World in 80 Days*), black and white—Joseph Ruttenberg (*Somebody Up There Likes Me*); Art Direction: color—Lyle R. Wheeler, John DeCuir, Walter M. Scott, Paul S. Fox (*The King and I*), black and white—Cedric Gibbons, Malcolm F. Brown, Edwin B. Willis, F. Keogh Gleason (*Somebody Up There Likes Me*); Costume Design: color—Irene Sharaff (*The King and I*), black and white—Jean Louis (*The Solid Gold Cadillac*); Film Editing: Gene Riggiero, Paul Weatherwax (*Around the World in 80 Days*); Sound Recording: Carl Faulkner, sound director, Twentieth Century-Fox Sound Department (*The King and I*); Special Effects: John Fulton (*The Ten Commandments*).

Documentary: *The Silent World*; Documentary Short Subject: *The True Story of the Civil War*; One-Reel Short Subject: *Crashing the Water Barrier*; Two-Reel Short Subject: *The Bespoke Overcoat*; Animated Short Subject: *Mister Magoo's Puddle Jumper*.

SPECIAL AWARDS

Eddie Cantor; Y. Frank Freeman (Jean Hersholt Award); Buddy Adler (Irving Thalberg Award).

Oscar continued to be driven by the folks at Oldsmobile with Jerry Lewis in the Hollywood driver's seat and Celeste Holm piloting the New York podium. This year there were only three commercials instead of four. Aside from Hermione Gingold's humorous accepting for S. J. Perelman, critics had few kind words for the 1956 Oscars. "A million dollars worth of talent in search of a format," sneered *Variety*. *The New York Times* dubbed the ceremony "a colossally listless affair . . . a coaxial wake" and suggested showing clips from the nominated films. Future Oscarcasts would take the hint.

NATIONAL BOARD OF REVIEW

Picture: *Around the World in 80 Days*; Actor: Yul Brynner (*The King and I, Anastasia,* and *The Ten Commandments*); Actress: Dorothy McGuire (*Friendly Persuasion*); Supporting Actor: Richard Basehart (*Moby Dick*); Supporting Actress: Debbie Reynolds (*The Catered Affair*); Director: John Huston (*Moby Dick*); Foreign Film: *The Silent World* (France).

BEST AMERICAN FILMS

Around the World in 80 Days, Moby Dick, The King and I, Lust for Life, Friendly Persuasion, Somebody Up There Likes Me, The Catered Affair, Anastasia, The Man Who Never Was, Bus Stop.

BEST FOREIGN FILMS

The Silent World (France), *War and Peace* (USA/Italy), *Richard III* (Britain), *La Strada* (Italy), *Rififi* (France).

The Board chose a documentary, the French-made *The Silent World*, as its best foreign film. The feature was the first of many from aquatic explorer Jacques Costeau and also won the Oscar for Best Documentary and the Golden Palm at Cannes.

NEW YORK FILM CRITICS CIRCLE

Picture: *Around the World in 80 Days*; Actor: Kirk Douglas (*Lust for Life*); Actress: Ingrid Bergman (*Anastasia*); Director: John Huston (*Moby Dick*); Foreign-Language Film: *La Strada* (Italy).

Twentieth Century-Fox bought out three performances of the Paris production of *Tea and Sympathy* so that its star Ingrid Bergman could fly to New York and accept the Film Critics' prize. It was the actress's first trip to the US after her affair with Roberto Rossellini and she was greeted with mobs of fans and photographers.

HOLLYWOOD FOREIGN PRESS ASSOCIATION GOLDEN GLOBE AWARDS

Picture (Drama): *Around the World in 80 Days*; Picture (Comedy or Musical): *The King and I*; Actor (Drama): Kirk Douglas (*Lust for Life*); Actress (Drama): Ingrid Bergman (*Anastasia*); Actor (Comedy or Musical): Cantinflas (*Around the World in 80 Days*); Actress (Comedy or Musical): Deborah Kerr (*The King and I*); Supporting Actor: Earl Holliman (*The Rainmaker*); Supporting Actress: Eileen Heckart (*The Bad Seed*); Most Promising Newcomers (Male): John Kerr, Paul Newman, Tony Perkins; Most Promising Newcomers (Female): Carroll Baker, Jayne Mansfield, Natalie Wood; Foreign Newcomer (Male): Jacques Bergerac; Foreign Newcomer (Female): Taina Elg; Director: Elia Kazan (*Baby Doll*); Foreign-Language Foreign Films (five winners): *The White Reindeer* (Finland), *Before Sundown* (Germany), *The Girls in Black* (Greece), *Rose on the Arm* (Japan), *War and Peace* (USA/Italy); English-Language Foreign Film: *Richard III*; Film Promoting International Understanding: *Battle Hymn*; World Film Favorite (Male); James Dean; World Film Favorite (Female): Kim Novak.

SPECIAL AWARDS

Dimitri Tiomkin (recognition award for music); Edwin Schallert (for advancing the film industry); Ronald Reagen (Hollywood Citizenship award); Elizabeth Taylor (for consistent performance); Mervyn LeRoy (Cecil B. DeMille Award).

With *Around the World in 80 Days*, the Hollywood Foreign Press wanted it both ways. They voted it as Best Dramatic Picture, but gave one of its stars, Cantinflas, the award for Best Actor in a Comedy or Musical.

CANNES FILM FESTIVAL

Golden Palm: *The Silent World* (France); Actor: No award; Actress: Susan Hayward (*I'll Cry Tomorrow*); Director: Sergei Yutkevich (*Othello*) (USSR); Special Jury Prize: *The Mystery of Picasso* (France); Other Awards: *Smiles of a Summer Night* (Sweden) for poetic humor; *Pather Panchali* (India) for best "human document."

ACADEMY AWARDS (OSCARS)

PICTURE
The Bridge on the River Kwai
Peyton Place
Sayonara
Twelve Angry Men
Witness for the Prosecution

A British film with American financing, *The Bridge on the River Kwai* brilliantly depicted the ravages of war through the struggle of wills between two equally stubborn commanders—a Japanese prisoner-of-war commandant (Sessue Hayakawa) and his British counterpart (best Actor Alec Guinness).

Both spectacle and message picture, *Bridge* seemed a likely favorite for best Picture. The death of Harry Cohn, head of the picture's distributor Columbia, made the film a sentimental favorite as well.

ACTOR
Marlon Brando (*Sayonara*)
Anthony Franciosa (*A Hatful of Rain*)

Alec Guinness (*The Bridge on the River Kwai*)
Charles Laughton (*Witness for the Prosecution*)
Anthony Quinn (*Wild Is the Wind*)

ACTRESS
Deborah Kerr (*Heaven Knows, Mr. Allison*)
Anna Magnani (*Wild Is the Wind*)
Elizabeth Taylor (*Raintree County*)
Lana Turner (*Peyton Place*)
Joanne Woodward (*The Three Faces of Eve*)

Playing a Georgia housewife afflicted with multiple personalities in *The Three Faces of Eve* paid off big for Joanne Woodward. While everyone praised her performance, not all were enchanted with her Oscar dress. Going against the tradition of Hollywood glamour, the new Mrs. Paul Newman bought the material, designed, and made the gown herself, all for the cost of about $100. Self-appointed fashion czarina Joan Crawford condemned the young actress, saying, "Joanne Woodward is setting the cause of Hollywood glamour back 20 years by making her own clothes."

While Woodward was triumphing at a post-Oscar party, loser Lana Turner was being savagely beaten by her lover Johnny Stompanato for not taking him to the ceremony. Ten days later, Turner's daughter Cheryl stabbed Stompanato during another of his fights with her mother. The scandalous murder trial echoed Turner's recent Oscar-nominated, soap opera-ish film *Peyton Place*. Cheryl was acquitted of murder.

SUPPORTING ACTOR
Red Buttons (*Sayonara*)
Vittorio de Sica (*A Farewell to Arms*)
Sessue Hayakawa (*The Bridge on the River Kwai*)
Arthur Kennedy (*Peyton Place*)
Russ Tamblyn (*Peyton Place*)

SUPPORTING ACTRESS
Carolyn Jones (*The Bachelor Party*)
Elsa Lanchester (*Witness for the Prosecution*)
Hope Lange (*Peyton Place*)
Miyohsi Umeki (*Sayonara*)
Diane Varsi (*Peyton Place*)

DIRECTOR
David Lean (*The Bridge on the River Kwai*)

Joshua Logan (*Sayonara*)
Sidney Lumet (*Twelve Angry Men*)
Mark Robson (*Peyton Place*)
Billy Wilder (*Witness for the Prosecution*)

ORIGINAL SCREENPLAY
Federico Fellini, Ennio Flaiano, Tullio Pinelli (*Vitelloni*)
Leonard Gershe (*Funny Face*)
Barney Slater, Joel Kane, Dudley Nichols (*The Tin Star*)
George Wells (*Designing Woman*)
Ralph Wheelright, R. Wright Campbell, Ivan Goff, Ben Roberts (*Man of a Thousand Faces*)

ADAPTED SCREENPLAY
Pierre Boulle (*The Bridge on the River Kwai*)
John Michael Hayes (*Peyton Place*)
John Lee Mahin, John Huston (*Heaven Knows, Mr. Allison*)
Paul Osborn (*Sayonara*)
Reginald Rose (*Twelve Angry Men*)

Although he wrote the novel upon which the film was based, French author Pierre Boulle did not pen the screenplay for *The Bridge on the River Kwai*. He could not even write in English. When he won the British Academy Award for Best Screenplay, Boulle told the English audience he didn't know why he was honored because he didn't write the script.

The true scriptwriters, Carl Foreman and Michael Wilson, were both victims of the Hollywood blacklist and would have been ineligible for nominations under the Academy's no-pinko by-laws. Boulle was not present at the ceremony and Columbia starlet Kim Novak picked up the statuette. The Academy did not acknowledge Wilson and Foreman as the true winners until 1985. Both had died by that time and their widows accepted posthumous Oscars.

FOREIGN-LANGUAGE FILM
The Devil Came at Night (Germany)
Gates of Paris (France)
Mother India (India)
The Nights of Cabiria (Italy)
Nine Lives (Norway)

OTHER AWARDS

Orignal Score: Malcolm Arnold (*The Bridge on the River Kwai*); Song: "All the Way" from *The Joker's Wild*, music by James Van Heusen, lyrics by Sammy Cahn; Cinematography: Jack Hildyard (*The Bridge on the River Kwai*); Art Direction: Ted Haworth, Robert Priestley (*Sayonara*); Costume Design: Orry-Kelly (*Les Girls*); Film Editing: Peter Taylor (*The Bridge on the River Kwai*); Sound: George Groves, sound director, Warner Brothers Sound Department (*Sayonara*); Special Effects: Walter Rossi (*The Enemy Below*).

Documentary: *Albert Schweitzer*; Documentary Short Subject: No award given; Live-Action Short Subject: *The Wetback Hound*; Animated Short Subject: *Birds Anonymous*.

SPECIAL AWARDS

Charles Brackett for services to the Academy; B. B. Kahne for service to the motion picture industry; movie pioneer Gilbert M. Anderson; The Society of Motion Picture and Television Engineers; Samuel Goldwyn (Jean Hersholt Humanitarian Award).

Sponsorship of the Oscar telecast returned to the motion picture industry for the 1957 awards. There were no more long car commercials to interrupt the show. One star not too enthusiastic about the change was Spencer Tracy, who told columnist Joe Hyams, "What's wrong with the commercials? Do you think our producers and actors are attractive? I, for one, would rather look at a pretty Oldsmobile or a Thunderbird than some of them."

Since there was no longer a conflict of interest for Bob Hope, whose TV program was financed by a rival car manufacturer, Old Ski-Nose returned for his eighth stint as host. The first hour and fifteen minutes were emceed by James Stewart, Rosalind Russell, David Niven, and Jack Lemmon, with Hope taking over for the rest of the show.

Entertainment included a medley of past Oscar-winning songs. The highlight was a suggestive rendering of "Baby, It's Cold Outside" delivered by the sultry, sixty-five-year-old Mae West and the stolid, young Rock Hudson. Donald Duck was featured in a humorous short on the history of the movies. Burt Lancaster and Kirk Douglas warbled a satiric specialty number "It's Great Not To Be Nominated."

In an attempt to streamline the proceedings, several categories were combined. The divisions of Art Direction, Costume Design, and Cinematography into two separate awards for black-and-white and color were eliminated (but they would be back the following year). Awards for screenwriting were reduced from three to two and Live-Action Short Subjects and Musical Scoring from two to one. Despite the trimming, the program still ran long so Bette Davis's presentation of special awards was not broadcast. Davis angrily vented to the press that there was time enough for Donald Duck, but not for her.

The number of Oscar nominators was also cut back. Formerly, members of the various film guilds and Academy members could nominate while only Academy members voted for the winners. Now only those belonging to the Academy could nominate and vote. This reduced the nominating pool from about 15,000 to 1,800.

NATIONAL BOARD OF REVIEW

Picture: *The Bridge on the River Kwai*; Actor: Alec Guinness (*The Bridge on the River Kwai*); Actress: Joanne Woodward (*The Three Faces of Eve* and *No Down Payment*); Supporting Actor: Sessue Hayakawa (*The Bridge on the River Kwai*); Supporting Actress: Dame Sybil Thorndyke (*The Princess and the Showgirl*); Director: David Lean (*The Bridge on the River Kwai*); Foreign Film: *Ordet* (Denmark); Special Award: *Funny Face* for its photographic effects.

BEST AMERICAN FILMS
The Bridge on the River Kwai, Twelve Angry Men, The Spirit of St. Louis, Albert Schweitzer, Funny Face, The Bachelor Party, The Enemy Below, A Hatful of Rain, A Farewell to Arms.

BEST FOREIGN FILMS
Ordet (Denmark), *Gervaise* (France), *Torero!* (Mexico), *The Red Balloon* (France), *A Man Escaped* (France).

NEW YORK FILM CRITICS CIRCLE

Picture: *The Bridge on the River Kwai*; Actor: Alec Guinness (*The Bridge on the River Kwai*); Actress:

Deborah Kerr (*Heaven Knows, Mr. Allison*); Director: David Lean (*The Bridge on the River Kwai*); Foregin-Language Film: *Gervaise* (France).

HOLLYWOOD FOREIGN PRESS ASSOCIATION GOLDEN GLOBE AWARDS

Picture (Drama): *The Bridge on the River Kwai*; Picture (Comedy or Musical): *Les Girls*; Actor (Drama): Alec Guinness (*The Bridge on the River Kwai*); Actress (Drama): Joanne Woodward (*The Three Faces of Eve*); Actor (Comedy or Musical): Frank Sinatra (*Pal Joey*); Actress (Comedy or Musical): Kay Kendall (*Les Girls*); Supporting Actor: Red Buttons (*Sayonara*); Supporting Actress: Elsa Lanchester (*Witness for the Prosecution*); Most Promising Newcomers (Male): James Garner, John Saxon, Patrick Wayne; Most Promising Newcomers (Female): Sandra Dee, Carolyn Jones, Diane Varsi; Director: David Lean (*The Bridge on the River Kwai*); English-Language Foreign Film: *Woman in a Dressing Gown*; Foreign-Language Foreign Film (three winners): *The Confessions of Felix Krull* (Federal Republic of Germany), *Yellow Crow* (Japan), *Tizoc* (Mexico); Film Promoting International Understanding: *The Happy Road*; World Film Favorite (Male): Tony Curtis; World Film Favorite (Female): Doris Day.

SPECIAL AWARDS
Buddy Adler (Cecil B. DeMille Award); George Sidney (Best World Entertainment through Musical Films); Jean Simmons (Most Versatile Actress); Zsa Zsa Gabor (Most Glamourous Actress); Hugo Friedhofer (for bettering the standard of motion picture music); LeRoy Prinz (choreography); Bob Hope (Good Will Ambassador).

CANNES FILM FESTIVAL

Golden Palm: *Friendly Persuasion*; Actor: John Kitzmiller (*Valley of Peace*) (Yugoslavia); Actress: Giulietta Masina (*Nights of Cabiria*) (Italy); Director: Robert Bresson (*A Man Escaped*) (France); Screenplay: Grigori Chukhrai (*The 41st*) (USSR); Special Jury Prize (tie): *The Seventh Seal* (Sweden), *Kanal* (Poland).

OTHER AWARDS
Exceptional Mention: *Gautama the Buddha* (India); Romantic Documentary Prize: *Shiroi Sammyaku* (Japan) and *Qivitoq* (France).

ACADEMY AWARDS (OSCARS)

PICTURE
Auntie Mame
Cat on a Hot Tin Roof
The Defiant Ones
Gigi
Separate Tables

Gigi, a musical collaboration between Broadway songwriters Alan Jay Lerner and Frederic Loewe and Hollywood director Vincente Minnelli, dominated the 1958 Oscars with nine wins. The sweep broke the record of eight previously established by *Gone with the Wind* and later tied by *From Here to Eternity* and *On the Waterfront*.

ACTOR
Tony Curtis (*The Defiant Ones*)
Paul Newman (*Cat on a Hot Tin Roof*)
David Niven (*Separate Tables*)
Sidney Poitier (*The Defiant Ones*)
Spencer Tracy (*The Old Man and the Sea*)

ACTRESS
Susan Hayward (*I Want to Live!*)
Deborah Kerr (*Separate Tables*)
Shirley MacLaine (*Some Came Running*)
Rosalind Russell (*Auntie Mame*)
Elizabeth Taylor (*Cat on a Hot Tin Roof*)

Not only was her *I Want to Live!* Oscar a long-delayed triumph for Susan Hayward (she had lost four times before), it also spelled comeback for her producer Walter Wanger. A former Academy president and convict for shooting his wife's agent (non-fatally), Wanger was now back in the business thanks to Hayward's win.

SUPPORTING ACTOR
Theodore Bikel (*The Definat Ones*)
Lee J. Cobb (*The Brothers Karamazov*)
Burl Ives (*The Big Country*)
Arthur Kennedy (*Some Came Running*)
Gig Young (*Teacher's Pet*)

SUPPORTING ACTRESS
Peggy Cass (*Auntie Mame*)
Wendy Hiller (*Separate Tables*)
Martha Hyer (*Some Came Running*)
Maureen Stapleton (*Lonelyhearts*)
Cara Williams (*The Defiant Ones*)

British actress Wendy Hiller wasn't interested in praise for her performance as a lonely hotel-keeper in *Separate Tables*. She wanted to be sure her Oscar would translate into more job offers. "Never mind the honor," she told *The London News-Chronicle*, "although I'm sure it's very nice of them. I hope this award means cash—hard cash."

DIRECTOR
Richard Brooks (*Cat on a Hot Tin Roof*)
Stanley Kramer (*The Defiant Ones*)
Vincente Minnelli (*Gigi*)
Mark Robson (*The Inn of the Sixth Happiness*)
Robert Wise (*I Want to Live!*)

ORIGINAL SCREENPLAY
Paddy Chayefsky (*The Goddess*)
Nathan E. Douglas, **Harold Jacob Smith**
    (*The Defiant Ones*)
James Edward Grant, William Bowers
    (*The Sheepmen*)
Fay and Michael Kanin (*Teacher's Pet*)
Melville Shavelson, Jack Rose (*Houseboat*)

Once again, an Oscar for screenwriting went to a victim of the blacklist. Nathan E. Douglas was a pseudonym for Ned Young, a blacklistee. But before the nominations came out, the Academy removed its anti-Communist clause and Young was eligible. Ultraconservative gossip columnist Hedda Hopper fumed that all red-blooded, American movie writers should now return their Oscars. Nobody followed her advice.

ADAPTED SCREENPLAY
Richard Brooks, James Poe (*Cat on a
    Hot Tin Roof*)
Nelson Gidding, Don Mankiewicz
    (*I Want to Live!*)
Alec Guinness (*The Horse's Mouth*)
Alan Jay Lerner (*Gigi*)
Terrence Rattigan, John Gay (*Separate Tables*)

FOREIGN-LANGUAGE FILMS
Arms and the Man (Germany)
La Venganza (Spain)
My Uncle (France)
The Road a Year Long (Yugoslavia)
Big Deal on Madonna Street (Italy)

OTHER AWARDS
Score of a Dramatic or Comedy Picture: Dimitri Tiomkin (*The Old Man and the Sea*); Score of a Musical Picture: Andre Previn (*Gigi*); Song: "Gigi" from *Gigi*, music by Frederick Loewe, lyrics by Alan Jay Lerner; Cinematography: color—Joseph Ruttenberg (*Gigi*), black and white—Sam Leavitt (*The Defiant Ones*); Art Direction: William Horning, Preston Ames, Henry Grace, Keogh Gleason (*Gigi*); Costume Design: Cecil Beaton (*Gigi*); Film Editing: Adrienne Fazan (*Gigi*); Sound: Fred Hynes, sound director, Todd-AO Sound Department (*South Pacific*); Special Effects: Tom Howard (*Tom Thumb*).

Note: Cinematography went back to two awards (one for color, one for black-and-white), while Art Direction and Costume Design remained a single honor regardless of the film's color or lack thereof.

Documentary: *White Wilderness*; Documentary Short Subject: *AMA Girls*; Live-Action Short Subject: *Grand Canyon*; Animated Short Subject: *Knighty Knight Bugs*.

SPECIAL AWARDS
Maurice Chevalier; Jack L. Warner (Irving Thalberg Award).

While the previous year's Oscars were praised as one of the best in thirty years, the 1958 edition was blasted from coast to coast. *The New York Times* called it a "bewildering potpourri . . . a tasteless disaster, a forlorn study of glamour in a state of disarray." According to *Variety*, the show was "a new nadir in the use of the talent—plus said talent's indifference." Columnist Joe Hyams quoted one wag who described the event as "the greatest galaxy of stars every to be assembled under one goof." Hyams went on to report a crackpot had phoned in a threat to throw a bomb in the theater. "The bomb was the show itself. It ended 20 minutes too early and was 100 minutes too long," he explained.

The program did in fact finish early. Producer Jerry Wald was so frantic to get the program off the air on time; he cut too much and was left with twenty minutes of airtime to fill. Jerry Lewis, the last of six emcees (including Bob Hope) for the evening, ad-libbed like crazy and attempted to get the other stars to join him in a sing-along of "There's No Business Like Show Business." He came across looking like a drunken boor at a party. Loser Rosalind Russell coldly snubbed him and walked offstage. After long minutes of Lewis' shenanigans, NBC cut the feed and unreeled a short film on guns to fill the remaining time.

The Oscars were beginning to take on the status of divine monsterhood which surrounds them today. Each ceremony is an event so tacky, so gauche, so unapologetically crass, you have to watch it.

NATIONAL BOARD OF REVIEW

Picture: *The Old Man and the Sea*; Actor: Spencer Tracy (*The Old Man and the Sea* and *The Last Hurrah*); Actress: Ingrid Bergman (*The Inn of the Sixth Happiness*); Supporting Actor: Albert Salmi (*The Brothers Karamazov* and *The Bravados*); Supporting Actress: Kay Walsh (*The Horse's Mouth*); Director: John Ford (*The Last Hurrah*); Foreign Film: *Pather Panchali* (India).

BEST AMERICAN FILMS
The Old Man and the Sea, Separate Tables, The Last Hurrah, The Long Hot Summer, Windjammer, Cat on a Hot Tin Roof, The Goddess, The Brother Karamazov, Me and the Colonel, Gigi.

BEST FOREIGN FILMS
Pather Panchali (India), *The Red and the Black* (France/Italy), *The Horse's Mouth* (Britain), *My Uncle* (France), *A Night to Remember* (Britain).

SPECIAL CITATION
For the valor of Robert Donat's last performance in *The Inn of the Sixth Happiness*.

The Board continued to disagree with the Oscars. As in recent years, the choice for Best Picture (*The Old Man and the Sea*) and a majority of the acting winners (Ingrid Bergman, Albert Salmi, and Kay Walsh) weren't even nominated by the Academy.

NEW YORK FILM CRITICS CIRCLE

Picture: *The Defiant Ones*; Actor: David Niven (*Separate Tables*); Actress: Susan Hayward (*I Want to Live!*); Director: Stanley Kramer (*The Defiant Ones*); Screenplay: Nathan E. Douglas, Harold Jacob Smith (*The Defiant Ones*); Foreign-Language Film: *My Uncle* (France).

The Circle began rewarding screenwriting. But the award officially went to the film itself since, according to the critics, the credited authors weren't always the ones who actually wrote the entire script.

HOLLYWOOD FOREIGN PRESS ASSOCIATION GOLDEN GLOBE AWARDS

Picture (Drama): *The Defiant Ones*; Picture (Comedy): *Auntie Mame*; Picture (Musical): *Gigi*; Actor (Drama): David Niven (*Separate Tables*); Actress (Drama): Susan Hayward (*I Want to Live!*); Actor (Comedy or Musical): Danny Kaye (*Me and the Colonel*); Actress (Comedy or Musical): Rosalind Russell (*Auntie Mame*); Supporting Actor: Burl Ives (*The Big Country*); Supporting Actress: Hermione Gingold (*Gigi*); Most Promising Newcomers (Male): Bradford Dillman, John Gavin, Efrem Zimbalist, Jr.; Most Promising Newcomers (Female): Linda Cristal, Susan Kohner, Tina Louise; Director: Vincente Minnelli (*Gigi*); English-Language Foreign Film: *A Night to Remember*; Foreign-Language Foreign Film (three winners): *The Road a Year Long* (Yugoslavia), *The Girl and the River* (France), *The Girl Rose Marie* (Germany); Film Promoting International Understanding: *The Inn of the Sixth Happiness*; World Film Favorite (Male): Rock Hudson; World Film Favorite (Female): Deborah Kerr.

SPECIAL AWARDS
Two Eyes, Twelve Hands (Samuel Goldwyn Award); Maurice Chevalier (Cecil B. DeMille Award); David Ladd (outstanding juvenile performance); Shirley MacLaine (most versatile actress).

CANNES FILM FESTIVAL

Golden Palm: *The Cranes Are Flying* (USSR); Actor: Paul Newman (*The Long, Hot Summer*); Actress: collective prize for Eva Dahlbeck, Ingrid Thulin, Bibi Andersson, Barbro Ornas (*Brink of Life*) (Sweden); Director: Ingmar Bergman (*Brink of Life*); Screenplay: Mauro Bolognini (*Newlyweds*) (Italy); Special Jury Prize: *My Uncle* (France).

OTHER AWARDS
Documentary: *Bronze Faces* (Switzerland) and *Goha* (Tunisia); International Critics Prize: *Vengeance* (Spain).

The Cranes Are Flying was the first Soviet film to win the Golden Palm. The prize gave the film enough press to ensure an American release and the Cold-War USA got a look at everyday life behind the Iron Curtain.

1959

ACADEMY AWARDS (OSCARS)

PICTURE
Anatomy of a Murder
Ben-Hur
The Diary of Anne Frank
The Nun's Story
Room at the Top

The Oscar record of *Gigi* (nine) didn't last very long. The very next year the three-and-a-half-hour epic *Ben-Hur* raced past the musical with eleven wins. Many criticized this trend of "sweep-itis" in which a single picture grabbed the lion's share of awards. It eliminated the suspense when the same theme song kept playing over and over again.

ACTOR
Laurence Harvey (*Room at the Top*)

Charlton Heston (*Ben-Hur*)
Jack Lemmon (*Some Like It Hot*)
Paul Muni (*The Last Angry Man*)
James Stewart (*Anatomy of a Murder*)

The selection of Charlton Heston in the title role of *Ben-Hur* for Best Actor was another bone of contention. His best acting moments were taking off his tunic to expose an impressive physique and whipping his horse in the climactic chariot race. Jack Lemmon's hysterical drag turn, Laurence Harvey's complex social climber, and James Stewart's folksy yet foxy defense lawyer would have been better choices.

ACTRESS
Doris Day (*Pillow Talk*)
Audrey Hepburn (*The Nun's Story*)
Katharine Hepburn (*Suddenly, Last Summer*)
Simone Signoret (*Room at the Top*)
Elizabeth Taylor (*Suddenly, Last Summer*)

"I wanted to be dignified, but I can't," wept Simone Signoret at the Oscar podium. The French actress's emotive limning as a bored housewife engaging in an adulterous affair with cad Laurence Harvey had triumphed over Hollywood favorites. Insiders speculated that Elizabeth Taylor and both Hepburns had split the vote, allowing Signoret a clear path to victory.

SUPPORTING ACTOR
Hugh Griffith (*Ben-Hur*)
Arthur O'Connell (*Anatomy of a Murder*)
George C. Scott (*Anatomy of a Murder*)
Robert Vaughn (*The Young Philadelphians*)
Ed Wynn (*The Diary of Anne Frank*)

SUPPORTING ACTRESS
Hermione Baddeley (*Room at the Top*)
Susan Kohner (*Imitation of Life*)
Juanita Moore (*Imitation of Life*)
Thelma Ritter (*Pillow Talk*)
Shelley Winters (*The Diary of Anne Frank*)

Shelley Winters gained 35 pounds for the role of the selfish Mrs. Van Daan who hides from the Nazis in Anne Frank's attic. The actress later donated her statuette to the Anne Frank museum in Amsterdam.

Stephen Boyd and Charlton Heston in the spectacular chariot race scene from *Ben-Hur* **(1959), winner of eleven Oscars, the most for any picture.**

DIRECTOR

Jack Clayton (*Room at the Top*)
George Stevens (*The Diary of Anne Frank*)
Billy Wilder (*Some Like It Hot*)
William Wyler (*Ben-Hur*)
Fred Zinnemann (*The Nun's Story*)

ORIGINAL SCREENPLAY

Ingmar Bergman (*Wild Strawberries*)
Paul King, Joseph Stone, Stanley Shapiro,
    Maurice Richlin (*Operation Petticoat*)
Ernest Lehman (*North by Northwest*)
Russell Rouse, Clarence Greene, Stanley Shapiro,
    Maurice Richlin (*Pillow Talk*)
Francois Truffaut, Marcel Moussy (*The 400 Blows*)

ADAPTED SCREENPLAY

Robert Anderson (*The Nun's Story*)
Wendell Mayes (*Anatomy of a Murder*)

Neil Paterson (*Room at the Top*)
Karl Tunberg (*Ben-Hur*)
Billy Wilder, I. A. L. Diamond (*Some Like It Hot*)

FOREIGN-LANGUAGE FILM

Black Orpheus (France/ Brazil)
The Bridge (Germany)
The Great War (Italy)
Paw (Denmark)
The Village on the River (The Netherlands)

OTHER AWARDS

Score of a Dramatic or Comedy Picture: Miklos
Rozsa (*Ben-Hur*); Score of a Musical Picture:
Andre Previn, Ken Darby (*Porgy and Bess*); Song:
"High Hopes" from *A Hole in the Head*, music by
James Van Heusen, lyrics by Sammy Cahn;
Cinematography: color—Robert L. Surtees (*Ben-Hur*), black and white—William C. Mellor (*The*

Diary of Anne Frank); Art Direction: color—William A. Horning, Edward Carfango, Hugh Hunt (*Ben-Hur*), black and white—Lyle R. Wheeler, George W. Davis, Walter M. Scott, Stuart A. Reiss (*The Diary of Anne Frank*); Costume Design: color—ELizabeth Haffenden (*Ben-Hur*), black and white—Orry-Kelly (*Some Like It Hot*); Film Editing: Ralph E. Winters, John D. Dunning (*Ben-Hur*); Sound: Franklin E. Milton, sound director, MGM Sound Department (*Ben-Hur*); Special Effects: A. Arnold Gillespie, Robert MacDonald (visual), Milo Lory (audio) (*Ben-Hur*).

Documentary: *Serengeti Shall Not Die*; Documentary Short Subject: *Glass*; Live-Action Short Subject: *The Golden Fish*; Animated Short Subject: *Moonbird*.

SPECIAL AWARDS

Sound pioneer Lee de Forest; Buster Keaton; Bob Hope (Jean Hersholt Humanitarian Award).

After the disaster of the 1958 awards, the 1959 Oscarcast was given high marks just for being competently produced. *Variety* gave it qualified praise: "Neither the funniest nor the most exciting of the Oscar derbies to be telecast, but nonetheless, it stacked up beaucoup entertainment values. The absence of awkwardness in itself was an achievement."

Both Jerry Wald and Jerry Lewis, producer and ad-libber of the previous Academy goof-fest, begged off for a repeat performance. Arthur Freed, mastermind behind many of MGM's classic musicals, would organize the shindig. He recruited top talent for the broadcast: director Vincente Minnelli and director/producer John Houseman. An avid baseball fan, Freed explained the line-up to *TV Guide*: "I am the manager. Minnelli and Houseman are my pitchers, you might say."

Bob Hope returned as host for another commercial-free Oscar night. All of the major studios paid for the show, except Universal which refused on principle. Why should they pay so a TV network can get their stars to appear and garner big ratings, the reasoning went. The networks should be paying the studios.

ABC outbid NBC for the broadcast rights. The program was preceded by a Oscar pre-show with Tony Randall going from table to table at Hollywood's Brown Derby restaurant asking if there were any celebrities in the house. He was often greeted with a chorus of "no's." A strike by the Screen Actors Guild did not prevent the stars from attending the subsequent ceremony in force.

While the previous year's show ended twenty minutes early, the 1959 edition went twenty minutes over the hour-and-a-half time slot.

NATIONAL BOARD OF REVIEW

Picture: *The Nun's Story*; Actor: Victor Sjostrom (*Wild Strawberries*); Actress: Simone Signoret (*Room at the Top*); Supporting Actor: Hugh Griffith (*Ben-Hur*); Supporting Actress: Edith Evans (*The Nun's Story*); Director: Fred Zinnemann (*The Nun's Story*); Foreign Film: *Wild Strawberries* (Sweden).

BEST AMERICAN FILMS

The Nun's Story, Ben-Hur, Anatomy of a Murder, The Diary of Anne Frank, Middle of the Night, The Man Who Understood Women, Some Like It Hot, Suddenly, Last Summer, On the Beach, North by Northwest.

BEST FOREIGN FILMS

Wild Strawberries (Sweden), *Room at the Top* (Britain), *Aparajito* (India), *The Roof* (Italy), *Look Back in Anger* (Britain).

SPECIAL AWARDS

Ingmar Bergman; Andrew Martin and Yakima Canutt for the direction of the chariot race in *Ben-Hur*.

NEW YORK FILM CRITICS CIRCLE

Picture: *Ben-Hur*; Actor: James Stewart (*Anatomy of a Murder*); Actress: Audrey Hepburn (*The Nun's Story*); Director: Fred Zinnemam (*The Nun's Story*); Screenplay: Wendell Mayes (*Anatomy of a Murder*); Foreign-Language Film: *The 400 Blows* (France).

Audrey Hepburn's nun defeated Simone Signoret's adulteress by one vote on the sixth ballot.

HOLLYWOOD FOREIGN PRESS ASSOCIATION GOLDEN GLOBE AWARDS

Picture (Drama): *Ben-Hur*; Picture (Comedy):

Some Like It Hot; Picture (Musical): *Porgy and Bess*; Actor (Drama): Anthony Franciosa (*Career*); Actress (Drama): Elizabeth Taylor (*Suddenly, Last Summer*); Actor (Comedy or Musical): Jack Lemmon (*Some Like It Hot*); Actress (Comedy or Musical): Marilyn Monroe (*Some Like It Hot*); Supporting Actor: Stephen Boyd (*Ben-Hur*); Supporting Actress: Susan Kohner (*Imitation of Life*); Most Promising Newcomers (Male): James Shigeta, Barry Coe, Troy Donahue, George Hamilton; Most Promising Newcomers (Female): Tuesday Weld, Angie Dickenson, Janet Munro, Stella Stevens; Director: William Wyler (*Ben-Hur*); Foreign-Language Films (five winners): *Black Orpheus* (France/Brazil), *Odd Obsession* (Japan), *The Bridge* (Federal Republic of Germany), *Wild Strawberries* (Sweden), *Aren't We Wonderful?* (Federal Republic of Germany); Score: Ernest Gold (*On the Beach*); Film Promoting Internationl Understanding: *The Diary of Anne Frank*; World Film Favorite (Male): Rock Hudson; World Film Favorite (Female): Doris Day.

SPECIAL AWARDS

The Nun's Story (award for outstanding merit); *Room at the Top* (Samuel Goldwyn Award); Bing Crosby (Cecil B. DeMille Award); Andrew Marton (for directing the chariot race scene in *Ben-Hur*); Francis X. Bushman, Ramon Navarro (original stars of the 1926 silent *Ben-Hur*); Hedda Hopper, Louella Parsons (journalistic merit).

CANNES FILM FESTIVAL

Golden Palm: *Black Orpheus* (France/Brazil); Actor (collective award): Bradford Dillman, Dean Stockwell, and Orson Welles (*Compulsion*); Actress: Simone Signoret (*Room at the Top*) (Britain); Director: Francois Truffaut (*The 400 Blows*) (France); Special Jury Prize: *Stars* (Bulgaria/East Germany).

OTHER AWARDS

Comedy Prize: *Policarpo dei Tappeti* (Italy); International Prize: Luis Bunuel for *Nazarin* (Mexico) and the body of his work; Special Mention: *Shirasagi* (Japan); International Critics Prize: *Hiroshima, Mon Amour* (France), *Araya* (Venezuela); Best Selection: Czechoslovakia.

Alain Resnais' *Hiroshima, Mon Amour* was almost pulled from the festival. Its depiction of a French woman having an affair with a Nazi soldier during World War II was considered potentially offensive to too much of the European community. But the Minister of Culture intervened and the film was shown on closing night.

1960

ACADEMY AWARDS (OSCARS)

PICTURE

The Alamo
The Apartment
Elmer Gantry
Sons and Lovers
The Sundowners

The Apartment is one of the few comedies to win Best Picture. Oscar voters tend to take themselves and the little golden guy pretty seriously. The only other humorous pictures to take the top Oscar have been *It Happened One Night, You Can't Take It with You, Tom Jones, Annie Hall*, and *Forest Gump*. Winning dramas with strong comedy elements include *Terms of Endearment* and *Driving Miss Daisy*.

Among those who did not want to see *The Apartment* added to this short list was John Wayne. It had taken the Western star fourteen years to produce *The Alamo*, and he spent $75,000 on a take-no-prisoners Oscar campaign. His most tasteless trade ad featured a tombstone with an epitath for Hollywood in the year 3000 A.D. In the ad, Wayne asked Academy voters if they wanted to be remembered for honoring a silly sex comedy (*The Apartment*) or his own timeless epic. There was also a banner hung across Sunset Boulevard proclaiming *The Alamo* as the most important picture ever made. The voters felt otherwise.

ACTOR

Trevor Howard (*Sons and Lovers*)
Burt Lancaster (*Elmer Gantry*)
Jack Lemmon (*The Apartment*)
Laurence Olivier (*The Entertainer*)
Spencer Tracy (*Inherit the Wind*)

ACTRESS

Greer Garson (*Sunrise at Campobello*)
Deborah Kerr (*The Sundowners*)
Shirley MacLaine (*The Apartment*)
Melina Mercouri (*Never on a Sunday*)
Elizabeth Taylor (*Butterfield 8*)

"Elizabeth Taylor finally won an Academy Award for having a tracheotomy after losing one for marrying Eddie Fisher," quipped columnist John Crosby. Taylor had endured a rash of negative publicity when she broke up Eddie Fisher's marriage to angelic Debbie Reynolds. All was forgiven when Taylor nearly died of pneumonia a few weeks before the ceremony and underwent surgery. She got the Sympathy Oscar for playing a call-girl in MGM's ultra-trashy adaptation of *Butterfield 8*, a soap-y John O'Hara novel. "I think it stinks," the star said of the film.

SUPPORTING ACTOR

Peter Falk (*Murder, Inc.*)
Jack Kruschen (*The Apartment*)
Sal Mineo (*Exodus*)
Peter Ustinov (*Spartacus*)
Chill Wills (*The Alamo*)

If John Wayne's campaign for *The Alamo* was the cavalry charging on the Academy voters as if they were the Indians, the Chills Wills run for Supporting Actor was the comedy relief. Wills, a raspy-voiced character actor mostly employed as the hero's sidekick, hired his own publicist and went all out. Ads appeared daily in the trades. One series included an alphabetical listing of all Academy members with a picture of Wills and the words: "Win, lose, or draw, you're all my cousins and I love you all."

Groucho Marx replied with an ad of his own: "Dear Mr. Chill Wills, I'm delighted to be your cousin, but I voted for Sal Mineo."

In the same edition of *The Hollywood Reporter* which ran Groucho's ad, there appeared a picture spread featuring the *Alamo* players with copy reading, "We of the *Alamo* cast are praying harder—than the real Texans prayed for their lives in the Alamo—for Chill Wills to win. . . ." Wayne bought yet another ad condemning Wills and his press agent for their bad taste.

Elizabeth Taylor, recovered from pneumonia, with her 1960 Oscar for *Butterfield 8*.

SUPPORTING ACTRESS

Glynis Johns (*The Sundowners*)
Shirley Jones (*Elmer Gantry*)
Shirley Knight (*The Dark at the Top of the Stairs*)
Janet Leigh (*Psycho*)
Mary Ure (*Sons and Lovers*)

Like Elizabeth Taylor, Shirley Jones was Oscared for playing a hooker. Ironically, she would follow the path of another movie bad-girl Donna Reed and wind up as an idealized TV mom—on the '70s sitcom *The Partridge Family*.

DIRECTOR

Jack Cardiff (*Sons and Lovers*)
Jules Dassin (*Never on a Sunday*)
Alfred Hitchcock (*Psycho*)
Billy Wilder (*The Apartment*)

Fred Zinnemann (*The Sundowners*)

ORIGINAL SCREENPLAY
Jules Dassin (*Never on a Sunday*)
Marguerite Duras (*Hiroshima, Mon Amour*)
Richard Gregson, Michael Craig, Bryan Forbes
(*The Angry Silence*)
Norman Panama, Melvin Frank (*The Facts of Life*)
Billy Wilder, I. A. L. Diamond (*The Apartment*)

ADAPTED SCREENPLAY
Richard Brooks (*Elmer Gantry*)
Nathan E. Douglas, Harold Jacob Smith
(*Inherit the Wind*)
James Kennaway (*Tunes of Glory*)
Gavin Lambert, T. E. B. Clarke (*Sons and Lovers*)
Isobel Lannart (*The Sundowners*)

FOREIGN-LANGUAGE FILM
Kapo (Italy)
La Vérité (France)
Macario (Mexico)
The Ninth Circle (Yugoslavia)
The Virgin Spring (Sweden)

OTHER AWARDS
Score of a Dramatic or Comedy Picture: Ernest
Gold (*Exodus*); Score of a Musical Picture: Morris
Stoloff, Harry Sukman (*Song without End*); Song:
"Never on a Sunday" from *Never on a Sunday*,
music and lyrics by Manos Hadjidakis; Cinema-
tography: color—Russell Metty (*Spartacus*), black
and white—Freddie Francis (*Sons and Lovers*); Art
Direction: color—Alexander Golitzen, Eric Orbom,
Russell A. Gausman, Julia Heron (*Spartacus*), black
and white—Alexander Trauner, Edward G. Boyle
(*The Apartment*); Costume Design: color—Valles
and Bill Thomas (*Spartacus*), black and white—
Edith Head, Edward Stevenson (*The Facts of Life*);
Film Editing: Daniel Mandell (*The Apartment*);
Sound: Samuel Goldwyn and Todd-AO Sound
Departments (*The Alamo*); Special Effects: Gene
Warren, Tim Baar (*The Time Machine*).

Documentary: *The Horse with the Flying Tail*;
Documentary Short Subject: *Giuseppina*; Live-
Action Short Subject: *Day of the Painter*; Animated
Short Subject: *Munro*.

SPECIAL AWARDS
Gary Cooper; Stan Laurel; Hayley Mills
(oustanding juvenile performance); Sol Lesser
(Jean Hersholt Humanitarian Award).

Arthur Freed, Vincente Minnelli, and Bob Hope
returned as producer, director, and host, respectively, for the 1960 Oscars. The personnel was the
same as the previous year, but the venue changed.
The ceremony moved from the Pantages Theatre
where the awards had been presented since 1950 to
the Santa Monica Civic Auditorium. Why the
move out of Hollywood? In remodeling for a
screening of the big-screen epic *Spartacus*, the
Pantages had lost too many seats. The Santa
Monica site was the only space deemed large
enough to hold the spectacle.

NATIONAL BOARD OF REVIEW

Picture: *Sons and Lovers*; Actor: Robert Mitchum
(*The Sundowners* and *Home from the Hill*); Actress:
Greer Garson (*Sunrise at Campobello*); Supporting
Actor: George Peppard (*Home from the Hill*);
Supporting Actress: Shirley Jones (*Elmer Gantry*);
Director: Jack Cardiff (*Sons and Lovers*); Foreign
Film: *The World of Apu* (India).

BEST ENGLISH-LANGUAGE FILMS
*Sons and Lovers, The Alamo, The Sundowners,
Inherit the Wind, Sunrise at Campobello, Elmer
Gantry, Home from the Hill, The Apartment, Wild
River, The Dark at the Top of the Stairs.*

BEST FOREIGN-LANGUAGE FILMS:
The World of Apu (India), *General Della Rovere*
(Italy/France), *The Angry Silence* (Britain), *I'm All
Right, Jack* (Britain), *Hiroshima, Mon Amour*
(France/Japan).

Though it was made in Britain with principally
British talent, *Sons and Lovers* based on D. H.
Lawrence's novel, was financed with American
money. The Board classified it as an American
release.

NEW YORK FILM CRITICS CIRCLE

Picture (tie): *The Apartment* and *Sons and Lovers*;
Actor: Burt Lancaster (*Elmer Gantry*); Actress:

Deborah Kerr (*The Sundowners*); Director (tie): Jack Cardiff (*Sons and Lovers*) and Billy Wilder (*The Apartment*); Screenplay: Billy Wilder, I. A. L. Diamond (*The Apartment*); Foreign-Language FIlm: *Hiroshima, Mon Amour*) (France/Japan).

This was the first time in the Circle's history there was a tie for best Picture and best Director.

HOLLYWOOD FOREIGN PRESS ASSOCIATION GOLDEN GLOBE AWARDS

Picture (Drama): *Spartacus*; Picture (Comedy): *The Apartment*; Picture (Musical): *Song without End*; Actor (Drama): Burt Lancaster (*Elmer Gantry*); Actress (Drama): Greer Garson (*Sunrise at Campobello*); Actor (Comedy or Musical): Jack Lemmon (*The Apartment*); Actress (Comedy or Musical): Shirley MacLaine (*The Apartment*); Supporting Actor: Sal Mineo (*Exodus*); Supporting Actress: Janet Leigh (*Psycho*); Most Promising Newcomers (Male): Michael Callen, Mark Damon, Brett Halsey; Most Promising Newcomers (Female): Ina Balin, Nancy Kwan, Hayley Mills; Director: Jack Cardiff (*Sons and Lovers*); Score: Dimitri Tiomkin (*The Alamo*); Foreign-Language Foreign Films (two winners): *La Vérité* (France), *The Virgin Spring* (Sweden); English-Language Foreign Film: *The Man with the Green Carnation*; Film Promoting International Understanding: *Hand in Hand*; World Film Favorite (Male) (tie): Rock Hudson, Tony Curtis; World Film Favorite (Female): Gina Lollobrigida.

SPECIAL AWARDS

The Sundowners (Merit Award); *Never on a Sunday* (Samuel Goldwyn Award); Fred Astaire (Cecil B. DeMille Award); Stanley Kubrick (artistic integrity); Cantinflas (special award for comedy).

CANNES FILM FESTIVAL

Golden Palm: *La Dolce Vita* (Italy); Actor: No award given; Actress (tie): Melina Mercouri (*Never on a Sunday*) (Greece), Jeanne Moreau (*Moderato Cantabile*) (France); Jury Prize: *L'Avventura* (Italy); Best Selection: USSR; Special Awards: *Kagi* (Japan), *The Virgin Spring* (Sweden), *The Young One* (Mexico).

It was booed and hissed at the Cannes screening, but Michelangelo Antonioni's existentialist *L'Avventura* was cited with a special jury prize for its "contribution towards seeking a new language of cinema."

1961

ACADEMY AWARDS (OSCARS)

PICTURE
Fanny
The Guns of Navarone
The Hustler
Judgment at Nuremberg
West Side Story

The fourth musical to win Best Picture, *West Side Story*, the Broadway update of the Romeo and Juliet story to the streets of New York, also took nine additional awards. Its total of ten surpassed *Gigi*'s eight, but came up short of *Ben-Hur*'s all-time record of eleven.

ACTOR
Charles Boyer (*Fanny*)
Paul Newman (*The Hustler*)
Maximilian Schell (*Judgment at Nuremberg*)
Spencer Tracy (*Judgment at Nuremberg*)
Stuart Whitman (*The Mark*)

Oscar went international this year with the leading performance awards going to a Swiss unknown (Maximilian Schell re-creating his defense lawyer role from the TV version of *Judgment at Nuremberg*) and a glamorous Italian star (Sophia Loren).

ACTRESS
Audrey Hepburn (*Breakfast at Tiffany's*)
Piper Laurie (*The Hustler*)
Sophia Loren (*Two Women*)
Geraldine Page (*Summer and Smoke*)
Natalie Wood (*Splendor in the Grass*)

The dazzling Sophia Loren proved she was more than just a pretty face—and body—with a raw, powerful performance as a mother struggling to survive in war-torn Europe in the Italian feature *Two Women*. Appearing in the spectacular *El Cid* during Oscar nominating time helped her get on the golden guy's short list. But she wasn't sure of taking the statuette home to Rome. Since an actress in a foreign-language film had never copped the Oscar, Loren elected to remain in Italy on the big night. But that did not stop her from sitting up with her husband, producer Carlo Ponti, until 6 a.m. as the ceremony was taking place. There was no Oscar broadcast to Europe at the time so the news was delivered on the phone by Cary Grant at 6:45 a.m., three-quarters of an hour after the actress had given up and gone to bed.

Some years later, Loren's Oscar was stolen by thieves who mistook it for solid gold. She sent the Academy $60 and was furnished with a replacement.

SUPPORTING ACTOR

George Chakiris (*West Side Story*)
Montgomery Clift (*Judgment at Nuremberg*)
Peter Falk (*Pocketful of Miracles*)
Jackie Gleason (*The Hustler*)
George C. Scott (*The Hustler*)

In a move foreshadowing trouble in the years ahead, George C. Scott requested that his name be withdrawn from the list of nominees, protesting that Oscar campaigning was too commercial. The Academy did not comply.

SUPPORTING ACTRESS

Fay Bainter (*The Children's Hour*)
Judy Garland (*Judgment at Nuremberg*)
Lotte Lenya (*The Roman Spring of Mrs. Stone*)
Una Merkel (*Summer and Smoke*)
Rita Moreno (*West Side Story*)

DIRECTOR

Federico Fellini (*La Dolce Vita*)
Stanley Kramer (*Judgment at Nuremberg*)
Robert Rossen (*The Hustler*)
J. Lee Thompson (*The Guns of Navarone*)
Robert Wise, Jerome Robbins (*West Side Story*)

This is the first instance of co-directors taking the best helmer Oscar. The collaborators did not get along. Wise banned Robbins—the stager and choreographer of the original Broadway version of *West Side*—from the set because he was taking too long getting his dancers warmed up and ready. Neither winner thanked or even mentioned the other in his acceptance speech.

ORIGINAL SCREENPLAY

Sergio Amidei, Diego Fabbri, Indro Montandelli (*General Della Rosse*)
Federico Fellini, Tullio Pinelli, Ennio Flaiano, Brunello Rondi (*La Dolce Vita*)
William Inge (*Splendor in the Grass*)
Stanley Shapiro, Paul Henning (*Lover Come Back*)
Valentin Yoshov, Grigori Chukhrai (*Ballad of a Soldier*)

ADAPTED SCREENPLAY

George Axelrod (*Breakfast at Tiffany's*)
Sidney Carroll, Robert Rossen (*The Hustler*)
Carl Foreman (*The Guns of Navarone*)
Abby Mann (*Judgment at Nuremberg*)
Ernest Lehman (*West Side Story*)

FOREIGN-LANGUAGE FILM

Harry and the Butler (Denmark)
Immortal Love (Japan)
The Important Man (Mexico)
Placido (Spain)
Through a Glass, Darkly (Sweden)

OTHER AWARDS

Score of a Dramatic or Comedy Picture: Henry Mancini (*Breakfast at Tiffany's*); Score of a Musical Picture: Saul Chaplin, Johnny Green, Sid Ramion, Irwin Kotel (*West Side Story*); Song: "Moon River" from *Breakfast at Tiffany's*, music by Henry Mancini, lyrics by Johnny Mercer; Cinematography: color—Daniel A. Fapp (*West Side Story*), black and white—Eugen Shuftan (*The Hustler*); Art Direction: color—Boris Leven, Victor A. Gangelin (*West Side Story*), black and white—Harry Horner, Gene Callahan (*The Hustler*); Costume Design: color—Irene Sharaff (*West Side Story*), black and white—Pierro Gherardi (*La Dolce Vita*); Film Editing: Thomas Stanford (*West Side Story*); Sound: Todd-AO and Samuel Goldwyn Studios Sound Departments (*West Side Story*); Special Effects: Bill Warrington (visual),

Vivian C. Greenham (audible) (*The Guns of Navarone*).

Documentary: *Sky Above and Mud Beneath*; Documentary Short Subject: *Project Hope*; Live-Action Short Subject: *Seawards the Great Ships*; Animated Short Subject: *Ersatz (The Substitute)*.

SPECIAL AWARDS
William Hendricks for writing and producing the Marine Corps film *A Force in Readiness*; Fred L. Metzler for service to the Academy; Jerome Robbins for achievements in choreography on film; Stanley Kramer (Irving Thalberg Award); George Seaton (Jean Hersholt Humanitarian Award).

The 1961 Oscars heralded the demise of the old Hollywood studios. The winners of the top acting awards were foreign stars and all five of the nominated Best Pictures were made by independent producers (although some were distributed by the studios). Much of the old guard skipped the ceremony, with Louella Parsons, doyenne of movieland gossip, missing the event for the first time since the premiere ceremony in 1929. (She was stricken with shingles.) A hefty percentage of the nominees were also absent. "The panning cameraman had trouble finding well-known faces," *Variety* grumbled. The star factor was made up with names from movies' rival medium, television. But there were flashes of the old Hollywood with presenters like Joan Crawford, Fred Astaire, and Rosalind Russell exuding their charms.

In addition to the erosion of the old glamour factory and the encroachment of the independents and foreigners, Oscar faced another challenge from the modern world. Ten protesters from an organization called the Hollywood Race Relations Bureau picketed the ceremony, citing American cinema's negligible representation of blacks. Academy president Wendell Corey had them arrested for trespassing. Caleb Peterson, the demonstrators' leader, was fined $26.50 and hit the Academy with a $1 million lawsuit for infringement for his Constitutional right of assembly. Ironically, two years later, Sidney Poitier would become the first African-American to win the best Actor award. But his triumph did not have much of influence since major portrayals of blacks in Hollywood films would continue to be scarce for many years.

Though the protestors failed to make much of an impact, a gate-crasher without a political message made it to the broadcast. As Shelley Winters and Vince Edwards were presenting the cinematography awards, a man suddenly walked to the podium and announced, "I'm the world's greatest gate-crasher and I just came here to present Bob Hope with his 1938 trophy." With that he handed Winters a tiny prop Oscar and walked off. Emcee Hope returned to the stage with the quip "Who needs Price Waterhouse? All we need is a doorman." The unexpected guest was later identified as Stan Berman, who would later pull similar stunts at the Tony Awards. One commentator enjoying the spontaneity of Berman's appearance was Jim Bacon of the Associated Press. "If it hadn't been for gate-crasher Stan Berman, it would have been a completely dull affair," the reporter commented.

NATIONAL BOARD OF REVIEW

Picture: *Question 7*; Actor: Albert Finney (*Saturday Night and Sunday Morning*); Actress: Geraldine Page (*Summer and Smoke*); Supporting Actor: Jackie Gleason (*The Hustler*); Supporting Actress: Ruby Dee (*A Raisin in the Sun*; Director: Jack Clayton (*The Innocents*); Foreign Film: *The Bridge* (Federal Republic of Germany).

BEST ENGISH-LANGUAGE FILMS
Question 7, The Hustler, West Side Story, The Innocents, The Hoodlum Priest, Summer and Smoke, The Young Doctors, Judgment at Nuremberg, One, Two, Three, Fanny.

BEST FOREIGN-LANGUAGE FILMS
The Bridge (Federal Republic of Germany), *La Dolce Vita* (Italy/France), *Two Women* (France/Italy), *Saturday Night and Sunday Morning* (Britain), *Seryozha* (USSR).

The NRB's choice for Best Picture, *Question 7*, was a propaganda film sponsored by the Lutheran Church about an East German youth torn between his religion and the desire for a state-funded education in a Communist country. It has since faded into obscurity.

NEW YORK FILM CRITICS CIRCLE

Picture: *West Side Story*; Actor: Maximilian Schell (*Judgment at Nuremberg*); Actress: Sophia Loren (*Two Women*); Director: Robert Rossen (*The Hustler*); Screenplay: Abby Mann (*Judgment at Nuremberg*); Foreign-Language Film: *La Dolce Vita*.

West Side Story was the first musical to win the Critics' Best Picture award.

Conflict of interest?: Critic Joseph Morgenstern of the *Herald-Tribune* voted for Piper Laurie of *The Hustler* for best actress. He was engaged to her at the time.

HOLLYWOOD FOREIGN PRESS ASSOCIATION GOLDEN GLOBE AWARDS

Picture (Drama): *The Guns of Navarone*; Picture (Comedy): *A Majority of One*; Picture (Musical): *West Side Story*; Actor (Drama): Maximilian Schell (*Judgment at Nuremberg*); Actress (Drama): Geraldine Page (*Summer and Smoke*); Actor (Comedy or Musical): Glenn Ford (*A Pocketful of Miracles*); Actress (Comedy or Musical): Rosalind Russell (*A Majority of One*); Supporting Actor: George Chakiris (*West Side Story*); Supporting Actress: Rita Moreno (*West Side Story*); Most Promising Newcomers (Male): Richard Beymer, Bobby Darrin, Warren Beatty; Most Promising Newcomers (Female): Christine Kaufman, Ann-Margret, Jane Fonda; Director: Stanley Kramer (*Judgment at Nuremberg*); Score: Dimitri Tiomkin (*Judgment at Nuremberg*); Song: "Town without Pity" from *Town without Pity*, music by Dimitri Tiomkin, lyrics by Ned Washington; Foreign-Language Film Golden Globe: *Two Women* (Italy), Silver Globes: *The Important Man* (Mexico), *The Good Soldier Schweik* (Federal Republic of Germany); Film Promoting International Understanding: *A Majority of One*; World Film Favorite (Male): Charlton Heston; World Film Favorite (Female): Marilyn Monroe.

SPECIAL AWARDS

Judy Garland (Cecil B. DeMille Award); *The Mark* (Samuel Goldwyn Award for Best English Picture); *El Cid* (Special Merit Award); Army Archerd of *Daily Variety* and Mike Connolly of *The Hollywood Reporter* (special journalistic merit awards).

CANNES FILM FESTIVAL

Golden Palm (tie): *Viridiana* (Spain) and *Such a Long Absence* (France); Actor: Anthony Perkins (*Goodbye Again*); Actress: Sophia Loren (*Two Women*) (Italy); Director: Yulia Solntseva for continuing the work of Alexander Dovzhenko (*Story of the Flaming Years*); Special Jury Prize: *Mother Joan of the Angels* (Poland); International Critics Prize: *The Hand in the Trap* (Argentina).

SPECIAL AWARDS

Best Selection: Italy; *A Raisin in the Sun* (Gary Cooper Award for the human valor of the film's content and treatment).

ACADEMY AWARDS (OSCARS)

PICTURE
Lawrence of Arabia
The Longest Day
The Music Man
Mutiny on the Bounty
To Kill a Mockingbird

The studios reasserted their power by grabbing best Picture nominations for three home-grown products: *The Longest Day, The Music Man,* and a remake of *Mutiny on the Bounty*. It's significant to note that this trio did not receive a single nomination in the acting, writing, or directing categories.

The Oscar did go to a spectacle—*Lawrence of Arabia*—but an independently made one with mostly British talent. The other nonstudio best Picture nominee, *To Kill a Mockingbird*, garnered two major prizes—best Actor and best Adapted Screenplay.

ACTOR
Burt Lancaster (*Birdman of Alcatraz*)
Jack Lemmon (*Days of Wine and Roses*)
Marcello Mastroianni (*Divorce—Italian Style*)

Peter O'Toole (*Lawrence of Arabia*)
Gregory Peck (*To Kill a Mockingbird*)

ACTRESS

Anne Bancroft (*The Miracle Worker*)
Bette Davis (*Whatever Happened to Baby Jane?*)
Katharine Hepburn (*Long Day's Journey into Night*)
Geraldine Page (*Sweet Bird of Youth*)
Lee Remick (*Days of Wine and Roses*)

Though relative newcomer Anne Bancroft was the ultimate winner, this category became a battleground between veteran stars Bette Davis and Joan Crawford. Both film divas had headlined *Whatever Happened to Baby Jane?*, a ghoulishly campy thriller which hit big and resulted in a comeback for the duo. But to call their relationship on the set rancorous would have been an understatement.

If the legendary ladies were at odds while *Baby Jane* was lensing, the daggers were out when Davis got an Oscar nomination for the showier role of Looney Tunes Jane and Crawford was shut out for her more subtle limning of wheelchair-bound Blanche. While Davis was campaigning for her third Oscar, Crawford petitioned all the other nominees to be their stand-in should they be unable to attend the ceremony. She was taken up on the generous offer by Bancroft, up for re-creating her Broadway triumph in *The Miracle Worker* as Anne Sullivan, teacher of the young deaf-mute Helen Keller.

On the big night, both Davis and Crawford were backstage smoking and waiting. Last year's Best Actor Maximilian Schell announced the winner—Anne Bancroft. But Bancroft was in New

Joan Crawford (right) presents Anne Bancroft (in costume after a performance of *Mother Courage* on Broadway) with her 1962 Oscar for *The Miracle Worker*.

York appearing onstage in *Mother Courage*. Crawford stamped out her cigarette, grabbed the stage manager's hand, nearly breaking his fingers, and strode onstage to accept Bancroft's award and the center spotlight while Davis fumed.

Davis later claimed Crawford kept the Oscar for a year, taking it on a round-the-world trip. But in fact, Crawford delivered it to its rightful owner a week later on the stage of *Mother Courage*.

SUPPORTING ACTOR
Ed Begley (*Sweet Bird of Youth*)
Victor Buono (*Whatever Happened to Baby Jane?*)
Telly Savalas (*Birdman of Alcatraz*)
Omar Sharif (*Lawrence of Arabia*)
Terence Stamp (*Billy Budd*)

SUPPORTING ACTRESS
Mary Badham (*To Kill a Mockingbird*)
Patty Duke (*The Miracle Worker*)
Shirley Knight (*Sweet Bird of Youth*)
Angela Lansbury (*The Manchurian Candidate*)
Thelma Ritter (*Birdman of Alcatraz*)

Sixteen-year-old Patty Duke brought a chihuahua in a bowling bag to the ceremony. Press releases stated the dog was hers, but it really belonged to her managers. They thought the pet would make good copy. As a result of the Oscar for her silent, intense portrayal of Helen Keller, and maybe the press about the dog, Duke began starring in her own television series that fall.

DIRECTOR
Pietro Germi (*Divorce—Italian Style*)
David Lean (*Lawrence of Arabia*)
Robert Mulligan (*To Kill a Mockingbird*)
Arthur Penn (*The Miracle Worker*)
Frank Perry (*David and Lisa*)

ORIGINAL SCREENPLAY
Ingmar Bergman (*Through a Glass, Darkly*)
Ennio de Concini, Alfredo Gianetti, Pietro Germi (*Divorce—Italian Style*)
Charles Kaufman, Wolfgang Reinhardt (*Freud*)
Alain Robbe-Grillet (*Last Year at Marienbad*)
Stanley Shapiro, Nate Monaster (*That Touch of Mink*)

Bette Davis announced the winners in this category as "those three difficult Italian names for *Divorce—Italian Style*."

ADAPTED SCREENPLAY
Robert Bolt (*Lawrence of Arabia*)
William Gibson (*The Miracle Worker*)
Horton Foote (*To Kill a Mockingbird*)
Vladimir Nabokov (*Lolita*)
Eleanor Perry (*David and Lisa*)

FOREIGN-LANGUAGE FILM
Electra (Greece)
The Four Days of Naples (Italy)
The Keeper of Promises (Brazil)
Sundays and Cybele (France)
Tlayican (Mexico)

OTHER AWARDS
Original Musical Score: Maurice Jarre (*Lawrence of Arabia*); Adapted Musical Score: Ray Heindorf (*The Music Man*); Song: "Days of Wine and Roses" from *Days of Wine and Roses*, music by Henry Mancini, lyrics by Johnny Mercer; Cinematography: color—Fred A. Young (*Lawrence of Arabia*), black and white—Jean Bourgoin, Walter Wottitz (*The Longest Day*); Art Direction: color—John Box, John Stoll, Dario Simoni (*Lawrence of Arabia*), black and white—Alexander Golitzen, Henry Bumstead, Oliver Emert (*To Kill a Mockingbird*); Costume Design: color—Mary Wills (*The Wonderful World of the Brothers Grimm*), black and white—Norma Koch (*Whatever Happened to Baby Jane?*); Film Editing: Anne Coates (*Lawrence of Arabia*); Sound: John Cox, sound director, Shepperton Studio Sound Department (*Lawrence of Arabia*); Special Effects: Robert MacDonald (visual), Jacques Maumont (audible) (*The Longest Day*).

Documentary: *Black Fox*; Documentary Short Subject: *Dylan Thomas*; Live-Action Short Subject: *Heureux Anniversaire* (*Happy Anniversary*); Animated Short Subject: *The Hole*.

SPECIAL AWARDS
Steve Broidy (Jean Hersholt Humanitarian Award).

Once again, sponsor conflicts prevented Bob Hope

from hosting. Procter and Gamble was one of the Oscar backers. The comedian's new corporate boss was rival Lever Brothers. Hope was replaced by Frank Sinatra, whose charms were lost on *New York Daily News* TV critic Kay Gardella. In her review she snapped, "Not even Mr. Sinatra's entourage of friends, referred to unflatteringly as 'The Rat Pack,' could have helped their buddy out of this one." The Chairman of the Board opened the show not with a song, but with an obscure monologue about the Mona Lisa ("That chick just sits there and smiles"), comparing the famous painting to motion pictures. "Frankie boy, we're afraid, was a bit obtuse," commented Gardella.

To make up for the absence of many stars, filmed appearances from various European capitals were made by Ingrid Bergman and Simone Sigornet (both in Paris), and Audrey Hepburn and Laurence Olivier (in London).

Despite Sinatra's "obtuse" performance, the reviews were more complimentary for this year's Oscarcast because of the surprise results (Golden Globe winners Omar Shariff and Angela Lansbury were expected to defeat Ed Begley and Patty Duke) and the Davis-Crawford backstage drama.

NATIONAL BOARD OF REVIEW

Picture: *The Longest Day*; Actor: Jason Robards (*Long Day's Journey into Night* and *Tender Is the Night*); Actress: Anne Bancroft (*The Miracle Worker*); Supporting Actor: Burgess Meredith (*Advise and Consent*); Supporting Actress: Angela Lansbury (*The Manchurian Candidate* and *All Fall Down*); Director: David Lean (*Lawrence of Arabia*); Foreign Film: *Sundays and Cybele* (France).

BEST ENGLISH-LANGUAGE FILMS
The Longest Day, Billy Budd, The Miracle Worker, Lawrence of Arabia, Long Day's Journey into Night, Whistle Down the Wind, Requiem for a Heavyweight, A Taste of Honey, Birdman of Alcatraz, War Hunt.

BEST FOREIGN-LANGUAGE FILMS
Sundays and Cybele (France), *Barabas* (Italy), *Divorce—Italian Style* (Italy), *The Isalnd* (Japan), *Through a Glass, Darkly* (Sweden).

NEW YORK FILM CRITICS CIRCLE

Because of a newspaper strike, the Circle announced it would delay voting on its choices for the year's best until after the dispute was settled. The critics didn't want the results broadcast on television and radio and thereby scooping the papers for which they worked. When the strike dragged on, it was decided to scrap the award for 1961.

HOLLYWOOD FOREIGN PRESS ASSOCIATION GOLDEN GLOBE AWARDS

Picture (Drama): *Lawrence of Arabia*; Picture (Comedy): *That Touch of Mink*; Picture (Musical): *The Music Man*; Actor (Drama): Gregory Peck (*To Kill a Mockingbird*); Actress (Drama): Geraldine Page (*Sweet Bird of Youth*); Actor (Comedy or Musical): Marcello Mastroianni (*Divorce—Italian Style*); Actress (Comedy or Musical): Rosalind Russell (*Gypsy*); Supporting Actor: Omar Sharif (*Lawrence of Arabia*); Supporting Actress: Angela Lansbury (*The Manchurian Candidate*); Most Promsing Newcomers (Male): Keir Dullea, Omar Sharif, Terence Stamp; Most Promising Newcomers (Female): Patty Duke, Sue Lyon, Rita Tushingham; Director: David Lean (*Lawrence of Arabia*); Score: Elmer Bernstein (*To Kill a Mockingbird*); Cinematography: color—Freddie Young (*Lawrence of Arabia*); black and white—Henri Persin, Walter Wottitz, Jean Bourgoin (*The Longest Day*); Foreign-Language Film (tie): *Divorce—Italian Style* (Italy) and *Best of Enemies* (Italy); Film Promoting International Understanding: *To Kill a Mockingbird*; World Film Favorite (Male): Rock Hudson; World Film Favorite (Female): Doris Day.

SPECIAL AWARDS
Bob Hope (Cecil B. DeMille Award); *Sundays and Cybele* (Samuel Goldwyn Award).

CANNES FILM FESTIVAL

Golden Palm: *The Given Word* (Brazil); Collective Acting Awards: Katharine Hepburn, Ralph Richardson, Jason Robards, Dean Stockwell (*Long Day's Journey into Night*), Rita Tushingham, Murray Melvin (*A Taste of Honey*); Special Jury Prize: *The Trial of Joan of Arc* (France), *The Eclipse* (Italy);

International Critics Prize: *The Exterminating Angel* (Spain).

SPECIAL AWARDS
Best Adaptation of a Stage Play: *Elektra* (Greece); Best Comedy: *Divorce—Italian Style* (Italy); Short Film Golden Palm: *An Occurence at Owl Creek* (France).

ACADEMY AWARDS (OSCARS)

PICTURE
America, America
Cleopatra
How the West Was Won
Lilies of the Field
Tom Jones

The Hollywood studios continued to muscle into the Best Picture category with monumental mediocrities. This year the two home-grown spectacles, the Elizabeth Taylor version of *Cleopatra* and the seemingly endless *How the West Was Won*, competed with independent sleeper *Lilies of the Field*, Elia Kazan's studio-financed immigrant drama *America, America*, and the bawdy British hit *Tom Jones*.

Based on Henry Fielding's ribald eighteenth-century novel, *Jones* was rollicking adult entertainment, innovatively filmed. An anti-English backlash led by columnist Hedda Hopper did not prevent the film from taking home four Oscars including best Picture.

The *Tom Jones* triumvirate—star Albert Finney, director Tony Richardson, and author John Osborne—was also triumphing on Broadway with *Luther*, an historical drama about the leader of the Reformation. A month after the Oscars, Osborne won the Tony Award for best Play.

ACTOR
Albert Finney (*Tom Jones*)
Richard Harris (*This Sporting Life*)
Rex Harrison (*Cleopatra*)
Paul Newman (*Hud*)
Sidney Poitier (*Lilies of the Field*)

Sidney Poitier's win, the first leading acting award to go to an African-American, was given for three reasons: (1) It was deserved; (2) to prevent a total sweep by *Tom Jones*; and (3) for Hollywood to prove its liberal credentials at the height of the Civil Rights movement.

Poitier was the only acting winner present. Patricia Neal was pregnant in London and unable to travel. Melvyn Douglas and Margaret Rutherford remained in the same country but for vastly different reasons than Neal. Douglas was making a movie and the British Rutherford did not want to leave her homeland.

ACTRESS
Leslie Caron (*The L-Shaped Room*)
Shirley MacLaine (*Irma La Douce*)
Patricia Neal (*Hud*)
Rachel Roberts (*This Sporting Life*)
Natalie Wood (*Love with the Proper Stranger*)

SUPPORTING ACTOR
Nick Adams (*Twilight of Honor*)
Bobby Darin (*Captain Newman, M.D.*)
Melvyn Douglas (*Hud*)
Hugh Griffith (*Tom Jones*)
John Huston (*The Cardinal*)

SUPPORTING ACTRESS
Diane Cilento (*Tom Jones*)
Edith Evans (*Tom Jones*)
Joyce Redman (*Tom Jones*)
Margaret Rutherford (*The V.I.P.s*)
Lilia Skala (*Lilies of the Fields*)

DIRECTOR
Federico Fellini (*8 1/2*)
Elia Kazan (*America, America*)
Otto Preminger (*The Cardinal*)
Tony Richardson (*Tom Jones*)
Martin Ritt (*Hud*)

ORIGINAL SCREENPLAY
Pasquale Festa Campanile, Massino Franciosa, Nanni Loy, Vasco Pratolini, Carlo Bernari (*The Four Days of Naples*)
Federico Fellini, Ennio Flaiano, Tullio Pinelli, Brunello Rondi (*8 1/2*)

Elia Kazan (*America, America*)
Arnold Schulman (*Love and the Proper Stranger*)
James R. Webb (*How the West Was Won*)

ADAPTED SCREENPLAY
Serge Bourguigon, Antoine Tudal
 (*Sundays and Cybele*)
Richard L. Breen, Phoebe and Henry Ephron
 (*Captain Newman, M.D.*)
John Osborne (*Tom Jones*)
James Poe (*Lillies of the Field*)
Irving Ravetch, Harriet Frank, Jr. (*Hud*)

FOREIGN-LANGUAGE FILMS
8 1/2 (Italy)
Knife in the Water (Poland)
Los Tarantos (Spain)
The Red Lanterns (Greece)
Twin Sisters of Kyoto (Japan)

OTHER AWARDS
Original Score: John Addison (*Tom Jones*);
Adapted Score: Andre Previn (*Irma La Douce*);
Song: "Call Me Irresponsible" from *Papa's Delicate Condition*, music by James Van Heusen, lyrics by Sammy Cahn; Cinematography: color—Leon Shamroy (*Cleopatra*), black and white—James Wong Howe (*Hud*); Art Direction: color—John DeCuir, Jack Martin Smith, Hilyard Brown, Herman Blumenthal, Elven Webb, Maurice Pelling, Boris Juraga, Walter M. Scott, Paul S. Fox, Ray Moyer (*Cleopatra*), black and white—Gene Callahan (*America, America*); Costume Design: color—Irene Sharaff, Vittorio Nino Novarese, Renie (*Cleopatra*), black and white—Piero Gherardi (*8 1/2*); Film Editing: Harold F. Kress (*How the West Was Won*); Sound: Franklin E. Milton, sound director, MGM Studio Sound Department (*How the West Was Won*); Special Visual Effects: Emil Kosa, Jr. (*Cleopatra*); Sound Effects: Walter G. Elliott (*It's a Mad, Mad, Mad, Mad World*).

Documentary: *Robert Frost: A Lover's Quarrel with the World*; Documentary Short Subject: *Chagall*; Live-Action Short Subject: *An Occurence at Owl Creek*; Animated Short Subject: *The Critic*.

SPECIAL AWARDS
Sam Spiegel (Irving Thalberg Award).

Bob Hope was still frozen out of hosting duties due to a sponsor conflict. Jack Lemmon gave a low-key performance as the compere for the Oscar evening. Columnist Mike Conolly reported the actor was so relaxed that fifteen minutes before the broadcast, he was in a red sweatshirt and corduroys talking on the telephone to his nine-year-old son about the lad's report card. The absence of Hope's razor wit was keenly felt. *The New York Times* sniped that Lemmon was "woefully miscast" and "burdened with wretched gags" such as introducing Steve McQueen as "President Johnson's driving instructor" and Tuesday Weld as "young lady with a day all to herself."

Lemmon was not helped out by the missing winners. The broadcast was saved by Sammy Davis, Jr., delivering a medley of past losing best Songs. They were better than any of that year's nominated best tunes, according to more than one critic. Davis further enlivened the ceremony when he quickly recovered from a flub. After being handed the wrong envelope by the representative from Price Waterhouse, the singer-dancer-comedian slyly ad-libbed, "Wait 'til the NAACP hears about this."

NATIONAL BOARD OF REVIEW

Picture: *Tom Jones*; Actor: Rex Harrison (*Cleopatra*); Actress: Patricia Neal (*Hud*); Supporting Actor: Melvyn Douglas (*Hud*); Supporting Actress: Margaret Rutherford (*The V.I.P.s*); Director: Tony Richardson (*Tom Jones*); Foreign-Language Picture: *8 1/2* (Italy).

BEST ENGLISH-LANGUAGE FILMS
Tom Jones, Lilies of the Field, All the Way Home, Hud, This Sporting Life, Lord of the Flies, The L-Shaped Room, The Great Escape, How the West Was Won, The Cardinal.

BEST FOREIGN-LANGUAGE FILMS
8 1/2 (Italy), *The Four Days of Naples* (Italy), *Winter Light* (Sweden), *The Leopard* (Italy), *Any Number Can Win* (France/Italy).

NEW YORK FILM CRITICS CIRCLE

Picture: *Tom Jones*; Actor: Albert Finney (*Tom Jones*); Actress: Patricia Neal (*Hud*); Director: Tony Richardson (*Tom Jones*); Screenplay: Irving Ravetch, Harriet Frank, Jr. (*Hud*); Foreign-Language Film: *8 1/2*.

Albert Finney defeated Sidney Poitier on the sixth and final ballot, eight votes to six. Also in the running were Paul Newman and Melvyn Douglas (both for *Hud*), Jason Robards (*Act One*), Richard Harris (*This Sporting Life*), and Gregory Peck who received a few votes for *To Kill a Mockingbird* from the previous year when the Circle did not meet. Patricia Neal's only competition came from Leslie Caron in *The L-Shaped Room*.

HOLLYWOOD FOREIGN PRESS ASSOCIATION GOLDEN GLOBE AWARDS

Picture (Drama): *The Cardinal*; Picture (Comedy or Musical): *Tom Jones*; Actor (Drama): Sidney Poitier (*Lilies of the Field*); Actress (Drama): Leslie Caron (*The L-Shaped Room*); Actor (Comedy or Musical): Alberto Sordi (*To Bed or Not to Bed*); Actress (Comedy or Musical): Shirley MacLaine (*Irma La Douce*); Supporting Actor: John Houston (*The Cardinal*); Supporting Actress: Margaret Rutherford (*The V.I.P.s*); Most Promising Newcomers (Male): Albert Finney, Robert Walker, Stathis Giallelis; Most Promsing Newcomers (Female): Ursula Andress, Tippi Hedren, Elke Sommer; Director: Elia Kazan (*America, America*); Foreign-Language Film: *Any Number Can Win*; English-Language Foreign Film: *Tom Jones*; Film Promoting International Understanding: *Lilies of the Field*; World Film Favorite (Male): Paul Newman; World Film Favorite (Female): Sophia Loren.

SPECIAL AWARDS
Joseph E. Levine (Cecil B. DeMille Award); *Yesterday, Today, and Tomorrow* (Samuel Goldwyn International Award).

The Golden Globes diplomatically solved the problem of the anti-British backlash with its category of best English-Language Foreign Film. This way an English product would get an award without slighting a Hollywood production. It didn't quite work out this year when *Tom Jones* won for both Best Comedy and the English-Language Foreign prize.

CANNES FILM FESTIVAL

Golden Palm: *The Leopard* (Italy); Actor: Richard Harris (*This Sporting Life*); Actress: Marina Vlady (*The Conjugal Bed/Queen Bee*) (Italy); Director: Not awarded; Screenplay: Yves Jamiaque, Dimitriu Carabat, Henri Colpi (*Codine*) (France/Romania); Special Jury Prize: *Seppuku (Harakiri)* (Japan), *One Day, a Cat* (Czechoslovakia); International Critics Prize: *This Sporting Life* (Britain), *Les Abysses* (France), and *Le Joli Mai* (France).

SPECIAL AWARDS
To Kill a Mockingbird (Gary Cooper Award); *The Optimistic Tragedy* (USSR) (Best Evocation of a Revolutionary Epic).

ACADEMY AWARDS (OSCARS)

PICTURE
Becket
Dr. Strangelove, or How I Learned to Stop Worrying and Love the Bomb
Mary Poppins
My Fair Lady
Zorba the Greek

It was traditional Hollywood versus a bold new style of American filmmaking. Warner Brothers' filmization (some critics might say embalming) of the Broadway hit musical *My Fair Lady* was pitted against the black doomsday comedy *Dr. Strangelove*. Each of the remaining nominees had Hollywood financing but employed a good deal of British and European talent. Predictably *Lady* trounced *Strangelove*.

While the American studios won big, American actors did not. For the first time, all four performance Oscars went to foreign talent—three Brits and the Russian-French Lila Kedrova.

ACTOR

Richard Burton (*Becket*)
Rex Harrison (*My Fair Lady*)
Peter O'Toole (*Becket*)
Anthony Quinn (*Zorba the Greek*)
Peter Sellers (*Dr. Strangelove*)

Though Julie Andrews, the original stage Eliza Doolittle in *My Fair Lady*, was replaced by Audrey Hepburn, Rex Harrison was the Henry Higgins of both versions and the best Actor favorite.

Patricia Neal, winner of the previous year's best Actress award, had suffered a series of strokes and was unable to present the prize for best Actor. Audrey Hepburn was asked to fill in. After being presented with the statuette by his *Fair Lady* co-star, Harrison expressed "deep love for two fair ladies."

ACTRESS

Julie Andrews (*Mary Poppins*)
Anne Bancroft (*The Pumpkin Eater*)
Sophia Loren (*Marriage, Italian Style*)
Debbie Reynolds (*The Unsinkable Molly Brown*)
Kim Stanley (*Seance on a Wet Afternoon*)

The biggest controversy at the 1964 Oscars was the nomination of Julie Andrews and the omission of Audrey Hepburn. Andrews was passed over for the chance to re-create her Broadway triumph as the Cockney flower-seller who could have danced all night in *My Fair Lady*. But producer Jack Warner didn't think she was a big enough box office name and gave the part to Hepburn. The only glitch was Hepburn couldn't sing. No problem. All Warner had to do was get Marni Nixon to dub in the songs as she had done for Deborah Kerr in *The King and I* and Natalie Wood in *West Side Story*. Academy insiders explained that Hepburn's lack of pipes cost her a nomination.

Andrews didn't have much time for grieving over the loss of *Lady*. Walt Disney signed her up for *his* big musical, *Mary Poppins*. Andrews' starchy but lovable intrepretation of the magical nanny, plus some sympathy votes from those who thought she should have had the chance to star in *Lady*, not to mention the fact that her second film *The Sound of Music* was in release just as the nomination came out, made her a cinch for best Actress.

"I know you Americans are famous for your hospitality, but this is really ridiculous," she joked upon receiving her award. Her only expressed regret was the no-win status of her husband Tony Walton, whose costumes for *Poppins* lost to those of Cecil Beaton for *Lady*.

Gossip columnists were salivating over the possibility of an off-stage Oscar cat-fight between Hepburn and Andrews, but the two stars were all smiles as they posed for photographers with Rex Harrison.

SUPPORTING ACTOR

John Gielgud (*Becket*)
Stanley Holloway (*My Fair Lady*)
Edmond O'Brien (*Seven Days in May*)
Lee Tracy (*The Best Man*)
Peter Ustinov (*Topkapi*)

SUPPORTING ACTRESS

Gladys Cooper (*My Fair Lady*)
Dame Edith Evans (*The Chalk Garden*)
Grayson Hall (*The Night of the Iguana*)
Lila Kedrova (*Zorba the Greek*)
Agnes Moorehead (*Hush . . . Hush, Sweet Charlotte*)

Lila Kedrova later won a Tony Award for playing the same role—an aging courtesan wooed by philosophical bum Anthony Quinn—in a 1984 revival of the musical version of *Zorba* also starring Quinn. There is a small club of actors who have copped the Tony and Oscar for enacting the identical parts on stage and screen, but Kedrova is so far the only one the win for the movie first and then the play.

DIRECTOR

Michael Cacoyannis (*Zorba the Greek*)
George Cukor (*My Fair Lady*)
Peter Glenville (*Becket*)
Stanley Kubrick (*Dr. Strangelove*)
Robert Stevenson (*Mary Poppins*)

ORIGINAL SCREENPLAY

S. H. Barnett, Peter Stone, Frank Tarloff (*Father Goose*)
Orville H. Hampton, Raphael Hayes (*One Potato, Two Potato*)

Age, Scarpelli, and Mario Monicelli
(*The Organizer*)
Alan Owen (*A Hard Day's Night*)
Jean-Paul Rappeneau, Ariane Mnouchkine,
Daniel Boulanger, Philippe De Broca
(*That Man from Rio*)

ADAPTED SCREENPLAY
Edward Anhalt (*Becket*)
Michael Cacoyannis (*Zorba the Greek*)
Stanley Kubrick, Peter George, Terry Southern
(*Dr. Strangelove*)
Alan Jay Lerner (*My Fair Lady*)
Bill Walsh, Don DaGradi (*Mary Poppins*)

FOREIGN-LANGUAGE FILM
Raven's End (Sweden)
Sallah (Israel)
The Umbrellas of Cherbourg (France)
Woman in the Dunes (Japan)
Yesterday, Today, and Tomorrow (Italy)

OTHER AWARDS
Original Score: Richard M. and Robert B. Sherman (*Mary Poppins*); Adapted Score: Andre Previn (*My Fair Lady*); Song: "Chim Chim Cheree" from *Mary Poppins*, music and lyrics by Richard M. and Robert B. Sherman; Cinematography: color—Harry Stradling (*My Fair Lady*), black and white—Walter Lassaly (*Zorba the Greek*); Art Direction: color—Gene Allen, Cecil Beaton, George James Hopkins (*My Fair Lady*), black and white—Vassilis Fotopoulos (*Zorba the Greek*); Costume Design: color—Cecil Beaton (*My Fair Lady*), black and white—Dorothy Jenkins (*Night of the Iguana*); Film Editing: Cotton Warburton (*Mary Poppins*); Sound: George R. Groves, sound director, Warner Brothers Studio Sound Department (*My Fair Lady*); Special Visual Effects: Peter Ellenshaw, Hamilton Luske, Eustace Lycett (*Mary Poppins*); Sound Effects: Norman Wanstall (*Goldfinger*).

Documentary: *World without Sun*; Documentary Short Subject: *Nine from Little Rock*; Live-Action Short Subject: *Casals Conducts: 1964*; Animated Short Subject: *The Pink Phink*.

SPECIAL AWARD
William Tuttle for the make-up in *The Seven Faces of Dr. Lao.*

Maybe it was the expected Andrews-Hepburn contretemps, but more nominees and stars showed up for this Oscar show than any in recent memory. "This was undoubtedly the most glittering star assemblage at an Oscar occasion in the past ten years," bubbled columnist Sheilah Graham. Bob Hope's return might have had something to do with the high turn-out as well. "With the return of Bob Hope as emcee, the Academy Awards program regained some of its pep, vim, and vigor noticeably absent when Hope was away," *Variety* enthused.

The comedian set the tone for the evening with his opening gag: "Welcome to Santa-Monica-on-the-Thames," referring to the high number of English nominees. He concluded the broadcast on a similar note: "The losers will lock arms and march on the British Embassy." In between, the production ran much more smoothly than usual. Teleprompters were employed for the reading of the nominees rather than hand-held lists and there were more clips from the nominated films. The drama of the duelling fair ladies was heightened by some clever direction. Every time *My Fair Lady* won, the public got a shot of Andrews' reaction, and for every *Mary Poppins* victory, we were treated to Hepburn's visage. Reviews for the program were among the most positive in years.

Andrew Sarris of The Village Voice had a more cycnical view—"My theory here is not that the award ceremonies have gotten so much better but that the rest of television has gotten so much worse."

NATIONAL BOARD OF REVIEW

Picture: *Becket*; Actor: Anthony Quinn (*Zorba the Greek*); Actress: Kim Stanley (*Seance on a Wet Afternoon*); Supporting Actor: Martin Balsam (*The Carpetbaggers*); Supporting Actress: Dame Edith Evans (*The Chalk Garden*); Director: Desmond Davis (*The Girl with Green Eyes*); Foreign-Language Film: *World without Sun.*

BEST ENGLISH-LANGUAGE FILMS
Becket, My Fair Lady, The Girl with Green Eyes, The World of Henry Orient, Zorba the Greek,

Topkapi, The Chalk Garden, The Finest Hour, Four Days in November, Seance on a Wet Afternoon.

BEST FOREIGN-LANGUAGE FILMS

World without Sun (France/Italy), *The Organizer* (France/Italy/Yugoslavia), *Anatomy of a Marriage* (France/Italy), *Seduced and Abandoned* (France/Italy); *Yesterday, Today, and Tomorrow* (Italy).

NEW YORK FILM CRITICS CIRCLE

Picture: *My Fair Lady*; Actor: Rex Harrison (*My Fair Lady*); Actress: Kim Stanley (*Seance on a Wet Afternoon*); Director: Stanley Kubrick (*Dr. Strangelove*); Screenplay: Harold Pinter (*The Servant*); Foreign-Language Film: *That Man from Rio* (France); Special Citation: *To Be Alive!* (New York World's Fair film).

At the Oscars, it was no contest between the big studios and the new Hollywood. But in the Film Critics' Circle, the battle was more closely joined. In a hotly contested vote, *My Fair Lady* beat out *Dr. Strangelove* by eight votes to five on the sixth and final ballot.

HOLLYWOOD FOREIGN PRESS ASSOCIATION GOLDEN GLOBE AWARDS

Picture (Drama): *Becket*; Picture (Comedy or Musical): *My Fair Lady*; Actor (Drama): Peter O'Toole (*Becket*); Actress (Drama): Anne Bancroft (*The Pumpkin Eater*); Actor (Comedy or Musical): Rex Harrison (*My Fair Lady*); Actress (Comedy or Musical): Julie Andrews (*Mary Poppins*); Supporting Actor: Edmond O'Brien (*Seven Days in May*); Supporting Actress: Agnes Moorehead (*Hush . . . Hush, Sweet Charlotte*); Most Promising Newcomers (Male): Harv Presnell, George Segal, Chaim Topol; Most Promising Newcomers (Female): Mia Farrow, Celia Kaye, Mary Ann Mobley; Director: George Cukor (*My Fair Lady*); Original Score: Dimitri Tiomkin (*The Fall of the Roman Empire*); Song: "Circus World" from *Circus World*, music by Dimitri Tiomkin, lyrics by Ned Washington; English-Language Foreign Film: *The Girl with Green Eyes*; Foreign-Language Films: *Marriage, Italian Style* (Italy), *Sallah* (Israel); World Film Favorite (Male): Marcello Mastroianni; World Film Favorite (Female): Sophia Loren.

Julie Andrews was a little less restrained at the Golden Globes than she was at the Oscars. At the Hollywood Foreign Press's gala, Andrews thanked Jack Warner for making her *Mary Poppins* win possible since he did not cast her in *My Fair Lady*.

CANNES FILM FESTIVAL

Golden Palm: *The Umbrellas of Cherbourg* (France); Actor (tie): Antel Pager (*The Lark*) (Hungary) and Saro Urzi (*Seduced and Abandoned*) (Italy); Actress (tie): Anne Bancroft (*The Pumpkin Eater*) and Barbara Barrie (*One Potato, Two Potato*); Director: Not awarded; Special Jury Prize: *Woman in the Dunes* (Japan).

SPECIAL AWARDS

The Passenger (Poland) (special tribute and International Critics Prize); Jaromil Jires (*The Cry*) (Czechoslovakia), Georgui Danelia (*Romance in Moscow*) (USSR), and Manuel Summers (*La Nina du Luto*) (Spain) (promising young directors).

1965

ACADEMY AWARDS (OSCARS)

PICTURE

Darling
Doctor Zhivago
Ship of Fools
The Sound of Music
A Thousand Clowns

Big pictures were in at the 1965 Oscars. The pot was divided evenly between Twentieth Century-Fox's adaptation of the Broadway hit *The Sound of Music* and MGM's sweeping filmization of *Doctor Zhivago*, Boris Pasternak's novel of the Russian revolution. Each epic took five awards.

ACTOR

Richard Burton (*The Spy Who Came in from the Cold*)
Lee Marvin (*Cat Ballou*)
Laurence Olivier (*Othello*)

Rod Steiger (*The Pawnbroker*)
Oskar Werner (*Ship of Fools*)

Lee Marvin was a popular winner for a dual role of a tipsy gunslinger and his nasty twin brother in the parody Western *Cat Ballou*. He was accompanied on Oscar night by his lover Michelle Triola who would later become famous as a legal precedent for her "palimony" suit against Marvin. Rod Steiger's wrenching turn as a withdrawn Holocaust survivor in *The Pawnbroker* was thought to be a shoo-in in some quarters, but his stunning performance was in an independent production and Hollywood decided to honor its own with a win for Marvin's studio-produced comedy.

ACTRESS
Julie Andrews (*The Sound of Music*)
Julie Christie (*Darling*)
Samantha Eggar (*The Collector*)
Elizabeth Hartman (*A Patch of Blue*)
Simone Signoret (*Ship of Fools*)

It was the battle of the Julies for best Actress. The previous year's winner Julie Andrews as the whole-some postulant nun in *The Sound of Music* was pitted against fellow Brit Julie Christie as a much more worldly, bed-hopping model in *Darling*. When Christie won, she shocked the staid Academy audience and fashion consultant Edith Head with her slinky, shimmering, golden pajama suit. The film *Darling* also revolutionized the fashion world with its introduction of the mini-skirt, soon to be a staple of the Oscar ceremonies.

SUPPORTING ACTOR
Martin Balsam (*A Thousand Clowns*)
Ian Bannen (*The Flight of the Phoenix*)
Tom Courtenay (*Doctor Zhivago*)
Michael Dunn (*Ship of Fools*)
Frank Finlay (*Othello*)

SUPPORTING ACTRESS
Ruth Gordon (*Inside Daisy Clover*)
Joyce Redman (*Othello*)
Maggie Smith (*Othello*)
Shelley Winters (*A Patch of Blue*)
Peggy Wood (*The Sound of Music*)

Winters stated that she gained twenty pounds for her role as a frumpy, abusive mother in *A Patch of Blue*, just as she had for her other Oscar-winning role in *The Diary of Anne Frank*.

DIRECTOR
David Lean (*Doctor Zhivago*)
John Schlesinger (*Darling*)
Hiroshi Teshigahara (*Woman in the Dunes*)
Robert Wise (*The Sound of Music*)
William Wyler (*The Collector*)

ORIGINAL SCREENPLAY
Age, Scarpelli, Mario Monicello, Tonino Guerra, Giorgio Salvioni, Suso Cecchi D'Amico (*Casanova '70*)
Franklin Coen, Frank Davis (*The Train*)
Jack Davies, Ken Annakin (*Those Magnificent Men in Their Flying Machines*)
Jacques Demy (*The Umbrellas of Cherbourg*)
Frederic Raphael (*Darling*)

ADAPTED SCREENPLAY
Robert Bolt (*Doctor Zhivago*)
Herb Gardner (*A Thousand Clowns*)
Abby Mann (*Ship of Fools*)
Stanley Mann, John Kohn (*The Collector*)
Walter Newman, Frank R. Pierson (*Cat Ballou*)

FOREIGN-LANGUAGE FILM
Blood on the Land (Greece)
Dear John (Sweden)
Kwaidan (Japan)
Marriage, Italian Style (Italy)
The Shop on Main Street (Czechoslovakia)

OTHER AWARDS
Original Musical Score: Maurice Jarre (*Doctor Zhivago*); Adapted Musical Score: Irwin Kostal (*The Sound of Music*); Original Song: "The Shadow of Your Smile" from *The Sandpiper*, music by Johnny Mandel, lyrics by Paul Francis Webster; Cinematography: color—Freddie Young (*Doctor Zhivago*), black and white—Ernest Laszlo (*Ship of Fools*); Art Direction: color—John Box, Terry Marsh, Dario Simoni (*Doctor Zhivago*), black and white—Robert Clatworthy, Joseph Kish (*Ship of Fools*); Costume Design: color—Phyllis Dalton (*Doctor Zhivago*), black and white—Julie Harris

(*Darling*); Film Editing: William Reynolds (*The Sound of Music*); Sound: Twentieth Century-Fox Studio Sound Department, James P. Corcoran, sound director, and Todd-AO Sound Department, Fred Hynes, sound director (*The Sound of Music*); Sound Effects: Tregoweth Brown (*The Great Race*); Special Visual Effects: John Stears (*Thunderball*).

Documentary: *The Eleanor Roosevelt Story*; Documentary Short Subject: *To Be Alive!*; Live-Action Short Subject: *The Chicken* (*Le Poulet*); Animated Short Subject: *The Dot and the Line*.

SPECIAL AWARDS
Bob Hope; William Wyler (Irving Thalberg Award); Edmond L. DePatie (Jean Hersholt Humanitarian Award).

Building on a return of glamour in the '64 Oscars, the '65 ceremony was as glittering as ever. For the first time, the Oscars were broadcast in color (the heat from the extra camera lights caused many a winner and presenter to sweat profusely). In a stroke of good fortune, all of the acting winners were present for the first time in years. Favorite host Bob Hope returned to act as master of ceremonies. The set was dazzling display of forty-two sprinkling fountains. "Looks like Lloyd Bridges' rumpus room," Hope quipped. The fountains turned out to be so loud, they had to be shut off during the acceptance speeches.

But all the Tinseltown opulence was upstaged by the presence of First Daughter Lynda Byrd Johnson, arriving on the arm of George Hamilton. Hope joked that if the young actor were lucky he might end up as the second Hamilton in the White House. The comic's history was a little off since Alexander Hamilton was shot by Aaron Burr before reaching the White House.

NATIONAL BOARD OF REVIEW

English-Language Film: *The Eleanor Roosevelt Story*; Foreign-Language Film: *Juliet of the Spirits*; Actor: Lee Marvin (*Cat Ballou* and *Ship of Fools*); Actress: Julie Christie (*Darling* and *Doctor Zhivago*); Supporting Actor: Harry Andrews (*The Agony and the Ecstasy* and *The Hill*); Supporting Actress: Joan Blondell (*The Cincinnatti Kid*); Director: John Schlesinger (*Darling*).

BEST ENGLISH-LANGUAGE FILMS
The Eleanor Roosevelt Story, The Agony and the Ecstasy, Doctor Zhivago, Ship of Fools, The Spy Who Came in from the Cold, Darling, The Greatest Story Ever Told, A Thousand Clowns, The Train, The Sound of Music.

BEST FOREIGN-LANGUAGE FILMS
Juliet of the Spirits (France/Italy/Federal Republic of Germany), *The Overcoat* (USSR), *La Boheme* (Switzerland), *La Tia Tula* (Spain), *Gertrud* (Denmark).

Once again, the National Board bucked Hollywood by giving its best English-Language Film award to *The Eleanor Roosevelt Story*, a documentary.

NEW YORK FILM CRITICS CIRCLE

Picture: *Darling*; Actor: Oskar Werner (*Ship of Fools*); Actress: Julie Christie (*Darling*); Director: John Schlesinger (*Darling*); Foreign Film: *Juliet of the Spirits*.

The Film Critics reflected a wide diversity of opinion, with eight films receiving votes for best Picture. The sixth and final ballot resulted in *Darling*, the mod character study of swinging London, winning by eight votes. Its nearest rivals were the dark drama *The Pawnbroker* (five votes) and the wacky comedy *Those Magnificent Men in Their Flying Machines* (three). Ten directors were in the running and the acting categories contained eight contenders each.

HOLLYWOOD FOREIGN PRESS ASSOCIATION GOLDEN GLOBE AWARDS

Picture (Drama): *Doctor Zhivago*; Picture (Comedy or Musical): *The Sound of Music*; English-Language Foreign Film: *Darling*; Foreign-Language Foreign Film: *Juliet of the Spirits*; Actor (Drama): Omar Sharif (*Doctor Zhivago*); Actress (Drama): Samantha Eggar (*The Collector*); Actor (Comedy or Musical): Lee Marvin (*Cat Ballou*); Actress (Comedy or Musical): Julie Andrews (*The Sound of Music*); Supporting Actor: Oskar Werner (*The Spy Who Came in from the Cold*); Supporting Actress:

Ruth Gordon (*Inside Daisy Clover*); Most Promising Newcomer (Male): Robert Redford (*Inside Daisy Clover*); Most Promising Newcomer (Female): Elizabeth Hartman (*A Patch of Blue*); Director: David Lean (*Doctor Zhivago*); Screenplay: Robert Bolt (*Doctor Zhivago*); Original Score: Maurice Jarre (*Doctor Zhivago*); Original Song: "Forget Domani" from *The Yellow Rolls Royce*, music by Riz Ortolani, lyrics by Norman Newel; World Film Favorite (Male): Paul Newman; World Film Favorite (Female): Natalie Wood.

SPECIAL AWARDS
John Wayne (Cecil B. DeMille Award).

CANNES FILM FESTIVAL

Golden Palm: *The Knack and How to Get It*; Actor: Terence Stamp (*The Collector*); Actress: Samantha Eggar (*The Collector*); Director: Liviu Ciulei (*The Forest of Hanged Men*) (Romania); Screenplay: Ray Rigby (*The Hill*) and Pierre Schondorffer (*Platoon 317*) (France); Special Jury Prize: *Kwaidan* (Japan).

SPECIAL AWARDS
Special Mention of Actors: Ida Kaminska, Josef Kroner (*The Shop on Main Street*), Vera Kuznetsova (*There Was an Old Man and an Old Woman*) (USSR); International Critics Prize: *Tarahumara* (Mexico).

ACADEMY AWARDS (OSCARS)

PICTURE
Alfie
A Man for All Seasons
The Russians Are Coming, The Russians Are Coming
The Sand Pebbles
Who's Afraid of Virginia Woolf?

Hollywood was changing with the times and so was Oscar. The 1966 Oscar derby was dominated by British films like *Alfie* and *A Man for All Seasons*, and the work of foreign directors Claude Lelouch (*A Man and a Woman*) and Michelangelo Antonioni (*Blow Up*). Even the studios' most nominated production was an adaptation of a stage hit which broke all the previous standards for language and subject matter. Warner Brothers' version of Edward Albee's *Who's Afraid of Virginia Woolf?* employed adult language in its blistering portrayal of an embattled marriage. It won five accolades out of thirteen nominations.

But the big winner was the more dignified English production of another Broadway hit *A Man for All Seasons*. The stately story of Sir Thomas More and his battle of conscience with King Henry VIII took six Oscars including best Picture and best Actor for Paul Scofield as More. It was only the fourth film for the renowned stage actor who also won the Tony Award for the theater version.

ACTOR
Alan Arkin (*The Russians Are Coming The Russians Are Coming*)
Richard Burton (*Who's Afraid of Virginia Woolf?*)
Michael Caine (*Alfie*)
Steve McQueen (*The Sand Pebbles*)
Paul Scofield (*A Man for All Seasons*)

ACTRESS
Anouk Aimee (*A Man and a Woman*)
Ida Kaminska (*The Shop on Main Street*)
Lynn Redgrave (*Georgy Girl*)
Vanessa Redgrave (*Morgan!*)
Elizabeth Taylor (*Who's Afraid of Virginia Woolf?*)

The only American in the pack, Elizabeth Taylor won her second—and more deserved—Oscar for an unexpectedly powerful performance as the shrewish Martha in *Who's Afraid of Virginia Woolf?* The beautiful star proved she could act by taking on Albee's frowsy, alcoholic faculty wife and standing toe to toe with real-life husband Richard Burton in this no-prisoners-taken battle of the sexes. She failed to attend the ceremony, even though she had time off from her filming assignment on the French Riviera. Rumor had it Burton was not expected to win and Taylor did not want to be present for another loss for her spouse.

British sisters Lynn and Vanessa Redgrave followed Olivia de Havilland and Joan Fontaine as the second set of siblings nominated in the same year. French Anouk Aimee and Polish Ida Kaminska rounded out the international nominees.

SUPPORTING ACTOR
Mako (*The Sand Pebbles*)
James Mason (*Georgy Girl*)
Walter Matthau (*The Fortune Cookie*)
George Segal (*Who's Afraid of Virginia Woolf?*)
Robert Shaw (*A Man for All Seasons*)

Despite a motorcycle accident, Walter Matthau made it to the Oscars and was the only acting winner present. Elizabeth Taylor and Paul Scofield disdained to make the trip from Europe, while Sandy Dennis was filming a movie in New York. Reacting to the cast on Matthau's arm and the bruises on his face, presenter Shelley Winters quipped, "You had a hard time getting here." This was Matthau's first humorous role after a slew of villains. He took the hint and concentrated on comedy thereafter.

SUPPORTING ACTRESS
Sandy Dennis (*Who's Afraid of Virginia Woolf?*)
Wendy Hiller (*A Man for All Seasons*)
Jocelyn LaGarde (*Hawaii*)
Vivien Merchant (*Alfie*)
Geraldine Page (*You're a Big Boy Now*)

DIRECTOR
Michelangelo Antonioni (*Blow Up*)
Richard Brooks (*The Professionals*)
Claude Lelouch (*A Man and a Woman*)
Mike Nichols (*Who's Afraid of Virginia Woolf?*)
Fred Zinnemann (*A Man for All Seasons*)

ORIGINAL SCREENPLAY
Michelangelo Antonioni, Tonino Guerra, Edward Bond (*Blow Up*)
Robert Ardrey (*Khartoum*)
Clint Johnston, Don Peters (*The Naked Prey*)
Claude Lelouch, Pierre Uytterhoeven (*A Man and a Woman*)
Billy Wilder, I. A. L. Diamond (*The Fortune Cookie*)

ADAPTED SCREENPLAY
Robert Bolt (*A Man for All Seasons*)
Richard Brooks (*The Professionals*)
Ernest Lehman (*Who's Afraid of Virginia Woolf?*)

Bill Naughton (*Alfie*)
William Rose (*The Russians Are Coming, The Russians Are Coming*)

FOREIGN-LANGUAGE FILM
The Battle of Algiers (Italy)
Loves of a Blonde (Czechoslovakia)
A Man and a Woman (France)
Pharaoh (Poland)
Three (Yugoslavia)

OTHER AWARDS
Original Music Score: John Barry (*Born Free*); Adapted Score: Ken Thorne (*A Funny Thing Happened on the Way to the Forum*); Original Song: Title song from *Born Free*, music by John Barry, lyrics by Don Black; Cinematography: color—Ted Moore (*A Man for All Seasons*), black and white—Haskell Wesler (*Who's Afraid of Virginia Woolf?*); Art Direction: color—Jack Martin Smith, Dale Hennesy, Walter M. Scott, Stuart A. Reiss (*Fantastic Voyage*), black and white—Richard Sylbert, George James Hopkins (*Who's Afraid of Virginia Woolf?*); Costume Design: color—Elizabeth Huffenden, Joan Bridge (*A Man for All Seasons*), black and white—Irene Sharaff (*Who's Afraid of Virginia Woolf?*); Film Editing: Frederic Steinkamp, Henry Berman, Stewart Linder, Frank Santillo (*Grand Prix*); Sound: MGM Sound Department, Franklin E. Milton, sound director (*Grand Prix*); Sound Effects: Gordon Daniel (*Grand Prix*); Visual Effects: Art Cruickshank (*Fantastic Voyage*).

Documentary: *The War Game*; Documentary Short Subject: *A Year toward Tomorrow*; Live-Action Short Subject: *Wild Wings*; Animated Short Subject: *Herb Albert and the Tijuana Brass Double Feature*.

SPECIAL AWARDS
Stuntman Yakima Canutt; Y. Frank Freeman for service to the Academy; George Bagnall (Jean Hersholt Humanitarian Award); Robert Wise (Irving Thalberg Award).

The biggest drama of the 1966 Oscars took place off-camera. A strike by AFTRA, the television actors' union, could have resulted in a boycott or postponement of the ceremony. A settlement was rushed through just in time to get the show on the air. As for the program itself, Leo Mishkin of the *New York Morning-Telegram* summed up the prevailing critical sentimental by labeling it "a crashing bore." Bob Hope's trademark witticisms helped somewhat, but not enough. Even the commericals for Eastman Kodak film got better reviews. *The Christian Science Monitor* called them "spectacular."

The most dramatic moment of the program came when Patricia Neal, recently recovered from a series of strokes, appeared to present the Foreign-Language Film award. She received a sustained standing ovation. "It was a lovely, touching moment—and the only one in the two-and-a-half-hour show," commented Harriet Van Horne of the *New York Journal-Tribune*.

There were moments of entertaining flubs (Candice Bergen rushing down the aisle to accept an award for someone who was already there) and nostalgia (Fred Astaire and Ginger Rogers launching into a brief, ad-lib dance routine), but they were few and far between. Despite the lacklustre quality of the show, it did respectably in the ratings. As Andrew Sarris of *The Village Voice* noted, "Who among us could bear to miss a moment of the annual fiasco?"

NATIONAL BOARD OF REVIEW

English-Language Film: *A Man for All Seasons*; Foreign-Language Film: *The Sleeping Car Murders*; Actor: Paul Scofield (*A Man for All Seasons*); Actress: Elizabeth Taylor (*Who's Afraid of Virginia Woolf?*); Supporting Actor: Robert Shaw (*A Man for All Seasons*); Supporting Actress: Vivien Merchant (*Alfie*); Director: Fred Zinnemann (*A Man for All Seasons*).

BEST ENGLISH-LANGUAGE FILMS

A Man for All Seasons, Born Free, Alfie, Who's Afraid of Virginia Woolf?, The Bible, Georgy Girl, Years of Lightning, Day of Drums, It Happened Here, The Russians Are Coming..., Shakespeare Wallah.

BEST FOREIGN-LANGUAGE FILMS

The Sleeping Car Murders (France), *The Gospel According to St. Matthew* (France/Italy), *The Shameless Old Lady* (France), *A Man and a Woman* (France), *Hamlet* (USSR).

NEW YORK FILM CRITICS CIRCLE

Picture: *A Man for All Seasons*; Actor: Paul Scofield (*A Man for All Seasons*); Actress: (tie) Lynn Redgrave (*Georgy Girl*) and Elizabeth Taylor (*Who's Afraid of Virginia Woolf?*); Director: Fred Zinnemann (*A Man for All Seasons*); Screenplay: Robert Bolt (*A Man for All Seasons*); Foreign Film: *The Shop on Main Street*.

John Lindsay was the first Gotham mayor to host the New York Film Critics Circle ceremony since Fiorella LaGuardia emceed the premiere event in 1935. Lindsay co-hosted with Judith Crist, chair of the Circle. In the third tie in Circle history, Elizabeth Taylor and Lynn Redgrave received seven votes apiece.

NATIONAL SOCIETY OF FILM CRITICS

Picture: *Blow Up*; Actor: Michael Caine (*Alfie*); Actress: Sylvie (*The Shameless Old Lady*); Director: Michelangelo Antonioni (*Blow Up*).

The newly formed National Society was created to provide an alternative voice to that of the Film Critics Circle, regarded as "middle-brow" and too close to the Oscars by the fledgling group. The Society eliminated the distinction between English-language and foreign films for best Picture. Its choices have often differed from those of the Academy and other groups, usually going to foreign, independent, and off-beat films.

Though the Society was National in name, most of its charter members were New York-based critics working for magazines with a national circulation. An effort was made in 1972 to recruit reviewers from other cities.

HOLLYWOOD FOREIGN PRESS ASSOCIATION GOLDEN GLOBE AWARDS

Picture (Drama): *A Man for All Seasons*; Picture (Comedy or Musical): *The Russians Are Coming...*; English-Language Foreign Film: *Alfie*; Foreign-Language Foreign Film: *A Man and a Woman*; Actor (Drama): Paul Scofield (*A Man for All Seasons*); Actress (Drama): Anouk Aimee (*A Man and a Woman*); Actor (Comedy or Musical): Alan

Arkin (*The Russians Are Coming . . .*); Actress (Comedy or Musical): Lynn Redgrave (*Georgy Girl*); Supporting Actor: Richard Attenborough (*The Sand Pebbles*); Supporting Actress: Jocelyn LaGarde (*Hawaii*); Most Promising Newcomer (Male): James Farentino (*The Pad*); Most Promising Newcomer (Female): Camilla Spary (*Dead on a Merry Go Round*); Director: Fred Zinnemann (*A Man for All Seasons*); Screenplay: Robert Bolt (*A Man for All Seasons*); Original Score: Elmer Bernstein (*Hawaii*); Original Song: "Strangers in the Night" from *A Man Could Get Killed*, music by Bert Kaempfert, lyrics by Charles Singleton and Eddie Snyder; World Film Favorite (Male): Steve McQueen; World Film Favorite (Female): Julie Andrews.

SPECIAL AWARD

Charlton Heston (Cecil B. DeMille Award).

The Golden Globes were aired on NBC and featured TV canine Lassie delivering the envelope with the winners' names to presenter John Wayne.

CANNES FILM FESTIVAL

Golden Palm Award (tie): *A Man and a Woman* (France) and *The Birds, the Bees, and the Italians* (France/Italy); Actor: Per Oscarsson (*Hunger*) (Denmark/Norway/Sweden); Actress: Vanessa Redgrave (*Morgan*); Director: Sergei Yutkevich (*Lenin in Poland*) (USSR); Special Jury Prize: *Alfie*; Cannes 20th Anniversary Prize: Orson Welles.

ACADEMY AWARDS (OSCARS)

PICTURE

Bonnie and Clyde
Doctor Doolittle
The Graduate
Guess Who's Coming to Dinner?
In the Heat of the Night

"It was a vote against youth," stated Mike Nichols in response to the win of the studio-backed crime melodrama *In the Heat of the Night* over indepen-

dent films made by younger directors such as his own comedy *The Graduate* and Arthur Penn's ultra-violent *Bonnie and Clyde*.

Musical monstrosity *Doctor Doolittle* managed to squeeze into the best Picture ranks due to an aggressive Oscar campaign by Twentith Century-Fox. It was telling that *Doolittle* failed to receive nominations in any of the other major categories. It did receive eight other nominations in the design, technical, and music area. When its "Talk to the Animals" won for best Song, the cries of "Oh, no!" were quite audible.

ACTOR

Warren Beatty (*Bonnie and Clyde*)
Dustin Hoffman (*The Graduate*)
Paul Newman (*Cool Hand Luke*)
Rod Steiger (*In the Heat of the Night*)
Spencer Tracy (*Guess Who's Coming to Dinner*)

"Thank you and we shall overcome," Rod Steiger exuded to the Academy audience on his triumph for playing the bigoted southern sheriff who comes to respect a black police officer from up north in *In the Heat of the Night*. Carroll O'Connor would later win an Emmy Award for playing the same role in the TV series version.

Sidney Poitier co-starred with both leading Oscar winners Steiger and Katharine Hepburn as well as turning in a sterling performance in *To Sir with Love*, but was overlooked at Oscar nomination time.

ACTRESS

Anne Bancroft (*The Graduate*)
Faye Dunaway (*Bonnie and Clyde*)
Edith Evans (*The Whisperers*)
Audrey Hepburn (*Wait Until Dark*)
Katharine Hepburn (*Guess Who's Coming to Dinner?*)

Katharine Hepburn was the unexpected winner of a second Oscar. She was honored for her drily witty turn in *Guess Who's Coming to Dinner?* as a white liberal whose views are put to the test when her daughter announces she's marrying a black man. It was her ninth performance opposite Spencer Tracy, who died shortly after the film was completed. When informed she had won but Tracy had not, she said, "I'm glad I won it for Spence."

SUPPORTING ACTOR
John Cassavetes (*The Dirty Dozen*)
Gene Hackman (*Bonnie and Clyde*)
Cecil Kellaway (*Guess Who's Coming to Dinner?*)
George Kennedy (*Cool Hand Luke*)
Michael J. Pollard (*Bonnie and Clyde*)

Former stuntman George Kennedy spent $5,000 of his own money on trade ads for his Oscar bid. The clever self-made campaign featured a picture of Kennedy carrying star Paul Newman in a scene from *Cool Hand Luke*. The caption read "George Kennedy—Supporting."

SUPPORTING ACTRESS
Carol Channing (*Thoroughly Modern Millie*)
Mildred Natwick (*Barefoot in the Park*)
Estelle Parsons (*Bonnie and Clyde*)
Beah Richards (*Guess Who's Coming to Dinner?*)
Katharine Ross (*The Graduate*)

In view of the recent spate of no-shows by winners, the Academy begged all the nominees to be present. Academy president Gregory Peck pleaded with Broadway producer David Merrick to allow Estelle Parsons to take a night off from Merrick's New York production of *The Seven Descents of Myrtle* in order to attend the Oscars.

"Okay," Merrick told Peck, "if you'll agree to appear on the Tony Awards."

"You've got a deal," Peck responded.

DIRECTOR
Richard Brooks (*In Cold Blood*)
Norman Jewison (*In the Heat of the Night*)
Stanley Kramer (*Guess Who's Coming to Dinner?*)
Mike Nichols (*The Graduate*)
Arthur Penn (*Bonnie and Clyde*)

ORIGINAL SCREENPLAY
Robert Kaufman, Norman Lear (*Divorce American Style*)
David Newman, Robert Benton (*Bonnie and Clyde*)
Frederic Raphael (*Two for the Road*)
William Rose (*Guess Who's Coming to Dinner?*)
Jorge Semprun (*La Guerre Est Finie*)

ADAPTED SCREENPLAY
Richard Brooks (*In Cold Blood*)
Donn Pearce, Frank R. Pierson (*Cool Hand Luke*)
Stirling Silliphant (*In the Heat of the Night*)
Joseph Strick, Fred Haines (*Ulysses*)
Calder Willingham, Buck Henry (*The Graduate*)

FOREIGN-LANGUAGE FILM
Closely Watched Trains (Czechoslovakia)
El Amor Brujo (Spain)
I Even Met Happy Gypsies (Yugoslavia)
Live for Life (France)
Portrait of Chieko (Japan)

OTHER AWARDS
Original Score: Elmer Bernstein (*Thoroughly Modern Millie*); Adapted Score: Alfred Newman, Ken Darby (*Camelot*); Original Song: "Talk to the Animals" from *Doctor Doolittle*, music and lyrics by Leslie Bricusse; Cinematography: Burnett Guffey (*Bonnie and Clyde*); Art Direction: John Truscott, Edward Carrere, John W. Brown; Costume Design: John Truscott (*Camelot*); Film Editing: Hal Ashby (*In the Heat of the Night*); Sound: Samuel Goldwyn Studio Sound Department (*In the Heat of the Night*); Sound Effects: John Pyner (*The Dirty Dozen*); Visual Effects: L. B. Abbott (*Doctor Doolittle*).

Separate awards for color and black-and-white films in the categories of Art Direction, Costume Design, and Cinematography were eliminated.

Documentary: *The Anderson Platoon*; Documentary Short Subject: *The Redwoods*; Live-Action Short Subject: *A Place to Stand*; Animated Short Subject: *The Box*.

SPECIAL AWARDS
Arthur Freed, for service to the Academy and producing six award telecasts; Gregory Peck (Jean Hersholt Humanitarian Award); Alfred Hitchcock (Irving Thalberg Award).

For the first time in its history, the Academy Awards were postponed. Dr. Martin Luther King, Jr. was assassinated four days before the ceremony. The funeral was set for the day after the Oscarcast. African-American performers like Sidney Poitier, Diahann Carroll, Sammy Davis, Jr., and Louis

Angela Lansbury performs "Thoroughly Modern Millie" at the 1967 Oscars.

Armstrong as well as white actors like Rod Steiger had announced they would boycott the program if it went off as originally planned.

Academy president Gregory Peck told the press: "We are trying to do the appropriate thing, to suit the mood of the people." The ceremony was delayed by two days. (History would repeat itself thirteen years later when another Oscar show would be delayed due to assassination. The 1980 ceremony was postponed by one day when John Hinckley, Jr., unsuccesfully attempted to murder President Ronald Reagan, a former actor and Oscar show announcer.)

Peck opened the program with a dignified tribute to King. He was followed by Bob Hope making his fourteenth tour of duty as host. Hope toned down the potentially offensive political jibes in his opening monologue, but many critics still found his jokes about the two-day delay, the bombing in Hanoi, and Lyndon Johnson's recent decision not to seek a second term as President tasteless.

The proceedings were enlivened by some excep-tionally spirited deliveries of the best Song nominees. Angela Lansbury gave "Thoroughly Modern Millie" the Broadway razzle-dazzle treatment; a Nehru-jacketed Sammy Davis, Jr., put across "Talk to the Animals"; and Louis Armstrong cavorted with dancers costumed as a bear, a gorilla, and an elephant for "The Bare Necessities."

The turbulent events of the late '60s were evident at this Oscarcast. A French anti-Vietnam War feature took the best Documentary award. There were references to "peace and love" in acceptance speeches and Hope concluded the broadcast with the maxim "rioting and indifference are equal sins."

NATIONAL BOARD OF REVIEW

English-Language Film: *Far from the Madding Crowd*; Foreign-Language Film: *Elvira Madigan*: Actor: Peter Finch (*Far from the Madding Crowd*); Actress: Edith Evans (*The Whisperers*); Supporting Actor: Paul Ford (*The Comedians*); Supporting Actress: Marjorie Rhodes (*The Family Way*); Director: Richard Brooks (*In Cold Blood*).

BEST ENGLISH-LANGUAGE FILMS
Far from the Madding Crowd, The Whisperers, Ulysses, In Cold Blood, The Family Way, The Taming of the Shrew, Doctor Doolittle, The Graduate, The Comedians, Accident.

BEST FOREIGN-LANGUAGE FILMS
Elvira Madigan (Sweden), *The Hunt* (Spain), *Africa Addio* (Italy), *Persona* (Sweden), *The Great British Train Robbery* (Federal Republic of Germany).

NEW YORK FILM CRITICS CIRCLE

Picture: *In the Heat of the Night*; Actor: Rod Steiger (*In the Heat of the Night*); Actress: Edith Evans (*The Whisperers*); Director: Mike Nichols (*The Graduate*); Screenplay: David Newman, Robert Benton (*Bonnie and Clyde*); Foreign Film: *La Guerre Est Finie*; Special Award: Retiring *New York Times* film critic Bosley Crowther.

Senator Robert Kennedy appeared at the Critics' ceremony, presenting the Best Picture award to *In the Heat of the Night*. Retiring *New York Times* critic Bosley Crowther hosted the event and received a special award for his service to the Circle.

When presenting the award for best Screenplay to David Newman and Robert Benton for *Bonnie and Clyde*, Crowther called their work a "highly imaginative and indisputably original script." He was referring to his published remarks that the film did not capture the true Bonnie and Clyde, but glamorized them and their violent careers. Word had it that that the powerful reviewer had prevented *B & C* from receiving the Circle's best Picture nod.

With Crowther's retirement, the Circle would become bolder and more unconventional in its selections.

NATIONAL SOCIETY OF FILM CRITICS

Picture: *Persona*; Actor: Rod Steiger (*In the Heat of the Night*); Actress: Bibi Andersson (*Persona*); Supporting Actor: Gene Hackman (*Bonnie and Clyde*); Supporting Actress: Marjorie Rhodes (*The Family Way*); Director: Ingmar Bergman (*Persona*); Screenplay: David Newman, Robert Benton

(*Bonnie and Clyde*); Cinematography: Haskell Wexler (*In the Heat of the Night*).

HOLLYWOOD FOREIGN PRESS ASSOCIATION GOLDEN GLOBE AWARDS

Picture (Drama): *In the Heat of the Night*; Picture (Comedy or Musical): *The Graduate*; English-Language Foreign Film: *The Fox*; Foreign-Language Foreign Film: *Live for Life* (France); Actor (Drama): Rod Steiger (*In the Heat of the Night*); Actress (Drama): Edith Evans (*The Whisperers*); Actor (Comedy or Musical): Dustin Hoffman (*The Graduate*); Actress (Comedy or Musical): Anne Bancroft (*The Graduate*); Supporting Actor: Richard Attenborough (*Doctor Doolittle*); Supporting Actress: Carol Channing (*Thoroughly Modern Millie*); Most Promising Newcomer (Male): Dustin Hoffman (*The Graduate*); Most Promising Newcomer (Female): Katharine Ross (*The Graduate*); Director: Mike Nichols (*The Graduate*); Screenplay: Sterling Silliphant (*In the Heat of the Night*); Original Score: Frederick Loewe (*Camelot*); Original Song: "If Ever I Would Leave You" from *Camelot*, music by Frederick Loewe, lyrics by Alan Jay Lerner; World Film Favorite (Male): Paul Newman; World Film Favorite (Female): Julie Andrews.

SPECIAL AWARD
Kirk Douglas (Cecil B. DeMille Award).

The announced winner of the World Film Favorite (Male) Golden Globe had been Frank Sinatra. But when Old Blue Eyes informed the Hollywood Foreign Press Association he would not be attending the ceremony, the membership demanded a recount. It turned out Paul Newman—who had agreed to be present—was the correct winner after all.

The Federal Communications Commission and NBC (which aired the show) began investigating the GG voting procedures. The HFPA later stated the World Film Favorites were chosen by a Reuters News Agency survey and hired the accounting firm of Ernst and Young to keep the balloting on the level.

The 1967 GGs were rife with other disasters. Sally Field, dressed as her TV character, the Flying

Nun, was supposed to swoop in with an envelope containing a winner's name. She got tangled in the wiring and had to stay near the ceiling.

To add to the confusion, the rules in the music categories were stretched. Both the score for *Camelot* and the song "If Ever I Would Leave You" were not orignally composed for the film, but were first heard in the 1960 Broadway stage version. Despite this, the HFPA awarded them Golden Globes for Original Score and Song.

CANNES FILM FESTIVAL

Golden Palm Award: *Blow-Up* (Britain/Italy); Actor: Odded Kotler (*Three Days and a Child*) (Israel); Actress: Pia Degermark (*Elvira Madigan*) (Sweden); Director: Ferenc Kosa (*Ten Thousand Suns*) (Hungary); Screenplay: Alain Jessua (*The Killing Game/Comic-Strip Hero*) (France), Elio Petri, Ugo Pirro (*We Still Kill the Old Way*) (Italy); Special Jury Prize: *Accident* and *I Even Met Happy Gypsies* (Yugoslavia).

SPECIAL AWARDS

Best First Film: *Les Vents des Aures* (Algeria); Internationl Critics Prize: *Accident* (UK), *Earth in Revolt* (Brazil), *I Even Met Happy Gypsies*; Special tribute to the work of Robert Bresson.

ACADEMY AWARDS (OSCARS)

PICTURE
Funny Girl
The Lion in Winter
Oliver!
Rachel, Rachel
Romeo and Juliet

The last hurrah of film musicals *Oliver!*, derived from Charles Dickens' *Oliver Twist* and a stage hit in London and on Broadway, was a surprise winner. *The Lion in Winter*, the New York Film Critics Circle's choice for best picture, was thought to have the edge. After *Oliver!*, few singing films would make it big.

Most glaring omission: Stanley Kubrick's *2001: A Space Odyssey*, a favorite with youthful audiences, a dazzling glimpse into the near future, and the year's second-highest grosser, was shut out of the best Picture field. Many attributed this to the advancing age of the Academy electorate. Academy president Gregory Peck attempted to replenish the greying ranks by recruiting new members.

ACTOR
Alan Arkin (*The Heart Is a Lonely Hunter*)
Alan Bates (*The Fixer*)
Ron Moody (*Oliver!*)
Peter O'Toole (*The Lion in Winter*)
Cliff Robertson (*Charly*)

Cliff Robertson was shooting *Too Late the Hero*, a World War II film, in the Philippines on Oscar night. A dozen Japanese actors, playing his captors, tossed him in the air three times. His Oscar did not save Robertson from outcast status when he exposed Columbia's David Begelman in a 1977 financial scandal.

ACTRESS (TIE)
Katharine Hepburn (*The Lion in Winter*)
Patricia Neal (*The Subject Was Roses*)
Vanessa Redgrave (*Isadora*)
Barbra Streisand (*Funny Girl*)
Joanne Woodward (*Rachel, Rachel*)

In the first best Actress tie ever, newcomer Barbra Streisand's repeat of her Broadway triumph as Fanny Brice in the musical biopic *Funny Girl* tied legend Katharine Hepburn's interpretation of the steely twelfth-century monarch Eleanor of Aquitaine in *The Lion in Winter*. As usual, Hepburn was not present. Streisand saluted her award with a line from her film ("Hello, gorgeous") and shocked viewers—and Oscar fashion consultant Edith Head—with her see-through pajama outfit. "The first script of *Funny Girl* was written when I was 11 years old," she said. "Thank God it took so long to get it right."

SUPPORTING ACTOR
Jack Albertson (*The Subject Was Roses*)
Seymour Cassel (*Faces*)
Daniel Massey (*Star!*)

Jack Wild (*Oliver!*)
Gene Wilder (*The Producers*)

Veteran Jack Albertson had toiled for decades as a second banana in burlesque, vaudeville, and television before landing the role of the disillusioned father in Frank Gilroy's play *The Subject Was Roses*. He won the Tony and the Oscar for the stage and film versions.

SUPPORTING ACTRESS

Lynn Carlin (*Faces*)
Ruth Gordon (*Rosemary's Baby*)
Sondra Locke (*The Heart Is a Lonely Hunter*)
Kay Medford (*Funny Girl*)
Estelle Parsons (*Rachel, Rachel*)

"I made my first movie in 1915 and here it is 1969," Ruth Gordon told the Academy audience. "You have no idea how encouraging a thing like this is." The seventy-two-year-old actress won for her role as a housewife-y Satan worshipper in *Rosemary's Baby*. She had been nominated twice in the screenwriting categories for *A Double Life* (1947) and *Pat and Mike* (1952), both collaborations with her husband Garson Kanin.

DIRECTOR

Anthony Harvey (*The Lion in Winter*)
Stanley Kubrick (*2001: A Space Odyssey*)
Gillo Pontecorvo (*The Battle of Algiers*)
Carol Reed (*Oliver!*)
Franco Zeffirelli (*Romeo and Juliet*)

ORIGINAL SCREENPLAY

Mel Brooks (*The Producers*)
John Cassavetes (*Faces*)
Stanley Kubrick, Arthur C. Clarke
    (*2001: A Space Odyssey*)
Franco Solinas, Gillo Pontecorvo
    (*The Battle of Algiers*)
Ira Wallach, Peter Ustinov (*Hot Millions*)

ADAPTED SCREENPLAY

James Goldman (*The Lion in Winter*)
Vernon Harris (*Oliver!*)
Roman Polanski (*Rosemary's Baby*)
Neil Simon (*The Odd Couple*)
Stewart Stern (*Rachel, Rachel*)

FOREIGN-LANGUAGE FILM

The Boys of Paul Street (Hungary)
The Fireman's Ball (Czechoslovakia)
The Girl with the Pistol (Italy)
Stolen Kisses (France)
War and Peace (USSR)

OTHER AWARDS

Original Score (Non-Musical Film): John Barry (*The Lion in Winter*); Original or Adapted Score (Musical Film): John Green (*Oliver!*); Original Song: "The Windmills of Your Mind" from *The Thomas Crown Affair*, music by Michel LeGrand, lyrics by Alan and Marilyn Bergman; Cinematography: Pasqualino De Santis (*Romeo and Juliet*); Art Direction: John Box, Terrence Marsh, Vernon Dixon, Ken Muggleston (*Oliver!*); Costume Design: Danilo Donati (*Romeo and Juliet*); Film Editing: Frank P. Keller (*Bullitt*); Sound: Shepperton Studio Sound Department (*Oliver!*); Visual Effects: Stanley Kubrick (*2001: A Space Odyssey*).

Documentary: *Journey into Self*; Documentary Short Subject: *Why Man Creates*; Live-Action Short Subject: *Robert Kennedy Remembered*; Animated Short Subject: *Winnie the Pooh and the Blustery Day*.

SPECIAL AWARDS

Martha Raye (Jean Hersholt Humanitarian Award); John Chambers for his make-up achievement in *Planet of the Apes*; Onna White for her choreography in *Oliver!*.

Oscar hit age 40 and made several mid-life changes. He got a new producer-director (Broadway's Gower Champion), a new musical director (Henry Mancini), and after eight years in suburban Santa Monica, the ceremony was moved to the Dorothy Chandler Pavillion in downtown Los Angeles.

"We're aiming for a 90-minute show," Champion told the *Sunday Boston Globe*. "At the most it will not run over two hours." Champion made several adjustments to ensure a fast-paced, modern show. There was no overture, no shots of the stars arriving, and no alternative acceptors were allowed if the winner was not present (although *Lion in Winter* director Anthony Harvey did pick

Don Rickles (right) coaches Frank Sinatra at the 1968 Academy Awards.

up Hepburn's prize). Jane Fonda introduced a choreographed number highlighting the nominees for best Costume Design, set to the music of The Soul Rascals. Henry Mancini and Marni Nixon performed a mini-operetta while presenting the musical nominees. Prickly comedian Don Rickles, who had made a hit at that year's Emmy Awards, juiced up the proceedings by barging in on Frank Sinatra's reading of the Screenplay candidates.

Bob Hope was not employed as emcee. Instead, the hosting duties were shared by ten "friends of Oscar" including Ingrid Bergman, Sidney Poitier, Natalie Wood, and Burt Lancaster. Hope did present the Jean Hersholt Humanitarian Award to Martha Raye for entertaining American troops in Southeast Asia. She was the first woman to be so honored. "It's the first time I haven't emceed in about four years and I dropped by to see how I

wasn't doing," the comic quipped.

Oscar's new look drew mixed notices. Kay Gardella of the *New York Daily News* found the show "streamlined, but sterile," with Hope's brief appearance the highlight. Vincent Canby, film critic for *The New York Times*, felt otherwise. "I must say, it was great," he wrote.

The show was televised worldwide for the first time. It was broadcast live in Canada and Mexico and delayed videotapes were seen in thirty other countries within hours.

NATIONAL BOARD OF REVIEW

English-Language Film: *The Shoes of the Fisherman*; Foreign-Language Film: *War and Peace*; Actor: Cliff Robertson (*Charly*); Actress: Liv Ullmann (*Shame* and *Hour of the Wolf*); Supporting Actor: Leo McKern (*The Shoes of the Fisherman*); Supporting

Actress: Virginia Maskell (*Interlude*); Director: Franco Zeffirelli (*Romeo and Juliet*).

BEST ENGLISH-LANGUAGE FILMS
The Shoes of the Fisherman, Romeo and Juliet, Yellow Submarine, Charly, Rachel, Rachel, The Subject Was Roses, The Lion in Winter, Planet of the Apes, Oliver!, 2001: A Space Odyssey.

BEST FOREIGN-LANGUAGE FILMS
War and Peace (USSR), *Hagbard and Signo* (Denmark/Iceland/Sweden), *Hunger* (Denmark/Norway/Sweden), *The Two of Us* (France), *The Bride Wore Black* (France/Italy).

NEW YORK FILM CRITICS CIRCLE

Picture: *The Lion in Winter*; Actor: Alan Arkin (*The Heart Is a Lonely Hunter*); Actress: Joanne Woodward (*Rachel, Rachel*); Director: Paul Newman (*Rachel, Rachel*); Screenplay: Lorenzo Semple, Jr. (*Pretty Poison*); Foreign Film: *War and Peace* (USSR).

The first post-Crowther Circle voting erupted in controversy. In an attempt to pump new blood into the organization, members of the radical National Society of Film Critics were admitted into the Circle. The battle lines between old and new schools of criticism were drawn over the best Picture ballot. Four new members—Crowther's replacement at the *Times* Renada Adler, her colleague at the same paper Vincent Canby, Richard Schickel of *Life Magazine*, and Stefan Kanfer of *Time*—all threatened to resign when the award went to the conventional costume drama *The Lion in Winter* over John Cassavetes' quirky, independent, character study *Faces*.

New rules were introduced for the next year and the Movie Critics Gang of Four did not resign.

NATIONAL SOCIETY OF FILM CRITICS

Picture: *Shame*; Actor: Per Oscarsson (*Hunger*); Actress: Liv Ullmann (*Shame*); Supporting Actor: Seymour Cassel (*Faces*); Supporting Actress: Billie Whitelaw (*Charlie Bubbles*); Director: Ingmar Bergman (*Shame* and *Hour of the Wolf*); Screenplay: John Cassavetes (*Faces*); Cinematography: William

A. Fraker (*Bullitt*); Special Awards: *Warrendale* and *A Face of War*, outstanding documentaries, *Yellow Submarine*, outstanding animation.

While Oscar played it safe with the adorable dancing orphans of *Oliver!* and the New York Film Critics voted for the stately and conventional dignity of *The Lion in Winter*, the National Society went for the bleak alienation of Ingmar Bergman. Their best Picture award went to the Swedish director's *Shame*, a shattering study of the effects of war on an ordinary couple played by two of Bergman's regular leads, Max von Sydow and Liv Ullmann.

HOLLYWOOD FOREIGN PRESS ASSOCIATION GOLDEN GLOBE AWARDS

Picture (Drama): *The Lion in Winter*; Picture (Musical or Comedy): *Oliver!*; English-Language Foreign Film: *Romeo and Juliet*; Foreign-Language Foreign Film: *War and Peace*; Actor (Drama): Peter O'Toole (*The Lion in Winter*); Actress (Drama): Joanne Woodward (*Rachel, Rachel*); Actor (Comedy or Musical): Ron Moody (*Oliver!*); Actress (Comedy or Musical): Barbra Striesand (*Funny Girl*); Supporting Actor: Daniel Massey (*Star!*); Supporting Actress: Ruth Gordon (*Rosemary's Baby*); Most Promising Newcomer (Male): Leonard Whiting (*Romeo and Juliet*); Most Promising Newcomer (Female): Olivia Hussey (*Romeo and Juliet*); Director: Paul Newman (*Rachel, Rachel*); Screenplay: Stirling Silliphant (*Charly*); Original Score: Alex North (*The Shoes of the Fisherman*); Original Song: "The Windmills of Your Mind" from *The Thomas Crown Affair*, by Michel Legrand and Alan and Marilyn Bergman; World Film Favorite (Male): Sidney Poitier; World Film Favorite (Female): Sophia Loren.

SPECIAL AWARDS
Gregory Peck (Cecil B. DeMille Award).

CANNES FILM FESTIVAL

The spirit of rebellion swept the world in 1968. Even the Cannes Film Festival fell victim to the international protest movement. When the French government fired the beloved Henri Langlois from his post as director of the Cinémathèque Française, film personalities including Simone Signoret, Yves Montand, and Francois Truffaut took to the streets with shouts and placards. The movement spread to engulf other issues including American involvement in Vietnam. There was a general strike and the gathering of movie folk at Cannes was canceled as a result.

ACADEMY AWARDS (OSCARS)

PICTURE
Anne of the Thousand Days
Butch Cassidy and the Sundance Kid
Hello, Dolly!
Midnight Cowboy
Z

Nineteen sixty-nine saw the motion picture industry institute a ratings system to allow filmgoers to know the basic content of pictures. An X rating was originally intended to be used for general-release films with adult themes wherein no one under age 18 would be admitted. But it came to denote unadulterated pornography.

By 1990 standards, *Midnight Cowboy* is mild. The dramatic buddy story of two drifters, a would-be male prostitute (Jon Voight) and a dying con artist (Dustin Hoffman), contained some nudity and sexual situations but none you wouldn't find in any R-rated movie made twenty-five years later.

Not only did it have an X rating against it, but *Midnight Cowboy* was filmed on location in New York and directed by an Englishman. One would think these three anti-Hollywood strikes would have sent *Cowboy* home Oscarless, particularly since Universal launched a $20,000 campaign for *Anne of the Thousand Days* which included a free filet mignon dinner with every screening.

Cowboy's win was attributed to the infusion of new, younger members Gregory Peck had campaigned so hard to join the Academy.

ACTOR
Richard Burton (*Anne of the Thousand Days*)
Dustin Hoffman (*Midnight Cowboy*)
Peter O'Toole (*Goodbye, Mr. Chips*)
Jon Voight (*Midnight Cowboy*)
John Wayne (*True Grit*)

While a *Midnight Cowboy* took best Picture, an old-time cowboy—John Wayne—took best Actor. Despite Dustin Hoffman's highly praised performance as Ratso Rizzo in the top film winner and Richard Burton's sixth Oscar-nominated performance (as Henry VIII in *Anne of the Thousand Days*), Academy voters went for sentiment, honoring Wayne for his long career. According to Burton biographer Melvyn Bragg, Wayne went to Burton's and Elizabeth Taylor's hotel room after the awards, thrust the Oscar at his losing fellow nominee and said, "You deserve this. Not me." The two actors proceeded to spend the night drinking.

ACTRESS
Genevieve Bujold (*Anne of the Thousand Days*)
Jane Fonda (*They Shoot Horses, Don't They?*)
Liza Minnelli (*The Sterile Cuckoo*)
Jean Simmons (*The Happy Ending*)
Maggie Smith (*The Prime of Miss Jean Brodie*)

Maggie Smith's theatrically precise performance as Jean Brodie, the eccentric Scottish teacher, was not released in Oscar prime time. The film opened in March and only played a few weeks. Voters were reminded of her brilliance when she appeared in Los Angeles with the English National Theatre's touring production of *The Beaux Strategem* the following January.

Smith was in London on the big night. The award was accepted by comedienne Alice Ghostley (who wasn't even identified on the show). Ghostley had co-starred with Smith on Broadway in *New Faces of 1956.*

Jane Fonda was also a favorite, but insiders predicted she had squashed her chances when she toked marijuana while being interviewed by Rex Reed for the *New York Post.*

SUPPORTING ACTOR
Rupert Crosse (*The Reivers*)
Elliott Gould (*Bob & Carol & Ted & Alice*)

Jack Nicholson (*Easy Rider*)
Anthony Quayle (*Anne of the Thousand Days*)
Gig Young (*They Shoot Horses, Don't They?*)

Jack Nicholson earned stunning reviews and awards from both the New York Film Critics Circle and National Society of Film Critics for his drop-out lawyer in the cult hit *Easy Rider*. But the Oscar went to Hollywood character actor Gig Young as the hard-bitten dance-marathon emcee in *They Shoot Horses, Don't They?* Young shot his wife and himself eight years later.

SUPPORTING ACTRESS
Catherine Burns (*Last Summer*)
Dyan Cannon (*Bob & Carol & Ted & Alice*)
Goldie Hawn (*Cactus Flower*)
Sylvia Miles (*Midnight Cowboy*)
Susannah York (*They Shoot Horses, Don't They?*)

Laugh-In regular Goldie Hawn was a surprise winner as Walter Matthau's young girlfriend in *Cactus Flower*. Raquel Welch accepted for Hawn who, like Maggie Smith, was in London.

DIRECTOR
Costa-Gravas (*Z*)
George Roy Hill (*Butch Cassidy and the Sundance Kid*)
Arthur Penn (*Alice's Restaurant*)
Sydney Pollack (*They Shoot Horses, Don't They?*)
John Schlesinger (*Midnight Cowboy*)

ORIGINAL SCREENPLAY
Nicola Badalucco, Enrico Medioli, Luchino Visconti (*The Damned*)
Peter Fonda, Dennis Hopper, Terry Southern (*Easy Rider*)
William Goldman (*Butch Cassidy and the Sundance Kid*)
Walon Green, Roy N. Sickner, Sam Peckinpah (*The Wild Bunch*)
Paul Mazursky, Larry Tucker (*Bob & Carol & Ted & Alice*)

ADAPTED SCREENPLAY
John Hale, Bridget Boland, Richard Sokolove (*Anne of the Thousand Days*)
James Poe, Robert E. Thompson (*They Shoot Horses, Don't They?*)
Waldo Salt (*Midnight Cowboy*)
Arnold Schulman (*Goodbye, Columbus*)
Jorge Semprun, Costa-Gravas (*Z*)

FOREIGN-LANGUAGE FILM
Adalen '31 (Sweden)
The Battle of Neretva (Yugoslavia)
The Brothers Karamazov (USSR)
My Night at Maud's (France)
Z (Algeria)

Z was the first picture to be nominated for both best Picture and best Foreign-Language Film.

OTHER AWARDS
Original Score (Non-Musical Picture): Burt Bacharach (*Butch Cassidy and the Sundance Kid*); Score for a Musical Picture: Lennie Hayton, Lionel Newman (*Hello, Dolly!*); Original Song: "Raindrops Keep Fallin' on My Head" from *Butch Cassidy and the Sundance Kid*, music by Burt Bacharach, lyrics by Hal David; Cinematography: Conrad Hall (*Butch Cassidy and the Sundance Kid*); Art Direction: John DeCuir, Jack Martin Smith, Herman Blumenthal, Walter M. Scott, George Hopkins, Raphael Bretton (*Hello, Dolly!*); Costume Design: Margaret Furse (*Anne of the Thousand Days*); Film Editing: Francoise Bonnot (*Z*); Sound: Jack Solomon, Murray Spivack (*Hello, Dolly!*); Visual Effects: Robbie Robertson (*Marooned*).

Documentary: *Arthur Rubinstein: The Love of Life*; Documentary Short Subject: *Czechoslovakia 1968*; Live-Action Short Subject: *The Magic Machines*; Animated Short Subject: *It's Tough to Be a Bird*.

SPECIAL AWARDS
Cary Grant; George Jessel (Jean Hersholt Humanitarian Award).

It was the Old Hollywood mixing with the New at the 1969 Oscars. John Wayne, Cary Grant, and George Jessel were honored along with the first X-rated best Film while radicals like Jane and Peter Fonda were nominated. Bob Hope made his sixteenth Academy Awards appearance, but was only one of fifteen "friends of Oscar." His comedy monologue was chock full of references to the new open sexuality of current films. "It's such a novelty to see actors with their clothes on" was a typical zinger. Like grade-schoolers snickering over a *Playboy*, the Oscar presenters continued with the slightly ribald, slightly tasteless innuendoes all evening. "I'm here for Special Visual Effects . . . and there are two of them," said the voluptuous Raquel Welch. Even John Wayne joined in. "I work with my clothes on. I have to, horses are rough on your legs" was his contribution.

Elizabeth Taylor got the most press. Though disappointed that husband Richard Burton had lost to Wayne, she dazzled the audience with the $1 million diamond Burton had given her, made into a necklace for the occasion, as she presented the best Picture award.

NATIONAL BOARD OF REVIEW

English-Language Film: *They Shoot Horses, Don't They?*; Foreign-Language Film: *Shame*; Actor: Peter O'Toole (*Goodbye, Mr. Chips*); Actress: Geraldine Page (*Trilogy*); Supporting Actor: Phillippe Noiret (*Topaz*); Supporting Actress: Pamela Franklin (*The Prime of Miss Jean Brodie*); Director: Alfred Hitchcock (*Topaz*).

BEST ENGLISH-LANGUAGE FILMS

They Shoot Horses, Don't They?, Ring of Bright Water, Topaz, Goodbye, Mr. Chips, Battle of Britain, The Loves of Isadora, The Prime of Miss Jean Brodie, Support Your Local Sheriff, True Grit, Midnight Cowboy.

BEST FOREIGN-LANGUAGE FILMS

Shame (Sweden), *Stolen Kisses* (France), *The Damned* (Italy), *Le Femme Infidele* (France/Italy), *Adalen '31* (Sweden).

NEW YORK FILM CRITICS CIRCLE

Picture: *Z*; Actor: Jon Voight (*Midnight Cowboy*); Actress: Jane Fonda (*They Shoot Horses, Don't They?*); Supporting Actor: Jack Nicholson (*Easy Rider*); Supporting Actress: Dyan Cannon (*Bob & Carol & Ted & Alice*); Director: Costa-Gravas (*Z*); Screenplay: *Bob & Carol & Ted & Alice*—awarded to the film itself, not the individual writers.

In response to last year's threat of resignation by four new members, the Circle spruced itself up and made some rule changes similar to those of the younger National Society of Film Critics. A new weighted voting system with critics putting down their top three choices was instituted to eliminate the need for numerous ballots in order for a candidate to achieve a clear majority. Supporting acting honors were added. The Best Picture category was now open to both English-language and foreign-language films. Costa-Gravas' Algerian-French-made political thriller *Z* became the first beneficary of this rule change, taking the scribes' Best Picture honor. It was followed in the voting by the English musical *Oh! What a Lovely War*, the Italian *The Damned*, and *Midnight Cowboy*.

NATIONAL SOCIETY OF FILM CRITICS

Picture: *Z*; Actor: Jon Voight (*Midnight Cowboy*); Actress: Vanessa Redgrave (*The Loves of Isadora*); Supporting Actor: Jack Nicholson (*Easy Rider*); Supporting Actress: Sian Philips (*Goodbye, Mr. Chips*); Director: Francois Truffaut (*Stolen Kisses*); Screenplay: Paul Mazursky, Larry Tucker (*Bob & Carol & Ted & Alice*); Cinematography: Lucien Ballard (*The Wild Bunch*); Special Awards: Ivan Passer for *Intimate Lightning*, Dennis Hopper for directing, co-writing and co-starring in *Easy Rider*.

HOLLYWOOD FOREIGN PRESS ASSOCIATION GOLDEN GLOBE AWARDS

Picture (Drama): *Anne of the Thousand Days*; Picture (Comedy or Musical): *The Secret of Santa Vittoria*; English-Language Foreign Film: *Oh, What a Lovely War!*; Foreign-Language Foreign Film: *Z*; Actor (Drama): John Wayne (*True Grit*); Actress (Drama): Genevieve Bujold (*Anne of the Thousand Days*); Actor (Comedy or Musical): Peter O'Toole (*Goodbye, Mr. Chips*); Actress (Comedy or Musical): Patty Duke (*Me, Natalie*); Supporting Actor: Gig Young (*They Shoot Horses, Don't They?*); Supporting Actress: Goldie Hawn (*Cactus Flower*); Most Promising Newcomer (Male): Jon Voight (*Midnight Cowboy*); Most Promising Newcomer (Female): Ali MacGraw (*Goodbye, Columbus*);

Director: Charles Jarrot (*Anne of the Thousand Days*); Screenplay: John Hale, Bridget Boland, Richard Sokolove (*Anne of the Thousand Days*); Original Score: Burt Bacharach (*Butch Cassidy and the Sundance Kid*); Original Song: "Jean" from *The Prime of Miss Jean Brodie*, by Rod McKuen; World Film Favorite (Male): Steve McQueen; World Film Favorite (Female): Barbra Streisand.

SPECIAL AWARD
Joan Crawford (Cecil B. DeMille Award).

CANNES FILM FESTIVAL

Golden Palm Award: *If*; Actor: Jean-Louis Trintignant (*Z*) (France/Algeria); Actress: Vanessa Redgrave (*The Loves of Isadora*); Director (tie): Glauber Rocha (*Antonio Das Mortes*) (Brazil) and Vojtech Jasny (*All My Countrymen*) (Czechoslovakia); Special Jury Prize: *Z* and *Adalen '31* (Sweden).

SPECIAL AWARDS
Easy Rider (Best First Film); *All My Countrymen* (*Technical Award); Andrei Rublev* (USSR) (International Critics Prize).

ACADEMY AWARDS (OSCARS)

PICTURE
Airport
Five Easy Pieces
Love Story
M*A*S*H
Patton

Slick studio fodder like *Airport* and *Love Story* vied with quirky tales of nonconformism like *M*A*S*H* and *Five Easy Pieces*. Oscar got the best of both worlds by giving best Picture to an epic about a rebel, *Patton*. But its lead actor, George C. Scott, proved to be a rebel with a cause—against the Academy.

ACTOR
Melvyn Douglas (*I Never Sang for My Father*)
James Earl Jones (*The Great White Hope*)
Jack Nicholson (*Five Easy Pieces*)
Ryan O'Neal (*Love Story*)
George C. Scott (*Patton*)

George C. Scott had previously refused an Oscar nomination—for his supporting role in 1961's *The Hustler*. A volcano of publicity and controversy erupted over the rough-hewn, maverick actor's next unwanted Oscar bid. In *Patton*, Scott's limning of the title role was a flawless impression of the five-star general. He was bound to make the short list of best Actor Oscar contenders. But once again, he derided the Academy Awards. They were a "meat parade" with Oscar hopefuls shamelessly vying for the little golden guy in a horserace which rewarded box office clout, popularity, and dollars spent in expensive advertising campaigns rather than artistic excellence. If nominated, he would refuse. If awarded, he would not accept.

A swirl of anticipation accompanied the forty-third Academy Awards. The tension was the highest in years. Would the Academy grant Scott an award even though he had insulted the whole process? Would they reward what was undoubtedly the best performance despite the controversy? The tension was broken when Goldie Hawn broke the seal on the envelope and shouted "Oh my God…. The winner is George C. Scott." *Patton* producer Frank McCarthy accepted the award which now resides, unclaimed, in an Academy storehouse.

ACTRESS
Jane Alexander (*The Great White Hope*)
Glenda Jackson (*Women in Love*)
Ali McGraw (*Love Story*)
Sarah Miles (*Ryan's Daughter*)
Carrie Snodgrass (*Diary of a Mad Housewife*)

Like Maggie Smith, the previous year's best Actress winner, Glenda Jackson was in her native London at the time of the awards. She stated that United Artists, the studio which made *Women in Love*, had refused to cover the airfare and she couldn't afford to pay her own way (although she did attend the New York Film Critics ceremony). Perhaps it's just as well since the actress stated that she felt she was "watching a public hanging" when she saw the ceremony on TV. The boob tube helped Jackson to

George C. Scott accepted accolades from critics' groups but rejected the Oscar for *Patton* (1970).

her first Oscar. She was playing the title role in *Elizabeth R* on public television's *Masterpiece Theatre* during the voting season.

SUPPORTING ACTOR
Richard Castellano (*Lovers and Other Strangers*)
Chief Dan George (*Little Big Man*)
Gene Hackman (*I Never Sang for My Father*)
John Marley (*Love Story*)
John Mills (*Ryan's Daughter*)

The only acting winner present, John Mills followed previous Oscar recipients Jane Wyman and Patty Duke by playing a deaf-mute. "I was speechless in Ireland for a year and I'm speechless now," he said, referring to the location of *Ryan's Daughter*.

SUPPORTING ACTRESS
Karen Black (*Five Easy Pieces*)

Lee Grant (*The Landlord*)
Helen Hayes (*Airport*)
Sally Kellerman (*M*A*S*H*)
Maureen Stapleton (*Airport*)

The longest gap between acting Oscars was recorded by Helen Hayes. She won for playing an unwed mother in *The Sin of Madelon Claudet* (1931–32) and a pixie-ish stowaway in *Airport* alomst forty years later. She was also the first Best Actress to win a second award in the Supporting category.

DIRECTOR
Robert Altman (*M*A*S*H*)
Federico Fellini (*Fellini Satryicon*)
Arthur Hiller (*Love Story*)
Ken Russell (*Women in Love*)
Franklin J. Schaffner (*Patton*)

ORIGINAL SCREENPLAY

Francis Ford Coppola, Edmund M. North (*Patton*)
Bob Rafelson, Adrien Joyce (*Five Easy Pieces*)
Eric Rohmer (*My Night at Maud's*)
Erich Segal (*Love Story*)
Norman Wexler (*Joe*)

ADAPTED SCREENPLAY

Robert Anderson (*I Never Sang for My Father*)
Larry Kramer (*Women in Love*)
Ring Lardner, Jr. (*M*A*S*H*)
George Seaton (*Airport*)
Renee Taylor, Joseph Bologna, David Zelig Goodman (*Lovers and Other Strangers*)

"At long last, a pattern has been established in my life," Ring Lardner, Jr., said upon accepting his *M*A*S*H* Oscar. "At the end of every 28 years, I win one of these. So I will see you all again in 1999." Lardner had won a Screenwriting Oscar for 1942's *Woman of the Year*. In the interim he was blacklisted for leftist leanings.

FOREIGN-LANGUAGE FILM

First Love (Switzerland)
Hoa-Binh (France)
Investigation of a Citizen Above Suspicion (Italy)
Paix Sur Les Champs (Belgium)
Tristana (Spain)

OTHER AWARDS

Original Score: Francis Lai (*Love Story*); Original Song Score: The Beatles (*Let It Be*); Original Song: "For All We Know" from *Lovers and Other Strangers*, music by Fred Karlin, lyrics by Robb Royer and James Griffin; Cinematography: Freddie Young (*Ryan's Daughter*); Art Direction: Urie McCleary, Gil Parrondo, Antonio Mateos, Pierre-Louis Thevent (*Patton*); Costume Design: Nino Novarese (*Cromwell*); Film Editing: Hugh S. Fowler (*Patton*); Sound: Douglas Williams, Don Bassman (*Patton*); Visual Effects: A. D. Flowers, L. B. Abbott (*Tora! Tora! Tora!*).

Documentary: *Woodstock*; Documentary Short Subject: *Interviews with My Lai Veterans*; Live-Action Short Subject: *The Resurrection of Bronco Billy*; Animated Short Subject: *Is It Always Right to Be Right?*.

SPECIAL AWARDS

Lillian Gish; Orson Welles; Ingmar Bergman (Irving Thalberg Award); Frank Sinatra (Jean Hersholt Humanitarian Award).

George C. Scott's rejection was only one of several indications that the Oscars and Hollywood were beginning to lose some of their glitter. The big traditional studios were were selling famous props like Judy Garland's ruby slippers from *The Wizard of Oz* in order to stay solvent. More production was going to independents and foreign companies. Hollywood, and by extension the Oscars, were seen as middle-aged, failing, and out of touch with the youth market. *Variety*'s headline said it all—"Age Beginning To Tell on Oscar as Hollywood Blows Its Big Scene." The ceremony was reviewed as bloated, boring, and hopelessly dated.

In addition to Scott, many of the winners failed to show up. Glenda Jackson was in London. Helen Hayes was performing *Long Day's Journey into Night* at Catholic University in Washington, D.C. Best Director Franklin J. Schaeffer was filming *Nicholas and Alexandra* in Europe. Best Screenplay author Francis Ford Coppola was likewise occupied with *The Godfather*. The Beatles had broken up and did not reassemble to collect their Oscar for the songs in *Let It Be*. Honorary honorees Ingmar Bergman and Orson Welles also declined to attend. Welles claimed to be in Europe shooting *The Other Side of the Wind*, a feature which he never completed. Presenter John Huston introduced a film clip of the director/author/actor expressing his thanks. In fact, Welles was at home in Hollywood, having a joke on the Academy.

Welles' prank got about as many laughs as Bob Hope's tired monologue. The Oscar reliable's gags were showing signs of age. Typical patter: "I go back to the kind of movie when a girl says 'I love you,' it's a declaration, not a demonstration"; and referring to Native American nominee Chief Dan George: "He was all right; but why couldn't they give that part to an American?" For the first time, an Oscar audience booed the comedian's material.

Once again, Hope was not the emcee but only one of several "Friends of Oscar." This year, the friends amounted to a small army—thirty-four in all. The ceremony had switched networks from ABC to NBC.

NATIONAL BOARD OF REVIEW

English-Language Film: *Patton*; Foreign-Language Film: *The Wild Child*; Actor: George C. Scott (*Patton*); Actress: Glenda Jackson (*Women in Love*); Supporting Actor: Frank Langella (*Diary of a Mad Housewife* and *The Twelve Chairs*); Supporting Actress: Karen Black (*Five Easy Pieces*); Director: Francois Truffaut (*The Wild Child*).

BEST ENGLISH-LANGUAGE FILMS

Patton, Kes, Women in Love, Five Easy Pieces, Ryan's Daughter, I Never Sang for My Father, Diary of a Mad Housewife, Love Story, The Virgin and the Gypsy, Tora! Tora! Tora!.

BEST FOREIGN-LANGUAGE FILMS

The Wild Child (France), *My Night at Maud's* (France), *The Passion of Anna* (Sweden), *The Confession* (France/Italy), *This Man Must Die* (France/Italy).

NEW YORK FILM CRITICS CIRCLE

Picture: *Five Easy Pieces*; Actor: George C. Scott (*Patton*); Actress: Glenda Jackson (*Women in Love*); Supporting Actor: Chief Dan George (*Little Big Man*); Supporting Actress: Karen Black (*Five Easy Pieces*); Director: Bob Rafelson (*Five Easy Pieces*); Screenplay: Eric Rohmer (*My Night at Maud's*).

Though he rejected the Oscar, George C. Scott accepted awards from critics' groups, stating they were bestowed by impartial reviewers rather than the Hollywood studio system. His then-wife Colleen Dewhurst picked up his award from the New York Film Critics Circle because he was in Spain filming *The Last Run*. "George thinks this is the only film award worth having," Dewhurst stated when she accepted the prize. After accepting her citation from Bette Davis, Glenda Jackson said Davis should have the award "in perpetuity." Best Supporting Actor Chief Dan George attended in his ceremonial Native American robes.

NATIONAL SOCIETY OF FILM CRITICS

Picture: *M*A*S*H*; Actor: George C. Scott (*Patton*); Actress: Glenda Jackson (*Women in Love*); Supporting Actor: Chief Dan George (*Little Big Man*); Supporting Actress: Lois Smith (*Five Easy Pieces*); Director: Ingmar Bergman (*The Passion of Anna*); Screenplay: Eric Rohmer (*My Night at Maud's*); Cinematography: Nestor Almendros (*My Night at Maud's* and *The Wild Child*); Special Award: Donald Richie and the Film Department of the Museum of Modern art for the retrospective of Japanese films; Daniel Talbot of the New Yorker Theatre.

*M*A*S*H* was the Society's first American winner for best Picture. Ingmar Bergman won his third best Director prize from the group.

HOLLYWOOD FOREIGN PRESS ASSOCIATION GOLDEN GLOBE AWARDS

Picture (Drama): *Love Story*; Picture (Comedy or Musical): *M*A*S*H*; English-Language Foreign Film: *Women in Love*; Foreign-Language Foreign Film: *Rider on the Rain*; Actor (Drama): George C. Scott (*Patton*); Actress (Drama): Ali MacGraw (*Love Story*); Actor (Comedy or Musical): Albert Finney (*Scrooge*); Actress (Comedy or Musical): Carrie Snodgrass (*Diary of a Mad Housewife*); Supporting Actor: John Mills (*Ryan's Daughter*); Supporting Actress (tie): Karen Black (*Five Easy Pieces*), Maureen Stapleton (*Airport*); Most Promising Newcomer (Male): James Earl Jones (*The Great White Hope*); Most Promising Newcomer (Female): Carrie Snodgrass (*Diary of a Mad Housewife*); Director: Arthur Hiller (*Love Story*); Screenplay: Erich Segal (*Love Story*); Original Score: Francis Lai (*Love Story*); Original Song: "Whistling Away the Dark" from *Darling Lili* by Henry Mancini and Johnny Mercer; World Film Favorite (Male): Clint Eastwood; World Film Favorite (Female): Barbra Streisand.

SPECIAL AWARD

Frank Sinatra (Cecil B. DeMille Award)

CANNES FILM FESTIVAL

Golden Palm Award: *M*A*S*H*; Actor: Marcello Mastroianni (*Drama of Jealousy*) (Italy); Actress: Ottavia Piccolo (*Metello*) (Italy); Director: John Boorman (*Leo the Last*) (Britain); Special Jury

Prize: *Investigation of a Citizen above Suspicion* (Italy); Special Citations: *The Strawberry Statement* and *The Falcons* (Hungary).

ACADEMY AWARDS (OSCARS)

PICTURE
A Clockwork Orange
Fiddler on the Roof
The French Connection
The Last Picture Show
Nicholas and Alexandra

A well-filmed detective thriller (*The French Connection*) beat out a brilliant, X-rated vision of the future (*A Clockwork Orange*) and a sensitive, adult study of a boy's coming of age in a Texas town (*The Last Picture Show*).

ACTOR
Peter Finch (*Sunday, Bloody Sunday*)
Gene Hackman (*The French Connection*)
Walter Matthau (*Kotch*)
George C. Scott (*The Hospital*)
Topol (*Fiddler on the Roof*)

ACTRESS
Julie Christie (*McCabe & Mrs. Miller*)
Jane Fonda (*Klute*)
Glenda Jackson (*Sunday, Bloody Sunday*)
Vanessa Redgrave (*Mary, Queen of Scotland*)
Janet Suzman (*Nicholas and Alexandra*)

Academy officals were quaking in their boots in fear that Jane Fonda would blow the roof off the Dorothy Chandler Pavillion with a radical left-wing speech. Fonda decided discretion was the better part of valour and simply stated, "There's a great deal to say, but I'm not going to say it tonight."

SUPPORTING ACTOR
Jeff Bridges (*The Last Picture Show*)
Leonard Frey (*Fiddler on the Roof*)
Richard Jaeckel (*Sometimes a Great Notion*)

Ben Johnson (*The Last Picture Show*)
Roy Scheider (*The French Connection*)

Ben Johnson had been featured in numerous Westerns before grabbing the Oscar for his role as the small town sage Sam the Lion in *The Last Picture Show*. "It couldn't have happened to a nicer fella," he told the Academy audience.

SUPPORTING ACTRESS
Ellen Burstyn (*The Last Picture Show*)
Barbara Harris (*Who Is Harry Kellerman and Why Is He Saying Those Terrible Things about Me?*)
Cloris Leachman (*The Last Picture Show*)
Margaret Leighton (*The Go-Between*)
Ann-Margret (*Carnal Knowledge*)

"I fought all my life against cliches. And now I'm a hopeless cliche," blubbered Cloris Leachman. The versatile character actress's career spanned *Lassie* in 1957 to *The Mary Tyler Moore Show* in the 1970s. She would later win a slew of Emmy Awards.

DIRECTOR
Peter Bogdanovich (*The Last Picture Show*)
William Friedkin (*The French Connection*)
Norman Jewison (*Fiddler on the Roof*)
Stanley Kubrick (*A Clockwork Orange*)
John Schlesinger (*Sunday, Bloody Sunday*)

ORIGINAL SCREENPLAY
Paddy Chayefsky (*The Hospital*)
Penelope Gilliat (*Sunday, Bloody Sunday*)
Andy and Dave Lewis (*Klute*)
Elip Petri, Ugo Pirro (*The Investigation of a Citizen above Suspicion*)
Herman Raucher (*Summer of '42*)

ADAPTED SCREENPLAY
Bernardo Bertolucci (*The Conformist*)
Stanley Kubrick (*A Clockwork Orange*)
Larry McMurtry, Peter Bogdanavich (*The Last Picture Show*)
Ugo Pirro, Vittorio Bonicelli (*The Garden of the Finzi-Continis*)
Ernest Tidyman (*The French Connection*)

FOREIGN-LANGUAGE FILM
Dodes'Ka-Den (Japan)

The Emigrants (Sweden)
The Garden of the Finzi-Continis (Italy)
The Policeman (Italy)
Tchaichovsky (USSR)

OTHER AWARDS

Original Score: Michel Legrand (*Summer of '42*); Adapted or Song Score: John Williams (*Fiddler on the Roof*); Original Song: "Theme from *Shaft*," music and lyrics by Isaac Hayes; Cinematography: Oswald Morris (*Fiddler on the Roof*); Art Direction: John Box, Ernest Archer, Jack Maxsted, Gil Parrondo, Vernon Dixon (*Nicholas and Alexandra*); Costume Design: Yvonne Blake, Antonio Castillo (*Nicholas and Alexandra*); Film Editing: Jerry Greenberg (*The French Connection*); Sound: Gordon K. McCallum, David Hildyard (*Fiddler on the Roof*); Visual Effects: Alan Maley, Eustace Lycett, Danny Lee (*Bedknobs and Broomsticks*).

Documentary: *The Hellstrom Chronicle*; Documentary Short Subject: *Sentinels of Silence*; Live-Action Short Subject: *Sentinels of Silence*; Animated Short Subject: *The Crunch Bird*.

SPECIAL AWARD

Charles Chaplin.

Oscar took a cue from the Tony Awards by opening the show with a lavish, glitzy production number. It worked for Broadway's award show and it definitely livened up filmdom's top shindig. Joel Grey, a hit in the just-released film version of *Cabaret*, was featured in a tongue-in-cheek salute to Hollywood called "Lights! Camera! Action!" Another dazzling highlight was provided by Isaac Hayes, the first African-American to win a music Oscar, performing his winning song, the theme from *Shaft*. Choreographed by Tony-winner Ron Field, the number featured flashing lights, dozens of dancers, stage smoke, bright metallic costumes, and Hayes, wearing a shirt made of chains, arriving on stage playing a lit-up organ.

The emotional climax of the evening was provided by Charles Chaplin, absent from Tinseltown for thirty years, accepting an honorary award. He was greeted with a five-minute standing ovation. With tears in his eyes, the Little Tramp thanked "all you lovely people." Chaplin had been vilified and rejected by Hollywood for his alledged Communist sympathies. Ironically, the current best Actress winner Jane Fonda probably would have found herself in the same boat had she been born a few years earlier.

Four hosts shared the spotlight—Helen Hayes, Jack Lemmon, Sammy Davis, Jr., and Alan King, who mocked the glitzy set: "It's amazing what you can do with a roll of Reynolds Wrap."

Chaplin's homecoming and the show's slick production values pushed Oscar back into the good graces of the reviewers. *Variety* labeled the 1971 offering "an improvement" and "a pleasant surprise." *The New York Times* opined, "In many ways, this year's extravaganza was the best of the Oscar lot that has been carried on television."

NATIONAL BOARD OF REVIEW

English-Language Film: *Macbeth*; Foreign-Language Film: *Claire's Knee*; Actor: Gene Hackman (*The French Connection*); Actress: Irene Papas (*The Trojan Women*); Supporting Actor: Ben Johnson (*The Last Picture Show*); Supporting Actress: Cloris Leachman (*The Last Picture Show*); Director: Ken Russell (*The Boy Friend* and *The Devils*).

BEST ENGLISH-LANGUAGE FILMS

Macbeth, The Boy Friend, One Day in the Life of Ivan Denisovich, The French Connection, The Last Picture Show, Nicholas and Alexandra, The Go-Between, King Lear, Peter Rabbit and the Tales of Beatrix Potter, Death in Venice.

BEST FOREIGN-LANGUAGE FILMS

Claire's Knee (France), *Bed and Board* (France/Italy), *The Clowns* (Italy), *The Garden of the Finzi-Continis* (Italy), *The Conformist* (Italy).

NEW YORK FILM CRITICS CIRCLE

Picture: *A Clockwork Orange*; Actor: Gene Hackman (*The French Connection*); Actress: Jane Fonda (*Klute*); Supporting Actor: Ben Johnson (*The Last Picture Show*); Supporting Actress: Ellen Burstyn (*The Last Picture Show*); Director: Stanley Kubrick (*A Clockwork Orange*); Screenplay (tie): Peter Bogdanovich, Larry McMurtry (*The Last*

Picture Show) and Penelope Gilliat (*Sunday, Bloody Sunday*).

Anthony Burgess, author of the novel *A Clockwork Orange*, accepted the Circle's best Picture award on behalf of its director/producer Stanley Kubrick. A former critic himself, Burgess regaled the crowd of scribes with pointed observations on the profession of passing judgment on art. But the most memorable speech was delivered by Ellen Burstyn. This was her first award and she didn't know what to say. She had been seated at the same table as Peter Falk. Burstyn asked the veteran actor for advice. He wrote something on a slip of paper and told her it would get a laugh. When accepting her best Supporting Actress accolade, she read his note: "Please consider Peter Falk for all future work."

The critics honored their own. Penelope Gilliat, film critic for *The New Yorker*, was honored by both the Circle and the National Society of Film Critics for her screenplay of *Sunday, Bloody Sunday.*

NATIONAL SOCIETY OF FILM CRITICS

Picture: *Claire's Knee*; Actor: Peter Finch (*Sunday, Bloody Sunday*); Actress: Jane Fonda (*Klute*); Supporting Actor: Bruce Dern (*Drive, He Said*); Supporting Actress: Ellen Burstyn (*The Last Picture Show*); Director: Bernardo Bertolucci (*The Conformist*); Screenplay: Penelope Gilliat (*Sunday, Bloody Sunday*); Cinematography: Vittorio Storaro (*The Conformist*); Special Award: *The Sorrow and the Pity.*

HOLLYWOOD FOREIGN PRESS ASSOCIATION GOLDEN GLOBE AWARDS

Picture (Drama): *The French Connection*; Picture (Comedy or Musical): *Fiddler on the Roof*; English-Language Foreign Film: *Sunday, Bloody Sunday*; Foreign-Language Foreign Film: *The Policeman*; Actor (Drama): Gene Hackman (*The French Connection*); Actress (Drama): Jane Fonda (*Klute*); Actor (Comedy or Musical): Topol (*Fiddler on the Roof*); Actress (Comedy or Musical): Twiggy (*The Boy Friend*); Supporting Actor: Ben Johnson (*The Last Picture Show*); Supporting Actress: Ann-Margret (*Carnal Knowledge*); Most Promising

Newcomer (Male): Desi Arnaz, Jr. (*Red Sky at Morning*); Most Promising Newcomer (Female): Twiggy (*The Boy Friend*); Director: William Friedkin (*The French Connection*); Screenplay: Paddy Chayefsky (*The Hospital*); Original Score: Isaac Hayes (*Shaft*); Original Song: "Life Is What You Make It," from *Kotch* by Marvin Hamlisch and Johnny Mercer; World Film Favorite (Male) (tie): Charles Bronson, Sean Connery; World Film Favorite (Female): Ali McGraw.

SPECIAL AWARD
Alfred Hitchcock (Cecil B. DeMille Award).

CANNES FILM FESTIVAL

Golden Palm Award: *The Go-Between*; Actor: Ricardo Cucciolla (*Sacco and Venzetti*) (Italy) ; Actress: Kitty Winn (*Panic in Needle Park*); Cannes Twenty-Fifth Anniversary Prize: Lucino Visconti for the body of his work and *Death in Venice*; Special Jury Prize: *Johnny Got His Gun* and *Taking Off.*

1972

ACADEMY AWARDS (OSCARS)

PICTURE
Cabaret
Deliverance
The Emigrants
The Godfather
Sounder

Though *The Godfather* took best Picture and had surpassed *Gone with the Wind* as top box-office champ, the lion's share of Oscars went to *Cabaret* which won eight awards. The film version of the Broadway musical has the unusual distinction of having won the most Oscars without being named best Picture.

ACTOR
Marlon Brando (*The Godfather*)
Michael Caine (*Sleuth*)
Laurence Olivier (*Sleuth*)

Marlon Brando won an Oscar for playing Don Corleone in *The Godfather*.

Peter O'Toole (*The Ruling Class*)
Paul Winfield (*Sounder*)

Still reeling from George C. Scott's rejection two years ago, the Academy was dealt another blow by Marlon Brando. The iconoclastic star had made a comeback as Don Corleone, the title character of *The Godfather*. After a decade of obscure pictures, his genius had once more resurfaced. But so did his penchant for controversy.

The alarm bells went off in Oscarcast producer Howard Koch's head when a young lady named Sacheen Littlefeather, dressed in Indian garb, introduced herself as Brando's representative just before the show began. She showed Koch a fifteen-page manifesto the actor had written to be delivered by her if he won. Koch informed her she would only have forty-five seconds to make her statement and then she would be removed from the stage. When Roger Moore and Liv Ullmann announced that *The Godfather* star had been named Best Actor, Littlefeather mounted the stage, shook her head when Moore proffered the award, and announced Brando was refusing the prize because of Hollywood's treatment of the American Indian. Boos and scattered applause greeted her brief speech. She promised to read the entirety of Brando's remarks to the press and then left the stage.

The program lumbered along with lame attempts at ad-lib humor. "Let's hope the winner doesn't have a cause," quipped Raquel Welch as she presented the next award. "What about an award for all those poor cowboys killed in John Ford's westerns?" proposed that great wit Clint Eastwood.

Reaction was mixed, with most of the Academy establishment against Brando. "It was childish," said Charlton Heston. "The American Indian needs better friends than that."

"I think if the man wants to make a gesture, I agree entirely with what he did," opined Michael Caine, "but I think he should have stood up and done it himself instead of letting some poor little Indian girl take the boos."

Academy president Daniel Taradash compared last year's radical winner Jane Fonda, who had accepted her award, with Brando: "It's the difference between a real person and a gifted fool." Meanwhile, Fonda chimed in with "I thought what he did was wonderful."

ACTRESS
Liza Minnelli (*Cabaret*)
Diana Ross (*Lady Sings the Blues*)
Maggie Smith (*Travels with My Aunt*)
Cicely Tyson (*Sounder*)
Liv Ullmann (*The Emigrants*)

"Bloodlines count," said Rock Hudson as he presented the best Actress award to Liza Minelli. Her mother Judy Garland won an honorary Oscar in 1939 and her father Vincente Minnelli was a winner in 1958 for his direction of *Gigi*. She won an Emmy later the same year for her TV special *Liza with a "Z"*.

The nominations of Diana Ross and Cicely Tyson marked the first time two African-American performers were in the running in the same acting category.

SUPPORTING ACTOR
Eddie Albert (*The Heartbreak Kid*)
James Caan (*The Godfather*)
Robert Duvall (*The Godfather*)
Joel Grey (*Cabaret*)
Al Pacino (*The Godfather*)

Part of the *Cabaret* sweep, Joel Grey claimed an Oscar for his sinister Emcee, a role he originated on Broadway and for which he also won a Tony.

SUPPORTING ACTRESS
Jeannie Berlin (*The Heartbreak Kid*)
Eileen Heckart (*Butterflies Are Free*)
Geraldine Page (*Pete 'n' Tillie*)
Susan Tyrell (*Fat City*)
Shelley Winters (*The Poseidon Adventure*)

Returning to the East Coast after the Oscar ceremony, Eileen Heckart went to her local unemployment office to file for benefits.

DIRECTOR
John Boorman (*Deliverance*)
Francis Ford Coppola (*The Godfather*)
Bob Fosse (*Cabaret*)
Joseph L. Mankiewicz (*Sleuth*)
Jan Troell (*The Emigrants*)

Bob Fosse had won a Tony Award for his direction and choreography of *Pippin* the previous Sunday.

"This might turn me into an optimist," said the dark-humored director. He would later win a Emmy Award for his television special *Liza with a "Z"*, making him the only person to win the top awards in film, theater, and television in the same year.

ORIGINAL SCREENPLAY

Luis Buñuel, Jean-Claude Carriere (*The Discreet Charm of the Bourgeoisie*)
Carl Foreman (*Young Winston*)
Jeremy Larner (*The Candidate*)
Louis Malle (*Murmur of the Heart*)
Terence McCloy, Chris Clark, Suzanne De Passe (*Lady Sings the Blues*)

ADAPTED SCREENPLAY

Jay Presson Allen (*Cabaret*)
Lonnie Elder III (*Sounder*)
Julius J. Epstein (*Pete 'n' Tillie*)
Mario Puzo, Francis Ford Coppola (*The Godfather*)
Jan Troell, Bengt Forslund (*The Emigrants*)

FOREIGN-LANGUAGE FILM

The Dawns Here Are Quiet (USSR)
The Discreet Charm of the Bourgeoisie (France)
I Love You Rosa (Israel)
My Dearest Senorita (Spain)
The New Land (Sweden)

OTHER AWARDS

Original Score: Charles Chaplin, Raymond Rasch, Larry Russell (*Limelight*); Adapted or Song Score: Ralph Burns (*Cabaret*); Original Song: "The Morning After" from *The Poseidon Adventure*, music and lyrics by Al Kasha and Joel Hirschhorn; Cinematography: Geoffrey Unsworth (*Cabaret*); Art Direction: Rolf Zehetbauer, Jurgen Kiebach, Herbert Strabel (*Cabaret*); Costume Design: Anthony Powell (*Travels with My Aunt*); Film Editing: David Bretherton (*Cabaret*); Sound: Robert Knudson, David Hildyard (*Cabaret*).

Documentary: *Marjoe*; Documentary Short Subject: *This Tiny World*; Live-Action Short Subject: *Norman Rockwell's World . . . An American Dream*; Animated Short Subject: *A Christmas Carol*.

SPECIAL AWARDS

Charles S. Boren, film industry labor negotiator; Edward G. Robinson; Rosalind Russell (Jean Hersholt Humanitarian Award); L. B. Abbott, A. D. Flowers for the visual effects in *The Poseidon Adventure*, presented as a special achievement award.

Marlon Brando's snub was not the only unexpected incident at the 1972 Oscar ceremony. Host Charlton Heston was delayed in traffic and Clint Eastwood was plucked out of the audience to read his material which kicked off the show. There were references to Heston hits like *The Ten Commandments* and *Ben-Hur* which made no sense with Eastwood delivering them. Since he is not a stand-up comedian, Eastwood stumbled his way through the bit until Heston strode on stage. The tight-lipped Western star did not return to the Oscars until 1992, when he received his first nominations and wins (for producing and directing *Unforgiven*).

NATIONAL BOARD OF REVIEW

English-Language Film: *Cabaret*; Foreign-Language Film: *The Sorrow and the Pity*; Actor: Peter O'Toole (*The Ruling Class* and *Man of La Mancha*); Actress: Cicely Tyson (*Sounder*); Supporting Actor (tie): Joel Grey (*Cabaret*) and Al Pacino (*The Godfather*); Supporting Actress: Marisa Berenson (*Cabaret*); Director: Bob Fosse (*Cabaret*).

BEST ENGLISH-LANGUAGE FILMS

Cabaret, Man of La Mancha, The Godfather, Sounder, 1776, The Effect of Gamma Rays on Man-in-the-Moon Marigolds, Deliverance, The Ruling Class, The Candidate, Frenzy.

BEST FOREIGN-LANGUAGE FILMS

The Sorrow and the Pity (Switzerland), *The Emigrants* (Sweden), *The Discreet Charm of the Bourgeoisie* (France), *Chloe in the Afternoon* (France), *Uncle Vanya* (USSR).

NEW YORK FILM CRITICS CIRCLE

Picture: *Cries and Whispers*; Actor: Laurence Olivier (*Sleuth*); Actress: Liv Ullmann (*Cries and Whispers* and *The Emigrants*); Supporting Actor: Robert

Duvall (*The Godfather*); Supporting Actress: Jeannie Berlin (*The Heartbreak Kid*); Director: Ingmar Bergman (*Cries and Whispers*); Special Citation: *The Sorrow and the Pity*.

Variety reported that Stacy Keach as a broken-down boxer in *Fat City* was robbed of the Circle's best Actor accolade. On the second round of balloting, Keach had twenty votes and Marlon Brando seventeen. A reviewer from an unnamed national magazine pointed out that twenty votes out a possible sixty hardly seemed a group endorsement. (There were twenty critics present, voting for their first three choices. The first received three points, the second two, and the third one. Thus there were sixty first-place points available.)

The dissenting scribe proposed a rule change: in order to win, a candidate must receive at least half of the potential first-place votes. As a result, there were three more ballots with Olivier as a duplictous mystery novelist in *Sleuth* finally emerging triumphant.

NATIONAL SOCIETY OF FILM CRITICS

Picture: *The Discreet Charm of the Bourgeoisie*; Actor: Al Pacino (*The Godfather*); Actress: Cicely Tyson (*Sounder*); Supporting Actor (tie): Eddie Albert (*The Heartbreak Kid*) and Joel Grey (*Cabaret*); Supporting Actress: Jeannie Berlin (*The Heartbreak Kid*); Director: Luis Buñuel (*The Discreet Charm of the Bourgeoisie*); Screenplay: Ingmar Bergman (*Cries and Whispers*); Cinematography: Sven Nykvist (*Cries and Whispers*); Special Awards: *My Uncle Antoine*, Iavan Passer, director of *Intimate Lighting*, and Robert Kaylor, director of *Derby* (Richard and Hilda Rosenthal Foundation Awards).

Ten members were added to the Society in order to broaden its "national" base, but only two—Charles Champlin of *The Los Angeles Times* and Roger Ebert of *The Chicago Tribune*—were not residing in New York. The cantankerous John Simon of *The New Leader* promptly resigned from the Society, in protest over what he called the "lack of critical competence" of the additions. Stanley Kauffman of *The New Republic* soon followed. There were now eleven scribes belonging to both the Society and the New York Film Critics Circle. *Variety* published an article postulating a merger between the two groups since there was so much overlap. But the following years have shown a wide divergence in opinion between the two organizations.

Winning for his screenplay of *Cries and Whispers*, Ingmar Bergman became the Society's first four-time winner.

HOLLYWOOD FOREIGN PRESS ASSOCIATION GOLDEN GLOBE AWARDS

Picture (Drama): *The Godfather*; Picture (Comedy or Musical): *Cabaret*; English-Language Foreign Film: *Young Winston*; Foreign-Language Foreign Film: *The Emigrants: The New Land*; Actor (Drama): Marlon Brando (*The Godfather*); Actress (Drama): Liv Ullmann (*The Emigrants*); Actor (Comedy or Musical): Jack Lemmon (*Avanti!*); Actress (Comedy or Musical): Liza Minnelli (*Cabaret*); Supporting Actor: Joel Grey (*Cabaret*); Supporting Actress: Shelley Winters (*The Poseidon Adventure*); Most Promising Newcomer (Male); Edward Albert (*Butterflies Are Free*); Most Promising Newcomer (Female): Diana Ross (*Lady Sings the Blues*); Director: Francis Ford Coppola (*The Godfather*); Screenplay: Francis Ford Coppola, Mario Puzo (*The Godfather*); Score: Nino Rota (*The Godfather*); Original Song: "Ben" from *Ben*, music by Walter Schraf, lyrics by Don Black; World Film Favorite (Male): Marlon Brando; World Film Favorite (Female): Jane Fonda.

SPECIAL AWARD

Samuel Goldwyn (Cecil B. DeMille Award).

Early warning: Marlon Brando refused the Golden Globe's best Actor (Drama) and World Film Favorite Awards.

CANNES FILM FESTIVAL

Golden Palm: *The Working Class Goes to Heaven* (Italy) and *The Mattei Affair* (Italy), special mention of Gian Maria Volonte's performances in both films; Actor: Jean Yanne (*We Will Not Grow Old Together*) (France); Actress: Susannah York (*Images*) (USA); Director: Miklos Jancso (*Red Psalm*) (Hungary); Jury Prize: *Slaughterhouse-Five* (USA);

Special Jury Prize: *Solaris* (USSR); International Critics Prize: *Avoir 20 Ans dans les Aures* (France).

ACADEMY AWARDS (OSCARS)

PICTURE
American Graffiti
Cries and Whispers
The Exorcist
The Sting
A Touch of Class

Julia Philips, one of the three producers of *The Sting*, was the first woman to win the Oscar for best Picture.

ACTOR
Marlon Brando (*Last Tango in Paris*)
Jack Lemmon (*Save the Tiger*)
Jack Nicholson (*The Last Detail*)
Al Pacino (*Serpico*)
Robert Redford (*The Sting*)

ACTRESS
Ellen Burstyn (*The Exorcist*)
Glenda Jackson (*A Touch of Class*)
Marsha Mason (*Cinderella Liberty*)
Barbra Streisand (*The Way We Were*)
Joanne Woodward (*Summer Wishes,*
    Winter Dreams)

Glenda Jackson missed the Oscars for her second win. Her response when she received the news of a double triumph: "Now my mother has a nice pair of bookends." Like Ronald Reagan before her, she gave up acting in the early 1990s to pursue a career in politics. Jackson now uses her performing skills as a member of Parliament.

SUPPORTING ACTOR
Vincent Gardenia (*Bang the Drum Slowly*)
Jack Gilford (*Save the Tiger*)
John Houseman (*The Paper Chase*)
Jason Miller (*The Exorcist*)
Randy Quaid (*The Last Detail*)

When presenting the Supporting Actor Oscar, Cybill Shepard slipped in plugs for her beau, director Peter Bogdanovich. She substituted *Paper Moon* and *The Last Picture Show*, two of Bogdanovich's films, for *The Paper Chase* and *The Last Detail*.

SUPPORTING ACTRESS
Linda Blair (*The Exorcist*)
Candy Clark (*American Graffiti*)
Madeline Kahn (*Paper Moon*)
Tatum O'Neal (*Paper Moon*)
Sylvia Sydney (*Summer Wishes, Winter Dreams*)

At age 10, Tatum O'Neal was (and remains) the youngest person to win an Oscar. The nomination of fellow youthful thespian Linda Blair stirred controversy when it was revealed the voice of the demon which possessed her in *The Exorcist* was supplied by an uncredited Mercedes McCambridge. Since the devilish vocals were felt to be an intregral part of the character, many protested Blair's placement in the Oscar derby.

DIRECTOR
Ingmar Bergman (*Cries and Whispers*)
Bernardo Bertolucci (*Last Tango in Paris*)
William Friedkin (*The Exorcist*)
George Roy Hill (*The Sting*)
George Lucas (*American Graffiti*)

ORIGINAL SCREENPLAY
Ingmar Bergman (*Cries and Whispers*)
Melvin Frank, Jack Rose (*A Touch of Class*)
George Lucas, Gloria Katz, Willard Huyck
    (*American Graffiti*)
Steve Shagan (*Save the Tiger*)
David S. Ward (*The Sting*)

ADAPTED SCREENPLAY
James Bridges (*The Paper Chase*)
William Peter Blatty (*The Exorcist*)
Waldo Salt, Norman Wexler (*Serpico*)
Alvin Sargent (*Paper Moon*)
Robert Towne (*The Last Detail*)

FOREIGN-LANGUAGE FILM
Day for Night (France)
The House on Chelouche Street (Israel)
L'Invitation (Switzerland)

The Pedestrian (Federal Republic of Germany)
Turkish Delight (The Netherlands)

OTHER AWARDS

Original Musical Score: Marvin Hamlisch (*The Way We Were*); Adapted or Song Score: Marvin Hamlisch (*The Sting*); Original Song: "The Way We Were" from *The Way We Were*, music by Marvin Hamlisch, lyrics by Alan and Marilyn Bergman; Cinematography: Sven Nykvist (*Cries and Whispers*); Art Direction: Henry Bumstead, James Payne (*The Sting*); Costume Design: Edith Head (*The Sting*); Film Editing: William Reynolds (*The Sting*); Sound: Robert Knudson, Chris Newman (*The Exorcist*).

Documentary: *The Great American Cowboy*; Documentary Short Subject: *Princeton: A Search for Answers*; Live-Action Short Subject: *The Bolero*; Animated Short Subject: *Frank Film*.

SPECIAL AWARDS

Groucho Marx; Henri Langlois, founder of Cinémathèque Français; Lawrence Weingarten (Irving Thalberg Award); Lew Wasserman (Jean Hersholt Humanitarian Award).

All images of the 1973 Oscars pale in comparison to a young man wearing nothing but a peace sign running past David Niven. The urbane actor rose to the occasion and ad-libbed, "Just think, the only laugh that man will ever get is for stripping and showing off his shortcomings." Elizabeth Taylor came out next and stated, "That's a pretty tough act to follow."

The fad of speeding through public places in the altogether, known as "streaking," briefly swept the country in the 1970s and Robert Opel had his fifteen minutes of fame as the Oscar streaker. He was shot to death in 1979 when his San Francisco sex shop was robbed.

Katharine Hepburn made a rare appearance to present the Irving Thalberg Award to former MGM producer Larry Weingarten. "Katharine Hepburn, Elizabeth Taylor, and a streaker. Does a show need anything else to be a smash?" asked *The Hollywood Reporter*.

The streaker wasn't the only scene-stealer that night. Porn star Linda Lovelace was wearing pristine Victorian white lace and arrived in a horse-drawn carriage. Edy Williams, star of the underground sleaze-fest *Beyond the Valley of the Dolls* wore a leopard-skin cape and a bikini. She brought along an enormous Great Dane. When asked if the dog had a ticket, the actress responded, "He doesn't need a ticket. He's got me, baby." This apparently was not enough and the canine was not admitted.

NATIONAL BOARD OF REVIEW

English-Language Film: *The Sting*; Foreign-Language Film: *Cries and Whispers*; Actor (tie): Al Pacino (*Serpico*) and Robert Ryan (*The Iceman Cometh*); Actress: Liv Ullman (*The New Land*); Supporting Actor: John Housmean (*The Paper Chase*); Supporting Actress: Sylvia Sydney (*Summer Wishes, Winter Dreams*); Director: Ingmar Bergman (*Cries and Whispers*).

BEST ENGLISH-LANGUAGE FILMS

The Sting, Paper Moon, The Homecoming, Bang the Drum Slowly, Serpico, O Lucky Man, The Last American Hero, The Hireling, The Day of the Dolphin, The Way We Were.

BEST FOREIGN-LANGUAGE FILMS

Cries and Whispers (Sweden), *Day for Night* (France), *The New Land* (Sweden), *The Tall Blonde Man with One Black Shoe* (France), *Alfredo, Alfredo* (Italy), *Traffic* (France/Italy).

SPECIAL CITATIONS

American Film Theater and Ely Landau; Woody Allen for the script of *Sleeper*; Walt Disney Productions for *Robin Hood*; Paramount for *Charlotte's Web*.

NEW YORK FILM CRITICS CIRCLE

Picture: *Day for Night*; Actor: Marlon Brando (*Last Tango in Paris*); Actress: Joanne Woodward (*Summer Wishes, Winter Dreams*); Supporting Actor: Robert De Niro (*Bang the Drum Slowly*); Supporting Actress: Valentina Cortese (*Day for Night*); Director: Francois Truffaut (*Day for Night*); Screenplay: George Lucas, Gloria Katz, William Huyack (*American Graffiti*).

NATIONAL SOCIETY OF FILM CRITICS

Picture: *Day for Night*; Actor: Marlon Brando (*Last Tango in Paris*); Actress: Liv Ullmann (*The New Land*); Supporting Actor: Robert De Niro (*Mean Streets*); Supporting Actress: Valentina Cortese (*Day for Night*); Director: Francois Truffaut (*Day for Night*); Screenplay: George Lucas, Gloria Katz, William Huyck (*American Graffiti*); Cinematography: Vilmos Zsigmond (*The Long Goodbye*). Special Awards: *Memories of Underdevelopment* and Darly Duke (director of *Payday*) (Richard and Hilda Rosenthal Foundation Awards); Robert Ryan (posthumous award for his performance in *The Iceman Cometh*).

Cuban filmmaker Tomas Gutierrez Alea was denied a visa to the US to accept his special award for *Memories of Underdevelopment* from the National Society. The State Department claimed the group was honoring Communism with its prize. Society chairman Andrew Sarris of *The Village Voice* stated at the awards ceremony that honoring *Memories* was no more celebrating Cuban Communism than saluting *American Graffiti* was cheering American capitalism or *Day for Night* French capitalism. The $2,000 cash prize had to be placed in a blocked bank account or the Society would face a $10,000 fine or a jail sentence.

HOLLYWOOD FOREIGN PRESS ASSOCIATION GOLDEN GLOBE AWARDS

Picture (Drama): *The Exorcist*; Picture (Comedy or Musical): *American Graffiti*; Actor (Drama): Al Pacino (*Serpico*); Actress (Drama): Marsha Mason (*Cinderella Liberty*); Actor (Comedy or Musical): George Segal (*A Touch of Class*); Actress (Comedy or Musical): Glenda Jackson (*A Touch of Class*); Supporting Actor: John Houseman (*The Paper Chase*); Supporting Actress: Linda Blair (*The Exorcist*); Most Promising Newcomer (Male): Paul Le Mat (*American Graffiti*); Most Promising Newcomer (Female): Tatum O'Neal (*Paper Moon*); Director: William Friedkin (*The Exorcist*); Screenplay: William Peter Blatty (*The Exorcist*); Original Score: Neil Diamond (*Jonathan Livingston Seagull*); Original Song: "The Way We Were" from *The Way We Were*, music by Marvin Hamlish, lyrics by Alan and Marilyn Bergman; Documentary: *Visions of Eight*; World Film Favorite (Male): Marlon Brando; World Film Favorite (Female): Elizabeth Taylor.

SPECIAL AWARD
Bette Davis (Cecil B. DeMille Award).

CANNES FILM FESTIVAL

Golden Palm Award (tie): *The Hireling* and *Scarecrow* with special mention of performances by Sarah Miles (*The Hireling*) and Gene Hackman and Al Pacino (*Scarecrow*); Actor: Giancarlo Giannini (*Love and Anarchy*) (Italy); Actress: Joanne Woodward (*The Effect of Gamma Rays on Man-in-the-Moon Marigolds*); Special Jury Prize: *La Maman et la Puritan* (France); Jury Prize: *L'Invitation* (Switzerland) and *The Sandglass* (Poland); International Critics Prize: *La Maman et la Puritan* and *La Grande Bouffe* (France).

SPECIAL AWARDS
Jermey (First Film); *Fantastic Planet* (France); Ingmar Bergman for *Cries and Whispers* (Sweden) (Technical Prize for use of color).

ACADEMY AWARDS (OSCARS)

PICTURE
Chinatown
The Conversation
The Godfather Part II
Lenny
The Towering Inferno

This was the first instance of a sequel to an Oscar-winning Best Picture also taking the same prize. The *Godfather* saga is Oscar's only two-part victor. Francis Ford Coppola received two nominations for Best Picture (*The Godfather Part II* and *The Conversation*).

ACTOR

Art Carney (*Harry and Tonto*)
Albert Finney (*Murder on the Orient Express*)
Dustin Hoffman (*Lenny*)
Jack Nicholson (*Chinatown*)
Al Pacino (*The Godfather Part II*)

Art Carney (*Harry and Tonto*) as an eccentric retired teacher traveling cross-country with his cat was the surprise winner. Jack Nicholson was thought to be a shoe-in by the oddsmakers.

ACTRESS

Ellen Burstyn (*Alice Doesn't Live Here Anymore*)
Diahann Carroll (*Claudine*)
Faye Dunaway (*Chinatown*)
Valerine Perrine (*Lenny*)
Gena Rowlands (*A Woman under the Influence*)

Ellen Burstyn did not attend the ceremonies. She was busy in New York appearing on Broadway in *Same Time, Next Year*, for which she would win a Tony Award the next week. She would later make the film version of the play and receive another shot at Oscar. Burstyn also had a small part as Art Carney's daughter in *Harry and Tonto*.

Liv Ullmann had won citations from both the New York Film Critics Circle and the National Society of Film Critics. She was deemed ineligibile for an Oscar nomination because her film *Scenes from a Marriage* was an edited version of a limited series which had been broadcast on Swedish television. Ullmann's director Ingmar Bergman was also out of the running. A letter protesting the Academy's decision signed by dozens of prominent actresses including nominees Gena Rowlands, Ellen Burstyn, and Diahann Carroll was sent to *The Los Angeles Times*. A similar missive signed by such directors as Francis Ford Coppola, Martin Scorsese, and Federico Fellini was also sent on behalf of Bergman. The Academy did not change its mind.

SUPPORTING ACTOR

Fred Astaire (*The Towering Inferno*)
Jeff Bridges (*Thunderbolt and Lightfoot*)
Robert De Niro (*The Godfather Part II*)

Robert De Niro won an Oscar for playing the young Don Corleone in *The Godfather II*.

Michael V. Gazzo (*The Godfather Part II*)
Lee Strasberg (*The Godfather Part II*)

Newcomer Robert De Niro defeated old pro Fred Astaire, whom many thought would be a sentimental favorite. De Niro's triumph was the first Oscar-winning performance delivered in Italian since Sophia Loren's in *Two Women*. He played the Marlon Brando role, Don Corleone, as a young man.

SUPPORTING ACTRESS

Ingrid Bergman (*Murder on the Orient Express*)
Valentina Cortese (*Day for Night*)
Madeline Kahn (*Blazing Saddles*)
Diane Ladd (*Alice Doesn't Live Here Anymore*)
Talia Shire (*The Godfather Part II*)

The Academy presented Ingrid Bergman with an "apology" Oscar for a miniscule cameo as one of a dozen stellar suspects in *Murder on the Orient Express*. It was Hollywood's way of saying "We're sorry for slamming you while you were living in sin with Roberto Rossellini." The star had an apology of her own on Oscar night when she asked forgiveness of Valentina Cortese of the French film *Day for Night*. Bergman felt Cortese should have won instead of her.

DIRECTOR

John Cassavetes (*A Woman under the Influence*)
Francis Ford Coppola (*The Godfather Part II*)
Bob Fosse (*Lenny*)
Roman Polanski (*Chinatown*)
Francois Truffaut (*Day for Night*)

ORIGINAL SCREENPLAY

Francis Ford Coppola (*The Conversation*)
Robert Getchell (*Alice Doesn't Live Here Anymore*)
Paul Mazursky, Josh Greenfield (*Harry and Tonto*)
Francois Truffaut, Jean-Louis Richard,
   Suzanne Schiffman (*Day for Night*)
Robert Towne (*Chinatown*)

ADAPTED SCREENPLAY

Julian Barry (*Lenny*)
Francis Ford Coppola, Mario Puzo
   (*The Godfather Part II*)
Paul Dehn (*Murder on the Orient Express*)

Mordecai Richler, Lionel Chetwynd
   (*The Apprenticeship of Duddy Kravitz*)
Gene Wilder, Mel Brooks (*Young Frankenstein*)

FOREIGN-LANGUAGE FILM

Amarcord (Italy)
Catsplay (Hungary)
The Deluge (Poland)
Lacombe, Lucien (France)
The Truce (Argentina)

OTHER AWARDS

Original Musical Score: Nino Rota, Carmine Coppola (*The Godfather Part II*); Original Song Score or Adapted Score: Nelson Riddle (*The Great Gatsby*); Original Song: "We May Never Love Like This Again" from *The Towering Inferno*, music by Elmer Bernstein, lyrics by Don Black; Cinematography: Fred Koenekamp, Joseph Biroc (*The Towering Inferno*); Art Direction: Dean Tavoularis, Angelo Graham, George R. Nelson (*The Godfather Part II*); Costume Design: Theoni V. Aldredge (*The Great Gatsby*); Editing: Harold F. Kress, Carl Kress (*The Towering Inferno*); Sound: Ronald Pierce, Melvin Metcalfe, Sr. (*Earthquake*).

Documentary: *Hearts and Minds*; Documentary Short Subject: *Don't*; Live-Action Short Subject: *One-Eyed Men Are Kings*; Animated Short Subject: *Closed Mondays*.

SPECIAL AWARDS

Howard Hawks; Jean Renoir; Arthur B. Krim (Jean Hersholt Humanitarian Award); Frank Brendel, Glen Robinson, Albert Whitlock for the visual effects of *Earthquake* (given as a special achievement award).

Hollywood's political wars continued at the Oscars as left and right publicly clashed. Peter Davis and Bert Schneider won for their documentary *Hearts and Minds*, a harsh examination of America's role in the Vietnam War. During their acceptance speech, Schneider read a telegram of greeting from the North Vietnamese delegation to the Paris Peace Talks.

Conservative Bob Hope demanded producer Howard Koch make some kind of statement disassociating the Academy from the telegram while liberal Shirley MacLaine screamed at him not to.

Hope later dictated a brief announcement to Frank Sinatra off-stage. Sinatra then read it on the air: "[The Academy is] not responsible for any political references made on the program and we are sorry they had to take place this evening." MacLaine exploded at Sinatra offstage, "You said you were speaking on behalf of the Academy. Well, I'm a member of the Academy and you didn't ask me." Academy president Walter Mirisch claimed to know nothing of Hope's statement.

For the finale, hosts Sinatra, MacLaine, Hope, and Sammy Davis, Jr., were supposed to enter arm in arm, singing "That's Entertainment." Sinatra was furious with MacLaine and refused to go onstage with her until Davis dragged him out.

The Academy's Board of Governors later met and, after two hours of deliberation, issued a five-line disclaimer: "Although the Academy discourages political use of the Oscar, a winner may say whatever they deem appropriate with the Academy disclaiming responsibility for the statements."

NATIONAL BOARD OF REVIEW

English-Language Film: *The Conversation*; Foreign-Language Film: *Amarcord*; Actor: Gene Hackman (*The Conversation*); Actress: Gena Rowlands (*A Woman under the Influence*); Supporting Actor: Holger Lowenadler (*Lacombe, Lucien*); Supporting Actress: Valerine Perrine (*Lenny*); Director: Francis Ford Coppola (*The Godfather Part II*).

BEST ENGLISH-LANGUAGE FILMS

The Conversation, Murder on the Orient Express, Chinatown, The Last Detail, Harry and Tonto, A Woman under the Influence, Thieves like Us, Lenny, Daisy Miller, The Three Musketeers.

BEST FOREIGN-LANGUAGE FILMS

Amarcord (Italy), *Lacombe, Lucien* (France), *Scenes from a Marriage* (Sweden), *The Phantom of Liberte* (France), *The Pedestrian* (Federal Republic of Germany).

SPECIAL CITATIONS

Special effects in *The Golden Voyage of Sinbad, Earthquake,* and *The Towering Inferno;* the film industry for increasing care in subsidiary casting of many films; film compiler Robert G. Youngson.

NEW YORK FILM CRITICS CIRCLE

Picture: *Amacord*; Actor: Jack Nicholson (*Chinatown* and *The Last Detail*); Actress: Liv Ullmann (*Scenes from a Marriage*); Supporting Actor: Charles Boyer (*Stravinsky*); Supporting Actress: Valerie Perrine (*Lenny*); Director: Federico Fellini (*Amacord*); Screenplay: Ingmar Bergman (*Scenes from a Marriage*); Special Award: Fabiano Canosa, for his innovative programs at the First Ave. Screening Room.

Jack Nicholson tied himself in the Circle voting, receiving thirty-two votes apiece for *The Last Detail* and *Chinatown*. *Detail* had been released in early 1974 in time for the 1973 Oscar nominations, but too late for the critics' prizes, which are awarded in December.

NATIONAL SOCIETY OF FILM CRITICS

Picture: *Scenes from a Marriage*; Actor: Jack Nicholson (*Chinatown* and *The Last Detail*); Actress: Liv Ullmann (*Scenes from a Marriage*); Supporting Actor: Holger Lowenadler (*Lacombe, Lucien*); Supporting Actress: Bibi Andersson (*Scenes from a Marriage*); Director: Francis Ford Coppola (*The Conversation* and *The Godfather Part II*); Screenplay: Ingmar Bergman (*Scenes from a Marriage*); Cinematography: Gordon Willis (*The Godfather Part II* and *The Parallax View*); Special Award: Jean Renoir.

The National Society had run out of money. There was no ceremony. The winners received their citations in the mail.

HOLLYWOOD FOREIGN PRESS ASSOCIATION GOLDEN GLOBE AWARDS

Picture (Drama): *Chinatown*; Picture (Comedy or Musical): *The Longest Yard*; Actor (Drama): Jack Nicholson (*Chinatown*); Actress (Drama): Gena Rowlands (*A Woman under the Influence*); Actor (Comedy or Musical): Art Carney (*Harry and Tonto*); Actress (Comedy or Musical): Raquel Welch (*The Three Musketeers*); Supporting Actor: Fred Astaire (*The Towering Inferno*); Supporting Actress: Karen Black (*The Great Gatsby*); Most

Promising Newcomer (Male): Joseph Bottoms (*The Dove*); Most Promising Newcomer (Female): Susan Flannery (*The Towering Inferno*); Director: Roman Polanski (*Chinatown*); Screenplay: Robert Towne (*Chinatown*); Foreign-Language Film: *Scenes from a Marriage*; Documentary: *Beautiful People*; Original Score: Alan Jay Lerner, Frederick Loewe (*The Little Prince*); Original Song: "I Feel Love" from *Benji* by Euel and Betty Box; World Film Favorite (Male): Robert Redford; World Film Favorite (Female): Barbra Streisand.

SPECIAL AWARD
Hal Wallis (Cecil B. DeMille Award).

CANNES FILM FESTIVAL

Golden Palm Award: *The Conversation*; Actor: Jack Nicholson (*The Last Detail*); Actress: Marie-Jose Nat (*Les Violins du Bal*) (France); Director: no award; Screenplay: Steven Spielberg (*The Sugarland Express*); Special Jury Prize: *One Thousand and One Nights* (Italy); Jury Prize: *Cousin Angelica* (Spain); International Critics Prize: *Ali: Fear Eats the Soul* (Federal Republic of Germany) and *Lancelot du Lac* (France); Technical Prize: *Mahler* (UK).

1975

ACADEMY AWARDS (OSCARS)

PICTURE
Barry Lyndon
Dog Day Afternoon
Jaws
Nashville
One Flew over the Cuckoo's Nest

In the first clean sweep of the top awards since 1934's *It Happened One Night*, *One Flew over the Cuckoo's Nest* took best Picture, Actor, Actress, Director, and Screenplay. Ken Kesey, author of the original novel about nonconformism in a mental institution, was publicly miffed that none of the winners acknowledged him in their acceptance speeches.

ACTOR
Walter Matthau (*The Sunshine Boys*)
Jack Nicholson (*One Flew over the Cuckoo's Nest*)
Al Pacino (*Dog Day Afternoon*)
Maximillian Schell (*The Man in the Glass Booth*)
James Whitmore (*Give 'em Hell, Harry*)

"Well, I guess this proves there are as many nuts in the Academy as anywhere else," Jack Nicholson declared upon receiving his Oscar for his blazingly intense Randall P. McMurphy, the rebel who may or may not be insane. Many felt the honor was long overdue and that the iconoclastic star had deserved it for *Chinatown* and *The Last Detail*.

ACTRESS
Isabelle Adjani (*The Story of Adele H*)
Ann-Margret (*Tommy*)
Louise Fletcher (*One Flew over the Cuckoo's Nest*)
Glenda Jackson (*Hedda*)
Carol Kane (*Hester Street*)

The emotional high spot of the '75 ceremony was provided by Louise Fletcher, who gave her speech in sign language as well as speaking it for the benefit of her deaf parents. Fletcher's role was really a

Louise Fletcher gave part of her acceptance speech as best Actress in 1975 in sign language for her deaf parents.

supporting one, that of the domineering nurse who breaks Jack Nicholson's spirit in *Cuckoo's Nest*. But the lack of meaty roles for women propelled her into the leading category.

SUPPORTING ACTOR
George Burns (*The Sunshine Boys*)
Brad Dourif (*One Flew over the Cuckoo's Nest*)
Burgess Meredith (*The Day of the Locust*)
Chris Sarandon (*Dog Day Afternoon*)
Jack Warden (*Shampoo*)

Octogeranian George Burns remarked to the Oscar audience, "I made my last picture in 1939. This is so exciting. I've decided to keep making one movie every thirty-six years."

SUPPORTING ACTRESS
Ronee Blakley (*Nashville*)
Lee Grant (*Shampoo*)
Sylvia Miles (*Farewell, My Lovely*)
Lily Tomlin (*Nashville*)
Brenda Vaccaro (*Once Is Not Enough*)

Nominees Lee Grant and Lily Tomlin both wore elaborate fantasy costumes to the ceremony—an old wedding gown for Grant and an idealized 1950s glamour star get-up for Tomlin. The Oscar provided winner Grant with some solace after taking some hard knocks. She was blacklisted in the '50s and her NBC sitcom *Fay* had been canceled just three weeks previously.

DIRECTOR
Robert Altman (*Nashville*)
Federico Fellini (*Amarcord*)
Milos Forman (*One Flew over the Cuckoo's Nest*)
Stanley Kubrick (*Barry Lyndon*)
Sidney Lumet (*Dog Day Afternoon*)

Oscar's long snub of Steven Speilberg began when he was not nominated for his work on *Jaws*, the only best Picture candidate that year which failed to pick up a nomination for its director. Almost two decades would pass before he finally won for *Schindler's List* (1993).

ORIGINAL SCREENPLAY
Ted Allan (*Lies My Father Told Me*)
Federico Fellini, Tonino Guerra (*Amarcord*)

Claude Lelouch, Pierre Uytterhoeven (*And Now My Love*)
Frank Pierson (*Dog Day Afternoon*)
Robert Towne, Warren Beatty (*Shampoo*)

ADAPTED SCREENPLAY
Lawrence Hauben, **Bo Goldman** (*One Flew over the Cuckoo's Nest*)
John Huston, Gladys Hill (*The Man Who Would Be King*)
Stanley Kubrick (*Barry Lyndon*)
Ruggero Maccari, Dino Risi (*Scent of a Woman*)
Neil Simon (*The Sunshine Boys*)

FOREIGN-LANGUAGE FILM
Dersu Uzala (USSR)
Land of Promise (Poland)
Letters from Marusia (Mexico)
Sandakan No. 8 (Japan)
Scent of a Woman (Italy)

OTHER AWARDS
Original Musical Score: John Williams (*Jaws*); Original Song Score or Adapted Score: Leonard Rosenman (*Barry Lyndon*); Original Song: "I'm Easy" from *Nashville*, music and lyrics by Keith Carradine; Cinematography: John Alcott (*Barry Lyndon*); Art Direction: Ken Adam, Roy Walker, Vernon Dixon (*Barry Lyndon*); Costume Design: Ulla-Britt Soderlund, Milena Canonero (*Barry Lyndon*); Editing: Verna Fields (*Jaws*); Sound: Robert L. Hoyt, Roger Heman, Earl Madery, John Carter (*Jaws*).

Documentary: *The End of the Game*; Documentary Short Subject: *The Man Who Skied Down Everest*; Live-Action Short Subject: *Angel and Big Joe*; Animated Short Subject: *Great*.

SPECIAL AWARDS
Mary Pickford; Mervyn LeRoy (Irving G. Thalberg Award); Jules C. Stein (Jean Hersholt Humanitarian Award); Peter Berkos for the sound effects of *The Hindenberg* and Albert Whitlock and Glen Robinson for the visual effects of *The Hindenberg* (presented as special achievement awards).

"The production lacked imagination, style, a sense of continuity, and a feeling for what the television audience expects from the Academy Award telecast," griped Kay Gardella in the *New York Daily News*. If the television audience expected celebrity goof-ups and big, gaudy production numbers, the 1975 Oscars delivered. Elizabeth Taylor made a grand entrance, asked the audience in the Dorothy Chandler Pavillion to join her in singing "America the Beautiful" (it was the year of the Bicentennial after all), and proceeded to demonstrate that she didn't know the words. As for elaborate spectacle, Ray Bolger opened the show with a number pre-taped outside the auditorium and then, live inside, Kelly Garret was half-hidden behind huge golden drapes. Diana Ross lip-synched "The Theme from *Mahogony*" live from Amsterdam (where it was 4:30 a.m.), and Bernadette Peters stopped the show with a nominated song from *Funny Lady*. By contrast, Keith Carradine's simple delivery of his Oscar-winning "I'm Easy" from *Nashville* accompanying himself on the guitar was a highlight.

The ceremony switched from NBC to ABC, a network which had no compunction about using the Oscar to promote itself. At the end of the telecast, a voice-over announced to the viewing public it could catch brand-new Oscar-winner Jack Nicholson in *Five Easy Pieces* right there on ABC the following week.

NATIONAL BOARD OF REVIEW

English-Language Film (tie): *Barry Lyndon* and *Nashville*; Actor: Jack Nicholson (*One Flew over the Cuckoo's Nest*); Actress: Isabelle Adjani (*The Story of Adele H*); Supporting Actor: Charles Durning (*Dog Day Afternoon*); Supporting Actress: Ronee Blakley (*Nashville*); Director (tie): Robert Altman (*Nashville*) and Stanley Kubrick (*Barry Lyndon*); Foreign-Language Film: *The Story of Adele H*; Special Citation: Ingmar Bergman's *The Magic Flute*.

BEST ENGLISH-LANGUAGE FILMS

Barry Lyndon, Nashville, Conduct Unbecoming, One Flew over the Cuckoo's Nest, Lies My Father Told Me, Dog Day Afternoon, Day of the Locust, The Passenger, Hearts of the West, Farewell, My Lovely, Alice Doesn't Live Here Anymore.

BEST FOREIGN-LANGUAGE FILMS

The Story of Adele H (France), *A Brief Vacation* (Italy), *Special Section* (France), *Stavinsky* (France), *Swept Away* (Italy).

NEW YORK FILM CRITICS CIRCLE

Picture: *Nashville*; Actor: Jack Nicholson (*One Flew over the Cuckoo's Nest*); Actress: Isabelle Adjani (*The Story of Adele H*); Supporting Actor: Alan Arkin (*Hearts of the West*); Supporting Actress: Lily Tomlin (*Nashville*); Director: Robert Altman (*Nashville*); Screenplay: François Truffaut, Jean Gruault, Suzanne Schiffman (*The Story of Adele H*).

In addition to its annual awards, the Circle voted a resolution condemning the imprisonment of Soviet filmmaker Sergei Paradjanov (*Shadows of Our Forgotten Ancestors*) for "homosexualism."

Nashville, Robert Altman's kaleidoscopic vision of the country-music capital, was the hands-down winner for best Picture with forty-five votes. *Barry Lyndon* (thirty votes), *Swept Away* (seventeen votes), and *The Story of Adele H* (thirteen votes) trailed far behind. Jack Nicholson was a popular choice for best Actor and even received some votes for another 1975 film, *The Passenger*. The awards ceremony at Sardi's was a literary affair, with Altman receiving his *Nashville* awards for Best Picture and Director from Kurt Vonnegut, Jr., and E. L. Doctorow. Both novelists were planning to have books of theirs filmed by Altman (Vonnegut's *Breakfast of Champions* and Doctorow's *Ragtime*), but neither project came to fruition. *Breakfast* was never filmed and *Ragtime* was helmed by Milos Forman, who had defeated Altman in this year's Oscar race.

NATIONAL SOCIETY OF FILM CRITICS

Picture: *Nashville*; Actor: Jack Nicholson (*One Flew over the Cuckoo's Nest*); Actress: Isabelle Adjani (*The Story of Adele H*); Supporting Actor: Henry Gibson (*Nashville*); Supporting Actress: Lily Tomlin (*Nashville*); Director: Robert Altman (*Nashville*); Screenplay: Robert Towne, Warren Beatty (*Shampoo*); Cinematography: John Alcott (*Barry Lyndon*); Special Award: Ingmar Bergman's *The Magic Flute*.

One absentee critic mailed in a proxy vote for best Supporting Actor: all the men in *Nashville*. The Society's most openly gay male member responded by nominating all the men in *Sex Tool*, a porno film.

LOS ANGELES FILM CRITICS ASSOCIATION

Picture (tie): *Dog Day Afternoon* and *One Flew over the Cuckoo's Nest*; Actor: Al Pacino (*Dog Day Afternoon*); Actress: Florinda Bolkan (*A Brief Vacation*); Director: Sidney Lumet (*Dog Day Afternoon*); Screenplay: Joan Tewkesbury (*Nashville*); Cinematography: John Alcott (*Barry Lyndon*); Foreign Film: *And Now, My Love*.

Reviewers from the film capital decided to band together and present their own awards in 1975. The Los Angeles Film Critics Association has grown in influence and is often an accurate precursor of the Oscars. Its choices are usually more mainstream than its New York and national counterparts, but occasionally its members go out on a limb, voting non-Hollywood films like *Brazil, Little Dorritt,* and *Do the Right Thing* as Best Picture.

HOLLYWOOD FOREIGN PRESS ASSOCIATION GOLDEN GLOBE AWARDS

Picture (Drama): *One Flew over the Cuckoo's Nest*; Picture (Comedy or Musical): *The Sunshine Boys*; Actor (Drama): Jack Nicholson (*One Flew over the Cuckoo's Nest*); Actress (Drama): Louise Fletcher (*One Flew over the Cuckoo's Nest*); Actor (Comedy or Musical): Walter Matthau (*The Sunshine Boys*); Actress (Comedy or Musical): Ann-Margret (*Tommy*); Supporting Actor: Richard Benjamin (*The Sunshine Boys*); Supporting Actress: Brenda Vaccaro (*Once Is Not Enough*); Most Promising Newcomer (Male): Brad Dourif (*One Flew over the Cuckoo's Nest*); Most Promising Newcomer (Female): Marilyn Hassett (*The Other Side of the Mountain*); Director: Milos Forman (*One Flew over the Cuckoo's Nest*); Screenplay: Lawrence Hauben, Bo Goldman (*One Flew over the Cuckoo's Nest*); Original Score: John Williams (*Jaws*); Original Song: "I'm Easy" from *Nashville*, music and lyrics by Keith Carradine; Documentary: *Youthquake*.

CANNES FILM FESTIVAL

Golden Palm: *Chronicle of the Burning Years* (Algeria); Actor: Vittorio Gassman (*Profumo di Donna*) (Italy); Actress: Valerie Perrine (*Lenny*); Director: Michel Brault (*Les Ordres*) (Canada), Costa-Gavras (*Special Section*) (France); Special Jury Prize: *Every Man for Himself and God against All/ The Mystery of Kaspar Hauser* (Federal Republic of Germany); International Critics Prize: in competition, *Every Man for Himself . . .*, out of competition, *The Traveling Players* (Greece); Special Mention: "the quality and presence of Delphine Seyrig in young cinema."

PICTURE
All the President's Men
Bound for Glory
Network
Rocky
Taxi Driver

Made for under $1 million, *Rocky* paralleled the underdog status of its lead character. Sylvester Stallone peddled his screenplay of a two-bit boxer who becomes a heavyweight contender to numerous studios. None would accept his condition of playing the lead himself. It was finally picked up by independent producers Robert Chartoff and Irwin Winkler and distributed by United Artists (which also produced another Oscar contender, *Network*). The film's rousing, feel-good appeal captured the public's heart, won three Oscars, and launched a string of sequels.

ACTOR
Robert De Niro (*Taxi Driver*)
Peter Finch (*Network*)
Giancarlo Giannini (*Seven Beauties*)
William Holden (*Network*)
Sylvester Stallone (*Rocky*)

The first posthumous acting Oscar went to Peter Finch for his mad-as-hell newscaster in the satirical comedy *Network*. Screenwriter Paddy Chayefsky was the official acceptor for the late Finch. Upon reaching the stage, he called out to the actor's widow, who was in the audience. Producer William Friedkin had nixed the idea of Mrs. Finch accepting on the grounds that it would be too sentimental.

ACTRESS
Marie-Christine Barrault (*Cousin, Cousine*)
Faye Dunaway (*Network*)
Talia Shire (*Rocky*)
Sissy Spacek (*Carrie*)
Liv Ullmann (*Face to Face*)

SUPPORTING ACTOR
Ned Beatty (*Network*)
Burgess Meredith (*Rocky*)
Laurence Olivier (*Marathon Man*)
Jason Robards (*All the President's Men*)
Burt Young (*Rocky*)

SUPPORTING ACTRESS
Jane Alexander (*All the President's Men*)
Jodie Foster (*Taxi Driver*)
Lee Grant (*Voyage of the Damned*)
Piper Laurie (*Carrie*)
Beatrice Straight (*Network*)

"If you blink, you miss it," said Beatrice Straight referring to her brief role in *Network* as the wife William Holden deserts for Faye Dunaway. But the veteran stage actress and Tony winner (for *The Crucible* in 1952–53) won for an intense five and a half minutes—the shortest performance to garner an Oscar.

DIRECTOR
John G. Avildsen (*Rocky*)
Ingmar Bergman (*Face to Face*)
Sidney Lumet (*Network*)
Alan J. Pakula (*All the President's Men*)
Lina Wertmulller (*Seven Beauties*)

Italian Lina Wertmuller was the first woman to be Oscar-nominated for best Director. The only other female up for this category was another non-Hollywood helmer, New Zealander Jane Campion for 1993's *The Piano*. Americans Penny Marshall and Barbra Streisand have yet to be so honored.

ORIGINAL SCREENPLAY
Walter Bernstein (*The Front*)
Paddy Chayefsky (*Network*)
Sylvester Stallone (*Rocky*)
Jean-Charles Tacchella, Daniele Thompson
(*Cousin, Cousine*)
Lina Wertmuller (*Seven Beauties*)

ADAPTED SCREENPLAY
Federico Fellini, Bernadino Zapponi
(*Fellini's Casanova*)
Robert Getchell (*Bound for Glory*)
William Goldman (*All the President's Men*)
Nicholas Meyer (*The Seven Percent Solution*)
Steve Shagan, David Butler (*Voyage of the Damned*)

FOREIGN-LANGUAGE FILM
Black and White in Color (Ivory Coast)
Cousin, Cousine (France)
Jacob, the Liar (German Democratic Republic)
Nights and Days (Poland)
Seven Beauties (Italy)

OTHER AWARDS
Original Score: Jerry Goldsmith (*The Omen*); Original Song Score or Adapted Score: Leonard Roseman (*Bound for Glory*); Original Song: "Evergreen (Love Theme from *A Star Is Born*)" from *A Star Is Born*, music by Barbra Streisand, lyrics by Paul Williams; Cinematography: Haskell Wexler (*Bound for Glory*); Art Direction: George Jenkins, George Gaines (*All the President's Men*); Costume Design: Danilo Doanti (*Fellini's Casanova*); Editing: Richard Halsey, Scott Conrad (*Rocky*); Sound: Arthur Piantadosi, Les Fresholts, Dick Alexander, Jim Webb (*All the President's Men*).
Documentary: *Harlan County, USA*; Documentary Short Subject: *Number Our Days*; Live-Action Short Subject: *In the Region of Ice*; Animated Short Subject: *Leisure*.

SPECIAL AWARDS
Pandro S. Berman (Irving Thalberg Award); Carlo Rambaldi, Glen Robinson, Frank Van Der Veer for the visual effects in *King Kong*; L. B. Abbott, Glen Robinson, Matthew Yuricich for the visual effects in *Logan's Run* (both visual effects awards given as special achievement awards).

William Friedkin took over the Oscar-producing reins from Howard Koch. The Oscar-winning director was determined to "bone down" the presentation and make it less "tacky." The slick, new Academy Awards featured four hosts representative of a young Hollywood—Ellen Burstyn (who wore a man's tuxedo), Warren Beatty, Jane Fonda, and Richard Pryor. There would be no audience reaction shots. If a winner was not present, no substitute acceptors were allowed. Instead of pairs of presentors, a single personality would give out the award, thus eliminating awkward dialogue. The usual opulent set was replaced by a spare, futuristic one.

There was somewhat raw material from Pryor and Chevy Chase, newly hot from his pratfalls on TV's *Saturday Night Live*. Norman Mailer spiced up his presentation of the writing awards with a reference to Voltaire's visit to a male brothel. Playwright/screenwriter Lillian Hellman, a victim of the 1950s blacklist, made a dignified re-entry into the Hollywood community by giving out the documentary awards. Comedian Marty Feldman was less dignified when he forgot to read the names of the Live-Action Short Subject nominees and smashed the Animated Short-Subject Oscar on the floor.

Variety's verdict—"Friedkin Classes Up Oscars But Feldman, Mailer Hit New Lows in Bad Taste; Hellman a Hit" ran the headline of the trade journal's review of the show.

NATIONAL BOARD OF REVIEW

English-Language Film: *All the President's Men*; Actor: David Carradine (*Bound for Glory*); Actress: Liv Ullmann (*Face to Face*); Supporting Actor: Jason Robards (*All the President's Men*); Supporting Actress: Talia Shire (*Rocky*); Director: Alan J. Pakula (*All the President's Men*); Foreign-Language Film: *The Marquise of O*.

BEST ENGLISH-LANGUAGE FILMS
All the President's Men, Network, Rocky, The Last Tycoon, The Seven-Per-Cent Solution, The Front, The Shootist, Family Plot, Silent Movie, Obsession.

BEST FOREIGN-LANGUAGE FILMS
The Marquise of O (France), *Face to Face* (Sweden), *Small Change, Cousin, Cousine, The Clockmaker* (all from France).

NEW YORK FILM CRITICS CIRCLE

Picture: *All the President's Men*; Actor: Robert De Niro (*Taxi Driver*); Actress: Liv Ullmann (*Face to Face*); Supporting Actor: Jason Robards (*All the President's Men*); Supporting Actress: Talia Shire (*Rocky*); Director: Martin Scorsese (*Taxi Driver*); Screenplay: Paddy Chayefsky (*Network*).

Elizabeth Taylor presented Robert Redford, producer of *All the President's Men*, with the award for best Picture and thanked him "for myself and all the women in America." She let out a girlish squeal after kissing him. *Washington Post* editor Ben Bradlee gave Jason Robards who played Bradlee in *All the President's Men* the Supporting Actor prize. The editor thanked the actor for not making him look like "a horse's ass."

NATIONAL SOCIETY OF FILM CRITICS

Picture: *All the President's Men*; Actor: Robert De Niro (*Taxi Driver*); Actress: Sissy Spacek (*Carrie*); Supporting Actor: Jason Robards (*All the President's Men*); Supporting Actress: Jodie Foster (*Taxi Driver*); Director: Martin Scorsese (*Taxi Driver*); Screenplay: Alain Tanner, John Berger (*Jonah Will Be 25 in the Year 2000*); Cinematography: Haskell Wexler (*Bound for Glory*).

LOS ANGELES FILM CRITICS ASSOCIATION

Picture (tie): *Network* and *Rocky*; Actor: Robert De Niro (*Taxi Driver*); Actress: Liv Ullmann (*Face to Face*); Director: Sidney Lumet (*Network*); Screenplay: Paddy Chayefsky (*Network*); Cinematography: Haskell Wexler (*Bound for Glory*); Music: Bernard Herrmann (*Taxi Driver*); Foreign Film: *Face to Face*; Special Award: *The Memory of Justice* (outstanding documentary).

Accepting the best Actress award for an absent Liv Ullmann, Carol Burnett broke the crowd up when she confided, "I can still see the tears running down Ingmar Bergman's face when I turned down the role."

HOLLYWOOD FOREIGN PRESS ASSOCIATION GOLDEN GLOBE AWARDS

Picture (Drama): *Rocky*; Picture (Comedy or Musical): *A Star Is Born*; Actor (Drama): Peter Finch (*Network*); Actress (Drama): Faye Dunaway (*Network*); Actor (Comedy or Musical): Kris Kristofferson (*A Star Is Born*); Actress (Comedy or Musical): Barbra Streisand (*A Star Is Born*); Supporting Actor: Laurence Olivier (*Marathon Man*); Supporting Actress: Katharine Ross (*Voyage of the Damned*); Acting Debut (Male): Arnold Schwarzenegger (*Stay Hungry*); Acting Debut (Female): Jessica Lange (*King Kong*); Director: Sidney Lumet (*Network*); Screenplay: Paddy Chayefsky (*Network*); Foreign Film: *Face to Face*; Original Score: Paul Williams, Kenny Ascher (*A Star Is Born*); Original Song: "Evergreen" from *A Star Is Born*, music by Barbra Streisand, lyrics by Paul Williams; Documentary: *Altars of the World*; World Film Favorite (Male): Robert Redford; World Film Favorite (Female): Sophia Loren.

SPECIAL AWARD
Walter Mirisch (Cecil B. DeMille Award).

CANNES FILM FESTIVAL

Golden Palm Award: *Taxi Driver*; Actor: Jorge-Luis Gomez (*La Familia de Pascual Duarte*) (Spain); Actress (tie): Mari Torocsik (*Dryne, Hol Van*) (Hungary) and Dominique Sanda (*The Inheritance*) (France/Italy); Director: Ettore Scola (*Ugly, Dirty, and Mean*) (Italy); Special Jury Award: *The Marquise of O* (France), *Cria Cuervos* (Spain); International Critics Prize: *In the Course of Time, Strongman Ferdinand* (both Federal Republic of Germany).

ACADEMY AWARDS (OSCARS)

PICTURE
Annie Hall
The Goodbye Girl
Julia
Star Wars
The Turning Point

Woody Allen nearly matched Orson Welles' one-year Oscar record by garnering nominations for best Actor, Director, and Screenplay. Welles had received nominations for those three categories as well as for producing *Citizen Kane*. Although he didn't produce *Annie Hall*, a quirky semi-autobiographical comedy about his relationship with Diane Keaton, Allen did win Oscars for his script (written with Marshall Brickman) and direction. He became the first person to win the golden guy in both categories in the same year since Joseph L. Mankiewicz in 1949 for *A Letter to Three Wives* and in 1950 for *All about Eve*. Allen was not present on the big night since it conflicted with his usual Monday night gig, playing clarinet with a Dixieland jazz band at Michael's Pub in Manhattan.

Future Oscar-winning writer/directors include Robert Benton, James L. Brooks, and Bernardo Bertolucci.

ACTOR
Woody Allen (*Annie Hall*)
Richard Burton (*Equus*)
Richard Dreyfuss (*The Goodbye Girl*)
Marcello Mastroianni (*A Special Day*)
John Travolta (*Saturday Night Fever*)

ACTRESS
Anne Bancroft (*The Turning Point*)
Jane Fonda (*Julia*)
Diane Keaton (*Annie Hall*)
Shirley MacLaine (*The Turning Point*)
Marsha Mason (*The Goodbye Girl*)

Her strong dramatic performance in *Looking for Mr. Goodbar* in the same year helped Diane Keaton take home an Oscar for her comic turn as the flighty title character based upon herself in *Annie Hall*.

SUPPORTING ACTOR
Mikhail Baryshnikov (*The Turning Point*)
Peter Firth (*Equus*)
Alec Guinness (*Star Wars*)
Jason Robards (*Julia*)
Maximilian Schell (*Julia*)

Best Supporting Actress Vanessa Redgrave launched a storm of controversy when she called her detractors "Zionist hoodlums" at the 1977 Oscars.

Jason Robards was the first consecutive winner of two Oscars in the Supporting Actor category.

SUPPORTING ACTRESS
Leslie Browne (*The Turning Point*)
Quinn Cummings (*The Goodbye Girl*)
Melinda Dillon (*Close Encounters of the Third Kind*)
Vanessa Redgrave (*Julia*)
Tuesday Weld (*Looking for Mr. Goodbar*)

Politics reared its ugly head once again during the Oscars as ultra-radical Vanessa Redgrave ignited a controversy. Protestors from the Jewish Defense League were gathering outside the Dorothy Chandler Pavillion objecting to Redgrave's nomination for *Julia* because of her pro-Palestinian views. There was also a faction of PLO supporters equally vocal in favor of the actress. In her acceptance speech, she called those who condemned her "Zionist hoodlums" and gave a brief explanation of her stand.

Later in the broadcast, Paddy Chayefsky chastised Redgrave for using the ceremony as a platform to advance her political agenda. "A simple thank you would have sufficed," he sniffed and then almost forgot to read the nominees for the writing awards.

DIRECTOR
Woody Allen (*Annie Hall*)
George Lucas (*Star Wars*)
Herbert Ross (*The Turning Point*)
Steven Spielberg (*Close Encounters of the Third Kind*)
Fred Zinnemann (*Julia*)

ORIGINAL SCREENPLAY
Woody Allen, Marshall Brickman (*Annie Hall*)
Robert Benton (*The Late Show*)
Arthur Laurents (*The Turning Point*)
George Lucas (*Star Wars*)
Neil Simon (*The Goodbye Girl*)

ADAPTED SCREENPLAY
Luis Buñuel, Jean-Claude Carriere (*That Obscure Object of Desire*)
Larry Gelbart (*Oh, God!*)
Gavin Lambert, John Lewis Carlino (*I Never Promised You a Rose Garden*)
Alvin Sargeant (*Julia*)
Peter Shaffer (*Equus*)

FOREIGN-LANGUAGE FILM
Iphigenia (Greece)
Madame Rosa (France)
Operation Thunderbolt (Israel)
A Special Day (Italy)
That Obscure Object of Desire (Spain)

OTHER AWARDS
Original Music Score: John Williams (*Star Wars*); Original Song Score or Adapted Score: Jonathan Tunick (*A Little Night Music*); Original Song: "You Light Up My Life" from *You Light Up My Life*, music and lyrics by Joseph Brooks; Cinematography: Vilmos Zsigmond (*Close Encounters of the Third Kind*); Art Direction: John Barry,

Norman Reynolds, Leslie Dilley, Roger Christian (*Star Wars*); Costume Design: John Mollo (*Star Wars*); Sound: Don MacDougall, Ray West, Bob Minkler, Derek Ball (*Star Wars*); Editing: Paul Hirsch, Marcia Lucas, Richard Chew (*Star Wars*); Visual Effects: John Staers, John Dykstra, Richard Edlund, Grant McCune, Robert Blalack (*Star Wars*).

Documentary: *Who Are the DeBolts? And Where Did They Get 19 Kids?*; Documentary Short Subject: *Gravity Is My Enemy*; Live-Action Short Subject: *I'll Find a Way*; Animated Short Subject: *Sand Castle*.

SPECIAL AWARDS

Walter Mirish (Irving Thalberg Award); Charlton Heston (Jean Hersholt Humanitarian Award); film editor Margaret Booth; Grodon E. Sawyer, Sidney P. Solow (service to the Academy); Frank Warner for sound effects editing of *Close Encounters of the Third Kind* and Benjamin Burtt, Jr., for sound effects of *Star Wars* (given as special achievement awards).

"Last year was a disaster," declared Alan Carr, new executive consultant to the Oscars. William Friedkin's slick, modern approach to the awards enraged the older guard who wanted a return to Hollywood glamour. Carr, a producer and personal manager who numbered Ann-Margret and Marvin Hamlisch among his clients, was famous for his weekly parties. He was hired to bring some of the elegance he injected into his soirees to Oscar's fiftieth anniversary.

Carr gathered a gaggle of glamour queens from yesterday including Barbara Stanwyck, Greer Garson, Bette Davis, Olivia de Havilland, Joan Fontaine, Cyd Charisse, and the first best Actress Janet Gaynor. Bob Hope returned for his fifteenth stint as host and twenty-second Oscar appearance.

"Bob Hope was back, but his writers must have died in 1940," grumbled Rex Reed. The caustic critic also slammed the opening number "Look How Far We've Come," which featured Debbie Reynolds, forty former Oscar winners, and twenty dancers milling about aimlessly. Reed called it "a masterpiece of clumsy confusion."

Another Debby, Debby Boone, sparked a controversy almost as big as Vanessa Regrave's pro-Palestinian polemic. While singing the Oscar-winning "You Light Up My Life," Boone was accompanied by a group of little girls, announced as hearing-impaired students, interpreting the song in sign language. It was later revealed in the press that none of the adorable tots had hearing loss and their signing was random gibberish.

NATIONAL BOARD OF REVIEW

English-Language Film: *The Turning Point*; Actor: John Travolta (*Saturday Night Fever*); Actress: Anne Bancroft (*The Turning Point*); Supporting Actor: Tom Skerritt (*The Turning Point*); Supporting Actress: Diane Keaton (*Annie Hall*); Director: Luis Buñuel (*That Obscure Object of Desire*); Foreign-Language Film: *That Obscure Object of Desire*.

BEST ENGLISH-LANGUAGE FILMS
The Turning Point, Annie Hall, Julia, Star Wars, Close Encounters of the Third Kind, The Late Show, Saturday Night Fever, Equus, The Picture Show Man, Harlan County, USA.

BEST FOREIGN-LANGUAGE FILMS
That Obscure Object of Desire (Spain), *The Man Who Loved Women* (France), *A Special Day* (Italy), *Cria* (Spain), *The American Friend* (Federal Republic of Germany).

SPECIAL AWARDS
Walt Disney Studios for *The Rescuers*; Columbia Pictures for the special effects in *Close Encounters of the Third Kind*.

NEW YORK FILM CRITICS CIRCLE

Picture: *Annie Hall*; Actor: John Gielgud (*Providence*); Actress: Diane Keaton (*Annie Hall*); Supporting Actor: Maximilian Schell (*Julia*); Supporting Actress: Sissy Spacek (*Three Women*); Director: Woody Allen (*Annie Hall*); Screenplay: Woody Allen, Marshall Brickman (*Annie Hall*).

The New York Critics' balloting predicted the Oscars' *Annie Hall* sweep with awards for best Picture, Actress, Director, and Screenplay. The best Picture tally ran as follows: *Annie Hall* (forty-six votes), *That Obscure Object of Desire* (twenty-eight votes), and *Close Encounters of the Third Kind* (twelve votes). Diane Keaton also received enough votes for *Looking for Mr. Goodbar* to place third behind herself in *Annie Hall* and Shelley Duvall in *Three Women*.

NATIONAL SOCIETY OF FILM CRITICS

Picture: *Annie Hall*; Actor: Art Carney (*The Late Show*); Actress: Diane Keaton (*Annie Hall*); Supporting Actor: Edward Fox (*A Bridge Too Far*); Supporting Actress: Anne Wedgeworth (*Handle with Care*); Director: Luis Buñuel (*That Obscure Object of Desire*); Screenplay: Woody Allen, Marshall Brickman (*Annie Hall*); Cinematography: Thomas Mauch (*Aguirre, The Wrath of God*).

The National Society's voting for best Picture duplicated that of the New York critics. *Annie Hall* took the award with forty-three votes. *Obscure Object* followed with twenty-seven, while *Close Encounters* racked up twelve.

LOS ANGELES FILM CRITICS ASSOCIATION

Picture: *Star Wars*; Actor: Richard Dreyfuss (*The Goodbye Girl*); Actress: Shelley Duvall (*Three Women*); Supporting Actor: Jason Robards (*Julia*); Supporting Actress: Vanessa Redgrave (*Julia*); Director: Herbert Ross (*The Turning Point*); Screenplay: Woody Allen, Marshall Brickman (*Annie Hall*); Cinematography: Douglas Siocombe (*Julia*); Music: John Williams (*Star Wars*); Foreign Film: *That Obscure Object of Desire*; Special Award: Gary Allison for *Fraternity Row*.

HOLLYWOOD FOREIGN PRESS ASSOCIATION GOLDEN GLOBE AWARDS

Picture (Drama): *The Turning Point*; Picture (Comedy or Musical): *The Goodbye Girl*; Actor (Drama): Richard Burton (*Equus*); Actress (Drama): Jane Fonda (*Julia*); Actor (Comedy or Musical): Richard Dreyfuss (*The Goodbye Girl*); Actress (Comedy or Musical) (tie): Diane Keaton (*Annie Hall*) and Marsha Mason (*The Goodbye Girl*); Supporting Actor: Peter Firth (*Equus*); Supporting Actress: Vanessa Redgrave (*Julia*);

Director: Herbert Ross (*The Goodbye Girl*); Screenplay: Neil Simon (*The Goodbye Girl*); Original Score: John Williams (*Star Wars*); Song: "You Light Up My Life" from *You Light Up My Life*, music and lyrics by Joseph Brooks; World Film Favorite (Male): Robert Redford; World Film Favorite (Female): Barbra Streisand.

SPECIAL AWARD
Red Skelton (Cecil B. DeMille Award).

CANNES FILM FESTIVAL

Golden Palm Award: *Padre, Padrone* (Italy); Actor: Fernando Rey (*Elissa, My Love*) (Spain); Actress (tie): Shelly Duvall (*Three Women*) and Monique Mercure (*J. A. Martin, Photographer*) (Canada); Special Jury Prize: *The Duellists* (UK); International Critics Prize: in competition, *Padre, Padrone*, out of competition, *Nine Months* (Hungary).

ACADEMY AWARDS (OSCARS)

PICTURE
Coming Home
The Deer Hunter
Heaven Can Wait
Midnight Express
An Unmarried Woman

Six years after American involvement ended, Hollywood was finally ready to deal with the Vietnam War. Two Vietnam dramas battled for box-office dollars and the Oscars. The spoils of war were split between *The Deer Hunter* (Picture, Director, Editing, Sound) and *Coming Home* (Actor, Actress, Original Screenplay). Jane Fonda, star of *Coming Home*, campaigned against *Deer Hunter*, stated she interpreted its portrayal of the Vietcong as racist.

Warren Beatty matched Orson Welles' *Citizen Kane* quadruple-play by receiving nominations for producing, writing, directing, and acting in *Heaven Can Wait*, a remake of a 1941 comic fantasy. His sister Shirley MacLaine gave the best line of the evening when, after praising his accomplishment, she stated, "Oh, Warren, think what you could accomplish if you tried celibacy."

ACTOR
Warren Beatty (*Heaven Can Wait*)
Gary Busey (*The Buddy Holly Story*)
Robert De Niro (*The Deer Hunter*)
Laurence Olivier (*The Boys from Brazil*)
Jon Voight (*Coming Home*)

ACTRESS
Ingrid Bergman (*Autumn Sonata*)
Ellen Burstyn (*Same Time, Next Year*)
Jill Clayburgh (*An Unmarried Woman*)
Jane Fonda (*Coming Home*)
Geraldine Page (*Interiors*)

At first it seemed as if Jane Fonda were parodying Louise Fletcher's speech of three years ago when she began signing her thanks. But she explained she had become more aware of the plight of handicapped people while filming *Coming Home*—which involved wounded Vietnam vets—and wanted to make sure all the hearing-impaired could understand her.

SUPPORTING ACTOR
Bruce Dern (*Coming Home*)
Richard Farnsworth (*Comes a Horseman*)
John Hurt (*Midnight Express*)
Christopher Walken (*The Deer Hunter*)
Jack Warden (*Heaven Can Wait*)

SUPPORTING ACTRESS
Dyan Cannon (*Heaven Can Wait*)
Penelope Milford (*Coming Home*)
Maggie Smith (*California Suite*)
Maureen Stapleton (*Interiors*)
Meryl Streep (*The Deer Hunter*)

Some of Maggie Smith's *California Suite* scenes were filmed at the previous year's Oscars. She played a witty British actress nominated for an Academy Award and became the only Oscar winner to play an Oscar loser.

DIRECTOR
Woody Allen (*Interiors*)

Hal Ashby (*Coming Home*)
Warren Beatty, Buck Henry (*Heaven Can Wait*)
Michael Cimino (*The Deer Hunter*)
Alan Parker (*Midnight Express*)

ORIGINAL SCREENPLAY
Woody Allen (*Interiors*)
Ingmar Bergman (*Autumn Sonata*)
Michael Cimino, Deric Washburn, Louis Garfinkle, Quinn K. Redeker (*The Deer Hunter*)
Nancy Dowd (story), **Waldo Salt**, **Robert C. Jones** (screenplay) (*Coming Home*)
Paul Mazurksky (*An Unmarried Woman*)

ADAPTED SCREENPLAY
Walter Newman (*Bloodbrothers*)
Elaine May, Warren Beatty (*Heaven Can Wait*)
Neil Simon (*California Suite*)
Bernard Slade (*Same Time, Next Year*)
Oliver Stone (*Midnight Express*)

FOREIGN-LANGUAGE FILM
Get Out Your Hankerchiefs (France)
The Glass Cell (German Federal Republic)
Hungarians (Hungary)
Viva Italia! (Italy)
White Bim Black Ear (USSR)

OTHER AWARDS
Original Music Score: Giorgorio Morricone (*Midnight Express*); Original Song Score or Adapted Score: Joe Renzetti (*The Buddy Holly Story*); Original Song: "Last Dance" from *Thank God It's Friday*, music and lyrics by Paul Jabara; Cinematography: Nestor Almendros (*Days of Heaven*); Art Direction: Paul Sylbert, Edwin O'Donovan, George Gaines (*Heaven Can Wait*); Costume Design: Anthony Powell (*Death on the Nile*); Editing: Peter Zinner (*The Deer Hunter*); Sound: Richard Portman, William McCaughey, Aaron Rochin, Darrin Knight (*The Deer Hunter*).

Documentary: *Scared Straight!*; Documentary Short Subject: *The Flight of the Gossamer Condor*; Live-Action Short Subject: *Teenage Father*; Animated Short Subject: *Special Delivery*.

SPECIAL AWARDS

Laurence Olivier; director King Vidor; animator Walter Lantz; The Museum of Modern Art Department of Film; Linwood G. Dunn, Loren L. Ryder, Waldon O. Watson (service to the Academy); Leo Jaffe (Jean Hersholt Humanitarian Award); Les Bowie, Colin Chilvers, Denys Coop, Roy Field, Derek Meddings, Zroan Perisic for the visual effects in *Superman* (given as a special achievement award).

Oscar acknowledged the power of television by inviting popular *Tonight Show* host Johnny Carson to host the ceremony. For the first time, a star of the small screen with no film credits whatsoever was judged the best draw for ratings on Hollywood's biggest night. In his opening monologue, Carson promised "two hours of sparkling entertainment spread out over four hours." Steve Martin and Robin Williams, comedians who had gained fame on TV and were just beginning to make their mark in films, made strong impressions as presenters. Steve Lawrence and Sammy Davis, Jr., pointed out Oscar's shortcomings by performing a medley of famous movie tunes which were not nominated for best Song—much to the embarrassment of the Academy's music branch.

Two former giants of the screen, now devastated by illness and frail shadows of their former selves, were given ovations. John Wayne presented the best Picture award and Laurence Olivier received a special honorary Oscar. Sir Larry beautifully delivered an incomprehensible speech. A reaction shot of Best Actor winner Jon Voight striking his forehead in admiration at Olivier's bizarre eloquence was a program high point.

Rex Reed, Oscar's harshest critic, acknowledged "I must admit in all fairness that this was one of the most dignified Oscar shows in memory. It wasn't good, just better than usual."

NATIONAL BOARD OF REVIEW

English-Language Film: *Days of Heaven*; Actor (tie): Jon Voight (*Coming Home*) and Laurence Olivier (*The Boys from Brazil*); Actress: Ingrid Bergman (*Autumn Sonata*); Supporting Actor: Richard Farnsworth (*Comes a Horseman*); Supporting Actress: Angela Lansbury (*Death on the Nile*); Director: Ingmar Bergman (*Autumn Sonata*); Foreign-Language Film: *Autumn Sonata*.

BEST ENGLISH-LANGUAGE FILMS

Days of Heaven, Coming Home, Interiors, Superman, Movie Movie, Midnight Express, An Unmarried Woman, Pretty Baby, Girlfriends, Comes a Horseman.

BEST FOREIGN-LANGUAGE FILMS

Autumn Sonata (Sweden), *Dear Detective* (France), *Madame Rosa* (France), *A Slave of Love* (USSR), *Bread and Chocolate* (Italy).

NEW YORK FILM CRITICS CIRCLE

Picture: *The Deer Hunter*; Actor: Jon Voight (*Coming Home*); Actress: Ingrid Bergman (*Autumn Sonata*); Supporting Actor: Christopher Walken (*The Deer Hunter*); Supporting Actress: Maureen Stapleton (*Interiors*); Director: Terrence Malick (*Days of Heaven*); Foreign-Language Film: *Bread and Chocolate*.

The policy of a separate award for best Foreign-Language Film was reinstated this year. Circle member Rex Reed received one Supporting Actor vote for a cameo appearance in *Superman*.

NATIONAL SOCIETY OF FILM CRITICS

Picture: *Get Out Your Handkerchiefs*; Actor: Gary Busey (*The Buddy Holly Story*); Actress: Ingrid Bergman (*Autumn Sonata*); Supporting Actor (tie): Richard Farnsworth (*Comes a Horseman*) and Robert Morley (*Who Is Killing the Great Chefs of Europe?*); Supporting Actress: Meryl Streep (*The Deer Hunter*); Director: Terrence Malick (*Days of Heaven*); Screenplay: Paul Mazursky (*An Unmarried Woman*); Cinematography: Nestor Almendros (*Days of Heaven*); Documentary: *The Battle of Chile*.

LOS ANGELES FILM CRITICS ASSOCIATION

Picture: *Coming Home*; Actor: Jon Voight (*Coming Home*); Actress: Jane Fonda (*Coming Home, Comes a Horseman,* and *California Suite*); Supporting

Actor: Robert Morley (*Who Is Killing the Great Chefs of Europe?*); Supporting Actress (tie): Maureen Stapleton (*Interiors*) and Mona Washbourne (*Stevie*); Director: Michael Cimino (*The Deer Hunter*); Screenplay: Paul Mazursky (*An Unmarried Woman*); Cinematography: Nestor Almendros (*Days of Heaven*); Music: Giorgio Moroder (*Midnight Express*); Foreign FIlm: *Madame Rosa*.

HOLLYWOOD FOREIGN PRESS ASSOCIATION GOLDEN GLOBE AWARDS

Picture (Drama): *Midnight Express*; Picture (Comedy or Musical): *Heaven Can Wait*; Actor (Drama): Jon Voight (*Coming Home*); Actress (Drama): Jane Fonda (*Coming Home*); Actor (Comedy or Musical): Warren Beatty (*Heaven Can Wait*); Actress (Comedy or Musical) (tie): Ellen Burstyn (*Same Time, Next Year*) and Maggie Smith (*California Suite*); Supporting Actor: John Hurt (*Midnight Express*); Supporting Actress: Dyan Cannon (*Heaven Can Wait*); Acting Debut (Male): Brad Davis (*Midnight Express*); Acting Debut (Female): Irene Miracle (*Midnight Express*); Director: Michael Cimino (*The Deer Hunter*); Screenplay: Oliver Stone (*Midnight Express*); Original Score: Giorgio Moroder (*Midnight Express*); Song: "Last Dance" from *Thank God It's Friday*, music and lyrics by Paul Jabara; World Film Favorite (Male): John Travolta; World Film Favorite (Female): Jane Fonda.

SPECIAL AWARD
Lucille Ball (Cecil B. DeMille Award).

After five years in syndication, the Golden Globes returned to network television on NBC.

CANNES FILM FESTIVAL

Golden Palm Award: *The Tree of Wooden Clogs* (Italy); Actor: Jon Voight (*Coming Home*); Actress (tie): Jill Clayburgh (*An Unmarried Woman*) and Isabelle Huppert (*Violette Noziere*) (France); Director: Nagisha Oshima (*Empire of Passion*) (Japan); Special Jury Prize: *Bye, Bye, Monkey* (Italy) and *The Shout* (UK); International Critics Prize: *Man of Marble* (Poland), *The Smell of Wild Flowers* (Yugoslavia).

1979

ACADEMY AWARDS (OSCARS)

PICTURE
All That Jazz
Apocalypse Now
Breaking Away
Kramer vs. Kramer
Norma Rae

Robert Benton's child-custody drama *Kramer vs. Kramer*, which was called "a soap opera" by its star Dustin Hoffman, defeated Francis Coppola's more revolutionary Vietnam film *Apocalypse Now*. Bob Fosse's *All That Jazz*, an autobiographical study of a driven director/choreographer, took most of the technical prizes.

ACTOR
Dustin Hoffman (*Kramer vs. Kramer*)
Jack Lemmon (*The China Syndrome*)
Al Pacino (*. . . And Justice for All*)
Roy Scheider (*All That Jazz*)
Peter Sellers (*Being There*)

He called the awards "vulgar" the last time he was nominated, but Dustin Hoffman showed to accept his *Kramer vs. Kramer* Oscar and gave a moving speech about the difficulties of being an actor.

ACTRESS
Jill Clayburgh (*Starting Over*)
Sally Field (*Norma Rae*)
Jane Fonda (*The China Syndrome*)
Marsha Mason (*Chapter Two*)
Bette Midler (*The Rose*)

Sally Field was unaccompanied by her then-current amour Burt Reynolds, who reportedly stayed home to sulk over his lack of a nomination for *Starting Over*.

SUPPORTING ACTOR
Melvyn Douglas (*Being There*)
Robert Duvall (*Apocalypse Now*)
Frederic Forrest (*The Rose*)
Justin Henry (*Kramer vs. Kramer*)

Dustin Hoffman and Meryl Streep in *Kramer vs. Kramer* (1979) (best Picture—Oscar, New York and Los Angeles Film Critics, Hollywood Foreign Press Association).

Mickey Rooney (*The Black Stallion*)

Melvyn Douglas, at age 78 one of the oldest actors to compete in this category, defeated the youngest nominee ever, eight-year-old Justin Henry who played the object of the custody battle in *Kramer*.

SUPPORTING ACTRESS
Jane Alexander (*Kramer vs. Kramer*)
Barbara Barrie (*Breaking Away*)
Candice Bergen (*Starting Over*)
Mariel Hemingway (*Manhattan*)
Meryl Streep (*Kramer vs. Kramer*)

"Holy mackerel!" cried Meryl Streep when she received her Oscar. Later in the evening, she left it in the ladies' room.

DIRECTOR
Robert Benton (*Kramer vs. Kramer*)
Francis Coppola (*Apocalypse Now*)
Bob Fosse (*All That Jazz*)
Edouard Molinaro (*La Cage aux Folles*)
Pater Yates (*Breaking Away*)

ORIGINAL SCREENPLAY
Woody Allen, Marshall Brickman (*Manhattan*)
Robert Allen Arthur, Bob Fosse (*All That Jazz*)
Valerie Curtin, Barry Levinson (*. . . And Justice for All*)
Mike Gray, T.S. Cook, James Bridges (*The China Syndrome*)
Steve Tesich (*Breaking Away*)

ADAPTED SCREENPLAY
Robert Benton (*Kramer vs. Kramer*)
Allan Burns (*A Little Romance*)
John Milius, Francis Coppola (*Apocalypse Now*)
Irving Ravetch, Harriet Frank, Jr. (*Norma Rae*)
Francis Veber, Edouard Molinaro, Marcello Danon, Jean Poiret (*La Cage aux Folles*)

FOREIGN-LANGUAGE FILM
The Maids of Wilko (Poland)
Mama Turns a Hundred (Spain)
A Simple Story (France)
The Tin Drum (Federal Repulic of Germany)
To Forget Venice (Italy)

OTHER AWARDS

Original Music Score: Georges Delerue (*A Little Romance*); Original Song or Adapted Score: Ralph Burns (*All That Jazz*); Original Song: "It Goes Like It Goes" from *Norma Rae*, music by David Shire, lyrics by Norman Gimbel; Cinematography: Vittorio Storaro (*Apocalypse Now*); Art Direction: Philip Rosenberg, Tony Walton, Edward Stewart, Gary Brink (*All That Jazz*); Editing: Alan Heim (*All That Jazz*); Sound: Walter Murch, Mark Berger, Richard Beggs, Nat Boxer (*Apocalypse Now*); Visual Effects: H.R. Ginger, Carlo Rambaldi, Brian Johnson, Nick Adler, Denys Ayling (*Alien*).

Documentary: *Best Boy*; Documentary Short Subject: *Paul Robeson: Tribute to an Artist*; Live-Action Short Subject: *Board and Care*; Animated Short Subject: *Every Child*.

SPECIAL AWARDS

Alec Guinness; Hal Elias for service to the Academy; John O. Aalberg, Charles G. Clarke, John G. Frayne for service to the Academy; Ray Stark (Irving Thalberg Award); Robert Benjamin (Jean Hersholt Humanitarian Award); Alan Splet for sound editing of *The Black Stallion* (given as special achievement award).

Miss Piggy saved the night, according to *The New York Daily News*'s Kay Gardella. Andrew Sarrris of *The Village Voice* agreed, suggesting the synthetic swine and her fellow Muppets should sing all the nominated songs and present all the awards in the future since they were more natural than the humans usually are on the Oscarcasts.

Host Johnny Carson got considerable mileage with no-show winner Alan Splet, who won a special award for his sound editing of *The Black Stallion*. "First George C. Scott doesn't show, and then Marlon Brando, and now Alan Splet," *The Tonight Show* desk jockey quipped. Throughout the evening, Carson gave the audience updates on Splet's whereabouts.

Documetary filmmaker Ira Wohl copped an Oscar for *Best Boy*, a feature about his mentally disabled brother, and proceeded to thank his entire family for nearly four minutes. "I'm glad he didn't have anymore relatives," presenter William Shatner tastelessly added after Wohl left the podium. Oscar

producer Howard Koch later blasted Wohl for his lengthy speech on a Los Angeles radio talk show. (Dustin Hoffman actually spoke a full minute longer than Wohl.)

Foreign-film winner Volker Schlondorff (*The Tin Drum*) pointed out his was the first German film to be so honored and came close to angrily accusing the Academy of discrimination against his country for its Nazi past.

Despite such outbursts, *Variety* labeled the ceremony "a quiet, dignified affair."

NATIONAL BOARD OF REVIEW

English-Language Film: *Manhattan*; Actor: Peter Sellers (*Being There*); Actress: Sally Field (*Norma Rae*); Supporting Actor: Paul Dooley (*Breaking Away*); Supporting Actress: Meryl Streep (*Kramer vs. Kramer, The Seduction of Joe Tynan,* and *Manhattan*); Director: John Schlesinger (*Yanks*).

BEST ENGLISH-LANGUAGE FILMS

Manhattan, Yanks, The Europeans, The China Syndrome, Breaking Away, Apocalypse Now, Being There, Time after Time, North Dallas Forty, Kramer vs. Kramer.

BEST FOREIGN-LANGUAGE FILMS

La Cage aux Folles (France/Italy), *The Tree of Wooden Clogs* (Italy), *The Marriage of Maria Braun* (Federal Republic of Germany), *Nosferatu* (Federal Republic of Germany), *Peppermint Soda* (France).

NEW YORK FILM CRITICS CIRCLE

Picture: *Kramer vs. Kramer*; Actor: Dustin Hoffman (*Kramer vs. Kramer*); Actress: Sally Field (*Norma Rae*); Supporting Actor: Melvyn Douglas (*Being There*); Supporting Actress: Meryl Streep (*Kramer vs. Kramer* and *The Seduction of Joe Tynan*); Director: Woody Allen (*Manhattan*); Screenplay: Steven Tesich (*Breaking Away*); Foreign-Language Film: *The Tree of Wooden Clogs* (Italy).

Melvyn Douglas was in competition with himself for the New York Film Critics Award. He received sixteen points for his performance as a senile senator in *The Seduction of Joe Tynan*, but won with thirty-three points for his work as a dying millionaire in *Being There*. Similarly Meryl Streep was a double favorite in the supporting actress field, garnering thirty-two points as Alan Alda's mistress in *The Seduction of Joe Tynan* and thirty-three for *Kramer vs. Kramer*. The Circle voted to award her for both films. She was unable to attend the ceremony at Sardi's because her newborn baby was sick. "Ah, poor baby," best Actress Sally Field was heard to murmur at the announcement.

NATIONAL SOCIETY OF FILM CRITICS

Picture: *Breaking Away*; Actor: Dustin Hoffman (*Kramer vs. Kramer* and *Agatha*); Actress: Sally Field (*Norma Rae*); Supporting Actor: Frederic Forrest (*The Rose*); Supporting Actress: Meryl Streep (*Kramer vs. Kramer, Manhattan*, and *The Seduction of Joe Tynan*); Director (tie): Woody Allen (*Manhattan* and Robert Benton (*Kramer vs. Kramer*); Screenplay: Steve Tesich (*Breaking Away*); Cinematography: Caleb Deschanel (*The Black Stallion* and *Being There*).

LOS ANGELES FILM CRITICS ASSOCIATION

Picture: *Kramer vs. Kramer*; Actor: Dustin Hoffman (*Kramer vs. Kramer*); Actress: Sally Field (*Norma Rae*); Supporting Actor: Melvyn Douglas (*Being There* and *The Seduction of Joe Tynan*); Supporting Actress: Meryl Streep (*Kramer vs. Kramer, The Seduction of Joe Tynan,* and *Manhattan*); Director: Robert Benton (*Kramer vs. Kramer*); Screenplay: Robert Benton (*Kramer vs. Kramer*); Cinematography: Caleb Deschanel (*The Black Stallion*); Music: Carmine Coppola (*The Black Stallion*); Foreign Film: *Soldier of Orange*.

HOLLYWOOD FOREIGN PRESS ASSOCIATION GOLDEN GLOBE AWARDS

Picture (Drama): *Kramer vs. Kramer*; Picture (Comedy or Musical): *Breaking Away*; Actor (Drama): Dustin Hoffman (*Kramer vs. Kramer*); Actress (Drama): Sally Field (*Norma Rae*); Actor (Comedy or Musical): Peter Sellers (*Being There*); Actress (Comedy or Musical): Bette Midler (*The Rose*); Supporting Actor (tie): Melvyn Douglas

(*Being There*) and Robert Duvall (*Apocalypse Now*); Supporting Actress: Meryl Streep (*Kramer vs. Kramer*); New Star of the Year (Male): Ricky Schroder (*The Champ*); New Star of the Year (Female): Bette Midler (*The Rose*); Director: Francis Coppola (*Apocalypse Now*); Screenplay: Robert Benton (*Kramer vs. Kramer*); Score: Carmine Coppola, Francis Coppola (*Apocalypse Now*); Song: "The Rose" from *The Rose*, by Amanda McBroom; World Film Favorite (Male): Roger Moore; World Film Favorite (Female): Jane Fonda.

SPECIAL AWARD
Henry Fonda (Cecil B. DeMille Award).

"I'll show you a pair of Golden Globes," cracked Bette Midler when she won a matched set of the prizes for playing a Janis Joplin-like rock star in *The Rose*. The Hollywood Foreign Press Association named her best Actress (Comedy or Musical) and best New Star of the Year. Not so lucky was little Justin Henry. When the eight-year-old actor lost New Star of the Year to 10-year-old Ricky Schroder and Supporting Actor to Melvyn Douglas, the child star burst into tears.

CANNES FILM FESTIVAL

Golden Palm Award: *Apocalypse Now* (USA) and *The Tin Drum* (Federal Republic of Germany); Actor: Jack Lemmon (*The China Syndrome*); Actress: Sally Field (*Norma Rae*); Supporting Actor: Stefano Madia (*Caro Papa*) (Italy); Supporting Actress: Eva Mattes (*Woyzeck*) (Federal Republic of Germany); Director: Terence Malik (*Days of Heaven*); Special Jury Prize: *Siberiade* (USSR); Young Cinema Prize: *La Drolesse* (France); Camera d'Or: *Northern Lights*; Technical Prize: *Norma Rae*; International Critics Prize: in competiton, *Apocalypse Now*, out of competition, *Angi Vera* (Hungary) and *Black Jack* (UK).

SPECIAL AWARD
Homage to Miklos Jancso for the body of his work.

1980

ACADEMY AWARDS (OSCARS)

PICTURE
Coal Miner's Daughter
The Elephant Man
Ordinary People
Raging Bull
Tess

Once again, Oscar favored a safe family drama over a brilliantly directed masterwork. In a repeat of last year's *Kramer vs. Kramer-Apocalypse Now* battle, Robert Redford's workman-like *Ordinary People* knocked out Martin Scorsese's extraordinary boxing film *Raging Bull*.

ACTOR
Robert De Niro (*Raging Bull*)
Robert Duvall (*The Great Santini*)
John Hurt (*The Elephant Man*)
Jack Lemmon (*Tribute*)
Peter O'Toole (*The Stunt Man*)

Not only were Robert De Niro and Sissy Spacek present at the Oscar ceremony, but so were the people they played in their Oscar-winning films—former prizefighter Jake LaMotta, the inspiration for *Raging Bull*, and country-western singer Loretta Lynn, the subject of *Coal Miner's Daughter*.

ACTRESS
Ellen Burstyn (*Resurrection*)
Goldie Hawn (*Private Benjamin*)
Mary Tyler Moore (*Ordinary People*)
Gena Rowlands (*Gloria*)
Sissy Spacek (*Coal Miner's Daughter*)

SUPPORTING ACTOR
Judd Hirsch (*Ordinary People*)
Timothy Hutton (*Ordinary People*)
Michael O'Keefe (*The Great Santini*)
Joe Pesci (*Raging Bull*)
Jason Robards (*Melvin and Howard*)

Timothy Hutton was the youngest individual ever to win the Supporting Actor Oscar. He was age 20 at victory time.

SUPPORTING ACTRESS
Eileen Brennan (*Private Benjamin*)
Eva La Gallienne (*Resurrection*)
Cathy Moriarty (*Raging Bull*)
Diana Scarwid (*Inside Moves*)
Mary Steenburgen (*Melvin and Howard*)

DIRECTOR
David Lynch (*The Elephant Man*)
Roman Polanski (*Tess*)
Robert Redford (*Ordinary People*)
Richard Rush (*The Stunt Man*)
Martin Scorsese (*Raging Bull*)

ORIGINAL SCREENPLAY
Bo Goldman (*Melvin and Howard*)
Christopher Gore (*Fame*)
Jean Gruault (*Mon Oncle d'Amerique*)
Nancy Myers, Charles Shyer, Harvery Miller
     (*Private Benjamin*)
W. D. Richter, Arthur Ross (*Brubaker*)

ADAPTED SCREENPLAY
Chistopher Devore, Eric Bergren, David Lynch
     (*The Elephant Man*)
Jonathan Hardy, David Stevens, Bruce Beresford
     (*Breaker Morant*)
Lawrence B. Marcus, Richard Rush
     (*The Stunt Man*)
Tom Rickman (*Coal Miner's Daughter*)
Alvin Sargeant (*Ordinary People*)

FOREIGN-LANGUAGE FILM
Confidence (Hungary)
Kagemusha (Japan)
The Last Metro (France)
Moscow Does Not Believe in Tears (USSR)
The Nest (Spain)

OTHER AWARDS
Original Music Score: Michael Gore (*Fame*); Original Song: "Fame" from *Fame*, music by Michael Gore, lyrics by Dean Pitchford; Cinematography: Geoffrey Unsworth, Ghislain Cloquet (*Tess*); Art Direction: Pierre Guffroy, Jack

Stevens (*Tess*); Costume Design: Anthony Powell (*Tess*); Editing: Thelma Schoonmaker (*Raging Bull*); Sound: Bill Varney, Steve Maslow, Gregg Landaker, Peter Sutton (*The Empire Strikes Back*).

Documentary: *From Mao to Mozart: Isaac Stern in China*; Documentary Short Subject: *Karl Hess: Toward Liberty*; Live-Action Short Subject: *The Dollar Bottom*; Animated Short Subject: *The Fly*.

SPECIAL AWARDS

Henry Fonda; Fred Hynes; Brian Johnson, Richard Edlund, Dennis Muren, Bruce Nicholson for the visual effects in *The Empire Strikes Back* (given as a special achievement award).

For the second time, the Oscars were delayed because of assassination. The 1967 ceremony was postponed when Martin Luther King, Jr., was gunned down. The tragedy was much closer to home for the 1980 show. Former actor/Oscar presenter and then President Ronald Reagen was gunned down but not killed on the afternoon of the Oscars by John Hinckley, a young man obsessed with actress Jodie Foster and one of her films *Taxi Driver*. In that Martin Scorsese picture, Robert De Niro attempts to assassinate a political figure in order to impress a woman. Best Actor De Niro stalked out of the post-show press room when was asked what he felt about Hinckley being influenced by the movie.

The Oscarcast was delayed one day and began with greetings from the President taped a week previously. In an attempt to enliven the reading of the voting rules, a chorus dressed as ushers sang and danced them. "They'll be back to sing the instructions on the 1040 form," host Johnny Carson quipped. The piece was remarkably similar to a number Tommy Tune had devised for the Broadway musical *A Day in Hollywood/A Night in the Ukraine* in which the ushers of Graumen's Chinese Theatre did a tap routine to the words of the 1930s' Hollywood Production Code. It was shown on the previous year's Tony Awards.

Lucianno Pavarotti sang "Torna a Sorrento" and gave out the best Song accolade with Angie Dickinson. The great operatic tenor was chosen as a presenter for no other reason than that he had a movie coming out that summer—which quickly flopped. Best Actor nominee Peter O'Toole

appeared totally disoriented and confused while presenting the Art Direction award with Sissy Spacek. He later claimed nervousness caused his flub.

New Oscar producer Norman Jewison was also stunned by the whole affair. After it was all over, he commented, "Doing this show is like dragging a dinosaur around behind you. Never again."

NATIONAL BOARD OF REVIEW

Picture: *Ordinary People*; Actor: Robert De Niro (*Raging Bull*); Actress: Sissy Spacek (*Coal Miner's Daughter*); Supporting Actor: Joe Pesci (*Raging Bull*); Supporting Actress: Eva La Galliene (*Resurrection*); Director: Robert Redford (*Ordinary People*).

BEST ENGLISH-LANGUAGE FILMS

Ordinary People, Raging Bull, Coal Miner's Daughter, Tess, Melvin and Howard, The Great Santini, The Elephant Man, The Stunt Man, My Bodyguard, Resurrection.

BEST FOREIGN-LANGUAGE FILMS

The Tin Drum (Federal Republic of Germany), *Kagemusha* (Japan), *Knife in the Head* (Federal Republic of Germany), *From the Life of Marionettes* (Federal Republic of Germany), *Eboli* (Italy).

NEW YORK FILM CRITICS CIRCLE

Picture: *Ordinary People*; Actor: Robert De Niro (*Raging Bull*); Actress: Sissy Spacek (*Coal Miner's Daughter*); Supporting Actor: Joe Pesci (*Raging Bull*); Supporting Actress: Mary Steenburgen (*Melvin and Howard*); Director: Jonathan Demme (*Melvin and Howard*); Screenplay: Bo Goldman (*Melvin and Howard*); Cinematography: Geoffrey Unsworth, Ghislaine Cloquet (*Tess*); Foreign-Language Film: *Mon Oncle d'Amerique*; Documentary: *Best Boy*.

Ruth Gordon left the Film Critics' awards dinner in a huff when she was informed that due to a mix-up in scheduling she would not be presenting the Supporting Actor award.

NATIONAL SOCIETY OF FILM CRITICS

Picture: *Melvin and Howard*; Actor: Peter O'Toole (*The Stunt Man*); Actress: Sissy Spacek (*Coal Miner's Daughter*); Supporting Actor: Joe Pesci (*Raging Bull*); Supporting Actress: Mary Steenburgen (*Melvin and Howard*); Director: Martin Scorsese (*Raging Bull*); Screenplay: Bo Goldman (*Melvin and Howard*); Cinematography: Michael Chapman (*Raging Bull*).

The best Picture award for *Melvin and Howard*, Jonathan Demme's character study of a man who claimed to have given recluse millionaire Howard Hughes a lift in his truck, gave the quirky comedy a big boost. Reportedly Universal, which owned the rights to the film, was planning the remove it from circulation, re-edit it, and release it under another name. The award brought attention and an audience to the film, which later won two Oscars.

LOS ANGELES FILM CRITICS ASSOCIATION

Picture: *Raging Bull*; Actor: Robert De Niro (*Raging Bull*); Actress: Sissy Spacek (*Coal Miner's Daughter*); Supporting Actor: Timothy Hutton (*Ordinary People*); Supporting Actress: Mary Steenburgen (*Melvin and Howard*); Director: Roman Polanski (*Tess*); Screenplay: John Sayles (*The Return of the Seacaucus 7*); Cinematography: Geoffrey Unsworth, Ghislain Cloquet (*Tess*); Music: Ry Cooder (*The Long Riders*); Foreign Film: *The Tin Drum*; Independent or Experimental Films: *Journeys to Berlin 1971* and *Demon Lover Diary*.

HOLLYWOOD FOREIGN PRESS ASSOCIATION GOLDEN GLOBE AWARDS

Picture (Drama): *Ordinary People*; Picture (Comedy or Musical): *Coal Miner's Daughter*; Actor (Drama): Robert De Niro (*Raging Bull*); Actress (Drama): Mary Tyler Moore (*Ordinary People*); Actor (Comedy or Musical): Ray Sharkey (*The Idolmaker*); Actress (Comedy or Musical): Sissy Spacek (*Coal Miner's Daughter*); Supporting

Actor: Timothy Hutton (*Ordinary People*); Supporting Actress: Mary Steenburgen (*Melvin and Howard*); Acting Debut (Male): Timothy Hutton (*Ordinary People*); Acting Debut (Female): Nastassja Kinski (*Tess*); Director: Robert Redford (*Ordinary People*); Screenplay: William Peter Blatty (*Twinkle, Twinkle, Killer Kane*); Original Score: Dominic Frontiere (*The Stunt Man*); Original Song: "Fame" from *Fame*, music by Michael Gore, lyrics by Dean Pitchford; Foreign Film: *Tess*.

SPECIAL AWARD
Gene Kelly (Cecil B. DeMille Award).

CANNES FILM FESTIVAL

Golden Palm Award: *All That Jazz* (USA) and *Kagemusha* (Japan); Actor: Michel Piccoli (*Leap into the Void*) (Italy/France); Actress: Anouk Aimee (*Leap into the Void*); Supporting Actor: Jack Thompson (*Breaker Morant*) (Australia); Supporting Actress (tie): Carla Gravina (*The Terrace*) (Italy), Milena Dravic (*Special Treatment*) (Yugoslavia); Director: Kryzstof Zanussi (*Constans*) (Poland); Screenplay: Ettore Scola, Age and Scarpelli (*The Terrace*); Camera d'Or: *Histoire d'Adrien*; Jury Prize: *The Constant Factor* (Poland); Special Jury Prize: *Mon Oncle d'Amerique* (France); Technical Prize: *Le Risque De Vivre*; International Critics Prize: in competition, *Mon Oncle d'Amerique*, out of competition, *Provincial Actors* (Poland).

1981

ACADEMY AWARDS (OSCARS)

PICTURE
Atlantic City
Chariots of Fire
On Golden Pond
Raiders of the Lost Ark
Reds

Janet Maslin of *The New York Times* called the 1981 Oscars "the most exciting in recent years." For once, the results were almost totally unexpected. Small-scale British import *Chariots of Fire* defeated *Reds*, Warren Beatty's $50 million, star-studded saga of American Communist John Reed. The ailing Henry Fonda was a shoe-in as best Actor in *On Golden Pond*. (His daughter and co-star Jane accepted for him—at length, speaking for four minutes.) But Katharine Hepburn was a surprise victor, making her collection of Oscars a quartet, the most won by any actor. Diane Keaton or Meryl Streep was thought to be the favorite.

The acting awards were a celebration of maturity with the average age of the four winners being 70½.

ACTOR
Warren Beatty (*Reds*)
Henry Fonda (*On Golden Pond*)
Burt Lancaster (*Atlantic City*)
Dudley Moore (*Arthur*)
Paul Newman (*Absence of Malice*)

ACTRESS
Katharine Hepburn (*On Golden Pond*)
Diane Keaton (*Reds*)
Marsha Mason (*Only When I Laugh*)
Susan Sarandon (*Atlantic City*)
Meryl Streep (*The French Lieutenant's Woman*)

When asked for a quote on copping her record-breaking fourth Oscar, crisp Kate Hepburn responded, "Thank you will suffice."

SUPPORTING ACTOR
James Coco (*Only When I Laugh*)
John Gielgud (*Arthur*)
Ian Holm (*Chariots of Fire*)
Jack Nicholson (*Reds*)
Howard E. Rollins, Jr. (*Ragtime*)

SUPPORTING ACTRESS
Melinda Dillon (*Absence of Malice*)
Jane Fonda (*On Golden Pond*)
Joan Hackett (*Only When I Laugh*)
Elizabeth McGovern (*Ragtime*)
Maureen Stapleton (*Reds*)

The only acting winner present, Maureen Stapleton stated she was "thrilled, happy, delighted—sober" and thanked "everyone I've ever met in my entire life."

DIRECTOR
Warren Beatty (*Reds*)
Hugh Hudson (*Chariots of Fire*)
Louis Malle (*Atlantic City*)
Mark Rydell (*On Golden Pond*)
Steven Spielberg (*Raiders of the Lost Ark*)

ORIGINAL SCREENPLAY
Warren Beatty, Trevor Griffiths (*Reds*)
Steve Gordon (*Arthur*)
John Guare (*Atlantic City*)
Kurt Luedtke (*Absence of Malice*)
Colin Welland (*Chariots of Fire*)

ADAPTED SCREENPLAY
Jay Presson Allen, Sideny Lumet
   (*Prince of the City*)
Harold Pinter (*The French Lieutenant's Woman*)
Dennis Potter (*Pennies from Heaven*)
Ernest Thompson (*On Golden Pond*)
Michael Weller (*Ragtime*)

FOREIGN-LANGUAGE FILM
The Boat Is Full (Switzerland)
Man of Iron (Poland)
Mephisto (Hungary)
Muddy River (Japan)
Three Brothers (Italy)

OTHER AWARDS
Original Musical Score: Vangelis (*Chariots of Fire*); Original Song: "The Best That You Can Do (Arthur's Theme)" from *Arthur*, music and lyrics by Burt Bacharach, Carole Bayer Sager, Christopher Cross, and Peter Allen; Cinematography: Vittorio Storaro (*Reds*); Art Direction: Norman Reynolds, Leslie Dilley, Michael Ford (*Raiders of the Lost Ark*); Costume Design: Milena Canonero (*Chariots of Fire*); Editing: Michael Kahn (*Raiders of the Lost Ark*); Sound: Bill Varney, Steve Maslow, Gregg Landaker, Roy Charman (*Raiders of the Lost Ark*); Visual Effects: Richard Edlund, Kit West, Bruce Nicholson, Joe Johnston (*Raiders of the Lost Ark*); Make-Up: Rick Baker (*An American Werewolf in London*).

Documentary: *Genocide*; Documentary Short Subject: *Close Harmony*; Live-Action Short Subject: *Violet*; Animated Short Subject: *Crac*.

SPECIAL AWARDS

Barbara Stanwyck; Danny Kaye (Jean Hersholt Humanitarian Award); Albert R. "Cubby" Broccoli (Irving Thalberg Award); Joseph B. Walker (Gordon E. Sawyer Award); Benjamin P. Burtt, Jr., Richard L. Anderson for the sound effects editing of *Raiders of the Lost Ark* (given as a special achievement award; Sound Effects Editing became a regular category the following year).

Despite an elaborate James Bond tribute complete with rockets and a lavish medley of Harry Warren tunes performed by Gregory Hines and Debbie Allen, the star of the evening was the irrepressible Bette Midler. Her task was to present the best Song award. In five hilarious minutes, she trashed all the nominees and the pretensions of the ceremony.

"This is the Oscars, we have to be dignified, as dignified as humanly possible," the Divine Miss M said from the podium. "That is why I have decided to rise to the occasion"—here she lifted her breasts and sarcastically continued—"and give the nominees all the dignity they deserve."

"Bette Midler emerged as the Mae West of the '80s with a nervy explosion of frankness that visibly shook up all the stuffed shirts, designer gowns, and frizzed hairdos," *The Village Voice* raved. "Without Bette, it would have been an endless evening," *Newsweek* opined. The greatest praise came from *Chariots of Fire* producer David Putnam. When the Oscar for best Picture was placed in his hands, the first thing he said was "Just for 30 seconds, I wish I were Bette Midler."

NATIONAL BOARD OF REVIEW

Picture: *Chariots of Fire*; Actor: Henry Fonda (*On Golden Pond*); Actress: Glenda Jackson (*Stevie*); Supporting Actor: Jack Nicholson (*Reds*); Supporting Actress: Mona Washbourne (*Stevie*); Director: Warren Beatty (*Reds*).

BEST ENGLISH-LANGUAGE FILMS

Chariots of Fire, Reds, Atlantic City, Stevie, Gallipoli, On Golden Pond, Prince of the City, Raiders of the Lost Ark, Heartland, Ticket to Heaven, Breaker Morant.

BEST FOREIGN-LANGUAGE FILMS

Oblomov (USSR), *The Boat Is Full* (Switzerland), *The Last Metro* (France), *Contract* (Poland), *Pixote* (Brazil).

NEW YORK FILM CRITICS CIRCLE

Picture: *Reds*; Actor: Burt Lancaster (*Atlantic City*); Actress: Glenda Jackson (*Stevie*); Supporting Actor: Jack Nicholson (*Reds*); Supporting Actress: Mona Washbourne (*Stevie*); Director: Sidney Lumet (*Prince of the City*); Screenplay: John Guare (*Atlantic City*); Cinematography: David Watkin (*Chariots of Fire*).

SPECIAL AWARDS

Napoleon, the restored 1926 silent film; Polish filmmakers Andrzej Wajda and Krzysztof Zanussi.

Burt Lancaster brought a tableful of relatives to the New York Film Critics awards dinner. An overly effusive William Hurt presented him with his prize. Columnist Arthur Bell of *The Village Voice* wrote, "Hurt's *Heaven's Gate*-like speech was the talk of the evening." Best Director Warren Beatty thanked his hosts by saying, "To receive recognition from such a mean, vitriolic, vituperative bunch is more than touching, it's paralyzing."

NATIONAL SOCIETY OF FILM CRITICS

Picture: *Atlantic City*; Actor: Burt Lancaster (*Atlantic City*); Actress: Marilia Pera (*Pixote*); Supporting Actor: Robert Preston (*S.O.B.*); Supporting Actress: Maureen Stapleton (*Reds*); Director: Louis Malle (*Atlantic City*); Screenplay: John Guare (*Atlantic City*); Cinematography: Gordon Willis (*Pennies from Heaven*).

LOS ANGELES FILM CRITICS ASSOCIATION

Picture: *Atlantic City*; Actor: Burt Lancaster (*Atlantic City*); Actress: Meryl Streep (*The French Lieutenant's Woman*); Supporting Actor: John Gielgud (*Arthur*); Supporting Actress: Maureen Stapleton (*Reds*); Director: Warren Beatty (*Reds*); Screenplay: John Guare (*Atlantic City*); Cinematography: Vittorio Storaro (*Reds*); Music:

Randy Newman (*Ragtime*); Foreign Film: *Pixote*; Independent or Experimental Film: *The Art of Worldly Wisdom*; Life Achievement: Barbara Stanwyck; New Generation Prize: John Guare for the screenplay of *Atlantic City*.

HOLLYWOOD FOREIGN PRESS ASSOCIATION GOLDEN GLOBE AWARDS

Picture (Drama): *On Golden Pond*; Picture (Comedy or Musical): *Arthur*; Actor (Drama): Henry Fonda (*On Golden Pond*); Actress (Drama): Meryl Streep (*The French Lieutenant's Woman*); Actor (Comedy or Musical): Dudley Moore (*Arthur*); Actress (Comedy or Musical): Bernadette Peters (*Pennies from Heaven*); Supporting Actor: John Gielgud (*Arthur*); Supporting Actress: Joan Hackett (*Only When I Laugh*); New Star of the Year: Pia Zadora (*Butterfly*); Director: Warren Beatty (*Reds*); Screenplay: Ernest Thompson (*On Golden Pond*); Original Song: "The Best That You Can Do (Arthur's Theme)" from *Arthur*, music and lyrics by Burt Bacharach, Carole Bayer Sager, Christopher Cross, Peter Allen; Foreign Film: *Chariots of Fire*.

SPECIAL AWARDS
Sidney Poitier (Cecil B. DeMille Award).

This was the year of the infamous Pia Zadora incident, which blackened the reputation of the Hollywood Foreign Press Association for years to come. Zadora was named New Star of the Year for her performance in the critically panned *Butterfly*. The starlet's chances were improved when her millionaire husband flew the entire HFPA on a junket to Las Vegas.

CANNES FILM FESTIVAL

Golden Palm: *Man of Iron* (Poland); Actor: Ugo Tognazzi (*Tragedy of a Ridiculous Man*) (Italy); Actress: Isabelle Adjani (*Quartet*) (UK/France) and *Possession* (France/Germany); Supporting Actor: Ian Holm (*Chariots of Fire*); Supporting Actress: Elena Solovei (*The Fact/Blood Type O*); Screenplay: Istvan Szabo (*Mephisto*) (Hungary/Federal Republic of Germany); Special Jury Prize: *Light Years Away* (Switzerland); Camera d'Or: *Desperado City*

(Federal Republic of Germany); Technical Prize: *Les Uns et les Autres* (France); International Critics Prize: in competition, *Mephisto*, critics' week, *Malou* (Federal Republic of Germany); American Critics Prize: *Chariots of Fire*; Artistic Contribution to Poetics of Cinema: *Excalibur* (UK).

The American Critics Prize, which was never given again, was dreamt up by Chicago reviewer Roger Ebert in order to reward *Chariots of Fire*, a favorite film of his that had been attacked by the French press. The unique Cannes award helped *Chariots* get American distribution and, subsequently, its best Picture Oscar.

ACADEMY AWARDS (OSCARS)

PICTURE
E.T.—The Extra-Terrestrial
Gandhi
Missing
Tootsie
The Verdict

A cute alien and an Indian leader were the top contendors for the 1982 best Picture Oscar. Steven Spielberg's *E.T.—The Extra-Terrestrial*, the top-grosser of all time (up to that point), and Richard Attenborough's epic biopic *Gandhi* were the only serious possibilities in the top category. *E.T.* was extremely popular, but by Oscar time there was a backlash against its relentless merchandising. Spielberg was still seen as getting too rich at too young an age. There was also the fatal accident on Spielberg's co-production of *The Twilight Zone* which resulted in the death of actor Vic Morrow and two child performers. Attenborough, on the other hand, had spent twenty years gathering the financing for *Gandhi*, a three-and-a-half-hour prestige project, the kind Oscar voters love to salute. Spielberg would have to get just as serious, by examining the Holocaust in *Schindler's List*, before he could collect a golden guy of his own.

Gandhi (Ben Kingsley in the title role, left) and *E.T.—The Extra-Terrestrial* (right) were the top contendors for the 1982 film awards.

ACTOR
Dustin Hoffman (*Tootsie*)
Ben Kingsley (*Gandhi*)
Jack Lemmon (*Missing*)
Paul Newman (*The Verdict*)
Peter O'Toole (*My Favorite Year*)

In his film debut, British actor Ben Kingsley in the title role of *Gandhi* defeated six-time nominee Paul Newman as a dissipated lawyer in *The Verdict* and five-time nominee Dustin Hoffman as a cross-dressing actor in *Tootsie*. The other entrants were equally battle-scarred from the Oscar wars: Jack Lemmon with eight Oscar nominations and Peter O'Toole achieving the dubious distinction of tying Richard Burton for the most nominations for an actor (seven) without a win.

ACTRESS
Julie Andrews (*Victor/Victoria*)
Jessica Lange (*Frances*)
Sissy Spacek (*Missing*)
Meryl Streep (*Sophie's Choice*)
Debra Winger (*An Officer and a Gentleman*)

Having already won every award possible, Meryl Streep was the clear favorite for her Polish concentration camp survivor in *Sophie's Choice*. After her British heroine in *The French Lieutenant's Woman*, this marked the beginning of a string of accent roles for the star.

SUPPORTING ACTOR
Charles Durning (*The Best Little Whorehouse in Texas*)
Louis Gossett, Jr. (*An Officer and a Gentleman*)
John Lithgow (*The World According to Garp*)
James Mason (*The Verdict*)
Robert Preston (*Victor/Victoria*)

Louis Gossett, Jr., was the second black actor to win an Oscar and the first to win in the Supporting Actor category.

SUPPORTING ACTRESS
Glenn Close (*The World According to Garp*)
Teri Garr (*Tootsie*)
Jessica Lange (*Tootsie*)
Kim Stanley (*Frances*)

Lesley Anne Warren (*Victor/Victoria*)

Jessica Lange was the third actress to be nominated for both leading and supporting Oscars in the same year. The first was Fay Bainter when the supporting category originated (see 1938). She was followed by Teresa Wright (see 1942). Sigourney Weaver, Emma Thompson, and Holly Hunter were later double nominees.

DIRECTOR
Richard Attenborough (*Gandhi*)
Sidney Lumet (*The Verdict*)
Wolfgang Peterson (*Das Boot*)
Sydney Pollack (*Tootsie*)
Steven Spielberg (*E.T.—The Extra-Terrestrial*)

ORIGINAL SCREENPLAY
John Briley (*Gandhi*)
Barry Levinson (*Diner*)
Melissa Matheson (*E.T.—The Extra-Terrestrial*)
Don McGuire, Larry Gelbart, Murray Schisgal (*Tootsie*)
Douglas Day Stewart (*An Officer and a Gentleman*)

ADAPTED SCREENPLAY
Costa-Gravas, Donald Stewart (*Missing*)
Blake Edwards (*Victor/Victoria*)
David Mamet (*The Verdict*)
Alan J. Pakula (*Sophie's Choice*)
Wolfgang Peterson (*Das Boot*)

FOREIGN-LANGUAGE FILM
Alsino and the Condor (Nicaragua)
Coup de Torchon (France)
The Flight of the Eagle (Sweden)
Private Life (USSR)
Volver a Empezar (Spain)

OTHER AWARDS
Original Musical Score: John Williams (*E.T.—The Extra-Terrestrial*); Original Song Score or Adapted Score: Leslie Bricusse, Henry Mancini (*Victor/Victoria*); Original Song: "Up Where We Belong" from *An Officer and a Gentleman*, music by Jack Nitzsche and Buffy Saint-Marie, lyrics by Will Jennings; Cinematography: Billy Williams, Ronnie Taylor (*Gandhi*); Art Direction: Stuart Craig, Bob Laing, Michael Seirton (*Gandhi*); Costume Design: John Mollo, Bhanu Athaiya (*Gandhi*); Editing: John Bloom (*Gandhi*); Sound: Gerry Humphreys, Robin O'Donoghue, Jonathan Bates, Simon Kaye (*Gandhi*); Visual Effects: Carlo Rambaldi, Dennis Murren, Kenneth F. Smith (*E.T.—The Extra-Terrestrial*); Sound Effects Editing: Charles L. Campbell, Ben Burtt (*E.T.—The Extra-Terrestrial*); Make-Up: *Quest for Fire* (credits in controversy).

Documentary: *Just Another Missing Kid*; Documentary Short Subject: *If You Love This Planet*; Live-Action Short Subject: *A Shocking Accident*; Animated Short Subject: *Tango*.

SPECIAL AWARDS
Mickey Rooney; Walter Mirisch (Jean Hersholt Humanitarian Award); John O. Aalberg (Gordon E. Sawyer Award).

"The Oscars seem to be confused with the Nobel Peace Prize, at least temporarily," observed Janet Maslin of *The New York Times*. As *Gandhi* continued to take award after award, the annual Hollywood ceremony became more like the annual one in Sweden with each *Gandhi* winner congratulating the Academy on its good taste and concern for world peace.

Returning to the ceremony were two-time winner Luise Rainer, who came out of retirement to present the Best Foreign Film award, and Oscar-refuser George C. Scott, who quietly sat in the audience. John Moschitta, the fast-talking star of numerous TV commercials, got the evening off to a rapid start by reading the Academy Award rules in twenty-five seconds. But the rest of the telecast was not to pass so quickly, clocking in at a staggering three and a half hours. "Is it still this year?" joked co-host Dudley Moore at the end of the show.

Mishaps prevailed, with Liza Minnelli getting shocked out of her wits by a descending screen, Richard Pryor speeding ahead of the cue cards, Charlton Heston introducing a film clip which never unreeled, and a technician falling off a set backstage.

The award for oddest couple went to Cher and Placido Domingo. The prize for worst luck would undoubtedly have been won by Animated Short

Subject winner Zbigniew Rybcyznski. The Polish filmmaker went outside of the Dorothy Chandler Pavillion for a smoke. When he attempted to return, a security guard stopped him. Rybcyznski had left his ticket inside, did not speak English, and tried to explain he was one of the honorees. A scuffle followed when the guard continued to bar his entry and the director was arrested. Rybcyznski asked for the only Hollywood lawyer he knew of, famous palimony attorney Marvin Mitchelson, who arranged for charges to be dropped and the director to be released.

NATIONAL BOARD OF REVIEW

Picture: *Gandhi*; Actor: Ben Kingsley (*Gandhi*); Actress: Meryl Streep (*Sophie's Choice*); Supporting Actor: Robert Preston (*Victor/Victoria*); Supporting Actress: Glenn Close (*The World According to Garp*); Director: Sidney Lumet (*The Verdict*).

BEST ENGLISH-LANGUAGE FILMS

Gandhi, The Verdict, Sophie's Choice, An Officer and a Gentleman, Missing, E.T.—The Extra-Terrestrial, The World According to Garp, Tootsie, Moonlighting, The Chosen.

BEST FOREIGN-LANGUAGE FILMS

Mephisto (Federal Republic of Germany), *Das Boot* (Federal Republic of Germany), *Three Brothers* (France/Italy), *Yol* (Turkey), *Siberiade* (USSR).

NEW YORK FILM CRITICS CIRCLE

Picture: *Gandhi*; Actor: Ben Kinglsey (*Gandhi*); Actress: Meryl Streep (*Sophie's Choice*); Supporting Actor: John Lithgow (*The World According to Garp*); Supporting Actress: Jessica Lange (*Tootsie*); Director: Sydney Pollack (*Tootsie*); Screenplay: Murray Schisgal, Larry Gelbart (*Tootsie*); Cinematography: Nestor Almendros (*Sophie's Choice*); Foreign-Language Film: *Time Stands Still*.

Among the critics' groups, Meryl Streep was everyone's choice for *Sophie's Choice*, but there was no agreement on best Picture, with New York going for *Gandhi*, Los Angeles electing *E.T.*, and the National Society voting for comedy with *Tootsie*.

At the New York Film Critics' ceremony, presenter Liv Ullmann stated she thought she had the edge over Meryl Streep since she already had an accent. And the other great female role went to Dustin Hoffman. "This has not been a great year for European actresses in their 40s," Ullmann quipped. In another cross-dressing role, John Lithgow won for best Supporting Actor as the transsexual former football player in *The World According to Garp*. Upon accepting, he chided the critics, "Only one person called me pretty. You used adjectives like 'alluring' and 'sensual' to describe Jessica Lange and Meryl Streep. But for me, it was beefy and hefty."

Hoffman had been asked to give Sydney Pollack the best Director prize. The request was greeted with laughter. Pollack and Hoffman did not get along on the set of *Tootsie*, and the cross-dressing star was the only major player in the film to go unrecognized by the New York Circle.

NATIONAL SOCIETY OF FILM CRITICS

Picture: *Tootsie*; Actor: Dustin Hoffman (*Tootsie*); Actress: Meryl Streep (*Sophie's Choice*); Supporting Actor: Mickey Rourke (*Diner*); Supporting Actress: Jessica Lange (*Tootsie*); Director: Steven Spielberg (*E.T.—The Extra-Terrestrial*); Screenplay: Murray Schisgal, Larry Gelbart (*Tootsie*); Cinematography: Philippe Rousselot (*Diva*).

LOS ANGELES FILM CRITICS ASSOCIATION

Picture: *E.T.—The Extra-Terrestrial*; Actor: Ben Kinglsey (*Gandhi*); Actress: Meryl Streep (*Sophie's Choice*); Supporting Actor: John Lithgow (*The World According to Garp*); Supporting Actress: Glenn Close (*The World Accoring to Garp*); Director: Steven Spielberg (*E.T.—The Extraterrestrial*); Screenplay: Murray Schisgal, Larry Gelbart (*Tootsie*); Cinematography: Jordan Cronenweth (*Blade Runner*); Music: James Homer and the Busboys (*48 Hours*); Foreign Film: *The Road Warrior*; Independent or Experimental Film: *Chan Is Missing*; Special Award: special effects technician Carlo Rambaldi.

HOLLYWOOD FOREIGN PRESS ASSOCIATION GOLDEN GLOBE AWARDS

Picture (Drama): *E.T.—The Extra-Terrestrial*; Picture (Comedy or Musical): *Tootsie*; Actor (Drama): Ben Kingsley (*Gandhi*); Actress (Drama): Meryl Streep (*Sophie's Choice*); Actor (Comedy or Musical): Dustin Hoffman (*Tootsie*); Actress (Comedy or Musical): Julie Andrews (*Victor/Victoria*); Supporting Actor: Louis Gosset, Jr. (*An Officer and a Gentleman*); Supporting Actress: Jessica Lange (*Tootsie*); New Star of the Year (Male): Ben Kingsley (*Gandhi*); New Star of the Year (Female): Sandahl Bergman (*Conan the Barbarian*); Director: Richard Attenborough (*Gandhi*); Screenplay: John Briley (*Gandhi*); Original Score: John Williams (*E.T.—The Extra-Terrestrial*); Original Song: "Up Where We Belong" from *An Officer and a Gentleman*, music by Jack Nitzche and Buffy Saint-Marie, lyrics by Will Jennings; Foreign Film: *Gandhi*.

SPECIAL AWARD
Laurence Olivier (Cecil B. DeMille Award).

Still reeling from the previous year's Pia Zadora incident, the Golden Globes sank even lower. Sir Laurence Olivier's Cecil B. DeMille Award came apart while he was delivering his acceptance speech and the ceremony was dropped from its berth on CBS. The show was taped for syndication instead.

CANNES FILM FESTIVAL

Golden Palm: *Missing* (USA) and *Yol* (Turkey); Actor: Jack Lemmon (*Missing*); Actress: Jadwiga Jankowska-Cieslak (*Another Way*) (Hungary); Director: Werner Herzog (*Fitzcarraldo*) (Federal Republic of Germany); Screenplay: Jerzy Skolimowski (*Moonlighting*) (UK); Special Jury Prize: *The Night of Shooting Stars* (Italy); Camera d'Or: *To Die at 30* (France); International Critics Prize: *Yol, Another Way,* and *Les Fleurs Sauvages* (Canada); Technical Prize: Raoul Coutard for the cinematography of *Passion* (France); Artistic Contribution: Bruno Nuytten for the the cinematography of *Invitation au Voyage* (France); Thirty-Fifth Anniversary Prize: Michelangelo Antonioni (*Identification of a Woman*) (Italy).

1983

ACADEMY AWARDS (OSCARS)

PICTURE
The Big Chill
The Dresser
The Right Stuff
Tender Mercies
Terms of Endearment

ACTOR
Michael Caine (*Educating Rita*)
Tom Conti (*Reuben, Reuben*)
Tom Courtenay (*The Dresser*)
Robert Duvall (*Tender Mercies*)
Albert Finney (*The Dresser*)

The only American in a Brit-heavy category, Robert Duvall won a long overdue Oscar after turning in amazingly life-like performances in *The Godfather, Apocalypse Now, The Seven Percent Solution,* and *The Great Santini.*

ACTRESS
Jane Alexander (*Testament*)
Shirley MacLaine (*Terms of Endearment*)
Meryl Streep (*Silkwood*)
Julie Walters (*Educating Rita*)
Debra Winger (*Terms of Endearment*)

Newly enlightened about the mystical side of life, Shirely MacLaine delivered a bizarre acceptance speech involving such occult topics as astral planes and reincarnation. The character she portrayed was more down to earth, a selfish mother coming to terms with the death of her daughter (Debra Winger) and a mid-life love affair with a former astronaut (Jack Nicholson).

In the pressroom afterward, her humor was also more earthy. When asked if she thought the Oscar was for her performance in *Terms of Endearment* or the entire body of her work, MacLaine replied, "For both . . . and for my body."

SUPPORTING ACTOR
Charles Durning (*To Be or Not to Be*)
John Lithgow (*Terms of Endearment*)

Jack Nicholson (*Terms of Endearment*)
Sam Shepard (*The Right Stuff*)
Rip Torn (*Cross Creek*)

Jack Nicholson became the second actor to win both a Leading and a Supporting Oscar. Jack Lemmon was the first and Gene Hackman was third to be double-honored.

SUPPORTING ACTRESS
Cher (*Silkwood*)
Glenn Close (*The Big Chill*)
Linda Hunt (*The Year of Living Dangerously*)
Amy Irving (*Yentl*)
Alfre Woodard (*Cross Creek*)

The previous year Julie Andrews, Dustin Hoffman, and John Lithgow were nominated for playing cross-dressers. This year Linda Hunt became the first Oscar winner to play a member of the opposite sex. The diminutive actress changed not only her gender but her race when she portrayed Billy Kwan, a Eurasian photographer who guides Mel Gibson through Indonesia in *The Year of Living Dangerously*.

DIRECTOR
Bruce Beresford (*Tender Mercies*)
Ingmar Bergman (*Fanny and Alexander*)
James L. Brooks (*Terms of Endearment*)
Mike Nichols (*Silkwood*)
Peter Yates (*The Dresser*)

James L. Brooks, winner of several Emmys for producing and writing *The Mary Tyler Moore Show* and *Taxi*, added three Oscars to his mantle as the producer, director, and author of *Terms of Endearment*.

Another hypenated talent, Barbra Striesand, did not receive a single nomination for producing, directing, or acting in *Yentl*. Babs and several of her fans cried sexism. On Oscar night, a group calling itself "Principals, Equality, and Professionalism in Film" staged a protest outside the Dorothy Chandler Pavillion. They carried signs reading "Oscar, Can You Hear Me?" and "Score, 1927–Present, Best Director Nominations: Men—273, Women—1."

ORIGINAL SCREENPLAY
Ingmar Bergman (*Fanny and Alexander*)
Nora Ephron, Alice Arlen (*Silkwood*)
Horton Foote (*Tender Mercies*)
Lawrence Kasden, Barbara Benedek
(*The Big Chill*)
Lawrence Lasker, Walter F. Parkes (*WarGames*)

ADAPTED SCREENPLAY
James L. Brooks (*Terms of Endearment*)
Julius J. Epstein (*Reuben, Reuben*)
Ronald Harwood (*The Dresser*)
Harold Pinter (*Betrayal*)
Willy Russell (*Educating Rita*)

FOREIGN-LANGUAGE FILM
Carmen (Spain)
Entre Nous (France)
Fanny and Alexander (Sweden)
Job's Revolt (Hungary)
Le Bal (Argentina)

OTHER AWARDS
Original Musical Score: Bill Conti (*The Right Stuff*); Original Song Score or Adaptation: Michel Legrand, Alan and Marilyn Bergman (*Yentl*); Original Song: "Flashdance . . . What a Feeling" from *Flashdance*, music by Giorgio Moroder, lyrics by Keith Forsey and Irene Cara; Cinematography: Sven Nykvist (*Fanny and Alexander*); Art Direction: Anna Asp, Susanne Lingheim (*Fanny and Alexander*); Costume Design: Marik Vos (*Fanny and Alexander*); Editing: Glenn Farr, Lisa Fruchtman, Stephen A. Rotter, Douglas Steward, Tom Rolf (*The Right Stuff*); Sound: Mark Berger, Tom Scott, Randy Thom, David MacMillan (*The Right Stuff*); Sound Effects Editing: Jay Boekelheide (*The Right Stuff*).

Documentary: *He Makes Me Feel Like Dancing*; Documentary Short Subject: *Flamenco at 5:15*; Live-Action Short Subject: *Boys and Girls*; Animated Short Subject: *Sundae in New York*.

SPECIAL AWARDS
M. J. "Mike" Frankovich (Jean Hersholt Humanitarian Award); Dr. John G. Frayn (Gordon E. Sawyer Award); Hal Roach; Richard Edulund, Dennis Muren, Ken Ralston, Phil

Tippett for the visual effects of *Return of the Jedi* (given as special achievement award).

"Watching the annual Academy Awards show is an obligation, like attending church, a friend's graduation, or the dentist," wrote Vincent Canby of *The New York Times.* "No one expects it to be a barrel of laughs, even when it's supposed to be funny, but it shouldn't be the endurance test that this year's function became." Indeed, the 1983 Oscars set a record for length at three hours and forty-seven minutes—and this despite the redesigning of the stage to make winners' walks up the steps faster. It was to no avail as acceptance speeches were lengthier than usual.

Host Johnny Carson joshed with the tired audience, "OK, folks, we're into our fourth hour. Let's check the tote board and see how much money we've raised." Best Actress Shirley MacLaine commented, "This show is longer than my career." Best Picture presenter and early Oscar sponsor Frank Capra did not express a majority opinion when he called the snoozefest "the greatest show ever put on."

NATIONAL BOARD OF REVIEW

Picture: *Betrayal*; Actor: Tom Conti (*Reuben, Reuben* and *Merry Christmas, Mr. Lawrence*); Actress: Shirley MacLaine (*Terms of Endearment*); Supporting Actor: Jack Nicholson (*Terms of Endearment*); Supporting Actress: Linda Hunt (*The Year of Living Dangerously*); Director: James L. Brooks (*Terms of Endearment*).

BEST ENGLISH-LANGUAGE FILMS
Betrayal, Terms of Endearment, Educating Rita, Tender Mercies, The Dresser, The Right Stuff, Testament, Local Hero, The Big Chill, Cross Creek, Yentl.

BEST FOREIGN-LANGUAGE FILMS
Fanny and Alexander (Sweden), *The Return of Martin Guerre* (France), *La Nuit de Varennes* (France), *La Traviata* (Italy), *The Boat People* (Hong Kong/China).

NEW YORK FILM CRITICS CIRCLE

Picture: *Terms of Endearment*; Actor: Robert Duvall (*Tender Mercies*); Actress: Shirley MacLaine (*Terms of Endearment*); Supporting Actor: Jack Nicholson

(*Terms of Endearment*); Supporting Actress: Linda Hunt (*The Year of Living Dangerously*); Director: Ingmar Bergman (*Fanny and Alexander*); Screenplay: Bill Forsyth (*Local Hero*); Cinematography: Gordon Willis (*Zelig*); Foreign Film: *Fanny and Alexander.*

NATIONAL SOCIETY OF FILM CRITICS

Picture: *The Night of Shooting Stars*; Actor: Gerard Depardieu (*Danton* and *The Return of Martin Guerre*); Actress: Debra Winger (*Terms of Endearment*); Supporting Actor: Jack Nicholson (*Terms of Endearment*); Supporting Actress: Sandra Bernhard (*King of Comedy*); Director: Paolo and Vittorio Tavian (*The Night of Shooting Stars*); Screenplay: Bill Forsyth (*Local Hero*); Cinematography: Hiro Narita (*Never Cry Wolf*).

LOS ANGELES FILM CRITICS ASSOCIATION

Picture: *Terms of Endearment*; Actor: Robert Duvall (*Tender Mercies*); Actress: Shirley MacLaine (*Terms of Endearment*); Supporting Actor: Jack Nicholson (*Terms of Endearment*); Supporting Actress: Linda Hunt (*The Year of Living Dangerously*); Director: James L. Brooks (*Terms of Endearment*); Screenplay: James L. Brooks (*Terms of Endearment*); Cinematography: Sven Nykvist (*Fanny and Alexander*); Music: Philip Glass (*Koyaanisqatsi*); Foreign Film: (*Fanny and Alexander*); Independent or Experimental Film: *So Is This*; Special Award: The studios that re-issued *A Star Is Born* and *The Leopard.*

HOLLYWOOD FOREIGN PRESS ASSOCIATION GOLDEN GLOBE AWARDS

Picture (Drama): *Terms of Endearment*); Picture (Comedy or Musical): *Yentl*; Actor (Drama) (tie): Tom Courtenay (*The Dresser*) and Robert Duvall (*Tender Mercies*); Actress (Drama): Shirley MacLaine (*Terms of Endearment*); Actor (Comedy or Musical): Michael Caine (*Educating Rita*); Actress (Comedy or Musical): Julie Walters (*Educating Rita*); Supporting Actor: Jack Nicholson (*Terms of Endearment*); Supporting Actress: Cher (*Silkwood*); Director: Barbra Streisand (*Yentl*);

Screenplay: James L. Brooks (*Terms of Endearment*); Original Score: Giorgio Moroder (*Flashdance*); Original Song: "Flashdance . . . What a Feeling" from *Flashdance*, music by Giorgio Moroder, lyrics by Keith Forsey and Irene Cara; Foreign Film: *Fanny and Alexander*.

SPECIAL AWARD

Paul Newman (Cecil B. DeMille Award).

CANNES FILM FESTIVAL

Golden Palm: *The Ballad of Narayama* (Japan); Actor: Gian Mario Volonte (*The Death of Mario Ricci*) (Switzerland); Actress: Hanna Schygulla (*Storia di Piera*) (Italy); Grand Prize for Creative Filmmaking (in lieu of best Director): Robert Bresson (*L'Argent*) (France), Andre Tarkovsky (*Nostlagia*) (Italy); Camera d'Or: *The Princess* (Hungary); Special Jury Prize: *Monty Python's The Meaning of Life* (UK); Jury Prize: *A Closed Case* (India); Technical Prize and Artistic Contribution: *Carmen* (Spain); International Critics Prize: in competiton, *Nostalgia*, Directors' Fortnight, *Daniel Takes a Train* (Hungary).

ACADEMY AWARDS (OSCARS)

PICTURE

Amadeus
The Killing Fields
A Passage to India
Places in the Heart
A Soldier's Story

Amadeus, Milos Forman's filmization of Peter Shaffer's London and Broadway stage hit, dominated the 1984 Oscars. The story of the rivalry between composers Mozart and Salieri won eight awards for eight nominations. Its closest competitor was *A Passage to India*, David Lean's adaptation of E. M. Forster's classic novel of Brits coping with the mysteries of the title country. This was seventy-six-year-old Lean's first film in fourteen years. He had been bitterly disappointed by the failure of

Ryan's Daughter. But *Passage* was seen as a good Oscar bet, having won the National Board of Review and New York Film Critics Circle awards.

Oscar voters were more influenced by the Los Angeles Critics awards and the Golden Globes, which favored *Amadeus*. The Mozart picture had also launched a massive campaign in the trades with fifty full pages of "For Your Consideration" ads. The subsequent Oscar sweep demonstrates that it pays to advertise.

ACTOR

F. Murray Abraham (*Amadeus*)
Jeff Bridges (*Starman*)
Albert Finney (*Under the Volcano*)
Tom Hulce (*Amadeus*)
Sam Waterston (*The Killing Fields*)

"I've known him since he was a fig leaf in the Fruit of the Loom underwear commercials," said the owner of a hardware store in F. Murray Abraham's Brooklyn neighborhood. The veteran stage actor was virtually unknown in films at the time of his portrayal of Salieri, the composer obsessed with jealousy of his rival Mozart.

ACTRESS

Judy Davis (*A Passage to India*)
Sally Field (*Places in the Heart*)
Jessica Lange (*Country*)
Vanessa Redgrave (*The Bostonians*)
Sissy Spacek (*The River*)

On the occasion of winning her second Oscar, Sally Field uttered those infamous and much-quoted words "You like me, you really like me."

SUPPORTING ACTOR

Adolph Caesar (*A Soldier's Story*)
John Malkovich (*Places in the Heart*)
Noriyuki "Pat" Morita (*The Karate Kid*)
Haing S. Ngor (*The Killing Fields*)
Ralph Richardson (*Greystoke: The Legend of Tarzan, Lord of the Apes*)

Haing S. Ngor was the first Asian and the second nonprofessional actor to win an Oscar (Harold Russell in *The Best Years of Our Lives*—see 1946—was the first). The Cambodian physician was cast in a role remarkably similar to his own life. Playing reporter Dith Prin in *The Killing Fields*, Ngor enacted scenes echoing his incarceration, torture, and eventual escape from the despotic Khmer Rouge in his native land. Ngor got a few subsequent acting jobs before tragically dying in 1996, during an attempted robbery.

SUPPORTING ACTRESS
Peggy Ashcroft (*A Passage to India*)
Glenn Close (*The Natural*)
Lindsay Crouse (*Places in the Heart*)
Christine Lahti (*Swing Shift*)
Geraldine Page (*The Pope of Greenwich Village*)

Dame Peggy Ashcroft was not present at the Oscars because of the funeral of her close friend Sir Michael Redgrave (his daughter, best Actress nominee Vanessa Redgrave was absent for the same reason). Ashcroft had designated her *Passage to India* co-star Victor Banerjee to accept for her. But it was Angela Lansbury who picked up Ashcroft's Oscar. Gregory Peck, who was co-producing the show, later apologized to the winner for the mix-up.

Ashcroft was also nominated for an Emmy the same year for *The Jewel in the Crown*, another British drama set in India. She lost to Joanne Woodward for *Do You Remember Love?*

DIRECTOR
Woody Allen (*Broadway Danny Rose*)
Robert Benton (*Places in the Heart*)
Milos Forman (*Amadeus*)
Roland Joffe (*The Killing Fields*)
David Lean (*A Passage to India*)

ORIGINAL SCREENPLAY
Woody Allen (*Broadway Danny Rose*)
Robert Benton (*Places in the Heart*)
Lowell Ganz, Babaloo Mandel, Bruce Jay Friedman (screenplay), Bruce Jay Friedman (screen story), Brian Grazer (story) (*Splash*)
Gregory Nava, Anna Thomas (*El Norte*)
Daniel Petrie, Jr. (screenplay), Danilo Bach, Daniel Petrie, Jr. (story) (*Beverly Hills Cop*)

ADAPTED SCREENPLAY
Charles Fuller (*A Soldier's Story*)
David Lean (*A Passage to India*)
Bruce Robinson (*The Killing Fields*)

Peter Shaffer (*Amadeus*)
P. H. Vazak, Michael Austin (*Greystoke: The Legend of Tarzan, Lord of the Apes*)

FOREIGN LANGUAGE FILM
Beyond the Walls (Israel)
Camila (Argentina)
Dangerous Moves (Switzerland)
Double Feature (Spain)
War-Time Romance (USSR)

OTHER AWARDS
Musical Score: Maurice Jarre (*A Passage to India*); Original Song: "I Just Called To Say I Love You" from *The Woman in Red*, music and lyrics by Stevie Wonder; Original Song Score: Prince (*Purple Rain*); Cinematography: Chris Menges (*The Killing Fields*); Art Direction: Karel Cerny (*Amadeus*); Costume Design: Theodor Pistek (*Amadeus*); Editing: Jim Clark (*The Killing Fields*); Sound: Mark Berger, Tom Scott, Todd Boekelheide, Chris Newman (*Amadeus*); Visual Effects: Dennis Muren, Michael McAlister, Lorne Peterson, George Gibbs (*Indiana Jones and the Temple of Doom*); Make-Up: Paul LeBlanc, Dick Smith (*Amadeus*).

Documentary: *The Times of Harvey Milk*; Documentary Short Subject: *The Stone Carvers*; Live-Action Short Subject: *Up*; Animated Short Subject: *Charade*.

SPECIAL AWARDS
National Endowment for the Arts; James Stewart; David L. Wolper (Jean Hersholt Humanitarian Award); Linwood G. Dunn (Gordon E. Sawyer Award); Kay Rose for the sound effects editing of *The River* (given as a special achievement award).

In reaction to the previous year's nearly four-hour show, the Oscars had to speed things up. Master of ceremonies Jack Lemmon, dispensing with an opening monologue, began the show by introducing ten young stars including William Hurt, Kathleen Turner, Jeff Bridges, and Glenn Close. They would be doing most of the award presenting, thus eliminating the need for introductions throughout the night. The clips from the nominated best Pictures were interspersed during the ceremony rather than bunched up at the end. In addition, the individual best Picture segments were short montages rather than extended scenes. When announcing the best Picture winner, Laurence Olivier was so rushed he didn't even bother reading the nominees. As a result, a whole half-hour was hacked off the previous year's seemingly endless length. "Even the baby elephant, on hand to show off the costume design for *A Passage to India*, managed to step lively," reported *The New York Times*.

To further tone up the show, Larry Gelbart, whose credits included TV's *M*A*S*H* and Broadway's *A Funny Thing Happened on the Way to the Forum*, was hired to co-produce and write the script. Scott Salmon (*La Cage aux Folles*) choreographed the production numbers and Tony-Oscar winning costumer Theoni V. Aldredge designed the clothes.

Despite all this, the national TV ratings dropped. Gelbart offered an explanation to *Variety*: "The audience didn't know all the big players. With all respect to such talents as Haing Ngor and F. Murray Abraham . . . they weren't Robert Redford and Dustin Hoffman. The marquee quotient was down. I think that may have been a factor." The marathon running time of the '83 Oscars probably turned off viewers as well.

NATIONAL BOARD OF REVIEW

Picture: *A Passage to India*; Actor: Victor Banerjee (*A Passage to India*); Actress: Peggy Ashcroft (*A Passage to India*); Supporting Actor: John Malkovich (*Places in the Heart*); Supporting Actress: Sabine Azema (*A Sunday in the Country*); Director: David Lean (*A Passage to India*).

BEST ENGLISH-LANGUAGE FILMS
A Passage to India, Paris, Texas, The Killing Fields, Places in the Heart, Mass Appeal, Country, A Soldier's Story, Birdy, Careful, He Might Hear You, Under the Volcano.

BEST FOREIGN-LANGUAGE FILMS
A Sunday in the Country (France), *Carmen* (Spain), *A Love in Germany* (Federal Republic of Germany), *The Fourth Man* (The Netherlands), *The Basileus Quartet* (France/Italy).

NEW YORK FILM CRITICS CIRCLE

Picture: *A Passage to India*; Actor: Steve Martin (*All of Me*); Actress: Peggy Ashcroft (*A Passage to India*); Supporting Actor: Ralph Richardson (*Greystoke: The Legend of Tarzan, Lord of the Apes*); Supporting Actress: Christine Lahti (*Swing Shift*); Director: David Lean (*A Passage to India*); Screenplay: Robert Benton (*Places in the Heart*); Cinematography: Chris Menges (*The Killing Fields*); Documentary: *The Times of Harvey Milk*; Foreign Film: *A Sunday in the Country*.

Comedian Steve Martin had the New York Film Critics Circle in stitches when he accepted their Best Actor award for his double-personality performance as a lawyer inhabited by the spirit of Lily Tomlin in *All of Me*. "It's a great honor for me to be given this award by so many distinguished critics—and Rex Reed," Martin quipped, referring to Reed's nasty review of the film. Though Martin won top honors from the New York scribes and the National Society of Film Critics, the Academy, historically snobbish about comedy performances, failed to nominate him for an Oscar.

NATIONAL SOCIETY OF FILM CRITICS

Picture: *Stranger Than Paradise*; Actor: Steve Martin (*All of Me*); Actress: Vanessa Redgrave (*The Bostonians*); Supporting Actor: John Malkovich (*Places in the Heart* and *The Killing Fields*); Supporting Actress: Melanie Griffith (*Body Double*); Director: Robert Bresson (*L'Argent*); Screenplay: Lowell Ganz, Babaloo Mandell, Bruce Jay Friedman (*Splash*); Cinematography: Chris Menges (*The Killing Fields* and *Comfort and Joy*); Documentary: *Stop Making Sense*.

LOS ANGELES FILM CRITICS ASSOCIATION

Picture: *Amadeus*; Actor (tie): F. Murray Abraham (*Amadeus*) and Albert Finney (*Under the Volcano*); Actress: Kathleen Turner (*Crimes of Passion* and *Romancing the Stone*); Supporting Actor: Adolph Caesar (*A Soldier's Story*); Supporting Actress: Peggy Ashcroft (*A Passage to India*); Director: Milos Foreman (*Amadeus*); Screenplay: Peter Shaffer

(*Amadeus*); Cinematography: Chris Menges (*The Killing Fields*); Music: Ennio Morricone (*Once Upon a Time in America*); Foreign Film: *The Fourth Man*; Independent or Experimental Film: The films of George Kuchar; New Generation Prize: Alan Rudolph, director and writer of *Choose Me*; Special Award: film critic Andrew Sarris, posthumous award to Francois Truffaut.

HOLLYWOOD FOREIGN PRESS ASSOCIATION GOLDEN GLOBE AWARDS

Picture (Drama): *Amadeus*; Picture (Comedy or Musical): *Romancing the Stone*; Actor (Drama): F. Murray Abraham (*Amadeus*); Actress (Drama): Sally Field (*Places in the Heart*); Actor (Comedy or Musical): Dudley Moore (*Mickey and Maude*); Actress (Comedy or Musical): Kathleen Turner (*Romancing the Stone*); Supporting Actor: Haing S. Ngor (*The Killing Fields*); Supporting Actress: Peggy Ashcroft (*A Passage to India*); Director: Milos Foreman (*Amadeus*); Screenplay: Peter Shaffer (*Amadeus*); Original Score: Maurice Jarre (*A Passage to India*); Original Song: "I Just Called To Say I Love You" from *The Woman in Red*, music and lyrics by Stevie Wonder; Foreign Film: *A Passage to India*.

SPECIAL AWARD
Elizabeth Taylor (Cecil B. DeMille Award).

CANNES FILM FESTIVAL

Golden Palm: *Paris, Texas* (USA/France/Federal Republic of Germany); Actor: Alfredo Landa, Francisco Rabal (*The Holy Innocents*) (Spain); Actress: Helen Mirren (*Cal*) (UK/Ireland); Director: Bertrand Tavernier (*A Sunday in the Country*); Screenplay: Theo Angelopolous, Th. Valtinos, Tonino Guerra (*Voyage to Cytherea*) (Greece); Special Jury Prize: *Diary for My Children* (Hungary); Artistic Contribution: Peter Bizion for the cinematography of *Another Country* (UK); Camera d'Or: *Stranger Than Paradise*; Technical Prize: *The Element of Crime* (Denmark); International Critics Prize: in competition, *Paris, Texas* and *Voyage to Cytherea*, out of competition, *Memorias do Cacere* (Brazil); Special Prize: John Huston.

1985

ACADEMY AWARDS (OSCARS)

PICTURE
The Color Purple
Kiss of the Spider Woman
Out of Africa
Prizzi's Honor
Witness

Oscar's long snub of Steven Spielberg continued. Just as the popular *E.T.* was defeated by the long and self-consciously noble *Gandhi*, Spielberg's *The Color Purple*, based on Alice Walker's Pulitzer Prize-winning novel, was crushed by the long and self-consciously noble *Out of Africa*. *Purple* tied *The Turning Point* as the film to garner the most nominations (eleven) without winning a single award. To add insult to injury, Spielberg was not even nominated as best Director, though he did win the Directors' Guild award.

ACTOR
Harrison Ford (*Witness*)
James Garner (*Murphy's Romance*)
William Hurt (*Kiss of the Spider Woman*)
Jack Nicholson (*Prizzi's Honor*)
Jon Voight (*Runaway Train*)

ACTRESS
Anne Bancroft (*Agnes of God*)
Whoopi Goldberg (*The Color Purple*)
Jessica Lange (*Sweet Dreams*)
Geraldine Page (*The Trip to Bountiful*)
Meryl Streep (*Out of Africa*)

Geraldine Page had taken off her shoes and was looking for them when her name was called as best Actress. This win on her eighth try (four leading and four supporting) at Oscar rescued her from the record books as the Most Losing Nominee. Richard Burton and Peter O'Toole are now tied for that dubious distinction with seven nominations apiece.

SUPPORTING ACTOR
Don Ameche (*Cocoon*)

Klaus Maria Brandauer (*Out of Africa*)
William Hickey (*Prizzi's Honor*)
Robert Loggia (*Jagged Edge*)
Eric Roberts (*Runaway Train*)

The winner Don Ameche was upstaged by the presenter Cher, who failed to receive an expected best Actress nomination for *Mask*. Described as looking like a "futuristic Daffy Duck" (*The New York Times*) and a "1956 Pontiac hood ornament" (*Newsweek*), the singer-actress dazzled the crowd in a $12,000 Bob Mackie gown featuring a bare midriff and a crown of 800 hackle feathers. "As you can see," she said upon her entrance, "I have received and read my Academy brochure on how to dress as a *serious* actress."

SUPPORTING ACTRESS

Margaret Avery (*The Color Purple*)
Anjelica Huston (*Prizzi's Honor*)
Amy Madigan (*Twice in a Lifetime*)
Meg Tilly (*Agnes of God*)
Oprah Winfrey (*The Color Purple*)

The first third-generation Oscar winner, Anjelica Huston is both the daughter of one winner (John Huston) and granddaughter of another (Walter Huston).

Another nominee, Margaret Avery, spent $3,500 of her own money on a controversial advertising campaign. Avery's ads adopted the style of *The Color Purple*'s prose which was written in the form of letters to God.

DIRECTOR

Hector Babenco (*Kiss of the Spider Woman*)
John Huston (*Prizzi's Honor*)
Akira Kurosawa (*Ran*)
Sydney Pollack (*Out of Africa*)
Peter Weir (*Witness*)

ORIGINAL SCREENPLAY

Woody Allen (*The Purple Rose of Cairo*)
Terry Gilliam, Tom Stoppard, Charles McKeown (*Brazil*)
Luis Puenzo, Aida Bortnik (*The Official Story*)
Earl W. Wallace, William Kelley (screenplay), **Earl W. Wallace, Pamela Wallace,** and **William Kelley** (story) (*Witness*)

ADAPTED SCREENPLAY

Richard Condon, Janet Roach (*Prizzi's Honor*)
Horton Foote (*The Trip to Bountiful*)
Kurt Luedtke (*Out of Africa*)
Menno Meyjes (*The Color Purple*)
Leonard Schrader (*Kiss of the Spider Woman*)

FOREIGN-LANGUAGE FILM

Angry Harvest (Federal Republic of Germany)
Colonel Redl (Hungary)
The Official Story (Argentina)
3 Men and a Cradle (France)
When Father Was Away on Business (Yugoslavia)

OTHER AWARDS

Musical Score: John Barry (*Out of Africa*); Original Song: "Say You, Say Me" from *White Knights*, music and lyrics by Lionel Richie; Cinematography: David Watkin (*Out of Africa*); Art Direction: Josie MacAvin (*Out of Africa*); Costume Design: Emi Wada (*Ran*); Editing: Thom Noble (*Witness*); Sound: Chris Jenkins, Gary Alexander, Larry Stensvold, Peter Handford (*Out of Africa*); Visual Effects: Ken Ralston, Ralph McQuarrie, Scott Farrar, David Berry (*Cocoon*); Sound Effects Editing: Charles L. Campbell, Robert Rutledge (*Back to the Future*); Make-Up: Michael Westmore, Zoltan Elek (*Mask*).

Documentary: *Broken Rainbow*; Documentary Short Subject: *Witness to War: Dr. Charlie Clements*; Live-Action Short Subject: *Molly's Pilgrim*; Animated Short Subject: *Anna & Bella*.

SPECIAL AWARDS

Paul Newman; composer Alex North; film pioneer John H. Whitney; Charles "Buddy" Rogers (Jean Hersholt Humanitarian Award).

Oscar was on the rebound. After the clunky, endless telecast of 1983, the 1984 edition moved right along, and 1985 was one of the best received ceremonies in Oscar's long history. Apart from a wacko opening featuring Teri Garr and a brace of chorus girls dancing on the wing of a plane à la *Flying Down to Rio*, the show had pace, energy, and wit. The new surge of fun was provided by host Robin Williams. He began the evening by saying to the representatives of Price Waterhouse who carried the briefcases containing all the winners' names, "You have all the envelopes right in there? What do you say we open those suckers up right now?" Co-hosts Jane Fonda and Alan Alda leavened Williams' insanity with more dignified demeanors. Having the script written by veteran TV scribes like Glen Gordon Caron (*Moonlighting*), Douglas Wyman (*Family Ties*), and Larry Gelbart (*M*A*S*H*) didn't hurt matters either.

For once, the performers who actually delivered the best Song nominees in their respective films presented them on the broadcast. This allowed pop stars like Huey Lewis and the News and Lionel Richie to add to the ceremony's marquee value. For the older viewers, eighty-two-year-old Bob Hope made his twenty-fifth Oscar appearance, and there was a salute to classic MGM musicals featuring stars of those films including Howard Keel, June Allyson, Leslie Caron, Cyd Charisse, and Debbie Reynolds. For added class, the best Picture award was presented by veteren directors Billy Wilder, Akira Kurosawa, and an ailing John Huston, who was taking whiffs from an oxygen tank while off-stage.

NATIONAL BOARD OF REVIEW

English-Language Film: *The Color Purple*; Actor (tie): William Hurt and Raul Julia (*Kiss of the Spider Woman*; Actress: Whoopi Goldberg (*The Color Purple*); Supporting Actor: Klaus Maria Brandauer (*Out of Africa*); Supporting Actress: Anjelica Huston (*Prizzi's Honor*); Director: Akira Kurosawa (*Ran*).

BEST ENGLISH-LANGUAGE FILMS
The Color Purple, Out of Africa, The Trip to Bountiful, Witness, Kiss of the Spider Woman, Prizzi's Honor, Back to the Future, The Shooting Party, Blood Simple, Dreamchild.

BEST FOREIGN-LANGUAGE FILMS
Ran (Japan), *The Official Story* (Argentina), *When Father Was Away on Business* (Yugoslavia), *La Chèvre* (France), *The Home and the World.*

NEW YORK FILM CRITICS CIRCLE

Picture: *Prizzi's Honor*; Actor: Jack Nicholson (*Prizzi's Honor*); Actress: Norma Aleandro (*The Official Story*); Supporting Actor: Klaus Maria Brandauer (*Out of Africa*); Supporting Actress: Anjelica Huston (*Prizzi's Honor*); Director: John Huston (*Prizzi's Honor*); Screenplay: Woody Allen (*The Purple Rose of Cairo*); Cinematography: David Watkin (*Out of Africa*); Foreign Film: *Ran*; Documentary: *Shoah*.

There was a pitched battle in the New York Film Critics Circle as to whether the eight-hour Holocaust documentary *Shoah* should be named as best Picture or best Documentary. A bitter round of close voting resulted in *Prizzi's Honor* winning best Picture and *Shoah* being relegated to the documentary category. In a *Village Voice* piece, J. Hoberman practically accused those who voted against the Holocaust film of anti-Semitism.

The ceremony itself was something of a family affair with Anjelica Huston winning for Supporting Actress for *Prizzi's Honor*. She also accepted her father's best Director accolade, and her then housemate Jack Nicholson took the best Actor prize.

NATIONAL SOCIETY OF FILM CRITICS

Picture: *Ran*; Actor: Jack Nicholson (*Prizzi's Honor*); Actress: Vanessa Redgrave (*Wetherby*); Supporting Actor: John Gielgud (*Plenty* and *The Shooting Party*); Supporting Actress: Anjelica Huston (*Prizzi's Honor*); Director: John Huston (*Prizzi's Honor*); Screenplay: Albert Brooks, Monica Johnson (*Lost in America*); Cinematography: Takao Saito, Masaharu Ueda, Asakazu Nakai (*Ran*); Documentary: *Shoah*.

LOS ANGELES FILM CRITICS ASSOCIATION

Picture: *Brazil*; Actor: William Hurt (*Kiss of the Spider Woman*); Actress: Meryl Streep (*Out of Africa*); Supporting Actor: John Gielgud (*Plenty* and *The Shooting Party*); Supporting Actress: Anjelica Huston (*Prizzi's Honor*); Director: Terry Gilliam (*Brazil*); Screenplay: Terry Gilliam, Tom Stoppard, Charles McKeown (*Brazil*); Cinematography: David Watkin (*Out of Africa*); Music: Toru Takemitsu (*Ran*); Foreign Film (tie): *Ran* and *The Official Story*; Independent or

Experimental Film: *Fear of Emptiness*; Life Achievement: Akira Kurosawa; New Generation Prize: Laura Dern, performances in *Mask* and *Smooth Talk*; Special Award: *Shoah*.

The Los Angeles critics chose *Brazil*, an Orwellian futuristic fantasy directed by former *Monty Python* animator Terry Gilliam, for best Picture, Director, and Screenplay. Universal, unsatisfied with what they regarded as the esoteric film's lack of box office appeal, had refused to release it in the United States. With the critics' stamp of approval, they changed their minds.

HOLLYWOOD FOREIGN PRESS ASSOCIATION GOLDEN GLOBE AWARDS

Picture (Drama): *Out of Africa*; Picture (Comedy or Musical): *Prizzi's Honor*; Actor (Drama): Jon Voight (*Runaway Train*); Actress (Drama): Whoopi Goldberg (*The Color Purple*); Actor (Comedy or Musical): Jack Nicholson (*Prizzi's Honor*); Actress (Comedy or Musical): Kathleen Turner (*Prizzi's Honor*); Supporting Actor: Klaus Maria Brandauer (*Out of Africa*); Supporting Actress: Meg Tilly (*Agnes of God*); Director: John Huston (*Prizzi's Honor*); Screenplay: Woody Allen (*The Purple Rose of Cairo*); Original Score: "Say You, Say Me" from *White Nights*, music and lyrics by Lionel Richie; Foreign Film: *The Official Story* (Argentina).

SPECIAL AWARD

Barbara Stanwyck (Cecil B. DeMille Award).

Jon Voight in *Runaway Train* as best Dramatic Actor? A poorly reviewed action picture winning a top honor? What gives? Canon Films splurged $200,000 in trade ads for its two big releases *Runaway Train* and the Yugoslavian import *When Father Was Away on Business*. More pages were taken out to promote *Train* for awards than any other film. With the Golden Globe voters, it worked. It also helped *Train* earn two Oscar nominations—for Voight and Supporting Actor Eric Roberts.

    Train's Oscar nods showed the influence of the Globes and increased their respectability in the Hollywood community.

CANNES FILM FESTIVAL

Palme d'Or: *When Father Was Away on Business* (Yugoslavia); Actor: William Hurt (*Kiss of the Spider Woman*); Actress (tie): Norma Aleandro (*The Official Story*) (Argentina) and Cher (*Mask*); Director: Andre Techine (*Rendez-Vous*) (France); Special Jury Prize (*Birdy*); Jury Prize: *Colonel Redl* (Hungary); Artistic Contribution: John Bailey (visual concept), Eiko Ishioka (production design), Philip Glass (musical score) (*Mishima*); Career Achievement: James Stewart; Camera d'Or: *Oriane* (Venezuela); Technical Prize: *Insignificance* (UK); International Critics Prize: in competition, *When Father Was Away on Business*, out of competition, *The Purple Rose of Cairo*, *Visages de Femme* (Ivory Coast).

1986

ACADEMY AWARDS (OSCARS)

PICTURE
Children of a Lesser God
Hannah and Her Sisters
The Mission
Platoon
A Room with a View

The Oscars were evenly distributed in 1986, with Oliver Stone's Vietnam drama *Platoon* taking four and Woody Allen's comedy *Hannah and Her Sisters* and James Ivory's adaptation of E. M. Forster's *A Room with a View* taking three apiece. Each had been made and distributed by a small studio while the larger studios were concentrating on mass-appeal blockbusters like *Top Gun*, which was recognized by the Academy only for its original song and special effects.

ACTOR
Dexter Gordon (*'Round Midnight*)
Bob Hoskins (*Mona Lisa*)
William Hurt (*Children of a Lesser God*)
Paul Newman (*The Color of Money*)
James Woods (*Salvador*)

Not wanting to sit through another Oscarless

night, Paul Newman stayed home for his seventh bid as best Actor. Traditionally, the previous year's best Actress winner presents the best Actor award, but Geraldine Page had died. Bette Davis was chosen to bestow the honor. A frail Davis, ravaged by a stroke and mastectomy, made an embarrassing spectacle of herself by missing her cues in reading the nominees so that the clips from their films were out of sync with Davis' reading. Director Marty Pasetta cut off her microphone and the names were unheard. The legendary actress compounded the fiasco by interrupting Robert Wise who was accepting for Newman. Pasetta again cut off the microphone and switched to the other side of the stage where Goldie Hawn and Chevy Chase continued with the show.

ACTRESS
Jane Fonda (*The Morning After*)
Marlee Matlin (*Children of a Lesser God*)
Sissy Spacek (*Crimes of the Heart*)
Kathleen Turner (*Peggy Sue Got Married*)
Sigourney Weaver (*Aliens*)

Although Jane Wyman, Patty Duke, and John Mills had won Academy Awards for portraying deaf-mute characters. Marlee Matlin was the first hearing-impaired performer to take Oscar home. The award was presented to her by her live-in lover (at the time) William Hurt. Phylliss Frelich won a Tony Award for playing the same part on stage.

SUPPORTING ACTOR
Tom Berenger (*Platoon*)
Michael Caine (*Hannah and Her Sisters*)
Willem Dafoe (*Platoon*)
Denholm Elliott (*A Room with a View*)
Dennis Hopper (*Hoosiers*)

The constantly employed Michael Caine was in the Bahamas filming *Jaws: The Revenge* on Oscar night. The morning after his win, the film crew serenaded him with a chorus of "Rule Britannia" outside his dressing room.

SUPPORTING ACTRESS
Tess Harper (*Crimes of the Heart*)
Piper Laurie (*Children of a Lesser God*)
Mary Elizabeth Mastrantonio (*The Color of Money*)

Maggie Smith (*A Room with a View*)
Dianne Wiest (*Hannah and Her Sisters*)

When asked what effect she thought the Oscar would have on her career, Dianne Wiest replied, "Maybe I'll work for somebody besides Woody." The actress had been known primarily for her stage work and a few small roles in Allen's films. She would later win a second Oscar for another Allen movie, *Bullets over Broadway*.

DIRECTOR
Woody Allen (*Hannah and Her Sisters*)
James Ivory (*A Room with a View*)
Roland Joffe (*The Mission*)
David Lynch (*Blue Velvet*)
Oliver Stone (*Platoon*)

Once again a woman was overlooked in the best Director category. *Children of a Lesser God* earned a best Picture nomination, but its director Randa Haines was not among the Oscar finalists.

ORIGINAL SCREENPLAY
Woody Allen (*Hannah and Her Sisters*)
Paul Hogan (story), Paul Hogan, Ken Shadie, John Cornell (screenplay) (*Crocodile Dundee*)
Hanif Kureishi (*My Beautiful Laundrette*)
Oliver Stone (*Platoon*)
Oliver Stone, Richard Boyle (*Salvador*)

ADAPTED SCREENPLAY
Hesper Anderson, Mark Medoff (*Children of a Lesser God*)
Raynold Gideon, Bruce A. Evans (*Stand By Me*)
Beth Henley (*Crimes of the Heart*)
Ruth Prawer Jhabvala (*A Room with a View*)
Richard Price (*The Color of Money*)

FOREIGN-LANGUAGE FILM
The Assault (The Netherlands)
Betsy Blue (France)
The Decline of the American Empire (Canada)
My Sweet Little Village (Czechoslovakia)
"38" (Austria)

OTHER AWARDS
Musical Score: Herbie Hancock (*'Round Midnight*); Original Song: "Take My Breath Away"

from *Top Gun*, music by Giorgio Moroder, lyrics by Tom Whitlock; Cinematography: Chris Menges (*The Mission*); Art Direction: Brian Savegar, Elio Altramura (*A Room with a View*); Costume Design: Jenny Beaven, John Bright (*A Room with a View*); Editing: Claire Simpson (*Platoon*); Sound: John "Doc" Wilkinson, Richard Rodgers, Charles "Bud" Grenzbach, Simon Kaye (*Platoon*); Visual Effects: Robert Skotak, Stan Winston, John Richardson, Suzanne Benson (*Aliens*); Sound Effects Editing: Don Sharpe (*Aliens*); Make-Up: Chris Walas, Stephan Dupuis (*The Fly*).

Documentary (tie): *Artie Shaw: Time Is All You've Got* and *Down and Out in America*; Documentary Short Subject: *Women—For America, for the World*; Live-Action Short Subject: *Precious Images*; Animated Short Subject: *A Greek Tragedy*.

SPECIAL AWARDS
Ralph Bellamy; E. M. "Al" Lewis; Steven Spielberg (Irving Thalberg Award).

Oscar continued on an upward swing with a national rating of 27.5, two-tenths of a point higher than the previous year. This stopped a four-year ratings decline. Even with competition from CBS's two-hour NCAA championship basketball game between Indiana and Syracuse, the Oscarcast was a hit.

Comedy was the keynote, with funny film stars like Chevy Chase, Goldie Hawn, and Australian Paul Hogan hosting. Hogan advised the winners of "The Three Gs": "Be gracious, be grateful, and get off." Shirley MacLaine arrived in a mock spaceship and made several self-deprecating gags about her much publicized mystical beliefs. The usually draggy best Song sequences were dispensed with quickly in a medley presided over by Bernadette Peters. There were several lively presenters including Bette Midler, Rodney Dangerfield, and Bugs Bunny. Lauren Bacall narrated a fashion show demonstrating how film influences public tastes in clothing. The Steven Spielberg slight of last year was glossed over by giving the director the Irving Thalberg Award.

Reviews were the most positive in years. "Director Marty Pasetta found more life in this outing than in recent years," declared *Variety*.

NATIONAL BOARD OF REVIEW

English-Language Film: *A Room with a View*; Actor: Paul Newman (*The Color of Money*); Actress: Kathleen Turner (*Peggy Sue Got Married*); Supporting Actor: Daniel Day-Lewis (*My Beautiful Laundrette* and *A Room with a View*); Supporting Actress: Dianne Wiest (*Hannah and Her Sisters*); Director: Woody Allen (*Hannah and Her Sisters*).

BEST ENGLISH-LANGUAGE FILMS
A Room with a View, Hannah and Her Sisters, My Beautiful Laundrette, The Fly, Stand By Me, The Color of Money, Children of a Lesser God, 'Round Midnight, Peggy Sue Got Married, The Mission.

BEST FOREIGN-LANGUAGE FILMS
Otello (Italy), *Miss Mary* (Argentina), *Ginger and Fred* (Italy), *Menage* (France), *Men* (Federal Republic of Germany).

NEW YORK FILM CRITICS CIRCLE

Picture: *Hannah and Her Sisters*; Actor: Bob Hoskins (*Mona Lisa*); Actress: Sissy Spacek (*Crimes of the Heart*); Supporting Actor: Daniel Day-Lewis (*My Beautiful Laundrette* and *A Room with a View*); Supporting Actress: Dianne Wiest (*Hannah and Her Sisters*); Director: Woody Allen (*Hannah and Her Sisters*); Screenplay: Hanif Kureishi (*My Beautiful Laundrette*); Cinematography: Tony Pierce-Roberts (*A Room with a View*); Foreign Film: *The Decline of the American Empire*; Documentary: *Marlene*.

Best Director Woody Allen did not show up for the New York Film Critics Awards, nor did Bob Hoskins or Daniel Day-Lewis, both of whom remained at home in England. Lynn Redgrave was in rare form when she accepted Hoskins' award. "Elizabeth Taylor and I tied for the New York Critics' Best Actress Award in 1966 and she wasn't here," Redgrave recalled, "but fuck her, really. This is better than the Tonys where you're locked up in the Shubert Theatre with [Tony producer] Alexander Cohen screaming at you." She thanked the critics on behalf of Hoskins because "you haven't shit on his work."

NATIONAL SOCIETY OF FILM CRITICS

Picture: *Blue Velvet*; Actor: Bob Hoskins (*Mona Lisa*); Actress: Chloe Webb (*Sid and Nancy*); Supporting Actor: Dennis Hopper (*Blue Velvet*); Supporting Actress: Dianne Wiest (*Hannah and Her Sisters*); Director: David Lynch (*Blue Velvet*); Screenplay: Hanif Kureishi (*My Beautiful Laundrette*); Cinematography: Frederick Elmes (*Blue Velvet*); Documentary: *Marlene*.

LOS ANGELES FILM CRITICS ASSOCIATION

Picture: *Hannah and Her Sisters*; Actor: Bob Hoskins (*Mona Lisa*); Actress: Sandrine Bonnaire (*Vagabond*); Supporting Actor: Dennis Hopper (*Blue Velvet* and *Hoosiers*); Supporting Actress (tie): Cathy Tyson (*Mona Lisa*) and Dianne Wiest (*Hannah and Her Sisters*); Director: David Lynch (*Blue Velvet*); Screenplay: Woody Allen (*Hannah and Her Sisters*); Cinematography: Chris Menges (*The Mission*); Music: Herbie Hancock, Dexter Gordon, et al. (*'Round Midnight*); Foreign Film: *Vagabond*; Independent or Experimental Film (tie): *Magdalena Viraga* and *Stands in the Desert Counting the Seconds of His Life*; Life Achievement: John Cassavetes; New Generation Prize: Spike Lee; Special Award: Rafigh Pooya for venturesome film programming at the Fox International Theatre in Venice and Chuck Workman and the Directors Guild of America for the short *Precious Images*.

In addition to their awards, the Los Angeles critics issued a statement condemning the alteration of films by editing, computer color, and "other means that subvert the look, the content, and the original intent of the filmmaker."

HOLLYWOOD FOREIGN PRESS ASSOCIATION GOLDEN GLOBE AWARDS

Picture (Drama): *Platoon*; Picture (Comedy or Musical): *Hannah and Her Sisters*; Actor (Drama): Bob Hoskins (*Mona Lisa*); Actress (Drama): Marlee Matlin (*Children of a Lesser God*); Actor (Comedy or Musical): Paul Hogan (*Crocodile Dundee*); Actress (Comedy or Musical): Sissy Spacek (*Crimes of the Heart*); Supporting Actor: Tom Berenger (*Platoon*); Supporting Actress: Maggie Smith (*A Room with a View*); Director: Oliver Stone (*Platoon*); Screenplay: Robert Bolt (*The Mission*); Original Score: Ennio Morricone (*The Mission*); Original Song: "Take My Breath Away" from *Top Gun*, music by Giorgio Moroder, lyrics by Tom Whitlock; Foreign Film: *The Assault* (The Netherlands).

SPECIAL AWARD
Anthony Quinn (Cecil B. DeMille Award).

CANNES FILM FESTIVAL

Palme d'Or: *The Mission* (UK); Actor (tie): Michel Blanc (*Menage*) (France) and Bob Hoskins (*Mona Lisa*) (UK); Actress (tie): Barbara Sukowa (*Rosa Lusemburg*) and Fernanda Torres (*Love Me Forever or Never*) (Brazil); Director: Martin Scorsese (*After Hours*); Special Jury Prize: *The Sacrifice* (Sweden/France); Artistic Contribution: Sven Nykvist for the cinematography of *The Sacrifice*; Palme d'Or for Short Film: *Peel* (Australia); Camera d'Or: Claire Devers (*Noir et Blanc*) (France); Technical Prize: *The Mission*; International Critics Prize: in competition, *The Sacrifice*, out of competition, *The Decline of the American Empire* (Canada).

1987

ACADEMY AWARDS (OSCARS)

PICTURE
Broadcast News
Fatal Attraction
Hope and Glory
The Last Emperor
Moonstruck

A British-produced epic about a Chinese emperor directed by an Italian unexpectedly swept the 1987 Oscars. *The Last Emperor* won all nine awards for which it was nominated, tying *Gigi* as the third most Oscared film in history (following *Ben-Hur* and *West Side Story*). "If New York is the Big Apple, to me Hollywood tonight is the Big

Richard Vuu played the title role in the gigantic epic *The Last Emperor* (1987), winner of nine Oscars and four Golden Globes.

Nipple," said a euphoric Bernardo Bertolucci after receiving two of the statuettes for his direction and screenplay (with Mark Peploe).

Emperor details the story of the final supreme ruler of China whose life ends in degradation after he is deposed. Ironically, Columbia chief David Puttnam was also deposed after he had brought the film to the studio. Puttnam's successors at Columbia had no interest in pushing the project since it wouldn't benefit them, making its Oscar triumph all the more surprising. The voters probably went for its size and spectacle (like *Gandhi* and *Out of Africa*) and because of a lack of enthusiasm for the critics' choices *Broadcast News*, *Hope and Glory*, and *The Dead* (which wasn't even nominated).

ACTOR
Michael Douglas (*Wall Street*)
William Hurt (*Broadcast News*)
Marcello Mastroianni (*Dark Eyes*)
Jack Nicholson (*Ironweed*)
Robin Williams (*Good Morning, Vietnam*)

Michael Douglas picked up an Oscar, a prize denied his father Kirk, for his role as a slimy financial wizard in *Wall Street*. Douglas was helped by his starring performance in *Fatal Attraction*, a top-grossing thriller released the same year. Steve Martin was not among his competitors. The comedian was again passed up for a nomination, despite the Los Angeles Film Critics and the National Society of Film Critics awards for *Roxanne*, his modern version of *Cyrano de Bergerac*.

ACTRESS
Cher (*Moonstruck*)
Glenn Close (*Fatal Attraction*)
Holly Hunter (*Broadcast News*)
Sally Kirkland (*Anna*)
Meryl Streep (*Ironweed*)

Once again making the boldest fashion statement of the evening, Cher mounted the steps to the stage, half-naked in a skimpy, clinging, transparent black number. She thanked "everyone I worked with on this picture" along with her fellow nominee "Mary Louise Streep . . . I did my first picture with her." Actually, Cher had appeared in three films before co-starring with Streep in *Silkwood*.

Though Cher won Best Actress, the award for Hardest Campaigner would have to go to Sally Kirkland. She starred in an ultra-low-budget independent film, *Anna*, about an expatriate Czech actress struggling in the New York theater world. Spending her own money, she bought ads, mailed letters to every Academy member, hired publicists, won a Golden Globe, and got the nomination.

SUPPORTING ACTOR
Albert Brooks (*Broadcast News*)
Sean Connery (*The Untouchables*)
Morgan Freeman (*Street Smart*)
Vincent Gardenia (*Moonstruck*)
Denzel Washington (*Cry Freedom*)

SUPPORTING ACTRESS
Norma Aleandro (*Gaby—A True Story*)
Anne Archer (*Fatal Attraction*)
Olympia Dukakis (*Moonstruck*)
Anne Ramsey (*Throw Momma from the Train*)
Anne Sothern (*The Whales of August*)

Olympia Dukakis concluded her acceptance speech by cheering, "Let's go, Michael," giving her cousin—Democratic Presidential candidate Michael Dukakis—a ringing endorsement on worldwide television. Dukakis, the governor of Massachusetts, was not a winner like his thespian cousin, later losing the race for the White House to George Bush.

DIRECTOR
Bernardo Bertolucci (*The Last Emperor*)
John Boorman (*Hope and Glory*)
Lasse Hallstrom (*My Life as a Dog*)
Norman Jewison (*Moonstruck*)
Adrian Lyne (*Fatal Attraction*)

"The winner gets a green card," joked Robin Williams of the best Director nominees, who included Italian Bertolucci, Swedish Hallstrom, Canadian Jewison, and Brits Boorman and Lyne.

ORIGINAL SCREENPLAY
John Boorman (*Hope and Glory*)
James L. Brooks (*Broadcast News*)
Louis Malle (*Au Revoir, les Enfants*)
John Patrick Shanley (*Moonstruck*)

ADAPTED SCREENPLAY
James Dearden (*Fatal Attraction*)
Lasse Hallstrom, Reidar Jonsson, Brasse
    Brannstrom, Per Berglund (*My Life as a Dog*)
Tony Huston (*The Dead*)
Stanley Kubrick, Michael Herr, Gustav Hasford
    (*Full Metal Jacket*)
Mark Peploe, Bernardo Bertolucci
    (*The Last Emperor*)

FOREIGN-LANGUAGE FILM:
Au Revoir, les Enfants (France)
Babette's Feast (Denmark)
Course Completed (Spain)
The Family (Italy)
Pathfinder (Norway)

OTHER AWARDS
Musical Score: Ryuichi Sakamoto, David Bryne, Cong Su (*The Last Emperor*); Original Song: "(I've Had) The Time of My Life" from *Dirty Dancing*, music by Franke Previte, John DeNicola, Donald Markowitz, lyrics by Franke Previte; Cinematography: Vittorio Storaro (*The Last Emperor*); Art Direction: Ferdinando Scarfiotti, Bruno Cesari (*The Last Emperor*); Costume Design: James Acheson (*The Last Emperor*); Editing: Gabriella Cristiani (*The Last Emperor*); Sound: Bill Rowe, Ivan Sharrock (*The Last Emperor*); Visual Effects: Dennis Muren, William George, Harley Jessup, Kenneth Smith (*Innerspace*); Make-Up: Rick Baker (*Harry and the Hendersons*).

Documentary: *The Ten-Year Lunch: The Wit and Legend of the Algonquin Round Table*; Documentary Short Subject: *Young at Heart*; Live-Action Short Subject: *Ray's Male Heterosexual Dance Hall*; Animated Short Subject: *The Man Who Planted Trees*.

Chevy Chase lent his customary good taste and sense of elegance to his role as host of the 1987 Oscars.

SPECIAL AWARDS

Billy Wilder (Irving Thalberg Award); Stephen Flick, John Pospisil for sound effects editing of *Robocop* (presented as a Special Achievement Oscar).

"Good evening, Hollywood phonies," said Chevy Chase at the top of the sixtieth Academy Awards. The ceremony was laboring under a Writers' Guild strike, so comedians like Chase, Billy Crystal, and Robin Williams were hired for their ability to ad-lib. Fortunately, creative consultant Ernest Lehman (whose credits included the screenplays for *North by Northwest, West Side Story,* and *The Sound of Music*) had completed eighty percent of the ceremony's working script before the strike went into effect. Highlights included a bizarre display of special effects with Pee Wee Herman flying through the air, later to be rescued by Robocop, and the annual spark of controversy, this time provided by Eddie Murphy who protested Oscar's lack of recognition of blacks before he handed out the best Picture award.

Reviews were mostly positive. "The 60th annual Oscar show was surprisingly lively," cheered Marvin Kitman in *Newsday*. Kay Gardella of *The New York Daily News* was among the naysayers. "I taped it so I'd never have to take another sleeping pill again," she sneered. "All I'll have to do is replay it."

NATIONAL BOARD OF REVIEW

English-Language Film: *Empire of the Sun*; Actor: Michael Douglas (*Wall Street*); Actress (tie): Lillian Gish (*The Whales of August*) and Holly Hunter (*Broadcast News*); Supporting Actor: Sean Connery (*The Untouchables*); Supporting Actress: Olympia Dukakis (*Moonstruck*); Director: Steven Spielberg (*Empire of the Sun*); Juvenile Performance: Christian Bale (*Empire of the Sun*).

BEST ENGLISH-LANGUAGE FILMS

Empire of the Sun, The Last Emperor, Broadcast News, The Untouchables, Gaby—A True Story, Cry Freedom, Fatal Attraction, Hope and Glory, Wall Street, Full Metal Jacket.

BEST FOREIGN-LANGUAGE FILMS

Jean de Florette (France), *Manon of the Spring* (France), *My Life as a Dog* (Sweden), *Au Revoir, les Enfants* (France), *Tampopo* (Japan), *Dark Eyes* (Italy).

NEW YORK FILM CRITICS CIRCLE

Picture: *Broadcast News*; Actor: Jack Nicholson (*Broadcast News, Ironweed,* and *The Witches of Eastwick*); Actress: Holly Hunter (*Broadcast News*); Supporting Actor: Morgan Freeman (*Street Smart*); Supporting Actress: Vanessa Redgrave (*Prick Up Your Ears*); Director: James L. Brooks (*Broadcast News*); Screenplay: James L. Brooks (*Broadcast News*); Cinematography: Vittorio Storaro (*The Last Emperor*); Foreign Film: *My Life as a Dog*.

When presenting the NYFCC award for best Picture to *Broadcast News*, playwright/actor Wallace Shawn launched into a rather lengthy harangue about the untrustworthiness of contemporary media, a subject not unrelated to the film being honored. However, Shawn's remarks were becoming a bit tedious for the cantankerous John Simon, film critic for *The National Review*, who shouted out, "Shut up, you fool!" Richard Freeman of Newhouse newspapers responded to Simon with a succinct "Fuck off!"

Broadcast News received a total of five awards (if you count Jack Nicholson's best Actor citation for *Ironweed, The Witches of Eastwick,* and an unbilled cameo in *News*). This is the most any film has received from the Circle. Incidentally, this was Nicholson's seventh prize from the New York scribes.

As she presented Holly Hunter with the best Actress award, Maureen Stapleton quipped, "She's young, attractive, beautiful, and rich. I can't stand her. But she'll get older and richer, so what the hell."

NATIONAL SOCIETY OF FILM CRITICS

Picture: *The Dead*; Actor: Steve Martin (*Roxanne*); Actress: Emily Lloyd (*Wish You Were Here*); Supporting Actor: Morgan Freeman (*Street Smart*); Supporting Actress: Kathy Baker (*Street Smart*); Director: John Boorman (*Hope and Glory*); Screenplay: John Boorman (*Hope and Glory*); Cinematography: Philippe Rousselot (*Hope and Glory*); Special Prize: Richard Roud, former director of the New York Film Festival.

LOS ANGELES FILM CRITICS ASSOCIATION

Picture: *Hope and Glory*; Actor (tie): Steve Martin (*Roxanne*) and Jack Nicholson (*The Witches of Eastwick* and *Ironweed*); Actress (tie): Holly Hunter (*Broadcast News*) and Sally Kirkland (*Anna*); Supporting Actor: Morgan Freeman (*Street Smart*); Supporting Actress: Olympia Dukakis (*Moonstruck*); Director: John Boorman (*Hope and Glory*); Screenplay: John Boorman (*Hope and Glory*); Cinematography: Vittorio Storaro (*The Last Emperor*); Music: Ryuichi Sakamoto, David Byrne, Cong Su (*The Last Emperor*); Documentary: *Weapons of the Spirit*; Independent/Experimental Film: *Mala Noche*; New Generation Prize: Pedro Almodovar; Life Achievement: Joel McCrea, Samuel Fuller; Special Citation: Film Forum Theater.

HOLLYWOOD FOREIGN PRESS ASSOCIATION GOLDEN GLOBE AWARDS

Picture (Drama): *The Last Emperor*; Picture (Comedy or Musical): *Hope and Glory*; Actor (Drama): Michael Douglas (*Wall Street*); Actress (Drama): Sally Kirkland (*Anna*); Actor (Comedy or Musical): Robin Williams (*Good Morning, Vietnam*); Actress (Comedy or Musical): Cher (*Moonstruck*); Supporting Actor: Sean Connery (*The Untouchables*); Supporting Actress: Olympia Dukakis (*Moonstruck*); Director: Bernardo Bertolucci (*The Last Emperor*); Screenplay: Bernardo Bertolucci, Mark Peploe (*The Last Emperor*); Original Score: Ryuichi Sakamoto, David Bryne, Cong Su (*The Last Emperor*); Original Song: "(I've Had) The Time of My Life" from *Dirty Dancing*, music by Frank Previte, John DeNicola, Donald Markowitz, lyrics by Frank Previte; Foreign Film: *My Life as a Dog*.

SPECIAL AWARD
Clint Eastwood (Cecil B. DeMille Award).

CANNES FILM FESTIVAL

Palme d'Or: *Under the Sun of Satan* (France); Actor: Marcello Mastroianni (*Dark Eyes*) (Italy); Actress: Barbara Hershey (*Shy People*); Director: Wim Wenders (*Wings of Desire*) (Federal Republic of Germany); Special Jury Prize: *Repentance* (USSR); Jury Prize: Souleymane Cisse for *Yeelen (Brightness)* (Mali), Rentano Mikuni for *Shinran: Path to Purity* (Japan); Fortieth Anniversary Prize: *Intervista* (Italy); Artisitic Contribution: Stanley Myers for the musical score of *Prick Up Your Ears*; Tributes: Jean Simmons, Jane Russell; Camera d'Or: *Robinson, My English Grandfather* (USSR); Technical Prize: *Le Cinema dans les Yeux* (France); Youth Prize: *I've Heard the Mermaids Singing* (Canada); International Critics Prize: in competition, *Repentance*, out of competition, *Wish You Were Here* (UK) and *Wedding in Galilee* (Belgium/France/Palestine).

ACADEMY AWARDS (OSCARS)

PICTURE
The Accidental Tourist
Dangerous Liaisons
Mississippi Burning

Rain Man
Working Girl

Illness flick met comedy met buddy-picture in *Rain Man*, Barry Levinson's box-office hit of a selfish young man (bankable Tom Cruise) reunited with his autistic older brother (second-Oscar-bait Dustin Hoffman). The combination helped the film win four top prizes. It won best Picture over two comedies without the benefit of a physically or mentally impaired main character (*The Accidental Tourist* and *Working Girl*), a liberal message-picture (*Mississippi Burning*), and a costume drama (*Dangerous Liaisons*).

ACTOR
Gene Hackman (*Mississippi Burning*)
Tom Hanks (*Big*)
Dustin Hoffman (*Rain Man*)
Edward James Olmos (*Stand and Deliver*)
Max von Sydow (*Pelle the Conqueror*)

ACTRESS
Glenn Close (*Dangerous Liaisons*)
Jodie Foster (*The Accused*)
Melanie Griffith (*Working Girl*)
Meryl Streep (*A Cry in the Dark*)
Sigourney Weaver (*Gorillas in the Mist*)

Glenn Close's evil French noblewoman in *Dangerous Liaisons* was thought to be a surefire winner (it was her fifth nomination without a walk to the podium). But the Academy rarely goes in for villains and Jodie Foster had been robbed in 1976 when her quirky *Taxi Driver* child-hooker was defeated by Beatrice Straight's quickie cameo in *Network*. In addition, Foster was playing a victim—of gang rape—in *The Accused*.

Note: Sigourney Weaver is the fourth actress to receive nominations in both Leading and Supporting categories in the same year (for *Gorillas in the Mist* and *Working Girl*). Previous double nominees Fay Bainter, Teresa Wright, and Jessica Lange got the supporting statuette as a consolation prize. Weaver was the first to lose both.

SUPPORTING ACTOR
Alec Guinness (*Little Dorrit*)
Kevin Kline (*A Fish Called Wanda*)
Martin Landau (*Tucker: The Man and His Dream*)
River Phoenix (*Running on Empty*)
Dean Stockwell (*Married to the Mob*)

Kevin Kline was another surprise winner. Odds favored New York, Los Angeles, and National Society winner Dean Stockwell or Golden Globe favorite Martin Landau. Both actors were also sentimental choices since they were making comebacks after years of obscurity. Stockwell and Landau probably split the vote and Kline squeaked in for his grandly egotistical bank robber in *A Fish Called Wanda*, a rare example of the Academy honoring a superb comedy performance.

SUPPORTING ACTRESS
Joan Cusack (*Working Girl*)
Geena Davis (*The Accidental Tourist*)
Frances McDormand (*Mississippi Burning*)
Michelle Pfeiffer (*Dangerous Liaisons*)
Sigourney Weaver (*Working Girl*)

DIRECTOR
Charles Crichton (*A Fish Called Wanda*)
Barry Levinson (*Rain Man*)
Mike Nichols (*Working Girl*)
Alan Parker (*Mississippi Burning*)
Martin Scorsese (*The Last Temptation of Christ*)

ORIGINAL SCREENPLAY
Ronald Bass, Barry Morrow (*Rain Man*)
John Cleese, Charles Crichton (*A Fish Called Wanda*)
Naomi Foner (*Running on Empty*)
Gary Ross, Anne Spielberg (*Big*)
Ron Shelton (*Bull Durham*)

ADAPTED SCREENPLAY
Jean-Claude Carriere, Philip Kaufman (*The Unbearable Lightness of Being*)
Christine Edzard (*Little Dorrit*)
Frank Galati, Lawrence Kasdan (*The Accidental Tourist*)
Anna Hamilton Phelan, Tab Murphy (*Gorillas in the Mist*)
Christopher Hampton (*Dangerous Liaisons*)

FOREIGN-LANGUAGE FILM
Hanussen (Hungary)

The Music Teacher (Belgium)
Pelle the Conqueror (Denmark)
Salaam Bombay! (India)
Women on the Verge of a Nervous Breakdown (Spain)

OTHER AWARDS

Musical Score: Dave Grusin (*The Milagro Beanfield War*); Original Song: "Let the River Run" from *Working Girl*, music and lyrics by Carly Simon; Cinematography: Peter Biziou (*Mississippi Burning*); Art Direction: Stuart Craig (*Dangerous Liaisons*); Costume Design: James Acheson (*Dangerous Liaisons*); Editing: Arthur Schmidt (*Who Framed Roger Rabbit?*); Sound: Les Fresholtz, Dick Alexander, Vern Poore, Willie D. Burton (*Bird*); Visual Effects: Ken Ralston, Richard Williams, Edward Jones, George Gibbs (*Who Framed Roger Rabbit?*); Sound Effects Editing: Charles L. Campbell, Louis L. Edelman (*Who Framed Roger Rabbit?*); Make-Up: Ve Neill, Steve LaPorte, Robert Short (*Beetlejuice*).

Documentary: *Hotel Terminus: The Life and Times of Klaus Barbie*; Documentary Short Subject: *You Don't Have To Die*; Live-Action Short Subject: *The Appointments of Dennis Jennings*; Animated Short Subject: *Tin Toy*.

SPECIAL AWARDS

Eastman Kodak; The National Film Board of Canada; Richard Williams for the animation direction of *Who Framed Roger Rabbit?*.

The evening began like any other Oscarcast: with a terrible production number. But the 1988 Academy Awards would go down in history as hitting an all-time Lowe (Rob Lowe, that is). A young actress (Eileen Bowman) dressed as Snow White stepped onstage and began singing "There Are Stars Out Tonight," a parody lyric set to the tune of "I Only Have Eyes for You." Then Snow was surprised (as was the audience) by the entrance of her dancing partner Rob Lowe (not exactly the Gene Kelly of his generation). What followed was a bizarre combination of Hollywood schmaltz and well-meaning, but off-target satire as Snow and Rob danced through a series of ill-conceived routines involving big hats and song-belting waitresses.

That year's Oscarcast producer Allan Carr derived this outlandish melange from *Beach*

Blanket Babylon, a long-running San Francisco stage revue. *Babylon*'s gay camp sensibility with its drag performers in enormous hats did not translate well to Hollywood's biggest night. To add to the bad taste, couples such as Don Johnson and Melanie Griffith and Goldie Hawn and Kurt Russell made adolescent references to their unmarried, live-in status. Carr even tried to get Russell to propose marriage to Hawn on the air, but thankfully they only joked about it.

The New York Times stated it "deserves a place in the annals of Oscar embarrassment." Several Academy members, including Gregory Peck, wrote letters of protest, Steve Martin dissed the opening number at the Tonys later that year, and the Walt Disney Corporation threatened to sue for infringement of a copyrighted character. (The matter was settled out of court.)

Despite the criticism, the 1988 Oscars was the highest rated Academy ceremony in five years.

NATIONAL BOARD OF REVIEW

English-Language Film: *Mississippi Burning*; Actor: Gene Hackman (*Mississippi Burning*); Actress: Jodie Foster (*The Accused*); Supporting Actor: River Phoenix (*Running on Empty*); Supporting Actress: Frances McDormand (*Mississippi Burning*); Director: Alan Parker (*Mississippi Burning*); Documentary: *The Thin Blue Line*.

BEST ENGLISH-LANGUAGE FILMS

Mississippi Burning, Dangerous Liaisons, The Accused, The Unbearable Lightness of Being, The Last Temptation of Christ, Tucker: The Man and His Dream, Big, Running on Empty, Gorillas in the Mist, Midnight Run.

BEST FOREIGN-LANGUAGE FILMS

Women on the Verge of a Nervous Breakdown (Spain), *Pelle the Conqueror* (Denmark), *Le Grand Chemin* (France), *Salaam Bombay!* (India), *A Taxing Woman* (Japan).

NEW YORK FILM CRITICS CIRCLE

Picture: *The Accidental Tourist*; Actor: Jeremy Irons (*Dead Ringers*); Actress: Meryl Streep: (*A Cry in the Dark*); Supporting Actor: Dean Stockwell (*Married* to the Mob and *Tucker: The Man and His Dream*); Supporting Actress: Diane Venora (*Bird*); Director: Chris Menges (*A World Apart*); Screenplay: Ron Shelton (*Bull Durham*); Cinematography: Henri Alekan (*Wings of Desire*); Foreign Film: *Women on the Verge of a Nervous Breakdown*; Documentary: *The Thin Blue Line*.

Meryl Streep wanted Dustin Hoffman to present her with the outstanding Actress NYFCC award. Hoffman had refused to attend because he lost the top actor race by a narrow margin to Jeremy Irons as evil twins in *Dead Ringers*. (Irons also won the 1983–84 Tony Award over Hoffman, who was egregiously not nominated that year despite his acclaimed performance in *Death of a Salesman*.) So Wendy Wasserstein made the presentation. Streep had appeared in her play *Uncommon Women and Others* on television.

Irons was late arriving at the affair because his Concorde flight from England was delayed. Dean Stockwell entertained the crowd during the wait by singing "It's a Burger King World," which he had warbled in *Married to the Mob*.

NATIONAL SOCIETY OF FILM CRITICS

Picture: *The Unbearable Lightness of Being*; Actor: Michael Keaton (*Beetlejuice* and *Clean and Sober*); Actress: Judy Davis (*High Tide*); Supporting Actor: Dean Stockwell (*Married to the Mob*); Supporting Actress: Mercedes Ruehl (*Married to the Mob*); Director: Philip Kaufman (*The Unbearable Lightness of Being*); Screenplay: Ron Shelton (*Bull Durham*); Cinematography: Henri Alekan (*Wings of Desire*); Documenatary: *The Thin Blue Line*; Special Award: Pedro Almodovar.

LOS ANGELES FILM CRITICS ASSOCIATION

Picture: *Little Dorrit*; Actor: Tom Hanks (*Big* and *Punchline*); Actress: Christine Lahti (*Running on Empty*); Supporting Actor: Alec Guinness (*Little Dorrit*; Supporting Actress: Genevieve Bujold (*Dead Ringers* and *The Moderns*); Director: David Cronenberg (*Dead Ringers*); Screenplay: Ron Shelton (*Bull Durham*); Cinematography: Henri Alekan (*Wings of Desire*); Music: Mark Isham (*The Moderns*); Foreign

Film: *Wings of Desire*; Documentary: *Hotel Terminus: The Life and Times of Klaus Barbie*; Independent or Experimental Film (tie): *The Last of England* and *Amerika*; Life Achievement: Don Siegel; New Generation Prize: director/writer Mira Nair.

Little Dorritt, a two-part adaptation of the Charles Dickens novel, was the surprise winner of the Los Angeles Critics' award for best Picture since it had a limited release in only New York and L.A.

HOLLYWOOD FOREIGN PRESS ASSOCIATION GOLDEN GLOBE AWARDS

Picture (Drama): *Rain Man*; Picture (Comedy or Musical): *Working Girl*; Actor (Drama): Dustin Hoffman (*Rain Man*); Actress (Drama) (three-way tie): Jodie Foster (*The Accused*), Shirley MacLaine (*Madame Sousatzka*), Sigourney Weaver (*Gorillas in the Mist*); Actor (Comedy or Musical): Tom Hanks (*Big*); Actress (Comedy or Musical): Melanie Griffith (*Working Girl*); Supporting Actor: Martin Landau (*Tucker: The Man and His Dream*); Supporting Actress: Sigourney Weaver (*Working Girl*); Director: Clint Eastwood (*Bird*); Screenplay: Naomi Foner (*Running on Empty*); Original Score: Maurice Jarre (*Gorillas in the Mist*); Original Song (tie): "Let the River Run" from *Working Girl*, music and lyrics by Carly Simon, and "Two Hearts" from *Buster*, music by Lamont Dozier, lyrics by Phil Collins; Foreign Film: *Pelle the Conqueror*.

SPECIAL AWARD
Doris Day (Cecil B. DeMille Award).

The relatively small membership of the Hollywood Foreign Press Association (about eighty) resulted in numerous ties. There were two winners for best Song and three for best Actress in a Drama. Sigourney Weaver won two awards for different films, but would later lose in both categories at the Oscars. The winner for best Actress (Comedy or Musical) was Melanie Griffith, a former Miss Golden Globe, a position employing young starlets handing awards to the presenters.

CANNES FILM FESTIVAL

Palme d'Or: *Pelle the Conqueror* (Denmark),

emphasizing Max Von Sydow's contribution; Actor: Forrest Whitaker (*Bird*); Actress (collective award): Barbara Hershey, Jodhi May, Linda Mvusi (*A World Apart*) (UK); Director: Fernando Solanas (*South*) (Argentina); Special Jury Prize: *A World Apart*; Jury Prize: Krzysztof Kieslowski for *A Short Film About Killing* from *The Decalogue* (Poland); Artistic Contribution: Peter Greenaway (*Drowning by Numbers*) (UK); Camera d'Or: *Salaam, Bombay!*; Techinical Prize: *Bird* for the quality of its soundtrack.

ACADEMY AWARDS (OSCARS)

PICTURE
Born on the Fourth of July
Dead Poets Society
Driving Miss Daisy
Field of Dreams
My Left Foot

A feel-good drama in the liberal tradition, *Driving Miss Daisy* won best Picture, but its director Bruce Beresford was the first helmer since Edmund Goulding in 1931–32 (for *Grand Hotel*) to have directed a best Picture without himself being nominated for an Oscar. Also missing from the category was Spike Lee, whose *Do the Right Thing* was slighted in the best Picture category as well.

ACTOR
Kenneth Branagh (*Henry V*)
Tom Cruise (*Born on the Fourth of July*)
Daniel Day-Lewis (*My Left Foot*)
Morgan Freeman (*Driving Miss Daisy*)
Robin Williams (*Dead Poets Society*)

Day-Lewis was an unexpected winner and began a three-year streak of Brits triumphing in the best Actor category (Jeremy Irons and Anthony Hopkins followed). Pretty boy Cruise was the 1989 favorite since he was a Hollywood actor and his performance in the previous year's Oscar winner *Rain Man* had been overshadowed by Dustin Hoffman. Both Day-Lewis and Cruise played physically impaired characters based on real-life heroes.

ACTRESS
Isabelle Adjani (*Camille Claudel*)
Pauline Collins (*Shirley Valentine*)
Jessica Lange (*The Music Box*)
Michelle Pfeiffer (*The Fabulous Baker Boys*)
Jessica Tandy (*Driving Miss Daisy*)

At age 80, Jessica Tandy became the oldest Academy Award winner. Her reaction when informed she was now an Oscar statistic: "Am I the oldest? Well, good for me!"

SUPPORTING ACTOR
Danny Aiello (*Do the Right Thing*)
Dan Aykroyd (*Driving Miss Daisy*)
Marlon Brando (*A Dry White Season*)
Martin Landau (*Crimes and Misdemeanors*)
Denzel Washington (*Glory*)

SUPPORTING ACTRESS
Brenda Fricker (*My Left Foot*)
Anjelica Huston (*Enemies—A Love Story*)
Lena Olin (*Enemies—A Love Story*)
Julia Roberts (*Steel Magnolias*)
Dianne Wiest (*Parenthood*)

DIRECTOR
Woody Allen (*Crimes and Misdemeanors*)
Kenneth Branagh (*Henry V*)
Jim Sheridan (*My Left Foot*)
Oliver Stone (*Born on the Fourth of July*)
Peter Weir (*Dead Poets Society*)

ORIGINAL SCREENPLAY
Woody Allen (*Crimes and Misdemeanors*)
Nora Ephron (*When Harry Met Sally . . .*)
Spike Lee (*Do the Right Thing*)
Tom Schulman (*Dead Poets Society*)
Steven Soderbergh (*sex, lies, and videotape*)

ADAPTED SCREENPLAY
Phil Alden Robinson (*Field of Dreams*)
Jim Sheridan, Shane Connaughton (*My Left Foot*)
Roger L. Simon, Paul Mazursky (*Enemies—A Love Story*)
Oliver Stone, Ron Kovic (*Born on the Fourth of July*)
Alfred Uhry (*Driving Miss Daisy*)

FOREIGN-LANGUAGE FILM

Camille Claudel (France)
Cinema Paradiso (Italy)
Jesus of Montreal (Canada)
Waltzing Regitze (Denmark)
What Happened to Santiago (Puerto Rico)

OTHER AWARDS

Musical Score: Alan Menken (*The Little Mermaid*); Original Song: "Under the Sea" from *The Little Mermaid*, music by Alan Menken, lyrics by Howard Ashman; Cinematography: Freddie Francis (*Glory*); Art Direction: Anton Furst (*Batman*); Costume Design: Phillis Dalton (*Henry V*); Editing: David Brenner, Joe Hutshing (*Born on the Fourth of July*); Sound: Gregg C. Rudloff, Elliott Tyson, Russell Williams II (*Glory*); Visual Effects: John Bruno, Dennis Muren, Hoyt Yeatman, Dennis Skotak (*The Abyss*); Sound Effects Editing: Ben Burtt, Richard Hymns (*Indiana Jones and the Last Crusade*); Make-Up: Manilo Rochetti, Lynn Barber, Kevin Haney (*Driving Miss Daisy*).

Documentary: *Common Threads, Stories from the Quilt*; Documentary Short Subject: *The Johnstown Flood*; Live-Action Short Subject: *Work Experience*; Animated Short Subject: *Balance*.

SPECIAL AWARDS

Akira Kurosawa; Howard W. Koch (Jean Hersholt Humanitarian Award).

In the wake of the previous year's disastrous "Snow White Meets Rob Lowe" Oscars, producer Alan Carr was replaced by Gilbert Cates (whose brother Joseph was producing the Tony Awards). Cates hired a new host—Billy Crystal, who had proven himself capable of taking on the job by emceeing the Grammys. The new producer took a leaf from his brother's book by giving the evening a "theme," a concept frequently employed at the Tonys. The unifying umbrella for the ceremony would be Oscar Goes Global. To emphasize the international appeal and influence of the movies, awards would be presented from around the world via satellite links. Stars were flown to London, Moscow, Tokyo, Buenos Aires, and Sydney, Australia. The stunt was self-defeating. In addition to technical flaws—the sound feed from Moscow was faulty—almost all of the winners were in Hollywood. "We were going to go live from Malaysia," joked presenter Steve

Martin, "but the TV crew was hanged at the airport." The press reaction to the international theme was negative. "Advice to Oscar the Diplomat, stay home," sneered *The New York Times*.

If the main concept was a bomb, the host was a hit. Billy Crystal ripped into Oscar conventions and clichés with razor-sharp wit. In place of the usual horrible Best-Song-Nominees medley, he warbled a parody of each of the nominated best Pictures to the tune of popular songs ("Gee but it's great/In a segregated state/Driving Miss Daisy back home").

Most embarassing presenter: A bizarrely dressed and somewhat spacey Kim Basinger chiding the Academy for failing to nominate Spike Lee's *Do the Right Thing* for Best Picture.

NATIONAL BOARD OF REVIEW

English-Language Film: *Driving Miss Daisy*; Actor: Morgan Freeman (*Driving Miss Daisy*); Actress: Michelle Pfeiffer (*The Fabulous Baker Boys*); Supporting Actor: Alan Alda (*Crimes and Misdemeanors*); Supporting Actress: Mary Stuart Masterson (*Immediate Family*); Director: Kenneth Branagh (*Henry V*): Documentary: *Roger and Me*.

SPECIAL AWARDS

Robert Girouz, for six decades of distinguished efforts on behalf of film; Robert A. Harris, for the restoration of *Lawrence of Arabia*; critics Andrew Sarris and Molly Haskell.

BEST ENGLISH-LANGUAGE FILMS

Driving Miss Daisy, Henry V, sex, lies, and videotape, The Fabulous Baker Boys, My Left Foot, Dead Poets Society, Crimes and Misdemeanors, Born on the Fourth of July, Glory, Field of Dreams.

BEST FOREIGN-LANGUAGE FILMS

The Story of Women (France), *Camille Claudel* (France), *Le Lectrice* (France), *Chocolat* (France/Federal Republic of Germany/Cameroon), *The Little Thief* (France).

NEW YORK FILM CRITICS CIRCLE

Picture: *My Left Foot*; Actor: Daniel Day-Lewis (*My Left Foot*); Actress: Michell Pfeiffer (*The Fabulous Baker Boys*); Supporting Actor: Alan Alda

(*Crimes and Misdemeanors*); Supporting Actress: Lena Olin (*Enemies—A Love Story*); Director: Paul Mazursky (*Enemies—A Love Story*); Screenplay: Gus Van Sant, Daniel Yost (*Drugstore Cowboy*); Cinematography: Ernest Dickerson (*Do the Right Thing*); Documentary: *Roger and Me*; New Director: Kenneth Branagh (*Henry V*); Foreign Film: *The Story of Women*.

NATIONAL SOCIETY OF FILM CRITICS

Picture: *Drugstore Cowboy*; Actor: Daniel Day-Lewis (*My Left Foot*); Actress: Michelle Pfeiffer (*The Fabulous Baker Boys*); Supporting Actor: Beau Bridges (*The Fabulous Baker Boys*); Supporting Actress: Anjelica Huston (*Enemies—A Love Story*); Director: Gus Van Sant (*Drugstore Cowboy*); Screenplay: Gus Van Sant, Dan Yost (*Drugstore Cowboy*); Cinematography: Michael Balhuas (*The Fabulous Baker Boys*); Documentary: *Roger and Me*.

LOS ANGELES FILM CRITICS ASSOCIATION

Picture: *Do the Right Thing*; Actor: Daniel Day-Lewis (*My Left Foot*); Actress (tie): Andie MacDowell (*sex, lies, and videotape*) and Michelle Pfeiffer (*The Fabulous Baker Boys*); Supporting Actor: Danny Aiello (*Do the Right Thing*); Supporting Actress: Brenda Fricker (*My Left Foot*); Director: Spike Lee (*Do the Right Thing*); Screenplay: Gus Van Sant, Daniel Yost (*Drugstore Cowboy*); Cinematography: Michael Ballhaus (*The Fabulous Baker Boys*); Music: Bill Lee, et al (*Do the Right Thing*); Foreign Film: *Distant Voices, Still Lives* and *The Story of Women*; Documentary: *Roger and Me*; Animated Film: *The Little Mermaid*; Independent or Experimental Film: *The Long Weekend o' Despair*; Life Achievement: Stanley Donen; New Generation Prize: Laura San Giacomo, for her performance in *sex, lies, and videotape*; Special Award: Margaret Herrick Library of the Academy of Motion Picture Arts & Sciences.

HOLLYWOOD FOREIGN PRESS ASSOCIATION GOLDEN GLOBE AWARDS

Picture (Drama): *Born on the Fourth of July*; Picture (Comedy or Musical): *Driving Miss Daisy*; Actor (Drama): Tom Cruise (*Born on the Fourth of July*); Actress (Drama): Michelle Pfeiffer (*The Fabulous Baker Boys*); Actor (Comedy or Musical): Morgan Freeman (*Driving Miss Daisy*); Actress (Comedy or Musical): Jessica Tandy (*Driving Miss Daisy*); Supporting Actor: Denzel Washington (*Glory*); Supporting Actress: Julia Roberts (*Steel Magnolias*); Director: Oliver Stone (*Born on the Fourth of July*); Screenplay: Ron Kovic, Oliver Stone (*Born on the Fourth of July*); Original Score: Alan Menken (*The Little Mermaid*); Original Song: "Under the Sea" from *The Little Mermaid*, music by Alan Menken, lyrics by Howard Ashman; Foreign Film: *Cinema Paradiso*.

SPECIAL AWARD
Audrey Hepburn (Cecil B. DeMille Award).

CANNES FILM FESTIVAL

Palme d'Or: *sex, lies, and videotape*; Actor: James Spader (*sex, lies, and videotape*); Actress: Meryl Streep (*A Cry in the Dark*); Director: Emir Kusturica (*Time of the Gypsies*) (Yugoslavia); Special Jury Prize: *Cinema Paradiso* (Italy), *Too Beautiful for You* (France); Jury Prize: *Jesus of Montreal* (Canada); Artistic Contribution: *Mystery Train*; Camera d'Or: *My Twentieth Century* (Hungary); Technical Prize: *Black Rain* (Japan); International Critics Prize: in competition, *sex, lies, and videotape*, out of competition, *Yaaba* (Burkina Faso).

Foreshadowing the Oscars, *Do the Right Thing* was snubbed for the Palme d'Or at Cannes—in favor of Steven Soderbergh's *sex, lies, and videotape*, which the Academy ignored as well.

1990

ACADEMY AWARDS (OSCARS)

PICTURE
Awakenings
Dances with Wolves
Ghost
The Godfather, Part III
Goodfellas

Novice director Kevin Costner dominated the Oscars and Golden Globes, while veteran Martin Scorsese took the lion's share of the critics' awards. *Dance with Wolves*, Costner's three-hour epic in which he directed himself as a Union soldier who lives among a Sioux tribe, won seven out of twelve Oscars and three Golden Globes. *Wolves* was the first Western to take the best Picture Oscar since *Cimarron* in 1930–31.

Goodfellas, Scorsese's stylish study of a career Mafia man, was named top film by the National Society of Film Critics and the New York and Los Angeles scribes—the first film to win best Picture from all three groups. However, save for a Supporting Actor nod to Joe Pesci, the film was shut out of the Oscar winners' circle. Another director snubbed by the golden guy was Penny Marshall, who failed to receive a nomination for *Awakenings*. The fact that her film was up for best Picture caused some to call the rejection sexist.

ACTOR
Kevin Costner (*Dances with Wolves*)
Robert De Niro (*Awakenings*)
Gerard Depardieu (*Cyrano de Bergerac*)
Jeremy Irons (*Reversal of Fortune*)
Richard Harris (*The Field*)

ACTRESS
Kathy Bates (*Misery*)
Anjelica Huston (*The Grifters*)
Julia Roberts (*Pretty Woman*)
Meryl Streep (*Postcards from the Edge*)
Joanne Woodward (*Mr. and Mrs. Bridge*)

The best Actor and best Actress Oscars usually go to performers playing sympathetic characters. In a depature from tradition, movie villains Jeremy Irons and Kathy Bates took the top acting Oscars. Irons won for his cold-as-ice portrayal of Klaus von Bulow, who is accused of attempting to murder his wife in *Reversal of Fortune*, while Kathy Bates triumphed for her twisted romance fan in *Misery*.

Many Oscarwatchers saw Irons' win as a consolation prize for his nonnominated performance as psychotic twins in 1988's *Dead Ringers*. Bates benefited from a split vote between front-runners and previous Oscar winners Anjelica Huston and Joanne Woodward.

SUPPORTING ACTOR
Bruce Davison (*Longtime Companion*)
Andy Garcia (*The Godfather, Part III*)
Graham Greene (*Dances with Wolves*)
Joe Pesci (*Goodfellas*)
Al Pacino (*Dick Tracy*)

Another villain won the Supporting Actor award. "It's my privilege, thank you" were Joe Pesci's only words when accepting his Oscar. His *Goodfellas* performance was bolstered by comic supporting turns in the more mainstream comedies *Home Alone* and *Lethal Weapon 2* during the voting period.

SUPPORTING ACTRESS
Annette Bening (*The Grifters*)
Lorraine Bracco (*Goodfellas*)
Whoopi Goldberg (*Ghost*)
Diane Ladd (*Wild at Heart*)
Mary McDonnell (*Dances With Wolves*)

Best Supporting Actress Whoopi Goldberg, who played a phony medium in the surprise hit *Ghost*, became the first black woman to win an Oscar since Hattie MacDaniel in 1939 for *Gone with the Wind*.

DIRECTOR
Francis Ford Coppola (*The Godfather, Part III*)
Kevin Costner (*Dances with Wolves*)
Stephen Frears (*The Grifters*)
Martin Scorsese (*Goodfellas*)
Barbet Schroeder (*Reversal of Fortune*)

ORIGINAL SCREENPLAY
Woody Allen (*Alice*)
Barry Levinson (*Avalon*)
Bruce Joel Rubin (*Ghost*)
Whit Stillman (*Metropolitan*)
Peter Weir (*Green Card*)

ADAPTED SCREENPLAY
Michael Blake (*Dances with Wolves*)
Nicholas Kazan (*Reversal of Fortune*)
Nicholas Pileggi, Martin Scorsese (*Goodfellas*)
Donald E. Westlake (*The Grifters*)
Steven Zaillian (*Awakenings*)

FOREIGN-LANGUAGE FILM

Cyrano de Bergerac (France)
Journey of Hope (Switzerland)
Ju Dou (People's Republic of China)
The Nasty Girl (Federal Republic of Germany)
Open Doors (Italy)

OTHER AWARDS

Musical Score: John Barry (*Dances with Wolves*); Original Song: "Sooner or Later (I Always Get My Man)" from *Dick Tracy*, music and lyrics by Stephen Sondheim; Cinematography: Dean Semler (*Dances with Wolves*); Art Direction: Richard Sylbert, Rick Simpson (*Dick Tracy*); Costume Design: Franca Squarciapino (*Cyrano de Bergerac*); Editing: Neil Travis (*Dances with Wolves*); Sound: Russell Williams II, Jeffrey Perkins, Bill W. Benton, Greg Watkins (*Dances with Wolves*); Visual Effects: Eric Brevig, Rob Bottin, Tom McGovern, Alex Funke (*Total Recall*); Sound Effects Editing: Cecelia Hall, George Watters II (*The Hunt for Red October*); Make-Up: John Caglone, Jr., Doug Drexler (*Dick Tracy*).

Documentary: *American Dream*; Documentary Short Subject: *Days of Waiting*; Live-Action Short Subject: *The Lunch Date*; Animated Short Subject: *Creature Comforts*.

SPECIAL AWARDS

Sophia Loren; Myrna Loy; Richard Zanuck and David Brown (Irving Thalberg Award).

For the second consecutive year, Billy Crystal hosted the Oscar ceremonies. Pop star/media icon Madonna was the hottest piece of entertainment, warbling Stephen Sondheim's "Sooner or Later (I Always Get My Man)" from *Dick Tracy*, which won the best Original Song award. Ironically, Madonna and her escort Michael Jackson were the two biggest attractions on Oscar night, but neither was a nominee.

The most spontaneous moment occured off-camera when an audience member cried out "AIDS action! 102,000 dead!"

NATIONAL BOARD OF REVIEW

English-Language Film: *Dances with Wolves*; Actor: Robert De Niro, Robin Williams (*Awakenings*); Actress: Mia Farrow (*Alice*); Supporting Actor: Joe Pesci (*Goodfellas*); Supporting Actress: Winona Ryder (*Mermaids*); Director: Kevin Costner (*Dances with Wolves*).

BEST ENGLISH-LANGUAGE FILMS

Dances with Wolves, Hamlet, Goodfellas, Awakenings, Reversal of Fortune, Miller's Crossing, Metropolitan, Mr. and Mrs. Bridge, Avalon, The Grifters.

BEST FOREIGN-LANGUAGE FILMS

Cyrano de Bergerac (France); *Jesus of Montreal* (Canada); *The Nasty Girl* (Federal Republic of Germany); *Monsieur Hire* (France); *Tie Me Up! Tie Me Down!* (Spain).

NEW YORK FILM CRITICS CIRCLE

Picture: *Goodfellas*; Actor: Robert De Niro (*Awakenings* and *Goodfellas*); Actress: Joanne Woodward (*Mr. and Mrs. Bridge*); Supporting Actor: Bruce Davison (*Longtime Companion*); Supporting Actress: Jennifer Jason Leigh (*Miami Blues* and *Last Exit to Brooklyn*); Director: Martin Scorsese (*Goodfellas*); Screenplay: Ruth Prawer Jhabvala (*Mr. and Mrs. Bridge*); Cinematography: Vittorio Storraro (*The Sheltering Sky*); New Director: Whit Stillman (*Metropolitan*); Foreign Film: *The Nasty Girl*.

Caustic critic Rex Reed hosted the 1990 NYFCC Awards and came in for some harsh criticism from his fellow pundits for his controversial handling of his emcee duties. The normally two-and-a-half-hour event dragged on for four and a half hours. In addition, Reed added his own commentary on some of the nonwinners. In an obvious swipe at *The Godfather, Part III*, Reed sniped, "*Goodfellas* is the only gangster picture made this year that doesn't look as if it was shot through a lens covered with marinara sauce."

NATIONAL SOCIETY OF FILM CRITICS

Picture: *Goodfellas*; Actor: Jeremy Irons (*Reversal of Fortune*); Actress: Anjelica Huston (*The Grifters* and *The Witches*); Supporting Actor: Bruce Davison (*Longtime Companion*); Supporting Actress: Annette Bening (*The Grifters*); Director: Martin Scorsese (*Goodfellas*); Screenplay: Charles

Burnett (*To Sleep with Anger*); Cinematography: Peter Suschitzky (*Where the Heart Is*); Foreign Film: *Ariel*; Documentary: *Berkeley in the Sixties*.

LOS ANGELES FILM CRITICS ASSOCIATION

Picture: *Goodfellas*; Actor: Jeremy Irons (*Reversal of Fortune*); Actress: Anjelica Huston (*The Grifters* and *The Witches*); Supporting Actor: Joe Pesci (*Goodfellas*); Supporting Actress: Lorraine Bracco (*Goodfellas*); Director: Martin Scorsese (*Goodfellas*); Screenplay: Nicholas Kazan (*Reversal of Fortune*); Cinematography: Michael Ballhaus (*Goodfellas*); Music: Ryuichi Sakamoto (*The Sheltering Sky*); Foreign Film: *Life and Nothing But*; Documentary (tie): *Paris Is Burning* and *Pictures of the Old World*; Animated Film: *The Rescuers Down Under*; Independent or Experimental Film: *Tongues Untied*; Life Achievement: Chuck Jones, Blake Edwards; New Generation Prize: Jane Campion, director of *Sweetie*; Special Award: Charles Burnett.

HOLLYWOOD FOREIGN PRESS ASSOCIATION GOLDEN GLOBE AWARDS

Picture (Drama): *Dances with Wolves*; Picture (Comedy or Musical): *Green Card*; Actor (Drama): Jeremy Irons (*Reversal of Fortune*); Actress (Drama): Kathy Bates (*Misery*); Actor (Comedy or Musical): Gerard Depardieu (*Green Card*); Actress (Comedy or Musical): Julia Roberts (*Pretty Woman*); Supporting Actor: Bruce Davison (*Longtime Companion*); Supporting Actress: Whoopi Goldberg (*Ghost*); Director: Kevin Costner (*Dances with Wolves*); Screenplay: Michael Blake (*Dances with Wolves*); Original Score: Ryuichi Sakamoto, Richard Horowitz (*The Sheltering Sky*); Original Song: "Blaze of Glory" from *Young Guns II*, music and lyrics by Jon Bon Jovi; Foreign Film: *Cyrano de Bergerac*.

SPECIAL AWARD
Jack Lemmon (Cecil B. DeMille Award).

CANNES FILM FESTIVAL

Palme d'Or: *Wild at Heart*; Actor: Gerard Depardieu (*Cyrano de Bergerac*); Actress: Krystyna Janda (*Interrogation*) (Poland); Director: Pavel

Lounguine (*Taxi Blues*) (France/USSR); Special Jury Prize: *The Sting of Death* (Japan), *Tilai* (Burkina Faso); Jury Prize: *Hidden Agenda* (UK); Artistic Contribution: *The Mother* (USSR/Italy); Special Mention: to Manoel de Oliveira and Andrzej Wadja; Camera d'Or: *Freeze—Die—Come to Life* (Russia); Technical Prize: Pierre Lhomme for the cinematography in *Cyrano de Bergerac*; International Critics Prize: in competition, *The Sting of Death*, out of competition, *Swan Lake: The Zone* (USSR), special mention to Manoel de Oliveira.

ACADEMY AWARDS (OSCARS)

PICTURE
Beauty and the Beast
Bugsy
JFK
The Prince of Tides
The Silence of the Lambs

The new Hollywood made its voice heard by voting the horrifying thriller *The Silence of the Lambs* the top five Oscars (Picture, Actor, Actress, Director, and Screenplay). *Lambs* was the first to take all five top prizes since *One Flew over the Cuckoo's Nest* in 1975. *Lambs* was also the first best Picture winner to be released on cable and video before winning.

Drawing power: *Beauty and the Beast* was the first animated feature to be nominated for best Picture.

ACTOR
Warren Beatty (*Bugsy*)
Robert De Niro (*Cape Fear*)
Anthony Hopkins (*The Silence of the Lambs*)
Nick Nolte (*The Prince of Tides*)
Robin Williams (*The Fisher King*)

ACTRESS
Geena Davis (*Thelma and Louise*)
Laura Dern (*Rambling Rose*)
Jodie Foster (*The Silence of the Lambs*)
Bette Midler (*For the Boys*)
Susan Sarandon (*Thelma and Louise*)

Laura Dern and Diane Ladd (lead and supporting actresses in *Rambling Rose*) were the first mother and daughter to be nominated in the same year. Host Billy Crystal joked, "They are the first mother-daughter team ever nominated if you don't count Faye Dunaway in *Chinatown*." When the audience was a trifle slow on the uptake, he commanded, "Rent it!"

SUPPORTING ACTOR
Tommy Lee Jones (*JFK*)
Harvey Keitel (*Bugsy*)
Ben Kingsley (*Bugsy*)
Michael Lerner (*Barton Fink*)
Jack Palance (*City Slickers*)

The seventy-two-year-old Jack Palance earned a place in Oscar history with a spontaneous exhibition of one-armed push-ups. This provided Billy Crystal, who had co-starred with Palance in *City Slickers*, with ample fodder for running gags. Samples of the Crystal-on-Palance patter: "Jack Palance just bungeed-jumped off the Hollywood sign"; "This just in: Jack Palance has won the New York primary"; and, after a musical number featuring numerous kids, "Jack Palance fathered all those children in his spare time."

SUPPORTING ACTRESS
Diane Ladd (*Rambling Rose*)
Juliette Lewis (*Cape Fear*)
Kate Nelligan (*The Prince of Tides*)
Mercedes Ruehl (*The Fisher King*)
Jessica Tandy (*Fried Green Tomatoes*)

DIRECTOR
Jonathan Demme (*The Silence of the Lambs*)
Barry Levinson (*Bugsy*)
Ridley Scott (*Thelma and Louise*)
John Singleton (*Boyz N the Hood*)
Oliver Stone (*JFK*)

At age 23, John Singleton was the youngest best Director nominee ever. Despite seven nomations for her film, Barbra Streisand failed to receive a best Director nomination for *The Prince of Tides*. With Randa Heller, Penny Marshall, and now for the second time, Streisand frozen out, the directors' branch of the Academy was appearing more and

more guilty of the sexist charges hurled at them.

ORIGINAL SCREENPLAY
Lawrence Kasdan, Meg Kasdan (*Grand Canyon*)
Callie Khouri (*Thelma and Louise*)
Richard La Gravenese (*The Fisher King*)
John Singleton (*Boyz N the Hood*)
James Tobak (*Bugsy*)

ADAPTED SCREENPLAY
Pat Conroy, Becky Johnson (*The Prince of Tides*)
Fannie Flagg, Carol Sobieski
    (*Fried Green Tomatoes*)
Agnieska Holland (*Europa, Europa*)
Oliver Stone, Zachary Sklar (*JFK*)
Ted Tally (*Silence of the Lambs*)

FOREIGN-LANGUAGE FILM
Children of Nature (Iceland)
The Elementary School (Czechoslovakia)
Mediterraneo (Italy)
The Ox (Sweden)
Raise the Red Lantern (Hong Kong)

OTHER AWARDS
Musical Score: Alan Menken (*Beauty and the Beast*); Original Song: "Beauty and the Beast" from *Beauty and the Beast*, music by Alan Menken, lyrics by Howard Ashman; Cinematography: Ralph Richardson (*JFK*); Art Direction: Dennis Gassner (*Bugsy*); Costume Design: Albert Wolsky (*Bugsy*); Editing: John Williams (*JFK*); Sound: Tom Johnson, Gary Rydstrom, Gary Summers, Lee Orloff (*Terminator 2*); Visual Effects: Dennis Muren, Stan Winston (*Terminator 2*); Sound Effects Editing: Gary Rydstrom, Gloria S. Borders (*Terminator 2*); Make-Up: Stan Winston, Jeff Dawn (*Terminator 2*).

    Documentary: *In the Shadow of the Stars*; Documentary Short Subject: *Deadly Deception: General Electric, Nuclear Weapons, and Our Environment*; Live-Action Short Subject: *Session Man*; Animated Short Subject: *Manipulation*.

SPECIAL AWARDS
Satyajit Ray; George Lucas (Irving Thalberg Award).

Battling the flu, Billy Crystal served as Oscar emcee for the third time and put on his best performance ever. "I had a 102-degree fever the morning of the show," he related to *TV Guide*. "I wasn't sure I could do it. I called Tom Hanks to put him on stand-by." Fortified with chicken soup, the actor/comedian made his entrance, tied up in a straight-jacket and wearing a face-mask à la Hannibal Lechter in *Silence of the Lambs*, and proceeded to slay the audience. Not only was the prepared material clever—his usual musical parodies of the nominated Best Pictures—but the spontaneous ad libs sizzled. Jack Palance's push-ups provided a running gag for the evening and, when film pioneer Hal Roach gave a rambling speech with no mike, Crystal saved the situation. "I think that's fitting because Mr. Roach started out in silent films," he quipped. The *New York Post* declared Crystal the best Oscar host ever.

Controversy of the year: Gay demonstrators threatened to disrupt the awards to protest negative and/or trivial portrayals of gay characters in films like *Basic Instinct, JFK, The Prince of Tides,* and *Silence of the Lambs*, and the passing over of films such as *Paris Is Burning*, a documentary on drag queens, and performances such as River Phoenix's sensitive portrayal of a gay hustler in *My Own Private Idaho*. There were sign-carriers outside the theater, but nothing happened during the telecast.

NATIONAL BOARD OF REVIEW

English-Language Film: *The Silence of the Lambs*; Actor: Warren Beatty (*Bugsy*); Actress: Geena Davis, Susan Sarandon (*Thelma and Louise*); Supporting Actor: Anthony Hopkins (*The Silence of the Lambs*); Supporting Actress: Kate Nelligan (*Frankie and Johnny*); Director: Jonathan Demme (*The Silence of the Lambs*).

BEST ENGLISH-LANGUAGE FILMS

Silence of the Lambs, Bugsy, Grand Canyon, Thelma and Louise, Homicide, Dead Again, Boyz N the Hood, Rambling Rose, Frankie and Johnny, Jungle Fever.

BEST FOREIGN-LANGUAGE FILMS

Europa, Europa (Germany/France), *The Vanishing, La Femme Nikita* (France), *My Father's Glory* and *My Mother's Castle, Toto les Heros* (Belgium).

While the Oscar considered him a leading man, the National Board of Review gave Anthony Hopkins a supporting actor award for *Silence of the Lambs*.

NEW YORK FILM CRITICS CIRCLE

Picture: *The Silence of the Lambs*; Actor: Anthony Hopkins (*The Silence of the Lambs*); Actress: Jodie Foster (*The Silence of the Lambs*); Supporting Actor: Samuel L. Jackson (*Jungle Fever*); Supporting Actress: Judy Davis (*Barton Fink* and *Naked Lunch*); Director: Jonathan Demme (*The Silence of the Lambs*); Screenplay: David Cronenberg (*Naked Lunch*); Cinematography: Roger Deakins (*Barton Fink*); Foreign Film: *Europa, Europa*; Documentary: *Paris Is Burning*; First Film: John Singleton (*Boyz N the Hood*).

Anthony Heald, who played a victim of Anthony Hopkins' cannibalism in *The Silence of the Lambs*, presented Hopkins with the NYFCC award. "My pleasure at being here was heightened when I found out my name was not on the menu," Heald said. Unexpected drama occurred when protestors from Action Tours, an ACT UP-affiliated organization, stormed the Pegasus Room in Rockefeller Center where the awards ceremony was being held. They distributed leaflets calling *Silence*, the critics' choice for best picture, homophobic and bigoted in its portrayal of a murderous transvestite.

NATIONAL SOCIETY OF FILM CRITICS

Picture: *Life Is Sweet*; Actor: River Phoenix (*My Own Private Idaho*); Actress: Alison Stedman (*Life Is Sweet*); Supporting Actor: Harvey Keitel (*Bugsy, Thelma and Louise,* and *Mortal Thoughts*); Supporting Actress: Jane Horrocks (*Life Is Sweet*); Director: David Cronenberg (*Naked Lunch*); Screenplay: David Cronenberg (*Naked Lunch*); Cinematography: Roger Deakins (*Barton Fink*); Documentary: *Paris Is Burning*; Experimental Film: *Archangel*; Special Citation: for film preservation to Peter Delpeut for his compilation film *Lyrical Nitrate* (The Netherlands).

LOS ANGELES FILM CRITICS ASSOCIATION

Picture: *Bugsy*; Actor: Nick Nolte (*The Prince of Tides*); Actress: Mercedes Ruehl (*The Fisher King*);

Supporting Actor: Michael Lerner (*Barton Fink*); Supporting Actress: Jane Horrocks (*Life Is Sweet*); Director: Barry Levinson (*Bugsy*); Screenplay: James Toback (*Bugsy*); Cinematography: Roger Deakins (*Barton Fink* and *Homicide*); Music: Zbigniew Preisner (*Europa, Europa, The Double Life of Veronique,* and *At Play in the Fields of the Lord*); Documentary: *American Dream*; Animated Film: *Beauty and the Beast*; Independent/ Experimental Film: *All the Vermeers in New York*; New Generation Prize: John Singleton (*Boyz N the Hood*); Life Achievement: Vincent Price, Elmer Bernstein; Special Citation: The National FIlm Board of Canada on its fiftieth anniversary.

HOLLYWOOD FOREIGN PRESS ASSOCIATION GOLDEN GLOBE AWARDS

Picture (Drama): *Bugsy*; Picture (Comedy or Musical): *Beauty and the Beast*; Actor (Drama): Nick Nolte (*The Prince of Tides*); Actress (Drama): Jodie Foster (*The Silence of the Lambs*); Actor (Comedy or Musical): Robin Williams (*The Fisher King*); Actress (Comedy or Musical): Bette Midler (*For the Boys*); Supporting Actor: Jack Palance (*City Slickers*); Supporting Actress: Mercedes Ruehl (*The Fisher King*); Director: Oliver Stone (*JFK*); Screenplay: Callie Khouri (*Thelma and Louise*); Original Score: Alan Menken (*Beauty and the Beast*); Original Song: "Beauty and the Beast" from *Beauty and the Beast*, music by Alan Menken, lyrics by Howard Ashman; Foreign Film: *Europa, Europa*.

CANNES FILM FESTIVAL

Palme d'Or: *Barton Fink*; Actor: John Turturro (*Barton Fink*); Actress: Irene Jacob (*The Double Life of Veronique*) (France); Supporting Actor: Samuel L. Jackson (*Jungle Fever*); Director: Joel Coen (*Barton Fink*); Special Jury Prize: *La Belle Noiseuse* (France); Jury Prize: *Europa, Europa* (Denmark), *Hors la Vie* (Lebanon); Camera d'Or: *Toto les Heros* (Belgium), special mentions to *Proof* (Australia) and *Sam and Me* (Canada); Technical Prize: Lars von Trier (*Europa, Europa*); International Critics Prize: in competition, *The Double Life of Veronique*, out of competition, *Riff-Raff* (UK).

Spike Lee was again overlooked at Cannes when his fiery film on interracial romance, *Jungle Fever*, failed to pick up any major recognition from the Cannes jury. As a consolation prize, the jury did vote Samuel L. Jackson who, played the hero's drug-addicted brother in the film, a Supporting Actor award. Supporting performances are rarely given honors at Cannes.

ACADEMY AWARDS (OSCARS)

PICTURE
The Crying Game
A Few Good Men
Howards End
Scent of a Woman
Unforgiven

Clint Eastwood almost single-handedly revived the Western and took two Oscars for producing and directing *Unforgiven*. The tight-lipped star won for his first nominations and also took the Los Angeles Film Critics Association and the National Society of Film Critics awards for best Picture. Andrew Sarris observed in the *New York Observer* that *Unforgiven* was stopped from grabbing the New York scribes' prize by "a cabal of die-hard, anti-Eastwood, anti-Western, [*New Yorker* film critic Pauline] Kaelians, who circled their wagons around Robert Altman's *The Player*."

Major oversight: Spike Lee's epic biopic *Malcolm X* was not nominated for best Picture.

ACTOR
Robert Downey, Jr. (*Chaplin*)
Clint Eastwood (*Unforgiven*)
Al Pacino (*Scent of a Woman*)
Stephen Rea (*The Crying Game*)
Denzel Washington (*Malcolm X*)

ACTRESS
Catherine Deneuve (*Indochine*)
Mary McDonnell (*Passion Fish*)
Michelle Pfeiffer (*Love Field*)
Susan Sarandon (*Lorenzo's Oil*)
Emma Thompson (*Howards End*)

Emma Thompson made a clean sweep of the acting awards, winning the Oscar, Golden Globe, and all the critics' prizes. The British star's uncontested triumph indicated the dearth of good roles for women in American films.

SUPPORTING ACTOR
Jaye Davidson (*The Crying Game*)
Gene Hackman (*Unforgiven*)
Jack Nicholson (*A Few Good Men*)
Al Pacino (*Glengarry Glen Ross*)
David Paymer (*Mr. Saturday Night*)

SUPPORTING ACTRESS
Judy Davis (*Husbands and Wives*)
Joan Plowright (*Enchanted April*)
Vanessa Redgrave (*Howards End*)
Miranda Richardson (*Damage*)
Marisa Tomei (*My Cousin Vinny*)

Tomei was the sole American nominee against a field of three Brits (Plowright, Redgrave, and Richardson) and an Australian (Davis). Her win for a mediocre comedy was seen by many as a Hollywood backlash against the invasion of quality British films.

DIRECTOR
Robert Altman (*The Player*)
Martin Brest (*Scent of a Woman*)
Clint Eastwood (*Unforgiven*)
James Ivory (*Howard's End*)
Neil Jordan (*The Crying Game*)

ORIGINAL SCREENPLAY
Woody Allen (*Husbands and Wives*)
Neil Jordan (*The Crying Game*)
George Miller, Nick Enright (*Lorenzo's Oil*)
David Webb Peoples (*Unforgiven*)
John Sayles (*Passion Fish*)

ADAPTED SCREENPLAY
Peter Barnes (*Enchanted April*)
Richard Friedenberg (*A River Runs through It*)
Bo Goldman (*Scent of a Woman*)
Ruth Prawer Jhabvala (*Howards End*)
Michael Tolkin (*The Player*)

FOREIGN-LANGUAGE FILM
Close to Eden (Russia)

Daens (Belgium)
Indochine (France)
A Place in the World (Uruguay)
Schtonk (Germany)

A Place in the World was declared ineligible after it was discovered most of the production elements were Argentinian rather than from Uruguay, the official country of its origin.

OTHER AWARDS
Musical Score: Alan Menken (*Aladdin*); Original Song: "A Whole New World" from *Aladdin*, music by Alan Menken, lyrics by Tim Rice; Cinematography: Philippe Rousselot (*A River Runs through It*); Art Direction: Luciana Arrighi (*Howards End*); Costume Design: Eiko Ishioka (*Dracula*); Editing: Joel Cox (*Unforgiven*); Sound: Chris Jenkins, Doug Hemphill, Mark Smith, Simon Kaye (*The Last of the Mohicans*); Visual Effects: Ken Ralston, Michael Lantieri (*Death Becomes Her*); Sound Effects Editing: Tom McCarthy, David Stone (*Dracula*); Make-Up: Michele Burke (*Dracula*).

Documentary: *The Panama Deception*; Documentary Short Subject: *Education Peter*; Live-Action Short Subject: *Omnibus*; Animated Short Subject: *Mona Lisa Descending a Staircase*.

SPECIAL AWARDS
Federico Fellini; Audrey Hepburn (posthumous); Elizabeth Taylor (Jean Hersholt Humanitarian Award).

In a year with so few good roles for women in American films, the Academy unintentionally shot itself in the foot by declaring 1992 "The Year of the Woman." During the ceremonies, Liza Minnelli sang a perfectly awful and condescending number called "Ladies' Day." "A celebration of women? Blow me," carped Cynthia Hamel in *The Village Voice*. "Could they please just cut out the patronizing smarminess and just call it 'A Celebration of Testosterone and Just Try to Stop Us'?"

Billy Cyrstal was unsure if he wanted to host again. Oscar producer Gilbert Cates was so desperate he sent the comic a funeral wreath with the message, "It's dead without you." Crystal told *TV Guide*, "Then he escalates and sends me a fake horse's head before Valentine's Day."

Once again Crystal hosted and made a potentially tedious three and a half hours bearable. In a hilarious reference to last year's Jack Palance running jokes, Crystal made his entrance atop a giant Oscar statue pulled by Palance in a harness. One anonymous agent quoted in *Variety* was less than enchanted with the ceremony, writing, "Bring back Alan Carr. His show was fun bad. This show was just pathetic and boring bad."

Most embarrassing presenter: Richard Gere speculating if Chinese ruler Deng Xiaoping was watching and pleading with him for civil rights in China and Tibet.

NATIONAL BOARD OF REVIEW

English-Language Film: *Howards End*; Actor: Jack Lemmon (*Glengarry Glen Ross*); Actress: Emma Thompson (*Howard's End*); Supporting Actor: Jack Nicholson (*A Few Good Men*); Supporting Actress: Judy Davis (*Husbands and Wives*); Director: James Ivory (*Howard's End*); Foreign Film: *Indochine*.

BEST ENGLISH-LANGUAGE FILMS

Howards End, The Crying Game, Glengarry Glen Ross, A Few Good Men, The Player, Unforgiven, One False Move, Peter's Friends, Bob Roberts, Malcolm X.

BEST FOREIGN-LANGUAGE FILMS:

Indochine (France), *Raise the Red Lantern* (Hong Kong), *Tous les Matins du Monde (*All the Mornings in the World) (France), *Mediterraneo* (Italy), *Like Water for Chocolate* (Mexico).

NEW YORK FILM CRITICS CIRCLE

Picture: *The Player*; Actor: Denzel Washington (*Malcolm X*); Actress: Emma Thompson (*Howards End*); Supporting Actor: Gene Hackman (*Unforgiven*); Supporting Actress: Miranda Richardson (*The Crying Game, Damage,* and *Enchanted April*); Director: Robert Altman (*The Player*); Screenplay: Neil Jordan (*The Crying Game*); Cinematography: Jean Lapine (*The Player*); Foreign Film: *Raise the Red Lantern*; Documentary: *Brother's Keeper*; New Director: Allison Anders (*Gas Food Lodging*).

NATIONAL SOCIETY OF FILM CRITICS

Picture: *Unforgiven*; Actor: Stephen Rea (*The Crying Game*); Actress: Emma Thompson (*Howards End*); Supporting Actor: Gene Hackman (*Unforgiven*); Supporting Actress: Judy Davis (*Husbands and Wives*); Director: Clint Eastwood (*Unforgiven*); Screenplay: David Webb Peoples (*Unforgiven*); Cinematography: Zhao Fei (*Raise the Red Lantern*); Foreign Film: *Raise the Red Lantern*; Documentary: *American Dream*; Special Citation: *Another Girl, Another Planet.*

LOS ANGELES FILM CRITICS ASSOCIATION

Picture: *Unforgiven*; Actor: Clint Eastwood (*Unforgiven*); Actress: Emma Thompson (*Howards End*); Supporting Actor: Gene Hackman (*Unforgiven*); Supporting Actress: Judy Davis (*Husbands and Wives*); Director: Clint Eastwood (*Unforgiven*); Screenplay: David Webb Peoples (*Unforgiven*); Cinematography: Zhao Fei (*Raise the Red Lantern*); Music: Zbigniew Preisner (*Damage*); Documentary: *The Threat, Black Harvest*; Foreign Film: *The Crying Game*; Animated Film: *Aladdin*; Independent/Experimental Film: Sadie Benning; Career Achievement: Budd Boetticher; New Generation Award: Carl Franklin (*One False Move*).

HOLLYWOOD FOREIGN PRESS ASSOCIATION GOLDEN GLOBE AWARDS

Picture (Drama): *Scent of a Woman*; Picture (Comedy or Musical): *The Player*; Actor (Drama): Al Pacino (*Scent of a Woman*); Actress (Drama): Emma Thompson (*Howards End*); Actor (Comedy or Musical): Tim Robbins (*The Player*); Actress (Comedy or Musical): Miranda Richardson (*Enchanted April*); Supporting Actor: Gene Hackman (*Unforgiven*); Supporting Actress: Joan Plowright (*Enchanted April*); Director: Clint Eastwood (*Unforgiven*); Screenplay: Bo Goldman (*Scent of a Woman*); Original Score: Alan Menken (*Aladdin*); Original Song: "A Whole New World" from *Aladdin*, music by Alan Menken, lyrics by Tim Rice; Foreign Film: *Indochine*.

SPECIAL AWARDS

Robin Williams for his voice-over work in

Aladdin; Lauren Bacall (Cecil B. Demille Award).

Controversy struck the Golden Globes again when accusations of "votes for sale" were hurled at the Hollywood Foreign Press Association. There were allegations in the press that Universal, the studio behind *Scent of a Woman*, paid for the members of the HFPA to fly to New York for the premiere of the film and a group interview with star Al Pacino. The trip occurred very close to the Globe voting. No one could argue that Al Pacino didn't deserve his best Actor GG (after all, he took the Oscar as well). But did this hokey remake of an Italian film about a blind ex-soldier's sojourn to the Big Apple merit the best Picture (Drama) and best Screenplay prizes? No other group bestowed these accolades on *Scent*.

It was later reported in *The New York Times* that thirty-four of the eighty-six members took the trip and it was unclear who paid for what. No one at Universal seemed to remember. Marianne Ruuth, a journalist for *La Figaro* and HFPA member who handled media relations for the group, told the *Times*, "We took the red-eye and went back the next afternoon. That was no luxury junket." Mirjan Van Blaricom, then president of the organization, stated, "What difference does it make if we paid or not? Most of the time we take care of our trips. Sometimes we pay. It depends. The important thing for us is the interview. Who paid for what is irrelevant."

CANNES FILM FESTIVAL

Palme d'Or: *The Best Intentions* (Sweden); Actor: Tim Robbins (*Bob Roberts*); Actress: Pernilla August (*The Best Intentions*); Director: Robert Altman (*The Player*); Forty-Fifth Anniversary Prize: *Howards End*; Special Jury Prize: *Stolen Children* (Italy); Jury Prize: *El Sol del Membrillo* (*The Dream of Light*) (Spain) and *An Independent Life* (Russia); Camera d'Or: *Mac*; Technical Prize: *El Viaje* (Argentina).

ACADEMY AWARDS (OSCARS)

PICTURE
The Fugitive

In the Name of the Father
The Piano
The Remains of the Day
Schindler's List

Finally, it was Steven Spielberg's year, with a high-brow, mature Holocaust drama (*Schindler's List*) and a crowd-pleasing science-fiction/special effects feast (*Jurassic Park*) taking a total of ten Oscars (seven for *Schindler* and three for *Jurassic*).

ACTOR
Daniel Day-Lewis (*In the Name of the Father*)
Laurence Fishburne (*What's Love Got to Do with It?*)
Tom Hanks (*Philadelphia*)
Anthony Hopkins (*The Remains of the Day*)
Liam Neeson (*Schindler's List*)

Tom Hanks gave a disjointed but ultimately moving acceptance speech for his win playing a lawyer with AIDS in *Philadelphia*. He pleaded for tolerance and sympathy for gays, acknowledged his gay high-school drama teacher, and ended by stating "God Bless America."

ACTRESS
Angela Bassett (*What's Love Got to Do with It?*)
Stockard Channing (*Six Degrees of Separation*)
Holly Hunter (*The Piano*)
Emma Thompson (*The Remains of the Day*)
Debra Winger (*Shadowlands*)

This was the first time two nominees for best Actress—Holly Hunter and Emma Thompson—were also nominated for best Supporting Actress. Hunter won for *The Piano* as a mute young bride caught in a romantic triangle in nineteenth- century New Zealand.

SUPPORTING ACTOR
Leonardo DiCaprio (*What's Eating Gilbert Grape?*)
Ralph Fiennes (*Schindler's List*)
Tommy Lee Jones (*The Fugitive*)
John Malkovich (*In the Line of Fire*)
Pete Postlethwaite (*In the Name of the Father*)

Tommy Lee Jones, who had shaved his head for a role, said upon accepting his *Fugitive* Oscar, "At a moment like this, all I can say is I'm not really bald."

SUPPORTING ACTRESS
Holly Hunter (*The Firm*)
Anna Paquin (*The Piano*)
Rosie Perez (*Fearless*)
Winona Ryder (*The Age of Innocence*)
Emma Thompson (*In the Name of the Father*)

At age 11, Anna Paquin was one of the youngest Oscar winners. But the record is still held by Tatum O'Neal, who copped her *Paper Moon* Oscar at age 10.

DIRECTOR
Robert Altman (*Short Cuts*)
Jane Campion (*The Piano*)
James Ivory (*The Remains of the Day*)
Jim Sheridan (*In the Name of the Father*)
Steven Spielberg (*Schindler's List*)

New Zealander Jane Campion is only the second woman to be nominated for best Director. The only other female nominee was Italian Lina Wurtmuller.

ORIGINAL SCREENPLAY
Jane Campion (*The Piano*)
Nora Ephron, David S. Ward, Jeff Arch (screenplay), Jeff Arch (story) (*Sleepless in Seattle*)
Jeff Maguire (*In the Line of Fire*)
Ron Nyswaner (*Philadelphia*)
Gary Ross (*Dave*)

ADAPTED SCREENPLAY
Jay Cocks, Martin Scorsese (*The Age of Innocence*)
Terry George, Jim Sheridan (*In the Name of the Father*)
Ruth Prawer Jhabvala (*The Remains of the Day*)
William Nicholson (*Shadowlands*)
Steve Zaillian (*Schindler's List*)

FOREIGN-LANGUAGE FILM
Belle Epoque (Spain)
Farewell, My Concubine (Hong Kong)
Hedd Wyn (UK)
The Scent of Green Papaya (Vietnam)
The Wedding Banquet (Tawain)

Though from the United Kingdom, *Hedd Wynn* qualified as a foreign-language film because its dialogue was in Welsh.

OTHER AWARDS
Musical Score: John Williams (*Schindler's List*); Original Song: "The Streets of Philadelphia" from *Philadelphia*, music and lyrics by Bruce Springsteen; Cinematography: Janusz Kaminski (*Schindler's List*); Art Direction: Allan Starski, Ewa Braun (*Schindler's List*); Costume Design: Gabriella Pesucci (*The Age of Innocence*); Editing: Michael Kahn (*Schindler's List*); Sound: Gary Summers, Gary Rydstrom, Shawn Murphy, Ron Judkins (*Jurassic Park*); Visual Effects: Dennis Muren, Stan Winston, Phil Tippett, Michael Lantieri (*Jurassic Park*); Sound Effects Editing: Gary Rydstrom, Richard Hymns (*Jurassic Park*); Make-Up: Greg Cannon, Ve Neill, Yolanda Toussieng (*Mrs. Doubtfire*).

Documentary: *I Am a Promise: The Children of the Stanton Elementary School*; Documentary Short Subject: *Defending Our Lives*; Live-Action Short Subject: *Black Rider*; Animated Short Subject: *The Wrong Trousers*.

SPECIAL AWARDS
Deborah Kerr; Paul Newman (Jean Hersholt Humantarian Award).

After four years of hosting Hollywood's biggest night and being called the best ever at the job, Billy Crystal called it quits. Speculation through Tinseltown had it that Crystal was disgruntled with the lack of Oscar recognition for his work in *When Harry Met Sally . . .*, *City Slickers*, and *Mr. Saturday Night*. Whoopi Goldberg took over to become the first woman to solo-host the ceremony. More of a character actress than a stand-up comic, Goldberg was slightly amusing but failed to garner the big-time laughs Crystal had been getting.

NATIONAL BOARD OF REVIEW

English-Language Film: *Schindler's List*; Actor: Anthony Hopkins (*The Remains of the Day* and *Shadowlands*); Actress: Holly Hunter (*The Piano*); Supporting Actor: Leonardo DiCaprio (*What's Eating Gilbert Grape?*); Winona Ryder (*The Age of Innocence*); Director: Martin Scorsese (*The Age of Innocence*); Documentary: *The War Room*.

BEST ENGLISH-LANGUAGE FILMS

Schindler's List, The Age of Innocence, The Remains of the Day, The Piano, Shadowlands, In the Name of the Father, Philadelphia, Much Ado about Nothing, Short Cuts, The Joy Luck Club.

BEST FOREIGN-LANGUAGE FILMS

Farewell, My Concubine (Hong Kong), *El Mariachi* (Mexico), *Un Coeur en Hiver* (France), *The Story of Qiu Ju* (China), *The Accompanist* (France).

NEW YORK FILM CRITICS CIRCLE

Picture: *Schindler's List*; Actor: David Thewlis (*Naked*); Actress: Holly Hunter (*The Piano*); Supporting Actor: Ralph Fiennes (*Schindler's List*); Supporting Actress: Gong Li (*Farewell, My Concubine*); Director: Jane Campion (*The Piano*); Screenplay: Jane Campion (*The Piano*); Cinematography: Janusz Kaminski (*Schindler's List*); Documentary: *Visions of Light: The Art of Cinematography*; Foreign Film: *Farewell, My Concubine*.

Though the New York and Los Angeles critics voted *Schindler's List* best Picture, they gave best Director to Jane Campion in close voting. Steven Spielberg did cop the best Director prize from the National Society of Film Critics. *Schindler* is the first film to win best Picture from all four critics' groups (New York, Los Angeles, National Society, and National Board of Review) as well as the Oscar.

NATIONAL SOCIETY OF FILM CRITICS

Picture: *Schindler's List*; Actor: David Thewlis (*Naked*); Actress: Holly Hunter (*The Piano*); Supporting Actor: Ralph Fiennes (*Schindler's List*); Supporting Actress: Madeleine Stowe (*Short Cuts*); Director: Steven Spielberg (*Schindler's List*); Screenplay: Jane Campion (*The Piano*); Cinematography: Janusz Kaminski (*Schindler's List*); Documentary: *Visions of Light: The Art of Cinematography*; Foreign Film: *The Story of Qiu Ju*; Special Citations: *It's All True* and *Rock Hudson's Home Movies*.

LOS ANGELES FILM CRITICS ASSOCIATION

Picture: *Schindler's List*; Actor: Anthony Hopkins

(*The Remains of the Day* and *Shadowlands*); Actress: Holly Hunter (*The Piano*); Supporting Actor: Tommy Lee Jones (*The Fugitive*); Supporting Actress (tie): Anna Paquin (*The Piano*) and Rosie Perez (*Fearless*); Director: Jane Campion (*The Piano*); Screenplay: Jane Campion (*The Piano*); Cinematography (tie): Janusz Kaminski (*Schindler's List*) and Stuart Dryburgh (*The Piano*); Music: Zbigniew Preisner (*Blue, The Secret Garden,* and *Olivier, Olivier*); Production Design: Allan Starski (*Schindler's List*); Documentary: *It's All True*; Foreign Film: *Farewell, My Concubine*; Animated Film: *The Mighty River*; Independent/Experimental Film: *Silverlake Life: The View from Here*; Career Achievement: cinematographer John Alton; New Generation Award: Leonardo DiCaprio for performances in *This Boy's Life* and *What's Eating Gilbert Grape?*

HOLLYWOOD FOREIGN PRESS ASSOCIATION GOLDEN GLOBE AWARDS

Picture (Drama): *Schindler's List*; Picture (Comedy or Musical): *Mrs. Doubtfire*; Actor (Drama): Tom Hanks (*Philadelphia*); Actress (Drama): Holly Hunter (*The Piano*); Actor (Comedy or Musical): Robin Williams (*Mrs. Doubtfire*); Actress (Comedy or Musical): Angela Bassett (*What's Love Got to Do with It?*); Supporting Actor: Tommy Lee Jones (*The Fugitive*); Supporting Actress: Winona Ryder (*The Age of Innocence*); Director: Steven Spielberg (*Schindler's List*); Screenplay: Steven Zillian (*Schindler's List*); Original Score: Kitaro (*Heaven and Earth*); Original Song: "Streets of Philadelphia" from *Philadelphia*, music and lyrics by Bruce Springsteen; Foreign Film: *Farewell, My Concubine*.

SPECIAL AWARDS

The cast of *Short Cuts*; Robert Redford (Cecil B. DeMille Award).

CANNES FILM FESTIVAL

Palme d'Or: *The Piano* (Australia) and *Farewell, My Concubine* (Hong Kong); Actor: David Thewlis (*Naked*) (UK); Actress: Holly Hunter (*The Piano*); Director: Mike Leigh (*Naked*); Special Jury Prize: *Faraway, So Close* (Germany); Jury Prize: *The*

Puppetmaster (Taiwan); Palme d'Or (Short Film): *Coffee and Cigarettes (Somewhere in California)* (USA); Camera d'Or: *The Scent of Green Papaya* (Vietnam), special mention to *Friends* (UK/France); Technical Prize: *Mazeppa* (France), special mention to the short *The Singing Trophy* (New Zealand); International Critics Prize: in competition, *Farewell, My Concubine*, out of competition, *Child Murders* (Hungary) and the short *The Debt* (USA).

Note: In addition to being the second woman nominated for a best Director Oscar, Jane Campion was the first woman to win the Palme d'Or at Cannes.

1994

ACADEMY AWARDS (OSCARS)

PICTURE
Forrest Gump
Four Weddings and a Funeral
Pulp Fiction
Quiz Show
The Shawshank Redemption

There was no clear favorite going into the 1994 Oscars. The critics had split between *Quiz Show* (New York), *Pulp Fiction* (National Society and Los Angeles), and *Forrest Gump* (tied for first place with *Pulp* in the National Board of Review running).

But as tabulation time drew near, *Forrest Gump* appeared to have the edge. It won the Golden Globe (an increasingly likely indicator of Oscar's choice). Also Hollywood was reeling from accusations by politicians of producing degrading and immoral films. By giving the Oscar to a warm-hearted story of a simple-minded hero who triumphs in the face of radical excesses in American society (*Gump*) instead of a nihilistic black comedy of violence, drugs, and crime (*Pulp*), the film community could say, "Look, we've got family values, too."

ACTOR
Morgan Freeman (*The Shawshank Redemption*)
Tom Hanks (*Forrest Gump*)
Nigel Hawthorne (*The Madness of King George*)

Paul Newman (*Nobody's Fool*)
John Travolta (*Pulp Fiction*)

With his triumphs for playing a lawyer with AIDS in 1993's *Philadelphia* and the endearing, mentally challenged *Forrest Gump*, Tom Hanks became the second person in Oscar history to win two consecutive awards for best Actor. The only other performer to duplicate this feat was Spencer Tracy for *Captains Courageous* (1937) and *Boys Town* (1938).

Actors who took home Oscar twice in a row in other categories include leading actresses Luise Rainer and Katharine Hepburn and supporting actor Jason Robards, Jr.

ACTRESS
Jodie Foster (*Nell*)
Jessica Lange (*Blue Sky*)
Miranda Richardson (*Tom and Viv*)
Winona Ryder (*Little Women*)
Susan Sarandon (*The Client*)

Jessica Lange was the expected winner, but her film *Blue Sky* was anything but a Hollywood mainstreamer. Made in 1991, it sat in a bank vault for three years when its studio Orion ran into financial difficulties. The director Tony Richardson died of AIDS soon after the film was completed, and when it was finally released, it only played for a few weeks. Lange's win in a little-seen, three-year-old movie indicated the lack of solid cinematic roles for women.

SUPPORTING ACTOR
Samuel L. Jackson (*Pulp Fiction*)
Martin Landau (*Ed Wood*)
Chazz Palminteri (*Bullets over Broadway*)
Paul Scofield (*Quiz Show*)
Gary Sinise (*Forrest Gump*)

SUPPORTING ACTRESS
Rosemary Harris (*Tom and Viv*)
Helen Mirren (*The Madness of King George*)
Uma Thurman (*Pulp Fiction*)
Jennifer Tilly (*Bullets over Broadway*)
Dianne Wiest (*Bullets over Broadway*)

DIRECTOR
Woody Allen (*Bullets over Broadway*)
Krzysztof Kieslowski (*Red*)

Robert Redford (*Quiz Show*)
Quentin Tarantino (*Pulp Fiction*)
Robert Zemeckis (*Forrest Gump*)

ORIGINAL SCREENPLAY
Woody Allen, Douglas McGrath
   (*Bullets over Broadway*)
Richard Curtis (*Four Weddings and a Funeral*)
Krzystof Piesiewicz, Krzysztof Kieslowski (*Red*)
Quentin Tarantino, Roger Avary (*Pulp Fiction*)
Frances Walsh, Peter Jackson (*Heavenly Creatures*)

ADAPTED SCREENPLAY
Paul Attanasio (*Quiz Show*)
Alan Bennett (*The Madness of King George*)
Robert Benton (*Nobody's Fool*)
Frank Darabont (*The Shawshank Redemption*)
Eric Roth (*Forrest Gump*)

FOREIGN-LANGUAGE FILM
Before the Rain (Macedonia)
Burnt by the Sun (Russia)
Eat Drink Man Woman (Taiwan)
Farinelli: Il Castrato (Belgium)
Strawberry and Chocolate (Cuba)

OTHER AWARDS
Musical Score: Hans Zimmer (*The Lion King*);
Original Song: "Can You Feel the Love Tonight?"
from *The Lion King*, music by Elton John, lyrics
by Tim Rice; Cinematography: John Toll (*Legends
of the Fall*); Art Direction: Ken Adam, Carolyn
Scott (*The Madness of King George*); Costume
Design: Lizzy Gardiner, Tim Chappel (*The
Adventures of Priscilla, Queen of the Desert*); Film
Editing: Arthur Schmidt (*Forest Gump*); Sound:
Gregg Landaker, Steve Maslow, Bob Beemer,
David R. B. MacMillan (*Speed*); Visual Effects:
Ken Ralston, George Murphy, Stephen
Rosenbaum, Allen Hall (*Forrest Gump*); Sound
Effects Editing: Stephen Hunter Flick (*Speed*);
Make-Up: Rick Baker, Ve Neill, Yolanda Toussieng
(*Ed Wood*).
   Documentary Feature: *Maya Lin: A Strong Clear
Vision*; Documentary Short Subject: *A Time for
Justice*; Live-Action Short Subject (tie): *Franz
Kafka's It's a Wonderful Life* and *Trevor*; Animated
Short Subject: *Bob's Birthday*.

SPECIAL AWARDS
Michelangelo Antonioni; Quincy Jones (Jean
Hearsholt Humantarian Award); Clint Eastwood
(Irving Thalberg Award).

Late-night talk-show wiseguy David Letterman
hosted the 1994 Academy Awards, inheriting the
position from his mentor Johnny Carson. Unfortunately, Letterman's edgy humor just didn't cut it
with the Oscar crowd. Taped segments, including
Dave interviewing New York cab drivers on the
current crop of nominees, went over well. But the
Letterman patter introducing presenters and a limp
opening monologue were not on the Oscar Top
Ten List.
   Most striking fashion statement: Winning costume designer Lizzie Gardiner in a dress made of
American Express gold cards.
   Major controversy of the year: *Hoop Dreams*, a
cinema vérité documentary of two NBA hopefuls,
wound up on almost every critic's Ten Best List,
but failed to garner a nomination for best
Documentary. This oversight led to a complete re-
examination of the Documentary Committee and
its nominating procedures.

NATIONAL BOARD OF REVIEW

English-Language Film (tie): *Forrest Gump* and
Pulp Fiction; Actor: Tom Hanks (*Forrest Gump*);
Actress: Miranda Richardson (*Tom and Viv*);
Supporting Actor: Gary Sinise (*Forrest Gump*);
Supporting Actress: Rosemary Harris (*Tom and
Viv*); Director: Quentin Tarantino (*Pulp Fiction*);
Documentary: *Hoop Dreams*; Family Film: *The
Lion King*; TV Movie: *The Last Seduction*; Special
Award for Ensemble Acting: *Ready-to-Wear*.

BEST ENGLISH-LANGUAGE FILMS:
Forrest Gump and *Pulp Fiction* (tie for first place),
*Quiz Show, Four Weddings and a Funeral, Bullets
over Broadway, Ed Wood, The Shawshank
Redemption, Nobody's Fool, The Madness of King
George, Tom & Viv, Heavenly Creatures.*

BEST FOREIGN-LANGUAGE FILMS
Eat Drink Man Woman (Tawain), *To Live* (Hong
Kong/China), *Strawberry and Chocolate* (Cuba),
Red (France), *Queen Margot* (France).

NEW YORK FILM CRITICS CIRCLE

Picture: *Quiz Show*; Actor: Paul Newman (*Nobody's Fool*); Actress: Linda Fiorentino (*The Last Seduction*); Supporting Actor: Martin Landau (*Ed Wood*); Supporting Actress: Dianne Wiest (*Bullets over Broadway*); Director: Quentin Tarantino (*Pulp Fiction*); Screenplay: Quentin Tarantino, Roger Avary (*Pulp Fiction*); Cinematography: Stefan Czapsky (*Ed Wood*); Documentary: *Hoop Dreams*; Foreign Film: *Red*; New Director: Darnell Martin (*I Like It Like That*); Special Award: Jean-Luc Godard.

Robert Redford left his Sundance Film Festival in order to attend the NYFCC dinner and pick up the best Picture prize for *Quiz Show*, which he directed and co-produced. The lure? The award was being presented by Paul Newman, his co-star in *Butch Cassidy and the Sundance Kid* and *The Sting*. Redford returned the favor by presenting Newman with the best Actor award for *Nobody's Fool*.

Linda Fiorentinto was not nominated for an Oscar because her film *The Last Seduction* was originally made for cable television.

NATIONAL SOCIETY OF FILM CRITICS

Picture: *Pulp Fiction*; Actor: Paul Newman (*Nobody's Fool*); Actress: Jennifer Jason Leigh (*Mrs. Parker and the Vicious Circle*); Supporting Actor: Martin Landau (*Ed Wood*); Supporting Actress: Dianne Wiest (*Bullets over Broadway*); Director: Quentin Tarantino (*Pulp Fiction*); Screenplay: Quentin Tarantino, Roger Avary (*Pulp Fiction*); Cinematography: Stefan Czapsky (*Ed Wood*); Documentary: *Hoop Dreams*; Foreign Film: *Red*; Special Citation: *Satantango* (Hungary), *The Pharoah's Belt*.

Samuel L. Jackson, the philosophisizing hit man of *Pulp Fiction*, was a runner-up in both the Leading Actor and Supporting Actor categories in the National Society voting.

LOS ANGELES FILM CRITICS ASSOCIATION

Picture: *Pulp Fiction*; Actor: John Travolta (*Pulp Fiction*); Actress: Jessica Lange (*Blue Sky*); Supporting Actor: Martin Landau (*Ed Wood*); Supporting Actress: Dianne Wiest (*Bullets over Broadway*); Director: Quentin Tarantino (*Pulp Fiction*); Screenplay: Quentin Tarantino, Roger Avary (*Pulp Fiction*); Cinematography: Stefan Czapsky (*Ed Wood*); Music: Howard Shore (*Ed Wood*); Foreign Film: *Red*; Documentary: *Hoop Dreams*; Animated Film: *The Lion King*; Independent/Experimental Film: *Rememberance of Things Fast*; Career Achievement: Billy Wilder; Special Achievement for Film Criticism: Pauline Kael; New Generation Award: John Dahl (*Red Rock West* and *The Last Seduction*).

HOLLYWOOD FOREIGN PRESS ASSOCIATION GOLDEN GLOBE AWARDS

Picture (Drama): *Forrest Gump*; Picture (Comedy or Musical): *The Lion King*; Actor (Drama): Tom Hanks (*Forrest Gump*); Actress (Drama): Jessica Lange (*Blue Sky*); Actor (Comedy or Musical): Hugh Grant (*Four Weddings and a Funeral*); Actress (Comedy or Musical): Jamie Lee Curtis (*True Lies*); Supporting Actor: Martin Landau (*Ed Wood*); Supporting Actress: Dianne Wiest (*Bullets over Broadway*); Director: Robert Zemeckis (*Forrest Gump*); Screenplay: Quentin Tarantino, Roger Avary (*Pulp Fiction*); Original Score: Hans Zimmer (*The Lion King*); Original Song: "Can You Feel the Love Tonight?" from *The Lion King*, music by Elton John, lyrics by Tim Rice; Foreign Film: *Farinelli*.

SPECIAL AWARD
Sophia Loren (Cecil B. DeMille Award).

CANNES FILM FESTIVAL

Palme d'Or: *Pulp Fiction*; Actor: Ge You (*To Live*) (Hong Kong/China); Actress: Virna Lisi (*Queen Margot*) (France); Director: Nanni Moretti [*Caro Diario (Dear Diary)*]; Screenplay: Michael Blanc (*Dead Tired*) (France); Special Jury Prize: *Burnt by the Sun* (Russia), *To Live*; Jury Prize: *Queen Margot*; Camera d'Or: *Coming to Terms with the Dead* (France), special mention to *The Silences of the Palace* (Tunisia/France); Technical Prize: special effects director Pitof for *Dead Tired*; International Critics Prize: in competition, *Exotica* (Canada), out of competition, *Bab El-Oued City* (Algeria).

ACADEMY AWARDS (OSCARS)

PICTURE
Apollo 13
Babe
Braveheart
The Postman (*Il Postino*)
Sense and Sensibility

"Now that I'm a bona fide director with a golden boy," said Mel Gibson looking at his Oscar for helming the medieval-action epic *Braveheart*, "I suppose, like most directors, what I really want to do is act." Gibson joined Warren Beatty, Robert Redford, and Clint Eastwood as actors who did not win Oscars until they started directing.

There was no one film dominating the 1995 Oscars. The best Picture *Braveheart* won a total of four awards and the other major categories were split among *Leaving Las Vegas*, *Dead Man Walking*, *Mighty Aphrodite*, *The Usual Suspects*, and *Sense and Sensibility*.

ACTOR
Nicolas Cage (*Leaving Las Vegas*)
Richard Dreyfuss (*Mr. Holland's Opus*)
Anthony Hopkins (*Nixon*)
Sean Penn (*Dead Man Walking*)
Massimo Troisi (*The Postman*)

ACTRESS
Susan Sarandon (*Dead Man Walking*)
Elizabeth Shue (*Leaving Las Vegas*)
Sharon Stone (*Casino*)
Meryl Streep (*The Bridges of Madison County*)
Emma Thompson (*Sense and Sensibility*)

SUPPORTING ACTOR
James Cromwell (*Babe*)
Ed Harris (*Apollo 13*)
Brad Pitt (*12 Monkeys*)

Tim Roth (*Rob Roy*)
Kevin Spacey (*The Usual Suspects*)

SUPPORTING ACTRESS
Joan Allen (*Nixon*)
Kathleen Quinlan (*Apollo 13*)
Mira Sorvino (*Mighty Aphrodite*)
Mare Winningham (*Georgia*)
Kate Winslet (*Sense and Sensibility*)

DIRECTOR
Mike Figgis (*Leaving Las Vegas*)
Mel Gibson (*Braveheart*)
Chris Noonan (*Babe*)
Michael Radford (*The Postman*)
Tim Robbins (*Dead Man Walking*)

ORIGINAL SCREENPLAY
Woody Allen (*Mighty Aphrodite*)
Christopher McQuarrie (*The Usual Suspects*)
Stephen J. Rivele, Christopher Wilkinson, Oliver Stone (*Nixon*)
Randall Wallace (*Braveheart*)
Joss Whedon, Andrew Stanton, Joel Cohen, Alec Sokolow; John Lasseter, Peter Docter, Andrew Stanton, Joe Ranft (story) (*Toy Story*)

ADAPTED SCREENPLAY
William Broyles, Jr., Al Reinert (*Apollo 13*)
George Miller, Chris Noonan (*Babe*)
Mike Figgis (*Leaving Las Vegas*)
Anna Pavignano, Michael Radford, Furio Scarpelli, Giacomo Scarpelli, Massimo Troisi (*The Postman*)
Emma Thompson (*Sense and Sensibility*)

FOREIGN-LANGUAGE FILM
All Things Fair (Sweden)
Antonia's Line (The Netherlands)
Dust of Life (Algeria)
O Quatrilho (Brazil)
The Star Maker (Italy)

OTHER AWARDS
Original Dramatic Score: Luis Bacalov (*The Postman*); Original Musical or Comedy Score: Alan Menken, Stephen Schwartz (*Pocahontas*); Original Song: "Colors of the Wind" from

Pocahontas, music by Alan Menken, lyrics by Stephen Schwartz; Cinematography: John Toll (*Braveheart*); Art Direction: Eugenio Zanetti (*Restoration*); Costume Design: James Acheson (*Restoration*); Film Editing: Mike Hill, Dan Hanley (*Apollo 13*); Sound: Rick Dior, Steve Pederson, Scott Millan, David MacMillan (*Apollo 13*); Sound Effects Editing: Lon Beder, Pat Halberg (*Braveheart*); Visual Effects: Scott Anderson, Charles Gibson, Neal Scanlan, John Cox (*Babe*); Make-Up: Peter Frampton, Paul Pattison, Lois Burwell (*Braveheart*).

Documentary: *Anne Frank Remembered*; Documentary Short Subject: *One Survivor Remembers*; Live-Action Short Subject: *Lieberman in Love*; Animated Short Subject: *A Close Shave*.

SPECIAL AWARDS

Kirk Douglas; animated cartoon director Chuck Jones; John Lasseter for his direction of *Toy Story*.

Less than enthused with David Letterman's poor showing as the previous year's host, Oscar producer Quincy Jones asked Whoopi Goldberg back to emcee the show. "Did you miss me?" were her first words to the Academy audience. Evidently they did, receiving Goldberg and her sharp barbs much more warmly than those of Letterman. The comedienne took aim at everyone including the Rev. Jesse Jackson, who had criticized the awards ceremony for only nominating one black person. The Reverend advised African-Americans not to view the show. In the middle of her monologue, Goldberg quipped, "I had something to say to Jesse right here, but he's not watching, so why bother?"

Jones also spiced things up with several clever production ideas. Among the producer's innovations were having the percussion-dance group Stomp perform a number in rhythm to short film clips to introduce the sound effects award. The Oscar for costume design was preceded by a fashion show featuring a clutch of gorgeous supermodels, both male and female.

The best ad-lib of the night was delivered by presenter Sharon Stone. When the envelope containing the winner's name in her catogory was missing, she said to the audience, "All right, let's all have a psychic moment." The emotional high point came when Christopher Reeve, recently paralyzed in a riding accident, introduced a series of scenes from movies with social messages.

The event was ranked as the second most watched program of the year. (The Super Bowl was first.) Despite this, there was a seven percent drop in veiwership from the previous year. Among the causes cited for the decline were a glut of pre-Oscar award shows (including the Golden Globes, the Screen Actors Guild Awards, the Blockbuster Entertainment Awards, and the People's Choice) and the lack of Letterman. Despite his much disparaged performance, Letterman brought along his young audience, who failed to watch this year.

NATIONAL BOARD OF REVIEW

English-Language Film: *Sense and Sensibility*; Actor: Nicolas Cage (*Leaving Las Vegas*); Actress: Emma Thompson (*Sense and Sensibility* and *Carrington*); Supporting Actor: Kevin Spacey (*Seven* and *The Usual Suspects*); Supporting Actress: Mira Sorvino (*Mighty Aphrodite*); Director: Ang Lee (*Sense and Sensibility*); Breakthrough Performer: Alicia Silverstone (*Clueless*); Foreign Film: *Shanghai Triad*; Documentary: *Crumb*.

SPECIAL AWARDS

Zhang Yimou (Freedom of Expression Award); James Earl Jones, Mel Gibson (Career Achievement); Stanley Donen (Billy Wilder Award); cast of *The Usual Suspects* (ensemble acting).

BEST ENGLISH-LANGUAGE FILMS

Sense and Sensibility, Apollo 13, Carrington, Leaving Las Vegas, The American President, Mighty Aphrodite, Smoke, Persuasion, Braveheart, The Usual Suspects.

BEST FOREIGN-LANGUAGE FILMS

Shanghai Triad (Hong Kong/China); *Les Miserables* (France); *The Postman* (*Il Postino*) (Italy); *Farinelli* (Belgium); *Lamerica* (Italy).

NEW YORK FILM CRITICS CIRCLE

Picture: *Leaving Las Vegas*; Actor: Nicolas Cage (*Leaving Las Vegas*); Actress: Jenifer Jason Leigh (*Georgia*); Supporting Actor: Kevin Spacey

(*Outbreak, Seven, Swimming with Sharks,* and *The Usual Suspects*); Supporting Actress: Mira Sorvino (*Mighty Aphrodite*); Director: Ang Lee (*Sense and Sensibility*); Screenplay: Emma Thompson (*Sense and Sensibility*); Cinematography: Lu Yue (*Shanghai Triad*); Foreign Film: *Wild Reeds*; Documentary: *Crumb*; First Feature: *Babe*; Special Award: Fabiano Canosa, head of the film program at the Joseph Papp Public Theater.

Winners braved a snowstorm in order to collect their prizes from the NYFCC. The only recipient not present was Best Actress Jenifer Jason Leigh, who couldn't get a flight into snowbound Manhattan from her location shoot.

NATIONAL SOCIETY OF FILM CRITICS

Picture: *Babe*; Actor: Nicolas Cage (*Leaving Las Vegas*); Actress: Elizabeth Shue (*Leaving Las Vegas*); Supporting Actor: Don Cheadle (*Devil in a Blue Dress*); Supporting Actress: Joan Allen (*Nixon*); Director: Mike Figgis (*Leaving Las Vegas*); Screenplay: Amy Heckerling (*Clueless*); Cinematography: Tak Fujimoto (*Devil in a Blue Dress*); Foreign-Language Film: *Wild Reeds*; Documentary: *Crumb*; Experimental Film: *Latcho Drom*; Special Archival Award: *I Am Cuba.*

Babe, the Australian family feature about a plucky talking pig, was the surprise Best Picture winner for the usually highbrow National Society of Film Critics.

LOS ANGELES FILM CRITICS ASSOCIATION

Picture: *Leaving Las Vegas*; Actor: Nicolas Cage (*Leaving Las Vegas*); Actress: Elizabeth Shue (*Leaving Las Vegas*); Supporting Actor: Don Cheadle (*Devil in a Blue Dress*); Supporting Actress: Joan Allen (*Nixon*); Director: Mike Figgis (*Leaving Las Vegas*); Screenplay: Emma Thompson (*Sense and Sensibility*); Cinematography: Lu Yue (*Shanghai Triad*); Production Design: Bo Welch (*A Little Princess*); Musical Score: Patrick Doyle (*A Little Princess*); Foreign Film: *Wild Reeds*; Animated Film: *Toy Story*; Documentary: *Crumb*; New Generation Award: Alfonso Cuaron (*A Little Princess*); Career Achievement Award: Andre de Toth; Independent/Experimental Film/Video Award: *From the Journals of Jean Seberg.*

HOLLYWOOD FOREIGN PRESS ASSOCIATION GOLDEN GLOBE AWARDS

Film (Drama): *Sense and Sensibility*; Film (Comedy or Musical): *Babe*; Actor (Drama): Nicolas Cage (*Leaving Las Vegas*); Actress (Drama): Sharon Stone (*Casino*); Actor (Comedy or Musical): John Travolta (*Get Shorty*); Actress (Comedy or Musical): Nicole Kidman (*To Die For*); Supporting Actor: Brad Pitt (*12 Monkeys*); Supporting Actress: Mira Sorvino (*Mighty Aphrodite*); Director: Mel Gibson (*Braveheart*); Screenplay: Emma Thompson (*Sense and Sensibility*); Musical Score: Maurice Jarre (*A Walk in the Clouds*); Original Song: "Colors of the Wind" from *Pocahontas*, music by Alan Menken, lyrics by Stephen Schwartz; Foreign-Language Film: *Les Miserables* (France); Cecil B. DeMille Award: Sean Connery.

As a sign of their growing respectability, the Golden Globes switched from years of airing on cable, in syndication, and late-night network berths to a prime-time spot on its former home NBC. Presented just as Academy voters are filling out their ballots, the GGs have become a fairly accurate predictor of the Oscars.

Emma Thompson delivered the cleverest acceptance speech of the evening by reading an account of the ceremony as Jane Austen, the nineteenth-century author of the novel on which Thompson's *Sense and Sensibilty* was based, might have written it had she been there.

CANNES FILM FESTIVAL

Palme d'Or: *Underground* (Bosnia); Actor: Jonathan Pryce (*Carrington*); Actress: Helen Mirren (*The Madness of King George*); Director: Mathieu Kassovitz (*Hate*) (France); Screenplay: Christopher Hampton (*Carrington*); Special Jury Prize: *Ulysses' Gaze* (Greece); Jury Prize: *Don't Forget You're Going to Die* (Iran); Camera d'Or: *The White Balloon* (Iran); Technical Prize: *Shanghai Triad* (Hong Kong), mention to *Denise Calls Up* (USA); International Critics Prize: in competition, *Land*

and Freedom (UK), *Ulysses' Gaze*, out of competition, *The White Balloon*.

ACADEMY AWARDS (OSCARS)

PICTURE
The English Patient
Fargo
Jerry Maguire
Secrets and Lies
Shine

It was Independents Day at the Oscars. Four out of the five nominees for best Picture were made by small, independent studios; only *Jerry Maguire* was from Hollywood. *The English Patient*, Oscar's favorite type of film—a huge epic with a British accent—took nine awards, tying it with *Gigi* and *The Last Emperor* as the third most awarded film ever. "Thank goodness there wasn't a song in *The English Patient*," quipped Andrew Lloyd Webber, who won an Original Song Oscar for "You Must Love Me," a new tune added to the film adaptation of *Evita*.

ACTOR
Tom Cruise (*Jerry Maguire*)
Ralph Fiennes (*The English Patient*)
Woody Harrelson (*The People vs. Larry Flynt*)
Geoffrey Rush (*Shine*)
Billy Bob Thornton (*Sling Blade*)

ACTRESS
Brenda Blethyn (*Secrets and Lies*)
Diane Keaton (*Marvin's Room*)
Frances McDormand (*Fargo*)
Kristin Scott Thomas (*The English Patient*)
Emily Watson (*Breaking the Waves*)

SUPPORTING ACTOR
Cuba Gooding, Jr. (*Jerry Maguire*)
William H. Macy (*Fargo*)
Armin Mueller-Stahl (*Shine*)
Edward Norton (*Primal Fear*)
James Woods (*Ghosts of Mississippi*)

SUPPORTING ACTRESS
Joan Allen (*The Crucible*)
Lauren Bacall (*The Mirror Has Two Faces*)
Juliette Binoche (*The English Patient*)
Barbara Hershey (*The Portrait of a Lady*)
Marianne Jean-Baptiste (*Secrets and Lies*)

Veteran Lauren Bacall was the expected winner. She had taken the Golden Globe for her performance as Barbra Streisand's mother in *The Mirror Has Two Faces*. But the award went to Juliette Binoche as the sympathetic nurse of the title charcter in *The English Patient*. "I thought Lauren was going to get it, and I think she deserved it," Binoche said. The camera caught Bacall frowning and then quickly smiling as the winner praised her.

DIRECTOR
Joel Coen (*Fargo*)
Milos Forman (*The People vs. Larry Flynt*)
Scott Hicks (*Shine*)
Mike Leigh (*Secrets and Lies*)
Anthony Minghella (*The English Patient*)

ORIGINAL SCREENPLAY
Ethan and **Joel Coen** (*Fargo*)
Cameron Crowe (*Jerry Maguire*)
Mike Leigh (*Secrets and Lies*)
Jan Sardi (screenplay), Scott Hicks (story) (*Shine*)
John Sayles (*Lone Star*)

ADAPTED SCREENPLAY
Kenneth Branagh (*Hamlet*)
John Hodge (*Trainspotting*)
Arthur Miller (*The Crucible*)
Anthony Minghella (*The English Patient*)
Billy Bob Thornton (*Sling Blade*)

FOREIGN-LANGUAGE FILM
A Chef in Love (Georgia)
Kolya (Czech Republic)
The Other Side of Sunday (Norway)
Prisoner of the Mountains Russia)
Ridicule (France)

OTHER AWARDS
Musical Score (Dramatic): Gabriel Yared (*The English Patient*); Musical Score (Musical or Comedy): Rachel Portman (*Emma*); Original

Song: "You Must Love Me" from *Evita*, music by Andrew Lloyd Webber, lyrics by Tim Rice; Cinematography: John Seale (*The English Patient*); Art Direction: Stuart Craig, Stephanie McMillan (*The English Patient*); Costume Design: Ann Roth (*The English Patient*); Editing: Walter Murch (*The English Patient*); Sound: Walter Murch, Mark Berger, David Parker, Chris Newman (*The English Patient*); Visual Effects: Volker Engel, Douglas Smith, Clay Pinney, Joseph Viskocil (*Twister*); Sound Effects Editing: Bruce Stambler (*The Ghost and the Machine*); Make-Up: Rick Baker, David Leroy Anderson (*The Nutty Professor*).

Documentary: *When We Were Kings*; Documentary Short Subject: *Breathing Lessons: The Life and Work of Mark O'Brien*; Live-Action Short Subject: *Dear Diary*; Animated Short Subject: *Quest*.

"Who are you people?" host Billy Crystal asked. Many of the nominees were in small and foreign films including Geoffrey Rush in the Australian feature *Shine*, based on the life of a musician troubled by mental illness, Frances McDormand as a pregnant and perky police officer in the Coen brothers' black comedy *Fargo*, and Brenda Blethyn and Marianne Jean-Baptiste in Mike Leigh's British drama *Secrets and Lies*.

Crystal returned to hosting the event after a three-year absence. In addition to his traditional musical medley mocking the Best Picture nominees, the comedian starred in a satiric compilation of clips from the top films. Emotional moments included an aged Muhammad Ali and George Foreman mounting the stage when a movie based on their 1974 title bout *When We Were Kings* won for best Documentary, and a performance of "Flight of the Bumblebee" by concert pianist David Helfgott (the subject of *Shine*).

Grammy winner Celine Dion pulled double duty. She was scheduled to warble Best Song nominee "Because You Loved Me" from *Up Close and Personal*. But Natalie Cole, who was slated to croon "I Finally Found Someone" from Barbra Streisand's *The Mirror Has Two Faces*, was sick. So Dion stood in for Cole in addition to singing her own song. Ironically, Streisand was in the audience but had refused to perform the song she co-wrote. The star was evidently displeased her film had not received more nominations.

NATIONAL BOARD OF REVIEW

English-Language Film: *Shine*; Actor: Tom Cruise (*Jerry Maguire*); Actress: Frances McDormand (*Fargo*); Supporting Actor: Edward Norton (*Everyone Says I Love You, The People vs. Larry Flynt,* and *Primal Fear*); Supporting Actress (tie): Juliette Binoche and Kristin Scott-Thomas (*The English Patient*); Director: Joel Coen (*Fargo*); Breakthrough Performer: Renee Zellweger (*Jerry Maguire*); Foreign-Language Film: *Ridicule* (France); Documentary: *Wild Bill.*

SPECIAL AWARDS

Billy Bob Thornton (achievement in filmmaking); Gena Rowlands (career achievement); *The First Wives Club* (ensemble performance).

BEST ENGLISH-LANGUAGE FILMS

Shine, The English Patient, Fargo, Secrets and Lies, Everyone Says I Love You, Evita, Sling Blade, Trainspotting, The People vs. Larry Flynt, Breaking the Waves, Jerry Maguire.

BEST FOREIGN-LANGUAGE FILMS

Ridicule (France), *Les Voleurs* (France), *Bitter Sugar* (Cuba), *La Ceremonie* (France), *Kolya* (Czech Republic).

NEW YORK FILM CRITICS CIRCLE

Picture: *Fargo*; Actor: Geoffrey Rush (*Shine*); Actress: Emily Watson (*Breaking the Waves*); Supporting Actor: Harry Belafonte (*Kansas City*); Supporting Actress: Courtney Love (*The People vs. Larry Flynt*); Director: Lars Von Trier (*Breaking the Waves*); Screenplay: Albert Brooks, Monica Johnson (*Mother*); Cinematography: Robby Muller (*Breaking the Waves* and *Dead Man*); Foreign Film: *White Balloon* (Iran); Documentary: *When We Were Kings*); First Film: *Big Night.*

SPECIAL AWARDS

Jonas Mekas, president of the Anthology Film Archives; *Vertigo* (distinguished reissue).

NATIONAL SOCIETY OF FILM CRITICS

Picture: *Breaking the Waves*; Actor: Eddie Murphy

(*The Nutty Professor*); Actress: Emily Watson (*Breaking the Waves*); Supporting Actor: Martin Donovan (*The Portrait of a Lady*); Supporting Actress: Barbara Hershey (*The Portrait of a Lady*); Director: Lars von Trier (*Breaking the Waves*); Screenplay: Albert Brooks, Monica Johnson (*Mother*); Cinematography: Robby Muller (*Breaking the Waves*); Foreign-Language Film: *La Ceremonie*; Documentary: *When We Were Kings*; Special Award: James Katz, Robert Harris, for their restoration of *Vertigo*.

LOS ANGELES FILM CRITICS ASSOCIATION

Picture: *Secrets and Lies*; Actor: Geoffrey Rush (*Shine*); Actress: Brenda Blethyn (*Secrets and Lies*); Supporting Actor: Edward Norton (*Everyone Says I Love You, The People vs. Larry Flynt,* and *Primal Fear*); Supporting Actress: Barbara Hershey (*The Portrait of a Lady*); Director: Mike Leigh (*Secrets and Lies*); Screenplay: Ethan and Joel Coen (*Fargo*); Cinematography (tie): Chris Menges (*Michael Collins*) and John Seale (*The English Patient*); Production Design (tie): Brian Morris (*Evita*) and Janet Patterson (*The Portrait of a Lady*); Musical Score: Hal Willner, The Hey Hey Club Musicians (*Kansas City*); New Generation Award: Emily Watson (*Breaking the Waves*); Foreign Film: *La Cermonie* (France); Documentary: *When We Were Kings*; Independent/Experimental Film/Video: *Sonic Outlaws*; Career Achievement Award: Roger Corman; Special Award: animator Nick Park.

HOLLYWOOD FOREIGN PRESS ASSOCIATION GOLDEN GLOBE AWARDS

Picture (Drama): *The English Patient*; Picture (Comedy or Musical): *Evita*; Actor (Drama): Geoffrey Rush (*Shine*); Actress (Drama): Brenda Blethyn (*Secrets and Lies*); Actor (Comedy or Musical): Tom Cruise (*Jerry Maguire*); Actress (Comedy or Musical): Madonna (*Evita*); Supporting Actor: Edward Norton (*Primal Fear*); Supporting Actress: Lauren Bacall (*The Mirror Has Two Faces*); Director: Milos Foreman (*The People vs. Larry Flynt*); Screenplay: Scott Alexander, Larry Karaszewski (*The People vs. Larry Flynt*); Score: Gabriel Yared (*The English Patient*); Original Song: "You Must Love Me" from *Evita*, music by Andrew Lloyd Webber, lyrics by Tim Rice; Foreign-Language Film: *Kolya* (Czech Republic).

SPECIAL AWARD

Dustin Hoffman (Cecil B. DeMille Award).

CANNES FILM FESTIVAL

Palme d'Or: *Secrets and Lies* (UK); Grand Prize: *Breaking the Waves* (Denmark); Actors: Pascal Duquenne, Daniel Auteuil (*Eighth Day*) (France); Actress: Brenda Blethyn (*Secrets and Lies*); Director: Joel Coen (*Fargo*); Screenplay: Alain le Henry (*A Self-Made Man*); Special Jury Prize: *Crash* (Canada); Camera d'Or for Film Debut: Shirley Barrett (*Love Serenade*) (Australia); Technique: *Microcosmos* (France); Palme d'Or for Short Film: *The Wind* (Hungary); Special Jury Prize for Short Film: *Small Deaths* (UK).

1997

CANNES FILM FESTIVAL

Palme d'Or (tie): *Unagi* (*The Eel*) (Japan) and *Ta'm E Guilass* (*The Taste of Cherry*) (Iran); Grand Prix and International Critics' Prize: *The Sweet Hereafter* (Canada); Actor: Sean Penn (*She's So Lovely*) (US); Actress: Cathy Burke (*Nil by Mouth*) (UK); Director: Wong Kar-Wai (*Happy Together*) (Hong Kong/Taiwain); Screenplay: James Schamus (*The Ice Age*) (US); Camera d'Or (for first feature): *Suzaku* (Japan), special mention Camera d'Or: *La Vie de Jesus* (France); Technical Achievement: *The Fifth Element* and *She's So Lovely*; Short Film: *Is It the Design or the Wrapper?*; Jury Prize Short Film (tie): *Leonie* and *Les Vacances*; Cannes Fiftieth Anniversary Prize: *Al Massir* (*Destiny*) (Egypt).

At the 1963 awards ceremony Barbra Streisand became the youngest artist to win the Best Album Grammy at the age of 22.

PART 2

Music

OF ALL THE MAJOR show-business awards, the one to receive the most pot-shots is undoubtedly the Grammy. The highest accolade in the music industry has long been accused of being woefully out of step with the medium it purports to honor. Created in 1958 at the height of the hard-driving, youth-oriented rock era, the Grammys honored such soft-edged, easy-listening artists as Frank Sinatra, Bobby Darin, and Perry Como. In the 1960s, white-hot groups like the Beatles were grudgingly honored while the Rolling Stones and Bob Dylan were totally ignored.

In recent years, the National Academy of Recording Arts and Sciences which administers the Grammys has recruited younger members and the awards have reflected a more cutting-edge sensibility.

Other awards have since cropped up. Both the American Music Awards (first presented in 1974) and the *Billboard* Music Awards (originated in 1990) are based on sales charts and public opinion.

1958

THE GRAMMY AWARDS

RECORD OF THE YEAR
"Catch a Falling Star" (Perry Como)
"The Chipmunk Song" (David Seville)
"Fever" (Peggy Lee)
"Nel Blu Dipinto Di Blu (Volare)"
    (Domenico Modugno)
"Witchcraft" (Frank Sinatra)

The first year of the Grammys looked like it would be a sweep for Frank Sinatra. The Chairman of the Board had received five individual nominations and his recordings garnered a total of twelve. But the premiere Grammys would prove to be a vanquishing of the Voice. Sinatra failed to take home a single vocal Grammy and the only prize his work won was for Best Album Cover.

The crooner's dominance of some categories had worked against him. He was nominated twice for both Album of the Year and Best Vocal Performance, Male. This split the vote and afforded a win to Henry Mancini's *Music from Peter Gunn* in the album category and to Perry Como for "Catch a Falling Star" in the male vocalist slot. Sinatra lost Record of the Year to one-hit wonder Domenico Modugno, an Italian singer whose spritely "Nel Blu Dipinto Di Blu (Volare)" was the No. 7 hit on *Billboard*'s chart for 1958.

Sinatra was so angry at losing big time that "he refused to let any of the photographers take our picture that night," his date, actress Sandra Giles, later told Sinatra biographer Kitty Kelly. "He was very moody and drank a lot afterwards. . . . I guess I should've been grateful Elvis didn't win anything."

Sinatra was particularly passionate in his denunciation of the popular Presley.

SONG OF THE YEAR
(AWARD TO SONGWRITER)
"Catch a Falling Star" (Paul Vance, Lee Pockriss)
"Fever" (Johnny Davenport, Eddie Conley)
"Gigi" (Alan Jay Lerner, Frederick Loewe)
"Nel Blu Dipinto Di Blu (Volare)"
    (Domenico Modugno; lyric collaborator

Frank Sinatra lost big at the first Grammys but bounced back at the second.

Franco Migliacci not noted)
"Witchcraft" (Cy Coleman, Carolyn Leigh)

ALBUM OF THE YEAR
Come Fly with Me (Frank Sinatra)
Ella Fitzgerald Sings the Irving Berlin Songbook
  (Ella Fitzgerald)
The Music from Peter Gunn (Henry Mancini)
Only the Lonely (Frank Sinatra)
*Tchaikovsky: Concerto No. 1 in B Flat Minor,
  Op. 23* (Van Cliburn)

VOCAL PERFORMANCE, MALE
Perry Como ("Catch a Falling Star")
Domenico Modugno ["Nel Blu Dipinto
  Di Dlu (Volare)"]
Frank Sinatra ("Come Fly with Me")
Frank Sinatra ("Witchcraft")
Andy Williams ("Hawaiian Wedding Song")

VOCAL PERFORMANCE, FEMALE
Doris Day ("Everybody Loves a Lover")
Ella Fitzgerald (*Ella Fitzgerald Sings the Irving
  Berlin Songbook*)
Edyie Gormé ("Eydie in Love")
Peggy Lee ("Fever")
Keely Smith ("I Wish You Love")

VOCAL PERFORMANCE,
GROUP OR CHORUS
The King Sisters ("Imagination")
The Kingston Trio ("Tom Dooley")
Kirby Stone Four ("Baubles, Bangles,
  and Beads")
Lambert, Hendricks, and Ross
  (*Sing a Song of Basie*)
Louis Prima, Keely Smith
  ("That Old Black Magic")

RHYTHM AND BLUES
PERFORMANCE
Harry Belafonte (*Belafonte Sings the Blues*)
The Champs ("Tequila")
Nat "King" Cole (*Looking Back*)
Earl Grant (*The End*)
Pérez Prado ("Patricia")

COUNTRY AND WESTERN
PERFORMANCE
The Everly Brothers ("All I Have to
  Do Is Dream")
The Everly Brothers ("Bird Dog")
Don Gibson ("Oh Lonesome Me")
The Kingston Trio ("Tom Dooley")
Jimmie Rodgers ("Oh, Oh, I'm Falling
  in Love Again")

Confusions of classification plagued the first
Grammys. Preferring to concentrate on pop standards, the National Academy of Recording Arts
and Sciences threw a bone to genres like country
and western and rhythm and blues with catch-all
performance categories. But even these were woefully inadequate at recognizing these vital segments
of the recording industry. While the 1958 R&B
field had seen hits by such artists as Little Richard,
Little Anthony, Chuck Berry, the Coasters, and
Jerry Butler and the Impressions, the Grammy
went to a thrown-together band called the Champs
for "Tequila," an instrumental recorded only so
there would be something to play on Side B of guitarist Dave Burgess's "Train to Nowhere."

As for country and western, most of the nominees and the winner (the Kingston Trio) were folk-
and pop-flavored rather than Nashville-nourished.

OTHER AWARDS
Jazz Performance, Individual: Ella Fitzgerald (*Ella
Fitzgerald Sings the Duke Ellington Songbook*); Jazz
Performance, Group: Count Basie (*Basie*);
Original Cast Album, Broadway or TV: *The Music
Man*; Soundtrack Album, Dramatic Picture Score
or Original Cast: *Gigi*; Comedy Performance:
David Seville ("The Chipmunk Song");
Documentary or Spoken Word Recording: Stan
Freberg (*The Best of the Stan Freberg Shows*);
Classical Performance, Orchestra (conductor's
award): Felix Slatkin conducting the Hollywood
Bowl Symphony, *Gaite Parisienne*

The Grammys were created by a group of conservative record executives to save American music
from the horror that was rock and roll. The new
driving, youth-oriented sound was dominating the
charts and threatened to drown out the melodic
tones of Gershwin and Porter as sung by the likes

of Frank Sinatra and Ella Fitzgerald.

The National Academy of Recording Arts and Sciences, the governing body which presents the Grammys, was formed in the backroom at the Brown Derby restaurant in Los Angeles. In 1955, the Hollywood Beautification Committee had drafted five record executives to come up with a list of names from the industry to be included in the brand-new Hollywood Walk of Fame. During its meetings, the quintet fantasized about an award for music similar to the Oscar, Emmy, and Tony which would be based on quality rather than chart performance. Employing the Motion Picture Academy as its model, this group officially formed the NARAS in 1957. Paul Weston of Columbia Records was elected the first president of the Los Angeles chapter. New York, Chicago, Nashville, and other music cities would soon have their own branches. The debut board of governors included jazz musician Benny Carter, lyricist Sammy Cahn, singer Nat "King" Cole, bandleader Stan Kenton, and songstress Jo Stafford (Weston's wife). There was a notable absence of rock artists. Though Elvis Presley and his ilk were responsible for an overwhelming majority of record sales, rock was seen by the NARAS as a passing fad. So there were no rock categories in the first Grammys. In later years, the Academy would have to admit rock's permanence on the scene and grudgingly allow it to be recognized.

With an organization set up, all that remained was the award itself. Marvin Schwartz, an art director with Capitol Records, designed the trophy, a miniature grammophone based on a combination of early Edison, Victor, and Columbia models. But what to call it? The Eddie (in tribute to Thomas Edison) and the Berliner (for Emile Berliner, who refined Edison's invention) were rejected. A contest was held to choose a proper moniker. Dozens of entries suggested Grammy (short for grammophone), but a Mrs. Jay Dana of New Orleans got her idea in first and won twenty-five albums as a prize.

The first Grammys were held in the Grand Ballroom of the Beverly Hills Hilton on May 4, 1959 (for recordings released during 1958). Comedian Mort Sahl acted as emcee. It was an informal affair, with Weston and Stafford lining up presenters among those present while they ate their dinners. These included Frank Sinatra, Henry Mancini, Peggy Lee, Sammy Davis, Jr., and Milton Berle. The winners were chosen in twenty-eight categories by the 700 NARAS members.

THE GRAMMY AWARDS

RECORD OF THE YEAR
"A Fool Such as I" (Elvis Presley)
"High Hopes" (Frank Sinatra)
"Like Young" (Andre Previn)
"Mack the Knife" (Bobby Darin)
"The Three Bells" (the Browns)

Upstart Bobby Darin was challenging Frank Sinatra as Top Crooner. The twenty-three-year-old was being called a young version of the elder statesman of song, and the two dominated the 1959 Grammys. Each won a pair of awards. Although he had been on the scene for two years (with rock hits "Splish Splash" and "Dream Lover"), Darin won the first New Artist Grammy as well as Record of the Year for his swinging interpretation of "Mack the Knife" from Kurt Weill's *The Threepenny Opera*.

Stung by his defeat the previous year, Sinatra failed to show, but did win this time, for Album of the Year and Vocal Performane, Male.

The rivalry between the two erupted into the headlines, with Darin reportedly stating, "I hope to surpass Frank Sinatra in everything he does" (Darin later denied making this boast.) Sinatra countered with "Bobby Darin does my prom dates." A photograph of the Chairman of the Board and pal Dean Martin throwing darts at a Darin 8×10 was later circulated throughout the country.

SONG OF THE YEAR
(AWARD TO SONGWRITER)
"The Battle of New Orleans" (Jimmy Driftwood)
"High Hopes" (Sammy Cahn, Jimmy Van Heusen)
"I Know" (Karl Stutz, Edith Linderman)
"Like Young" (Paul Francis Webster, Andre Previn)
"Small World" (Jule Styne, Stephen Sondheim)

ALBUM OF THE YEAR

Belafonte at Carnegie Hall (Harry Belafonte)
Come Dance with Me (Frank Sinatra)
More Music from Peter Gunn (Henry Mancini)
Rachmaninoff Piano Concerto No. 3 (Van Cliburn)
Victory at Sea, Vol. I (Robert Russell Bennett)

NEW ARTIST

Edd Byrnes
Bobby Darin
Mark Murphy
Johnny Restivo
Mavis Rivers

VOCAL PERFORMANCE, MALE

Harry Belafonte (*Belafonte at Carnegie Hall*)
Jesse Belvin ("Guess Who")
Bobby Darin ("Mack the Knife")
Robert Merrill (*An Evening with Lerner and Loewe*)
Frank Sinatra (*Come Dance with Me*)

VOCAL PERFORMANCE, FEMALE

Ella Fitzgerald ("But Not for Me")
Lena Horne (*Porgy and Bess*)
Peggy Lee ("Alright, Okay")
Pat Suzuki (*Broadway '59*)
Caterina Valenta (*La Starda del Amore*)

VOCAL PERFORMANCE, GROUP OR CHORUS

The Ames Brothers (*The Ames Brothers Sing Famous Hits of Famous Quartets*)
The Browns ("The Three Bells")
The Kingston Trio (*The Kingston Trio at Large*)
The Mormon Tabernacle Choir ("The Battle Hymn of the Republic")

PERFORMANCE BY A TOP 40 ARTIST

The Coasters ("Charlie Brown")
Nat "King" Cole ("Midnight Flyer")
Elvis Presley ("A Big Hunk o' Love")
Floyd Robinson ("Makin' Love")
Neil Sedaka (*Neil Sedaka*)
Sarah Vaughan ("Broken-Hearted Melody")

In a concession to the existence of rock and roll, members of the NARAS created one category for the genre. Not being able to bring themselves to honor R&R as such, they called it Performance by a Top 40 Artist. But the winner, Nat "King" Cole's "Midnight Flyer," had not cracked *Billboard*'s Top 40 chart and was not a rock song. This was Cole's only Grammy.

RHYTHM AND BLUES PERFORMANCE

Jesse Belvin ("Guess Who")
The Coasters ("Charlie Brown")
Nat "King" Cole ("Midnight Flyer")
Elvis Presley ("A Big Hunk 'o Love")
Dinah Washington ("What a Diff'rence a Day Makes")

COUNTRY AND WESTERN PERFORMANCE

Eddy Arnold ("Tennessee Stud")
Skeeter Davis ("Set Him Free")
Don Gibson ("Don't Tell Me Your Troubles")
Johnny Horton ("The Battle of New Orleans")
Jim Reeves ("Home")

OTHER AWARDS

Jazz Performance, Soloist: Ella Fitzgerald (*Ella Swings Lightly*); Jazz Performance, Group: Jonah Jones (*I Dig Chicks*); Folk Performance: the Kingston Trio (*The Kingston Trio at Large*); Broadway Show Album (tie): *Gypsy* and *Redhead*; Soundtrack Album, Original Cast: *Porgy and Bess*; Soundtrack Album, Background Score: *Anatomy of a Murder*; Comedy Performance, Spoken Word: Shelley Berman (*Inside Shelley Berman*); Comedy Performance, Musical: Homer and Jethro (*The Battle of Kookamonga*); Documentary or Spoken Word: Carl Sandburg (*A Lincoln Portrait*); Classical Performance, Orchestra (conductor's award): Charles Munch conducting the Boston Symphony (*Debussy: Images for Orchestra*)

The second Grammys were the first to be televised. Broadway songwriter Meredith Willson (*The Music Man*) presided over an hour-long program on NBC, broadcast on Thanksgiving weekend. Nominations had been announced on October 5, just four months after the first Grammys were handed out. Classical pianist Van Cliburn was a presenter. Willson and Bobby Darin musically announced the winners in technical areas in a duet. The winners had been previously announced in twin ceremonies at Los Angeles' Beverly Hilton Hotel and New York's Waldorf Astoria. Nine new Grammy recipients participated in the live show, telecast from a Burbank studio. Duke Ellington and Nat "King" Cole were on tape, but in-person performers included the Kingston Trio, Bobby Darin, and comedian Shelley Berman.

Variety called the show "a fairly solid hour of entertainment by some of the top names in the platter field."

Grammy got its first taste of controversy when RCA was accused of bloc voting. The record label received over 100 nominations, more than the other labels put together. The Academy attempted to offset large companies voting for their own products by an extensive membership drive so no one label would dominate.

1960

THE GRAMMY AWARDS

RECORD OF THE YEAR
"Are You Lonesome Tonight?" (Elvis Presley)
"Georgia on My Mind" (Ray Charles)
"Mack the Knife" (Ella Fitzgerald)
"Nice 'n' Easy" (Frank Sinatra)
"Theme from *A Summer Place*" (Percy Faith)

SONG OF THE YEAR (AWARD TO SONGWRITER)
"He'll Have to Go" (Charles Grean, Joe and Audrey Allison)
"Nice 'n' Easy" (Lew Spence, Marilyn Keith, Alan Bergman)
"Second Time Around" (Sammy Cahn, Jimmy Van Heusen)
"Theme from *Exodus*" (Ernest Gold)
"Theme from *A Summer Place*" (Max Steiner)

Grammy continued to take it nice and easy, awarding its top two accolades of Record of the Year and Song of the Year to unchallenging movie themes from *A Summer Place* and *Exodus*. Today, both are extremely popular choices for supermarkets and dentists' offices.

ALBUM OF THE YEAR
Belafonte Returns to Carnegie Hall (Harry Belafonte)
Brahams: Concerto No. 2 in B Flat (Sviatoslav Richter)
Button Down Mind (Bob Newhart)
Nice 'n' Easy (Frank Sinatra)
Puccini: Turandot (Erich Leinsdorf)
Wild Is Love (Nat "King" Cole)

If variety is the spice of life, the 1960 Album of the Year category was as spicy as they come. The nominees ran the gamut from classical to pop to comedy. The winner was Bob Newhart's *Button Down Mind*, a stand-up satire on middle-class woes such as driving schools and airlines. It is only one of two comedy platters to take the award (the other being Vaugh Meader's *The First Family*). Newhart was also named best New Artist, the only comic to be so honored. The comedian was on a roll. He had made a hit on the Emmys the previous June and would start his own NBC series in the fall.

NEW ARTIST
Brothers Four
Miriam Makeba
Bob Newhart
Leontyne Pryce
Joanie Sommers

VOCAL PERFORMANCE, ALBUM (MALE)
Harry Belafonte (*Belafonte Returns to Carnegie Hall*)
Ray Charles (*The Genius of Ray Charles*)
Nat "King" Cole (*Wild Is Love*)
Elvis Presley (*GI Blues*)
Frank Sinatra (*Nice 'n' Easy*)

VOCAL PERFORMANCE, ALBUM (FEMALE)
Rosemary Clooney (*Clap Hands, Here Comes Rosie*)
Ella Fitzgerald (*Mack the Knife, Ella in Berlin*)
Peggy Lee (*Latin à la Lee*)
Miriam Makeba (*Miriam Makeba*)
Della Reese (*Della*)

VOCAL PERFORMANCE, SINGLE OR TRACK (MALE)
Ray Charles ("Georgia on My Mind")
Johnny Mathis ("Misty")
Elvis Presley ("Are You Lonesome Tonight?")
Jim Reeves ("He'll Have to Go")
Frank Sinatra ("Nice 'n' Easy")

VOCAL PERFORMANCE, SINGLE OR TRACK (FEMALE)
Doris Day ("The Sound of Music")
Ella Fitzgerald ("Mack the Knife")
Eileen Farrell ("I've Gotta Right to Sing the Blues")
Brenda Lee ("I'm Sorry")
Peggy Lee ("I'm Gonna Go Fishin'")

VOCAL PERFORMANCE, POP SINGLE ARTIST
Ray Charles ("Georgia on My Mind")
Ella Fitzgerald ("Mack the Knife")
Peggy Lee ("Heart")
Elvis Presley ("Are You Lonesome Tonight?")
Frank Sinatra ("Nice 'n' Easy")

The Top 40 category, Grammy's concession to the existence of rock, was dropped and replaced by Pop Single Artist. Once again, the NARAS was without a clue and nominated traditional crooners like Sinatra, Peggy Lee, and Ella Fitzgerald along with Elvis. The award went to Ray Charles' "Georgia on My Mind," a cover of a 1930s' Hoagy Carmichael ballad. Charles won a total of four 1960 Grammys. His other wins were for Male Vocalist, Single (also for "Georgia on My Mind"), Vocal Performance, Album (*The Genius of Ray Charles*), and Rhythm and Blues Performance ("Let the Good Times Roll").

VOCAL GROUP
Brothers Four ("Greenfields")
Edyie Gormé, Steve Lawrence ("We Got Us")
The Hi-Los ("All over the Place")
The Kingston Trio ("Here We Go Again")
The Swe-Danes ("Scandinavian Shuffle")

RHYTHM AND BLUES PERFORMANCE
LaVerne Baker ("Shake a Hand")
Hank Ballard ("Finger Poppin' Time")
Ray Charles ("Let the Good Times Roll")
Bo Diddley ("Walkin' and Talkin'")
John Lee Hooker ("Travelin' ")
Etta James ("All I Could Do Was Cry")
Muddy Waters ("Got My Mojo Working")
Jackie Wilson ("Lonely Teardrops")

COUNTRY AND WESTERN PERFORMANCE
Johnny Horton ("North to Alaska")
Ferlin Husky ("Wings of a Dove")
Hank Locklin ("Please Help Me, I'm Falling")
Jim Reeves ("He'll Have to Go")
Marty Robbins ("El Paso")

OTHER AWARDS
Jazz Performance (Soloist or Small Group): André Previn (*West Side Story*); Jazz Performance (Large Group): Henry Mancini (*The Blues and the Beat*); Original Cast Show Album: *The Sound of Music*; Soundtrack Album from a Motion Picture or TV Special (Original Cast): *Can-Can*; Soundtrack Album from a Motion Picture or TV Special (Background Music): *Exodus*; Spoken Word: Franklin Delano Roosevelt (*FDR Speaks*); Comedy (Spoken Word): Bob Newhart (*Button Down Mind Strikes Back*); Comedy (Musical): Paul Weston, Jo Stafford (*Jonathan and Darlene Edwards in Paris*); Classical Performance, Orchestra: Fritz Reiner conducting the Chicago Symphony, *Bartok: Music for Strings, Percussion, and Celeste*

The previous year's awards telecast was indifferently received, so the 1960 Grammys were not seen on the small screen. Dual banquets were held in New York and Los Angeles. A transcontinental telephone would keep both coasts informed of the winners. Unfortunately, the connection failed before the ceremony started. The line was never fixed, so the NARAS's secret winners' list was read to learn the results.

Complaints of bloc voting persisted when recording giants RCA, Capitol, and Columbia copped the most awards. In response, the voting procedures were slightly changed, with a supposedly impartial Academy nominating committee adding nominees to those of the general membership.

1961

THE GRAMMY AWARDS

RECORD OF THE YEAR
"Big Bad John" (Jimmy Dean)
"Moon River" (Henry Mancini)
"The Second Time Around" (Frank Sinatra)
"Take Five" (Dave Brubeck)
"Up a Lazy River" (Si Zentner)

SONG OF THE YEAR
(AWARD TO SONGWRITER)
"Big Bad John" (Jimmy Dean)
"A Little Bitty Tear" (Hank Cochran)
"Lollipops and Roses" (Tony Velona)
"Make Someone Happy" (Jule Styne,
     Betty Comden, Adolph Green)
"Moon River" (Henry Mancini)

Henry Mancini not only dominated the Grammys with the score for the film *Breakfast at Tiffany's* and its hit single "Moon River," but he also won two Oscars (Song and Score) the same year. The music from the film, which starred Audrey Hepburn as Truman Capote's eccentric and glamorous Holly Golightly, netted a total of five awards. Mancini had written "Moon River" within one octave so the nonmusical Hepburn could warble it.

Mancini's career total of Grammys eventually reached twenty. The composer had amassed so many statues a few years later that when director George Schlatter needed extra trophies to decorate the set for a "Best on Record" Grammy special, he had to borrow them from Mancini.

ALBUM OF THE YEAR
Breakfast at Tiffany's (Henry Mancini)
Genius + Soul = Jazz (Ray Charles)
Great Band with Great Voices (Si Zentner,
     Johnny Mann Singers)
Judy at Carnegie Hall (Judy Garland)
The Nat "King" Cole Story (Nat "King" Cole)
West Side Story (Soundtrack, Johnny Green,
     music director)

The musical event of the year was Judy Garland's triumphant concert at Carnegie Hall. After suc-cumbing to drugs and alcohol, her film career had fizzled, but the singer came back at the top of her form with an unforgettable performance. The album recording the event was named Album of the Year and also won for Solo Vocal Performance, Female, Engineering Contribution, Popular, and Album Cover. The wins helped Garland re-estab-lish her career and launched her on a brief foray into television variety.

NEW ARTIST
Ann-Margret
Dick Gregory
The Lettermen
Peter Nero
Timi Yuro

SOLO VOCAL PERFORMANCE, MALE
Jimmy Dean ("Big Bad John")
Burl Ives ("A Little Bitty Tear")
Jack Jones ("Lollipops and Roses")
Steve Lawrence ("Portrait of My Love")
Andy Williams ("Danny Boy")

SOLO VOCAL PERFORMANCE, FEMALE
Ella Fitzgerald (*Mr. Paganini*)
Judy Garland (*Judy at Carnegie Hall*)
Billie Holiday [*The Essential Billie Holiday
     (Carnegie Hall Concert)*]
Lena Horne (*Lena at the Sands*)
Peggy Lee (*Basin Street East*)

VOCAL GROUP
The Four Freshmen (*Voices in Fun*)
The Kingston Trio (*Close Up*)
Lambert, Hendricks, and Ross (*Flying High*)
The Lettermen (*The Way You Look Tonight*)
The Limeliters (*The Slightly Famous Limeliters*)

ROCK AND ROLL RECORDING
"Goodbye Cruel World" (James Darren)
"I Like It Like That" (Chris Kenner)
"It's Gonna Work Out Fine" (Ike and
     Tina Turner)
"Let's Twist Again" (Chubby Checker)
"The Lion Sleeps Tonight" (the Tokens)

Finally, rock and roll was officially recognized by the Grammys with an award of its own. They even managed to name it properly (rather than 1959's Performance by a Top 40 Artists, or 1960's best Vocal Performance by a Pop Artist). The NARAS appointed a special panel of genre producers, agents, and arrangers to make sure the nominations accurately reflected rock music.

RHYTHM AND BLUES RECORDING

"Bright Lights, Big City" (Jimmy Reed)
"Fool That I Am" (Etta James)
"Hit the Road, Jack" (Ray Charles)
"Mother-in-Law" (Ernie K-Doe)
"Saved" (Laverne Baker)

COUNTRY AND WESTERN RECORDING

"Big Bad John" (Jimmy Dean)
"Hello Walls" (Faron Young)
"Hillbilly Heaven" (Tex Ritter)
"A Little Bitty Tear" (Burl Ives)
"Walk On By" (Leroy Van Dyke)

OTHER AWARDS

Jazz Performance (Soloist or Small Group): André Previn (*André Previn Plays Harold Arlen*); Jazz Performance (Large Group): Stan Kenton (*West Side Story*); Folk Recording: *The Belafonte Folk Singers at Home and Abroad* (The Belafonte Folk Singers); Original Cast Show Album: *How to Succeed in Business without Really Trying*; Soundtrack Album (Original Cast): *West Side Story*; Soundtrack Album (Score): *Breakfast at Tiffany's*; Comedy Performance: Mike Nicholas, Elaine May (*An Evening with Mike Nichols and Elaine May*); Spoken Word: Leonard Bernstein (*Humor in Music*); Classical Album: *Stravinsky Conducts, 1960: La Sacre du Printemps; Petruchka*

Television and the Grammys were still strangers in 1961. The New York-Los Angeles awards dinners were without cameras. The Gotham bash featured Tony Bennett and Buddy Hackett while Bob Newhart (last year's Album of the Year and New Artist winner) held sway in L.A.

1962

THE GRAMMY AWARDS

RECORD OF THE YEAR

"Desafinado" (Stan Getz, Charlie Byrd)
"Fly Me to the Moon Bossa Nova"
    (Joe Harnell and His Orchestra)
"I Can't Stop Loving You" (Ray Charles)
"I Left My Heart in San Francisco"
    (Tony Bennett)
"What Kind of Fool Am I" (Sammy Davis, Jr.)

SONG OF THE YEAR (AWARD TO SONGWRITER)

"As Long as He Needs Me" (Lionel Bart)
"I Left My Heart in San Francisco"
    (Douglass Cross, George Cory)
"My Coloring Book" (John Kander, Fred Ebb)
"The Sweetest Sounds" (Richard Rodgers)
"What Kind of Fool Am I" (Leslie Bricusse,
    Anthony Newley)

Best song "What Kind of Fool Am I" from the musical *Stop the World—I Want To Get Off* was also nominated for Solo Vocalist, Male—in two versions, by co-composer Anthony Newley and by Sammy Davis, Jr. Both lost to Tony Bennett's "I Left My Heart in San Francisco."

ALBUM OF THE YEAR

The First Family (Vaughn Meader)
I Left My Heart in San Francisco (Tony Bennett)
Jazz Samba (Stan Getz, Charlie Byrd)
Modern Sounds in Country and Western Music
    (Ray Charles)
My Son, the Folk Singer (Allan Sherman)

For the second (and so far) last time, a comedy album was named Album of the Year. Vaughn Meader had risen to fame with an affectionate imitation of President John F. Kennedy. *The First Family* featured Meader and a small cast enacting gently humorous parodies of the enormous Kennedy clan. The album sold over five million copies and was listed in *The Guinness Book of World Records* as the fast-selling album of the time. (Ironically, this record was later broken by a recorded BBC tribute to JFK.) But Kennedy's assassination in 1963 killed Meader's career as well.

NEW ARTIST
The Four Seasons
Robert Goulet
Vaughn Meader
The New Christy Minstrels
Peter, Paul and Mary
Allan Sherman

SOLO VOCAL PERFORMANCE, MALE
Tony Bennett ("I Left My Heart in San Francisco")
Ray Charles ("I Can't Stop Loving You")
Sammy Davis, Jr. ("What Kind of Fool Am I")
Anthony Newley ("What Kind of Fool Am I")
Mel Tormé ("Comin' Home Baby")

SOLO VOCAL PERFORMANCE, FEMALE
Diahann Carroll (*No Strings*)
Ella Fitzgerald (*Ella Swings Brightly with Nelson Riddle*)
Lena Horne (*Lena . . . Lovely and Alive*)
Peggy Lee ("I'm a Woman")
Kitty Lester (*Love Letters*)
Sandy Stewart ("My Coloring Book")
Pat Thomas ("Slightly Out of Tune")

PERFORMANCE BY A VOCAL GROUP
The Four Freshmen (*The Swingers*)
The Hi-Los (*The Hi-Los Happen to Folk Songs*)
The Lettermen (*A Song for Young Love*)
The Limeliters (*Through Children's Eyes*)
Peter, Paul and Mary ("If I Had a Hammer")

The smooth vocalizing of Peter, Paul and Mary brought the politcally charged folk sound of the early '60s into the mainstream and won over conservative Grammy voters. The trio (once described by a record executive as "two rabbis and a hooker") won two 1962 awards (Performance by a Vocal Group and Folk Recording) for Pete Seeger's "If I Had a Hammer" and another two the following year for Bob Dylan's "Blowin' in the Wind." The harder-edged Dylan would have to undergo a religious conversion before Grammy recognized him in 1979 for his born-again track "Gotta Serve Somebody."

ROCK AND ROLL RECORDING
"**Alley Cat**" (Bent Fabric)
"Big Girls Don't Cry" (the Four Seasons)
"Breaking Up Is Hard To Do" (Neil Sedaka)
"Twistin' the Night Away" (Sam Cooke)
"Up on the Roof" (the Drifters)
"You Beat Me to the Punch" (Mary Wells)

After honoring Chubby Checker in the new rock category the year before, the Grammy voters slipped back into their old ways. The 1961 rock prize went to Bent Fabric, a Danish pianist, for his soft-as-yogurt instrumental "Alley Cat," best known today as the background for line dances at weddings and bar mitzvahs.

RHYTHM AND BLUES RECORDING
"Bring It on Home to Me" (Sam Cooke)
"Comin' Home Baby" (Mel Torme)
"**I Can't Stop Loving You**" (Ray Charles)
"Loco-Motion" (Little Eva)
"Nut Rocker" (B. Bumble and the Stingers)
"What'd I Say" (Bobby Darin)

COUNTRY AND WESTERN RECORDING
"Devil Woman" (Marty Robbins)
"**Funny Way of Laughin'**" (Burl Ives)
"It Keeps Right on A-Hurtin'" (Johnny Tillotson)
"P.T. 109" (Jimmy Dean)
"She Still Thinks I Can" (George Jones)
"Wolverton Mountain" (Claude King)

OTHER AWARDS
Jazz Performance (Soloist or Small Group): Stan Getz ("Desafinado"); Jazz Performance (Large Group): Stan Kenton (*Adventures in Jazz*); Folk Recording: "If I Had a Hammer" (Peter, Paul and Mary); Original Cast Show Album: *No Strings*; Comedy Performance: Vaughn Meader (*The First Family*); Spoken Word: Charles Laughton (*The Story-Teller: A Session with Charles Laughton*); Classical Album: *Columbia Records Presents Vladimir Horowitz*

Without a TV network, the NARAS was running out of money to present its awards. Producer Ted Bergmann vainly attempted to pitch a live ceremony to indifferent programmers. They wanted stars and performances by the winners. Bergmann could guarantee neither since the Grammys were seen as inconsequential in the recording industry. Then the producer hit upon a compromise. Why not air a special featuring taped performances of the winners after the awards were revealed? Timex sponsored the event, Frank Sinatra, Bing Crosby, and Bob Hope were signed to guarantee star power, and NBC bought it. The New York-L.A. Grammy banquets (for work produced during 1962) were held in May 1963. The special, titled *The Best on Record*, was set to air November 24, 1963. President Kennedy was killed two days before the scheduled broadcast and the special was postponed. It was finally shown on December 8 but with some changes. Comedian Vaughn Meader, whose JFK impressions had won him Album of the Year and Comedy Performance Grammys, was set to perform and offered to do a serious tribute to Kennedy instead of a comedy routine. The network nixed the idea. Diahann Carroll sang a medley from Broadway Show Album of the Year winner *No Strings* in Meader's time-slot.

In typical Grammy fashion, rock was ignored. Middle-of-the-road crooners Steve Lawrence, Edyie Gormé, Connie Francis, and Dean Martin were among the *Best on Record* headliners.

1963

THE GRAMMY AWARDS

RECORD OF THE YEAR
"**The Days of Wine and Roses**" (Henry Mancini)
"Dominique" (The Singing Nun)
"Happy Days Are Here Again" (Barbra Streisand)
"I Wanna Be Around" (Tony Bennett)
"Wives and Lovers" (Jack Jones)

SONG OF THE YEAR
(AWARD TO SONGWRITER)
"Call Me Irresponsible" (Sammy Cahn, Jimmy Van Heusen)
"**The Days of Wine and Roses**" (Johnny Mercer, Henry Mancini)
"The Good Life" (Sacha Distel, Jack Reardon)

"I Wanna Be Around" (Sadie Vimmerstedt, Johnny Mercer)
"Wives and Lovers" (Burt Bacharach, Hal David)

As he did two years ago, Henry Mancini won both Record of the Year and Song of the Year as well as an Oscar for the same song. This time it was the title tune from *The Days of Wine and Roses*. In contrast to the romantic comedy *Breakfast at Tiffany's*, the last Manicini Oscar-Grammy winner, *Wine and Roses* was a heavy drama starring Jack Lemmon and Lee Remick as an alcoholic couple.

ALBUM OF THE YEAR
Bach's Greatest Hits (Swingle Singers)
The Barbra Streisand Album (Barbra Streisand)
The Days of Wine and Roses (Henry Mancini)
Honey in the Horn (Al Hirt)
The Singing Nun (the Singing Nun)

At age 22, Barbra Streisand became the youngest recording artist to win the Album of the Year Grammy (an honor she still holds). She also won for Vocal Performance, Female. These were the first of many accolades for La Streisand. In addition to a career total of eight Grammys, she has netted two Oscars (Actress and best Original Song), four Emmys (for two TV specials thirty years apart), and an honorary Tony as well as countless Golden Globes and American Music Awards.

NEW ARTIST
Vicki Carr
John Gary
The J's with Jamie
Trini Lopez
The Swingle Singers

VOCAL PERFORMANCE, MALE
Tony Bennett ("I Wanna Be Around")
Ray Charles ("Busted")
John Gary ("Catch a Rising Star")
Jack Jones ("Wives and Lovers")
Andy Williams ("The Days of Wine and Roses")

VOCAL PERFORMANCE, FEMALE
Eydie Gormé ("Blame It on the Bossa Nova")
Peggy Lee (*I'm a Woman*)
Miriam Makeba (*The World of Miriam Makeba*)

The Singing Nun ("Dominique")
Barbra Streisand (*The Barbra Streisand Album*)

PERFORMANCE BY A VOCAL GROUP
The Hi-Los (*The Hi-Los Happen to Bossa Nova*)
The J's with Jamie (*Hey Look Us Over!*)
The Anita Kerr Quartet (*Waitin' for the Evening Train*)
Jackie and Ray Kral (*Like Sing—Jackie and Ray Kral*)
Peter, Paul and Mary ("Blowin' in the Wind")

ROCK AND ROLL RECORDING
"Another Saturday Night" (Sam Cooke)
"Deep Purple" (Nino Tempo, April Stevens)
"I Will Follow Him" (Little Peggy March)
"It's My Party" (Lesley Gore)
"Our Day Will Come" (Ruby and the Romantics)
"Teen Scene" (Chet Atkins)

Grammy continued to play it safe in the rock category, opting for a re-recording of "Deep Purple," a tune from the 1930s, over teen-scream numbers like "It's My Party" and "I Will Follow Him." Sam Cooke's classic "Another Saturday Night" was thought to be a shoe-in by the eventual co-winner of the category Nino Tempo.

RHYTHM AND BLUES RECORDING
"Busted" (Ray Charles)
"Frankie and Johnny" (Sam Cooke)
"(Love Is Like a) Heat Wave" (Martha and the Vandellas)
"Hey, Little Girl" (Major Lance)
"Hello Stranger" (Barbara Lewis)
"Part Time Love" (Little Johnny Taylor)
"Since I Fell for You" (Lenny Welch)

COUNTRY AND WESTERN RECORDING
"Detroit City" (Bobby Bare)
Flatt and Scruggs at Carnegie Hall (Flatt and Scruggs)
"Love's Gonna Live Here" (Buck Owens)
"Ninety Miles an Hour (Down a Dead End Street)" (Hank Snow)
The Porter Wagoner Show (Porter Wagoner)
"Ring of Fire" (Johnny Cash)
"Saginaw, Michigan" (Lefty Frizzell)

OTHER AWARDS
Jazz Performance (Soloist or Small Group): Bill Evans (*Conversations with Myself*); Jazz Performance (Large Group): Woody Herman Band (*Encore: Woody Herman, 1963*); Folk Recording: "Blowin' in the Wind" (Peter, Paul, and Mary); Original Cast Show Album: *She Loves Me*; Soundtrack Score: *Tom Jones*; Comedy Performance: Allan Sherman (*Hello Muddah, Hello Faddah*); Spoken Word: *Who's Afraid of Virginia Woolf?* (original Broadway cast); Classical Album: *Britten: War Requiem*

Most of the winners failed to show at the Los Angeles Grammy ceremonies while most were present in New York. Losing New Artist nominees Vicki Carr and John Gary carried the night in L.A. by performing the five nominees for Record of the Year. NBC continued its *Best on Record* wrap-up special with taped renditions of some of the winning songs.

THE GRAMMY AWARDS

RECORD OF THE YEAR
"Downtown" (Petula Clark)
"The Girl from Ipanema" (Stan Getz, Astrud Gilberto)
"Hello, Dolly" (Louis Armstrong)
"I Want To Hold Your Hand" (the Beatles)
"People" (Barbra Streisand)

SONG OF THE YEAR (AWARD TO SONGWRITER)
"A Hard Day's Night" (John Lennon, Paul McCartney)
"Hello, Dolly" (Jerry Herman)
"Dear Heart" (Henry Mancini, Ray Evans, Jay Livingston)
"People" (Jule Styne, Bob Merrill)
"Who Can I Turn To?" (Leslie Bricusse, Anthony Newley)

ALBUM OF THE YEAR
Cotton Candy (Al Hirt)
Funny Girl (Jule Styne, Robert Merrill)

Getz/Gilberto (Stan Getz, Joao Gilberto)
People (Barbra Streisand)
The Pink Panther (Henry Mancini)

NEW ARTIST
The Beatles
Petula Clark
Astrud Gilberto
Antonio Carlos Jobim
Morgana King

The NARAS could no longer deny the rock writing on the wall. Rock and roll was taking over the music industry and they had to accept it, or at least acknowledge the fact. Nothing brought this truth home harder than the arrival of the Beatles. Beginning in January 1964, the Lads from Liverpool obliterated any competition when their first US release "I Wanna Hold Your Hand" took the No. 1 spot on *Billboard*'s chart. By April, they became the first and only artists to hold all five top spots on *Billboard*'s hit parade. (The other four singles were "Can't Buy Me Love," "Twist and Shout," "She Loves You," and "Please, Please Me.")

The NARAS did not embarrass itself too badly where the Beatles were concerned in 1964. The group was named best New Artist and won the Performance by a Vocal Group accolade for the album *A Hard Day's Night*. (That's better than Elvis Presley, whose only Grammys came for his gospel recordings way past his heyday.) But the Fab Four were passed up in the Rock and Roll Recording and, Record of the Year, Song of the Year, and Album of the Year categories.

VOCAL PERFORMANCE, MALE
Louis Armstrong ("Hello, Dolly")
Tony Bennett ("Who Can I Turn To?")
João Gilberto (*Getz/Gilberto*)
Dean Martin ("Everybody Loves Somebody Sometime")
Andy Williams (*Call Me Irresponsible*)

The Beatles won Grammys for best New Artist and best Vocal Group in 1964, but never took Record of the Year.

VOCAL PERFORMANCE, FEMALE

Petula Clark ("Downtown")
Gale Garnett ("We'll Sing in the Sunshine")
Astrud Gilberto ("The Girl from Ipanema")
Barbra Streisand ("People")
Nancy Wilson ("How Glad I Am")

PERFORMANCE BY A VOCAL GROUP

The Beatles (*A Hard Day's Night*)
The Browns (*Grand Ole Opry Favorites*)
The Double Six of Paris (*The Double Six of Paris Sing Ray Charles*)
The Four Freshmen (*More Four Freshmen and Five Trombones*)
Peter, Paul and Mary (*Peter, Paul and Mary in Concert*)

ROCK AND ROLL RECORDING

"Downtown" (Petula Clark)
"A Hard Day's Night" (the Beatles)
"Mr. Lonely" (Bobby Vinton)
"Oh, Pretty Woman" (Roy Orbison)
"You've Lost That Lovin' Feeling" (the Righteous Brothers)

RHYTHM AND BLUES RECORDING

"Baby Love" (the Supremes)
"Good Times" (Sam Cooke)
"Hold What You've Got" (Joe Tex)
"How Glad I Am" (Nancy Wilson)
"Keep On Pushing" (the Impressions)
"Walk On By" (Dionne Warwicke)

COUNTRY AND WESTERN

Single: "Dang Me" (Roger Miller); Song (award to songwriter): "Dang Me" (Roger Miller); Album: *Dang Me/Chug-a-Lug* (Roger Miller); Vocal Performance, Male: Roger Miller ("Dang Me"); Vocal Performance, Female: Dottie West ("Here Comes My Baby"); New Artist: Roger Miller

The growing popularity of country music led the NARAS to establish a Nashville chapter. Country music publisher Wesley Rose negotiated with the Academy for a bigger slice of the Grammy pie. As a result, country wound up with six categories all its own, more than rock, jazz, and R&B put together.

OTHER AWARDS

Jazz Performance (Soloist or Small Group): Stan Getz (*Getz/Gilberto*); Jazz Performance (Large Group): Laurindo Almeida (*Guitar from Ipanema*); Folk Recording: Gale Garnett (*We'll Sing in the Sunshine*); Original Cast Show Album: *Funny Girl*; Soundtrack Album: *Mary Poppins*; Comedy Performance: Bill Cosby (*I Started Out as a Child*); Spoken Word: The cast of *That Was the Week That Was* (*BBC Tribute to John F. Kennedy*); Classical Album: *Bernstein: Symphony No. 3* ("Kaddish")

Bill Cosby began his six-year winning streak in the comedy category with *I Started Out as a Child*. The following year, he would begin a similar three-year streak of wins at the Emmys for *I Spy*.

Once again, nontelevised Grammy dinners were given in L.A. and New York and NBC presented a suspense-less, post mortem compilation *Best on Record* special. Only this time, there was at least a touch of contemporary sound with the Beatles performing "I'm So Happy Just To Dance with You" from London's Twickenham Studios. They received their Grammys from fellow Brit Peter Sellers. *Best on Record* host Steve Allen may have been expressing the true feelings of the older NARAS members in his sniping jokes about beatles and chipmunks (referring to Dave Seville's cartoon singing animals) making hits while "real" performers had it tougher.

1965

THE GRAMMY AWARDS

With its 1965 list of nominees, NARAS attempted to appease critics who accused them of being out of touch with contemporary tastes. Four new categories for rock and roll were created, leaving the "general" slots open to the kind of softer, "old-fashioned" music the Academy seemed to prefer. But this did not stop the squawking. Popular artists like the Beach Boys, the Rolling Stones, and Bob Dylan were still ignored.

If the nominations caused grousing, the awards themselves elicited screams. The year-old Nashville chapter flexed its considerable musical muscle and dominated the rock categories as well as its own country division. C&W favorites Roger Miller, The Statler Brothers, and Anita Kerr (who happened to be vice president of the Nashville NARAS chapter) rolled over rock contendors like the Beatles and Herman's Hermits.

The general categories were no better. In one of the most glaring Grammy gaffes, Kerr's quartet won the Performance by a Vocal Group award over the Beatles' classic "Help!"

RECORD OF THE YEAR
"The 'In' Crowd" (The Ramsey Lewis Trio)
"King of the Road" (Roger Miller)
"The Shadow of Your Smile (Theme from *The Sandpiper*)" (Tony Bennett)
"A Taste of Honey" (Herb Alpert and the Tijuana Brass)
"Yesterday" (Paul McCartney)

SONG OF THE YEAR (AWARD TO SONGWRITER)
"I Will Wait for You (Theme from *The Umbrellas of Cherbourg*)" (Michel Legrand, Norman Gimbel, Jacques Demy)
"King of the Road" (Roger Miller)
"September of My Years" (Jimmy Van Heusen, Sammy Cahn)
"The Shadow of Your Smile (Theme from *The Sandpiper*)" (Paul Francis Webster, Johnny Mandel)
"Yesterday" (John Lennon, Paul McCartney)

ALBUM OF THE YEAR
Help! (the Beatles)
My Name Is Barbra (Barbra Streisand)
My World (Eddy Arnold)
September of My Years (Frank Sinatra)
The Sound of Music (Julie Andrews and cast)

NEW ARTIST
The Byrds
Herman's Hermits
Horst Jankowski
Tom Jones
Marilyn Maye
Sonny and Cher
Glenn Yarbrough

VOCAL PERFORMANCE, MALE
Tony Bennett ["The Shadow of Your Smile (Theme from *The Sandpiper*)"]
Paul McCartney ("Yesterday")
Roger Miller ("King of the Road")
Frank Sinatra ("It Was a Very Good Year")
Glenn Yarbrough ("Baby the Rain Must Fall")

The introduction of several separate rock categories allowed the triumph of old-style crooners like Frank Sinatra in the more general categories. Sinatra would win again the next year in Vocal Performance, Male, for "Strangers in the Night."

VOCAL PERFORMANCE, FEMALE
Petula Clark ("Downtown")
Jackie DeShannon ("What the World Needs Now Is Love")
Astrud Gilberto (*The Astrud Gilberto Album*)
Barbra Streisand (*My Name Is Barbra*)
Nancy Wilson (*Gentle Is My Love*)

PERFORMANCE BY A VOCAL GROUP
The Beatles ("Help!")
Herman's Hermits ("Mrs. Brown, You've Got a Lovely Daughter")
The Anita Kerr Quartet (*We Dig Mancini*)
The Statler Brothers ("Flowers on the Wall")
We Five ("You Were on My Mind")

CONTEMPORARY (R&R) SINGLE
"Baby the Rain Must Fall" (Glenn Yarbrough)
"It's Not Unusual" (Tom Jones)
"King of the Road" (Roger Miller)
"What the World Needs Now Is Love" (Jackie DeShannon)
"Yesterday" (Paul McCartney)

Roger Miller nabbed six Grammys, a record for the most won in a single year that stood until Michael Jackson was more of a thriller than Miller in 1983 by taking home eight awards.

CONTEMPORARY (R&R) VOCAL PERFORMANCE, MALE
Len Barry ("1-2-3")
Tom Jones ("What's New, Pussycat?")
Paul McCartney ("Yesterday")
Roger Miller ("King of the Road")

Johnny Tillotson ("Heartaches by the Number")

CONTEMPORARY (R&R) VOCAL PERFORMANCE, FEMALE
Fontella Bass ("Rescue Me")
Petula Clark ("I Know a Place")
Jackie DeShannon ("What the World Needs Now Is Love")
Lesley Gore ("Sunshine, Lollipops, and Rainbows")
Barbara Lewis ("Baby, I'm Yours")

CONTEMPORARY (R&R) VOCAL PERFORMANCE, GROUP
The Beatles ("Help!")
Herman's Hermits ("Mrs. Brown, You've Got a Lovely Daughter")
Sam the Sham and the Pharaohs ("Wooly Bully")
The Statler Brothers ("Flowers on the Wall")
The Supremes ("Stop in the Name of Love")

RHYTHM AND BLUES RECORDING
"In the Midnight Hour" (Wilson Pickett)
"My Girl" (the Temptations)
"Papa's Got a Brand New Bag" (James Brown)
"Shake" (Sam Cooke)
"Shotgun" (Jr. Walker and the All Stars)

COUNTRY AND WESTERN
Single: "King of the Road" (Roger Miller); Song (award to songwriter): "King of the Road" (Roger Miller); Album: *The Return of Roger Miller*; Vocal Performance, Male: Roger Miller ("King of the Road"); Vocal Performance, Female: Jody Miller ("Queen of the House"); New Artist: the Statler Brothers

OTHER AWARDS
Jazz Performance (Soloist or Small Group): the Ramsey Lewis Trio (*The 'In' Crowd*); Jazz Performance (Large Group): the Duke Ellington Orchestra (*Ellington '66*); Folk Recording: *An Evening with Belafonte/Makeba* (Harry Belafonte, Miriam Makeba); Original Cast Show Album: *On a Clear Day You Can See Forever*; Soundtrack Album: *The Sandpiper*; Comedy Performance: Bill Cosby (*Why Is There Air?*); Spoken Word: *John F. Kennedy: As We Remember Him*; Classical Album:

Horowitz at Carnegie Hall, An Historic Return (Vladimir Horowitz)

Chicago and Nashville held their own Grammy dinners in addition to those in New York and Los Angeles. NBC aired another *Best on Record* special, again hosted by Steve Allen, who made more anti-rock quips.

THE GRAMMY AWARDS

RECORD OF THE YEAR
"Almost Persuaded" (David Houston)
"Monday, Monday" (the Mamas and the Papas)
"Strangers in the Night" (Frank Sinatra)
"What Now My Love" (Herb Alpert and the Tijuana Brass)
"Winchester Cathedral" (the New Vaudeville)

As the '60s passed the mid-way point, the NARAS held fast to its love of traditional pop, but began to give a little to the youngsters. Grammy favorite Frank Sinatra dominated the 1966 awards, after an early '60s slump, with three major wins—Record of the Year and Vocal Performance, Male, for "Strangers in the Night" and Album of the Year for *Sinatra: A Man and His Music*, a retrospective of the Chairman of the Board's biggest hits. A TV special version of the album also won an Emmy. This brought the saloon singer's Grammy total to eight. He would make yet another Grammy comeback almost thirty years later in 1995 with a win for his *Duets II* album.

The younger generation was rewarded with accolades for two of the Beatles [Paul McCartney and John Lennon's Song of the Year "Michelle" and McCartney's Contemporary (R&R) Solo Vocal Performance, Male or Female, of "Eleanor Rigby"] and the Mamas and the Papas [Contemporary (R&R) Performance by a Group for "Monday, Monday"]. It should be noted that the Academy was rewarding the Beatles and the M&Ps for softer tunes while the driving, jagged songs of Mick Jagger and the Rolling Stones were still Grammy orphans.

SONG OF THE YEAR (AWARD TO SONGWRITER)

"Born Free" (John Barry, Don Black)
"The Impossible Dream" (Mitch Leigh, Joe Darion)
"Michelle" (John Lennon, Paul McCartney)
"Somewhere, My Love (Love Theme from *Dr. Zhivago*)" (Paul Francis Webster, Maurice Jarre)
"Strangers in the Night" (Bert Kaempfert, Charles Singleton, Eddie Snyder)

ALBUM OF THE YEAR

Color Me Barbra (Barbra Streisand)
Dr. Zhivago (soundtrack, Maurice Jarre)
Revolver (the Beatles)
Sinatra: A Man and His Music (Frank Sinatra)
What Now My Love (Herb Alpert and the Tijuana Brass)

VOCAL PERFORMANCE, MALE

David Houston ("Almost Persuaded")
Jack Jones ("The Impossible Dream")
Paul McCartney ("Eleanor Rigby")
Jim Reeves ("Distant Drums")
Frank Sinatra ("Strangers in the Night")
Andy Williams (*The Shadow of Your Smile*)

VOCAL PERFORMANCE, FEMALE

Ella Fitzgerald (*Ella at Duke's Place*)
Edyie Gormé ("If He Walked into My Life Today")
Sandy Posey ("Born a Woman")
Nancy Sinatra ("These Boots Are Made for Walkin'")
Barbra Streisand (*Color Me Barbra*)

PERFORMANCE BY A VOCAL GROUP

The Association ("Cherish")
The Beach Boys ("Good Vibrations")
The Anita Kerr Quartet ("A Man and a Woman")
The Mamas and the Papas ("Monday, Monday")
The Sandpipers ("Guantanamera")

CONTEMPORARY (R&R) RECORDING

"Cherish" (the Association)
"Eleanor Rigby" (Paul McCartney)
"Good Vibrations" (the Beach Boys)
"Last Train to Clarksville" (the Monkees)
"Monday, Monday" (the Mamas and the Papas)
"Winchester Cathedral" (the New Vaudeville Band)

The NARAS was making some progress in the rock categories, but was still out to lunch on the big one. Its 1966 "Contemporary" (R&R) Recording of the year was "Winchester Cathedral," a lilting, ready-made-for-Muzak tribute to the late 1920s' sound of vaudeville.

CONTEMPORARY (R&R) SOLO VOCAL PERFORMANCE, MALE OR FEMALE

Bobby Darin ("If I Were a Carpenter")
Paul McCartney ("Eleanor Rigby")
Sandy Posey ("Born a Woman")
Nancy Sinatra ("These Boots Are Made for Walkin'")
Dusty Springfield ("You Don't Have to Say You Love Me")

CONTEMPORARY (R&R) PERFORMANCE BY A GROUP

The Association ("Cherish")
The Beach Boys ("Good Vibrations")
The Mamas and the Papas ("Monday, Monday")
The Monkees ("Last Train to Clarksville")
The Sandpipers ("Guantanamera")

RHYTHM AND BLUES

Recording: "Crying Time" (Ray Charles); Solo Vocal Performance, Male or Female: Ray Charles ("Crying Time"); Performance by a Group: Ramsey Lewis ("Hold It Right There")

COUNTRY AND WESTERN

Recording: "Almost Persuaded" (David Houston); Song (award to songwriter): "Almost Persuaded" (Billy Sherrill, Glenn Sutton); Vocal Performance, Male: David Houston ("Almost Persuaded"); Vocal Performance, Female: Jeannie Seely ("Don't Touch Me")

OTHER AWARDS

Jazz Performance: Wes Montgomery ("Goin' Out of My Mind"); Folk Recording: *Blues in the Street* (Cortelia Clark); Original Cast Show Album: *Mame*; Soundtrack Album: *Dr. Zhivago*; Comedy Performance: Bill Cosby (*Wonderfulness*); Spoken Word: Edward R. Murrow (*Edward R. Murrow, A*

Reporter Remembers—Vol. I, The War Years);
Classical Album: *Ives: Symphony No. 1 in D Minor*
(Morton Gould conducting the Chicago
Symphony)

In one of the most bizarre wins in Grammy history, the folk recording prize went to Cortelia Clark, a blind, African-American street singer who plied his trade on the avenues of Nashville. His album was recorded on the street, complete with sounds of traffic and passers-by. It did not sell well and was soon forgotten. But the Nashville chapter pushed for a nomination and voted solidly for one of its citizens, handing Clark a victory over the likes of Pete Seeger and Peter, Paul and Mary. Clark was famous for the proverbial fifteen minutes, but no recording contracts followed. He continued performing in the street to earn a living and never made another album. Three years after winning the Grammy, a kerosone heater exploded in his tiny trailer home and he died of third-degree burns.

The split between the NARAS and the rock world was made painfully clear at the New York Grammy ceremony at the Waldorf-Astoria. Tony Randall was the host and legendary jazz bandleader Woody Herman and his musicians provided the entertainment. To prove that its members weren't old fuddie-duddies, the Academy invited long-hair rocker Frank Zappa and his band the Mothers of Invention to perform. Following Herman's traditional rendition of Duke Ellington's "Satin Doll," Zappa and his crew gave out with a heavy-metal rock version of the same song. While whaling out the number, the Mothers ripped apart baby dolls and handed their remains to the shocked audience.

THE GRAMMY AWARDS

RECORD OF THE YEAR
"By the Time I Get to Phoenix" (Glen Campbell)
"My Cup Runneth Over" (Ed Ames)
"Ode To Billie Joe" (Bobbie Gentry)
"Somethin' Stupid" (Nancy and Frank Sinatra)
"Up, Up, and Away" (the 5th Dimension)

The 5th Dimension was a perfect Grammy candidate. It was an African-American vocal group specializing in sweet harmony. Its sound was aimed at

The 5th Dimension
with one of five 1967
Grammys won for their
hit "Up, Up, and Away."

Glen Campbell and Bobbie Gentry display country's influence on the 1967 Grammys as they performed on "The Best on Record," the NARAS's after-the-fact award show.

the youth market, but was easy-listening for the older, conservative NARAS voters. The group's hit single "Up, Up, and Away" by Jimmy Webb garnered seven nominations and four awards.

The other big winners this year were Glen Campbell and Bobbie Gentry, two country-flavored artists who crossed over into the mainstream with "By the Time I Get to Phoenix" (another Jimmy Webb tune) for Campbell and "Ode to Billie Joe" (Gentry's story-form ballad of a mysterious suicide which was later made into a movie). Campbell was a popular choice, having served as background guitarist for many previous Grammy winners. He later starred in his own TV variety series. Gentry never had a another hit the size of "Billie Joe."

The Beatles were thrown a bone with the Album of the Year and Contemporary Album Grammys for *Sgt. Pepper's Lonely Hearts Club Band.*

SONG OF THE YEAR (AWARD TO SONGWRITER)

"By the Time I Get to Phoenix" (Jimmy Webb)

"Gentle on My Mind" (John Hartford)

"My Cup Runneth Over" (Tom Jones, Harvey Schmidt)

"Ode to Billie Joe" (Bobbie Gentry)

"Up, Up, and Away" (Jimmy Webb)

ALBUM OF THE YEAR

Francis Albert Sinatra/Antonio Carlos Jobim (Frank Sinatra, Antonio Carlos Jobim)

It Must Be Him (Vikki Carr)

My Cup Runneth Over (Ed Ames)

Ode to Billie Joe (Bobbie Gentry)

Sgt. Pepper's Lonely Hearts Club Band (the Beatles)

NEW ARTIST

Lana Cantrell
The 5th Dimension
Bobbie Gentry
Harpers Bizarre
Jefferson Airplane

VOCAL PERFORMANCE, MALE

Ed Ames (*My Cup Runneth Over*)
Glen Campbell ("By the Time I Get to Phoenix")
Ray Charles ("Yesterday")
Frank Sinatra (*Francis Albert Sinatra/
    Antonio Carlos Jobim*)
Joe South ("Can't Take My Eyes Off You")

VOCAL PERFORMANCE, FEMALE

Vikki Carr ("It Must Be Him")
Petula Clark ("Don't Sleep in the Subway")
Aretha Franklin ("Respect")
Bobbie Gentry ("Ode to Billie Joe")
Dionne Warwick ("Alfie")

VOCAL PERFORMANCE, GROUP

The Association ("Never My Love")
The Beatles ("Sgt. Pepper's Lonely Hearts
    Club Band")
The Box Tops ("The Letter")
The 5th Dimension ("Up, Up, and Away")
The Monkees ("I'm a Believer")

CONTEMPORARY SINGLE

"By the Time I Get to Phoenix" (Glen Campbell)
"Don't Sleep in the Subway" (Petula Clark)
"Ode to Billie Joe" (Bobbie Gentry)
"Up, Up, and Away" (the 5th Dimension)
"Yesterday" (Ray Charles)

NARAS was still trying to downplay rock. Rock and roll was dropped as a part of the "contemporary" category titles. In a case of Grammy double exposure, all of the general winners triumphed in the separate contemporary counterpart slots.

CONTEMPORARY ALBUM

Insight Out (the Association)
It Must Be Him (Vikki Carr)
Ode to Billie Joe (Bobbie Gentry)
Sgt. Pepper's Lonely Hearts Club Band
    (the Beatles)

Up, Up and Away (the 5th Dimension)

CONTEMPORARY VOCAL SOLO, MALE

Glen Campbell ("By the Time I Get to Phoenix")
Ray Charles ("Yesterday")
Scott MacKenzie ["San Francisco (Be Sure to
    Wear Some Flowers in Your Hair)"]
Jimmie Rodgers ("Child of Clay")
Frankie Valli ("Can't Take My Eyes Off You")

CONTEMPORARY VOCAL SOLO, FEMALE

Vikki Carr ("It Must Be Him")
Petula Clark ("Don't Sleep in the Subway")
Aretha Franklin ("A Natural Woman")
Bobbie Gentry ("Ode to Billie Joe")
Dionne Warwick ("I Say a Little Prayer")

CONTEMPORARY VOCAL GROUP

The Association ("Windy")
The Beatles ("Sgt. Pepper's Lonely Hearts
    Club Band")
The Box Tops ("The Letter")
The 5th Dimension ("Up, Up, and Away")
The Monkees ("I'm a Believer")
Procol Harum ("A Whiter Shade of Pale")

RHYTHM AND BLUES

Recording: "Respect" (Aretha Franklin); Vocal Solo Performance, Male: Lou Rawls ("Dead End Street"); Vocal Performance, Female: Aretha Franklin ("Respect"); Vocal Group: Sam and Dave ("Soul Man")

Aretha Franklin began an eight-year winning streak in the Female Vocalist (R&B) category. Her career Grammy total is fifteen.

COUNTRY AND WESTERN

Recording: "Gentle on My Mind" (Glen Campbell); Song (award to songwriter): "Gentle on My Mind" (John Hartford); Vocal Solo Performance, Male: Glen Campbell ("Gentle on My Mind"); Vocal Solo Performance, Female: Tammy Wynette ("I Don't Wanna Play House"); Vocal Group: Johnny Cash, June Carter ("Jackson")

OTHER AWARDS

Jazz Performance (Soloist or Small Group): Cannonball Adderly Quintet (*Mercy, Mercy, Mercy*); Jazz Performance (Large Group): Duke Ellington ("Far East Suite"); Folk Recording: "Gentle on my Mind" (John Hartford); Original Cast Show Album: *Cabaret*; Soundtrack Album: *Mission: Impossible*; Comedy Performance: Bill Cosby (*Revenge*); Spoken Word: Senator Everett M. Dirksen (*Gallant Men*); Classical Album (tie): *Berg: Wozzeck* (Pierre Boulez conducting the Paris National Opera Orchestra and Chorus) and *Mahler: Symphony No. 8 in E Flat Major* (Leonard Bernstein conducting the London Symphony)

Satirist Stan Freberg (1958 Spoken Word winner) hosted the Los Angeles Grammy banquet, which drew the most winners and nominees including Glen Campbell, Bobbie Gentry, the 5th Dimension, and Ed Ames, all of whom performed their nominated songs. Steve Allen emceed the New York shindig, while separate soirees were held in Chicago and Nashville.

COUNTRY MUSIC ASSOCIATION AWARDS

Entertainer: Eddy Arnold; Single: "There Goes My Everything" (Jack Green); Song: "There Goes My Everything" (Dallas Frazier, songwriter); Album: *There Goes My Everything* (Jack Green); Male Vocalist: Jack Green; Female Vocalist: Loretta Lynn; Vocal Group: the Stoneman Family; Musician: Chet Atkins

The previous year, the Grammys cut country categories from six to four. In retaliation, Nashville executives and artists created the Country Music Association Awards. As the country sound has grown in popularity, these prizes have grown in importance. They are now presented in an annual televised special.

1968

THE GRAMMY AWARDS

RECORD OF THE YEAR
"Harper Valley PTA" (Jeannie C. Riley)
"Hey Jude" (the Beatles)
"Honey" (Bobby Goldsboro)
"Mrs. Robinson" (Simon and Garfunkel)
"Witchita Lineman" (Glen Campbell)

SONG OF THE YEAR (AWARD TO SONGWRITER)
"Harper Valley PTA" (Tom T. Hall)
"Honey" (Bobby Russell)
"Hey Jude" (John Lennon, Paul McCartney)
"Little Green Apples" (Bobby Russell)
"Mrs. Robinson" (Paul Simon)

ALBUM OF THE YEAR
Bookends (Simon and Garfunkel)
By the Time I Get to Phoenix (Glen Campbell)
Felicano! (Jose Felicano)
Magical Mystery Tour (the Beatles)
A Tramp Shining (Richard Harris)

Though Glen Campbell had won the Contemporary Vocal Solo, Male, Grammy the year before for the single of "Phoenix," the album was released during the 1968 eligibility period. It won Campbell another prize, beating the Beatles and Simon and Garfunkel.

NEW ARTIST
Cream
José Feliciano
Gary Puckett and the Union Gap
Jeannie C. Riley
O. C. Smith

MALE VOCALIST (CONTEMPORARY POP)
Glen Campbell ("Wichita Lineman")
José Feliciano ("Light My Fire")
Bobby Goldsboro ("Honey")
Richard Harris ("MacArthur Park")
O.C. Smith ("Little Green Apples")

Former winner Edyie Gormé with Dionne Warwick (Female Pop Contemporary Vocalist for "Do You Know the Way to San Jose?") at the 1968 Grammys.

The contemporary and general categories were merged into "Contemporary Pop," thereby eliminating any reference to rock, just as R&R had firmly established itself as the predominant force in the music industry.

FEMALE VOCALIST (CONTEMPORARY POP)

Aretha Franklin ("I Say a Little Prayer")
Mary Hopkins ("Those Were the Days")
Merrilee Rush ("Angel of the Morning")
Barbra Streisand (*Funny Girl*)
Dionne Warwick ("Do You Know the Way to San Jose")

VOCAL GROUP

The Beatles ("Hey Jude")
Blood, Sweat, and Tears ("Child Is Father to the Man")
The Lettermen ("Goin' Out of My Head/ Can't Take My Eyes Off You")
Sergio Mendes and Brasil '66 ("Fool on the Hill")
Gary Puckett and the Union Gap (*Woman, Woman*)
Simon and Garfunkel ("Mrs. Robinson")

RHYTHM AND BLUES

Song (award to songwriter): "(Sittin' on) The Dock of the Bay" (Otis Redding, Steve Cropper);
Male Vocalist: Otis Redding ["(Sittin' on) The

Dock of the Bay"]; Female Vocalist: Aretha Franklin ("Chain of Fools"); Vocal Group: the Temptations ("Cloud Nine")

COUNTRY AND WESTERN
Song (award to songwriter): "Little Green Apples" (Bobby Russell); Male Vocalist: Johnny Cash ("Folsom Prison Blues"); Female Vocalist: Jeannie C. Riley ("Harper Valley PTA"); Vocal Group: Flatt and Scruggs ("Foggy Mountain Breakdown")

OTHER AWARDS
Jazz Performance (Soloist or Small Group): Bill Evans Trio (*Bill Evans at the Montreux Jazz Festival*); Jazz Performance (Large Group): Duke Ellington ("And His Mother Called Him Bill"); Folk Performance: Judy Collins ("Both Sides Now"); Original Cast Show Album: *Hair*; Soundtrack Album: *The Graduate*; Comedy Performance: Bill Cosby (*To Russell, My Brother, Whom I Slept With*); Spoken Word: Rod McKuen (*Lonesome Cities*); Classical Performance (Orchestra): Pierre Boulez conducting the New York Philharmonic Orchestra (*Boulez Conducts Debussy*)

Dan Rowan and Dick Martin, hosts of the hit series *Laugh-In*, acted as emcees for the *Best on Record* program broadcast on NBC months after the Grammy ceremonies. Flip Wilson, Lou Rawls, Bobbie Gentry, Mama Cass, Don Rickles, and Tiny Tim introduced a selection of recipients who performed their winning songs. There was a concession to the contemporary with appearances by the Beatles performing "Hey, Jude," the Los Angeles cast of *Hair*, and José Feliciano.

To add a measure of suspense to the post mortem proceedings, the announcement of the Record of the Year award was saved for the broadcast. Attendees at the Los Angeles Grammy ceremony booed when they heard this. The winner was "Mrs. Robinson," Simon and Garfunkel's satiric swipe at sururban values from the Oscar-winning film *The Graduate*. Rather than simply perform the number for the *Best on Record*, S&G put together a prehistoric music video. *The New York Times* described it as "surrealistic bits of a slapstick, silent movie with Simon and Garfunkel playing baseball. . . . Joe DiMaggio (who was mentioned in the song) joined them."

COUNTRY MUSIC ASSOCIATION AWARDS
Entertainer: Glen Campbell; Single: "Harper Valley PTA" (Jeannie C. Riley); Song: "Honey" (Bobby Russell, songwriter); Album: *Johnny Cash at Folsom Prison* (Johnny Cash); Male Vocalist: Glen Campbell; Female Vocalist: Tammy Wynette; Vocal Group: Porter Wagoner and Dolly Parton; Musician: Chet Atkins

THE GRAMMY AWARDS

RECORD OF THE YEAR
"Aquarius/Let the Sunshine In"
   (the 5th Dimension)
"A Boy Named Sue" (Johnny Cash)
"Is That All There Is" (Peggy Lee)
"A Time for Us (Love Theme from *Romeo and Juliet*)" (Henry Mancini)
"Spinning Wheel" (Blood, Sweat and Tears)

The 5th Dimension, 1967's Grammy stars, came back with another mainstream hit, making rock palatable for the NARAS. "Aquarius" and "Let the Sunshine In," the group's easy medley of two songs from the Broadway rock musical *Hair*, was No. 1 for the year according to *Billboard*. The group received six nominations and won two.

The other champs of the 1969 Grammys were newcomers Blood, Sweat and Tears, who combined jazz, rock, gospel, and blues. BS&T sweated out ten nominations for three awards. The Beatles were left in the dust, despite having produced their ultimate musical statement *Abbey Road*. The group broke up the following year, but took an Original Soundtrack award for *Let It Be*. Their career total of Grammys: eight (including three 1996 Grammys for "Free as a Bird," based on a tape left by the late John Lennon).

SONG OF THE YEAR (AWARD TO SONGWRITER)
"Games People Play" (Joe South)
"I'll Never Fall in Love Again" (Burt Bacharach, Hal David)

"Raindrops Keep Fallin' on My Head"
(Burt Bacharach, Hal David)
"Spinning Wheel" (David Clayton Thomas)
"A Time for Us (Love Theme from *Romeo and Juliet*)" (Larry Kusik, Eddie Snyder, Nino Rota)

ALBUM OF THE YEAR
Abbey Road (the Beatles)
The Age of Aquarius (the 5th Dimension)
Blood, Sweat and Tears (Blood, Sweat and Tears)
Crosby, Stills and Nash (Crosby, Stills and Nash)
Johnny Cash at San Quentin (Johnny Cash)

NEW ARTIST
Chicago
Crosby, Stills and Nash
Led Zeppelin
Oliver
The Neon Philharmonic

MALE VOCALIST (CONTEMPORARY)
Harry Nilsson ("Everybody's Talkin'")
Frank Sinatra ("My Way")
Joe South ("Games People Play")
Ray Stevens ("Guitarzan")
B.J. Thomas ("Raindrops Keep Fallin' on My Head")

FEMALE VOCALIST (CONTEMPORARY)
Vikki Carr ("With Pen in Hand")
Jackie DeShannon ("Put a Little Love
in Your Heart")
Brenda Lee ("Johnny One Time")
Peggy Lee ("Is That All There Is")
Dusty Springfield ("Son of a Preacher Man")
Dionne Warwick ("This Girl's in Love with You")

As a last hurrah for the traditional pop sound, the NARAS oldsters voted establishment star Peggy Lee the Female Vocalist (Contemporary) award, her first and only Grammy. This was not a totally out-of-left field win. "Is That All There Is" did make it into the Top 40.

VOCAL GROUP (CONTEMPORARY)
The Beatles (*Abbey Road*)
Blood, Sweat and Tears (*Blood, Sweat and Tears*)
Crosby, Stills and Nash (*Crosby, Stills and Nash*)
The 5th Dimension ("Aquarius/
Let the Sunshine In")

The Neon Philharmonic (*Morning Girl*)

CONTEMPORARY SONG (AWARD TO SONGWRITER)
"Games People Play" (Joe South)
"In the Ghetto" (Mac Davis)
"Jean" (Rod McKuen)
"Raindrops Keep Fallin' on My Head"
(Burt Bacharach, Hal David)
"Spinning Wheel" (David Clayton Thomas)

A separate award for Contemporary Song was reinstated this year. Once again, as in 1967, the winner for Song of the Year was also winner of Contemporary Song. Joe South, a popular background guitarist, won both prizes for his country-pop comment on hypocrisy, "Games People Play."

RHYTHM AND BLUES
Song (award to songwriter): "Color Him Father" (Richard Spencer); Male Vocalist: Joe Simon ("The Chokin' Kind"); Female Vocalist: Aretha Franklin ("Share Your Love with Me"); Vocal Group: the Isley Brothers ("It's Your Thing")

COUNTRY
Song (award to songwriter): "A Boy Named Sue" (Shel Silverstein); Male Vocalist: Johnny Cash ("A Boy Named Sue"); Female Vocalist: Tammy Wynette ("Stand By Your Man"); Vocal Group: Waylon Jennings and the Kimberlys ("MacArthur Park")

OTHER AWARDS
Jazz Performance (Soloist or Small Group): Wes Montgomery (*Willow Weep for Me*); Jazz Performance (Large Group): Quincy Jones ("Waling in Space"); Folk Performance: Joni Mitchell (*Clouds*); Original Cast Show Album: *Promises, Promises*; Soundtrack Album: *Butch Cassidy and the Sundance Kid*; Comedy Performance: Bill Cosby (*The Best of Bill Cosby*); Spoken Word: Art Linkletter and Diane (*We Love You, Call Collect*); Classical Album: *Switched-On Bach* (Walter Carlos)

Host Bill Cosby, winner of six consecutive comedy Grammys, kept the audience laughing at the Hollywood awards dinner, which featured many winners including Peggy Lee, Harry Nilsson, and

Burt Bacharach. Conversely, the New York ceremony at Alice Tully Hall was an unmitigated fiasco, featuring cheap food and numerous sound problems.

The Grammys' after-the-award TV special wasn't doing much better. Previous ratings were low and reviews were nasty. Nineteen sixty-nine marked the last year of the *Best on Record* specials. Producer Ted Bergmann quit after NARAS and record company officials harshly criticized the program and attempted to influence the format. The CBS Records president pushed Bergmann to include a long tribute to the Moog Synthesizer, a fadish new instrument featured on the Classical Album winner *Switched-On Bach* (a CBS Records release). Bergmann balked at being told what to put on his show. The Moog was briefly mentioned, but Bergmann was through with the Grammys. Pierre Cossette and Burt Sugarman subsequently took over the producing reigns and sold ABC on presenting the Grammys as a live ceremony.

COUNTRY MUSIC
ASSOCIATION AWARDS

Entertainer: Johnny Cash; Single: "A Boy Named Sue" (Johnny Cash); Song: "Carroll County Accident" (Bob Ferguson, songwriter); Album: *Johnny Cash at San Quentin Prison* (Johnny Cash); Male Vocalist: Johnny Cash; Female Vocalist: Tammy Wynette; Vocal Group: Johnny Cash and June Carter; Musician: Chet Atkins

THE GRAMMY AWARDS

RECORD OF THE YEAR
"Bridge over Troubled Water" (Simon and
     Garfunkel)
"Close to You" (the Carpenters)
"Everything Is Beautiful" (Ray Stevens)
"Fire and Rain" (James Taylor)
"Let It Be" (the Beatles)

With "Bridge over Troubled Water," Simon and Garfunkel became the first artists to win the

Grammy Triple Crown of Record of the Year, Song of the Year, and Album of the Year. Carole King and Christopher Cross are the only other Grammy winners to take the top three in one year. "Bridge" also won in the short-lived category Contemporary Song (award to songwriter) and for Arrangement Accompanying Vocalist(s) and Engineered Recording. The gentle ballad reflected the national need for healing as the turbulent '60s came to a close. More than the decade was ending. In addition to the deaths of Janis Joplin and Jim Morrison, Simon and Garfunkel and the Beatles broke up. Hard-edged rock rage gave way to a smoother '70s' sound.

"Bridge" won again the next year when Aretha Franklin continued her dominance of the R&B Vocal Performance, Female, category with her cover of the song.

SONG OF THE YEAR
(AWARD TO SONGWRITER)
"Bridge over Troubled Water" (Paul Simon)
"Everything Is Beautiful" (Ray Stevens)
"Fire and Rain" (James Taylor)
"Let It Be" (John Lennon, Paul McCartney)
"We've Only Just Begun" (Roger Nichols,
     Paul Williams)

ALBUM OF THE YEAR
Bridge over Troubled Water (Simon and
     Garfunkel)
Chicago (Chicago)
Close to You (the Carpenters)
Deja Vu (Crosby, Stills, Nash and Young)
Elton John (Elton John)
Sweet Baby James (James Taylor)

NEW ARTIST
The Carpenters
Elton John
Melba Moore
Anne Murray
The Partridge Family

MALE VOCALIST (CONTEMPORARY)
Joe Cocker (*Mad Dogs and Englishmen*)
Brook Benton ("Rainy Night in Georgia")
Elton John (*Elton John*)

Art Garfunkel and Paul Simon with an armful of 1970 Grammys for "Bridge over Troubled Water." The duo split up soon afterwards.

Ray Stevens ("Everything Is Beautiful")
James Taylor (*Sweet Baby James*)

FEMALE VOCALIST (CONTEMPORARY)
Bobbie Gentry (*Fancy*)
Anne Murray ("Snowbird")
Linda Ronstadt (*Long, Long Time*)
Diana Ross ("Ain't No Mountain High Enough")
Dionne Warwick ("I'll Never Fall in Love Again")

VOCAL GROUP (CONTEMPORARY)
The Beatles ("Let It Be")
The Carpenters ("Close to You")
Chicago (*Chicago*)
The Jackson 5 ("ABC")
Simon and Garfunkel ("Bridge over
    Troubled Water")

CONTEMPORARY SONG
(AWARD TO SONGWRITER)
"Bridge over Troubled Water" (Paul Simon)
"Everything Is Beautiful" (Ray Stevens)
"Fire and Rain" (James Taylor)
"Let It Be" (John Lennon, Paul McCartney)

"We've Only Just Begun" (Roger Nichols,
    Paul Williams)

RHYTHM AND BLUES
Song (award to songwriter): "Patches" (Ronald
Dunbar, General Johnson); Male Vocalist: B. B.
King ("The Thrill Is Gone"); Female Vocalist:
Aretha Franklin ("Don't Play That Song"); Vocal
Group: the Delfonics ["Didn't I (Blow Your Mind
This Time)"]

COUNTRY
Song (award to songwriter): "My Woman, My
Woman, My Wife" (Marty Robbins); Male
Vocalist: Ray Price ("For the Good Times");
Female Vocalist: Lynn Anderson ("Rose Garden");
Vocal Group: Johnny Cash, June Carter ("If I
Were a Carpenter")

OTHER AWARDS
Jazz Performance (Soloist or Small Group): Bill
Evans (*Alone*); Jazz Performance (Large Group):
Miles Davis (*Bitches Brew*); Original Cast Show
Album: *Company*; Soundtrack Album: *Let It Be*;

Comedy Performance: Flip Wilson (*The Devil Made Me Buy This Dress*); Spoken Word: Rev. Martin Luther King, Jr. (*Why I Oppose the War in Vietnam*); Classical Album: *Berlioz: Les Troyens* (Colin Davis conducting the Royal Opera House Orchestra and Chorus)

For the first time, the Grammys were accorded the same treatment as the Oscars, Emmys, and Tonys with a full-scale network award show. When the NARAS wanted to switch from the *Best on Record* special to a live ceremony, NBC told them to take a hike. Producers Pierre Cossette and Burt Sugarman bought the licensing rights from the Academy and persuaded last-place ABC to pick up the program. The NARAS made only one condition, that the show be rotated between Los Angeles, New York City, and Nashville, the three music capitals where most of the members lived. This stipulation would later cause trouble for Cossette.

The first Grammycast was ninety minutes long and came under criticism for its soft-and-mellow talent roster. Andy Williams, the king of middle American music, was the host. Cossette had produced Williams' Emmy-winning TV series. The talent included the Carpenters, Anne Murray, the Osmond Brothers, and many country acts. Rock was represented by Paul McCartney accepting the last Grammy for the just-dissolved Beatles (for the soundtrack of *Let It Be*, which also won an Oscar). McCartney received the award from an unlikely presenter—John Wayne.

Because of the time limit, only seventeen of the forty-three awards were presented on the live show. The rest were handed out in a separate ceremony earlier in the day. With Grammy categories reaching almost ninety by the '90s, that practice has continued to this day.

The premiere TV Grammys had the expected quota of mishaps. Minutes before airtime the celebrities were still socializing in the lobby of the Hollywood Palladium and had to be hurriedly herded into the auditorium. Even after all those attending were present and accounted for, there were still too many empty seats. Parking lot attendants were used as "chair fillers." A hanging light shorted out, sending sparks over the wife of a record company executive.

COUNTRY MUSIC ASSOCIATION AWARDS

Entertainer: Merle Haggard; Single: "Okie from Muskogee" (Merle Haggard); Song: "Sunday Morning Coming Down" (Kris Kristofferson, songwriter); Album: *Okie from Muskogee* (Merle Haggard); Male Vocalist: Merle Haggard; Female Vocalist: Tammy Wynette; Vocal Group: the Glaser Brothers; Vocal Duo: Porter Wagoner and Dolly Parton; Musician: Jerry Reed

1971

THE GRAMMY AWARDS

RECORD OF THE YEAR
"It's Too Late" (Carole King)
"Joy to the World (Three Dog Night)
"My Sweet Lord" (George Harrison)
"Theme from *Shaft*" (Isaac Hayes)
"You've Got a Friend" (James Taylor)

Carole King repeated Simon and Garfunkel's triple win of 1970 by taking Record of the Year, Song of the Year, and Album of the Year for 1971. She bested S & G's win by also taking an award for her performance of the title track of *Tapestry*. (Simon and Garfunkel had lost their vocal category to the saccharine Carpenters.) King's influence was felt in other categories as well. James Taylor triumphed in the Male Vocalist (Pop) category for his rendition of King's "You've Got a Friend" while Quincy Jones took the Pop Instrumental Performance award for his spin on her composition "Smackwater Jack."

Old-guard Grammy voters embraced King because she was both hip and soft. A veteran of the music business, King wrote (with her then husband Gerry Goffin) numerous R&B and pop-rock hits of the '60s including "The Locomotion" (Grammy-nominated in 1962), "He's a Rebel," and "Will You Still Love Me Tomorrow." With her emergence as a singer-songwriter, King made the transition from teenage crush tunes to mature melodies about adult relationships. She never won another Grammy after 1971, but was nominated for "Jazzman" (1974).

Carole King dominated the 1971 Grammys with her *Tapestry* album.

SONG OF THE YEAR
(AWARD TO SONGWRITER)
"Help Me Make It Through the Night"
   (Kris Kristofferson)
"It's Impossible" (Sid Wayne, Armando Manzanero)
"Me and Bobby McGee" (Kris Kristofferson,
   Fred Foster)
"Rose Garden" (Joe South)
"You've Got a Friend" (Carole King)

ALBUM OF THE YEAR
All Things Must Pass (George Harrison)
The Carpenters (the Carpenters)
Jesus Christ Superstar (London Production)
Shaft (Isaac Hayes)
Tapestry (Carole King)

Tapestry remains one of the top-selling albums by a female soloist of all time, at 10 million units sold.

NEW ARTIST
Chase
Emerson, Lake and Palmer
Hamilton, Joe Frank and Reynolds
Carly Simon
Bill Withers

New Artist winner Carly Simon married Male Vocalist (Pop) winner James Taylor six months after their respective Grammy wins.

MALE VOCALIST (POP)
Perry Como ("It's Impossible")
Neil Diamond ("I Am . . . I Said")
Gordon Lightfoot ("If You Could Read My
   Mind")
James Taylor ("You've Got a Friend")
Bill Withers ("Ain't No Sunshine")

FEMALE VOCALIST (POP)
Joan Baez ("The Night They Drove Old
   Dixie Down")
Cher ("Gypsies, Tramps and Thieves")
Janis Joplin ("Me and Bobby McGee")
Carole King ("Tapestry")
Carly Simon ("That's the Way I've Always Heard
   It Should Be")

The Contemporary categories were changed to Pop this year.

VOCAL GROUP (POP)
The Bee Gees ("How Can You Mend a
   Broken Heart")
The Carpenters (*the Carpenters*)
Jesus Christ Superstar London cast
   (*Jesus Christ Superstar*)
Sonny and Cher ("All I Ever Need Is You")
Three Dog Night ("Joy to the World")

RHYTHM AND BLUES
Song (award to songwriter): "Ain't No Sunshine"
(Bill Withers); Male Vocalist: Lou Rawls ("A
Natural Man"); Female Vocalist: Aretha Franklin
("Bridge over Troubled Water"); Vocal Group: Ike
and Tina Turner ("Proud Mary")

COUNTRY
Song (award to songwriter): "Help Me Make It
Through the Night" (Kris Kristofferson); Male
Vocalist: Jerry Reed ("When You're Hot, You're
Hot"); Female Vocalist: Sammi Smith ("Help Me
Make It Through the Night"); Vocal Group:
Conway Twitty, Loretta Lynn ("After the Fire Is
Gone")

OTHER AWARDS

Jazz Performance (Soloist): Bill Evans (*The Bill Evans Album*); Jazz Performance (Group): the Bill Evans Trio (*The Bill Evans Album*); Jazz Performance (Big Band): Duke Ellington ("New Orleans Suite"); Original Cast Show Album: *Godspell*; Soundtrack Album: *Shaft*; Comedy Performance: Lily Tomlin (*This Is a Recording*); Spoken Word: Les Crane (*Desiderata*); Classical Album: *Horowitz Plays Rachmaninoff* (Vladimir Horowitz)

The Grammys moved to New York for its second telecast. The show became the first to be broadcast from Madison Square Garden's Felt Forum. "After checking out the absymal sightlines and backstage wiring, I could guess why," producer Pierre Cosette told *TV Guide*.

Once again, the NARAS came under fire for virtually ignoring rock artists. Though Isaac Hayes' soundtrack album for *Shaft*, which combined R&B with hard rock, garnered the most nominations (eight) and three awards, acts such as The Rolling Stones, Alice Cooper, and Jefferson Airplane were not even in the running. Easy-listening groups like the Carpenters were still Grammy favorites.

Leonard Bernstein sounded a "sour note" when he said he was leaving the Grammys in order to watch his *West Side Story* on another network. The film (on NBC) trounced the awards (on ABC) in the ratings.

COUNTRY MUSIC ASSOCIATION AWARDS

Entertainer: Charley Pride; Single: "Help Me Make It Through the Night" (Sammi Smith); Song: "Easy Loving" (Freddie Hart, songwriter); Album: *I Won't Mention It Again* (Ray Price); Male Vocalist: Charley Pride; Female Vocalist: Lynn Anderson; Vocal Group: the Osborne Brothers; Vocal Duo: Porter Wagoner and Dolly Parton; Musician: Jerry Reed

One of the few black singers in country music, Charley Pride, was named Entertainer of the Year and won the Male Vocalist award. He also took Grammys for Sacred Performance (Musical) and Gospel Performance (Other Than Soul Gospel).

1972

RECORD OF THE YEAR

"Alone Again (Naturally)" (Gilbert O'Sullivan)
"American Pie" (Don McLean)
"The First Time Ever I Saw Your Face" (Roberta Flack)
"Song Sung Blue" (Neil Diamond)
"Without You" (Nilsson)

Roberta Flack dominated the 1972 Grammys. Her slow, sensuous rendering of "The First Time Ever I Saw Your Face" won her Record of the Year, the first time a black soloist had done so. "First Time" also won Song of the Year for its author Ewan MacColl (who originally wrote the tune for his wife Peggy Seeger, daughter of folksinger Pete). Flack also took Pop Vocal Performance, Duo, Group, or Chorus, for her duet with Danny Hathaway, "Where Is the Love." This was, however, not the first time for "The First Time." Flack had recorded it in 1969 for her *First Take* album. The song did not become a hit until Clint Eastwood used it in his film *Play Misty for Me*, in which he played a disc jockey plagued by an obsessed fan. As a result of the exposure in the Eastwood film, Atlantic released it as a single. It hit the No. 1 spot on *Billboard's* chart and held it for six weeks.

The same week Flack won her two Grammys for "First Time," she was No. 1 again for "Killing Me Softly with His Song," which won her another pair of awards the following year.

SONG OF THE YEAR (AWARD TO SONGWRITER)

"Alone Again (Naturally)" (Gilbert O'Sullivan)
"American Pie" (Don McLean)
"The First Time Ever I Saw Your Face" (Ewan MacColl)
"Song Sung Blue" (Neil Diamond)
"The Summer Knows" (Marilyn and Alan Bergman, Michel Legrand)

ALBUM OF THE YEAR

American Pie (Don McClean)
The Concert for Bangladesh (George Harrison and Friends: Ravi Shankar, Bob Dylan,

Leon Russell, Ringo Starr, Billy Preston, Eric Clapton, Klaus Voorman, others)
Jesus Christ Superstar (Original Broadway Cast)
Moods (Neil Diamond)
Nilsson Schmilsson (Nilsson)

NEW ARTIST
America
Harry Chapin
The Eagles
Loggins and Messina
John Prine

MALE VOCALIST (POP)
Mac Davis ("Baby, Don't Get Hooked on Me")
Sammy Davis, Jr. ("Candy Man")
Don McLean ("American Pie")
Nilsson ("Without You")
Gilbert O'Sullivan ["Alone Again (Naturally)"]

FEMALE VOCALIST (POP)
Roberta Flack (*Quiet Fire*)
Aretha Franklin ("Day Dreaming")
Helen Reddy ("I Am Woman")
Carly Simon (*Anticipation*)
Barbra Streisand ("Sweet Inspiration/
   Where You Lead")

"I Am Woman" was the unofficial anthem of the Women's Liberation movement. Helen Reddy touched off a minor controversy when, during her acceptance speech, she thanked God "because She makes everything possible." The Australian songstress was besieged with complaints from religious conservatives.

VOCAL GROUP (POP)
America ("A Horse with No Name")
Bread (*Baby I'm-a Want You*)
Roberta Flack, Donny Hathaway
   ("Where Is the Love")
The New Seekers ["I'd Like to Teach the World
   to Sing (in Perfect Harmony)"]
Seals and Croft ("Summer Breeze")

RHYTHM AND BLUES
Song (awarded to songwriter): "Papa Was a Rolling Stone" (Barrett Strong, Norman Whitfield); Male Vocalist: Billy Paul ("Me and

Mrs. Jones"); Female Vocalist: Aretha Franklin (*Young, Gifted and Black*); Vocal Group: the Temptations and Paul Riser, conducting ("Papa Was a Rolling Stone")

COUNTRY
Song (awarded to songwriter): "Kiss an Angel Good Mornin'" (Ben Peters); Male Vocalist: Charley Pride (*Charley Pride Sings Heart Songs*); Female Vocalist: Donna Fargo ("The Happiest Girl in the Whole USA"); Vocal Group: the Statler Brothers ("Class of '57")

OTHER AWARDS
Jazz Performance (Soloist): Gary Burton (*Alone at Last*); Jazz Performance (Group): Freddie Hubbard (*First Light*); Jazz Performance (Big Band): Duke Ellington ("Togo Brava Suite"); Original Cast Show Album: *Don't Bother Me, I Can't Cope*; Soundtrack Album: *The Godfather*; Comedy Performance: George Carlin (*FM & AM*); Spoken Word: *Lenny* (original Broadway cast); Classical Album: *Mahler: Symphony No. 8 in E Flat Major (Symphony of a Thousand)* (Georg Solti conducting the Chicago Symphony, Vienna Boys Choir, Vienna State Opera Chorus)

After two years, ABC decided to drop the Grammys. Because of a contractual agreement with the NARAS, the 1972 awards were scheduled to be broadcast from Nashville. The network felt the country music audience was too small and dropped its option. Producer Pierre Cosette (now presenting the event alone since his partner Burt Sugarman split) was desperate. He was obligated to put on a show, but had no network to broadcast it.

"NBC and CBS didn't want the Grammys because ABC had dropped them," Cosette told *Emmy Magazine*. "I had to guarantee the show or lose it. . . . I committed everything I owned in life and I came up with the $1,750,000. Then I went desperately back to CBS and climbed into bed with [then CBS president] Bob Wood and his wife. I climbed right into bed with them and said, 'Bob, you've got to buy this goddamned show, because if you don't, I'm ruined.' And he yelled 'Get out of my bed, you asshole,' and he bought the show."

Cosette's troubles didn't end there. There was a frantic search for an appropriate site in Nashville.

Roberta Flack repeated her triumph of the previous year at 1973's Grammys for "Killing Me Softly with His Song."

The Grand Ole Opry was unavailable, so the Tennessee Theatre, an aging movie house was rented. But there was no backstage space and no orchestra pit.

The producer continued the story for *TV Guide*: "Somehow, I convinced the minister of a Methodist church next door to let my 31-piece ensemble perform inside the building while we piped the sound across. I had rock musicians—many of whom must have scared this God-fearing man to death—wait inside the church also."

To add to the confusion, ten minutes before airtime, there was a total black-out. Cosette asked Joe Hamilton, the producer of *The Carol Burnett Show* and Burnett's husband, which one of Carol's shows they could rerun if the power didn't return.

Fortunately, the power did return. The ceremony went relatively smoothly until host Andy Williams introduced Curtis Mayfield to sing his anti-drug hit "Freddie's Dead." To create atmosphere, Cosette had planted a smoke machine backstage. But in the unventilated Tennessee Theatre

there was nowhere for the smoke to dissipate. The camera couldn't even find Mayfield in the ensuing fog bank and had to shoot him from behind. Afterwards, according to Cosette, "the whole theatre smelled like a wet sock."

Despite the glitches, the first CBS Grammys were a ratings hit. The annual ceremony has remained on the Big Eye network ever since. To get back the pop music crowd, ABC countered with the American Music Awards, first presented in 1974.

COUNTRY MUSIC ASSOCIATION AWARDS

Entertainer: Loretta Lynn; Single: "The Happiest Girl in the Whole USA" (Donna Fargo); Song: "Easy Loving" (Freddie Hart, songwriter); Album: *Let Me Tell You about a Song* (Merle Haggard); Male Vocalist: Charley Pride; Female Vocalist: Loretta Lynn; Vocal Group: the Statler Brothers; Vocal Duo: Conway Twitty and Loretta Lynn; Musician: Charlie McCoy

1973

THE GRAMMY AWARDS

RECORD OF THE YEAR
"Bad, Bad Leroy Brown" (Jim Croce)
"Behind Closed Doors" (Charlie Rich)
"Killing Me Softly with His Song" (Roberta Flack)
"You Are the Sunshine of My Life" (Stevie Wonder)
"You're So Vain" (Carly Simon)

Once again, a Roberta Flack release won both Record of the Year and Song of the Year. "Killing Me Softly with His Song" repeated the triumph of "The First Time Ever I Saw Your Face."

SONG OF THE YEAR (AWARD TO SONGWRITER)
"Behind Closed Doors" (Kenny O'Dell)
"Killing Me Softly with His Song" (Norman Gimbel, Charles Fox)
"Tie a Yellow Ribbon Round the Ole Oak Tree" (Irwin Levine, L. Russell Brown)

"You Are the Sunshine of My Life" (Stevie Wonder)

ALBUM OF THE YEAR
Behind Closed Doors (Charlie Rich)
The Divine Miss M (Bette Midler)
Innervisions (Stevie Wonder)
Killing Me Softly (Roberta Flack)
There Goes Rhymin' Simon (Paul Simon)

At age 23, Stevie Wonder was the second youngest artist to win Album of the Year (Barbra Streisand at age 22 holds the honor). But he has plenty of other Grammy records. Previously ignored by the NARAS for his Motown hits as a teenager, Wonder broke down that indifference in 1973 with a total of four Grammys (Album of the Year, Male Vocalist (Pop), R&B Male Vocalist, R&B Song). He almost broke down something else when he was in a near fatal auto accident just months before the awards ceremony.

He is one of only three artists to win Album of the Year three times. (Frank Sinatra and Paul Simon are the others.) His career total of Grammys so far is seventeen.

NEW ARTIST
Eumir Deodato
Maureen McGovern
Bette Midler
Marie Osmond
Barry White

Upon receiving her Grammy for New Artist from the white-bread Karen Carpenter, the raucous Bette Midler broke up the crowd with her brief acceptance speech: "Isn't that a hoot? Me up here with Miss Karen."

MALE VOCALIST (POP)
Perry Como ("And I Love You So")
Jim Croce ("Bad, Bad Leroy Brown")
Elton John ("Daniel")
Paul Simon (*There Goes Rhymin' Simon*)
Stevie Wonder ("You Are the Sunshine of My Life")

FEMALE VOCALIST (POP)
Roberta Flack ("Killing Me Softly with His Song")
Bette Midler ("Boogie Woogie Bugle Boy")
Anne Murray ("Danny's Song")

Diana Ross ("Touch Me in the Morning")
Carly Simon ("You're So Vain")

VOCAL GROUP (POP)
The Carpenters ("Sing")
Dawn featuring Tony Orlando ("Tie a Yellow Ribbon Round the Ole Oak Tree")
Gladys Knight and the Pips ["Neither One of Us (Wants to Be the First to Say Goodbye)"]
Paul McCartney and Wings ("Live and Let Die")
Seals and Croft ("Diamond Girl")

RHYTHM AND BLUES
Song (award to songwriter): "Superstition" (Stevie Wonder); Male Vocalist: Stevie Wonder ("Superstition"); Female Vocalist: Aretha Franklin ("Master of Eyes"); Vocal Group: Gladys Knight and the Pips ("Midnight Train to Georgia")

COUNTRY
Song (award to songwriter): "Behind Closed Doors" (Kenny O'Dell); Male Vocalist: Charlie Rich ("Behind Closed Doors"); Female Vocalist: Olivia Newton-John ("Let Me Be There"); Vocal Group: Kris Kristofferson, Rita Coolidge ("From the Bottle to the Bottom")

OTHER AWARDS
Jazz Performance (Soloist): Art Tatum (*God Is in the House*); Jazz Performance (Group): Supersax (*Supersax Plays Bird*); Jazz Performance (Big Band): Woody Herman (*Giant Steps*); Original Show Cast Album: *A Little Night Music*; Soundtrack Album: *Jonathan Livingston Seagull*; Comedy Performance: Cheech and Chong (*Los Cochinos*); Spoken Word: Richard Harris (*Jonathan Livingston Seagull*); Classical Album: *Bartok: Concerto for Orchestra* (Pierre Boulez conducting the New York Philharmonic)

The Grammys shifted back to Los Angeles for their second year on CBS. They were upstaged by ABC's new show *The American Music Awards*. Created in response to the Grammy ratings triumph of last year (after ABC had let the Grammys go), the AMAs were promoted with great fanfare and broadcast several weeks before the rival CBS show. *Variety* commented that the Grammys had several of the same artists that appeared on the AMAs, including Stevie Wonder, Tony Orlando and Dawn, and Roberta Flack, "so the Grammys couldn't escape that *deja vu* feeling." As a result the more established Grammy show lost the ratings war to the upstart American Music Awards program.

Grammy presenters were paired as "odd couples." Helen Reddy and Alice Cooper traded quips about Cooper's snake. Moms Mabley reduced Kris Kristofferson to helpless laughter by removing her false teeth.

Little Richard and Chuck Berry, neither of whom had ever won a Grammy, rocked several of their 1950s' hits. During the number Little Richard's microphone went dead, but even with a kaput mike they were judged the most dynamic act on the bill. Perennial host Andy Williams coolly crooned the five nominees for best Song.

THE AMERICAN MUSIC AWARDS

POP/ROCK
Single: "Tie a Yellow Ribbon" (Tony Orlando and Dawn); Album: *Lady Sings the Blues* (Diana Ross); Male Artist: Jim Croce; Female Artist: Helen Reddy; Band, Duo, or Group: the Carpenters

SOUL/RHYTHM AND BLUES
Single: "Superstition" (Stevie Wonder); Album: *I'm Still in Love with You* (Al Green); Male Artist: Stevie Wonder; Female Artist: Roberta Flack; Band, Duo, or Group: the Temptations

COUNTRY
Single: "Behind Closed Doors" (Charlie Rich); Album: *A Sun Shiny Day* (Charley Pride); Male Artist: Charley Pride; Female Artist: Lynn Anderson; Band, Duo, or Group: the Carter Family

SPECIAL AWARD
Bing Crosby

As noted above, the American Music Awards were created by ABC to gain back the audience it lost when CBS snapped up the Grammys. The show was (and still is) produced by Dick Clark, the ageless entrepreneur behind the popular *American Bandstand* program. Relying on sales charts and public opinion polls rather than votes by industry

insiders, the AMAs categories begin with "Favorite" rather than "Best."

COUNTRY MUSIC ASSOCIATION AWARDS

Entertainer: Roy Clark; Single: "Behind Closed Doors" (Charlie Rich); Song: "Behind Closed Doors" (Kenny O'Dell, songwriter); Album: *Behind Closed Doors* (Charlie Rich); Male Vocalist: Charlie Rich; Female Vocalist: Loretta Lynn; Vocal Group: the Statler Brothers; Vocal Duo: Conway Twitty and Loretta Lynn; Musician: Charlie McCoy

THE GRAMMY AWARDS

RECORD OF THE YEAR
"Don't Let the Sun Go Down on Me" (Elton John)
"Feel Like Makin' Love" (Roberta Flack)
"Help Me" (Joni Mitchell)
"I Honestly Love You" (Olivia Newton-John)
"Midnight at the Oasis" (Maria Muldaur)

Middle-road popsters Olivia Newton-John and Marvin Hamlisch triumphed over the likes of soft-rockers Elton John, Maria Muldaur, Phoebe Snow, and Joni Mitchell at the '74 Grammys—while harder and hotter acts like Bruce Springsteen (coverman for both *Time* and *Newsweek*), Van Morrison, and Jackson Browne weren't even nominated.

Australian songstress Newton-John's "I Honestly Love You" (co-authored by fellow Aussie and Liza Minnelli's ex Peter Allen) won for Record of the Year and Female Vocalist (Pop).

Composer Hamlisch garnered a total of four awards: Song of the Year and Soundtrack Album (for *The Way We Were*), Pop Instrumental Performance (for his recording of Scott Joplin's "The Entertainer" from the film *The Sting*), and New Artist. The last win triggered criticism since the award traditionally had gone to a performer. But Hamlisch did play the piano for "The Entertainer."

Hamlisch was having a Henry Mancini-like career, conquering movies, Broadway, and the music business. One year previous to his double-Grammy victory, he took home three Oscars (two for *The Way We Were,* and one for *The Sting*). At the 1976 Tonys, the youthful composer collected another prize. He won for his score (with lyricist Ed Kleban) for *A Chorus Line*, the second-longest running show in Broadway history.

SONG OF THE YEAR (AWARD TO SONGWRITER)
"Feel Like Makin' Love" (Eugene McDaniels)
"I Honestly Love You" (Jeff Barry, Peter Allen)
"Midnight at the Oasis" (David Nichtern)
"The Way We Were" (Marilyn and Alan Bergman, Marvin Hamlisch)
"You and Me against the World" (Paul Williams, Ken Ascher)

ALBUM OF THE YEAR
Back Home Again (John Denver)
Band on the Run (Paul McCartney and Wings)
Caribou (Elton John)
Court and Spark (Joni Mitchell)
Fulfillingness' First Finale (Stevie Wonder)

Repeating his success of the year before, Stevie Wonder copped four Grammys. This time it was for *Fulfillingness' First Finale*, his first one-hit album since 1963's *Little Stevie Wonder—The 10-Year-Old Genius.*

NEW ARTIST
Bad Company
Johnny Bristol
David Essex
Graham Central Station
Marvin Hamlisch
Phoebe Snow

MALE VOCALIST (POP)
Harry Chapin ("Cat's in the Cradle")
Elton John ("Don't Let the Sun Go Down on Me")
Dave Loggins ("Please Come to Boston")
Billy Preston ("Nothing from Nothing")
Stevie Wonder (*Fulfillingness' First Finale*)

FEMALE VOCALIST (POP)
Roberta Flack ("Feel Like Makin' Love")
Carole King ("Jazzman")

Cleo Laine (*Cleo Laine Live at Carnegie Hall*)
Joni Mitchell ("Court and Spark")
Olivia Newton-John ("I Honestly Love You")

VOCAL GROUP (POP)
Quincy Jones ("Body Heat")
Paul McCartney and **Wings** ("Band on the Run")
Steely Dan ("Ricky, Don't Lose That Number")
The Stylistics ("You Make Me Feel Brand New")
Dionne Warwick and the Spinners ("Then Came You")

RHYTHM AND BLUES
Song (awarded to songwriter): "Living for the City" (Stevie Wonder); Male Vocalist: Stevie Wonder ("Boogie on Reggae Woman"); Female Vocalist: Aretha Franklin ("Ain't Nothing Like the Real Thing"); Vocal Group: Rufus ("Tell Me Something Good")

COUNTRY
Song (awarded to songwriter): "A Very Special Love Song" (Norris Wilson, Billy Sherrill); Male Vocalist: Ronnie Milsap ("Please Don't Tell Me How the Story Ends"); Female Vocalist: Anne Murray ("Love Song"); Vocal Group: the Pointer Sisters ("Fairy Tale")

OTHER AWARDS
Jazz Performance (Soloist): Charlie Parker (*First Recordings!*); Jazz Performance (Group): Oscar Peterson, Joe Pass, Niels Pederson (*The Trio*); Jazz Performance (Big Band): Woody Herman (*Thundering Herd*); Original Cast Show Album: *Raisin*; Soundtrack Album: *The Way We Were*; Comedy Recording: Richard Pryor (*That Nigger's Crazy*); Spoken Word: Peter Cook, Dudley Moore (*Good Evening*); Classical Album: *Berlioz: Symphonie Fantastique* (Georg Solti conducting the Chicago Symphony)

Andy Williams continued his hosting chores. The 1974 show originated from the Uris (later renamed the Gershwin) Theatre on Broadway in New York. The site was chosen in honor of Scott Joplin, the early 1900s' ragtime composer whose work was having a renaissance through the popularity of *The Sting* which employed Joplin's melodies in its background score. The theater housed a production of the composer's previously unseen opera *Treemonisha*. An additional ceremony for awards not presented on the broadcast was held at New York's Americana Hotel. The previous year's New Artist winner Bette Midler was one of 1974's most memorable presenters. She appeared wearing a 45 rpm platter on her head. "It was a great record, but it's a better hat," the Divine Miss M joked.

THE AMERICAN MUSIC AWARDS

POP/ROCK
Single: "I Honestly Love You" (Olivia Newton-John); Album: *Behind Closed Doors* (Charlie Rich); Male Artist: John Denver; Female Artist: Olivia Newton-John; Band, Duo, or Group: Gladys Knight and the Pips

SOUL/RHYTHM AND BLUES
Single: "Midnight Train to Georgia" (Gladys Knight and the Pips); Album: *Imagination* (Gladys Knight and the Pips); Male Artist: Stevie Wonder; Female Artist: Diana Ross; Band, Duo, or Group: Gladys Knight and the Pips

COUNTRY
Single: "The Most Beautiful Girl" (Charlie Rich); Album: *Let Me Be There* (Olivia Newton-John); Male Artist: Charley Pride; Female Artist: Olivia Newton-John; Band, Duo, or Group: Conway Twitty and Loretta Lynn

SPECIAL AWARD
Berry Gordy, Jr.

COUNTRY MUSIC ASSOCIATION AWARDS

Entertainer: Charlie Rich; Single: "Country Bumpkin" (Cal Smith); Song: "Country Bumpkin" (Don Wayne, songwriter); Album: *A Very Special Love Song* (Charlie Rich); Male Vocalist: Ronnie Milsap; Female Vocalist: Olivia Newton-John; Vocal Group: the Statler Brothers; Vocal Duo: Conway Twitty and Loretta Lynn; Musician: Don Rich

1975

THE GRAMMY AWARDS

RECORD OF THE YEAR
"At Seventeen" (Janis Ian)
"Love Will Keep Us Together" (the Captain and Tenille)
"Lyin' Eyes" (the Eagles)
"Mandy" (Barry Manilow)
"Rhinestone Cowboy" (Glen Campbell)

The Captain and Tenille were the mildest of a mild set of nominees for Record of the Year. Their easy-listening hit "Love Will Keep Us Together" was the top-selling single on the *Billboard* charts.

SONG OF THE YEAR (AWARD TO SONGWRITER)
"At Seventeen" (Janis Ian)
"Feelings" (Morris Albert)
"Love Will Keep Us Together" (Neil Sedaka, Howard Greenfield)
"Rhinestone Cowboy" (Larry Weiss)
"Send in the Clowns" (Stephen Sondheim)

Though it was first heard in the score of Stephen Sondheim's musical *A Little Night Music* in 1973, "Send in the Clowns" was released as a single by Judy Collins in 1975. The bittersweet ballad of two lovers who just miss each other garnered the Broadway composer-lyricist his first (and so far only) Song of the Year Grammy.

ALBUM OF THE YEAR
Between the Lines (Janis Ian)
Captain Fantastic and the Dirt Brown Cowboy (Elton John)
Heart like a Wheel (Linda Ronstadt)
One of These Nights (the Eagles)
Still Crazy after All These Years (Paul Simon)

Nineteen seventy-five was the Grammy year of the comeback. Three stars of the '60s earned multiple nominations. The biggest victor was Paul Simon. After breaking up with Art Garfunkel, Simon established himself as a solo act with his humorous twist on reaching maturity, *Still Crazy after All*

These Years. The LP won Album of the Year and Simon took Male Vocalist (Pop) honors, adding two awards to the seven he had garnered in previous years with Garfunkel. Simon and Garfunkel, together in a brief reunion, were also nominated for Vocal Group (Pop) for "My Little Town," but they lost to the Eagles for "Lyin' Eyes." Upon receiving his *Still Crazy* Grammy, the thirty-four-year-old singer/songwriter thanked Stevie Wonder "for not releasing an album this year."

Also making new hits were Janis Ian, a teen star who had retired in 1967, with her album of adolescent loneliness *Between the Lines*, and folk heroine Judy Collins crooning the Song of the Year "Send in the Clowns."

NEW ARTIST
Morris Albert
Amazing Rhythm Aces
The Brecker Brothers
Natalie Cole
K. C. and the Sunshine Band

MALE VOCALIST (POP)
Morris Albert ("Feelings")
Glen Campbell ("Rhinestone Cowboy")
Elton John (*Captain Fantastic and the Brown Dirt Cowboy*)
Neil Sedaka ("Bad Blood")
Paul Simon (*Still Crazy after All These Years*)

FEMALE VOCALIST (FEMALE)
Judy Collins ("Send in the Clowns")
Janis Ian ("At Seventeen")
Olivia Newton-John ("Have You Never Been Mellow?")
Helen Reddy ("Ain't No Way to Treat a Lady")
Linda Ronstadt (*Heart like a Wheel*)

Natalie Cole, daughter of Nat "King" Cole, was the first black performer to win the New Artist award. She also interrupted Aretha Franklin's until then unbroken winning streak in the R&B Female Vocalist category. She would return to the Grammy stage in 1991 when *Unforgettable*, her engineered collaboration with her late father, would win her three awards.

VOCAL GROUP (POP)
The Captain and Tenille ("Love Will Keep Us Together")
The Eagles ("Lyin' Eyes")
Gladys Knight and the Pips ("The Way We Were/ Try to Remember")
Simon and Garfunkel ("My Little Town")
Singers Unlimited (*A Capella 2*)

RHYTHM AND BLUES
Song (awarded to songwriter): "Where Is the Love?" (H. W. Casey, Richard Finch, Willie Clarke, Betty Wright); Male Vocalist: Ray Charles ("Living for the City"); Female Vocalist: Natalie Cole ("This Will Be"); Vocal Group: Earth, Wind and Fire ("Shining Star")

COUNTRY
Song (awarded to songwriter): "(Hey Won't You Play) Another Somebody Done Somebody Wrong Song" (Chips Moman, Larry Butler); Male Vocalist: Willie Nelson ("Blue Eyes Crying in the Rain"); Female Vocalist: Linda Rondstadt ["I Can't Help It (If I'm Still in Love With You)"]; Vocal Group: Kris Kristofferson, Rita Coolidge ("Lover, Please")

OTHER AWARDS
Jazz Performance (Soloist): Dizzy Gillespie (*Oscar Peterson and Dizzy Gillespie*); Jazz Performance (Group): Return to Forever featuring Chick Corea (*No Mystery*); Jazz Performance (Big Band): Phil Woods with Michel Legrand and His Orchestra (*Images*); Original Cast Show Album: *The Wiz*; Soundtrack Album: *Jaws*; Comedy Recording: Richard Pryor (*Is It Something I Said?*); Spoken Word: James Whitmore (*Give 'em Hell, Harry*); Classical Album of the Year: *Beethoven: Symphonies (9) Complete* (Sir Georg Solti conducting the Chicago Symphony)

Andy Williams continued hosting the Grammys (this time from the Hollywood Palladium), though he was drifting further and further away from the heartbeat of contemporary music. *Variety* did commend Williams for having the good sense to kid himself about his "less than daring, commercially bent image."

With the Captain and Tenille honored and Bruce Springsteen and Bob Dylan ignored, the Grammys were still seen as being as much out of the current musical loop as the awards ceremony's host.

THE AMERICAN MUSIC AWARDS

POP/ROCK
Single: "Rhinestone Cowboy" (Glen Campbell); Album: *Have You Never Been Mellow* (Olivia Newton-John); Male Artist: John Denver; Female Artist: Olivia Newton-John; Band, Duo, or Group: Tony Orlando and Dawn

SOUL/RHYTHM AND BLUES
Single: "Get Down Tonight" (KC and the Sunshine Band); Album: *A Song for You* (the Temptations); Male Artist: Barry White; Female Artist: Aretha Franklin; Band, Duo, or Group: Gladys Knight and the Pips

COUNTRY
Single: "Rhinestone Cowboy" (Glen Campbell); Album: *Back Home Again* (John Denver); Male Artist: John Denver; Female Artist: Olivia Newton-John; Band, Duo, or Group: Donny and Marie Osmond

SPECIAL AWARD
Irving Berlin

COUNTRY MUSIC ASSOCIATION AWARDS

Entertainer: John Denver; Single: "Before the Next Teardrop Falls" (Freddie Fender); Song: "Back Home Again" (John Denver, songwriter); Album: *A Legend in My Time* (Ronnie Milsap); Male Vocalist: Waylon Jennings; Female Vocalist: Dolly Parton; Vocal Group: the Statler Brothers; Vocal Duo: Conway Twitty and Loretta Lynn; Musician: Johnny Gimble

THE GRAMMY AWARDS

RECORD OF THE YEAR
"Afternoon Delight" (the Starland Vocal Band)

"50 Ways to Leave Your Lover" (Paul Simon)
"I Write the Songs" (Barry Manilow)
"If You Leave Me Now" (Chicago)
"This Masquerade" (George Benson)

SONG OF THE YEAR (AWARD TO SONGWRITER)
"Afternoon Delight" (Bill Danoff)
"Breaking Up Is Hard To Do" (Neil Sedaka, Howard Greenfield)
"I Write the Songs" (Bruce Johnson)
"This Masquerade" (Leon Russell)
"The Wreck of the Edmund Fitzgerald" (Gordon Lightfoot)

ALBUM OF THE YEAR
Breezin' (George Benson)
Chicago X (Chicago)
Frampton Comes Alive (Peter Frampton)
Silk Degrees (Boz Scaggs)
Songs in the Key of Life (Stevie Wonder)

Stevie Wonder followed up his 1973 and 1974 wins with a total of five 1976 Grammys for *Songs in the Key of Life*. [He won two as producer and singer-songwriter on the album, as well as accolades for Male Vocalist (Pop), R&B Male Vocalist, and Producer of the Year.] This brought his Grammy total to fifteen.

Wonder was performing in Lagos, Nigeria, on Grammy night, so a satellite transmission was set up. There was a problem with the broadcast. During the ceremony, the signal broke up. Grammy host Andy Williams committed one of the most famous goofs in awards show history by asking the blind Wonder, "If you can't hear me, can you *see* me?" Williams quickly apologized.

NEW ARTIST
Boston
Dr. Buzzard's Original "Savannah" Band
The Brothers Johnson
The Starland Vocal Band
Wild Cherry

One-hit wonders the Starland Vocal Band formerly served as back-up singers for John Denver. The group's smash single "Afternoon Delight" was its only No. 1 song. Upon accepting the New Artist award, one group member thanked her mother who had told her to keep her day job. Perhaps she should have listened to mom. The group disbanded in 1980.

MALE VOCALIST (POP)
George Benson ("This Masquerade")
Gordon Lightfoot ("The Wreck of the Edmund Fitzgerald")
Lou Rawls ("You'll Never Find Another Love Like Mine")
Boz Scaggs (*Silk Degrees*)
Stevie Wonder (*Songs in the Key of Life*)

FEMALE VOCALIST (POP)
Natalie Cole (*Natalie*)
Emmylou Harris ("Here, There and Everywhere")
Joni Mitchell (*The Hissing of Summer Lawns*)
Vicki Sue Robinson ("Turn the Beat Around")
Linda Ronstadt (*Hasten Down the Wind*)

VOCAL GROUP (POP)
Chicago ("If You Leave Me Now")
Elton John, Kiki Dee ("Don't Go Breaking My Heart")
England Dan and John Ford Coley ("I'd Really Love to See You Tonight")
The Starland Vocal Band ("Afternoon Delight")
Queen ("Bohemian Rhapsody")

RHYTHM AND BLUES
Song (award to songwriter): "Lowdown" (Boz Scaggs, David Paich); Male Vocalist: Stevie Wonder ("I Wish"); Female Vocalist: Natalie Cole ["Sophisticated Lady (She's a Different Lady)"]; Vocal Group: Marilyn McCoo, Billy Davis, Jr. ["You Don't Have To Be a Star (To Be in My Show)"]

COUNTRY
Song (songwriter's award): "Broken Lady" (Larry Gatlin); Male Vocalist: Ronnie Milsap ["(I'm a) Stand By My Woman Man"]; Female Vocalist: Emmylou Harris (*Elite Hotel*); Vocal Group: the Amazing Rhythm Aces ["The End Is Not in Sight (The Cowboy Tune)"]

JAZZ
Vocal Performance: Ella Fitzgerald (*Fitzgerald and Pass . . . Again*); Soloist: Count Basie (*Basie and Zoot*); Group: Chick Corea (*The Leprechaun*); Big Band: Duke Ellington (*The Ellington Suites*)

OTHER AWARDS
Original Cast Show Album: *Bubbling Brown Sugar*; Soundtrack Album: *Car Wash*; Comedy Performance: Richard Pryor (*Bicentennial Nigger*); Spoken Word: Orson Welles, Henry Fonda, Helen Hayes, James Earl Jones (*Great American Documents*); Classical Album: *Beethoven: The Five Piano Concertos* (Daniel Barenboim conducting the London Philharmonic)

Andy Williams' Stevie Wonder slip-up spelled the end of his days as a Grammy host. At the other end of the taste spectrum, Bette Midler was the evening's hippest presenter. She slowly made her entrance, stunning the audience with a brilliant red dress featuring a train that never ended. When she reached the podium she wrapped herself up in the seemingly mile-long garment and said "I am the ghost of Grammys past. . . . It's great to be back in L.A., the home of *absolutely nothing*!"

The New York Times commented, "Paul Williams and Ringo Starr insisted on performing like 12-year-old cut-ups and succeeded in vastly amusing only each other. . . . On the whole, though, the Grammys provided one of television's better award extravaganzas."

THE AMERICAN MUSIC AWARDS

POP/ROCK
Single: "Don't Go Breaking My Heart" (Elton John, Kiki Dee); Album: *The Eagles' Greatest Hits* (the Eagles); Male Artist: Elton John; Female Artist: Olivia Newton-John; Band, Duo, or Group: Chicago

SOUL/RHYTHM AND BLUES
Single (tie): "Play That Funky Music" (Wild Cherry) and "You'll Never Find Another Love Like Mine" (Lou Rawls); Album: *Songs in the Key of Life* (Stevie Wonder); Male Artist: Stevie Wonder; Female Artist: Aretha Franklin; Band, Duo, or Group: Earth, Wind and Fire

COUNTRY

Single: "Blue Eyes Cryin' in the Rain" (Willie Nelson); Album: *Rhinestone Cowboy* (Glen Campbell); Male Artist: Charley Pride; Female Artist: Loretta Lynn; Band, Duo, or Group: Conway Twitty, Loretta Lynn

SPECIAL AWARD

Johnny Cash

COUNTRY MUSIC ASSOCIATION AWARDS

Entertainer: Mel Tillis; Single: "Good Hearted Woman" (Waylon Jennings, Willie Nelson); Song: "Rhinestone Cowboy" (Larry Weiss, songwriter); Album: *Wanted—The Outlaws* (Waylon Jennings, Willie Nelson, Tompall Glaser, Jessi Cotler); Male Vocalist: Ronnie Milsap; Female Vocalist: Dolly Parton; Vocal Group: the Statler Brothers; Vocal Duo: Waylong Jennings, Willie Nelson; Musician: Hargus "Pig" Robbins

THE GRAMMY AWARDS

RECORD OF THE YEAR

"Blue Bayou" (Linda Ronstadt)
"Don't It Make My Brown Eyes Blue" (Crystal Gayle)
"Hotel California" (the Eagles)
"Love Theme From *A Star Is Born* (Evergreen)" (Barbra Streisand)
"You Light Up My Life" (Debby Boone)

Soft rock groups like the Eagles and Fleetwood Mac dominated the '77 Grammys, while Debby Boone, daughter of Pat and herself a saccharine singer in the traditional Grammy mode, took the New Artist award.

SONG OF THE YEAR (AWARD TO SONGWRITER) (TIE)

"Don't It Make My Brown Eyes Blues" (Richard Leigh)
"Hotel California" (Don Felder, Don Henley, Glenn Frey)

"Love Theme from *A Star Is Born* (Evergreen)" (Barbra Streisand, Paul Williams)
"Nobody Does It Better" (Marvin Hamlisch, Carole Bayer Sager)
"Southern Nights" (Allen Toussaint)
"You Light Up My Life" (Joe Brooks)

Grammy continued its soft-focus approach by splitting the best Song award between two easy-listening movie themes: "Evergreen" from *A Star Is Born* and "You Light Up My Life" from the picture of the same name. This was the only tie in a major category in Grammy history. Both tunes had won the Oscar for Original Song in successive years.

Co-winner Paul Williams jibed, "I want to thank Barbra [Streisand] for writing a beautiful melody amd Dr. Jack Wallstader for the valium that got me through the whole experience." Streisand, who had not won a Grammy since 1965, also copped the Female Vocalist (Pop) award for her performance of the song.

ALBUM OF THE YEAR

Aja (Steely Dan)
Hotel California (the Eagles)
J. T. (James Taylor)
Rumours (Fleetwood Mac)
Star Wars (John Williams conducting the London Symphony)

Fleetwood Mac's *Rumours* was No. 1 on the *Billboard* charts for seven months and contained four Top 10 singles—"Dreams," "Go Your Own Way," "You Make Loving Fun," and "Don't Stop" (later to become Bill Clinton's 1992 Presidential campaign theme song). Ironically, this smash hit was recorded while the two couples in the group—Lindsay Buckingham and Stevie Nicks and Christine and John McVie—were splitting up. This turned out to be the group's only Grammy.

NEW ARTIST

Stephen Bishop
Debby Boone
Shaun Cassidy
Foreigner
Andy Gibb

MALE VOCALIST (POP)
Stephen Bishop ("On and On")
Andy Gibb ("I Just Want To Be Your Everything")
Engelbert Humperdinck ("After the Lovin'")
Leo Sayer ("When I Need You")
James Taylor ("Handy Man")

FEMALE VOCALIST (POP)
Debby Boone ("You Light Up My Life")
Dolly Parton ("Here You Come Again")
Linda Ronstadt ("Blue Bayou")
Carly Simon ("Nobody Does It Better")
Barbra Streisand ["Love Theme from *A Star Is Born* (Evergreen)"]

VOCAL GROUP (POP)
The Bee Gees ("How Deep Is Your Love")
Crosby, Stills and Nash (*CSN*)
The Eagles (*Hotel California*)
Fleetwood Mac (*Rumours*)
Steely Dan (*Aja*)

RHYTHM AND BLUES
Song (award to songwriter): "You Make Me Feel Like Dancing" (Leo Sayer, Vini Poncia); Male Vocalist: Lou Rawls (*Unmistakable Lou*); Female Vocalist: Thelma Houston ("Don't Leave Me This Way"); Vocal Group: the Emotions ("The Best of My Love")

COUNTRY
Song (award to songwriter): "Don't It Make My Brown Eyes Blue" (Richard Leigh); Male Vocalist: Kenny Rogers ("Lucille"); Female Vocalist: Crystal Gayle ("Don't It Make My Brown Eyes Blue"); Vocal Group: the Kendalls ("Heaven's Just a Sin Away")

JAZZ
Vocal Performance: Al Jarreau (*Look to the Rainbow*); Soloist: Oscar Peterson (*The Giants*); Group: Phil Woods (*The Phil Woods Six—Live from the Showboat*); Big Band: Count Basie and His Orchestra (*Prime Time*)

OTHER AWARDS
Original Cast Show Album: *Annie*; Soundtrack Album: *Star Wars*; Comedy Performance: Steve Martin (*Let's Get Small*); Spoken Word: Julie Harris (*The Belle of Amherst*); Classical Album: *Concert of the Century* (recorded live at Carnegie Hall, May 18, 1976)

After his Stevie Wonder gaffe of the previous year, Andy Williams was removed as host of the Grammys. The NARAS TV Committee was clammering for an emcee more in tune with the contemporary music industry, not an old crooner like Williams. Glamorous rocker David Bowie was briefly considered, but he was too far-out for CBS. The compromise choice, country singer/songwriter John Denver, may have been only slightly more hip than Williams, but he was younger and had proven his telegenic qualities in a series of TV specials, one of which had won an Emmy. Denver continued as the Grammys' main host into the '80s.

Performances from the likes of Denver, Debby Boone, Shaun Cassidy, and Crystal Gayle gave 1977 a distinctly middle-of-the-road sound, even without Andy Williams. The Eagles, up for several awards, had agreed to perform and give the show a rock edge. But they would only appear if they could be guaranteed a win. Producer Pierre Cossette refused to give out the results of the voting prior to the broadcast (and besides, he wasn't privy to the information). The group's members later reversed themselves and stated they would perform without the assurance of a win, but never showed up. The rock press hailed them for their boycott.

For the first time, the ceremony was open to the public and the balcony of the Shrine Auditorium contained hundreds of shrieking music fans.

The New York Times was harsh in its criticism of the show: "The awards telecast was fraught with mistakes, clumsiness, and vulgarity. Halfway through the proceedings, the audience had stopped even trying to laugh at the jokes John Denver, the host, was asked to recite."

POP/ROCK
Single: "You Light Up My Life" (Debby Boone); Album: *Rumours* (Fleetwood Mac); Male Artist: Barry Manilow; Female Artist: Linda Ronstadt; Band, Duo, or Group: Fleetwood Mac

SOUL/RHYTHM AND BLUES
Single: "The Best of My Love" (the Emotions); Album: *Songs in the Key of Life* (Stevie Wonder); Male Artist: Stevie Wonder; Female Artist: Natalie Cole; Band, Duo, or Group: Earth, Wind and Fire

COUNTRY
Single: "Lucille" (Kenny Rogers); Album: *New Harvest—First Gathering* (Dolly Parton); Male Vocalist: Conway Twitty; Female Vocalist: Loretta Lynn; Band, Duo, or Group: Conway Twitty, Loretta Lynn

SPECIAL AWARD
Ella Fitzgerald

COUNTRY MUSIC ASSOCIATION AWARDS

Entertainer: Ronnie Milsap; Single: "Lucille" (Kenny Rogers); Song: "Lucille" (Roger Bowling, Hal Bynum, songwriters); Album: Ronnie Milsap (*Ronnie Milsap Live*); Male Vocalist: Ronnie Milsap; Female Vocalist: Crystal Gayle; Vocal Group: the Statler Brothers; Vocal Duo: Jim Ed Brown, Helen Cornelius; Musician: Roy Clark

THE GRAMMY AWARDS

RECORD OF THE YEAR
"Baker Street" (Gerry Rafferty)
"Feels So Good" (Chuck Mangione)
"Just the Way You Are" (Billy Joel)
"Stayin' Alive" (the Bee Gees)
"You Needed Me" (Anne Murray)

SONG OF THE YEAR (AWARD TO SONGWRITER)
"Just the Way You Are" (Billy Joel)
"Stayin' Alive" (Barry, Robin, and Maurice Gibb)
"Three Times a Lady" (Lionel Ritchie)
"You Don't Bring Me Flowers" (Neil Diamond, Alan and Marilyn Bergman)
"You Needed Me" (Randy Goodrum)

Billy Joel began a three-year Grammy streak in 1978. His sweetly lyrical "Just the Way You Are" took both Record of the Year and Song of the Year (preventing a total take-over of the awards by the Bee Gees). Joel would win Album of the Year and Male Vocalist (Pop) in 1979 (for *52nd Street*) and Male Vocalist (Rock) in 1980 (for *Glass Houses*).

ALBUM OF THE YEAR
Even Now (Barry Manilow)
Grease (Original Soundtrack Album)
Running on Empty (Jackson Browne)
Saturday Night Fever (Soundtrack Album)
Some Girls (the Rolling Stones)

The disco beat was dominating American consciousness and the Grammys. High-voiced, Australian brother-act the Bee Gees (Maurice, Andy, and Barry Gibb) took home five prizes for their contributions to the *Saturday Night Fever* album [Album of the Year as both artists and producers, Producers of the Year, Arrangements, and Vocal Group (Pop)]. *Fever* starred John Travolta as a working-class Brooklyn teenager whose only glory comes on the dance floor. Although it was released late in 1977, the soundtrack missed the Grammy eligibilty cut-off date for that year. By the time of the '78 Grammys, *Saturday Night Fever* was fifteen months old. But it was still selling strong (it eventually sold 11 million units) and featured three No. 1 hits: "Stayin' Alive," "Night Fever," and "How Deep Is Your Love?"

SNF was the first soundtrack LP to take Album of the Year since the *Peter Gunn* TV album won the prize in 1958, Grammy's first year. *Fever* is still the sole film soundtrack album to be named best of the year. Among the albums it defeated was another film score, *Grease*, which also starred John Travolta. Bee Gee Barry Gibb and *SNF* album co-producers Albhy Galuten and Karl Richardson were competing against themselves as producers of the *Grease* recording. Another notable nominee was *Some Girls*, the first Grammy bid for the Rolling Stones.

Other disco winners of '78 were R&B Female Vocalist Donna Summer and New Artist A Taste of Honey.

NEW ARTIST
The Cars
Elvis Costello
Chris Rea
A Taste of Honey
Toto

MALE VOCALIST (POP)
Jackson Browne (*Running on Empty*)
Dan Hill ("Sometimes When We Touch")
Barry Manilow ["Copacabana (At the Copa)"]
Gerry Rafferty ("Baker Street")
Gino Vannelli ("I Just Wanna Stop")

FEMALE VOCALIST (POP)
Anne Murray ("You Needed Me")
Olivia Newton-John ("Hopelessly Devoted
   to You")
Carly Simon ("You Belong to Me")
Barbra Streisand ("You Don't Bring Me Flowers,"
   solo version)
Donna Summer ("MacArthur Park")

VOCAL GROUP (POP)
The Bee Gees (*Saturday Night Fever*)
The Commodores ("Three Times a Lady")
Earth, Wind and Fire ("Got to Get You
   into My Life")
Roberta Flack, Donny Hathaway ("The Closer
   I Get to You")
Steely Dan ["FM (No Static at All)"]

RHYTHM AND BLUES
Song (award to songwriter): "Last Dance" (Paul
Jabara); Male Vocalist: George Benson ("On
Broadway"); Female Vocalist: Donna Summer
("Last Dance"); Vocal Group: Earth, Wind and
Fire (*All 'n' All*)

Disco diva Donna Summer won in the R&B
Female Vocalist category for "Last Dance." She
lobbied the NARAS hard for a separate disco
award, which was created in 1979. Ironically,
Summer's *Bad Girls* album lost in the new Disco
Recording slot to Gloria Gaynor's "I Will Survive."
Disco did not survive and the new award was dis-
continued after one year.

   The American Music Awards anticipated the
Grammys by creating a Disco category in 1978—

and then dropping it in '79. Summer won three
Disco AMAs.

COUNTRY
Song (award to songwriter): "The Gambler" (Don
Schlitz); Male Vocalist: Willie Nelson ("Georgia
on My Mind"); Female Vocalist: Dolly Parton
(*Here You Come Again*); Vocal Group: Waylon
Jennings, Willie Nelson ("Mamas, Don't Let Your
Babies Grow Up To Be Cowboys")

JAZZ
Vocal Performance: Al Jarreau (*All Fly Home*);
Soloist: Oscar Peterson (*Montreux '77, Oscar
Peterson Jam*); Group: Chick Corea (*Friends*); Big
Band: Thad Jones, Mel Lewis (*Live in Munich*)

OTHER AWARDS
Original Cast Show Album: *Ain't Misbehavin'*;
Soundtrack Album: *Close Encounters of the Third
Kind*; Comedy Performance: Steve Martin (*A Wild
and Crazy Guy*); Spoken Word: Orson Welles
(*Citizen Kane* Original Motion Picture
Soundtrack); Classical Album: *Brahms: Concerto
for Violin in D Major* (Carlo Maria Giulini
conducting the Chicago Symphony)

John Denver returned as host and the technical
snafus of the previous year appeared to be smoothed
over. The comic highlight of the night was provided
by Steve Martin, who accepted an award for his *A
Wild and Crazy Guy* album in a formal tuxedo—
with no pants. In a later interview, Martin revealed
his trouserless appeearence was meant as a comment
on awards in general. "The history of awards is that
they're usually wrong," he said.

   There was an interesting contest in the normally
overlooked Spoken Word category. Orson Welles
defeated former President Richard Nixon. Welles
won for a recording of his performance in the
1941 film classic *Citizan Kane*. Nixon was up for
his interviews conducted with David Frost after
having resigned as Commander in Chief.

THE AMERICAN MUSIC AWARDS

POP/ROCK
Single: "Three Times a Lady" (the Commodores);
Album: *Grease* (Soundtrack Album); Male Artist:

Barry Manilow; Female Artist: Linda Ronstadt; Band, Duo, or Group: the Bee Gees

SOUL/RHYTHM AND BLUES
Single: "Too Much, Too Little, Too Late" (Johnny Mathis, Deniece Williams); Album: *Saturday Night Fever* (Soundtrack); Male Artist (tie): Teddy Pendergrass and Lou Rawls; Female Artist: Natalie Cole; Band, Duo, or Group: Earth, Wind and Fire

COUNTRY
Single: "Blue Bayou" (Linda Ronstadt); Album: *Ten Years of Gold* (Kenny Rogers); Male Artist: Kenny Rogers; Female Artist: Crystal Gayle; Band, Duo, or Group: the Statler Brothers

DISCO (PRESENTED THIS YEAR ONLY)
Single: "Last Dance" (Donna Summer); Album: *Live and More* (Donna Summer); Male Artist: Isaac Hayes; Female Artist: Donna Summer; Group: the Village People

SPECIAL AWARD
Perry Como

COUNTRY MUSIC ASSOCIATION AWARDS

Entertainer: Dolly Parton; Single: "Heaven's Just a Sin Away" (the Kendalls); Song: "Don't It Make My Brown Eyes Blue" (Richard Leigh, songwriter); Album: *It Was Almost Like a Song* (Ronnie Milsap); Male Vocalist: Don Williams; Female Vocalist: Crystal Gayle; Musician: Roy Clark

1979

THE GRAMMY AWARDS

RECORD OF THE YEAR
"After the Love Has Gone" (Earth, Wind and Fire)
"The Gambler" (Kenny Rogers)
"I Will Survive" (Gloria Gaynor)
"What a Fool Believes" (the Doobie Brothers)
"You Don't Bring Me Flowers" (Barbra Streisand, Neil Diamond)

The Doobie Brothers reaped the most '79 nominations, with six nods, and won four—Record of the Year, Song of the Year, Vocal Group (Pop), and Arrangements. They won for their hit single "What a Fool Believes" and the album *Minute by Minute*, which was No. 3 for the year on *Billboard*'s charts.

SONG OF THE YEAR (AWARD TO SONGWRITER)
"After the Love Has Gone" (David Foster, Jay Graydon, Bill Champlin)
"Chuck E.'s in Love" (Rickie Lee Jones)
"Honesty" (Billy Joel)
"I Will Survive" (Dino Fekaris, Freddie Perren)
"Minute by Minute" (Lester Abrams, Michael McDonald)
"Reunited" (Dino Fekaris, Freddie Perren)
"She Believes in Me" (Steve Gibb)
"What a Fool Believes" (Kenny Loggins, Michael McDonald)

ALBUM OF THE YEAR
Bad Girls (Donna Summer)
Breakfast in America (Supertramp)
52nd Street (Billy Joel)
The Gambler (Kenny Rogers)
Minute by Minute (the Doobie Brothers)

NEW ARTIST
The Blues Brothers
Dire Straits
The Knack
Rickie Lee Jones
Robin Williams

MALE VOCALIST (POP)
Billy Joel (*52nd Street*)
Robert John ("Sad Eyes")
Kenny Rogers ("She Believes in Me")
Rod Stewart ("Do Ya Think I'm Sexy?")
James Taylor ("Up on the Roof")

FEMALE VOCALIST (POP)
Gloria Gaynor ("I Will Survive")
Rickie Lee Jones ("Chuck E.'s in Love")
Melissa Manchester ("Don't Cry Out Loud")
Donna Summer (*Bad Girls*)
Dionne Warwick ("I'll Never Love This Way Again")

VOCAL GROUP (POP)
The Commodores ("Sail On")
The Doobie Brothers (*Minute by Minute*)
The Little River Band ("Lonesome Loner")
Barbra Streisand, Neil Diamond ("You Don't Bring Me Flowers")
Supertramp (*Breakfast in America*)

MALE VOCALIST (ROCK)
Bob Dylan ("Gotta Serve Somebody")
Joe Jackson ("Is She Really Going Out with Him?")
Robert Palmer ["Bad Case of Loving You (Doctor, Doctor)"]
Rod Stewart ["Blondes (Have More Fun)"]
Frank Zappa ("Dancin' Fool")

After ignoring him for fifteen years, the NARAS finally honored Bob Dylan with a Grammy. He did have to go through a religious conversion to get one, though. His "Gotta Serve Somebody" was a statement of his "born-again" status. Nineteen seventy-nine was the year of righting Grammy wrongs. Rock was restored as a separate category for Male, Female, and Group Vocals. But in typical NARAS fashion, the winners were announced before the TV broadcast.

FEMALE VOCALIST (ROCK)
Cindy Bullens ("Survivor")
Rickie Lee Jones ("The Last Chance Texaco")
Bonnie Raitt ("You're Gonna Get What's Coming")
Carly Simon ("Vengeance")
Donna Summer ("Hot Stuff")
Tanya Tucker (*TNT*)

Though she lost in the new and short-lived Disco Recording category, Donna Summer, an evangelical convert like Bob Dylan, won in the Female Vocalist (Rock) category.

VOCAL GROUP (ROCK)
The Blues Brothers (*Briefcase Full of Blues*)
The Cars (*Candy-O*)
Dire Straits ("Sultans of Swing")
The Eagles ("Heartache Tonight")
The Knack ("My Sharona")
Styx (*Cornerstone*)

RHYTHM AND BLUES
Song (award to songwriter): "After the Love Has Gone" (David Foster, Jay Garydon, Bill Champlin); Male Vocalist: Michael Jackson ("Don't Stop 'Til You Get Enough"); Female Vocalist: Dionne Warwick ("Deja Vu"); Vocal Group: Earth, Wind and Fire ("After the Love Has Gone")

COUNTRY
Song (award to songwriter): "You Decorated My Life" (Bob Morrison, Debbie Hupp); Male Vocalist: Kenny Rogers ("The Gambler"); Female Vocalist: Emmylou Harris (*Blue Kentucky Girl*); Vocal Group: the Charlie Daniels Band ("The Devil Went Down to Georgia")

JAZZ
Jazz Fusion Performance: Weather Report (*8:30*); Vocal Performance: Ella Fitzgerald (*Fine and Mellow*); Soloist: Oscar Peterson (*Jousts*); Group: Gary Burton, Chick Corea (*Duet*); Big Band: Duke Ellington (*At Fargo, 1940 Live*)

OTHER AWARDS
Disco Recording: "I Will Survive" (Gloria Gaynor); Original Cast Show Album: *Sweeney Todd*; Soundtrack Album: *Superman*; Comedy Performance: Robin Williams (*Reality . . . What a Concept*); Spoken Word: Sir John Gielgud (*The Ages of Man*); Classical Album: *Brahms Symphonies (4) Complete* (Sir Georg Solti conducting the Chicago Symphony Orchestra)

In an evening otherwise dominated by the Doobie Brothers, Barbra Streisand and Neil Diamond stopped the show with a passionate performance of their duo hit "You Don't Bring Me Flowers." There was even talk of making a film version of the ballad of a couple who have drifted apart starring the singers, but these plans never came to fruition.

Streisand's solo version of the song had been released in time for the 1978 Grammys [and received nominations for Song of the Year and Female Vocalist (Pop)]. But the duet came out after the deadline. Streisand and Diamond were defeated in their Grammy bids for Record of the Year and Vocal Group (Pop) by the unstoppable Doobies.

Kenny Rogers became the third host of the Grammy telecast, succeeding Andy Williams and

John Denver. Rogers was nominated for five awards, but only won one. In addition to his podium duties as emcee, he made a trip to the stage to accept a Grammy for Male Country Vocalist (for "The Gambler"). He took home similar prizes from the American Music Awards and the Country Music Association Awards.

THE AMERICAN MUSIC AWARDS

POP/ROCK
Single: "Bad Girls" (Donna Summer); Album: *Spirits Having Flown* (the Bee Gees); Male Artist: Barry Manilow; Female Artist: Donna Summer; Band, Duo, or Group: the Bee Gees

SOUL/RHYTHM AND BLUES
Single: "Don't Stop 'Til You Get Enough" (Michael Jackson); Album: *Off the Wall* (Michael Jackson); Male Artist: Michael Jackson; Female Artist: Donna Summer; Band, Duo, or Group: the Commodores

COUNTRY
Single: "Sleeping Single in a Double Bed" (Barbara Mandrell); Album: *The Gambler* (Kenny Rogers); Male Artist: Kenny Rogers; Female Artist: Crystal Gayle; Band, Duo, or Group: the Statler Brothers

SPECIAL AWARD
Benny Goodman

COUNTRY MUSIC ASSOCIATION AWARDS

Entertainer: Willie Nelson; Single: "The Devil Went Down to Georgia" (the Charlie Daniels Band); Song: "The Gambler" (Don Schlitz, songwriter); Album: *The Gambler* (Kenny Rogers); Male Vocalist: Kenny Rogers; Female Vocalist: Barbara Mandrell; Vocal Group: the Statler Brothers; Vocal Duo: Kenny Rogers, Dottie West; Musician: Charlie Daniels

1980

THE GRAMMY AWARDS

RECORD OF THE YEAR
"Lady" (Kenny Rogers)
"The Rose" (Bette Midler)
"Sailing" (Christopher Cross)
"Theme from *New York, New York*" (Frank Sinatra)
"Woman in Love" (Barbra Streisand, Barry Gibb)

In one of the biggest upsets in Grammy history, newcomer Christopher Cross took the Triple Crown of Record of the Year, Song of the Year, and Album of the Year. Only Simon and Garfunkel and Carole King have pulled off a similar triple play and Cross is the only first-time artist to do so. In addition, Cross took Grammys for New Artist and Arrangements Accompanying Vocalist (with producer/arranger Michael Omartian), bringing his total take to five.

The recording industry was up in arms over the Cross quintuple victory. Not only had this mellow upstart defeated such middle-of-the-road musical legends as Frank Sinatra and Barbra Streisand, but he also won in a year which had produced such innovative voices as the Clash, Prince, and the Talking Heads, as well as new work from Bruce Springsteen, Michael Jackson, Billy Joel, and Pink Floyd. Cross's "Sailing," a smooth paean to life on the water so relaxing it could be used as a tranquilizer, seemed to be an unhappy compromise choice for NARAS voters. They didn't wish to seem too old-fashioned by honoring Sinatra or Streisand, nor did they want to go too far into the rock world with the Clash or Pink Floyd. So Cross was canonized, satisfying neither the traditionalists nor the advocates of new sounds.

Cross would win a 1981 best Song Oscar for "Arthur's Theme" (a collaboration with Peter Allen, Carole Bayer Sager, and Burt Bacharach). The song from the Dudley Moore comedy would also garner four Grammy nominations, but fail to win in any of those categories. Cross has not been nominated since.

Christopher Cross sailed away with an unexpected four Grammys at the 1980 ceremony.

SONG OF THE YEAR (AWARD TO SONGWRITER)
"Fame" (Michael Gore, Dean Pitchford)
"Lady" (Lionel Richie)
"Theme from *New York, New York*" (John Kander, Fred Ebb)
"The Rose" (Amanda McBroom)
"Sailing" (Christopher Cross)
"Woman in Love" (Barry and Robin Gibb)

ALBUM OF THE YEAR
Christopher Cross (Christopher Cross)
Glass Houses (Billy Joel)
Guilty (Barbra Streisand, Barry Gibb)
Trilogy: Past, Present, Future (Frank Sinatra)
The Wall (Pink Floyd)

NEW ARTIST
Irene Cara
Christopher Cross
Robbie Dupree
Amy Holland
The Pretenders

MALE VOCALIST (POP)
Christopher Cross (*Christopher Cross*)
Kenny Loggins ("This Is It")
Kenny Rogers ("Lady")
Paul Simon ("Late in the Evening")
Frank Sinatra ("Theme from *New York, New York*")

FEMALE VOCALIST (POP)
Irene Cara ("Fame")
Bette Midler ("The Rose")
Olivia Newton-John ("Magic")
Barbra Streisand ("Woman in Love")
Donna Summer ("On the Radio")

VOCAL GROUP (POP)
Ambrosia ("Biggest Part of Me")
The Pointer Sisters ("He's So Shy")
Kenny Rogers, Kim Carnes ("Don't Fall in Love with a Dreamer")
Bob Seger and the Silver Bullet Band ("Against the Wind")
Barbra Streisand, Barry Gibb ("Guilty")

MALE VOCALIST (ROCK)
Jackson Browne ("Boulevard")
Billy Joel (*Glass Houses*)
Kenny Loggins ["I'm Alright (Theme from *Caddyshack*)"]
Paul McCartney ["Coming Up (Live at Glasgow)"]
Bruce Springsteen ("Medley: Devil with the Blue Dress/Good Golly Miss Molly/ Jenny Take a Ride")

FEMALE VOCALIST (ROCK)
Joan Armatrading (*How Cruel*)
Pat Benatar (*Crimes of Passion*)
Marianne Faithful (*Broken English*)
Linda Ronstadt ("How Do I Make You")
Grace Slick (*Dreams*)

VOCAL GROUP (ROCK)
Blondie ("Call Me")
Pink Floyd (*The Wall*)
The Pretenders ["Brass in Pocket (I'm Special)"]
Queen ("Another One Bites the Dust")
Bob Seger and the Silver Bullet Band (*Against the Wind*)

RHYTHM AND BLUES

Song (award to songwriter): "Never Knew Love Like This Before" (Reggie Lucas, James Mtume); Male Vocalist: George Benson (*Give Me the Night*); Female Vocalist: Stephanie Mills ("Never Knew Love Like This Before"); Vocal Group: the Manhattans ("Shining Star")

COUNTRY

Song (award to songwriter): "On the Road Again" (Willie Nelson); Male Vocalist: George Jones ("He Stopped Loving Her Today"); Female Vocalist: Anne Murray ("Could I Have This Dance"); Vocal Group: Roy Orbison, Emmylou Harris ("That Lovin' You Feelin' Again")

JAZZ

Jazz Fusion Performance: the Manhattan Transfer ("Birdland"); Male Vocalist: George Benson ("Moody's Mood"); Female Vocalist: Ella Fitzgerald (*A Perfect Match/Ella and Basie*); Soloist: Bill Evans (*I Will Say Goodbye*); Group: Bill Evans (*We Will Meet Again*); Big Band: Count Basie and his Orchestra (*On the Road*)

OTHER AWARDS

Original Cast Show Album: *Evita*; Soundtrack Album: *The Empire Strikes Back*; Comedy Performance: Rodney Dangerfield (*No Respect*); Spoken Word: Pat Carroll (*Gertrude Stein Gertrude Stein Gertrude Stein*); Classical Album: *Berg: Lulu* (Pierre Boulez conducting the Orchestre de l'Opera de Paris)

The Grammys returned to New York City (Radio City Music Hall, to be specific) after a five-year absence. In a rare nod to the composers and lyricists, the nominees for Song of the Year were performed by the people who wrote them, many of whom were also performers. Highlights included Patti LuPone singing "Don't Cry for Me, Argentina" from best Original Cast Show Album winner *Evita*, and host Paul Simon's moving tribute to John Lennon. The ex-Beatle had been slain by an obsessed fan only two months previously.

The Grammycast received mixed notices. *Billboard* stated it "maintained a degree of elegance." while *Variety* labeled the show "one of the most flawed in recent years, with technical problems plaguing the evening throughout. On the other hand, Paul Simon, himself a victim of a technical foul-up, proved a witty emcee." Kay Gardella of the *New York Daily News* was unequivocal in her review: "What a sham! What an abomination!"

THE AMERICAN MUSIC AWARDS

POP/ROCK

Single: "Another One Bites the Dust" (Queen); Album: *Glass Houses* (Billy Joel); Male Artist: Kenny Rogers; Female Artist: Barbra Streisand; Band, Duo, or Group: the Eagles

SOUL/RHYTHM AND BLUES

Single: "Upside Down" (Diana Ross); Album: *Off the Wall* (Michael Jackson); Male Artist: Michael Jackson; Female Artist: Diana Ross; Band, Duo, or Group: Earth, Wind and Fire

COUNTRY

Single: "Coward of the County" (Kenny Rogers); Album: *The Gambler* (Kenny Rogers); Male Artist: Kenny Rogers; Female Artist: Barbara Mandrell; Band, Duo, or Group: the Statler Brothers

SPECIAL AWARD

Chuck Berry

COUNTRY MUSIC ASSOCIATION AWARDS

Entertainer: Barbara Mandrell; Single: "He Stopped Loving Her Today" (George Jones); Song: "He Stopped Loving Her Today" (Bobby Braddock, Curly Putman, songwriters); Album: Original Soundtrack, *Coal Miner's Daughter*; Male Vocalist: George Jones; Female Vocalist: Emmylou Harris; Vocal Group: the Statler Brothers; Vocal Duo: Moe Bandy, Joe Stampley; Musician: Roy Clark

1981

THE GRAMMY AWARDS

RECORD OF THE YEAR

"Arthur's Theme (The Best That You Can Do)" (Christopher Cross)

"**Bette Davis Eyes**" (Kim Carnes)
"Endless Love" (Diana Ross, Lionel Richie)
"(Just Like) Starting Over" (John Lennon)
"Just the Two of Us" (Bill Withers, Grover Washington, Jr.)

SONG OF THE YEAR (AWARD TO SONGWRITER)
"Arthur's Theme (The Best That You Can Do)" (Peter Allen, Burt Bacharach, Carole Bayer Sager, Christopher Cross)
"**Bette Davis Eyes**" (Donna Weiss, Jackie DeShannon)
"Endless Love" (Lionel Richie)
"Just the Two of Us" (Bill Withers, William Salter, Ralph MacDonald)
"9 to 5" (Dolly Parton)

ALBUM OF THE YEAR
Breakin' Away (Al Jarreau)
Double Fantasy (John Lennon, Yoko Ono)
The Dude (Quincy Jones)
Gaucho (Steely Dan)
Mistaken Identity (Kim Carnes)

NEW ARTIST
Adam and the Ants
Sheena Easton
The Go-Gos
James Ingram
Luther Vandross

MALE VOCALIST (POP)
Christopher Cross ["Arthur's Theme (The Best That You Can Do)"]
James Ingram ("Just Once")
Al Jarreau (*Breakin' Away*)
John Lennon ["Double Fantasy" (Lennon tracks only)]
Bill Withers ("Just the Two of Us")

FEMALE VOCALIST (POP)
Kim Carnes ("Bette Davis Eyes")
Sheena Easton ("For Your Eyes Only")
Lena Horne (*Lena Horne: The Lady and Her Music*)
Juice Newton ("Angel of the Morning")
Olivia Newton-John ("Physical")

VOCAL GROUP (POP)
Daryl Hall, John Oates (*Private Eyes*)
Manhattan Transfer ("Boy From New York City")
The Pointer Sisters ("Slow Hand")
Diana Ross, Lionel Richie ("Endless Love")
Steely Dan (*Gaucho*)

MALE VOCALIST (ROCK)
Gary "U.S." Bonds (*Dedication*)
Rick James ("Super Freak")
Rick Springfield ("Jesse's Girl")
Bruce Springsteen (*The River*)
Rod Stewart ("Young Turks")

FEMALE VOCALIST (ROCK)
Pat Benatar ("Fire and Ice")
Lulu ("Who's Foolin' Who")
Stevie Nicks ("Edge of Seventeen")
Yoko Ono ("Walking on Thin Ice")
Donna Summer ("Cold Love")

VOCAL GROUP (ROCK)
Foreigner (*4*)
The Police ("Don't Stand So Close to Me")
REO Speedwagon (*Hi Fidelity*)
Stevie Nicks with Tom Petty and the Heartbreakers ("Stop Draggin' My Heart Around")
The Rolling Stones (*Tattoo You*)

RHYTHM AND BLUES
Song (award to songwriter): "Just the Two of Us" (Bill Withers, William Salter, Ralph MacDonald); Male Vocalist: James Ingram ("One Hundred Ways"); Female Vocalist: Aretha Franklin ("Hold On, I'm Comin'"); Vocal Group: Quincy Jones with Guest Artists (*The Dude*)

COUNTRY
Song (award to songwriter): "9 to 5" (Dolly Parton); Male Vocalist: Ronnie Milsap ["(There's) No Gettin' Over Me"]; Female Vocalist: Dolly Parton ("9 to 5"); Vocal Group: The Oak Ridge Boys ("Elvira")

JAZZ
Jazz Fusion Performance: Grover Washington, Jr. (*Winelight*); Male Vocalist: Al Jarreau ("Blue Rondo à la Turk"); Female Vocalist: Ella Fitzgerald

(*Digital III at Montreux*); Vocal Group: Manhattan Transfer ["Until I Met You (Corner Pocket)"]; Soloist: John Coltrane (*Bye, Bye Blackbird*); Group: Chick Corea, Gary Burton (*Chick Corea and Gary Burton in Concert, Zurich, October 28, 1979*); Big Band: Gerry Mulligan and His Orchestra (*Walk on the Water*)

OTHER AWARDS
Original Cast Show Album: *Lena Horne: The Lady and Her Music*; Soundtrack Album: *Raiders of the Lost Ark*; Comedy Performance: Richard Pryor (*Rev. Du Rite*); Spoken Word: Orson Welles (*Donovan's Brain*); Classical Album: *Mahler: Symphony No. 2 in C Major* (Sir Georg Solti conducting the Chicago Symphony Orchestra and Chorus); Video of the Year: *Michael Nesmith in Elephant Parts* (Michael Nesmith)

The Grammys moved back to Los Angeles's Shrine Auditorium, with John Denver hosting. The Oak Ridge Boys, Rick Springfield, and the Pointer Sisters were among the entertainers. But the emotional highpoint of the evening, and of the decade for the Grammy's, was provided by Yoko Ono, widow of John Lennon who had been slain a year ago. The couple's joint album *Double Fantasy* won for Album of the Year. Ono and Sean Lennon (her son with John Lennon) accepted the prize and received a sustained standing ovation. "I think John is here with us here tonight," she said to the audience. Lennon's single "(Just Like) Starting Over" lost to Kim Carnes; "Bette Davis Eyes" for Record of the Year.

THE AMERICAN MUSIC AWARDS

POP/ROCK
Single: "Endless Love" (Diana Ross, Lionel Richie); Album: *Kenny Rogers' Greatest Hits* (Kenny Rogers); Male Artist: Kenny Rogers; Female Artist: Pat Benatar; Band, Duo, or Group: Air Supply

SOUL/RHYTHM AND BLUES
Single: "Endless Love" (Diana Ross, Lionel Richie); Album: *Street Songs* (Rick James); Male Artist: Stevie Wonder; Female Artist: Stephanie Mills; Band, Duo, or Group: Kool and the Gang

COUNTRY
Single (tie): "Could I Have This Dance" (Anne Murray) and "On the Road Again" (Willie Nelson); Album: *Kenny Rogers' Greatest Hits* (Kenny Rogers); Male Artist: Willie Nelson; Female Artist: Barbara Mandrell; Band, Duo, or Group: the Oak Ridge Boys

SPECIAL AWARD
Stevie Wonder.

COUNTRY MUSIC ASSOCIATION AWARDS

Entertainer: Barbara Mandrell; Single: "Elvira" (the Oak Ridge Boys); Song: "He Stopped Loving Her Today" (Bobby Braddock, Curly Putman, songwriters); Album: *I Believe in You* (Don Williams); Male Vocalist: George Jones; Female Vocalist: Barbara Mandrell; Vocal Group: Alabama; Vocal Duo: David Frizzell, Shelley West; Musician: Chet Atkins; Horizon Award: Terri Gibbs

1982
THE GRAMMY AWARDS

RECORD OF THE YEAR
"Always on My Mind" (Willie Nelson)
"Ebony and Ivory" (Paul McCartney, Stevie Wonder)
"Rosanna" (Toto)
"Steppin' Out" (Joe Jackson)
"Theme from *Chariots of Fire*" (Vangelis)

Hackles were raised in the music industry when routine rockers Toto swept the '82 Grammys with five wins. Recalling the multiple triumph of the bland Christopher Cross, grousers cried the NARAS was hopelessly out of step with reality. Toto's music had been labeled shallow and ordinary. Yet it grabbed the awards for Record of the Year and Album of the Year (the first band to do so in the same year) as well prizes for Producer of the Year, Vocal Arrangements, and Instrumental Arrangement Accompanying Vocals. This was especially surprising when veterans like Paul

The NARAS was criticized for canonizing Toto, a "safe" group, with five 1982 Grammys.

McCartney and Stevie Wonder came up Grammyless. In response to Toto's total take-over, the Academy launched a membership drive for younger artists.

Not all the old-timers went empty-handed. Marvin Gaye, Sarah Vaughan, Mel Tormé, and blues guitarist Clarence "Gatemouth" Brown copped their first Grammys after long careers.

SONG OF THE YEAR
(AWARD TO SONGWRITER)
"Always on My Mind" (Johnny Christopher, Mark James, Wayne Thompson)
"Ebony and Ivory" (Paul McCartney)
"Eye of the Tiger" (Frankie Sullivan, Jim Peternik)
"IGY (What a Beautiful World)" (Donald Fagen)
"Rosanna" (David Paich)

Despite the fact that it was written for Elvis Presley and released by the King in 1971, "Always on My Mind" won Song of the Year as well as best Country Song and Country Male Vocalist for Willie Nelson. The Country Music Association honored it as best Single and best Song, and the American Music Awards crowned Nelson's album featuring "Mind" as tops in both pop and country.

Previously recorded songs were permitted to compete in this category with new tunes as long as they had never been nominated before. In 1992 the rules were changed to allow only recent songs to compete for Song of the Year.

ALBUM OF THE YEAR
American Fool (John Cougar)
The Nightfly (Donald Fagen)
The Nylon Curtain (Billy Joel)
Tug of War (Paul McCartney)
Toto IV (Toto)

NEW ARTIST
Asia
Jennifer Holliday
The Human League
Men at Work
Stray Cats

MALE VOCALIST (POP)
Donald Fagen ["IGY (What a Beautiful World)"]

Joe Jackson ("Steppin' Out")
Elton John ("Blue Eyes")
Michael McDonald ["I Keep Forgetting
   (Every Time You're Near)"]
Lionel Richie ("Truly")
Rick Springfield ("Don't Talk to Strangers")

FEMALE VOCALIST (POP)
Laura Branigan ("Gloria")
Melissa Manchester ("You Should Hear How
   She Talks about You")
Juice Newton ("Love's Been a Little Bit Hard
   on Me")
Olivia Newton-John ("Heart Attack")
Linda Ronstadt ("Get Closer")

VOCAL GROUP (POP)
Chicago ("Hard to Say I'm Sorry")
Joe Cocker, **Jennifer Warnes** ("Up Where
   We Belong")
Daryl Hall, John Oates ("Maneater")
Paul McCartney, Stevie Wonder ("Ebony and Ivory")
Toto ("Rosanna")

MALE VOCALIST (ROCK)
John Cougar ("Hurts So Good")
Peter Gabriel ("Shock the Monkey")
Don Henley ("Dirty Laundry")
Rick Springfield ("I Get Excited")
Rod Stewart (*Tonight I'm Yours*)

FEMALE VOCALIST (ROCK)
Pat Benatar ("Shadows of the Night")
Kim Carnes ("Voyeur")
Bonnie Raitt ("Green Light")
Linda Ronstadt ("Get Closer")
Donna Summer ("Protection")

VOCAL GROUP (ROCK)
Asia (*Asia*)
J. Geils Band ("Centerfold")
Kenny Loggins with Steve Perry ("Don't Fight It")
Survivor ("Eye of the Tiger")
Frank and Moon Zappa ("Valley Girl")

RHYTHM AND BLUES
Song (award to songwriter): "Turn Your Love
Around" (Jay Graydon, Steve Lukather, Bill

Champlin); Male Vocalist: Marvin Gaye ("Sexual
Healing"); Female Vocalist: Jennifer Holliday
("And I Am Telling You I'm Not Going"); Vocal
Group (tie): Dazz Band ("Let It Whip") and
Earth, Wind and Fire ("Wanna Be with You")

Jennifer Holliday knocked out audiences at both
the Grammys and the Tonys with her powerful
rendition of "And I Am Telling You I'm Not
Going" from the musical *Dreamgirls*. (She performed the number at the 1981 Grammys.)
Holliday won a Tony as best Actress in a Musical
and a Grammy for Rhythm and Blues Female
Vocalist for the recording of the song in which her
character begs her lover not to leave.

COUNTRY
Song (award to songwriter): "Always on My
Mind" (Johnny Christopher, Wayne Thompson,
Mark James); Male Vocalist: Willie Nelson
("Always on My Mind"); Female Vocalist: Juice
Newton ("Break It to Me Gently"); Vocal Group:
Alabama (*Mountain Music*)

JAZZ
Jazz Fusion Performance: Pat Methany Group
(*Offramp*); Male Vocalist: Mel Tormé (*An Evening
with Mel Tormé and George Shearing*); Female
Vocalist: Sarah Vaughan (*Gershwin Live!*); Vocal
Group: Manhattan Transfer ("Route 66"); Soloist:
Miles Davis (*We Want Miles*); Group: Phil Woods
Quartet (*"More" Live*); Big Band: Count Basie and
His Orchestra (*Warm Breeze*)

OTHER AWARDS
Original Cast Show Album: *Dreamgirls*;
Soundtrack Album: *E. T.—The Extra-Terrestrial*;
Comedy Performance: Richard Pryor (*Live on the
Sunset Strip*); Spoken Word: *Raiders of the Lost
Ark: The Movie on Record*; Classical Album: *Bach:
The Goldberg Variations* (Glenn Gould); Video of
the Year: *Olivia Physical* (Olivia Newton-John)

E. T.—The Extra-Terrestrial had lost the big prize of
best Picture at the Oscars, but Steven Spielberg's
cuddly alien won three Grammys for soundtrack
composer John Williams (Soundtrack Album,
Instrumental Arrangement, and Instrumental
Composition). Other winning film-related songs

included "Up Where We Belong" from *An Officer and a Gentleman*, crooned by Joe Cocker and Jennifer Warnes [Vocal Group (Pop)] and Survivor's "The Eye of the Tiger," Slyvester Stallone's fight song in *Rocky III* [Vocal Group (Rock)]. In addition, a Spoken Word award went to a recording of *Raiders of the Lost Ark*.

John Denver hosted the Grammy ceremony, once again from the Shrine Auditorium in L.A., expanded from two hours to three. Many categories were still left out of the broadcast so that more production numbers could be squeezed in. Performers ranged from opera diva Leontyne Pryce to comeback queen Lena Horne to New Artist winners Men at Work. Many critics found the show bloated, but all praised a rousing medley by Count Basie, Ray Charles, Jerry Lee Lewis, and Little Richard.

THE AMERICAN MUSIC AWARDS

POP/ROCK
Single: "Truly" (Lionel Richie); Album: *Always on My Mind* (Willie Nelson); Male Artist (tie): John Cougar and Rick Springfield; Female Artist: Olivia Newton-John; Band, Duo, or Group: Daryl Hall, John Oates

SOUL/RHYTHM AND BLUES
Single: "Sexual Healing" (Marvin Gaye); Album: *Jump to It* (Aretha Franklin); Male Artist: Lionel Richie; Female Artist: Diana Ross; Band, Duo, or Group: Kool and the Gang

COUNTRY
Single: "Love Will Turn You Around" (Kenny Rogers); Album: *Always on My Mind* (Willie Nelson); Male Artist: Kenny Rogers; Female Artist: Barbara Mandrell; Band, Duo, or Group: Alabama

SPECIAL AWARD
Kenny Rogers

COUNTRY MUSIC ASSOCIATION AWARDS

Entertainer: Alabama; Single: "Always on My Mind" (Willie Nelson); Song: "Always on My Mind" (Johnny Christopher, Wayne Carson, Mark James, songwriters); Album: *Always on My Mind* (Willie Nelson); Male Vocalist: Ricky Skaggs; Female Vocalist: Janie Fricke; Vocal Group: Alabama; Vocal Duo: David Frizzell, Shelly West; Musician: Chet Atkins; Horizon Award: Ricky Skaggs

1983

THE GRAMMY AWARDS

RECORD OF THE YEAR
"All Night Long (All Night)" (Lionel Richie)
"Beat It" (Michael Jackson)
"Every Breath You Take" (the Police)
"Flashdance . . . What a Feeling" (Irene Cara)
"Maniac" (Michael Sembello)

It was Michael Jackson-mania at the 1983 Grammys. The Gloved One received twelve nominations and won eight of them, beating Roger Miller's record of most awards taken in one year. Jackson's Album of the Year *Thriller* sold over 40 million copies worldwide, making it the top-seller of all time.

The King of Pop arrived at the ceremony looking like royalty. Dressed in a bespangled admiral's uniform, eyes covered by sunglasses, he was accompanied by starlet Brooke Shields and Emmanuel Lewis, the diminutive young star of the ABC sitcom *Webster*. The three resembled a reigning royal family of pop culture, King, Queen, and Heir Apparent.

The Jackson sweep included Record of the Year (for "Beat It"), Male Vocalist (Pop) (for *Thriller*), Male Vocalist (Rock)(again for "Beat It"), and Rhythm and Blues Song (for "Billie Jean"). Jackson was even featured in several Pepsi-Cola commercials during the breaks. Upon receiving his final Grammy of the night, Jackson removed his sunglasses, stating he was doing so on the advice of his "dear friend" Katharine Hepburn.

SONG OF THE YEAR (AWARD TO SONGWRITER)
"All Night Long (All Night)" (Lionel Richie)
"Beat It" (Michael Jackson)

Michael Jackson's eight 1983 Grammys obliterated Roger Miller's record of six for most awards won by a single artist in one year.

"Billie Jean" (Michael Jackson)
"Every Breath You Take" (Sting)
"Maniac" (Michael Sembello, Dennis Matkosky)

ALBUM OF THE YEAR
Flashdance (Original Soundtrack)
An Innocent Man (Billy Joel)
Let's Dance (David Bowie)
Synchronicity (the Police)
Thriller (Michael Jackson)

NEW ARTIST
Big Country
Culture Club
The Eurythmics
Men without Hats
Musical Youth

"Thank you, America," exuded Boy George, androgynous leader of the British group Culture Club as he accepted the New Artist award. "You've got good taste, style, and you know a good drag queen when you see one." Earlier in the evening, Joan Rivers joked with George, "You look like Brooke Shields on steroids."

MALE VOCALIST (POP)
Billy Joel ("Uptown Girl")
Michael Jackson (*Thriller*)
Prince (*1999*)
Lionel Richie ["All Night Long (All Night)"]
Michael Sembello ("Maniac")

FEMALE VOCALIST (POP)
Irene Cara ("Flashdance . . . What a Feeling")

Sheena Easton ["Telefone (Long Distance Love Affair)"]
Linda Ronstadt (*What's New*)
Donna Summer ("She Works Hard for the Money")
Bonnie Tyler ("Total Eclipse of the Heart")

VOCAL GROUP (POP)
Culture Club ("Do You Really Want to Hurt Me")
James Ingram, Patti Austin ("How Do You Keep the Music Playing")
Michael Jackson, Paul McCartney ("The Girl Is Mine")
The Police ("Every Breath You Take")
Kenny Rogers, Dolly Parton ("Islands in the Stream")

MALE VOCALIST (ROCK)
David Bowie ["Cat People (Putting Out Fire)"]
Phil Collins ("I Don't Care Anymore")
Michael Jackson ("Beat It")
Bob Seger (*The Distance*)
Rick Springfield ("Affair of the Heart")

FEMALE VOCALIST (ROCK)
Joan Armatrading (*The Key*)
Pat Benatar ("Love Is a Battlefield")
Kim Carnes (*Invisible Hands*)
Stevie Nicks (*Stand Back*)
Bonnie Tyler (*Faster Than the Speed of Night*)

VOCAL GROUP (ROCK)
Big Country ("In a Big Country")
Huey Lewis and the News (*Heart and Soul*)
The Police (*Synchonicity*)
The Talking Heads ("Burning Down the House")
ZZ Top (*Eliminator*)

RHYTHM AND BLUES
Song (award to songwriter): "Billie Jean" (Michael Jackson); Male Vocalist: Michael Jackson ("Billie Jean"); Female Vocalist: Chaka Khan (*Chaka Khan*); Vocal Group: Rufus and Chaka Khan ("Ain't Nobody")

COUNTRY
Song (award to songwriter): "Stranger in My House" (Mike Reed); Male Vocalist: Lee Greenwood ("IOU"); Female Vocalist: Anne Murray ("A Little Good News"); Vocal Group: Alabama (*The Closer You Get*)

JAZZ
Jazz Fusion Performance: Pat Metheny Group (*Travels*); Male Vocalist: Mel Tormé (*Top Drawer*); Female Vocalist: Ella Fitzgerald (*The Best Is Yet To Come*); Group: Manhattan Transfer ("Why Not!"); Soloist: Wynton Marsalis (*Think of One*); Group: Phil Woods Quartet (*At the Vanguard*); Big Band: Rob McConnel and the Boss Brass (*All in Good Time*)

OTHER AWARDS
Original Cast Show Album: *Cats*; Soundtrack Album: *Flashdance*; Comedy Performance: Eddie Murphy (*Eddie Murphy: Comedian*); Spoken Word: William Warfield (*Copland: Lincoln Portrait*); Classical Album: *Mahler: Symphony No. 9 in D Major* (Sir Georg Solti conducting the Chicago Symphony); Video of the Year: *Duran Duran* (Duran Duran)

The 1983 Grammys was both a critical and ratings success. The enormous popularity of Michael Jackson drew viewers to the show like a magnet. The program was the second most watched program of the year, with only the Super Bowl drawing more viewers. *The New York Times* commended the program on the "sheer variety of the material" presented. Wynton Marsalis, nominated in both jazz and classical categories, Lifetime Achievement winner Chuck Berry, Donna Summer, Annie Lennox of the Eurythmics, and the cast of *La Cage aux Folles* were among the entertainers. After the appearance of Boy George and the transvestites of *La Cage*, the camera caught host John Denver looking stunned.

The only major gaffe of the evening occured when Joan Rivers stated how happy she was to be part of the Emmys.

THE AMERICAN MUSIC AWARDS

POP/ROCK
Single: "Billie Jean" (Michael Jackson); Album: *Thriller* (Michael Jackson); Male Artist: Michael Jackson; Female Artist: Pat Benatar; Band, Duo, or

Group: Daryl Hall, John Oates; Video: "Beat It" (Michael Jackson)

SOUL/RHYTHM AND BLUES

Single: "All Night Long (All Night)" (Lionel Richie); Album: *Thriller* (Michael Jackson); Male Artist: Michael Jackson; Female Artist: Aretha Franklin; Band, Duo, or Group: Gladys Knight and the Pips; Video: "Beat It" (Michael Jackson)

COUNTRY

Single: "Islands in the Stream" (Kenny Rogers, Dolly Parton); Album: *The Closer You Get* (Alabama); Male Artist: Willie Nelson; Female Artist: Barbara Mandrell; Band, Duo, or Group: Alabama; Video: "Dixieland Delight" (Alabama)

SPECIAL AWARD

Michael Jackson

COUNTRY MUSIC ASSOCIATION AWARDS

Entertainer: Alabama; Single: "Swingin'" (John Anderson); Song: "Always on My Mind" (Johnny Christopher, Wayne Carson, Mark James, songwriters); Album: Alabama (*The Closer You Get*); Male Vocalist: Lee Greenwood; Female Vocalist: Janie Fricke; Vocal Group: Alabama; Vocal Duo: Merle Haggard, Willie Nelson; Musician: Chet Atkins; Horizon Award: John Anderson

1984

THE GRAMMY AWARDS

RECORD OF THE YEAR

"Dancing in the Dark" (Bruce Springsteen)
"Girls Just Want To Have Fun" (Cyndi Lauper)
"Hard Habit to Break" (Chicago)
"The Heart of Rock and Roll" (Huey Lewis and the News)
"What's Love Got To Do with It?" (Tina Turner)

After his eight-award blitz of '83, Michael Jackson did not attend the '84 Grammys. He won only one

Comeback queen Tina Turner was named top Female Vocalist in both the rock and pop Grammy categories in 1984. She also won Record of the Year for "What's Love Got to Do with It?"

prize this time, in the relatively new Music Video Album category.

Though she did not win as many awards as Jackson last year, Tina Turner was the unquestionable queen of the 1984 Grammys. After breaking up with her abusive husband and stage partner Ike in 1976, she fought to make an individual name for herself. It finally happened with her *Private Dancer* album. It remained on the charts for seventy-one weeks and three of the songs were in the Top 10.

On Grammy night, Turner (called "two sensational legs topped by an explosion of hair" by *The New York Times*) went to the podium three times—

After a decade of snubs from the the NARAS, Bruce Springsteen won his first Grammy for 1984's "Dancing in the Dark."

for Record of the Year ("What's Love Got To Do with It?"), Female Vocalist (Pop) (also for "What's Love"), and Female Rock Vocalist (for "Better Be Good to Me"). In addition, "What's Love" was named Song of the Year. Each award and her performance of the winning song was greeted with a standing ovation. Even Leonard Bernstein deferred to Turner, hurrying his acceptance speech for a Lifetime Achievement award to give her more time.

Other big winners coming back after defeats included Bruce Springsteen, who was taking home his first Grammy despite his red-hot career, and Lionel Ritchie, after losing in 1980, 1981, and 1983.

SONG OF THE YEAR
(AWARD TO SONGWRITER)
"Against All Odds (Take a Look at Me Now)" (Phil Collins)

"Hello" (Lionel Richie)
"I Just Called To Say I Love You" (Stevie Wonder)
"Time after Time" (Cyndi Lauper, Rob Hyman)
"What's Love Got To Do with It?" (Graham Lyle, Terry Britten)

ALBUM OF THE YEAR
Born in the USA (Bruce Springsteen)
Can't Slow Down (Lionel Richie)
Private Dancer (Tina Turner)
Purple Rain—Music from the Motion Picture (Prince and the Revolution)
She's So Unusual (Cyndi Lauper)

NEW ARTIST
Sheila E.
Frankie Goes to Hollywood
Corey Hart

The Judds
Cyndi Lauper

MALE VOCALIST (POP)
Phil Collins ["Against All Odds (Take a Look at Me Now)"]
Kenny Loggins ("Footloose")
Lionel Richie ("Hello")
John Waite ("Missing You")
Stevie Wonder ("I Just Called To Say I Love You")

FEMALE VOCALIST (POP)
Sheila E. ("The Glamorous Life")
Sheena Easton ("Strut")
Cyndi Lauper ("Girls Just Wanna Have Fun")
Tina Turner ("What's Love Got To Do with It?")
Deniece Williams ("Let's Hear It for the Boy")

VOCAL GROUP (POP)
The Cars ("Drive")
Chicago ("Hard Habit to Break")
The Pointer Sisters ["Jump (For My Love)"]
Wham! ("Wake Me Up Before You Go-Go")
Yes ("Owner of a Lonely Heart")

MALE VOCALIST (ROCK)
David Bowie ("Blue Jean")
Billy Idol ("Rebel Yell")
Elton John ("Restless")
John Cougar Mellencamp ("Pink Houses")
Bruce Springsteen ("Dancing in the Dark")

FEMALE VOCALIST (ROCK)
Lita Ford (*Dancin' on the Edge*)
Tina Turner ("Better Be Good to Me")
Bonnie Tyler ("Here She Comes")
Wendy O. Williams (*Wow*)
Pia Zadora ("Rock It Out")

VOCAL GROUP (ROCK)
The Cars (*Heatbreak City*)
Genesis (*Genesis*)
Prince and the Revolution (*Purple Rain— Music from the Motion Picture*)
Van Halen ("Jump")
Yes (*90125*)

RHYTHM AND BLUES
Song (award to songwriter): "I Feel for You" (Prince); Male Vocalist: Billy Ocean ["Caribbean Queen (No More Love on the Run)"]; Female Vocalist: Chaka Khan ("I Feel for You"); Vocal Group: James Ingram, Michael McDonald ("Yah Mo B There")

COUNTRY
Song (award to songwriter): *City of New Orleans* (Steve Goodman); Male Vocalist: Merle Haggard ("That's the Way Love Goes"); Female Vocalist: Emmylou Harris ("In My Dreams"); Vocal Group: the Judds ("Mama He's Crazy")

JAZZ
Jazz Fusion Performance: Pat Metheny Group (*First Circle*); Vocal Performance: Joe Williams (*Nothin' but the Blues*); Soloist: Wynton Marsalis (*Hot House Flowers*); Group: Art Blakey and the Jazz Messengers ("New York Scene"); Big Band: Count Basie and His Orchestra (*88 Basie Street*)

OTHER AWARDS
Original Cast Show Album: *Sunday in the Park with George*; Soundtrack Album: *Purple Rain*; Comedy Performance: "Weird Al" Yankovic ("Eat It" from *"Weird Al" Yankovic in 3-D*); Spoken Word: Ben Kingsley (*The Words of Gandhi*); Classical Album: *Amadeus (Original Soundtrack)*; Video, Short Form: *David Bowie* (David Bowie); Video Album: *Making Michael Jackson's Thriller* (Michael Jackson)

The Grammys opened with Huey Lewis and the News performing "The Heart of Rock and Roll." Then host John Denver reminded the crowd in the Shrine Auditorium that this was the thirtieth anniversary of the month that Bill Haley and the Comets released "Rock around the Clock." Quite a change from the early days of the awards when rock was thought of by the NARAS elders as the rantings of spoiled teenagers.

Though rock was given the most attention, the entire range of the music industry was included. Stevie Wonder led a synthesizer session. Julia Migenes-Johnson performed an aria from *Carmen*. Andrae Crouch, Pop Staples, and Deneice Williams warbled a gospel number. Kenny Loggins showed he was "Footloose." The direction featured numerous close-ups of the musicians and the audience. "Technically, this was the most impressive display yet for the Grammys," hailed *The New York Times*.

THE AMERICAN MUSIC AWARDS

POP/ROCK
Single: "Dancing in the Dark" (Bruce Springsteen); Album: *Purple Rain* (Prince); Male Artist: Lionel Richie; Female Artist: Cyndi Lauper; Band, Duo, or Group: Daryl Hall, John Oates; Video Single: "Hello" (Lionel Richie); Male Video Artist: Lionel Richie; Female Video Artist: Cyndi Lauper; Video Duo or Group: Huey Lewis and the News

SOUL/RHYTHM AND BLUES
Single: "When Doves Cry" (Prince); Album: *Purple Rain* (Prince); Male Artist: Lionel Richie; Female Artist: Tina Turner; Band, Duo, or Group: the Pointer Sisters; Video Single: "Hello" (Lionel Richie); Male Video Artist: Lionel Richie; Female Video Artist: Tina Turner; Video Duo or Group: the Pointer Sisters

COUNTRY
Single: "Islands in the Stream" (Kenny Rogers, Dolly Parton); Album: *Eyes That See in the Dark* (Kenny Rogers); Male Artist: Kenny Rogers; Female Artist: Barbara Mandrell; Band, Duo, or Group: Alabama; Video Single: "A Little Good News" (Anne Murray); Male Video Artist: Willie Nelson; Female Video Artist: Anne Murray; Video Duo or Group: the Oak Ridge Boys

SPECIAL AWARD
Loretta Lynn

COUNTRY MUSIC ASSOCIATION AWARDS

Entertainer: Alabama; Single: "A Little Good News" (Anne Murray); Song: "Wind beneath My Wings" (Larry Henley, Jeff Silbar, songwriters); Album: *A Little Good News* (Anne Murray); Male Vocalist: Lee Greenwood; Female Vocalist: Reba McEntire; Vocal Group: the Statler Brothers; Vocal Duo: Willie Nelson, Julio Iglesias; Musician: Chet Atkins; Horizon Award: the Judds

MTV VIDEO MUSIC AWARDS

Video of the Year: *You Might Think* (the Cars); Male Video: David Bowie (*China Girl*); Female Video: Cyndi Lauper (*Girls Just Wanna Have Fun*); Group Video: ZZ Top (*Legs*); Concept Video: Herbie Hancock (*Rockit*); New Artist in a Video: the Eurythmics [*Sweet Dreams (Are Made of This)*]; Special Effects: Herbie Hancock's *Rockit*; Director: Tim Newman (ZZ Top's *Sharp Dressed Men*); Viewers' Choice Award: Michael Jackson (*Thriller*); Video Vanguard Award: the Beatles, David Bowie, Richard Lester

A new form of entertainment—the music video—had burst onto the scene. A combination of sales promotion and mini-motion picture, these short pieces were becoming as influential and distinctive as the songs they accompanied. Of course, they had to have their own award. MTV (Music Television), the network devoted to showcasing music videos, filled the gap with yet another prize-giving ceremony.

THE GRAMMY AWARDS

RECORD OF THE YEAR
"Born in the USA" (Bruce Springsteen)
"The Boys of Summer" (Don Henley)
"Money for Nothing" (Dire Straits)
"The Power of Love" (Huey Lewis and the News)
"We Are the World" (USA for Africa)

Written by Michael Jackson and Lionel Richie, "We Are the World" was the first of many joint efforts by the American music industry to charitably contribute to a variety of worthy causes. In this case, it was African famine. Harry Belafonte was inspired by Bob Geldorf's Band-Aid release "Do They Know It's Christmas," which featured vocals by a host of British pop stars.

Belafonte set the wheels in motion to produce an American all-star single to benefit the starving continent. The single involved forty-five big names including Bruce Springsteen, Bob Dylan, Cyndi Lauper, Diana Ross, and Tina Turner. It was recorded immediately after the American Music Awards for 1984 on January 28, 1985, when the singers were all in one place at one time. The Grammys attempted to cash in on the event by premiering the song a month later, but there wasn't enough time to prepare a properly mixed final version.

"We Are the World" went on to raise $60 million for African hunger relief and won four Grammys [Record of the Year, Song of the year, Vocal Group (Pop), and Short-Form Music Video].

SONG OF THE YEAR (AWARD TO SONGWRITER)
"The Boys of Summer" (Don Henley, Mike Campbell)
"Everytime You Go Away" (Daryl Hall)
"I Want to Know What Love Is" (Mick Jones)
"Money for Nothing" (Mark Koopfler, Sting)
"We Are the World" (Michael Jackson, Lionel Richie)

ALBUM OF THE YEAR
Brothers in Arms (Dire Straits)
The Dream of the Blue Turtles (Sting)
No Jacket Required (Phil Collins)
We Are the World (USA for Africa)
Whitney Houston (Whitney Houston)

NEW ARTIST
a-ha
Freddie Jackson
Katrina and the Waves
Julian Lennon
Sade

MALE VOCALIST (POP)
Phil Collins (*No Jacket Required*)
Glenn Frey ("The Heat Is On")
Sting (*The Dream of the Blue Turtles*)
Stevie Wonder ("Part-Time Lover")
Paul Young ("Everytime You Go Away")

FEMALE VOCALIST (POP)
Pat Benatar ("We Belong")
Whitney Houston ("Saving All My Love for You")
Madonna ("Crazy for You")

Linda Ronstadt (*Lush Life*)
Tina Turner ["We Don't Need Another Hero (Thunderdome)"]

VOCAL GROUP (POP)
Phil Bailey, Phil Collins ("Easy Lover")
Foreigner ("I Want to Know What Love Is")
Huey Lewis and the News ("The Power of Love")
Mr. Mister ("Broken Wings")
USA for Africa ("We Are the World")

MALE VOCALIST (ROCK)
Bryan Adams (*Reckless*)
John Fogerty (*Centerfold*)
Don Henley ("The Boys of Summer")
Mick Jagger ("Just Another Night")
John Cougar Mellencamp (*Scarecrow*)

FEMALE VOCALIST (ROCK)
Pat Benatar ["Invincible (Theme from *The Legend of Billie Jean*)"]
Nona Hendryx ("Rock This House")
Cyndi Lauper ("What a Thrill")
Melba Moore ("Read My Lips")
Tina Turner ("One of the Living")

VOCAL GROUP (ROCK)
Bryan Adams, Tina Turner ("It's Only Love")
Dire Straits ("Money for Nothing")
Heart (*Heart*)
The Eurythmics ("Would I Lie to You")
Starship ("We Built This City")

RHYTHM AND BLUES
Song (award to songwriter): "Freeway of Love" (Narada Michael Walden, Jeffrey Cohen); Male Vocalist: Stevie Wonder (*In Square Circle*); Female Vocalist: Aretha Franklin ("Freeway of Love"); Vocal Group: the Commodores ("Nightshift")

COUNTRY
Song (award to songwriter): "Highwayman" (Jimmy L. Webb); Male Vocalist: Ronnie Milsap ["Lost in the Fifties Tonight (In the Still of the Night)"]; Female Vocalist: Rosanne Cash ("I Don't Know Why You Don't Want Me"); Vocal Group: the Judds (*Why Not Me*)

The Rolling Stones were one of many pioneering rock groups the NARAS ignored during the heyday of the movement in the 1960s. The Academy compensated the Stones with a 1985 Lifetime Achievement Award.

JAZZ

Male Vocalist: Jon Hendricks, Bobby McFerrin ("Another Night in Tunisia"); Female Vocalist: Cleo Laine (*Cleo at Carnegie the 10th Anniversary Concert*); Vocal Group: Manhattan Transfer (*Vocalese*); Soloist: Wynton Marsalis (*Black Codes from the Underground*); Group: Wynton Marsalis (*Black Codes from the Underground*); Big Band: John Barry, Bob Wilber (*The Cotton Club— Original Motion Picture Soundtrack*)

OTHER AWARDS

Cast Show Album: *West Side Story* (new version); Soundtrack Album: *Beverly Hills Cop*; Comedy Performance: Whoopi Goldberg (*Whoopi Goldberg—Original Broadway Show Recording*); Spoken Word: *Ma Rainey's Black Bottom* (Original Broadway Cast); Classical Album: *Berlioz: Requiem* (Robert Shaw conducting the Atlanta Symphony); Video (Short Form): *We Are the World: The Video Event* (USA for Africa); Video (Long Form): *Huey*

Lewis and the News: The Heart of Rock and Roll (Huey Lewis and the News)

Kenny Rogers wasn't sure if he'd be able to host the 1985 Grammys since he was recovering from throat surgery. About ten minutes before airtime Dionne Warwick was reading cue cards in case she had to go on. But Rogers made it.

Fans of jazz, a genre usually left out of the on-air Grammy ceremony, were appeased with an extended medley featuring B. B. King, Buddy Rich, Tony Williams, Ron Carter, Herbie Hancock, Dizzy Gillespie, Gerry Mulligan, Joe Williams, Sarah Vaughan, the Manhattan Transfer, and a dozen others. This did not satsify jazz critic and frequent Grammy grouser Leonard Feather. "It was too much in too short a time," he complained to *Emmy Magazine*. "They had a total of eight minutes of music with 24 people. Nobody got more than 30 seconds. Outrageous."

Among the nonjazz performers were Sting, Huey Lewis and the News, Whitney Houston (who was later nominated for an Emmy for her soulful warbling of "Saving All My Love for You"), and Norweigan rockers a-ha, a studio group which had never previously performed before a live audience. Their hit single "Take Me On" was made into an innovative music video combining live action with animation. The short won five MTV awards the following year, but the group's popularity soon fizzled.

Another group whose staying power was about as strong as a-ha's was weak garnered a Lifetime Achievement award. The Rolling Stones had never received a competitive Grammy. Judged more jarring and jagged than their comtemporaries the Beatles, Mick Jagger and his cohorts were snubbed by conservative Grammy voters of the '60 and '70s. "The joke is on you," Jagger jibed at the group's critics upon accepting the award.

THE AMERICAN MUSIC AWARDS

POP/ROCK
Single: "The Power of Love" (Huey Lewis and the News); Album: *Born in the USA* (Bruce Springsteen); Male Artist: Bruce Springsteen; Female Artist: Tina Turner; Band, Duo, or Group: Chicago; Video Single: "The Power of Love" (Huey Lewis and the News); Male Video Artist: Bruce Springsteen; Female Video Artist: Pat Benatar; Video Duo or Group: Wham

SOUL/RHYTHM AND BLUES
Single: "You Give Good Love" (Whitney Houston); Album: *Emergency* (Kool and the Gang); Male Artist: Stevie Wonder; Female Artist: Aretha Franklin; Band, Duo, or Group: Kool and the Gang; Video Single: "Saving All My Love for You" (Whitney Houston); Male Video Artist: Stevie Wonder; Female Video Artist: Aretha Franklin; Video Duo or Group: the Pointer Sisters

COUNTRY
Single: "Forgiving You Was Easy" (Willie Nelson); Album: *40 Hour Week* (Alabama); Male Artist: Willie Nelson; Female Artist: Crystal Gayle; Band, Duo, or Group: Alabama; Video Single: "Highwayman" (Willie Nelson, Wayland Jennings, Kris Kristofferson, Johnny Cash); Male Video Artist: Hank Williams, Jr.; Female Video Artist: Crystal Gayle; Video Duo or Group: the Highwaymen (Nelson, Jennings, Kristofferson, Cash)

SPECIAL AWARD
Paul McCartney

COUNTRY MUSIC ASSOCIATION AWARDS

Entertainer: Ricky Skaggs; Single: "Why Not Me" (the Judds); Song: "God Bless the USA" (Lee Greenwood, songwriter); Album: *Does Fort Worth Ever Cross Your Mind* (George Strait); Male Vocalist: George Strait; Female Vocalist: Reba McEntire; Vocal Group: the Judds; Vocal Duo: Anne Murray, Dave Loggins; Musician: Chet Atkins; Music Video: "All My Rowdy Friends Are Coming Over" (Hank Williams, Jr.); Horizon Award: Sawyer Brown

MTV VIDEO MUSIC AWARDS

Video of the Year: *The Boys of Summer* (Don Henley); Male Video: Bruce Springsteen (*I'm on Fire*); Female Video: Tina Turner (*What's Love Got To Do with It*); Group Video: USA for Africa (*We Are the World*); Concept Video: Glenn Frey

(*Smuggler's Blues*); New Artist in a Video: 'Til Tuesday (*Voices Carry*); Special Effects: Tony Mitchell, Kathy Dougherty, Peter Cohen (Tom Petty and the Heartbreakers, (*Don't Come Around Here No More*); Director: John Baptiste Mondino (Don Henley, *The Boys of Summer*); Video Vanguard Award: David Bryne, Kerin Godley and Lol Creme, Russell Mulcahy; Viewers' Choice Award: USA for Africa (*We Are the World*)

THE GRAMMY AWARDS

RECORD OF THE YEAR
"Addicted to Love" (Robert Palmer)
"The Greatest Love of All" (Whitney Houston)
"Higher Love" (Steve Winwood)
"Sledgehammer" (Peter Gabriel)
"That's What Friends Are For" (Dionne Warwick, Elton John, Gladys Knight, Stevie Wonder)

SONG OF THE YEAR
(AWARD TO SONGWRITER)
"Addicted to Love" (Robert Palmer)
"Graceland" (Paul Simon)
"Higher Love" (Steve Winwood, Will Jennings)
"Sledgehammer" (Peter Gabriel)
"That's What Friends Are For" (Burt Bacharach, Carole Bayer Sager)

"We Are the World" was followed up by "That's What Friends Are For," a pop anthem against AIDS by husband and wife Burt Bacharach and Carole Bayer Sager. The single featured vocals by Elton John, Dionne Warwick, Stevie Wonder, and Gladys Knight and raised $1 million by Grammy night. (Amazingly, this was John's first Grammy.) Like "World," "Friends" won for Song of the Year and Vocal Group (Pop) performance.

ALBUM OF THE YEAR
Back in the High Life (Steve Winwood)
The Broadway Album (Barbra Streisand)
Control (Janet Jackson)
Graceland (Paul Simon)
So (Peter Gabriel)

Paul Simon won his third Album of the Year Grammy for *Graceland* (his previous wins were for *Bridge over Troubled Water* with Art Garfunkel and his solo *Still Crazy after All These Years*). Only Frank Sinatra and Stevie Wonder have achieved similar triple plays. Simon collaborated with South African vocal group Ladysmith Black Mambazo on *Graceland*. He was criticized by anti-apartheid organizations for traveling to South Africa and thus breaking the boycott of the country. Simon countered that he did not perform in the country and only went to work with Ladysmith, an anti-apartheid group.

NEW ARTIST
Glass Tiger
Bruce Hornsby and the Range
Nu Shooz
Simply Red
Timbuk 3

MALE VOCALIST (POP)
Peter Cetera ["Glory of Love (Theme from *The Karate Kid, Part II*)"]
Kenny Loggins ("Danger Zone")
Michael McDonald ["Sweet Freedom (Theme from *Running Scared*)"]
Paul Simon (*Graceland*)
Steve Winwood ("Higher Love")

FEMALE VOCALIST (POP)
Cyndi Lauper ("True Colors")
Madonna ("Papa Don't Preach")
Barbra Streisand (*The Broadway Album*)
Tina Turner ("Typical Male")
Dionne Warwick (*Dionne and Friends*)

Barbra Streisand copped her eighth Grammy for *The Broadway Album*, a collection of her favorite show tunes. It was commerically risky since theater music had been losing ground to pop and rock for two decades. But the album was a best-seller. For the project, Streisand persuaded Stephen Sondheim to rewrite his Grammy winning "Send in the Clowns."

VOCAL GROUP (POP)
Peter Cetera, Amy Grant ("The Next Time I Fall")
Patti LaBelle, Michael McDonald ("On My Own")

Mike and the Mechanics ("All I Needs Is a Miracle")
Simply Red ("Holding Back the Years")
Dionne Warwick, **Elton John**, **Gladys Knight**, **Stevie Wonder** ("That's What Friends Are For")

MALE VOCALIST (ROCK)
John Fogerty (*Eye of the Zombie*)
Peter Gabriel ("Sledgehammer")
Billy Idol ("To Be a Lover")
Eddie Money ("Take Me Home Tonight")
Robert Palmer ("Addicted to Love")

FEMALE VOCALIST (ROCK)
Pat Benatar ("Sex as a Weapon")
Cyndi Lauper ("911")
Stevie Nicks ("Talk to Me")
Bonnie Raitt ("No Way to Treat a Lady")
Tina Turner ("Back Where You Started")

VOCAL GROUP (ROCK)
Artists United against Apartheid ("Sun City")
The Eurythmics ("Missionary Man")
The Fabulous Thunderbirds ("Tuff Enuff")
The Rolling Stones ("Harlem Shuffle")
ZZ Top (*Afterburner*)

RHYTHM AND BLUES
Song (award to songwriter): "Sweet Love" (Anita Baker, Louis A. Johnson, Gary Bias); Male Vocalist: James Brown ("Living in America"); Female Vocalist: Anita Baker (*Rapture*); Vocal Group: Prince and the Revolution ("Kiss")

COUNTRY
Song (award to songwriter): "Grandpa (Tell Me 'Bout the Good Old Days)" (Jamie O'Hara); Male Vocalist: Ronnie Milsap (*Lost in the Fifties Tonight*); Female Vocalist: Reba McEntire ("Whoever's in New England"); Vocal Group: the Judds ["Grandpa (Tell Me 'Bout the Good Old Days)"]

JAZZ
Male Vocalist: Bobby McFerrin ("'Round Midnight"); Female Vocalist: Diane Schuur (*Timeless*); Vocal Group: 2 + 2 Plus (Clare Fischer and His Latin Sextet) (*Free Fall*); Soloist: Miles Davis (*Tutu*); Group: Wynton Marsalis (*J Mood*);

Big Band: the Tonight Show Band with Doc Severinsen (*The Tonight Show Band with Doc Severinsen*)

OTHER AWARDS
Cast Show Album: *Follies in Concert*; Comedy Performance: Bill Cosby (*Those of You with or without Children, You'll Understand*); Spoken Word: Carl Perkins, Jerry Lee Lewis, Roy Orbison, Johnny Cash, Sam Phillips, Rick Nelson, Chips Moman (*Interviews from the Class of '55, Recording Sessions*); Classical Album: *Horowitz: The Studio Recordings, New York 1985* (Vladimir Horowitz); Music Video (Short Form): *Dire Straits Brothers in Arms* (Dire Straits); Music Video (Long Form): *Bring on the Night* (Sting)

Taking a cue from Oscar, Grammy switched from hosts with a middle-of-the-road musical background (Andy Williams, John Denver, Kenny Rogers) to a quick-witted comedian (Billy Crystal). Crystal gave a much needed charge to the proceedings and set the stage for his eventual emceeing of the Academy Awards. Performance highlights included a blues jam session with Robert Cray, B. B. King, Etta James, and others; Dionne Warwick, Stevie Wonder, and Gladys Knight rendering "That's What Friends Are For" in a performance judged by many critics as better than the recorded version; and the finale: "Stand By Me," newly popular because of the film of the same name, sung by original Drifter Ben E. King and joined by over 150 of the evening's winners and nominees.

Michael Jackson had no new recordings in competition, but his presence was still felt. A Pepsi-Cola ad campaign featuring the Gloved One was premiered during the broadcast.

THE AMERICAN MUSIC AWARDS

POP/ROCK
Single: "There'll Be Sad Songs" (Billy Ocean); Album: *Whitney Houston* (Whitney Houston); Male Artist: Lionel Richie; Female Artist: Whitney Houston; Band, Duo, or Group: Huey Lewis and the News; Video Single: "Dancing on the Ceiling" (Lionel Richie); Male Video Artist: Billy Ocean; Female Video Artist: Madonna; Video Duo or Group: Huey Lewis and the News

SOUL/RHYTHM AND BLUES

Single: "Nasty" (Janet Jackson); Album: *Whitney Houston* (Whitney Houston); Male Artist: Lionel Richie; Female Artist: Whitney Houston; Band, Duo, or Group: New Edition; Video Single: "The Greatest Love of All" (Whitney Houston); Male Video Artist: Lionel Richie; Female Video Artist: Janet Jackson; Video Duo or Group: Kool and the Gang

COUNTRY

Single: "Grandpa" (the Judds); Album: *Alabama's Greatest Hits* (Alabama); Male Artist: Willie Nelson; Female Artist: Barbara Mandrell; Band, Duo, or Group: Alabama; Video Single: "Grandpa" (the Judds); Male Video Artist: George Jones; Female Video Artist: Reba McEntire; Video Duo or Group: Alabama

SPECIAL AWARD

Elvis Presley (posthumous)

COUNTRY MUSIC ASSOCIATION AWARDS

Entertainer: Reba McEntire; Single: "Bop" (Dan Seals); Song: "On the Other Hand" (Paul Overstreet, Don Schlitz, songwriters); Album: *Lost in the Fifties Tonight* (Ronnie Milsap); Male Vocalist: George Strait; Female Vocalist: Reba McEntire; Vocal Group: the Judds; Vocal Duo: Dan Seals, Marie Osmond; Musician: Johnny Gimble; Horizon Award: Randy Travis; Music Video: "Who's Gonna Fill Their Shoes" (George Jones)

MTV VIDEO MUSIC AWARDS

Video of the Year: *Money for Nothing* (Dire Straits); Male Video: Robert Palmer (*Addicted to Love*); Female Video: Whitney Houston (*How Will I Know*); Group Video: Dire Straits (*Money for Nothing*); Concept Video: *Take Me On* (a-ha); New Artist in a Video: a-ha (*Take Me On*); Special Effects: Michael Patterson (a-ha, *Take Me On*); Director: Steve Barron (a-ha, *Take Me On*); Video Vanguard Award: Madonna, Zbigniew Rybeznski; Viewers' Choice Award: a-ha (*Take Me On*)

1987

THE GRAMMY AWARDS

RECORD OF THE YEAR

"Back in the High Life Again" (Steve Winwood)
"Graceland" (Paul Simon)
"I Still Haven't Found What I'm Looking For" (U2)
"La Bamba" (Los Lobos)
"Luka" (Suzanne Vega)

What? Didn't Paul Simon's *Graceland* win Album of the Year in 1986? Yes, but the single "Graceland" was released after the album, during the 1987 eligibilty period.

SONG OF THE YEAR (AWARD TO SONGWRITER)

"Didn't We Almost Have It All" (Michael Masser, Will Jennings)
"I Still Haven't Found What I'm Looking For" (U2)
"La Bamba" (adapted by Richie Valens)
"Luka" (Suzanne Vega)
"Somewhere Out There" (James Horner, Barry Mann)

ALBUM OF THE YEAR

Bad (Michael Jackson)
The Joshua Tree (U2)
Sign O' the Times (Prince)
Trio (Dolly Parton, Linda Ronstadt, Emmylou Harris)
Whitney (Whitney Houston)

The high-spot of the '87 Grammys and perhaps of the past ten Grammycasts was Michael Jackson's electric performance of "Man in the Mirror." He then went to his seat in Radio City Music Hall and lost all four nominations for *Bad*, his first album since *Thriller*, which had won him a record number of Grammys in 1983. *Bad*'s luck wasn't all bad. It did win one prize for engineering.

Album of the Year went to *The Joshua Tree* by underground Irish band U2, whose lead guitarist The Edge thanked everyone from Bob Dylan to Morris the Cat and Batman and Robin.

Irish band U2 surprisingly defeated Michael Jackson for Album of the Year at the '87 Grammys.

NEW ARTIST
The Breakfast Club
Cutting Crew
Terence Trent D'Arby
Swing Out Sister
Jody Watley

The most memorable presentation of the night was given by Little Richard in the New Artist category. After Richard and Buster Poindexter read the nominees, Richard opened the envelope and declared, "And the winner is . . . me!" The veteran rock-and-roller went on to laughingly state he had never won a Grammy even though he was a pioneer in the field. "I am the *architect* of rock and roll," he shouted with equal measures of humor and anger. After several tense moments, Richard announced the winner was Jody Watley.

MALE VOCALIST (POP)
Michael Jackson (*Bad*)
Al Jarreau ("*Moonlighting* Theme")
Elton John ("Candle in the Wind")
Bruce Springsteen ("Brilliant Disguise")
Sting (*Bring on the Night*)

FEMALE VOCALIST (POP)
Belinda Carlisle ("Heaven Is a Place on Earth")
Whitney Houston ["I Wanna Dance with Somebody (Who Loves Me)"]
Carly Simon (*Coming Around Again*)
Barbra Streisand (*One Voice*)
Suzanne Vega ("Luka")

VOCAL GROUP (POP)
Heart ("Alone")
Los Lobos ("La Bamba")

Bill Medley, Jennifer Warnes ["(I've Had) The Time of My Life"]
Linda Ronstadt, James Ingram ("Somewhere Out There")
Swing Out Sister ("Breakout")

VOCAL PERFORMANCE (ROCK, MALE OR FEMALE)
Joe Cocker ("Unchain My Heart")
Richard Marx ("Don't Mean Nothing")
Bob Seger ("Shakedown")
Bruce Springsteen (*Tunnel of Love*)
Tina Turner ("Better Be Good to Me")

VOCAL GROUP (ROCK)
The Georgia Satellites ("Keep Your Hand to Yourself")
Heart (*Bad Animals*)
Los Lobos (*By the Light of the Moon*)
U2 (*The Joshua Tree*)
Yes (*Big Generator*)

RHYTHM AND BLUES
Song (award to songwriter): "Lean on Me" (Bill Withers); Male Vocalist: Smokey Robinson ("Just to See Her"); Female Vocalist: Aretha Franklin (*Aretha*); Vocal Group: Aretha Franklin, George Michael ["I Knew You Were Waiting (for Me)"]

Aretha Franklin became the most Grammyed female artist this year, winning her thirteenth and fourteenth awards. Her career total stands at fifteen.

COUNTRY
Song (award to songwriter): "Forever and Ever, Amen" (Paul Overstreet, Don Schlitz); Male Vocalist: Randy Travis (*Always and Forever*); Female Vocalist: K. T. Oslin ("'80s Ladies"); Vocal Group: Dolly Parton, Linda Ronstadt, Emmylou Harris (*Trio*); Vocal Duet: Ronnie Milsap, Kenny Rogers ("Make No Mistake, She's Mine")

JAZZ
Jazz Fusion Performance: Pat Metheny Group [*Still Life (Talking)*]; Male Vocalist: Bobby McFerren ("What Is This Thing Called Love"); Female Vocalist: Diane Schuur (*Diane Schuur and the Count Basie Orchestra*); Soloist: Dexter Gordon (*The Other Side of 'Round Midnight*); Group: Wynton Marsalis (*Marsalis Standard Time, Volume I*); Big Band: Duke Ellington Orchestra conducted by Mercer Ellington (*Digital Duke*)

OTHER AWARDS
Cast Show Album: *Les Miserables* (Broadway cast); Soundtrack Album: *The Untouchables*; Song Written for a Motion Picture or Television: "Somewhere Out There" (from *An American Tail*); Comedy Performance: Robin Williams (*A Night at the Met*); Spoken Word: Garrison Keillor (*Lake Wobegon Days*); Classical Album: *Horowitz in Moscow* (Vladimir Horowitz); Performance Music Video: *The Prince's Trust All-Star Rock Concert*; Concept Music Video: *Land of Confusion* (Genesis)

For the thirtieth anniversary ceremony, Grammy switched from the traditional Shrine Auditorium in Los Angeles to New York City's Radio City Music Hall. This would be the first time the Grammys played Gotham since the 1980 awards. A back-and-forth battle began between Tinseltown and the Big Apple over which metropolis would play host to the music industry's big night. Billy Crystal hosted for the second year in a row.

THE AMERICAN MUSIC AWARDS

POP/ROCK
Single: "I Wanna Dance with Somebody (Who Loves Me)" (Whitney Houston); Album: *Graceland* (Paul Simon); Male Artist: Paul Simon; Female Artist: Whitney Houston; Band, Duo, or Group: Bon Jovi; Video (Pop/Rock or Soul/Rhythm and Blues): "When I Think of You" (Janet Jackson)

SOUL/RHYTHM AND BLUES
Single: "Bad" (Michael Jackson); Album: *Rapture* (Anita Baker); Male Artist: Luther Vandross; Female Artist: Anita Baker; Band, Duo, or Group: Cameo

COUNTRY
Single: "Forever and Ever, Amen" (Randy Travis); Album: *Always and Forever* (Randy Travis); Male Artist: Randy Travis; Female Artist: Reba

McEntire; Band, Duo, or Group: Alabama; Video: "Forever and Ever, Amen" (Randy Travis)

SPECIAL AWARD
The Beach Boys

COUNTRY MUSIC ASSOCIATION AWARDS

Entertainer: Hank Williams, Jr.; Single: "Forever and Ever, Amen" (Randy Travis); Song: "Forever and Ever, Amen" (Paul Overstreet, Don Schlitz, songwriters); Album: *Always and Forever* (Randy Travis); Male Vocalist: Randy Travis; Female Vocalist: Reba McEntire; Vocal Group: the Judds; Vocal Duo: Ricky Skaggs, Sharon Mhite; Musician: Johnny Gimble; Horizon Award: Holly Dunn; Music Video: "My Name Is Bocephus" (Hank Williams, Jr.)

MTV VIDEO MUSIC AWARDS

Video of the Year: *Sledgehammer* (Peter Gabriel); Male Video: Peter Gabriel (*Sledgehammer*); Female Video: Madonna (*Papa Don't Preach*); Group Video: Talking Heads (*Wild Wild Life*); Concept Video: Peter Gabriel/Stephen Johnson (*Sledgehammer*); New Artist in a Video: Crowded House (*Don't Dream It's Over*); Video from a Film: the Talking Heads (*Wild Wild Life*); Special Effects: Stephen Johnson, Peter Lord (Peter Gabriel, *Sledgehammer*); Director: Stephen Johnson (Peter Gabriel, *Sledgehammer*); Video Vanguard Award: Julien Temple, Peter Gabriel; Viewers' Choice Award: U2 (*With or without You*)

THE GRAMMY AWARDS

RECORD OF THE YEAR
"Don't Worry, Be Happy" (Bobby McFerrin)
"Fast Car" (Tracy Chapman)
"Giving You the Best That I Got" (Anita Baker)
"Man in the Mirror" (Michael Jackson)
"Roll with It" (Steve Winwood)

Though folk-pop balladeer Tracy Chapman had

the most nominations (six), jazz a cappella vocalist Bobbie McFerrin swept the '88 Grammys, winning four out of the five categories in which he was a contender. McFerrin's catchy ditty "Don't Worry, Be Happy" featured the singer recreating the sounds of a full orchestra. The popular tune was introduced in the Tom Cruise film *Cocktail* and won Record of the Year, Song of the Year, and Male Vocalist (Pop) awards. McFerrin reaped a fourth Grammy for Jazz Male Vocalist for "Brothers," a track from *Rob Wasserman's Duets* album.

SONG OF THE YEAR (AWARD TO SONGWRITER)
"Be Still My Beating Heart" (Sting)
"Don't Worry, Be Happy" (Bobby McFerrin)
"Fast Car" (Tracy Chapman)
"Giving You the Best That I Got" (Anita Baker, Skip Scarborough, Randy Holland)
"Piano in the Dark" (Brenda Russell, Jeff Hall, Scott Cutler)

ALBUM OF THE YEAR
Faith (George Michael)
. . . Nothing Like the Sun (Sting)
Roll with It (Steve Winwood)
Simple Pleasures (Bobby McFerrin)
Tracy Chapman (Tracy Chapman)

NEW ARTIST
Rick Astley
Tracy Chapman
Toni Childs
Take 6
Vanessa Williams

MALE VOCALIST (POP)
Phil Collins ("A Groovy Kind of Love")
Bobby McFerrin ("Don't Worry, Be Happy")
George Michael ("Father Figure")
Sting ("Be Still My Beating Heart")
Steve Winwood ("Roll with It")

FEMALE VOCALIST (POP)
Tracy Chapman ("Fast Car")
Taylor Dane (*Tell It to My Heart*)
Whitney Houston ("One Moment in Time")

Joni Mitchell (*Chalk Mark in a Rain Storm*)
Brenda Russell (*Get Here*)

VOCAL GROUP (POP)
The Beach Boys ("Kokomo")
The Escape Club ("Wild, Wild West")
Gloria Estefan and the Miami Sound Machine
    ("Anything for You," Spanish/English version)
The Manhattan Transfer (*Brasil*)
Brenda Russell, Joe Esposito ("Piano in the Dark")

The Beach Boys, top-selling purveyors of surf music in the '60s, had an '80s comeback with "Kokomo." Like "Don't Worry, Be Happy," "Kokomo" was featured in *Cocktail*. The song earned the Beach Boys their first Grammy nomination. But they lost to the jazz-pop quartet, the Manhattan Transfer, for the latter's venture into Latin sounds, the *Brasil* album.

MALE VOCALIST (ROCK)
Eric Clapton ("After Midnight")
Joe Cocker (*Unchain My Heart*)
Robert Palmer ("Simply Irresistible")
Robbie Robertson (*Robbie Robertson*)
Rod Stewart ("Forever Young")

FEMALE VOCALIST (ROCK)
Pat Benatar ("All Fired Up")
Toni Childs ("Don't Walk Away")
Melissa Etheridge ("Show Me Some Water")
Sinead O'Connor (*The Lion and the Cobra*)
Tina Turner (*Tina Live in Europe*)

VOCAL GROUP (ROCK)
INXS (*Kick*)
Joan Jett and the Blackhearts ("I Hate Myself
    for Loving You")
Little Feat (*Let It Roll*)
Midnight Oil ("Beds Are Running")
U2 ("Desire")

RHYTHM AND BLUES
Song (award to songwriter): "Giving You the Best That I Got" (Anita Baker, Skip Scarborough, Randy Holland); Male Vocalist: Terence Trent D'Arby (*Introducing the Hard Line According to Terence Trent D'Arby*); Female Vocalist: Anita Baker ("Giving You the Best That I Got"); Vocal Group:

Gladys Knight and the Pips ("Love Overboard")

COUNTRY
Song (award to songwriter): "Hold Me" (K. T. Oslin); Male Vocalist: Randy Travis (*Old 8 × 10*); Female Vocalist: K. T. Oslin ("Hold Me"); Vocal Group: the Judds ("Give a Little Love"); Vocal Collaboration: Roy Orbison, k. d. lang ("Crying")

JAZZ
Jazz Fusion Performance: the Yellowjackets (*Politics*); Male Vocalist: Bobby McFerrin ("Brothers"); Female Vocalist: Betty Carter (*Look What I Got!*); Vocal Group: Take 6 ("Spread Love"); Soloist: Michael Brecker (*Don't Try This at Home*); Group: McCoy Tyner, Pharoah Sanders, David Murray, Cecil McBee, Roy Haynes (*Blues for Coltrane: A Tribute to John Coltrane*); Big Band: Gil Evans and the Monday Night Orchestra (*Bud and Bird*)

OTHER AWARDS
Hard Rock/Metal Performance: Jethro Tull (*Crest of a Wave*); Rap Performance: D.J. Jazzy Jeff and the Fresh Prince ("Parents Just Don't Understand"); Cast Show Album: *Into the Woods*; Soundtrack Album: *The Last Emperor*; Song Written for a Motion Picture or Television: "Two Hearts" (from *Buster*); Comedy Performance: Robin Williams (*Good Morning, Vietnam*); Spoken Word: Rev. Jesse Jackson ("Speech by Rev. Jesse Jackson, July 27," on Aretha Franklin's *One Lord, One Faith, One Baptism*); Classical Album: *Verdi: Requiem and Operatic Choruses* (Robert Shaw conducting the Atlanta Symphony Orchestra and Chorus); Performance Music Video: *Where the Streets Have No Name* (U2); Concept Music Video: *Fat* ("Weird Al" Yankovic)

Back to Los Angeles's Shrine Auditorium after the previous year's outing at New York City's Radio City Music Hall. Once again, Billy Crystal presided. But this would be his last year as Grammy host before moving on to a bigger award-show gig (namely the Oscars).

A curiously flat telecast featured two bizarre performers. Rock nominee Sinead O'Connor appeared in "combat boots, ripped jeans, and black halter top to go with her shaven head" (*Variety*). As if to complete the picture of nonmainstream hipness, O'Connor's bald skull sported a tattoo. Kool Moe Dee recited an angry poem about the NARAS not including the new rap category on the air. The winners were D.J. Jazzy Jeff and the Fresh Prince, who boycotted the ceremony in protest of rap's off-air status. Another new category indicated the Academy's half-hearted attempts to keep up with current music trends. The freshly minted Hard Rock/Metal Performance award went to veteran Jethro Tull rather than the popular band Metallica. This announcement was greeted with boos by the crowd. Grammy was at least trying to court cutting-edge artists with nominations, but still playing it safe by giving awards to middle-of-the-roaders.

THE AMERICAN MUSIC AWARDS

POP/ROCK
Single: "Sweet Child O' Mine" (Guns 'N' Roses); Album: *Dirty Dancing* (Original Soundtrack); Male Artist: George Michael; Female Artist: Whitney Houston; Band, Duo, or Group: Gloria Estefan and the Miami Sound Machine; New Artist: Tracy Chapman

SOUL/RHYTHM AND BLUES
Single: "Nice 'N' Slow" (Freddie Jackson); Album: *Faith* (George Michael); Male Artist: George Michael; Female Artist: Whitney Houston; Band, Group, or Duo: Gladys Knight and the Pips; New Artist: Al B. Sure!

COUNTRY
Single: "I Told You So" (Randy Travis); Album: *Always and Forever* (Randy Travis); Male Artist: Randy Travis; Female Artist: Reba McEntire; Band, Duo, or Group: Alabama; New Artist: Patty Loveless

RAP/HIP HOP
Album: *He's the DJ, I'm the Rapper* (D.J. Jazzy Jeff and the Fresh Prince); Artist: D.J. Jazzy Jeff and the Fresh Prince

HEAVY METAL/HARD ROCK
Album: *Hysteria* (Def Leppard); Artist: Def Leppard

SPECIAL AWARDS
Willie Nelson; Michael Jackson

COUNTRY MUSIC ASSOCIATION AWARDS

Entertainer: Hank Williams, Jr.; Single: "Eighteen Wheels and a Dozen Roses" (Kathy Mattea); Song: "'80s Ladies" (K. T. Oslin, songwriter); Album: *Born to Boogie* (Hank Williams, Jr.); Male Vocalist: Randy Travis; Female Vocalist: K. T. Oslin; Vocal Group: Highway 101; Vocal Duo: the Judds; Vocal Event: Dolly Parton, Linda Ronstadt, Emmylou Harris (*Trio*); Musician: Chet Atkins

MTV VIDEO MUSIC AWARDS

Video of the Year: INXS (*Need You Tonight/Mediate*); Male Video: Prince (*U Got the Look*); Female Video: Suzanne Vega (*Luka*); Group Video: INXS (*Need You Tonight/Mediate*); Concept Video: Pink Floyd (*Learning to Fly*); New Artist in a Video: Guns 'N' Roses (*Welcome to the Jungle*); Video from a Film: Los Lobos (*La Bamba*); Special Effects: Jim Francis, Dave Barton (Squeeze, *Hourglass*); Director: Andy Morahan, George Michael (George Michael, *Father Figure*); Breakthrough Video: INXS (*Need You Tonight/Mediate*); Video Vanguard Award: Michael Jackson; Viewers' Choice Award: INXS (*Need You Tonight/Mediate*)

THE GRAMMY AWARDS

RECORD OF THE YEAR
"The End of Innocence" (Don Henley)
"The Living Years" (Mike and the Mechanics)
"She Drives Me Crazy" (Fine Young Cannibals)
"We Didn't Start the Fire" (Billy Joel)
"Wind Beneath My Wings" (Bette Midler)

In typical fashion, Grammy bypassed a hard-edged hit like Don Henley's "The End of Innocence" and a fast-paced social history lesson of the past thirty years like Billy Joel's "We Didn't Start the Fire," in favor of a gooey-centered ballad—"Wind Beneath

Bonnie Raitt's four 1989 Grammys boosted her career tremendously.

My Wings," warbled by Bette Midler in the weepy film melodrama *Beaches*. "Wings" won both Record of the Year and Song of the Year. "Hey, Bonnie Raitt, I got one, too," the irrepressible Miss M shouted when she picked up her Record of the Year award.

Midler was referring to Raitt's sweep of all the categories for which she was nominated. After twenty years, ten albums of middling success, and a battle with alcoholism, the raspy-voiced Raitt, daughter of Broadway star John Raitt, won her first Grammys for Female Vocalist (Pop) and Female Vocalist (Rock), Album of the Year (*Nick of Time*), and Traditional Blues Duo for "I'm in the Mood," a collaboration with John Lee Hooker on his *The Healer* LP.

Nick of Time was "my first sober album," she informed the Grammy audience at the Shrine Auditorium. "My sobriety means I'm going to feel great tomorrow."

SONG OF THE YEAR
(AWARD TO SONGWRITER)

"Don't Know Much" (Barry Mann, Cynthia Weil, Tom Snow)

"The End of Innocence" (Don Henley, Bruce Hornsby)

"The Living Years" (Mike Rutherford, Brian A. Robertson)

"We Didn't Start the Fire" (Billy Joel)

"Wind beneath My Wings" (Larry Henley, Jeff Silbar)

ALBUM OF THE YEAR

The End of Innocence (Don Henley)
Full Moon Fever (Tom Petty)
Nick of Time (Bonnie Raitt)
The Raw and the Cooked (Fine Young Cannibals)
The Traveling Wilburys, Volume I (the Traveling Wilburys)

NEW ARTIST

Milli Vanilli
Neneh Cherry
Indigo Girls
Soul II Soul
Tone Loc

In the biggest scandal in Grammy history, the West German pair Milli Vanilli garnered the New Artist award for a fake act. The win wasn't too popular to begin with. Critics charged the dreadlocked duo (Fab Morvan and Rob Pilatus) specialized in mindless pop and flashy music videos with no substance. A year after their triumph, the two were revealed to have lip-synced their entire album *Girl You Know It's True.* Even their vocal performance of the title track on the '89 Grammys was provided by others. Soon after the story broke, the Academy took back the award, the only time a Grammy has been rescinded. The two were also relieved of their American Music Awards.

MALE VOCALIST (POP)

Michael Bolton ("How Am I Supposed to Live without You")
Billy Joel ("We Didn't Start the Fire")
Richard Marx ("Right Here Waiting")
Roy Orbison ("You Got It")
Prince (*Batman, Motion Picture Soundtrack*)

FEMALE VOCALIST (POP)

Paula Abdul ("Straight Up")
Gloria Estefan ("Don't Wanna Lose You")
Bette Midler ("Wind beneath My Wings")
Bonnie Raitt ("Nick of Time")
Linda Ronstadt (*Cry Like a Rainstorm, Howl Like the Wind*)

VOCAL GROUP (POP)

The B-52s ("Love Shack")
Fine Young Cannibals ("She Drives Me Crazy")

Mike and the Mechanics ("The Living Years")
Linda Ronstadt, Aaron Neville ("Don't Know Much")
Simply Red ("If You Don't Know Me By Now")

MALE VOCALIST (ROCK)

Joe Cocker ("When the Night Comes")
Don Henley (*The End of Innocence*)
Tom Petty ("Free Fallin'")
Lou Reed (*New York*)
Neil Young (*Freedom*)

FEMALE VOCALIST (ROCK)

Pat Benatar ("Let's Stay Together")
Melissa Etheridge (*Brave and Crazy*)
Cyndi Lauper ("I Drove All Night")
Bonnie Raitt (*Nick of Time*)
Tina Turner (*Foreign Affair*)

VOCAL GROUP (ROCK)

Living Colour ("Glamour Boys")
The Rolling Stones ("Mixed Emotions")
The Traveling Wilburys (*The Traveling Wilburys, Volume I*)
U2 (*Rattle and Hum*)
U2, B. B. King ("When Love Comes to Town")

RHYTHM AND BLUES

Song (award to songwriter): "If You Don't Know Me By Now" (Kenny Gamble, Leon Huff); Male Vocalist: Bobby Brown ("Every Little Step"); Female Vocalist: Anita Baker (*Giving You the Best That I Got*); Vocal Group: Soul II Soul, Caron Wheeler ("Back to Life")

COUNTRY

Song (award to songwriter): "After All This Time" (Rodney Crowell); Male Vocalist: Lyle Lovett (*Lyle Lovett and His Large Band*); Female Vocalist: k. d. lang (*Absolute Torch and Twang*); Vocal Group: the Nitty Gritty Dirt Band (*Will the Circle Be Unbroken, Volume II*); Vocal Collaboration: Hank Williams, Jr., Hank Williams, Sr. ("There's a Tear in My Beer")

JAZZ

Jazz Fusion Performance: Pat Metheny Group (*Letter from Home*); Male Vocalist: Harry Connick,

Jr. (*When Harry Met Sally . . .*); Female Vocalist: Ruth Brown (*Blues on Broadway*); Vocal Group: Dr. John, Rickie Lee Jones ("Makin' Whoopee"); Soloist: Miles Davis (*Aura*); Group: Chick Corea Akoustic Band (*Chick Corea Akoustic Band*); Big Band: Miles Davis (*Aura*)

OTHER AWARDS

Hard Rock Performance: Living Colour ("Cult of Personality"); Metal Performance: Metallica ("One"); Rap Performance: Young MC ("Bust a Move"); Musical Cast Show Album: *Jerome Robbins' Broadway*; Soundtrack Album: *The Fabulous Baker Boys*; Song for a Motion Picture or Television: "Let the River Run" from *Working Girl*; Comedy Performance: "Professor" Peter Schickele and the Greater Hoople Area Off-Season Philharmonic (*PDQ Bach: 1712 Overture and Other Musical Assaults*); Spoken Word: Gilda Radner (*It's Always Something*); Classical Album: *Bartok: 6 String Quartets* (the Emerson String Quartet); Music Video (Short Form): *Leave Me Alone* (Michael Jackson); Music Video (Long Form): *Rhythm Nation* (Janet Jackson)

Comedian Gary Shandling was called in to replace Billy Crystal as host. Performers included Billy Joel, the controversial Milli Vanilli, and, in a tribute to Paul McCartney, Ray Charles and Stevie Wonder.

THE AMERICAN MUSIC AWARDS

POP/ROCK

Single: "Girl You Know It's True" (Milli Vanilli); Album: *Hangin' Tough* (New Kids on the Block); Male Artist: Bobby Brown; Female Artist: Paula Abdul; Band, Duo, or Group: Aerosmith; New Artist: Milli Vanilli

SOUL/RHYTHM AND BLUES

Single: "Miss You Much" (Janet Jackson); Album: *Don't Be Cruel* (Bobby Brown); Male Artist: Luther Vandross; Female Artist: Anita Baker; Band, Duo, or Group: The O'Jays; New Artist: Milli Vanilli

COUNTRY

Single: "Deeper Than the Holler" (Randy Travis); Album: *Reba Live* (Reba McEntire); Male Artist:

Randy Travis; Female Artist: Reba McEntire; Band, Duo, or Group: Alabama; New Artist: Clint Black

RAP/HIP-HOP

Album: *Let's Get It Started* (M. C. Hammer); Artist: M. C. Hammer; New Artist: Young MC

HEAVY METAL/HARD ROCK

Album: *Appetite for Destruction* (Guns 'N' Roses); Artist: Guns 'N' Roses

DANCE MUSIC

Single: "Miss You Much" (Janet Jackson); Artist: Paula Abdul; New Artist: Tone Loc

SPECIAL AWARDS

Neil Diamond; Prince

COUNTRY MUSIC ASSOCIATION AWARDS

Entertainer: George Strait; Single: "I'm No Stranger to the Rain" (Keith Whitley); Song: "Chiseled in Stone" (Max D. Barnes, Vern Gosdin, songwriters); Album: *Will the Circle Be Unbroken, Volume II* (the Nitty Gritty Dirt Band); Male Vocalist: Ricky Van Shelton; Female Vocalist: Kathy Mattea; Vocal Group: Highway 101; Vocal Duo: the Judds; Vocal Event: Hank Williams, Jr., Hank Williams, Sr.; Musician: Johnny Gimble; Horizon Award: Clint Black; Music Video: "There's a Tear in My Beer" (Hank Williams, Jr., Hank Williams, Sr.)

MTV VIDEO MUSIC AWARDS

Video of the Year: Neil Young (*This Note's for You*); Male Video: Elvis Costello (*Veronica*); Female Video: Paula Abdul (*Straight Up*); Group Video: Living Colour (*Cult of Personality*); New Artist in a Video: Living Colour (*Cult of Personality*); Rap Video: D.J. Jazzy Jeff and the Fresh Prince (*Parents Just Don't Understand*); Dance Video: Paula Abdul (*Straight Up*); Metal/Hard Rock Video: Guns 'N' Roses (*Sweet Child O' Mine*); Video from a Film: U2, B. B. King (*When Love Comes to Town*); Special Effects: Jim Blashfield (Michael Jackson, *Leave Me Alone*); Director: David Fincher

(Madonna, *Express Yourself*); Breakthrough Video: Art of Noise Featuring Tom Jones (*Kiss*); Video Vanguard Award: George Michael; Viewers' Choice Award: Madonna (*Like a Prayer*)

1990

THE GRAMMY AWARDS

RECORD OF THE YEAR
"Another Day in Paradise" (Phil Collins)
"From a Distance" (Bette Midler)
"Nothing Compares 2 U" (Sinead O'Connor)
"U Can't Touch This" (M. C. Hammer)
"Vision of Love" (Mariah Carey)

SONG OF THE YEAR
(AWARD TO SONGWRITER)
"Another Day in Paradise" (Phil Collins)
"From a Distance" (Julie Gold)
"Hold On" (Chynna Philips, Glen Ballard, Carnie Wilson)
"Nothing Compares 2 U" (Prince)
"Vision of Love" (Mariah Carey, Ben Margulies)

Following 1989's "Wind beneath My Wings," "From a Distance" was voted Song of the Year, making it two years in a row that a ballad sung by Bette Midler won the category. "Distance" was originally recorded in 1985 by Irish folksinger Nanci Griffith. Its anti-violence message then applied to conflicts in Northern Ireland. Midler's rendition came out at the time of the Persian Gulf War.

ALBUM OF THE YEAR
Back on the Block (Quincy Jones)
. . . But Seriously (Phil Collins)
Mariah Carey (Mariah Carey)
Please Hammer Don't Hurt 'Em (M. C. Hammer)
Wilson Philips (Wilson Philips)

Producer/arranger/composer/musician Quincy Jones' *Back on the Block* album, a survey of African-American music from the 1940s to the 1990s featuring such diverse artists as Ella Fitzgerald, Ray Charles, Kool Moe Dee, James Ingram, and Ice T,

brought his Grammy total to twenty-five. This broke Henry Mancini's record of twenty for most awards won by a popular artist. (Chicago Symphony conductor Sir Georg Solti held—and still holds—the record for most Grammys overall with thirty awards in the classical field.) Jones won six individual accolades for *Block*, including Producer of the Year and Album of the Year. The album also won for engineering and R&B Vocal Duo for Ray Charles and Chaka Khan's intrepretation of "I'll Be Good to You."

Jones remains the pop artist with the most Grammys. His total is twenty-six as of this writing.

NEW ARTIST
Black Crowes
Mariah Carey
The Kentucky Headhunters
Lisa Stansfield
Wilson Philips

MALE VOCALIST (POP)
Michael Bolton ("Georgia on My Mind")
Phil Collins ("Another Day in Paradise")
James Ingram ("I Don't Have the Heart")
Billy Joel (*Storm Front*)
Roy Orbison ("Oh, Pretty Woman")
Rod Stewart ("Downtown Train")

FEMALE VOCALIST (POP)
Mariah Carey ("Vision of Love")
Whitney Houston ("I'm Your Baby Tonight")
Bette Midler ("From a Distance")
Sinead O'Connor ("Nothing Compares 2 U")
Lisa Stansfield ("All Around the World")

VOCAL GROUP (POP)
The B-52s ("Roam")
Heart ("All I Wanna Do Is Make Love to You")
Bruce Hornsby and the Range ("Across the River")
The Righteous Brothers ("Unchained Melody," 1990 re-recording)
Linda Ronstadt, Aaron Neville ("All My Life")

MALE VOCALIST (ROCK)
Eric Clapton ("Bad Love")
Joe Cocker ("You Can Leave Your Hat On")
Billy Idol ("Cradle of Love")

Jon Bon Jovi ("Blaze of Glory")
Neil Young ("Rockin' on the Free World")

FEMALE VOCALIST (ROCK)
Melissa Etheridge ("The Angels")
Janet Jackson ("Black Cat")
Alannah Myles ("Black Velvet")
Stevie Nicks ("Whole Lotta Trouble")
Tina Turner ("Steamy Windows")

VOCAL GROUP (ROCK)
Aerosmith ("Janie's Got a Gun")
INXS ("Suicide Blonde")
Midnight Oil (*Blue Sky Morning*)
Red Hot Chili Peppers ("Higher Ground")
The Rolling Stones ("Almost Hear You Sigh")

RHYTHM AND BLUES
Song (award to songwriter): "U Can't Touch This" (James Miller, M. C. Hammer); Male Vocalist: Luther Vandross ("Here and Now"); Female Vocalist: Anita Baker (*Compositions*); Vocal Group: Ray Charles, Chaka Khan ("I'll Be Good to You")

COUNTRY
Song (award to songwriter): "Where've You Been" (Jon Vezner, Don Henry); Male Vocalist: Vince Gill ("When I Call Your Name"); Female Vocalist: Kathy Mattea ("Where've You Been"); Vocal Group: the Kentucky Headhunters (*Pickin' on Nashville*); Vocal Collaboration: Chet Atkins, Mark Knopfler ("Poor Boy Blues")

JAZZ
Male Vocalist: Harry Connick, Jr. (*We Are in Love*); Female Vocalist: Ella Fitzgerald (*All That Jazz*); Soloist: Oscar Peterson (*The Legendary Oscar Peterson Trio Live at the Blue Note*); Group: The Oscar Peterson Trio (*The Legendary Oscar Peterson Trio Live at the Blue Note*); Big Band: Frank Foster, conductor ("Basie's Bag," *Big Boss Band*)

OTHER AWARDS
Hard Rock Performance: Living Colour (*Time's Up*); Metal Performance: Metallica ("Stone Cold Crazy"); Rap Performance (Solo): M. C. Hammer ("U Can't Touch This"); Rap Performance (Group): Ice-T, Melle Mel, Big Daddy Kane, Kool Moe

Dee, Quincy Jones III ("Back on the Block"); Musical Show Cast Album: *Les Miserables, The Complete Symphonic Recording*; Soundtrack Album: *Glory*; Song from a Motion Picture or Television: "Under the Sea" from *The Little Mermaid*; Comedy Performance: "Professor" Peter Schickele (*PDQ Bach: Oedipus Tex and Other Choral Calamities*); Spoken Word: George Burns (*Gracie: A Love Story*); Classical Album: *Ives: Symphony No. 2* (Leonard Bernstein conducting the New York Philharmonic); Music Video (Short Form): *Opposites Attract* (Paula Abdul); Music Video (Long Form): *Please Hammer Don't Hurt 'Em the Movie* (M. C. Hammer)

This year the Grammys shifted back to Gotham after the previous year's return to L.A. The ceremony was hosted by Gary Shandling at Radio City Music Hall. *Variety* commented that "the most exciting competition was among the performers vying for the most embarassing display." Among those cited in this hot contest were Garth Brooks in jeans and cowboy hat "trapped in an overblown production number that had him singing in the middle of what looked like a set for a Noel Coward play"; Billy Idol who added the new lyric "This song is so cheesy" to his performance of "Cradle of Love"; and M. C. Hammer, attired in what appeared to be a suit made of tin foil.

Sinead O'Connor made an even bigger display without even showing up. Nominated in four categories, the controversial Irish singer stated she would refuse to accept any Grammy she might win and called the whole idea of the awards crass and commercial. Grammy producer Pierre Cossette stated that O'Connor had appeared on the show two years previously and the exposure was her "first big break." She did win in the new category of Alternative Music Performance and true to her word did not collect the miniature gramophone prize. O'Connor would raise the ire of the public again when she tore up a picture of the Pope on national television.

Other highlights of the 1990 Grammys included vocal groups En Vogue and Take 6 singing the nominees for New Artist a capella and Jack Nicholson presenting the Lifetime Achievement award to Bob Dylan. With this presentation, the NARAS seemed to be apologizing to Dylan for ignoring him for so many years.

Sinead O'Connor (1990 winner) was the first artist to refuse a Grammy.

THE AMERICAN MUSIC AWARDS

POP/ROCK
Single: "Blaze of Glory" (Jon Bon Jovi); Album: *... But Seriously* (Phil Collins); Male Artist: Phil Collins; Female Artist: Janet Jackson; Band, Duo, or Group: Aerosmith; New Artist: Vanilla Ice

SOUL/RHYTHM AND BLUES
Single: "U Can't Touch This" (M. C. Hammer); Album: *Please Hammer Don't Hurt 'Em the Movie* (M. C. Hammer); Male Artist: M. C. Hammer; Female Artist: Janet Jackson; Band, Duo, or Group: Tony! Toni! Tone!; New Artist: Bell Biv DeVoe

COUNTRY
Single: "If Tomorrow Never Comes" (Garth Brooks); Album: *No Fences* (Garth Brooks); Male Artist: George Strait; Female Artist: Reba McEntire; Band, Duo, or Group: Alabama; New Artist: the Kentucky Headhunters

RAP/HIP-HOP
Album: *Please Hammer Don't Hurt 'Em the Movie* (M. C. Hammer); Artist: M. C. Hammer; New Artist: Vanilla Ice

HEAVY METAL/HARD ROCK
Album: *Dr. Feelgood* (Motley Crue); Artist: Aerosmith; New Artist: Skid Row

DANCE MUSIC
Single: "Vogue" (Madonna); Artist: Janet Jackson; New Artist: Bell Biv DeVoe

SPECIAL AWARD
Merle Haggard

BILLBOARD MUSIC AWARDS

Top Worldwide Single: "Nothing Compares 2 U" (Sinead O'Connor); Top Worldwide Album: *... But Seriously* (Phil Collins); Top Male Artist: Phil Collins; Top Female Artist: Janet Jackson

Pop Album: *Rhythm Nation 1814* (Janet Jackson); Pop Artist: New Kids on the Block; Rock Album Artist: Aerosmith; Rock Male Artist: Michael Penn; Rock Female Artist: Sinead O'Connor; R&B Female Artist: Janet Jackson; R&B Male Artist: M. C. Hammer; R&B Duo or Group: After 7; Male Country Artist: Randy Travis; Female Country Artist: Reba McEntire; Country Group or Duo: Alabama; Adult Contemporary Male Artist: Phil Collins; Adult Contemporary Female Artist: Gloria Estefan; Jazz Artist: Harry Connick, Jr.; New Male Artist: Young MC; New Female Artist: Lisa Stansfield

This year *Billboard* got into the act by presenting its own awards based on its famous sales charts and frequency of radio airplay. Fox broadcast the first ceremony. (Categories vary from year to year.)

COUNTRY MUSIC ASSOCIATION AWARDS

Entertainer: George Strait; Single: "When I Call Your Name" (Vince Gill); Song: "Where've You Been" (Jon Vezner, Don Henry, songwriters);

Album: *Pickin' on Nashville* (the Kentucky Headhunters); Male Vocalist: Clint Black; Female Vocalist: Kathy Mattea; Vocal Group: the Kentucky Headhunters; Vocal Duo: the Judds; Vocal Event: Lorrie Morgan, Keith Whitley; Musician: Johnny Gimble; Horizon Award: Garth Brooks; Music Video: "The Dance" (Garth Brooks)

MTV VIDEO MUSIC AWARDS

Video of the Year: *Nothing Compares 2 U* (Sinead O'Connor); Male Video: Don Henley (*The End of Innocence*); Female Video: Sinead O'Connor (*Nothing Compares 2 U*); Group Video: *Love Shack* (the B-52s); New Artist in a Video: Michael Penn (*No Myth*); Rap Video: *Mama Said Knock You Out* (L.L. Cool J); Dance Video: *U Can't Touch This* (M.C. Hammer); Metal/Hard Rock Video: Aerosmith ("Janie's Got a Gun"); Video from a Movie: *Cradle of Love (Ford Fairlane)* (Billy Idol); Special Effects: Jim Blashfield (Tears for Fears, *Sowing the Seeds of Love*); Director: David Fincher (Madonna, *Vogue*); Breakthrough Video: Tears for Fears (*Sowing the Seeds of Love*); Video Vanguard Award: Janet Jackson; Viewers' Choice Award: Aerosmith (*Janie's Got a Gun*)

THE GRAMMY AWARDS

RECORD OF THE YEAR
"Baby Baby" (Amy Grant)
"(Everything I Do) I Do It for You" (Bryan Adams)
"Losing My Religion" (REM)
"Something to Talk About" (Bonnie Raitt)
"Unforgettable" (Natalie Cole with
   Nat "King" Cole)

Just as the Grammys were gaining credibility as a barometer of current music trends, the NARAS heaped major awards on new recordings of old songs. The Record of the Year and Song of the Year was a forty-year-old tune "Unforgettable," an engineered duet between Natalie Cole and her late father Nat "King" Cole on one of his classic performances. While he was alive, the senior Cole had

won only one Grammy—in 1959 for "Midnight Flyer" in the short-lived Performance by a Top 40 Artist category. The new recording also triumphed in the freshly minted category of Traditional Pop Performance. (Ironically, the Academy was now creating a special award for an area that had dominated the Grammys when they originated.) The single was a track from Natalie Cole's LP tribute to her father also titled *Unforgettable* featuring her renditions of twenty-two of Nat's songs. It took Album of the Year as well as accolades for engineering, arrangements, and Producer of the Year for David Foster.

In this year of old winning over new, the Male Vocalist (Pop) honors went to a cover of a 1960s' standard, "When a Man Loves a Woman."

SONG OF THE YEAR
(AWARD TO SONGWRITER)
"Baby Baby" (Amy Grant, Keith Thomas)
"(Everything I Do) I Do It for You" (Bryan Adams,
   Robert John "Mutt" Lange, Michael Kamen)
"Losing My Religion" (Bill Berry, Peter Buck,
   Mike Mills, Michael Stipe)
"Unforgettable" (Irving Gordon)
"Walking in Memphis" (Marc Cohn)

Seventy-seven-year-old Irving Gordon thanked the Grammy voters for choosing a song "where you don't get a hernia when you sing it." The fact that Gordon's forty-year-old "Unforgettable" was competing with brand-new tunes did give some Grammy critics a hernia. The rules were changed the following year so that only current melodies could run for Song of the Year.

ALBUM OF THE YEAR
Heart in Motion (Amy Grant)
Luck of the Draw (Bonnie Raitt)
Out of Time (REM)
The Rhythm of the Saints (Paul Simon)
Unforgettable (Natalie Cole)

NEW ARTIST
Boyz II Men
Marc Cohn
C + C Music Factory
Color Me Badd
Seal

MALE VOCALIST (POP)
Bryan Adams ["(Everything I Do) I Do It for You"]
Michael Bolton ("When a Man Loves a Woman")
Marc Cohn ("Walking in Memphis")
George Michael ("Freedom 90")
Aaron Neville (*Warm Your Heart*)
Seal ("Crazy")

Soft-pop star Michael Bolton drew the ire of rock purists when he won the Male Vocalist (Pop) award for his version of the '60s' rock ballad "When a Man Loves a Woman." He forgot to thank Percy Sledge, co-author and original crooner of the song. To add insult to injury, he refused to apologize when the error was pointed out backstage.

FEMALE VOCALIST (POP)
Oleta Adams ("Get Here")
Mariah Carey (*Emotions*)
Amy Grant ("Baby Baby")
Whitney Houston ("All the Man That I Need")
Bonnie Raitt ("Something to Talk About")

VOCAL GROUP (POP)
The Commitments (*The Commitments—Original Motion Picture Soundtrack*)
Extreme ("More Than Words")
Jesus Jones ("Right Here, Right Now")
REM ("Losing My Religion")
Wilson Philips ("You're in Love")

TRADITIONAL POP PERFORMANCE
Natalie Cole (with Nat "King" Cole) ("Unforgettable")
Harry Connick, Jr. (*Blue Light, Red Light*)
Johnny Mathis (*In a Sentimental Mood: Mathis Sings Ellington*)
Diane Schuur (*Pure Schuur*)
Barbra Streisand ("Warm All Over")

ROCK SONG (AWARD TO SONGWRITER)
"Been Caught Stealing" (Jane's Addiction)
"Can't Stop This Thing We Started" (Bryan Adams, Robert John "Mutt" Lange)
"Enter Sandman" (James Hetfield, Lars Ulrich, Kirk Hammett)
"Learning to Fly" (Tom Petty, Jeff Lynne)
"Silent Lucidity" (Chris DeGarmo)
"Soul Cages" (Sting)

SOLO VOCAL PERFORMANCE (ROCK, MALE OR FEMALE)
Bryan Adams ("Can't Stop This Thing We Started")
Eric Clapton (*24 Hours*)
John Mellencamp (*Whenever We Wanted*)
Bonnie Raitt (*Luck of the Draw*)
Robbie Robertson (*Storyville*)
Bob Seger (*The Fire Inside*)

VOCAL GROUP (ROCK)
Jane's Addiction ("Been Caught Stealing")
Tom Petty and the Heartbreakers (*Into the Great Wide Open*)
Queensryche ("Silent Lucidity")
Bonnie Raitt, Delbert McClinton ("Good Man, Good Woman")
REM ("Radio Song")

RHYTHM AND BLUES
Song (award to songwriter): "Power of Love/Love Power" (Luther Vandross, Marcus Miller, Teddy Vann); Male Vocalist: Luther Vandross (*Power of Love*); Female Vocalist: Lisa Fischer ("How Can I Ease the Pain"); Vocal Group: Boyz II Men (*Cooleyhighharmony*)

COUNTRY
Song (award to songwriter): "Love Can Build a Bridge" (Naomi Judd, John Jarvis, Paul Overstreet); Male Vocalist: Garth Brooks (*Reapin' the Wind*); Female Vocalist: Mary-Chapin Carpenter ("Down at the Twist and Shout"); Vocal Group: the Judds ("Love Can Build a Bridge"); Vocal Collaboration: Steve Wariner, Ricky Skaggs, Vince Gill ("Restless")

JAZZ
Contemporary Jazz Performance: the Manhattan Transfer ("Sassy"); Jazz Vocal Performance: Take 6 (*He Is Christmas*); Soloist: Stan Getz ("I Remember You"); Group: Oscar Peterson Trio (*Saturday Night at the Blue Note*); Large Ensemble: Dizzy Gillespie and the United Nations Orchestra (*Live at the Royal Festival Hall*)

OTHER AWARDS

Hard Rock Performance: Van Halen (*For Unlawful Carnal Knowledge*); Metal Performance: Metallica (*Metallica*); Alternative Music Album: *Out of Time* (REM); Rap Performance (Solo): L.L. Cool J ("Mama Said Knock You Out"); Rap Performance (Group): D.J. Jazzy Jeff and the Fresh Prince ("Summertime")

In their acceptance remarks for Metal Performance, band members of Metallica sarcastically thanked mainstream radio disc jockeys and MTV "for nothing" since the group claimed they were ignored by these mass-market outlets.

Cast Show Album: *The Will Rogers Follies*; Soundtrack Album: *Avalon*; Song from a Motion Picture or Television: "(Everything I Do) I Do It for You" from *Robin Hood, Prince of Thieves*; Comedy Performance: "Professor" Peter Schickele (*PDQ Bach: WTWP Classical Talkity-Talk Radio*); Spoken Word: *The Civil War (Geoffrey Ward with Rick and Ken Burns*); Classical Album: *Bernstein: Candide*; Music Video (Short Form): *Losing My Religion* (REM); Music Video (Long Form): *Madonna: Blonde Ambition World Tour Live* (Madonna)

Whoopi Goldberg emceed the '91 Grammys as the show's first black female host. She was following in the footsteps of Billy Crystal and would later succeed Crystal as compere of the Oscars. The awards remained in New York for the second consecutive year and hit an all-time record length of four hours.

THE AMERICAN MUSIC AWARDS

POP/ROCK

Single: "(Everything I Do) I Do It for You" (Bryan Adams); Album: *Time, Love, and Tenderness* (Michael Bolton); Male Artist: Michael Bolton; Female Artist: Paula Abdul; Band, Group, or Duo: C + C Music Factory; New Artist: C + C Music Factory

SOUL/RHYTHM AND BLUES

Single: "I Wanna Sex You Up" (Color Me Badd); Album: *Power of Love* (Luther Vandross); Male Artist: Luther Vandross; Female Artist: Mariah Carey; Band, Group, or Duo: Bell Biv DeVoe; New Artist: Boyz II Men

COUNTRY

Single: "The Thunder Rolls" (Garth Brooks); Album: *No Fences* (Garth Brooks); Male Artist: Garth Brooks; Female Artist: Reba McEntire; Band, Duo, or Group: Alabama; New Artist: Trisha Yearwood

RAP/HIP-HOP

Album: *Homebase* (D.J. Jazzy Jeff and the Fresh Prince); Artist: M. C. Hammer; New Artist: Naughty by Nature

HEAVY METAL/HARD ROCK

Album: *For Unlawful Carnal Knowledge* (Van Halen); Artist: Guns 'N' Roses; New Artist: Firehouse

DANCE MUSIC

Album: *Gonna Make You Sweat (Everybody Dance Now)* (C + C Music Factory); Artist: C + C Music Factory; New Artist: C + C Music Factory

ADULT CONTEMPORARY

Album: *Unforgettable* (Natalie Cole); Artist: Natalie Cole; New Artist: Michael W. Smith

SPECIAL AWARDS

James Brown; Michael Jackson (International Artist Award)

BILLBOARD MUSIC AWARDS

Top World Album: *Out of Time* (REM); Top World Single: "Everything I Do (I Do It for You)" (Bryan Adams); Top Albums Artist: Garth Brooks; Top Pop Artist: Mariah Carey; Top Pop Album: *Mariah Carey* (Mariah Carey); Top Adult Contemporary Artist: Mariah Carey; Top New Pop Artist: C + C Music Factory; Top R&B Artist: Whitney Houston; Top R&B Album: *I'm Your Baby Tonight* (Whitney Houston); Top Country Artist: Garth Brooks; Top Country Album: *No Fences* (Garth Brooks)

COUNTRY MUSIC ASSOCIATION AWARDS

Entertainer: Garth Brooks; Single: "Friends in Low Places" (Garth Brooks); Song: "When I Call Your Name" (Vince Gill, Tim DuBois, songwriters); Album: *No Fences* (Garth Brooks); Male Vocalist: Vince Gill; Female Vocalist: Tanya Tucker; Vocal Group: the Kentucky Headhunters; Vocal Duo: the Judds; Vocal Event: Mark O'Connor and the Nashville Cats (featuring Vince Gill, Ricky Skaggs, Steve Wariner); Musician: Mark O'Connor; Horizon Award: Travis Tritt; Music Video: *The Thunder Rolls* (Garth Brooks)

MTV VIDEO MUSIC AWARDS

Video of the Year: *Losing My Religion* (REM); Male Video: Chris Isaak (*Wicked Game*, concept version); Female Video: Janet Jackson (*Love Will Never Do without You*); Group Video: *Losing My Religion* (REM); New Artist in a Video: Jesus Jones (*Right Here, Right Now*); Rap Video: *Mama Said Knock You Out* (L.L. Cool J); Dance Video: *Gonna Make You Sweat (Everybody Dance Now)* (C + C Music Factory); Metal/Hard Rock Video: *The Other Side* (Aerosmith); Video from a Movie: *Wicked Game*, from *Wild at Heart* (Chris Isaak); Alternative Video: *Been Caught Stealing* (Jane's Addiction); Special Effects: David Faithful, Ralph Ziman (Faith No More, *Falling to Pieces*); Director: Tarsem (REM, *Losing My Religion*); Breakthrough Video: *Losing My Religion* (REM); Michael Jackson Video Vanguard Award: Bon Jovi, Wayne Isham

1992

THE GRAMMY AWARDS

RECORD OF THE YEAR
"Achy Breaky Heart" (Billy Ray Cyrus)
"Beauty and the Beast" (Celine Dion, Peabo Bryson)
"Constant Craving" (k. d. lang)
"Save the Best for Last" (Vanessa Williams)
"Tears in Heaven" (Eric Clapton)

After decades of fame as a hard-rock guitar legend, Eric Clapton garnered a shelf full of Grammys for the tender ballad "Tears in Heaven." The song was written after the British superstar's 4-year-old son Conor was killed in an accidental fall from their high-rise New York apartment. In addition to Song of the Year, Record of the Year, and Male Vocalist (Pop), Clapton took awards for Rock Song ("Layla"), Album of the Year (*Unplugged*, from an MTV special), and Male Vocalist (Rock).

Half-way through the evening host Garry Shandling joked, "I'm going to go out on a limb. If you're up against Eric Clapton in any other categories, I'd go home now."

Clapton's six-award triumph tied Quincy Jones (1990) and Roger Miller (1965) for the second most Grammys taken in one year. Michael Jackson still held the record with eight in 1983.

SONG OF THE YEAR (AWARD TO SONGWRITER)
"Achy Breaky Heart" (Don Von Tress)
"Beauty and the Beast" (Alan Menken, Howard Ashman)
"Constant Craving" (k. d. lang, Ben Mink)
"Save the Best for Last" (Wendy Waldman, Jon Lind, Phil Galdston)
"Tears in Heaven" (Eric Clapton)

ALBUM OF THE YEAR
Achtung Baby (U2)
Beauty and the Beast (Original Soundtrack)
Diva (Annie Lennox)
Ingenue (k. d. lang)
Unplugged (Eric Clapton)

NEW ARTIST
Arrested Development
Billy Ray Cyrus
Sophie B. Hawkins
Kris Kross
Jon Secada

MALE VOCALIST (POP)
Eric Clapton ("Tears in Heaven")
Peter Gabriel (*US*)
Michael Jackson ("Black or White")
Elton John ("The One")
Lyle Lovett (*Joshua Judges Ruth*)

FEMALE VOCALIST (POP)
Mariah Carey (*MTV Unplugged EP*)
Celine Dion (*Celine Dion*)
k. d. lang ("Constant Craving")
Annie Lennox (*Diva*)
Vanessa Williams ("Save the Best for Last")

VOCAL GROUP (POP)
Celine Dion, Peabo Bryson ("Beauty and the Beast")
Genesis ("I Can't Dance")
George Michael, Elton John ("Don't Let the Sun Go Down on Me")
Prince and the New Power Generation ("Diamonds and Pearls")
Patty Smyth, Don Henley ("Sometimes Love Just Ain't Enough")

TRADITIONAL POP PERFORMANCE
Tony Bennett (*Perfectly Frank*)
Rosemary Clooney (*Girl Singer*)
Michael Feinstein (*Michael Feinstein Sings the Jule Styne Songbook*)
Bobby Short (*Late Night at the Cafe Carlyle*)
Nancy Wilson (*My Lover beside Me*)

ROCK SONG (AWARD TO SONGWRITER)
"Digging in the Dirt" (Peter Gabriel)
"Human Touch" (Bruce Springsteen)
"Jeremy" (Eddie Vedder, Jeff Ament)
"Layla" (Eric Clapton, Jim Gordon)
"Smells Like Teen Spirit" (Kurt Cobain, Nirvana)

MALE VOCALIST (ROCK)
Bryan Adams ("There Will Never Be Another Tonight")
Eric Clapton (*Unplugged*)
Tom Cochrane ("Life Is a Highway")
Peter Gabriel ("Digging in the Dirt")
Bob Seger ("The Fire Inside")
Bruce Springsteen (*Human Touch*)

FEMALE VOCALIST (ROCK)
Melissa Etheridge ("Ain't It Heavy")
Lita Ford ("Shot of Poison")
Alison Moyet ("It Won't Be Long")

Alannah Myles (*Rockinghorse*)
Tina Turner ("The Bitch Is Back")

VOCAL GROUP (ROCK)
En Vogue ("Free Your Mind")
Little Village (*Little Village*)
Los Lobos (*Kiko*)
Red Hot Chili Peppers ("Under the Bridge")
U2 (*Achtung Baby*)

RHYTHM AND BLUES
Song (award to songwriter): "End of the Road" (L. A. Reid, Babyface, Daryl Simmons); Male Vocalist: Al Jarreau (*Heaven and Earth*); Female Vocalist: Chaka Khan (*The Woman I Am*); Vocal Group: Boyz II Men ("End of the Road")

COUNTRY
Song (award to songwriter): "I Still Believe in You" (Vince Gill, John Barlow Jarvis); Male Vocalist: Vince Gill (*I Still Believe in You*); Female Vocalist: Mary-Chapin Carpenter ("I Feel Lucky"); Vocal Group: Emmylou Harris and the Nash Ramblers at the Ryman (*Emmylou Harris and the Nash Ramblers at the Ryman*); Vocal Collaboration: Travis Tritt, Marty Stuart ("The Whiskey Ain't Workin'")

JAZZ
Vocal Performance: Bobbie McFerrin ("'Round Midnight"); Instrumental Solo: Joe Henderson ("Lush Life"); Instrumental Individual or Group: Branford Marsalis (*I Heard You Twice the First Time*); Large Ensemble: McCoy Tyner Big Band (*The Turning Point*); Contemporary Jazz Performance: Pat Metheny (*Secret Story*)

OTHER AWARDS
Hard Rock Performance: Red Hot Chili Peppers ("Give It Away"); Metal Performance: Nine Inch Nails ("Wish"); Alternative Music Performance: Tom Waits ("Bone Machine"); Rap Solo: Sir Mix-a-Lot ("Baby Got Back"); Rap Group: Arrested Development ("Tennessee"); Musical Show Album: *Guys and Dolls*; Song Written for a Motion Picture or Television: "Beauty and the Beast" from *Beauty and the Beast* (Alan Menken, Howard Ashman); Comedy Performance: Prof.

Peter Schickele, PDQ Bach (*Music for an Awful Lot of Winds and Percussion*); Spoken Word: Earvin "Magic" Johnson, Robert O'Keefe (*What You Can Do To Avoid AIDS*); Classical Album: *Mahler: Symphony No. 9* (Leonard Bernstein conducting the Berlin Philharmonic Orchestra); Music Video (Short Form): *Digging in the Dirt* (Peter Gabriel); Music Video (Long Form): *Diva* (Annie Lennox)

In addition to Eric Clapton's dominance of the evening, highlights of the 1992 Grammys included Peter Gabriel opening the show with an elaborate production number of his "Steam" featuring acrobats from Cirque du Soleil; a duet from Tony Bennett and Natalie Cole; the L.A. Master Chorale and a gospel group in alternative versions of Handel's *Messiah*.

But the flashiest personage on stage didn't even sing. Michael Jackson gave a spoken acceptance speech for a Grammy Legend award presented to him by his sister Janet. "This puts to rest another rumor that has been in the press for too many years," the Gloved One joked. "Me and Janet are two different people." Another Legend winner Little Richard was not invited to accept his honor on stage. (The other Legend recipients were given taped tributes.) Richard griped about the omission on Howard Stern's national radio program. NARAS president Michael Greene responded that the Academy respected the rock and roll veteran, but there was not enough time to include his remarks in the ceremony. Richard had briefly disrupted the 1987 awards by complaining that he had never won a Grammy.

THE AMERICAN MUSIC AWARDS

POP/ROCK
Single: "End of the Road" (Boyz II Men); Album: *Dangerous* (Michael Jackson); Male Artist: Michael Bolton; Female Artist: Mariah Carey; Band, Duo, or Group: Genesis; New Artist: Pearl Jam

SOUL/RHYTHM AND BLUES
Single: "Remember the Time" (Michael Jackson); Album: *Funky Divas* (En Vogue); Male Artist: Bobby Brown; Female Artist: Patti LaBelle; Band, Duo, or Group: Boyz II Men; New Artist: Kris Kross

COUNTRY
Single: "Achy Breaky Heart" (Billy Ray Cyrus); Album: *For My Broken Heart* (Reba McEntire); Male Artist: Garth Brooks; Female Artist: Reba McEntire; Band, Duo, or Group: Alabama; New Artist: Billy Ray Cyrus

OTHER AWARDS
Rap/Hip-Hop Artist: Sir Mix-A-Lot; New Rap/Hip-Hop Artist: Naughty by Nature; Heavy Metal/Hard Rock Artist: Metallica; New Heavy Metal/Hard Rock Artist: Pearl Jam; Adult Contemporary Artist: Michael Bolton; New Adult Contempopary Artist: k. d. lang; Adult Contemporary Album: *Unplugged* (Mariah Carey)

SPECIAL AWARDS
Bill Graham (posthumous); Michael Jackson (International Artist Award)

BILLBOARD MUSIC AWARDS

No. 1 Pop Artist: Garth Brooks; No. 1 Worldwide Single: "Black or White" (Michael Jackson); No. 1 Worldwide Album: *Dangerous* (Michael Jackson); No. 1 Hot 100 Single: "End of the Road" (Boyz II Men); No. 1 *Billboard* 200 Album: *Ropin' the Wind* (Garth Brooks); No. 1 *Billboard* 200 Artist: Garth Brooks; No. 1 Hot 100 Singles Artist: Boyz II Men

No. 1 Album Tracks Artist: U2; No. 1 Album Rock Track: *Mysterious Ways* (U2); No. 1 Hot Rhythm and Blues Single: "Come and Talk to Me" (Jodeci); No. 1 R&B Album: *Forever My Lady* (Jodeci); No. 1 R&B Artist: Jodeci; No. 1 R&B Singles Artist: Jodeci; No. 1 Rap Single: "The Phuncky Feel One" (Cypress Hill); No. 1 Country Artist: Garth Brooks; No. 1 Country Single: "I Saw the Light" (Wynonna); No. 1 Hot Country Album: *Ropin' the Wind* (Garth Brooks)

BILLBOARD CENTURY AWARD
George Harrison

COUNTRY MUSIC ASSOCIATION AWARDS

Entertainer: Garth Brooks; Single: "Achy Breaky Heart" (Billy Ray Cyrus); Song: "Just Look at Us" (Vince Gill, Max D. Barnes, songwriters); Album:

Ropin' the Wind (Garth Brooks); Male Vocalist: Vince Gill; Female Vocalist: Mary-Chapin Carpenter; Vocal Group: Diamond Rio; Vocal Event: Marty Stuart, Travis Tritt; Vocal Duo: Brooks and Dunn; Musician: Mark O'Connor; Music Video: Alan Jackson (*Midnight in Montgomery*); Horizon Award: Suzy Bogguss

MTV VIDEO MUSIC AWARDS

Video of the Year: *Right Now* (Van Halen); Male Video: Eric Clapton ("Tears in Heaven" performance); Female Video: Annie Lennox (*Why*); Group Video: *Even Better Than the Real Thing* (U2); New Artist in a Video: Nirvana (*Smells Like Teen Spirit*); Rap Video: *Tennessee* (Arrested Development); Dance Video: *Cream* (Prince and the New Power Generation); Metal/Hard Rock Video: *Enter Sandman* (Metallica); Video from a Film: *Bohemian Rhapsody*, from *Wayne's World* (Queen); Alternative Video: Nirvana ("Smells Like Teen Spirit"); Special Effects: Simon Taylor (U2, *Even Better Than the Real Thing*); Direction: Mark Fenske (Van Halen, *Right Now*); Breakthrough Video: *Give It Away* (Red Hot Chili Peppers); Michael Jackson Video Vanguard Award: Guns 'N' Roses

1993

THE GRAMMY AWARDS

RECORD OF THE YEAR
"Harvest Moon" (Neil Young)
"I Will Always Love You" (Whitney Houston)
"If I Ever Lose My Faith in You" (Sting)
"The River of Dreams" (Billy Joel)
"A Whole New World (Aladdin's Theme)" (Peabo Bryson, Regina Belle)

Sting received the most nominations (six), but Whitney Houston was the big winner at the 1993 Grammys. The songstress took Album of the Year for the soundtrack of *The Bodyguard* (which also featured her motion picture acting debut) as well as Record of the Year and Female Vocalist (Pop) (both for "I Will Always Love You," originally recorded

by Dolly Parton). Sting took home only one award—Male Vocalist (Pop) for his "If I Ever Lose My Faith in You." Houston also dominated the American Music Awards and the *Billboard* Music Awards, copping six of the former and a record eleven of the latter.

SONG OF THE YEAR (AWARD TO SONGWRITER)
"Harvest Moon" (Neil Young)
"I'd Do Anything for Love (But I Won't Do That)" (Jim Steinman)
"If I Ever Lose My Faith in You" (Sting)
"The River of Dreams" (Billy Joel)
"A Whole New World (Aladdin's Theme)" (Alan Menken, Tim Rice)

ALBUM OF THE YEAR
The Bodyguard (Original Soundtrack)
For the People (REM)
Kamakiriad (Donald Fagen)
River of Dreams (Billy Joel)
Ten Summoner's Tales (Sting)

NEW ARTIST
Belly
Blind Melon
Toni Braxton
Digable Planets
SWV (Sisters with Voices)

MALE VOCALIST (POP)
Boy George ("The Crying Game")
Billy Joel ("The River of Dreams")
Aaron Neville ("Don't Take Away My Heaven")
Rod Stewart ("Have I Told You Lately")
Sting ("If I Ever Lose My Faith in You")

FEMALE VOCALIST (POP)
Mariah Carey ("Dreamlover")
Shawn Colvin ("I Don't Know Why")
Whitney Houston ("I Will Always Love You")
k. d. lang ("Miss Chatelaine")
Tina Turner ("I Don't Wanna Fight")

VOCAL GROUP (POP)
Peabo Bryson, Regina Belle ["A Whole New World (Aladdin's Theme)"]

Celine Dion, Clive Griffin ("When I Fall in Love")
REM ("Man on the Moon")
Barbra Streisand, Michael Crawford
 ("The Music of the Night")
Vanessa Williams, Brian McKnight ("Love Is")

TRADITIONAL POP VOCAL PERFORMANCE
Tony Bennett (*Steppin' Out*)
Rosemary Clooney (*Do You Miss New York?*)
Michael Crawford (*A Touch of Music in the Night*)
Diane Schuur (*Love Songs*)
Barbra Streisand (*Back to Broadway*)

ROCK SONG (AWARD TO SONGWRITER)
"Are You Gonna Go My Way?" (Lenny Kravitz, Craig Ross)

"Cryin'" (Steven Tyler, Joe Perry, Taylor Rhodes)
"I'd Do Anything for Love (But I Won't Do
 That)" (Jim Steinman)
"Livin' on the Edge" (Steven Tyler, Joe Perry,
 Mark Hudson)
"Runaway Train" (David Pirner)

ROCK VOCAL PERFORMANCE (SOLO)
Peter Gabriel ("Steam")
Lenny Kravitz ("Are You Gonna Go My Way?")
Meat Loaf ["I'd Do Anything for Love (But I
 Won't Do That)"]
Sting ("Demolition Man")
Neil Young ("All Along the Watchtower")

ROCK VOCAL PERFORMANCE (GROUP)
Aerosmith ("Livin' on the Edge")
Blind Melon ("No Rain")

Bob Dylan, Roger McGuinn, Tom Petty, Neil Young, Eric Clapton, George Harrison ("My Back Pages")
Soul Asylum ("Runaway Train")
The Spin Doctors ("Two Princes")

RHYTHM AND BLUES
Song (award to songwriter): "That's the Way Love Goes" (Janet Jackson, James Harris III, Terry Lewis); Male Vocalist: Ray Charles ("A Song for You"); Female Vocalist: Toni Braxton ("Another Sad Love Song"); Vocal Group: Sade ("No Ordinary Love")

COUNTRY
Song (award to songwriter): "Passionate Kisses" (Lucinda Williams); Male Vocalist: Dwight Yoakim ("Ain't That Lonely Yet"); Female Vocalist: Mary-Chapin Carpenter ("Passionate Kisses"); Vocal Group: Brooks and Dunn ("Hard Workin' Man"); Vocal Collaboration: Reba McEntire, Linda Davis ("Does He Love You")

JAZZ
Vocal Performance: Natalie Cole (*Take a Look*); Solo Instrumentalist: Joe Henderson ("Miles Ahead"); Individual or Group Instrumentalist: Joe Henderson [*So Near, So Far (Musings for Miles)*]; Large Ensemble: Miles Davis, Quincy Jones (*Miles and Quincy Live at Montreux*); Contemporary Jazz Performance: Pat Metheny Group (*The Road to You*)

OTHER AWARDS
Hard Rock Performance: Stone Temple Pilots ("Plush"); Metal Performance: Ozzy Osbourne ("I Don't Want to Change the World"); Alternative Music Performance: U2 (*Zooropa*); Rap Solo Performance: Dr. Dre ("Let Me Ride"); Rap Group Performance: Digable Planets ["Rebirth of Slick (Cool Like Dat)"]; Musical Show Album: *The Who's Tommy*; Song Written for a Motion Picture or Television: "A Whole New World (Aladdin's Theme)" from *Aladdin* (Alan Menken, Tim Rice); Comedy Peformance: George Carlin (*Jammin' in New York*); Spoken Word: Maya Angelou (*On the Pulse of Morning*); Classical Album: *Bartok: The Wooden Prince and Cantata*

Profana (Pierre Boulez conducting the Chicago Symphony Orchestra and Chorus); Music Video (Short Form): *Steam* (Peter Gabriel); Music Video (Long Form): *Ten Summoner's Tales* (String)

New met old as Bono, lead singer of the Irish rock band U2, introduced Frank Sinatra to the Grammy audience of 4,000 at Radio City Music Hall. The veteran singer was receiving a Grammy Legend honor. "Frank's the Chairman of the Board," Bono said, "the boss of bosses, the *man*. I'm not gonna mess with him. Are *you*?" Well, somebody was gonna, because three minutes into Sinatra's rambling acceptance remarks, which included bad jokes about being skinny, backstage booze, and New York City, the screen cut to a list of other Grammy winners and then a commercial break.

A game of Wheel of Blame was played by behind-the-scenes personnel to find the party responsible for cutting off the Chairman of the Board. Mike Greene, president of the NARAS, stated that Sinatra staffers made the call. Grammy executive producer Pierre Cossette agreed. "Sinatra's people were saying, 'Get him off, get him off now, he can't remember what he was going to say,'" Cosette told *The New York Daily News*. Sinatra spokesperson Susan Reynolds countered that Cossette and his crew made the decision because of time constraints.

Gossip columnists later reported that Sinatra left the post-Grammy party at the Museum of Modern Art in a huff, complaining that the temperature was too cold.

THE AMERICAN MUSIC AWARDS

POP/ROCK
Single: "I Will Always Love You" (Whitney Houston); Album: *The Bodyguard* (Original Soundtrack); Male Artist: Eric Clapton; Female Artist: Whitney Houston; Band, Duo, or Group: Aerosmith; New Artist: Stone Temple Pilots

SOUL/RHYTHM AND BLUES
Single: "I Will Always Love You" (Whitney Houston); Album: *The Bodyguard* (Original Soundtrack); Male Vocalist: Luther Vandross; Female Vocalist: Whitney Houston; Band, Duo, or Group: En Vogue; New Artist: Toni Braxton

COUNTRY

Single: "Chattahoochee" (Alan Jackson); Album: *A Lot about Livin' (And a Little about Love)* (Alan Jackson); Male Vocalist: Garth Brooks; Female Vocalist: Reba McEntire; Band, Duo, or Group: Alabama; New Artist: John Michael Montgomery

OTHER AWARDS

Rap/Hip-Hop Artist: Dr. Dre; New Rap/Hip-Hop Artist: Dr. Dre; Heavy Metal/Hard Rock Artist: Aerosmith; New Heavy Metal/Hard Rock Artist: Stone Temple Pilots; Adult Contemporary Artist: Kenny G; New Adult Contemporary Artist: Toni Braxton; Adult Contemporary Album: *The Bodyguard* (Original Soundtrack)

SPECIAL AWARDS

Whitney Houston; Rod Stewart (International Artist Award)

BILLBOARD MUSIC AWARDS

No. 1 World Artist: Whitney Houston; No. 1 World Single: "I Will Always Love You" (Whitney Houston); No. 1 Album of the Year: *The Bodyguard* (Original Soundtrack); No. 1 Pop Artist: Garth Brooks; No. 1 Rock Single: "Plush" (Stone Temple Pilots); No. 1 Rock Artist: Aerosmith; No. 1 Adult Contemporary Artist: Jon Secada; No. 1 Adult Contemporary Single: "Love Is" (Brian McKnight, Vanessa Williams)

No. 1 R&B Single: "I Will Always Love You" (Whitney Houston); No. 1 R&B Artist: Dr. Dre; No. 1 Country Artist: Garth Brooks; No. 1 Rap Single: "We Getz Buzy/Head or Gut" (Illegal)

BILLBOARD CENTURY AWARD

Buddy Guy

COUNTRY MUSIC ASSOCIATION AWARDS

Entertainer: Vince Gill; Single: "Chattahoochee" (Alan Jackson); Song: "I Still Believe in You" (Vince Gill, songwriter); Album: *I Still Believe in You* (Vince Gill); Male Vocalist: Vince Gill; Female Vocalist: Mary-Chapin Carpenter; Vocal Group: Diamond Rio; Vocal Duo: Brooks and Dunn; Vocal Event: George Jones with Vince Gill, Mark

Chesnutt, Garth Brooks, Travis Tritt, Joe Diffie, Alan Jackson, Pam Tillis, T. Graham Brown, Patty Loveless, Clint Black; Musician: Mark O'Connor; Horizon Award: Mark Chesnutt; Music Video: Alan Jackson ("Chattahoochee")

MTV VIDEO MUSIC AWARDS

Video of the Year: *Jeremy* (Pearl Jam); Male Video: Lenny Kravitz (*Are You Gonna Go My Way?*); Female Video: k. d. lang (*Constant Craving*); Group Video: *Jeremy* (Pearl Jam); New Artist in a Video: Stone Temple Pilots (*Plush*); Rap Video: *People Everyday* (Arrested Development); Dance Video: *Free Your Mind* (En Vogue); Metal/Hard Rock Video: *Jeremy* (Pearl Jam); R&B Video: *Free Your Mind* (En Vogue); Video From a Film: Alice in Chains ("Would?" from *Singles*); Alternative Video: *In Bloom (Version 1—Dresses)* (Nirvana); Special Effects: Real World Productions/Colossal Pictures (Peter Gabriel, *Steam*); Direction: Mark Pellington (Pearl Jam, *Jeremy*); Breakthrough Video: *Kiko and the Lavender Man* (Los Lobos)

1994

THE GRAMMY AWARDS

RECORD OF THE YEAR

"All I Wanna Do" (Sheryl Crow)
"He Thinks He'll Keep Her" (Mary-Chapin Carpenter)
"I'll Make Love to You" (Boyz II Men)
"Love Sneakin' Up on You" (Bonnie Raitt)
"Streets of Philadelphia" (Bruce Springsteen)

SONG OF THE YEAR (AWARD TO SONGWRITER)

"All I Wanna Do" (David Baerwald, Bill Bottrell, Wynn Cooper, Sheryl Crow, Kevin Gilbert)
"Can You Feel the Love Tonight" (Elton John, Tim Rice)
"The Circle of Life" (Elton John, Tim Rice)
"I Swear" (Gary Baker, Frank J. Meyers)
"Streets of Philadelphia" (Bruce Springsteen)

ALBUM OF THE YEAR
From the Cradle (Eric Clapton)
Longing in Their Hearts (Bonnie Raitt)
MTV Unplugged (Tony Bennett)
Seal (Seal)
The 3 Tenors in Concert, 1994 (Jose Carreras, Placido Domingo, Luciano Pavarotti with Zubin Mehta)

Tony Bennett, singing idol of the 1950s, was enjoying an amazing comeback in the 1990s. A recording of his *Unplugged* special on MTV received both Album of the Year and Traditional Pop Performance Grammys. After making his acceptance speech for the first award (the second was announced off the air), Bennett encouraged his son and his producer to make their own remarks, but they were drowned out by the orchestra.

Bennett and company were not the only ones to be cut off as the show was running out of time. The final number, Luther Vandross singing "Love the One You're With" accompanied by several stars, was chopped in half. This despite the fact that one of the stars scheduled to join in was David Crosby in his first public appearance since a liver transplant. The program simply came to a halt, without a good night from host Paul Reiser or ending credits.

NEW ARTIST
Ace of Base
Counting Crows
Crash Test Dummies
Sheryl Crow
Green Day

POP ALBUM
I Love Everybody (Lyle Lovett)
Longing in Their Hearts (Bonnie Raitt)
Seal (Seal)
The Sign (Ace of Base)
The 3 Tenors in Concert, 1994 (Jose Carreras, Placido Domingo, Luciano Pavarotti with Zubin Mehta)

Grammy critics had often complained that in the vocalist categories one could be nominated for either a single or an entire album. This was seen as unfair since a singer with an album nomination had an unfair advantage over a crooner for just one song. To quell the criticism, top album categories were introduced into each of the major genres—Pop, Rock, R&B, and Country. Singers could now only be nominated for single tracks.

MALE VOCALIST (POP)
The Artist Formerly Known as Prince ("The Most Beautiful Girl in the World")
Michael Bolton ("Said I Loved You . . . But I Lied")
Elton John ("Can You Feel the Love Tonight")
Seal ("Prayer for the Dying")
Luther Vandross ("Love the One You're With")

This was Elton John's first Grammy as a soloist (he had previously won for his contribution to the fund-raising anthem against AIDS, "That's What Friends Are For," in 1986). The Rolling Stones, another act largely ignored by the NARAS, won their first competitive Grammys for their *Voodoo Lounge* in the Rock Album category and their *Love Is Strong* in the Music Video (Short Form) category.

FEMALE VOCALIST (POP)
Mariah Carey ("Hero")
Sheryl Crow ("All I Wanna Do")
Celine Dion ("The Power of Love")
Bonnie Raitt ("Longing in Their Hearts")
Barbra Streisand ("Ordinary Miracles")

VOCAL GROUP (POP)
Ace of Base ("The Sign")
All-4-One ("I Swear")
Crash Test Dummies ("MMM MMM MMM MMM")
Lisa Loeb and Nine Stories ["Stay (I Missed You)"]
The Pretenders ("I'll Stand By You")

VOCAL COLLABORATION (POP)
Bryan Adams, Rod Stewart, Sting ("All for Love")
Tony Bennett, k. d. lang ("Moonglow")
Al Green, Lyle Lovett ("Funny How Time Slips Away")
John Mellencamp, Me'Shell NdegeOcello ("Wild Night")
Luther Vandross, Mariah Carey ("Endless Love")

TRADITIONAL POP PERFORMANCE
Tony Bennett (*MTV Unplugged*)
Roberta Flack (*Roberta*)
Willie Nelson (*Moonlight Becomes You*)
Frank Sinatra (*Duets*)
Barbra Streisand (*The Concert*)

ROCK SONG (AWARD TO SONGWRITER)
"All Apologies" (Kurt Cobain)
"Black Hole Sam" (Chris Cornell)
"Come to My Window" (Melissa Etheridge)
"I'm the Only One" (Melissa Etheridge)
"Streets of Philadelphia" (Bruce Springsteen)

ROCK ALBUM
Monster (REM)
Sleeps with Angels (Neil Young and Crazy Horse)
Superunknown (Soundgarden)
Voodoo Lounge (The Rolling Stones)
Vs. (Pearl Jam)

MALE VOCALIST (ROCK)
Beck ("Loser")
Peter Gabriel ("Red Rain")
Van Morrison ("In the Garden/You Send Me/Allegeny")
Bruce Springsteen ("The Streets of Philadelphia")
Neil Young ("Philadelphia")

FEMALE VOCALIST (ROCK)
Sheryl Crow ("I'm Gonna Be a Wheel Someday")
Melissa Etheridge ("Come to My Window")
Liz Phair ("Supernova")
Sam Philips ("Circle of Fire")
Bonnie Raitt ("Love Sneakin' Up on You")

VOCAL GROUP (ROCK)
Aerosmith ("Crazy")
Counting Crows ("Round Here")
Green Day ("Basket Case")
Nirvana ("All Apologies")
Pearl Jam ("Daughter")

RHYTHM AND BLUES
Song (award to songwriter): "I'll Make Love to You" (Babyface); Album: *II* (Boyz II Men); Male Vocalist: Babyface ("When Can I See You");
Female Vocalist: Toni Braxton ("Breathe Again"); Vocal Group: Boyz II Men ("I'll Make Love to You")

COUNTRY
Song (award to songwriter): "I Swear" (Gary Baker, Frank J. Meyers); Album: *Stones in the Road* (Mary-Chapin Carpenter); Male Vocalist: Vince Gill ("When Love Finds You"); Female Vocalist: Mary-Chapin Carpenter ("Shut Up and Kiss Me"); Vocal Group: Asleep at the Wheel with Lyle Lovett ("Blues for Dixie"); Vocal Collaboration: Aaron Neville, Trisha Yearwood ("I Fall to Pieces")

JAZZ
Vocal Performance: Etta James [*Mystery Lady (Songs of Billie Holliday)*]; Solo Instrumentalist: Benny Carpenter ("Prelude to a Kiss"); Individual or Group Instrumentalist: Ron Carter, Herbie Hancock, Wallace Roney, Wayne Shorter, Tony Williams (*A Tribute to Miles*); Large Ensemble: McCoy Tyne Big Band ("Journey"); Contemporary Jazz Performance: the Brecker Brothers ("Out of the Loop")

OTHER AWARDS
Hard Rock Performance: Soundgarden ("Black Hole Sun"); Metal Performance: Soundgarden ("Spoonman"); Alternative Music Performance: Green Day (*Dookie*); Rap Solo Performance: Queen Latifah ("UNITY"); Rap Group Performance: Salt-N-Pepa ("None of Your Business"); Musical Show Album: *Passion*; Song Written for a Motion Picture or Television: "Streets of Philadelphia" from *Philadelphia* (Bruce Springsteen); Comedy Performance: Sam Kinison (*Live from Hell*); Spoken Word: Henry Rollins (*Get in the Van: On the Road with Black Flag*); Classical Album: *Bartok: Concerto for Orchestra; Four Orchestral Pieces, Op. 12* (Pierre Boulez conducting the Chicago Symphony Orchestra); Music Video (Short Form): the Rolling Stones (*Love Is Strong*); Music Video (Long Form): U2 (*Zoo TV: Live from Sydney*)

The 1994 ceremony received the lowest rating for the Grammys ever: an 11.8 rating (percentage of the nation's TV homes) and a 19 share (percentage of sets in use). The program finished second overall behind ABC's roster of sitcoms, but narrowly came in first with the all-important demographic audience of 18- to-49-year-olds.

The three-hour show dragged, even for the usually long Grammys. Host Paul Reiser unintentionally characterized the whole evening when he was forced to ad-lib while Bonnie Raitt's band set up to perform. The *Mad about You* star stopped in the middle of his off-the-cuff remarks and said, "I'm boring myself. This has never happened before."

Among the few performance highlights were Bruce Springsteen delivering his award-winning "Streets of Philadelphia," which also won an Oscar, and the unusual pairing of Tony Bennett and k. d. lang crooning "Moonglow," nominated in the new Vocal Collaboration (Pop) category.

The program was rescued from total blandness by NARAS president Michael Greene, who injected the proceedings with a touch of controversy. Against broadcaster CBS's wishes, Greene made an on-air plea for viewers to phone a 1-800 number to protest cuts in federal arts funding. Network executives had made it clear to the NARAS president that CBS would not take a position on such a volatile topic. They even went so far as to remove the 1-800 phone number from the screen and excise Greene's speech from the teleprompter. Nevertheless, Greene went ahead and got his message out.

THE AMERICAN MUSIC AWARDS

POP/ROCK
Single: "I'll Make Love to You" (Boyz II Men); Album: *The Lion King* (Original Soundtrack); Male Artist: Michael Bolton; Female Vocalist: Mariah Carey; Band, Duo, or Group: Ace of Base; New Artist: Ace of Base

SOUL/RHYTHM AND BLUES
Single: "I'll Make Love to You" (Boyz II Men); Album: *Toni Braxton* (Toni Braxton); Male Artist: Babyface; Female Artist: Anita Baker; Band, Duo, or Group: Boyz II Men; New Artist: All-4-One

COUNTRY
Single: "Whenever You Come Around" (Vince Gill); Album: *Read My Mind* (Reba McEntire); Male Artist: Garth Brooks; Female Artist: Reba McEntire; Band, Duo, or Group: Alabama; New Artist: Tim McGraw

OTHER AWARDS
Rap/Hip-Hop Artist: Snoop Doggy Dogg; Heavy Metal/Hard Rock Artist: Nirvana; Alternative Music Artist: Counting Crows; Adult Contemporary Artist: Michael Bolton

SPECIAL AWARDS
The Artist Formerly Known as Prince; Led Zeppelin (International Artist Award)

BILLBOARD MUSIC AWARDS

No. 1 Single: "The Sign" (Ace of Base); Top Male Artist: Snoop Doggy Dogg; Top Female Artist: Mariah Carey; Top R&B Artist: R. Kelly; Top New Artist: Ace of Base; Top Album Rock Track: "Shine" (Collective Soul); Top Modern Rock Act: Stone Temple Pilots

BILLBOARD CENTURY AWARD
Billy Joel

SPECIAL AWARDS
The Rolling Stones; Eric Clapton

COUNTRY MUSIC ASSOCIATION AWARDS

Entertainer: Vince Gill; Single: "I Swear" (John Michael Montgomery); Song: "Chattahoochee" (Alan Jackson, songwriter); Album: *Common Threads: The Songs of the Eagles* (John Anderson, Clint Black, Suzy Bogguss, Brooks and Dunn, Billy Dean, Diamond Rio, Vince Gill, Alan Jackson, Little Texas, Lorrie Morgan, Travis Tritt, Tanya Tucker, Trisha Yearwood); Male Vocalist: Vince Gill; Female Vocalist: Pam Tillis; Vocal Group: Diamond Rio; Vocal Duo: Brooks and Dunn; Vocal Event: Reba McEntire, Linda Davis; Musician: Mark O'Connor; Horizon Award: John Michael Montgomery; Music Video: *Independence Day* (Martina McBride)

MTV VIDEO MUSIC AWARDS

Video of the Year: *Cryin'* (Aerosmith); Male Video: Tom Petty and the Heartbreakers (*Mary Jane's Last*

Dance); Female Video: Janet Jackson (*If*); Group Video: *Cryin'* (Aerosmith); New Artist in a Video: Counting Crows (*Mr. Jones*); Rap Video: Snoop Doggy Dogg (*Doggy Dogg World*); Dance Video: *What a Man* (Salt-N-Peppa, En Vogue); Metal /Hard Rock Video: *Black Hole Sun* (Soundgarden); R&B Video: *What a Man* (Salt-N-Peppa, En Vogue); Video from a Film: Bruce Springsteen (*Streets of Philadelphia* from *Philadelphia*); Choreography: Frank Gatson, Randy Connors (Salt-N-Peppa and En Vogue, *What a Man*); Alternative Video: *Heart-Shaped Box* (Nirvana); Special Effects: Brett Leonard/Angel Studios (Peter Gabriel, *Kiss That Frog*); Direction: Jake Scott (REM, *Everybody Hurts*); Breakthrough Video: REM, *Everybody Hurts* (REM); Video Vanguard Award: Tom Petty; Viewer's Choice Award: Aerosmith (*Cryin'*)

1995
THE GRAMMY AWARDS

RECORD OF THE YEAR
"Gangsta's Paradise" (Coolio)
"Kiss from a Rose" (Seal)
"One of Us" (Joan Osborne)
"One Sweet Day" (Mariah Carey, Boyz II Men)
"Waterfalls" (TLC)

SONG OF THE YEAR
(AWARD TO SONGWRITER)
"I Can Love You Like That" (Maribeth Derry, Sam Diamond, Jennifer Kimball)
"Kiss from a Rose" (Seal)
"One of Us" (Eric Bazilian)
"You Are Not Alone" (R. Kelly)
"You Oughta Know" (Glen Ballard, Alanis Morisette)

ALBUM OF THE YEAR
Daydream (Mariah Carey)
HIStory: Past, Present, and Future, Book I (Michael Jackson)
Jagged Little Pill (Alanis Morissette)
Relish (Joan Osborne)
Vitalogy (Pearl Jam)

NEW ARTIST
Brandy
Hootie and the Blowfish
Alanis Morisette
Joan Osborne
Shania Twain

In a major rule change, nominees for the biggest awards— Record of the Year, Song of the Year, Album of the Year, and New Artist—were no longer chosen by popular vote of the NARAS membership. The five nominees in each of the top four categories would now be selected from the top twenty choices of the membership by a secret twenty-five-member panel of music industry executives. The Academy instituted these rules in response to charges that only top-selling rather than top-quality selections were being made. A prime example was Hole, Courtney Love's band, failing to receive any Grammy recognition in 1994 when its album *Live through This* headed the lists of most rock critics' choices for best of the year. It was hoped a smaller, more discerning electorate would include lesser-known but noteworthy artists.

POP ALBUM
Bedtime Stories (Madonna)
Daydream (Mariah Carey)
Hell Freezes Over (the Eagles)
Medusa (Annie Lennox)
Turbulent Indigo (Joni Mitchell)

MALE VOCALIST (POP)
Bryan Adams ("Have You Ever Really Loved a Woman?")
Michael Jackson ("You Are Not Alone")
Elton John ("Believe")
Seal ("Kiss from a Rose")
Sting ("When We Dance")

FEMALE VOCALIST (POP)
Mariah Carey ("Fantasy")
Dionne Farris ("I Know")
Annie Lennox ("No More 'I Love Yous' ")
Joan Osborne ("One of Us")
Bonnie Raitt ("You Got It")
Vanessa Williams ("Colors of the Wind")

VOCAL GROUP (POP)
All-4-One ("I Can Love You Like That")
The Eagles ("Love Will Keep Us Alive")
Hootie and the Blowfish ("Let Her Cry")
The Rembrandts ["I'll Be There for You (Theme from *Friends*)"]
TLC ("Waterfalls")

VOCAL COLLABORATION (POP)
Jon B. featuring Babyface ("Someone to Love")
Anita Baker, James Ingram ("When You Love Someone")
Mariah Carey, Boyz II Men ("One Sweet Day")
The Chieftans, **Van Morrison** ("Have I Told You Lately That I Love You")
Michael and Janet Jackson ("Scream")

TRADITIONAL POP PERFORMANCE
Julie Andrews (*Julie Andrews—Broadway—The Music of Richard Rodgers*)
Rosemary Clooney (*Demi-Centennial*)
Eartha Kitt (*Back in Business*)
John Raitt (*Broadway Legend*)
Frank Sinatra (*Duets II*)

ROCK SONG (AWARD TO SONGWRITER)
"Dignity" (Bob Dylan)
"Downtown" (Neil Young)
"Hold Me, Thrill Me, Kiss Me, Kill Me" (Bono, U2)
"Hurt" (Trent Reznor)
"You Oughta Know" (Glen Ballard, Alanis Morissette)

ROCK ALBUM
Forever Blue (Chris Isaak)
Jagged Little Pill (Alanis Morissette)
Mirror Ball (Neil Young)
Vitalogy (Pearl Jam)
Wildflowers (Tom Petty)

MALE VOCALIST (ROCK)
Bob Dylan ("Knockin' on Heaven's Door")
Chris Isaak ("Somebody's Crying")
Lenny Kravitz ("Rock and Roll Is Dead")
Tom Petty ("You Don't Know How It Feels")
Neil Young ("Peace and Love")

FEMALE VOCALIST (ROCK)
Toni Childs ("Lay Down Your Pain")
P. J. Harvey ("Down by the Water")
Alanis Morissette ("You Oughta Know")
Joan Osborne ("St. Teresa")
Liz Phair ("Don't Have Time")

VOCAL GROUP (ROCK)
Blues Traveler ("Run-Around")
The Eagles ("Hotel California")
The Dave Matthews Band ("What Would You Say")
Jimmy Page, Robert Plant ("Kashmir")
U2 ("Hold Me, Thrill Me, Kiss Me, Kill Me")

RHYTHM AND BLUES
Song (award to songwriter): "For Your Love" (Stevie Wonder); Album: *CrazySexyCool* (TLC); Male Vocalist: Stevie Wonder ("For Your Love"); Female Vocalist: Anita Baker ("I Apologize"); Vocal Group: TLC ("Creep")

COUNTRY
Song (award to songwriter): "Go Rest High on That Mountain" (Vince Gill); Album: *The Woman in Me* (Shania Twain); Male Vocalist: Vince Gill ("Go Rest High on That Mountain"); Female Vocalist: Alison Krauss ("Baby, Now That I've Found You"); Vocal Group: the Mavericks ("Here Comes the Rain"); Vocal Collaboration: Shenandoah, Alison Krauss ("Somewhere in the Vicinity of the Heart")

JAZZ
Vocal Performance: Lena Horne (*An Evening with Lena Horne*); Solo Instrumentalist: Michael Brecker ("Impressions"); Individual or Group Instrumentalist: McCoy Tyner Trio featuring Michael Brecker ("Infinity"); Large Ensemble: GRP All-Star Big Band and Tom Scott ("All Blues"); Contemporary Jazz Performance: Pat Metheny Group ("We Live Here")

OTHER AWARDS
Hard Rock Performance: Pearl Jam ("Spin the Black Circle"); Metal Performance: Nine Inch Nails ("Happiness Is Slavery"); Alternative Music Performance: Nirvana (*MTV Unplugged in New*

York); Rap Album: *Poverty's Paradise* (Naughty by Nature); Rap Solo Performance: Coolio ("Gangsta's Paradise"); Rap Group Performance: Method Man/Mary J. Blige ("I'll Be There for You"/"You're All I Need to Get By"); Musical Show Album: *Smokey Joe's Cafe: The Songs of Leiber and Stoller*; Song Written for a Motion Picture or Television: "Colors of the Wind" from *Pocohontas* (Alan Menken, Steven Schwartz); Comedy Performance: Jonathan Winters (*Crank Calls*); Spoken Word; Maya Angelou (*Phenomenal Woman*); Classical Album: *Debussy: La Mer; Nocturnes; Jeux, etc.* (Pierre Boulez conducting the Chicago Symphony Orchestra); Music Video (Short Form): *Scream* (Michael and Janet Jackson); Music Video (Long Form): *Secret World Live* (Peter Gabriel)

The threat of censorship hung over the 1995 Grammys. Performances of potentially controversial song lyrics had CBS nervous. Alanis Morissette's "You Oughta Know" contained the f-word and a reference to oral sex. Michael Greene, president of the NARAS, stated she could sing the song as written while CBS countered they would bleep any offensive lyrics since the "live" show was on a seven-second delay. The network did blank out a few seconds of Morrissette's song.

Joan Osborne's "One of Us" was another source of controversy, but not as great. The thought-provoking tune contained lyrics imagining God as an everyday person, riding the bus and going to work. The network received some complaints that the song was sacrilegious but CBS did not find it so.

Ellen DeGeneres, a previous Emmy host, proved a popular choice for emceeing the music industry's biggest night. "This is like being in a record store," she quipped, "except you would all be seated in alphabetical order and according to your musical styles. And the classical people, no offense, would be in a separate room all by yourselves." The comedienne was nominated for an Emmy for her performance and returned the following year.

THE AMERICAN MUSIC AWARDS

POP/ROCK
Album: *Hell Freezes Over* (the Eagles); Male Artist: Michael Jackson; Female Artist: Mariah Carey; Band, Duo, or Group: the Eagles; New Artist: Hootie and the Blowfish

SOUL/RHYTHM AND BLUES
Album: *II* (Boyz II Men); Male Artist: Luther Vandross; Female Artist: Mariah Carey; Band, Duo, or Group: Boyz II Men; New Artist: Brandy

COUNTRY
Album: *Garth Brooks' Greatest Hits* (Garth Brooks); Male Artist: Garth Brooks; Female Artist: Reba McEntire; Band, Duo, or Group: Alabama; New Artist: Shania Twain

OTHER AWARDS
Rap/Hip-Hop Artist: Coolio; Heavy Metal/Hard Rock Artist: Pearl Jam; Alternative Music Artist: Pearl Jam; Soundtrack Album: *The Lion King*; Adult Contemporary Artist: the Eagles

SPECIAL AWARDS
Tammy Wynette; Garth Brooks (Favorite Artist of the Year)

The normally uneventful American Music Awards were rocked by controversy when country superstar Garth Brooks turned down the newly created Favorite Artist of the Year award. Brooks, who had been named Favorite Male Country Artist for five consecutive years, stated he thought new group Hootie and the Blowfish deserved the honor more than he and left the pyramid-shaped prize on the podium.

Vince Gill joked about the incident at the Grammys. Upon winning his Country Male Vocalist award, he said "Hootie and the Blowfish did not deserve this award. . . . I'm just kidding, they're my golfing buddies."

BILLBOARD MUSIC AWARDS

Artist of the Year: TLC; Album of the Year: *Cracked Rear View* (Hootie and the Blowfish); Single of the Year: "Gangsta's Paradise" (Coolio); New Artist of the Year: Real McCoy; Rock Artist of the Year: Live; Top Rock Album Track: "December" (Collective Soul); R&B Artist of the Year: TLC; New R&B Artist: Brandy; Top R&B Single: "Creep" (TLC); Top Adult Contemporary

Single: "In the House of Light and Stone" (Martin Page)

BILLBOARD CENTURY AWARD
Joni Mitchell

SPECIAL AWARDS
Michael and Janet Jackson

COUNTRY MUSIC ASSOCIATION AWARDS

Entertainer: Alan Jackson; Single: "When You Say Nothing at All" (Alison Krauss, Union Station); Song: "Independence Day" (Gretchen Peters, songwriter); Album: *When Fallen Angels Fly* (Patty Loveless); Male Vocalist: Vince Gill; Female Vocalist: Alison Kraus; Vocal Group: the Mavericks; Vocal Duo: Brooks and Dunn; Vocal Event: Alison Krauss, Shenandoah; Musician: Mark O'Connor; Horizon Award: Alison Krauss; Music Video: the Tractors ("Baby Likes to Rock It")

MTV VIDEO MUSIC AWARDS

Video of the Year: *Waterfalls* (TLC); Male Video: Tom Petty and the Heartbreakers ("You Don't Know How It Feels"); Female Video: Madonna ("Take a Bow"); Group Video: *Waterfalls* (TLC); New Artist in a Video: Hootie and the Blowfish (*Hold My Hand*); Rap Video: *Keep Their Heads Ringin'* (Dr. Dre); Dance Video: *Scream* (Michael and Janet Jackson); Metal/Hard Rock Video: *More Human Than Human* (White Zombie); R&B Video: *Waterfalls* (TLC); Video from a Film: *Kiss from a Rose* from *Batman Forever* (Seal); Choreography: Lavelle Smith, Travis Payne, Tina Landon, Sean Cheeseman (Michael and Janet Jackson, *Scream*); Alternative Video: *Buddy Holly* (Weezer); Special Effects: Fred Raimondi (The Rolling Stones, *Love Is Strong*); Direction: Spike Jonze (Weezer, *Buddy Holly*); Breakthrough Video: *Buddy Holly* (Weezer); Video Vanguard Award: REM; Viewers' Choice Award: TLC (*Waterfalls*)

1996

THE GRAMMY AWARDS

RECORD OF THE YEAR
"Because You Loved Me (Theme from *Up Close and Personal*)" (Celine Dion)
"Change the World" (Eric Clapton)
"Give Me One Reason" (Tracy Chapman)
"Ironic" (Alanis Morissette)
"1979" (the Smashing Pumpkins)

In a repeat of his 1992 sweep, Eric Clapton dominated the 1996 Grammys. His "Change the World" took Record of the Year, Song of the Year, and Male Vocalist (Pop)—the same prizes that his "Tears in Heaven" took four years previously. Clapton's producer on the song, Babyface, earned a record twelve nominations for his work as a performer, songwriter, and producer. He took home three awards—one as Producer of the Year, another for producing "Change the World," and the third for writing the top R&B song "Exhale (Shoop Shoop)" sung by Whitney Houston in the film *Waiting to Exhale.*

SONG OF THE YEAR
(AWARD TO SONGWRITER)
"Because You Loved Me (Theme from *Up Close and Personal*)" (Diane Warren)
"Blue" (Bill Mack)
"Change the World" (Gordon Kennedy, Wayne Kirkpatrick, Tommy Sims)
"Exhale (Shoop Shoop)" (Babyface)
"Give Me One Reason" (Tracy Chapman)

ALBUM OF THE YEAR
Falling Into You (Celine Dion)
Mellon Collie and the Infinite Sadness (the Smashing Pumpkins)
Odelay (Beck)
The Score (the Fugees)
Waiting to Exhale (Original Soundtrack)

NEW ARTIST
Garbage
Jewel

No Doubt
The Tony Rich Project
LeAnn Rimes

Fourteen-year-old LeAnn Rimes is the youngest Grammy winner and the first country singer to be named New Artist. She also won as top Country Female Vocalist for "Blue," a song originally written for Patsy Cline.

POP ALBUM
A Few Small Repairs (Shawn Colvin)
Falling into You (Celine Dion)
Mercury Falling (Sting)
New Beginning (Tracy Chapman)
Secrets (Toni Braxton)

MALE VOCALIST (POP)
Bryan Adams ("Let's Make a Night to Remember")
Eric Clapton ("Change the World")
John Mellencamp ["Key West Intermezzo (I Saw You First)"]
The Tony Rich Project ("Nobody Knows")
Sting ("Let Your Soul Be Your Pilot")

FEMALE VOCALIST (POP)
Toni Braxton ("Un-break My Heart")
Shawn Colvin ("Get Out of This House")
Celine Dion ["Because You Loved Me (Theme from *Up Close and Personal*)"]
Gloria Estefan ("Reach")
Jewel ("Who Will Save Your Soul")

VOCAL GROUP (POP)
The Beatles ("Free as a Bird")
The Gin Blossoms ("As Long as It Matters")
Journey ("When You Love a Woman")
The Neville Brothers ("Fire on the Mountain")
The Presidents of the United States of America ("Peaches")
Take 6 ("When You Wish upon a Star")

Twenty-six years after winning their last Grammy (1970's *Let It Be*), the Beatles collected another award for "Free as a Bird," a song engineered by the three surviving members based on a tape made by the late John Lennon. In addition, the briefly reconstituted Fab Four took Grammys for both Music Video (Long Form) and Music Video (Short Form).

VOCAL COLLABORATION (POP)
Burt Bacharach, Elvis Costello ("God Give Me Strength")
Brandy, Tamia, Gladys Knight, Chaka Khan ("Missing You")
Natalie Cole, Nat "King" Cole ("When I Fall in Love")
Whitney Houston, CeCe Winans ("Count on Me")
Frank Sinatra, Luciano Pavarotti ("My Way")
Sting, John McLaughlin, Dominic Miller, Vinnie Colaiuta ("The Wind Cries Mary")

TRADITIONAL POP PERFORMANCE
Tony Bennett (*Here's to the Ladies*)
Rosemary Clooney (*Dedicated to Nelson*)
Natalie Cole (*Stardust*)
Liza Minnelli (*Gently*)
Bernadette Peters (*I'll Be Your Baby Tonight*)

ROCK SONG (AWARD TO SONGWRITER)
"Cry Love" (John Hiatt)
"Give Me One Reason" (Tracy Chapman)
"6th Avenue Heartache" (Jakob Dylan)
"Stupid Girl" (Garbage)
"Too Much" (Dave Matthews Band)
"Wonderwall" (Noel Gallagher)

ROCK ALBUM
Broken Arrow (Neil Young With Crazy Horse)
Crash (Dave Matthews Band)
Road Tested (Bonnie Raitt)
Sheryl Crow (Sheryl Crow)
Tragic Kingdom (No Doubt)

MALE VOCALIST (ROCK)
Bryan Adams ("The Only Thing That Looks Good on Me Is You")
Beck ("Where It's At")
Eric Clapton ("Ain't Gone 'N' Give Up on Your Love")
John Hiatt ("Cry Love")
Bruce Springsteen ("Dead Man Walkin'")

FEMALE VOCALIST (ROCK)
Tracy Bonham ("Mother Mother")
Tracy Chapman ("Give Me One Reason")
Sheryl Crow ("If It Makes You Happy")

Joan Osborne ("Spider Web")
Bonnie Raitt ("Burning Down the House")

VOCAL GROUP (ROCK)
Garbage ("Stupid Girl")
Dave Matthews Band ("So Much To Say")
Oasis ("Wonderwell")
The Smashing Pumpkins ("1979")
The Wallflowers ("6th Avenue Heartache")

RHYTHM AND BLUES
Song (award to songwriter): "Exhale (Shoop Shoop)" (Babyface); Album: *Words* (the Tony Rich Project); Male Vocalist: Luther Vandross ("Your Secret Love"); Female Vocalist: Toni Braxton ("You're Makin' Me High"); Vocal Group: the Fugees ("Killing Me Softly with His Song")

COUNTRY
Song (award to songwriter): "Blue" (Bill Mack); Album: *The Road to Ensenada* (Lyle Lovett); Male Vocalist: Vince Gill ("Worlds Apart"); Female Vocalist: LeAnn Rimes ("Blue"); Vocal Group: Brooks and Dunn ("My Maria"); Vocal Collaboration: Vince Gill featuring Alison Krause and Union Station ("High Lonesome Sound")

JAZZ
Vocal Performance: Cassandra Wilson (*New Moon Daughter*); Instrumental Solo: Michael Brecker ("Cabin Fever"); Solo or Group: Michael Brecker (*Tales from the Hudson*); Large Ensemble: Count Basie Orchestra (*Live at Manchester Craftsmen's Guild*); Contemporary Jazz Performance: Wayne Shorter (*High Life*)

OTHER AWARDS
Hard Rock Performance: the Smashing Pumpkins (*Bullet with Butterfly Wings*); Metal Performance: Rage against the Machine (*Tire Me*); Alternative Music Performance: Beck (*Odelay*); Rap Album: *The Score* (the Fugees); Rap Solo Performance: L.L. Cool J ("Hey Lover"); Rap Group Performance: Bone Thugs-n-Harmony ("The Crossroads"); Musical Show Album: *Riverdance*; Song Written for a Motion Picture or Television: "Because You Loved Me (Theme from *Up Close and Personal*)" (Diane Warren); Comedy Performance: Al Franken (*Rush Limbaugh Is a Big Fat Idiot*); Spoken Word: Hilary Rodham Clinton (*It Takes a Village*); Classical Album: *Corigliano: Of Rage and Rememberance (Symphony No. 1)* (Leonard Slatkin conducting the National Symphony Orchestra); Music Video (Short Form): *Free as a Bird* (the Beatles); Music Video (Long Form): *The Beatles Anthology* (the Beatles)

Presented at New York's Madison Square Garden, the Grammys had one of their best nights. The enormous sports arena was converted into a theater with a three-quarter stage. Ellen DeGeneres returned for a second year to host. "This is sort of like a second date," she joked. The program opened with DeGeneres leading an all-female band consisting of Bonnie Raitt, Chaka Khan, Sheila E., Me'Shell Ndegeocello, Shawn Colvin, and Fiona Apple.

The high-spot was provided by cast members of *Riverdance* and *Bring in 'da Noise, Bring in 'da Funk*. Both dance-oriented productions were nominated for the Musical Show Album Grammy and energetic numbers from the pieces were performed. Natalie Cole be-bopped a thrilling tribute to Ella Fitzgerald with "Mr. Paganini." R&B divas Whitney Houston, CeCe Winans, Brandy, Mary J. Blige, and Aretha Franklin gave a stirring medley of songs from the nominated soundtrack of *Waiting to Exhale*.

But the most famous winner wasn't a singer at all. First Lady Hillary Rodham Clinton won a Spoken-Word Grammy for the audio version of her book *It Takes a Village*. "I didn't know they gave these to people who are tone-deaf," Mrs. Clinton quipped.

Even the New York City police got into the musical act. Gotham's men in blue chose this highly publicized occasion to protest outside MSG for a pay hike. "All We Are Saying Is Give Us a Raise" they sang to the tune of "Give Peace a Chance."

THE AMERICAN MUSIC AWARDS

POP/ROCK
Album: *Jagged Little Pill* (Alanis Morissette); Male Artist: Eric Clapton; Female Artist: Alanis Morissette; Band, Duo, or Group: Hootie and the Blowfish; New Artist: Jewel

SOUL/RHYTHM AND BLUES

Album: *Secrets* (Toni Braxton); Male Artist: Keith Sweat; Female Artist: Toni Braxton; Band, Duo, or Group: New Edition; New Artist: D'Angelo

COUNTRY

Album: *Blue Clear Sky* (George Strait); Male Artist: Garth Brooks; Female Artist: Shania Twain; Band, Duo, or Group: Brooks and Dunn; New Artist: LeAnn Rimes

OTHER AWARDS

Heavy Metal/Hard Rock Artist: Metallica; Rap/Hip-Hop Artist: Tupac Shakur; Adult Contemporary Artist: Whitney Houston; Alternative Artist: the Smashing Pumpkins; Soundtrack Album: *Waiting to Exhale*

SPECIAL AWARD

Little Richard

BILLBOARD MUSIC AWARDS

Artist of the year: Alanis Morissette; Album of the Year: *Jagged Little Pill* (Alanis Morissette); Single of the Year: "Macarena" (Los Del Rio); New Artist of the Year: Tony Rich; Hot 100 Artist of the Year: Mariah Carey; Rock Track Single of the Year: "Counting Blue Cars" (Dishwalla); R&B Artist of the Year: R. Kelly; R&B Single of the Year: "You're Makin' Me High"/ "Let It Flow" (Toni Braxton); Country Artist of the Year: George Strait; Country Single of the Year: "My Maria" (Brooks and Dunn)

BILLBOARD CENTURY AWARD

Carlos Santana

ARTIST ACHIEVEMENT AWARD

Madonna

SPECIAL HOT 100 AWARD

Mariah Carey; Boyz II Men

For the first time, the *Billboard* awards originated from Las Vegas. A fire during rehearsal almost prevented the show from airing at all, but only one act (Bone Thugs-N-Harmony) had to cancel because of damage from the blaze.

COUNTRY MUSIC ASSOCIATION AWARDS

Entertainer: Brooks and Dunn; Single: "Check Yes or No" (George Strait); Song: "Go Rest High on That Mountain" (Vince Gill, songwriter); Album: *Clear Blue Sky* (George Strait); Male Vocalist: George Strait; Female Vocalist: Patty Loveless; Vocal Group: the Mavericks; Vocal Duo: Brooks and Dunn; Vocal Event: Vince Gill, Dolly Parton; Musician: Mark O'Connor; Horizon Award: Bryan White; Music Video: Junior Brown ("My Wife Thinks You're Dead")

MTV VIDEO MUSIC AWARDS

Video of the Year: *Tonight, Tonight* (the Smashing Pumpkins); Male Video: Beck (*Where It's At*); Female Video: Alanis Morissette (*Ironic*); Group Video: *Big Me* (Foo Fighters); New Artist in a Video: Alanis Morissette (*Ironic*); Rap Video: Coolio featuring LV (*Gangsta's Paradise*); Dance Video: *1,2,3,4 (Sumpin' New)* (Coolio); Metal/Hard Rock Video: *Until It Sleeps* (Metallica); R&B Video: *Killing Me Softly* (the Fugees); Video from a Film: *Gangsta's Paradise* from *Dangerous Minds* (Coolio featuring LV); Choreography: Michael Rooney (Bjork, *It's Oh So Quiet*); Alternative Video: *1979* (the Smashing Pumpkins); Special Effects: Chris Staves (the Smashing Pumpkins, *Tonight, Tonight*); Direction: Jonathan Dayton, Valerie Faris (the Smashing Pumpkins, *Tonight, Tonight*); Breakthrough Video: *Tonight, Tonight* (the Smashing Pumpkins); Viewers' Choice Award: Bush (*Glycerine*)

Emmy loved *Lucy* in 1953.
Desi Arnaz is flanked by winners
Lucille Ball and Vivian Vance.

PART 3

Television

THE EMMY, the top honor in television, has often been compared unfavorably to its more exciting sister awards. The Oscars have glamorous movie stars. The Grammys have dynamic recording artists. The Tonys have show-stopping musical numbers. The Emmys have familiar faces, which the viewing audience sees week after week, and a mind-numbing number of categories.

As the medium of television has expanded to gargantuan proportions so have the Emmys. Starting out by only honoring local programming in six categories, they now encompass broadcast, cable, and syndication in over seventy separate areas. And that's just for prime time. Don't forget the Emmys for daytime, news, sports, and international programs.

Despite their overabundance of accolades and lack of dazzle, the Emmys are probably the fairest of all the major awards. Nominations are made by the entire membership of the Academy of Television Arts and Sciences, but the winners are chosen by select peer, blue-ribbon panels of judges. (Actors judging actors, directors picking directors, etc.). The Oscars and the Tonys are voted on by several hundred film and theater professionals. With the film and theater honors, there is no way to verify that each voter has seen every nominee.

The Emmy judges view all the nominated shows over a marathon weekend of TV-watching (nominees in continuing series submit a sample of their best work.) Representatives of the Academy can assure the public that every judge has seen every candidate. As a result, the judges make their choices while all the nominees are fresh in their minds, as opposed to the Oscar and Tony voters who view nominated work over the course of a year.

Because of these rules, developed over several decades, the Emmy is seen as a measure of quality rather than popularity. Nor is it viewed merely as a tool to strengthen a show's ratings. In fact, Emmy awards have gone to several canceled series (*My World and Welcome to It, The Julie Andrews Hour, The Seven Lively Arts*). But Emmys have occasionally rescued a worthy program from the axe (*Hill Street Blues, Cagney & Lacey, Mission: Impossible*).

Emmy has come in for heavy criticism for its bewildering array of changes. Its rules have shifted more times than for any other show business prize. But many media watchers agree its current criteria are probably the most equitable.

Only the major Emmy categories are included in this section. Also included are winners of the television Golden Globe awards, the prestigous Peabody awards for entertainment and news, and the Cable ACE awards.

1948

THE EMMY AWARDS

MOST POPULAR TELEVISION PROGRAM
Armchair Detective, KTLA
Don Lee Music Hall, KTLA
Felix de Cola Show, KTSL
Judy Splinters, KTLA
Mabel's Fables, KTLA
The Masked Spooner, KTSL
Pantomime Quiz, KTLA
The Treasure of Literature, KFI-TV
Tuesday Varietie, KTLA
What's the Name of That Song? KTSL

BEST FILM MADE FOR TELEVISION
Christopher Columbus (Emerson Film Corp.)
Hollywood Brevities (Tele-Features)
It Could Happen to You (Vallee Video)
The Necklace (*Your Show Time* series)
   (Marshall Grant-Realm Prods.)
The Tell-Tale Heart (Telepak)
Time Signal (Centaur Productions)

OUTSTANDING TELEVISION PERSONALITY
Shirley Dinsdale and her puppet Judy Splinters,
   KTLA
Rita LeRoy, KTLA
Patricia Morison
Mike Stokey, KTLA
Bill Welsh, KTLA

TECHNICAL AWARD
Charles Mesak, Don Lee Television for the
introduction of the phasefader

STATION AWARD
KTLA

SPECIAL AWARD
Louis McManus, designer of the Emmy statuette

The first six of what over the years would eventually amount to almost 5,000 Emmy awards were handed out on January 15, 1949, for the 1948 television year. The awards were presented by the Academy of Television Arts and Sciences, founded in 1946 by Syd Cassyd. The infant ATAS was meant to serve the new video industry as the Academy of Motion Picture Arts and Sciences did the cinema, but with a few differences. While both organizations handed out annual awards for excellence, the TV academy planned to stress the "academic" part of its monicker and become a source of ideas, discussions, and papers on the industry. The first ATAS president was Edgar Bergen, whose daughter Candice would later win a total of five Emmys for her performance on the sitcom *Murphy Brown*.

The initial name for the awards was "Ike," short for iconoscope tube. But this was discarded because of its similarity to General (and future President) Eisenhower's popular nickname. Emmy was finally chosen for its abbreviation of the image orthicon camera tube. The form of the statuette was chosen in a contest. The winner, Louis McManus, an engineer, was one of the first recipients of the prizes he designed.

The Emmys were presented to Los Angeles programs since almost all TV was generated locally at that time. Walter O'Keefe was the host of the show broadcast over local L.A. station KTSL. The first award went to Shirley Dinsdale, a ventriloquist who had a daily fifteen-minute program.

THE PEABODY AWARDS

OUTSTANDING CONTRIBUTION TO THE ART OF TELEVISION
Actors' Studio (ABC)

OUTSTANDING CHILDREN'S PROGRAM
Howdy Doody (NBC)

The George Foster Peabody Awards were originally intended to honor excellence in radio journalism and programming. Named for a prominent Georgia philanthropist, they were first presented in 1940 and administered (as they still are) by the Henry W. Grady School of Journalism at the University of Georgia. The 1948 awards included the first two for the new medium of television.

From 1948 to 1971 and in 1973, categories were flexible. In 1972 and from 1974 on, there were no specific categories. The Peabodys honor entertainment and news programs, both national and local.

THE EMMY AWARDS

LIVE SHOW
The Ed Wynn Show, KTTV (CBS)
Pantomime Quiz, KTTV (CBS)
Your Witness, KECA-TV (ABC)

KINESCOPE SHOW
Fred Waring, KTTV (CBS)
The Goldbergs, KTTV (CBS)
Studio One, KTTV (CBS)
Texaco Star Theater, KNBH (NBC)

In their second year, the Emmys began to achieve national prominence. The Television Academy dropped the requirement that all nominees originate in Los Angeles. In addition to West Coast programming, entries were accepted from New York and Chicago, the two other principal centers of television production.

East Coast and Chicago transmissions were not yet powerful enough to reach Hollywood. In order to get these programs, kinescopes were made. This process involved shooting a film of the actual TV picture and then shipping the film to the West Coast where it would air the next day.

In order to accommodate this new method, the Emmy categories were divided between live shows (those made in Los Angeles and aired as they were performed) and kinescopes (those shipped from New York and elsewhere).

Most early television programming was provided by variety hours, which were mixes of comedy sketches and musical numbers. The awards reflected this by naming Ed Wynn and Milton Berle, clowns with roots in vaudeville, the top winners. Wynn was hailed as top live personality and Berle copped the kinescope category. Wynn's show lensed in Los Angeles while Berle's *Texaco Star Theater* came out of New York. Thus began the great East-

West Emmy rivalry, with both coasts vying for top honors. Chicago eventually faded as a national TV base. During the 1950s, New York would continue to play host to much distinguished video fare (particularly dramatic anthologies). But by the 1960s, production would move primarily to the West with only an occasional program based in the Big Apple.

FILM MADE FOR AND VIEWED ON TELEVISION
Guiding Star, KTTV (CBS)
The Life of Riley, KNBH (NBC)
The Lone Ranger, KECA-TV (ABC)
Time Bomb, KNBH (NBC)
Vain Glory, KNBH (NBC)
Your Show Time, KNBH (NBC)

CHILDREN'S SHOW
Cyclone Malone, KNBH (NBC)
Kukla, Fran and Ollie, KNBH (NBC)
Time for Beany, KTLA

LIVE PERSONALITY
Tom Harmon, KFI-TV, KECA-TV (ABC), KTTV (CBS)
Mike Stokey, KTTV (CBS), KTLA
Bill Welsh, KFI-TV, KTLA
Ed Wynn, KTTV (CBS)

Ed Wynn knew he was a winner before the envelope was even opened at the Los Angeles Ambassador Hotel. Word of the winners had leaked out earlier in the afternoon of the Emmy ceremony. All the previous recipients kept mum about the leak, but Wynn blurted out he had known he was taking home the statuette for five weeks. After he got his laugh, Wynn stated "I was only kidding, I just learned about it twenty minutes ago." This lack of secrecy started Emmy's reputation of being a shady lady.

KINESCOPE PERSONALITY
Fran Allison, KNBH (NBC)
Milton Berle, KNBH (NBC)
Arthur Godfrey, KTTV (CBS)

OTHER AWARDS
Public Service, Cultural, or Educational Program:
Crusade in Europe, KECA-TV (ABC) and KTTV

(CBS); Technical Award: Harold W. Jury of KTSL, Los Angeles, for the synchronizing coordinator device which allows two locations to be shown at once; Sports Coverage: *Wrestling*, KTLA; Commercial: Lucky Strike cigarettes, N. W. Ayer for American Tobacco Co.; Station Achievement: KTLA, Los Angeles (honorable mention to KECA-TV)

THE PEABODY AWARDS

ENTERTAINMENT
The Ed Wynn Show (CBS)

EDUCATION
Crusade in Europe (ABC)

REPORTING AND INTERPRETATION OF THE NEWS
The United Nations in Action (CBS)

CHILDREN'S PROGRAM
Kukla, Fran, and Ollie (NBC)

THE EMMY AWARDS

DRAMATIC SHOW
Fireside Theatre, KTLA
I Remember Mama, KTTV (CBS)
Philco TV Playhouse, KNBH (NBC)
Pulitzer Prize Playhouse, KECA-TV (ABC)
Studio One, KTTV (CBS)

VARIETY SHOW
The Alan Young Show, KTTV (CBS)
Four Star Revue, KNBH (NBC)
Ken Murray, KTTV (CBS)
Texaco Star Theater, KNBH (NBC)
Your Show of Shows, KNBH (NBC)

CULTURAL SHOW
Campus Chorus and Orchestra, KTSL
Designed for Women, KNBH (NBC)
Sunset Service, KNBH (NBC)

Vienna Philharmonic, KTTV (CBS)
The Woman's Voice, KTTV (CBS)

CHILDREN'S SHOW
Cisco Kid, KNBH (NBC)
Jump Jump, KTTV (CBS)
Kukla, Fran & Ollie, KNBH (NBC)
The Lone Ranger, KTLA
Time for Beany, KTLA

GAME AND AUDIENCE PARTICIPATION SHOW
Kay Kyser's College of Musical Knowledge, KNBH (CBS)
Life with Linkletter, KECA-TV (ABC)
Pantomime Quiz, KTTV (CBS)
Truth or Consequences, KTTV (CBS)
You Bet Your Life, KNBH (NBC)

PERSONALITY
Sid Caesar, KNHB (NBC)
Faye Emerson, KTTV (CBS) and KECA-TV (ABC)
Dick Lane, KTLA
Groucho Marx, KNHB (NBC)
Alan Young, KTTV (CBS)

Film funnyman Groucho Marx found a new audience for his zany antics as the host of a game show called *You Bet Your Life* wherein he traded quips with hapless contestants. Upon receiving his Emmy award, he picked up the former Miss America who presented it to him, walked off stage with her, and left the statuette behind.

ACTOR
Sid Caesar, KNBH (NBC)
Jose Ferrer
Stan Freberg (as voice of Cecil the Sea-Sick Sea Serpent), KTLA
Charles Ruggles, KECA-TV
Alan Young, KTTV (CBS)

ACTRESS
Judith Anderson
Gertrude Berg, KTTV (CBS)
Imogene Coca, KNBH (NBC)
Helen Hayes, KECA-TV (ABC)
Betty White, KLAC

Acting awards were added for the 1950 Emmys. But there was no taking into account the type of program for which the performer was nominated. In fact, there were no specific shows cited, only the performer's names. This led to some odd "apples-and-oranges" competition. Commediennes Gertrude Berg and Imogene Coca vied for top honors with dramatic actresses Helen Hayes and Judith Anderson. Meanwhile on the male side, Oscar and Tony winner Jose Ferrer was pitted against Stan Freeberg, who provided the voice for Cecil the Sea Serpent on the *Time for Beany* puppet show. Neither won. The award went to a young Canadian comedian named Alan Young, star of his own CBS series which was named top variety show. Young would later become better known as straight man to a talking horse on the sitcom *Mr. Ed.*

OTHER AWARDS
News Program: *KTLA Newsreel*, KTLA; Sports Coverage: *Rams Football*, KNBH (NBC); Educational Show: *KFI-TV University*, KFI-TV; Special Event: *Departure of Marines for Korea*, KFMB-TV, San Diego, and KTLA; Public Service: *City at Night*, KTLA; Station Achievement: KTLA; Technical Achievement: Orthogram TV Amplifier by KNBH (NBC)

The kinescope-versus-live distinction was dropped from the 1950 Emmys, but the ATAS rules still stated a program had to be shown on a Los Angeles station for award eligibility. Thirteen of the fifteen prizes went to either local or West Coast-based programs, leading New York producers to cry foul. The criticisms of bias toward L.A. and the mixing of drama and comedy performers in the acting categories would lead to a major revamping of TV's top award.

THE PEABODY AWARDS

ENTERTAINMENT
Jimmy Durante (NBC)

CHILDREN'S PROGRAMS
Saturday at the Zoo (ABC); *Zoo Parade* (NBC)

SPECIAL AWARD
To ABC president Robert Kintner and associates

Robert Saudek and Joseph McDonald "for their courageous stand in resisting organized pressures and their reaffirmation of basic American principles"

THE EMMY AWARDS

DRAMATIC SHOW
Celanese Theatre (ABC)
Philco-Goodyear TV Playhouse (NBC)
Pulitzer Prize Playhouse (ABC)
Robert Montgomery Presents (NBC)
Studio One (CBS)

COMEDY SHOW
The George Burns and Gracie Allen Show (CBS)
The Herb Shriner Show (ABC)
I Love Lucy (CBS)
Red Skelton Show (CBS)
You Bet Your Life (NBC)

VARIETY SHOW:
All Star Revue (NBC)
Comedy Hour (NBC)
The Fred Waring Show (CBS)
Toast of the Town (CBS)
Your Show of Shows (NBC)

ACTOR
Sid Caesar
Walter Hampden
Charlton Heston
Robert Montgomery
Thomas Mitchell
Vaughn Taylor

ACTRESS
Imogene Coca
Helen Hayes
Maria Riva
Mary Sinclair
Margaret Sullavan

In response to criticism of the previous year's combining of comic and dramatic performers, there were now separate categories for actors and comedians. But comedians still found their way into the actors' group. Sid Caesar and Imogene Coca, the stars of NBC's hit comedy revue *Your Show of Shows*, were named best actor and actress over the likes of Charlton Heston and Helen Hayes. Both Caesar and Coca were in New York to tape their show and unable to attend the Los Angeles ceremony. Presenter Ed Wynn attempted to speak with them by telephone. His call to Caesar went off without a hitch, but Wynn had to deal with an uncooperative operator to get through to Coca.

COMEDIAN OR COMEDIENNE
Lucille Ball (CBS)
Sid Caesar (NBC)
Imogene Coca (NBC)
Jimmy Durante (NBC)
Dean Martin and Jerry Lewis (NBC)
Herb Shriner (ABC)
Red Skelton (NBC)

"Ladies and gentlemen, you've given this to the wrong redhead," Red Skelton told the Emmy audience. "It should go to Lucille Ball." The comedian then took his Emmy and tried to hand it to Ball, who was co-hosting the program with her husband and co-star Desi Arnaz. She waved him away through tears. *The Hollywood Reporter* stated, "There wasn't a dry eye in the house."

Though Lucy lost both the Comedian or Comedienne and Comedy Show awards to Skelton in 1951, she would later take Emmy home a total of four times.

SPECIAL AWARDS
U.S. Senator Estes Kefauver for outstanding public service on television; American Telephone and Telegraph Company for the transcontinental Microwave Relay System; Jack Burrel of station KNBH, Los Angeles, for the development of an independent transmission mobile unit

To answer cries of Hollywood bias, the Television Academy changed its rules to give the Emmys a more national flavor. The Academy's executive committee would now accept nominations from impartial TV newspaper editors all across the country, with the Academy membership voting on the winners. Also awards would now go to network rather than local programming.

THE PEABODY AWARDS

ENTERTAINMENT (NONMUSICAL)
Celanese Theatre (ABC)

ENTERTAINMENT (MUSICAL)
Gian Carlo Menotti for *Amahl and the Night Visitors* (NBC) (the first opera written specifically for TV)

EDUCATION
What in the World (WCAU-TV, Philadelphia)

NEWS AND INTERPRETATION
Edward R. Murrow and *See It Now* (CBS)

MERITORIOUS REGIONAL PUBLIC SERVICE BY RADIO AND TELEVISION
WSB, Atlanta for *The Pastor's Study and Our World Today*

1952
THE EMMY AWARDS

DRAMATIC PROGAM
Celanese Theatre (ABC)
Kraft Television Theatre (ABC)
Philco-Goodyear TV Playhouse (NBC)
Robert Montgomery Presents (NBC)
Studio One (CBS)

SITUATION COMEDY
The Adventures of Ozzie and Harriet (ABC)
Amos 'n' Andy (CBS)
The George Burns and Gracie Allen Show (CBS)
I Love Lucy (CBS)
Mr. Peepers (NBC)
Our Miss Brooks (CBS)

MYSTERY, ACTION, OR ADVENTURE PROGRAM
Big Story (NBC)

Dragnet (NBC)
Foreign Intrigue (Syndicated)
Martin Kane, Private Eye (NBC)
Racket Squad (CBS)

VARIETY PROGRAM
Arthur Godfrey and His Friends (CBS)
Colgate Comedy Hour (NBC)
The Jackie Gleason Show (CBS)
Toast of the Town (CBS)
Your Show of Shows (NBC)

PUBLIC AFFAIRS PROGRAM
Camel News Caravan (NBC)
Life Is Worth Living (DuMont)
Meet the Press (NBC)
See It Now (CBS)
Victory at Sea (NBC)

CHILDREN'S PROGRAM
Big Top (CBS)
Gabby Hayes
Howdy Doody (NBC)
Kukla, Fran and Ollie (NBC)
Super Circus (NBC)
Time for Beany, KTLA
Zoo Parade (NBC)

AUDIENCE PARTICIPATION, QUIZ OR PANEL SHOW
Down You Go (Du Mont)
This Is Your Life (NBC)
Two for the Money (NBC)
What's My Line? (CBS)
You Bet Your Life (NBC)

ACTOR
John Forsthye
Charlton Heston
Thomas Mitchell
John Newland
Vaughn Taylor
Jack Webb

ACTRESS
Sarah Churchill
Helen Hayes
June Lockhart

Maria Riva
Peggy Wood

Helen Hayes had previously won an Oscar (for *The Sin of Madelon Claudet*) and a Tony (for *Happy Birthday*). With her 1952 Emmy, she became the first performer to win the Triple Crown of acting honors in film, theater, and television.

Thomas Mitchell who won for best TV actor that year, soon joined the triple club. He had an Oscar on his mantle for his supporting performance in 1939's *Stagecoach*. Then one month after the 1952 Emmy ceremony, he copped the Tony for best actor in a musical for *Hazel Flagg*.

Since most video performers appeared on numerous anthology series, no specific programs were cited in the Emmy nominations.

COMEDIAN
Sid Caesar (NBC)
Wally Cox (NBC)
Jimmy Durante (NBC)
Jackie Gleason (CBS)
Herb Shriner (ABC)

COMEDIENNE
Eve Arden (CBS)
Lucille Ball (CBS)
Imogene Coca (NBC)
Joan Davis (NBC)
Martha Raye (NBC)

PERSONALITY
Lucille Ball (CBS)
Arthur Godfrey (CBS)
Jimmy Durante (NBC)
Edward R. Murrow (CBS)
Donald O'Connor (NBC)
Bishop Fulton J. Sheen (Du Mont)
Adlai Stevenson (NBC)

Though she won for best Comedienne, Lucille Ball lost the outstanding Personality award to Bishop Fulton J. Sheen who appeared on *Life Is Worth Living*, a weekly inspirational program on the short-lived Du Mont network. One of the few religious shows ever aired in prime time, it was popular enough to go against Milton Berle's *Texaco Star Theater*. When Du Mont folded in 1955,

Sheen moved to ABC.

The bizarre catch-all category of outstanding Personality continued the Emmy tradition of comparing dissimilar nominees. The wacky redhead and the paternalistic clergyman were in competition with folksy host Arthur Godfrey, lovable comic Jimmy Durante, song-and-dance man Donald O'Connor, hard-hitting news reporter Edward R. Murrow, and erudite Presidential candidate/commentator Adlai Stevenson.

As the Emmy became more national, several West Coast-based Academy members either resigned or did not renew their memberships in protest. They wanted the awards to remain a strictly Los Angeles affair. To keep the ranks full, the Academy presented separate awards for local L.A. programs. Betty White and Liberace were among the winners of 1952 local Emmys.

THE PEABODY AWARDS

ENTERTAINMENT
Mr. Peepers (NBC); *Your Hit Parade* (NBC)

EDUCATION
The Johns Hopkins Science Review (Du Mont)

NEWS
Meet the Press (NBC)

YOUTH AND CHILDREN'S PROGRAMS
Ding Dong School (NBC)

SPECIAL AWARD
Victory at Sea (NBC)

LOCAL PUBLIC SERVICE
WEWS-TV, Cleveland

1953

THE EMMY AWARDS

DRAMATIC PROGRAM
Kraft Television Theatre (NBC)
Philco-Goodyear TV Playhouse (NBC)

Robert Montgomery Presents (NBC)
Studio One (CBS)
U.S. Steel Hour (ABC)

SITUATION COMEDY
The George Burns and Gracie Allen Show (CBS)
I Love Lucy (CBS)
Mr. Peepers (NBC)
Our Miss Brooks (CBS)
Topper (CBS)

VARIETY PROGRAM
Colgate Comedy Hour (NBC)
The Jackie Gleason Show (CBS)
Omnibus (CBS)
Toast of the Town (CBS)
Your Show of Shows (NBC)

NEW PROGRAM (TIE)
Adventure (CBS)
Ding Dong School (NBC)
A Letter to Loretta (NBC)
Make Room for Daddy (ABC)
Person to Person (CBS)
U.S. Steel Hour (ABC)

MALE STAR, REGULAR SERIES
Sid Caesar (*Your Show of Shows*) (NBC)
Wally Cox (*Mr. Peepers*) (NBC)
Jackie Gleason (*The Jackie Gleason Show*) (CBS)
Donald O'Connor (*Colgate Comedy Hour*) (NBC)
Jack Webb (*Dragnet*) (NBC)

FEMALE STAR, REGULAR SERIES
Eve Arden (*Our Miss Brooks*) (CBS)
Lucille Ball (*I Love Lucy*) (CBS)
Imogene Coca (*Your Show of Shows*) (NBC)
Dinah Shore (*The Dinah Shore Shore*) (NBC)
Loretta Young (*A Letter to Loretta*) (NBC)

Neither Donald O'Connor nor Eve Arden were at the Hollywood Palladium to accept their awards. O'Connor was taping a segment of the *Colgate Comedy Hour* while Arden stayed home. She had a slight cold and didn't think she had a chance anyway, so she spent Emmy night hooking a rug in her living room.

SUPPORTING ACTOR (SERIES)
Ben Alexander (*Dragnet*) (NBC)
Art Carney (*The Jackie Gleason Show*) (CBS)
William Frawley (*I Love Lucy*) (CBS)
Tony Randall (*Mr. Peepers*) (NBC)
Carl Reiner (*Your Show of Shows*) (NBC)

SUPPORTING ACTRESS (SERIES)
Bea Benedaret (*The George Burns and Gracie Allen Show*) (CBS)
Ruth Gilbert (*Texaco Star Theater*) (NBC)
Marion Lorne (*Mr. Peepers*) (NBC)
Audrey Meadows (*The Jackie Gleason Show*) (CBS)
Vivian Vance (*I Love Lucy*) (CBS)

For the first time supporting performances were recognized. Art Carney won the first of five Emmys for his portrayal of the ingratiating sewer worker Ed Norton on *The Jackie Gleason Show*. Gleason himself never won the coveted prize.

Another sidekick, Vivian Vance, accomplice to Lucy Ricardo and her crazy schemes on *I Love Lucy*, was also honored. William Frawley, who played her grumpy husband on the series, did not get to join her at the podium. Angry over his loss, he groused within Vance's earshot, "It goes to prove that the whole vote is rigged."

PERSONALITY
Arthur Godfrey (NBC)
Edward R. Murrow (CBS)
Martha Raye (NBC)
Bishop Fulton J. Sheen (Syndicated)
Jack Webb (NBC)

OTHER AWARDS
Mystery, Adventure, or Action Program: *Dragnet* (NBC); Children's Program: *Kukla, Fran and Ollie* (NBC); Audience Participation, Quiz or Panel Program (tie): *This Is Your Life* (NBC) and *What's My Line* (CBS); News or Sports Program: *See It Now* (CBS); Public Affairs Program: *Victory at Sea* (NBC)

For the first time, the ceremony to honor television's top achievements was not broadcast. Local Los Angeles stations balked at footing the bill.

For their roles on *The Jackie Gleason Show* and *The Honeymooners*, Art Carney won five Emmys, Audrey Meadows took home one, but Gleason himself never received the winged lady.

They were losing interest in the Emmys since the awards were turning national.

According to UPI, the four-hour banquet went smoothly except for one slight mishap: "The only slip-up [occured] when Desi Arnaz stalked scowling for the stage. The audience had laughed at his heavy Cuban accent. 'Darn it, they're laughing at me,' he said as he walked to his seat. But later he insisted, 'I was only kidding.'" *I Love Lucy*'s win as best situation comedy must have improved his humor.

THE PEABODY AWARDS

ENTERTAINMENT
Philco Television Playhouse (NBC); Imogene Coca (*Your Show of Shows*) (NBC)

MUSIC
NBC Television Opera Theatre

EDUCATION
Cavalcade of Books, KNXT-TV, Los Angeles; *Camera Three*, WCBS-TV, New York

NEWS
Gerald W. Johnson, WAAM-TV, Baltimore

YOUTH AND CHILDREN'S PROGRAM
Mr. Wizard (NBC)

SPECIAL AWARD
Edward R. Murrow (CBS)

PROMOTION OF INTERNATIONAL UNDERSTANDING THROUGH TELEVISION
British Broadcasting Corporation (BBC) for coverage of Queen Elizabeth II's coronation

1954

THE EMMY AWARDS

As television expanded, so did the Emmys. Categories jumped from fourteen in 1953 to thirty-four in 1954 (technical awards are not listed in

this section). The selection of nominees was now removed from the hands of TV editors and returned to the full ATAS membership (technical awards were judged by peer members within the particular craft).

INDIVIDUAL PROGAM
Diamond Jubilee of Light (Four networks)
"Operation Undersea," *Disneyland* (ABC)
"White Is the Color," *Medic* (NBC)
A Christmas Carol, Shower of Stars (CBS)
Twelve Angry Men, Studio One (CBS)

DRAMA SERIES
Four Star Playhouse (CBS)
Medic (NBC)
Philco TV Playhouse (NBC)
Studio One (CBS)
U.S. Steel Hour (ABC)

SITUATION COMEDY SERIES
The George Burns and Gracie Allen Show (CBS)
I Love Lucy (CBS)
Make Room for Daddy (ABC)
Mr. Peepers (NBC)
Our Miss Brooks (CBS)
Private Secretary (CBS)

VARIETY SERIES
Disneyland (ABC)
The George Gobel Show (NBC)
The Jack Benny Show (CBS)
The Jackie Gleason Show (CBS)
Toast of the Town (CBS)
Your Hit Parade (NBC)

ACTOR IN A SERIES
Richard Boone (*Medic*) (NBC)
Robert Cummings (*My Hero*) (Syndicated)
Jackie Gleason (*The Jackie Gleason Show*) (CBS)
Danny Thomas (*Make Room for Daddy*) (ABC)
Jack Webb (*Dragnet*) (NBC)

ACTRESS IN A SERIES
Eve Arden (*Our Miss Brooks*) (CBS)
Gracie Allen (*The George Burns and Gracie Allen Show* (CBS)
Lucille Ball (*I Love Lucy*) (CBS)

1954 Emmy winners Danny Thomas (*Make Room for Daddy*) and Loretta Young (*The Loretta Young Show*).

Ann Sothern (*Private Secretary*) (CBS)
Loretta Young (*The Loretta Young Show*) (NBC)

ACTOR IN A SINGLE PERFORMANCE
Robert Cummings (*Twelve Angry Men, Studio One*) (CBS)
Frank Lovejoy (*Double Indemnity, Lux Video Theatre*) (CBS)
Frederic March (*A Christmas Carol, Shower of Stars*) (CBS)
Frederic March (*Royal Family, Best of Broadway*) (CBS)
Thomas Mitchell (*Good of His Soul, Ford Theatre*) (NBC)
David Niven (*The Answer, Four Star Playhouse*) (CBS)

ACTRESS IN A SINGLE PERFORMANCE
Judith Anderson (*Macbeth, Hallmark Hall of Fame*) (NBC)
Ethel Barrymore ("The 13th Chair," *Climax*) (CBS)
Beverly Garland ("White Is the Color," *Medic*) (NBC)
Ruth Hussey (*Craig's Wife, Lux Video Theatre*) (NBC)
Dorothy McGuire ("The Giaconda Smile," *Climax*) (CBS)
Eva Marie Saint (*Middle of the Night, Philco TV Playhouse*) (NBC)
Claire Trevor (*Ladies in Retirement, Lux Video Theatre*) (NBC)

Judith Anderson would repeat her performance as Lady Macbeth in the 1960–61 remake of Shakespeare's classic for *Hallmark Hall of Fame* and again win an Emmy. She is unique in Emmy annals as the only performer to win two awards for playing the same role in two different versions of the same play.

SUPPORTING ACTOR (SERIES)
Ben Alexander (*Dragnet*) (NBC)
Art Carney (*The Jackie Gleason Show*) (CBS)
Don DeFore (*The Adventures of Ozzie and Harriet*) (CBS)
William Frawley (*I Love Lucy*) (CBS)
Gale Gordon (*Our Miss Brooks*) (CBS)

SUPPORTING ACTRESS (SERIES)
Bea Benaderet (*The George Burns and Gracie Allen Show*) (CBS)
Jean Hagen (*Make Room for Daddy*) (ABC)
Marion Lorne (*Mr. Peepers*) (NBC)
Audrey Meadows (*The Jackie Gleason Show*) (CBS)
Vivian Vance (*I Love Lucy*) (CBS)

MALE SINGER
Perry Como (CBS)
Eddie Fisher (NBC)
Frankie Lane (Syndicated)
Tony Martin (NBC)
Gordon MacRae (NBC)

FEMALE SINGER
Jane Froman (CBS)
Peggy King (NBC)
Gisele Mackenzie (NBC)
Dinah Shore (NBC)
Jo Stafford (CBS)

NEW PERSONALITY
Richard Boone (NBC)
Walt Disney (ABC)
Tennessee Ernie Ford (CBS)
George Gobel (NBC)
Preston Foster (Syndicated)
Michael O'Shea (NBC)
Fess Parker (ABC)

OTHER AWARDS
Mystery or Intrigue Series: *Dragnet* (NBC); Western or Adventure Series: *Stories of the Century* (Syndicated); Cultural, Religious or Educational Program: *Omnibus* (ABC); Audience, Guest Participation or Panel Program: *What's My Line* (CBS); Children's Program: *Lassie* (CBS); Writing (Dramatic): Reginald Rose (*Twelve Angry Men, Studio One*) (CBS); Writing (Comedy): James Allardice, Jack Douglas, Hal Kanter, Harry Winkler (*The George Gobel Show*) (NBC); Director: Franklin Schaffner (*Twelve Angry Men, Studio One*) (CBS); News Reporter or Commentator: John Daly (ABC); Daytime Program: *Art Linkletter's House Party*; Sports Program: *Gillette Cavalcade of Sports*

With the 1954 ceremony, the Emmys became truly national. The program was broadcast from coast to coast on NBC from the Moulin Rogue restaurant in Los Angeles and Nino's LaRue eatery in New York. With the loss of support from the Los Angeles stations, Academy president Don DeFore (best known as *Hazel*'s boss) went to NBC to sell the Emmys as an annual entertainment show. Steve Allen hosted in Los Angeles while *The Today Show*'s Dave Garroway held sway in Gotham. The Peacock network would continue to broadcast the awards until 1966.

THE PEABODY AWARDS

ENTERTAINMENT
George Gobel (NBC)

EDUCATION
Adventure (CBS)

NEWS (RADIO AND TELEVISION)
John Daly (ABC)

YOUTH AND CHILDREN'S PROGRAM
Disneyland (ABC)

SPECIAL AWARDS
Omnibus (CBS); *The Search* (CBS)

NATIONAL PUBLIC SERVICE
Industry on Parade (National Association of Manufacturers)

REGIONAL PUBLIC SERVICE
WJAR-TV, Providence (for hurricane coverage)

1955

THE EMMY AWARDS

SINGLE PROGRAM
"The American West," *Wide Wide World* (NBC)
*The Caine Muntiny Court-Martial,
Ford Star Jubilee* (CBS)
"Davy Crockett and the River Pirates,"
Disneyland (ABC)
No Time for Sergeants, The U.S. Steel Hour (ABC)
Peter Pan, *Producers' Showcase* (NBC)
"Peter Pan Meets Rusty Williams," *Make Room
for Daddy* (ABC)
The Sleeping Beauty, Producers' Showcase (NBC)

DRAMA SERIES
The Alcoa Hour/Goodyear Playhouse (NBC)
Climax (CBS)
Producers' Showcase (NBC)
Studio One (CBS)
U.S. Steel Hour (ABC)

COMEDY SERIES
The Bob Cummings Show (CBS)
The Jack Benny Show (CBS)
Caesar's Hour (NBC)
The George Gobel Show (NBC)
Make Room for Daddy (ABC)
The Phil Silvers Show (CBS)

The big winner of 1955 was Phil Silvers, copping
two winged ladies [for Actor (Continuing Series)
and Comedian]. His eponymous program also
received the Comedy Series award. Silvers played
Sergeant Bilko, a fast-talking con man who surrep-
titiously rules the roost at a Kansas army base. *The
New York Times* stated the comedian deserved
"another handful [of awards] for poking fun at
Saturday night's tedious affair." The *Times* critic
went on to call the Emmy attendees "perhaps the
coldest and most unenthuiastic studio audience
ever seen on TV."

VARIETY SERIES
The Dinah Shore Show (NBC)
The Ed Sullivan Show (CBS)

Ford Star Jubilee (CBS)
The Perry Como Show (NBC)
Shower of Stars (CBS)

MUSIC SERIES
Coke Time with Eddie Fisher (NBC)
The Dinah Shore Show (NBC)
The Perry Como Show (NBC)
The Voice of Firestone (ABC)
Your Hit Parade (NBC)

ACTOR (SINGLE PERFORMANCE)
Ralph Bellamy (*Fearful Decision,
The U.S. Steel Hour*) (CBS)
Jose Ferrer (*Cyrano de Bergerac,
Producers' Showcase*) (NBC)
Lloyd Nolan (*The Caine Mutiny Court-Martial,
Ford Star Jubilee*) (CBS)
Everett Sloane (*Patterns, Kraft Television Theatre*)
(NBC)
Barry Sullivan (*The Caine Mutiny Court-Martial*)
(CBS)

ACTRESS (SINGLE PERFORMANCE)
Julie Harris (*Wind from the South,
The U.S. Steel Hour*) (CBS)
Mary Martin (*Peter Pan, Producers' Showcase*) (NBC)
Eva Marie Saint (*Our Town, Producers' Showcase*)
(NBC)
Jessica Tandy (*The Fourposter, Producers' Showcase*)
(NBC)
Loretta Young ("Christmas Stopover,"
The Loretta Young Show) (NBC)

Both Lloyd Nolan as the neurotic Captain Queeg
of the *USS Caine* and Mary Martin as Peter Pan,
the boy who wouldn't grow up, had created their
Emmy-winning roles on Broadway. Martin had
won a Tony for the stage version of *Pan* a year earlier, making her the first to receive the top awards
in video and theater for the same character. The
only other performers with this dual honor are Ed
Flanders (for *Moon for the Misbegotten*), Jessica
Tandy (for *Foxfire*), and Robert Morse (for *Tru*).

ACTOR (CONTINUING SERIES)
Bob Cummings (*The Bob Cummings Show*) (CBS)
Jackie Gleason (*The Honeymooners*) (CBS)
Phil Silvers (*The Phil Silvers Show*) (CBS)

Danny Thomas (*Make Room for Daddy*) (ABC)
Robert Young (*Father Knows Best*) (CBS)

ACTRESS (CONTINUING SERIES)
Gracie Allen (*The George Burns and
   Gracie Allen Show*) (CBS)
Eve Arden (*Our Miss Brooks*) (CBS)
Lucille Ball (*I Love Lucy*) (CBS)
Jean Hagen (*Make Room for Daddy*) (ABC)
Ann Sothern (*Private Secretary*) (CBS)

For the first time since its premiere, *I Love Lucy* was not nominated for Best Comedy Series. An angry Lucille Ball refused to attend the awards. When she won for Actress (Continuing Series), the prize was accepted by Madelyn Pugh, one of the show's writers.

SUPPORTING ACTOR
Ed Begley (*Patterns, Kraft Television Theatre*) (NBC)
Art Carney (*The Honeymooners*) (CBS)
William Frawley (*I Love Lucy*) (CBS)
Carl Reiner (*Caesar's Hour*) (NBC)
Cyril Ritchard (*Peter Pan, Producers' Showcase*)
   (NBC)

SUPPORTING ACTRESS
Ann B. Davis (*The Bob Cummings Show*) (CBS)
Nanette Fabray (*Caesar's Hour*) (NBC)
Jean Hagen (*Make Room for Daddy*) (ABC)
Audrey Meadows (*The Honeymooners*) (CBS)
Thelma Ritter (*The Catered Affair, The Alcoa
   Hour/Goodyear Playhouse*) (NBC)

Nanette Fabray took home two Emmys (as Supporting Actress and Best Commedienne) for her work as Sid Caesar's leading lady on *Caesar's Hour*, the comic's new vehicle after the demise of *Your Show of Shows*. She took over for Imogene Coca when the latter started her own short-lived sitcom. Ironically, when Fabray won she was no longer employed by Caesar. She had left the series due to "artisitic differences."

OTHER AWARDS
Comedian: Phil Silvers (CBS); Comedienne: Nanette Fabray (NBC); Male Singer: Perry Como (NBC); Female Singer: Dinah Shore (NBC); MC or Program Host (Male or Female): Perry Como

(NBC); Specialty Act—Single or Group: Marcel Marceau

Action or Adventure Series: *Disneyland* (ABC); Special Event or News Program: *A-Bomb Test Coverage* (CBS); News Commentator: Edward R. Murrow (CBS); Documentary Program: *Omnibus* (CBS); Daytime Program: *Matinee Theatre* (NBC); Audience Participation Series: *The $64,000 Question* (CBS); Children's Series: *Lassie*

The Emmy-winning *$64,000 Question* toppled *I Love Lucy* as America's favorite program. The suspenseful quiz show allowed ordinary people with arcane knowledge the chance to win big money. Or so it seemed. It was later revealed that the show, along with several similar series, was fixed with contestants being provided the answers before airtime.

Producer (Live Series): Fred Coe (*Producers' Showcase*); Producer (Film Series): Walt Disney (*Disneyland*) (ABC); Director (Live Series): Franklin Schaffner (*The Caine Mutiny Court-Martial, Ford Star Jubilee*) (CBS); Director (Film Series): Nat Hiken (*The Phil Silvers Show*) (CBS); Writing (Original Teleplay): Rod Serling (*Patterns, Kraft Television Theatre*) (NBC); Television Adaptation: Paul Gregory, Franklin Schaffner (*The Caine Mutiny Court-Martial, Ford Star Jubilee*) (CBS); Writing (Comedy): Nat Hiken, Barry Blitser, Arnold Auerbach, Harvey Orkin, Vincent Bogert, Arnold Rosen, Coleman Jacoby, Tony Webster, Terry Ryan (*The Phil Silvers Show*) (CBS)

Emmy was now definitely a sophisticated, bicoastal lady rather than a local gal. For the second year, the ceremony was broadcast nationwide (with Art Linkletter emceeing from Hollywood's Pan Pacific Auditorium and John Daly in charge at the Waldorf-Astoria in Manhattan). One of the main motivators behind the push for a national scope to the Emmys was Ed Sullivan. The popular TV host and Broadway columnist had set up his own New York-based video awards to rival the Emmys. The Sullivan prizes were called the Michaels (short for microphone). By 1955, the Michaels fizzled and Sullivan campaigned for a New York chapter of the Television Academy, equal in importance and stature to the L.A. branch. After much haranguing, the stone-faced host got a Gotham outlet from the Academy.

Rule changes: several categories were divided into live and filmed shows. With the advent of coast-to-coast TV, kinescopes were no longer necessary, but most New York dramatic programs were still telecast as they were performed while L.A. fare was largely recorded on film. This stretched the number of categories from the previous year's thirty-four to a confusing forty-one. John Crosby of the *New York Herald-Tribune* wryly commented, "Next thing you know, they'll be giving an Emmy for Best Inter-Office Memo."

Party pooper: Jerry Lewis loudly and publicly refused to host the Emmys because he and Dean Martin failed to receive a nomination for their antics on *The Colgate Comedy Hour*. Lewis made a hit hosting the Oscars a week after the Emmys.

THE PEABODY AWARDS

ENTERTAINMENT
Jackie Gleason (CBS); Perry Como (NBC)

DRAMATIC ENTERTAINMENT
Producers' Showcase (NBC)

MUSIC (RADIO AND TELEVISION)
The Voice of Firestone (ABC)

EDUCATION
Dr. Frank Baxter (KNXT-TV, Los Angeles)

NEWS
Douglas Edwards (CBS)

YOUTH AND CHILDREN'S PROGRAMS
Lassie (CBS)

The dignified Peabodys indulged in a bit of show-biz glitz when the canine winner Lassie trotted up to the podium, barked, and returned to his seat with the award in his mouth.

PUBLIC SERVICE (RADIO AND TELEVISION)
Sylvester Weaver, Jr. (NBC) "for pioneering Program concepts"

PROMOTION OF INTERNATIONAL UNDERSTANDING (RADIO AND TELEVISION)
Quincy Howe (ABC)

THE GOLDEN GLOBE AWARDS

Dinah Shore; *I Love Lucy* (CBS); *The American Comedy*; *Davy Crockett, Disneyland* (ABC)

The Hollywood Foreign Press Association began honoring television as well as film work this year. The awards were presented in 1956 for the previous year and until 1961 cited individuals and series without specific categories. Nominations and winners are voted on by the general membership.

1956

THE EMMY AWARDS

In an effort to streamline the Emmys, the numbers of categories were cut from an unwieldy forty-one to a more managable twenty-nine. There were still some unusual pairings such as Tennessee Ernie Ford, Bishop Fulton J. Sheen, and Leonard Bernstein all up for Male Personality (Continuing Performance).

SINGLE PROGRAM OF THE YEAR
A Night to Remember, Kraft Television Theatre (NBC)
"Leonard Bernstein," *Omnibus* (CBS)
***Requiem for a Heavyweight**, Playhouse 90* (CBS)
"The Secret Life of Danny Kaye,"
    See It Now (CBS)
The Victor Borge Show (CBS)

Though its subject was a losing fighter, *Requiem for a Heavyweight* was the undisputed champ of the 1956 Emmys, winning all five of the awards for which it was nominated. *Caesar's Hour* scored an equal knockout record with a quintet of Emmys as well, but *Playhouse 90*, the drama anthology series which presented *Requiem*, also won an Emmy for New Series.

Rod Serling's powerful drama of a punch-drunk boxer was later made into a film (with Anthony Quinn) and a play (starring John Lithgow).

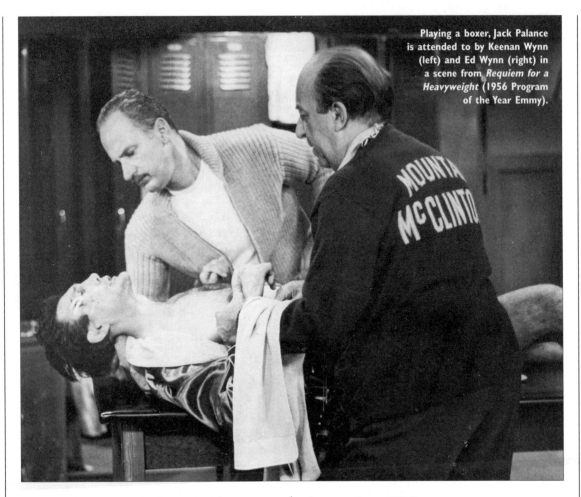

SERIES (ONE HOUR OR MORE)
Caesar's Hour (NBC)
Climax (CBS)
The Ed Sullivan Show (NBC)
Omnibus (CBS)
The Perry Como Show (NBC)

As noted, *Caesar's Hour* won an impressive five 1956 Emmys, taking the awards for Series (One Hour or More) and four of the series acting categories. This must have been gratifying to Sid Caesar since the variety show was losing ratings to Lawrence Welk. Despite the accolades, *Caesar's Hour* was canceled two months later.

SERIES (HALF-HOUR OR LESS)
Alfred Hitchcock Presents (CBS)
Father Knows Best (NBC)
The Jack Benny Show (CBS)

Person to Person (CBS)
The Phil Silvers Show (CBS)

NEW PROGRAM
Air Power (CBS)
The Dinah Shore Chevy Show (CBS)
The Ernie Kovacs Show (CBS)
Playhouse 90 (CBS)
The Steve Allen Sunday Show (NBC)

ACTOR (SINGLE PERFORMANCE)
Lloyd Bridges (*Tragedy in a Temporary Town, The Alcoa Hour/Goodyear Playhouse*) (NBC)
Frederic March (*Dodsworth, Producers' Showcase*) (NBC)
Sal Mineo (*Dino, Studio One*) (CBS)
Jack Palance (*Requiem for a Heavyweight, Playhouse 90*) (CBS)

Red Skelton (*The Big Slide, Playhouse 90*) (CBS)

ACTRESS (SINGLE PERFORMANCE)

Edna Best (*This Happy Breed, Ford Star Jubilee*) (CBS)

Gracie Fields (*The Old Lady Shows Her Medals, The U.S. Steel Hour*) (CBS)

Nancy Kelly (*The Pilot, Studio One*) (CBS)

Evelyn Rudie (*Eloise, Playhouse 90*) (CBS)

Claire Trevor (*Dodsworth, Producers' Showcase*) (NBC)

ACTOR (DRAMA SERIES)

James Arness (*Gunsmoke*) (CBS)

Charles Boyer (*Four Star Playhouse*) (CBS)

David Niven (*Four Star Playhouse*) (CBS)

Hugh O'Brien (*The Life and Legend of Wyatt Earp*) (ABC)

Robert Young (*Father Knows Best*) (NBC)

Although *Father Knows Best* was a comedy series, Robert Young was nominated in the Actor (Drama Series) category. He won a second Emmy in 1957 for Actor (Comedy or Drama Series), and a third in 1969–70 as one of America's favorite physicans, *Marcus Welby, MD.* He is the first actor to win leading Emmys for both comedy and dramatic series. Carroll O'Connor was the second for *All in the Family* and *In the Heat of the Night.* (Note: In 1955 *Father Knows Best* had switched from CBS to NBC.)

ACTRESS (DRAMA SERIES)

Jan Clayton (*Lassie*) (CBS)

Ida Lupino (*Four Star Playhouse*) (CBS)

Peggy Wood (*Mama*) (CBS)

Jane Wyman (*Fireside Theatre*) (CBS)

Loretta Young (*The Loretta Young Show*) (CBS)

COMEDIAN IN A SERIES

Jack Benny (*The Jack Benny Show*) (CBS)

Sid Caesar (*Caesar's Hour*) (NBC)

Bob Cummings (*The Bob Cummings Show*) (CBS)

Ernie Kovacs (*The Ernie Kovacs Show*) (NBC)

Phil Silvers (*The Phil Silvers Show*) (CBS)

COMEDIENNE IN A SERIES

Edie Adams (*The Ernie Kovacs Show*) (NBC)

Gracie Allen (*The George Burns and Gracie Allen Show*) (CBS)

Lucille Ball (*I Love Lucy*) (CBS)

Nanette Fabray (*Caesar's Hour*) (NBC)

Ann Sothern (*Private Secretary*) (CBS)

Fabray repeated her win of the previous year, but critics cried she was not even performing on *Caesar's Hour* at the time of the awards, having left at the end of the previous season. The Academy Board of Governors pointed out that eligibilty was based on the calendar year rather than the TV season of September to the following spring. Fabray was still a cast member in the spring of 1956 and therefore her award was not in dispute. Two years later, the Emmys would switch to following the video season to avoid conflicts of a similar nature.

SUPPORTING ACTOR

Art Carney (*The Jackie Gleason Show*) (CBS)

Paul Ford (*The Phil Silvers Show*) (CBS)

William Frawley (*I Love Lucy*) (CBS)

Carl Reiner (*Caesar's Hour*) (NBC)

Ed Wynn (*Requiem for a Heavyweight, Playhouse 90*) (CBS)

SUPPORTING ACTRESS

Pat Carroll (*Caesar's Hour*) (NBC)

Ann B. Davis (*The Bob Cummings Show*) (CBS)

Audrey Meadows (*The Jackie Gleason Show*) (CBS)

Mildred Natwick (*Blithe Spirit, Ford Star Jubilee*) (CBS)

Vivian Vance (*I Love Lucy*) (CBS)

MALE PERSONALITY (CONTINUING PERFORMANCE)

Steve Allen (NBC)

Leonard Bernstein (CBS)

Perry Como (NBC)

Tennessee Ernie Ford (NBC)

Alfred Hitchcock (CBS)

Bishop Fulton J. Sheen (ABC)

FEMALE PERSONALITY (CONTINUING PERFORMANCE)

Rosemary Clooney (Syndicated)

Faye Emerson (CBS)

Arlene Francis (CBS)

Gisele Mackenzie (NBC)

Dinah Shore (NBC)

OTHER AWARDS

News Coverage/News Event: *Years of Crisis*, year-end report with Edward R. Murrow and other correspondents (CBS); News Commentator: Edward R. Murrow (CBS); Public Service Series: *Omnibus* (CBS); Directing (One Hour or More): Ralph Nelson (*Requiem for a Heavyweight, Playhouse 90*) (CBS); Directing (Half-Hour or Less): Sheldon Leonard ("Danny's Comeback," *Make Room for Daddy*) (CBS); Teleplay Writing (One Hour or More): Rod Serling (*Requiem for a Heavyweight, Playhouse 90*) (CBS); Teleplay Writing (Half-Hour or Less): James P. Kavanagh ("Fog Closing In," *Alfred Hitchcock Presents*) (CBS); Comedy Writing: Nat Hiken, Billy Friedberg, Tony Webster, Leonard Stern, Arnold Rosen, Coleman Jacoby (*The Phil Silvers Show*) (CBS)

Attempting to garner more interest in the Emmys, the announcement of the nominees was made into a separate entertainment show of its own. (The Oscars put together a similar nominees' program for the previous two years, but abandoned the idea.) Steve Allen, Ernie Kovacs, Phil Silvers, and Kukla-and-Ollie puppeteer Burr Tilstrom appeared on the nominations show which boasted a script by Rod Serling.

The awards themselves were presented in color for the first time and sponsored by General Motors. This precluded appearances by several TV stars whose shows' bills were paid by rival car companies. Among the no-shows were Emmy Awards Committee chairman Ed Sullivan (a Ford-Mercury man), Jack Benny (Chrysler), and Lawrence Welk (Dodge-Chrysler). Welk pleaded a heavy work schedule as the real reason for his absence. But many conjectured it was a lack of a nomination for his champagne-music show that kept the bandleader away.

Another disgruntled performer was Ann Sothern. Though her performance in *Private Secretary* was in the running, the series itself was not among the best sitcom finalists.

The nominating procedure consisted of Academy members submitting candidates in their respective fields. The top twenty in each category were put on a reminder list and sent out with a nominating ballot. The top five vote-getters received the nominations.

"I'm not a crusader, but I'm really burned up about this," Sothern told *TV Guide*. "For the Emmy nominations, they sent us a reminder list of just 20 half-hour shows. They claim they sent everybody a letter asking us to submit names of shows to be put on the reminder list. But I never got one and I know other people who never got one." The Academy checked out Sothern's claim and found the letter had been sent to her business manager.

THE PEABODY AWARDS

ENTERTAINMENT
The Ed Sullivan Show (CBS)

EDUCATION
You Are There (CBS)

NEWS
ABC, John Daly, and associates for convention coverage

YOUTH AND CHILDREN'S PROGRAMS
Youth Wants to Know (NBC)

PUBLIC SERVICE
World in Crisis (CBS)

LOCAL AND REGIONAL PUBLIC SERVICE
"Regimental Raindrops" (WOW, Omaha)

WRITING
Rod Serling

PROMOTION OF INTERNATIONAL UNDERSTANDING
The Secret Life of Danny Kaye (UNICEF)

PROMOTION OF INTERNATIONAL UNDERSTANDING (SPECIAL AWARD)
United Nations Radio and Television

SPECIAL AWARD
Jack Gould of *The New York Times* (for writings on radio and television)

THE GOLDEN GLOBE AWARDS

Cheyenne (ABC); *Mickey Mouse Club* (ABC); *Playhouse 90* (CBS); *Matinee Theatre* (NBC); *This Is Your Life* (NBC)

THE EMMY AWARDS

SINGLE PROGRAM OF THE YEAR
The Comedian, Playhouse 90 (CBS)
The Edsel Show (CBS)
The Green Pastures, Hallmark Hall of Fame (NBC)
The Helen Morgan Story, Playhouse 90 (CBS)

For the third year in a row, a Rod Serling-scripted show dominated the drama division of the Emmys. *Patterns* and *Requiem for a Heavyweight* were followed by *The Comedian*, an unflattering portrait of a sadistic television comic. Ironically, the award was presented by Milton Berle, a rumored role model for the program's title character. "I wonder who they wrote that about," Berle quipped as he read the name of the winner.

DRAMA SERIES (CONTINUING CHARACTERS)
Gunsmoke (CBS)
Lassie (CBS)
Maverick (ABC)
Perry Mason (CBS)
Wagon Train (CBS)

DRAMA SERIES (ANTHOLOGY)
Alfred Hitchcock Presents (CBS)
Climax (CBS)
Hallmark Hall of Fame (NBC)
Playhouse 90 (CBS)
Studio One (CBS)

COMEDY SERIES
The Bob Cummings Show (CBS, NBC)
Caesar's Hour (NBC)
Father Knows Best (NBC)
The Jack Benny Show (CBS)
The Phil Silvers Show (CBS)

MUSICAL, VARIETY, AUDIENCE PARTICIPATION, OR QUIZ SHOW
The Dinah Shore Chevy Show (NBC)
The Ed Sullivan Show (CBS)
The Jack Paar Tonight Show (NBC)
The Perry Como Show (NBC)
The Steve Allen Show (NBC)

NEW PROGRAM OF THE YEAR
Leave It to Beaver (CBS)
The Jack Paar Tonight Show (NBC)
Maverick (ABC)
The Seven Lively Arts (CBS)
Wagon Train (NBC)

ACTOR (SINGLE PERFORMANCE, LEAD OR SUPPORTING)
Lee J. Cobb (*No Deadly Medicine, Studio One*) (CBS)
Mickey Rooney (*The Comedian, Playhouse 90*) (CBS)
Peter Ustinov (*The Life of Samuel Johnson, Omnibus*) (CBS)
David Wayne (*Heartbeat, Suspicion*) (NBC)
Ed Wynn (*On Borrowed Time, Hallmark Hall of Fame*) (NBC)

ACTRESS (SINGLE PERFORMANCE, LEAD OR SUPPORTING)
Julie Andrews (*Cinderella*) (CBS)
Polly Bergen (*The Helen Morgan Story, Playhouse 90*) (CBS)
Helen Hayes (*Mrs. Gilling and the Skyscraper, Alcoa Hour*) (NBC)
Piper Laurie (*The Deaf Heart, Studio One*) (CBS)
Teresa Wright (*The Miracle Worker, Playhouse 90*) (CBS)

ACTOR (DRAMA OR COMEDY SERIES)
James Arness (*Gunsmoke*) (CBS)
Bob Cummings (*The Bob Cummings Show*) (CBS, NBC)
Phil Silvers (*The Phil Silvers Show*) (CBS)
Danny Thomas (*The Danny Thomas Show*) (ABC, CBS)
Robert Young (*Father Knows Best*) (NBC)

Bob Cummings and Danny Thomas switched networks. *Make Room for Daddy* moved from ABC to

CBS and was renamed *The Danny Thomas Show*. Bob Cummings' sitcom shifted from CBS to NBC, as had Robert Young's *Father Knows Best* two years previously.

ACTRESS (DRAMA OR COMEDY SERIES)
Eve Arden (*The Eve Arden Show*) (CBS)
Spring Byington (*December Bride*) (CBS)
Jan Clayton (*Lassie*) (CBS)
Ida Lupino (*Mr. Adams and Eve*) (CBS)
Jane Wyatt (*Father Knows Best*) (NBC)

SUPPORTING ACTOR (DRAMA OR COMEDY SERIES)
Paul Ford (*The Phil Silvers Show*) (CBS)
William Frawley (*I Love Lucy*) (CBS)
Louis Nye (*The Steve Allen Show*) (NBC)
Carl Reiner (*Caesar's Hour*) (NBC)
Dennis Weaver (*Gunsmoke*) (CBS)

SUPPORTING ACTRESS (DRAMA OR COMEDY SERIES)
Ann B. Davis (*The Bob Cummings Show*) (CBS, NBC)
Pat Carroll (*Caesar's Hour*) (NBC)
Verna Felton (*December Bride*) (CBS)
Marion Lorne (*Sally*) (NBC)
Vivian Vance (*I Love Lucy*) (CBS)

OTHER AWARDS
Continuing Performance in a Series by a Comedian, Singer, Host, Dancer, MC, Announcer, Narrator, Panelist or Any Person Who Essentially Plays Him or Herself (Male): Jack Benny (*The Jack Benny Show*) (CBS); (Female): Dinah Shore (*The Dinah Shore Chevy Show*) (NBC)

Public Service Program or Series: *Omnibus* (CBS); Coverage of an Unscheduled Newsworthy Event: Coverage of the Rikers Island, New York, plane crash, *World News Round-Up* (CBS); News Commentary: Edward R. Murrow (*See It Now*) (CBS); Direction (One Hour or More): Bob Banner (*The Dinah Shore Chevy Show*) (NBC); Direction (Half-Hour or Less): Robert Stevens ("The Glass Eye," *Alfred Hitchcock Presents*) (CBS); Teleplay Writing (One Hour or More): Rod Serling (*The Comedian, Playhouse 90*) (CBS); Teleplay Writing (Half-Hour or Less): Paul Monash (*The Lonely Wizard, Schlitz Playhouse of Stars*) (CBS); Comedy Writing: Nat Hiken, Billy Friedberg, Phil Sharp, Terry Ryan, Coleman Jacoby, Arnold Rosen, Sidney Zelinka, A. J. Russell, Tony Webster (*The Phil Silvers Show*) (CBS)

"The Academy show was the biggest mess these eyes have encountered in nine straight years of tele-viewing; and let me tell you, I've seen some beauts," tartly commented Jo Coppola of the *New York Post* on the 1957 Emmys. Mistakes plagued the ceremony. Milton Berle took up so much extra time with his lengthy comedy monologue that a planned video montage of previous Emmy shows had to be scrapped. Eddie Cantor yelled at the teleprompter when he couldn't read it. A split screen musical number featuring James Garner and Shirley MacLaine in Hollywood singing and dancing simultaneously with Jill Corey and Louis Nye in New York did not come off well. The lyrics became jumbled because of a sound delay between the two coasts and the twin pictures never meshed properly.

Phil Silvers, the host for the East Coast portion of the show, provided the few comic highlights. When a platoon of his writers came on stage to collect their awards, the comic quipped, "But I'm a great ad-libber." Then shaking the hand of one of the nine scribes, Silvers said, "I don't think I've ever had the pleasure."

Despite the numerous flubs, the Emmys received their highest ratings to date, with seventy-three percent of the nation's sets tuned to the show.

Off-screen, the Academy of Television Arts and Sciences was dissolved and rechristened the National Academy of Television Arts and Sciences, with dual headquarters in Hollywood and New York. Ed Sullivan, who had campaigned for a bigger East Coast participation in the original Academy, was elected the new president.

THE PEABODY AWARDS

ENTERTAINMENT (NONMUSICAL)
Playhouse 90 (CBS)

ENTERTAINMENT (MUSICAL)
The Dinah Shore Chevy Show (NBC)

EDUCATION
The Heritage Series (WQED-TV, Pittsburgh)

NEWS
ABC for *Prologue '58* and other significant news coverage

NEWS (RADIO AND TELEVISION)
CBS for "depth and range"

LOCAL NEWS (RADIO AND TELEVISION)
Louis M. Lyons (WGBH, Boston)

YOUTH AND CHILDREN'S PROGRAMS
Captain Kangaroo (CBS)

LOCAL YOUTH AND CHILDREN'S PROGRAMS
Wunda Wunda (KING-TV, Seattle)

PUBLIC SERVICE
The Last Word (CBS)

LOCAL PUBLIC SERVICE
Panorama (KLZ-TV, Denver)

CONTRIBUTION TO INTERNATIONAL UNDERSTANDING
Bob Hope (NBC)

SPECIAL AWARDS
NBC for "outstanding contribution to education"; Westinghouse Broadcasting Company, Inc., for "its Boston Conference and the high quality of its public service broadcasting"

THE GOLDEN GLOBE AWARDS

Eddie Fisher; Alfred Hitchcock; Jack Benny; Mike Wallace

THE EMMY AWARDS

In an effort to match the Emmy eligibility period to the television season, programs broadcast between January of 1958 and February of 1959 were placed in award consideration. Another element to be extended was the number of categories. With new types of shows growing like weeds all over the television landscape, the Academy rushed to keep up with them. In response to the bewildering array of new classifications of awards, columnist Leo Mishkin called the nominees' list "the most complicated document since the federal government invented Form 1040 for registering income tax returns." There were now 197 nominees in forty-two categories—and on Emmy night it seemed as if *An Evening with Fred Astaire* won all of them.

SINGLE PROGRAM OF THE YEAR
An Evening with Fred Astaire (NBC)
Child of Our Time, Playhouse 90 (CBS)
Little Moon of Alban, Hallmark Hall of Fame (NBC)
The Old Man, Playhouse 90 (CBS)

Fred Astaire's first video special was a delightful hour of song and dance, but the Academy treated it as if it were the Second Coming. The special garnered a total of nine Emmys, winning in every category for which it was nominated. Objections were raised when Astaire himself won in the category of Actor (Single Performance). Why was a variety performer placed with the dramatic stars? His show was composed entirely of musical numbers with no dialogue scenes at all.

After an avalanche of letters, columns, and articles decrying the dancer's triumph in the dramatic category, Astaire offered to return the award. The Academy stuck by its guns and told him to keep it. But at the following year's ceremony, Astaire was nominated with the musical artists for his second special.

SPECIAL DRAMATIC PROGRAM (ONE HOUR OR LONGER)
The Bridge of San Luis Rey, The DuPont Show of the Month (CBS)

Fred Astaire and Barrie Chase in *An Evening with Fred Astaire*, which won nine 1958–59 Emmys.

Hamlet, The DuPont Show of the Month (CBS)
*The Hasty Heart, The DuPont Show
    of the Month* (CBS)
Johnny Belinda, Hallmark Hall of Fame (NBC)
Little Moon of Alban, *Hallmark Hall
    of Fame* (NBC)

DRAMATIC SERIES
(ONE HOUR OR LONGER)
Playhouse 90 (CBS)
The U.S. Steel Hour (CBS)

DRAMATIC SERIES
(LESS THAN ONE HOUR)
Alcoa-Goodyear Theatre (NBC)
Alfred Hitchcock Presents (CBS)
General Electric Theater (CBS)
The Loretta Young Show (NBC)
Naked City (ABC)
Peter Gunn (NBC)

COMEDY SERIES
The Bob Cummings Show (NBC)
The Danny Thomas Show (CBS)
Father Knows Best (NBC, CBS)
The Jack Benny Show (CBS)
The Phil Silvers Show (CBS)
The Red Skelton Show (CBS)

Note: This season *Father Knows Best* switched back to CBS from NBC.

MUSICAL OR VARIETY SERIES
The Dinah Shore Chevy Show (NBC)
The Perry Como Show (NBC)
The Steve Allen Show (NBC)

SPECIAL MUSICAL OR VARIETY
PROGRAM (ONE HOUR OR LONGER)
Art Carney Meets Peter and the Wolf (ABC)
An Evening with Fred Astaire (NBC)

WESTERN SERIES
Gunsmoke (CBS)
Have Gun Will Travel (CBS)
Maverick (ABC)
The Rifleman (ABC)
Wagon Train (NBC)

ACTOR (SINGLE PERFORMANCE)
Fred Astaire (*An Evening with Fred Astaire*) (NBC)
Robert Crawford (*Child of Our Time,
    Playhouse 90*) (CBS)
Paul Muni (*Last Clear Chance, Playhouse 90*)
    (CBS)
Christopher Plummer (*Little Moon of Alban,
    Hallmark Hall of Fame*) (CBS)
Mickey Rooney (*Eddie, Alcoa-Goodyear Theatre*)
    (CBS)
Rod Steiger (*A Town Has Turned to Dust,
    Playhouse 90*) (CBS)

ACTRESS (SINGLE PERFORMANCE)
Judith Anderson (*The Bridge of San Luis Rey, DuPont Show of the Month*) (CBS)
Julie Harris (*Little Moon of Alban, Hallmark Hall of Fame*) (NBC)
Helen Hayes (*One Red Rose for Christmas, The U.S. Steel Hour*) (CBS)
Piper Laurie (*The Days of Wine and Roses, Playhouse 90*) (CBS)
Geraldine Page (*The Old Man, Playhouse 90*) (CBS)
Maureen Stapleton (*All the King's Men, Kraft Television Theatre*) (NBC)

ACTOR (DRAMATIC SERIES)
James Arness (*Gunsmoke*) (CBS)
Richard Boone (*Have Gun Will Travel*) (CBS)
Raymond Burr (*Perry Mason*) (CBS)
James Garner (*Maverick*) (ABC)
Craig Stevens (*Peter Gunn*) (NBC)

Efrem Zimbalist, Jr. (*77 Sunset Strip*) (ABC)

When Raymond Burr grasped his new Emmy—for his portrayal of the dynamic attorney Perry Mason—one of the wings broke. It was returned to be repaired. When the actor clasped the repaired statuette with joy—the other wing broke.

ACTRESS (DRAMATIC SERIES)
Phyllis Kirk (*The Thin Man*) (NBC)
June Lockhart (*Lassie*) (CBS)
Jane Wyman (*Jane Wyman Theatre*) (NBC)
Loretta Young (*The Loretta Young Show*) (NBC)

ACTOR (COMEDY SERIES)
Jack Benny (*The Jack Benny Show*) (CBS)
Walter Brennan (*The Real McCoys*) (ABC)
Bob Cummings (*The Bob Cummings Show*) (NBC)
Phil Silvers (*The Phil Silvers Show*) (CBS)

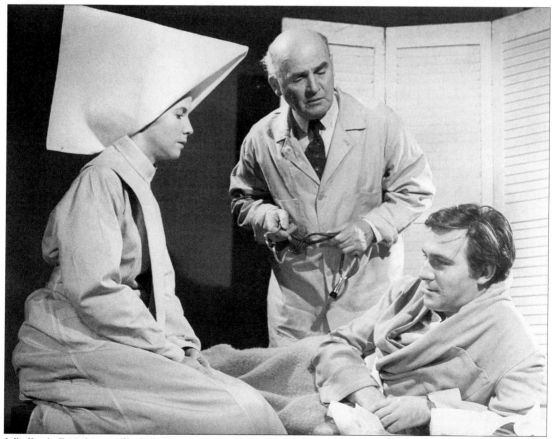

Julie Harris [best Actress (Single Performance) Emmy], Barry Jones, and Christopher Plummer in the *Hallmark Hall of Fame* presentation of *Little Moon of Alban* [1958–59 Emmy for best Special Dramatic Program (One Hour or Longer)].

Danny Thomas (*The Danny Thomas Show*) (CBS)
Robert Young (*Father Knows Best*) (NBC, CBS)

ACTRESS (COMEDY SERIES)
Gracie Allen (*The George Burns and Gracie Allen Show*) (CBS)
Spring Byington (*December Bride*) (CBS)
Ida Lupino (*Mr. Adams and Eve*) (CBS)
Donna Reed (*The Donna Reed Show*) (ABC)
Ann Sothern (*Private Secretary*) (CBS)
Jane Wyatt (*Father Knows Best*) (NBC, CBS)

ACTOR (MUSICAL OR VARIETY SERIES)
Steve Allen (*The Steve Allen Show*) (NBC)
Perry Como (*The Perry Como Show*) (NBC)
Jack Paar (*The Tonight Show*) (NBC)

ACTRESS (MUSICAL OR VARIETY SERIES)
Patti Page (*The Patti Page Show*) (ABC)
Dinah Shore (*The Dinah Shore Chevy Show*) (NBC)

SUPPORTING ACTOR (DRAMA SERIES)
Herschel Bernardi (*Peter Gunn*) (NBC)
Johnny Crawford (*The Rifleman*) (ABC)
William Hopper (*Perry Mason*) (CBS)
Dennis Weaver (*Gunsmoke*) (CBS)

SUPPORTING ACTRESS (DRAMA SERIES)
Lola Albright (*Peter Gunn*) (NBC)
Amanda Blake (*Gunsmoke*) (CBS)
Hope Emerson (*Peter Gunn*) (NBC)
Barbara Hale (*Perry Mason*) (CBS)

SUPPORTING ACTOR (COMEDY SERIES)
Richard Crenna (*The Real McCoys*) (ABC)
Paul Ford (*The Phil Silvers Show*) (CBS)
Maurice Gosfield (*The Phil Silvers Show*) (CBS)
Billy Gray (*Father Knows Best*) (ABC)
Harry Morgan (*December Bride*) (CBS)
Tom Poston (*The Steve Allen Show*) (NBC)

SUPPORTING ACTRESS (COMEDY SERIES)
Ann B. Davis (*The Bob Cummings Show*) (NBC)

Rosemary DeCamp (*The Bob Cummings Show*) (NBC)
Elinor Donahue (*Father Knows Best*) (NBC, CBS)
Verna Felton (*December Bride*) (CBS)
Kathy Nolan (*The Real McCoys*) (ABC)
Zasu Pitts (*Oh! Susanna*) (CBS)

DIRECTING AWARDS
Single Dramatic Program (One Hour or More): George Schaefer (*Little Moon of Alban, Hallmark Hall of Fame*) (NBC); Single Dramatic Program (Less Than One Hour): Jack Smight (*Eddie, Alcoa-Goodyear Theatre*) (NBC); Single Program of a Comedy Series: Peter Tewksbury ("Medal for Margaret," *Father Knows Best*) (CBS); Single Musical or Variety Program: Bud Yorkin (*An Evening with Fred Astaire*) (NBC)

WRITING AWARDS
Single Dramatic Program (One Hour or More): James Costigan (*Little Moon of Alban, Hallmark Hall of Fame*); Single Dramatic Program (Less Than One Hour): Alfred Brenner, Ken Hughes (*Eddie, Alcoa-Goodyear Theatre*) (NBC); Single Program of a Comedy Series: Sam Perrin, George Balzer, Hal Goodman, Al Gordon (*The Jack Benny Show* with guest star Ernie Kovacs) (CBS); Single Musical or Variety Program: Bud Yorkin, Herbert Baker (*An Evening with Fred Astaire*) (NBC)

For the first time, the Emmys were broadcast from three sites: the Moulin Rogue in Hollywood, the Ziegfeld Theatre in New York, and the Mayflower Hotel in Washington, DC, where many of the nominees in the news categories worked. Technical employees on strike against NBC (the network telecasting the program) picketed outside the various locations, many of them holding up Emmys that they had won in previous years. In Washington, several political figures, fearing to upset unions, refused to cross the picket line. Vice-President Richard Nixon cleverly solved the problem by showing up at the Mayflower before the protesters gathered.

The comedy team of Mike Nichols and Elaine May provided a savage satire on the whole awards process and on television itself. In a brief sketch, they presented a prize for Outstanding Mediocrity.

THE PEABODY AWARDS (FOR 1958)

DRAMATIC ENTERTAINMENT
Playhouse 90 (CBS)

ENTERTAINMENT WITH HUMOR
The Steve Allen Show (NBC)

MUSICAL ENTERTAINMENT
Lincoln Center Presents Leonard Bernstein and the New York Philharmonic (CBS)

EDUCATION
Continental Classroom (NBC)

NEWS
The Huntley-Brinkley Report (NBC)

PROGRAM FOR YOUTH
College News Conference (ABC)

PROGRAM FOR CHILDREN
The Blue Fairy (WGN-TV, Chicago)

PUBLIC SERVICE
CBS

WRITING
James Costigan (*Little Moon of Alban, Hallmark Hall of Fame*) (NBC)

CONTRIBUTION TO INTERNATIONAL UNDERSTANDING
M.D. International (NBC)

SPECIAL AWARDS
An Evening with Fred Astaire (NBC); Orson Welles (*Fountain of Youth, Colgate Theatre*) (NBC)

THE PEABODY AWARDS (FOR 1959)

ENTERTAINMENT (NONMUSICAL)
The Play of the Week (WNTA-TV, Newark); *The Moon and Sixpence* (NBC)

ENTERTAINMENT (MUSICAL)
The Bell Telephone Hour (NBC); *Great Music from Chicago* (WGN-TV, Chicago)

EDUCATION
"Decisions" (WGBH-TV, Boston, and the World Affairs Council); "The Population Explosion" (CBS)

NEWS
"Khrushchev Abroad" (ABC)

LOCAL PUBLIC SERVICE
WDSU-TV, New Orleans

CONTRIBUTIONS TO INTERNATIONAL UNDERSTANDING
The Ed Sullivan Show (CBS); *Small World* (CBS)

SPECIAL AWARDS
Dr. Frank Stanton (CBS); "The Lost Class of '59" (CBS)

THE GOLDEN GLOBE AWARDS (FOR 1958)

Paul Oates; Ann Sothern; Loretta Young; Red Skelton; Ed Sullivan; William Orr

THE GOLDEN GLOBE AWARDS (FOR 1959)

David Susskind; Chuck Connors; Pat Boone; *77 Sunset Strip* (ABC); Dinah Shore; Ed Sullivan; Edward R. Murrow

1959-60

THE EMMY AWARDS

PROGRAM ACHIEVEMENT IN DRAMA
Ethan Frome, DuPont Show of the Month (CBS)
The Moon and Sixpence (NBC)
Playhouse 90 (CBS)
The Turn of the Screw, Ford Startime (NBC)
The Untouchables (ABC)

PROGRAM ACHIEVEMENT IN HUMOR
VIP—Art Carney Special (NBC)
The Danny Thomas Show (CBS)
Father Knows Best (CBS)

The Jack Benny Show (CBS)
The Red Skelton Show (NBC)

PROGRAM ACHIEVEMENT IN VARIETY
Another Evening with Fred Astaire (NBC)
The Dinah Shore Chevy Show (NBC)
The Fabulous Fifties (CBS)
The Garry Moore Show (CBS)
Tonight with Belafonte: The Revlon Revue (CBS)

ACTOR (SINGLE PERFORMANCE, LEAD OR SUPPORTING)
Lee J. Cobb (*Project Immortality, Playhouse 90*) (CBS)
Alec Guinness (*The Wicked Scheme of Jebal Deeks, Ford Startime*) (NBC)
Laurence Olivier (*The Moon and Sixpence*) (NBC)

The leading single-performance actor and actress awards were taken by film stars in adaptations of literary classics. Laurence Olivier was heralded for his portrayal of a Paul Gaugin-like artist in Somerset Maugham's *The Moon and Sixpence*, while Ingrid Bergman won as the governess in a presentation based on Henry James's suspense story *The Turn of the Screw*.

Neither was present to accept the prize. Sir Laurence had asked his *Moon* co-star Hume Cronyn to accept for him, but NBC wanted Charlton Heston (a movie actor with larger marquee value than the stage veteran Cronyn). Heston stated, "I will say something that Larry never would say himself—he deserves it."

ACTRESS (SINGLE PERFORMANCE, LEAD OR SUPPORTING)
Ingrid Bergman (*The Turn of the Screw, Ford Startime*) (NBC)
Julie Harris (*Ethan Frome, DuPont Show of the Month*) (CBS)
Teresa Wright (*The Margaret Bourke-White Story, Breck Sunday Showcase*) (NBC)

ACTOR (SERIES, LEAD OR SUPPORTING)
Richard Boone (*Have Gun Will Travel*) (CBS)
Raymond Burr (*Perry Mason*) (CBS)
Robert Stack (*The Untouchables*) (ABC)

Desi Arnaz, the producer of Robert Stack's *Untouchables* series, had a $12,000 Mercedes Benz waiting for the star in the parking lot of the Emmy show as a reward. "I was going to give it to you win or lose," the producer/actor told Stack after the latter's victory for his portrayal of the tough FBI agent Elliott Ness. The series had begun life as a segment of *Desilu Playhouse*, an anthology series from the studio owned by Arnaz and Lucille Ball.

ACTRESS (SERIES, LEAD OR SUPPORTING)
Donna Reed (*The Donna Reed Show*) (ABC)
Jane Wyatt (*Father Knows Best*) (CBS)
Loretta Young (*The Loretta Young Show*) (NBC)

PERFORMANCE IN A VARIETY SERIES OR SPECIAL
Fred Astaire (*Another Evening with Fred Astaire*) (NBC)
Harry Belafonte (*Tonight with Belafonte, The Revlon Revue*) (CBS)
Dinah Shore (*The Dinah Shore Chevy Show*) (NBC)

Learning a lesson from the 1958–59 Astaire uproar, the Emmy nominators placed Fred Astaire with the musical variety performers rather than the actors for his second special. But Astaire lost to Calypso singer Harry Belafonte, the first African-American to win an Emmy.

OTHER AWARDS
Directing (Drama): Robert Mulligan (*The Moon and Sixpence*) (NBC); Directing (Comedy): Ralph Levy, Bud Yorkin (*The Jack Benny Specials*) (CBS); Writing (Drama): Rod Serling (*The Twilight Zone*) (CBS); Writing (Comedy): Sam Perrin, George Balzer, Al Gordon, Hal Goldman (*The Jack Benny Show*) (CBS); Writing (Documentary): Howard K. Smith, Av Westin ("The Population Explosion," *CBS Reports*) (CBS)

Variety called the 1959–60 Emmys "easily the best of the series." In an effort to speed up the proceedings and quell cracks about confusing categories, the NATAS cut the number of categories from the previous year's forty-two to a more managable twenty-three. Former winner Jack Webb was among those who heaved a sigh of relief. "There were so many categories, you'd get dizzy just scanning the ballot," he told *The New York Herald-Tribune.* Leading and supporting acting categories were combined and the Outstanding Program of the Year slot was eliminated altogether.

The show was hosted by Fred Astaire in Hollywood and Arthur Godfrey in New York. But the real star was Bob Newhart, an unknown Chicago comic whose dry humor satirized everyday frustrations. Newhart got to perform two of his monologues when a sketch by Mike Nichols and Elaine May was pulled from the broadcast.

As a result of this lucky break and the subsequent exposure, the comedian got his own NBC series (later to win a Peabody and an Emmy) and a solo comedy album (a Grammy winner).

THE PEABODY AWARDS (FOR 1960)

ENTERTAINMENT
The Fabulous Fifties (CBS)

EDUCATION
White Paper series (NBC)

NEWS
The Huntley-Brinkley Report (NBC)

PROGRAM FOR YOUTH
GE College Bowl (CBS)

PROGRAM FOR CHILDREN
The Shari Lewis Show (NBC)

PUBLIC SERVICE
CBS Reports (CBS)

CONTRIBUTION TO INTERNATIONAL UNDERSTANDING
CBS for its Olympic coverage

EDUCATION (RADIO AND TELEVISION)
Broadcasting and Film Commission, National Council of Churches of Christ in the USA

LOCALLY PRODUCED PROGRAMS
WOOD and WOOD-TV, Grand Rapids; WCKT-TV, Miami; WCCO-TV, Minneapolis; KPFR-FM, Los Angeles

SPECIAL AWARD
Dr. Frank Stanton (CBS)

THE GOLDEN GLOBE AWARDS (FOR 1960)

Hanna-Barbera Presents (Syndicated); *Perry Mason* (CBS); *Bell Telephone Hour* (NBC); *Hong Kong* (ABC); Walter Cronkite

1960–61

THE EMMY AWARDS

PROGRAM OF THE YEAR
Astaire Time (NBC)
Convention Coverage (NBC)
An Hour with Danny Kaye (CBS)
Macbeth, Hallmark Hall of Fame (NBC)
Sacco-Vanzetti (NBC)

In theatrical circles, it's considered bad luck to mention *Macbeth.* But for the *Hallmark Hall of Fame,* Shakespeare's play of the ambitious Scottish king was extremely good luck. A lavish color production, filmed on location in Scotland, took five awards—six if you count a special prize to Hallmark Cards, the show's sponsor. "Only the author failed to garner one of the coveted statuettes," joked *The New York Times.* In 1954, Hallmark had previously presented a live version of the play with the same leads, Maurice Evans and Judith Anderson.

There was some criticism that this new *Macbeth* should not have been considered for a TV prize because it was shot and produced as if it were a film. Indeed, it was shown in selected movie theaters in the U.S. and abroad.

In addition to *Macbeth,* many of the '60–'61 Emmy winners were filmed shows, pointing the way to the future of TV. Many critics lamented the loss of the intimacy of live broadcasts.

Judith Anderson
and Maurice Evans
in the elaborate
1960–61 *Hallmark
Hall of Fame*
remake of
Macbeth..

PROGRAM ACHIEVEMENT IN DRAMA
Naked City (ABC)
Macbeth, Hallmark Hall of Fame (NBC)
Sacco-Vanzetti (NBC)
The Twilight Zone (CBS)
The Untouchables (ABC)

PROGRAM ACHIEVEMENT IN HUMOR
The Andy Griffith Show (CBS)
The Bob Hope Buick Show (NBC)
Candid Camera (CBS)
The Flintstones (ABC)
The Jack Benny Show (CBS)

On the day of the Emmys, Jack Benny served as a pallbearer at Gary Cooper's funeral and elected not to attend the awards cermony.

Sidelight: *The Flintstones* was the first animated program to be nominated in a prime-time category.

PROGRAM ACHIEVEMENT IN VARIETY
Astaire Time (NBC)
Belafonte (CBS)
The Garry Moore Show (CBS)
An Hour with Danny Kaye (CBS)
The Jack Paar Tonight Show (NBC)

ACTOR (SINGLE PERFORMANCE)
Maurice Evans (*Macbeth, Hallmark Hall of Fame*) (NBC)
Cliff Robertson (*The Two Worlds of Charlie Gordon, The U.S. Steel Hour*) (CBS)
Ed Wynn (*The Man in the Funny Suit, Westinghouse-Desilu Playhouse*) (CBS)

ACTRESS (SINGLE PERFORMANCE)
Judith Anderson (*Macbeth, Hallmark Hall of Fame*) (NBC)
Ingrid Bergman (*24 Hours in a Woman's Life*) (CBS)
Elizabeth Montgomery ("The Rusty Heller Story," *The Untouchables*) (ABC)

ACTOR (SERIES, LEAD)
Raymond Burr (*Perry Mason*) (CBS)
Jackie Cooper (*Hennesey*) (CBS)
Robert Stack (*The Untouchables*) (ABC)

ACTRESS (SERIES, LEAD)
Donna Reed (*The Donna Reed Show*) (ABC)
Barbara Stanwyck (*The Barbara Stanwyck Show*) (NBC)
Loretta Young (*The Loretta Young Show*) (NBC)

As she was leaving her seat to accept her award, Barbara Stanwyck ripped the back of her gown. A gentleman in the audience helped her on with a coat while the audience continued applauding. Host Joey Bishop later cracked, "The guy who helped Barbara Stanwyck on with her coat was on camera longer than I was!"

SUPPORTING ACTOR OR ACTRESS (SINGLE PERFORMANCE)
Charles Bronson (*Memory in White, General Electric Theatre*) (CBS)
Peter Falk ("Cold Turkey," *The Law and Mr. Jones*) (ABC)
Roddy McDowall (*Not without Honor, Equitable's American Heritage*) (NBC)

SUPPORTING ACTOR OR ACTRESS (SERIES)
Abby Dalton (*Hennesey*) (ABC)
Barbara Hale (*Perry Mason*) (CBS)
Don Knotts (*The Andy Griffith Show*) (CBS)

Rule change: Supporting performances were once again divided from leading ones. Don Knotts of *The Andy Griffith Show* would win a total of five Emmys for his portrayal of Barney Fife, the scrawny, lovable blowhard deputy of Mayberry, North Carolina. His co-star Andy Griffith failed to collect a single Emmy.

VARIETY OR MUSICAL PERFORMANCE (SERIES OR SPECIAL)
Fred Astaire (*Astaire Time*) (NBC)
Harry Belafonte (*Belafonte N.Y.*) (CBS)
Dinah Shore (*The Dinah Shore Chevy Show*) (NBC)

OTHER AWARDS
Directing (Drama): George Schaefer (*Macbeth, Hallmark Hall of Fame*) (NBC); Directing (Comedy): Sheldon Leonard (*The Danny Thomas Show*) (CBS); Writing (Drama): Rod Serling (*The Twilight Zone*) (CBS); Writing (Comedy): Sherwood Schwartz, Dave O'Brien, Al Schwartz, Martin Ragaway, Red Skelton (*The Red Skelton Show*) (CBS); Writing (Documentary): Victor Wolfson (*Winston Churchill: The Valiant Years*)

The Emmycast was chockful of comedy routines which were performed with varying results. Dan Blocker and Lorne Greene acted out spoofy foreign versions of their Western *Bonanza*. In another sketch, the *Dobie Gillis* cast became members of the Nielsen ratings family. From New Mexico, *Route 66* stars Martin Milner and George Maharis demonstrated the advantages of on-location filming. Cartoon characters Huckleberry Hound and Yogi Bear got mixed up in a ratings machine. The best received bit was a parody of Shakespeare performed by *Gunsmoke*'s Dennis Weaver. With deadpan seriousness, he asked "TV or not TV."

THE PEABODY AWARDS (FOR 1961)

ENTERTAINMENT
The Bob Newhart Show (NBC)

EDUCATION
An Age of Kings (BBC); *Vincent Van Gogh: A Self-Portrait* (NBC)

NEWS
David Brinkley's Journal (NBC)

YOUTH AND CHILDREN'S PROGRAMS
Expedition! (ABC)

PUBLIC SERVICE
Let Freedom Ring! (KSL-TV, Salt Lake City)

CONTRIBUTION TO INTERNATIONAL UNDERSTANDING
Walter Lippmann and CBS

SPECIAL AWARDS
Fred W. Friendly, CBS; Newton N. Minow, chairman, Federal Communications Commission; Capital Cities Broadcasting Corporation, for "Verdict for Tomorrow: The Eichmann Trial on Television"

THE GOLDEN GLOBE AWARDS (FOR 1961)

Outstanding Programs: *What's My Line?* (CBS), *My Three Sons* (CBS); Male Television Stars: Bob Newhart, John Daly; Female Television Star: Pauline Fredericks

1961-62

THE EMMY AWARDS

PROGRAM OF THE YEAR
"Biography of a Bookie Joint," *CBS Reports* (CBS)
The Judy Garland Show (CBS)
Victoria Regina, Hallmark Hall of Fame (NBC)
Vincent Van Gogh: A Self-Portrait (NBC)
"Walk in My Shoes," *Bell and Howell Closeup* (ABC)

The TV Academy came under fire once again for its confusing categories. The diverse nominees for Program of the Year included three documentaries, a variety special starring the great Judy Garland, and *Hallmark Hall of Fame*'s ninety-minute version of Laurence Housman's biodrama on Queen Victoria. Critics cried Emmy voters would be com-

paring apples and oranges. There was an even louder outcry when *Victoria Regina* won for outstanding overall program, but lost in the drama category to CBS's legal series *The Defenders*. How fair was it to compare a single program to an entire series?

PROGRAM ACHIEVEMENT IN DRAMA
Ben Casey (ABC)
The Defenders (CBS)
Dick Powell Theatre (NBC)
Naked City (ABC)
People Need People, Alcoa Premiere (ABC)
Victoria Regina, Hallmark Hall of Fame (NBC)

Despite its controversial subject matter (including an episode on abortion), *The Defenders* won all four of the Emmys for which it was nominated. The critically praised courtroom drama about a father-and-son law firm would go on to win nine more statuettes.

PROGRAM ACHIEVEMENT IN HUMOR
The Andy Griffith Show (CBS)
The Bob Newhart Show (NBC)
Car 54, Where Are You? (NBC)
Hazel (NBC)
The Red Skelton Show (NBC)

This Emmy victory was bittersweet for Bob Newhart. His unconventional variety series had been canceled by NBC a month before the awards. To add ironic insult to injury, the program had also copped a prestigous Peabody Award in 1961. Newhart would return to the airwaves as a Chicago psychologist (*The Bob Newhart Show*) and a Vermont innkeeper (*Newhart*). Neither long-running, popular sitcom would win an Emmy.

PROGRAM ACHIEVEMENT IN VARIETY
The Garry Moore Show (CBS)
Here's Edie (ABC)
The Judy Garland Show (CBS)
The Kraft Music Hall (NBC)
Walt Disney's Wonderful World of Color (NBC)

PROGRAM ACHIEVEMENT IN MUSIC
The Bell Telephone Hour (NBC)
Leonard Bernstein and the New York Philharmonic in Japan (CBS)

NBC Opera (NBC)
The Thief and the Hangman (ABC)

ACTOR (SINGLE PERFORMANCE)
Milton Berle ("Doyle against the House," *Dick Powell Theatre*) (NBC)
James Donald (*Victoria Regina, Hallmark Hall of Fame*) (NBC)
Peter Falk ("The Price of Tomatoes," *Dick Powell Theatre*) (NBC)
Lee Marvin (*People Need People, Alcoa Premiere*) (ABC)
Mickey Rooney ("Somebody's Waiting," *Dick Powell Theatre*) (NBC)

ACTRESS (SINGLE PERFORMANCE)
Geraldine Brooks ("Call Back Yesterday," *Bus Stop*) (ABC)
Julie Harris (*Victoria Regina, Hallmark Hall of Fame*) (NBC)
Suzanne Pleshette ("Shining Image," *Dr. Kildare*) (NBC)
Inger Stevens ("The Price of Tomatoes," *Dick Powell Theatre*) (NBC)
Ethel Waters ("Goodnight, Sweet Blues," *Route 66*) (CBS)

Ethel Waters was the first black woman to be nominated in the drama category.

ACTOR (SERIES)
Paul Burke (*Naked City*) (ABC)
Jackie Cooper (*Hennesey*) (CBS)
Vincent Edwards (*Ben Casey*) (ABC)
George Maharis (*Route 66*) (CBS)
E. G. Marshall (*The Defenders*) (CBS)

ACTRESS (SERIES)
Gertrude Berg (*The Gertrude Berg Show*) (CBS)
Shirley Booth (*Hazel*) (NBC)
Donna Reed (*The Donna Reed Show*) (ABC)
Mary Stuart (*Search for Tomorrow*) (CBS)
Cara Williams (*Pete and Gladys*) (CBS)

With her triumph as the no-nonsense sitcom maid *Hazel*, Shirley Booth became the third performer to place an Oscar, Tony, and Emmy on her mantle (Helen Hayes and Thomas Mitchell preceded her). Mary Stuart of the soap opera *Search for Tomorrow*

was the first daytime performer to receive an Emmy nomination.

SUPPORTING ACTOR
Sam Jaffe (*Ben Casey*) (ABC)
Don Knotts (*The Andy Griffith Show*) (CBS)
Barry Jones (*Victoria Regina, The Hallmark Hall of Fame*) (NBC)
Horace McMahon (*Naked City*) (ABC)
George C. Scott ("I Remember a Lemon Tree," *Ben Casey*) (ABC)

SUPPORTING ACTRESS
Pamela Brown (*Victoria Regina, Hallmark Hall of Fame*) (NBC)
Jeanne Cooper ("But Linda Only Smiled," *Ben Casey*) (ABC)
Colleen Dewhurst (*Focus*) (NBC)
Joan Hackett ("A Certain Time, A Certain Darkness," *Ben Casey*) (ABC)
Mary Wickes (*The Gertrude Berg Show*) (CBS)

PERFORMANCE IN VARIETY OR MUSICAL PROGRAM OR SERIES
Edie Adams (*Here's Edie*) (ABC)
Carol Burnett (*The Garry Moore Show*) (CBS)
Perry Como (*The Kraft Music Hall*) (NBC)
Judy Garland (*The Judy Garland Show*) (CBS)
Yves Montand (*Yves Montand on Broadway*) (ABC)

OTHER AWARDS
Directing (Drama): Franklin Schaffner (*The Defenders*) (CBS); Directing (Comedy): Nat Hiken (*Car 54, Where Are You?*) (NBC); Writing (Drama): Reginald Rose (*The Defenders*) (CBS); Writing (Comedy): Carl Reiner (*The Dick Van Dyke Show*) (CBS); Writing (Documentary): Lou Hazam (*Vincent Van Gogh: A Self-Portrait*) (NBC)

The two biggest stars of the 1961–62 TV season didn't even have their own shows. Astronaut Colonel John Glenn making the first orbit around the Earth and First Lady Jacqueline Kennedy's tour of the White House were the most significant video events of the year. The NATAS acknowledged both historic occasions with special Emmys. All three networks received an award for their pooled coverage of Col. Glenn's space journey. Mrs. Kennedy and CBS, which produced the

White House program, were also honored. Neither the astronaut nor the First Lady was present at the awards ceremony, which was broadcast from three locations: Hollywood (hosted by Bob Newhart), New York (Johnny Carson), and Washington, DC (David Brinkley).

The show was streamlined and devoid of forced humor in the form of TV stars performing specialty sketches. *Variety* had called previous Emmy sketches "more deadly than funny." So instead of a series of tired comedy bits, producer Fred Coe assembled a montage of clips featuring video highlights of the past season. These included Jack Paar's tearful farewell as he ended his reign as *The Tonight Show* host to be succeeded by Johnny Carson; Judy Garland's stunning performance on her variety special; Edie Adams imitating Marilyn Monore; and a tribute to Adams' late husband, the innovative comedian Ernie Kovacs who had recently died in an automobile accident.

Best acceptance speech: Carl Reiner for his *Dick Van Dyke Show* scripts, saying, "I wish someone had told me. I would have worn my hair."

Rule changes: Academy members could now submit candidates for nominees on a monthly basis rather than only once in the spring. It was thought this would give a fairer chance to programs aired earlier in the year. The supporting category would be split between women and men rather than having members of both sexes compete against each other. Daytime categories were added.

THE PEABODY AWARDS (FOR 1962)

ENTERTAINMENT
Carol Burnett (CBS); *The DuPont Show of the Week* (NBC)

EDUCATION
Biography (Official Films, Inc.)

NEWS
Walter Cronkite (CBS)

YOUTH AND CHILDREN'S PROGRAMS
Exploring (NBC); *Walt Disney's Wonderful World of Color* (NBC)

PUBLIC SERVICE
A Tour of the White House With Mrs. John F. Kennedy (CBS)

CONTRIBUTION TO INTERNATIONAL UNDERSTANDING
Adlai Stevenson Reports (ABC)

LOCALLY PRODUCED PROGRAMS
Books of Our Time (WNDT-TV, New York); *Elliott Norton Reviews* (WGBH-TV, Boston); *San Francisco Paegant* (KPIX-TV, San Francisco)

SPECIAL AWARDS
William McAndrew and NBC News; Television Information Office of the National Association of Broadcasting (for a study of local children's programming)

THE GOLDEN GLOBE AWARDS (FOR 1962)

Outstanding TV Programs: *The Dick Powell Theatre* (NBC); *The Defenders* (CBS); *Mister Ed* (CBS); Male TV Stars: Richard Chamberlain, Rod Serling; Female TV Star: Donna Reed; Special Award to the Telstar communications satellite

1962-63

THE EMMY AWARDS

PROGRAM OF THE YEAR
The Danny Kaye Show with Lucille Ball (NBC)
"The Madman," *The Defenders* (CBS)
The Tunnel (NBC)
The Voice of Charlie Pont, Alcoa Premiere (ABC)

For the first time, a news show was named Program of the Year. *The Tunnel* was an NBC, ninety-minute documentary following the efforts of a group of West German students to dig under the Berlin Wall. NBC financed the diggers, which led to some ethical questions in the press about manufacturing news. The State Department initially objected to the program as not being in the best interests of America. After it was broadcast, the objection was withdrawn and *The Tunnel* was shown overseas by the U.S. Information Agency.

PROGRAM ACHIEVEMENT IN DRAMA
Alcoa Premiere (ABC)
The Defenders (CBS)
The Dick Powell Show (NBC)
The Eleventh Hour (NBC)
Naked City (ABC)

PROGRAM ACHIEVEMENT IN HUMOR
The Beverly Hillbillies (CBS)
The Danny Kaye Show with Lucille Ball (NBC)
The Dick Van Dyke Show (CBS)
McHale's Navy (ABC)

In its second season, *The Dick Van Dyke Show* swept the comedy awards, winning for writing, directing, and as outstanding comedy series. The sharp sitcom dealt with the adventures of TV comedy writer Rob Petrie. It went on to win the top award a total of four times, tying with *All in the Family* and *Cheers* for most wins in that category.

The *DVD Show* was nearly canceled in its first season and faced stiff Emmy competition from *The Beverly Hillbillies*, a lowbrow concoction which ranked No. 1 in the Nielsen ratings for several years. But quality did win out and the *Hillbillies* went home Emmyless.

PROGRAM ACHIEVEMENT IN VARIETY
The Andy Williams Show (NBC)
Carol & Company (CBS)
The Garry Moore Show (CBS)
Here's Edie (ABC)
The Red Skelton Hour (CBS)

Bob Finkel briefly took time off from the hectic backstage job of producing the Emmy broadcast in order to accept the award for *The Andy Williams Show*, which he also produced. Prior to the ceremony, NBC had announced Williams' program would not be returning the following fall. The Emmy win may have influenced the network brass to reverse their decision and pick up the series, which lasted until 1967. Williams would go on to have a total of three prime-time and one syndicated series which bore his name.

PROGRAM ACHIEVEMENT IN MUSIC
The Bell Telephone Hour (NBC)
Julie and Carol at Carnegie Hall (CBS)
Judy Garland (CBS)
The Lively Ones (NBC)
NBC Opera (NBC)

ACTOR (SINGLE PERFOMANCE)
Bradford Dillman (*The Voice of Charlie Pont, Alcoa Premiere*) (ABC)
Don Gordon ("The Madman," *The Defenders*) (CBS)
Trevor Howard (*The Invincible Mr. Disraeli, Hallmark Hall of Fame* (NBC)
Walter Matthau (*Big Deal in Laredo, DuPont Show of the Week*) (NBC)
Jospeh Schildkraut ("Hear the Mellow Wedding Bells," *Sam Benedict*) (NBC)

ACTRESS (SINGLE PERFORMANCE)
Diahann Carroll ("A Horse Has a Big Head, Let Him Worry," *Naked City*) (ABC)
Diana Hyland (*The Voice of Charlie Pont, Alcoa Premiere*) (ABC)
Eleanor Parker ("Why Am I Grown So Cold?" *The Eleventh Hour*) (NBC)
Kim Stanley ("A Cardinal Act of Mercy," *Ben Casey*) (ABC)
Sylvia Sidney ("The Madman," *The Defenders*) (CBS)

Anthology shows were on the wane, as can be seen by the increasing number of single-performance nominees for guest shots on continuing doctor and lawyer series. Trevor Howard won for playing Queen Victoria's Prime Minister Benjamin Disraeli on a *Hallmark Hall of Fame* drama, while Kim Stanley triumphed for a segment of the medical show *Ben Casey* in which she played a drug-addicted lawyer. Former film star Glenda Farrell won a supporting Emmy for the same episode.

ACTOR (SERIES)
Ernest Borgnine (*McHale's Navy*) (ABC)
Paul Burke (*Naked City*) (ABC)
E. G. Marshall (*The Defenders*) (CBS)
Vic Morrow (*Combat*) (ABC)
Dick Van Dyke (*The Dick Van Dyke Show*) (CBS)

Carol Burnett and
E. G. Marshall with
their 1962–63
Emmys.

ACTRESS (SERIES)
Lucille Ball (*The Lucy Show*) (CBS)
Shirley Booth (*Hazel*) (NBC)
Shirl Conway (*The Nurses*) (CBS)
Mary Tyler Moore (*The Dick Van Dyke Show*)
(CBS)
Irene Ryan (*The Beverly Hillbillies*) (CBS)

SUPPORTING ACTOR
Tim Conway (*McHale's Navy*) (ABC)
Paul Ford (*The Teahouse of the August Moon,
Hallmark Hall of Fame*) (NBC)

Hurd Hatfield (*The Invincible Mr. Disraeli,
Hallmark Hall of Fame*) (NBC)
Don Knotts (*The Andy Griffith Show*) (CBS)
Robert Redford (*The Voice of Charlie Pont,
Alcoa Premiere*) (ABC)

SUPPORTING ACTRESS
Davey Davison ("Of Roses and Nightingales
and Other Lovely Things," *The Eleventh Hour*)
(NBC)
Glenda Farrell ("A Cardinal Act of Mercy,"
Ben Casey) (ABC)

Nancy Malone (*Naked City*) (ABC)
Rose Marie (*The Dick Van Dyke Show*) (CBS)
Kate Reid (*The Invincible Mr. Disraeli*,
    The Hallmark Hall of Fame) (NBC)

PERFORMANCE IN VARIETY OR MUSICAL SERIES OR PROGRAM

Edie Adams (*Here's Edie*) (ABC)
Carol Burnett (*Julie and Carol at Carnegie Hall*
    and *Carol & Company*) (CBS)
Merv Griffin (*The Merv Griffin Show*) (NBC)
Danny Kaye (*The Danny Kaye Show with*
    Lucille Ball) (NBC)
Andy Williams (*The Andy Williams Show*) (NBC)

OTHER AWARDS

News Program: *The Huntley-Brinkley Report*
(NBC); News Commentary or Public Affairs
Program: *David Brinkley's Journal* (NBC);
Documentary Program: *The Tunnel* (NBC);
International Reporting or Commentary: Piers
Anderton (*The Tunnel*) (NBC); Panel, Quiz or
Audience Participation Program: *G.E. College Bowl*
(CBS); Children's Program: *Walt Disney's
Wonderful World of Color* (NBC)

Directing (Drama): Stuart Rosenberg ("The
Madman," *The Defenders*) (CBS); Directing
(Comedy): John Rich (*The Dick Van Dyke Show*)
(CBS); Writing (Drama): Robert Thom, Reginald
Rose ("The Madman," *The Defenders*) (CBS);
Writing (Comedy): Carl Reiner (*The Dick Van
Dyke Show*) (CBS)

"This is where you find out that the shows you
turned off all winter were the best TV has to offer."
So ran New York host Arthur Godfrey's opening
remarks to the 1962–63 Emmys. He was referring
to the fact that many of the winning shows
(including last year's *The Bob Newhart Show*) had
been axed due to low ratings. Joey Bishop, emcee
in Hollywood, put it more succinctly: "I'd like to
let the winners get their awards before their shows
are canceled."

Once again, Emmy came to TV viewers from
three cities (NBC's Chet Huntley was the
Washington host). One of the highlights was a
greeting from London via the new Telstar communications satellite. Unfortunately, Telstar's pass
occurred at the wrong time. Ironically, America's

introduction to transatlantic transmission had to be
taped.

THE PEABODY AWARDS (FOR 1963)

ENTERTAINMENT
The Danny Kaye Show (CBS); *Mr. Novack* (NBC)

EDUCATION
The American Revolution '63 (NBC); *Saga of
Western Man* (ABC)

NEWS
Eric Sevareid (CBS)

PROGRAM FOR YOUTH
The Dorothy Gordon Forum (WNBC-TV,
New York)

PROGRAM FOR CHILDREN
Treetop House (WGN-TV, Chicago)

PUBLIC SERVICE
"Storm over the Supreme Court," *CBS Reports*
(CBS)

CONTRIBUTION TO INTERNATIONAL UNDERSTANDING
"Town Meeting of the World," CBS and Dr.
Frank Stanton, president

SPECIAL AWARD
To the Broadcasting industry for its coverage of
President John F. Kennedy and related events

THE GOLDEN GLOBE AWARDS (FOR 1963)

Outstanding Programs: *The Richard Boone Show*
(NBC), *The Danny Kaye Show* (CBS), *The Dick
Van Dyke Show* (CBS); Male TV Star: Mickey
Rooney; Female TV Star: Inger Stevens

THE EMMY AWARDS

PROGRAM OF THE YEAR
The American Revolution of '63 (NBC)
"Blacklist," *The Defenders* (CBS)
The Kremlin (NBC)
The Making of the President (ABC)
Town Meeting of the World (CBS)

News overwhelmed this category for 1963–64. Four out of the five nominees were documentary programs. Despite the presence of a CBS program among the nominees, Fred Friendly, president of the news division of the Big Eye network, announced a boycott of the Emmys. (Many industry insiders stated that CBS was merely jealous because NBC's *The Huntley-Brinkley Report* had won so many times.) In an inter-office memo to news employees, Friendly was most unfriendly to the awards: "Although they purport to be the best judgement of the TV industry about its own best work, in reality they are the end result of pressure, politics, and, in the case of news, lack of professional judgement."

Thomas W. Moore, president of ABC, followed suit and pulled his entire network out of the Emmys. James Aubrey, head of CBS, soon followed, taking the entertainment division along with the news department. Independent producers David Susskind (*East Side, West Side*) and Herbert Brodkin (*The Defenders, The Nurses*) also critized the awards and resigned from the Academy. The boycott was largely symbolic, with only CBS and ABC network executives not attending the NBC-broadcast ceremony. (Ironically, CBS came out on top with thirteen awards.) Even George C. Scott, who had previously refused an Oscar nomination and would later refuse the Oscar itself, stated he would accept the Emmy (for his role as a social worker on the canceled *East Side, West Side*) if he won. The entire nominating system was revamped as a result of the controversy.

PROGRAM ACHIEVEMENT IN DRAMA
Bob Hope Presents the Chrysler Theater (NBC)

The Defenders (CBS)
East Side, West Side (CBS)
Mr. Novack (NBC)
The Richard Boone Show (NBC)

PROGRAM ACHIEVEMENT IN COMEDY
The Bill Dana Show (NBC)
The Dick Van Dyke Show (CBS)
The Farmer's Daughter (ABC)
McHale's Navy (ABC)
That Was the Week That Was (NBC)

PROGRAM ACHIEVEMENT IN VARIETY
The Andy Williams Show
The Danny Kaye Show (CBS)
The Garry Moore Show (CBS)
The Judy Garland Show (CBS)
The Tonight Show Starring Johnny Carson (NBC)

PROGRAM ACHIEVEMENT IN MUSIC
The Bell Telephone Hour (NBC)
The Lively Ones (NBC)
New York Philharmonic Young People's Concerts with Leonard Bernstein (CBS)

ACTOR (SINGLE PERFORMANCE)
James Earl Jones ("Who Do You Kill?" *East Side, West Side*) (CBS)
Jack Klugman ("Blacklist," *The Defenders*) (CBS)
Roddy McDowall ("Journey into Darkness," *Arrest and Trial*) (ABC)
Jason Robards, Jr. (*Abe Lincoln in Illinois, Hallmark Hall of Fame*) (NBC)
Rod Steiger (*A Slow Fade to Black, Bob Hope Presents the Chrysler Theatre*) (NBC)
Harold J. Stone ("Nurse Is a Feminine Noun," *The Nurses*) (CBS)

ACTRESS (SINGLE PERFORMANCE)
Ruby Dee ("Express Stop from Lenox Avenue," *The Nurses* (CBS)
Bethel Leslie ("Statement of Fact," *The Richard Boone Show*) (NBC)
Jeanette Nolan ("Vote No on 11!" *The Richard Boone Show*) (NBC)
Diana Sands ("Who Do You Kill?" *East Side, West Side*) (CBS)

Rob Petrie (Dick Van Dyke) pops the question to his future wife Laura (Mary Tyler Moore) in a flashback scene from *The Dick Van Dyke Show* (1961–66) (winner of fifteen Emmys).

Shelley Winters (*Two Is the Number, Bob Hope Presents the Chrysler Theater*) (NBC)

Two-time Oscar winner Shelley Winters got her award shows confused and thanked "the entire Motion Picture Academy" for her Emmy.

ACTOR (SERIES)
Richard Boone (*The Richard Boone Show*) (CBS)
Dean Jagger (*Mr. Novak*) (NBC)
David Jansen (*The Fugitive*) (ABC)
George C. Scott (*East Side, West Side*) (CBS)
Dick Van Dyke (*The Dick Van Dyke Show*) (CBS)

ACTRESS (SERIES)
Shirley Booth (*Hazel*)
Patty Duke (*The Patty Duke Show*)
Mary Tyler Moore (*The Dick Van Dyke Show*) (CBS)
Irene Ryan (*The Beverly Hillbillies*) (CBS)
Inger Stevens (*The Farmer's Daughter*) (ABC)

SUPPORTING ACTOR
Sorrell Booke ("What's God to Julius?" *Dr. Kildare*) (NBC)
Conlan Carter ("The Hostages," *Combat*) (ABC)

Carl Lee ("Express Stop from Lenox Avenue," *The Nurses*) (CBS)

Albert Paulsen (*One Day in the Life of Ivan Denisovich, Bob Hope Presents the Chrysler Theater*)

SUPPORTING ACTRESS

Martine Bartlett ("Journey into Darkness," *Arrest and Trial*) (ABC)

Anjanette Comer ("Journey into Darkness," *Arrest and Trial*) (ABC)

Rose Marie (*The Dick Van Dyke Show*) (CBS)

Claudia McNeil ("Express Stop from Lenox Avenue," *The Nurses*) (CBS)

Ruth White (*Little Moon of Alban, Hallmark Hall of Fame*) (NBC)

Ruth White won for a remake of *Little Moon of Alban*, which had been named outstanding Drama Special in 1958–59.

PERFORMANCE IN A VARIETY OR MUSIC PROGRAM OR SERIES

Judy Garland (*The Judy Garland Show*) (CBS)

Danny Kaye (*The Danny Kaye Show*) (NBC)

Barbra Streisand (*The Judy Garland Show*) (CBS)

Burr Tillstrom (*That Was the Week That Was*) (NBC)

Andy Williams (*The Andy Williams Show*) (NBC)

OTHER AWARDS

Directing (Drama): Tom Gries ("Who Do You Kill?" *East Side, West Side*) (CBS); Directing (Comedy): Jerry Paris (*The Dick Van Dyke Show*) (CBS); Directing (Variety or Music): Robert Scherer (*The Danny Kaye Show*) (CBS); Writing (Drama—Original): Ernest Kinoy ("Blacklist," *The Defenders*) (CBS); Writing (Drama—Adaptation): Rod Serling (*It's Mental Work, Bob Hope Presents the Chrysler Theater*) (NBC); Writing (Comedy or Variety): Carl Reiner, Sam Denoff, Bill Persky (*The Dick Van Dyke Show*) (CBS)

Outgoing Academy president and NBC vice president Mort Werner opened the controversial 1963–64 Emmys by saying of TV's golden girl, "Her wings might be a little damp this year, her feathers a little ruffled, but I can assure you she will continue to fly." The opening remarks of New York host E. G. Marshall were only heard by those in the studio audience because of a failure of the sound equipment. In Hollywood, Joey Bishop kidded the boycott situation: "I bid you welcome to one of the greatest fights of the century. The NBC peacock got its feather in CBS's eye. . . . Win or lose, the secret word is jealousy."

Entertainment was provided by Carl Reiner and Mel Brooks, who performed their 2,000-year-old man routine and the cast of NBC's satirical revue series *That Was the Week That Was*. Both segments chastised CBS's Fred Friendly and ABC's Thomas Moore. In an opening sketch, Mary Tyler Moore played the scandal-ridden Emmy while Dick Van Dyke was got up as the more prestigious Oscar. Emmy producer Bob Finkel reported it was the first time the Motion Picture Academy had ever permitted a spoof of its award. Johnny Carson got off the best line of the night when he said, "I've never played a mutiny before."

Incoming Academy president and previous Emmy winner Rod Serling soon launched a study to improve the awards. The 1964–65 ceremony would be radically different, but drew as much fire as the Emmys of 1963–1964.

THE PEABODY AWARDS (FOR 1964; NO SPECIFIC CATEGORIES)

Joyce Hall (president of Hallmark Cards, sponsor of *Hallmark Hall of Fame*, NBC); *Profiles in Courage* (NBC); *CBS Reports* (CBS); *The Louvre* (NBC); Julia Child (*The French Chef*) (NET and WGBH-TV, Boston); Intertel (International Television Federation); Burr Tillstrom; the networks and broadcasting industry for "inescapably confronting the American public with the realities of racial discrimination"

THE GOLDEN GLOBE AWARDS (FOR 1964)

The Rogues (NBC); *Burke's Law* (ABC); Male Television Star: Gene Barry; Female Television Star: Mary Tyler Moore

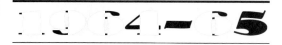

THE EMMY AWARDS

PROGRAM ACHIEVEMENT IN ENTERTAINMENT (MULTIPLE WINNERS)

The Andy Williams Show (NBC)
Bob Hope Presents the Chrysler Theater (NBC)
The Defenders (CBS)
The Dick Van Dyke Show (CBS)
Hallmark Hall of Fame (NBC)
The Magnificent Yankee, *Hallmark Hall of Fame* (NBC)
The Man from UNCLE (NBC)
Mr. Novak (NBC)
My Name Is Barbra (CBS)
Profiles in Courage (NBC)
That Wonderful World of Burlesque (NBC)
Walt Disney's Wonderful World of Color (NBC)
"What Is Sonata Form?" *New York Philharmonic Young People's Concerts with Leonard Bernstein* (CBS)
Xerox Specials—"Carol for Another Christmas" and "Who Has Seen the Wind?" (ABC)

INDIVIDUAL ACHIEVEMENT IN ENTERTAINMENT (MULTIPLE WINNERS)

Julie Andrews (*The Andy Williams Show*) (NBC)
Leonard Bernstein (*New York Philharmonic Young People's Concerts with Leonard Bernstein*) (CBS)
Johnny Carson (*The Tonight Show Starring Johnny Carson*) (NBC)
Gladys Cooper (*The Rogues*) (NBC)
Robert Coote (*The Rogues*) (NBC)
Richard Crenna (*Slattery's People*) (CBS)
Lynn Fontanne (*The Magnificent Yankee, Hallmark Hall of Fame*) (NBC)
Julie Harris (*The Holy Terror, Hallmark Hall of Fame*) (NBC)
Bob Hope (*The Bob Hope Special*) (NBC)
Dean Jagger (*Mr. Novak*) (NBC)
Danny Kaye (*The Danny Kaye Show*) (NBC)
Alfred Lunt (*The Magnificent Yankee, Hallmark Hall of Fame*) (NBC)
David McCallum (*The Man from UNCLE*) (NBC)
Red Skelton (*The Red Skelton Show*) (NBC)
Barbra Streisand (*My Name Is Barbra*) (CBS)
Dick Van Dyke (*The Dick Van Dyke Show*) (CBS)

OTHER AWARDS

Program Achievements in News, Documentaries, Information and Sports (multiple winners): "I, Leonardo da Vinci," *Saga of Western Man* (ABC), and *The Louvre* (NBC); Directing: Paul Bogart ("The 700-Year-Old Gang," *The Defenders*) (CBS); Writing: David Karp ("The 700-Year-Old Gang," *The Defenders*) (CBS)

In response to the boycott of '64, the National Academy of Television Arts and Sciences overhauled the awards procedure. After an exhaustive study, an entirely new system was proposed. Throughout the television season, the 6,000 Academy members, plus producers who were not members, would submit suggestions for nominees in four broad areas—program and individual achievement in entertainment and program and individual achievement in news, documentaries, information, and sports. Three "screening committees" in each of the broad areas would determine the nominees. Then five-member blue-ribbon panels would view all the nominated shows and vote for the winners. The names of the blue-ribbon judges would be witheld to prevent "pressure" from the networks. There could be more than one winner in each area, or there could be none. In addition, the awards program would now be rotated among the three networks so that each would benefit from its huge ratings.

The boycotting networks (CBS and ABC) supported the new plan. But Fred Friendly of CBS News still didn't care for the Emmys, even though the entertainment division of CBS was playing ball. He refused to submit any CBS news programs for consideration.

Academy president Rod Serling began the Emmy broadcast by calling for the elevation of television. The distinguished live drama shows Serling had won Emmys for were dead and the airwaves were dominated by silly sitcoms like *The Beverly Hillbillies, Petticoat Junction, Gilligan's Island,* and *The Munsters.* "It's time we became not just an industry, but an art form," he said. Ironically, *The Twilight Zone* creator and host had stated in an earlier interview he was frustrated with the tube and intended to concentrate on writing for the movies.

There was no suspense to the ceremony since there was the possibility of multiple winners. There was also no glamour or stars. Only five performers won and just one showed up. Barbra Streisand picked up her Emmy for her first special *My Name Is Barbra*. Dick Van Dyke, Leonard Bernstein, and Broadway's legendary acting couple Alfred Lunt and Lynn Fontanne sent proxies to accept for them.

The headline in *The New York Herald-Tribune* ran "Emmy Lays Biggest Egg Ever—Back to the Drawing Board." *The New York Daily News* declared the show "a bore" and "honest but dull." *Newsweek* labeled the proceedings "a 90-minute exercise in tedium." Hollywood host Sammy Davis, Jr., confided to *Newsweek*, "For the first time in my life, I felt like the captain of the Titanic."

"It didn't work on any level," Serling admitted to *The New York Herald-Tribune*. "I will say we tried to lend some kind of dignity to the award, but we failed and we failed miserably."

The Emmys went back to competitive categories for entertainment shows the following year. But in crafts, news, and documentaries, "an indeterminate number" of winners would be chosen, and anonymous blue-ribbon panels would continue to determine the final prize recipients in all areas.

THE PEABODY AWARDS (FOR 1965)

ENTERTAINMENT
Frank Sinatra—A Man and His Music (NBC); *The Julie Andrews Show* (NBC); *My Name Is Barbra* (CBS)

EDUCATION
National Educational Television

NEWS
Frank McGee (NBC); Morley Safer (CBS); KTLA-TV, Los Angeles

YOUTH AND CHILDREN'S PROGRAMS
A Charlie Brown Christmas (CBS)

PUBLIC SERVICE
"KKK—The Invisible Empire," *CBS Reports* (CBS)

CONTRIBUTION TO INTERNATIONAL UNDERSTANDING
Xerox Corporation

INNOVATION
The National Driver's Test (CBS)

MOST INVENTIVE ART DOCUMENTARY
The Mystery of Stonehenge (CBS)

SPECIAL AWARD
A Visit to Washington with Mrs. Lyndon B. Johnson —On Behalf of a More Beautiful America (ABC)

THE GOLDEN GLOBE AWARDS (FOR 1965)

The Man from UNCLE (CBS); Male Television Star: David Janssen; Female Television Star: Anne Francis

1965-66

THE EMMY AWARDS

SINGLE DRAMATIC PROGRAM
The Ages of Man (CBS)
Eagle in a Cage, Hallmark Hall of Fame (NBC)
Inherit the Wind, Hallmark Hall of Fame (NBC)
"Rally 'Round Your Own Flag, Mister," *Slattery's People* (CBS)

DRAMA SERIES
Bonanza (NBC)
The Fugitive (ABC)
I Spy (NBC)
The Man from UNCLE (NBC)
Slattery's People (CBS)

COMEDY SERIES
Batman (ABC)
Bewitched (ABC)
The Dick Van Dyke Show (CBS)

Get Smart (NBC)
Hogan's Heroes (CBS)

VARIETY SERIES
The Andy Williams Show (NBC)
The Danny Kaye Show (CBS)
The Hollywood Palace (ABC)
The Red Skelton Hour (CBS)
The Tonight Show Starring Johnny Carson (NBC)

VARIETY SPECIAL
Chrysler Presents the Bob Hope Christmas Special (NBC)
An Evening with Carol Channing (CBS)
Jimmy Durante Meets the Lively Arts (ABC)
The Julie Andrews Show (NBC)
The Swinging World of Sammy Davis, Jr. (Syndicated)

MUSICAL PROGRAM
The Bell Telephone Hour (NBC)
The Bolshoi Ballet (Syndicated)
Color Me Barbra (CBS)
Frank Sinatra: A Man and His Music (NBC)
New York Philharmonic Young People's Concerts with Leonard Bernstein (CBS)

ACTOR (SINGLE PERFORMANCE)
Ed Begley (*Inherit the Wind, Hallmark Hall of Fame*) (NBC)
Melvyn Douglas (*Inherit the Wind, Hallmark Hall of Fame*) (NBC)
Trevor Howard (*Eagle in a Cage, Hallmark Hall of Fame*) (NBC)
Christopher Plummer (*Hamlet*) (Syndicated)
Cliff Robertson (*The Game, Bob Hope Presents the Chrysler Theater*) (NBC)

ACTRESS (SINGLE PERFORMANCE)
Eartha Kitt ("The Loser," *I Spy*) (NBC)
Margaret Leighton ("Behold the Great Man," "A Life for a Life," "Web of Hate," and "Horizontal Hero," *Dr. Kildare*) (NBC)
Simone Signoret (*A Small Rebellion, Bob Hope Presents the Chrysler Theater*) (NBC)
Shelley Winters (*Back to Back, Bob Hope Presents the Chrysler Theater*) (NBC)

ACTOR (DRAMA SERIES)
Bill Cosby (*I Spy*) (NBC)
Richard Crenna (*Slattery's People*) (CBS)
Robert Culp (*I Spy*) (NBC)
David Jansen (*The Fugitive*) (ABC)
David McCallum (*The Man from UNCLE*) (NBC)

Bill Cosby won the first of his three Emmys for *I Spy*, an action adventure series. Cosby was the first black actor to receive star billing in a continuing drama show. Previous series headlined by African-American performers like *Beulah* and *Amos and Andy* were comedies. In addition, the characters in those shows were stereotypical clowns and domestics. Cosby was a powerful, clever espionage agent on an equal level with his white co-star Robert Culp.

ACTRESS (DRAMA SERIES)
Ann Francis (*Honey West*) (ABC)
Barbara Parkins (*Peyton Place*) (ABC)
Barbara Stanwyck (*The Big Valley*) (ABC)

ACTOR (COMEDY SERIES)
Don Adams (*Get Smart*) (NBC)
Bob Crane (*Hogan's Heroes*) (CBS)
Dick Van Dyke (*The Dick Van Dyke Show*) (CBS)

ACTRESS (COMEDY SERIES)
Lucille Ball (*The Lucy Show*) (CBS)
Elizabeth Montgomery (*Bewitched*) (ABC)
Mary Tyler Moore (*The Dick Van Dyke Show*) (CBS)

SUPPORTING ACTOR (DRAMA)
David Burns (*The Trials of O'Brien*) (CBS)
James Daly (*Eagle in a Cage, Hallmark Hall of Fame*) (NBC)
Leo G. Carroll (*The Man from UNCLE*) (NBC)

SUPPORTING ACTRESS (DRAMA)
Diane Baker (*Inherit the Wind, Hallmark Hall of Fame*) (NBC)
Pamela Franklin (*Eagle in a Cage, Hallmark Hall of Fame*) (NBC)
Lee Grant (*Peyton Place*) (ABC)
Jeanette Nolan ("The Conquest of Maude Murdock," *I Spy* (NBC)

SUPPORTING ACTOR (COMEDY)
Morey Amsterdam (*The Dick Van Dyke Show*) (CBS)
Frank Gorshin ("Hi Diddle Diddle," *Batman*) (ABC)
Don Knotts ("The Return of Barney Fife," *The Andy Griffith Show*) (CBS)
Werner Klemperer (*Hogan's Heroes*) (CBS)

Even though he had left *The Andy Griffith Show*, Don Knotts won a fourth Emmy for a single guest-star shot in which he returned for a visit.

SUPPORTING ACTRESS (COMEDY)
Agnes Moorehead (*Bewitched*) (ABC)
Rose Marie (*The Dick Van Dyke Show*) (CBS)
Alice Pearce (*Bewitched*) (ABC)

Character actress Alice Pearce, who played the snoopy neighbor Gladys Kravitz on the supernatural comedy *Bewitched*, had died of cancer. Her husband accepted the award. Pearce was replaced on the show by Sandra Gould. Ironically, two years later, *Bewitched* would win another posthumous acting award in the same category. The prize would go to the late Marion Lorne for her characterization of the befuddled Aunt Clara.

OTHER AWARDS
Directing (Drama): Sidney Pollack (*The Game*, *Bob Hope Presents the Chrysler Theater*) (NBC); Directing (Comedy): William Asher (*Bewitched*) (ABC); Directing (Variety or Music): Alan Hadley (*The Julie Andrews Show*) (NBC); Writing (Drama): Millard Lampert (*Eagle in a Cage*, *Hallmark Hall of Fame*) (NBC); Writing (Comedy): Bill Persky, Sam Denoff ("Coast to Coast Big Mouth," *The Dick Van Dyke Show*) (CBS); Writing (Variety): Al Gordon, Hal Goldman, Sheldon Keller (*An Evening with Carol Channing*) (CBS)

With the return of competitive categories, the Emmys received improved reviews. "A better program than last year's," conceded Cynthia Lowry of Associated Press, "but [the show] still lacks the glamour and excitement of the movies' Oscars." Tom Mackin of the *Newark Evening News* objected to the constant interuption of commercials: "The moving tribute to Edward R. Murrow was profaned by an instant switch to a youngster winning a footrace because he used the right toothpaste."

Winning writer Millard Lampert provided a rare moment of drama when he reminded the audience of a grim period in recent history: "Everyone here ought to know I was blacklisted for ten years."

CBS News continued its boycott of the awards even though perennial Emmy critic Fred Friendly had resigned as president of the department. His replacement Richard Salant continued the boycott despite the fact that CBS was host to the awards in the first year of the rotation agreement between the three networks.

THE PEABODY AWARDS (FOR 1966)

ENTERTAINMENT
A Christmas Memory, ABC Stage 67 (ABC)

EDUCATION
American White Paper: Organized Crime in the United States (NBC); *National Geographic Specials* (CBS)

NEWS
Harry Reasoner (CBS)

YOUTH AND CHILDREN'S PROGRAMS
The World of Stuart Little (NBC)

PROMOTION OF INTERNATIONAL UNDERSTANDING
ABC's Wide World of Sports (ABC); *Siberia: A Day in Irkutsk* (NBC)

LOCAL NEWS AND ENTERTAINMENT
Kup's Show (WBKB-TV, Chicago)

LOCAL MUSIC PROGRAMS
Artists' Showcase (WGN-TV, Chicago); *A Polish Millennium Concert* (WTMJ-TV, Milwaukee)

LOCAL PUBLIC SERVICE
Assignment Four (KRON-TV, San Francisco)

SPECIAL AWARDS
The Bell Telephone Hour (NBC); Tom John (CBS) for art direction of *Death of a Salesman, The*

Strollin' Twenties and *Color Me Barbra*; National Educational Television; and "The Poisoned Air," *CBS Reports* (CBS)

THE GOLDEN GLOBE AWARDS (FOR 1966)

I Spy (NBC); Male Television Star: Dean Martin; Female Televsion Star: Marlo Thomas

THE EMMY AWARDS

SINGLE DRAMATIC PROGRAM
A Christmas Memory, ABC Stage 67 (ABC)
Death of a Salesman (CBS)
The Final War of Olly Winter,
    CBS Playhouse (CBS)
The Glass Menagerie, CBS Playhouse (CBS)
The Love Song of Barney Kempinski,
    ABC Stage 67 (ABC)
Mark Twain Tonight! (CBS)

The highbrows of Broadway and the literary world were honored along with sitcoms and action shows. Numerous video adaptations of stage plays and novels were nominated and won in the special program divisions while more mainstream fare reaped the prizes among the series categories. Arthur Miller (*Death of a Salesman*), Truman Capote (*A Christmas Memory*), Tennessee Williams (*The Glass Menagerie*), and Mark Twain (*Mark Twain Tonight!*) were cheek by jowl with *Mission: Impossible, The Monkees, Get Smart, The Lucy Show,* and *Bewitched*. Many observers commented on the schizophrenic nature of the '66–'67 Emmys, which reflected the wide array of offerings available to the TV viewer.

DRAMA SERIES
The Avengers (ABC)
I Spy (NBC)
Mission: Impossible (CBS)
Run for Your Life (NBC)
Star Trek (NBC)

Mission: Impossible was almost defeated by the ultimate TV villain, the ratings box. The fast-paced

action series was faring poorly in its first year. Ironically, its main competition was NBC's *Get Smart*, a wild spoof on spy shows like *Mission*. The drama-series win for the series was one of the rare instances of an Emmy helping an ailing show. CBS gave the show a better time slot and the ratings improved.

COMEDY SERIES
The Andy Griffith Show (CBS)
Bewitched (ABC)
Get Smart (NBC)
Hogan's Heroes (CBS)
The Monkees (NBC)

VARIETY SERIES
The Andy Williams Show (NBC)
The Dean Martin Show (NBC)
The Hollywood Palace (ABC)
The Jackie Gleason Show (CBS)
The Smothers Brothers Comedy Hour (CBS)
The Tonight Show Starring Johnny Carson (NBC)

VARIETY SPECIAL
Chrysler Presents the Bob Hope Christmas
    Special (NBC)
The Sid Caesar, Imogene Coca, Carl Reiner,
    Howard Morris Special (CBS)
A Time for Laughter: A Look at Negro Humor
    in America, ABC Stage 67 (ABC)
Dick Van Dyke (CBS)

MUSICAL PROGRAM
Brigadoon (ABC)
Frank Sinatra: A Man and His Music,
    Part II (CBS)
"Toscanini: The Maestro Revisited,"
    The Bell Telephone Hour (NBC)

ACTOR (SINGLE PERFORMANCE)
Alan Arkin (*The Love Song of Barney Kempinski,*
    ABC Stage 67) (ABC)
Lee J. Cobb (*Death of a Salesman*) (CBS)
Ivan Dixon (*The Final War of Olly Winter,*
    CBS Playhouse) (CBS)
Hal Holbrook (*Mark Twain Tonight!*) (CBS)
Peter Ustinov (*Barefoot in Athens, Hallmark*
    Hall of Fame) (NBC)

Barbara Bain garnered three Emmys for *Mission: Impossible* (1966–67, 1967–68, 1968–69) while her husband at the time Martin Landau lost three times. He would later take home an Oscar for *Ed Wood*.

ACTRESS (SINGLE PERFORMANCE)
Shirley Booth (*The Glass Menagerie, CBS Playhouse*) (CBS)
Mildred Dunnock (*Death of a Salesman*) (CBS)
Lynn Fontanne (*Anastasia, Hallmark Hall of Fame*) (NBC)
Julie Harris (*Anastasia, Hallmark Hall of Fame*) (NBC)
Geraldine Page (*A Christmas Memory, ABC Stage 67*) (ABC)

ACTOR (DRAMA SERIES)
Bill Cosby (*I Spy*) (NBC)
Robert Culp (*I Spy*) (NBC)
Ben Gazzara (*Run for Your Life*) (NBC)
David Jansen (*The Fugitive*) (ABC)
Martin Landau (*Mission: Impossible*) (CBS)

ACTRESS (DRAMA SERIES)
Barbara Bain (*Mission: Impossible*) (CBS)
Diana Rigg (*The Avengers*) (ABC)
Barbara Stanwyck (*The Big Valley*) (CBS)

ACTOR (COMEDY SERIES)
Don Adams (*Get Smart*) (NBC)
Bob Crane (*Hogan's Heroes*) (CBS)
Brian Keith (*Family Affair*) (CBS)
Larry Storch (*F Troop*) (ABC)

ACTRESS (COMEDY SERIES)
Lucille Ball (*The Lucy Show*) (CBS)
Elizabeth Montgomery (*Bewitched*) (ABC)
Agnes Moorehead (*Bewitched*) (ABC)
Marlo Thomas (*That Girl*) (ABC)

"The last time I got it, I thought it was because I had a baby," enthused Lucille Ball upon winning her third Emmy. "That baby is now 14 years old." Actually, the baby, Desi Arnaz, Jr., was three years old when Lucy won her last Emmy [in 1955 for Actress (Continuing Series)].

SUPPORTING ACTOR (DRAMA)
Leo G. Carroll (*The Man from UNCLE*) (NBC)
Leonard Nimoy (*Star Trek*) (NBC)
Eli Wallach (*The Poppy Is Also a Flower, Xerox Special*) (ABC)

SUPPORTING ACTRESS (DRAMA)
Tina Chen (*The Final War of Olly Winter, CBS Playhouse*) (CBS)
Agnes Moorehead ("The Night of the Vicious Valentine," *The Wild, Wild West*) (CBS)
Ruth Warrick (*Peyton Place*) (ABC)

SUPPORTING ACTOR (COMEDY)
Gale Gordon (*The Lucy Show*) (CBS)
Werner Klemperer (*Hogan's Heroes*) (CBS)
Don Knotts ("Barney Comes to Mayberry," *The Andy Griffith Show*) (CBS)

SUPPORTING ACTRESS (COMEDY)
Francis Bavier (*The Andy Griffith Show*) (CBS)
Nancy Kulp (*The Beverly Hillbillies*) (CBS)
Marion Lorne (*Bewitched*) (ABC)

SPECIAL CLASSIFICATIONS OF INDIVIDUAL ACHIEVEMENT
Art Carney (*The Jackie Gleason Show*); Truman Capote, Eleanor Perry for the adaptation of *A Christmas Memory, ABC Playhouse 67* (ABC); Arthur Miller for the adaptation of *Death of a Salesman* (CBS)

OTHER AWARDS
Directing (Drama): Alex Segal (*Death of a Salesman*) (CBS); Directing (Comedy): James Frawley ("Royal Flush," *The Monkees*) (NBC); Directing (Variety or Music): Fielder Cook (*Brigadoon*) (ABC)
   Writing (Drama): Bruce Geller (*Mission: Impossible*) (CBS); Writing (Comedy): Buck Henry, Leonard Stern ("Ship of Spies," *Get Smart*) (NBC);

Writing (Variety): Mel Brooks, Sam Denoff, Bill Persky, Carl Reiner, Mel Tolkin (*The Sid Caesar, Imogene Coca, Carl Reiner, Howard Morris Special*) (CBS)

"At 19, Emmy was a lady," declared *Variety*. "The 19th annual Emmy Awards telecast had grace, glamour, and good fun." The grace was supplied by the numerous distinguished lights of the literary world whose work was honored. The glamour by the numerous stars appearing as presenters. The good fun came in the form of humorous moments, the best being when Jimmy Durante and little Annisa Jones, "Buffy" of the sitcom *Family Affair*, rubbed noses while presenting the best comedy series award.

Joey Bishop in Hollywood and Hugh Downs in New York hosted the ceremony, which moved at a much faster clip than usual. Usherettes in the audience bestowed the many technical awards, helping to save time. There were the inevitable glitches. As variety-writing winner Carl Reiner was about to explain why his co-winner Mel Brooks was not present, the program abruptly cut to a commercial. When the show was back, Hugh Downs quipped, "We'll have to wait 'til next year to find out why Mel Brooks wasn't here."

Among those who took a new shine to Emmy was CBS News, which ended its long boycott of the awards in September of 1967.

THE PEABODY AWARDS (FOR 1967)

ENTERTAINMENT
CBS Playhouse (CBS); *An Evening at Tanglewood* (NBC)

NEWS ANALYSIS AND COMMENTARY (RADIO AND TELEVISION)
Eric Sevareid (CBS)

YOUTH OR CHILDREN'S PROGRAMS
CBS Children's Film Festival (CBS); *Mr. Knozit* (WIS-TV, Columbia, SC)

PUBLIC SERVICE
The Opportunity Line (WBBM-TV, Chicago)

PROMOTION OF INTERNATIONAL UNDERSTANDING
Africa (ABC)

SPECIAL AWARDS
The Ed Sullivan Show (CBS); Bob Hope (NBC); Dr. James R. Killian, Jr., Massachusettes Institute of Technology for broadcasting education; *Meet the Press* (NBC)

THE GOLDEN GLOBE AWARDS (FOR 1967)

Mission: Impossible (CBS); Male Television Star: Martin Landau; Female Television Star: Carol Burnett

THE EMMY AWARDS

DRAMATIC PROGRAM
Do Not Go Gentle into That Good Night, CBS Playhouse (CBS)
Dear Friends, CBS Playhouse (CBS)
Dr. Jekyll and Mr. Hyde (ABC)
Elizabeth the Queen, *Hallmark Hall of Fame* (NBC)
Luther, Xerox Special (ABC)
Uncle Vanya, NET Playhouse (NET)

DRAMA SERIES
The Avengers (CBS)
I Spy (NBC)
Mission: Impossible (CBS)
NET Playhouse (NET)
Run for Your Life (NBC)
Star Trek (NBC)

COMEDY SERIES
Bewitched (ABC)
Family Affair (CBS)
Get Smart (NBC)
Hogan's Heroes (CBS)
The Lucy Show (CBS)

MUSICAL OR VARIETY SERIES
The Bell Telephone Hour (NBC)
The Carol Burnett Show (CBS)
The Dean Martin Show (NBC)
Rowan and Martin's Laugh-In (NBC)
The Smothers Brothers Comedy Hour (CBS)

MUSICAL OR VARIETY PROGRAM
Chrysler Presents the Bob Hope Christmas Special (NBC)
"Five Ballets of the Five Senses," *Lincoln Center/Stage 5* (NET)
Frank Sinatra (NBC)
The Fred Astaire Show (NBC)
Herb Alpert and the Tijuana Brass Special (CBS)
Rowan and Martin's Laugh-In Special (NBC)

The 1967–68 TV season was dominated by the wildly inventive variety series *Rowan and Martin's Laugh-In*. Combining elements of vaudeville, the visual electronic humor pioneered by Ernie Kovacs, and the satiric wit of *That Was the Week That Was*, *Laugh-In* rattled its audience with nonstop puns, sketches, off-beat continuing characters, and songs. There were about 250 jokes in every one-hour segment.

The show won four Emmys in its first year, for Musical or Variety Series, Musical or Variety Program (for the special which acted as a pilot), Tape Editing, and Writing (Music or Variety).

NBC would once again dominate the variety categories eight years later with a similarly wild series: *Saturday Night Live*.

ACTOR (SINGLE PERFORMANCE)
Raymond Burr (*Ironside*) (NBC)
Melvyn Douglas (*Do Not Go Gentle into That Good Night, CBS Playhouse*) (CBS)
Van Heflin (*A Case of Libel*) (ABC)
George C. Scott (*The Crucible*) (CBS)
Eli Wallach (*Dear Friends, CBS Playhouse*) (CBS)

ACTRESS (SINGLE PERFORMANCE)
Dame Judith Anderson (*Elizabeth the Queen, Hallmark Hall of Fame*) (NBC)
Genevieve Bujold (*Saint Joan, Hallmark Hall of Fame*) (NBC)
Colleen Dewhurst (*The Crucible*) (CBS)
Anne Jackson (*Dear Friends, CBS Playhouse*) (CBS)

Maureen Stapleton (*Among the Paths to Eden, Xerox Special*) (ABC)

ACTOR (DRAMA SERIES)
Raymond Burr (*Ironside*) (NBC)
Bill Cosby (*I Spy*) (NBC)
Robert Culp (*I Spy*) (NBC)
Ben Gazzara (*Run for Your Life*) (NBC)
Martin Landau (*Mission: Impossible*) (CBS)

ACTRESS (DRAMA SERIES)
Barbara Bain (*Mission: Impossible*) (CBS)
Diana Rigg (*The Avengers*) (ABC)
Barbara Stanwyck (*The Big Valley*) (ABC)

ACTOR (COMEDY SERIES)
Don Adams (*Get Smart*) (NBC)
Richard Benjamin (*He & She*) (CBS)
Sebastian Cabot (*Family Affair*) (CBS)
Brian Keith (*Family Affair*) (CBS)
Dick York (*Bewitched*) (ABC)

ACTRESS (COMEDY SERIES)
Lucille Ball (*The Lucy Show*) (CBS)
Barbara Feldon (*Get Smart*) (CBS)
Elizabeth Montgomery (*Bewitched*) (ABC)
Paula Prentiss (*He & She*) (ABC)
Marlo Thomas (*That Girl*) (ABC)

For the first, and so far only, time all four lead series winners—Bill Cobsy, Barbara Bain, Don Adams, and Lucille Ball—repeated from the previous year.

SUPPORTING ACTOR (DRAMA)
Jospeh Campanella (*Mannix*) (CBS)
Lawrence Dobkin (*Do Not Go Gentle into That Good Night, CBS Playhouse*) (CBS)
Leonard Nimoy (*Star Trek*) (NBC)
Milburn Stone (*Gunsmoke*) (CBS)

SUPPORTING ACTRESS (DRAMA)
Barbara Anderson (*Ironside*) (NBC)
Linda Cristal (*The High Chaparral*) (NBC)
Tessie O'Shea (*Dr. Jekyll and Mr. Hyde*) (ABC)

SUPPORTING ACTOR (COMEDY SERIES)
Jack Cassidy (*He & She*) (CBS)

William Demarest (*My Three Sons*) (CBS)
Gale Gordon (*The Lucy Show*) (CBS)
Werner Klemperer (*Hogan's Heroes*) (CBS)

SUPPORTING ACTRESS (COMEDY SERIES)
Agnes Mooorehead (*Bewitched*) (ABC)
Marion Lorne (*Bewitched*) (ABC)
Marge Redmond (*The Flying Nun*) (ABC)
Nita Talbot ("The Hostage," *Hogan's Heroes*) (CBS)

SPECIAL CLASSIFICATION OF OUTSTANDING INDIVIDUAL ACHIEVEMENT
Art Carney (*The Jackie Gleason Show*) (CBS); Pat Paulsen (*The Smothers Brothers Comedy Hour*) (CBS)

In one of the most bizarre Emmy categories ever, Art Carney and Pat Paulsen won Special Classification awards over the special effects in *Star Trek*.

OTHER AWARDS
Directing (Drama): Paul Bogart (*Dear Friends, CBS Playhouse*) (CBS); Directing (Comedy): Bruce Bilson ("Maxwell Smart, Private Eye," *Get Smart*) (NBC); Directing (Music or Variety): Jack Haley, Jr. (*Movin' with Nancy*) (NBC)

Writing (Drama): Loring Mandel (*Do Not Go Gentle into That Good Night, CBS Playhouse*) (CBS); Writing (Comedy): Alan Burns, Chris Hayward ("The Coming-Out Party," *He & She*) (CBS); Writing (Music or Variety): Paul Keyes, Hugh Wedlock, Allan Manings, Chris Beard, David Panich, Phil Hahn, Jack Hanrahan, Coslough Johnson, Marc London, Digby Wolfe (*Rowan and Martin's Laugh-In*) (NBC)

The 1967–68 Emmys opened with co-host Frank Sinatra (in Los Angeles) singing "Luck Be a Lady Tonight." She was not a lady for Sinatra's New York partner in emcee duties, Dick Van Dyke. The three-time Emmy winner had problems reading the cue cards and at one point had to borrow a script from a production assistant in order to find his place. When a cameraman was gesturing to speed things up, Van Dyke said to him, "I can't tell the winners to say whoopee and sit down." There were periods when the sound went dead. By the program's end, the comedian stated that he deserved an Emmy for "outstanding achievement in the field of total confusion."

Insult specialist Don Rickles enlivened the proceedings with his acidic humor. After reading off a long list of nominated variety show writers, Rickles snapped, "Who cares?"

CBS News rejoined the Emmys after its boycott, but the news and documentary awards were given short shrift, with winners remaining in their seats and having their prizes brought to them. Reviewers slammed the Emmys for this slight since events like the assassinations of Robert Kennedy and Martin Luther King, Jr., the Vietnam War, student protests, and the civil rights movement made news coverage of paramount importance.

Jack Gould of *The New York Times* was especially scathing: "For an inept snafu in full color, there is clearly only one place to turn: the National Academy of Television Arts and Sciences."

THE PEABODY AWARDS (FOR 1968)

ENTERTAINMENT
NET Playhouse (NET)

EDUCATION
Robert Cromie and *Book Beat* (WTTW, Chicago); ABC for its "creative 1968 documentaries"

NEWS
Charles Kurault and "On the Road" (CBS)

YOUTH OR CHILDREN'S PROGRAMS
Mister Rogers' Neighborhood (NET)

PUBLIC SERVICE
Westinghouse Broadcasting for *One Nation Indivisible*

PROMOTION OF INTERNATIONAL UNDERSTANDING
ABC for coverage of 1968 Olympic Games

SPECIAL AWARDS
Hunger in America, CBS Reports (CBS)

THE GOLDEN GLOBE AWARDS (FOR 1968)

Rowan and Martin's Laugh-In (NBC); Male Television Star: Carl Betz (*Judd for the Defense*) (ABC); Female Television Star: Diahann Carroll (*Julia*) (NBC)

THE EMMY AWARDS

DRAMATIC PROGRAM
"The Execution," *Mission: Impossible* (CBS)
Heidi (NBC)
A Midsummer Night's Dream (CBS)
The People Next Door, CBS Playhouse (CBS)
Talking to a Stranger, NET Playhouse (NET)
Teacher, Teacher, Hallmark Hall of Fame (NBC)

DRAMA SERIES
The FBI (ABC)
Judd for the Defense (ABC)
Mission: Impossible (CBS)
The Name of the Game (NBC)
NET Playhouse (NET)

COMEDY SERIES
Bewitched (ABC)
Family Affair (CBS)
Get Smart (NBC)
The Ghost and Mrs. Muir (NBC)
Julia (NBC)

MUSICAL OR VARIETY SERIES
The Carol Burnett Show (CBS)
The Dean Martin Show (NBC)
Rowan and Martin's Laugh-In (NBC)
The Smothers Brothers Comedy Hour (CBS)
That's Life (ABC)

MUSICAL OR VARIETY SPECIAL
Barbra Streisand: A Happening in Central Park (CBS)
The Bill Cosby Special (NBC)
Duke Ellington Concert of Sacred Music, NET Playhouse (NET)

Francis Albert Sinatra Does His Thing (CBS)
The Rite of Spring, NET Festival (NET)
Rowan and Martin's Laugh-In with guest star Marcel Marceau (NBC)
Vladimir Horowitz: A Television Concert at Carnegie Hall (CBS)

ACTOR (SINGLE PERFORMANCE)
Ossie Davis (*Teacher, Teacher, Hallmark Hall of Fame*) (NBC)
David McCallum (*Teacher, Teacher, Hallmark Hall of Fame*) (NBC)
Paul Scofield (*Male of the Species, Prudential's On Stage*) (NBC)
Bill Travers (*The Admirable Crichton, Hallmark Hall of Fame*) (NBC)

ACTRESS (SINGLE PERFORMANCE)
Anne Baxter ("The Bobbie Currier Story," *The Name of the Game*) (NBC)
Lee Grant ("The Gates of Cerberus," *Judd for the Defense*) (ABC)
Geraldine Page (*The Thanksgiving Visitor*) (ABC)

ACTOR (DRAMA SERIES)
Carl Betz (*Judd for the Defense*) (ABC)
Raymond Burr (*Ironside*) (NBC)
Peter Graves (*Mission: Impossible*) (CBS)
Martin Landau (*Mission: Impossible*) (CBS)
Ross Martin (*The Wild, Wild West*) (CBS)

Almost every winner in the series acting categories was in a canceled show or was leaving a program. Carl Betz's *Judd for the Defense* had been axed by ABC. Barbara Bain was in her last year of *Mission: Impossible*. She and her husband Martin Landau were leaving the esponiage program because of a contract dispute. "There are a lot of people I'd like to thank," she said. "There are a couple of people I'd like not to thank. Since they each know their names, I won't call them."

In the comedy division, Don Adams and Hope Lange were starring in sitcoms not returning to NBC's schedule the following fall. *Get Smart* was picked up by CBS, while *The Ghost and Mrs. Muir* had made the trip to ABC. Both shows would last one more year on their new networks before the blade of cancellation fell.

ACTRESS (DRAMA SERIES)
Barbara Bain (*Mission: Impossible*) (CBS)
Joan Blondell (*Here Come the Brides*) (ABC)
Peggy Lipton (*The Mod Squad*) (ABC)

ACTOR (COMEDY SERIES)
Don Adams (*Get Smart*) (NBC)
Brian Keith (*Family Affair*) (CBS)
Edward Mulhare (*The Ghost and Mrs. Muir*) (NBC)
Lloyd Nolan (*Julia*) (NBC)

ACTRESS (COMEDY SERIES)
Diahann Carroll (*Julia*) (NBC)
Barbara Feldon (*Get Smart*) (NBC)
Hope Lange (*The Ghost and Mrs. Muir*) (NBC)
Elizabeth Montgomery (*Bewitched*) (ABC)

SUPPORTING ACTOR (SINGLE PERFORMANCE)
No award given
Ned Glass ("A Little Chicken Soup Never Hurt Anybody," *Julia*) (NBC)
Hal Holbrook (*The Whole World Is Watching*) (NBC)
Billy Schulman (*Teacher, Teacher, Hallmark Hall of Fame*) (NBC)

One of the TV Academy's most unpopular rule changes was the stipulation that no award could be given in some categories if none of the nominees were judged worthy of honor. The single-performance supporting actor Emmy was the first major award to be deemed unwinnable.

One of the nominees was Billy Schulman, a fourteen-year-old retarded boy who played a similarly impaired child in *Teacher, Teacher,* a *Hallmark Hall of Fame* drama. Academy official Peter Cott stated, "Billy might trip or make an error on stage." Rather than risk such an incident, they had an announcer state Billy was the recipient of a special award and showed a close-up of him in his seat. Moments before, producer George Lefferts, in accepting the Emmy for *Teacher* in the Dramatic Program category, angrily denounced the Academy for not allowing Schulman "to compete and win or lose with dignity."

SUPPORTING ACTRESS (SINGLE PERFORMANCE)
Anna Calder-Marshall (*Male of the Species, Prudential's On Stage*) (NBC)

Pamela Brown (*The Admirable Crichton, Hallmark Hall of Fame*) (NBC)
Irene Hervey ("The O'Casey Scandal," *My Three Sons*) (CBS)
Nancy Kovack ("The Girl Who Came In with the Tide," *Mannix*) (CBS)

SUPPORTING ACTOR (SERIES)
Werner Klemperer (*Hogan's Heroes*) (CBS)
Greg Morris (*Mission: Impossible*) (CBS)
Leonard Nimoy (*Star Trek*) (NBC)

SUPPORTING ACTRESS (SERIES)
Barbara Anderson (*Ironside*) (NBC)
Susan Saint James (*The Name of the Game*) (NBC)
Agnes Moorehead (*Bewitched*) (ABC)

Another rule change combined all supporting comedy and drama series performers into one category, regardless of their genre.

SPECIAL CLASSIFICATION OF OUTSTANDING INDIVIDUAL ACHIEVEMENT
Arte Johnson (*Rowan and Martin's Laugh-In*) (NBC); Harvey Korman (*The Carol Burnett Show*) (CBS)

OTHER AWARDS
Directing (Drama): David Greene (*The People Next Door, CBS Playhouse*) (CBS); Directing (Comedy, Variety or Music): no winners

Writing (Drama): J. P. Miller (*The People Next Door, CBS Playhouse*) (CBS); Writing (Comedy, Variety or Music): Alan Blye, Bob Einstein, Murray Roman, Carl Gottlieb, Jerry Music, Steve Martin, Cecil Tuck, Paul Wayne, Cy Howard, Mason Williams (*The Smothers Brothers Comedy Hour*) (CBS)

Once again, the Emmy rules were revamped in order to streamline the ceremony. Several categories were combined with some odds results. Vladimir Horowitz was up against *Rowan and Martin's Laugh-In*, while an episode of *Mission: Impossible* vied with *A Midsummer Night's Dream*. Comedy and variety directors and writers were thrown together in the same category. The directors were frozen out altogether when the blue-ribbon panel decided none of the three nominees had done particularly exciting work.

In order to avoid multiple repeat winners, it was announced that only the first season of a program would be eligible for consideration and, if an actor or actress won for a role in a series, he or she could not be nominated again for the same part. The networks screamed bloody murder and threatened a boycott if these new rules went into effect. The Academy quickly retreated on the first-season requirements, but kept the possibility of giving no award in some cases. That too was dropped after one year.

The news awards were announced two weeks before the ceremony so that excerpts could be shown and the winners would have time to make speeches. Coretta Scott King presented two of the news Emmys, including one to CBS for coverage of the assassination of her husband, civil rights leader Martin Luther King, Jr. Apollo 10 astronauts Tom Stafford, John Young, and Gene Cernan were given a special Trustees Award. The astronauts and Mrs. King "brought the excitement of real life" to the program, stated the *New York Daily News*.

Despite the squawking about the rule changes, the Emmys were well received, perhaps because there were no technical screw-ups like those which had so marred last year's ceremony. Bill Cosby hosted from the Santa Monica Civic Auditorium while Merv Griffin presided from the swanky stage of Carnegie Hall in New York.

THE PEABODY AWARDS (FOR 1969)

ENTERTAINMENT
Experiment in Television (NBC); Curt Gowdy, sportscaster

EDUCATION
The Advocates (WGBH-TV, Boston, KCET-TV, Los Angeles); *Who Killed Lake Erie?* (NBC)

NEWS
Newsroom (KQED-TV, San Francisco); Frank Reynolds (ABC)

YOUTH OR CHILDREN'S PROGRAMS
Sesame Street (Children's Television Workshop)

PUBLIC SERVICE
Tom Petit (NBC)

PROMOTION OF INTERNATIONAL UNDERSTANDING
The Japanese (CBS)

LOCAL PUBLIC SERVICE
The Negro in Indianapolis (WFBM-TV, Indianapolis)

SPECIAL AWARDS
Bing Crosby (outstanding service to television); Chet Huntley (contributions to television news); *J.T., CBS Children's Hour* (CBS)

THE GOLDEN GLOBE AWARDS (FOR 1969)

Drama Series: *Marcus Welby, MD* (ABC); Comedy or Musical Series: *The Governor and JJ* (CBS)

Actor (Drama Series): Mike Connors (*Mannix*) (CBS); Actress (Drama Series): Linda Cristal (*The High Chaparral*) (NBC); Actor (Comedy or Musical Series): Dan Dailey (*The Governor and JJ*) (CBS); Actress (Comedy or Musical Series) (tie): Carol Burnett (*The Carol Burnett Show*) (CBS) and Julie Sommers (*The Governor and JJ*) (CBS)

Starting with this year, the Golden Globes divided their categories between drama and comedy or musical series.

THE EMMY AWARDS

DRAMATIC PROGRAM
David Copperfield (NBC)
"Hello, Goodbye, Hello," *Marcus Welby, MD* (ABC)
My Sweet Charlie, NBC World Premiere Movie (NBC)
A Storm in Summer, Hallmark Hall of Fame (NBC)

DRAMA SERIES
The Forsyte Saga (NET)
Ironside (NBC)

Marcus Welby, MD (ABC)
The Mod Squad (ABC)
The Name of the Game (NBC)
NET Playhouse (NET)

COMEDY SERIES
The Bill Cosby Show (NBC)
The Courtship of Eddie's Father (ABC)
Love, American Style (ABC)
My World and Welcome to It (NBC)
Room 222 (ABC)

VARIETY OR MUSICAL SERIES
The Carol Burnett Show (CBS)
The David Frost Show (Syndicated)
The Dean Martin Show (NBC)
The Dick Cavett Show (ABC)
Rowan and Martin's Laugh-In (NBC)

VARIETY OR MUSICAL SPECIAL (POPULAR MUSIC)
Annie, the Women in the Life of a Man (CBS)
The Friars Club 'Roasts' Jack Benny, The Kraft Music Hall (NBC)
The Second Bill Cosby Special (NBC)
Sinatra (CBS)
The Sound of Burt Bacharach, The Kraft Music Hall (NBC)

NEW SERIES
The Bill Cosby Show (NBC)
The Forsyte Saga (NET)
Marcus Welby, MD (ABC)
Room 222 (ABC)
Sesame Street (NET)

To offset the numerous repeat winners preventing freshmen series from winning, the Best New Series category was introduced. NET's innovative children's series *Sesame Street* was expected to be the first winner of the new category, but the prize went to ABC's *Room 222*, a half-hour show about an intregrated high school which combined elements of comedy and drama.

ACTOR (SINGLE PERFORMANCE)
Al Freeman, Jr. (*My Sweet Charlie, NBC World Premiere Movie*) (NBC)
Laurence Olivier (*David Copperfield*) (NBC)

Peter Ustinov (*A Storm in Summer, Hallmark Hall of Fame*) (NBC)

ACTRESS (SINGLE PERFORMANCE)
Patty Duke (*My Sweet Charlie, NBC World Premiere Movie*) (NBC)
Edith Evans (*David Copperfield*) (NBC)
Shirley Jones (*Silent Night, Lonely Night*) (NBC)

In one of the most rambling acceptance speeches of any award, a disoriented Patty Duke veered from topic to topic. She thanked fellow nominee Dame Edith Evans, congratulated her mother on her birthday, and recited her three favorite words, "yes," "thank you," and "enthusiasm" (which were actually four words). Her incoherent remarks were punctuated with long pauses and vacant stares. Off-stage she announced she was rejecting the award, quitting acting, and taking up the study of medicine (none of which she did). Many observers concluded she was as high as a kite. She revealed in her autobiography she was suffering from manic depression at the time.

The program for which she won, *My Sweet Charlie*, had received a total of eight nominations and won three. The story of a runaway pregnant white girl and a black fugitive from justice had earlier been a novel and an unsuccessful Broadway play. It was the first made-for-television movie (if you don't count *Macbeth* in 1961) to receive such attention. Soon TV movies would totally replace shot-on-tape, in-studio productions.

ACTOR (DRAMA SERIES)
Raymond Burr (*Ironside*) (NBC)
Mike Connors (*Mannix*) (CBS)
Robert Wagner (*It Takes a Thief*) (ABC)
Robert Young (*Marcus Welby, MD*) (ABC)

Robert Young was the first performer to win leading Emmys in both comedy (*Father Knows Best*) and drama (*Marcus Welby, MD*).

ACTRESS (DRAMA SERIES)
Joan Blondell (*Here Come the Brides*) (ABC)
Susan Hampshire (*The Forsyte Saga*) (NET)
Peggy Lipton (*The Mod Squad*) (ABC)

Brit Susan Hampshire was the first performer in an National Education Television (NET) program to win an Emmy. She was honored for her selfish Fleur Forsyte in the British Broadcasting Corporation import *The Forsyte Saga* based on the novels by John Galsworthy. NET won a total of eight Emmys, a trend which the three commercial networks did not like one bit.

ACTOR (COMEDY SERIES)
Bill Cosby (*The Bill Cosby Show*) (NBC)
Lloyd Haynes (*Room 222*) (ABC)
William Windom (*My World and Welcome to It*) (NBC)

"I am sober, have tux, and will travel," William Windom informed the Emmy audience. His series *My World and Welcome to It*, based on the writings and drawings of James Thurber, had just been canceled.

ACTRESS (COMEDY SERIES)
Hope Lange (*The Ghost and Mrs. Muir*) (ABC)
Elizabeth Montgomery (*Bewitched*) (ABC)
Marlo Thomas (*That Girl*) (ABC)

SUPPORTING ACTOR (DRAMA)
Tige Andrews (*The Mod Squad*) (ABC)
James Brolin (*Marcus Welby, MD*) (ABC)
Greg Morris (*Mission: Impossible*) (CBS)

SUPPORTING ACTRESS (DRAMA)
Barbara Anderson (*Ironside*) (NBC)
Gail Fisher (*Mannix*) (CBS)
Susan Saint James (*The Name of the Game*) (NBC)

SUPPORTING ACTOR (COMEDY)
Michael Constantine (*Room 222*) (ABC)
Werner Klemperer (*Hogan's Heroes*) (CBS)
Charles Nelson Reilly (*The Ghost and Mrs. Muir*) (ABC)

SUPPORTING ACTRESS (COMEDY)
Agnes Moorehead (*Bewitched*) (ABC)
Lurene Tuttle (*Julia*) (NBC)
Karen Valentine (*Room 222*) (ABC)

OTHER AWARDS
Directing (Drama): Paul Bogart (*Shadow Game, CBS Playhouse*) (CBS); Directing (Comedy, Music or Variety): Dwight Hemion (*The Sound of Burt*

Bacharach, The Kraft Music Hall) (NBC)

Writing (Drama): Richard Levinson, William Link (*My Sweet Charlie, NBC World Premiere Movie*) (NBC); Writing (Comedy, Music or Variety): Gary Belkin, Peter Bellwood, Herb Sargeant, Thomas Meehan, Judith Viorst (*Annie, the Women in the Life of a Man*) (CBS)

New York host Dick Cavett drew glowing reviews for his witty ad-libs. When pictures of the moon landing during a montage of news highlights got scrambled, Cavett quipped, "One small step for mankind and one giant leap for radio." Mike Connors of *Mannix* was mistakenly identified as Chuck Connors during the credit crawl. Cavett saved the situation by asking, "Who's doing Chuck Connors' make-up these days? He looks great." Los Angeles emcee Bill Cosby also drew laughs. When his variety special and his new NBC sitcom (in which he played a bachelor-gym instructor) failed to win any awards, Cosby sighed, "The only thing left for me to do is go into politics."

For the first time, technical awards were presented in a separate ceremony. Despite the cutting of the tech prizes and a lack of production numbers, the program still ran seventeen minutes over its allotted two hours.

THE PEABODY AWARDS (FOR 1970)

ENTERTAINMENT
The Andersonville Trial, Hollywood Television Theatre (PBS); *Evening at Pops* (PBS); *The Flip Wilson Show* (NBC)

EDUCATION
Eye of the Storm (ABC)

NEWS
60 Minutes (CBS); *Polithon '70* (WPBT-TV, Miami)

YOUTH OR CHILDREN'S PROGRAMS
The "Dr. Seuss" programs (NBC); *Hot Dog* (NBC)

PUBLIC SERVICE
Peace . . . On Our Time: KMEX-TV and the Death of Reuben Salazar (KMEX-TV, Los Angeles); *Migrant: An NBC White Paper* (NBC)

PROMOTION OF INTERNATIONAL UNDERSTANDING
Civilisation (BBC); *This New Frontier* (WWL-TV, New Orleans)

SPECIAL AWARD
The Selling of the Pentagon (CBS)

THE GOLDEN GLOBE AWARDS (FOR 1970)

Drama Series: *Medical Center* (CBS); Comedy or Musical Series: *The Carol Burnett Show* (CBS)

Actor (Drama Series): Peter Graves (*Mission: Impossible*) (CBS); Actress (Drama Series): Peggy Lipton (*The Mod Squad*) (ABC); Actor (Comedy or Musical Series): Flip Wilson (*The Flip Wilson Show*) (NBC); Actress (Comedy or Musical Series): Mary Tyler Moore (*The Mary Tyler Moore Show*) (CBS)

THE EMMY AWARDS

SINGLE PROGRAM
The Andersonville Trial, Hollywood Television Theatre (PBS)
Hamlet, Hallmark Hall of Fame (NBC)
The Price, Hallmark Hall of Fame (NBC)
"They're Tearing Down Tim Reilly's Bar," *Night Gallery, Four-in-One* (NBC)
Vanished, World Premiere NBC Monday and *Tuesday Night at the Movies* (NBC)

DRAMA SERIES
The First Churchills, Masterpiece Theatre (PBS)
Ironside (NBC)
Marcus Welby, MD (ABC)
NET Playhouse (PBS)
The Senator, The Bold Ones (NBC)

Once again, Emmy was not stronger than Nielsen. *The Senator*, one of three segments of the rotating NBC series *The Bold Ones*, copped a total of five awards. But the Peacock network dropped the story of an idealistic legislator because of poor ratings.

(Left to right) Rob Reiner, Sally Struthers, Jean Stapleton, and Carroll O'Connor would all cop Emmys for their roles on *All in the Family* (1971–83).

COMEDY SERIES
All in the Family (CBS)
Arnie (CBS)
Love, American Style (ABC)
The Mary Tyler Moore Show (CBS)
The Odd Couple (ABC)

The 1970–71 Emmys opened with a sketch featuring the cast of *All in the Family* settling in to watch the ceremony on TV. The new sitcom broke ground in its frank portrayal of the bigotry of the lead character, Archie Bunker, and in addressing controversial issues. But it would gradually move beyond politics to become a moving depiction of the Bunker household—crusty, but basically good-hearted Archie, his endearingly naive wife Edith, his daughter Gloria, and son-in-law Mike (whom Archie disparagingly referred to as "Meathead"). Each member of this quartet would win at least two Emmys each.

This was also the first year for *The Mary Tyler Moore Show* to garner a shelf full of golden ladies. Moore made the transition from suburban housewife in *The Dick Van Dyke Show* to independent career woman in her own series, which would eventually win twenty-nine awards, a record for a prime-time series.

VARIETY SERIES (MUSICAL)
The Carol Burnett Show (CBS)
The Flip Wilson Show (NBC)
Rowan and Martin's Laugh-In (NBC)

VARIETY SERIES (TALK)
The David Frost Show (Syndicated)
The Dick Cavett Show (ABC)
The Tonight Show Starring Johnny Carson (NBC)

VARIETY OR MUSICAL PROGRAM

Another Evening with Burt Bacharach (NBC)
Harry and Lena (ABC)
Singer Presents Burt Bacharach (CBS)

NEW SERIES

All in the Family (CBS)
The Flip Wilson Show (NBC)
The Mary Tyler Moore Show (CBS)
The Odd Couple (ABC)
The Senator, The Bold Ones (NBC)

ACTOR (SINGLE PERFORMANCE)

Jack Cassidy (*The Andersonville Trial,*
  Hollywood Television Theatre) (PBS)
Hal Holbrook (*A Clear and Present Danger,*
  World Premiere NBC Saturday Night
  at the Movies) (NBC)
George C. Scott (*The Price, Hallmark Hall*
  of Fame) (NBC)
Richard Widmark (*Vanished, World Premiere*
  NBC Monday and *Tuesday Night at the Movies*)
  (NBC)
Gig Young (*The Neon Ceiling, World Premiere*
  NBC Monday Night at the Movies) (NBC)

"Oh my God! It's George C. Scott," cried Suzanne
Pleshette as she opened the envelope. Her cry was
an echo of Goldie Hawn, who had opened a similar envelope on Oscar night just one month earlier.
Scott had refused to accept the Academy Award for
his performance in *Patton*, stating that the top prize
of filmdom was nothing but a popularity contest.

Although he was not present at the Emmy ceremony, Scott did accept the TV award for his performance as a policeman confronting his estranged
brother in Arthur Miller's *The Price*. The reason?
The Oscars were voted on by the entire Motion
Picture Academy membership, who were subject to
campaigning and persuasion by the film studios.
The Emmys were awarded by select blue-ribbon
panels of experts whose identities remained anonymous so there was no pressure on them from television executives.

It was quite a night for Scott. His then wife
Colleen Dewhurst was also nominated for *The Price*,
and a production he directed, *The Andersonville
Trial*, won for outstanding dramatic special. Jack
Cassidy, who was nominated for *Andersonville*,

accepted the Actor (Single Performance) award for
the maverick star.

ACTRESS (SINGLE PERFORMANCE)

Colleen Dewhurst (*The Price, Hallmark Hall*
  of Fame) (NBC)
Lee Grant (*The Neon Ceiling, World Premiere*
  NBC Monday Night at the Movies) (NBC)
Lee Grant (*Ransom for a Dead Man, World*
  Premiere NBC Monday Night at the Movies)

ACTOR (DRAMA SERIES)

Raymond Burr (*Ironside*) (NBC)
Mike Connors (*Mannix*) (CBS)
Hal Holbrook (*The Senator, The Bold Ones*) (NBC)
Robert Young (*Marcus Welby, MD*) (ABC)

ACTRESS (DRAMA SERIES)

Linda Cristal (*The High Chaparral*) (NBC)
Susan Hampshire (*The First Churchills,*
  Masterpiece Theatre) (PBS)
Peggy Lipton (*The Mod Squad*) (ABC)

ACTOR (COMEDY SERIES)

Ted Bessell (*That Girl*) (ABC)
Bill Bixby (*The Courtship of Eddie's Father*) (ABC)
Jack Klugman (*The Odd Couple*) (ABC)
Carroll O'Connor (*All in the Family*) (CBS)
Tony Randall (*The Odd Couple*) (ABC)

ACTRESS (COMEDY SERIES)

Jean Stapleton (*All in the Family*) (CBS)
Mary Tyler Moore (*The Mary Tyler Moore Show*)
  (CBS)
Marlo Thomas (*That Girl*) (ABC)

SUPPORTING ACTOR (DRAMA)

James Brolin (*Marcus Welby, MD*) (ABC)
David Burns (*The Price, Hallmark Hall of Fame*)
  (NBC)
Robert Young (*Vanished, World Premiere NBC*
  Monday and *Tuesday Night at the Movies*) (NBC)

Veteran Broadway comedian David Burns died a
few weeks before the Emmy ceremony. He had
originated the role of Solomon, the eighty-nine-
year-old furniture dealer, in *The Price* when it was
trying out in Philadelphia before playing New
York. Burns fell ill before the production reached

the Main Stem, but thanks to television his sterling performance has been preserved.

SUPPORTING ACTRESS (DRAMA)
Gail Fisher (*Mannix*) (CBS)
Margaret Leighton (*Hamlet, Hallmark Hall of Fame*) (NBC)
Susan Saint James (*The Name of the Game*) (NBC)
Elena Verdugo (*Marcus Welby, MD*) (ABC)

The *Hallmark* production of *Hamlet* received thirteen nominations—the most for any program that year—and won five. Margaret Leighton's magisterial portrayal of Gertrude was honored along with awards in four technical categories. Richard Chamberlain in the title role of the Melancholy Dane was not nominated.

SUPPORTING ACTOR (COMEDY)
Edward Asner (*The Mary Tyler Moore Show*) (CBS)
Michael Constantine (*Room 222*) (ABC)
Gale Gordon (*Here's Lucy*) (CBS)

SUPPORTING ACTRESS (COMEDY)
Valerie Harper (*The Mary Tyler Moore Show*) (CBS)
Agnes Moorehead (*Bewitched*) (ABC)
Karen Valentine (*Room 222*) (ABC)

SPECIAL CLASSIFICATION OF OUTSTANDING ACHIEVEMENT
Harvey Korman (*The Carol Burnett Show*) (CBS)

OTHER AWARDS
Directing (Drama, Series): Daryl Duke ("The Day the Lion Died," *The Senator, The Bold Ones*) (NBC); Directing (Drama, Special): Fielder Cook (*The Price, Hallmark Hall of Fame*) (NBC); Directing (Comedy): Jay Sandrich ("Toulouse-Lautrec Is One of My Favorite Artists," *The Mary Tyler Moore Show*) (CBS); Directing (Variety or Music, Series): Mark Warren (*Rowan and Martin's Laugh-In* with Orson Welles) (NBC); Directing (Variety or Music, Special): Sterling Johnson (*Timex Presents Peggy Fleming at Sun Valley*) (NBC)

Mark Warren of *Rowan and Martin's Laugh-In* was the first African-American director to win an Emmy.

Writing (Drama, Series): Joel Oliansky ("To Taste of Death but Once," *The Senator, The Bold Ones*)

(NBC); Writing (Drama, Special—Original): Tracy Keenan Wynn, Marvin Schwartz (*Tribes, Movie of the Week*) (ABC); Writing (Drama, Special—Adaptation): Saul Levitt (*The Andersonville Trial, Hollywood Television Theatre* (PBS); Writing (Comedy): James L. Brooks, Allan Burns ("Support Your Local Mother," *The Mary Tyler Moore Show*) (CBS); Writing (Variety or Music, Series): Herbert Baker, Hal Goodman, Larry Klein, Bob Weiskopf, Bob Schiller, Norman Steinberg, Flip Wilson (*The Flip Wilson Show* with Lena Horne and Tony Randall) (NBC); Writing (Variety or Music, Special): Bob Ellison, Marty Farrell (*Singer Presents Burt Bacharach*) (CBS)

With almost all production of prime-time entertainment now based on the West Coast, the Emmys dropped New York as a location. Starting with the 1970–71 awards, the entire ceremony would originate from Los Angeles. Johnny Carson, host of *The Tonight Show* and so far Emmy-less, served as host for the first of many times. He eventually graduated to the Oscars.

THE PEABODY AWARDS (FOR 1971)

ENTERTAINMENT
The American Revolution: 1770–1783, A Conversation with Lord North (CBS); *Brian's Song, ABC Movie of the Week* (ABC); NBC for its dramatic programming

EDUCATION
The Turned On Crisis (WQED-TV, Pittsburgh)

NEWS
John Rich (NBC Radio and Television)

YOUTH OR CHILDREN'S PROGRAM
Make a Wish (ABC)

PUBLIC SERVICE
This Child Is Rated X (NBC)

PROMOTION OF INTERNATIONAL UNDERSTANDING
United Nations Day Concert with Pablo Casals (United Nations Television)

SPECIAL AWARDS

George Heinemann of NBC for contributions to children's programming; Mississippi Authority for Educational Television and William Smith, executive director; Dr. Frank Stanton, president, CBS, Inc.

THE GOLDEN GLOBE AWARDS (FOR 1971)

Drama Series: *Mannix* (CBS); Comedy or Musical Series: *All in the Family* (CBS)

Actor (Drama): Robert Young (*Marcus Welby, MD*) (ABC); Actress (Drama): Patricia Neal (*The Homecoming*) (CBS); Actor (Comedy or Musical): Carroll O'Connor (*All in the Family*) (CBS); Actress (Comedy or Musical): Carol Burnett (*The Carol Burnett Show*) (CBS); Supporting Actor: Edward Asner (*The Mary Tyler Moore Show*) (CBS); Supporting Actress: Sue Ann Langdon (*Arnie*) (CBS)

1971-72

THE EMMY AWARDS

SINGLE PROGRAM (DRAMA OR COMEDY)

Brian's Song, ABC Movie of the Week (ABC)
"Jane Seymour," *The Six Wives of Henry VIII* (CBS)
"The Lion's Cub," *Elizabeth R, Masterpiece Theatre* (PBS)
"Sammy's Visit," *All in the Family* (CBS)
The Snow Goose, Hallmark Hall of Fame (NBC)

DRAMA SERIES

Columbo, NBC Mystery Movie (NBC)
Elizabeth R, *Masterpiece Theatre* (PBS)
Mannix (CBS)
Marcus Welby, MD (ABC)
The Six Wives of Henry VIII (CBS)

The 1971–72 Emmys were dominated by the British, with imported English shows winning Drama Series and New Series (*Elizabeth R* showcased on PBS's new anthology program *Masterpiece Theatre*), Actor (Single Performance) (Keith

Michell as Elizabeth I's father, Henry VIII, in CBS's *The Six Wives of Henry VIII*), Actress (Single Performance) and Actress (Drama Series) (both to Glenda Jackson as the Virgin Queen), Supporting Actress (Drama) (Jenny Agutter in *The Snow Goose*), and Docu-drama (*The Search for the Nile*). You could even count *All in the Family* and *Sanford and Son* as part of the British invasion because they were based on English shows. American producers bristled and the Academy responded three days after the awards by creating a new category for the following year: limited series. Most of the British programs were relegated there since their series usually contained no more than six or seven episodes.

COMEDY SERIES

All in the Family (CBS)
The Mary Tyler Moore Show (CBS)
The Odd Couple (ABC)
Sanford and Son (NBC)

VARIETY SERIES (MUSICAL)

The Carol Burnett Show (CBS)
The Dean Martin Show (NBC)
The Flip Wilson Show (NBC)
The Sonny and Cher Show (CBS)

"I won my first Emmy ten years ago and here I am one year older," Carol Burnett told the audience upon winning the first of three Emmys for her variety series. Her previous wins were for her supporting role on *The Garry Moore Moore Show* and a special she did with Julie Andrews.

VARIETY SERIES (TALK)

The David Frost Show (Syndicated)
The Dick Cavett Show (ABC)
The Tonight Show Starring Johnny Carson (NBC)

SINGLE PROGRAM (VARIETY OR MUSICAL)

The Flip Wilson Show (NBC)
Jack Lemmon in 'S Wonderful, 'S Marvelous, 'S Gershwin (NBC)
Julie and Carol at Lincoln Center (CBS)
The Sonny and Cher Comedy Hour (CBS)

"This is wonderful, especially when you're out of work," enthused Martin Charnin when he won for

Glenda Jackson (right) as Elizabeth I (in *Masterpiece Theatre's Elizabeth R*) and Keith Michell (left) as Elizabeth I's father Henry VIII (in CBS's *The Six Wives of Henry VIII*). Both were crowned for Emmy honors at the 1972–73 ceremony.

co-directing the Jack Lemmon special saluting the music of George Gershwin. Later in the evening when he copped another award for producing the same show, he stated, "I just got a job off-stage."

NEW SERIES

Columbo, NBC Mystery Movie (NBC)
Elizabeth R, Masterpiece Theatre (PBS)
Sanford and Son (NBC)
The Six Wives of Henry VIII (CBS)
The Sonny and Cher Comedy Hour (CBS)

ACTOR (SINGLE PERFORMANCE)

James Caan (*Brian's Song, ABC Movie of the Week*) (ABC)
Richard Harris (*The Snow Goose, Hallmark Hall of Fame*) (NBC)
Keith Michell ("Catherine Howard," *The Six Wives of Henry VIII*) (CBS)
George C. Scott (*Jane Eyre*) (NBC)
Billy Dee Williams (*Brian's Song, ABC Movie of the Week*) (ABC)

ACTRESS (SINGLE PERFORMANCE)

Helen Hayes (*Do Not Fold, Spindle or Mutilate, ABC Movie of the Week*) (ABC)
Glenda Jackson ("The Lion's Cub," *Elizabeth R, Masterpiece Theatre*) (PBS)
Glenda Jackson ("Shadow in the Sun," *Elizabeth R, Masterpiece Theatre*) (PBS)
Patricia Neal (*The Homecoming*) (CBS)
Susannah York (*Jane Eyre*) (NBC)

ACTOR (DRAMA SERIES)

Raymond Burr (*Ironside*) (NBC)
Mike Connors (*Mannix*) (CBS)
Peter Falk (*Columbo, NBC Mystery Movie*) (NBC)
Keith Michell (*The Six Wives of Henry VIII*) (CBS)
Robert Young (*Marcus Welby, MD*) (ABC)

ACTRESS (DRAMA SERIES)

Glenda Jackson (*Elizabeth R, Masterpiece Theatre*) (PBS)
Peggy Lipton (*The Mod Squad*) (ABC)
Susan Saint James (*McMillan and Wife, NBC Mystery Movie*) (NBC)

ACTOR (COMEDY SERIES)

Redd Foxx (*Sanford and Son*) (NBC)
Jack Klugman (*The Odd Couple*) (ABC)
Carroll O'Connor (*All in the Family*) (CBS)
Tony Randall (*The Odd Couple*) (ABC)

ACTRESS (COMEDY SERIES)

Sandy Duncan (*Funny Face*) (CBS)
Mary Tyler Moore (*The Mary Tyler Moore Show*) (CBS)
Jean Stapleton (*All in the Family*) (CBS)

SUPPORTING ACTOR (DRAMA)

James Brolin (*Marcus Welby, MD*) (ABC)
Greg Morris (*Mission: Impossible*) (CBS)
Jack Warden (*Brian's Song, ABC Movie of the Week*) (ABC)

SUPPORTING ACTRESS (DRAMA)

Jenny Agutter (*The Snow Goose, Hallmark Hall of Fame*) (NBC)
Gail Fisher (*Mannix*) (CBS)
Elena Verdugo (*Marcus Welby, MD*) (ABC)

SUPPORTING ACTOR (COMEDY)

Edward Asner (*The Mary Tyler Moore Show*) (CBS)
Ted Knight (*The Mary Tyler Moore Show*) (CBS)
Rob Reiner (*All in the Family*) (CBS)

SUPPORTING ACTRESS (COMEDY) (TIE)

Valerie Harper (*The Mary Tyler Moore Show*) (CBS)
Cloris Leachman (*The Mary Tyler Moore Show*) (CBS)
Sally Struthers (*All in the Family*) (CBS)

PERFORMER IN MUSIC OR VARIETY

Ruth Buzzi (*Rowan and Martin's Laugh-In*) (NBC)
Harvey Korman (*The Carol Burnett Show*) (CBS)
Lily Tomlin (*Rowan and Martin's Laugh-In*) (NBC)

The previous year, Harvey Korman, Carol Burnett's versatile second banana, refused to accept a special award because it would be presented at a separate technical Emmy awards presentation. For 1971–72 the Academy promised his category would be shown on the prime-time broadcast. Korman agreed to take the award if he won. At the last minute, the show ran over and his category was cut.

OTHER AWARDS

Directing (Drama, Single Program): Tom Gries (*The Glass House, The New CBS Friday Night Movies*) (CBS); Directing (Drama, Series): Alexander Singer ("The Invasion of Kevin Ireland," *The Lawyers, The Bold Ones*) (NBC); Directing (Comedy): John Rich ("Sammy's Visit," *All in the Family*) (CBS); Directing (Variety or Music, Series): Art Fisher (*The Sonny and Cher Comedy Hour* with Tony Randall); Directing (Variety or Music, Single Program): Walter C. Miller, Martin Charnin (*Jack Lemmon in 'S Wonderful, 'S Marvelous, 'S Gershwin*) (NBC)

Writing (Drama, Single Program—Original Teleplay): Allan Sloane (*To All My Friends on Shore*) (CBS); Writing (Drama, Single Program—Adaptation): William Blinn (*Brian's Song, ABC Movie of the Week*) (ABC); Writing (Drama, Series): Richard L. Levinson, William Link ("Death Lends a Hand," *Columbo, NBC Mystery Movie*) (NBC); Writing (Comedy, Series): Burt Styler ("Edith's Problem," *All in the Family*) (CBS); Writing (Variety or

Music, Series): Don Hinkley, Stan Hart, Larry Siegel, Woody Kling, Roger Beatty, Art Baer, Ben Joelson, Stan Burns, Mike Marmer, Arnie Rosen (*The Carol Burnett Show* with Tim Conway and Ray Charles) (CBS); Writing (Variety or Music, Single Program): Anne Howard Bailey (*The Trial of Mary Lincoln, NET Opera*) (PBS)

"The Emmys made Hollywood's self-conscious Oscars look like Broadway's brilliant Tonys," sneered *The New York Times* in response to the twenty-third annual Emmys. Johnny Carson repeated his hosting chores and attempted to inject much-needed humor into the proceedings. Toward the end of the evening, he advised the attendees, "Please keep your seats. The waiters will be around soon with breakfast." After a long-winded acceptance speech by Norman Lear, the profilic producer of *All in the Family* and *Sanford and Son*, Carson quipped, "I understand Norman just sold that speech as a new series."

But most of the entertainment was not sparkling, the nadir being reached when Paul Lynde presented an award with an ape (the chimp from an awful short-lived series *The Chimp and Me*). Lynde made a tasteless joke about the animal forgetting to use a deordorant.

A big patriotic musical number was provided by the Johnny Mann Singers. As the choir belted out "You're a Grand Old Flag," a giant American flag unfurled. Mann turned from his singers to the audience and said, "We're all partners and, partner, this is no time to sell out." His meaning was presumably to support the Vietnam War, which was still raging. Carson added irony to the saccharine moment by sarcastically stating after the song that "war bonds are on sale in the lobby."

THE PEABODY AWARDS (FOR 1972; NO SPECIFIC CATEGORIES)

The Waltons (CBS); NBC for the musical specials *Jack Lemmon in 'S Wonderful, 'S Marvelous, 'S Gershwin, Singer Presents Liza with a "Z,"* and *The Timex All-Star Swing Festival*; *The Search for the Nile* (BBC, NBC); *Pensions: The Broken Promise* (NBC); Bill Monroe, NBC-TV, Washington editor of *Today*; Alistair Cooke; *ABC Afterschool Specials* (ABC); *Captain Kangaroo* (CBS); WHRO-TV,

Norfolk, "for its overall classroom programming"; *The Restless Earth* (WNET, New York, and BBC); *China '72: A Hole in the Bamboo Curtain* (WWL-TV, New Orleans); *Willowbrook: The Last Disgrace* (WABC-TV, New York); ABC for sports coverage of the Olympics

THE GOLDEN GLOBE AWARDS (FOR 1972)

Made-for-TV Movie: *That Certain Summer* (ABC); Drama Series: *Columbo* (NBC); Comedy or Musical Series: *All in the Family* (CBS).

Actor (Drama): Peter Falk (*Colombo, NBC Sunday Mystery Movie*) (NBC); Actress (Drama): Gail Fisher (*Mannix*) (CBS); Actor (Comedy or Musical): Red Foxx (*Sanford and Son*) (NBC); Actress (Comedy or Musical): Jean Stapleton (*All in the Family*) (CBS); Supporting Actor: James Brolin (*Marcus Welby, MD* (ABC); Supporting Actress: Ruth Buzzi (*Rowan and Martin's Laugh-In*) (NBC)

THE EMMY AWARDS

SINGLE PROGRAM (DRAMA OR COMEDY)
Long Day's Journey into Night (ABC)
The Marcus-Nelson Murders, The CBS Thursday Night Movies (CBS)
The Red Pony, The Bell System Family Theatre (NBC)
That Certain Summer, Wednesday Movie of the Week (ABC)
A War of Children, *The New CBS Tuesday Night Movies* (CBS)

DRAMA SERIES
Cannon (CBS)
Columbo, NBC Sunday Mystery Movie (NBC)
Hawaii Five-O (CBS)
Kung Fu (ABC)
The Waltons (CBS)

According to Emmy host Johnny Carson, *The Waltons* was a show "with no homosexuals, no atheists, and nobody had an abortion. Who'd think a bunch of weirdos like that would win?" The Depression-era family series received twelve Emmy nominations, the most for 1972–73. The show won a total of six statuettes—three for acting, one for best drama series, one for writing, and another for film editing. It was in an uphill ratings struggle against *The Flip Wilson Show*, but its warm depiction of an earlier, simpler time soon earned it a long run. Perhaps its popularity was a reaction to the proliferation of issue-oriented, contemporary shows and specials like *Maude* (in which the main charcter had an abortion), *All in the Family*, and the TV-movie *That Certain Summer*, the story of a gay father telling his son about his sexuality.

Waltons writer John McGreevy gave the funniest acceptance speech of the night by thanking "the man who did so much to make the Depression possible—Herbert Hoover."

COMEDY SERIES
All in the Family (CBS)
The Mary Tyler Moore Show (CBS)
*M*A*S*H* (CBS)
Maude (CBS)
Sanford and Son (NBC)

LIMITED SERIES
The Last of the Mohicans, Masterpiece Theatre (PBS)
The Life of Leonardo Da Vinci (CBS)
Tom Brown's Schooldays, Masterpiece Theatre (PBS)

Take that, Brits! After a sweep of the 1971–72 Emmys, the English were relegated to the new limited series categories. They dominated this area, but their triumphs were not even broadcast on the ceremony because of time constraints. The winner of the best new series award *America* was also British-made. The BBC documentary series narrated by Alistair Cooke was announced before the Emmys went on the air.

VARIETY MUSICAL SERIES
The Carol Burnett Show (CBS)
The Dick Cavett Show (ABC)
The Flip Wilson Show (NBC)
The Julie Andrews Hour (ABC)
The Sonny and Cher Comedy Hour (CBS)

The Julie Andrews Hour won a total of seven Emmys, including Variety Series, Directing (Variety or Music, Series), and five technical citations. This set a record for the most Emmys for any series in one year which lasted until 1980–81 when *Hill Street Blues* collared eight. ABC and the public did not agree with the Academy on Andrews' show. The series was axed after only one Emmy-laden, but low-rated season.

SINGLE PROGRAM (VARIETY OR MUSICAL)
Applause (CBS)
Once upon a Mattress (NBC)
Singer Presents Liza with a "Z" (NBC)

Award history was made when Bob Fosse won three awards for directing, producing, and choreographing *Liza with a "Z"*, a Singer-sponsored special featuring Liza Minnelli. Just a few weeks earlier, Fosse had garnered an Oscar for directing Minnelli in *Cabaret* and two Tonys for staging and directing *Pippin*. He is the only person in history to cop the top awards in film, theater, and TV in the same year.

NEW SERIES
America (NBC)
The Julie Andrews Hour (ABC)
Kung Fu (ABC)
*M*A*S*H* (CBS)
Maude (CBS)
The Waltons (CBS)

ACTOR (SINGLE PERFORMANCE)
Henry Fonda (*The Red Pony, The Bell System Family Theatre*) (NBC)
Hal Holbrook (*That Certain Summer, Wednesday Movie of the Week*) (ABC)
Laurence Olivier (*Long Day's Journey into Night*) (ABC)
Telly Savalas (*The Marcus-Nelson Murders, The CBS Thursday Night Movies*) (CBS)

ACTRESS (SINGLE PERFORMANCE)
Lauren Bacall (*Applause*) (CBS)
Hope Lange (*That Certain Summer, Wednesday Movie of the Week*) (ABC)
Cloris Leachman (*A Brand New Life, Tuesday Movie of the Week*) (ABC)

ACTOR (DRAMA SERIES)
David Carradine (*Kung Fu*) (ABC)
Mike Connors (*Mannix*) (CBS)
William Conrad (*Cannon*) (CBS)
Peter Falk (*Columbo, NBC Sunday Mystery Movie*) (NBC)
Richard Thomas (*The Waltons*) (CBS)

ACTRESS (DRAMA SERIES)
Lynda Day George (*Mission: Impossible*) (CBS)
Susan Saint James (*McMillan and Wife, NBC Sunday Mystery Movie*) (NBC)
Michael Learned (*The Waltons*) (CBS)

ACTOR (COMEDY SERIES)
Alan Alda (*M*A*S*H*) (CBS)
Redd Foxx (*Sanford and Son*) (NBC)
Jack Klugman (*The Odd Couple*) (ABC)
Carroll O'Connor (*All in the Family*) (CBS)
Tony Randall (*The Odd Couple*) (ABC)

ACTRESS (COMEDY SERIES)
Beatrice Arthur (*Maude*) (CBS)
Jean Stapleton (*All in the Family*) (CBS)
Mary Tyler Moore (*The Mary Tyler Moore Show*) (CBS)

After two years of watching her supporting cast, writers, and directors win Emmys, Mary Tyler Moore finally won a statuette of her own for her spunky, independent, but somewhat shy Mary Richards.

ACTOR (LIMITED SERIES)
John Abineri (*The Last of the Mohicans, Masterpiece Theatre*) (PBS)
Philippi LeRoy (*The Life of Leonardo Da Vinci*) (CBS)
Anthony Murphy (*Tom Brown's School Days, Masterpiece Theatre*) (PBS)

ACTRESS (LIMITED SERIES)
Susan Hampshire (*Vanity Fair, Masterpiece Theatre*) (PBS)
Vivien Heilbron (*The Moonstone, Masterpiece Theatre*) (PBS)
Margaret Tyzack (*Cousin Bette, Masterpiece Theatre*) (PBS)

SUPPORTING ACTOR (DRAMA)
James Brolin (*Marcus Welby, MD*) (CBS)
Will Geer (*The Waltons*) (CBS)
Scott Jacoby (*That Certain Summer, Wednesday Movie of the Week*) (ABC)

SUPPORTING ACTRESS (DRAMA)
Ellen Corby (*The Waltons*) (CBS)
Gail Fisher (*Mannix*) (CBS)
Nancy Walker (*McMillan and Wife, NBC Sunday Mystery Movie*) (NBC)

SUPPORTING ACTOR (COMEDY)
Edward Asner (*The Mary Tyler Moore Show*) (CBS)
Gary Burghoff (*M*A*S*H*) (CBS)
Ted Knight (*The Mary Tyler Moore Show*) (CBS)
Rob Reiner (*All in the Family*) (CBS)
McLean Stevenson (*M*A*S*H*)

SUPPORTING ACTRESS (COMEDY)
Valerie Harper (*The Mary Tyler Moore Show*) (CBS)
Cloris Leachman (*The Mary Tyler Moore Show*) (CBS)
Sally Struthers (*All in the Family*) (CBS)

SUPPORTING PERFORMER (VARIETY OR MUSIC)
Tim Conway (*The Carol Burnett Show*) (CBS)
Harvey Korman (*The Carol Burnett Show*) (CBS)
Liza Minnelli (*A Royal Gala Variety Performance in the Presence of Her Majesty the Queen*) (ABC)
Lily Tomlin (*Rowan and Martin's Laugh-In*) (NBC)

OTHER AWARDS
Directing (Drama, Single Program): Joseph Sargent (*The Marcus-Nelson Murders, The CBS Thursday Night Movies*) (CBS); Directing (Drama, Series): Jerry Thorpe ("An Eye for an Eye," *Kung Fu*) (ABC); Directing (Comedy): Jay Sandrich ("It's Whether You Win or Lose," *The Mary Tyler Moore Show*) (CBS); Directing (Variety or Music, Series): Bill Davis (*The Julie Andrews Hour* with "Eliza Doolittle" and "Mary Poppins"); Directing (Variety or Music, Single Program): Bob Fosse (*Singer Presents Liza with a "Z"*)

Writing (Drama, Single Program—Original Teleplay): Abby Mann (*The Marcus-Melson Murders, The CBS Thursday Night Movies*) (CBS); Writing (Drama, Single Program—Adaptation): Eleanor Perry (*The House without a Christmas Tree*) (CBS); Writing (Comedy): Michael Ross, Bernie West, Lee Kalchiem ("The Bunkers and the Swingers," *All in the Family*) (CBS); Writing (Variety or Music, Series): Stan Hart, Larry Siegel, Gail Parent, Woody Kling, Roger Beatty, Tom Patchett, Jay Tarses, Robert Hilliard, Arnie Kogen, Bill Angelos, Buz Kohan (*The Carol Burnett Show* with Steve Lawrence and Lily Tomlin) (CBS); Writing (Variety or Music, Single Program): Renee Taylor, Joseph Bologna (*Acts of Love—and Other Comedies*) (ABC)

"Welcome to ABC's Wide World of Egos. This is an event second only in importance to the Golddiggers' auditions." So began Johnny Carson's opening monologue for his third stint as host of the Emmys. Don Rickles than proceeded to make mincemeat of the award procedures by putting them through the grinder of his comic venom. The program switched gears when Arthur Hill recited a tribute to TV scribes called "What Is a Writer?" while a silhouette of a actor typing away was shown on screen. Choreographer Tony Charmoli staged a salute to the TV dancer. A film montage satirizing cop shows had to be cut because of a Writers' Guild strike.

On the whole, the program moved smoothly, with producer Bob Finkel and director Marty Pasetta grouping the award presentations by category rather than giving out each one separately. *Variety* liked the show: "All things considered . . . [the Emmys] played rather well as live entertainment." But Kay Gardella of *The New York Daily News* found them "duller than dull."

THE PEABODY AWARDS (FOR 1973)

ENTERTAINMENT
Myshkin (WTIU-TV, Bloomington, IN); NBC, ABC, and CBS for "outstanding contribution to television drama as evidenced by *The Red Pony* (NBC), *Pueblo* and *The Glass Menagerie* (ABC), and *The Catholics, CBS Playhouse 90* (CBS)

EDUCATION
ABC "as evidenced by *The First and Essential Freedom* and *Learning Can Be Fun*"; *Dusty's Treehouse* (KNXT-TV, Los Angeles)

NEWS
Close-Up (ABC)

YOUTH AND CHILDREN'S PROGRAMS
The Borrowers, Hallmark Hall of Fame (NBC); *Street of the Flower Boxes, NBC Children's Theatre* (NBC)

PUBLIC SERVICE
Home Rule Campaign (WRC-TV, Washington, DC); Pamela Ilott (CBS), executive producer, *Lamp Unto My Feet* and *Look Up and Live*

PROMOTION OF INTERNATIONAL UNDERSTANDING
Overture to Friendship: The Philadelphia Orchestra in China (WCAU-TV, Philadelphia)

SPECIAL AWARDS
The Energy Crisis . . . An American White Paper (NBC); Joe Garagiola (*The Baseball World of Joe Garagiola*) (NBC); Peter Lisagor, *Chicago Daily News*, for contributions to broadcast news

THE GOLDEN GLOBE AWARDS (FOR 1973)

Drama Series: *The Waltons* (CBS); Comedy or Musical Series: *All in the Family* (CBS)

Actor (Drama Series): James Stewart (*Hawkins*) (CBS); Actress (Drama Series): Lee Remick (*The Blue Knight*) (NBC); Actor (Comedy or Musical Series): Jack Klugman (*The Odd Couple*) (ABC); Actress (Comedy or Musical Series) (tie): Jean Stapleton (*All in the Family*) (CBS) and Cher (*The Sonny and Cher Comedy Hour*) (CBS); Supporting Actor: McLean Stevenson (*M*A*S*H*); Supporting Actress: Ellen Corby (*The Waltons*) (CBS)

THE EMMY AWARDS

SINGLE PROGRAM
(DRAMA OR COMEDY)

The Autobiography of Miss Jane Pittman (CBS)
The Migrants, Playhouse 90 (CBS)
*The Execution of Private Slovik, NBC Wednesday
    Night at the Movies* (NBC)
Steambath, Hollywood Television Theatre (PBS)
6 Rms Riv Vu (CBS)

The most nominated program of the year, *The Autobiography of Miss Jane Pittman*, was up for twelve Emmys and collected a total of nine. The CBS special was a tour-de-force for Cicely Tyson, who portrayed a 110-year-old woman recalling her life from slavery to the Civil Rights movement.

DRAMA SERIES

Kojak (CBS)
Police Story (NBC)
The Streets of San Francisco (ABC)
Upstairs, Downstairs, *Masterpiece Theatre* (PBS)
The Waltons (CBS)

A surprise winner in the drama series category, the British import *Upstairs, Downstairs* charmed American audiences with its detailed depiction of the lives of the lords and servants in an Edwardian household. Since it was shown on *Masterpiece Theatre* in installments of thirteen episodes, it was not considered a limited series as previous English entries had been.

In the year of the "Super Emmy," Cicely Tyson won two awards for the same performance in *The Autobiography of Miss Jane Pittman* (1973–74).

COMEDY SERIES
All in the Family (CBS)
*M*A*S*H* (CBS)
The Mary Tyler Moore Show (CBS)
The Odd Couple (ABC)

LIMITED SERIES
The Blue Knight (NBC)
Columbo, *NBC Sunday Mystery Movie* (NBC)
McCloud, NBC Sunday Mystery Movie (NBC)

VARIETY OR MUSICAL SERIES
The Carol Burnett Show (CBS)
The Sonny and Cher Show (CBS)
The Tonight Show Starring Johnny Carson (NBC)

SINGLE PROGRAM (VARIETY OR MUSICAL)
Barbra Streisand . . . and Other Musical Instruments (CBS)
Lily Tomlin (CBS)
The John Denver Show (ABC)
Magnavox Presents Frank Sinatra (NBC)

In yet another attempt to pare down the gargantuan number of Emmy categories, the Academy proposed a new system: Winners would be announced before the ceremony and the victors in like categories would vie for a "Best of the Year" Award—the Super Emmy. For example, the outstanding actors in drama, comedy, limited series, and specials were to duke it out for top prize. Alan Alda from *M*A*S*H* might be up against Laurence Olivier in a dramatic special. "The number of categories was reaching an almost unmanageable level," explained Academy national president Robert Levine, "and it was felt therefore that the Emmy itself would begin to be so commonly distributed it would lose its meaning and significance."

A dissident block of 100 Academy members, representing such popular shows as *All in the Family, The Waltons, The Bob Newhart Show,* and *Maude*, quickly formed a committee to protest this radical innovation. Bob Sweeney, producer of *Hawaii Five-O*, was chairman of the committee. Grant Tinker, Mary Tyler Moore's husband and president of MTM Productions, resigned as chairman of the Emmy TV show (but remained as an Academy trustee).

There were threats of a boycott. "I would just as soon not attend. The new system is unfair," Moore told the press. The Academy compromised. Series winners would compete among themselves while outstanding performers in specials would be pitted against those from limited series. There was still some grumbling on Emmy night. "I feel like an apple that's been chosen over an orange," Moore said after she was named Actress of the Year in a Series over Michael Learned of *The Waltons*.

ACTOR (SINGLE PERFORMANCE)
Alan Alda (*6 Rms Riv Vu*) (CBS)
Hal Holbrook (*Pueblo, ABC Theatre*) (ABC)
Laurence Olivier (*The Merchant of Venice, ABC Theatre*) (ABC)
Martin Sheen (*The Execution of Private Slovik, NBC Wednesday Night at the Movies*) (NBC)
Dick Van Dyke (*The Morning After, Wednesday Movie of the Week*) (ABC)

ACTRESS (SINGLE PERFORMANCE)
Carol Burnett (*6 Rms Riv Vu*) (CBS)
Katharine Hepburn (*The Glass Menagerie*) (ABC)
Cloris Leachman (*The Migrants, Playhouse 90*) (CBS)
Elizabeth Montgomery (*A Case of Rape, NBC Wednesday Night at the Movies*) (NBC)
Cicely Tyson (*The Autobiography of Miss Jane Pittman*) (CBS)

ACTOR (LIMITED SERIES)
Peter Falk (*Columbo, NBC Sunday Mystery Movie*) (NBC)
William Holden (*The Blue Knight*) (NBC)
Dennis Weaver (*McCloud, NBC Sunday Mystery Movie*) (NBC)

ACTRESS (LIMITED SERIES)
Helen Hayes (*The Snoop Sisters, NBC Wednesday Mystery Movie*) (NBC)
Mildred Natwick (*The Snoop Sisters, NBC Wednesday Mystery Movie*) (NBC)
Lee Remick (*The Blue Knight*) (NBC)

ACTOR OF THE YEAR (SPECIAL)
Hal Holbrook (*Pueblo, ABC Theatre*) (ABC)

Carol Burnett and Harvey Korman (here parodying *Sunset Boulevard*) both won Emmys for *The Carol Burnett Show* (1967–79).

ACTRESS OF THE YEAR (SPECIAL)
Cicely Tyson (*The Autobiography of Miss Jane Pittman*) (CBS)

ACTOR (DRAMA SERIES)
William Conrad (*Cannon*) (CBS)
Karl Malden (*The Streets of San Francisco*) (ABC)
Telly Savalas (*Kojak*) (CBS)
Richard Thomas (*The Waltons*)

ACTRESS (DRAMA SERIES)
Michael Learned (*The Waltons*) (CBS)
Jean Marsh (*Upstairs, Downstairs, Masterpiece Theatre*) (PBS)
Jeanette Nolan (*Dirty Sally*) (CBS)

ACTOR (COMEDY SERIES)
Alan Alda (*M*A*S*H*) (CBS)
Redd Foxx (*Sanford and Son*) (NBC)
Jack Klugman (*The Odd Couple*) (ABC)
Carroll O'Connor (*All in the Family*) (CBS)
Tony Randall (*The Odd Couple*) (NBC)

ACTRESS (COMEDY SERIES)
Beatrice Arthur (*Maude*) (CBS)

Mary Tyler Moore (*The Mary Tyler Moore Show*) (CBS)
Jean Stapleton (*All in the Family*) (CBS)

ACTOR OF THE YEAR (SERIES)
Alan Alda (*M*A*S*H*) (CBS)

ACTRESS OF THE YEAR (SERIES)
Mary Tyler Moore (*The Mary Tyler Moore Show*) (CBS)

SUPPORTING ACTOR (DRAMA)
Michael Douglas (*The Streets of San Francisco*) (ABC)
Will Geer (*The Waltons*) (CBS)
Michael Moriarty (*The Glass Menagerie*) (ABC)
Sam Waterston (*The Glass Menagerie*) (CBS)

Just a month previously, Michael Moriarty had won a Tony Award for his performance as a British gay hustler in *Find Your Way Home*. His Emmy win for his sensitive limning of the Gentleman Caller in Tennessee Williams' *The Glass Menagerie* made him the first actor to garner the Tony and the Emmy in the same year.

SUPPORTING ACTRESS (DRAMA)
Ellen Corby (*The Waltons*) (CBS)
Joanna Miles (*The Glass Menagerie*) (ABC)
Nancy Walker (*McMillan and Wife, NBC Sunday Mystery Movie*) (NBC)

SUPPORTING ACTOR (COMEDY)
Edward Asner (*The Mary Tyler Moore Show*) (CBS)
Gary Burghoff (*M*A*S*H*) (CBS)
Ted Knight (*The Mary Tyler Moore Show*) (CBS)
Rob Reiner (*All in the Family*) (CBS)
McLean Stevenson (*M*A*S*H*) (NBC)

SUPPORTING ACTRESS (COMEDY)
Valerie Harper (*The Mary Tyler Moore Show*) (CBS)
Cloris Leachman ("The Lars Affair," *The Mary Tyler Moore Show*) (CBS)
Sally Struthers (*All in the Family*) (CBS)

SUPPORTING ACTOR (COMEDY/ VARIETY, VARIETY OR MUSIC)
Foster Brooks (*The Dean Martin Comedy Hour*) (NBC)
Tim Conway (*The Carol Burnett Show*) (CBS)
Harvey Korman (*The Carol Burnett Show*) (CBS)

SUPPORTING ACTRESS (COMEDY/ VARIETY, VARIETY OR MUSIC)
Ruth Buzzi (*The Dean Martin Comedy Hour*) (NBC)
Lee Grant (*The Shape of Things*) (CBS)
Vicki Lawrence (*The Carol Burnett Show*) (CBS)
Brenda Vaccaro (*The Shape of Things*) (CBS)

SUPPORTING ACTOR OF THE YEAR
Michael Moriarty (*The Glass Menagerie*) (ABC)

SUPPORTING ACTRESS OF THE YEAR
Joanna Miles (*The Glass Menagerie*) (ABC)

SPECIAL CLASSIFICATION OF OUTSTANDING PROGRAM AND INDIVIDUAL ACHIEVEMENT
The Dick Cavett Show (ABC); Tom Snyder, host *Tomorrow* (NBC)

Dick Cavett turned down his special classification Emmy because it was not mentioned during the broadcast. The witty talk-show host sent a telegram to the Academy: "If you could not find time for my award in your two-and-a-half-hour program, I cannot find room for your award in my four-and-a-half room apartment." Ironically, Cavett would host the news Emmys that September.

DAYTIME SHOWS
Drama Series: *The Doctors* (NBC); Daytime Special: *The Other Woman, ABC Matinee Today* (ABC); Actor (Daytime Special): Pat O'Brien (*The Other Woman, ABC Matinee Today*) (ABC); Actress (Daytime Special): Cathleen Nesbitt (*The Mask of Love, ABC Matinee Today*) (ABC); Actor (Series): MacDonald Carey (*Days of Our Lives*) (NBC); Actress (Series): Elizabeth Hubbard (*The Doctors*) (NBC); Daytime Actor of the Year: Pat O'Brien (*The Other Woman, ABC Matinee Today*); Daytime Actress of the Year: Cathleen Nesbitt (*The Mask of Love, ABC Matinee Today*) (ABC); Game Show: *Password* (ABC); Talk Show: *The Merv Griffin Show* (Syndicated)

For the first time, Emmys for daytime shows were presented in a separate ceremony. (There were now three Emmy prizefests—daytime, nighttime, and news, documentaries, and sports). The debut daytime fest was broadcast by NBC in an outdoor ceremony from New York's Rockefeller Center at noon on the same day as the prime-time show. The same rules applied for daytime as for the evening program. Winners in similar cateogries would compete for a "Best of the Year" prize. Daytime dramatic specials went out of vogue after a few years and categories to honor them were soon dropped.

OTHER PRIME-TIME AWARDS
Directing (Drama or Comedy, Single Program): John Korty (*The Autobiography of Miss Jane Pittman*) (CBS); Directing (Drama, Series): Robert Butler (*The Blue Knight*, Part III) (NBC); Directing (Comedy, Series): Jackie Cooper ("Carry On, Hawkeye," *M*A*S*H*) (CBS); Directing (Variety or Music, Series): Dave Powers ("The Australia Show," *The Carol Burnett Show*) (CBS); Directing (Variety or Music, Single Program): Dwight Hemion (*Barbra Streisand . . . and Other Musical Instruments*) (CBS)

Director of the Year (Series): Robert Butler (*The Blue Knight*, Part III) (NBC); Director of the Year

(Special): Dwight Hemion (*Barbra Streisand . . . and Other Musical Instruments*) (CBS)

Writing (Drama, Single Program—Original Teleplay): Fay Kanin (*Tell Me Where It Hurts, GE Theater*) (CBS); Writing (Drama, Single Program—Adaptation): Tracy Keenan Wynn (*The Autobiography of Miss Jane Pittman* (CBS); Writing (Drama, Series): Joanna Lee ("The Thanksgiving Story," *The Waltons*) (CBS); Writing (Comedy, Series): Treva Silverman ("The Lou and Edie Story," *The Mary Tyler Moore Show*) (CBS); Writing (Variety or Music, Series): Ed Simmons, Gary Belkin, Roger Beatty, Arnie Kogen, Bill Richmond, Gene Perret, Rudy DeLuca, Barry Levinson, Dick Clair, Jenna McMahon, Barry Harman (*The Carol Burnett Show* with Tim Conway and Bernadette Peters); Writing (Variety or Music, Single Program): Herb Sargent, Rosalyn Drexler, Lorne Michaels, Richard Pryor, Jim Rusk, James R. Stein, Robert Iles, Lily Tomlin, George Yanok, Jane Wagner, Rod Warren, Ann Elder, Karyl Geld (*Lily*) (CBS)

Writer of the Year (Special): Fay Kanin (*Tell Me Where It Hurts, GE Theater*) (CBS); Writer of the Year (Series): Treva Silverman ("The Lou and Edie Story," *The Mary Tyler Moore Show*) (CBS)

Shades of the category-less 1965 Emmys! The first and last ceremony featuring the "super Emmy" was an "orderly, almost subdued telecast that was practically devoid of suspense" declared *Variety*. Since the outstanding actors, actresses, directors, and writers were competing with each other, the winners in the various categories had been announced two weeks before the show. Despite the presence of Johnny Carson as host, the trade publication stated the proceedings were as exciting as "college commencement exercises."

The new system was lambasted in the press. Where was the logic in pitting sitcom writers with scribes for drama shows? How can one judge the direction of a Barbra Streisand musical special over that of a moving drama like *The Autobiography of Miss Jane Pittman*? The latest effort to streamline the Emmys was scrapped and the next year there was an explosion of categories.

THE PEABODY AWARDS (FOR 1974)
(No specific categories from this year on)

NBC for "distinguished dramatic programs, as evidenced by *The Execution of Private Slovik, The Law* and *IBM Presents Clarence Darrow*"; *Benjamin Franklin* (CBS); *Theater in America* (PBS, WNET, New York); *Nova* (PBS, WGBH, Boston); Carl Stern of NBC News; Fred Graham of CBS News; *Free to Be . . . You and Me* (ABC); *Sadat: Action Biography* (NBC); *Tornado! 4:40 p.m., Xenia, Ohio* (NBC); *From Belfast with Love*, news documentary, (WCCO-TV, Minneapolis); *The Right Man*, news documentary, (KPRC-TV, Houston); WCKT-TV, Miami, for local investigative reporting; Marilyn Baker, KQED-TV, San Francisco for local investigative reporting; *How Come?*, local children's series, (KING-TV, Seattle); The National Public Affairs Center for Television (NPACT); Julian Goodman, chairman of the board of NBC for "outstanding work in the area of first amendment rights and privileges for broadcasting"

THE GOLDEN GLOBE AWARDS (FOR 1974)

Drama Series: *Upstairs, Downstairs, Masterpiece Theatre* (PBS); Comedy or Musical Series: *Rhoda* (CBS)

Actor (Drama Series): Telly Savalas (*Kojak*) (CBS); Actress (Drama Series): Angie Dickinson (*Police Woman*) (NBC); Actor (Comedy or Musical Series): Alan Alda (*M*A*S*H*) (CBS); Actress (Comedy or Musical Series): Valerie Harper (*Rhoda*) (CBS); Supporting Actor: Harvey Korman (*The Carol Burnett Show*) (CBS); Supporting Actress: Betty Garrett (*All in the Family*) (CBS)

THE EMMY AWARDS

SINGLE PROGRAM
The Law, NBC World Premiere Movie (NBC)
Love among the Ruins, ABC Theatre (ABC)
The Missiles of October, ABC Theatre (ABC)
QB VII, ABC Theatre (ABC)
Queen of the Stardust Ballroom (CBS)

DRAMA SERIES

Kojak (CBS)
Police Story (NBC)
The Streets of San Francsico (ABC)
Upstairs, Downstairs, *Masterpiece*
  Theatre (PBS)
The Waltons (CBS)

COMEDY SERIES

All in the Family (CBS)
The Mary Tyler Moore Show (CBS)
M*A*S*H (CBS)
Rhoda (CBS)

"I'm really in trouble," cried Lucille Ball as she opened the envelope for outstanding Comedy Series. Unable to read the name of the winning show, she called out, "Glasses! Glasses!" Milton Berle and Art Carney, ready for a laugh, rushed to her aid with drinking glasses. Ball finally found her spectacles and read the victor, *The Mary Tyler Moore Show.* "Now can we help you off," quipped Berle.

The MTM Show had won a number of awards over the past four years but this was its first win as best comedy series (it lost three times to *All in the Family* and once to *M*A*S*H*). This year its total Emmy haul was twenty-one, the most for any prime-time series up to that point. If spin-offs counted, *MTM* would have an even higher Emmy count. Ironically, the star of the show, Mary Tyler Moore, would lose to Valerie Harper in the best comedy Actress category. Harper triumphed for *Rhoda*, a spin-off from *MTM*. Cloris Leachman would be nominated the following year for *Phyllis*, another show based on one of Mary's friends. After the original ended, Edward Asner went on to win two more Emmys to add to his previous three as *Lou Grant*, Mary's former boss who would edit a Los Angeles newspaper in a new one-hour drama. "With all the spin-offs, the zero population people think the MTM cat should be spayed," Asner commented.

LIMITED SERIES

Benjamin Franklin (CBS)
Columbo, NBC Sunday Mystery Movie (NBC)
McCloud, NBC Sunday Mystery Movie (NBC)

COMEDY-VARIETY OR MUSIC SERIES

The Carol Burnett Show (CBS)
Cher (CBS)

COMEDY-VARIETY OR MUSIC SPECIAL

An Evening with John Denver (ABC)
Lily (ABC)
Shirley MacLaine: If They Could See Me Now (CBS)

ACTOR (SINGLE PERFORMANCE)

Richard Chamberlain (*The Count of Monte Cristo, Bell System Family Theatre*) (NBC)
William Devane (*The Missiles of October, ABC Theatre*) (ABC)
Charles Durning (*The Queen of the Stardust Ballroom*) (CBS)
Henry Fonda (*IBM Presents Clarence Darrow*) (NBC)
Laurence Olivier (*Love among the Ruins, ABC Theatre*) (ABC)

ACTRESS (SINGLE PERFORMANCE)

Jill Clayburgh (*Hustling, ABC Saturday Night Movie*) (ABC)
Katharine Hepburn (*Love among the Ruins, ABC Theatre*) (ABC)
Elizabeth Montgomery (*The Legend of Lizzie Borden, Special World Premiere ABC Monday Night Movie*) (ABC)
Diana Rigg (*In This House of Brede, G.E. Theatre*) (CBS)
Maureen Stapleton (*Queen of the Stardust Ballroom*) (CBS)

ACTOR (DRAMA SERIES)

Robert Blake (*Baretta*) (ABC)
Karl Malden (*The Streets of San Francisco*) (ABC)
Barry Newman (*Petrocelli*) (NBC)
Telly Savalas (*Kojak*) (CBS)

Robert Blake's acceptance speech ranked with Patty Duke's as one of the most confusing in Emmy history. In addition to thanking personnel on his show, the detective series *Baretta*, he rambled on at length about a number of topics including welcoming Vietnamese boat people to our shores.

Katharine Hepburn and Laurence Olivier added Emmys to their collection of awards for *Love among the Ruins* (1974–75).

ACTRESS (DRAMA SERIES)
Angie Dickinson (*Police Woman*) (NBC)
Michael Learned (*The Waltons*) (CBS)
Jean Marsh (*Upstairs, Downstairs, Masterpiece Theatre*) (PBS)

ACTOR (COMEDY SERIES)
Alan Alda (*M*A*S*H*) (CBS)
Jack Albertson (*Chico and the Man*) (NBC)
Jack Klugman (*The Odd Couple*) (ABC)
Carroll O'Connor (*All in the Family*) (CBS)
Tony Randall (*The Odd Couple*) (ABC)

Winning for his persnickety Felix Ungar in the last year of *The Odd Couple*, Tony Randall remarked, "I sure am glad I won. Now if only I had a job."

ACTRESS (COMEDY SERIES)
Valerie Harper (*Rhoda*) (CBS)
Mary Tyler Moore (*The Mary Tyler Moore Show*) (CBS)
Jean Stapleton (*All in the Family*) (CBS)

ACTOR (LIMITED SERIES)
Peter Falk (*Columbo, NBC Sunday Mystery Movie*) (NBC)
Dennis Weaver (*McCloud, NBC Sunday Mystery Movie*) (NBC)

ACTRESS (LIMITED SERIES)
Susan Saint James (*McMillan and Wife, NBC Sunday Mystery Movie*) (NBC)
Jessica Walter (*Amy Prentiss, NBC Sunday Mystery Movie*) (NBC)

SUPPORTING ACTOR (SINGLE PERFORMANCE, DRAMA OR COMEDY SPECIAL)
Ralph Bellamy (*The Missiles of October*) (ABC)
Jack Hawkins (*QB VII, ABC Theatre*) (ABC)
Trevor Howard (*The Count of Monte Cristo, Bell System Family Theatre*) (NBC)
Anthony Quayle (*QB VII, ABC Theatre*) (ABC)

SUPPORTING ACTRESS (SINGLE PERFORMANCE, DRAMA OR COMEDY SPECIAL)
Eileen Heckart (*Wedding Band, ABC Theatre*) (ABC)
Juliet Mills (*QB VII, ABC Theatre*) (ABC)
Charlotte Rae (*Queen of the Stardust Ballroom*) (CBS)
Lee Remick (*QB VII, ABC Theatre*) (ABC)

SUPPORTING ACTOR (DRAMA SERIES)
J. D. Cannon (*McCloud, NBC Sunday Mystery Movie*) (NBC)

Michael Douglas (*The Streets of San Francisco*) (ABC)
Will Geer (*The Waltons*) (CBS)

SUPPORTING ACTRESS
(DRAMA SERIES)
Angela Baddeley (*Upstairs, Downstairs, Masterpiece Theatre*) (PBS)
Ellen Corby (*The Waltons*) (CBS)
Nancy Walker (*McMillan and Wife, NBC Sunday Mystery Movie*) (NBC)

SUPPORTING ACTOR
(COMEDY SERIES)
Edward Asner (*The Mary Tyler Moore Show*) (CBS)
Gary Burghoff (*M*A*S*H*) (CBS)
Ted Knight (*The Mary Tyler Moore Show*) (CBS)
Rob Reiner (*All in the Family*) (CBS)
McLean Stevenson (*M*A*S*H*) (CBS)

SUPPORTING ACTRESS
(COMEDY SERIES)
Julie Kavner (*Rhoda*) (CBS)
Loretta Swit (*M*A*S*H*) (CBS)
Nancy Walker (*Rhoda*) (CBS)
Betty White (*The Mary Tyler Moore Show*) (CBS)

SUPPORTING ACTOR
(SINGLE PERFORMANCE,
COMEDY OR DRAMA SERIES)
Lew Ayres ("The Vanishing Image," *Kung Fu*) (ABC)
Harold Gould ("Fathers and Sons," *Police Story*) (NBC)
Patrick McGoohan ("By Dawn's Early Light," *Columbo, NBC Sunday Mystery Movie*) (NBC)
Harry Morgan ("The General Flipped at Dawn," *M*A*S*H*) (CBS)

SUPPORTING ACTRESS
(SINGLE PERFORMANCE,
COMEDY OR DRAMA SERIES) (TIE)
Zohra Lampert ("The Queen of the Gypsies," *Kojak*) (CBS)
Cloris Leachman ("Phyllis Whips Inflation," *The Mary Tyler Moore Show*) (CBS)
Shelley Winters ("The Barefoot Girls of Bleecker Street," *McCloud, NBC Sunday Mystery Movie*) (NBC)

SUPPORTING ACTOR
(VARIETY OR MUSIC)
Jack Albertson (*Cher*) (CBS)
Tim Conway (*The Carol Burnett Show*) (CBS)
John Denver (*Doris Day Today*) (CBS)

SUPPORTING ACTRESS
(VARIETY OR MUSIC)
Vicki Lawrence (*The Carol Burnett Show*) (CBS)
Cloris Leachman (*Cher*) (CBS)
Rita Moreno (*Out to Lunch*) (ABC)

DAYTIME AWARDS
Daytime Series: *The Young and the Restless* (CBS); Drama Special: *The Girl Who Couldn't Lose, ABC Afternoon Playbreak* (ABC); Actor (Drama Series): MacDonald Carey (*Days of Our Lives*) (NBC); Actress (Drama Series): Susan Flannery (*Days of Our Lives*) (NBC); Actor (Daytime Special): Bradford Dillman (*The Last Bride of Salem, ABC Afternoon Playbreak*) (ABC); Actress (Daytime Special): Kay Lenz (*Heart in Hiding, ABC Afternoon Playbreak*) (ABC)

The second annual daytime Emmys were presented on board a Hudson River Day Liner in the New York Harbor.

OTHER PRIME-TIME AWARDS
Directing (Drama or Comedy, Single Program): George Cukor (*Love among the Ruins, ABC Theatre*) (ABC); Directing (Drama, Series): Bill Bain ("A Sudden Storm," *Upstairs, Downstairs, Masterpiece Theatre*) (PBS); Directing (Comedy, Series): Gene Reynolds ("O.R.," *M*A*S*H*) (CBS); Directing (Comedy-Variety or Music, Series): Dave Powers (*The Carol Burnett Show* with Alan Alda) (CBS); Directing (Comedy-Variety or Music, Single Program): Bill Davis (*An Evening with John Denver*) (ABC)

Writing (Drama, Single Program—Original Teleplay): James Costigan (*Love among the Ruins, ABC Theatre*) (ABC); Writing (Drama, Single Program—Adaptation): David W. Rintels (*IBM Presents Clarence Darrow*) (NBC); Writing (Drama, Series): Howard Fast ("The Ambassador," *Benjamin Franklin*) (CBS); Writing (Comedy, Series): Ed Weinberger, Stan Daniels ("Mary Richards Goes to Jail," *The Mary Tyler Moore Show*) (CBS); Writing

(Comedy-Variety or Music, Series): Ed Simmons, Gary Belkin, Roger Beatty, Arnie Kogen, Bill Richmond, Gene Perret, Rudy De Luca, Barry Levinson, Dick Clair, Jenna McMahon (*The Carol Burnett Show* with Alan Alda); Writing (Comedy-Variety or Music, Single Program): Bob Wells, John Bradford, Cy Coleman (*Shirley MacLaine: If They Could See Me Now*) (CBS)

As if to make up for the previous year's disastrous "Super Emmys," the television academy decided it was time to give Emmys to everybody by expanding the categories exponentially. There were 231 nominations for night- and daytime Emmys. (Because of a dispute over the rules and a lack of network support to carry them over the air during the awards show, there were no news Emmys presented.)

The prime-time show opened with a parade of thirty-five nominees in the ten supporting acting categories—single performances in series and specials were now given separate awards. Johnny Carson had declined to participate since he felt his gabfest *The Tonight Show* was improperly placed in competition with variety series like *The Carol Burnett Show* and *Cher*. As a result, *The Tonight Show* was withdrawn from Emmy consideration (the show won a special Emmy the following year). To replace Carson as emcee, ten leading ladies of the videowaves, including Mary Tyler Moore, Carol Burnett, and Beatrice Arthur, were recruited.

The program was devoid of staged entertainment save for Cloris Leachman's gown coming unhooked and Jack Albertson crooning "I've Grown Accustomed to His Face" to his *Chico and the Man* co-star Freddie Prinze. To save time, it was announced that writers and directors would not be allowed to make acceptance speeches. Another threatened boycott scotched this notion. The writers and directors got to have their say.

THE PEABODY AWARDS (FOR 1975)

*M*A*S*H* (CBS); *Love among the Ruins, ABC Theatre* (ABC); *Mr. Rooney Goes to Washington* (CBS News); *The American Assassins* (CBS); *Weekend* (NBC); Charles Kurault, CBS News, for "On the Road to '76"; The ABC Afterschool Specials (ABC), *Call It Macaroni* (Group W), *Big*

Blue Marble (Alphaventure), and *Snippets* (Kaiser Broadcasting), all outstanding children's programs; WCVB, Boston, for excellence in viewer-oriented programming; WTOP-TV, Washington, DC, for "overall public service effort"; WCKT-TV, Miami, for "outstanding investigative reporting"; *The Dale Car: A Dream or a Nightmare*, local news documenatary (KABC-TV, Los Angeles); *A Sunday Journal*, local news magazine (WWL-TV, New Orleans); *Las Rosas Blancas*, local dramatic program (WAPA-TV, San Juan); Dr. James Killian, Boston, for "outstanding contribution to educational television"

THE GOLDEN GLOBE AWARDS (FOR 1975)

Made-for-TV Movie: *Babe* (CBS); Drama Series: *Kojak* (CBS); Comedy or Musical Series: *Barney Miller* (ABC)

Actor (Drama Series) (tie): Robert Blake (*Baretta*) (ABC) and Telly Savalas (*Kojak*) (CBS); Actress (Drama Series): Lee Remick (*Jennie: Lady Randolph Churchill, Great Performances*) (PBS); Actor (Comedy or Musical Series): Alan Alda (*M*A*S*H*) (CBS); Actress (Comedy or Musical Series): Cloris Leachman (*Phyllis*) (CBS); Supporting Actor (tie): Edward Asner (*The Mary Tyler Moore Show*) (CBS) and Tim Conway (*The Carol Burnett Show*) (CBS); Supporting Actress: Hermione Baddeley (*Maude*) (CBS)

1975-76

THE EMMY AWARDS

SINGLE PROGRAM (DRAMA OR COMEDY)
Babe (CBS)
***Eleanor and Franklin, ABC Theatre* (ABC)**
Fear on Trial (CBS)
The Lindbergh Kidnapping Case, NBC Thursday Night at the Movies (NBC)
A Moon for the Misbegotten, ABC Theatre (ABC)

Eleanor and Franklin, a two-part drama special centering on the Roosevelts, received sixteen nominations and won eleven, the most for any made-for-

TV movie. Ironically, the leading actors, Edward Herrmann and Jane Alexander, lost to performers playing other real-life figures from the same era: Anthony Hopkins as accused kidnapper Bruno Hauptmann in *The Lindbergh Kidnapping Case* and Susan Clark as athlete Babe Didrikson Zaharias in *Babe*.

DRAMA SERIES
Baretta (ABC)
Columbo, NBC Sunday Mystery Movie (NBC)
Police Story (NBC)
The Streets of San Francisco (ABC)

COMEDY SERIES
All in the Family (CBS)
Barney Miller (ABC)

The Mary Tyler Moore Show (CBS)
*M*A*S*H* (CBS)
Welcome Back, Kotter (ABC)

LIMITED SERIES
The Adams Chronicles (PBS)
*Jennie: Lady Randolph Churchill,
    Great Performances* (PBS)
The Law (NBC)
Rich Man, Poor Man (ABC)
Upstairs, Downstairs, *Masterpiece Theatre* (PBS)

Even though it was still running in braces of thirteen episodes, *Upstairs, Downstairs* was moved from the regular Drama Series category to the Limited Series slot. Many columnists conjectured this shift was made to allow an American program to win

the Drama Series award since the British *Upstairs* had dominated the category for the last two years. In a parallel switch, *Columbo*, which ran a small number of segments per season, was relocated from the Limited Series to the regular Drama series category.

COMEDY-VARIETY OR MUSIC SERIES

The Carol Burnett Show (CBS)
NBC's Saturday Night Live (NBC)

Lorne Michaels, producer of the irreverent, youth-oriented, late-night series *Saturday Night Live*, thanked the city where it was filmed, New York, "for providing the rejection and alienation that keeps the comedy spirit alive." That spirit was seen in acceptance speeches by winners from the show. Chevy Chase did his trademark pratfall on the way to the stage. Once there, he said, "This is totally expected on my part." The army of winning *SNL* writers joked about writing a sketch for their next show about a group of scribes who couldn't come up with a sketch because they all went to the Emmys.

SINGLE PROGRAM (COMEDY-VARIETY OR MUSIC)

Gypsy in My Soul (CBS)
John Denver Rocky Mountain Christmas (ABC)
Lily Tomlin (ABC)
The Monty Python Show, Wide World Special (ABC)
Steve and Edyie: Our Love Is Here To Stay (CBS)

ACTOR (SINGLE PERFORMANCE, SPECIAL)

William Devane (*Fear on Trial*) (CBS)
Edward Herrmann (*Eleanor and Franklin, ABC Theatre*) (ABC)
Anthony Hopkins (*The Lindbergh Kidnapping Case, NBC Thursday Night at the Movies*) (NBC)
Jack Lemmon (*The Entertainer*) (NBC)

Jason Robards (*A Moon for the Misbegotten, ABC Theatre*) (ABC)

ACTRESS (SINGLE PERFORMANCE, SPECIAL)
Jane Alexander (*Eleanor and Franklin, ABC Theatre*) (ABC)
Susan Clark (*Babe*) (CBS)
Colleen Dewhurst (*A Moon for the Misbegotten, ABC Theatre*) (ABC)
Sada Thompson (*The Entertainer*) (NBC)

ACTOR (DRAMA SERIES)
Peter Falk (*Columbo, NBC Sunday Mystery Movie*) (NBC)
James Garner (*The Rockford Files*) (NBC)
Karl Malden (*The Streets of San Francisco*) (ABC)

ACTRESS (DRAMA SERIES)
Angie Dickinson (*Police Woman*) (NBC)
Michael Learned (*The Waltons*) (CBS)
Anne Meara (*Kate McShane*) (CBS)
Brenda Vaccaro (*Sara*) (CBS)

ACTOR (COMEDY SERIES)
Jack Albertson (*Chico and the Man*) (NBC)
Alan Alda (*M*A*S*H*) (CBS)
Hal Linden (*Barney Miller*) (ABC)
Henry Winkler (*Happy Days*) (ABC)

"It's fitting that I should win this because I've been doing straight lines for a 21-year-old Puerto Rican kid for two years, and I ought to get something for that," Jack Albertson jokingly said of his *Chico and the Man* co-star Freddie Prinze. Less than a year later, Prinze would commit suicide. The series would continue briefly without him but soon ended its run.

ACTRESS (COMEDY SERIES)
Beatrice Arthur (*Maude*) (CBS)
Lee Grant (*Fay*) (NBC)
Valerie Harper (*Rhoda*) (CBS)
Cloris Leachman (*Phyllis*) (CBS)
Mary Tyler Moore (*The Mary Tyler Moore Show*) (NBC)

ACTOR (LIMITED SERIES)
George Grizzard (*The Adams Chronicles*) (PBS)
Hal Holbrook (*Sandburg's Lincoln*) (NBC)
Nick Nolte (*Rich Man, Poor Man*) (ABC)
Peter Strauss (*Rich Man, Poor Man*) (ABC)

ACTRESS (LIMITED SERIES)
Susan Blakely (*Rich Man, Poor Man*) (ABC)
Rosemary Harris (*Notorious Woman, Masterpiece Theatre*) (PBS)
Jean Marsh (*Upstairs, Downstairs, Masterpiece Theatre*) (PBS)
Lee Remick (*Jennie: Lady Randolph Churchill, Great Performances*) (PBS)

ACTOR (SINGLE PERFORMANCE, DRAMA OR COMEDY SERIES)
Edward Asner (*Rich Man, Poor Man*) (ABC)
Bill Bixby ("Police Buff," *The Streets of San Francisco*) (ABC)
Tony Musante ("The Quality of Mercy," *Medical Story*) (NBC)
Robert Reed ("The Fourth Sex," *Medical Center*) (CBS)

"I want to thank to the U.S. postal service for eliminating competition," joked Edward Asner in his acceptance speech. Numerous performers, including Carroll O'Connor, Jean Stapleton, and Robert Blake, were not nominated because their entry ballots did not arrive on time due to a mail-room snafu. Asner won as the domineering immigrant father in the ABC mini-series *Rich Man, Poor Man*.

ACTRESS (SINGLE PERFORMANCE, DRAMA OR COMEDY SERIES)
Helen Hayes ("Retire in Sunny Hawaii . . . Forever," *Hawaii Five-O*) (CBS)
Sheree North ("How Do You Know What Hurts Most," *Marcus Welby, MD*) (ABC)
Pamela Payton-Wright ("John Quincy Adams, Diplomat," *The Adams Chronicles*) (PBS)
Martha Raye ("Greed," *McMillan and Wife, NBC Sunday Mystery Movie*) (NBC)
Kathryn Walker ("John Adams, Lawyer," *The Adams Chronicles*) (PBS)

SUPPORTING ACTOR (SINGLE PERFORMANCE, DRAMA OR COMEDY SPECIAL)

Ray Bolger (*The Entertainer*) (NBC)

Art Carney (*Katherine, ABC Sunday Night Movie*) (ABC)

Ed Flanders (*A Moon for the Misbegotten, ABC Theatre*) (ABC)

SUPPORTING ACTRESS (SINGLE PERFORMANCE, DRAMA OR COMEDY SPECIAL)

Rosemary Murphy (*Eleanor and Franklin, ABC Theatre*) (ABC)

Lois Nettleton (*Fear on Trial*) (CBS)

Lilia Skala (*Eleanor and Franklin, ABC Theatre*) (ABC)

Irene Tedrow (*Eleanor and Fraklin, ABC Theatre*) (ABC)

SUPPORTING ACTOR (DRAMA SERIES)

Michael Douglas (*The Streets of San Francisco*) (ABC)

Will Geer (*The Waltons*) (CBS)

Ray Milland (*Rich Man, Poor Man*) (ABC)

Robert Reed (*Rich Man, Poor Man*) (ABC)

Anthony Zerbe (*Harry O*) (ABC)

SUPPORTING ACTRESS (DRAMA SERIES)

Angela Baddeley (*Upstairs, Downstairs, Masterpiece Theatre*) (PBS)

Ellen Corby (*The Waltons*) (CBS)

Susan Howard (*Petrocelli*) (NBC)

Dorothy McGuire (*Rich Man, Poor Man*) (CBS)

Sada Thompson (*Sandburg's Lincoln*) (NBC)

SUPPORTING ACTOR (COMEDY SERIES)

Edward Asner (*The Mary Tyler Moore Show*) (CBS)

Gary Burghoff (*M*A*S*H*) (CBS)

Ted Knight (*The Mary Tyler Moore Show*) (CBS)

Harry Morgan (*M*A*S*H*) (CBS)

Abe Vigoda (*Barney Miller*) (ABC)

SUPPORTING ACTRESS (COMEDY SERIES)

Georgia Engel (*The Mary Tyler Moore Show*) (CBS)

Julie Kavner (*Rhoda*) (CBS)

Loretta Swit (*M*A*S*H*) (CBS)

Nancy Walker (*Rhoda*) (CBS)

Betty White (*The Mary Tyler Moore Show*) (CBS)

Offering a refreshing change from the usual sugar-sweet acceptance speeches and reflecting her bitchy Sue Ann Nivens character, Betty White thanked "the evil, wonderful, nasty business of television."

SUPPORTING ACTOR (SINGLE PERFORMANCE, COMEDY OR DRAMA SERIES)

Bill Bixby (*Rich Man, Poor Man*) (ABC)

Roscoe Lee Browne ("The Escape Artist," *Barney Miller*) (ABC)

Norman Fell (*Rich Man, Poor Man*) (ABC)

Gordon Jackson ("The Beastly Hun," *Upstairs, Downstairs, Masterpiece Theatre*) (PBS)

Van Johnson (*Rich Man, Poor Man*) (ABC)

SUPPORTING ACTRESS (SINGLE PERFORMANCE, COMEDY OR DRAMA SERIES)

Kim Darby (*Rich Man, Poor Man*) (ABC)

Fionnula Flanagan (*Rich Man, Poor Man*) (ABC)

Ruth Gordon ("Kiss Your Epaulets Goodbye," *Rhoda*) (CBS)

Eileen Heckart ("Mary's Aunt," *The Mary Tyler Moore Show*) (CBS)

Kay Lenz (*Rich Man, Poor Man*) (ABC)

SUPPORTING ACTOR (VARIETY OR MUSIC)

Chevy Chase (*NBC's Saturday Night Live*) (NBC)

Tim Conway (*The Carol Burnett Show*) (CBS)

Harvey Korman (*The Carol Burnett Show*) (CBS)

SUPPORTING ACTRESS (VARIETY OR MUSIC)

Vicki Lawrence (*The Carol Burnett Show*) (CBS)

Cloris Leachman (*Telly . . . Who Loves Ya, Baby?*) (CBS)

SPECIAL CLASSIFICATION OF ACHIEVEMENT

Bicentennial Minutes (CBS); *The Tonight Show Starring Johnny Carson* (NBC); Ann Marcus, Jerry Adelman, Daniel Gregory Browne, writers (pilot episode, *Mary Hartman, Mary Hartman*) (Syndicated)

DAYTIME AWARDS

Drama Series: *Another World* (NBC); Drama Special: *First Ladies' Diaries: Edith Wilson* (NBC); Actor (Drama Series): Larry Haines (*Search for Tomorrow*) (CBS); Actress (Drama Series); Helen Gallagher (*Ryan's Hope*) (ABC); Actor (Drama Special) (tie): Gerald Gordon (*First Ladies' Diaries: Rachel Jackson*) (NBC) and James Luisi (*First Ladies' Diaries: Martha Washington*) (NBC); Actress (Drama Special): Elizabeth Hubbard (*First Ladies' Diaries: Edith Wilson*) (NBC); Game Show: *The $20,000 Pyramid* (ABC); Talk Show: *Dinah!*

OTHER PRIME-TIME AWARDS

Directing (Drama or Comedy, Single Program): Daniel Petrie (*Eleanor and Franklin, ABC Theatre*) (ABC); Directing (Drama, Series): David Greene ("Episode 8," *Rich Man, Poor Man*) (ABC); Directing (Comedy, Series): Gene Reynolds ("Welcome to Korea," *M*A*S*H*) (CBS); Directing (Comedy-Variety or Music, Series): Dave Wilson (*NBC's Saturday Night Live* with Paul Simon) (NBC); Directing (Comedy-Variety or Music, Single Program): Dwight Hemion (*Steve and Eydie: Our Love Is Here To Stay*) (CBS)

Writing (Drama or Comedy, Single Program—Original Teleplay): James Costigan (*Eleanor and Franklin, ABC Theatre*) (ABC); Writing (Drama or Comedy, Single Program—Adaptation): David W. Rintels (*Fear on Trial*) (CBS); Writing (Drama, Series): Sherman Yellen ("John Adams, Lawyer," *The Adams Chronicles*) (PBS); Writing (Comedy, Series): David Lloyd ("Chuckles Bites the Dust," *The Mary Tyler Moore Show*) (CBS); Writing (Variety or Music, Series): Ann Beatts, Chevy Chase, Al Franken, Tom Davis, Lorne Michaels, Marilyn Suzanne Miller, Michael O'Donoghue, Herb Sargent, Tom Schiller, Rosie Schuster, Alan Zweibel (*NBC's Saturday Night Live* with Elliott Gould) (NBC); Writing (Variety or Music, Single Program): Jane Wagner, Lorne Michaels, Ann Elder, Christopher Guest, Earl Pomerantz, Jim Rusk, Lily Tomlin, Rod Warren, George Yanok (*Lily Tomlin*) (CBS)

As if it didn't have enough already, the Academy added on even more Emmy categories. There were now awards for single appearances by both leading and supporting actors in regular series (shows with limited episodes were included).

Meanwhile, viewers were becoming disenchanted with the ever-expanding Emmys. Audiences had shrunk by 2 million over the past five years. ABC, whose turn it was to carry the ceremony in a rotating network policy, threatened not to broadcast the awards if they could not be guaranteed higher ratings. (Ironically, ABC won the most Emmys of any network that year.) The Academy did its best by handing out fifty awards on the air instead of a possible seventy. Once again, the news awards were not presented at all and daytime prizes were given in a separate ceremony.

The prime-time show was hosted by John Denver and Mary Tyler Moore, who won her third Best Actress in a Comedy Series award for her popular CBS series.

THE PEABODY AWARDS (FOR 1976)

Sybil (NBC); *Eleanor and Franklin, ABC Theatre* (ABC); *Visions* (KCET-TV, Los Angeles); *In Performance at Wolf Trap* (WETA-TV, Washington, DC); Perry Como, "with especial reference to *Perry Como's Christmas in Austria* (NBC)"; *Judge Horton and the Scottsboro Boys* (Tomorrow Entertainment, Inc.); *60 Minutes* (CBS); *The Adams Chronicles* (WNET-TV, New York); *Suddenly an Eagle* (ABC News); *Animals Animals Animals* (ABC News); Hughes Rudd and Bruce Morton, writer/reporters for *The CBS Morning News* (CBS); Sy Pearlman, producer of *Weekend's* "Sawyer Brothers" segment (NBC); "In Celebration of US," CBS News coverage of July 4, 1976; *1976 Presidental Debates* (Jim Karayn and the League of Women Voters); *A Conversation with Jimmy Carter* (WETA-TV, Washington, DC); *In the News* (CBS News); ABC Sports for its Olympic coverage; *Power Politics in Mississippi* (WLBT-TV, Jackson, MS); *A Thirst in the Garden* (KERA-TV, Dallas, TX); Franklin McMahon, reporter, WBBM-TV, Chicago, for *Primary Colors, an Artist on the Campaign Trial*; Charles Barthold, WHO-TV, Des Moines, IA, for "his filming of a powerful and destructive tornado in action"

THE GOLDEN GLOBE AWARDS
(FOR 1976)

TV Movie: *Eleanor and Franklin, ABC Theatre* (ABC); Drama Series: *Rich Man, Poor Man* (ABC); Comedy or Musical Series: *Barney Miller* (ABC)

Actor (Drama Series): Richard Jordan (*Captains and the Kings, Best Sellers*) (NBC); Actress (Drama Series): Susan Blakely (*Rich Man, Poor Man*) (ABC); Actor (Comedy or Musical Series): Henry Winkler (*Happy Days*) (ABC); Actress (Comedy or Musical Series): Carol Burnett (*The Carol Burnett Show*) (CBS); Supporting Actor: Edward Asner (*Rich Man, Poor Man*) (ABC); Supporting Actress: Josette Banzet (*Rich Man, Poor Man*) (ABC)

How did unknown Josette Banzet, who had a tiny, walk-on role in the mini-series *Rich Man, Poor Man*, receive a Golden Globe Award as Best Supporting Actress? Her press-agent husband threw a series of parties for the Hollywood Foreign Press Association and they gave her one, that's how.

1976-77

THE EMMY AWARDS

"It's warfare. I don't see any peace in the cards," Hollywood Academy chapter president Larry Stewart stated to *The New York Times*. He was explaining the tense relationship between the Los Angeles and New York chapters of the TV Academy. The Hollywood group had 5,000 of the Academy's total membership of 12,000 and was responsible for the majority of prime-time television programming. Spokesmen for the faction claimed the Academy was dominated by the national board of trustees in New York. The Los Angelenos wanted a bigger say in national decisions. The Gotham chapter resisted and threatened to expel the rebel Californians. Several L.A. dissidents like Alan Alda, Edward Asner, David Wolper, producer of the smash *Roots*, and *M*A*S*H* producer Burt Metcalfe responded by announcing the withdrawal of their shows from Emmy consideration.

The Hollywood chapter sued to dissolve the National Academy and for the right to start its own Emmy awards. The Big Apple chapter countersued,

claiming it had exclusive rights to the name Emmy. The awards ceremony was scheduled for May 15, but because of the threatened boycott and conflicting lawsuits, the show was postponed.

The situation was in a stalemate. The East had the name Emmy, but the West Coast had the stars America wanted to see. The entire ugly matter was settled in July. There would now be two separate organizations and two sets of Emmys. The West Coast group would be called the Academy of Television Arts and Sciences and be responsible for the prime-time and local Los Angeles awards. In New York, the National Academy of Television Arts and Sciences would present the accolades for daytime, news, and sports shows, documentaries, and local shows outside of L.A. In the first year of this new arrangement, the news awards were presented by the new Academy in Los Angeles during a luncheon along with technical and craft prizes. The group did not have the right to the name Emmy and so the winners were given plaques called Achievement in Broadcast Journalism Awards. Thereafter, the New York group presented actual news Emmys.

SPECIAL (DRAMA OR COMEDY) (TIE)
Eleanor and Franklin: The White House Years,
　　ABC Theatre (ABC)
Harry S. Truman: Plain Speaking (PBS)
Raid on Entebbe, The Big Event (NBC)
Sybil, *The Big Event* (NBC)
21 Hours at Munich (ABC)

DRAMA SERIES
Baretta (ABC)
Columbo, NBC Sunday Mystery Movie (NBC)
Family (ABC)
Police Story (NBC)
Upstairs, Downstairs, *Masterpiece Theatre* (PBS)

Upstairs, Downstairs was switched back from the Limited Series slot where it won the previous year to the regular Drama Series competition where it triumphed yet again.

COMEDY SERIES
All in the Family (CBS)
Barney Miller (NBC)
The Bob Newhart Show (CBS)

Louis Gossett, Jr., and LeVar Burton in *Roots* (1977), winner of nine Emmys, the Peabody, and the Golden Globe.

The Mary Tyler Moore Show (CBS)
M*A*S*H (CBS)

LIMITED SERIES
The Adams Chronicles (PBS)
Captains and the Kings, Best Sellers (NBC)
Madame Bovary, Masterpiece Theatre (PBS)
The Moneychangers, The Big Event (NBC)
Roots (ABC)

The ABC mini-series *Roots* captured the American imagination and a record total of thirty-seven Emmy nominations. It won nine awards, the most for any mini-series. The series' hefty share of nominations can be attributed to multiple citations in both the drama and limited series categories.

Based on Alex Haley's best-selling account of the search for his African-American ancestry, the multi-part special was broadcast over seven consecutive nights and earned big ratings. A sequel *Roots:*

The Next Generations was broadcast two seasons later and also won the Emmy for best Limited Series.

COMEDY-VARIETY OR MUSIC SERIES
The Carol Burnett Show (CBS)
Evening at Pops (PBS)
The Muppet Show (Syndicated)
NBC's Saturday Night Live (NBC)
Van Dyke and Company (NBC)

COMEDY-VARIETY OR MUSIC SPECIAL
The Barry Manilow Special (ABC)
Doug Henning's World of Magic (NBC)
The Neil Diamond Special (NBC)
The Shirley MacLaine Special: Where Do We Go from Here? (CBS)
Sills and Burnett at the Met (CBS)

ACTOR (SINGLE PERFORMANCE, COMEDY OR DRAMA SPECIAL)

Peter Boyle (*Tail Gunner Joe, The Big Event*) (NBC)
Peter Finch (*Raid on Entebbe, The Big Event*) (NBC)
Ed Flanders (*Harry S. Truman: Plain Speaking*) (PBS)
Edward Herrmann (*Eleanor and Franklin: The White House Years, ABC Theatre*) (ABC)
George C. Scott (*Beauty and the Beast, Hallmark Hall of Fame*) (NBC)

ACTRESS (SINGLE PERFORMANCE, COMEDY OR DRAMA SPECIAL)

Jane Alexander (*Eleanor and Franklin: The White House Years, ABC Theatre*) (ABC)
Susan Clark (*Amelia Earhart, NBC Monday Night at the Movies*) (NBC)
Sally Field (*Sybil, The Big Event*) (NBC)
Julie Harris (*The Last of Mrs. Lincoln, Hollywood Television Theatre*) (PBS)
Joanne Woodward (*Sybil, The Big Event*) (NBC)

Sally Field's multi-faceted portrayal of a victim of multiple personality disorder in *Sybil* won her an Emmy. She was nominated against Joanne Woodward, who played her psychiatrist and had won a 1957 Oscar for playing a similarly disturbed young woman in *The Three Faces of Eve.*

ACTOR (DRAMA SERIES)

Robert Blake (*Baretta*) (ABC)
Peter Falk (*Columbo, NBC Sunday Mystery Movie*) (NBC)
James Garner (*The Rockford Files*) (NBC)
Jack Klugman (*Quincy*) (ABC)
Karl Malden (*The Streets of San Francisco*) (ABC)

ACTRESS (DRAMA SERIES)

Angie Dickinson (*Police Woman*) (NBC)
Kate Jackson (*Charlie's Angels*) (ABC)
Michael Learned (*The Waltons*) (CBS)
Sada Thompson (*Family*) (ABC)
Lindsay Wagner (*The Bionic Woman*) (ABC)

ACTOR (COMEDY SERIES)

Jack Albertson (*Chico and the Man*) (NBC)
Alan Alda (*M*A*S*H*) (CBS)
Hal Linden (*Barney Miller*) (ABC)

Carroll O'Connor (*All in the Family*) (CBS)
Henry Winkler (*Happy Days*) (ABC)

ACTRESS (COMEDY SERIES)

Beatrice Arthur (*Maude*) (CBS)
Valerie Harper (*Rhoda*) (CBS)
Mary Tyler Moore (*The Mary Tyler Moore Show*) (CBS)
Suzanne Pleshette (*The Bob Newhart Show*) (CBS)
Jean Stapleton (*All in the Family*) (CBS)

ACTOR (LIMITED SERIES)

Stanley Baker (*How Green Was My Valley, Masterpiece Theatre*) (PBS)
Richard Jordan (*Captain and the Kings, Best Sellers*) (NBC)
Steven Keats (*Seventh Avenue, Best Sellers*) (NBC)
Christopher Plummer (*The Moneychangers, The Big Event*) (NBC)

ACTRESS (LIMITED SERIES)

Patty Duke Astin (*Captains and the Kings, Best Sellers*) (NBC)
Dori Brenner (*Seventh Avenue, Best Sellers*) (NBC)
Susan Flannery (*The Moneychangers, The Big Event*) (NBC)
Eva Marie Saint (*How the West Was Won*) (ABC)
Jane Seymour (*Captains and the Kings, Best Sellers*) (NBC)

ACTOR (SINGLE PERFORMANCE, DRAMA OR COMEDY SERIES)

John Amos (*Roots, Part 5*) (ABC)
LeVar Burton (*Roots, Part 1*) (ABC)
Louis Gossett, Jr. (*Roots, Part 2*) (ABC)
Ben Vereen (*Roots, Part 6*) (ABC)

ACTRESS (SINGLE PERFORMANCE, DRAMA OR COMEDY SERIES)

Susan Blakely (*Rich Man, Poor Man—Book II, Chapter 1*) (ABC)
Beulah Bondi ("The Pony Cart," *The Waltons*) (CBS)
Madge Sinclair (*Roots, Part 4*) (ABC)
Leslie Uggams (*Roots, Part 6*) (ABC)
Jessica Walter ("'Til Death Do Us Part," *The Streets of San Francisco*) (ABC)

At age 85, Beulah Bondi was the oldest Emmy

winner ever. She received a tremendous ovation as she slowly made her way to the stage. Once there she thanked the Academy for honoring her "while I'm still alive."

SUPPORTING ACTOR (SINGLE PERFORMANCE, COMEDY OR DRAMA SPECIAL)
Martin Balsam (*Raid on Entebbe, The Big Event*) (NBC)
Mark Harmon (*Eleanor and Franklin: The White House Years, ABC Theatre*) (ABC)
Yaphet Kotto (*Raid on Entebbe, The Big Event*) (NBC)
Walter McGinn (*Eleanor and Franklin: The White House Years, ABC Theatre*) (ABC)
Burgess Meredith (*Tail Gunner Joe, The Big Event*) (NBC)

SUPPORTING ACTRESS (SINGLE PERFORMANCE, COMEDY OR DRAMA SPECIAL)
Ruth Gordon (*The Great Houdinis, ABC Friday Night Movie*) (ABC)
Diana Hyland (*The Boy in the Plastic Bubble, ABC Friday Night Movie*) (ABC)
Rosemary Murphy (*Eleanor and Franklin: The White House Years, ABC Theatre*) (ABC)
Patricia Neal (*Tail Gunner Joe, The Big Event*) (NBC)
Susan Oliver (*Amelia Earhart, NBC Monday Night at the Movies*) (NBC)

John Travolta accepted the award for the late Diana Hyland, who played his mother in the ABC TV-movie about an immune-deficent young man forced to live in plastic isolation. Hyland and Travolta had been romantically linked.

SUPPORTING ACTOR (DRAMA SERIES)
Noah Beery (*The Rockford Files*) (NBC)
David Doyle (*Charlie's Angels*) (ABC)
Tom Ewell (*Baretta*) (ABC)
Gary Frank (*Family*) (ABC)
Will Geer (*The Waltons*) (CBS)

SUPPORTING ACTRESS (DRAMA SERIES)
Meredith Baxter Birney (*Family*) (ABC)
Ellen Corby (*The Waltons*) (CBS)

Kristy McNichol (*Family*) (ABC)
Lee Meriwether (*Barnaby Jones*) (CBS)
Jacqueline Tong (*Upstairs, Downstairs, Masterpiece Theatre*) (PBS)

SUPPORTING ACTOR (COMEDY SERIES)
Edward Asner (*The Mary Tyler Moore Show*) (CBS)
Gary Burghoff (*M*A*S*H*) (CBS)
Ted Knight (*The Mary Tyler Moore Show*) (CBS)
Harry Morgan (*M*A*S*H*) (CBS)
Abe Vigoda (*Barney Miller*) (ABC)

SUPPORTING ACTRESS (COMEDY SERIES)
Georgia Engel (*The Mary Tyler Moore Show*) (CBS)
Julie Kavner (*Rhoda*) (CBS)
Mary Kay Place (*Mary Hartman, Mary Hartman*) (Syndicated)
Loretta Swit (*M*A*S*H*) (CBS)
Betty White (*The Mary Tyler Moore Show*) (CBS)

SUPPORTING ACTOR (SINGLE PERFORMANCE, COMEDY OR DRAMA SERIES)
Edward Asner (*Roots*, Part 1) (ABC)
Charles Durning (*Captain and the Kings, Best Sellers*, Chapter 2) (NBC)
Moses Gunn (*Roots*, Part 1) (ABC)
Robert Reed (*Roots*, Part 5) (ABC)
Ralph Waite (*Roots*, Part 1) (ABC)

SUPPORTING ACTRESS (SINGLE PERFORMANCE, COMEDY OR DRAMA SERIES)
Olivia Cole (*Roots*, Part 8) (ABC)
Sandy Duncan (*Roots*, Part 5) (ABC)
Eileen Heckart ("Lou Proposes," *The Mary Tyler Moore Show*) (CBS)
Cicely Tyson (*Roots*, Part 1) (ABC)
Nancy Walker ("The Separation," *Rhoda*) (CBS)

SUPPORTING ACTOR (VARIETY OR MUSIC)
John Belushi (*NBC's Saturday Night Live*) (NBC)
Chevy Chase (*NBC's Saturday Night Live*) (NBC)
Tim Conway (*The Carol Burnett Show*) (CBS)
Harvey Korman (*The Carol Burnett Show*) (CBS)

Ben Vereen (*The Bell Telephone Jubilee*) (NBC)

SUPPORTING ACTRESS (VARIETY OR MUSIC)
Vicki Lawrence (*The Carol Burnett Show*) (CBS)
Rita Moreno (*The Muppet Show*) (Syndicated)
Gilda Radner (*NBC's Saturday Night Live*) (NBC)

SPECIAL CLASSIFICATION OF OUTSTANDING ACHIEVEMENT
The Tonight Show Starring Johnny Carson (NBC)

DAYTIME AWARDS
Drama Series: *Ryan's Hope* (ABC); Actor (Drama Series): Val Dufour (*Search for Tomorrow*) (CBS); Actress (Drama Series): Helen Gallagher (*Ryan's Hope*) (ABC); Game Show: *Family Feud* (ABC); Talk or Variety Series: *The Merv Griffin Show* (Syndicated)

OTHER PRIME-TIME AWARDS
Directing (Special, Drama or Comedy): Daniel Petrie (*Eleanor and Franklin: The White House Years, ABC Theatre*) (ABC); Directing (Drama, Series): David Greene (*Roots*, Part 2) (ABC); Directing (Comedy, Series): Alan Alda ("Dear Sigmund," *M*A*S*H*) (CBS); Directing (Variety or Music, Series): Dave Powers (*The Carol Burnett Show* with Edyie Gormé) (CBS); Directing (Variety or Music, Special): Dwight Hemion (*America Salutes Richard Rodgers: The Sound of His Music*) (CBS)

Writing (Special, Comedy or Drama—Original Teleplay): Lane Slate (*Tail Gunner Joe, The Big Event*) (NBC); Writing (Special, Comedy or Drama—Adaptation): Stewart Stern (*Sybil, The Big Event*) (NBC); Writing (Drama, Series): William Blinn (*Roots*, Part 2); Writing (Comedy, Series): Allan Burns, James L. Brooks, Ed Weinberger, Stan Daniels, David Lloyd, Bob Ellison ("The Final Show," *The Mary Tyler Moore Show*) (CBS); Writing (Variety or Music, Series): Anne Beatts, Dan Aykroyd, Al Franken, Tom Davis, James Downey, Lorne Michaels, Marilyn Suzanne Miller, Michael O'Donoghue, Herb Sargent, Tom Schiller, Rosie Schuster, Alan Zweibel, John Belushi, Bill Murray (*NBC's Saturday Night Live* with host Sissy Spacek) (NBC); Writing (Comedy or Variety,

Special): Alan Buz Kohan, Ted Strauss (*America Salutes Richard Rodgers: The Sound of His Music*) (CBS)

Despite the big split between the New York and Hollywood chapters of the Academy, the Emmys went on. Producer Don Ohlmeyer, formerly of ABC Sports, covered the show like an athletic event. He employed nine cameras and numerous video clips to give the audience a brief idea of the nominated work. In a striking visual move, Doc Severinsen's orchestra was suspended over the stage on a U-shaped platform. There were tributes to *The Tonight Show* and *The Mary Tyler Moore Show*, which had completed its last season and brought its Emmy total to twenty-nine, the most for any prime-time series.

Angie Dickinson and Robert Blake hosted. The show was allotted a generous two and half hours by NBC, but ran a staggering three hours and twenty-seven minutes—one of the longest Emmy presentations up to that point. Dickinson explained the overage by pointing out they had 2,300 hours of programming to cover. In spite of the length, John J. O'Connor of *The New York Times* called the telecast "one of the best award shows of the year," while *Variety* found it "innovative, sometimes funny, and dramatic." NBC still lost the night in ratings, coming in second to ABC's Watergate-inspired mini-series *Washington: Behind Closed Doors*—an Emmy winner the following year.

THE PEABODY AWARDS (FOR 1977)

Roots (ABC); Norman Lear for *All in the Family*; *Upstairs, Downstairs* (London Weekend Television); *The Mary Tyler Moore Show* (CBS); *The MacNeil-Lehrer Report* (WNET/13, New York, WETA, Arlington, VA); *Camera Three* (WCBS-TV, New York); Steve Allen for *Meeting of Minds*; *Green Eyes* (CBS); *The Hobbit* (NBC); *Tut: The Boy King* (NBC); *Live from the Met* (Metropolitan Opera Association); *FIND Investigative Reports* (WNBC-TV); *Buyline: Betty Furness* (WNBC-TV); *A Good Dissonance like a Man* (WNET-TV); *Police Tapes* (WNET-TV); *The Lifers' Group—I Am My Brother's Keeper* (WPIX, New York); *Police Accountability* (KABC-TV, Los Angeles); *Where Have All the Flood Cars Gone?* (KCMO-TV,

Betty White, Gavin MacLeod, Edward Asner, Georgia Engle, Ted Knight, and Mary Tyler Moore in a scene from the last episode of *The Mary Tyler Moore Show*, aired one week before the 1976–77 Emmys.

Fairway, KS); *The Rowe String Quartet Plays on Your Imagination* (WBTV, Charlotte, NC); *Joshua's Confusion* (Multimedia Productions)

THE GOLDEN GLOBE AWARDS (FOR 1977)

Made-for-TV Movie or Mini-Series: *Raid on Entebbe* (NBC); Drama Series: *Roots* (ABC); Comedy or Musical Series: *All in the Family* (CBS)

Actor (Drama Series): Edward Asner (*Lou Grant*) (CBS); Actress (Drama Series): Lesley Anne Warren (*79 Park Avenue*) (NBC); Actor (Comedy or Musical Series): Henry Winkler (*Happy Days*) (ABC); Actress (Comedy or Musical Series): Carol Burnett (*The Carol Burnett Show*) (CBS)

NBC was carrying the Golden Globes and demanded the show come in at two hours. The categories of Supporting Actor and Supporting Actress were dropped because of the time constraint.

THE EMMY AWARDS

SPECIAL (COMEDY OR DRAMA)
A Death in Canaan (CBS)
The Gathering (ABC)
Jesus of Nazareth (NBC)
Our Town, The Bell System Special (NBC)
Young Joe, The Forgotten Kennedy (ABC)

DRAMA SERIES
Columbo, NBC Mystery Movie (NBC)
Family (ABC)
Lou Grant (CBS)
Quincy (NBC)
The Rockford Files (NBC)

COMEDY SERIES
All in the Family (CBS)

Barney Miller (ABC)
M*A*S*H (CBS)
Soap (ABC)
Three's Company (ABC)

LIMITED SERIES
Anna Karenina, Masterpiece Theatre (PBS)
Holocaust, *The Big Event* (NBC)
King (NBC)
Washington: Behind Closed Doors (ABC)

The Limited Series format continued to deal with formerly taboo subjects. Last year's winner in this category, *Roots*, examined the legacy of slavery in America. It was succeeded by *Holocaust*, a fictional account of one family's suffering during the Nazi persecution of Jews. Many critics, including Nobel Prize-winning author Elie Weisel, accused the series of cheapening the Holocaust experience by bringing it to the level of a melodramatic soap opera. Others countered that the program made millions aware of the horrors of the era.

COMEDY-VARIETY OR MUSIC SERIES
America 2Night (Syndicated)
The Carol Burnett Show (CBS)
Evening at Pops (PBS)
The Muppet Show (Syndicated)
NBC's Saturday Night Live (NBC)

Turned down by all three networks, *The Muppet Show* featuring Jim Henson's crazy cloth creations was a hit in syndication and was the first nonnetwork show to win as best Comedy-Variety or Music Series.

SPECIAL (COMEDY-VARIETY OR MUSIC)
Bette Midler—Ol' Red Hair Is Back (NBC)
Doug Henning's World of Magic (NBC)
The George Burns One-Man Show (CBS)
Neil Diamond: I'm Glad You're Here with Me Tonight (NBC)
The Second Barry Manilow Special (ABC)

ACTOR (SINGLE PERFORMANCE, DRAMA OR COMEDY SPECIAL)
Alan Alda (*Kill Me If You Can*) (NBC)
Fred Astaire (*A Family Upside Down*) (NBC)

Hal Holbrook (*Our Town, The Bell System Special*) (NBC)
Martin Sheen (*Taxi!!!, Hallmark Hall of Fame*) (NBC)
James Stacy (*Just a Little Inconvenience*) (NBC)

ACTRESS (SINGLE PERFORMANCE, DRAMA OR COMEDY SPECIAL)
Helen Hayes (*A Family Upside Down*) (NBC)
Eva Marie Saint (*Taxi!!!, Hallmark Hall of Fame*) (NBC)
Maureen Stapleton (*The Gathering*) (ABC)
Sada Thompson (*Our Town, Bell System Theatre*) (NBC)
Joanne Woodward (*See How She Runs, G.E. Theatre*) (CBS)

ACTOR (DRAMA SERIES)
Edward Asner (*Lou Grant*) (CBS)
James Broderick (*Family*) (ABC)
Peter Falk (*Columbo, NBC Sunday Mystery Movie*) (NBC)
James Garner (*The Rockford Files*) (NBC)
Jack Klugman (*Quincy*) (NBC)
Ralph Waite (*The Waltons*) (CBS)

Edward Asner won his fourth Emmy for portraying Lou Grant. The first three were as a supporting charcter on *The Mary Tyler Moore Show*, and now he won for a leading role in a new spin-off series. Asner also starred in the Emmy-winning dramatic special *The Gathering* as a dying businessman who reunites his estranged family.

ACTRESS (DRAMA SERIES)
Melissa Sue Anderson (*Little House on the Praire*) (NBC)
Fionnula Flanagan (*How the West Was Won*) (ABC)
Kate Jackson (*Charlie's Angels*) (ABC)
Michael Learned (*The Waltons*) (CBS)
Susan Sullivan (*Julie Farr, MD*) (ABC)
Sada Thompson (*Family*) (ABC)

ACTOR (COMEDY SERIES)
Alan Alda (*M*A*S*H*) (CBS)
Hal Linden (*Barney Miller*) (ABC)
Carroll O'Connor (*All in the Family*) (CBS)
John Ritter (*Three's Company*) (ABC)
Henry Winkler (*Happy Days*) (ABC)

Edward Asner continued to win awards for his *Lou Grant* character in a new eponymous series while Nancy Marchand took home four Emmys for her portrayal of his patrician publisher, Mrs. Pynchon. The series aired from 1977 to 1982.

ACTRESS (COMEDY SERIES)
Beatrice Arthur (*Maude*) (CBS)
Cathryn Damon (*Soap*) (ABC)
Valerie Harper (*Rhoda*) (CBS)
Katherine Helmond (*Soap*) (ABC)
Suzanne Pleshette (*The Bob Newhart Show*) (CBS)
Jean Stapleton (*All in the Family*) (CBS)

ACTOR (LIMITED SERIES)
Hal Holbrook (*The Awakening Land*) (NBC)
Michael Moriarty (*Holocaust, The Big Event*) (NBC)
Jason Robards (*Washington: Behind Closed Doors*) (ABC)
Fritz Weaver (*Holocaust, The Big Event*) (NBC)
Paul Winfield (*King*) (NBC)

ACTRESS (LIMITED SERIES)
Rosemary Harris (*Holocaust, The Big Event*) (NBC)
Elizabeth Montgomery (*The Awakening Land*) (NBC)
Lee Remick (*Wheels*) (NBC)
Meryl Streep (*Holocaust, The Big Event*) (NBC)
Cicely Tyson (*King*) (NBC)

ACTOR (SINGLE PERFORMANCE, DRAMA OR COMEDY SERIES)
David Cassidy ("A Chance To Live," *Police Story*) (NBC)
Will Geer ("The Old Man and the Runaway," *The Love Boat*) (ABC)
Judd Hirsch ("Rhoda Likes Mike," *Rhoda*) (CBS)

Barnard Hughes ("Judge," *Lou Grant*) (CBS)
John Rubinstein ("And Baby Makes Three," *Family*) (ABC)
Keenan Wynn ("Good Old Uncle Ben," *Police Woman*) (NBC)

ACTRESS (SINGLE PERFORMANCE, DRAMA OR COMEDY SERIES)
Patty Duke Astin ("Having Babies III," *Having Babies*) (ABC)
Kate Jackson ("James at 15," *James at 15/16*) (NBC)
Jayne Meadows ("Luther, Voltaire, Plato, Nightengale," *Meeting of Minds*) (PBS)
Rita Moreno ("The Paper Palace," *The Rockford Files*) (NBC)
Irene Tedrow ("Ducks," *James at 15/16*) (NBC)

SUPPORTING ACTOR (SINGLE PERFORMANCE, DRAMA OR COMEDY SPECIAL)
Howard Da Silva (*Verna: USO Girl, Great Performances*) (PBS)
James Farentino (*Jesus of Nazareth*) (NBC)
Burgess Meredith (*The Last Hurrah, Hallmark Hall of Fame*) (NBC)
Donald Pleasance (*The Defection of Simas Kudirka*) (CBS)
Efrem Zimbalist, Jr. (*A Family Upside Down*) (NBC)

SUPPORTING ACTRESS (SINGLE PERFORMANCE, DRAMA OR COMEDY SPECIAL)
Patty Duke Astin (*A Family Upside Down*) (NBC)
Tyne Daly (*Intimate Strangers*) (ABC)
Mariette Hartley (*The Last Hurrah, Hallmark Hall of Fame*) (NBC)
Eva La Galliene (*The Royal Family, Great Performances*) (PBS)
Cloris Leachman (*It Happened One Christmas*) (ABC)
Viveca Lindfors (*A Question of Guilt*) (CBS)

SUPPORTING ACTOR (DRAMA SERIES)
Ossie Davis (*King*) (NBC)
Will Geer (*The Waltons*) (CBS)
Robert Vaughn (*Wasington: Behind Closed Doors*) (ABC)

Sam Wanamaker (*Holocaust, The Big Event*) (NBC)
David Warner (*Holocaust, The Big Event*) (NBC)

SUPPORTING ACTRESS (DRAMA SERIES)
Meredith Baxter Birney (*Family*) (ABC)
Tovah Feldshuh (*Holocaust, The Big Event*) (NBC)
Linda Kelsey (*Lou Grant*) (CBS)
Nancy Marchand (*Lou Grant*) (CBS)
Kristy McNichol (*Family*) (ABC)

SUPPORTING ACTOR (COMEDY SERIES)
Tom Bosley (*Happy Days*) (ABC)
Gary Burghoff (*M*A*S*H*) (CBS)
Harry Morgan (*M*A*S*H*) (CBS)
Rob Reiner (*All in the Family*) (CBS)
Vic Tayback (*Alice*) (CBS)

SUPPORTING ACTRESS (COMEDY SERIES)
Polly Holliday (*Alice*) (CBS)
Julie Kavner (*Rhoda*) (CBS)
Sally Struthers (*All in the Family*) (CBS)
Loretta Swit (*M*A*S*H*) (CBS)
Nancy Walker (*Rhoda*) (CBS)

SUPPORTING ACTOR (SINGLE PERFORMANCE, DRAMA OR COMEDY SERIES)
Will Geer ("Yes, Nicholas . . . There Is a Santa Claus," *Eight Is Enough*) (ABC)
Larry Gelman ("Goodbye, Mr. Fish, Part II," *Barney Miller*) (ABC)
Harold Gould ("Happy Anniversary," *Rhoda*) (CBS)
Ricardo Montalban (*How the West Was Won*, Part II) (ABC)
Abe Vigoda ("Goodbye, Mr. Fish, Part II," *Barney Miller*) (ABC)

SUPPORTING ACTRESS (SINGLE PERFORMANCE, DRAMA OR COMEDY SERIES)
Blanche Baker (*Holocaust, The Big Event*, Part 1) (NBC)
Ellen Corby ("Grandma Comes Home," *The Waltons*) (CBS)

Jeanette Nolan (*The Awakening Land*) (NBC)
Beulah Quo ("Douglass, T'zu-Hsi, Beccariu, De Sade," *Meeting of Minds*) (PBS)
Beatrice Straight (*The Dain Curse*, Part 2) (CBS)

SUPPORTING ACTOR (VARIETY OR MUSIC)
Dan Aykroyd (*NBC's Saturday Night Live*) (NBC)
John Belushi (*NBC's Saturday Night Live*) (NBC)
Tim Conway (*The Carol Burnett Show*) (CBS)
Louis Gossett, Jr. (*The Sentry Collection Presents Ben Vereen—His Roots*) (ABC)
Peter Sellers (*The Muppet Show*) (Syndicated)

SUPPORTING ACTRESS (VARIETY OR MUSIC)
Beatrice Arthur (*Laugh-In*) (NBC)
Jane Curtin (*NBC's Saturday Night Live*) (NBC)
Dolly Parton (*Cher . . . Special*) (CBS)
Bernadette Peters (*The Muppet Show*) (Syndicated)
Gilda Radner (*NBC's Saturday Night Live*) (NBC)

SPECIAL CLASSIFICATION OF OUTSTANDING PROGRAM ACHIEVEMENT
The Tonight Show Starring Johnny Carson (NBC)

DAYTIME AWARDS
Drama Series: *Days of Our Lives* (NBC); Actor (Drama Series): James Pritchett (*The Doctors*) (NBC); Actress (Drama Series): Laurie Heinnemann (*Another World*) (NBC); Game Show: *The Hollywood Squares* (NBC); Talk or Variety Series: *Donahue* (Syndicated)

OTHER PRIME-TIME AWARDS
Directing (Drama or Comedy, Special): David Lowell Rich (*The Defection of Simas Kudirka*) (CBS); Directing (Drama, Series): Marvin J. Chomsky (*Holocaust, The Big Event*) (NBC); Directing (Comedy, Series): Paul Bogart ("Edith's 50th Birthday," *All in the Family*) (CBS); Directing (Variety or Music, Series): Dave Powers (*The Carol Burnett Show* with Steve Martin and Betty White) (CBS); Directing (Variety or Music, Special): Dwight Hemion (*The Sentry Collection Presents Ben Vereen—His Roots*) (ABC)
　Writing (Comedy or Drama, Special—Original Teleplay): George Rubino (*The Last Tenant*) (ABC); Writing (Comedy or Drama, Special—Adaptation): Caryl Ledner (*Mary White*) (ABC); Writing (Drama, Series): Gerald Green (*Holocaust, The Big Event*) (NBC); Writing (Comedy, Series): Bob Weiskopf, Bob Schiller (teleplay), Barry Harman, Harve Brosten (story) ("Cousin Liz," *All in the Family*) (CBS); Writing (Variety or Music, Series): Ed Simmons, Roger Beatty, Rick Hawkins, Liz Sage, Robert Iles, James Stein, Franelle Silver, Larry Siegel, Tim Conway, Bill Richmond, Gene Perret, Dick Clair, Jenna McMahon (*The Carol Burnett Show* with Steve Martin and Betty White) (CBS); Writing (Variety or Music, Special): Lorne Michaels, Paul Simon, Chevy Chase, Tom Davis, Al Franken, Charles Grodin, Lily Tomlin, Alan Zweibel (*The Paul Simon Special*) (NBC)

The odds were against the 1977–78 Emmys. The ceremony was being telecast on CBS and the other two networks were not showing restraint in counterprogramming. NBC was running the Disney film *Dumbo*, followed by the broadcast premiere of the remake of *King Kong*. Meanwhile, ABC was debuting its new expensive space opera *Battlestar Galatica*. As if that weren't enough, President Jimmy Carter, Egyptian leader Anwar Sadat, and Israeli Prime Minister Menachem Begin interrupted the Emmys for a thirty-minute news conference to announce a new Middle East peace accord. Host Alan Alda handled the situation with aplomb, picking up right where he left off before the newsbreak.

Alexander Cohen, the producer who turned out so many dazzling Tony shows, was signed to put on the Emmys. He wasn't given much of an opportunity to stage the kind of razzle-dazzle production numbers which distinguished the Broadway Tonys because so many awards had to be squeezed in. With the Carter/Sadat/Begin interruption, the program ran over four hours. Cohen did open the show with a flashy dance number featuring Pamela Myers, employed many backstage elements in the presentations, and recruited an unusual group of presenters including Jacques Costeau, Julia Child, "Roots" author Alex Haley, and comedy writer Gail Parent.

THE PEABODY AWARDS (FOR 1978)

Lou Grant (CBS); *Barney Miller* (ABC); *30 Minutes* (CBS News); *Cartoon-A-Torial* (Newsweek Broadcasting); *Over Easy* (KQED-TV, San Francisco); *Holocaust* (NBC); *The Battle for South Africa* (CBS News); *Mysterious Cities of Clay* (NBC); *A Connecticut Yankee in King Arthur's Court, Once Upon a Classic* (WQED-TV, Pittsburgh, PA); *The Body Human: The Vital Connection* (CBS); Bob Keeshan for his role as *Captain Kangaroo*; Richard S. Salant, president of CBS News; The Muppets; *Race War in Rhodesia* (WDVM-TV, Washington, DC); *Your Health and Your Wallet* (WDVM-TV, Washington, DC); *A River to the Sea* (The Baptist Radio-TV Commission of Fort Worth, TX); *Arts in New Hampshire* (WENH-TV, Durham, NH); *Old Age: Do Not Go Gentle* (KGO-TV, San Francisco); *Damien* (KHET, Honolulu); *Whose Child Is This?* (WAVE-TV, Louisville, KY)

THE GOLDEN GLOBE AWARDS (FOR 1978)

TV-Movie or Mini-Series: *A Family Upside Down* (NBC); Drama Series: *60 Minutes* (CBS); Comedy or Musical Series: *Taxi* (ABC)

Actor (Drama Series): Michael Moriarty (*Holocaust*) (NBC); Actress (Drama Series): Rosemary Harris (*Holocaust*) (NBC); Actor (Comedy or Musical Series): Robin Williams (*Mork and Mindy*) (ABC); Actress (Comedy or Musical Series): Linda Lavin (*Alice*) (CBS); Supporting Actor: Norman Fell (*Three's Company*) (ABC); Supporting Actress: Polly Holliday (*Alice*) (CBS)

The Hollywood Foreign Press Association made an unusual choice by nominating CBS News' investigative journalism show *60 Minutes* for best Drama Series. Producer Don Hewitt refused to accept the nomination, stating it was ridiculous to place his documentary show in competition with fictional series such as *Dynasty* and *Lou Grant*. On the night of the awards, *60 Minutes* did win, no one came up to accept the prize, and Golden Globe host Chevy Chase took possesion of it.

THE EMMY AWARDS

DRAMA OR COMEDY SPECIAL
Dummy (CBS)
First You Cry (CBS)
Friendly Fire, ABC Theatre (ABC)
The Jericho Mile (ABC)
Summer of My German Soldier (NBC)

DRAMA SERIES
Lou Grant (CBS)
The Paper Chase (CBS)
The Rockford Files (NBC)

COMEDY SERIES
All in the Family (CBS)
Barney Miller (ABC)
M*A*S*H (CBS)
Mork & Mindy (ABC)
Taxi (ABC)

LIMITED SERIES
Backstairs at the White House (NBC)
Blind Ambition (CBS)
Roots: The Next Generations (ABC)

COMEDY-VARIETY MUSIC PROGRAM (SERIES OR SPECIAL)
Arthur Fiedler: Just Call Me Maestro (PBS)
The Muppet Show (Syndicated)
NBC's Saturday Night Live (NBC)
Shirley MacLaine at the Lido (CBS)
Steve and Edyie Celebrate Irving Berlin (NBC)

The comedy-variety series format was dying on network television. With the ending of *The Carol Burnett Show*, there were few high-quality weekly variety shows during prime time on any of the three commercial networks. Because of the dearth of nominees, series and specials were lumped together in one category. Thus the entire seasons of the late-night *Saturday Night Live* and the syndicated *Muppet Show* competed with one-time specials starring Boston Pops conductor Arthur Fiedler,

Tony Danza, Marilu Henner, Christopher Lloyd, and Judd Hirsch in *Taxi* (outstanding Comedy Series for three consecutive years, 1978–79 to 1980–81).

Shirley MacLaine, and Steve Lawrence and Edyie Gormé. The latter won.

ACTOR (LIMITED SERIES OR SPECIAL)
Ned Beatty (*Friendly Fire, ABC Theatre*) (ABC)
Louis Gossett, Jr. (*Backstairs at the White House*) (NBC)
Kurt Russell (*Elvis*) (ABC)
Peter Strauss (*The Jericho Mile*) (ABC)

ACTRESS (LIMITED SERIES OR SPECIAL)
Carol Burnett (*Friendly Fire, ABC Theatre*) (ABC)
Bette Davis (*Strangers: The Story of a Mother and Daughter*) (CBS)
Olivia Cole (*Backstairs at the White House*) (NBC)
Katharine Hepburn (*The Corn Is Green*) (CBS)
Mary Tyler Moore (*First You Cry*) (CBS)

ACTOR (DRAMA SERIES)
Edward Asner (*Lou Grant*) (CBS)
James Garner (*The Rockford Files*) (NBC)
Jack Klugman (*Quincy*) (NBC)
Ron Leibman (*Kaz*) (CBS)

Ron Leibman's series *Kaz*, in which he starred as an ex-con-turned-lawyer, had been canceled by CBS. "Here we are another Sunday night and *Kaz* has been pre-empted again," he said with bittersweet humor upon accepting his Emmy. Meanwhile, his wife Linda Lavin's series *Alice* was enjoying a long run on the same network. *Alice*, based on the Oscar-winning film *Alice Doesn't Live Here Anymore*, would win several Golden Globes, but no Emmys. Leibman would later divorce Lavin and marry fellow Emmy-winner Jessica Walter.

ACTRESS (DRAMA SERIES)
Barbara Bel Geddes (*Dallas*) (CBS)
Mariette Hartley ("Married," *The Incredible Hulk*) (CBS)
Rita Moreno ("Rosendahl and Gilda Stern Are Dead," *The Rockford Files*) (NBC)
Sada Thompson (*Family*) (ABC)

Here we go again. Categories were recombined in yet another effort to streamline the Emmys. The acting categories for specials and limited series were merged. Single and continuing perfomers in series were now in competition. Thus Mariette Hartley, who appeared in one segment of *The Incredible Hulk*, and Ruth Gordon, a guest on *Taxi*, were named best actresses in drama and comedy series.

ACTOR (COMEDY SERIES)
Alan Alda (*M*A*S*H*) (CBS)
Judd Hirsch (*Taxi*) (ABC)
Hal Linden (*Barney Miller*) (ABC)
Carroll O'Connor (*All in the Family*) (CBS)
Robin Williams (*Mork & Mindy*) (ABC)

ACTRESS (COMEDY SERIES)
Ruth Gordon ("Sugar Mama," *Taxi*) (ABC)
Katherine Helmond (*Soap*) (ABC)
Linda Lavin (*Alice*) (CBS)
Isabel Sanford (*The Jeffersons*) (CBS)
Jean Stapleton (*All in the Family*) (CBS)

SUPPORTING ACTOR (SPECIAL OR LIMITED SERIES)
Marlon Brando (*Roots: The Next Generations*) (ABC)
Ed Flanders (*Backstairs at the White House*) (NBC)
Al Freeman, Jr. (*Roots: The Next Generations*) (ABC)
Robert Vaughn (*Backstairs at the White House*) (NBC)
Paul Winfield (*Roots: The Next Generations*) (ABC)

SUPPORTING ACTRESS (SPECIAL OR LIMITED SERIES)
Ruby Dee (*Roots: The Next Generations*) (ABC)
Colleen Dewhurst (*Silent Victory: The Kitty O'Neill Story*) (NBC)
Eileen Heckart (*Backstairs at the White House*) (NBC)
Celeste Holm (*Backstairs at the White House*) (NBC)
Esther Rolle (*Summer of My German Soldier*) (NBC)

SUPPORTING ACTOR (DRAMA SERIES)
Mason Adams (*Lou Grant*) (CBS)
Noah Beery (*The Rockford Files*) (NBC)
Stuart Margolin (*The Rockford Files*) (NBC)
Joe Santos (*The Rockford Files*) (NBC)
Robert Walden (*Lou Grant*) (CBS)

SUPPORTING ACTRESS (DRAMA SERIES)
Linda Kelsey (*Lou Grant*) (CBS)
Nancy Marchand (*Lou Grant*) (CBS)
Kristy McNichol (*Family*) (ABC)

SUPPORTING ACTOR (COMEDY OR COMEDY-VARIETY OR MUSIC SERIES)
Gary Burghoff (*M*A*S*H*) (CBS)
Danny DeVito (*Taxi*) (ABC)
Max Gail (*Barney Miller*) (ABC)
Robert Guillaume (*Soap*) (ABC)
Harry Morgan (*M*A*S*H*) (ABC)

SUPPORTING ACTRESS (COMEDY OR COMEDY-VARIETY OR MUSIC SERIES)
Polly Holliday (*Alice*) (CBS)
Marion Ross (*Happy Days*) (ABC)
Sally Struthers ("California, Here We Are," *All in the Family*) (CBS)
Loretta Swit (*M*A*S*H*) (CBS)

DAYTIME AWARDS
Drama Series: *Ryan's Hope* (ABC); Actor (Drama Series): Al Freeman, Jr. (*One Life to Live*) (ABC); Actress (Drama Series): Irene Dailey (*Another World*) (NBC); Supporting Actor (Drama Series): Peter Hansen (*General Hospital*) (ABC); Supporting Actress (Drama Series): Suzanne Rogers (*Another World*) (ABC); Game Show: *The Hollywood Squares* (NBC); Talk or Variety Show: *Donahue* (Syndicated)

OTHER PRIME-TIME AWARDS
Directing (Special or Limited Series): David Greene (*Friendly Fire, ABC Theatre*) (ABC); Directing (Drama Series): Jackie Cooper (*The White Shadow,* pilot episode) (CBS); Directing (Comedy or Comedy-Variety or Music Series): Noam Pitlik ("The Harris Incident," *Barney Miller*) (ABC)

Writing (Special or Limited Series): Patrick Nolan, Michael Mann (*The Jericho Mile*) (ABC); Writing (Drama Series): Michele Gallery ("Dying," *Lou Grant*) (CBS); Writing (Comedy or Comedy-Variety or Music Series): Alan Alda ("Inga," *M*A*S*H*) (CBS)

With his win for a script of *M*A*S*H*, Alan Alda

earned a place in the Emmy record books. He became the first person to win the winged lady in three different cartegories—acting, directing, and writing. To celebrate, he turned a cartwheel in the aisle.

ABC was now dominating the airwaves as the No. 1 network. The formerly No. 3 web was boss of the Emmys as well. Not only did ABC carry the awards, but the hosts were stars of two of the network's shows—Henry Winkler of *Happy Days* and Cheryl Ladd from *Charlie's Angels*. The Emmys were on top of the ratings heap as well, with an audience of 60 million, the highest since 1973. President Jimmy Carter interrupted the show again—but this time only briefly to pay tribute to three TV newsmen who lost their lives in Guyana and Nicaragua.

THE PEABODY AWARDS (FOR 1979)

CBS News Sunday Morning (CBS News); Sylvia Fine Kaye, producer/hostess, for *Musical Comedy Tonight* (PBS); *Valentine* (ABC); *Friendly Fire* (ABC); *When Hell Was in Session* (NBC); *Dummy* (NBC); *Treasures of the British Crown* (NBC and BBC); *A Special Gift, ABC Afterschool Special* (ABC); Roger Mudd "for his searching questions of Senator Edward Kennedy in the *CBS Reports* program *Teddy*"; *The Boston Goes to China* (CBS News); Robert Trout of ABC News; *World* (WGBH-TV, Boston); *The Adventures of Whistling Sam* (KTVI, St. Louis, MO); *Strip and Search* (WMAQ-TV, Chicago); *The Long Eyes of Kit Peak* (KOOL-TV, Phoeniz, AZ); *Politics of Poison* (KRON-TV, San Francisco); *Miles to Go Before We Sleep* (WTTW-TV, Chicago); *Little Rock Central High School* (WTTW-TV, Chicago); *Down at the Dunbar* (KNXT, Hollywod)

THE GOLDEN GLOBE AWARDS (FOR 1979)

Made-for-TV Movie: *All Quiet on the Western Front* (CBS); Drama Series: *Lou Grant* (CBS); Comedy or Musical Series (tie): *Alice* (CBS) and *Taxi* (ABC)

Actor (Drama Series): Edward Asner (*Lou Grant*) (CBS); Actress (Drama Series): Natalie Wood (*From Here to Eternity*) (NBC); Actor (Comedy or Musical Series): Alan Alda (*M*A*S*H*)

(CBS); Actress (Comedy or Musical Series); Linda Lavin (*Alice*) (CBS); Supporting Actor (tie): Danny DeVito (*Taxi*) (ABC) and Vic Tayback (*Alice*) (CBS); Supporting Actress: Polly Holliday (*Alice*) (CBS)

THE CABLE ACE AWARDS (FOR 1979)

SRO: Gladys Knight and the Pips (HBO); *Emmet Otter's Jug Band Christmas* (HBO)

Cable was beginning to make inroads in the traditional broadcast television audience. The new industry wanted to be part of the Emmys, but Academy rules stipulated shows must reach at least fifty-one percent of all American TV sets to qualify for award nominations. The nonbroadcast networks banded together to create their own awards, the Cable ACEs. Cable shows became eligible for Emmys in 1987–88.

THE EMMY AWARDS

DRAMA OR COMEDY SPECIAL
All Quiet on the Western Front, Hallmark Hall of Fame (CBS)
Amber Waves (ABC)
Gideon's Trumpet, Hallmark Hall of Fame (CBS)
Guyana Tragedy: The Story of Jim Jones (CBS)
The Miracle Worker, *NBC Theatre* (NBC)

DRAMA SERIES
Dallas (CBS)
Family (ABC)
Lou Grant (CBS)
The Rockford Files (NBC)
The White Shadow (CBS)

In its third season, *Lou Grant* garnered the most Emmy nominations of any program for 1979–80 with fifteen citations. It swept the night by taking six awards—for Drama Series, Writing (Drama Series) and Directing (Drama Series) (both for the same epsiode about a gay cop who is forced to reveal his sexuality), Music Composition (Series), Actor (Drama Series) (Edward Asner as the tough titular editor), and Supporting Actress (Drama Series) (Nancy Marchand as the imperious publisher). Neither Asner, Marchand, nor most of that year's Emmy acting winners were present to collect their accolades since there was a performers' boycott of the awards because of a strike against the networks by the Screen Actors Guild (SAG) and the American Federation of Television and Radio Artists (AFTRA), the actors' unions.

COMEDY SERIES
Barney Miller (ABC)
M*A*S*H (CBS)
Soap (ABC)
Taxi (ABC)
WKRP in Cincinnati (CBS)

LIMITED SERIES
Disraeli, Portrait of a Romantic,
    Masterpiece Theatre (PBS)
The Duchess of Duke Street,
    Masterpiece Theatre (PBS)
Edward and Mrs. Simpson (Syndicated)
Moviola (NBC)

VARIETY OR MUSIC PROGRAM
Baryshnikov on Broadway (ABC)
The Benny Hill Show (Syndicated)
Goldie and Liza Together (CBS)
The Muppet Show (Syndicated)
Shirley MacLaine …"Every Little Movement" (CBS)

ACTOR (SPECIAL OR LIMITED SERIES)
Powers Boothe (*Guyana Tragedy: The Story of Jim Jones*) (CBS)
Tony Curtis (*Moviola: The Scarlett O'Hara War*) (NBC)
Henry Fonda (*Gideon's Trumpet, Hallmark Hall of Fame*) (CBS)
Jason Robards (*FDR: The Last Year*) (NBC)

"This is either the most courageous moment of my life or the stupidest," said Powers Boothe as he accepted his award for his performance as the demonic Reverend Jim Jones in *Guyana Tragedy*. He was the only actor to break the Emmy boycott.

ACTRESS (SPECIAL OR LIMITED SERIES)
Patty Duke Astin (*The Miracle Worker, NBC Theatre*) (NBC)
Bette Davis (*White Mama*) (CBS)
Melissa Gilbert (*The Miracle Worker, NBC Theatre*) (NBC)
Lee Remick (*Haywire*) (CBS)

As a child, Patty Duke Astin had played the young deaf and blind Helen Keller in the both the stage and film versions of *The Miracle Worker*. She revisited the story as an adult when she played Helen's heroic teacher Annie Sullivan in this TV-movie remake.

ACTOR (DRAMA SERIES)
Edward Asner (*Lou Grant*) (CBS)
James Garner (*The Rockford Files*) (NBC)
Larry Hagman (*Dallas*) (CBS)
Jack Klugman (*Quincy*) (NBC)

ACTRESS (DRAMA SERIES)
Lauren Bacall ("Lions, Tigers, Monkeys, and Dogs," *The Rockford Files*) (NBC)
Barbara Bel Geddes (*Dallas*) (CBS)
Mariette Hartley ("Paradise Cove," *The Rockford Files*) (CBS)
Kristy MacNichol (*Family*) (ABC)
Sada Thompson (*Family*) (ABC)

ACTOR (COMEDY SERIES)
Alan Alda (*M*A*S*H*) (CBS)
Robert Guillaume (*Benson*) (ABC)
Judd Hirsch (*Taxi*) (ABC)
Hal Linden (*Barney Miller*) (ABC)
Richard Mulligan (*Soap*) (ABC)

ACTRESS (COMEDY SERIES)
Cathryn Damon (*Soap*) (ABC)
Katherine Helmond (*Soap*) (ABC)
Polly Holliday (*Flo*) (CBS)
Sheree North (*Archie Bunker's Place*) (CBS)
Isabel Sanford (*The Jeffersons*) (CBS)

SUPPORTING ACTOR (SPECIAL OR LIMITED SERIES)
Ernest Borgnine (*All Quiet on the Western Front, Hallmark Hall of Fame*) (CBS)

John Cassavetes (*Flesh and Blood*) (CBS)
Charles Durning (*Attica*) (ABC)
Harold Gould (*Moviola*) (NBC)
George Grizzard (*The Oldest Living Graduate*) (NBC)

SUPPORTING ACTRESS (SPECIAL OR LIMITED SERIES)
Eileen Heckart (*FDR: The Last Year*) (NBC)
Patricia Neal (*All Quiet on the Western Front, Hallmark Hall of Fame*) (CBS)
Carrie Nye (*Moviola: The Scarlett O'Hara War*) (NBC)
Mare Winningham (*Amber Waves*) (ABC)

SUPPORTING ACTOR (DRAMA SERIES)
Mason Adams (*Lou Grant*) (CBS)
Noah Beery (*The Rockford Files*) (NBC)
Stuart Margolin (*The Rockford Files*) (NBC)
Robert Walden (*Lou Grant*) (CBS)

SUPPORTING ACTRESS (DRAMA SERIES)
Nina Foch ("Hollywood," *Lou Grant*) (CBS)
Linda Kelsey (*Lou Grant*) (CBS)
Nancy Marchand (*Lou Grant*) (CBS)
Jessica Walter (*Trapper John, MD*) (CBS)

SUPPORTING ACTOR (COMEDY, VARIETY, OR MUSIC SERIES)
Mike Farrell (*M*A*S*H*) (CBS)
Max Gail (*Barney Miller*) (ABC)
Howard Hesseman (*WKRP in Cincinnati*) (CBS)
Harry Morgan (*M*A*S*H*) (CBS)
Steve Landesberg (*Barney Miller*) (ABC)

SUPPORTING ACTRESS (COMEDY, VARIETY, OR MUSIC SERIES)
Loni Anderson (*WKRP in Cincinnati*) (CBS)
Polly Holliday (*Alice*) (CBS)
Inga Swenson (*Benson*) (ABC)
Loretta Swit (*M*A*S*H*) (CBS)

DAYTIME AWARDS
Drama Series: *Guiding Light* (CBS); Actor: Douglass Watson (*Another World*) (NBC); Actress: Judith Light (*One Life to Live*) (ABC); Supporting Actor: Warren Burton (*All My Children*) (ABC); Supporting Actress: Francesca James (*All My Children*) (ABC); Game Show (tie): *The Hollywood Squares* (NBC) and *The $20,000 Pyramid* (ABC); Talk or Variety Series: *Donahue* (Syndicated)

OTHER PRIME-TIME AWARDS
Directing (Special or Limited Series): Marvin J. Chomsky (*Attica*) (ABC); Directing (Drama Series): Robert Young ("Cop," *Lou Grant*) (CBS); Directing (Comedy Series): James Burrows ("Louie and the Nice Girl," *Taxi*) (ABC); Directing (Variety or Music Program): Dwight Hemion (*Baryshnikov on Broadway*) (ABC)

Writing (Special or Limited Series): David Chase (*Off the Minnesota Strip*) (ABC); Writing (Drama Series): Seth Freeman ("Cop," *Lou Grant*) (CBS); Writing (Comedy Series): Bob Colleary ("Photographer," *Barney Miller*) (ABC); Writing (Variety or Music Program): Buz Kohan (*Shirley MacLaine . . . "Every Little Movement"*) (CBS)

September 7, 1980, was the night none of the stars came out. A strike by SAG and AFTRA against all three networks resulted in a boycott of the Emmys. Scheduled hosts Bob Newhart, Michael Landon, and Lee Remick dropped out but were replaced by Steve Allen and Dick Clark. As both performers and producers, Allen and Clark could legitimately appear, but they donated their $10,000 fees to the SAG strike fund.

Allen provided much needed humor for the potentially embarassing broadcast. He opened with an acknowledgement of the boycott: "We have a star-studded audience tonight—three stars and fourteen studs."

Substitute presenters had to be found and some interesting choices were made. Among those doling out the Emmys were figure skater Peggy Fleming, former evangelist Marjoe Gortner, former *Playboy* playmate Barbie Benton, newscaster Kelly Lange, illusionist David Copperfield, sportscaster Jayne Kennedy, and a covey of network executives and producers.

Because of the lack of star power and AFTRA's forbidding the use of taped clips showing its members, the program emphasized craftspeople with film and tape segments of behind-the-scenes personnel. The Smothers Brothers crossed the boycott line in order to entertain.

The *New York Post* called the show "a lifeless flop," while *Variety* found it a "smooth three-hour telecast that reflected the professional excellence that the awards themselves are supposed to be celebrating."

NBC, the Emmy network for 1980, was having a bad year. The Peacock web was also set to broadcast the Olympics from Moscow, but the United States announced it was boycotting the event.

THE PEABODY AWARDS (FOR 1980)

Universe (CBS News); *Gideon's Trumpet* (CBS); *Shogun* (NBC); *IBM Presents Baryshnikov on Broadway* (ABC); *Amber Waves* (ABC); *Playing for Time* (CBS); *All Creatures Great and Small* (PBS); Carroll O'Connor for "Edith's Death," *All in the Family*; Phil Donahue; Walter Cronkite; radio/TV reporter Sol Taishoff; *The American Short Story* (PBS); Mary Nissenson for *Poland: Changing Nation*; Elaine Green of WCPO-TV, Cincinatti, OH, for *The Hoskins Interview*; *Cosmos* (KCET, Los Angeles, Adrian Malone, and Carl Sagan); *Terra: Our World* (Maryland Instructional Television); *National Geographic Specials (WQED and National Geographic Society);* The Battle of the Wetlands (KTEH, San Jose, CA, Carol Mon Pere, and Sandra Nichols); *Broken Arrow: Can a Nuclear Weapons Accident Happen Here?* (KQED-TV, San Francisco); *The MX Debate, Bill Moyers' Journal* (KUED-TV, Salt Lake City, UT, WNET/13, New York)

THE GOLDEN GLOBE AWARDS (FOR 1980)

Made-for-TV Movie: *The Shadow Box* (ABC); Drama Series: *Shogun* (NBC); Comedy or Musical Series: *Taxi* (ABC)

Actor (Drama Series): Richard Chamberlain (*Shogun*) (NBC); Actress (Drama Series): Yoko Shimada (*Shogun*) (NBC); Actor (Comedy or Musical Series): Alan Alda (*M*A*S*H*) (CBS); Actress (Comedy or Musical Series): Katherine Helmond (*Soap*) (ABC); Supporting Actor (tie): Pat Harrington (*One Day at a Time*) (CBS) and Vic Tayback (*Alice*) (CBS); Supporting Actress (tie): Diane Ladd (*Alice*) (CBS) and Valerie Bertinelli (*One Day at a Time*) (CBS)

THE CABLE ACE AWARDS (FOR 1980)

General Entertainment: *Standing Room Only: Here It Is, Burlesque* (HBO); Music Entertainment: *On Tour: Willie Nelson Plays Lake Tahoe* (Showtime)

THE EMMY AWARDS

DRAMA SPECIAL
Evita Peron (NBC)
Fallen Angel (CBS)
Playing for Time (CBS)
The Shadow Box (ABC)
The Women's Room (ABC)

Pulitzer Prize-winning playwright Arthur Miller adapted *Playing for Time*, Fania Fenelon's memoir of her experiences in the women's orchestra of the Auschwitz concentration camp. The casting of pro-Palestinian activist Vanessa Redgrave as the Jewish Fenelon sparked a controversy. Nevertheless, the searing drama was named outstanding Drama Special and Redgrave best Actress (Special or Limited Series). Jane Alexander also won in the Supporting Actress (Special or Limited Series) category as the conductor.

DRAMA SERIES
Dallas (CBS)
Hill Street Blues (NBC)
Lou Grant (CBS)
Quincy (NBC)
The White Shadow (CBS)

The gritty, ultra-realistic *Hill Street Blues*, set in an active, urban police precinct, was praised by critics as one of the best cop shows ever. But audiences weren't paying attention. The NBC series came in eighty-seventh in the ratings out of a total of ninety-six programs. But Emmy agreed with the critics and gave *Hill Street* a record twenty-one nominations, the most ever for a prime-time series.

On the big night, the roll call was all *Hill Street*. The series won eight Emmys, breaking the record previously held by *The Julie Andrews Hour* for the

most awards won by a series in one season. A shelf full of golden ladies did not rescue the Andrews series from extinction, but *Hill Street* was saved from a similar fate. NBC renewed it before the nominations came out. The series set another record as the lowest-rated program ever to be picked up for a second year.

While the Emmys did not directly save the show from the axe, they did get viewers to give the program a try. *Hill Street* ultimately gained a loyal following and went on to win a total of twenty-six Emmys and ninety-eight nominations (making it the third most nominated show ever behind *Cheers* and *M*A*S*H*). It also took the best series title for four years in a row—a record it shares with *The Dick Van Dyke Show* and *All in the Family*.

COMEDY SERIES

Barney Miller (ABC)
M*A*S*H (CBS)
Soap (ABC)
Taxi (ABC)
WKRP in Cincinnati (CBS)

LIMITED SERIES

East of Eden (ABC)
Masada (ABC)
Rumpole of the Bailey, Mystery! (PBS)
Shogun (NBC)
Tinker, Tailor, Soldier, Spy, Great Performances (PBS)

VARIETY OR MUSIC PROGRAM

*The American Film Institute Salute
    to Fred Astaire* (CBS)
The Benny Hill Show (Syndicated)
Lily: Sold Out (CBS)
The Muppet Show (Syndicated)
*The Tonight Show Starring
    Johnny Carson* (NBC)

ACTOR (SPECIAL OR LIMITED SERIES)

Richard Chamberlain (*Shogun*) (NBC)
Anthony Hopkins (*The Bunker*) (CBS)
Toshiro Mifune (*Shogun*) (NBC)
Peter O'Toole (*Masada*) (ABC)
Peter Strauss (*Masada*) (ABC)

ACTRESS (SPECIAL OR LIMITED SERIES)

Ellen Burstyn (*The People vs. Jean Harris*) (NBC)
Catherine Hicks (*Marilyn: The Untold Story*) (ABC)
Vanessa Redgrave (*Playing for Time*) (CBS)
Yoko Shimada (*Shogun*) (NBC)
Joanne Woodward (*Crisis at Central
    High*) (CBS)

ACTOR (DRAMA SERIES)

Edward Asner (*Lou Grant*) (CBS)
Jim Davis (*Dallas*) (CBS)
Louis Gossett, Jr. ("Future City,"
    Palmerstown, USA) (CBS)
Larry Hagman (*Dallas*) (CBS)
Pernell Roberts (*Trapper John, M.D.*) (CBS)
Daniel J. Travanti (*Hill Street Blues*) (NBC)

ACTRESS (DRAMA SERIES)

Barbara Babcock ("Fecund Hand Rose,"
    Hill Street Blues) (NBC)
Barbara Bel Geddes (*Dallas*) (CBS)
Linda Gray (*Dallas*) (CBS)
Veronica Hamel (*Hill Street Blues*) (NBC)
Michael Learned (*Nurse*) (CBS)
Stefanie Powers (*Hart to Hart*) (ABC)

ACTOR (COMEDY SERIES)

Alan Alda (*M*A*S*H*) (CBS)
Judd Hirsch (*Taxi*) (ABC)
Hal Linden (*Barney Miller*) (ABC)
Richard Mulligan (*Soap*) (ABC)
John Ritter (*Three's Company*) (ABC)

ACTRESS (COMEDY SERIES)

Eileen Brennan ("Thy Boss's Wife,"
    Taxi) (ABC)
Cathryn Damon (*Soap*) (ABC)
Katherine Helmond (*Soap*) (ABC)
Lynn Redgrave (*House Calls*) (CBS)
Isabel Sanford (*The Jeffersons*) (CBS)

While munching a piece of cheese she started eating backstage, Isabel Sanford exclaimed, "I've been waiting for so long, my humility is just gone." She had been playing the role of Louise Jefferson, first as a neighbor of the Bunkers on *All in the Family* and then in her own spin-off series, for a decade.

SUPPORTING ACTOR
(SPECIAL OR LIMITED SERIES)

Andy Griffith (*Murder in Texas*) (NBC)
Yuki Meguro (*Shogun*) (NBC)
Anthony Quayle (*Masada*) (ABC)
John Rhys-Davies (*Shogun*) (NBC)
David Warner (*Masada*) (ABC)

SUPPORTING ACTRESS
(SPECIAL OR LIMITED SERIES)

Jane Alexander (*Playing for Time*) (CBS)
Patty Duke Astin (*The Women's Room*) (ABC)
Colleen Dewhurst (*The Women's Room*) (ABC)
Shirley Knight (*Playing for Time*) (CBS)
Piper Laurie (*The Bunker*) (CBS)

SUPPORTING ACTOR (DRAMA SERIES)

Mason Adams (*Lou Grant*) (CBS)
Michael Conrad (*Hill Street Blues*) (NBC)
Charles Haid (*Hill Street Blues*) (NBC)
Robert Walden (*Lou Grant*) (CBS)
Bruce Weitz (*Hill Street Blues*) (NBC)

SUPPORTING ACTRESS
(DRAMA SERIES)

Barbara Barrie (*Breaking Away*) (ABC)
Barbara Bosson (*Hill Street Blues*) (NBC)
Linda Kelsey (*Lou Grant*) (CBS)
Nancy Marchand (*Lou Grant*) (CBS)
Betty Thomas (*Hill Street Blues*) (NBC)

SUPPORTING ACTOR (COMEDY,
VARIETY OR MUSIC SERIES)

Danny DeVito (*Taxi*) (ABC)
Howard Hesseman (*WKRP in Cincinnati*) (CBS)
Steve Landesberg (*Barney Miller*) (ABC)
Harry Morgan (*M*A*S*H*) (CBS)
David Ogden Stiers (*M*A*S*H*) (CBS)

SUPPORTING ACTRESS (COMEDY,
VARIETY OR MUSIC SERIES)

Loni Anderson (*WKRP in Cincinnati*) (CBS)
Eileen Brennan (*Private Benjamin*) (CBS)
Marla Gibbs (*The Jeffersons*) (CBS)
Anne Meara (*Archie Bunker's Place*) (CBS)
Loretta Swit (*M*A*S*H*) (CBS)

In March, Eileen Brennan had been nominated for a Supporting Actress Oscar for her role as the tough commanding officer in the film version of *Private Benjamin*. She lost to Mary Steenbergen for *Melvin and Howard*. Her Emmy win is one of the few instances of a performer taking the TV award for a part also played in the movie edition.

DAYTIME AWARDS

Drama Series: *General Hospital* (ABC); Actor: Douglass Watson (*Another World*) (NBC); Actress: Judith Light (*One Life To Live*) (ABC); Supporting Actor: Larry Haines (*Search for Tomorrow*) (CBS); Supporting Actress: Jane Elliot (*General Hospital*) (ABC); Game Show: *The $20,000 Pyramid* (ABC); Talk/Service Series: *Donahue* (Syndicated); Variety Series: *The Merv Griffin Show* (Syndicated)

OTHER PRIME-TIME AWARDS

Directing (Special or Limited Series): James Goldstone (*Kent State*) (NBC); Directing (Drama Series): Robert Butler ("Hill Street Station," *Hill Street Blues*) (NBC); Directing (Comedy Series): James Burrows ("Elaine's Strange Triangle," *Taxi*) (ABC); Directing (Variety or Music Program): Don Mischer (*The Kennedy Center Honors: A National Celebration of the Performing Arts*) (CBS)

Writing (Special or Limited Series): Arthur Miller (*Playing for Time*) (CBS); Writing (Drama Series): Michael Kozoll, Stephen Bochco ("Hill Street Station," *Hill Street Blues*) (NBC); Writing (Comedy Series): Michael Leeson ("Tony's Sister and Jim," *Taxi*) (ABC); Writing (Variety or Music Progam): Jerry Juhl, David Odell, Chris Langham, Jim Henson, Don Hinkley (*The Muppet Show* with Carol Burnett) (Syndicated)

The 1980–81 Emmys opened with the collected casts of sixteen prime-time series singing that TV was "One Big Happy Family," an ironic choice in light of the previous year's boycott by the performers. The program was hosted by Shirley MacLaine and Edward Asner, one of the leaders of the 1980 boycott. Dwight Hemion and Gary Smith, producers of numerous Emmy-winning musical specials, worked their magic behind the scenes of the telecast.

In addition to the opening number, twelve daytime drama stars sang the praises of their genre with an "Ode to the Soaps." Two late leading lights of 1950s' TV were paid homage. Sid Caesar and

Imogene Coca eulogized Max Leibman, their producer on *Your Show of Shows*, while video playwright Paddy Chayefsky was remembered by Peter O'Toole and Rod Steiger (the original *Marty*, Chayefsy's landmark TV drama). The still-very-much-alive Lucille Ball received a special award and a standing ovation.

NBC, aided by the eight *Hill Street Blues* wins, began a long reign of dominance over the Emmys with a total of twenty awards to CBS's eighteen, ABC's twelve, PBS's eight, and the syndicated *Muppet Show*'s one. Despite its embarrassment of riches, the Peacock network was ranked third in overall ratings for the season.

THE PEABODY AWARDS (FOR 1981)

Hill Street Blues (NBC); *Bill* (CBS); *The Wave* (ABC); ABC News for *Viewpoint, Nightline,* and *America Held Hostage: The Secret Negotiations*; *The Red Army, World* (WGBH, Boston); *Dance in America* (PBS and WNET/Thirteen); *The Private History of a Campaign That Failed* (The Nebraska Educational Television Network and The Great Amwell Company); *She's Nobody's Baby: The History of the American Woman in the 20th Century* (HBO and *Ms. Magazine*) (the first Peabody given to a cable network); Bill Leonard, CBS News; Danny Kaye for *An Evening with Danny Kaye and the New York Philharmonic* and *Skokie*; *Eyewitness News* (WLS-TV, Chicago); John Goldsmith, WDVM-TV (Washington, DC), for *Now That We've Got Your Interest*; *Project: China* (KJRH-TV, Tulsa, OK); WSMV, Nashville, and KATU-TV, Portland, OR, for a series of significant television documentaries; The Eight Decade Consortium for *Fed Up with Fear*; *The Day after Trinity: J. Robert Oppenheimer and the Atomic Bomb* (KTEH, San Jose, CA)

THE GOLDEN GLOBE AWARDS (FOR 1981)

Made-for-TV Movie or Limited Series (tie): *Bill* (CBS) and *East of Eden* (ABC); Drama Series: *Hill Street Blues* (NBC); Comedy or Musical Series: *M*A*S*H* (CBS); Variety or Music Special: *The Kennedy Center Honors: A Celebration of the Performing Arts* (CBS)

Actor (Telefilm/Limited Series): Mickey Rooney (*Bill*) (CBS); Actress (Telefilm/Limited Series): Jane Seymour (*East of Eden*) (ABC); Actor (Drama Series): Daniel J. Travanti (*Hill Street Blues*) (NBC); Actress (Drama Series) (tie): Barbara Bel Geddes (*Dallas*) (CBS) and Linda Evans (*Dynasty*) (ABC); Actor (Comedy or Musical Series): Alan Alda (*M*A*S*H*); Actress (Comedy or Musical Series): Eileen Brennan (*Private Benjamin*) (CBS); Supporting Actor: John Hillerman (*Magnum, PI*) (CBS); Supporting Actress: Valerie Bertinelli (*One Day at a Time*) (CBS)

THE CABLE ACE AWARDS (FOR 1981)

Dramatic Special: *Broadway on Showtime: Passion of Dracula* (Showtime); General Entertainment (Music): *SRO: Diana Ross* (HBO); General Entertainment (Unclassified): *Little Johnny Jones* (Showtime)

THE EMMY AWARDS

DRAMA SPECIAL
Bill (CBS)
The Elephant Man (ABC)
Inside the Third Reich (ABC)
Skokie (CBS)
A Woman Called Golda (Syndicated)

A Woman Called Golda, a bio-drama about Israeli Prime Minister Golda Meir, was the first syndicated program to win an Emmy for outstanding Drama Special. The title role was played by Ingrid Bergman in a rare television performance which also turned out to be her last. The lengendary film star died a few weeks before the Emmy voting. Bergman's posthumous Emmy for best Actress (Special or Mini-Series) was accepted by her daughter, broadcaster Pia Lindstrom. "I really do think she deserved this award," Lindstrom said, "not only for her performance on camera, but her performance off camera." She was referring to her mother's bout with cancer during the filming.

DRAMA SERIES
Dynasty (ABC)
Fame (NBC)
Hill Street Blues (NBC)
Lou Grant (CBS)
Magnum, PI (CBS)

COMEDY SERIES
Barney Miller (ABC)
Love, Sidney (NBC)
*M*A*S*H* (CBS)
Taxi (ABC)
WKRP in Cincinnati (CBS)

Barney Miller, a lighter take on police work than *Hill Street* but with a similar sharp edge, was in its last year of a five-year run when it finally won the Emmy as outstanding comedy series. Other winning and nominated series facing cancellation included *Lou Grant* (inside gossip had it the show was killed by CBS because of star Edward Asner's controversial support of left-wing causes), *Police Squad, WKRP in Cincinnati, Nurse*, and *Taxi*, which was axed by ABC but picked up by NBC.

LIMITED SERIES
Brideshead Revisited, Great Performances (PBS)
Flickers, Masterpiece Theatre (PBS)
Marco Polo (NBC)
Oppenheimer, American Playhouse (PBS)
A Town like Alice, Masterpiece Theatre (PBS)

VARIETY, MUSIC OR COMEDY PROGRAM (SERIES OR SPECIAL)
Ain't Misbehavin' (NBC)
American Film Institute Salute to Frank Capra (CBS)
Baryshnikov in Hollywood (CBS)
Night of 100 Stars (ABC)
SCTV Comedy Network (NBC)

ACTOR (SPECIAL OR MINI-SERIES)
Anthony Andrews (*Brideshead Revisited, Great Performances*) (PBS)
Philip Anglim (*The Elephant Man*) (ABC)
Anthony Hopkins (*The Hunchback of Notre Dame, Hallmark Hall of Fame*) (CBS)
Jeremy Irons (*Brideshead Revisited, Great Performances*) (PBS)
Mickey Rooney (*Bill*) (CBS)

ACTRESS (SPECIAL OR MINI-SERIES)
Ingrid Bergman (*A Woman Called Golda*) (Syndicated)
Glenda Jackson (*The Patricia Neal Story*) (CBS)
Ann Jillian (*Mae West*) (CBS)
Jean Stapleton (*Eleanor, First Lady of the World*) (CBS)
Cicely Tyson (*The Marva Collins Story, Hallmark Hall of Fame*) (CBS)

ACTOR (DRAMA SERIES)
Edward Asner (*Lou Grant*) (CBS)
John Forsythe (*Dynasty*) (ABC)
James Garner (*Bret Maverick*) (NBC)
Tom Selleck (*Magnum, PI*) (CBS)
Daniel J. Travanti (*Hill Street Blues*) (NBC)

ACTRESS (DRAMA SERIES)
Debbie Allen (*Fame*) (NBC)
Veronica Hamel (*Hill Street Blues*) (NBC)
Michael Learned (*Nurse*) (CBS)
Michele Lee (*Knots Landing*) (CBS)
Stefanie Powers (*Hart to Hart*) (ABC)

ACTOR (COMEDY SERIES)
Alan Alda (*M*A*S*H*) (CBS)
Robert Guillaume (*Benson*) (ABC)
Judd Hirsch (*Taxi*) (ABC)
Hal Linden (*Barney Miller*) (ABC)
Leslie Nielsen (*Police Squad!*) (ABC)

ACTRESS (COMEDY SERIES)
Nell Carter (*Gimme a Break*) (NBC)
Bonnie Franklin (*One Day at a Time*) (CBS)
Carol Kane ("Simka Returns," *Taxi*) (ABC)
Swoosie Kurtz (*Love, Sidney*) (NBC)
Charlotte Rae (*The Facts of Life*) (NBC)
Isabel Sanford (*The Jeffersons*) (CBS)

SUPPORTING ACTOR (SPECIAL OR LIMITED SERIES)
Jack Albertson (*My Body, My Child*) (ABC)
John Gielgud (*Brideshead Revisited, Great Performances*) (PBS)
Derek Jacobi (*Inside the Third Reich*) (ABC)
Leonard Nimoy (*A Woman Called Golda*) (Syndicated)

Laurence Olivier (*Brideshead Revisited, Great Performances*) (PBS)

SUPPORTING ACTRESS (SPECIAL OR LIMITED SERIES)

Claire Bloom (*Brideshead Revisited, Great Performances*) (PBS)
Judy Davis (*A Woman Called Golda*) (Syndicated)
Penny Fuller (*The Elephant Man*) (ABC)
Vicki Lawrence (*Eunice*) (CBS)
Rita Moreno (*Portrait of a Showgirl*) (CBS)

SUPPORTING ACTOR (DRAMA SERIES)

Tauren Blacque (*Hill Street Blues*) (NBC)
Michael Conrad (*Hill Street Blues*) (NBC)
Charles Haid (*Hill Street Blues*) (NBC)
Michael Warren (*Hill Street Blues*) (NBC)
Bruce Weitz (*Hill Street Blues*) (NBC)

SUPPORTING ACTRESS (DRAMA SERIES)

Barbara Bosson (*Hill Street Blues*) (NBC)
Julie Harris (*Knots Landing*) (CBS)
Linda Kelsey (*Lou Grant*) (CBS)
Nancy Marchand (*Lou Grant*) (CBS)
Betty Thomas (*Hill Street Blues*) (NBC)

SUPPORTING ACTOR (COMEDY, VARIETY OR MUSIC SERIES)

Danny DeVito (*Taxi*) (ABC)
Ron Glass (*Barney Miller*) (ABC)
Steve Landesberg (*Barney Miller*) (ABC)
Christopher Lloyd (*Taxi*) (ABC)
Harry Morgan (*M*A*S*H*) (CBS)
David Ogden Stiers (*M*A*S*H*) (CBS)

SUPPORTING ACTRESS (COMEDY, VARIETY OR MUSIC SERIES)

Eileen Brennan (*Private Benjamin*) (CBS)
Marla Gibbs (*The Jeffersons*) (CBS)
Andrea Martin (*SCTV Comedy Network*) (NBC)
Anne Meara (*Archie Bunker's Place*) (CBS)
Inga Swenson (*Benson*) (CBS)
Loretta Swit (*M*A*S*H*) (CBS)

INDIVIDUAL ACHIEVEMENT— SPECIAL CLASSIFICATION

Nell Carter, Andre De Shields, performers (*Ain't Misbehavin'*) (NBC)

DAYTIME AWARDS

Drama Series: *The Guiding Light* (CBS); Actor: Anthony Geary (*General Hospital*) (ABC); Actress: Robin Strasser (*One Life To Live*) (ABC); Supporting Actor: David Lewis (*General Hospital*) (ABC); Supporting Actress: Dorothy Lyman (*All My Children*) (ABC); Game Show: *Password Plus* (NBC); Variety Series: *The Regis Philbin Show* (NBC); Talk or Service Series: *The Richard Simmons Show* (Syndicated)

OTHER PRIME-TIME AWARDS

Directing (Special or Limited Series): Marvin J. Chomsky (*Inside the Third Reich*) (ABC); Directing (Drama Series): Harry Harris ("To Soar and Never Falter," *Fame*) (NBC); Directing (Comedy Series): Alan Rafkin ("Barbara's Crisis," *One Day at a Time*) (CBS); Directing (Variety or Music Program): Dwight Hemion (*Goldie and Kids . . . Listen to Us*) (ABC)

Writing (Special or Limited Series): Corey Blechman (teleplay), Barry Morrow (story) (*Bill*) (CBS); Writing (Drama Series): Steven Bochco, Anthony Yerkovich, Jeffrey Lewis, Michael Wagner (teleplay), Michael Kozoll, Steven Bochco (story) ("Freedom's Last Stand," *Hill Street Blues*) (NBC); Writing (Comedy Series): Ken Estin ("Elegant Iggy," *Taxi*) (ABC); Writing (Variety or Music Program): John Candy, Joe Flaherty, Eugene Levy, Andrea Martin, Rick Moranis, Catherine O'Hara, Dave Thomas, Dick Blasucci, Paul Flaherty, Bob Dolman, John McAndrew, Doug Steckler, Mert Rich, Jeffrey Barron, Michael Short, Chris Cluess, Stuart Kreisman, Brian McConnachie ("Moral Majority Show," *SCTV Comedy Network*) (NBC)

NBC was still in the ratings basement, but was on top of the heap in Emmy's eyes. The Peacock network claimed several of the night's winners including *Fame, Hill Street Blues, Marco Polo, SCTV Comedy Network,* and ABC's rejected *Taxi.*

Marlo Thomas and John Forsythe hosted the ABC-broadcast ceremony, once again produced by Dwight Hemion and Gary Smith. Entertainment came in the form of tributes to early children's shows, pioneering newscaster Edward R. Murrow, Dave Garroway (the first host of the *Today* show), and Bob Hope. To lend variety to the tedious obligatory reading of the Emmy rules, they were barked out by a Marine drill sargeant from California's Camp Pendleton. The program ended on an emotional note with Kate Smith pushed onstage in a wheelchair by Hope. The crowd sang Smith's theme song "God Bless America."

The daytime Emmys, televised on CBS, received their highest ratings ever, but the news and sports awards were not broadcast. NBC, the biggest prime-time winner, boycotted the news accolades, claiming the rules and awards procedures were sloppy. The Peacock network did allow individuals to submit their work independently and three NBC shows took home awards.

THE PEABODY AWARDS (FOR 1982)

Skeezer (NBC); *The Wall* (CBS); *The Electric Grandmother, Project Peacock* (NBC); *The Man Who Shot the Pope: A Study in Terrorism, NBC White Paper* (NBC News); *ABC News Closeup/Vietnam Requiem* (ABC News); *Juilliard and Beyond: A Life in Music* (CBS News); *Blood and Honor: Youth under Hitler* (Daniel Wilson Productions and Taurus Films); *784 Days That Changed America—from Watergate to Resignation* (The Television Corporation of America); Nickelodeon: The First Channel for Kids (Warner Amex Satellite Entertainment Company); Texaco, Inc., the Texaco Foundation, and the Metropolitan Opera Association for TV and radio opera presentations; *Smiley's People* (BBC, Paramount, and Operation Prime Time); *Stravinsky's Firebird, Dance Theatre of Harlem* (WQED, Pittsburgh); *Current Affairs/The Case of Dashiell Hammett* (KQED-TV, San Francisco); *Oklahoma Shame* (KOCO-TV, Oklahoma City); *Ground Zero: Victory Road* (WCVB-TV, Boston); *Sweet Nothing* (KYW-TV, Philadelphia); *The Search for Alexander* (WWL-TV, New Orleans); *Beyond the Great Wall: Journey to the End of China* (KGMB-TV, Honolulu and Lee Productions, Inc.); *Paradise Saved* (WAGA-TV, Atlanta); *Killing Crime: A Police Cop-Out* (WBBM-TV, Chicago); *Prisoners of the Harvest* (WTSP-TV, St. Petersburg, FL); Alistair Cooke

THE GOLDEN GLOBE AWARDS (FOR 1982)

Made-for-TV Movie or Mini-Series: *Brideshead Revisited, Great Performances* (PBS); Drama Series: *Hill Street Blues* (NBC); Comedy or Musical Series: *Fame* (NBC)

Actor (Teleflim/Mini-Series): Anthony Andrews (*Brideshead Revisited, Great Performances*) (PBS); Actress (Teleflim/Mini-Series): Ingrid Bergman (*A Woman Called Golda*) (Syndicated); Actor (Drama Series): John Forsythe (*Dynasty*) (ABC); Actress (Drama Series): Joan Collins (*Dynasty*) (ABC); Actor (Comedy or Musical Series): Alan Alda (*M*A*S*H*) (CBS); Actress (Comedy or Musical Series): Debbie Allen (*Fame*) (NBC); Supporting Actor: Lionel Stander (*Hart to Hart*) (ABC); Supporting Actress: Shelley Long (*Cheers*) (NBC)

THE CABLE ACE AWARDS (FOR 1982)

Theatrical Special: *Purlie* (Showtime); Dramatic Special: *Hugie* (Showtime); General Entertainment or Variety (Music): *Marvin Hamlisch: They're Playing My Song* (Showtime); General Entertainment or Variety (Comedy): *Tush: Late Night TV Parody* (WTBS)

1982-83

THE EMMY AWARDS

DRAMA SPECIAL
Little Gloria . . . Happy at Last (NBC)
M.A.D.D.: Mothers against Drunk Drivers (NBC)
The Scarlet Pimpernel (CBS)
Special Bulletin (NBC)
Who Will Love My Children? (ABC)

DRAMA SERIES
Cagney & Lacey (CBS)
Fame (NBC)
Hill Street Blues (NBC)
Magnum, P.I. (CBS)
St. Elsewhere (NBC)

The cast of *M*A*S*H*, which concluded its eleven-year run in 1983 after ninety-nine Emmy nominations.

COMEDY SERIES

Buffalo Bill (NBC)
Cheers (NBC)
*M*A*S*H* (CBS)
Newhart (CBS)
Taxi (ABC)

Like NBC's previous big Emmy winner *Hill Street Blues*, *Cheers* started out at the bottom of the ratings pile. The sitcom set in a Boston barroom gathered criticial kudos and thirteen Emmy nominations its first low-rated year (seventy-fourth out of a possible ninety-eight shows). Emmy cheered and the series garnered six awards including outstand-

ing Comedy Series. It eventually beat *Hill Street* for the second-most Emmy wins at twenty-seven and received the most nominations with 117.

LIMITED SERIES

Nicholas Nickleby (Syndicated)
Smiley's People (Syndicated)
The Thorn Birds (ABC)
To Serve Them All My Days,
    Masterpiece Theatre (PBS)
The Winds of War (ABC)

All three networks had turned down the video adaptation of *Nicholas Nickleby*, the Royal

Shakespeare Company's eight-hour stage version of Charles Dickens' novel. On Broadway, the two-part evening had won a Tony as best play, but executives feared viewers would be bored by the four-part TV version. So it was sold to syndication and defeated the expected winner, ABC's expensive *The Winds of War*, for outstanding Limited Series.

VARIETY OR MUSIC PROGRAM
Kennedy Center Honors: A Celebration of the Performing Arts (CBS)
Motown 25: Yesterday, Today, Forever (NBC)
SCTV Comedy Network (NBC)
The Tonight Show Starring Johnny Carson (NBC)
The 37th Annual Tony Awards (CBS)

ACTOR (SPECIAL OR LIMITED SERIES)
Robert Blake (*Blood Feud*) (Syndicated)
Richard Chamberlain (*The Thorn Birds*) (ABC)
Sir Alec Guinness (*Smiley's People*) (Syndicated)
Tommy Lee Jones (*The Executioner's Song*) (NBC)
Roger Rees (*Nicholas Nickleby*) (Syndicated)

ACTRESS (SPECIAL OR LIMITED SERIES)
Ann-Margret (*Who Will Love My Children?*) (ABC)
Roseanna Arquette (*The Executioner's Song*) (NBC)
Mariette Hartley (*M.A.D.D.: Mothers against Drunk Drivers*) (NBC)
Angela Lansbury (*Little Gloria …Happy at Last*) (NBC)
Barbara Stanwyck (*The Thorn Birds*) (ABC)

Winner Barbara Stanwyck paid an unexpected tribute to fellow nominee Ann-Margret. Stanwyck praised Margret's performance as a dying mother in *Who Will Love My Children?* "You were superb," she exclaimed. Cameras caught a shocked and tearful Ann-Margret in the audience.

ACTOR (DRAMA SERIES)
William Daniels (*St. Elsewhere*) (NBC)
Ed Flanders (*St. Elsewhere*) (NBC)
John Forsythe (*Dynasty*) (ABC)
Tom Selleck (*Magnum, P.I.*) (CBS)
Daniel J. Travanti (*Hill Street Blues*) (NBC)

St. Elsewhere was even further down in the ratings than *Cheers*. Described as "*Hill Street Blues* in a hospital," the medical drama was eighty-eighth in the ratings, but critics praised its real-life grittiness and black humor. Despite its low viewership, *St. Elsewhere* won Emmys for Ed Flanders as the harried chief of staff and supporting actors James Coco and Doris Roberts, who guest-starred on one episode as a homeless couple. Like it did for *Hill Street* and *Cheers*, NBC gave the series a prescription of renewal.

ACTRESS (DRAMA SERIES)
Debbie Allen (*Fame*) (NBC)
Tyne Daly (*Cagney & Lacey*) (CBS)
Linda Evans (*Dynasty*) (ABC)
Sharon Gless (*Cagney & Lacey*) (CBS)
Veronica Hamel (*Hill Street Blues*) (NBC)

Tyne Daly won the first of her four *Cagney & Lacey* Emmys when CBS had canceled the series about a pair of policewomen. The Big Eye network was considering trying out a few more episodes the following season. Daly's win, plus a letter-writing campaign by fans of the show, saved the series. It later won several more Emmys including the outstanding Drama Series prize twice.

ACTOR (COMEDY SERIES)
Alan Alda (*M*A*S*H*) (CBS)
Dabney Coleman (*Buffalo Bill*) (NBC)
Ted Danson (*Cheers*) (NBC)
Robert Guillaume (*Benson*) (ABC)
Judd Hirsch (*Taxi*) (NBC)

After being canceled by ABC, *Taxi* was acquired by NBC, which in turn also dropped the multi-award-winning sitcom. Judd Hirsch did not conceal his anger about the cancellation when he picked up his second Emmy: "There are people I don't wish to thank at all tonight." He even appealed directly to NBC president Grant Tinker to reconsider's the show demise. "We'll come back anytime you say," he practically begged the executive. Despite the pleas, *Taxi's* meter had run out.

ACTRESS (COMEDY SERIES)
Nell Carter (*Gimme a Break*) (NBC)
Mariette Hartley (*Goodnight, Beantown*) (CBS)
Swoosie Kurtz (*Love, Sidney*) (NBC)
Shelley Long (*Cheers*) (NBC)

Rita Moreno (*9 to 5*) (ABC)
Isabel Sanford (*The Jeffersons*) (CBS)

SUPPORTING ACTOR (SPECIAL OR LIMITED SERIES)
Ralph Bellamy (*The Winds of War*) (ABC)
Bryan Brown (*The Thorn Birds*) (ABC)
Richard Kiley (*The Thorn Birds*) (ABC)
Christopher Plummer (*The Thorn Birds*) (ABC)
David Threlfall (*Nicholas Nickleby*) (Syndicated)

SUPPORTING ACTRESS (SPECIAL OR LIMITED SERIES)
Dame Judith Anderson (*Medea, Kennedy Center Tonight*) (PBS)
Polly Bergen (*The Winds of War*) (ABC)
Bette Davis (*Little Gloria . . . Happy at Last*) (NBC)
Piper Laurie (*The Thorn Birds*) (ABC)
Jean Simmons (*The Thorn Birds*) (ABC)

SUPPORTING ACTOR (DRAMA SERIES)
Ed Begley, Jr. (*St. Elsewhere*)
James Coco ("Cora and Arnie," *St. Elsewhere*) (NBC)
Michael Conrad (*Hill Street Blues*) (NBC)
Joe Spano (*Hill Street Blues*) (NBC)
Bruce Weitz (*Hill Street Blues*) (NBC)

SUPPORTING ACTRESS (DRAMA SERIES)
Barbara Bosson (*Hill Street Blues*) (NBC)
Christina Pickles (*St. Elsewhere*) (NBC)
Doris Roberts ("Cora and Arnie," *St. Elsewhere*) (NBC)
Madge Sinclair (*Trapper John, M.D.*) (CBS)
Betty Thomas (*Hill Street Blues*) (NBC)

SUPPORTING ACTOR (COMEDY, VARIETY, OR MUSIC SERIES)
Nicholas Colasanto (*Cheers*) (NBC)
Danny DeVito (*Taxi*) (NBC)
Christopher Lloyd (*Taxi*) (NBC)
Harry Morgan (*M*A*S*H*) (CBS)
Eddie Murphy (*NBC's Saturday Night Live*) (NBC)

PERFORMER (VARIETY OR MUSIC PROGRAM)
Carol Burnett (*Texaco Star Theater*) (NBC)
Michael Jackson (*Motown 25: Yesterday, Today, Forever*) (NBC)
Luciano Pavarotti (*Luciano Pavarotti and the New York Philharmonic, Live from Lincoln Center*) (PBS)
Leontyne Price (*Leontyne Price, Zubin Mehta, and the New York Philharmonic, Live from Lincoln Center*) (PBS)
Richard Pryor (*Motown 25: Yesterday, Today, Forever*) (NBC)

DAYTIME AWARDS
Drama Series: *The Young and the Restless* (CBS); Actor: Robert Woods (*One Life To Live*) (ABC); Actress: Dorothy Lyman (*All My Children*) (ABC); Supporting Actor: Darnell Williams (*All My Children*) (ABC); Supporting Actress: Louise Shaffer (*Ryan's Hope*) (ABC); Game Show: *The New $25,000 Pyramid* (CBS); Talk/Service Series: *This Old House* (PBS); Variety Series: *The Merv Griffin Show* (Syndicated)

It was NBC's turn to broadcast the daytime Emmys as part of a rotating commitment, but the Peacock network declined to do so and the ceremony was not broadcast.

OTHER PRIME-TIME AWARDS
Directing (Special or Limited Series): John Erman (*Who Will Love My Children?*) (ABC); Directing (Drama Series): Jeff Bleckner ("Life in the Minors," *Hill Street Blues*) (NBC); Directing (Comedy Series): James Burrows ("Showdown, Part 2," *Cheers*) (NBC); Directing (Variety or Music Program): Dwight Hemion (*Sheena Easton, Act I*) (NBC)

Writing (Special or Limited Series): Marshall Herskovitz (teleplay), Edward Zwick, Marshall Herskovitz (story) (*Special Bulletin*) (NBC); Writing (Drama Series): David Milch ("Trial by Fury," *Hill Street Blues*) (NBC); Writing (Comedy Series): Glen Charles, Les Charles ("Give Me a Ring Sometime," *Cheers*) (NBC); Writing (Variety or Music Program): John Candy, Joe Flaherty, Eugene Levy, Andrea Martin, Martin Short, Dick Blasucci, Paul Flaherty, John McAndrew, Doug

Steckler, Bob Dolman, Michael Short, Mary Charlotte Wilcox ("The Energy Ball/Sweeps Week," *SCTV Network*) (NBC)

Joan Rivers and Eddie Murphy played hosts to what many felt was the most tasteless Emmy show in years. Rivers' lewd jokes got plenty of press and numerous complaints as viewers phoned NBC switchboards to complain. In a typical quip, she stated Joan Collins had "more hands up her dress than the Muppets." The comedienne also made cracks about hookers, gays, and controversial Secretary of the Interior James Watt ("The man is an idiot!").

Meanwhile, NBC local affiliates used commercial time to cut in and boast about their network's wins. For the third year in a row, NBC swept the awards, taking thirty-three prizes to ABC's fourteen and CBS's eleven. But the Peacock network still remained mired in low ratings.

THE PEABODY AWARDS
(FOR 1983)

The Woman Who Willed a Miracle, ABC Afterschool Specials (ABC); *What Have We Learned, Charlie Brown?* (CBS); *Romeo and Juliet on Ice, The CBS Festival of Lively Arts for Young People* (CBS); *The Plane That Fell from the Sky* (CBS News); "Lenell Geter's in Jail," *60 Minutes* (CBS News); *Motown 25: Yesterday, Today, Forever* (NBC); *Prisoner without a Name, Cell without a Number* (NBC); *He Makes Me Feels Like Dancin'* (NBC); *Vietnam: A Television History* (WGBH-TV, Boston, Central Independent TV, and Antenne-2); *The Miracle of Life, Nova* (WGBH-TV, Boston); *The Making of a Continent* (WTTW/Chicago and the BBC); *The Merry Widow* (WTTW/Chicago); *The Great Space Coaster* (Sunbow Productions, New York); *Portrait of America* (WTBS, Atlanta); Cable News Network (CNN); *Asylum in the Streets* (WNBC-TV, New York); *I-TEAM: Ambulances* (WCCO-TV, Minneapolis); *Studebaker: Less Than They Promised* (WBBM-TV, Chicago); *Give Me That Bigtime Religion* (WBRZ-TV, Baton Rouge); *Climate of Death* (KRON-TV, San Francisco); *Diagnosis: AIDS* (KCTS, Seattle); Westinghouse stations executive Don McGannon; The Grand Ole Opry

THE GOLDEN GLOBE AWARDS
(FOR 1983)

Made-for-TV Movie or Mini-Series: *The Thorn Birds* (ABC); Drama Series: *Dynasty* (ABC); Comedy or Musical Series: *Fame* (NBC)

Actor (Telefilm/Mini-Series): Richard Chamberlain (*The Thorn Birds*) (ABC); Actress (Telefilm/Mini-Series): Ann-Margret (*Who Will Love My Children?*) (ABC); Actor (Drama Series): John Forsythe (*Dynasty*) (ABC); Actress (Drama Series): Jane Wyman (*Falcon Crest*) (CBS); Actor (Comedy or Musical Series): John Ritter (*Three's Company*) (ABC); Actress (Comedy or Musical Series): Joanna Cassidy (*Buffalo Bill*) (NBC); Supporting Actor: Richard Kiley (*The Thorn Birds*) (ABC); Supporting Actress: Barbara Stanwyck (*The Thorn Birds*) (ABC)

THE CABLE ACE AWARDS
(FOR 1983)

Theatrical/Musical Special: *Sweeney Todd* (The Entertainment Channel); Theatrical/Non-Musical Special: *The Deadly Game* (HBO); Dramatic Special (60 Minutes or Less): *The Paper Chase: The Second Year: The Birthday Party*; Dramatic Special (60 Minutes or More) (tie): *Long Day's Journey into Night* (Hearst/ABC Arts) and *The Terry Fox Story* (HBO); General Entertainment or Variety (Music): *Seventh International Tchaikowsky Competition* (Hearst/ABC Arts); General Entertainment or Variety (Comedy): *Not Necessarily the News #2* (HBO)

Actor (Theatrical/Musical Program): George Hearn (*Sweeney Todd*) (The Entertainment Channel); Actress (Theatrical/Musical Program): Angela Lansbury (*Sweeney Todd*) (The Entertainment Channel); Actor (Theatrical/Non-Musical Program): Alan Bates (*Separate Tables*) (HBO); Actress (Theatrical/Non-Musical Program): Julie Christie (*Separate Tables*) (HBO); Actor (Dramatic Special): Earle Hyman (*Long Day's Journey into Night*) (Hearst/ABC Arts); Actress (Dramatic Special): Ruby Dee (*Long Day's Journey into Night*) (Hearst/ABC Arts)

THE EMMY AWARDS

DRAMA OR COMEDY SPECIAL
Adam (NBC)
The Day After, ABC Theatre (ABC)
The Dollmaker, ABC Theatre (ABC)
Something about Amelia, *ABC Theatre* (ABC)
A Streetcar Named Desire, ABC Theatre (ABC)

DRAMA SERIES
Cagney and Lacey (CBS)
Fame (Syndicated)
Hill Street Blues (NBC)
Magnum, P.I. (CBS)
St. Elsewhere (NBC)

COMEDY SERIES
Buffalo Bill (NBC)
Cheers (NBC)
Family Ties (NBC)
Kate & Allie (CBS)
Newhart (CBS)

LIMITED SERIES
Chiefs (CBS)
Concealed Enemies, *American Playhouse* (PBS)
George Washington (CBS)
Nancy Astor, Masterpiece Theatre (PBS)
Reilly: Ace of Spies, Mystery! (PBS)

VARIETY, MUSIC OR COMEDY PROGRAM
*The American Film Institute Salute to
    Lillian Gish* (CBS)
Late Night with David Letterman (NBC)
The 1984 Tony Awards (CBS)
**The 6th Annual Kennedy Center Honors: A
    Celebration of the Performing Arts** (CBS)
The Tonight Show Starring Johnny Carson (NBC)

ACTOR (SPECIAL OR LIMITED SERIES)
Ted Danson (*Something about Amelia,
    ABC Theatre*) (ABC)
Louis Gossett, Jr. (*Sadat*) (Syndicated)
Laurence Olivier (*King Lear*) (Syndicated)

Mickey Rooney (*Bill: On His Own*) (CBS)
Daniel J. Travanti (*Adam*) (NBC)

ACTRESS (SPECIAL OR LIMITED SERIES)
Jane Alexander (*Calamity Jane*) (CBS)
Ann-Margret (*A Streetcar Named Desire, ABC
    Theatre*) (ABC)
Glenn Close (*Sonething about Amelia,
    ABC Theatre*) (ABC)
Jane Fonda (*The Dollmaker, ABC Theatre*) (ABC)
JoBeth Williams (*Adam*) (NBC)

ACTOR (DRAMA SERIES)
William Daniels (*St. Elsewhere*) (NBC)
John Forsythe (*Dynasty*) (ABC)
Tom Selleck (*Magnum, P.I.*) (CBS)
Daniel J. Travanti (*Hill Street Blues*) (NBC)

ACTRESS (DRAMA SERIES)
Debbie Allen (*Fame*) (Syndicated)
Joan Collins (*Dynasty*) (ABC)
Tyne Daly (*Cagney & Lacey*) (CBS)
Sharon Gless (*Cagney & Lacey*) (CBS)
Veronica Hamel (*Hill Street Blues*) (NBC)

ACTOR (COMEDY SERIES)
Dabney Coleman (*Buffalo Bill*) (NBC)
Ted Danson (*Cheers*) (NBC)
Robert Guillaume (*Benson*) (ABC)
Sherman Hemsley (*The Jeffersons*) (CBS)
John Ritter (*Three's Company*) (ABC)

ACTRESS (COMEDY SERIES)
Joanna Cassidy (*Buffalo Bill*) (NBC)
Jane Curtin (*Kate & Allie*) (CBS)
Shelley Long (*Cheers*) (NBC)
Susan Saint James (*Kate & Allie*) (CBS)
Isabel Sanford (*The Jeffersons*) (CBS)

SUPPORTING ACTOR (SPECIAL OR LIMITED SERIES)
Art Carney (*Terrible Joe Moran,
    ITT Theatre*) (CBS)
Keith Carradine (*Chiefs*) (CBS)
John Gielgud (*The Master of Ballantrae,
    Hallmark Hall of Fame*) (CBS)
John Lithgow (*The Day After*) (ABC)

Randy Quaid (*A Streetcar Named Desire, ABC Theatre*) (ABC)

David Ogden Stiers (*The First Olympics— Athens 1896*) (NBC)

SUPPORTING ACTRESS (SPECIAL OR LIMITED SERIES)

Patty Duke Astin (*George Washington*) (CBS)

Beverly D'Angelo (*A Streetcar Named Desire, ABC Theatre*) (ABC)

Cloris Leachman (*Between the Laughter*) (ABC)

Tuesday Weld (*The Winter of Our Discontent, Hallmark Hall of Fame*) (CBS)

Roxanna Zal (*Something about Amelia, ABC Theatre*) (ABC)

SUPPORTING ACTOR (DRAMA SERIES)

Ed Begley, Jr. (*St. Elsewhere*) (NBC)

Michael Conrad (*Hill Street Blues*) (NBC)

John Hillerman (*Magnum, P.I.*) (CBS)

James B. Sikking (*Hill Street Blues*) (NBC)

Bruce Weitz (*Hill Street Blues*) (NBC)

SUPPORTING ACTRESS (DRAMA SERIES)

Barbara Bosson (*Hill Street Blues*) (NBC)

Piper Laurie ("Lust Et Veritas," *St. Elsewhere*) (NBC)

Madge Sinclair (*Trapper John, M.D.*) (CBS)

Betty Thomas (*Hill Street Blues*) (NBC)

Alfre Woodard ("Doris in Wonderland," *Hill Street Blues*) (NBC)

SUPPORTING ACTOR (COMEDY SERIES)

Rene Auberjonois (*Benson*) (ABC)

Nicholas Colasanto (*Cheers*) (NBC)

Pat Harrington (*One Day at a Time*) (CBS)

Tom Poston (*Newhart*) (CBS)

George Wendt (*Cheers*) (NBC)

SUPPORTING ACTRESS (COMEDY SERIES)

Julia Duffy (*Newhart*) (CBS)

Marla Gibbs (*The Jeffersons*) (CBS)

Paula Kelly (*Night Court*) (NBC)

Rhea Pearlman (*Cheers*) (NBC)

Marion Ross (*Happy Days*) (ABC)

INDIVIDUAL PERFORMANCE (VARIETY OR MUSIC)

Debbie Allen (*Live . . . and in Person*) (NBC)

George Burns (*George Burns Celebrates 80 Years in Show Business*) (NBC)

Cloris Leachman (*Screen Actors Guild 50th Anniversary Celebration*) (CBS)

Eddie Murphy (*Saturday Night Live*) (NBC)

Joe Piscopo (*Saturday Night Live*) (NBC)

Lily Tomlin (*Live . . . and in Person*) (NBC)

Cloris Leachman won in the Individual Performance (Variety or Music) category, but lost her bid in the Supporting Actress (Special or Limited Series) field. As Leachman walked off with her sixth Emmy, the camera caught nominee Lily Tomlin, dressed as her Ernestine the Telephone Operator character, acting like a bitter loser by feigning tears.

DAYTIME AWARDS

Drama Series: *General Hospital* (ABC); Actor: Larry Bryggman (*As the World Turns*) (CBS); Actress: Erika Slezak (*One Life To Live*) (ABC); Supporting Actor: Justin Deas (*As the World Turns*) (ABC); Supporting Actress: Judi Evans (*Guiding Light*) (CBS); Game Show: *The $25,000 Pyramid* (CBS); Talk/Service Series: *Woman to Woman* (Syndicated); Variety Series: *The Merv Griffin Show* (Syndicated)

OTHER PRIME-TIME AWARDS

Directing (Special or Limited Series): Jeff Bleckner (*Concealed Enemies, American Playhouse*) (PBS); Directing (Drama Series): Corey Allen ("Goodbye, Mr. Scripps," *Hill Street Blues*) (NBC); Directing (Comedy Series): Bill Persky ("A Very Loud Family," *Kate & Allie*) (CBS); Directing (Variety or Music Program): Dwight Hemion (*Here's Television Entertainment*) (PBS)

Writing (Special or Limited Series): William Hanley (*Something about Amelia*) (ABC); Writing (Drama Series): John Ford Noonan (teleplay), John Masius, Tom Fontana (story) ("The Women," *St. Elsewhere*) (NBC); Writing (Comedy Series): David Angell ("Old Flames," *Cheers*) (NBC); Writing (Variety or Music Program): Steve O'Donnell, Gerard Mulligan, Sandy Frank, Joe Toplyn, Chris Elliott, Matt Wickline, Jeff Martin,

Todd Greenberg, David Yazbek, Merill Markoe, David Letterman (*Late Night with David Letterman* with Dr. Ruth Westheimer and Teri Garr) (NBC)

It was the fourth year in a row the Emmys were produced by Dwight Hemion and Gary Smith. Tom Selleck and Carol Burnett were announced to co-host the Emmys, but Burnett had to bow out due to a bout with the flu. Selleck smoothly handled the hosting task solo, particularly when he won for outstanding Actor (Drama Series) as the hunky, Hawaii-based investigator *Magnum, P.I.* The surprised Selleck uttered a quick "thank you" and then crossed to the other side of the stage to continue with the show.

At three hours and thirty-four minutes, this Emmycast tied 1978's as the longest ever. In addition to all the awards, there were four production numbers. They featured Charles Nelson Reilly and writer-producer Stephen J. Cannel explaining what goes on behind the scenes; trumpeter Wynton Marsalis playing "Carnival in Venice"; a tribute to familiar TV faces; and a dance sequence staged by Tony-winner Ron Field performed by such video choreographers as Peter Gennaro, Debbie Allen, June Taylor, and Lester Flatt. There was also a montage of film clips from PBS series and tribute to the late Rod Serling by Richard Kiley and Keenan Wynn, actors who performed in his early TV plays *Patterns* and *Requiem for a Heavyweight*.

THE PEABODY AWARDS (FOR 1984)

The Protestant Hour (Protestant Radio and Television Center); *Heartsounds, ABC Theatre*; *Heritage: Civilization and the Jews* (WNET/Thirteen, New York); *To Save Our Schools, To Save Our Children, ABC News Closeup*; *Frontline*; *The Brain* (WNET/Thirteen, New York); *George Washington* (CBS); *St. Elsewhere* (NBC); *Seeds of Despair* (Central Independent Television of England); *Faerie Tale Theatre* (Showtime); *Cousteau/Amazon* (TBS); Ted Koppel/*Nightline* (ABC); "The Roger Rosenblatt Essays" presented on *The MacNeil-Lehrer NewsHour*; *A Walk through the 20th Century with Bill Moyers* (Corporation for Entertainment and Learning); *The Jewel in the Crown, Masterpiece Theatre* (Granada Television of England); Roone Arledge of ABC Sports and News

THE GOLDEN GLOBE AWARDS (FOR 1984)

Made-for-TV Movie or Mini-Series: *Something about Amelia* (ABC); Drama Series: *Murder, She Wrote* (CBS); Comedy or Musical Series: *The Cosby Show* (NBC)

Actor (Teleflim/Mini-Series): Ted Danson (*Something about Amelia*) (ABC); Actress (Teleflim/Mini-Series): Ann-Margret (*A Streetcar Named Desire*) (ABC); Actor (Drama Series): Tom Selleck (*Magnum, P.I.*) (CBS); Actress (Drama Series): Angela Lansbury (*Murder, She Wrote*) (CBS); Actor (Comedy or Musical Series): Bill Cosby (*The Cosby Show*) (NBC); Actress (Comedy or Musical Series): Shelley Long (*Cheers*) (NBC); Supporting Actor: Paul Le Mat (*The Burning Bed*) (NBC); Supporting Actress: Faye Dunaway (*Ellis Island*) (CBS)

THE CABLE ACE AWARDS (FOR 1984)

Dramatic Special: *Tiger Town* (The Disney Channel); Theatrical Special: *A Case of Libel* (Showtime); Drama Series: *Stage* (A&E); Comedy Series: *Not Necessarily the News* (HBO)

Actor (Dramatic/Theatrical Program): Laurence Olivier (*Mr. Halpern & Mr. Johnson*) (HBO); Actress (Dramatic/Theatrical Program): Carol Burnett (*Between Friends*) (HBO); Actor (Comedy or Music Program): Billy Joel (*Billy Joel in Concert: A Television First*) (HBO); Actress (Comedy or Music Program): Lee Remick (*I Do! I Do!*) (A&E)

THE EMMY AWARDS

DRAMA OR COMEDY SPECIAL
The Burning Bed (NBC)
Do You Remember Love? (CBS)
Fatal Vision (NBC)
Heartsounds (ABC)
Wallenberg: A Hero's Story (NBC)

Bill Cosby, seen here with his TV family (from left) Tempestt Bledsoe, Keshia Knight Pulliam, Lisa Bonet, and Phylicia Rashad, did not submit his name for Emmy consideration. But *The Cosby Show* was named outstanding Comedy Series for 1984–85.

DRAMA SERIES
Cagney & Lacey (CBS)
Hill Street Blues (NBC)
Miami Vice (NBC)
Murder, She Wrote (CBS)
St. Elsewhere (NBC)

The four-time champ *Hill Street Blues* and the trendy newcomer *Miami Vice* were both defeated in the Drama Series category by another cop show. *Cagney & Lacey*, CBS's unusual police show about two female officers, had been brought back from cancellation *twice* and was still low in the ratings. Once again, Emmy proved she didn't give a hoot for Nielsen and awarded *C&L* six statuettes.

COMEDY SERIES
Cheers (NBC)
The Cosby Show (NBC)
Family Ties (NBC)
Kate & Allie (CBS)
Night Court (NBC)

The Cosby Show, a family sitcom starring the five-time Emmy winner Bill Cosby, was one of the year's top-rated shows and won as outstanding Comedy Series as well in the categories Writing (Comedy Series) and Directing (Comedy Series). Cobsy himself, claiming he had enough prizes already, declined to participate in the nomination process.

LIMITED SERIES

Barbara Taylor Bradford's "A Woman of Substance" (Syndicated)
Ellis Island (CBS)
The Jewel in the Crown, *Masterpiece Theatre* (PBS)
Robert Kennedy and His Times (CBS)
Space (CBS)

VARIETY, MUSIC OR COMEDY PROGRAM

The American Film Institute Salute to Gene Kelly (CBS)
Late Night with David Letterman (NBC)
Lena Horne: The Lady and Her Music, Great Performances (PBS)
Motown Returns to the Apollo (NBC)
The Tonight Show Starring Johnny Carson (NBC)

ACTOR (SPECIAL OR LIMITED SERIES)

Richard Chamberlain (*Wallenberg: A Hero's Story*) (NBC)
Richard Crenna (*The Rape of Richard Beck, ABC Theatre*) (ABC)
James Garner (*Heartsounds, ABC Theatre*) (ABC)
Richard Kiley (*Do You Remember Love?*) (ABC)
George C. Scott (*A Christmas Carol*) (CBS)

ACTRESS (SPECIAL OR LIMITED SERIES)

Jane Alexander (*Malice in Wonderland*) (CBS)
Peggy Aschcroft (*The Jewel in the Crown, Masterpiece Theatre*) (PBS)
Farrah Fawcett (*The Burning Bed*) (NBC)
Mary Tyler Moore (*Heartsounds, ABC Theatre*) (ABC)
Joanne Woodward (*Do You Remember Love?*) (CBS)

ACTOR (DRAMA SERIES)

William Daniels (*St. Elsewhere*) (NBC)
Ed Flanders (*St. Elsewhere*) (NBC)
Don Johnson (*Miami Vice*) (NBC)
Tom Selleck (*Magnum, P.I.*) (CBS)
Daniel J. Travanti (*Hill Street Blues*) (NBC)

With a look of disgust worthy of the domineering Dr. Craig, his *St. Elsewhere* character, William Daniels informed the audience his limo had broken down on the way to the ceremony.

ACTRESS (DRAMA SERIES)

Debbie Allen (*Fame*) (Syndicated)
Tyne Daly (*Cagney & Lacey*) (CBS)
Sharon Gless (*Cagney & Lacey*) (CBS)
Veronica Hamel (*Hill Street Blues*) (NBC)
Angela Lansbury (*Murder, She Wrote*) (CBS)

Upon winning her third consecutive Emmy for *Cagney & Lacey*, a very pregnant Tyne Daly thanked her husband Georg Stanford Brown for his "outstanding work." Earlier in the evening, Brown lost in the directing category for a segment of *Hill Street Blues*.

ACTOR (COMEDY SERIES)

Harry Anderson (*Night Court*) (NBC)
Ted Danson (*Cheers*) (NBC)
Robert Guillaume (*Benson*) (ABC)
Bob Newhart (*Newhart*) (CBS)
Jack Warden (*Crazy Like a Fox*) (CBS)

Robert Guillaume thanked Bill Cosby for not submitting his name in nomination.

ACTRESS (COMEDY SERIES)

Phylicia Ayers-Allen (*The Cosby Show*) (NBC)
Jane Curtin (*Kate & Allie*) (CBS)
Shelley Long (*Cheers*)
Susan Saint James (*Kate & Allie*) (CBS)
Isabel Sanford (*The Jeffersons*) (CBS)

SUPPORTING ACTOR (SPECIAL OR LIMITED SERIES)

Richard Burton (*Ellis Island*) (CBS)
John Gielgud (*Romance on the Orient Express*) (NBC)
Karl Malden (*Fatal Vision*) (NBC)
Richard Masur (*The Burning Bed*) (NBC)
Rip Torn (*The Atlanta Child Murders*) (CBS)

SUPPORTING ACTRESS (SPECIAL OR LIMITED SERIES)

Penny Fuller (*Cat on a Hot Tin Roof, American Playhouse*) (PBS)
Ann Jillian (*Ellis Island*) (CBS)
Deborah Kerr (*Barbara Taylor Bradford's "A Woman of Substance"*) (Syndicated)
Kim Stanley (*Cat on a Hot Tin Roof, American Playhouse*) (PBS)

Alfre Woodard (*Words by Heart, Wonderworks*) (PBS)

SUPPORTING ACTOR (DRAMA SERIES)
Ed Begley, Jr. (*St. Elsewhere*) (NBC)
John Hillerman (*Magnum, P.I.*) (CBS)
John Karlen (*Cagney & Lacey*) (CBS)
Edward James Olmos (*Miami Vice*) (NBC)
Bruce Weitz (*Hill Street Blues*) (NBC)

SUPPORTING ACTRESS (DRAMA SERIES)
Barbara Bosson (*Hill Street Blues*) (NBC)
Christina Pickles (*St. Elsewhere*) (NBC)
Doris Roberts (*Remington Steele*) (NBC)
Madge Sinclair (*Trapper John, M.D.*) (CBS)
Betty Thomas (*Hill Street Blues*) (NBC)

When Peter Graves read Betty Thomas's name as the outstanding Supporting Actress (Drama Series), a gentleman in a tuxedo ascended to the stage and stated that Thomas was not present and he would accept on her behalf. As the unknown man was thanking sports announcer Dick Schaap, the camera picked out the *Hill Street* actress making her way to the podium. It was later revealed the mysterious accepter was named Barry Bremer, a gate-crasher with a history of breaking into sporting events and pretending to be an athlete.

After the network cut to a commercial, Bremer was arrested for grand theft of an Emmy. Thomas was onstage when the break ended and joked, "Well, it's definitely hard to follow an act like that." She would get to make a fuller acceptance speech when she won an Emmy in 1993 for her direction of HBO's *Dream On*.

SUPPORTING ACTOR (COMEDY SERIES)
Nicholas Colasanto (*Cheers*) (NBC)
Michael J. Fox (*Family Ties*) (NBC)
John Larroquette (*Night Court*) (NBC)
John Ratzenberger (*Cheers*) (NBC)
George Wendt (*Cheers*) (NBC)

SUPPORTING ACTRESS (COMEDY SERIES)
Selma Diamond (*Night Court*) (NBC)
Julia Duffy (*Newhart*) (CBS)

Marla Gibbs (*The Jeffersons*) (CBS)
Rhea Pearlman (*Cheers*) (NBC)
Inga Swenson (*Benson*) (ABC)

"I have two and you have one! Ha-Ha-Ha," Rhea Pearlman, the sharp-tongued barmaid of *Cheers*, teased her husband Danny DeVito on the occasion of her second Emmy win. DeVito garnered a single statuette for his role as the equally vociferous cab dispatcher on *Taxi*. Pearlman would win another two Emmys for *Cheers* (in 1985–86 and 1988–89).

INDIVIDUAL PERFORMANCE (VARIETY OR MUSIC)
Billy Crystal (*Saturday Night Live*) (NBC)
Gregory Hines (*Motown Returns to the Apollo*) (NBC)
George Hearn (*Sweeney Todd, Great Performances*) (PBS)
Patti La Belle (*Motown Returns to the Apollo*) (NBC)
Angela Lansbury (*Sweeney Todd, Great Performances*) (PBS)

DAYTIME AWARDS
Drama Series: *The Young and the Restless* (CBS); Actor: Darnell Williams (*All My Children*) (ABC); Actress: Kim Zimmer (*Guiding Light*) (CBS); Supporting Actor: Larry Gates (*Guiding Light*) (CBS); Supporting Actress: Beth Maitland (*The Young and the Restless*) (CBS); Game Show: *The $25,000 Pyramid* (CBS); Talk/Service Series: *Donahue* (Syndicated)

After a three-year hiatus, the daytime Emmys were finally back on the air. CBS broadcast the ceremony from New York's Waldorf-Astoria Hotel.

OTHER PRIME-TIME AWARDS
Directing (Special or Limited Series): Lamont Johnson (*Wallenberg: A Hero's Story*) (NBC); Directing (Drama Series): Karen Arthur ("Heat," *Cagney & Lacey*) (CBS) Directing (Comedy Series): Jay Sandrich ("The Younger Woman," *The Cosby Show*) (NBC); Directing (Variety or Music Program): Terry Hughes (*Sweeney Todd, Great Performances*) (PBS).

Writing (Special or Limited Series): Vickie Patik (*Do You Remember Love?*) (CBS); Writing (Drama Series): Patricia M. Green ("Who Said It's Fair,

Part 2," *Cagney & Lacey*) (CBS); Writing (Comedy Series): Ed Weinberg, Michael Leeson (premiere episode, *The Cosby Show*); Writing (Variety or Music Program): Gerard Mulligan, Sandy Frank, Joe Toplyn, Chris Elliott, Matt Wickline, Jeff Martin, Eddie Gorodetsky, Randy Cohen, Larry Jacobson, Kevin Curran, Fred Graver, Merrill Markoe, David Letterman ("Christmas with the Lettermans," show #491 *Late Night with David Letterman*) (NBC)

After years of finishing first in the Emmys and last in the Nielsens, NBC finally pulled ahead in both races. Thanks to the high viewership of *The Cosby Show*, the Peacock network was out of its ratings slump. It also swept the awards, taking a total of twenty-five golden ladies. CBS and PBS tied with seventeen each and ABC brought up the rear with eight.

Alexander Cohen, producer of the Tony Awards and 1978's Emmys, came back to produce this year's awards. There were multiple hosts with Carol Burnett, John Forsythe, and Mary Tyler Moore playing "recurring roles" throughout the evening. In keeping with the high number of nominations for police programs like *Cagney and Lacey, Hill Street Blues,* and *Miami Vice,* there was a musical tribute to detective shows of the past featuring such TV crimebusters as Hal Linden, Robert Stack, Mike Connors, Peter Graves, and Telly Savalas.

THE PEABODY AWARDS (FOR 1985)

"Apartheid's People," *The MacNeil-Lehrer NewsHour*; *Vietnam: Ten Years After* (NBC News); *Whose America Is It?* (CBS News); *Do You Remember Love?* (CBS); *An Early Frost* (NBC); *The American West: Steinbeck Country* (KGO-TV, San Francisco); *Braingames* (Spinning Reels and HBO); *The Final Chapter?*; *Crisis in Central America, Frontline*; *The Times of Harvey Milk* (The Harvey Milk Project, Inc., and WNET/Thirteen); *Live from Lincoln Center* (Lincoln Center for the Performing Arts); Bob Geldorf and *Live Aid*; Lawrence Fraiberg for "outstanding contributions to broadcasting"; Johnny Carson

THE GOLDEN GLOBE AWARDS (FOR 1985)

TV-Movie or Mini-Series: *The Jewel in the Crown* (PBS); Drama Series: *Murder, She Wrote* (CBS); Comedy or Musical Series: *The Golden Girls* (NBC)

Actor (Telefilm/Mini-Series): Dustin Hoffman (*Death of a Salesman*) (CBS); Actress (Telefilm /Mini-Series): Liza Minnelli (*A Time to Love*) (NBC); Actor (Drama Series): Don Johnson (*Miami Vice*) (NBC); Actress (Drama Series): Sharon Gless (*Cagney & Lacey*) (CBS); Actor (Comedy or Musical Series): Bill Cosby (*The Cosby Show*) (NBC); Actress (Comedy or Musical Series) (tie): Estelle Getty (*The Golden Girls*) (NBC) and Cybill Shepherd (*Moonlighting*) (ABC); Supporting Actor: Edward James Olmos (*Miami Vice*) (NBC); Supporting Actress: Sylvia Sydney (*An Early Frost*) (NBC)

THE CABLE ACE AWARDS (FOR 1985)

Movie/Mini-Series: *Sakharov* (HBO); Theatrical Special: *Master Harold . . . and the Boys* (Showtime); Dramatic Special: *Countdown to Looking Glass* (HBO); Drama Series: *The Paper Chase (Second and Third Years)* (Showtime); Comedy Series: Brothers (Showtime)

Actor (Movie/Mini-Series): Art Carney (*The Undergrads*) (The Disney Channel); Actress (Movie/Mini-Series): Glenda Jackson (*Sakharov*) (HBO); Actor (Dramatic/Theatrical Special): Alan Bates (*An Englishman Abroad*) (A&E); Actress (Dramatic/Theatrical Special): Amy Madigan (*The Laundromat*) (HBO); Actor (Drama Series): James Coco (*Ray Bradbury Theatre*) (USA); Actress (Drama Series): Ann Bell (*Tenko*) (A&E); Actor (Comedy Series): Stuart Pankin (*Not Necessarily the News*); Actress (Comedy Series): Lucy Webb (*Not Necessarily the News*) (HBO)

1985-86

THE EMMY AWARDS

DRAMA OR COMEDY SPECIAL
Amos (CBS)
Death of a Salesman (CBS)
An Early Frost (NBC)
Love Is Never Silent, *Hallmark Hall of Fame* (NBC)
Mrs. Delafield Wants To Marry (CBS)

DRAMA SERIES
Cagney & Lacey (CBS)
Hill Street Blues (NBC)
Moonlighting (ABC)
Murder, She Wrote (CBS)
St. Elsewhere (NBC)

The previous year *Cagney & Lacey* defeated flashy newcomer *Miami Vice* as outstanding Drama Series. This year, it won over another highly touted freshmen series, *Moonlighting*, an innovative detective series which lightheartedly played with the conventions of the genre. *Moonlighting* received a whopping sixteen nominations but only won a single prize—for editing. The series had more than a touch of humor and the members of the Hollywood Foreign Press Association placed it in the Comedy or Musical categories for their Golden Globe Awards. Though it lost at the Emmys, *Moonlighting* was not eclipsed at the GGs.

COMEDY SERIES
Cheers (NBC)
The Cosby Show (NBC)
Family Ties (NBC)
The Golden Girls (NBC)
Kate & Allie (CBS)

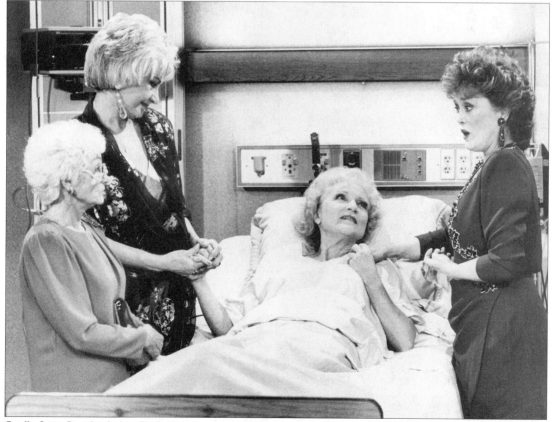

Estelle Getty, Beatrice Arthur, Betty White, and Rue McClanahan of *The Golden Girls* (1985–92) each won a golden girl (Emmy) of their own.

LIMITED SERIES
Dress Grey (NBC)
The Long Hot Summer (NBC)
Lord Mountbatten: The Last Viceroy, Masterpiece Theatre (PBS)
On Wings of Eagles (NBC)
Peter the Great (NBC)

VARIETY, MUSIC, OR COMEDY PROGRAM
The American Film Institute Salute to Billy Wilder (CBS)
The Kennedy Center Honors: A Celebration of the Performing Arts (CBS)
Late Night with David Letterman (NBC)
The 1986 Tony Awards (CBS)
The Tonight Show Starring Johnny Carson (NBC)

ACTOR (SPECIAL OR LIMITED SERIES)
Kirk Douglas (*Amos*) (CBS)
Ben Gazzara (*An Early Frost*) (NBC)
Dustin Hoffman (*Death of a Salesman*) (CBS)
John Lithgow (*Resting Place, Hallmark Hall of Fame*) (CBS)
Aidan Quinn (*An Early Frost*) (NBC)

ACTRESS (SPECIAL OR LIMITED SERIES)
Katharine Hepburn (*Mrs. Delafield Wants To Marry*) (CBS)
Vanessa Redgrave (*Second Serve*) (CBS)
Gena Rowlands (*An Early Frost*) (NBC)
Marlo Thomas (*Nobody's Child*) (CBS)
Mare Winningham (*Love Is Never Silent, Hallmark Hall of Fame*) (NBC)

ACTOR (DRAMA SERIES)
William Daniels (*St. Elsewhere*) (NBC)
Ed Flanders (*St. Elsewhere*) (NBC)
Tom Selleck (*Magnum, P.I.*) (CBS)
Bruce Willis (*Moonlighting*) (ABC)
Edward Woodward (*The Equalizer*) (CBS)

Williams Daniels and Bonnie Bartlett, outstanding Actor (Drama Series) and Supporting Actress (Drama Series) for *St. Elsewhere*, are the only husband and wife to win Emmys for playing a married couple.

ACTRESS (DRAMA SERIES)
Tyne Daly (*Cagney & Lacey*) (CBS)
Sharon Gless (*Cagney & Lacey*) (CBS)
Angela Lansbury (*Murder, She Wrote*) (CBS)
Cybill Shepherd (*Moonlighting*) (ABC)
Alfre Woodard (*St. Elsewhere*) (NBC)

After losing three years in a row to her *Cagney & Lacey* co-star Tyne Daly, Sharon Gless got to take home an Emmy. She thanked Daly "who I'm sure is the most relieved woman in this room tonight."

Though Daly lost, both her husbands won. John Karlen, who played her spouse on the series was named outstanding Supporting Actor (Drama Series), while real-lifemate Georg Stanford Brown copped an Emmy for directing an episode of his wife's show.

ACTOR (COMEDY SERIES)
Harry Anderson (*Night Court*) (NBC)
Ted Danson (*Cheers*) (NBC)
Michael J. Fox (*Family Ties*) (NBC)
Bob Newhart (*Newhart*) (CBS)
Jack Warden (*Crazy Like a Fox*) (CBS)

ACTRESS (COMEDY SERIES)
Beatrice Arthur (*The Golden Girls*) (NBC)
Shelley Long (*Cheers*) (NBC)
Rue McClanahan (*The Golden Girls*) (NBC)
Phylicia Rashad (*The Cosby Show*) (NBC)
Betty White (*The Golden Girls*) (NBC)

SUPPORTING ACTOR (SPECIAL OR LIMITED SERIES)
Charles Durning (*Death of a Salesman*) (CBS)
John Glover (*An Early Frost*) (NBC)
Harold Gould (*Mrs. Delafield Wants To Marry*) (CBS)
John Malkovich (*Death of a Salesman*) (CBS)
Pat Morita (*Amos*) (CBS)

SUPPORTING ACTRESS (SPECIAL OR LIMITED SERIES)
Colleen Dewhurst (*Between Two Women*) (ABC)
Phyllis Frelich (*Love Is Never Silent, Hallmark Hall of Fame*) (NBC)
Dorothy McGuire (*Amos*) (CBS)
Vanessa Redgrave (*Peter the Great*) (NBC)
Sylvia Sydney (*An Early Frost*) (NBC)

SUPPORTING ACTOR (DRAMA SERIES)
Ed Begley, Jr. (*St. Elsewhere*) (NBC)
John Hillerman (*Magnum, P.I.*) (CBS)
John Karlen (*Cagney & Lacey*) (CBS)
Edward James Olmos (*Miami Vice*) (NBC)
Bruce Weitz (*Hill Street Blues*) (NBC)

SUPPORTING ACTRESS (DRAMA SERIES)
Bonnie Bartlett (*St. Elsewhere*) (NBC)
Allyce Beasley (*Moonlighting*) (ABC)
Christina Pickles (*St. Elsewhere*) (NBC)
Betty Thomas (*Hill Street Blues*) (NBC)

SUPPORTING ACTOR (COMEDY SERIES)
John Larroquette (*Night Court*) (NBC)
Tom Poston (*Newhart*) (CBS)
John Ratzenberger (*Cheers*) (NBC)
Malcolm-Jamal Warner (*The Cosby Show*) (NBC)
George Wendt (*Cheers*) (NBC)

SUPPORTING ACTRESS (COMEDY SERIES)
Justine Bateman (*Family Ties*) (NBC)
Lisa Bonet (*The Cosby Show*) (NBC)
Julia Duffy (*Newhart*) (CBS)
Estelle Getty (*The Golden Girls*) (NBC)
Rhea Perlman (*Cheers*) (NBC)
Keshia Knight Pulliam (*The Cosby Show*) (NBC)

INDIVIDUAL PERFORMANCE (VARIETY OR MUSIC)
Debbie Allen (*An All-Star Celebration Honoring Dr. Martin Luther King, Jr.*) (NBC)
Whitney Houston (*The 28th Annual Grammy Awards*) (CBS)
Patti LaBelle (*Sylvia Fine Kaye's Musical Comedy Tonight III, Great Performances*) (PBS)
Jon Lovitz (*Saturday Night Live*) (NBC)
Sarah Vaughn (*The 28th Annual Grammy Awards*) (CBS)
Stevie Wonder (*An All-Star Celebration Honoring Dr. Martin Luther King, Jr.*) (NBC)

GUEST PERFORMERS
Comedy: Roscoe Lee Browne ("The Card Game," *The Cosby Show*) (NBC); Drama: John Lithgow ("The Doll," *Amazing Stories*) (NBC)

Guest performers were now separated from series regulars and given their own categories.

DAYTIME AWARDS
Drama Series: *The Young and the Restless* (CBS); Actor: David Canary (*All My Children*) (ABC); Actress: Erika Slezak (*One Life To Live*) (ABC); Supporting Actor: John Wesley Shipp (*As the World Turns*) (CBS); Supporting Actress: Leann Hunley (*Days of Our Lives*) (NBC); Game Show: *The $25,000 Pyramid* (CBS); Talk/Service Program: *Donahue* (Syndicated)

OTHER PRIME-TIME AWARDS
Directing (Special or Limited Series): Joseph Sargent (*Love Is Never Silent, Hallmark Hall of Fame*) (NBC); Directing (Drama Series): Georg Stanford Brown ("Parting Shots," *Cagney & Lacey*) (CBS); Directing (Comedy Series): Jay Sandrich ("Denise's Friend," *The Cosby Show*) (NBC); Directing (Variety or Music Program): Waris Hussein (*Copacabana*) (CBS)

Writing (Special or Limited Series): Ron Cowen, Daniel Lipman (teleplay), Sherman Yellen (story) (*An Early Frost*) (NBC); Writing (Drama Series): Tom Fontana, John Tinker, John Masius ("Time Heals," *St. Elsewhere*) (NBC); Writing (Comedy Series): Barry Fanaro, Mort Nathan ("A Little Romance," *The Golden Girls*) (NBC); Writing (Variety or Music Program): David Letterman, Joe O'Donnell, Sandy Frank, Joe Toplyn, Chris Elliott, Matt Wickline, Jeff Martin, Gerard Mulligan, Randy Cohen, Larry Jacobson, Kevin Curran, Fred Graver, Merrill Markoe (Fourth Anniversary Show, *Late Night with David Letterman*) (NBC)

Taking a cue from his succesful Tony Award ceremonies, Alexander Cohen presented an Emmy show with a theme—TV nostalgia. A horde of former video performers began the evening by delivering their familiar catch phrases. David Letterman brought his razor-sharp, sardonic humor to bear as host. Letterman refused to appear in a similar production number, but he did deliver one of his famous Top 10 lists. Co-hostess Shelley Long of *Cheers* was only too happy to perform musically and was featured in a tribute to women in TV.

At the 1951 Emmys, Red Skelton had attempted to give his Comedian or Comedienne award to Lucille Ball. Now the Queen of TV got to return the favor by presenting Skelton with a special Governors Award.

NBC was the top winner again, dominating both comedy and drama categories, with *The Golden Girls, The Cosby Show, Family Ties,* and *St. Elsewhere* triumphing. The Peacock network also took top honors among specials with winners *Love Is Never Silent,* a Hallmark Hall of Fame presentation about the daughter of deaf parents, and *An Early Frost,* one of the first TV-movies to address the then-taboo subject of AIDS.

THE PEABODY AWARDS (FOR 1986)

Sunday Morning: Vladimir Horowitz, with special reference to the contribution of Robert "Shad" Northshield (CBS News); *The Story of English* (MacNeil-Lehrer Productions and BBC); *Anne of Green Gables* (WQED, Pittsburgh); *The Mouse and the Motorcycle* (ABC); *Unknown Chaplin, American Masters* (Thames Television International and D.L. Taffner, Ltd); *The National Geographic Specials* (WQED, Pittsburgh, and the National Geographic Society); *CBS Reports: The Vanishing Family—Crisis in Black America* (CBS News); *The 1986 Kennedy Center Honors: A Celebration of the Performing Arts* (Kennedy Center for the Performing Arts); *Paradise Postponed, Masterpiece Theatre* (Thames Television International and WGBH-TV, Boston); *The Cosby Show* (NBC); *Promise, Hallmark Hall of Fame* (CBS); Jim Henson and the Muppets; *This Week with David Brinkley* (ABC News)

THE GOLDEN GLOBE AWARDS (FOR 1986)

TV-Movie or Mini-Series: *Promise, Hallmark Hall of Fame)* (CBS); Drama Series: *LA Law* (NBC); Comedy or Musical Series: *The Golden Girls* (NBC)

Actor (Telefilm/Mini-Series): James Woods (*Promise, Hallmark Hall of Fame*) (CBS); Actress (Telefilm/Mini-Series): Loretta Young (*Christmas Eve*) (NBC); Actor (Drama Series): Edward Woodward (*The Equalizer*) (CBS); Actress (Drama Series): Susan Dey (*LA Law*) (NBC); Actor (Comedy or Musical Series): Bruce Willis (*Moonlighting*) (ABC); Actress (Comedy or Musical Series):

Cybill Shepherd (*Moonlighting*) (ABC); Supporting Actor: Jan Niklas (*Anastasia: The Mystery of Anna*) (NBC); Supporting Actress: Olivia de Havilland (*Anastasia: The Mystery of Anna*) (NBC)

THE CABLE ACE AWARDS (FOR 1986)

Movie/Mini-Series: *Murrow* (HBO); Dramatic Special: *Knockback* (A&E); Theatrical Special: *Lady Windermere's Fan* (A&E); Drama Series: *Oxbridge Blues* (A&E); Comedy Series: *Brothers* (Showtime).

Actor (Movie/Mini-Series): Anthony Hopkins (*Mussolini*) (HBO); Actress (Movie/Mini-Series): Beah Richards (*As Summers Die*) (HBO); Actor (Dramatic/Theatrical Special): Mandy Patinkin (*Sunday in the Park with George*) (Showtime); Actress (Dramatic/Theatrical Special): Bernadette Peters (*Sunday in the Park with George*) (Showtime); Actor (Drama Series) (tie): Gary Busey (*The Hitchhiker: WGOD*) (HBO) and Peter O'Toole (*Ray Bradbudy Theatre: Banshee*) (USA); Actress (Drama Series): Susan Sarandon (*Oxbridge Blues: He'll See You Now*) (A&E); Actor (Comedy Series): Stuart Pankin (*Not Necessarily the News*) (HBO); Actress (Comedy Series): Lucy Webb (*Not Necessarily the News*) (HBO)

1986-87

THE EMMY AWARDS

DRAMA OR COMEDY SPECIAL
Escape from Sobibor (CBS)
LBJ: The Early Years (NBC)
Pack of Lies, Hallmark Hall of Fame (CBS)
Promise, Hallmark Hall of Fame (CBS)
Unnatural Causes (NBC)

DRAMA SERIES
Cagney & Lacey (CBS)
LA Law (NBC)
Moonlighting (ABC)
Murder, She Wrote (CBS)
St. Elsewhere (NBC)

The producers of two past Emmy-winning shows

Producer Stephen Bochco went from one award-winning series (*Hill Street Blues*) to another (*LA Law*) (1986–94). Most of the cast were either Emmy or Golden Globe winners or were at least nominated.

got together to create a third. Steven Bochco, the main man behind *Hill Street Blues*, and Terry Louise Fisher, one of the creators of *Cagney & Lacey*, joined forces to develop *LA Law*, sort of a legal *Hill Street* with multiple characters and story-lines running from week to week. The series won six awards its freshman year—including one for Bochco and Fisher for their script of the "Venus Butterfly" episode.

LA Law won the Drama Series Emmy four times (though not consecutively). Early in the show's long run, Fisher left the series because of creative differences with Bochco.

COMEDY SERIES

Cheers (NBC)
The Cosby Show (NBC)
Family Ties (NBC)
The Golden Girls (NBC)
Night Court (NBC)

MINI-SERIES

Anastasia: The Mystery of Anna (NBC)
Nutcracker: Money, Madness, Murder (NBC)
Out on a Limb (ABC)
The Two Mrs. Grenvilles (NBC)
A Year in the Life (NBC)

VARIETY, MUSIC OR COMEDY PROGRAM
Late Night with David Letterman (NBC)
Liberty Weekend—The Closing Ceremony (ABC)
The 1987 Tony Awards (CBS)
The Tonight Show Starring Johnny Carson (NBC)
The Tracey Ullman Show (Fox)

ACTOR (SPECIAL OR MINI-SERIES)
Alan Arkin (*Escape from Sobibor*) (CBS)
James Garner (*Promise, Hallmark Hall of Fame*) (CBS)
Louis Gossett, Jr. (*A Gathering of Old Men*) (CBS)
Randy Quaid (*LBJ: The Early Years*) (NBC)
James Woods (*Promise, Hallmark Hall of Fame*) (CBS)

ACTRESS (SPECIAL OR MINI-SERIES)
Ellen Burstyn (*Pack of Lies, Hallmark Hall of Fame*) (CBS)
Ann-Margret (*The Two Mrs. Grenvilles*) (NBC)
Lee Remick (*Nutcracker: Money, Madness, Murder*) (NBC)
Gena Rowlands (*The Betty Ford Story*) (ABC)
Alfre Woodard (*Unnatural Causes*) (NBC)

ACTOR (DRAMA SERIES)
Corbin Bernsen (*LA Law*) (NBC)
William Daniels (*St. Elsewhere*) (NBC)
Ed Flanders (*St. Elsewhere*) (NBC)
Bruce Willis (*Moonlighting*) (ABC)
Edward Woodward (*The Equalizer*) (CBS)

Ironically, Bruce Willis won a Drama Series Emmy for *Moonlighting*, a series with a strong comedic element, while Michael J. Fox took home his Comedy Series award for a heavy episode of *Family Ties* in which a close friend of his character is killed. Willis kept the comedy going when he won by sticking his tongue out at the camera and thanking Al Pacino and the Three Stooges.

ACTRESS (DRAMA SERIES)
Tyne Daly (*Cagney & Lacey*) (CBS)
Susan Dey (*LA Law*) (NBC)
Jill Eikenberry (*LA Law*) (NBC)
Sharon Gless (*Cagney & Lacey*) (CBS)
Angela Lansbury (*Murder, She Wrote*) (CBS)

ACTOR (COMEDY SERIES)
Harry Anderson (*Night Court*) (NBC)
Ted Danson (*Cheers*) (NBC)
Michael J. Fox (*Family Ties*) (NBC)
Bob Newhart (*Newhart*) (CBS)
Bronson Pinchot (*Perfect Strangers*) (ABC)

ACTRESS (COMEDY SERIES)
Beatrice Arthur (*The Golden Girls*) (NBC)
Blair Brown (*The Days and Nights of Molly Dodd*) (NBC)
Jane Curtin (*Kate & Allie*) (CBS)
Rue McClanahan (*The Golden Girls*) (NBC)
Betty White (*The Golden Girls*) (NBC)

SUPPORTING ACTOR (SPECIAL OR MINI-SERIES)
Dabney Coleman (*Sworn to Silence*) (ABC)
Stephen Collins (*The Two Mrs. Grenvilles*) (NBC)
John Glover (*Nutcracker: Money, Madness, Murder*) (NBC)
Laurence Olivier (*Lost Empires, Masterpiece Theatre*) (PBS)
Eli Wallach (*Something in Common*) (CBS)

SUPPORTING ACTRESS (SPECIAL OR MINI-SERIES)
Claudette Colbert (*The Two Mrs. Grenvilles*) (NBC)
Olivia de Havilland (*Anastasia: The Mystery of Anna*) (NBC)
Christine Lahti (*Amerika*) (ABC)
Piper Laurie (*Promise, Hallmark Hall of Fame*) (CBS)
Elizabeth Wilson (*Nutcracker: Money, Madness, Murder*) (NBC)

SUPPORTING ACTOR (DRAMA SERIES)
Ed Begley, Jr. (*St. Elsewhere*) (NBC)
John Hillerman (*Magnum, P.I.*) (CBS)
John Karlen (*Cagney & Lacey*) (CBS)
Jimmy Smits (*LA Law*) (NBC)
Michael Tucker (*LA Law*) (NBC)

Accepting the award for his absent *Magnum* co-star, Tom Selleck said, "I told the little fart he ought to be here."

SUPPORTING ACTRESS (DRAMA SERIES)
Bonnie Bartlett (*St. Elsewhere*) (NBC)
Allyce Beasley (*Moonlighting*) (ABC)
Christina Pickles (*St. Elsewhere*) (NBC)
Susan Ruttan (*LA Law*) (NBC)
Betty Thomas (*Hill Street Blues*) (NBC)

SUPPORTING ACTOR (COMEDY SERIES)
Woody Harrelson (*Cheers*) (NBC)
John Larroquette (*Night Court*) (NBC)
Tom Poston (*Newhart*) (CBS)
Peter Scolari (*Newhart*) (CBS)
George Wendt (*Cheers*) (CBS)

SUPPORTING ACTRESS (COMEDY SERIES)
Justine Bateman (*Family Ties*) (NBC)
Julia Duffy (*Newhart*) (CBS)
Estelle Getty (*The Golden Girls*) (NBC)
Jackee Harry (*227*) (NBC)
Rhea Perlman (*Cheers*) (NBC)

INDIVIDUAL PERFOMER (VARIETY OR MUSIC)
Billy Crystal (*The 29th Annual Grammy Awards*) (CBS)
Julie Kavner (*The Tracey Ullman Show*) (Fox)
Angela Lansbury (*The 1987 Tony Awards*) (CBS)
John Lovitz (*Saturday Night Live*) (NBC)
Robin Williams (*A Carol Burnett Special: Carol, Carl, Whoopi & Robin*) (ABC)

GUEST PERFORMER
Drama: Alfre Woodard (Pilot episode, *LA Law*) (NBC); Comedy: John Cleese ("Simon Says," *Cheers*) (NBC)

DAYTIME AWARDS
Drama Series: *As the World Turns* (CBS); Actor: Larry Bryggman (*As the World Turns*) (CBS); Actress: Kim Zimmer (*Guiding Light*) (CBS); Supporting Actor: Gregg Marx (*As the World Turns*) (CBS); Supporting Actress: Kathleen Noone (*All My Children*) (CBS); Game Show: *The $25,000 Pyramid* (CBS); Talk/Service Show: *The Oprah Winfrey Show* (Syndicated)

OTHER PRIME-TIME AWARDS
Directing (Special or Limited Series): Glenn Jordan (*Promise, Hallmark Hall of Fame*) (CBS); Directing (Drama Series): Gregory Hoblit (pilot episode, *LA Law*) (NBC); Directing (Comedy Series): Terry Hughes ("Isn't It Romantic?," *The Golden Girls*) (NBC); Directing (Variety or Music Program): Don Mischer (*The Kennedy Center Honors: A Celebration of the Performing Arts*) (CBS)

Writing (Special or Limited Series): Richard Friedenberg (teleplay), Kenneth Blackwell, Tennyson Flowers, Richard Friedenberg (story) (*Promise, Hallmark Hall of Fame*) (CBS); Writing (Drama Series): Steven Bochco, Terry Louise Fisher ("Venus Butterfly," *LA Law*) (NBC); Writing (Comedy Series): Gary David Goldberg, Alan Uger ("A, My Name Is Alex," *Family Ties*) (NBC); Writing (Variety or Music Program): Steve O'Donnell, Sandy Frank, Joe Toplyn, Chris Elliott, Matt Wickline, Jeff Martin, Gerard Mulligan, Randy Cohen, Larry Jacobson, Kevin Curran, Fred Graver, Adam Resnick, David Letterman (Fifth Anniversary Special, *Late Night with David Letterman*) (NBC)

Upstart network Fox outfoxed the competition by outbidding all three traditional webs for the rights to the Emmys. The newcomer won a three-year contract to broadcast the awards as well as the Academy's new annual TV Hall of Fame specials. The premiere Fox Emmy show was not only the lowest rated ever (a 10.2 rating and a 14 share), but also the longest at twenty seconds shy of four hours. The marathon length should have come as no surprise since the producer was Don Ohlmeyer, the gentleman behind the 1977 Emmys, a program which clocked in at three hours and thirty minutes.

Ohlmeyer was determined not to stint the ceremony, allowing the winners to go on as long as they liked. Like the '77 show, he would treat the '87 awards as a sporting competition. "We're going to cover the Emmys like an event," he said. "If something is going on backstage, we'll show it. . . . We'll have cameras backstage, in the press room, everywhere." And cover it he did. Phylicia Rashad and Alan Thicke conducted instant interviews with the winners as they came offstage, a narrator provided brief bios of the nominees as their categories came up, and commentatary was provided by columnist Marilyn Beck and fashion designer Mary McFadden. In addition, Jane Curtin interrupted the proceedings periodically with satirical news flashes and there were tributes to Jackie Gleason, Fred Astaire, and *Hill Street Blues.*

Joan Rivers was a presenter in her first public appearance since her husband committed suicide a month earlier. Her publicist stated she wanted to do it because it was the last booking her late spouse had made for her.

The longest Emmys in history drew mixed notices. Kay Gardella of the *New York Daily News* called them "punishment beyond the call of duty," while Fred Rothenberg of the *New York Post* found the telecast "more successful, smooth, and entertaining than most recent Emmy shows."

Once again NBC won the night, taking home thirty-two awards (including technical prizes). Fox, the Emmy broadcaster, came up empty-handed, though its *Tracey Ullman Show* did receive several nominations. The versatile Ullman, who played a broad range of characters every week, did cop a Golden Globe.

THE PEABODY AWARDS (FOR 1987)

CNN for live coverage of breaking news stories; *Hallmark Hall of Fame* and CBS for *Foxfire* and *Pack of Lies*; Japan Series, *The MacNeil-Lehrer NewsHour*; *LBJ: The Early Years* (NBC); *Corridos! Tales of Passion and Revolution* (KQED, San Francisco); *Mandela* (Titus Productions); *LA Law* (NBC); "The Big Goodbye," *Star Trek: The Next Generation*) (Paramount); *A Season in the Sun, Nature* (WNET/Thirteen, New York); *Eyes on the Prize: America's Civil Rights Years* (Blackside, Inc.); *Spy Machines, Nova* (WGBH-TV, Boston, and KCET, Los Angeles); *America Undercover: Drunk and Deadly* (Niemack Productions, Inc., and HBO); *American Tongues* (The Center for New American Media, Inc.); "Small Happiness: Women of a Chinese Village," part of *One Village in China* (Long Bow Productions and PBS); *Shoah* (Claude Lanzmann, WNET/Thirteen, New York, PBS); Levin Brownlow and David Gill, as evidenced by *Hollywood, Unknown Chaplin,* and *Buster Keaton: A Hard Act to Follow,* produced in association with Thames Television and D. L. Taffner, Ltd.

THE GOLDEN GLOBE AWARDS (FOR 1987)

Made-for-TV Movie or Mini-Series (tie): *Escape from Sobibor* (CBS) and *Poor Little Rich Girl: The Barbara Hutton Story* (NBC); Drama Series: *LA Law* (NBC); Comedy or Musical Series: *The Golden Girls* (NBC)

Actor (Drama Series): Richard Kiley (*A Year in the Life*) (NBC); Actress (Drama Series): Susan Dey (*LA Law*) (NBC); Actor (Comedy or Musical Series): Dabney Coleman (*The "Slap" Maxwell Story*) (ABC); Actress (Comedy or Musical Series): Tracey Ullman (*The Tracey Ullman Show*) (Fox); Supporting Actor: Rutger Hauer (*Escape from Sobibor*) (CBS); Supporting Actress: Claudette Colbert (*The Two Mrs. Grenvilles*) (NBC)

THE CABLE ACE AWARDS (FOR 1987)

Movie/Mini-Series: *Hotel Du Lac* (A&E); Dramatic Special: *HBO Showcase: Conspiracy: The Trial of the Chicago 8* (HBO); Theatrical Special: *The Browning Version* (A&E); Drama Series: *Alfred Hitchcock Presents* (USA); Comedy Series: *Blackadder II* (A&E)

Actor (Movie/Mini-Series): John Gielgud (*Time after Time*) (A&E); Actress (Movie/Mini-Series): Googie Withers (*Time after Time*) (A&E); Actor (Theatrical Special): Ian Holm (*The Browning Version*) (A&E); Actress (Theatrical Special): Judi Dench (*The Browning Version*) (A&E); Actor (Drama Series): Timothy Bottoms (*The Hitchhiker: The Joker*) (HBO); Actress (Drama Series): Barbara Babcock (*Alfred Hitchcock Presents: Conversation over a Corpse*) (USA); Actor (Comedy Series): Paul Eddington (*Yes, Prime Minister*) (A&E); Actress (Comedy Series): Lucy Webb (*Not Necessarily the News*) (HBO); Supporting Actor: Denholm Elliott (*Hotel Du Lac*) (A&E); Supporting Actress: Colleen Dewhurst (*Anne of Avonlea*) (The Disney Channel)

1987-88

THE EMMY AWARDS

DRAMA/COMEDY SPECIAL
The Ann Jillian Story (NBC)
The Attic: The Hiding of Anne Frank, General Foods' Golden Showcase (CBS)
Foxfire, Hallmark Hall of Fame (CBS)
Inherit the Wind, AT&T Presents (NBC)
The Taking of Flight 847: The Uli Derickson Story (NBC)

DRAMA SERIES
Beauty and the Beast (CBS)
LA Law (NBC)
Rumpole of the Bailey, Mystery! (PBS)
St. Elsewhere (NBC)
thirtysomething (ABC)

COMEDY SERIES
Cheers (NBC)
Frank's Place (CBS)
The Golden Girls (NBC)
Night Court (NBC)
The Wonder Years (ABC)

Two first-year ABC shows defeated long-run NBC favorites for top drama and comedy series. Favorite *LA Law* was defeated by *thirtysomething*, the weekly story of a group of Philadelphia friends which split the critics. Some found it an incisive portrayal of the difficulties of being an adult while others called the characters nothing but a bunch of whining yuppies. *Cheers* and *The Golden Girls* lost the comedy trophy to *The Wonder Years*, a nostalgic view of adolescence in the 1960s.

MINI-SERIES
Baby M (ABC)
Billionaire Boys Club (NBC)
The Bourne Identity (ABC)
Gore Vidal's Lincoln (ABC)
The Murder of Mary Phagan (NBC)

VARIETY, COMEDY OR MUSIC PROGRAM
Irving Berlin's 100th Birthday Celebration (CBS)
Late Night with David Letterman (NBC)
Late Night with David Letterman 6th Anniversary Special (NBC)
The Smothers Brothers Comedy Hour 20th Reunion (CBS)
The Tracey Ullman Show (Fox)

ACTOR (SPECIAL OR MINI-SERIES)
Hume Cronyn (*Foxfire, Hallmark Hall of Fame*) (CBS)
Danny Glover (*Mandela*) (HBO)
Stacy Keach (*Hemingway*) (Syndicated)
Jack Lemmon (*The Murder of Mary Phagan*) (NBC)
Jason Robards (*Inherit the Wind, AT&T*) (NBC)

ACTRESS (SPECIAL OR MINI-SERIES)
Ann Jillian (*The Ann Jillian Story*) (NBC)
Mary Tyler Moore (*Gore Vidal's Lincoln*) (NBC)
Mary Steenburgen (*The Attic: The Hiding of Anne Frank, General Foods' Golden Showcase*) (CBS)
Jessica Tandy (*Foxfire, Hallmark Hall of Fame*) (CBS)
JoBeth Williams (*Baby M*) (ABC)

ACTOR (DRAMA SERIES)
Corbin Bernsen (*LA Law*) (NBC)
Richard Kiley (*A Year in the Life*) (NBC)
Ron Perlman (*Beauty and the Beast*) (CBS)
Michael Tucker (*LA Law*) (NBC)
Edward Woodward (*The Equalizer*) (CBS)

ACTRESS (DRAMA SERIES)
Tyne Daly (*Cagney & Lacey*) (CBS)
Susan Dey (*LA Law*) (NBC)
Jill Eikenberry (*LA Law*) (NBC)
Sharon Gless (*Cagney & Lacey*) (CBS)
Angela Lansbury (*Murder, She Wrote*) (CBS)

ACTOR (COMEDY SERIES)
Dabney Coleman (*The "Slap" Maxwell Story*) (ABC)
Ted Danson (*Cheers*) (NBC)
Michael J. Fox (*Family Ties*) (NBC)
Tim Reid (*Frank's Place*) (CBS)
John Ritter (*Hooperman*) (ABC)

ACTRESS (COMEDY SERIES)
Kirstie Alley (*Cheers*) (NBC)
Beatrice Arthur (*The Golden Girls*) (NBC)
Blair Brown (*The Days and Nights of Molly Dodd*) (NBC)
Rue McClanahan (*The Golden Girls*) (NBC)
Betty White (*The Golden Girls*) (NBC)

SUPPORTING ACTOR (SPECIAL OR MINI-SERIES)
Dabney Coleman (*Baby M*) (ABC)
Anthony Quinn (*Onassis: The Richest Man in the World*) (ABC)
John Shea (*Baby M*) (ABC)
Ron Silver (*Billionaire Boys Club*) (NBC)
Bruce Weitz (*Baby M*) (NBC)

SUPPORTING ACTRESS (SPECIAL OR MINI-SERIES)
Stockard Channing (*Joseph Wambaugh's "Echoes in the Darkness"*) (CBS)
Ruby Dee (*Gore Vidal's Lincoln*) (NBC)
Julie Harris (*The Woman He Loved*) (CBS)
Lisa Jacobs (*The Attic: The Hiding of Anne Frank, General Foods' Golden Showcase*) (CBS)
Jane Seymour (*Onassis: The Richest Man in the World*) (ABC)

SUPPORTING ACTOR (DRAMA SERIES)
Ed Begley, Jr. (*St. Elsewhere*) (NBC)
Timothy Busfield (*thirtysomething*) (ABC)
Larry Drake (*LA Law*) (NBC)
Alan Rachins (*LA Law*) (NBC)
Jimmy Smits (*LA Law*) (NBC)

SUPPORTING ACTRESS (DRAMA SERIES)
Bonnie Bartlett (*St. Elsewhere*) (NBC)
Polly Draper (*thirtysomething*) (ABC)
Christina Pickles (*St. Elsewhere*) (NBC)
Susan Ruttan (*LA Law*) (NBC)
Patricia Wettig (*thirtysomething*) (ABC)

SUPPORTING ACTOR (COMEDY SERIES)
Kelsey Grammer (*Cheers*) (NBC)
Woody Harrelson (*Cheers*) (NBC)
John Larroquette (*Night Court*) (NBC)
Peter Scolari (*Newhart*) (CBS)
George Wendt (*Cheers*) (NBC)

SUPPORTING ACTRESS (COMEDY SERIES)
Julia Duffy (*Newhart*) (CBS)
Estelle Getty (*The Golden Girls*) (NBC)
Katherine Helmond (*Who's the Boss?*) (ABC)
Jackee (*227*) (NBC)
Rhea Perlman (*Cheers*) (NBC)

INDIVIDUAL PERFORMER (VARIETY OR MUSIC)
Mikhail Baryshkikov (*Celebrating Gershwin, Great Performances*) (PBS)
Billy Crystal (*All-Star Salute to the Improv*) (HBO)
Ray Charles (*Irving Berlin's 100th Birthday Celebration*) (CBS)
Julie Kavner (*The Tracey Ullman Show*) (Fox)
Robin Williams (*ABC Presents a Royal Gala*) (ABC)

GUEST PERFORMER
Drama: Shirley Knight ("The Parents Are Coming," *thirtysomething*) (ABC); Comedy: Beah Richards ("The Bridge," *Frank's Place*) (CBS)

DAYTIME AWARDS
Drama Series: *Santa Barbara* (NBC); Actor: David Canary (*All My Children*) (ABC); Actress: Helen Gallagher (*Ryan's Hope*) (ABC); Supporting Actor: Justin Deas (*Santa Barbara*) (NBC); Supporting Actress: Ellen Wheeler (*All My Children*) (ABC); Game Show: *The Price Is Right* (CBS); Talk/Service Show: *The Oprah Winfrey Show* (Syndicated)

OTHER PRIME-TIME AWARDS
Directing (Special or Mini-Series): Lamont Johnson (*Gore Vidal's Lincoln*) (NBC); Directing (Drama Series): Mark Tinker ("Weigh In, Way Out," *St. Elsewhere*) (NBC); Directing (Comedy Series): Gregory Hoblit (pilot episode, *Hooperman*); Directing (Variety or Music Program): Patricia Birch, Humphrey Burton (*Celebrating Gershwin, Great Performances*) (PBS)

Writing (Special or Mini-Series): William Hanley (*The Attic: The Hiding of Anne Frank, General Foods' Golden Showcase*) (CBS); Writing

(Drama Series): Paul Haggis, Marshall Hershovitz ["Business as Usual (Michael's Father's Death)," *thirtysomething*] (ABC); Writing (Comedy Series): Hugh Wilson ("The Bridge," *Frank's Place*) (CBS); Writing (Variety or Music Program): Jackie Mason (*Jackie Mason on Broadway*) (HBO)

The "sports coverage" of the 1987 Emmys was dropped in favor of a "hip comedy approach" for 1988. To give the show the desired contemporary humorous angle, the Academy hired Lorne Michaels of *Saturday Night Live* to produce and direct.

Michaels recruited two of his *SNL* cast members, Nora Dunn and Jan Hooks, to open the show. Playing the Sweeney Sisters, a pair of tacky lounge singers, Dunn and Hooks ran through a medley of TV theme songs. Other comic devices included Penn and Teller performing an elaborate magic trick while reading off the winners of the technical awards and *Taxi's* Tony Danza acting as "designated acceptor" for any winners not present. The joke backfired when a high number of absent Emmy recipients necessitated Danza making repeat trips to the podium. He ran out of funny material before the awards ended.

For the first time, cable programs were eligible. The first major cable winner was the HBO special *Jackie Mason on Broadway*. The fast-talking comedian won for the script of his one-man show, which also copped a special Tony Award when it was onstage. HBO gathered two more Emmys, as well as the prestigous Peabody, for the special *Dear America: Letters Home from Vietnam*, which was named Outstanding Informational Special.

Fox's second Emmycast showed improved viewership over the previous year's, with the brand-new network finishing in first place for the evening.

THE PEABODY AWARDS (FOR 1988)

The MacNeil-Lehrer NewsHour: Election '88 Coverage (MacNeil-Lehrer Productions); *Frontline—The Choice*; "Abortion Battle" and "On Runaway Street," *48 Hours* (CBS News); *The Attic: The Hiding of Anne Frank* (CBS); *The Singing Detective* (BBC and WNET/Thirteen, New York); *The Murder of Mary Phagan* (NBC); *thirtysomething* (ABC); *3-2-1 Contact Extra: I Have AIDS, A*

Teenager's Story (Children's Television Workshop); *Children's Express Newsmagazine: Campaign '88* (South Carolina ETV Network and the Mosiac Group, Inc.); *Islam in Turmoil* (Christian Science Monitor Reports); *Suzi's Story* (HBO and Pro Image Productions); *Dear America: Letters Home from Vietnam* (HBO); *The Making of a Legend: Gone with the Wind* (TNT); "Mr. Snow Goes to Washington," *60 Minutes* (CBS News); *Bill Moyers' World of Ideas* (Public Affairs Television); Jim McKay, ABC-TV sports commentator; Don Hewitt of CBS News; Ambassador Walter Annenberg

THE GOLDEN GLOBE AWARDS (FOR 1988)

Made-for-TV Movie or Mini-Series: *War and Remembrance* (ABC); Drama Series: *thirtysomething* (ABC); Comedy Series: *The Wonder Years* (ABC)

Actor (Telefilm/Mini-Series) (tie): Michael Caine (*Jack the Ripper*) (CBS) and Stacy Keach (*Hemingway*) (Syndicated); Actress (Telefilm/Mini-Series): Ann Jillian (*The Ann Jillian Story*) (NBC); Actor (Drama Series): Ron Perlman (*Beauty and the Beast*) (CBS); Actress (Drama Series): Jill Eikenberry (*LA Law*); Actor (Comedy or Musical Series) (three-way tie): Michael J. Fox (*Family Ties*) (NBC), Judd Hirsch (*Dear John*) (NBC), and Richard Mulligan (*Empty Nest*) (NBC); Actress (Comedy or Musical Series): Candice Bergen (*Murphy Brown*) (CBS); Supporting Actor (tie): Barry Bostwick and John Gielgud (both in *War and Remembrance*) (ABC); Supporting Actress: Katherine Helmond (*Who's the Boss*) (ABC)

THE CABLE ACE AWARDS (FOR 1988)

Movie/Mini-Series: *The Race for the Double Helix* (A&E); Dramatic/Theatrical Special: *HBO Showcase: Tidy Endings*; Drama Series: *Vietnam War Story* (HBO); Comedy Series: *Blackadder the Third* (A&E)

Actor (Movie/Mini-Series): Danny Glover (*Mandela*) (HBO); Actress (Movie/Mini-Series): Alfre Woodard (*Mandela*) (HBO); Actor (Dramatic/Theatrical Special): Daniel Massey (*HBO Showcase: Intimate Contact*); Actress

(Dramatic/Theatrical Special): Stockard Channing (*HBO Showcase: Tidy Endings*); Actor (Drama Series): Wesley Snipes (*Vietnam War Story: An Old Ghost Walks the Earth*) (HBO); Actress (Drama Series): Pamela Reed (*Tanner '88*) (HBO); Actor (Comedy Series): Billy Crystal (*HBO Comedy Hour Live: An All-Star Tribute to the Improv*) (HBO); Actress (Comedy Series): Lucy Webb (*Not Necessarily the News*) (HBO); Supporting Actor (Movie/Mini-Series): Rip Torn (*Laguana Heat*) (HBO); Supporting Actress (Movie/Mini-Series): Juliet Stevenson (*The Race for the Double Helix*) (A&E)

THE EMMY AWARDS

DRAMA OR COMEDY SPECIAL (TIE)
Day One, *AT&T Presents* (CBS)
David (ABC)
Murderers among Us: The Simon Wiesenthal Story (HBO)
My Name Is Bill W., Hallmark Hall of Fame (ABC)
Roe vs. Wade (NBC)

In a rare tie, two controversial TV-movies were named best of the year. *Day One*, about the events behind the making of the atomic bomb, took four years to make. *Roe vs. Wade*, on the historic abortion-rights Supreme Court case, was rewritten twenty times and incited protests from conservative anti-choice groups. Several advertisers threatened to pull out of the broadcast. Holly Hunter winning the Actress (Special or Mini-Series) Emmy as the anonymous Jane Roe, the subject of the case, thanked NBC for getting the movie on the air despite the pressure.

DRAMA SERIES
Beauty and the Beast (CBS)
China Beach (CBS)
LA Law (NBC)
thirtysomething (ABC)
Wiseguy (CBS)

COMEDY SERIES
Cheers (NBC)

Designing Women (CBS)
The Golden Girls (NBC)
Murphy Brown (CBS)
The Wonder Years (ABC)

MINI-SERIES
I Know My First Name Is Steven (NBC)
Lonesome Dove (CBS)
A Perfect Spy, Masterpiece Theatre (PBS)
War and Remembrance (ABC)
The Women of Brewster Place (ABC)

Another surprise outcome was the defeat of CBS's highly praised mini-series *Lonesome Dove*, based on Larry McMurty's Pulitzer Prize-winning western novel, by *War and Remembrance*, ABC's mammoth sequel to *The Winds of War*. *Dove* went into the competition with eighteen nominations, more than any other show. It did round up seven awards: six techical prizes, presented in a separate ceremony, and one "main-event" Emmy for Simon Wincer's direction.

VARIETY, MUSIC OR COMEDY PROGRAM
The Arsenio Hall Show (Syndicated)
Gregory Hines' Tap Dance in America, Great Performances (PBS)
Late Night with David Letterman (NBC)
Saturday Night Live (NBC)
The Tracey Ullman Show (Fox)

ACTOR (SPECIAL OR MINI-SERIES)
Robert Duvall (*Lonesome Dove*) (CBS)
Robert Mitchum (*War and Remembrance*) (ABC)
John Gielgud (*War and Remembrance*) (ABC)
Ben Kingsley (*Murderers among Us: The Simon Wiesenthal Story*) (HBO)
Tommy Lee Jones (*Lonesome Dove*) (CBS)
James Woods (*My Name Is Bill W., Hallmark Hall of Fame*) (ABC)

ACTRESS (SPECIAL OR MINI-SERIES)
Holly Hunter (*Roe vs. Wade*) (NBC)
Anjelica Huston (*Lonesome Dove*) (CBS)
Diane Lane (*Lonesome Dove*) (CBS)
Amy Madigan (*Roe vs. Wade*) (NBC)
Jane Seymour (*War and Remembrrance*) (ABC)

ACTOR (DRAMA SERIES)
Carroll O'Connor (*In the Heat of the Night*) (NBC)
Ron Perlman (*Beauty and the Beast*) (CBS)
Michael Tucker (*LA Law*) (NBC)
Ken Wahl (*Wise Guy*) (CBS)
Edward Woodward (*The Equalizer*) (CBS)

ACTRESS (DRAMA SERIES)
Dana Delaney (*China Beach*) (ABC)
Susan Dey (*LA Law*) (NBC)
Linda Hamilton (*Beauty and the Beast*) (CBS)
Angela Lansbury (*Murder, She Wrote*) (CBS)
Jill Eikenberry (*LA Law*) (NBC)

ACTOR (COMEDY SERIES)
Ted Danson (*Cheers*) (NBC)
Michael J. Fox (*Family Ties*) (NBC)
John Goodman (*Roseanne*) (ABC)
Richard Mulligan (*Empty Nest*) (NBC)
Fred Savage (*The Wonder Years*) (ABC)

ACTRESS (COMEDY SERIES)
Beatrice Arthur (*The Golden Girls*) (NBC)
Candice Bergen (*Murphy Brown*) (CBS)
Blair Brown (*The Days and Nights of Molly Dodd*) (Lifetime)
Rue McClanahan (*The Golden Girls*) (NBC)
Betty White (*The Golden Girls*) (NBC)

Candice Bergen won the first of five Emmys for the title role in *Murphy Brown*, a world-famous television reporter just back from drying out at the Betty Ford Clinic. Bergen's father, ventriloquist Edgar Bergen, was the first president of the television Academy. Stage actress Colleen Dewhurst, who had guest-starred as Murphy's mother, also won an Emmy in the now expanded guest performers' categories. In addition, she copped a second Emmy as outstanding Supporting Actress (Special or Mini-Series) for *Those She Left Behind*.

Roseanne Barr (later Arnold and then just plain Roseanne) was not nominated despite glowing reviews and the popularity of her eponymous ABC sitcom. Many felt the snub occurred either because Barr was perceived as a stand-up comedienne essentially playing herself or because of the proliferation of negative stories in the tabloid press surrounding her.

SUPPORTING ACTOR (SPECIAL OR MINI-SERIES)
Armante Assante (*Jack the Ripper*) (CBS)
James Garner (*My Name Is Bill W., Hallmark Hall of Fame*) (ABC)
Danny Glover (*Lonesome Dove*) (CBS)
Derek Jacobi (*The Tenth Man, Hallmark Hall of Fame*) (CBS)
Corky Nemec (*I Know My First Name Is Steven*) (NBC)

SUPPORTING ACTRESS (SPECIAL OR MINI-SERIES)
Peggy Ashcroft (*A Perfect Spy, Masterpiece Theatre*) (PBS)
Polly Bergen (*War and Remembrance*) (ABC)
Colleen Dewhurst (*Those She Left Behind*) (NBC)
Glenne Headly (*Lonesome Dove*) (CBS)
Paula Kelly (*The Women of Brewster Place*) (ABC)

SUPPORTING ACTOR (DRAMA SERIES)
Jonathan Banks (*Wiseguy*) (CBS)
Timothy Busfield (*thirtysomething*) (ABC)
Larry Drake (*LA Law*) (NBC)
Richard Dysart (*LA Law*) (NBC)
Jimmy Smits (*LA Law*) (NBC)

SUPPORTING ACTRESS (DRAMA SERIES)
Michele Greene (*LA Law*) (NBC)
Melanie Mayron (*thirtysomething*) (ABC)
Lois Nettleton (*In the Heat of the Night*) (NBC)
Amanda Plummer (*LA Law*) (NBC)
Susan Ruttan (*LA Law*) (NBC)

SUPPORTING ACTOR (COMEDY SERIES)
Woody Harrelson (*Cheers*) (NBC)
Joe Regalbuto (*Murphy Brown*) (CBS)
Peter Scolari (*Newhart*) (CBS)
Meschach Taylor (*Designing Women*) (CBS)
George Wendt (*Cheers*) (NBC)

After four wins, *Night Court's* John Larrouquette bowed out of the competition, leaving the field clear for Woody Harrelson, who played the dim-witted but cute bartender of *Cheers*, to take the prize. Unfortunately, Harrelson was not present to accept.

SUPPORTING ACTRESS (COMEDY SERIES)

Julia Duffy (*Newhart*) (CBS)
Faith Ford (*Murphy Brown*) (CBS)
Estelle Getty (*The Golden Girls*) (NBC)
Katharine Helmond (*Who's the Boss?*) (ABC)
Rhea Perlman (*Cheers*) (NBC)

INDIVIDUAL PERFORMER (VARIETY OR MUSIC PROGRAM)

Dana Carvey (*Saturday Night Live*) (NBC)
Julie Kavner (*The Tracey Ullman Show*) (Fox)
Maurice Lamarche, puppet voices, and puppeteers of *D.C. Follies* (Syndicated)
John Roarke, puppet voices, and puppeteers of *D.C. Follies* (Syndicated)
Linda Ronstadt (*Canciones de Mi Padre, Great Performances*) (PBS)

GUEST PERFORMERS

Actor (Drama): Joe Spano ("The Execution of John Saringo," *Midnight Caller*) (NBC); Actress (Drama): Kay Lenz ("After It Happened . . .," *Midnight Caller*) (NBC); Actor (Comedy): Cleavon Little ("Stand By Your Man," *Dear John*) (NBC); Actress (Comedy): Colleen Dewhurst ("Mama Said," *Murphy Brown*) (CBS)

DAYTIME AWARDS

Drama Series: *Santa Barbara* (NBC); Actor: David Canary (*All My Children*) (ABC); Actress: Marcy Walker (*Santa Barbara*) (NBC); Supporting Actor: Justin Deas (*Santa Barbara*) (NBC); Supporting Actress (tie): Debbie Morgan (*All My Children*) (ABC) and Nancy Lee Grahn (*Santa Barbara*) (NBC); Game Show: *The $25,000 Pyramid* (CBS); Talk/Service Show: *The Oprah Winfrey Show* (Syndicated)

OTHER PRIME-TIME AWARDS

Directing (Special or Mini-Series): Simon Wincer (*Lonesome Dove*) (CBS); Directing (Drama Series): Robert Altman ("The Boiler Room," *Tanner '88*) (HBO); Directing (Comedy Series): Peter Baldwin ("Our Miss White," *The Wonder Years*) (ABC); Directing (Variety or Music Program): Jim Henson ("Dog City," *The Jim Henson Hour*) (NBC)
Writing (Special or Mini-Series): Abby Mann, Robin Vote, Ron Hutchinson (*Murderers among Us: The Simon Wiesenthal Story*) (HBO); Writing (Drama Series): Joseph Dougherty ("First Day/Last Day," *thirtysomething*) (ABC); Writing (Comedy Series): Diane English ("Respect," *Murphy Brown*) (CBS); Writing (Music or Variety Program): James Downey (head writer), John Bowman, A. Whitney Brown, Gregory Daniels, Tom Davis, Al Franken, Shannon Gaughan, Jack Handey, Phil Hartman, Lorne Michaels, Mike Myers, Conan O'Brien, Bob Odenkirk, Herb Sargent, Tom Schiller, Robert Smigel, Bonnie Turner, Terry Turner, Christine Zander (writers), George Meyer (additional sketches) (*Saturday Night Live*) (NBC)

The comedy tone of the previous year's Emmys was carried over. The producers of the broadcast were John Moffitt and Pat Tourk Lee, who had worked on such yuckfests as HBO's *Not Necessarily the News* and *Comic Relief* specials. Comic bits included the cast of *Designing Women* airing their grievances over not being nominated and "dramatic recreations" of acceptances for winners who were not present. This was a satire on ABC News' controversial (and later abandoned) practice of "reenacting" news events. When the absent Woody Harrelson did not come to get his Emmy, a picture of him was flashed on the screen and his lips were animated to deliver a phony acceptance speech. The missing Carroll O'Connor was impersonated by an unidentified actor in a suit of armor.

As usual, there was a heavy emphasis on TV nostalgia, with clips of old shows to celebrate the medium's fiftieth anniversary. Standing ovations went to Milton Berle and Bob Hope. The latter presented a posthumous special award to Lucille Ball, who had died just six months previously.

The tables turned among the big three networks, with last-place CBS taking home the most Emmys. The Big Eye netted twenty-seven awards. Top-rated NBC, previously a ratings loser, but an Emmy champ, came in second this year with twenty-five. For the third year in a row, Fox telecast the ceremony, which received the second highest rating ever for a Fox program. (The No. 1 slot belonged to an episode of *Married with Children*.) The fledgling network finally won some awards. The off-beat *Tracey Ullman Show* copped four, including one for outstanding Variety, Music or Comedy Program.

THE PEABODY AWARDS (FOR 1989)

Cable News Network's coverage of China; *Cambodia: Year Ten* (Central Independent Television, London); *Decade* (MTV); *Lonesome Dove* (CBS); *The Wonder Years* (ABC); "Vets," *China Beach* (ABC); *Small Sacrifices* (ABC); *The Great Wall of Iron* (Beyond International Group, Sydney, Australia); *Common Threads: Stories from the Quilt* (HBO); *The Public Mind* (Alvin H. Perlmutter, Inc., Public Affairs Television); "Who Killed Vincent Chin?" (Film News Now, Detroit, WTVS, Detroit); *Sesame Street* (Children's Television Workshop); *NBC News Special: To Be an American* (NBC News); David Brinkley, ABC-TV; broadcasting pioneer J. Leonard Reinsch

THE GOLDEN GLOBE AWARDS (FOR 1989)

TV-Movie or Mini-Series: *Lonesome Dove* (CBS); Drama Series: *China Beach* (ABC); Comedy or Musical Series: *Murphy Brown* (CBS)

Actor (TV-Movie or Mini-Series): Robert Duvall (*Lonesome Dove*) (CBS); Actress (TV-Movie/Mini-Series): Christine Lahti (*No Place Like Home*) (CBS); Actor (Drama Series): Ken Wahl (*Wiseguy*) (CBS); Actress (Drama Series): Angela Lansbury (*Murder, She Wrote*) (CBS); Actor (Comedy or Musical Series): Ted Danson (*Cheers*) (NBC); Actress (Comedy or Musical): Jamie Lee Curtis (*Anything But Love*) (ABC); Supporting Actor: Dean Stockwell (*Quantum Leap*) (NBC); Supporting Actress: Amy Madigan (*Roe vs. Wade*) (NBC)

THE CABLE ACE AWARDS (FOR 1989)

Movie/Mini-Series: *Murderers among Us: The Simon Wiesenthal Story* (HBO); Dramatic/ Theatrical Special: *HBO Showcase: Lip Service* (HBO); Drama Series: *The Ray Bradbury Theatre* (USA); Comedy Series: *It's Garry Shandling's Show* (Showtime)

Actor (Movie/Mini-Series): Ruben Blades (*HBO Showcase: Dead Man Out*) (HBO); Actress (Movie/Mini-Series): Vanessa Redgrave (*A Man for All Seasons*) (TNT); Actor (Drama Series): Harold Gould (*The Ray Bradbury Theatre: To the Chicago Abyss*) (USA); Actress (Drama Series): Sydney

Walsh (*Vietnam War Story: Dirty Work*) (HBO); Actor (Comedy Series): Mark McKinney (*The Kids in the Hall*) (HBO); Actress (Comedy Series): Lucy Webb (*Not Necessarily the News*) (HBO); Supporting Actor (Movie/Mini-Series): James Whitmore (*Glory! Glory!*) (HBO); Supporting Actress (Movie/Mini-Series): Mimi Maynard (*The Forgotten*) (USA)

THE EMMY AWARDS

DRAMA/COMEDY SPECIAL (TIE)
Caroline?, Hallmark Hall of Fame (CBS)
The Final Days, AT&T Presents (CBS)
The Incident, AT&T Presents (CBS)
A Killing in a Small Town (CBS)
Murder in Mississippi (NBC)

Echoing the previous year's tie vote for outstanding Drama/Comedy Special, two telefilms received an equal number of votes for the '89–'90 Emmy in the same category. The winners were *Caroline?*, a presentation from *Hallmark Hall of Fame* about a woman presumed dead reappearing after fifteen years, and *The Incident*, a courtroom drama featuring Walter Matthau as a lawyer representing a German prisoner of war accused of homicide during World War II.

DRAMA SERIES
China Beach (ABC)
LA Law (NBC)
Quantum Leap (NBC)
thirtysomething (ABC)
Twin Peaks (ABC)

Twin Peaks, David Lynch's ultra-moody series noir about a murder in a bizarre Northwestern town, grabbed the attention of the press and the nation, but was ignored at Emmy time in favor of the tried and true *LA Law*. The legal series won its third Emmy for best Drama Series. *Peaks* only received two accolades (for costuming and editing) out of fourteen nominations. (But *Peaks* soared above the competition at the Golden Globes, winning three major awards.) The dissing of *Peaks* was likened to the previous year's snub of *Lonesome Dove*. Critics charged the Academy with being afraid of anything new and innovative.

COMEDY SERIES
Cheers (NBC)
Designing Women (CBS)
The Golden Girls (NBC)
Murphy Brown (CBS)
The Wonder Years (ABC)

MINI-SERIES
Blind Faith (NBC)
Drug Wars: The Camarena Story (NBC)
Family of Spies (CBS)
The Kennedys of Massachusetts (ABC)
Small Sacrifices (ABC)

VARIETY, MUSIC OR COMEDY SERIES
The Arsenio Hall Show (Syndicated)
In Living Color (Fox)
Late Night with David Letterman (NBC)
Saturday Night Live (NBC)
The Tracey Ullman Show (Fox)

VARIETY, MUSIC OR COMEDY SPECIAL
The Best of the Tracey Ullman Show (Fox)
Billy Crystal: Midnight Train to Moscow (HBO)
The 43rd Annual Tony Awards (CBS)
Sammy Davis, Jr.'s 60th Anniversary Celebration (ABC)
The 62nd Annual Academy Awards (ABC)

ACTOR (SPECIAL OR MINI-SERIES)
Michael Caine (*Jekyll and Hyde*) (ABC)
Art Carney (*Where Pigeons Go To Die*) (NBC)
Hume Cronyn (*Age-Old Friends*) (HBO)
Albert Finney (*The Image*) (HBO)
Tom Hulce (*Murder in Mississippi*) (NBC)

ACTRESS (SPECIAL OR MINI-SERIES)
Farrah Fawcett (*Small Sacrifices*) (ABC)
Barbara Hershey (*A Killing in a Small Town*) (CBS)

Christine Lahti (*No Place Like Home*) (CBS)
Annette O'Toole (*The Kennedys of Massachusetts*) (ABC)
Lesley Ann Warren (*Family of Spies*) (CBS)
Alfre Woodard (*A Mother's Courage: The Mary Thomas Story, The Magical World of Disney*) (NBC)

ACTOR (DRAMA SERIES)
Scott Bakula (*Quantum Leap*) (NBC)
Peter Falk (*Columbo, The ABC Monday Mystery Movie*) (ABC)
Robert Loggia (*Mancuso, FBI*) (NBC)
Kyle MacLachlan (*Twin Peaks*) (ABC)
Edward Woodward (*The Equalizer*) (CBS)

Winning his fourth Emmy for playing the trench-coated detective *Columbo*, Peter Falk informed the audience it was his birthday: "You know, to get one of these things at any age is nice, but when you hit 43. . . ." He had, in fact, turned 63.

ACTRESS (DRAMA SERIES)
Dana Delany (*China Beach*) (ABC)
Jill Eikenberry (*LA Law*) (NBC)
Angela Lansbury (*Murder, She Wrote*) (CBS)
Piper Laurie (*Twin Peaks*) (ABC)
Patricia Wettig (*thirtysomething*) (ABC)

ACTOR (COMEDY SERIES)
Ted Danson (*Cheers*) (NBC)
John Goodman (*Roseanne*) (ABC)
Richard Mulligan (*Empty Nest*) (NBC)
Craig T. Nelson (*Coach*) (ABC)
Fred Savage (*The Wonder Years*) (ABC)

After nine years of fruitless nominations, Ted Danson finally received an Emmy for his starring role as bartender Sam Malone on *Cheers*. "I guess you'll be saying 'You've been robbed' to some other boy," he quipped.

ACTRESS (COMEDY SERIES)
Kirstie Alley (Cheers) (NBC)
Blair Brown (*The Days and Nights of Molly Dodd*) (Lifetime)
Candice Bergen (*Murphy Brown*) (CBS)
Delta Burke (*Designing Women*) (CBS)
Betty White (*The Golden Girls*) (NBC)

SUPPORTING ACTOR (SPECIAL OR MINI-SERIES)

Ned Beatty (*Last Train Home*) (Family Channel)
Brian Dennehy (*A Killing in a Small Town*) (CBS)
Vincent Gardenia (*Age-Old Friends*) (HBO)
Anthony Hopkins (*Great Expectations*) (Disney Channel)
James Earl Jones (*By Dawn's Early Light*) (HBO)
Max Von Sydow (*Red King, White Knight*) (HBO)

SUPPORTING ACTRESS (SPECIAL OR MINI-SERIES)

Stockard Channing (*Perfect Witness*) (NBC)
Colleen Dewhurst (*Lantern Hill*) (Disney Channel)
Swoosie Kurtz (*The Image*) (HBO)
Eva Marie Saint (*People Like Us*) (HBO)
Irene Worth (*The Shell Seekers, Hallmark Hall of Fame*) (ABC)

SUPPORTING ACTOR (DRAMA SERIES)

Timothy Busfield (*thirtysomething*) (ABC)
Larry Drake (*LA Law*) (NBC)
Richard Dysart (*LA Law*) (NBC)
Jimmy Smits (*LA Law*) (NBC)
Dean Stockwell (*Quantum Leap*) (NBC)

SUPPORTING ACTRESS (DRAMA SERIES)

Sherilyn Fenn (*Twin Peaks*) (ABC)
Marg Helgenberger (*China Beach*) (ABC)
Melanie Mayron (*thirtysomething*) (ABC)
Diana Muldaur (*LA Law*) (NBC)
Susan Ruttan (*LA Law*) (NBC)

SUPPORTING ACTOR (COMEDY SERIES)

Kelsey Grammer (*Cheers*) (NBC)
Woody Harrelson (*Cheers*) (NBC)
Charles Kimbrough (*Murphy Brown*) (CBS)
Alex Rocco (*The Famous Teddy Z*) (CBS)
Jerry Van Dyke (*Coach*) (ABC)

SUPPORTING ACTRESS (COMEDY SERIES)

Julia Duffy (*Newhart*) (CBS)
Faith Ford (*Murphy Brown*) (CBS)
Estelle Getty (*The Golden Girls*) (NBC)

Bebe Neuwirth (*Cheers*) (NBC)
Rhea Perlman (*Cheers*) (NBC)

INDIVIDUAL PERFORMANCE (VARIETY OR MUSIC)

Dana Carvey (*Saturday Night Live*) (NBC)
Billy Crystal (*Billy Crystal: Midnight Train to Moscow*) (HBO)
Julie Kavner (*The Tracey Ullman Show*) (Fox)
Angela Lansbury (*The 43rd Annual Tony Awards*) (CBS)
Tracey Ullman (*The Best of the Tracey Ullman Show*) (Fox)

Tracey Ullman received two Emmys, one for writing and another for her performance, on a compilation special on her Fox series. The double honor was bittersweet for the versatile British comedienne since the show had filmed its last episode. "Maybe I should have taken that ten minutes in the middle of *The Simpsons*," she joked, referring to the fact that the smash-hit cartoon series started out as brief "filler" on her show.

GUEST PERFORMERS

Actor (Drama Series): Patrick McGoohan ("Agenda for Murder," *Columbo, The ABC Monday Mystery Movie*) (ABC); Actress (Drama Series): Viveca Lindfors ("Save the Last Dance for Me," *Life Goes On*) (ABC); Actor (Comedy Series): Jay Thomas ("Heart of Gold," *Murphy Brown*) (CBS); Actress (Comedy Series): Swoosie Kurtz ("Reunion," *Carol and Company*) (NBC)

DAYTIME AWARDS

Drama Series: *Santa Barbara* (NBC); Actor: A Martinez (*Santa Barbara*) (NBC); Actress: Kim Zimmer (*Guiding Light*) (CBS); Supporting Actor: Henry Darrow (*Santa Barbara*) (NBC); Supporting Actress: Julia Barr (*All My Children*) (ABC); Game Show: *Jeopardy!* (Syndicated); Talk/Service Show: *Sally Jessy Raphael* (Syndicated)

OTHER PRIME-TIME AWARDS

Directing: (Special or Mini-Series): Joseph Sargent (*Caroline?, The Hallmark Hall of Fame*) (CBS); Directing (Drama) (tie): Thomas Carter ("Promises to Keep," *Equal Justice*) (ABC) and Scott Winant (*thirtysomething*) (ABC); Directing

(Comedy): Michael Dinner ("Good-Bye," *The Wonder Years*) (ABC); Directing (Variety or Music): Dwight Hemion (*The Kennedy Center Honors: A Celebration of the Performing Arts*) (CBS)

Writing: (Special or Mini-Series): Terrence McNally (*Andre's Mother, American Playhouse*) (PBS); Writing (Drama): David E. Kelley ("Blood, Sweat, and Fears," *LA Law*) (NBC); Writing (Comedy): Bob Brush ("Good-Bye," *The Wonder Years*) (ABC); Writing (Variety or Music) (tie): Billy Crystal (*Billy Crystal: Midnight Train to Moscow*) (HBO) and James L. Brooks, Heidi Perlman, Sam Simon, Jerry Belson, Marc Flanagan, Dinah Kirgo, Jay Kogen, Wallace Wolodarsky, Ian Prasier, Marilyn Suzanne Miller, Tracey Ullman (*The Tracey Ullman Show*) (Fox)

The three-hour Emmycast featured a different host for each hour: Candice Bergen [winner as best Actress (Comedy Series) for *Murphy Brown*], Jay Leno, and Jane Pauley. Fox broadcast the ceremony again and the Emmys received their lowest rating yet (an 8.2 rating and a 14 share). Nevertheless, the scrappy underdog network successfully bid to retain exclusive Emmy rights for another three years.

Thanks to some special-effects wizardry, Ted Danson was presented with his Actor (Comedy Series) award by the Simpsons, Fox's gonzo animated family. Despite pleas from its legion of fans and the Fox network, the cartoon series was relegated to the Animated Series category and kept out of competition with live-action programming— although another animated prime-time series *The Flintstones* had been nominated in the Program Achievement in Humor against noncartoon competitors in 1960–61.

THE PEABODY AWARDS (FOR 1990)

The Civil War (PBS); *Twin Peaks* premiere episode (ABC); *Saturday Night Live* (NBC); *American Playhouse* (PBS); *Mother Goose Rock 'N' Rhyme* (Disney Channel); *Eyes on the Prize II: America at the Racial Crossroads (1965–1985)* (PBS); *POV: Days of Waiting* (PBS); *The Koppel Report: Death of a Dictator* (ABC News); *Peter Jennings Reporting: Guns* (ABC News); CNN coverage of the Persian Gulf War; *Backhauling: MacNeil-Lehrer News Hour*; *John Hammond: From Bessie Smith to Bruce Springsteen* (CBS Music Video Enterprises); *Mount*

St. Helens: A Decade Later (KPTV, Portland, OR); *Dick Fleagler Commentaries* (WKYC, Cleveland); *Futures* (FASE Productions); John D. and Catherine T. MacArthur Foundation; sportscaster Red Barber; documentary filmmaker Frederick Wiseman; reporters Paul and Holly Fine

THE GOLDEN GLOBE AWARDS: (FOR 1990)

Made-for-TV Movie or Mini-Series : *Decoration Day* (NBC); Drama Series: *Twin Peaks* (ABC); Comedy Series: *Cheers* (NBC)

Actor (Made-for-TV Movie or Miniseries): James Garner (*Decoration Day*) (NBC); Actress (Made-for-TV Movie or Mini-Series): Barbara Hershey (*A Killing in a Small Town*) (CBS); Actor (Drama Series); Kyle MacLachlan (*Twin Peaks*) (ABC); Actress (Drama Series) (tie): Sharon Gless (*The Trials of Rosie O'Neill*) (CBS) and Patricia Wettig (*thirtysomething*) (ABC); Actor (Comedy Series): Ted Danson (*Cheers*) (NBC); Actress (Comedy Series): Kirstie Alley (*Cheers*) (NBC); Supporting Actor: Charles Durning (*The Kennedys of Massachusetts*) (ABC); Supporting Actress: Piper Laurie (*Twin Peaks*) (ABC)

THE CABLE ACE AWARDS (FOR 1990)

Movie/Mini-Series: *Heat Wave* (TNT); Dramatic/Theatrical Special: *Women & Men: Stories of Seduction: The Man in the Brooks Brothers Shirt* (HBO); Drama Series: *Tales from the Crypt* (HBO); Comedy Series: *It's Garry Shandling's Show* (Showtime)

Actor (Movie/Mini-Series): Hume Cronyn (*Age-Old Friends*) (HBO); Actress (Movie/Mini-Series): Cicely Tyson (*Heat Wave*) (TNT); Actor (Drama Series): James Earl Jones (*American Playwrights Theatre: Third and Oak: The Pool Room*) (A&E); Actress (Drama Series): Blair Brown (*The Days and Nights of Molly Dodd*) (Lifetime); Actor (Comedy Series): Garry Shandling (*It's Garry Shandling's Show*) (Showtime); Actress (Comedy Series): Jessica Harper (*It's Garry Shandling's Show*) (Showtime); Supporting Actor (Movie/Mini-Series): James Earl Jones (*Heat Wave*) (TNT); Supporting Actress (Movie/Mini-Series): Colleen Dewhurst (*Lantern Hill*) (The Disney Channel)

THE EMMY AWARDS

DRAMA/COMEDY SPECIAL OR MINI-SERIES

Decoration Day, Hallmark Hall of Fame (NBC)
The Josephine Baker Story (HBO)
Paris Trout (Showtime)
Sarah, Plain and Tall, Hallmark Hall of Fame (CBS)
Separate but Equal (ABC)
Switched at Birth (NBC)

DRAMA SERIES

China Beach (ABC)
LA Law (NBC)
Northern Exposure (CBS)
Quantum Leap (NBC)
thirtysomething (ABC)

COMEDY SERIES

Cheers (NBC)
Designing Women (CBS)
The Golden Girls (NBC)
Murphy Brown (CBS)
The Wonder Years (ABC)

VARIETY OR MUSIC PROGRAM

In Living Color (Fox)
The Kennedy Center Honors: A Celebration of the Performing Arts (CBS)
Late Night with David Letterman (NBC)
The Muppets Celebrate Jim Henson (CBS)
The 63rd Annual Academy Awards (ABC)
The Tonight Show Starring Johnny Carson (NBC)

ACTOR (SPECIAL OR MINI-SERIES)

James Garner (*Decoration Day, Hallmark Hall of Fame*) (NBC)
John Gielgud (*Summer's Lease, Masterpiece Theatre*) (PBS)
Dennis Hopper (*Paris Trout*) (Showtime)
Sidney Poitier (*Separate but Equal*) (ABC)
Christopher Walken (*Sarah, Plain and Tall, Hallmark Hall of Fame*) (CBS)

ACTRESS (SPECIAL OR MINI-SERIES)

Glenn Close (*Sarah, Plain and Tall, Hallmark Hall of Fame*) (CBS)
Barbara Hershey (*Paris Trout*) (Showtime)
Suzanne Pleshette (*Leona Helmsley: The Queen of Mean*) (CBS)
Lee Purcell (*Long Road Home*) (NBC)
Lynn Whitfield (*The Josephine Baker Story*) (HBO)

The Josephine Baker Story, HBO's bio-pic on the black American entertainer who captivated French audiences from the 1930s to the 1960s, received the most nominations for a cable presentation with twelve. It won a total of five, displaying the growing influence of cable in the industry. Among *Baker*'s wins were outstanding Actress (Special or Mini-Series) for Lynn Whitfield in the title role and Directing (Special or Mini-Series) for Brian Gibson's direction. The film provided more than a pair of awards for the duo. Whitfield met Gibson during the filming, they married, and had a child three weeks before the Emmys.

ACTOR (DRAMA SERIES)

Scott Bakula (*Quantum Leap*) (NBC)
Peter Falk (*Columbo, The ABC Monday Mystery Movie*) (ABC)
James Earl Jones (*Gabriel's Fire*) (ABC)
Kyle MacLachlan (*Twin Peaks*) (ABC)
Michael Moriarty (*Law & Order*) (NBC)

The official theme of the 1990–91 Emmys was comedy. To get that message across, the baritone-voiced dramatic actor James Earl Jones was hit in the face with a pie at the top of the show. Almost as if to make up for his sacrifice of dignity in order to get a laugh, Jones won two Emmys later in the evening. (The previous year he had copped two Cable ACE Awards as well.) His two Emmys were for outstanding Actor (Dramatic Series) (for *Gabriel's Fire*, in which he played an ex-con crimefighter) and for outstanding Supporting Actor (Special or Mini-Series) (for *Heat Wave*, a TV-film on the 1965 Los Angeles race riots shown on the TNT cable network). Despite Jones' win and that of Madge Sinclair as outstanding Supporting Actress (Drama Series) for *Gabriel's Fire*, the show fell victim to low ratings. The following season ABC retooled it, brought in Richard Crenna as a co-star, and retitled the series *Pros and Cons*. The changes failed to help and cancellation soon followed.

ACTRESS (DRAMA SERIES)
Dana Delaney (*China Beach*) (ABC)
Sharon Gless (*The Trials of Rosie O'Neill*) (CBS)
Angela Lansbury (*Murder, She Wrote*) (CBS)
Patricia Wettig (*thirtysomething*) (ABC)

ACTOR (COMEDY SERIES)
Ted Danson (*Cheers*) (NBC)
John Goodman (*Roseanne*) (ABC)
Richard Mulligan (*Empty Nest*) (NBC)
Craig T. Nelson (*Coach*) (ABC)
Burt Reynolds (*Evening Shade*) (CBS)

ACTRESS (COMEDY SERIES)
Kirstie Alley (*Cheers*) (NBC)
Candice Bergen (*Murphy Brown*) (CBS)
Blair Brown (*The Days and Nights of Molly Dodd*) (Lifetime)
Delta Burke (*Designing Women*) (CBS)
Betty White (*The Golden Girls*) (NBC)

SUPPORTING ACTOR (SPECIAL OR MINI-SERIES)
Ruben Blades (*The Josephine Baker Story*) (HBO)
David Dukes (*The Josephine Baker Story*) (HBO)
Richard Kiley (*Separate but Equal*) (ABC)
James Earl Jones (*Heat Wave*) (TNT)
Leon Russom (*Long Road Home*) (NBC)

SUPPORTING ACTRESS (SPECIAL OR MINI-SERIES)
Ruby Dee (*Decoration Day, Hallmark Hall of Fame*) (NBC)
Olympia Dukakis (*Lucky Day*) (ABC)
Doris Roberts (*The Sunset Gang, American Playhouse*) (PBS)
Vanessa Redgrave (*Young Catherine*) (TNT)
Elaine Stritch (*An Inconvenient Woman*) (ABC)

SUPPORTING ACTOR (DRAMA SERIES)
Timothy Busfield (*thirtysomething*) (ABC)
David Clennon (*thirtysomething*) (ABC)
Richard Dysart (*LA Law*) (NBC)
Jimmy Smits (*LA Law*) (NBC)
Dean Stockwell (*Quantum Leap*) (NBC)

SUPPORTING ACTRESS (DRAMA SERIES)
Marg Helgenberger (*China Beach*) (ABC)
Piper Laurie (*Twin Peaks*) (ABC)
Melanie Mayron (*thirtysomething*) (ABC)
Diana Muldaur (*LA Law*) (NBC)
Madge Sinclair (*Gabriel's Fire*) (ABC)

SUPPORTING ACTOR (COMEDY SERIES)
Charles Durning (*Evening Shade*) (CBS)
Woody Harrelson (*Cheers*) (NBC)
Michael Jeter (*Evening Shade*) (CBS)
Jerry Van Dyke (*Coach*) (ABC)
Jonathan Winters (*Davis Rules*) (ABC)

SUPPORTING ACTRESS (COMEDY SERIES)
Elizabeth Ashley (*Evening Shade*) (CBS)
Faith Ford (*Murphy Brown*) (CBS)
Estelle Getty (*The Golden Girls*) (NBC)
Bebe Neuwirth (*Cheers*) (NBC)
Rhea Pearlman (*Cheers*) (NBC)

VARIETY OR MUSIC PERFORMER
Dana Carvey (*Saturday Night Live*) (NBC)
Harry Connick, Jr. (*Swinging Out with Harry, Great Performances*) (PBS)
Billy Crystal (*The 63rd Annual Academy Awards*) (ABC)
Damon Wayans (*In Living Color*) (Fox)
Keenen Ivory Wayans (*In Living Color*) (Fox)

GUEST PERFORMERS
Actor (Drama): David Opatoshu ("A Prayer for the Goldsteins," *Gabriel's Fire*) (ABC); Actress (Drama): Peggy McCay ("State of Mind," *The Trials of Rosie O'Neill*) (CBS); Actor (Comedy): Jay Thomas ("Gold Rush," *Murphy Brown*) (CBS); Actress (Comedy): Colleen Dewhurst ("Bob and Murphy and Ted and Avery," *Murphy Brown*) (CBS)

DAYTIME AWARDS
Drama Series: *As the World Turns* (CBS); Actor: Peter Bergman (*The Young and the Restless*) (CBS); Actress: Finola Hughes (*General Hospital*) (ABC); Supporting Actor: Bernie Barrow (*Loving*) (ABC);

Supporting Actress: Jess Walton (*The Young and the Restless*) (CBS); Game Show: *Jeopardy!* (Syndicated); Talk/Service Show: *The Ophrah Winfrey Show* (Syndicated)

OTHER PRIME-TIME AWARDS

Directing (Special or Mini-Series): Brian Gibson (*The Josephine Baker Story*) (HBO); Directing (Drama Series): Thomas Carter ("In Confidence," *Equal Justice*) (ABC); Directing (Comedy Series): James Burrows ("Woody Interruptus," *Cheers*) (NBC); Directing (Variety or Music Program): Hal Gurnee (*Late Night with David Letterman, Show #1425*) (NBC)

Writing (Special or Mini-Series): Andrew Davies (*House of Cards, Masterpiece Theatre*) (PBS); Writing (Drama Series): David E. Kelley ("On the Toad Again," *LA Law*) (NBC); Writing (Comedy Series): Gary Dontzig, Steven Peterman ("Jingle Hell, Jingle Hell, Jingle All the Way," *Murphy Brown*) (CBS); Writing (Variety or Music Program): Hal Kanter, Buz Kohan (writers), Billy Crystal, David Steinberg, Bruce Vilanch, Robert Wuhl (special material) (*The 63rd Annual Academy Awards*) (ABC)

The announced theme of the '90–'91 Emmys was comedy. But the humor turned off-color when winner Kirstie Alley thanked her husband Parker Stevenson for giving her "the big one." More risque jokes followed. Burt Reynolds thanked his wife Loni Anderson for giving him "two big ones," referring to her breasts. Comedian Gilbert Gottfried crossed even further over the line into tastelessness when he launched into a monologue about masturbation. Fox, the carrying network, edited Gottfried's remarks for the delayed West Coast airing of the show and the Television Academy issued a statement of apology. But the damage was done and the 1990–91 Emmys were labeled the dirtiest ever (even bluer than the 1983 awards when Joan Rivers cracked wise about prostitutes, gays, and Secretary of the Interior James Watt).

On a more serious note, the ceremony featured a tribute to performers who had died during the year including Danny Thomas, Lee Remick, Michael Landon, and Colleen Dewhurst, who had died just two days before the program. She posthumously won her fourth career Emmy—a Guest Actress (Comedy) prize for a guest shot as Candice Bergen's mother on *Murphy Brown*.

THE PEABODY AWARDS (FOR 1991)

KTLA-TV, Los Angeles, for its coverage of the Rodney King videotaped beating by police; *I'll Fly Away* (NBC); *Northern Exposure* (CBS); *Murphy Brown* (CBS); Armed Forces Radio and Television in honor of its fiftieth anniversary; WRAL Environmental Report (WRAL, Raleigh, NC); *Who's Watching the Store?* (KSTP-TV, St. Paul, MN); Brian Rossi Reports on BCCI (NBC News); "Friendly Fire," *60 Minutes* (CBS News); CNN for its coverage of the attempted Soviet coup; *When It Was a Game* (HBO Sports, Black Canyon Productions); "Everybody Dance Now!," *Dance in America* (Channel 13, New York); *Late Night with David Letterman* (NBC); "Heil Hitler: Confessions of a Hitler Youth," *America Undercover* (HBO); "It's Only Television," *Nickelodeon Special Edition* (Nickelodeon, MTV Network); *Coup d'Etat: The Week That Changed the World* (Turner Multimedia, Atlanta); *Soviets: Red Hot* (Central Independent Television, Nottingham, England, and WETA-TV, Washington, DC); *Pearl Harbor: Two Hours That Changed the World* (ABC News and NHK, Japan); *People of the Forest: The Chimps of Gombe* (The Discovery Channel); *Arkansas's Time Bomb: Teen Pregnancy* (KARK-TV, Little Rock, AR, Arkansas Dept. of Health); *The Masters* (CBS Sports); Peggy Charren, founder of Action for Children's Television

THE GOLDEN GLOBE AWARDS (FOR 1991)

Made-for-TV Movie or Mini-Series: *One against the Wind, Hallmark Hall of Fame* (CBS); Drama Series: *Northern Exposure* (CBS); Comedy or Musical Series: *Brooklyn Bridge* (CBS)

Actor (Made-for-TV Movie/Mini-Series): Beau Bridges (*Without Warning: The James Brady Story*) (HBO); Actress (Made-for-TV Movie/Mini-Series): Judy Davis (*One against the Wind, Hallmark Hall of Fame*) (CBS); Actor (Drama Series): Scott Bakula (*Quantum Leap*) (NBC); Actress (Drama Series): Angela Lansbury (*Murder, She Wrote*) (CBS); Actor (Comedy or Musical Series): Burt Reynolds

(*Evening Shade*) (CBS); Actress (Comedy or Musical Series): Candice Bergen (*Murphy Brown*) (CBS); Supporting Actor: Louis Gosset, Jr. (*The Josephine Baker Story*) (HBO); Supporting Actress: Amanda Donohue (*LA Law*) (NBC)

THE CABLE ACE AWARDS (FOR 1991)

Movie/Mini-Series: *Doublecrossed* (HBO); Dramatic/Theatrical Special: *Kurt Vonnegut's Monkey House: All the King's Horses* (Showtime); Drama Series: *Avonlea* (The Disney Channel); Comedy Series: *Dream On* (HBO)

Actor (Movie/Mini-Series): Beau Bridges (*Without Warning: The James Brady Story*) (HBO); Actress (Movie/Mini-Series): Christine Lahti (*Crazy from the Heart*) (TNT); Actor (Drama Series): Darren McGavin (*Clara*) (A&E); Actress (Drama Series): Olympia Dukakis (*The Last Act Is a Solo*) (A&E); Actor (Comedy Series): Bob Einstein (*Super Dave*) (Showtime); Actress (Comedy Series): Wendy Malick (*Dream On*) (HBO); Supporting Actor (Movie/Mini-Series): Arliss Howard (*Somebody Has to Shoot the Picture*) (HBO); Supporting Actress (Movie/Mini-Series): Vanessa Redgrave (*Young Catherine*) (TNT)

1991-92

THE EMMY AWARDS

MADE-FOR-TV MOVIE
Doing Time on Maple Drive (Fox)
Homefront (ABC)
I'll Fly Away (pilot) (NBC)
Miss Rose White, Hallmark Hall of Fame (NBC)
Without Warning: The James Brady Story (HBO)

DRAMA SERIES
I'll Fly Away (NBC)
LA Law (NBC)
Law & Order (NBC)
Northern Exposure (CBS)
Quantum Leap (NBC)

Like *Moonlighting*, *Northern Exposure* was heavily laced with humor though it was officially considered a drama because of its sixty-minute length. The show followed the adventures of the quirky citizens of the mythical Alaskan town of Cicely.

COMEDY SERIES
Brooklyn Bridge (CBS)
Cheers (NBC)
Home Improvement (ABC)
Murphy Brown (CBS)
Seinfeld (NBC)

Murphy Brown won the best Comedy Series Emmy for a second time partially due to some election year publicity. Vice-President Dan Quayle sharply criticized the series when Candice Bergen's unwed character, a high-powered news reporter, became pregnant. He cited Brown's unwed-mother status as contributing to the downfall of "traditional family values."

Upon winning, series producer-creator Diane English advised all single parents, "Don't let anyone tell you you're not a family." She also joked, "As Murphy herself said, 'I couldn't possibly do a worse job raising my kid alone than the Reagans did with theirs.'"

MINI-SERIES
Cruel Doubt (NBC)
Drug Wars: The Cocaine Cartel (NBC)
In a Child's Name (CBS)
Scott Turlow's "Burden of Proof" (ABC)
A Woman Called Jackie (NBC)

VARIETY OR MUSIC PROGRAM
Cirque du Soleil II: A New Experience (HBO)
Comic Relief V (HBO)
In Living Color (Fox)
Late Night with David Letterman (NBC)
The Tonight Show Starring Johnny Carson (NBC)
Unforgettable, with Love: Natalie Cole Sings the Songs of Nat King Cole, Great Performances (PBS)

ACTOR (SPECIAL OR MINI-SERIES)
Ruben Blades (*Crazy from the Heart*) (TNT)
Beau Bridges (*Without Warning: The James Brady Story*) (HBO)

Hume Cronyn (*Christmas on Division Street*) (CBS)

Brian Dennehy (*To Catch a Killer*) (Syndicated)

Maximilian Schell (*Miss Rose White, Hallmark Hall of Fame*) (NBC)

ACTRESS (SPECIAL OR MINI-SERIES)
Anne Bancroft (*Mrs. Cage, American Playhouse*) (PBS)

Meredith Baxter (*A Woman Scorned: The Betty Broderick Story*) (CBS)

Judy Davis (*One against the Wind, Hallmark Hall of Fame*) (CBS)

Laura Dern (*Afterburn*) (HBO)

Gena Rowlands (*Face of a Stranger*) (CBS)

ACTOR (DRAMA SERIES)
Scott Bakula (*Quantum Leap*) (NBC)

Kirk Douglas (guest) (*Tales from the Crypt*) (HBO)

Christopher Lloyd (guest) (*Avonlea*) (Disney Channel)

Michael Moriarty (*Law & Order*) (NBC)

Rob Morrow (*Northern Exposure*) (CBS)

Harrison Page (guest) (*Quantum Leap*) (NBC)

Sam Waterston (*I'll Fly Away*) (NBC)

Once again the Emmy rules were changed and guest performers were competing with series regulars. Thus, Christopher Lloyd in a single appearance on the Disney Channel's *Avonlea* beat out weekly stars Scott Bakula, Rob Morrow, Michael Moriarty, and Sam Waterston. There was such an uproar of criticism that the categories of regular and guest performers were divided again the following year.

ACTRESS (DRAMA SERIES)
Dana Delaney (*China Beach*) (ABC)

Sharon Gless (*The Trials of Rosie O'Neill*) (CBS)

Shirley Knight (guest) (*Law & Order*) (NBC)

Angela Lansbury (*Murder, She Wrote*) (CBS)

Kate Nelligan (guest) (*Avonlea*) (Disney Channel)

Regina Taylor (*I'll Fly Away*) (NBC)

ACTOR (COMEDY SERIES)
Ted Danson (*Cheers*) (NBC)

John Goodman (*Roseanne*) (ABC)

Kelsey Grammer (guest) (*Wings*) (NBC)

Craig T. Nelson (*Coach*) (ABC)

Burt Reynolds (*Evening Shade*) (ABC)

Jerry Seinfeld (*Seinfeld*) (NBC)

ACTRESS (COMEDY SERIES)
Kirstie Alley (*Cheers*) (NBC)

Roseanne Arnold (*Roseanne*) (ABC)

Candice Bergen (*Murphy Borwn*) (CBS)

Tyne Daly (guest) (*Wings*) (NBC)

Marion Ross (*Brooklyn Bridge*) (CBS)

Betty White (*The Golden Girls*) (ABC)

SUPPORTING ACTOR (SPECIAL OR MINI-SERIES)
Hume Cronyn (*Neil Simon's "Broadway Bound"*) (ABC)

Brian Dennehy (*Scott Turlow's "Burden of Proof"*) (ABC)

Hector Elizondo (*Mrs. Cage, American Playhouse*) (PBS)

Jerry Orbach (*Neil Simon's "Broadway Bound"*) (ABC)

Ben Vereen (*Intruders: They Are among Us*) (CBS)

Hume Cronyn lost in the leading Actor (Special or Mini-Series) category (for *Christmas on Division Street*), but won a Supporting Actor (Special or Mini-Series) Emmy for his role as the grandfather in the TV adaptation of Neil Simon's play *Broadway Bound*. John Randolph had won a Tony for playing the same role onstage. Other double nominees this year included Anne Bancroft and Brian Dennehy.

SUPPORTING ACTRESS (SPECIAL OR MINI-SERIES)
Anne Bancroft (*Neil Simon's "Broadway Bound"*) (ABC)

Bibi Besch (*Doing Time on Maple Drive*) (Fox)

Penny Fuller (*Miss Rose White, Hallmark Hall of Fame*) (CBS)

Amanda Plummer (*Miss Rose White, Hallmark Hall of Fame*) (CBS)

Maureen Stapleton (*Miss Rose White, Hallmark Hall of Fame*) (CBS)

SUPPORTING ACTOR (DRAMA SERIES)
Ed Asner (*The Trials of Rosie O'Neill*) (CBS)

John Corbett (*Northern Exposure*) (CBS)

Richard Dysart (*LA Law*) (NBC)

Richard Kiley (guest) (*The Ray Bradbury Theatre*) (USA)
Jimmy Smits (*LA Law*) (NBC)
Dean Stockwell (*Quantum Leap*) (NBC)

SUPPORTING ACTRESS (DRAMA SERIES)
Mary Alice (*I'll Fly Away*) (CBS)
Barbara Barrie (guest) (*Law & Order*) (NBC)
Conchata Ferrell (*LA Law*) (NBC)
Cynthia Geary (*Northern Exposure*) (CBS)
Kay Lenz (*Reasonable Doubts*) (NBC)
Valerie Mahaffey (*Northern Exposure*) (CBS)

SUPPORTING ACTOR (COMEDY SERIES)
Jason Alexander (*Seinfeld*) (NBC)
Charles Durning (*Evening Shade*) (CBS)
Harvey Fierstein (guest) (*Cheers*) (NBC)
Michael Jeter (*Evening Shade*) (CBS)
Jay Thomas (guest) (*Murphy Brown*) (CBS)
Jerry Van Dyke (*Coach*) (ABC)

SUPPORTING ACTRESS (COMEDY SERIES)
Faith Ford (*Murphy Brown*) (CBS)
Estelle Getty (*The Golden Girls*) (NBC)
Alice Ghostley (*Designing Women*) (CBS)
Julia Louis-Dreyfus (*Seinfeld*) (NBC)
Laurie Metcalfe (*Roseanne*) (ABC)
Frances Sternhagen (guest) (*Cheers*) (NBC)

INDIVIDUAL PERFORMER (VARIETY OR MUSIC)
George Carlin (*George Carlin Jammin' in New York*) (HBO)
Dana Carvey (*Saturday Night Live*) (NBC)
Natalie Cole (*Unforgettable, with Love: Natalie Cole Sings the Songs of Nat King Cole, Great Performances*) (PBS)
Billy Crystal (*The 64th Annual Academy Awards*) (ABC)
Bette Midler (*The Tonight Show Starring Johnny Carson*) (NBC)

DAYTIME AWARDS
Drama Series: *All My Children* (ABC); Actor: Peter Bergman (*The Young and the Restless*) (CBS); Actress: Erika Slezak (*One Life To Live*) (ABC); Supporting Actor: Thom Christopher (*One Life To Live*) (ABC); Supporting Actress: Maeve Kinkead (*Guiding Light*) (CBS); Game Show: *Jeopardy!* (Syndicated); Talk/Service Show: *The Oprah Winfrey Show* (Syndicated)

OTHER PRIME-TIME AWARDS
Directing (Special or Mini-Series): Daniel Petrie (*Mark Twain and Me*) (Disney Channel); Directing (Drama Series): Eric Lanueville ("All God's Children," *I'll Fly Away*) (NBC); Directing (Comedy Series): Barnet Kellman ("Birth 101," *Murphy Brown*) (CBS); Directing (Variety or Music Program): Patricia Birch (*Unforgettable, with Love: Natalie Cole Sings the Songs of Nat King Cole, Great Performances*) (PBS)

Writing (Special or Mini-Series): John Falsey, Joshua Brand (*I'll Fly Away* pilot) (NBC); Writing (Drama Series): Andrew Schneider, Diane Frolov ("Seoul Mates," *Northern Exposure*) (CBS); Writing (Comedy Series): Elaine Pope, Larry Charles ("The Fix-Up," *Seinfeld*) (NBC); Writing (Variety or Music Program): Hal Kanter, Buz Kohan (writers), Billy Crystal, Marc Shaiman, David Steinberg, Robert Wuhl, Bruce Vilanch (special material) (*The 64th Annual Academy Awards*) (ABC)

"Boy, Quayle is just getting stomped on here," commented Emmy host Dennis Miller. Vice President Dan Quayle, then running for re-election with President George Bush, had harshly criticized the entertainment industry for promoting lax moral values and characterized it as being peopled with the "cultural elite." In particular, Quayle cited *Murphy Brown* as a bad example to young viewers because the title character was going to have a child out of wedlock.

Hollywood responded on Emmy night by going Quayle-hunting. "Comedy was supposed to be the theme," the *New York Daily News* reported, "but Republican-bashing came to the forefront."

Numerous quips were made about the Vice President's famous spelling gaffe. Miller cracked that Quayle "had better learn how to spell potato because if the economy keeps going down the way it is, that's all we'll be eating."

Gags were the order of the day, with little entertainment other than Dan Quayle jokes and award presentations. The only production number was interrupted by the Energizer Bunny in a send-up of the Energizer battery commercials.

The Vice President responded the next day in a campaign speech by joking that *Murphy Brown* owed him "big time" for all the free publicity he gave the show. "They said I attacked single mothers," he added. "That is a lie. . . . Winning an Emmy is not a license to lie."

THE PEABODY AWARDS (FOR 1992)

Roseanne (ABC); *Seinfeld* (NBC); *Citizen Cohn* (HBO); Channel One for educational programming on AIDS; *72 Hours to Victory: Behind the Scenes with Bill Clinton* and *Moment of Crisis, ABC News Nightline Specials*; *The Donner Party, The American Experience* (WGBH-TV, Boston); *The Machine That Changed the World* (WGBH-TV, Boston, BBC); *Abortion: Desperate Choices* (HBO); *The Health Quarterly: The AIDS Report Series* (WGBH-TV, Boston); KTTV-TV, Los Angeles, for its coverage of the trial of the police officers accused of beating Rodney King; WTVJ-TV, Miami, for its coverage of Hurricane Andrew; *Where in the World Is Carmen Sandiego?* (WGBH-TV, Boston); *Rock the Vote* (Propaganda Films and

Fox Broadcasting Corporation); *When the Salmon Run Dry* (KIRO-TV, Seattle); *Surviving Columbus* (KNME-TV and the Institute for American Indian Arts, Albuquerque, NM); *Color Adjustment* (PBS and Signifyin' Work, Berkeley, CA); *Threads of Hope* (Canamedia Productions, Ltd., and TV Ontario, Canada); *Close to Home: The Tommy Boccomino Story* (HKO Media, Inc., and WKBD-TV, Detroit); *Reading Rainbow: The Wall* (GPN-Nebraska ETV Network, Lincoln, NE); *The Incredible Voyage of Bill Pickney* (WCVB-TV, Needham, MA); *The More You Know* (NBC); MTV's Choose or Lose Campaign; "Cicely," *Northern Exposure* (CBS); *Larry King Live* Election Coverage 1992 (CNN); *Seven Ages in America* (CBS and Granada Television, London); reporter Daniel Schorr; C-SPAN; Fred Rogers for twenty-five years of *Mister Rogers' Neighborhood*

THE GOLDEN GLOBE AWARDS (FOR 1992)

Made-for-TV Movie or Mini-Series: *Sinatra* (CBS); Drama Series: *Northern Exposure* (CBS); Comedy or Musical Series: *Roseanne* (ABC)

Actor (Telefilm/Mini-Series): Robert Duvall (*Stalin*) (HBO); Actress (Telefilm/Mini-Series): Laura Dern (*Afterburn*) (HBO); Actor (Drama

Sam Waterston and Regina Taylor of the short-lived, but highly praised *I'll Fly Away* were triumphant at the 1992 Golden Globes, but lost out at the Emmys. They are flanked by presenters Marilu Henner and Richard Dean Anderson.

Series): Sam Waterston (*I'll Fly Away*) (NBC);
Actress (Drama Series): Regina Taylor (*I'll Fly Away*) (NBC); Actor (Comedy or Musical Series): John Goodman (*Roseanne*) (ABC); Actress (Comedy or Musical Series): Roseanne Arnold (*Roseanne*) (ABC); Supporting Actor: Maximillian Schell (*Stalin*) (HBO); Supporting Actress: Joan Plowright (*Stalin*) (HBO)

THE CABLE ACE AWARDS (FOR 1992)

Movie/Mini-Series: *Citizen Cohn* (HBO); Dramatic/Theatrical Special: *Kurt Vonnegut's Monkey House: Fortitude* (Showtime); Drama Series: *The Ray Bradbury Theatre* (USA); Comedy Series: *The Larry Sanders Show* (HBO)

Actor (Movie/Mini-Series): Jon Voight (*The Last of His Tribe*) (HBO); Actress (Movie/Mini-Series): Patricia Arquette (*Wildflowers*) (Lifetime); Actor (Drama Series): Frank Langella (*Kurt Vonnegut's Monkey House: Fortitude*) (Showtime); Actress (Drama Series): Cathy Moriarty (*Tales from the Crypt: Seance*) (HBO); Actor (Comedy Series): Brian Benben (*Dream On*) (HBO); Actress (Comedy Series): Wendy Malick (*Dream On*) (HBO); Supporting Actor (Movie/Mini-Series): Martin Landau (*Legacy of Lies*) (USA); Supporting Actress (Movie/Mini-Series): Herta Ware (*Crazy in Love*) (TNT)

1992-93

THE EMMY AWARDS

MADE-FOR-TV MOVIE (TIE)
Barbarians at the Gate (HBO)
Citizen Cohn (HBO)
The Positively True Adventures of the Alleged Texas Cheerleader-Murdering Mom (HBO)
Stalin (HBO)
Tru, American Playhouse (PBS)

At the '92–'93 Emmys, cable was king. Once the outsiders at the ceremony, nonbroadcast networks this year received a total of seventy-six nominations. Home Box Office took seventeen awards

(including technical prizes), the most for any network, broadcast or cable. Four of the five nominees for Made-for-TV Movie were from HBO. (The fifth was a PBS videotaped version of *Tru*, Robert Morse's one-man stage performance as eccentric author Truman Capote.) Unrestricted by the need for ratings, cable films were able to tackle risky subject matter like the homophobic, closeted gay lawyer Roy Cohn (*Citizen Cohn*), the true case of a mother who attempted to assassinate her daughter's rival for a spot on a cheerleading squad (*. . . Texas Cheerleader-Murdering Mom*), a despotic Russian dictator (*Stalin*), and a satiric version of the takeover of the Nabisco corporation (*Barbarians at the Gate*).

DRAMA SERIES
Homefront (ABC)
I'll Fly Away (NBC)
Law & Order (NBC)
Northern Exposure (CBS)
Picket Fences (CBS)

Like *Northern Exposure*, the previous year's Drama Series winner, *Picket Fences* was a quirky CBS series about a small town. The hamlet of Rome, Wisconsin, was a microcosm of American society in which every major issue from homelessness to integration to violence on television was given play. In its first year it won three major awards: Series (Drama), along with Actor (Drama Series) and Actress (Drama Series) (Tom Skerritt and Kathy Baker as husband and wife and the town's sheriff and main doctor). The series was in a low-rated spot, searching for viewers. It never became a Top 10 show, but continued to win Emmys until its final season in 1995–96.

COMEDY SERIES
Cheers (NBC)
Home Improvement (ABC)
The Larry Sanders Show (HBO)
Murphy Brown (CBS)
Seinfeld (NBC)

Pitched to the networks as a show about nothing, *Seinfeld* started as extensions of Jerry Seinfeld's comedy routines about the annoying little details of life. It grew into one of the most popular sitcoms ever. In its second year, it won as outstanding Comedy Series; in addition a controversial episode about masturbation took the outstanding Writing (Comedy Series) Emmy.

MINI-SERIES
Alex Haley's "Queen" (CBS)
Family Pictures (ABC)
The Jacksons: An American Dream (ABC)
Prime Suspect 2, *Mystery!* (PBS)
Sinatra (CBS)

VARIETY OR MUSIC PROGRAM
Bob Hope: The First 90 Years (NBC)
The 1992 Tony Awards (CBS)
The Search for Signs of Intelligent Life in the Universe (Showtime)
The 65th Annual Academy Awards (ABC)
Sondheim: A Celebration at Carnegie Hall (PBS)

VARIETY OR MUSIC SERIES
Late Night with David Letterman (NBC)
MTV Unplugged (MTV)
Saturday Night Live (NBC)
The Tonight Show with Jay Leno (NBC)

ACTOR (SPECIAL OR MINI-SERIES)
Robert Blake (*Judgment Day: The John List Story*) (CBS)
Robert Duvall (*Stalin*) (HBO)
James Garner (*Barbarians at the Gate*) (HBO)
Robert Morse (*Tru, American Playhouse*) (PBS)
James Woods (*Citizen Cohn*) (HBO)

ACTRESS (SPECIAL OR MINI-SERIES)
Glenn Close (*Skylark, Hallmark Hall of Fame*) (CBS)
Holly Hunter (*The Positively True Adventures of the Alleged Texas Cheerleader-Murdering Mom*) (HBO)
Helen Mirren (*Prime Suspect 2, Mystery!*) (PBS)
Maggie Smith (*Suddenly Last Summer, Great Performances*) (PBS)
Joanne Woodward (*Blind Spot*) (CBS)

ACTOR (DRAMA SERIES)
Scott Bakula (*Quantum Leap*) (NBC)
Rob Morrow (*Northern Exposure*) (CBS)

Michael Moriarty (*Law & Order*) (NBC)
Tom Skerritt (*Picket Fences*) (CBS)
Sam Waterston (*I'll Fly Away*) (NBC)

ACTRESS (DRAMA SERIES)
Kathy Baker (*Picket Fences*) (CBS)
Swoosie Kurtz (*Sisters*) (NBC)
Angela Lansbury (*Murder, She Wrote*) (CBS)
Regina Taylor (*I'll Fly Away*) (NBC)
Janine Turner (*Northern Exposure*) (ABC)

ACTOR (COMEDY SERIES)
Tim Allen (*Home Improvement*) (ABC)
Ted Danson (*Cheers*) (NBC)
John Goodman (*Roseanne*) (CBS)
Jerry Seinfeld (*Seinfeld*) (NBC)
Garry Shandling (*The Larry Sanders Show*) (HBO)

ACTRESS (COMEDY SERIES)
Kirstie Alley (*Cheers*) (NBC)
Roseanne Arnold (*Roseanne*) (ABC)
Candice Bergen (*Murphy Brown*) (CBS)
Helen Hunt (*Mad about You*) (NBC)
Marion Ross (*Brooklyn Bridge*) (CBS)

After being ignored by the Academy, Roseanne Arnold (formerly Barr and later just plain old Roseanne) finally won an Emmy. The caustic comedienne's performance as a harried working mother on her eponymous sitcom failed to receive a nomination during the show's first three seasons. She was cited in 1991–92, but lost to Candice Bergen. When she won in 1992–93, she did not show up to collect her award.

SUPPORTING ACTOR (SPECIAL OR MINI-SERIES)
Beau Bridges (*The Positively True Adventures of the Alleged Texas Cheerleader-Murdering Mom*) (HBO)
Brian Dennehy (*Murder in the Heartland*) (ABC)
Jonathan Pryce (*Barbarians at the Gate*) (HBO)
Peter Reigert (*Barbarians at the Gate*) (HBO)
Maximillian Schell (*Stalin*) (HBO)

SUPPORTING ACTRESS (SPECIAL OR MINI-SERIES)
Ann-Margret (*Alex Haley's "Queen"*) (CBS)
Lee Grant (*Citizen Cohn*) (HBO)

Peggy McCay (*Woman on the Run: The Lawrencia Bembeneck Story*) (NBC)
Mary Tyler Moore (*Stolen Babies*) (Lifetime)
Joan Plowright (*Stalin*) (HBO)

This was Mary Tyler Moore's eighth Emmy, tying her with Dinah Shore for the most awards won by a performer. In the Lifetime original film *Stealing Babies*, Moore played the devious head of a shady adpotion agency—quite a change of pace from Laura Petrie and Mary Richards.

SUPPORTING ACTOR (DRAMA SERIES)
Barry Corbin (*Northern Exposure*) (CBS)
John Cullum (*Northern Exposure*) (CBS)
Chad Lowe (*Life Goes On*) (ABC)
Fyvush Finkel (*Picket Fences*) (CBS)
Dean Stockwell (*Quantum Leap*) (NBC)

SUPPORTING ACTRESS (DRAMA SERIES)
Mary Alice (*I'll Fly Away*) (NBC)
Cynthia Geary (*Northern Exposure*) (CBS)
Kay Lenz (*Reasonable Doubts*) (NBC)
Kellie Martin (*Life Goes On*) (ABC)
Peg Phillips (*Northern Exposure*) (CBS)

SUPPORTING ACTOR (COMEDY SERIES)
Jason Alexander (*Seinfeld*) (NBC)
Michael Jeter (*Evening Shade*) (CBS)
Michael Richards (*Seinfeld*) (NBC)
Jeffrey Tambor (*The Larry Sanders Show*) (HBO)
Rip Torn (*The Larry Sanders Show*) (HBO)

SUPPORTING ACTRESS (COMEDY SERIES)
Shelley Fabares (*Coach*) (ABC)
Sara Gilbert (*Roseanne*) (ABC)
Julia Louis-Dreyfus (*Seinfeld*) (NBC)
Laurie Metcalfe (*Roseanne*) (ABC)
Rhea Perlman (*Cheers*) (NBC)

INDIVIDUAL PERFORMER (VARIETY OR MUSIC)
Dana Carvey (*Saturday Night Live's Presidential Bash*) (NBC)
Cirque du Soleil (*The Tonight Show with Jay Leno*) (NBC)

Billy Crystal (*The 65th Annual Academy Awards*) (ABC)
Liza Minnelli (*Liza Minnelli Live from Radio City Music Hall*) (PBS)
Lily Tomlin (*The Search for Signs of Intelligent Life in the Universe*) (Showtime)

GUEST PERFORMERS
Actor (Drama Series): Laurence Fishburne ("The Box," *Tribeca*) (Fox); Actress (Drama Series): Elaine Stritch ("Point of View," *Law & Order*) (NBC); Actor (Comedy Series): David Clennon ("For Peter's Sake," *Dream On*) (HBO); Actress (Comedy Series): Tracey Ullman ("The Prima Dava," *Love and War*) (CBS)

DAYTIME AWARDS
Drama Series: *All My Children* (ABC); Actor: Michael Zaslow (*Guiding Light*) (CBS); Actress: Hillary B. Smith (*One Life To Live*) (ABC); Supporting Actor: Justin Deas (*Guiding Light*) (CBS); Supporting Actress: Susan Haskell (*One Life To Live*) (ABC); Talk/Service Show: *The Oprah Winfrey Show* (Syndicated)

OTHER PRIME-TIME AWARDS
Directing (Special or Mini-Series): James Sadwith (*Sinatra*) (CBS); Directing (Drama Series): Barry Levinson ("Gone for Goode," *Homicide: Life on the Streets*) (NBC); Directing (Comedy Series): Betty Thomas ("For Peter's Sake," *Dream On*) (HBO); Directing (Variety or Music Program): Walter C. Miller (*The 1992 Tony Awards*) (CBS)

Writing (Special or Mini-Series): Jane Anderson (*The Positively True Adventures of the Alleged Texas Cheerleader-Murdering Mom*) (HBO); Writing (Drama Series): Tom Fontana ("Three Men and Adena," *Homicide: Life on the Streets*) (NBC); Writing (Comedy Series): Larry David ("The Contest," *Seinfled*) (NBC); Writing (Variety or Music Program): Judd Apatow, Robert Cohen, David Cross, Brent Forrester, Jeff Kahn, Bruce Kirschbaum, Bob Odenkirk, Sultan Pepper, Dino Stamatopoulos, Ben Stiller (*The Ben Stiller Show*) (Fox)

In order to counteract the trashy sexual innuendos of the 1991–92 ceremony and the Quayle-bashing of 1992–93, the Academy decided to "go for class" with the 1993–94 Emmys. Don Mischer, producer of the prestigous Kennedy Center Honors and three Tony Awards shows, was hired to spiff up the ceremonies. Angela Lansbury, who had emceed all three of the Mischer Tony outings, smoothly handled the hostessing chores. La Lansbury never lost her cool, though she lost as Actress (Drama Series) in *Murder, She Wrote* for the thirteenth time. To redress recent criticism of TV as being too violent and sexual, she delivered a sermon on the medium as "life-enhancing" and "capable of nourishing our minds and spirits."

Comedienne Paula Poundstone balanced Lansbury's high-minded elegance by taking the viewing audience on a crazy backstage tour.

While the program itself proceeded relatively calmly, a backstage drama among the networks was raging. After Fox's four-year contract with the Academy to broadcast the awards expired, ABC immediately snatched up the ratings-grabbing ceremony for another four years. Fox, CBS, and NBC were furious because all four of the webs had agreed to negotiate for a rotation deal. Executives and employees from the three shut-out networks boycotted the awards. ABC agreed to cancel the exclusive deal after the 1993–94 Emmys and renegotiate to share the show with the others. Thereafter, the lucky web to get the right to telecast the accolades (and usually win the ratings race that night) was chosen by lottery. Ironically, the winner in 1994–95 was Fox and in 1995–96 was ABC.

THE PEABODY AWARDS (FOR 1993)

Animaniacs (Steven Spielberg and Amblin Entertainment); *Facing Reality: Politics, Drugs, and Waste* (WWL-TV, New Orleans); "Scarred for Life," *Day One* (ABC News); *Under the Influence* (WKRN-TV, Nashville); Robert Bazell for health and science reporting on NBC News; *Chuck Kraemer Reporting* (WCVB-TV, Boston); *Good Morning, Miss Toliver* (Fase Productions); *The New Explorers* (WTTW-TV, Chicago, and Kurtis Productions); Fox Children's Network and Churchill Entertainment, Ltd., Los Angeles, for a public service campaign about racial, gender, and general differences; *I Am a Promise* (HBO and Video Verte Films); *The Nineties* (BBC South, Bristol England); *Silverlake Life* (POV, Silverlake

Productions); *Angels of Change* (WTVM-TV, Birmingham, AL); "The CIA's Cocaine," *60 Minutes* (CBS News); *Kate and Eilish: Siamese Twins* (Yorkshire Television, Yorkshire, England, The Discovery Channel); *Homicide: Life on the Streets* (NBC); *The Ernest Green Story* (AML and The Disney Channel); *American Masters: Paul Simon* (Channel 13/WNET); *Mystery Science Theatre 3000* (Best Brains, Inc., and Comedy Central); *Prime Suspect* (Granada Television, England, and WGBH-TV, Boston); *The Larry Sanders Show* (HBO); The Discovery Network; CNN correspondent Christiane Amanpour for coverage of Bosnia and other world crises

THE GOLDEN GLOBE AWARDS (FOR 1993)

Made-for-TV Movie or Mini-Series: *Barbarians at the Gate* (HBO); Drama Series: *NYPD Blue* (ABC); Comedy Series: *Seinfeld* (NBC)

Actor (Made-for-TV Movie/Mini-Series): James Garner (*Barbarians at the Gate*) (HBO); Actress (Made-for-TV Movie/Mini-Series): Bette Midler (*Gypsy*) (CBS); Actor (Drama Series): David Caruso (*NYPD Blue*) (ABC); Actress (Drama Series): Kathy Baker (*Picket Fences*) (CBS); Actor (Comedy Series): Jerry Seinfeld (*Seinfeld*) (NBC); Actress (Comedy Series): Helen Hunt (*Mad about You*) (NBC); Supporting Actor: Beau Bridges (*The Positively True Adventures of the Alleged Texas Cheerleader-Murdering Mom*) (HBO); Supporting Actress: Julia Louis-Dreyfus (*Seinfeld*) (NBC)

THE CABLE ACE AWARDS (FOR 1993)

Movie/Mini-Series: *The Positively True Adventures of the Alleged Texas Cheerleader-Murdering Mom* (HBO); Dramatic/Theatrical Special: *The Search for Signs of Intelligent Life in the Universe* (Showtime); Drama Series: *Avonlea* (The Disney Channel); Comedy Series: *The Larry Sanders Show* (HBO)

Actor (Movie/Mini-Series): Brian Dennehy (*Foreign Affairs*) (TNT); Actress (Movie/Mini-Series): Holly Hunter (*The Positively True Adventures . . .*) (HBO); Actor (Drama Series): Gary Oldman (*Fallen Angels: Dead End for Delia*); Actress (Drama Series): Mariangela Pino (*The*

Showtime 30-Minute Movie: Evening Cross) (Showtime); Actor (Comedy Series): Rip Torn (*The Larry Sanders Show*) (HBO); Actress (Comedy Series): Wendy Malick (*Dream On*) (HBO); Supporting Actor (Movie/Mini-Series): Maximillian Schell (*Stalin*) (HBO); Supporting Actress (Movie/Mini-Series): Juanita Jennings (*Laurel Avenue*) (HBO)

THE EMMY AWARDS

TV-MOVIE
And the Band Played On (HBO)
Breathing Lessons, Hallmark Hall of Fame (CBS)
Gypsy (CBS)
A Place for Annie (ABC)
To Dance with the White Dog,
   Hallmark Hall of Fame (CBS)

Producer Aaron Spelling dedicated the Emmy he won for *And the Band Played On* to Randy Shilts, who had died of AIDS earlier that year. Shilts wrote the book upon which the HBO film was based. Featuring an all-star cast (Steve Martin, Lily Tomlin, Richard Gere, and Alan Alda were just a few of the performers), it detailed the history of the AIDS epidemic.

DRAMA SERIES
Law & Order (NBC)
Northern Exposure (CBS)
NYPD Blue (ABC)
Picket Fences (CBS)
Star Trek: The Next Generation (Syndicated)

Picket Fences won for the second year in a row, though the favorite was an explosive new police drama *NYPD Blue* from producer-writer Steven Bochco. The ABC series was peppered with strong expletives and nudity. Some stations refused to carry it.

   NYPD Blue got the most nominations with twenty-six, breaking the record for most nominations in a single season. The previous record-maker was another Steven Bochco cop series *Hill Street Blues*, which garnered twenty-one nominations in 1980–81.

COMEDY SERIES
Frasier (NBC)
Home Improvement (ABC)
The Larry Sanders Show (HBO)
Mad about You (NBC)
Seinfeld (NBC)

Frasier starred Kelsey Grammer as a pompous psychologist with a Seattle phone-in radio show. Playing the same role on *Cheers*, he had been nominated twice for Supporting Actor (Comedy Series). He won twice when he played the lead.

MINI-SERIES
Armistead Maupin's "Tales of the City,"
   American Playhouse (PBS)
Oldest Living Confederate Widow Tells All (CBS)
Prime Suspect 3, *Mystery!* (PBS)
Stephen King's The Stand (ABC)
World War II: When Lions Roared (NBC)

VARIETY, MUSIC OR COMEDY SPECIAL
Comic Relief VI (HBO)
The Kennedy Center Honors (CBS)
The 1994 Tony Awards (CBS)
The 66th Annual Academy Awards (ABC)
Tracey Ullman Takes on New York (HBO)

VARIETY, MUSIC OR COMEDY SERIES
Dennis Miller Live (HBO)
The Late Show with David Letterman (CBS)
MTV Unplugged (MTV)
Saturday Night Live (NBC)
The Tonight Show with Jay Leno) (NBC)

David Letterman transferred his cutting edge wit and sardonic take on talk shows from NBC to CBS and won the Emmy for his first year on his new network. He thanked "everyone drawing breath at this moment."

ACTOR (SPECIAL OR MINI-SERIES)
Michael Caine (*World War II:*
   When Lions Roared) (NBC)
Hume Cronyn (*To Dance with the White Dog,*
   Hallmark Hall of Fame) (CBS)
James Garner (*Breathing Lessons,*
   Hallmark Hall of Fame) (CBS)

Matthew Modine (*And the Band Played On*) (HBO)
Sam Waterston (*I'll Fly Away: Then and Now*) (PBS)

ACTRESS (SPECIAL OR MINI-SERIES)
Kirstie Alley (*David's Mother*) (CBS)
Bette Midler (*Gypsy*) (CBS)
Helen Mirren (*Prime Suspect 3, Mystery!*) (PBS)
Jessica Tandy (*To Dance with the White Dog, Hallmark Hall of Fame*) (CBS)
Joanne Woodward (*Breathing Lessons, Hallmark Hall of Fame*) (CBS)

One of the high points of the 1993–94 Emmys was a tribute to previous winner Jessica Tandy (*Foxire*, 1987–88) who died the day of the ceremony. Though she lost this year to Kirstie Alley in the Actress (Special or Mini-Series) category, her husband Hume Cronyn won. Ironically, Cronyn's performance in *To Dance with the White Dog* was as a man whose wife dies.

ACTOR (DRAMA SERIES)
David Caruso (*NYPD Blue*) (ABC)
Peter Falk (*Columbo*) (ABC)
Dennis Franz (*NYPD Blue*) (ABC)
Michael Moriarty (*Law & Order*) (NBC)
Tom Skerritt (*Picket Fences*) (CBS)

"What a shocker," Dennis Franz told reporters after being named outstanding Actor (Drama Series) for his tough, sometimes alcoholic Detective Sipowicz on *NYPD Blue*. The expected winner had been David Caruso, the actor who played his partner and who had recently announced he was leaving the series in order to persue a movie career. Caruso did not attend the Emmys. Caruso's films have failed at the box office, but *NYPD Blue* continues to be a hit. He was replaced by Jimmy Smits, an Emmy winner from yet another Bochco series *LA Law*.

ACTRESS (DRAMA SERIES)
Kathy Baker (*Picket Fences*) (CBS)
Swoosie Kurtz (*Sisters*) (NBC)
Angela Lansbury (*Murder, She Wrote*) (CBS)
Jane Seymour (*Dr. Quinn, Medicine Woman*) (CBS)
Sela Ward (*Sisters*) (NBC)

This year Angela Lansbury tied with Susan Lucci of ABC's daytime drama *All My Children* for the most Emmy nominations without a win at fourteen each.

ACTOR (COMEDY SERIES)
John Goodman (*Roseanne*) (ABC)
Kelsey Grammer (*Frasier*) (NBC)
John Larroquette (*The John Larroquette Show*) (NBC)
Paul Reiser (*Mad about You*) (NBC)
Jerry Seinfeld (*Seinfeld*) (NBC)

If David Caruso was the spoilsport of the '93–'94 Emmys, Tim Allen was Mr. Congeniality. The star of *Home Improvement* was not nominated for Actor (Comedy Series) because his staff failed to mail in his request for nomination by the deadline. He presented an award anyway, rushing in out of breath. "I almost didn't make it," he said, panting heavily. "My staff forgot to tell me what night it was."

ACTRESS (COMEDY SERIES)
Candice Bergen (*Murphy Brown*) (CBS)
Helen Hunt (*Mad about You*) (NBC)
Annie Potts (*Love & War*) (CBS)
Patricia Richardson (*Home Improvement*) (ABC)
Roseanne (*Roseanne*) (CBS)

SUPPORTING ACTOR (SPECIAL OR MINI-SERIES)
Alan Alda (*And the Band Played On*) (HBO)
Matthew Broderick (*A Life in the Theatre*) (TNT)
Richard Gere (*And the Band Played On*) (HBO)
Michael Goorjian (*David's Mother*) (CBS)
Ian McKellen (*And the Band Played On*) (HBO)

SUPPORTING ACTRESS (SPECIAL OR MINI-SERIES)
Anne Bancroft (*Oldest Living Confederate Widow Tells All*) (CBS)
Swoosie Kurtz (*And the Band Played On*) (HBO)
Lee Purcell (*Secret Sins of the Father*) (NBC)
Lily Tomlin (*And the Band Played On*) (HBO)
Cicely Tyson (*Oldest Living Confederate Widow Tells All*) (CBS)

SUPPORTING ACTOR (DRAMA SERIES)
Gordon Clapp (*NYPD Blue*) (ABC)
Barry Corbin (*Northern Exposure*) (CBS)
Fyvush Finkel (*Picket Fences*) (CBS)
Nick Turturro (*NYPD Blue*) (ABC)
Ray Walston (*Picket Fences*) (CBS)

SUPPORTING ACTRESS (DRAMA SERIES)
Amy Brenneman (*NYPD Blue*) (ABC)
Jill Eikenberry (*LA Law*) (NBC)
Sharon Lawrence (*NYPD Blue*) (ABC)
Gail O'Grady (*NYPD Blue*) (ABC)
Leigh Taylor-Young (*Picket Fences*) (CBS)

SUPPORTING ACTOR (COMEDY SERIES)
Jason Alexander (*Seinfeld*) (NBC)
David Hyde Pierce (*Frasier*) (NBC)
Michael Richards (*Seinfeld*) (NBC)
Rip Torn (*The Larry Sanders Show*) (HBO)
Jerry Van Dyke (*Coach*) (ABC)

SUPPORTING ACTRESS (COMEDY SERIES)
Shelley Fabares (*Coach*) (ABC)
Faith Ford (*Murphy Brown*) (CBS)
Sara Gilbert (*Roseanne*) (ABC)
Julia Louis-Dreyfuss (*Seinfeld*) (NBC)
Laurie Metcalfe (*Roseanne*) (ABC)
Liz Torres (*The John Larroquette Show*) (NBC)

INDIVIDUAL PERFORMER (VARIETY, MUSIC OR COMEDY)
Whoopi Goldberg (*The 66th Annual Academy Awards*) (ABC)
Phil Hartman (*Saturday Night Live*) (NBC)
Mike Myers (*Saturday Night Live*) (NBC)
Lily Tomlin (*Growing Up Funny*) (Lifetime)
Tracey Ullman (*Tracey Ullman Takes on New York*) (HBO)

GUEST PERFORMERS
Actor (Drama Series): Richard Kiley ("Buried Alive," *Picket Fences*) (CBS); Actress (Drama Series): Faye Dunaway ("It's All in the Game," *Columbo*) (ABC); Actor (Comedy Series): Martin Sheen ("Angst for the Memories," *Murphy Brown*) (CBS); Actress (Comedy Series): Eileen Heckart ("You Make Me Feel So Young," *Love & War*) (CBS)

DAYTIME AWARDS
Drama Series: *General Hospital* (ABC); Actor (Drama Series): Justin Deas (*Guiding Light*) (CBS); Actress (Daytime Drama): Erika Slezak (*One Life To Live*) (ABC); Supporting Actor (Drama Series): Jerry Van Dorn (*Guiding Light*) (CBS); Supporting Actress (Drama Series): Rena Sofer (*General Hospital*) (ABC); Game Show: *Jeopardy!* (Syndicated); Talk/Service Show: *The Oprah Winfrey Show* (Syndicated)

OTHER PRIME-TIME AWARDS
Directing (TV-Movie or Mini-Series): John Frankenheimer (*Against the Wall*) (HBO); Directing (Drama Series): Daniel Sackheim ("Tempest in a C-Cup," *NYPD Blue*) (ABC); Directing (Comedy Series): James Burrows ("The Good Son," *Frasier*) (NBC); Directing (Variety, Music or Comedy Program): Walter C. Miller (*The 1994 Tony Awards*) (CBS)

Writing (TV-Movie or Mini-Series): Bob Randall (*David's Mother*) (CBS); Writing (Drama Series): Ann Biderman ("Steroid Boy," *NYPD Blue*) (ABC); Writing (Comedy Series): David Angell, Peter Casey, David Lee ("The Good Son," *Frasier*) (NBC); Writing (Comedy, Music or Variety Program): Jeff Cesario, Mike Dugan, Eddie Feldmann, Greg Greenberg, Dennis Miller, Kevin Rooney (*Dennis Miller Live*) (HBO)

Just as Paula Poundstone did the year before, co-hostess Ellen DeGeneres broke up the monotony of awards and tributes with a whirlwind backstage tour of the Emmy site, the Pasadena Civic Auditorium. She went into the balcony, outdoors to the bleachers, to the directors' truck, and to the press-room, dispensing quips and gags as she went. Co-hostess Patricia Richardson of *Home Improvement* was pretty much upstaged. Musical entertainment was provided by Bette Midler, who opened the show with a medley of songs from *Gypsy*, and Jason Alexander of *Seinfeld*, who along with an a cappella quartet sang a medley of old TV themes from *All in the Family* to *Flipper*.

Variety missed the nasty, trashy fun of previous years, calling the program "smooth, if dull, sailing."

THE PEABODY AWARDS (FOR 1994)

ER (NBC); *Armistead Maupin's "Tales of the City,"* *American Playhouse* (Channel 4, London); *Frasier* (NBC); *MTV Unplugged* (MTV); *Mad about You* (NBC); *Barbra Streisand: The Concert* (HBO); *Moon Shot* (Turner Entertainment Network); *Nick News* (Nickelodeon); "Rush to Read," *Prime Time Live* (ABC); *D-Day, CBS Reports* (CBS News); *Rwanda* (KGO-TV, San Francisco); *The Atomic Bombshell* (KSEE-TV, Fresno, CA); *Fat Chance* (National Film Board of Canada); *Sewer Solvent Scandal* (KGAN-TV, Cedar Rapids, IA); "The Battle of the Bulge," "FDR," and "Malcolm X: Make It Plain," all broadcast on *The American Experience* (WGBH-TV, Boston); *Normandy: The Great Crusade* (Discovery Communications, Bethesda, MD); "The Hunger Inside," *20/20* (ABC News); *Just Because: Tales of Violence, Dreams of Peace* (KSBW-TV, Salinas, CA); *China: Beyond the Clouds* (WETA, Washington, DC, and Channel 4, London); *Buddy Check 12* (WTLV-TV, Jacksonville, FL); *Reflections on Elephants* (National Geographic Television, for the Public Broadcasting Service); *Fourways Farm* (Channel 4, London); *Kids against Child Abuse* (CBS)

THE GOLDEN GLOBE AWARDS (FOR 1994)

TV-Movie or Mini-Series: *The Burning Season* (HBO); Drama Series: *The X-Files* (Fox); Comedy or Musical Series (tie): *Frasier* (NBC) and *Mad about You* (NBC)

Actor (TV-Movie/Mini-Series): Raul Julia (*The Burning Season*) (HBO); Actress (TV-Movie/Mini-Series): Joanne Woodward (*Breathing Lessons, Hallmark Hall of Fame*) (CBS); Actor (Drama Series): Dennis Franz (*NYPD Blue*) (ABC); Actress (Drama Series): Claire Danes (*My So-Called Life*) (ABC); Actor (Comedy or Musical Series): Tim Allen (*Home Improvement*) (ABC); Actress (Comedy or Musical Series): Helen Hunt (*Mad about You*) (NBC); Supporting Actor: Edward James Olmos (*The Burning Season*) (HBO); Supporting Actress: Miranda Richardson (*Fatherland*) (HBO)

THE CABLE ACE AWARDS (FOR 1994)

Movie/Mini-Series: *Cracker: To Say I Love You* (A&E); Dramatic/Theatrical Special: *A Life in the Theatre* (TNT); Drama Series: *Avonlea* (The Disney Channel); Comedy Series: *The Larry Sanders Show* (HBO)

Actor (Movie/Mini-Series): Robbie Coltrane (*Cracker: To Say I Love You*) (A&E); Actress (Movie/Mini-Series): Amy Madigan (*And Then There Was One*) (Lifetime); Actor (Drama Series): David Packer (*Big Al*) (Showtime); Actress (Drama Series): Glenda Jackson (*The South Bank Show: The Secret of Arnold Bax*) (Bravo); Actor (Comedy Series): Rip Torn (*The Larry Sanders Show*) (HBO); Actress (Comedy Series): Denny Dillon (*Dream On*) (HBO); Supporting Actor (Movie/Mini-Series): Ian McKellen (*And the Band Played On*) (HBO); Supporting Actress (Movie/Mini-Series): Ja'Net DuBois (*Other Women's Children*) (Lifetime)

THE EMMY AWARDS

TV-MOVIE
The Burning Season (HBO)
Citizen X (HBO)
Indictment: The McMartin Trial (HBO)
The Piano Lesson, Hallmark Hall of Fame (CBS)
Serving in Silence: The Margarethe Cammermeyer Story (NBC)

DRAMA SERIES
Chicago Hope (CBS)
ER (NBC)
Law & Order (NBC)
NYPD Blue (ABC)
The X-Files (Fox)

In 1993–94, sophomore show *Picket Fences* won the Drama Series award over the more heavily favored freshman *NYPD Blue* despite more than twenty nominations for the jagged-edge cop show. In an odd case of Emmy symmetry, *NYPD Blue* was named best drama series in 1994–95, but at the expense of hot new medical show *ER* despite twenty-three nominations for the latter program. *ER*'s double-digit nomination count places it second after *NYPD* (twenty-six in 1993–94) for most nominations in a single season.

COMEDY SERIES
Frasier (NBC)
Friends (NBC)
The Larry Sanders Show (HBO)
Mad about You (NBC)
Seinfeld (NBC)

MINI-SERIES
Buffalo Girls (CBS)
Children of the Dust (CBS)
Joseph (TNT)
Martin Chuzzlewit, Masterpiece Theatre (PBS)
A Woman of Independent Means (NBC)

VARIETY, MUSIC OR COMEDY SERIES
The Late Show with David Letterman (CBS)
The Tonight Show with Jay Leno (NBC)
Dennis Miller Live (HBO)
Politically Incorrect with Bill Maher (Comedy Central)
MTV Unplugged (MTV)

When Jay Leno took over NBC's *The Tonight Show* from Johnny Carson, public sentiment was against him. His material was bad and he was losing ratings to David Letterman on CBS. In his second year, he had fired his producer, improved his routines, and was beginning to make headway with audiences. When he won the Emmy, he joked, "I guess this means HBO's gotta shoot a new ending for that movie." He was referring to a TV-movie version of *The Late Shift*, a tell-all book of the battle between Letterman and Leno which ended with the big-chinned comic still in the ratings basement.

VARIETY, MUSIC OR COMEDY SPECIAL
The American Film Institute Salute to Steven Spielberg (NBC)
Barbra Streisand: The Concert (HBO)
A Comedy Salute to Andy Kaufman (NBC)
Eagles: Hell Freezes Over (MTV)
The 67th Annual Academy Awards (ABC)

In another case of Emmy symmetry, HBO's television recording of Barbra Streisand's concert tour won five awards. It was thirty years ago that her first special, *My Name Is Barbra*, also grabbed a quintet of Emmys.

ACTOR (TV MOVIE OR MINI-SERIES)
Charles S. Dutton (*The Piano Lesson, Hallmark Hall of Fame*) (CBS)
John Goodman (*Kingfish: The Story of Huey P. Long*) (TNT)
Raul Julia (*The Burning Season*) (HBO)
John Lithgow (*My Brother's Keeper*) (CBS)
James Woods (*Indictment: The McMartin Trial*) (HBO)

ACTRESS (TV MOVIE OR MINI-SERIES)
Glenn Close (*Serving in Silence: The Margarethe Cammermeyer Story*) (NBC)
Sally Field (*A Woman of Independent Means*) (NBC)
Anjelica Huston (*Buffalo Girls*) (CBS)
Diane Keaton (*Amelia Earhart: The Final Flight*) (TNT)
Alfred Woodard (*The Piano Lesson, Hallmark Hall of Fame*) (CBS)

Earlier in the year, Glenn Close had copped the Tony Award as Outstanding Actress in a Musical for *Sunset Boulevard*. With her Emmy-winning performance as a lesbian medical officer who takes on the military's anti-gay policy in *Serving in Silence: The Margarethe Cammermeyer Story*, she became the first actress to take top honors in theater and television in the same year. Michael Moriarty was the first actor in 1973–74 for *The Glass Menagerie* [Supporting Actor (Drama) Emmy] and *Find Your Way Home* [Actor (Play) Tony].

ACTOR (DRAMA SERIES)
George Clooney (*ER*) (NBC)
Anthony Edwards (*ER*) (NBC)
Dennis Franz (*NYPD Blue*) (ABC)
Mandy Patinkin (*Chicago Hope*) (CBS)
Jimmy Smits (*NYPD Blue*) (ABC)

Mandy Patinkin, a Tony winner for *Evita* in 1979–80, was the only Emmy recipient from *Chicago Hope*, a CBS hospital drama which was not given a good prognosis for prolonged life when

Candice Bergen won a record five Emmys as *Murphy Brown* **while Colleen Dewhurst nabbed two for guest appearances as her mother.**

it lost the ratings battle opposite NBC's grittier *ER*. *Chicago* switched time periods, gained a new audience, and was renewed for another year. But Patinkin would not be back. Before winning his Emmy, the Broadway actor/singer had announced he was leaving the series. It seemed TV was more demanding of his time than the stage and he wanted to spend more time with his family.

ACTRESS (DRAMA SERIES)
Kathy Baker (*Picket Fences*) (CBS)
Claire Danes (*My So-Called Life*) (ABC)
Angela Lansbury (*Murder, She Wrote*) (CBS)
Sherry Stringfield (*ER*) (NBC)
Cicely Tyson (*Sweet Justice*) (NBC)

ACTOR (COMEDY SERIES)
John Goodman (*Roseanne*) (ABC)
Kelsey Grammer (*Frasier*) (NBC)

Paul Reiser (*Mad about You*) (NBC)
Jerry Seinfeld (*Seinfeld*) (NBC)
Garry Shandling (*The Larry Sanders Show*) (HBO)

ACTRESS (COMEDY SERIES)
Candice Bergen (*Murphy Brown*) (CBS)
Ellen DeGeneres (*Ellen*) (ABC)
Helen Hunt (*Mad about You*) (NBC)
Roseanne (*Roseanne*) (ABC)
Cybill Shepherd (*Cybill*)

With this fifth Emmy win, Candice Bergen set a record for the most awards for playing the same leading character on the same series. Edward Asner had won five for his Lou Grant character—three supporting Emmys for *The Mary Tyler Moore Show* and two leading awards for the eponymous spin-off. Don Knotts and Art Carney also won a quintet of Emmys apiece, but in the supporting category.

SUPPORTING ACTOR
(TV MOVIE OR MINI-SERIES)
Jeffrey De Munn (*Citizen X*) (HBO)
Sam Elliott (*Buffalo Girls*) (CBS)
Ben Kingsley (*Joseph*) (TNT)
Donald Sutherland (*Citizen X*) (HBO)
Edward James Olmos (*The Burning Season*) (HBO)

SUPPORTING ACTRESS (TV MOVIE OR
MINI-SERIES) (TIE)
Sonia Braga (*The Burning Season*) (HBO)
Judy Davis (*Serving in Silence: The Margarethe Cammermeyer Story*) (NBC)
Shirley Knight (*Indictment: The McMartin Trial*) (HBO)
Sissy Spacek (*The Good Old Boys*) (TNT)
Sada Thompson (*Indictment: The McMartin Trial*) (HBO)

SUPPORTING ACTOR (DRAMA SERIES)
Hector Elizondo (*Chicago*) (CBS)
James Earl Jones (*Under One Roof*) (CBS)
Eriq La Salle (*ER*) (NBC)
Ray Walston (*Picket Fences*) (CBS)
Noah Wylie (*ER*) (NBC)

"I have thirty seconds to tell you that I've been waiting sixty years to get up on this stage," a beaming Ray Walston informed the Emmy audience. Although he had won a Tony for the original production of *Damn Yankees* in 1956, Walston was best known as a whimsical extra-terrestial on the silly '60s' sitcom *My Favorite Martian*. That is, until he landed the role of the irrascible Judge Bone, who often delivered the moral of each episode of *Picket Fences*.

The year before, his co-star Fyvush Finkel made a similar acceptance speech: "I waited 51 years to get on this stage."

SUPPORTING ACTRESS
(DRAMA SERIES)
Barbara Babcock (*Dr. Quinn, Medicine Woman*) (CBS)
Tyne Daly (*Christy*) (CBS)
Sharon Lawrence (*NYPD Blue*) (ABC)
Juliana Marguiles (*ER*) (NBC)
Gail O'Grady (*NYPD Blue*) (ABC)

SUPPORTING ACTOR
(COMEDY SERIES)
Jason Alexander (*Seinfeld*) (NBC)
David Hyde Pierce (*Frasier*) (NBC)
Michael Richards (*Seinfeld*) (NBC)
David Schwimmer (*Friends*) (NBC)
Rip Torn (*The Larry Sanders Show*) (HBO)

SUPPORTING ACTRESS
(COMEDY SERIES)
Christine Baranski (*Cybill*) (CBS)
Lisa Kudrow (*Friends*) (NBC)
Julia Louis-Dreyfus (*Seinfeld*) (NBC)
Laurie Metcalf (*Roseanne*) (ABC)
Liz Torres (*The John Larroquette Show*) (NBC)

INDIVIDUAL PERFORMER
(VARIETY OR MUSIC)
Julie Andrews (*The Sound of Julie Andrews*) (Disney Channel)
Carol Burnett (*Men, Movies, and Carol*) (CBS)
Dennis Miller (*Dennis Miller Live*) (HBO)
Barbra Streisand (*Barbra Streisand: The Concert*) (HBO)
Tracey Ullman (*Women of the Night*) (HBO)

GUEST PERFORMERS
Actor (Drama): Paul Winfield ("Enemy Lines," *Picket Fences*) (CBS); Actress (Drama): Shirley Knight ("Large Mouth Bass," *NYPD Blue*) (ABC); Actor (Comedy): Carl Reiner ("The Alan Brady Show," *Mad about You*) (NBC); Actress (Comedy): Cyndi Lauper ("Money Changes Everything," *Mad about You*) (NBC)

DAYTIME AWARDS
Drama Series: *General Hospital* (ABC); Actor: Justin Deas (*Guiding Light*) (CBS); Actress: Erika Slezak (*One Life To Live*) (ABC); Supporting Actor: Jerry Van Dorn (*Guiding Light*) (CBS); Supporting Actress: Rena Sofer (*General Hospital*) (ABC); Game Show: *Jeopardy!* (Syndicated); Talk/Service Show: *The Oprah Winfrey Show* (Syndicated)

OTHER PRIME-TIME AWARDS
Directing (TV-Movie or Mini-Series): John Frankenheimer (*The Burning Season*) (HBO);

Directing (Drama Series): Mimi Leder ("Love's Labor Lost," *ER*) (NBC); Directing (Comedy Series): David Lee ("The Matchmaker," *Frasier*) (NBC); Directing (Variety or Music Program): Jeff Margolis (*The 67th Annual Academy Awards*) (ABC)

Writing (TV-Movie or Mini-Series): Alison Cross (*Serving in Silence: The Margarethe Cammermeyer Story*) (NBC); Writing (Drama Series): Lance A. Gentile ("Love's Labor Lost," *ER*) (NBC); Writing (Comedy Series): Chuck Ranberg, Anne Flett-Giordano ("An Affair To Remember," *Frasier*) (NBC); Writing (Variety or Music Program): Eddie Feldmann, writing supervisor, Jeff Cesario, Ed Driscoll, David Feldman, Gregory Greenberg, Dennis Miller, Kevin Rooney, writers (*Dennis Miller Live*) (HBO)

Cybill Shepherd and Jason Alexander took an irreverent attitude toward their roles as Emmy hosts. They began by handing out appetizers as if they were at a party. Later in the program, Alexander departed from the script, declaring his prepared material "lame," and went into the audience to ad-lib. He kidded multiple winner Barbra Streisand. "Would it have killed her to do a number?" he asked. "Bette Midler sang last year." Since Streisand was not in a chirping mood, the nominee from *Seinfeld* warbled a medley of old TV theme songs with an a cappella quartet (just as he did the year before).

Like Paula Poundstone and Ellen DeGeneres before her, Shepherd conducted a backstage tour—and wound up in a food fight with the caterer of the post-Emmy gala. "The two kept the proceedings fast-paced and funny," *TV Guide* exuded, giving the program a "Cheers" on the magazine's "Cheers and Jeers" page. Eric Mink of the *New York Daily News* called it "one of the best Emmy Awards in memory."

THE PEABODY AWARDS (FOR 1995)

Homicide: Life on the Streets (NBC); CBS News for its coverage of the assassination of Israeli Prime Minister Yitzhak Rabin; three local Oklahoma City stations for coverage of the Oklahoma City terrorist bombing; Barbara Walters for her interview with Christopher Reeve; Oprah Winfrey; *Hoop Dreams* (PBS); *Kevin's Sentence* (Canadian Broadcasting Company); *Wynton Marsalis: Making the Music: Marsalis on Music* (PBS); *The Peary Investigation* (WFAA-TV, Dallas, TX); "Truth on Trial," *20/20* (ABC News); *Target Seven: Armed and Angry* (WXYZ-TV, Detroit); *New York City School Corruption* (WCBS-TV, New York); *50 Years after the War* (Television Broadcasts, Ltd., Kowloon, Hong Kong); *The Dying Rooms* (Channel 4, London, Cinemax, New York); *Road Scholar* (PBS); *Rock and Roll* (WGBH-TV, Boston); *Peter Jennings Reporting: Hiroshima: Why the Bomb Was Dropped* (ABC News); *Yugoslavia: Death of a Nation* (The Discovery Channel); *CBS Reports: In the Killing Fields of America* (CBS News); *Complaints of a Dutiful Daughter* (PBS); *Hank Aaron: Chasing the Dream* (Turner Original Productions); *The Private Life of Plants* (Turner Original Productions); *Coming Out Under Fire* (PBS); *Wallace and Gromit* (Aardman Animations); *Frontline: Waco: The Inside Story* (WGBH-TV, Boston)

THE GOLDEN GLOBE AWARDS (FOR 1995)

Made-for-TV Movie or Mini-Series: *Indictment: The McMartin Trial* (HBO); Drama Series: *Party of Five* (Fox); Comedy or Musical Series: *Cybill* (CBS)

Actor (TV Movie/Mini-Series): Gary Sinise (*Truman*) (HBO); Actress (TV Movie/Mini-Series): Jessica Lange (*A Streetcar Named Desire*) (CBS); Actor (Drama Series): Jimmy Smits (*NYPD Blue*) (ABC); Actress (Drama Series): Jane Seymour (*Doctor Quinn, Medicine Woman*) (CBS); Actor (Comedy or Musical Series): Kelsey Grammer (*Frasier*) (NBC); Actress (Comedy or Musical Series): Cybill Shepherd (*Cybill*) (CBS); Supporting Actor: Donald Sutherland (*Citizen X*) (HBO); Supporting Actress: Shirley Knight (*Indictment: The McMartin Trial*) (HBO)

THE CABLE ACE AWARDS (FOR 1995)

Movie/Mini-Series: *Citizen X* (HBO); Dramatic/Theatrical Special: *Cosmic Slop: Space Traders* (HBO); Drama Series: *The Outer Limits* (Showtime); Comedy Series: *The Larry Sanders Show* (HBO)

Actor (Movie/Mini-Series): Raul Julia (*The Burning Season*) (HBO); Actress (Movie/Mini-

Series): Linda Hamilton (*A Mother's Prayer*) (USA); Actor (Drama Series/Special): John Hurt (*Picture Windows: Two Nudes Bathing*) (Showtime); Actress (Drama Series/Special): Paula Jai Parker (*Cosmic Slop: Tang*) (HBO); Actor (Comedy Series): Garry Shandling (*The Larry Sanders Show*) (HBO); Actress (Comedy Series): Wendie Malick (*Dream On*) (HBO); Supporting Actor (Movie/Mini-Series): Jeffrey DeMunn (*Citizen X*) (HBO); Supporting Actress (Movie/Mini-Series): Jean Marsh (*Fatherland*) (HBO).

1995-96

THE EMMY AWARDS

MADE-FOR-TELEVISION MOVIE
Almost Golden: The Jessica Savitch Story (Lifetime)
The Heidi Chronicles (TNT)
The Late Shift (HBO)
Truman (HBO)
Tuskegee Airmen (HBO)

Once again, cable dominated the TV-Movie and Mini-Series categories. All five of the telefilms and four out of the five mini-series nominees were from nonbroadcast networks. NBC took the most awards with twenty, but HBO made a strong showing in several major categories with fourteen prizes. In addition to taking awards for its telefilms about two very different world leaders, *Truman* and *Rasputin*, Home Box Office also won for Variety, Music or Comedy Series (*Dennis Miller Live*) and Supporting Actor (Comedy Series) (Rip Torn for *The Larry Sanders Show*).

DRAMA SERIES
Chicago Hope (CBS)
ER (NBC)
Law & Order (NBC)
NYPD Blue (ABC)
The X-Files (Fox)

COMEDY SERIES
Frasier (NBC)
Friends (NBC)
The Larry Sanders Show (HBO)

Mad about You (NBC)
Seinfeld (NBC)

MINI-SERIES
Andersonville (TNT)
Gulliver's Travels (NBC)
Hiroshima (Showtime)
Moses (TNT)
Pride and Prejudice (A&E)

VARIETY, MUSIC OR COMEDY SERIES
Dennis Miller Live (HBO)
The Late Show with David Letterman (CBS)
Muppets Tonight (ABC)
Politically Incorrect with Bill Maher (Comedy Central)
The Tonight Show with Jay Leno (NBC)

"If the Muppets win, Dennis Miller will kill himself," joked presenter Garry Shandling. Upon accepting his Emmy, the sharp-witted Miller retorted, "I guess Kermie is going to have to kill *himself*."

VARIETY, MUSIC OR COMEDY SPECIAL
The 68th Annual Academy Awards (ABC)
The Best of Tracey Takes On . . . (HBO)
Dennis Miller: Citizen Arcane (HBO)
The Kennedy Center Honors (CBS)
Sinatra: 80 Years My Way (ABC)

ACTOR (SPECIAL OR LIMITED SERIES)
Alec Baldwin (*A Streetcar Named Desire*) (CBS)
Beau Bridges (*Kissinger and Nixon*) (TNT)
Laurence Fishburne (*Tuskegee Airmen*) (HBO)
Alan Rickman (*Rasputin*) (HBO)
Gary Sinise (*Truman*) (HBO)

ACTRESS (SPECIAL OR LIMITED SERIES)
Ashley Judd (*Norma Jean and Marilyn*) (HBO)
Jessica Lange (*A Streetcar Named Desire*) (CBS)
Helen Mirren (*Prime Suspect: Scent of Darkness*) (PBS)
Mira Sorvino (*Norma Jean and Marilyn*) (HBO)
Sela Ward (*Almost Golden: The Jessica Savitch Story*) (Lifetime)

ACTOR (DRAMA SERIES)
Andre Braugher (*Homicide: Life on the Streets*) (NBC)
George Clooney (*ER*) (NBC)
Anthony Edwards (*ER*) (NBC)
Dennis Franz (*NYPD Blue*) (ABC)
Jimmy Smits (*NYPD Blue*) (ABC)

ACTRESS (DRAMA SERIES)
Gillian Anderson (*The X-Files*) (Fox)
Kathy Baker (*Picket Fences*) (CBS)
Christine Lahti (*Chicago Hope*) (CBS)
Angela Lansbury (*Murder, She Wrote*) (CBS)
Sherry Stringfield (*ER*) (NBC)

Angela Lansbury's last season as mystery author and amatuer detective Jessica Fletcher on *Murder, She Wrote* was not rewarded with an Emmy. Her record for the most nominations without a win (twelve for *Murder* and four for other TV work) remains unbroken. However, she does hold another record for the most wins—four Tonys for best Actress (Musical).

ACTOR (COMEDY SERIES)
Kelsey Grammer (*Frasier*) (NBC)
John Lithgow (*3rd Rock from the Sun*) (NBC)
Paul Reiser (*Mad about You*) (NBC)
Jerry Seinfeld (*Seinfeld*) (NBC)
Garry Shandling (*The Larry Sanders Show*) (HBO)

ACTRESS (COMEDY SERIES)
Ellen DeGeneres (*Ellen*) (ABC)
Fran Drescher (*The Nanny*) (CBS)
Helen Hunt (*Mad about You*) (NBC)
Patricia Richardson (*Home Improvement*) (ABC)
Cybill Shepherd (*Cybill*) (CBS)

SUPPORTING ACTOR (SPECIAL OR LIMITED SERIES)
Andre Braugher (*Tuskegee Airmen*) (HBO)
John Goodman (*A Streetcar Named Desire*) (CBS)
Tom Hulce (*The Heidi Chronicles*) (TNT)
Ian McKellen (*Rasputin*) (HBO)
Treat Williams (*The Late Shift*) (HBO)

Tom Hulce won his Emmy for *The Heidi Chronicles* as a gay pediatrician, the best friend of the lead character, a disillusioned feminist. Boyd

Gaines won a 1988–89 Tony for playing the same role in the stage version, which also won a Tony, the Pulitzer Prize, and the New York Drama Critics Circle Award for author Wendy Wasserstein.

SUPPORTING ACTRESS (SPECIAL OR LIMITED SERIES)
Kathy Bates (*The Late Shift*) (HBO)
Greta Scacchi (*Rasputin*) (HBO)
Diana Scarwid (*Truman*) (HBO)
Mare Winningham (*The Boys Next Door, Hallmark Hall of Fame*) (CBS)
Alfre Woodard (*Gulliver's Travels*) (NBC)

SUPPORTING ACTOR (DRAMA SERIES)
Hector Elizondo (*Chicago Hope*) (CBS)
James McDaniel (*NYPD Blue*) (ABC)
Stanley Tucci (*Murder One*) (ABC)
Ray Walston (*Picket Fences*) (CBS)
Noah Wylie (*ER*) (NBC)

SUPPORTING ACTRESS (DRAMA SERIES)
Barbara Bosson (*Murder One*) (ABC)
Tyne Daly (*Christy*) (CBS)
Sharon Lawrence (*NYPD Blue*) (ABC)
Julianna Marguiles (*ER*) (NBC)
Gail O'Grady (*NYPD Blue*) (ABC)

This Emmy for Tyne Daly, added to the four she won for *Cagney & Lacey*, made her the Academy's most honored dramatic actress.

SUPPORTING ACTOR (COMEDY SERIES)
Jason Alexander (*Seinfeld*) (NBC)
David Hyde Pierce (*Frasier*) (NBC)
Michael Richards (*Seinfeld*) (NBC)
Jeffrey Tambor (*The Larry Samders Show*) (HBO)
Rip Torn (*The Larry Sanders Show*) (HBO)

SUPPORTING ACTRESS (COMEDY SERIES)
Christine Baranski (*Cybill*) (CBS)
Janeane Garofalo (*The Larry Sanders Show*) (HBO)
Julia Louis-Dreyfus (*Seinfeld*) (NBC)
Jayne Meadows Allen (*High Society*) (CBS)
Renee Taylor (*The Nanny*) (CBS)

INDIVIDUAL PERFORMANCE (VARIETY OR MUSIC PROGRAM)

Tony Bennett (*Tony Bennett Live by Request: A Valentine Special*) (A&E)

Ellen DeGeneres (*The 38th Annual Grammy Awards*) (CBS)

Whoopi Goldberg (*The 68th Annual Academy Awards*) (ABC)

Tracey Ullman (*The Best of Tracey Takes On…*) (HBO)

Robin Williams, Whoopi Goldberg, Billy Crystal (joint nomination) (*Comic Relief VII*) (HBO)

GUEST PERFORMERS

Actor (Drama Series): Peter Boyle ("Clyde Bruckman's Final Repose," *The X-Files*) (Fox); Actress (Drama Series): Amanda Plummer ("A Stitch in Time," *The Outer Limits*) (Showtime); Actor (Comedy Series): Tim Conway ("The Gardener," *Coach*) (ABC); Actress (Comedy Series): Betty White ("Here We Go Again," *The John Larroquette Show*) (NBC)

DAYTIME AWARDS

Drama Series: *General Hospital* (ABC); Actor: Charles Keating (*Another World*) (NBC); Actress: Erika Slezak (*One Life To Live*) (ABC); Supporting Actor: Jerry Van Dorn (*Guiding Light*) (CBS); Supporting Actress: Anna Holbrook (*Another World*) (NBC); Talk Show: *The Oprah Winfrey Show* (Syndicated); Game Show: *The Price Is Right* (CBS)

OTHER PRIME-TIME AWARDS

Directing (TV-Movie or Mini-Series): John Frankenheimer (*Andersonville*) (TNT); Directing (Drama Series): Jeremy Kagan ("Leave of Absence," *Chicago Hope*) (CBS); Directing (Comedy Series): Michael Lembeck ("The One after the Superbowl," *Friends*) (NBC); Director (Variety or Music Program): Louis J. Horvitz (*The Kennedy Center Honors*) (CBS)

Winning director Louis J. Horvitz had to accept his award from the control booth since he was directing the Emmys. He continued to call camera angles during his acceptance speech and even managed to get in a shot of his parents.

Writing (TV-Movie or Mini-Series): Simon Moore (*Gulliver's Travels*) (NBC); Writing (Drama Series): Darin Morgan ("Clyde Bruckman's Final Repose," *The X-Files*) (Fox); Writing (Comedy Series): Joe Keenan, Christopher Lloyd, Rob Greenberg, Jack Burditt, Chuck Ranberg, Anne Flett-Giordano, Linda Morris, Vic Rauseo ("Moondance," *Frasier*) (NBC); Writing (Variety or Music Program): Dennis Miller, Eddie Feldman, David Feldman, Mike Gandolfi, Tom Hertz, Leah Krinsky, Rick Overton (*Dennis Miller Live*) (HBO)

David Hyde Pierce and Jane Leeves performed a comic tango before giving out an Emmy, recreating a scene from an award-winning episode of their series *Frasier*. "They gave us two choices," Pierce explained to the audience. "We could banter or tango," Leeves said. And without missing a beat, the two then launched into the nominees for their category. Unfortunately, that brief bit of fun was cited by many critics as the highlight of the evening. Host Paul Reiser (nominated for *Mad about You*) did his best to keep up the laughs, but too often his material fell flat. One good line came when Reiser pointed out that the show was being beamed to 600 million people in twenty countries. "As you know, everybody cares," he sarcastically added. Despite the tedium, some viewers must have cared, because the ceremony was the third-highest rated show of the week, up sixteen percent from the previous year's Emmys.

There was a film montage of TV characters opening doors, and Candice Bergen made a dignified announcement that it was the fiftieth anniversary of the TV Academy, co-founded by her father Edgar Bergen. She then presented a new Emmy citation. Called the President's Award, this category was for television which makes a social impact or statement. The first winner was the documentary film *Blacklist: Hollywood on Trial*, shown on American Movie Classics

THE PEABODY AWARDS (FOR 1996)

Law & Order (NBC); *NYPD Blue* (ABC); *The X-Files* (Fox); *The Simpsons* (Fox); *Pride and Prejudice* (A&E, BBC); *Mobil Masterpiece Theatre* for *House of Cards, To Play the King,* and *The Final Cut* (BBC and WGBH, Boston); *Edith Ann's Christmas*

(ABC); "Who's Guarding the Guardians?" (WCVB, Boston); "Newsnight Afghanistan" (BBC News, London); "Passport to Kill" (WNBC, New York); *Vote for Me: Politics in America* (WETA, Washington, DC); *The Celluloid Closet* (Telling Pictures HBO, Channel 4, London, ZDF-Arte, Germany/France); *Frontline: The Gate of Heavenly Peace* and *Frontline: The Choice '96* (WGBH, Boston); *Paradise Lost: The Child Murders at Robin Hood Hills* (HBO); KOMO, Seattle, for excellence in local programming; *Nova: Odysssey of Life* (WGBH, Boston); *People Century* (BBC and WGBH, Boston); *The American Experience: The Battle over 'Citizen Kane'* (American Experience and Lennon Documentary Group/WGBH, Boston); *The Great War and the Shaping of the 20th Century* (KCET, Los Angeles, BBC); *Surviviors of the Holocaust* (Turner Entertainment Group and Steven Spielberg); *Journey of the African-American Athlete* (HBO Sports); *How Do You Spell God?* (HBO); *Wise Up!* (Carlton Television for Channel 4, London); *One to One: Mentoring* (WCCO, Minneapolis); Bud Greenspan for sports documentary filmmaking

THE GOLDEN GLOBE AWARDS (FOR 1996)

Made-for-TV Movie/Mini-Series: *Rasputin* (HBO); Drama Series: *The X-Files* (Fox); Comedy or Musical Series: *3rd Rock from the Sun* (NBC)

Actor (TV-Movie/Mini-Series); Alan Rickman (*Rasputin*); Actress (TV-Movie/Mini-Series): Helen Mirren (*Losing Chase*) (Showtime); Actor (Drama Series): David Duchovny (*The X-Files*) (Fox); Actress (Drama Series): Gillian Anderson (*The X-Files*) (Fox); Actor (Comedy or Musical Series): John Lithgow (*3rd Rock from the Sun*) (NBC); Actress (Comedy or Musical Series): Helen Hunt (*Mad about You*) (NBC); Supporting Actor: Ian

McKellen (*Rasputin*) (HBO); Supporting Actress: Kathy Bates (*The Late Shift*) (HBO)

THE CABLE ACE AWARDS (FOR 1996)

Movie or Mini-Series: *Truman* (HBO); Dramatic or Theatrical Special: *America's Dream: Long Black Song* (HBO); Drama Series: *The Outer Limits* (Showtime); Comedy Series: *The Larry Sanders Show* (HBO)

Actor (Movie or Mini-Series): Gary Sinise (*Truman*) (HBO); Actress (Movie or Mini-Series): Sela Ward (*Almost Golden: The Jessica Savitch Story*) (Lifetime); Actor (Drama Special or Series): Danny Glover (*America's Dream: Long Black Song*) (HBO); Actress (Drama Special or Series): Donna Murphy (*Someone Had to Be Benny*) (HBO); Actor (Comedy Series): Garry Shandling (*The Larry Sanders Show*) (HBO); Actress (Comedy Series): Tracey Ullman (*Tracey Takes On . . .*) (HBO); Supporting Actor (Movie/Mini-Series): Tom Hulce (*The Heidi Chronicles*) (TNT); Supporting Actress (Movie/Mini-Series): Amanda Plummer (*The Right to Remain Silent*) (Showtime)

1996-97

THE EMMY AWARDS

DAYTIME AWARDS

Drama Series: *General Hospital*; Actor: Justin Deas (*Guiding Light*); Actress: Jess Walton (*The Young and the Restless*); Supporting Actor: Ian Buchanan (*The Bold and the Beautiful*); Supporting Actress: Michelle Stafford (*The Young and the Restless*); Talk Show: *The Oprah Winfrey Show*; Game Show: *The Price Is Right*

Yul Brynner [Tony Featured Actor (Musical)] and Gertrude Lawrence [Tony Actress (Musical)] in *The King and I* (1951–52).

PART 4

Theater

THE BEST-KNOWN ACCOLADE for live theater is the Tony Award. Thanks to its annual television broadcast, a national audience is treated to spectacular numbers from the nominated musicals.

Despite high production standards, the Tonys are frequently not as popular as other prize-giving specials. While anyone with the price of a movie ticket can see the films up for Oscars and any TV viewer has the opportunity to review the contenders for the Emmys, only those who live in the New York area or are willing to make the trek there will be able to catch the Tony nominees. And don't forget the average Broadway show charges $60 a seat. So these awards are by nature more limited in their appeal, but they are often the best produced and most professionally done of all the awards shows. Since the entertainment has already been tested in front of paying audiences rather than cobbled together, as is the case with many of the numbers on the Oscars and the Emmys, the end product is often superior.

The Tonys were first presented by the American Theatre Wing in 1947 as a tribute to director-producer Antoinette Perry. The debut ceremony was a relatively intimate dinner-dance for the theater community. In 1967, the adminstration of the awards was shared between the Wing and the League of New York Theaters and Producers (later renamed the League of American Theaters and Producers). Showman Alexander Cohen suggested the ceremony should be presented on television as a means of advertising Broadway. The resultant annual video presentation has broadened the public's awareness of and enthusiasm for theater.

But the Tonys are not the only, nor the most representative, major stage awards. They totally ignore the existence of Off-Broadway, the vital venue operating beyond the Times Square theater district which is honored by *The Village Voice*'s Obie Awards. The Drama Desk Awards consider both Broadway and Off-Broadway shows in all its categories, as does the Pulitzer Prize and the New York Drama Critics Circle. The Outer Critics Circle divides its top awards between Broadway and Off-Broadway productions.

1916-17

THE PULITZER PRIZE FOR DRAMA

No award

The Pulitzer Prize is presented annually by the Columbia School of Journalism thanks to a trust created by newspaper tycoon Joseph Pulitzer. The Pulitzers honor outstanding work in American journalism and literature including drama. The Columbia trustees present the awards but an Advisory Board made up of publishers and editors decides the winners based on the recommendations of juries in each field. The Board can reject the jurors' suggestions and, when it has, controversy has ensued. The author of the Pulitzer play receives a check for $1,000. The first year the awards were presented, no play was judged worthy enough for the distinction.

1917-18

THE PULITZER PRIZE FOR DRAMA

Why Marry? by Jesse Lynch Williams

The first play to win the Pulitzer was a slight comedy about a young woman who holds the "modern" view that couples should live together without benefit of clergy. Terribly outdated, its chief claim to fame is being the premiere Pulitzer winner.

1918-19

THE PULITZER PRIZE FOR DRAMA

No award

1919-20

THE PULITZER PRIZE FOR DRAMA

Beyond the Horizon by Eugene O'Neill

Eugene O'Neill, America's foremost playwright, won the first of his four Pulitzers for *Beyond the Horizon*, a drama of two brothers, each living the wrong life. The other three were for *Anna Christie* (1921–22), the tale of a reformed prostitute; *Strange Interlude* (1927–28), a nine-act marathon of psychological conflicts among a captivating woman and the three men in her life; and *Long Day's Journey into Night* (1956–57), an autobiographical study of O'Neill's own tortured family. The last Pulitzer was awarded posthumously.

1920-21

THE PULITZER PRIZE FOR DRAMA

Miss Lulu Bett by Zona Gale

A weepy melodrama concerning an old maid who finds happiness, *Miss Lulu Bett* was produced by Brock Pemberton, later the founder of the Tony Awards.

1921-22

THE PULITZER PRIZE FOR DRAMA

Anna Christie by Eugene O'Neill

1922-23

THE PULITZER PRIZE FOR DRAMA

Icebound by Owen Davis

1923-24

THE PULITZER PRIZE FOR DRAMA

Hell-Bent fer Heaven by Hatcher Hughes

The Pulitzer got its first taste of controversy when George Kelly's *The Show-Off*, a warm comedy of a Philadelphia family and the Pulitzer drama jury's selection, was passed over in favor of *Hell-Bent fer Heaven*, a creaky melodrama set in the Blue Ridge Mountains. The fact that *Heaven* was written by a Columbia professor and the award was presented by Columbia University did not go unnoticed by the press. George Abbott, who would become one

Earl Larimore and
Lynn Fontanne in
Strange Interlude,
Eugene O'Neill's
1928 Pulitzer
Prize winner.

of Broadway's most prolific producer/directors, had a supporting role in the play's cast.

adequate domestic drama which later provided Joan Crawford with one of her bitchier screen roles, was inferior to the previous Kelly play.

1924-25

THE PULITZER PRIZE FOR DRAMA

They Knew What They Wanted by Sidney Howard

1926-27

THE PULITZER PRIZE FOR DRAMA

In Abraham's Bosom by Paul Green

1925-26

THE PULITZER PRIZE FOR DRAMA

Craig's Wife by George Kelly

This award was a consolation prize to Kelly for being passed over for *The Show-Off*. *Craig's Wife*, an

1927-28

THE PULITZER PRIZE FOR DRAMA

Strange Interlude by Eugene O'Neill

A scene from the political satire *Of Thee I Sing* (1931–32), the first musical to win the Pulitzer Prize.

1928-29

THE PULITZER PRIZE FOR DRAMA

Street Scene by Elmer Rice

1929-30

THE PULITZER PRIZE FOR DRAMA

The Green Pastures by Marc Connelly

The Green Pastures, Marc Connelly's retelling of the Old Testament with an all-black cast, was a tremendous hit in its day, but would be shunned as condescending and insulting to African-Americans today for its depiction of them as simplistic innocents.

1930-31

THE PULITZER PRIZE FOR DRAMA

Alison's House by Susan Glaspell

Another controversial decision. Susan Glaspell's weak drama loosely based on the life of poet Emily Dickenson had a brief run in Eva La Galliene's Civic Repertory Theatre season. No one expected it to win the Pulitzer when stronger shows like *Elizabeth the Queen, Once in a Lifetime,* and *Tomorrow and Tomorrow* were in the running.

1931-32

THE PULITZER PRIZE FOR DRAMA

Of Thee I Sing by George S. Kaufman, Morris Ryskin, and Ira Gershwin

Of Thee I Sing, a political satire, was the first musical to be awarded the Pulitzer Prize for Drama. But the Pulitzer jury decided that the award should be for the words and not the music. So composer George Gershwin was omitted from the list of winners. The Prize of $1,000 was awarded to bookwriters George S. Kaufman and Morris Ryskind and lyricist Ira Gerswin, George's brother.

1932-33

THE PULITZER PRIZE FOR DRAMA

Both Your Houses by Maxwell Anderson

1933-34

THE PULITZER PRIZE FOR DRAMA

Men in White by Sidney Kingsley

All three jurors had recommended Maxwell Anderson's *Mary of Scotland.* The Advisory Board dismissed their choice and went for *Men in White,* Sidney Kingsley's medical drama and the first success of the Group Theatre. The jurors resigned their positions in protest.

1934-35

THE PULITZER PRIZE FOR DRAMA

The Old Maid by Zoe Akins

In the 1934–35 season, several plays were considered worthy of the Pulitzer. These included Lillian Hellman's *The Children's Hour,* Clifford Odets's *Awake and Sing,* Robert E. Sherwood's *The Petrified Forest,* and Maxwell Anderson's *Valley Forge.* All of these were bypassed in favor of *The Old Maid,* Zoe Akins's soap operatic adaptation of a story by Edith Wharton.

In protest, the Broadway reviewers banded together and formed the New York Drama Critics Circle in order to present their own awards. The first winner, presented the following season, was Maxwell Anderson's verse drama *Winterset.*

The initial presentation was made at a formal dinner at the Algonquin Hotel and broadcast over radio. In its early years, the Circle thought it only fair to allow members who did not support the majority choice to speak. Percy Hammond of the *New York Herald Tribune* voiced the minority opinion of Anderson's play, stating it was "spinach and I say to hell with it." In subsequent years, this custom of dissenting speeches was dropped. Despite Hammond's views, Anderson also won the following year for *High Tor.*

1935-36

THE NEW YORK DRAMA CRITICS CIRCLE AWARDS

BEST AMERICAN PLAY
Winterset by Maxwell Anderson

THE PULITZER PRIZE FOR DRAMA

Idiot's Delight by Robert E. Sherwood

1936-37

THE NEW YORK DRAMA CRITICS CIRCLE AWARDS

BEST AMERICAN PLAY
High Tor by Maxwell Anderson

THE PULITZER PRIZE FOR DRAMA

You Can't Take It with You by Moss Hart and George S. Kaufman

The Pulitzer's choosing the light humor of *You Can't Take It with You* over the lyrical drama of *High Tor* was met with some derision among critics, but the eccentric comedy by Kaufman and Hart has proved far more durable than Anderson's verse play. *You Can't Take It with You* is constantly

Henry Travers, Josephine Hull, and Hugh Rennie in *You Can't Take It with You,* winner of the 1936–37 Pulitzer Prize. The film version would win the Oscar for best Picture.

seen on community and regional stages while *High Tor* is hardly ever reproduced.

1937-38

THE NEW YORK DRAMA CRITICS CIRCLE AWARDS

BEST AMERICAN PLAY
Of Mice and Men by John Steinbeck

BEST FOREIGN PLAY
Shadow and Substance
by Paul Vincent Carroll

THE PULITZER PRIZE FOR DRAMA

Our Town by Thornton Wilder

1938-39

THE NEW YORK DRAMA CRITICS CIRCLE AWARDS

BEST AMERICAN PLAY
No award

BEST FOREIGN PLAY
The White Steed by Paul Vincent Carroll

For the first time in its four-year existence, the New York Drama Critics Circle failed to choose a winner for Best American Play. Lillian Hellman's *The Little Foxes* and Robert E. Sherwood's *Abe Lincoln in Illinois* were leaders in the voting, with Clifford Odets's *Rocket to the Moon* and William Saroyan's *My Heart's in the Highlands* trailing. But the Circle's by-laws required a three-quarters majority in order for a play to emerge victorious. After ten rounds of voting, *The Little Foxes*, an incisive study of a corrupt Southern family, was ahead but still lacked the necessary majority. Irish dramatist Paul Vincent Carroll's *The White Steed* was unanimously chosen as Best Foreign Play on the first ballot.

As a consolation, the four losing American playwrights were invited to the awards dinner.

THE PULITZER PRIZE FOR DRAMA

Abe Lincoln in Illinois by Robert E. Sherwood

1939-40

THE NEW YORK DRAMA CRITICS CIRCLE AWARDS

BEST AMERICAN PLAY
The Time of Your Life by William Saroyan

THE PULITZER PRIZE FOR DRAMA

The Time of Your Life by William Saroyan

1940-41

THE NEW YORK DRAMA CRITICS CIRCLE AWARDS

BEST AMERICAN PLAY
Watch on the Rhine by Lillian Hellman

BEST FOREIGN PLAY
The Corn Is Green by Emlyn Williams

THE PULITZER PRIZE FOR DRAMA

There Shall Be No Night by Robert E. Sherwood

Both *Watch on the Rhine* and *There Shall Be No Night* concerned the growing war in Europe and indirectly pleaded for American intervention in the conflict. *Watch* opened on April 1, 1941, missing the Pulitzer cut-off date of March 31. It was in the running for the 1941–42 award, but the Advisory Board decided not to give an award that year.

1941-42

THE NEW YORK DRAMA CRITICS CIRCLE AWARDS

BEST AMERICAN PLAY
No award

BEST FOREIGN PLAY
Blithe Spirit by Noel Coward

THE PULITZER PRIZE FOR DRAMA

No award

1942-43

THE NEW YORK DRAMA CRITICS CIRCLE AWARDS

BEST AMERICAN PLAY
The Patriots by Sidney Kingsley

THE PULITZER PRIZE FOR DRAMA

The Skin of Our Teeth by Thornton Wilder

1943-44

THE NEW YORK DRAMA CRITICS CIRCLE AWARDS

BEST FOREIGN PLAY
Jacobowsky and the Colonel by S. N. Behrman, adapted from Franz Werfel's play

THE PULITZER PRIZE FOR DRAMA

No award

Rodgers and Hammerstein's ground-breaking musical *Oklahoma!* was given a special "citation of excellence" from the Pulitzer judges, but was deemed ineligible for the Prize itself because it was based on an earlier play *Green Grow the Lilacs* by Lynn Riggs. Pulitzer winners have been derived from fiction, but not other dramas.

Laurette Taylor in *The Glass Menagerie*, the New York Drama Critics Circle Best American Play, 1944–45.

1944-45

THE NEW YORK DRAMA CRITICS CIRCLE AWARDS

BEST AMERICAN PLAY
The Glass Menagerie by Tennessee Williams

THE PULITZER PRIZE FOR DRAMA

Harvey by Mary Chase

Whimsy won over good playwrighting for the 1944–45 Pulitzer. Mary Chase's *Harvey* was a charming comedy about a lovable drunk and his relationship with an invisible six-foot rabbit. A popular, fun evening (it's the longest-running Pulitzer winner apart from *A Chorus Line*), but hardly a better work than Tennessee Williams' poetic *The Glass Menagerie*, which did win the New York Drama Critics Circle Award for Best American Play.

1945-46

THE NEW YORK DRAMA CRITICS CIRCLE AWARDS

BEST MUSICAL
Carousel by Richard Rodgers and Oscar Hammerstein II, based on *Liliom* by Ferenc Molnar

THE PULITZER PRIZE FOR DRAMA

State of the Union by Howard Lindsay and Russell Crouse

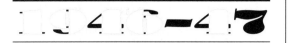

THE TONY AWARDS

OUTSTANDING PERFORMANCES
Ingrid Bergman (*Joan of Lorraine*)
Helen Hayes (*Happy Birthday*)
Jose Ferrer (*Cyrano de Bergerac*)
Frederic March (*Years Ago*)

DEBUT PERFORMANCE
Patricia Neal (*Another Part of the Forest*)

MUSICAL PERFORMANCE
David Wayne (*Finian's Rainbow*)

SCORE
Kurt Weill (*Street Scene*)

PLAYWRIGHT
Arthur Miller (*All My Sons*)

DIRECTOR
Elia Kazan (*All My Sons*)

OTHER AWARDS
Choreography: Agnes De Mille (*Brigadoon*),
Michael Kidd (*Finian's Rainbow*); Set Design:
David Ffolkes (*Henry VIII*); Costume Design:
Lucinda Ballard (*Happy Birthday, Another Part of
the Forest, Street Scene, John Loves Mary,* and *The
Chocolate Soldier*)

SPECIAL AWARDS
Ira and Rita Katzenberg, for enthusiasm as
inveterate first-nighters; restauranteur Vincent
Sardi, Sr.; Dora Chamberlain, treasurer of the
Martin Beck Theatre; Burn Mantle, editor of the
annual *Best Plays* volumes; Jules J. Leventhal, the
season's most prolific backer and producer; P. A.
McDonald for intricate construction for the
production of *If a Shoe Fits*

Ironically, it was a movie executive who indirectly
originated the Tony Awards—formally named the
Antoinette Perry Awards—which are the highest
honors for achievement on the Broadway stage.

Jacob Wilk of the Warner Brothers studios had an
idea there should be a memorial to Antoinette Perry,
who had died in 1946. A producer and director
whose hits included the long-running *Harvey*, Perry
was well loved for her volunteer work with the
National Experimental Theatre and the American
Theatre Wing. She was chair of the Wing's board,
whose activities included the operation of the Stage
Door Canteens for the entertainment of servicemen and -women during World War II. (The
Wing founded a theater school in 1946 and today
sponsors numerous programs and seminars.)

Brock Pemberton, Perry's partner on many pro-
jects, chaired a Wing committee to come up with a
fitting tribute. A tangible monument like a plaque,
statue, or building were rejected in favor of a per-
petual honor, annual awards for theater people presented by theater people. The Wing's board determined the winners, but nominees were not
announced. This practice continued until 1956.

The first awards were presented at a dinner-
dance held at the Waldorf-Astoria Hotel on Easter
Sunday, when most shows would be dark and performers could attend. (The Waldorf would be the
site of eleven subsequent Tony dinners.)

Entertainment was provided in the form of
songs from such then-running shows as *The
Chocolate Soldier, Street Scene, Brigadoon, Finian's
Rainbow, Oklahoma!, Carousel,* and *Sweethearts,* as
well as through appearances by Mickey Rooney,
Ethel Waters, and David Wayne. In fact, there was
so much entertainment the awards themselves were
not gotten to until midnight. The first Tony ceremony was broadcast on local radio station WOR
and nationally over the Mutual Network.

THE NEW YORK DRAMA CRITICS CIRCLE AWARDS

BEST AMERICAN PLAY
All My Sons by Arthur Miller

BEST FOREIGN PLAY
No Exit by Jean-Paul Sartre

BEST MUSICAL
Brigadoon by Alan Jay Lerner and
Frederick Loewe

THE PULITZER PRIZE FOR DRAMA

No award

THE TONY AWARDS

PLAY
Mister Roberts by Thomas Heggen
and Joshua Logan

While Tennessee Williams's simmering *A Streetcar Named Desire* had electrified the Great White Way and won the Pulitzer and Critics Circle Awards, the Tony for Outstanding Play went to *Mister Roberts*, a boisterous World War II service comedy.

The play was based on Thomas Heggen's best-selling series of short stories *Night Watch*. Director/playwright Joshua Logan collaborated with Heggen on the stage version. The show was a tremendous hit starring Henry Fonda but Heggen did not survive the success. Fearing he'd never be able to match the triumph of his first play, the young author plunged into numerous periods of depression. In 1949, just one year after *Mister Roberts* won the Tony, Heggen was found dead in his apartment, drowned in a bathtub, at the age of 29.

PERFORMANCES BY ACTORS
Henry Fonda (*Mister Roberts*);
Paul Kelly (*Command Decision*);
Basil Rathbone (*The Heiress*)

Twenty-four-year-old Marlon Brando's sizzling embodiment of the animalistic Stanley Kowlaski in *A Streetcar Named Desire* was overlooked by the Tonys much to the anger of many critics and columnists. Jessica Tandy's Blanche Du Bois was awarded, though. A similar snub occured when Brando lost the Oscar for the movie of *Streetcar*, but Vivien Leigh, the screen Blanche, took the statuette home.

PERFORMANCES BY ACTRESSES
Judith Anderson (*Medea*);
Katherine Cornell (*Antony and Cleopatra*);
Jessica Tandy (*A Streetcar Named Desire*)

In her acceptance speech, Judith Anderson memorably quoted Robinson Jeffers, author of the adaptation of *Medea* for which she won: "If God would lend me a touch of eloquence, I'd show you my heart."

MUSICAL PERFORMANCES
Grace and Paul Hartman (*Angel in the Wings*)

Dance team Grace and Paul Hartman, stars of the revue *Angel in the Wings*, were the first married couple to win Tony awards. The only other acting spouses in Tony's winner circle are Jessica Tandy [for *Streetcar Named Desire* (1947–48), *The Gin Game* (1977–78) and *Foxfire* (1982–83)] and Hume Cronyn [for *Hamlet* (1963–64)].

PERFORMANCES BY NEWCOMERS
June Lockhart (*For Love or Money*);
James Whitmore (*Command Decision*)

DIRECTOR
Joshua Logan (*Mister Roberts*)

FOREIGN COMPANY
The Importance of Being Earnest,
directed by John Gielgud

SPREADING THEATRE TO THE COUNTRY WHILE THE ORIGINAL PERFORMED IN NEW YORK
Mary Martin (*Annie Get Your Gun*);
Joe E. Brown (*Harvey*)

There was grumbling about conflict of interest in this new category since Brock Pemberton, one of the administrators of the Tonys, was the producer of the tour of *Harvey* for which Joe E. Brown was honored. This was the only time a Tony for starring in a touring production was presented.

OTHER AWARDS
Choreography: Jerome Robbins (*High Button Shoes*); Set Design: Horace Armistead (*The Medium*); Costume Design: Mary Percy Schenck (*The Heiress*); Orchestra Conductor: Max Meth (*Finian's Rainbow*); Backstage Technician: George Gebhart

Marlon Brando, Kim Hunter, and Jessica Tandy (Tony Award winner) in Tennessee Williams's *A Streetcar Named Desire* (1947–48 New York Drama Critics Circle Best American Play Award and Pulitzer Prize winner).

SPECIAL AWARDS

Theater operators Robert W. Dowling and Paul Beisman; Rosamond Gilder, editor of *Theatre Arts* magazine; Experimental Theatre, Inc.; Robert Porterfield, Virginia Barter Theatre; actress Vera Allen for distinguished volunteer work for the American Theatre Wing; backstage doorman George Pierce

After only one year, the Tony Awards were already beginning to grow. The first ceremony was briefly broadcast on radio. The second was shown for ninety minutes via the new medium of television on the short-lived Dumont Network. The program was also radio-broadcast by the Mutual Network. Instead of one host, there were now five: Harry Hershfield (of the radio show *Can You Top This?*), James Sauter (who arranged the entertainment), actors Bert Lytell and Hiram Sherman, and producer and Tony adminstrator Brock Pemberton.

Musical numbers were from *Look Ma, I'm Dancing, Make Mine Manhattan, Allegro, High Button Shoes,* and productions from the Metropolitan Opera. Male winners were given gold engraved bill clips, as in the previous year, but female winners were given gold bracelets instead of compact cases.

THE NEW YORK DRAMA CRITICS CIRCLE AWARDS

BEST AMERICAN PLAY
A Streetcar Named Desire
by Tennessee Williams

BEST FOREIGN PLAY
The Winslow Boy by Terrence Rattigan

THE PULITZER PRIZE FOR DRAMA

A Streetcar Named Desire
by Tennessee Williams

THE TONY AWARDS

PLAY
Death of a Salesman by Arthur Miller

MUSICAL
Kiss Me, Kate

ACTOR (PLAY)
Rex Harrison (*Anne of the Thousand Days*)

ACTRESS (PLAY)
Martita Hunt (*The Madwoman of Chaillot*)

MUSICAL PERFORMANCES
Ray Bolger (*Where's Charley?*);
Nanette Fabray (*Love Life*)

SUPPORTING PERFORMANCES
Arthur Kennedy (*Death of a Salesman*);
Shirley Booth (*Goodbye, My Fancy*)

DIRECTOR
Elia Kazan (*Death of a Salesman*)

OTHER AWARDS
Choreography: Gower Champion (*Lend an Ear*);

Conductor/Musical Director: Max Meth (*As the Girls Go*); Set Design: Jo Mielziner (work throughout the season including *South Pacific*); Costume Design: Lemuel Ayers (work throughout the season)

The year 1949 marked the first season the Tony medallion was awarded rather than bracelets and bill clips. The new award design by Herman Rosse was chosen out of twenty entries. The medallion was four inches in diameter with the masks of comedy and tragedy on one side and a raised profile of Antoinette Perry and the name of the winner on the other. The producers of the winning play and musical received scrolls rather than the medallions.

The awards dinner took place at the Waldorf-Astoria. Brock Pemberton, founder of the Tonys, and James Sauter, entertainment chairman, hosted. Entertainment was provided by such Broadway stars as Carol Channing, Alfred Drake, Lisa Kirk, Gene Nelson, and Tony winners Nanette Fabray and Ray Bolger.

THE NEW YORK DRAMA CRITICS CIRCLE AWARDS

BEST AMERICAN PLAY
Death of a Salesman by Arthur Miller

BEST FOREIGN PLAY
The Madwoman of Chaillot
by Jean Giraudoux

BEST MUSICAL
South Pacific by Richard Rodgers,
Oscar Hammerstein, II, and Joshua Logan

South Pacific opened too late in the season to be considered for the Tonys, which had a March 1 deadline, but it won the New York Critics Circle Award. The Rodgers and Hammerstein hit won a total of eight Tonys the following season.

THE PULITZER PRIZE FOR DRAMA

Death of a Salesman by Arthur Miller

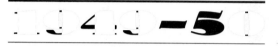

THE TONY AWARDS

PLAY
The Cocktail Party by T. S. Eliot

MUSICAL
South Pacific

ACTOR (PLAY)
Sidney Blackmer (*Come Back, Little Sheba*)

ACTRESS (PLAY)
Shirley Booth (*Come Back, Little Sheba*)

When Shirley Booth and Sidney Blackmer examined their Tony medallions, they found the engraver had mistakenly stated they had both won for *South Pacific*. This is understandable since *South Pacific* won a total of eight awards out of fifteen categories. The medals were later corrected. Booth later won an Oscar for the film version of *Come Back, Little Sheba*.

ACTOR (MUSICAL)
Ezio Pinza (*South Pacific*)

ACTRESS (MUSICAL)
Mary Martin (*South Pacific*)

Both Ezio Pinza and Mary Martin of *South Pacific* were on vacation the night of the Tonys. Their awards were accepted by Barbara Luna and Michael de Leon, who played Pinza's children in the show. Myron McCormick and Juanita Hall, also from *South Pacific*, took the Featured Actor and Featured Actress awards. This remains the only instance in which one show has won all the available performance categories.

FEATURED ACTOR
Myron McCormick (*South Pacific*)

FEATURED ACTRESS
Juanita Hall (*South Pacific*)

OTHER AWARDS
Director: Joshua Logan (*South Pacific*); Musical Score: Richard Rodgers (*South Pacific*); Libretto: Oscar Hammerstein, II, Joshua Logan (*South Pacific*); Choreography: Helen Tamaris (*Touch and Go*); Conductor/Musical Director: Maurice Abravanel (*Regina*); Set Design: Jo Mielziner (*The Innocents*); Costume Design: Aline Bernstein (*Regina*); Stage Technician: Joe Lynn (master propertyman for *Miss Liberty*)

SPECIAL AWARDS
Maurice Evans for the City Center Theatre Company's season; Philip Faversham, a volunteer for the American Theatre Wing's hospital program; Brock Pemberton (posthumous), founder of the awards

Brock Pemberton, the founder of the awards, died a few months before the 1950 ceremony. His memory was honored with a special Tony. James Sauter, the entertainment chair, once again presided. Those who performed at the event, held again at the Waldorf-Astoria, included Yvonne Adair of *Gentlemen Prefer Blondes*, William Tabbert of *South Pacific*, and Allyn Ann McLerie of *Miss Liberty* and her then husband, lyricist-writer Adolph Green.

THE NEW YORK DRAMA CRITICS CIRCLE AWARDS

BEST AMERICAN PLAY
The Member of the Wedding
by Carson McCullers

BEST FOREIGN PLAY
The Cocktail Party by T. S. Eliot

BEST MUSICAL
The Consul by Gian Carlo Menotti

THE PULITZER PRIZE FOR DRAMA

South Pacific by Richard Rodgers, Oscar Hammerstein, II, Joshua Logan

"Luck, Be a Lady Tonight" from *Guys and Dolls* (1950–1951 best Musical Tony and New York Drama Critics Circle Award).

THE OUTER CRITICS CIRCLE AWARDS

Play: *The Cocktail Party*; Musical: *The Consul*; Performances in Minor Roles: Daniel Reed (*Come Back, Little Sheba*), Sheila Guyse (*Lost in the Stars*)

The Outer Critics Circle, an organization of reviewers for out-of-town and national periodicals, was founded this season and gave out its first set of awards. Its categories have varied from year to year. Because of its early deadline, the winners of the Outer Critics Circle Awards often differ from those of the other awards.

THE TONY AWARDS

PLAY
The Rose Tattoo by Tennessee Williams

MUSICAL
Guys and Dolls

ACTOR (PLAY)
Claude Rains (*Darkness at Noon*)

ACTRESS (PLAY)
Uta Hagen (*The Country Girl*)

ACTOR (MUSICAL)
Robert Alda (*Guys and Dolls*)

ACTRESS (MUSICAL)
Ethel Merman (*Call Me Madam*)

FEATURED ACTOR (PLAY)
Eli Wallach (*The Rose Tattoo*)

FEATURED ACTRESS (PLAY)
Maureen Stapleton (*The Rose Tattoo*)

Because they were billed below the title in *The Rose Tattoo*, Maureen Stapleton and Eli Wallach were considered featured performers. Anna Magnani would win a leading actress Oscar when she did the film version in the role Stapleton originated.

FEATURED ACTOR (MUSICAL)
Russell Nype (*Call Me Madam*)

FEATURED ACTRESS (MUSICAL)
Isabel Bigley (*Guys and Dolls*)

OTHER AWARDS
Musical Score: Irving Berlin (*Call Me Madam*); Director: George S. Kaufman (*Guys and Dolls*); Choreography: Michael Kidd (*Guys and Dolls*); Musical Director: Lehman Engel (*The Consul*); Set Designer: Boris Aronson (*The Rose Tattoo, The Country Girl,* and *Season in the Sun*); Costume Design: Miles White (*Bless You All*); Stage Technician: Richard Raven (master electrician, *The Autumn Garden*)

SPECIAL AWARD
American Theatre Wing volunteer Ruth Green for her services in arranging the seating and reservations for the past five awards ceremonies

Once again James Sauter presided over a Tony dinner-dance at the Waldorf-Astoria. Performers at the ceremony included Celeste Holm, Anne Jeffreys, and Juanita Hall, who had won a Tony the year before for *South Pacific*. The event was broadcast on local radio station WOR and the Mutual Radio Network.

THE NEW YORK DRAMA CRITICS CIRCLE AWARDS

BEST AMERICAN PLAY
Darkness at Noon by Sidney Kingsley

BEST FOREIGN PLAY
The Lady's Not for Burning by Christopher Fry

BEST MUSICAL
Guys and Dolls by Frank Loesser, Jo Swerling, and Abe Burrows

THE PULITZER PRIZE FOR DRAMA

No award

THE OUTER CRITICS CIRCLE AWARDS

Play: *Billy Budd*; Musical: *Guys and Dolls*; Supporting Performance: Naomi Mitty (*A Tree Grows in Brooklyn*)

1951–52

THE TONY AWARDS

PLAY
The Fourposter by Jan de Hartog

MUSICAL
The King and I

ACTOR (PLAY)
Jose Ferrer (*The Shrike*)

Jose Ferrer also won the best Director Tony for his staging of *The Shrike*, a drama about a mental patient and his shrewish wife, and for two other shows, *The Fourposter* and *Stalag 17*. So far, he is the only person to direct himself to a Tony.

ACTRESS (PLAY)
Julie Harris (*I Am a Camera*)

ACTOR (MUSICAL)
Phil Silvers (*Top Banana*)

1951–52 Tony winners Oscar Hammerstein, Gertrude Lawrence, Richard Rodgers, Helen Hayes (mistress of ceremonies), Phil Silvers, Judy Garland, and Yul Brynner.

ACTRESS (MUSICAL)
Gertrude Lawrence (*The King and I*)

FEATURED ACTOR (PLAY)
John Cromwell (*Point of No Return*)

FEATURED ACTRESS (PLAY)
Marian Winters (*I Am a Camera*)

FEATURED ACTOR (MUSICAL)
Yul Brynner (*The King and I*)

When Rodgers and Hammerstein's *The King and I* first opened, Yul Brynner as the Siamese monarch was given second billing to Gertrude Lawrence as the British governess who tutors his royal children. Thus, Brynner won a featured Tony. During the run of the show, the Russian-born actor was elevated to star status, equal with Lawrence. When the film was made, he won a leading actor Oscar. Brynner would return to the role throughout his career. In 1984–85, he was awarded a special Tony for 4,525 performances as the powerful potentate puzzled by a changing world.

FEATURED ACTRESS (MUSICAL)
Helen Gallagher (*Pal Joey*)

OTHER AWARDS
Director: Jose Ferrer (*The Shrike, The Fourposter,* and *Stalag 17*); Choreography: Robert Alton (*Pal Joey*); Musical Director/Conductor: Max Meth (*Pal Joey*); Set Design: Jo Mielziner (*The King and I*); Costume Design: Irene Sharaff (*The King and I*); Stage Technician: Peter Feller (master electrician, *Call Me Madam*)

SPECIAL AWARDS
Judy Garland for her engagement at the Palace Theatre; lighting designer Edward Kook; Charles Boyer for his performance in *Don Juan in Hell*

Helen Hayes, president of the American Theatre Wing and a past Tony winner, took over as mistress of ceremonies for the event.

THE NEW YORK DRAMA CRITICS CIRCLE AWARDS

BEST AMERICAN PLAY
I Am a Camera by John Van Druten

BEST FOREIGN PLAY
Venus Observed by Christopher Fry

BEST MUSICAL
Pal Joey by Richard Rodgers, Lorenz Hart, and John O'Hara

SPECIAL CITATION
Don Juan in Hell

THE PULITZER PRIZE FOR DRAMA

The Shrike by Joseph Kramm

THE OUTER CRITICS CIRCLE AWARDS

Play: *Play of No Return*; Supporting Performance: Kim Stanley (*The Case*)

1952-53

THE TONY AWARDS

PLAY
The Crucible by Arthur Miller

This was Arthur Miller's third Tony. His previous wins were for *All My Sons* (1946–47) and *Death of a Salesman* (1948–49). The only other dramatic authors to be so honored are the British Tom Stoppard whose Tonys were for *Rosencrantz and Guildenstern Are Dead* (1967–68), *Travesties* (1975–76), and *The Real Thing* (1983–84) and Neil Simon for *The Odd Couple* (1964–65), *Biloxi Blues* (1984–85), and *Lost in Yonkers* (1990–91). [Simon won a best Author (Play) Tony as playwright for *The Odd Couple*, but the best Play Tony

that year went to *The Subject Was Roses*].

Terrence McNally is also a triple winner, but two of his were for his plays (*Love! Valour! Compassion!* in 1994–95 and *Master Class* in 1995–96) and one for the libretto of a musical (1992–93's *Kiss of the Spider Woman*).

MUSICAL
Wonderful Town

ACTOR (PLAY)
Tom Ewell (*The Seven Year Itch*)

ACTRESS (PLAY)
Shirley Booth (*Time of the Cuckoo*)

Earlier in the same month as the Tonys, Shirley Booth copped an Oscar for *Come Back, Little Sheba*, for which she had won a Tony for the stage version.

ACTOR (MUSICAL)
Thomas Mitchell (*Hazel Flagg*)

This Tony for character actor Thomas Mitchell, added to his 1939 Oscar for *Stagecoach* and a 1952 best Actor Emmy, made him the first performer to win the top awards in three different media.

ACTRESS (MUSICAL)
Rosalind Russell (*Wonderful Town*)

FEATURED ACTOR (PLAY)
John Williams (*Dial M for Murder*)

FEATURED ACTRESS (PLAY)
Beatrice Straight (*The Crucible*)

FEATURED ACTOR (MUSICAL)
Hiram Sherman (*Two's Company*)

FEATURED ACTRESS (MUSICAL)
Sheila Bond (*Wish You Were Here*)

OTHER AWARDS
Director: Joshua Logan (*Picnic*); Choreography: Donald Saddler (*Wonderful Town*); Musical Director/Conductor: Lehman Engel (*Wonderful Town* and Gilbert and Sullivan season); Set

Design: Raoul Pene du Bois (*Wonderful Town*); Costume Design: Miles White (*Hazel Flagg*); Stage Technician: Abe Kurnit (property man, *Wish You Were Here*)

SPECIAL AWARDS
Beatrice Lillie; Danny Kaye; Equity Community Theatre

Faye Emerson presided over this year's Tonys, which were radio-broadcast nationally by NBC.

THE NEW YORK DRAMA CRITICS CIRCLE AWARDS

BEST AMERICAN PLAY
Picnic by William Inge

BEST FOREIGN PLAY
The Love of Four Colonels by Peter Ustinov

BEST MUSICAL
Wonderful Town by Leonard Bernstein, Betty Comden, Adolph Green, Joseph Fields, and Jerome Chodorov

THE PULITZER PRIZE FOR DRAMA

Picnic by William Inge

THE OUTER CRITICS CIRCLE AWARDS

MUSICAL
Wonderful Town

1953-54

THE TONY AWARDS

PLAY
The Teahouse of the August Moon
   by John Patrick

MUSICAL
Kismet

ACTOR (PLAY)
David Wayne (*The Teahouse of the August Moon*)

ACTRESS (PLAY)
Audrey Hepburn (*Ondine*)

Hepburn had just won an Oscar for her performance in *Roman Holiday* four days earlier. Shirley Booth had pulled off the same-year Oscar-Tony double play the year before and Ellen Burstyn would also duplicate it in 1975.

ACTOR (MUSICAL)
Alfred Drake (*Kismet*)

ACTRESS (MUSICAL)
Dolores Gray (*Carnival in Flanders*)

Carnival in Flanders was a six-performance flop. Gray was praised for her performance as a seventeenth-century Flemish mayor's wife, but the show was panned. This is the shortest-running Tony win on record.

FEATURED ACTOR (PLAY)
John Kerr (*Tea and Sympathy*)

FEATURED ACTRESS (PLAY)
Jo Van Fleet (*The Trip to Bountiful*)

FEATURED ACTOR (MUSICAL)
Harry Belafonte (*John Murray Anderson's Almanac*)

FEATURED ACTRESS (MUSICAL)
Gwen Verdon (*Can-Can*)

OTHER AWARDS
Director: Alfred Lunt (*Ondine*); Set Design: Peter Larkin (*Ondine* and *The Teahouse of the August Moon*); Costume Design: Richard Whorf (*Ondine*); Choreography: Michael Kidd (*Can-Can*); Musical Conductor: Louis Adrian (*Kismet*); Stage Technician: John Davis (*Picnic*)

The Tonys switched from their usual venue at the Waldorf-Astoria and were held at the Plaza Hotel, with no radio or TV coverage. Helen Hayes, the Wing president, was chair of the dinner committee and handed out the prizes, but James Sauter, who had arranged the entertainment at many previous awards, was master of ceremonies. Hayes would take over that function the following year.

THE NEW YORK DRAMA CRITICS CIRCLE AWARDS

BEST AMERICAN PLAY
The Teahouse of the August Moon by John Patrick

BEST FOREIGN PLAY
Ondine by Jean Giradoux, adapted by Maurice Valency

BEST MUSICAL
The Golden Apple by John Latouche and Jerome Moross

THE PULITZER PRIZE FOR DRAMA

The Teahouse of the August Moon by John Patrick

THE OUTER CRITICS CIRCLE AWARDS

Play: *The Caine Munity Court-Martial*; Musical: *Kismet*; Supporting Performance (Drama): Eva Marie Saint (*The Trip to Bountiful*); Supporting Performance (Musical): Bibi Osterwald (*The Golden Apple*)

THE TONY AWARDS

PLAY
Anastasia by Marcelle Maurette, English
    adaptation by Guy Bolton
The Desperate Hours by Joseph Hayes
The Flowering Peach by Clifford Odets
The Rainmaker by N. Richard Nash
Witness for the Prosecution by Agatha Christie

MUSICAL
Fanny
The Pajama Game
Peter Pan
Plain and Fancy
Silk Stockings

For the first time, the nominees for the outstanding play and musical were announced before the awards were given out. The following year, all nominees in all categories would be made public.

ACTOR (PLAY)
Alfred Lunt (*Quadrille*)

ACTRESS (PLAY)
Nancy Kelly (*Bad Seed*)

ACTOR (MUSICAL)
Walter Slezak (*Fanny*)

ACTRESS (MUSICAL)
Mary Martin (*Peter Pan*)

Rosalind Russell accepted Mary Martin's Tony for the absent musical star, stating, "Mary has been flying high throughout her career, but this is the first time she's ever used wires!"

FEATURED ACTOR (PLAY)
Francis L. Sullivan (*Witness for the Prosecution*)

FEATURED ACTRESS (PLAY)
Patricia Jessel (*Witness for the Prosecution*)

FEATURED ACTOR (MUSICAL)
Cyril Ritchard (*Peter Pan*)

FEATURED ACTRESS (MUSICAL)
Carol Haney (*The Pajama Game*)

DIRECTOR
Robert Montgomery (*The Desperate Hours*)

Like Mary Martin, Robert Montgomery was unable to attend the ceremony, so he sent his daughter and future *Bewitched* star Elizabeth to pick up his prize. She reportedly ticked off a few actors in *The Desperate Hours* company with her acceptance speech: "Dad worked so hard with the cast to win this," implying the actors were not quite up to snuff and required Montgomery's guidance to give exceptional performances.

OTHER AWARDS
Choreography: Bob Fosse (*The Pajama Game*);

Musical Director/Conductor: Thomas Schippers (*The Saint of Bleecker Street*); Set Design: Oliver Messel (*House of Flowers*); Costume Design: Cecil Beaton (*Quadrille*); Stage Technician: Richard Rodda (*Peter Pan*)

SPECIAL AWARD
Proscenium Productions for its Off-Broadway productions

Helen Hayes, president of the American Theatre Wing, acted as mistress of ceremonies. She joked that Shirley Booth had won so many Tonys that it was a great Hayes year whenever Booth was out of town on tour. She then presented the Outstanding Play Award to the author of the suspense drama *The Desperate Hours* Joseph Hayes—no relation. A portion of the ceremony was broadcast as part of the NBC spectacular *Entertainment '55*.

Two of the hottest plays of the season, William Inge's *Bus Stop* and Tennessee Williams' *Cat on a Hot Tin Roof*, were ineligible since they opened after the March 1 Tony deadline. Both were considered for the Pulitzer and Drama Critics Awards, with *Cat* clawing its way to victory in both competitions. Radie Harris of *The Hollywood Reporter* criticized the early cut-off date for Tony nominations. She also called the entire Tony process unfair since the only voters were the fifty American Theatre Wing board members, many of whom were not theater professionals.

The awards did branch out by bestowing a special citation to an Off-Broadway company, Proscenium Productions. A few Tonys went to non-Broadway shows and companies in the next few years, but the practice was discontinued as the Tony officially became a "Broadway"-only prize.

THE VERNON RICE AWARDS

PRODUCTIONS
Proscenium Productions (*The Way of the World* and *A Thieves' Carnival*); The Shakespearewrights (*Twelfth Night* and *The Merchant of Venice*); David Ross (Fourth Street Theatre productions of *The Way of the World* and *The White Devil*)

PERFORMANCE
Nancy Wickwire (*The Way of the World* and *The White Devil*)

DIRECTION
Jack Landau (*The Clandestine Marriage* and *The White Devil*)

To honor distinguished work in the Off-Broadway theater, the Drama Desk, an organization of New York critics, editors, and reporters, inaugurated the Vernon Rice Awards. Named for the late critic of the *New York Post*, the prizes predated the similar Obie Awards by a year. The Rice Awards gradually evolved into the Drama Desk Awards, which honor both Broadway and Off-Broadway.

THE NEW YORK DRAMA CRITICS CIRCLE AWARDS

BEST AMERICAN PLAY
Cat on a Hot Tin Roof by Tennessee Williams

BEST FOREIGN PLAY
Witness for the Prosecution by Agatha Christie

BEST MUSICAL
The Saint of Bleecker Street by Gian Carlo Menotti

THE PULITZER PRIZE FOR DRAMA

Cat on a Hot Tin Roof by Tennessee Williams

THE OUTER CRITICS CIRCLE AWARDS

Play: *Inherit the Wind*; Musical: *Three for Tonight*; Performances in Supporting Roles: Crahan Denton (*Bus Stop*), Gretchen Wyler (*Silk Stockings*)

THE TONY AWARDS

PLAY
Bus Stop by William Inge
Cat on a Hot Tin Roof by Tennessee Williams
The Chalk Garden by Enid Bagnold

The Diary of Anne Frank by Frances Goodrich and Albert Hackett

Tiger at the Gates by Jean Giraudox, adapted by Christopher Fry

The season of 1955–56 was a banner year for plays. Even with five slots open, several highly praised works were not Tony-nominated for out-standing Play. Among the no-placers were *The Lark*, French author Jean Anouilh's drama of Joan of Arc, adapted by Lillian Hellman; *Inherit the Wind*, a dramatization of the Scopes monkey trial; *A Hatful of Rain*, the searing examination of a drug-addicted vet; and *Time Limit*, a thriller from the Theatre Guild. Two of the nominees were holdovers from 1954–55, *Bus Stop* and *Cat on a Hot Tin Roof*, because they were produced after the March 1 Tony cut-off date for that season.

MUSICAL
Damn Yankees
Pipe Dream

While there were numerous plays to chose from for the top Tony, just two productions were in the run-ning for the Musical award. The only competition was between *Damn Yankees*, the sports variation on the Faust legend, and *Pipe Dream*, an unsuccessful adaptation of a John Steinbeck novel and one of Rodgers and Hammerstein's few failures. The *Yankees* production team had also won the previous year for *The Pajama Game*.

My Fair Lady had opened in March, too late for this year's Tonys, but it did take the New York Drama Critics' Circle Award as Best Musical.

ACTOR (PLAY)
Ben Gazzara (*A Hatful of Rain*)
Boris Karloff (*The Lark*)
Paul Muni (*Inherit the Wind*)
Michael Redgrave (*Tiger at the Gates*)
Edward G. Robinson (*The Middle of the Night*)

ACTRESS (PLAY)
Barbara Bel Geddes (*Cat on a Hot Tin Roof*)
Gladys Cooper (*The Chalk Garden*)
Ruth Gordon (*The Matchmaker*)
Julie Harris (*The Lark*)
Siobhan McKenna (*The Chalk Garden*)

Susan Strasberg (*The Diary of Anne Frank*)

ACTOR (MUSICAL)
Stephen Douglass (*Damn Yankees*)
William Johnson (*Pipe Dream*)
Ray Walston (*Damn Yankees*)

ACTRESS (MUSICAL)
Carol Channing (*The Vamp*)
Gwen Verdon (*Damn Yankees*)
Nancy Walker (*Phoenix '55*)

FEATURED ACTOR (PLAY)
Ed Begley (*Inherit the Wind*)
Anthony Franciosa (*A Hatful of Rain*)
Andy Griffith (*No Time for Sargeants*)
Anthony Quayle (*Tamburlaine the Great*)
Fritz Weaver (*The Chalk Garden*)

FEATURED ACTRESS (PLAY)
Diane Cilento (*Tiger at the Gates*)
Anne Jackson (*The Middle of the Night*)
Una Merkel (*The Ponder Heart*)
Elaine Stritch (*Bus Stop*)

FEATURED ACTOR (MUSICAL)
Russ Brown (*Damn Yankees*)
Mike Kellin (*Pipe Dream*)
Will Mahoney (*Finian's Rainbow*)
Scott Merrill (*The Threepenny Opera*)

FEATURED ACTRESS (MUSICAL)
Rae Allen (*Damn Yankees*)
Pat Carroll (*Catch a Star*)
Lotte Lenya (*The Threepenny Opera*)
Judy Tyler (*Pipe Dream*)

Lotte Lenya won the Tony as Featured Actress (Musical) and Scott Merrill was nominated in the Featured Actor (Musical) category for the hit pro-duction of *The Threepenny Opera*, the dark musical by Bertolt Brecht and Lenya's late husband Kurt Weill. The show also was given a special citation as distinguished Off-Broadway production. In later years, as the Tonys became more prominent and influential, they came under the jurisdiction of the League of New York Theatres and Producers (later renamed the League of American Theatres and Producers). The League wanted the Tonys to be given only to shows presented in its member theatres, i.e., in Broadway houses. Its members did not want competition from Off-Broadway. As non-Broadway productions increased, the on and Off-Broadway dispute would serve as a constant source of controversy for the awards and their sponsors.

OTHER AWARDS
Director: Tyrone Guthrie (*The Matchmaker*); Musical Director/Conductor: Hal Hastings (*Damn Yankees*); Choreography: Bob Fosse (*Damn Yankees*); Set Design: Peter Larkin (*No Time for Sargeants*); Costume Design: Alvin Colt (*Pipe Dream*); Stage Technician: Harry Green (*The Middle of the Night* and *Damn Yankees*)

SPECIAL AWARDS
City Center; Fourth Street Chekhov Theatre; The Shakespearewrights; *The Threepenny Opera* (distinguished Off-Broadway production); The Theatre Collection of the New York Public Library

In an effort to boost general interest in the Tonys, the nominations were made public before the ceremony for the first time and the awards were shown on television. Helen Hayes, president of the American Theatre Wing, and comedian Jack Carter hosted the ceremony, which was seen on New York local Channel 5 and the Dumont Network.

Presenter Diane Cilento failed to show up and film starlet Linda Darnell was almost literally grabbed off the floor to sub at the last minute. This was also the Year of the Great Tony Mix-Up. Eileen Herlie, cast member of *The Matchmaker*, was accepting the award meant for Tyrone Guthrie, the show's director who was unable to attend. She got the Tony inscribed for Costume Design winner Alvin Colt. Colt received Peter Larkin's Set Design Tony. When Colt returned the mistaken award, he got back the prize intended to go to Richard Adler and Jerry Ross, the songwriters of *Damn Yankees*.

Meanwhile Ray Walston picked up his own Tony for leading Actor (Musical) in *Yankees* and the one for Russ Brown as Featured Actor (Musical) actor in the same show. What he was handed were Tonys for Ed Begley [Featured Actor (Play) for *Inherit the Wind*] and for Tyrone Guthrie (Director of *The Matchmaker*). Walston swapped

Tonys with Begley, but refused to return Guthrie's medal till he had Russ Brown's in his hands.

THE VERNON RICE AWARDS

PRODUCTION
The Iceman Cometh (Circle in the Square)

DIRECTION
Jose Quintero (*The Iceman Cometh*)

PERFORMANCES
Janine Manatis (*Village Wooing*); Pernell Roberts (*Macbeth*)

THE NEW YORK DRAMA CRITICS CIRCLE AWARDS

BEST AMERICAN PLAY
The Diary of Anne Frank by Frances Goodrich and Albert Hackett

BEST FOREIGN PLAY
Tiger at the Gates by Jean Giraudox

BEST MUSICAL
My Fair Lady by Alan Jay Lerner and Frederick Loewe

THE PULITZER PRIZE FOR DRAMA

The Diary of Anne Frank by Frances Goodrich and Albert Hackett

THE OBIE AWARDS

BEST NEW PLAY
Absalom by Lionel Abel

BEST ALL-AROUND PRODUCTION
Uncle Vanya

BEST MUSICAL
The Threepenny Opera

BEST DIRECTOR
Jose Quintero (*The Iceman Cometh*)

BEST ACTOR (TIE)
Jason Robards, Jr. (*The Iceman Cometh*) and George Voskovic (*Uncle Vanya*)

BEST ACTRESS
Julie Bovasso (*The Maids*)

BEST SUPPORTING ACTOR
Gerald Hiken (*The Cherry Orchard* and *Uncle Vanya*)

BEST SUPPORTING ACTRESS
Peggy McCay (*Uncle Vanya*)

DISTINGUISHED PERFORMANCES
Alan Ansara (*The Private Life of the Master Race*); Roberts Blossom (*Village Wooing*); Shirlee Emmons (*The Mother of Us All*); Addison Powell (*The Iceman Cometh*); Frances Sternhagen (*The Admirable Bashville*); Nancy Wickwire (*The Cherry Orchard*)

SETS, LIGHTING, AND COSTUME DESIGN
Klaus Holm and Alvin Colt (Phoenix Theatre)

SPECIAL CITATIONS
Phoenix Theatre; The Shakespearean Workshop Theatre; Tempo Playhouse

Off-Broadway was growing in importance and influence. Failed Broadway productions deserving of a second look, innovative work by new playwrights both foreign and domestic, and fresh reinterpretations of Ibsen, Chekhov, and Shakespeare were all being seen on small stages far from the Times Square theater district. Jerry Tallmer, associate editor and theater critic from the fledgling radical newspaper *The Village Voice*, decided this venue needed an award of its own. His paper began sponsoring the Obie (derived from OB, short for Off-Broadway) Awards. The selection process remains the same today as it did in 1956. The winners are decided on by a panel of *Voice* theater writers and guest judges. The panel can choose as many or as few receipients as it desires and the categories are equally flexible. There are no nominees, only recognition for outstanding work.

Shelley Winters, appearing on Broadway in *A Hatful of Rain*, was mistress of ceremonies for the first Obie Awards. The annual ceremony is uncorseted, wild, and unconventional, with the crowd appearing in everything from drag to casual wear and acceptance speeches often peppered with expletives.

THE OUTER CRITICS CIRCLE AWARDS

Play: *The Diary of Anne Frank*; Musical: *My Fair Lady*; Performance (Drama): Anthony Franciosa (*A Hatful of Rain*); Special citations: Alice Pearce (performance in *Fallen Angels*), Peter Larkin (designer for *No Time for Sargeants*)

1956-57

THE TONY AWARDS

PLAY
Long Day's Journey into Night by Eugene O'Neill
Separate Tables by Terrence Rattigan
The Potting Shed by Graham Greene
The Waltz of the Toreadors by Jean Anouilh, translated by Lucienne Hill

Long Day's Journey into Night, Eugene O'Neill's autobiographical drama of his tortured family, was completed in 1945. The author presented the manuscript to Random House publishers on the condition it not be released until twenty-five years after his death. Three years after O'Neill's death in 1953, his widow Carlotta secured the rights to the script and gave permission for its production, first in Stockholm, then on Broadway. The New York version, searingly directed by Jose Quintero, won the Triple Crown of Tony, Pulitzer, and New York Drama Critics Circle Awards.

MUSICAL
Bells Are Ringing
Candide
My Fair Lady
The Most Happy Fella

My Fair Lady, the elegant Lerner and Loewe adaptation of Shaw's *Pygmalion*, was Tony's favorite for 1956–57, winning a total of six awards including outstanding Musical. Rex Harrison's misanthropic linguist Henry Higgins won him an outstanding Actor (Musical) Tony, but Julie Andrews' Cockney flower girl Eliza Doolittle lost to Judy Holliday's warm-hearted phone operator in *Bells Are Ringing*.

ACTOR (PLAY)
Maurice Evans (*The Apple Cart*)
Wilfrid Hyde-White (*The Reluctant Debutante*)
Frederic March (*Long Day's Journey into Night*)
Eric Porter (*Separate Tables*)
Ralph Richardson (*The Waltz of the Toreadors*)
Cyril Ritchard (*A Visit to a Small Planet*)

ACTRESS (PLAY)
Florence Eldridge (*Long Day's Journey into Night*)
Margaret Leighton (*Separate Tables*)
Rosalind Russell (*Auntie Mame*)
Sybil Thorndike (*The Potting Shed*)

ACTOR (MUSICAL)
Rex Harrison (*My Fair Lady*)
Fernando Lamas (*Happy Hunting*)
Robert Weede (*The Most Happy Fella*)

ACTRESS (MUSICAL)
Julie Andrews (*My Fair Lady*)
Judy Holliday (*Bells Are Ringing*)
Ethel Merman (*Happy Hunting*)

FEATURED ACTOR (PLAY)
Frank Conroy (*The Potting Shed*)
Eddie Mayehoff (*A Visit to a Small Planet*)
William Podmore (*Separate Tables*)
Jason Robards, Jr. (*Long Day's Journey into Night*)

FEATURED ACTRESS (PLAY)
Peggy Cass (*Auntie Mame*)
Anna Massey (*The Reluctant Debutante*)
Beryl Measor (*Separate Tables*)
Mildred Natwick (*The Waltz of the Toreadors*)
Phyllis Neilson-Terry (*Separate Tables*)
Diana Van der Vlis (*The Happiest Millionaire*)

FEATURED ACTOR (MUSICAL)
Sydney Chaplin (*Bells Are Ringing*)
Robert Coote (*My Fair Lady*)
Stanley Holloway (*My Fair Lady*)

Victors at the 1956–57 Tonys: Judy Holliday, Rex Harrison, Margaret Leighton, and Frederic March.

FEATURED ACTRESS (MUSICAL)
Edith Adams (*L'il Abner*)
Virginia Gibson (*Happy Hunting*)
Irra Petina (*Candide*)
Jo Sullivan (*The Most Happy Fella*)

OTHER AWARDS

Director: Moss Hart (*My Fair Lady*); Musical Director/Conductor: Franz Allers (*My Fair Lady*); Choreography: Michael Kidd (*L'il Abner*); Set Design: Oliver Smith (*My Fair Lady*); Costume Design: Cecil Beaton (*My Fair Lady*); Stage Technician: Howard McDonald, posthumous (*Major Barbara*)

Choreographer Michael Kidd was the first person to accumulate four Tonys. His previous wins were for the dances of *Finian's Rainbow, Guys and Dolls,* and *Can Can.* He would later also win for *Destry Rides Again.* Bob Fosse surpassed Kidd's record with a total of eight Tonys.

SPECIAL AWARDS

American Shakespeare Festival, Stratford, CT; Jean-Louis Barrault, French Repertory; Robert Russell Bennett; William Hammerstein; Paul Shyre

Legendary stage actress Katherine Cornell and her director-husband Guthrie McClintock served as co-chairs of the Tony banquet at the usual stand of the Waldorf-Astoria, with Mrs. Martin Beck, the Wing's first vice president, as coordinator.

Presenters included Bert Lahr, Beatrice Lillie, Tom Ewell, Nancy Kelly, Lillian Gish, Cornelia Otis Skinner, Cliff Robertson, and Nancy Olson. The awards were to be telecast by CBS, but a juris-dictional dispute between two labor unions forced a cancellation.

THE VERNON RICE AWARDS

Paul Shyre for his adaptation of Sean O'Casey's *Pictures in the Hallway* and his production of *Purple Dust*

PERFORMANCES

Sada Thompson (*The River Line* and *The Misanthrope*); Arthur Malet (*Volpone* and *The Misanthrope*)

THE NEW YORK DRAMA CRITICS CIRCLE AWARDS

BEST AMERICAN PLAY
Long Day's Journey into Night by Eugene O'Neill

BEST FOREIGN PLAY
The Waltz of the Toreadors by Jean Anouilh

BEST MUSICAL
The Most Happy Fella by Frank Loesser

THE PULITZER PRIZE FOR DRAMA

Long Day's Journey into Night by Eugene O'Neill

THE OBIE AWARDS

BEST NEW PLAY
A House Remembered by Louis A. Lippa

BEST ALL-AROUND PRODUCTION
Exiles produced by Daniel S. Brown and Burry Frederik

BEST DIRECTOR
Gene Frankel (*Volpone*)

BEST ACTOR
William Smithers (*The Sea Gull*)

BEST ACTRESS
Colleen Dewhurst (*The Taming of the Shrew, The Eagle Has Two Heads,* and *Camille*)

DISTINGUISHED PERFORMANCES
Thayer David (*Saint Joan* and *Oscar Wilde*); Michael Kane, Betty Miller, Jutta Wolf (*Exiles*); Marguerite Lenert (*House of Breath*); Arthur Malet (*Volpone, The Misanthrope,* and *The Apollo of Bellac*)

SPECIAL CITATIONS
Paul Shyre, for bring O'Casey to Off-Broadway and his adaptations of *I Knock the Door, Pictures in the Hallway,* and *USA*

The second Obie ceremony had a particularly Irish flavor. Productions of O'Casey, Wilde, and Joyce were honored while Irish coffee was served. Radio humorist Jean Shepard and Geraldine Page were the hosts.

THE OUTER CRITICS CIRCLE AWARDS

Play: *Long Day's Journey into Night*; Musical: *My Fair Lady*; Performance (Drama): Inga Swenson (*The First Gentleman*); Performance (Musical): Stubby Kaye (*L'il Abner*); Special citations: New York City Center Light Opera Company, Osbert Lancaster for design of *Hotel Paradiso*.

THE TONY AWARDS

PLAY

The Dark at the Top of the Stairs
    by William Inge
Look Back in Anger by John Osborne
Look Homeward, Angel by Ketti Frings
Romanoff and Juliet by Peter Ustinov
The Rope Dancers by Morton Wishengrad
Sunrise at Campobello by Dore Schary
Time Remembered by Jean Anouilh,
    English version by Patricia Moyes
Two for the Seesaw by William Gibson

MUSICAL

Jamaica
The Music Man
New Girl in Town
Oh, Captain!
West Side Story

Tony was bursting at the seams this year with six to eight nominees in some categories. The voters went for the sentimental, with *Sunrise at Campobello*, a misty-eyed tribute to Franklin Delano Roosevelt, and *The Music Man*, a valentine to small-town America, taking outstanding Play and Musical, respectively. The innovative *West Side Story* won only two prizes, for outstanding Choreography and Stage Technician.

ACTOR (PLAY)

Ralph Bellamy (*Sunrise at Campobello*)
Richard Burton (*Time Remembered*)
Hugh Griffith (*Look Homeward, Angel*)
Laurence Olivier (*The Entertainer*)
Anthony Perkins (*Look Homeward, Angel*)
Peter Ustinov (*Romanoff and Juliet*)
Emlyn Williams (*A Boy Growing Up*)

ACTRESS (PLAY)

Helen Hayes (*Time Remembered*)
Wendy Hiller (*A Moon for the Misbegotten*)
Eugenie Leontovich (*The Cave Dwellers*)
Siobhann McKenna (*The Rope Dancers*)
Jo Van Fleet (*Look Homeward, Angel*)

ACTOR (MUSICAL)

Eddie Foy (*Rumple*)
Ricardo Montalban (*Jamaica*)
Tony Randall (*Oh, Captain*)
Robert Preston (*The Music Man*)

ACTRESS (MUSICAL) (TIE)

Lena Horne (*Jamaica*)
Beatrice Lillie (*Ziegfeld Follies*)
Thelma Ritter (*New Girl in Town*)
Gwen Verdon (*New Girl in Town*)

Not only was this the first tie in Tony history, but also the first instance of two actresses from the same production winning in the same category. Verdon won the third of four Tonys for her role as the reformed prostitute in *New Girl in Town*, a musical retelling of O'Neill's *Anna Christie*. Thelma Ritter was the older wharf slattern.

FEATURED ACTOR (PLAY)

Sig Arno (*Time Remembered*)
Theodore Bikel (*The Rope Dancers*)
Pat Hingle (*The Dark at the Top of the Stairs*)
Henry Jones (*Sunrise at Campobello*)
George Relph (*The Entertainer*)

FEATURED ACTRESS (PLAY)

Anne Bancroft (*Two for the Seesaw*)
Brenda de Banzie (*The Entertainer*)
Joan Blondell (*The Rope Dancers*)
Mary Fickett (*Sunrise at Campobello*)
Eileen Heckart (*The Dark at the Top of the Stairs*)

Joan Plowright (*The Entertainer*)

FEATURED ACTOR (MUSICAL)
David Burns (*The Music Man*)
Ossie Davis (*Jamaica*)
Cameron Prud'homme (*New Girl in Town*)
Iggie Wolfington (*The Music Man*)

FEATURED ACTRESS (MUSICAL)
Barbara Cook (*The Music Man*)
Susan Johnson (*Oh, Captain*)
Carol Lawrence (*West Side Story*)
Jacquelyn McKeever (*Oh, Captain*)
Josephine Premice (*Jamaica*)

OTHER AWARDS
Director: Vincent J. Donehue (*Sunrise at Campobello*); Musical Director: Herbert Green (*The Music Man*); Choreography: Jerome Robbins (*West Side Story*); Set Design: Oliver Smith (*West Side Story*); Costume Design: Motley (*The First Gentleman*); Stage Technician: Harry Romar (*Time Remembered*)

SPECIAL AWARD
New York Shakespeare Festival

For the second year, the Tonys were not televised. A strike by the International Brotherhood of Electrical Workers against local station WCBS prevented the broadcast. Despite the cancellation, the Pepsi-Cola Bottling Company, the sponsor of the program, contributed $5,000 to the Wing's activities. Mary Martin, Frederic March, and Mrs. Albert D. Lasker were co-chairs of the dinner dance.

THE VERNON RICE AWARDS

PERFORMANCES
Gerry Jedd (*Blood Wedding*); George C. Scott (*Children of Darkness*)

THE NEW YORK DRAMA CRITICS CIRCLE AWARDS

BEST AMERICAN PLAY
Look Homeward, Angel by Ketti Frings

BEST FOREIGN PLAY
Look Back in Anger by John Osborne

BEST MUSICAL
The Music Man by Meredith Willson and Franklin Lacey

THE PULITZER PRIZE FOR DRAMA

Look Homeward, Angel by Ketti Frings

THE OBIE AWARDS

BEST FOREIGN PLAY
Endgame by Samuel Beckett

BEST PLAY (ADAPTATION)
The Brothers Karamazov by Boris Tumarin and Jack Sydow

BEST REVIVAL
The Crucible by Arthur Miller, directed by Word Baker

BEST ONE-ACT PLAY
Guests of the Nation by Neil McKenzie

BEST COMEDY
Comic Strip by George Panetta

BEST DIRECTOR
Stuart Vaughn (New York Shakespeare Festival)

BEST ACTOR
George C. Scott (*Richard II, As You Like It,* and *Children of Darkness*)

BEST ACTRESS
Anne Meacham (*Garden District*)

DISTINGUISHED PERFORMANCES
Jack Cannon (New York Shakespeare Festival and *Children of Darkness*); Leonardo Cimino (*The Brothers Karamazov*); Robert Gerringer (New York Shakespeare Festival and *Guests of the Nation*); Tammy Grimes (*Clerambard*); Michael Higgins (*The Crucible*); Grania O'Malley (*Guests of the Nation*); Nydia Westman (*Endgame*)

SPECIAL CITATIONS
The Phoenix Theatre; The Theatre Club; Lucille Lortel

Hostess Maureen Stapleton presided over the third annual Obie Awards. Raymond S. Rubinow, chairman of a committee to close Washington Square to commercial traffic, made the first political speech at the Obies by stating Off-Broadway was an important element in the preservation of the Greenwich Village community.

THE OUTER CRITICS CIRCLE AWARDS

Play: *Look Homeward, Angel*; Musical: *The Music Man*; Performance (Drama): Henry Jones (*Sunrise at Campobello*); Performance (Musical): Jacquelyn McKeever (*Oh, Captain!*); Set Design: Rouben Ter-Arutunian (*Who Was That Lady I Saw You With?*); Special Award: Joseph Papp

1958-59

THE TONY AWARDS

PLAY
The Disenchanted by Budd Schulberg and Harvey Briet
Epitaph for George Dillon by John Osborne
JB by Archibald MacLeish
A Touch of the Poet by Eugene O'Neill
The Visit by Frederick Duerrenmatt

MUSICAL
Flower Drum Song
La Plume de Ma Tante
Redhead

ACTOR (PLAY)
Cedric Hardwicke (*A Majority of One*)
Alfred Lunt (*The Visit*)
Christopher Plummer (*JB*)
Cyril Ritchard (*The Pleasure of His Company*)
Jason Robards, Jr. (*The Disenchanted*)
Robert Stephens (*Epitaph for George Dillon*)

ACTRESS (PLAY)
Gertrude Berg (*A Majority of One*)
Claudette Colbert (*The Marriage-Go-Round*)
Lynn Fontanne (*The Visit*)

Kim Stanley (*A Touch of the Poet*)
Maureen Stapleton (*The Cold Wind and the Warm*)

ACTOR (MUSICAL)
Larry Blyden (*Flower Drum Song*)
Richard Kiley (*Redhead*)

ACTRESS (MUSICAL)
Miyoshi Umeki (*Flower Drum Song*)
Gwen Verdon (*Redhead*)

This was Gwen Verdon's fourth award, making her the performer with the most Tonys. Her previous wins were for a featured role in *Can-Can*, and the leads in *Damn Yankees* and *New Girl in Town*. She held the record until 1976–77, when Julie Harris surpassed her with five wins. Angela Lansbury tied Verdon in 1978–79 with a quartet of Tonys, as did Zoe Caldwell in 1995–96.

FEATURED ACTOR (PLAY)
Marc Connelly (*Tall Story*)
George Grizzard (*The Disenchanted*)
Walter Matthau (*Once More, with Feeling*)
Robert Morse (*Say, Darling*)
Charlie Ruggles (*The Pleasure of His Company*)
George C. Scott (*Comes a Day*)

FEATURED ACTRESS (PLAY)
Maureen Delaney (*God and Kate Murphy*)
Dolores Hart (*The Pleasure of His Company*)
Julie Newmar (*The Marriage-Go-Round*)
Nan Martin (*JB*)
Beatrice Reading (*Requiem for a Nun*)

FEATURED ACTOR (MUSICAL) (TIE)
Russell Nype (*Goldilocks*)
Leonard Stone (*Redhead*)
The male cast of *La Plume de Ma Tante*

FEATURED ACTRESS (MUSICAL) (TIE)
Julienne Marie (*Whoop-Up*)
Pat Stanley (*Goldilocks*)
The female cast of *La Plume de Ma Tante*

OTHER AWARDS
Director: Elia Kazan (*JB*); Choreography: Bob Fosse (*Redhead*); Musical Director: Salvatore Dell'Isolda (*Flower Drum Song*); Set Design:

Donald Oenslager (*A Majority of One*); Costume Design: Rouben Ter-Arutunian (*Redhead*); Stage Technician: Sam Knapp (*The Music Man*)

SPECIAL AWARDS

John Gielgud for *Ages of Man*; playwrights Howard Lindsay and Russell Crouse; *La Plume de Ma Tante*

The Tonys were back on the air (on local New York station WCBS) after being canceled the two previous years because of union troubles. The awards were presented in a fifty-five-minute ceremony at 11:15 p.m. under the sponsorship of Pepsi-Cola. TV game show host Bud Collyer was the emcee. Walter Cronkite spoiled some of the surprise of the evening by announcing four of the winners on the late evening news just before the show began.

THE VERNON RICE AWARDS

PERFORMANCES
Hal Holbrook (*Mark Twain Tonight!*); Jane McArthur (*Our Town*)

DIRECTION
William Ball (*Ivanov*)

THE NEW YORK DRAMA CRITICS CIRCLE AWARDS

BEST AMERICAN PLAY
A Raisin in the Sun by Lorraine Hansberry

BEST FOREIGN PLAY
The Visit by Friederich Duerrenmatt

BEST MUSICAL
La Plume de Ma Tante by Gerard Calvi, Ross Parker, and Robert Dhery

For the first time, the Circle voted a revue as its choice for Best Musical. *La Plume de Ma Tante*, a French entertainment featuring songs and sketches but no plot, also received a special Tony Award. In another first, *A Raisin in the Sun* was the first play by a black author to take the Circle's top prize. *Raisin*, the drama of an African-American Chicago family moving to an all-white suburb, opened too late to be considered for the Tonys, which had an earlier cut-off date, and was nominated for those awards the following season.

THE PULITZER PRIZE FOR DRAMA

JB by Archibald MacLeish

THE OBIE AWARDS

BEST NEW PLAY
The Quare Fellow by Brendan Behan

BEST ALL-AROUND PRODUCTION
Ivanov

BEST DIRECTION (FOREIGN PLAY)
William Ball (*Ivanov*)

BEST DIRECTION (AMERICAN PLAYS)
Jack Ragotzy (*The Time of the Cuckoo* and *A Clearing in the Woods*)

BEST ACTOR
Alfred Ryder (*I Rise in Flame, Cried the Phoenix*)

BEST ACTRESS
Kathleen Maguire (*The Time of the Cuckoo*)

DISTINGUISHED PERFORMANCES
Rosina Fernhoff (*Fashion* and *The Geranium Hut*); Anne Fielding (*Ivanov*); Zero Mostel (*Ulysses in Nighttown*); Lester Rawlins (*The Quare Fellow*); Harold Scott (*Deathwatch*); Nancy Wickwire (*A Clearing in the Woods*)

BEST MUSICAL
A Party with Betty Comden and Adolph Green

BEST REVUE
Steven Vinaver (*Diversions*)

SET DESIGN
Open Stage: David Hjas (*The Quare Fellow*); Proscenium: Will Steven Armstrong (*Ivanov*)

MUSIC
David Amram (many productions)

LIGHTING
Nikolai Cernovich (many productions)

SPECIAL CITATION
Hal Holbrook (*Mark Twain Tonight!*)

THE OUTER CRITICS CIRCLE AWARDS

Play: *The Vist*; Performance (Drama): Diana Sands (*A Raisin in the Sun*); Performance (Musical): Tommy Rall (*Juno*); Set Design: Oliver Messel (*Rashomon*); Special citation: Hal Holbrook (*Mark Twain Tonight!*)

THE TONY AWARDS

PLAY
The Best Man by Gore Vidal
The Miracle Worker by William Gibson
A Raisin in the Sun by Lorraine Hansberry
The Tenth Man by Paddy Chayefsky
Toys in the Attic by Lillian Hellman

MUSICAL (TIE)
Fiorello!
Gypsy
Once upon a Mattress
The Sound of Music
Take Me Along

ACTOR (PLAY)
Melvyn Douglas (*The Best Man*)
Jason Robards, Jr. (*Toys in the Attic*)
Sidney Poitier (*A Raisin in the Sun*)
George C. Scott (*The Andersonville Trial*)
Lee Tracy (*The Best Man*)

ACTRESS (PLAY)
Anne Bancroft (*The Miracle Worker*)
Margaret Leighton (*Much Ado about Nothing*)
Claudia MacNeil (*A Raisin in the Sun*)
Maureen Stapleton (*Toys in the Attic*)
Irene Worth (*Toys in the Attic*)

Winner Anne Bancroft wanted to share the good news with her parents. But by the time she got to their apartment, they were asleep. So she left her Tony medallion in their mailbox.

ACTOR (MUSICAL)
Jackie Gleason (*Take Me Along*)
Andy Griffith (*Destry Rides Again*)
Robert Morse (*Take Me Along*)
Anthony Perkins (*Greenwillow*)
Walter Pidgeon (*Take Me Along*)

ACTRESS (MUSICAL)
Carol Burnett (*Once upon a Mattress*)
Dolores Gray (*Destry Rides Again*)
Eileen Herlie (*Take Me Along*)
Mary Martin (*The Sound of Music*)
Ethel Merman (*Gypsy*)

FEATURED ACTOR (PLAY)
Warren Beatty (*A Loss of Roses*)
Harry Guardino (*One More River*)
Roddy McDowall (*The Fighting Cock*)
Rip Torn (*Sweet Bird of Youth*)
Lawrence Winters (*The Long Dream*)

FEATURED ACTRESS (PLAY)
Leora Dana (*The Best Man*)
Jane Fonda (*There Was a Little Girl*)
Sarah Marshall (*Goodbye, Charlie*)
Juliet Mills (*Five Finger Exercise*)
Anne Revere (*Toys in the Attic*)

FEATURED ACTOR (MUSICAL)
Theodore Bikel (*The Sound of Music*)
Tom Bosley (*Fiorello!*)
Howard Da Silva (*Fiorello!*)
Kurt Kaszner (*The Sound of Music*)
Jack Klugman (*Gypsy*)

FEATURED ACTRESS (MUSICAL)
Sandra Church (*Gypsy*)
Pert Kelton (*Greenwillow*)
Patricia Neway (*The Sound of Music*)
Lauri Peters and the Children
   (*The Sound of Music*)

In one of the oddest Tony nominations ever, all seven child actors in *The Sound of Music* were up for Featured Actress (Musical), even though two of them were boys.

OTHER AWARDS

Director (Play): Arthur Penn (*The Miracle Worker*); Director (Musical): George Abbott (*Fiorello!*); Choreography: Michael Kidd (*Destry Rides Again*); Musical Director/Conductor: Frederick Dvonch (*The Sound of Music*); Set Design (Play): Howard Bay (*Toys in the Attic*); Set Design (Musical): Oliver Smith (*The Sound of Music*); Costume Design: Cecil Beaton (*Saratoga*); Stage Technician: John Walters (chief carpenter, *The Miracle Worker*)

SPECIAL AWARDS

John D. Rockefeller, 3rd, for vision and leadership in creating Lincoln Center; Burgess Meredith and James Thurber for *A Thurber Carnival*

Once again, the Tonys were relegated to a late-night spot on a local New York channel (WCBS). There was a major uproar when Ethel Merman's dynamic portrayal of the ultimate stage mother Mama Rose in *Gypsy* lost to Mary Martin's performance in *The Sound of Music*. (Ironically, both Angela Lansbury and Tyne Daly would win Tonys for playing Rose in revivals.) Columnists like Earl Wilson and Leonard Lyons of the *New York Post* and Burt Boyar of the *Long Island Daily Press* protested the Tony results and stated the awards were not representative of the theater as a whole. Under the system as of 1960, the nominations and the final selection of winners were voted on only by the American Theatre Wing's board of directors, some of whom were not even directly involved in production. The controversy over Merman's loss resulted in an overhaul of the awards the following year.

THE VERNON RICE AWARDS

AUTHORS

Edward Albee (*The Zoo Story*); Rick Besoyan (for the musical *Little Mary Sunshine*); Jack Gelber (*The Connection*); Jack Richardson (*The Prodigal*)

THE NEW YORK DRAMA CRITICS CIRCLE AWARDS

BEST AMERICAN PLAY
Toys in the Attic by Lillian Hellman

BEST FOREIGN PLAY
Five Finger Exercise by Peter Shaffer

BEST MUSICAL
Fiorello! by Jerome Weidman, George Abbott, Sheldon Harnick, and Jerry Bock

THE PULITZER PRIZE FOR DRAMA

Fiorello! by Jerome Weidman, George Abbott, Sheldon Harnick, and Jerry Bock

THE OBIE AWARDS

BEST FOREIGN PLAY
The Balcony by Jean Genet

BEST ALL-AROUND PRODUCTION
The Connection

DISTINGUISHED PLAYS
Krapp's Last Tape by Samuel Beckett; *The Zoo Story* by Edward Albee; *The Prodigal* by Jack Richardson

BEST DIRECTOR
Gene Frankel (*Machinal*)

BEST ACTOR
Warren Finnerty (*The Connection*)

BEST ACTRESS
Eileen Brennan (*Little Mary Sunshine*)

DISTINGUISHED PERFORMANCES
William Daniels (*The Zoo Story*); Donald Davis (*Krapp's Last Tape*); Patricia Falkenhain (*Peer Gynt* and *Henry IV*); Vincent Gardenia (*Machinal*); John Heffernan (*Henry IV, Part 2*); Jack Livingston (*The Balcony*); Elisa Loti (*Come Share My House*); Nancy Marchand (*The Balcony*)

SETS
David Hays (*The Balcony*)

SPECIAL CITATION
Brooks Atkinson of *The New York Times*

THE OUTER CRITICS CIRCLE AWARDS

Play: *The Miracle Worker*; Musical: *Bye, Bye, Birdie*; Performance (Drama): Risa Schwartz (*The Tenth Man*); Performance (Musical): Cecil Kellaway (*Greenwillow*); Special Citations: National Phoenix Company, *Mary Stuart* on tour

1960-61

THE TONY AWARDS

PLAY
All the Way Home by Tad Mosel
Becket by Jean Anouilh
The Devil's Advocate by Dore Schary
The Hostage by Brendan Behan

MUSICAL
Bye, Bye, Birdie
Do Re Mi
Irma La Douce

ACTOR (PLAY)
Hume Cronyn (*Big Fish, Little Fish*)
Sam Levene (*The Devil's Advocate*)
Zero Mostel (*Rhinoceros*)
Anthony Quinn (*Becket*)

"The fellows at the zoo will be happy about this," joked Zero Mostel when he accepted his Tony for *Rhinoceros*, in which he played a boastful man who is transformed into the title creature.

ACTRESS (PLAY)
Tallulah Bankhead (*Midgie Purvis*)
Barbara Baxley (*Period of Adjustment*)
Barbara Bel Geddes (*Mary, Mary*)
Joan Plowright (*A Taste of Honey*)

ACTOR (MUSICAL)
Richard Burton (*Camelot*)
Maurice Evans (*Tenderloin*)
Phil Silvers (*Do Re Mi*)

ACTRESS (MUSICAL)
Julie Andrews (*Camelot*)
Carol Channing (*Show Girl*)
Elizabeth Seal (*Irma La Douce*)
Nancy Walker (*Do Re Mi*)

FEATURED ACTOR (PLAY)
Philip Bosco (*The Rape of the Lock*)
Eduardo Ciannelli (*The Devil's Advocate*)
Martin Gabel (*Big Fish, Little Fish*)
George Grizzard (*Big Fish, Little Fish*)

FEATURED ACTRESS (PLAY)
Colleen Dewhurst (*All the Way Home*)
Eileen Heckart (*Invitation to a March*)
Tresa Hughes (*The Devil's Advocate*)
Rosemary Murphy (*Period of Adjustment*)

FEATURED ACTOR (MUSICAL)
Dick Gautier (*Bye, Bye, Birdie*)
Ron Husmann (*Tenderloin*)
Clive Revill (*Irma La Douce*)
Dick Van Dyke (*Bye, Bye, Birdie*)

FEATURED ACTRESS (MUSICAL)
Nancy Dussault (*Do Re Mi*)
Tammy Grimes (*The Unsinkable Molly Brown*)
Chita Rivera (*Bye, Bye, Birdie*)

The Tony rules stated that performers billed below the show's title were considered featured players, even if they had leading roles. Thus Tammy Grimes and Dick Van Dyke, the stars of *The Unsinkable Molly Brown* and *Bye, Bye, Birdie*, respectively, won Featured Performer Tonys for those musicals.

OTHER AWARDS
Director (Play): Sir John Gielgud (*Big Fish, Little Fish*); Director (Musical): Gower Champion (*Bye, Bye, Birdie*); Choreography: Gower Champion (*Bye, Bye, Birdie*); Musical Director/Conductor: Franz Allers (*Camelot*); Set Design (Play): Oliver Smith (*Becket*); Set Design (Musical): Oliver Smith (*Camelot*); Costume Design (Play): Motley (*Becket*); Costume Design (Musical): Adrian and Tony Duquette (*Camelot*); Stage Technician: Teddy Van Bemmel (*Becket*)

Richard Burton congratulates Elizabeth Seal at the 1960–61 Tonys.

SPECIAL AWARDS

David Merrick; The Theatre Guild for organizing the first repertory to go abroad for the State Department

The 1960–61 Tonys were presented by local New York channel WCBS in the slot after the evening news at 11:15 p.m. Comedian and former Tony winner Phil Silvers hosted. The ceremony took place on the night before the Oscars were handed out. Presenter Frederic March quipped, "This is the curtain raiser to those other awards that will be presented on the West Coast tomorrow night."

In response to criticism over the previous year's results (particularly Ethel Merman in *Gypsy* losing to Mary Martin in *The Sound of Music*), the voting spread to include the entire American Theatre Wing membership. In addition, a committee representative of the theater industry as a whole rather than the board of the Wing chose the nominees. The committee would annually consist of one producer, one director, one playwright, and two critics.

THE VERNON RICE AWARDS

Joan Hackett for her performance in *Call Me By My Rightful Name*; Tom Jones and Harvey Schmidt for their musical *The Fantasticks*; Richard Barr and Clinton Wilder for their Theater '61 productions of new playwrights, especially Edward Albee and Jack Richardson; Boris Tumarin for direction of *Montserrat* and *The Idiot*; Theodore J. Flicker for *The Premise*

THE NEW YORK DRAMA CRITICS CIRCLE AWARDS

BEST AMERICAN PLAY
All the Way Home by Tad Mosel

BEST FOREIGN PLAY
A Taste of Honey by Shelagh Delaney

BEST MUSICAL
Carnival by Michael Stewart and Bob Merrill

THE PULITZER PRIZE FOR DRAMA

All the Way Home by Tad Mosel

THE OBIE AWARDS

BEST NEW PLAY
The Blacks by Jean Genet

BEST OVER-ALL PRODUCTION
Hedda Gabler

BEST OFF-OFF-BROADWAY PRODUCTION
The Premise

BEST DIRECTOR
Gerald Freedman (*The Taming of the Shrew*)

BEST ACTOR
Khigh Deigh (*In the Jungle of Cities*)

BEST ACTRESS
Anne Meacham (*Hedda Gabler*)

DISTINGUISHED PERFORMANCES
Godfrey M. Cambridge (*The Blacks*); James Coco (*The Moon in the Yellow River*); Joan Hackett (*Call Me By My Rightful Name*); Gerry Jedd (*She Stoops to Conquer*); Surya Kumari (*The King of the Darn Chamber*); Lester Rawlins (*Hedda Gabler*)

MUSIC
Teiji Ito (*In the Jungle of Cities, Three Modern Japanese Plays,* and *King Ubu*)

SPECIAL CITATION
Bernard Frechtman for his translation of *The Blacks*

THE OUTER CRITICS CIRCLE AWARDS

Creative Contributions to the Season: *Rhinoceros,* Gower Champion, *Carnival;* Ensemble Acting: *Big Fish, Little Fish;* Performance (Musical): Don Tompkins (*Wildcat*); Set Design: Oliver Smith (*Camelot*); Special citation: American Shakespeare Festival Theatre and Academy

1961-62

THE TONY AWARDS

PLAY
The Caretaker by Harold Pinter
Gideon by Paddy Chayefsky
A Man for All Season by Robert Bolt
Night of the Iguana by Tennessee Williams

Robert Bolt's *A Man for All Seasons,* a study of Sir Thomas More who lost his head but gained sainthood in a battle of wills with King Henry VIII, collected five Tonys, the most ever for a straight play. This record was later tied by *Who's Afraid of Virginia Woolf?, Child's Play,* and *The Real Thing.*

MUSICAL
Carnival
How to Succeed in Business without Really Trying
Milk and Honey
No Strings

ACTOR (PLAY)
Frederic March (*Gideon*)
John Mills (*Ross*)
Donald Pleasance (*The Caretaker*)
Paul Scofield (*A Man for All Seasons*)

ACTRESS (PLAY)
Gladys Cooper (*A Passage to India*)
Colleen Dewhurst (*Great Day in the Morning*)
Margaret Leighton (*Night of the Iguana*)
Kim Stanley (*A Far Country*)

ACTOR (MUSICAL)
Ray Bolger (*All American*)
Alfred Drake (*Kean*)
Richard Kiley (*No Strings*)
Robert Morse (*How to Succeed...*)

ACTRESS (MUSICAL) (TIE)
Anna Maria Alberghetti (*Carnival*)
Diahann Carroll (*No Strings*)
Molly Picon (*Milk and Honey*)
Elaine Stritch (*Sail Away*)

Anna Maria Alberghetti had left the lead role of *Carnival* by the time of the Tonys. Her producer David Merrick had stated in the press that he preferred her replacement Anita Gillette. To get back at him, Alberghetti did not show up at the ceremony and designated Merrick as her acceptor should she win. This meant the producer had to publicly acknowledge she had given a worthy performance.

FEATURED ACTOR (MUSICAL)
Godfrey M. Cambridge (*Purlie Victorious*)
Joseph Campanella (*A Gift of Time*)
Walter Matthau (*A Shot in the Dark*)
Paul Sparer (*Ross*)

FEATURED ACTRESS (PLAY)
Elizabeth Ashley (*Take Her, She's Mine*)
Zohra Lampert (*Look We've Come Through*)
Janet Margolin (*Daughter of Silence*)
Pat Stanley (*Sunday in New York*)

FEATURED ACTOR (MUSICAL)
Orson Bean (*Subways Are for Sleeping*)
Severn Darden (*From the Second City*)
Pierre Olaf (*Carnival*)
Charles Nelson Reilly (*How to Succeed...*)

FEATURED ACTRESS (MUSICAL)
Elizabeth Allen (*The Gay Life*)
Barbara Harris (*From the Second City*)

Diahann Carroll, Robert Morse, Margaret Leighton, and Paul Scofield at the 1961–62 Tonys. Anna Maria Alberghetti, who won in a tie with Carroll, was not present.

Phyllis Newman (*Subways Are for Sleeping*)
Barbra Streisand (*I Can Get It for You Wholesale*)

OTHER AWARDS
Director (Play): Noel Willman (*A Man for All Seasons*); Director (Musical): Abe Burrows (*How to Succeed…*); Producer (Play): Robert Whitehead, Roger L. Stevens (*A Man for All Seasons*); Composer: Richard Rodgers (*No Strings*); Book of a Musical: Abe Burrows, Jack Weinstock, Willie Gilbert (*How to Succeed…*); Choreography: Agnes De Mille (*Kwamina*); Musical Director/Conductor: Elliot Lawrence (*How to Succeed…*); Set Design: Will Steven Armstrong (*Carnival*); Costume Design: Lucinda Ballard (*The Gay Life*); Stage Technician: Michael Burns (*A Man for All Seasons*)

SPECIAL AWARDS
Brooks Atkinson, retired drama critic for *The New York Times*; Franco Zeffirelli for design and direction of the Old Vic's *Romeo and Juliet*; Richard Rodgers

The Tonys were again shown by local New York station WCBS at 11:15 p.m. in a one-hour format. Robert Preston and Ray Bolger hosted. American Theatre Wing president Helen Menken read a letter of congratulation from President Kennedy. Despite this, *Variety* labeled the show "a lifeless and labored affair."

THE VERNON RICE AWARDS

PLAYWRIGHT
Arthur Kopit for *Oh Dad, Poor Dad, Mamma's Hung You in the Closet and I'm Feelin' So Sad*; Performances: Barbara Harris (*Oh Dad, Poor Dad…*); Geoff Garland (*The Hostage*); Cicely Tyson (*Moon on a Rainbow Shawl*); Association of Producing Artists (APA) for its entire repertory season

THE NEW YORK DRAMA CRITICS CIRCLE AWARDS

BEST AMERICAN PLAY
Night of the Iguana by Tennessee Williams

BEST FOREIGN PLAY
A Man for All Seasons by Robert Bolt

BEST MUSICAL
How to Succeed in Business without Really Trying by Abe Burrows, Willie Gilbert, Jack Weinstock, and Frank Loesser

THE PULITZER PRIZE FOR DRAMA

How to Succeed in Business without Really Trying by Abe Burrows, Willie Gilbert, Jack Weinstock, and Frank Loesser

THE OBIE AWARDS

BEST AMERICAN PLAY
Who'll Save the Plowboy? by Frank D. Gilroy

BEST FOREIGN PLAY
Happy Days by Samuel Beckett

Obie judge Walter Kerr, critic for the *Herald-Tribune*, strongly objected to the award for Samuel Beckett's symbolic play *Happy Days*, in which a woman delivers a rambling monologue while buried up to her waist in the first act and up to her neck in the second. The citation read "Walter Kerr abstaining."

BEST MUSICAL
Fly Blackbird by C. Jackson, James Hatch, and Jerome Eskow

BEST ACTOR
James Earl Jones (New York Shakespeare Festival, *Clandestine on the Morning Line, The Apple,* and *Moon on a Rainbow Shawl*)

BEST ACTRESS
Barbara Harris (*Oh Dad, Poor Dad…*)

DISTINGUISHED PERFORMANCES
Sudie Bond (*Theatre of the Absurd*); Vinette Carroll (*Moon on a Rainbow Shawl*); Clayton Corzatte and Rosemary Harris (APA Repertory); Geoff Garland (*The Hostage*); Gerald O'Laughlin (*Who'll Save the Plowboy?*); Paul Roebling (*This Side of Paradise*); Ruth White (*Happy Days*)

SET
Norris Houghton (*Who'll Save the Plowboy?*)

SPECIAL CITATIONS
Ellis Rabb for conceiving and maintaining the Association of Producing Artists (APA); *The Hostage*

THE OUTER CRITICS CIRCLE AWARDS

Creative Contribution to the Season: *No Strings,* George Abbott for *A Funny Thing Happened…*; Revival: *Anything Goes*; Other Awards: Rudy Vallee for his contribution to *How to Succeed …*, *Oh Dad, Poor Dad…*, Margot Mosher, the first American to play Eliza in *My Fair Lady*; Special citations: George Freedley, National Repertory Theatre

1962-63

THE TONY AWARDS

PLAY
Mother Courage and Her Children
    by Bertolt Brecht
A Thousand Clowns by Herb Gardner
Tchin-Tchin by Sidney Michaels
Who's Afraid of Virginia Woolf? by Edward Albee

A scathing cauldron of love-hate, Edward Albee's *Who's Afraid of Virginia Woolf* shocked and startled Broadway with its frank portrayal of the embattled union of a college professor and his shrewish wife. The play took five Tonys, tying *A Man for All Seasons* record. The movie version would win six Oscars.

Albee's blunt dialogue proved too much for the Pulitzer judges. Though a three-man jury of critics recommended *Virginia Woolf* for the Pulitzer Prize, the judges decided not to give any award. The jury resigned in protest. Albee made up for the loss by winning three Pulitzers for later plays.

MUSICAL
A Funny Thing Happened on the Way to the Forum

Little Me
Oliver!
Stop the World—I Want to Get Off

ACTOR (PLAY)
Charles Boyer (*Lord Pengo*)
Paul Ford (*Never Too Late*)
Arthur Hill (*Who's Afraid of Virginia Woolf?*)
Bert Lahr (*The Beauty Part*)

ACTRESS (PLAY)
Hermione Baddeley (*The Milk Train Doesn't Stop Here Anymore*)
Uta Hagen (*Who's Afraid of Virginia Woolf?*)
Margaret Leighton (*Tchin-Tchin*)
Claudia McNeil (*Tiger, Tiger, Burning Bright*)

ACTOR (MUSICAL)
Sid Caesar (*Little Me*)
Zero Mostel (*A Funny Thing Happened…*)
Anthony Newley (*Stop the World—I Want to Get Off*)
Clive Revill (*Oliver!*)

ACTRESS (MUSICAL)
Georgia Brown (*Oliver!*)
Nanette Fabray (*Mr. President*)
Sally Ann Howes (*Brigadoon*)
Vivien Leigh (*Tovarich*)

FEATURED ACTOR (PLAY)
Alan Arkin (*Enter Laughing*)
Barry Gordon (*A Thousand Clowns*)
Paul Rogers (*Photo Finish*)
Frank Silvera (*The Lady of the Camelias*)

FEATURED ACTRESS (PLAY)
Sandy Dennis (*A Thousand Clowns*)
Melinda Dillon (*Who's Afraid of Virginia Woolf?*)
Alice Ghostley (*The Beauty Part*)
Zohra Lampert (*Mother Courage and Her Children*)

FEATURED ACTOR (MUSICAL)
David Burns (*A Funny Thing Happened…*)
Jack Gilford (*A Funny Thing Happened…*)
David Jones (*Oliver!*)
Swen Swenson (*Little Me*)

FEATURED ACTRESS (MUSICAL)
Ruth Kobart (*A Funny Thing Happened…*)
Virginia Martin (*Little Me*)
Anna Quayle (*Stop the World—I Want to Get Off*)
Louise Troy (*Tovarich*)

OTHER AWARDS
Director (Play): Alan Schneider (*Who's Afraid of Virginia Woolf?*); Director (Musical): George Abbott (*A Funny Thing Happened…*); Producer (Play): Richard Barr, Clinton Wilder (*Who's Afraid of Virginia Woolf?*); Producer (Musical): Harold Prince (*A Funny Thing Happened…*); Musical Score: Lionel Bart (*Oliver!*); Book of a Musical: Larry Gelbart, Burt Shevelove (*A Funny Thing Happened…*); Choreography: Bob Fosse (*Little Me*); Musical Director/Conductor: Donald Pippin (*Oliver!*); Set Design: Sean Kenny (*Oliver!*); Costume Design: Anthony Powell (*The School for Scandal*); Stage Technician: Solly Pernick (*Mr. President*)

SPECIAL AWARDS
Irving Berlin; W. McNeil Lowry of the Ford Foundation; Alan Bennett, Peter Cook, Jonathan Miller, Dudley Moore for *Beyond the Fringe*

The Tonys switched from WCBS to WOR, and were still seen only by a local New York TV audience. Abe Burrows and Robert Morse, the author and star, respectively, of *How To Succeed in Business without Really Trying*, the big musical winner of the previous year, were the emcees. At one point in the show, Burrows was interrupted by a man later identified as Ronnie Mills who came up on stage to complain he couldn't make a living because newspapers refused to take ads for his business (the then novel enterprise of a dating service). He was escorted from the stage. Mills had previously gatecrashed *The Tonight Show*, which was then filmed in New York.

THE VERNON RICE AWARDS

PLAYWRIGHTS
Oliver Hailey (*Hey You, Light Man*); William Hanley (*Whisper into My Good Ear* and *Mrs. Dally Has a Lover*); Murray Schisgal (*The Typists and The Tiger*)

BEST OVER-ALL PRODUCTIONS

The Boys from Syracuse and *The Coach with Six Insides*

THE NEW YORK DRAMA CRITICS CIRCLE AWARDS

BEST PLAY

Who's Afraid of Virginia Woolf? by Edward Albee

SPECIAL CITATION

Beyond the Fringe

The voting rules for the Critics Circle changed this year. Instead of chosing a Best American and Best Foreign Play, the Circle now voted first for the Best Play regardless of origin. Depending on the nationality of the winner, a top foreign or American play would then be elected (if there were any worthy candidates).

THE PULITZER PRIZE FOR DRAMA

No award

THE OBIE AWARDS

BEST PRODUCTION

Six Characters in Search of an Author

BEST MUSICAL PRODUCTION

The Boys from Syracuse

BEST ACTOR

George C. Scott (*Desire under the Elms*)

BEST ACTRESS

Colleen Dewhurst (*Desire under the Elms*)

BEST DIRECTOR

Alan Schneider (*The Pinter Plays*)

DISTINGUISHED PERFORMANCES

Jacqueline Brookes and Michael O'Sullivan (*Six Characters in Search of an Author*); Joseph Chaikin and Olympia Dukakis (*Man Is Man*); Anne Jackson and Eli Wallach (*The Typists and The Tiger*); James Patterson (*The Collection*); Madeline Sherwood (*Hey You, Light Man*)

SPECIAL CITATIONS

The Second City; Jean Erdman for *The Coach with Six Insides*

THE OUTER CRITICS CIRCLE AWARDS

Playwright of the Season: Edward Albee (*Who's Afraid of Virginia Woolf?*); Staging: Alan Schneider (*Who's Afraid of Virginia Woolf?*), William Ball (*Six Characters in Search of an Author*); New Playwright: Murray Schisgal (*The Tiger and The Typists*); Special Citations: Alexander H. Cohen, Helen Hayes, Maurice Evans, *Oliver!*

1963-64

THE TONY AWARDS

PLAY

The Ballad of the Sad Cafe
   by Edward Albee
Barefoot in the Park by Neil Simon
Dylan by Sidney Michaels
Luther by John Osborne

MUSICAL

Funny Girl
Hello, Dolly!
High Spirits
She Loves Me

Tony said *Hello, Dolly!* by awarding the musical about a lovable matchmaker ten prizes, the most for any show ever. The record still stands.

ACTOR (PLAY)

Richard Burton (*Hamlet*)
Albert Finney (*Luther*)
Alec Guinness (*Dylan*)
Jason Robards, Jr. (*After the Fall*)

Richard Burton joked he was angry that as a Welshman in a play by an Englishman (*Hamlet*), he had lost to an Englishman (Alec Guinness) playing a Welshman (poet Dylan Thomas).

David Burns and
Carol Channing in
Hello, Dolly!, winner
of a record ten
Tonys in 1963–64.

ACTRESS (PLAY)
Elizabeth Ashley (*Barefoot in the Park*)
Sandy Dennis (*Any Wednesday*)
Colleen Dewhurst (*The Ballad of the Sad Cafe*)
Julie Harris (*Marathon '33*)

ACTOR (MUSICAL)
Sydney Chaplin (*Funny Girl*)
Bob Fosse (*Pal Joey*)
Bert Lahr (*Foxy*)
Steve Lawrence (*What Makes Sammy Run?*)

ACTRESS (MUSICAL)
Carol Channing (*Hello, Dolly!*)
Beatrice Lillie (*High Spirits*)
Barbra Streisand (*Funny Girl*)
Inga Swenson (*110 in the Shade*)

FEATURED ACTOR (PLAY)
Lee Allen (*Marathon '33*)
Hume Cronyn (*Hamlet*)
Michael Dunn (*The Ballad of the Sad Cafe*)
Larry Gates (*A Case of Libel*)

FEATURED ACTRESS (PLAY)
Barbara Loden (*After the Fall*)
Rosemary Murphy (*Any Wednesday*)
Kate Reid (*Dylan*)
Diana Sands (*Blues for Mister Charlie*)

FEATURED ACTOR (MUSICAL):
Jack Cassidy (*She Loves Me*)
Will Geer (*110 in the Shade*)
Danny Meehan (*Funny Girl*)
Charles Nelson Reilly (*Hello, Dolly!*)

Alec Guinness, Sandy Dennis, Carol Channing, and Bert Lahr with their '63–'64 Tonys.

FEATURED ACTRESS (MUSICAL)

Julienne Marie (*Foxy*)
Kay Medford (*Funny Girl*)
Tessie O'Shea (*The Girl Who Came to Supper*)
Louise Troy (*High Spirits*)

OTHER AWARDS

Director (Play): Mike Nichols (*Barefoot in the Park*); Director (Musical): Gower Champion (*Hello, Dolly!*); Producer (Play): Herman Schumlin (*The Deputy*); Producer (Musical): David Merrick (*Hello, Dolly!*); Musical Score: Jerry Herman (*Hello, Dolly!*); Book of a Musical: Michael Stewart (*Hello, Dolly!*); Choreography: Gower Champion (*Hello, Dolly!*); Musical Director/Conductor: Shepard Coleman (*Hello, Dolly!*); Set Design: Oliver Smith (*Hello, Dolly!*); Costume Design: Freddy Wittop (*Hello, Dolly!*)

SPECIAL AWARD

Eva La Galliene

The Tonys were one month later than usual this year. The Wing had booked the Waldorf-Astoria for April 26. But they canceled when producer David Merrick announced he had gotten a deal for the awards to be presented nationally on NBC's *The Tonight Show*. Two days later, the Wing was informed the deal had fallen through. The Waldorf had been booked solid in the meantime. So the Tonys had to be given out on the next available date (May 24) at another hotel ballroom, the Hilton. Instead of a national audience, the Tonys had a local one. The show was aired on New York's WOR-TV. But at least it was on during prime time (at 8 p.m.), rather than the late-night spot of years past. Character actor Sydney Blackmer was master of ceremonies.

There were a few notable bloopers. Arthur Hill mispronounced Edward Albee's *The Ballad of the Sad Cafe* as *The Salad of the Bad Cafe*. After Carol Lawrence announced Barbara Loden of *After the Fall* as the winner for Featured Actress (Play), there were several seconds of silence. The winner was not present and had not designated an acceptor. Finally, Lawrence broke her frozen smile and accepted for Loden.

The Tony electorate was further widened to include first- and second-night theater critics and legitimate producers as well as members of the Wing.

THE DRAMA DESK-
VERNON RICE AWARDS

(The title of the award was changed this year.)

PERFORMANCES
Gloria Foster (*In White America*);
Imelda De Martin (*The Amourous Flea*)

PLAYWRIGHT
John Lewis Carlino (*Cages, Telemachus Clay,* and *Double Talk*)

BEST OVER-ALL PRODUCTIONS
In White America and *The Streets of New York*

THE NEW YORK DRAMA CRITICS
CIRCLE AWARDS

BEST PLAY
Luther by John Osborne

BEST MUSICAL
Hello, Dolly! by Michael Stewart and Jerry Herman

SPECIAL CITATION
The Trojan Women

THE PULITZER PRIZE FOR DRAMA

No award

THE OBIE AWARDS

BEST PLAY
Play by Samuel Beckett

BEST AMERICAN PLAY
Dutchman by LeRoi Jones

BEST PRODUCTION (PLAY)
The Brig (The Living Theatre)

BEST PRODUCTION (MUSICAL)
What Happened (Judson Poets Theatre)

DISTINGUISHED PLAYS
Home Movies by Rosalyn Drexler; *Funnyhouse of a Negro* by Adrienne Kennedy

BEST DIRECTOR
Judith Malina (*The Brig*)

DISTINGUISHED DIRECTION
Lawrence Kornfeld (*What Happened*)

BEST PERFORMANCE
Gloria Foster (*In White America*)

DISTINGUISHED PERFORMANCES
Philip Bruns (*Mr. Simian*); Joyce Ebert (*The Trojan Women*); Lee Grant (*The Maids*); David Hurst (*A Month in the Country*); Taylor Mead (*The General Returns from One Place to Another*); Estelle Parsons (*Next Time I'll Sing to You* and *In the Summer House*); Marian Seldes (*The Ginger Man*); Jack Warden (*Epiphany*); Ronald Weyand (*The Lesson*)

MUSIC
Al Carmines (*Home Movies* and *What Happened*)

DESIGN
Julian Beck (*The Brig*)

SPECIAL CITATION
The Judson Memorial Church for sponsorship of the Judson Poets' Theatre and Judson Dance Theatre

THE OUTER CRITICS
CIRCLE AWARDS

Performances: Lee Allen (*Marathon '33*), Inga Swenson (*110 in the Shade*); Revival of a Classic Play: *The Trojan Women*; Revival of a Modern Play: *The Lower Depths*; New Playwright: Frank D. Gilroy (*The Subject Was Roses*); Other Awards: Lincoln Center for the Performing Arts, Beatrice Lillie, Carol Burnett, Barbara Loden, Carol Haney (posthumous)

THE TONY AWARDS

PLAY
Luv by Murray Schisgal
The Odd Couple by Neil Simon

The Subject Was Roses by Frank D. Gilroy
Tiny Alice by Edward Albee

In order to spread as many awards around as possible, confusing Tony categories were added. *The Subject Was Roses* won for best Play, but Neil Simon was chosen as best Author (Play) for *The Odd Couple* and Clare Nechtern was voted best Producer (Play) for *Luv*. The following year, the three awards would be combined and the one award for best Play would be shared by the playwright and producer.

MUSICAL
Fiddler on the Roof
Golden Boy
Half a Sixpence
Oh, What a Lovely War

ACTOR (PLAY)
John Gielgud (*Tiny Alice*)
Walter Matthau (*The Odd Couple*)
Donald Pleasance (*Poor Bitos*)
Jason Robards (*Hughie*)

ACTRESS (PLAY)
Marjorie Rhodes (*All in Good Time*)
Beah Richards (*The Amen Corner*)
Diana Sands (*The Owl and the Pussycat*)
Irene Worth (*Tiny Alice*)

ACTOR (MUSICAL)
Sammy Davis (*Golden Boy*)
Zero Mostel (*Fiddler on the Roof*)
Cyril Ritchard (*The Roar of the Greasepaint—the Smell of the Crowd*)
Tommy Steele (*Half a Sixpence*)

Zero Mostel, winning for his portrayal of Tevye the milkman in *Fiddler on the Roof*, the hit musical based on the stories of Sholom Aleichem, gave his thanks in Yiddish.

ACTRESS (MUSICAL)
Elizabeth Allen (*Do I Hear a Waltz?*)
Nancy Dussault (*Bajour*)
Liza Minnelli (*Flora, the Red Menace*)
Inga Swenson (*Baker Street*)

FEATURED ACTOR (PLAY)
Jack Albertson (*The Subject Was Roses*)
Murray Hamilton (*Absence of a Cello*)
Martin Sheen (*The Subject Was Roses*)
Clarence Williams III (*Slow Dance on the Killing Ground*)

FEATURED ACTRESS (PLAY)
Rae Allen (*Traveller without Luggage*)
Alexandra Berlin (*All in Good Time*)
Carolan Daniels (*Slow Dance on the Killing Ground*)
Alice Ghostley (*The Sign in Sidney Brustein's Window*)

FEATURED ACTOR (MUSICAL)
Jack Cassidy (*Fade In-Fade Out*)
James Grout (*Half a Sixpence*)
Jerry Orbach (*Guys and Dolls*)
Victor Spinetti (*Oh, What a Lovely War*)

FEATURED ACTRESS (MUSICAL)
Maria Karnilova (*Fiddler on the Roof*)
Luba Lisa (*I Had a Ball*)
Carrie Nye (*Half a Sixpence*)
Barbara Windsor (*Oh, What a Lovely War*)

OTHER AWARDS
Director (Play): Mike Nichols (*Luv* and *The Odd Couple*); Director (Musical): Jerome Robbins (*Fiddler on the Roof*); Author (Play): Neil Simon (*The Odd Couple*); Producer (Play): Claire Nichtern (*Luv*); Producer (Musical): Harold Prince (*Fiddler on the Roof*); Musical Score: Jerry Bock, Sheldon Harnick (*Fiddler on the Roof*); Book of a Musical: Joseph Stein (*Fiddler on the Roof*); Choreography: Jerome Robbins (*Fiddler on the Roof*); Set Design: Oliver Smith (*Baker Street*); Costume Design: Patricia Zipprodt (*Fiddler on the Roof*)

SPECIAL AWARDS
Producer Gilbert Miller; set designer Oliver Smith

The Tonys were in trouble. The American Theatre Wing, sponsor of the awards, was running out of money and had closed its school. Wing president Helen Menken and her husband Wall Street financier George N. Richard were the principal backers of the annual Tony dinner. Menken had announced her retirement. She was persuaded by the Wing's board to postpone leaving her post so the '64–'65 awards could be held.

The voting expanded from only Wing members to include members of the League of New York Theatres and Producers, drama critics, and drama editors.

THE DRAMA DESK-VERNON RICE AWARDS

PLAYWRIGHTS
Robert Lowell (*The Old Glory*); Harold Willis (*A Sound of Silence*)

DIRECTOR
Ulu Grosbard (*A View from the Bridge*)

PERFORMANCES
James Earl Jones (*Othello*); Barbara Ann Teer (*Home Movies*); Susan Towers (*Shout from the Rooftops*)

THE NEW YORK DRAMA CRITICS CIRCLE AWARDS

BEST PLAY
The Subject Was Roses by Frank D. Gilroy

BEST MUSICAL
Fiddler on the Roof by Joseph Stein, Jerry Bock, and Sheldon Harnick

THE PULITZER PRIZE FOR DRAMA

The Subject Was Roses by Frank D. Gilroy

THE OBIE AWARDS

BEST AMERICAN PLAY
The Old Glory by Robert Lowell

DISTINGUISHED PLAYS
Promenade and *The Successful Life of Three* by Marie Irene Fornes

BEST MUSICAL PRODUCTION
The Cradle Will Rock

BEST DIRECTOR
Ulu Grosbard (*A View from the Bridge*)

BEST PERFORMANCES
Roscoe Lee Browne, Frank Langella, Lester Rawlins (*The Old Glory*)

DISTINGUISHED PERFORMANCES
Brian Bedford (*The Knack*); Roberts Blossom (*Do Not Pass Go*); Joseph Chaikin (*Victims of Duty* and *The Exception and the Rule*); Margaret De Priest (*The Place for Chance*); Dean Dittman (*The Cradle Will Rock*); Robert Duvall (*A View from the Bridge*); Rosemary Harris (APA Repertory); James Earl Jones (*Baal*); Frances Sternhagen (*The Room* and *A Slight Ache*); Sada Thompson (*Tartuffe*)

COSTUMES
Willa Kim (*The Old Glory*).

SPECIAL CITATIONS
The Paper Bag Players; Caffe Cino; Cafe La MaMa

THE OUTER CRITICS CIRCLE AWARDS

Productions: *Tartuffe, Oh, What a Lovely War*; Performances: Zero Mostel (*Fiddler on the Roof*), Tommy Steele (*Half a Sixpence*); Other Awards: City Center Light Opera Company, Mike Nichols for directing four hits, Sol Hurok for importing distinguished foreign attractions, William Hanley as outstanding new playwright, Association of Producing Artists (APA)

1965-66

THE TONY AWARDS

PLAY
Inadmissible Evidence by John Osborne
The Persecution and Assassination of Jean-Paul Marat as Performed by the Inmates of the Asylum of Charenton under the Direction of the Marquis de Sade by Peter Weiss
Philadelphia, Here I Come by Brian Friel

The Right Honourable Gentleman by Michael Dyne

The Tony rules changed this year. Previously, there were confusing separate categories for best Play, best Author (Play), and best Producer (Play). Now the Tony for best Play was presented to the author and the producer. With musicals, there had been a similar split with separate Tonys going to the producer, composer, lyricist, and book-writer. Starting this year, the best Musical Tony was shared by the producer and the author(s), but there was still a category for best Score of a Musical.

Accepting the Tony for best Play for the Royal Shakespeare Company's limited imported engagement of *Marat/Sade*, producer David Merrick stated that the way to win Tonys was "to bring shows over from England."

MUSICAL
Mame
Man of La Mancha
Skyscraper
Sweet Charity

Although it was playing in Greenwich Village at the ANTA Washington Square Theatre, *Man of La Mancha* was in the running for the Tonys. Its theater, which has since been torn down, was not in the Broadway theater district, but its cast was employed under the standard Broadway production contract.

ACTOR (PLAY)
Ronald Culver (*Ivanov*)
Donal Donnelly and Patrick Bedford (*Philadelphia, Here I Come*)
Hal Holbrook (*Mark Twain Tonight!*)
Nicol Williamson (*Inadmissible Evidence*)

Hal Holbrook countered David Merrick's claim that all the Tony-winning shows were British. "Well, Mr. Merrick," he challenged when he took his prize. Holbrook's one-man performance as Mark Twain was as American as possible. He went on to thank small towns in Ohio, Georgia, Iowa, and Texas where he tried the production out.

Donal Donnelly and Patrick Bedford received a joint, single nomination for playing two aspects of the same character in *Philadelphia, Here I Come*.

ACTRESS (PLAY)
Sheila Hancock (*Entertaining Mr. Sloane*)
Rosemary Harris (*The Lion in Winter*)
Kate Reid (*Slapstick Tragedy*)
Lee Remick (*Wait Until Dark*)

ACTOR (MUSICAL)
Jack Cassidy (*It's a Bird, It's a Plane, It's Superman*)
John Cullum (*On a Clear Day You Can See Forever*)
Richard Kiley (*Man of La Mancha*)
Harry Secombe (*Pickwick*)

ACTRESS (MUSICAL)
Barbara Harris (*On a Clear Day You Can See Forever*)
Julie Harris (*Skyscraper*)
Angela Lansbury (*Mame*)
Gwen Verdon (*Sweet Charity*)

FEATURED ACTOR (PLAY)
Burt Brinckerhoff (*Cactus Flower*)
A. Larry Haines (*Generation*)
Eamon Kelly (*Philadelphia, Here I Come*)
Patrick Magee (*Marat/Sade*)

FEATURED ACTRESS (PLAY)
Zoe Caldwell (*Slapstick Tragedy*)
Glenda Jackson (*Marat/Sade*)
Mairin D. O'Sullivan (*Philadelphia, Here I Come*)
Brenda Vaccaro (*Cactus Flower*)

FEATURED ACTOR (MUSICAL)
Roy Castle (*Pickwick*)
John McMartin (*Sweet Charity*)
Frankie Michaels (*Mame*)
Michael O'Sullivan (*...Superman*)

At age 10, Frankie Michaels, who played Angela Lansbury's nephew Patrick Dennis as a child in *Mame*, became the youngest person ever to win a Tony.

FEATURED ACTRESS (MUSICAL)
Beatrice Arthur (*Mame*)
Helen Gallagher (*Sweet Charity*)
Patricia Marand (*Superman*)
Charlotte Rae (*Pickwick*)

OTHER AWARDS

Director (Play): Peter Brook (*Marat/Sade*); Director (Musical): Albert Marre (*Man of La Mancha*); Score of a Musical: Mitch Leigh, Joe Darion (*Man of La Mancha*); Choreography: Bob Fosse (*Sweet Charity*); Set Design: Howard Bay (*Man of La Mancha*); Costume Design: Gunilla Palmstierna-Weiss (*Marat/Sade*)

SPECIAL AWARD

Helen Menken (posthumous)

It looked like the end of the Tony Awards. Because of the recent death of Helen Menken, president of the American Theatre Wing, the ceremony was held for the first and only time in the afternoon. It was a relatively sedate affair at the Rainbow Room in Rockefeller Center with no entertainment. Menken and her husband George N. Richard had been the principal financial backers of the annual Tony banquet and now its future was in doubt. The League of New York Theatres and Producers had taken over the administration of the awards from the Wing, which was practically inactive owing to a lack of funds. Tony voting shifted from Wing and League members, drama critics, and drama editors to members of the League, reviewers whose names appeared on the League's first- and second-night press list, and the governing boards of the Dramatists Guild, Actors' Equity, and the Society of Stage Directors and Choreographers.

Ginger Rogers, then appearing in *Hello, Dolly!*, and producer/director/writer George Abbott were the hosts. Abbott joked, "Next year, we are planning a nationwide television hook-up. … Suggestions should be made to the committee—if you can find them."

Ironically, the joke proved prophetic. The Tonys were televised the following year. The broadcast revitalized the awards and the Wing thanks to fees paid to them by the League for the use of the award.

THE DRAMA DESK- VERNON RICE AWARDS

PLAYWRIGHTS

Douglas Turner Ward (*Day of Absence/Happy Ending*); William Alfred (*Hogan's Goat*); John Arden (*Sargeant Musgrave's Dance*)

PERFORMANCES

Kevin O'Connor (*Six from La MaMa*); Irene Dailey (*Rooms*).

SPECIAL AWARD

The Living Theatre

THE NEW YORK DRAMA CRITICS CIRCLE AWARDS

BEST PLAY

Marat/Sade by Peter Weiss.

BEST MUSICAL

Man of La Mancha by Dale Wasserman, Mitch Leigh, and Joe Darion

THE PULITZER PRIZE FOR DRAMA

No award

THE OBIE AWARDS

BEST PLAY

Journey of the Fifth Horse by Ronald Ribman

DISTINGUISHED PLAYS

Good Day by Emanuel Peluso; *Chicago, Icarus's Mother,* and *Red Cross* by Sam Shepard

These were the first three plays by Sam Shepard to win Obies. His career total so far is eleven.

BEST ACTOR

Dustin Hoffman (*Journey of the Fifth Horse*)

BEST ACTRESS

Jane White (*Coriolanus* and *Love's Labour's Lost*)

DISTINGUISHED PERFORMANCES

Clarice Blackburn (*The Exhaustion of Our Son's Love*); Mari-Claire Charba (*Birdbath*); Gloria Foster (*Medea*); Sharon Gans (*Soon Jack November*); Frank Langella (*Good Day* and *The White Devil*); Kevin O'Connor (*Chicago*); Jess Osuna (*Bugs and Veronica*); Florence Turlow (*Istanbul, Red Cross,* and *A Beautiful Day*); Douglas Turner Ward (*Day of Absence*)

DISTINGUISHED DIRECTION
Jacques Levy (*You're Only as Old as Your Arteries, Red Cross,* and *The Next Thing*); Remy Charlip (*A Beautiful Day*)

SET DESIGN
Lindsey Decker (*Red Cross*); Ed Wittstein (*Sergeant Musgrave's Dance*)

SPECIAL CITATIONS
Joseph H. Dunn for his production of *The Automobile Graveyard*; playwright H.M. Koutoukas; Peter Schumann for his Bread and Puppet Theatre; Theatre of Ideas; Theatre in the Street

THE OUTER CRITICS CIRCLE AWARDS

Productions: *Man of La Mancha, Wait a Minit!*; Performances: Gwen Verdon (*Sweet Charity*), Angela Lansbury and Beatrice Arthur (*Mame*), Donal Donnelly and Patrick Bedford (*Philadelphia, Here I Come*); Frank Loesser for the revival of his work at City Center; Director: Peter Brook (*Marat/Sade*); Other awards: David Merrick, Institute for Advanced Studies in Theatre Arts for its revival of *Phaedra*

THE TONY AWARDS

PLAY
A Delicate Balance by Edward Albee
Black Comedy by Peter Shaffer
The Homecoming by Harold Pinter
The Killing of Sister George by Frank Marcus

This was the first year the Tony Awards were fully telecast on a national network. Broadway and London producer Alexander Cohen sold the idea of promoting Broadway through a television special to the League of New York Producers and Theatres, which now ran the awards, and to ABC, which broadcast the one-hour show. The impact of television on the Great White Way was immediately felt. The winner for best Play, Harold Pinter's darkly menacing *The Homecoming*, had taken in only $14,000 the week before the Tonys. The week after, the box-office jumped to $42,000.

MUSICAL
The Apple Tree
Cabaret
I Do! I Do!
Walking Happy

For the first TV Tonys, the entertainment was ready-made. Numbers from the nominated shows were a natural choice. Unlike the hokey diversions cooked up for the Oscars and Emmys, the Tony numbers had been tested before Broadway audiences. Joel Grey as the evil emcee from *Cabaret* opened the telecast with "Wilkommen." Co-hosts for the evening Robert Preston and Mary Martin performed "Nobody's Perfect" from the two-charatcer musical *I Do! I Do!* Barbara Harris re-created her performance as a chimney sweep dreaming of cinema glamor in *The Apple Tree* by singing "I Wanna Be a Movie Star." Norman Wisdom warbled the title song from *Walking Happy*.

ACTOR (PLAY)
Hume Cronyn (*A Delicate Balance*)
Donald Madden (*Black Comedy*)
Donald Moffat (*Right You Are* and *The Wild Duck*)
Paul Rogers (*The Homecoming*)

ACTRESS (PLAY)
Eileen Atkins (*The Killing of Sister George*)
Vivien Merchant (*The Homecoming*)
Rosemary Murphy (*A Delicate Balance*)
Beryl Reid (*The Killing of Sister George*)

Beryl Reid and Eileen Atkins had both been nominated for the London *Evening Standard* Award for the same roles, that of an alcoholic soap opera actress (Reid) and her child-like lover (Atkins) in *The Killing of Sister George*.

ACTOR (MUSICAL)
Alan Alda (*The Apple Tree*)
Jack Gilford (*Cabaret*)
Robert Preston (*I Do! I Do!*)
Norman Wisdom (*Walking Happy*)

Robert Preston was so stunned by winning that he forgot the lyrics to a song from *I Do! I Do!* to close the show. His co-star Mary Martin prompted him.

ACTRESS (MUSICAL)
Barbara Harris (*The Apple Tree*)
Lotte Lenya (*Cabaret*)
Mary Martin (*I Do! I Do!*)
Louise Troy (*Walking Happy*)

Stan Berman, a thirty-five-year-old Brooklyn cab driver, claimed he was the world's greatest gate crasher. He made good on his boast by walking into the Shubert Theatre, getting onstage, and kissing Barbara Harris as she was accepting her Tony Award.

FEATURED ACTOR (PLAY)
Clayton Corzatte (*The School for Scandal*)
Stephen Elliott (*Marat/Sade*)
Ian Holm (*The Homecoming*)
Sydney Walker (*The Wild Duck*)

FEATURED ACTRESS (PLAY)
Camila Ashland (*Black Comedy*)
Brenda Forbes (*The Loves of Cass McGuire*)
Marian Seldes (*A Delicate Balance*)
Maria Tucci (*The Rose Tattoo*)

FEATURED ACTOR (MUSICAL)
Leon Bibb (*A Hand Is on the Gate*)
Gordon Dilworth (*Walking Happy*)
Joel Grey (*Cabaret*)
Edward Winter (*Cabaret*)

Joel Grey also won a 1972 Oscar for playing the same role in the film version.

FEATURED ACTRESS (MUSICAL)
Peg Murray (*Cabaret*)
Leland Palmer (*A Joyful Noise*)
Josephine Premice (*A Hand Is on the Gate*)
Susan Watson (*A Joyful Noise*)

OTHER AWARDS
Director (Play): Peter Hall (*The Homecoming*); Director (Musical): Harold Prince (*Cabaret*); Score of a Musical: John Kander, Fred Ebb (*Cabaret*); Choreography: Ronald Field (*Cabaret*); Set Design: Boris Aronson (*Cabaret*); Costume Design: Patricia Zipprodt (*Cabaret*)

The Tonys were saved from extinction by television. After the death of Helen Menken, president of the American Theatre Wing, in 1966, it appeared the award had seen its last season. But Alexander Cohen's video presentation, scripted by his wife and partner Hildy Parks, was an immediate hit. *The New York Times* reported: "The first coast-to-coast telecast of the Antoinette Perry Awards was an auspicious occasion. . . . It gave the Broadway stage more national television attention in one night than it had received in years." *Variety* concurred: "Immediate indications are that the television show was one of the biggest exploitation lifts the theatre has ever had."

Cohen made sure the program garnered viewers by loading the marquee with names well known outside the relatively small world of theatre. Among the charter Tony presenters on TV were Lauren Bacall, Lee Remick, John Forsythe, Kirk Douglas, Harry Belafonte, Carol Burnett, Angela Lansbury, and Zero Mostel. Also presenting was David Merrick, the flamboyant theatrical producer, who thanked viewers for "not watching *Bonanza*."

The total budget for the show, provided by American Airlines, was $500,000, a hefty chunk of which went to publicity. Entertainment reporters from around the country were flown in for the entire Tony weekend and treated to two days of playgoing and receptions. In front of the Shubert Theatre, where the awards were held, a red carpet was rolled out, spotlights arced across the sky, fans filled bleachers, and a brass band played show tunes.

The Tonys were a national smash and the Cohens continued to produce them for the next twenty years.

THE DRAMA DESK- VERNON RICE AWARDS

PLAYWRIGHTS
Jean-Claude van Itallie (*America Hurrah*); Lanford Wilson (*The Rimers of Eldritch*)

PERFORMERS
Bill Hinnant (*You're a Good Man, Charlie Brown*);

Dustin Hoffman (*Eh?*); Stacy Keach (*MacBird!*); Will Lee (*The Deer Park*)

DIRECTOR
Joseph Hardy (*You're a Good Man, Charlie Brown*)

THE PULITZER PRIZE FOR DRAMA

A Delicate Balance by Edward Albee

THE NEW YORK DRAMA CRITICS CIRCLE AWARDS

BEST PLAY
The Homecoming by Harold Pinter

BEST MUSICAL
Cabaret by John Kander, Fred Ebb, and Joe Masteroff

THE OBIE AWARDS

DISTINGUISHED PLAYS
Eh? by Henry Livings; *Futz* by Rochelle Owens; *La Turista* by Sam Shepard

BEST DIRECTOR
Tom O'Horgan (*Futz*)

BEST ACTOR
Seth Allen (*Futz*)

DISTINGUISHED PERFORMANCES
Tom Aldredge (*Measure for Measure* and *Stock Up on Pepper Cause Turkey's Going to War*); Robert Bonnard (*The Chairs*); Alvin Epstein (*Dynamite Tonight*); Neil Flanagan (*The Madness of Lady Bright*); Bette Henritze (*Measure for Measure, The Wilder Plays, The Distinguished Person,* and *The Rimers of Eldritch*); Stacy Keach (*MacBird!*); Terry Kaiser (*Fortune and Men's Eyes*); Eddie McCarty (*Kitchenette*); Robert Salvio (*Hamp*); Rip Torn (*The Deer Park*)

BEST LIGHTING
John Dodd (*The White Whore and the Bit Player, The Madness of Lady Bright,* and *Charles Dickens' A Christmas Carol*)

SPECIAL CITATIONS
La MaMa Troupe for its European tour; The Open Theatre; Tom Sankey for conceiving, writing, and performing *The Golden Screw* at Theatre Grande; The Second Story Players; Jeff Weiss for writing and performing in *And That's How the Rent Gets Paid* and *A Funny Walk Home*

This year's Tony winner for best Actress (Musical) Barbara Harris presided over the Obie ceremonies, which featured entertainment from a new band called the Mothers of Invention led by a singer named Frank Zappa. Three of the winners described themselves as "paranoid" in their acceptance speeches.

THE OUTER CRITICS CIRCLE AWARDS

Productions: *Cabaret, America Hurrah, You're a Good Man, Charlie Brown, You Know I Can't Hear You When the Water's Running*; Performance: Martin Balsam (*You Know I Can't Hear You...*; New Personalities: Melina Mercouri (*Ilya, Darling*), Leslie Uggams (*Hallelujah, Baby*); Director: Joseph Hirsch (*Galileo*); Other Awards: Alexander H. Cohen, Constance Towers for her performance in *The Sound of Music* revival; Bill and Cora Baird for establishing a permanent puppet theater

THE TONY AWARDS

PLAY
A Day in the Death of Joe Egg by Peter Nichols
Plaza Suite by Neil Simon
Rosencrantz and Guildenstern Are Dead
   by Tom Stoppard
The Price by Arthur Miller

MUSICAL
Hallejulah, Baby!
The Happy Time
How Now, Dow Jones
Ilya, Darling

This was the year of the Tony lawsuit. Numerous

producers had rushed their shows to Broadway in order to qualify for the awards, only to be left out in the cold when the Tony eligibility cut-off date was pushed up. Two entrepreneurs went so far as to take the matter to court.

The cut-off date had been announced as April 11. When NBC picked up the ceremony, it wanted an earlier date to ensure a bigger audience. (TV viewership tends to fall off in the late spring-early summer.) To placate the Peacock network, the cut-off date was changed to March 15. David Black, whose musical *George M!* was scheduled to premiere in April, sued the League of New York Theatres and Producers, as did Michael Butler, the producer of *Hair*, another late entry. A New York Supreme Court judge tossed out Black's suit to force the League to consider *George M!* as a Tony candidate. Butler's case was also dismissed. Both shows received nominations the next season.

In a sideshow, Zev Bufman campaigned to get his *Your Own Thing* as a write-in choice. The updated version of Shakespeare's *Twelfth Night* won the New York Drama Critics Circle Award as Best Musical but was ineligible for a Tony since it was an Off-Broadway show. Bufman maintained there were few if any worthier shows on Broadway. All of the Best Musical nominees had received mixed to negative notices. The winner *Hallelujah, Baby!* had closed by the time of the awards.

Also ineligible were all productions by nonprofit repertory companies. In a controversial rule change, the League eliminated all shows operating under a LORT (League of Resident Theatres) Equity contract from Tony consideration, even though most were playing Broadway houses. Just in the previous year, productions from APA-Phoenix Repertory received multiple nominations. Many saw this as a crass attempt by the Broadway producers who ran the Tonys to keep shows not produced by them out of competition. As a peace offering, APA-Phoenix was given a special Tony. The following year, repertory shows were eligible again.

ACTOR (PLAY)
Martin Balsam (*You Know I Can't Hear You When the Water's Running*)
Albert Finney (*Joe Egg*)

Milo O'Shea (*Staircase*)
Alan Webb (*I Never Sang for My Father*)

ACTRESS (PLAY)
Zoe Caldwell (*The Prime of Miss Jean Brodie*)
Colleen Dewhurst (*More Stately Mansions*)
Maureen Stapleton (*Plaza Suite*)
Dorothy Tutin (*Portrait of a Queen*)

ACTOR (MUSICAL)
Robert Goulet (*The Happy Time*)
Robert Hooks (*Hallelujah, Baby!*)
Anthony Roberts (*How Now, Dow Jones*)
David Wayne (*The Happy Time*)

ACTRESS (MUSICAL) (TIE)
Melina Mercouri (*Ilya, Darling*)
Patricia Routledge (*Darling of the Day*)
Leslie Uggams (*Hallelujah, Baby!*)
Brenda Vaccaro (*How Now, Dow Jones*)

"I don't know where my feet are tonight," exclaimed an ecstatic Leslie Uggams. Presenter Groucho Marx brought the house down with his comeback, "Want me to look?"

FEATURED ACTOR (PLAY)
Paul Hecht (*Rosencrantz and Guildenstern Are Dead*)
Brian Murray (*Rosencrantz and Guildenstern Are Dead*)
James Patterson (*The Birthday Party*)
John Wood (*Rosencrantz and Guildenstern Are Dead*)

FEATURED ACTRESS (PLAY)
Pert Kelton (*Spofford*)
Zena Walker (*Joe Egg*)
Ruth White (*The Birthday Party*)
Eleanor Wilson (*Weekend*)

FEATURED ACTOR (MUSICAL)
Scott Jacoby (*Golden Rainbow*)
Nikos Kourkoulos (*Ilya, Darling*)
Mike Rupert (*The Happy Time*)
Hiram Sherman (*How Now, Dow Jones*)

FEATURED ACTRESS (MUSICAL)
Geula Gill (*The Grand Music Hall of Israel*)

Julie Gregg (*The Happy Time*)
Lillian Hayman (*Hallelujah, Baby!*)
Alice Playten (*Henry, Sweet Henry*)

OTHER AWARDS
Director (Play): Mike Nichols (*Plaza Suite*);
Director (Musical): Gower Champion (*The Happy Time*); Score of a Musical: Jule Styne, Betty Comden, Adolph Green (*Hallelujah, Baby!*); Choreography: Gower Champion (*The Happy Time*); Set and Costume Design: Desmond Heeley (*Rosencrantz and Guildenstern Are Dead*)

SPECIAL AWARDS
Audrey Hepburn; Carol Channing; Pearl Bailey; David Merrick; Maurice Chevalier; APA-Phoenix Repertory Theatre; Marlene Dietrich

The first Tonycast had gone over so well, it was expanded from an hour to ninety minutes and switched from ABC to NBC, which was willing to give it the extra half-hour. Peter Ustinov and Angela Lansbury hosted the event and Eastern Airlines was the sole sponsor. Presenters included stars from film and television such as Jack Benny, Shirley Booth, Alan King, Paul Newman, Gregory Peck, and Joanne Woodward. Tony producer Alexander Cohen stipulated that each presenter must have at least one major theatrical credit.

In addition to numbers from new musicals *Golden Rainbow, The Happy Time, How Now, Dow Jones,* and *Hallelujah, Baby!*, there were performances from holdover hits of previous seasons like *Hello, Dolly!, Cabaret, Man of La Mancha,* and *Fiddler on the Roof,* which featured Bette Midler making her television debut as one of Tevye's daughters singing "Matchmaker, Matchmaker."

In spite of the controversy over the early cut-off date and the freeze-out of repertory companies, the show was well received. Cynthia Lowry of the Associated Press wrote, "The Broadway theatre has about it an electricity and glamour that somehow motion pictures can't touch. It was evident Sunday in the Tony Award presentation…. It came off smoothly and with excitement."

Director Mike Nichols received the Oscar for *The Graduate* the same year. He gave a pre-taped thank you for his *Plaza Suite* Tony from Rome where he was shooting a picture. Another absentee,

best Author (Play) winner Tom Stoppard, gave his acceptance speech via video from London where he was rehearsing a new play. This was the first and last year this method was used for nonattendees. Because the Tonys are traditionally tight on time, there are no designated acceptors for those who cannot be present. The presenter merely says thanks on the winner's behalf and the show goes on.

THE DRAMA DESK-VERNON RICE AWARDS

PERFORMANCE BY AN ACTRESS IN A REPERTORY COMPANY
Helen Hayes (*The Show-Off,* APA-Phoenix Repertory)

PLAYWRIGHTS
Ed Bullins (*The Ed Bullins Plays*); Ron Cowen (*Summertree*); Israel Horovitz (*The Indian Wants the Bronx*); Donald Driver (book of *Your Own Thing*)

COMPOSERS
Al Carmines (*In Circles*); Galt MacDermot (*Hair*)

DIRECTORS
Robert Moore (*The Boys in the Band*); Tom O'Horgan (*Hair*)

THEATERS
The Negro Ensemble Company; Joseph Papp's Public Theater

THE NEW YORK DRAMA CRITICS CIRCLE AWARDS

BEST PLAY
Rosencrantz and Guildenstern Are Dead by Tom Stoppard

BEST MUSICAL
Your Own Thing by Donald Driver, Hal Hester, and Danny Apolinar (first Off-Broadway musical to win the Circle's award)

THE PULITZER PRIZE FOR DRAMA

No award

THE OBIE AWARDS

BEST FOREIGN PLAY
The Memorandum by Vaclav Havel

DISTINGUISHED PLAYS
The Indian Wants the Bronx by Israel Horovitz; *Muzeeka* by John Guare; *Forensic and the Navigators* and *Melodrama Play* by Sam Shepard

BEST MUSICAL
In Circles by Gertrude Stein and Al Carmines.

DIRECTION
Best Director: Michael A. Schultz (*Song of the Lusitanian Bogey*); Distinguished Direction: John Hancock (*A Midsummer Night's Dream*), Rip Torn (*The Beard*)

BEST ACTOR
Al Pacino (*The Indian Wants the Bronx*)

Pacino won an Obie for his stage debut as a brutal hoodlum in the harrowing one-act of urban violence *The Indian Wants the Bronx*. The next year he would win a Tony for his first Broadway show, the short-lived *Does a Tiger Wear a Necktie?*

BEST ACTRESS
Billie Dixon (*The Beard*)

DISTINGUISHED PERFORMANCES
John Cazale (*Line* and *The Indian Wants the Bronx*); James Coco (*Fragments*); Jean David (*Istanbul*); Cliff Gorman (*The Boys in the Band*); Mari Gorman (*The Memorandum* and *Walking to Waldheim*); Moses Gunn (Negro Ensemble Company); Peggy Pope (*Mama*); Roy R. Scheider (*Stephen D.*)

BEST DESIGN
Robert LaVigne (*A Midsummer Night's Dream* and *Endecott and the Red Cross*)

SPECIAL CITATIONS
El Teatro Campesino; The Fortune Society; The Negro Ensemble Company; San Francisco Mime Troupe

THE OUTER CRITICS CIRCLE AWARDS

Productions: *Rosencrantz and Guildenstern Are Dead, The Price, George M!, Your Own Thing*; Performances: Pearl Bailey, Cab Calloway (*Hello, Dolly!*), Harold Gray (*The Price*), Joel Grey (*George M!*), Helen Hayes (*The Show-Off*), Zena Jasper (*Saturday Night*); Other Awards: Herman Shumlin, Mike Nichols, The Forum and Public Theatres

THE TONY AWARDS

PLAY
The Great White Hope by Howard Sackler
Hadrian VII by Peter Luke
Lovers by Brian Friel
The Man in the Glass Booth by Robert Shaw

Responding to criticism that the Tonys downplayed straight plays in favor of musicals, producer Alexander Cohen included scenes from two best Play nominees. While self-contained musical numbers look great on television, scenes taken out of context from plays seldom prove effective. Tony winners James Earl Jones and Jane Alexander recreated dramatic sparks from *The Great White Hope*, the sprawling stage biography based on the life of Jack Johnson, the first black heavyweight boxing champion, but the excerpt from the Irish comedy *Lovers* fell flat.

The ninety-minute telecast had run thirty-five minutes overtime and it was agreed the best Play scenes were the most expendable. Extensive segments from nonmusicals nominees were not included until 1986–87.

MUSICAL
Hair
Promises, Promises
1776
Zorba

Hair, the free-form musical chronicling the counterculture revolution erupting on the streets outside the theatre, had opened too late in the 1967–68

season to qualify for that year's Tonys. The League of New York Theatres and Producers had also declared the show would be ineligible anyway since it originated Off-Broadway. In the intervening year, *Hair* grew to hit proportions and the League changed its mind, allowing the hippie musical to compete. It received one nomination, for best Musical. Ironically, it lost to a show about another revolution, one that took place almost 200 years earlier, *1776*, which documented the events leading to the signing of the Declaration of Independence.

In a rule change, the category of best Composer and Lyricist was eliminated and incorporated into the best Musical slot, which now went to the producers as well as the authors.

ACTOR (PLAY)
Art Carney (*Lovers*)
James Earl Jones (*The Great White Hope*)
Alec McCowen (*Hadrian VII*)
Donald Pleasence (*The Man in the Glass Booth*)

ACTRESS (PLAY)
Julie Harris (*Forty Carats*)
Estelle Parsons (*Seven Descents of Myrtle*)
Charlotte Rae (*Morning, Noon, and Night*)
Brenda Vaccaro (*The Goodbye People*)

ACTOR (MUSICAL)
Herschel Bernardi (*Zorba*)
Jack Cassidy (*Maggie Flynn*)

Joel Grey (*George M!*)
Jerry Orbach (*Promises, Promises*)

ACTRESS (MUSICAL)
Maria Karnilova (*Zorba*)
Angela Lansbury (*Dear World*)
Dorothy Loudon (*The Fig Leaves Are Falling*)
Jill O'Hara (*Promises, Promises*)

FEATURED ACTOR (PLAY)
Richard Castellano (*Lovers and Other Strangers*)
Al Pacino (*Does a Tiger Wear a Necktie?*)
Anthony Roberts (*Play It Again, Sam*)
Louis Zorich (*Hadrian VII*)

FEATURED ACTRESS (PLAY)
Jane Alexander (*The Great White Hope*)
Lauren Jones (*Does a Tiger Wear a Necktie?*)
Diane Keaton (*Play It Again, Sam*)
Anna Manahan (*Lovers*)

FEATURED ACTOR (MUSICAL)
William Daniels (*1776*) (nomination refused)
A. Larry Haines (*Promises, Promises*)
Ronald Holgate (*1776*)
Edward Winter (*Promises, Promises*)

William Daniels refused his nomination as a Featured Actor (Musical) in *1776*, stating his role as John Adams was a leading one. Indeed, as Adams, Daniels was the main motivator of the show's action, the signing of the Declaration of Independence, and was onstage almost constantly. He had been placed in the ranks of featured players since his name was not above the show's title. Daniels requested his name be taken off the Tony ballot. The League of New York Theatres and Producers complied. The prize ultimately went to Ronald Holgate from the same show who truly was a supporting player, appearing in only a few scenes.

FEATURED ACTRESS (MUSICAL)
Sandy Duncan (*Canterbury Tales*)
Marian Mercer (*Promises, Promises*)
Lorraine Serabian (*Zorba*)
Virginia Vestoff (*1776*)

OTHER AWARDS
Director: Peter Dews (*Hadrian VII*); Director

(Musical): Peter Hunt (*1776*); Choreography: Joe Layton (*George M!*); Set Design: Boris Aronson (*Zorba*); Costume Design: Louden Sainthill (*Canterbury Tales*)

SPECIAL AWARDS
The National Theatre Company of Great Britain; The Negro Ensemble Company; Rex Harrison; Leonard Bernstein; Carol Burnett

Interrupting a London run of the demanding lead role in Strindberg's *The Dance of Death*, Sir Laurence Olivier flew to New York to accept a special Tony Award for the National Theatre of Great Britain, gave a charming acceptance speech, rushed out of the stage door into a waiting limo which raced to Kennedy airport with a police escort, flew back to London, and went on stage the next day.

Diahann Carroll and Alan King were master of ceremonies for the 1968–69 Tonys on NBC. This was the first year there was significant campaigning for nominations and awards, demonstrating the growing importance of the prizes. Since the show was now broadcast, a Tony win meant an increased box office.

Unlike the previous years, there were plenty of still-running musicals and each of the nominated tuners was featured on the program. *Zorba* and *1776* presented one number each while *Hair* and *Promises, Promises* got in two apiece.

THE DRAMA DESK AWARDS

Under the leadership of its president Henry Hewes of the *Saturday Review*, the Drama Desk changed its awards to include Broadway as well as Off-Broadway. Productions originating anywhere in New York were given equal consideration. The Vernon Rice Award continued as a special citation for outstanding Off-Broadway work until 1973–74.

From 1968–69 through 1973–74, the organization employed a complicated form of proportional voting. The Drama Desk ballot asked each voter to check only those performances and productions he or she had actually seen. This made it possible to compute the proportion of those who voted for the show to those whose saw it, determining winners by percentages rather than total votes received.

During this period, Most Promising Playwrights were honored rather than Outstanding Plays.

In 1974–75, the system was switched to straight voting for a single winner among a small group of nominees.

OUTSTANDING PERFORMERS (IN ORDER OF PERCENTAGES RECEIVED)

James Earl Jones, Jane Alexander (*The Great White Hope*); Al Pacino (*Does a Tiger Wear a Necktie?*); James Coco (*Next*); Alec McCowen (*Hadrian VII*); Donald Pleasence (*The Man in the Glass Booth*); Nicol Williamson (*Hamlet*); Ron O'Neal (*No Place To Be Somebody*); Joseph Wiseman (*In the Matter of J. Robert Oppenheimer*); Marian Mercer (*Promises, Promises*); Bernadette Peters (*Dames at Sea*); Dustin Hoffman (*Jimmy Shine*); Dorothy Loudon (*The Fig Leaves Are Falling*); Nathan George (*No Place To Be Somebody*); Linda Lavin (*Little Murders*); Ron Leibman (*We Bombed in New Haven*); Douglas Truner Ward (*Ceremonies in Dark Old Men*); Jerry Orbach (*Promises, Promises*); Brian Bedford (*The Misanthrope*); Frank Langella (*A Cry of Players*)

OUTSTANDING DIRECTORS (IN ORDER OF PERCENTAGES RECEIVED)

Edwin Sherin (*The Great White Hope*); Gordon Davidson (*In the Matter of J. Robert Oppenheimer*); Tom O'Horgan (*Futz*): Neal Kenyon (*Dames at Sea*); Alan Arkin (*Little Murders*); Michael A. Schultz (*Does a Tiger Wear a Necktie?*)

MUSIC (IN ORDER OF PERCENTAGES RECEIVED)

Al Carmines (*Peace*), Burt Bacharach (*Promises, Promises*)

LYRICS (IN ORDER OF PERCENTAGES RECEIVED)

George Haimsohn, Robin Miller (*Dames at Sea*), Fred Ebb (*Zorba*)

BOOK

Peter Stone (*1776*)

CHOREOGRAPHY

Grover Dale (*Billy*)

SET DESIGN (IN ORDER OF PERCENTAGES RECEIVED)

Ming Cho Lee (*Invitation to a Beheading, Billy*), Boris Aronson (*Zorba*)

COSTUME DESIGN (IN ORDER OF PERCENTAGES RECEIVED)

Tanya Moiseiwitsch (*The House of Atreus*), Patricia Zipprodt (*1776, Zorba*)

MOST PROMISING PLAYWRIGHTS (IN ORDER OF PERCENTAGES RECEIVED)

Charles Gordone (*No Place To be Somebody*); Lonnie Elder III (*Ceremonies in Dark Old Men*); Elaine May (*Adaptation*)

VERNON RICE AWARD

Joseph Chaikin

THE NEW YORK DRAMA CRITICS CIRCLE AWARDS

BEST PLAY

The Great White Hope by Howard Sackler

BEST MUSICAL

1776 by Peter Stone and Sherman Edwards.

THE PULITZER PRIZE FOR DRAMA

The Great White Hope by Howard Sackler

THE OBIE AWARDS

(No separate categories, only citations for distinguished achievement.)

The Living Theatre (*Frankenstein*); Jeff Weiss (*The International Wrestling Match*); Julie Bovasso (*Gloria and Esperanza*); Judith Malina, Julian Beck (*Antigone*); Israel Horovitz (*The Honest-to-God Schnozzola*); Jules Feiffer (*Little Murders*); Ronald Tavel (*The Boy on the Straight-Back Chair*); Nathan George, Ron O'Neal (*No Place to Be Somebody*); Arlene Rothstein (*The Poor Little Matchgirl*); Theatre Genesis (sustained excellence); The Open Theatre (*The Serpent*); Om Theatre (*The Riot*); The Performance Group (*Dionysus in '69*)

Best acceptance speech: Richard Schechner for the Performance Group's *Dionysus in '69* proclaimed,

"We deserve it." Among the entertainers was Ching Yeh, who recited Hamlet's "To be or not to be" soliloquy in Chinese.

THE OUTER CRITICS CIRCLE AWARDS

Performances: Lorraine Serabian (*Zorba*), Linda Lavin (*Little Murders* and *Cop-Out*); Directors: Edwin Sherin (*The Great White Hope*), Elaine May (*Adaptation/Next*) (also cited as author of the first play); Composer/Lyricist: Sherman Edwards (*1776*); Off-Broadway Musical: *Dames at Sea*; Other awards: Jean Rosenthal (posthumous) for contributions to stage lighting, David Hays for work with the National Theatre of the Deaf

THE TONY AWARDS

PLAY

Borstal Boy by Frank McMahon
Child's Play by Robert Marasco
Indians by Arthur Kopit
Last of the Red Hot Lovers by Neil Simon

The official Tony eligibility cut-off date had been announced as March 15. This early date was instituted so that the Tony telecast on NBC could take place on April 19 since the sizes of TV audiences dropped by fifteen to twenty percent after Daylight Savings Time, which this year would go into effect on April 26. But as the Broadway season progressed, several shows were scheduled to open after the cut-off and would have missed the awards. These included *Borstal Boy* and *Applause*, the eventual winners of the best Play and best Musical Tonys.

So the League of New York Theatres and Producers pushed back the deadline to March 31. This also allowed shows which were in previews by that time to be eligible. This would be the first time the Tony nominating committee would consider productions which had not yet officially opened.

MUSICAL

Applause
Coco
Purlie

Excerpted scenes from *Applause* and *Purlie* were live, but Katharine Hepburn (who hated performing on television) taped "Always, Mademoiselle" from *Coco*.

ACTOR (PLAY)

James Coco (*Last of the Red Hot Lovers*)
Frank Grimes (*Borstal Boy*)
Stacy Keach (*Indians*)
Fritz Weaver (*Child's Play*)

ACTRESS (PLAY)

Geraldine Brooks (*Brightower*)
Tammy Grimes (*Private Lives*)
Helen Hayes (*Harvey*)

ACTOR (MUSICAL)

Len Cariou (*Applause*)
Cleavon Little (*Purlie*)
Robert Weede (*Cry for Us All*)

ACTRESS (MUSICAL)

Lauren Bacall (*Applause*)
Katharine Hepburn (*Coco*)
Dilys Watling (*Georgy*)

FEATURED ACTOR (PLAY)

Joseph Bova (*The Chinese and Dr. Fish*)
Ken Howard (*Child's Play*)
Dennis King (*A Patriot for Me*)

Ken Howard drew chuckles when he thanked "the deans of admissions at several law schools for inadvertently encouraging me to go into this business."

FEATURED ACTRESS (PLAY)

Blythe Danner (*Butterflies Are Free*)
Alice Drummond (*The Chinese and Dr. Fish*)
Eileen Heckart (*Butterflies Are Free*)
Linda Lavin (*Last of the Red Hot Lovers*)

FEATURED ACTOR (MUSICAL)

Rene Auberjonois (*Coco*)

Brandon Maggart (*Applause*)
George Rose (*Coco*)

Major oversight: There was great consternation when Lewis J. Stadlen was not nominated for his acclaimed portrayal of the young Groucho Marx in the musical *Minnie's Boys*. Stadlen's fellow cast members took out an ad in *Variety* to express their indignation on his behalf.

FEATURED ACTRESS (MUSICAL)
Bonnie Franklin (*Applause*)
Penny Fuller (*Applause*)
Melissa Hart (*Georgy*)
Melba Moore (*Purlie*)

OTHER AWARDS
Director (Play): Joseph Hardy (*Child's Play*);
Director (Musical): Ron Field (*Applause*);
Choreography: Ron Field (*Applause*); Set Design: Jo Mielziner (*Child's Play*); Costume Design: Cecil Beaton (*Coco*); Lighting Design: Jo Mielziner (*Child's Play*)

This was the first year an award for lighting design was presented.

SPECIAL AWARDS
Noel Coward; Alfred Lunt and Lynn Fontanne; New York Shakespeare Festival; Barbra Striesand

The fourth Tony telecast was the most stellar one yet. Not only were two of Hollywood's greatest ladies (Lauren Bacall and Katharine Hepburn) competing for the best Actress (Musical) award, but special honors were being presented to such legendary luminaries of the stage as Noel Coward and the acting couple Alfred Lunt and Lynn Fontanne. Relative newcomer Barbra Striesand was awarded a "Star of the Decade" prize though she had not appeared in a legitimate Broadway production since *Funny Girl* in 1964.

Bacall's high-energy comeback turn as the insecure star in *Applause*, the musicalization of the classic film *All About Eve*, triumphed over Hepburn's portrayal of the frosty designer Chanel in *Coco*. "This is the first prize I've ever won," Bacall exuded. When Cary Grant presented Noel Coward with his special Tony, the witty playwright/actor/composer made an ironic variation on Bacall's speech: "This is my first award, so please be kind."

George C. Scott, who would refuse an Oscar the following year, appeared to present the best

Play Tony. Julie Andrews, Shirley MacLaine, and Walter Matthau hosted the ninety-minute ceremony, which had its share of unforeseen glitches. At the eleventh hour, two presenters had fallen ill. Both Elliott Gould and Mia Farrow had come down with the flu. Jack Cassidy stepped in for Gould. Co-producer Hildy Parks found Claire Bloom in the audience before the broadcast and asked her to take Farrow's place. The actress consented and went on with a minimum of rehearsal.

THE DRAMA DESK AWARDS

OUTSTANDING PERFORMANCES (IN ORDER OF PERCENTAGES RECEIVED)

Zoe Caldwell (*Colette*); Sada Thompson (*The Effect of Gamma Rays on Man-in-the-Moon Marigolds*); Fritz Weaver (*Child's Play*); Frank Grimes (*Borstal Boy*); Lauren Bacall (*Applause*); Melba Moore (*Purlie*); Ryszard Cieslak (*The Constant Prince*); Lewis J. Stadlen (*Minnie's Boys*); Stacy Keach (*Indians*); Cleavon Little (*Purlie*); Tammy Grimes (*Private Lives*); Colleen Dewhurst (*Hello and Goodbye*); Stephen Elliott (*A Whistle in the Dark*); Niall Tobin (*Borstal Boy*); Ron Leibman (*Transfers*); Christopher Walken (*Lemon Sky*); Austin Pendleton (*The Last Sweet Days of Isaac*); Brian Bedford (*Private Lives*); Sandy Duncan (*The Boy Friend*); James Stewart (*Harvey*); Ethel Merman (*Hello, Dolly!*)

OUTSTANDING DIRECTORS (IN ORDER OF PERCENTAGES RECEIVED)

Harold Prince (*Company*); Jerzy Grotowski (*The Apocalypse*); Alan Arkin (*The White House Murder Case*); Joseph Hardy (*Child's Play*); Ron Field (*Applause*)

MUSIC (IN ORDER OF PERCENTAGES RECEIVED)

Stephen Sondheim (*Company*), Kurt Weill (*Mahagonny*)

LYRICS (IN ORDER OF PERCENTAGES RECEIVED)

Stephen Sondheim (*Company*), Bertolt Brecht (*Mahagonny*)

BOOK

George Furth (*Company*)

CHOREOGRAPHY

Ron Field (*Applause*)

SET DESIGN (IN ORDER OF PERCENTAGES RECEIVED)

Boris Aronson (*Company*); Jo Mielziner (*Child's Play*); Fred Voelpel (*The Memory Bank*)

COSTUME DESIGN (IN ORDER OF PERCENTAGES RECEIVED)

Freddy Wittop (*A Patriot for Me*); Willa Kim (*Promenade, Operation Sidewinder*); Theoni V. Aldredge (*Peer Gynt*)

MOST PROMISING PLAYWRIGHTS (IN ORDER OF PERCENTAGES RECEIVED)

Paul Zindel (*The Effect of Gamma Rays on Man-in-the-Moon Marigolds*); Stanley Eveling (*Dear Janet Rosenberg, Dear Mr. Kooning*); Susan Yankowitz (*Terminal*)

MOST PROMISING MUSICAL WRITERS (IN ORDER OF PERCENTAGES RECEIVED)

C. C. Courtney, Peter Link (*Salvation*); Nancy Ford, Gretch Cryer (*The Last Sweet Days of Isaac*); Gary William Friedman, Will Holt (*The Me Nobody Knows*)

BEST PLAY

Borstal Boy by Frank MacMahon

BEST AMERICAN PLAY

The Effect of Gamma Rays on Man-in-the-Moon Marigolds by Paul Zindel

BEST MUSICAL

Company by George Furth and Stephen Sondheim

THE PULITZER PRIZE FOR DRAMA

No Place to Be Somebody by Charles Gordone

This was the first Off-Broadway play to win the Pulitzer and Charles Gordone was the first African-American author to win.

THE OBIE AWARDS

BEST AMERICAN PLAYS
The Effect of Gamma Rays on Man-in-the-Moon Marigolds by Paul Zindel; *Approaching Simone* by Megan Terry

"I haven't been in a room with so much love and hate since high school English," declared Paul Zindel. The especially rowdy Obie crowd booed and jeered at several acceptance speeches. Late in the evening, an irate audience member yelled at a heckler, "Earn your right to be on stage, you loud-mouth." It turned out the heckler had earned it since he had won an Obie earlier that night.

BEST FOREIGN PLAY
What the Butler Saw by Joe Orton

BEST MUSICALS
The Last Sweet Days of Isaac by Gretchen Cryer and Nancy Ford; *The Me Nobody Knows* by Robert Livingston, Gary William Friedman, and Will Holt

DISTINGUISHED PLAYS
The Deer Kill by Murray Mednick; *The Increased Difficulty of Concentration* by Vaclav Havel

Czech playwright Havel would later become president of his country after the fall of Communism.

DISTINGUISHED DIRECTION
Alan Arkin (*The White House Murder Case*); Melvin Bernhardt (*The Effect of Gamma Rays...*); Maxine Kline (*Approaching Simone*); Gilbert Moses (*Slave Ship*)

BEST PERFORMANCE
Sada Thompson (*The Effect of Gamma Rays...*)

DISTINGUISHED PERFORMANCES
Beeson Carroll, Lee Kissman (*The Unseen Hand*); Vincent Gardenia (*Passing Through Exotic Places*); Harold Gould (*The Increased Difficulty of Concentration*); Anthony Holland (*The White House Murder Case*); Ron Leibman (*Transfers*); Rue McClanahan (*Who's Happy Now?*); Roberta Maxwell (*Whistle in the Dark*); Austin Pendleton, Fredericka Weber (*The Last Sweet Days of Isaac*);

Pamela Payton-Wright (*The Effect of Gamma Rays...*)

SPECIAL CITATIONS
Charles Ludlam, The Ridiculous Theatrical Company; John Vaccaro, Theatre of the Ridiculous; Richard Foreman, Stanley Silverman (*Elephant Steps*); Gardner Compton, Emile Ardolino (projected media for *Oh! Calcutta!*); Chelsea Theatre Center for distinguished production; Andre Gregory (*Alice in Wonderland*)

THE OUTER CRITICS CIRCLE AWARDS

Play: *Child's Play*; Musical: *Company*; Off-Broadway Play: *The White House Murder Case*; Off-Broadway Musical: *The Last Sweet Days of Isaac*; Performances: Brian Bedford (*Private Lives*); Sandy Duncan (*The Boy Friend*); Bonnie Franklin (*Applause*); Lewis J. Stadlen (*Minnie's Boys*); Frank Grimes and Niall Toibin (*Borstal Boy*)

THE TONY AWARDS

PLAY
Home by David Storey
Sleuth by Anthony Shaffer
Story Theatre by Paul Sills
The Philanthropist by Christopher Hampton

The English dominated the dramatic side of the Tony slate this year, taking three of the four best Play nominations, three of the four Director (Play) nominations, two of the four Featured Actors (Play) nominations, and all of the leading Actor (Play) slots (if you count Canadian Brian Bedford as a Brit). *Home, Sleuth,* and *The Philanthropist* all originated in London, while *Story Theatre* was Paul Sills' revue starring Second City comic actors in sketches based on fairy tales. *Sleuth*, Anthony Shaffer's intricate maze of a murder mystery, took the top prize.

MUSICAL
Company

The Me Nobody Knows
The Rothschilds

Previously the best Musical Tony went to the composer, lyricist, author of the book, and the producer. Beginning this year, the prize for top tuner went to the producer alone. The authors each had to compete in his or her own category. Both the producers and author of *Company*, a sharp-edged commentary on contemporary marriage, won. The musical had opened too late in the 1969–70 season to qualify for that year's Tonys.

ACTOR (PLAY)
Brian Bedford (*The School for Wives*)
John Gielgud (*Home*)
Alec McCowen (*The Philanthropist*)
Ralph Richardson (*Home*)

Canadian Brian Bedford triumphed against three formidable Englishman, including two knights (Sir Ralph Richardson and Sir John Gielgud), in the best Actor (Play) category. "You couldn't have made a wiser choice," he joked.

ACTRESS (PLAY)
Estelle Parsons (*And Miss Reardon Drinks a Little*)
Diana Rigg (*The Misanthrope*)
Marian Seldes (*Father's Day*)
Maureen Stapleton (*The Gingerbread Lady*)

"I wanted to spend my life in the theater, but not in one night," jibed Maureen Stapleton about the Tonycast's inordinate length.

ACTOR (MUSICAL)
David Burns (*Lovely Ladies, Kind Gentlemen*)
Larry Kert (*Company*)
Hal Linden (*The Rothschilds*)
Bobby Van (*No, No, Nanette*)

David Burns died a week before the nominations came out, making him the first posthumous Tony nominee. He was up for his role in *Lovely Ladies, Kind Gentlemen*, an unsuccessful musical version of *The Teahouse of the August Moon* which had folded after a week of performances. Burns also won an Emmy the same year for his supporting role in the *Hallmark Hall of Fame* version of Arthur Miller's *The Price*.

ACTRESS (MUSICAL)
Susan Browning (*Company*)
Sandy Duncan (*The Boy Friend*)
Helen Gallagher (*No, No, Nanette*)
Elaine Stritch (*Company*)

FEATURED ACTOR (PLAY)
Ronald Radd (*Abelard and Heloise*)
Donald Pickering (*Conduct Unbecoming*)
Paul Sand (*Story Theatre*)
Ed Zimmerman (*The Philanthropist*)

FEATURED ACTRESS (PLAY)
Rae Allen (*And Miss Reardon Drinks a Little*)
Lili Darvas (*Les Blancs*)
Joan Van Ark (*The School for Wives*)
Mona Washbourne (*Home*)

FEATURED ACTOR (MUSICAL)
Keene Curtis (*The Rothschilds*)
Charles Kimbrough (*Company*)
Walter Willison (*Two by Two*)

The totally bald Kenne Curtis said he was grateful he was following Yul Brynner, who had just performed a number from *The King and I*. "Touché," a spectator was heard to say, "or toupee."

FEATURED ACTRESS (MUSICAL)
Barbara Barrie (*Company*)
Pamela Myers (*Company*)
Patsy Kelly (*No, No, Nanette*)

OTHER AWARDS
Director (Play): Peter Brook (*A Midsummer Night's Dream*); Director (Musical): Harold Prince (*Company*); Music: Stephen Sondheim (*Company*); Lyrics: Stephen Sondheim (*Company*); Book of a Musical: George Furth (*Company*); Choreography: Donald Saddler (*No, No, Nanette*); Set Design: Boris Aronson (*Company*); Costume Design: Raoul Pene du Bois (*No, No, Nanette*); Lighting Design: H. R. Poindexter (*Story Theatre*)

SPECIAL AWARDS
Ingram Ash, president of Blaine-Thompson Advertising; drama critic Elliot Norton; producer Roger L. Stevens; *Playbill* magazine

The twenty-fifth anniversary of the Tony Awards was celebrated with a unprecedented star-filled extravangza. Alexander Cohen and Hildy Parks outdid themselves by presenting songs from each of the twenty-four previous best Musicals, many with the original players. The broadcast switched from NBC to ABC and expanded from ninety minutes to two hours. It ran over by twenty minutes, but that hardly seemed enough. The talent could have peopled twenty or thirty TV specials.

The program began with a production number set to "I'll Tell You What's Playing at the Roxy" from *Guys and Dolls* with special new lyrics by Betty Comden and Adolph Green explaining the rules of the Tonys. Then David Wayne in his leprechaun costume from *Finian's Rainbow*, seated in front of a giant sign reading 1947, sang "When I'm Not Near the Girl I Love." Among those that followed were Nanette Fabray (*High Button Shoes*), Alfred Drake (*Kiss Me, Kate* and *Kismet*), Vivian Blaine (*Guys and Dolls*), John Raitt (*The Pajama Game*), Robert Preston (*The Music Man*), Tom Bosley (*Fiorello*), Zero Mostel (*A Funny Thing . . .* and *Fiddler on the Roof*), and Carol Channing (*Hello, Dolly!*). As the hour grew late, Lauren Bacall interrupted her number from *Applause*, shouting, "Enough of this, let's get on with the awards." She then strode downstage to present the next prize.

In order to speed up the show and leave room for the cavalcade of musical numbers, hosts Bacall, Angela Lansbury, Anthony Quinn, and Anthony Quayle handed out all the Tonys.

There were a few setbacks. Angela Lansbury was introducing Gwen Verdon in a scene from *Damn Yankees* when a flashpot exploded prematurely. Lansbury had been mentioning Marilyn Monroe in her remarks. As the explosion went off, she quickly ad-libbed, "Well, that was Marilyn." The impromptu quip brought the house down.

Many reviewers called this the best Tony show ever and some went even further naming it the greatest award show of any kind ever presented. *Variety* called it "the largest spectacle in Tony history and clearly the most favorably received by critics and public alike." *The New York Times*: "The Tony show offered lessons in organization, pacing, use of talent and sheer excitement." *The Boston Globe*: "A milestone in television history."

THE DRAMA DESK AWARDS

OUTSTANDING PERFORMANCES (IN ORDER OF PERCENTAGES RECEIVED)
Ralph Richardson, John Gielgud (*Home*); Cliff Gorman (*Lenny*); Claire Bloom (*A Doll's House, Hedda Gabler*); Jack MacGowran (*The Works of Samuel Beckett*); Ruby Dee (*Boesman and Lena*); Alec McCowen (*The Philanthropist*); Brian Bedford (*The School for Wives*); Siobhan McKenna (*Here Are Ladies*); Marian Seldes (*Father's Day*); Madeleine Renaud (*L'Amante Anglaise*); Alexis Smith (*Follies*); Mildred Dunnock (*A Place without Doors*); Anthony Quayle (*Sleuth*); Helen Gallagher (*No, No, Nanette*); Keith Baxter (*Sleuth*); James Earl Jones (*Les Blancs*); Colleen Dewhurst (*All Over*); Maureen Stapleton (*The Gingerbread Lady*); Paul Sand (*Story Theatre, Metamorphosis*); Roberta Maxwell (*Slag*)

OUTSTANDING DIRECTORS (IN ORDER OF PERCENTAGES RECEIVED)
Peter Brook (*A Midsummer Night's Dream*); Harold Prince, Michael Bennett (*Follies*); Paul Sills (*Story Theatre, Metamorphosis*); Robert Wilson (*Deafman Glance*); Andre Gregory (*Alice in Wonderland*); Tom O'Horgan (*Lenny*)

MUSIC
Stephen Sondheim

LYRICS
Stephen Sondheim (*Follies*)

BOOK
Burt Shevelove (*No, No, Nanette*)

CHOREOGRAPHY (IN ORDER OF PERCENTAGES RECEIVED)
Michael Bennett (*Follies*), Donald Saddler (*No, No, Nanette*)

SET DESIGN (IN ORDER OF PERCENTAGES RECEIVED)
Boris Aronson (*Follies*); Sally Jacobs (*A Midsummer Night's Dream*); Robin Wagner (*Lenny*)

COSTUME DESIGN (IN ORDER OF PERCENTAGES RECEIVED)
Florence Klotz (*Follies*); Raoul Pene Du Bois (*No, No, Nanette*)

MOST PROMISING PLAYWRIGHTS (IN ORDER OF PERCENTAGES RECEIVED)
Kurt Vonnegut, Jr. (*Happy Birthday, Wanda June*); David Rabe (*The Basic Training of Pavlo Hummel*); Robert Montgomery (*Subject to Fits*); A. R. Gurney, Jr. (*Scenes from American Life*)

MOST PROMISING DIRECTORS (IN ORDER OF PERCENTAGES RECEIVED)
Jeff Bleckner (*The Basic Training of Pavlo Hummel*); John-Michael Tebelak (*Godspell*); Russel Treyz (*Whitsuntide*)

MOST PROMISING COMPOSERS (IN ORDER OF PERCENTAGES RECEIVED)
Stephen Schwartz (*Godspell*); Itsuro Shimoda (*Golden Bat*)

MOST PROMISING LYRICISTS (IN ORDER OF PERCENTAGES RECEIVED)
Stephen Schwartz (*Godspell*); Yutaka Higashi (*Golden Bat*)

MOST PROMISING SET DESIGN
Eugene Lee, Fred Newman (*Alice in Wonderland*).

MOST PROMISING COSTUME DESIGN
Susan Tsu (*Godspell*)

VERNON RICE AWARD
Long Day's Journey into Night, director: Arvin Brown; cast: Paddy Croft, Geraldine Fitzgerald, Stacy Keach, Robert Ryan, and James Naughton

THE NEW YORK DRAMA CRITICS CIRCLE AWARDS

BEST PLAY
Home by David Storey

BEST AMERICAN PLAY
The House of Blue Leaves by John Guare

BEST MUSICAL
Follies by James Goldman and Stephen Sondheim

THE PULITZER PRIZE FOR DRAMA

The Effect of Gamma Rays on Man-in-the-Moon Marigolds by Paul Zindel

THE OBIE AWARDS

BEST AMERICAN PLAY
The House of Blue Leaves by John Guare

BEST FOREIGN PLAYS
Boesman and Lena by Athol Fugard; *AC/DC* by Heathcote Williams; *Dream on Monkey Mountain* by Derek Walcott

DISTINGUISHED PLAYS
The Fabulous Miss Marie and *In New England Winter* by Ed Bullins; *The Basic Training of Pavlo Hummel* by David Rabe

DISTINGUISHED PRODUCTION
The Trial of the Catonsville Nine

DISTINGUISHED DIRECTION
John Berry (*Boesman and Lena*); John Hirsch (*AC/DC*); Gordon Davidson (*The Trial of the Catonsville Nine*); Jeff Bleckner (*The Basic Training of Pavlo Hummel*); Larry Kornfeld (*Dracula Sabbat*)

BEST PERFORMANCE BY AN ACTOR
Jack MacGowran (*The Works of Samuel Beckett*)

BEST PERFORMANCE BY AN ACTRESS
Ruby Dee (*Boesman and Lena*)

DISTINGUISHED PERFORMANCES
Susan Batson (*AC/DC*); Margaret Braidwood, Donald Ewer, James Woods (*Saved*); Hector Elizondo (*Steambath*); Sonny Jim (Gaines) (*The Fabulous Miss Marie*); Stacy Keach (*Long Day's Journey into Night*); Harris Laskawy (*Uncle Vanya*); Joan MacIntosh (*Commune*); William Schallert (*The Trial of the Catonsville Nine*); Kirk Kirksey (consistent excellence of performance)

SET DESIGN
John Scheffer (*AC/DC*)

SPECIAL CITATION
Orlando Furioso

Comedienne/playwright/actress/director Elaine May served as mistress of ceremonies for the 1970–71 Obies. "Does anyone have any questions?" she asked at the top of the show. "Anything at all?" "Can you find me an apartment?" shouted an audience member. Otto Preminger, who was directing a film for which May had written the screenplay, tagged along to present an award.

THE OUTER CRITICS CIRCLE AWARDS

Productions: *Follies, A Midsummer Night's Dream, No, No, Nanette*; Outstanding Achievement Awards: Joseph Papp and the New York Shakespeare Festival, Paul Sills of *Story Theatre*, The Phoenix Theatre productions of *The School for Wives* and *The Trial of the Catonsville 9*; Other Citations: John Guare (*The House of Blue Leaves*), Clare Bloom (*Hedda Gabbler* and *A Doll's House*)

THE TONY AWARDS

PLAY
Old Times by Harold Pinter
The Prisoner of Second Avenue by Neil Simon
Sticks and Bones by David Rabe
Vivat! Vivat Regina! by Robert Bolt

Joseph Papp's New York Shakespeare Festival produced both the Tony outstanding Play (David Rabe's antiwar *Sticks and Bones*) and Musical (a rock updating of Shakespeare's *Two Gentlemen of Verona*). This was the first time the same producer won both top awards.

Several nominees had opened too late in the 1970–71 season to qualify for the previous year's Tonys. *70 Girls 70* and *All Over* had already closed. *Follies*, Stephen Sondheim and James Goldman's innovative musical set at a reunion of former show-

girls, had won the New York Drama Critics Circle for '70–'71, but was faring poorly at the box office.

In the early part of the Tony ceremony, it appeared that *Follies* would make a clean sweep, picking up nearly every award it could. But at the end of evening, an element of suspense was introduced as *Two Gentlemen of Verona* won the outstanding Book of a Musical honor. The biggest surprise of all came when *Two Gentlemen* was announced as oustanding Musical over the Sondheim-Goldman collaboration. Despite winning seven '71–'72 Tonys, *Follies* folded at a loss two months after the awards ceremony.

MUSICAL
Ain't Supposed to Die a Natural Death
Follies
Grease
Two Gentlemen of Verona

Grease, the nostalgic tribute to the '50s, was playing Off-Broadway at the Eden Theatre. But its producers contended it should be in the running for Tonys since they were paying the cast under a standard Broadway production contract. The request was granted. Though the show failed to win a single award, the publicity helped *Grease* slide into a Broadway house and one of the longest runs on record.

ACTOR (PLAY)
Tom Aldredge (*Sticks and Bones*)
Cliff Gorman (*Lenny*)
Donald Pleasance (*Wise Child*)
Jason Robards (*The Country Girl*)

ACTRESS (PLAY)
Eileen Atkins (*Vivat! Vivat Regina!*)
Colleen Dewhurst (*All Over*)
Rosemary Harris (*Old Times*)
Sada Thompson (*Twigs*)

ACTOR (MUSICAL)
Barry Bostwick (*Grease*)
Clifton Davis (*Two Gentlemen of Verona*)
Raul Julia (*Two Gentlemen of Verona*)
Phil Silvers (*A Funny Thing Happened on the Way to the Forum*)

ACTRESS (MUSICAL)
Jonelle Allen (*Two Gentlemen of Verona*)
Dorothy Collins (*Follies*)
Mildred Natwick (*70 Girls 70*)
Alexis Smith (*Follies*)

FEATURED ACTOR (PLAY)
Vincent Gardenia (*The Prisoner of Second Avenue*)
Douglas Rain (*Vivat! Vivat Regina!*)
Lee Richardson (*Vivat! Vivat Regina!*)
Joe Silver (*Lenny*)

FEATURED ACTRESS (PLAY)
Cara Duff-MacCormick (*Moonchildren*)
Mercedes McCambridge (*The Love Suicide at Schofield Barracks*)
Frances Sternhagen (*The Sign in Sidney Brustein's Window*)
Elizabeth Wilson (*Sticks and Bones*)

FEATURED ACTOR (MUSICAL)
Larry Blyden (*A Funny Thing…*)
Timothy Myers (*Grease*)
Gene Nelson (*Follies*)
Ben Vereen (*Jesus Christ Superstar*)

FEATURED ACTRESS (MUSICAL)
Adrienne Barbeau (*Grease*)
Linda Hopkins (*Inner City*)
Bernadette Peters (*On the Town*)
Beatrice Winde (*Ain't Supposed to Die a Natural Death*)

OTHER AWARDS
Director: Mike Nichols (*The Prisoner of Second Avenue*); Director (Musical): Harold Prince, Michael Bennett (*Follies*); Score: Stephen Sondheim (*Follies*); Book of a Musical: John Guare, Mel Shapiro (*Two Gentlemen of Verona*); Choreography: Michael Bennett (*Follies*); Set Design: Boris Aronson (*Follies*); Costume Design: Florence Klotz (*Follies*); Lighting Design: Tharon Musser (*Follies*)

In 1970–71, the outstanding Score award was split into two separate categories, one for Music and another for Lyrics. They were merged again in 1971–72 into one prize, outstanding Score. Stephen Sondheim was the victor both years.

SPECIAL AWARDS
Richard Rodgers; Ethel Merman;
Fiddler on the Roof;
The Theatre Guild-American Theatre Society

The 1971–72 Tonys, hosted by Deborah Kerr, Henry Fonda, and Peter Ustinov, blended nostalgia and the contemporary scene by saluting two musical comedy legends and offering excerpts from currently playing shows.

The highlights were a tribute to special Tony winners Ethel Merman and Richard Rodgers. A company of "strolling players" (Hal Linden, Constance Towers, Janet Blair, Alfred Drake, Lisa Kirk, Larry Blyden, Helen Gallagher, and Barbara McNair) performed a medley of Rodgers tunes. Merman herself, with Blyden and Linden in support, belted out a series of her own standards. Both honorees received extended standing ovations.

Yesterday was also represented by two numbers from the hit revival of the 1925 tuner *No, No, Nanette* while scenes from *Jesus Christ Superstar* and the black urban musical *Ain't Supposed to Die a Natural Death* provided more modern sounds.

The program was scheduled to begin at 9 p.m. on ABC but was delayed by twenty minutes for coverage of the Apollo 16 space shot.

THE DRAMA DESK AWARDS

OUTSTANDING PERFORMANCES (IN ORDER OF PERCENTAGES RECEIVED)
Marilyn Chris (*Kaddish*); Sada Thompson (*Twigs*); Eileen Atkins (*Vivat! Vivat Regina!*); Raul Julia (*Two Gentlemen of Verona*); Julie Bovasso (*The Screens*); Richard A. Dysart (*That Championship Season*); Robert Morse (*Sugar*); Jonelle Allen (*Two Gentlemen of Verona*); Paul Sorvino (*That Championship Season*); George S. Irving (*An Evening with Richard Nixon*); Charles Durning, Walter McGinn, Michael McGuire (*That Championship Season*); Kain (*The Black Terror*); Rosemary Harris (*Old Times*); Ron Faber (*And They Put Handcuffs on the Flowers*); William Atherton (*Suggs*); Linda Hopkins (*Inner City*); Micki Grant (*Don't Bother Me, I Can't Cope*); Brock Peters (*Lost in the Stars*); Lester Rawlins (*Nightride*); Tom Aldredge (*Sticks and Bones*)

OUTSTANDING DIRECTORS (IN ORDER OF PERCENTAGES RECEIVED)

A. J. Antoon (*That Championship Season*); Mel Shapiro (*Two Gentlemen of Verona, Older People*); Jeff Bleckner (*Sticks and Bones*); Andrei Serban (*Medea*); Peter Hall (*Old Times*)

MUSIC

Galt MacDermot (*Two Gentlemen of Verona*)

LYRICS

John Guare (*Two Gentlemen of Verona*)

BOOK

John Guare, Mel Shapiro (*Two Gentlemen of Verona*)

CHOREOGRAPHY (IN ORDER OF PERCENTAGES RECEIVED)

Patricia Birch (*Grease*), Jean Erdman (*Two Gentlemen of Verona*)

SET DESIGN (IN ORDER OF PERCENTAGES RECEIVED)

Santo Loquasto (*Sticks and Bones, That Championship Season*); Robert U. Taylor (*The Beggar's Opera*); Kert Lundell (*Ain't Supposed to Die a Natural Death*)

COSTUME DESIGN (IN ORDER OF PERCENTAGES RECEIVED)

Willa Kim (*The Screens*); Theoni V. Aldredge (*Two Gentlemen of Verona*)

MOST PROMISING PLAYWRIGHTS (IN ORDER OF PERCENTAGES RECEIVED)

Jason Miller (*That Championship Season*); Michael Weller (*Moonchildren*); David Wiltse (*Suggs*); J. E. Franklin (*Black Girl*); Richard Wesley (*The Black Terror*); Philip Dean Hayes (*The Sty of the Blind Pig*); J. E. Gaines (*Don't Let It Go to Your Head*)

MOST PROMISING DIRECTORS (IN ORDER OF PERCENTAGES RECEIVED)

Dan Sullivan (*Suggs*); Gilbert Moses (*Ain't Supposed to Die a Natural Death*)

MOST PROMISING COMPOSER

Andrew Lloyd Webber (*Jesus Christ Superstar*).

MOST PROMISING LYRICIST

Micki Grant (*Don't Bother Me, I Can't Cope*)

MOST PROMISING BOOK

Melvin Van Pebbles (*Ain't Supposed to Die a Natural Death*)

MOST PROMISING SET DESIGN

Video Free America (*Kaddish*)

MOST PROMISING COSTUME DESIGN

Carrie F. Robbins (*Grease, The Beggar's Opera*).

VERNON RICE AWARD

Chelsea Theater Center

THE NEW YORK DRAMA CRITICS CIRCLE AWARDS

BEST PLAY

That Championship Season by Jason Miller

BEST FOREIGN PLAY

The Screens by Jean Genet

BEST MUSICAL

Two Gentlemen of Verona, adapted from Shakespeare's play by John Guare, Mel Shapiro, and Galt MacDermot

SPECIAL CITATIONS

Sticks and Bones and *Old Times*

It was the closest voting in the history of the New York Drama Critics Circle. The final tally for Best Play was thirty-six for David Rabe's *Sticks and Bones* and thirty-seven for Jason Miller's *That Championship Season*. Both were produced by Joseph Papp's New York Shakespeare Festival. Under the Circle's rules, if the best Play victor is American, there is then a vote for Best Foreign Play. This competition was equally nip and tuck, with Jean Genet's *The Screens* barely edging Harold Pinter's *Old Times* thirty-five to thirty-four.

Because of a mathematical error, *Season* was reported as garnering twenty-seven instead of thirty-seven votes, and *Sticks* was named the winner. The mistake was caught after the press announcement had been made and an embarrassing correction had to be issued. In view of the close competition, special citations were presented to the two runners-up.

Championship, a searingly realistic indictment of middle-class values which takes places at the reunion of a high-school basketball team, had opened too late in the season to qualify for the Tony or Pulitzer. It won both the following year.

THE PULITZER PRIZE FOR DRAMA

No award

THE OBIE AWARDS

BEST THEATRE PIECE
The Mutation Show by The Open Theatre

DIRECTION
Wilford Leach, John Braswell (*The Only Jealousy of Emer*); Mel Shapiro (*Two Gentlemen of Verona*); Michael Smith (*Country Music*); Tom Sydorick (*20th Century Tar*)

PERFORMANCES
Salome Bey (*Love Me, Love My Children*); Maurice Blanc (*The Celebrations: Joos/Guns/Movies/The Abyss*); Alex Bradford (*Don't Bother Me, I Can't Cope*); Marilyn Chris (*Kaddish*); Ron Faber (*And They Put Handcuffs on the Flowers*); Jeanne Hepple, Ed Zang (*The Reliquary of Mr. and Mrs. Potterfield*); Danny Sewell (*The Homecoming*); Marilyn Sokol, Kathleen Widdoes (*The Beggar's Opera*); Elizabeth Wilson (*Sticks and Bones*)

OTHER CITATIONS
Music and Lyrics: Micki Grant (*Don't Bother Me, I Can't Cope*); Composer: Elizabeth Swados (*Medea*); Visual Effects: Video Free America (*Kaddish*)

SPECIAL CITATIONS
Meredith Monk (*Vessel*); Charles Stanley, actor, dancer, choreographer, costume designer; *Free the Army*

Groucho Marx was the unlikely host of the 1971–72 Obies. The legendary comedian upstaged the awards, leering at the winning actresses and quipping like mad. At one point he asked co-host Madeleine LeRoux if she was a virgin. When pre-

senting an award to Charles Stanley, he was told the performer included Greta Garbo among his characters. "You don't look like Garbo," Marx observed. "No, but I often wear her clothes," Stanley replied.

THE OUTER CRITICS CIRCLE AWARDS

Plays: *That Championship Season, Sticks and Bones*; Actors: Robert Morse (*Sugar*), Brock Peters (*Lost in the Stars*); Actresses: Sada Thompson (*Twigs*), Marilyn Chris (*Kaddish*), Rosemary Harris (*Old Times*); John Gassner Playwriting Award: Jason Miller (*That Championship Season*); Special Awards: John Houseman, Chelsea Theatre Center, Equity Library Theatre

THE TONY AWARDS

PLAY
Butley by Simon Gray
That Championship Season by Jason Miller
The Changing Room by David Storey
The Sunshine Boys by Neil Simon

MUSICAL
A Little Night Music
Don't Bother Me, I Can't Cope
Pippin
Sugar

A Little Night Music and *Pippin* were the big winners at the 1972–73 Tonys. *Night Music* took six awards while *Pippin* copped five. The two shows were almost diametrically opposed. *Night Music* was a sophisticated, adult romp based on a film by Ingmar Bergman with an intricate, complex score by Stephen Sondheim. *Pippin* was saved from a thin book by Bob Fosse's slickly professional, razzle-dazzle staging. Fosse won the Director (Musical) award as an acknowledgment of his miraculous feat of transforming a skimpy show into an entertaining spectacle, but *Night Music* was judged the best overall production.

ACTOR (PLAY)
Jack Albertson (*The Sunshine Boys*)
Alan Bates (*Butley*)
Wilfrid Hyde-White (*The Jockey Club Stakes*)
Paul Sorvino (*That Championship Season*)

ACTRESS (PLAY)
Jane Alexander (*6 Rms Riv Vu*)
Colleen Dewhurst (*Mourning Becomes Electra*)
Julie Harris (*The Last of Mrs. Lincoln*)
Kathleen Widdoes (*Much Ado about Nothing*)

ACTOR (MUSICAL)
Len Cariou (*A Little Night Music*)
Robert Morse (*Sugar*)
Brock Peters (*Lost in the Stars*)
Ben Vereen (*Pippin*)

ACTRESS (MUSICAL)
Glynis Johns (*A Little Night Music*)
Leland Palmer (*Pippin*)
Debbie Reynolds (*Irene*)
Marica Rodd (*Shelter*)

FEATURED ACTOR (PLAY)
Barnard Hughes (*Much Ado About Nothing*)
John Lithgow (*The Changing Room*)
John McMartin (*Don Juan*)
Hayword Morse (*Butley*)

FEATURED ACTRESS (PLAY)
Maya Angelou (*Look Away*)
Leora Dana (*The Last of Mrs. Lincoln*)
Katherine Helmond (*The Great God Brown*)
Penelope Windust (*Elizabeth I*)

Both Maya Angelou and Penelope Windust appeared in plays which ran for one perfomance.

FEATURED ACTOR (MUSICAL)
Laurence Guittard (*A Little Night Music*)
George S. Irving (*Irene*)
Avon Long (*Don't Play Us Cheap*)
Gilbert Price (*Lost in the Stars*)

FEATURED ACTRESS (MUSICAL)
Patricia Elliot (*A Little Night Music*)
Hermione Gingold (*A Little Night Music*)

Patsy Kelly (*Irene*)
Irene Ryan (*Pippin*)

OTHER AWARDS
Director (Play): A. J. Antoon (*That Championship Season*); Director (Musical): Bob Fosse (*Pippin*); Score: Stephen Sondheim (*A Little Night Music*); Book of a Musical: Hugh Wheeler (*A Little Night Music*); Choreography: Bob Fosse (*Pippin*); Set Design: Tony Walton (*Pippin*); Costume Design: Florence Klotz (*A Little Night Music*); Lighting Design: Jules Fisher (*Pippin*)

SPECIAL AWARDS
John Lindsay; Actors' Fund of America; The Shubert Organization

The 1972–73 Tonys celebrated "The Wide World of Broadway." In order to demonstrate that Broadway has a life beyond the confines of midtown Manhattan, Alexander Cohen, Hildy Parks, and director Clark Jones spent three and a half months traveling through Europe to film foreign productions of Broadway musicals. In each capital, an international celebrity would narrate a segment on the city's theater life and present scenes from an American-born show. In London, Peter Ustinov introduced Cleo Laine in *Show Boat*. The Parisian excerpt featured Yul Brynner playing host to a Gallic-flavored *Hello, Dolly!*. There was also a Viennese *West Side Story*; a Serb-Croatian *Man of La Mancha*; the Milan production of *Ciao, Rudy*, an original Italian musical based on the life of silent-screen shiek Rudolph Valentino; a Tokyo rendition of *The King and I*; and, finally, a high-school mounting of *My Fair Lady* from Wichita Falls, Texas.

The whole affair was introduced by a quartet of veteran singer-dancers—Gwen Verdon, Helen Gallagher, Paula Kelly, and Donna MacKechnie—in a special theme song written by Jerry Herman. Hosts Rex Harrison, Celeste Holm, Jerry Orbach, and Sandy Duncan then presided over the awards and periodically introduced the international segments, which were shown on a giant video-box in the shape of a globe. Further demonstrating Broadway's reach, a brief montage of snippets from films based on Main Stem shows was screened.

In order to fit in all the international video clips, only one currently playing musical got to show off its wares in a live excerpt. This was "Magic to Do" from *Pippin*.

Reaction to the program was mixed. Some TV reviewers objected to the overuse of taped segments and the lack of live entertainment. The *New York Daily News* stated "the big bash . . . was a big bust," calling the program "a glorified travelogue." *Variety* qualified its negative review: "Chalk this one up as slightly below the Tony show standards which ain't bad at all considering those standards." But Clive Barnes writing in the *London Times* praised it, stating, "Year after year after year Hollywood comes off looking like a rank amateur, while Broadway's Tony emerges as one of the most effective and shrewdly produced spectaculars in America."

THE DRAMA DESK AWARDS

OUTSTANDING PERFORMANCES (IN ORDER OF PERCENTAGES RECEIVED)

Mari Gorman (*The Hot L Baltimore*); Christopher Plummer (*Cyrano*); Alan Bates (*Butley*); Julie Harris (*The Last of Mrs. Lincoln*); Sam Waterston (*Much Ado about Nothing*); Ben Vereen (*Pippin*); Jack Albertson (*The Sunshine Boys*); John McMartin (*The Great God Brown* and *Don Juan*); Stacy Keach (*Hamlet*); John Glover (*The Great God Brown*); Jessica Tandy (*Happy Days* and *Not I*); Christopher Lloyd (*Kaspar*); Ruby Dee (*Wedding Band*); Michele Lee (*Seesaw*); Glynis Johns (*A Little Night Music*); Rosemary Harris (*A Streetcar Named Desire, The Merchant of Venice*); John Lithgow (*The Changing Room*); Colleen Dewhurst (*Mourning Becomes Electra*); Douglass Watson (*Much Ado about Nothing*); James Earl Jones (*Hamlet, The Cherry Orchard*); Patricia Elliott (*A Little Night Music*); Pamela Payton-Wright (*Mourning Becomes Electra*)

MOST PROMISING PERFORMERS (IN ORDER OF PERCENTAGES RECEIVED)

Tom Atkins (*The Changing Room*); Ralph Carter (*Dude*); Bill Cobbs (*Freeman, What the Wine Sellers Buy*); Trish Hawkins (*The Hot L Baltimore*); D. Jamin-Bartlett (*A Little Night Music*); Mary Lou Rosato (*The School for Scandal*); Gail Strickland (*Status Quo Vadis*)

OUTSTANDING DIRECTORS (IN ORDER OF PERCENTAGES RECEIVED)

Michael Rudman (*The Changing Room*); Bob Fosse (*Pippin*); Victor Garcia (*Yerma*); Joseph Chaikin, Robert Sklar (*The Mutation Show*); Harold Prince (*The Great God Brown, A Little Night Music*)

MUSIC, LYRICS

Stephen Sondheim (*A Little Night Music*)

BOOK

Hugh Wheeler (*A Little Night Music*)

CHOREOGRAPHY

Bob Fosse (*Pippin*)

SET DESIGN (IN ORDER OF PERCENTAGES RECEIVED)

Victor Garcia, Fabian Puigserver (*Yerma*); Tony Walton (*Pippin, Shelter*); David Jenkins (*The Changing Room*)

COSTUME DESIGN (IN ORDER OF PERCENTAGES RECEIVED)

Theoni V. Aldredge (*Much Ado about Nothing*); Patricia Zipprodt (*Pippin*)

MOST PROMISING PLAYWRIGHTS (IN ORDER OF PERCENTAGES RECEIVED)

Joseph A. Walker (*The River Niger*); Robert Randall (*6 Rms Riv Vu*); James Prideaux (*The Last of Mrs. Lincoln*); Steve Tesich (*Baba Goya*)

MOST PROMISING COMPOSER

Stanley Silverman (*Dr. Selavy's Magic Theatre*)

MOST PROMISING LYRICIST

Jean Kelly (*National Lampoon Lemmings*)

MOST PROMISING BOOK

Ron House, Diz White (*El Grande de Coco-Cola*)

MOST PROMISING SET DESIGN

Jerry Rojo (*Endgame*)

MOST PROMISING COSTUME DESIGN

Laura Crow, Cookie Gluck (*Warp*)

THE NEW YORK DRAMA CRITICS CIRCLE AWARDS

BEST PLAY
The Changing Room by David Storey

BEST AMERICAN PLAY
The Hot L Baltimore by Lanford Wilson

BEST MUSICAL
A Little Night Music by Hugh Wheeler and Stephen Sondheim

THE PULITZER PRIZE FOR DRAMA

That Championship Season by Jason Miller

THE OBIE AWARDS

BEST AMERICAN PLAY (TIE)
The Hot L Baltimore by Lanford Wilson and *The River Niger* by Joseph A. Walker

BEST FOREIGN PLAY (TIE)
Not I by Samuel Beckett and *Kaspar* by Peter Handke

DISTINGUISHED PLAYS
The Tooth of Crime by Sam Shepard; *Bigfoot* by Ronald Tavel; *What If It Had Turned Up Heads?* by J. E. Gaines

DIRECTION
Jack Gelber (*The Kid*); William E. Lathan (*What If It Had Turned Up Heads?*); Marshall W. Mason (*The Hot L Baltimore*)

PERFORMANCES
Hume Cronyn (*Krapp's Last Tape*); Mari Gorman (*The Hot L Baltimore*); James Hilbrandt (*A Boy Named Dog*); Stacy Keach (*Hamlet*); Christopher Lloyd (*Kaspar*); Charles Ludlam (*Corn* and *Camille*); Lola Pashalinski (*Corn*); Alice Playten (*National Lampoon Lemmings*); Roxie Roker, Douglas Turner Ward (*The River Niger*); Jessica Tandy (*Not I*); Sam Waterston (*Much Ado about Nothing*)

Alice Playten thanked her psychiatrist for "convic-ing me not to quit when the going gets rough." Three members of the audience later asked her for his name.

SPECIAL CITATIONS
Richard Foreman (Ontological-Hysteric Theatre); Workshop of the Player's Art (WPA) for *The Dragon Lady's Revenge*; City Center Acting Company; Workshop of the Player's Art (WPA)

Harry Orzello of the WPA Theatre was surprised at his company's winning an Obie since the *Villlage Voice* hadn't given its productions a good review in six months. This prompted host Sylvia Miles to comment that "the *Voice* is like the Pentagon. First they bomb you, then they give you an award."

THE OUTER CRITICS CIRCLE AWARDS

Actor: Christopher Plummer (*Cyrano*); Actress (Play): Julie Harris (*The Last of Mrs. Lincoln*); Actresses (Musical): Michele Lee (*Seesaw*), Debbie Reynolds (*Irene*); Ensemble Performance: The entire cast of *The Women*; Directors: Ellis Rabb (*A Streetcar Named Desire*), Bob Fosse (*Pippin*)

THE TONY AWARDS

PLAY
The Au Pair Man by Hugh Leonard
Boom Boom Room by David Rabe
The River Niger by Joseph A. Walker
Ulysses in Nighttown by Marjorie Barkentin

The River Niger, Joseph A. Walker's black family drama, was originally produced Off-Broadway by the Negro Ensemble Company in December of 1972, then tranferred to Broadway in April of 1973. It was too late for that season's Tonys and had closed by the time of the 1973–74 awards.

Although *Ulysses in Nighttown*, an adaptation of James Joyce's literary masterpiece *Ulysses*, had first appeared Off-Broadway in 1958–59, this was its first Broadway production and was judged eligible as a best new Play candidate.

Christopher Plummer, Virginia Capers, Colleen Dewhurst, and Michael Moriarty (1973–74 Tonys).

MUSICAL
Over Here
Raisin
Seesaw

Although it had a totally new book, *Candide* was deemed ineligible for nomination in the best Musical category since it had been produced on Broadway in 1956. It received a special award instead. The New York Drama Critics Circle disagreed and awarded the adaptation of Voltaire's satire its honor for top new tuner.

ACTOR (PLAY)
Michael Moriarty (*Find Your Way Home*)
Zero Mostel (*Ulysses in Nighttown*)
Jason Robards (*A Moon for the Misbegotten*)
George C. Scott (*Uncle Vanya*)
Nicol Williamson (*Uncle Vanya*)

In the biggest upset of the evening, Michael Moriarty as the gay hustler in British import *Find Your Way Home* triumphed over Jason Robards in an acclaimed performance in the hit revival of *A Moon for the Misbegotten*.

ACTRESS (PLAY)
Jane Alexander (*Find Your Way Home*)
Colleen Dewhurst (*A Moon for the Misbegotten*)
Julie Harris (*The Au Pair Man*)
Madeline Kahn (*Boom Boom Room*)
Rachel Roberts (*New Phoenix Repertory*)

ACTOR (MUSICAL)
Alfred Drake (*Gigi*)
Joe Morton (*Raisin*)
Christopher Plummer (*Cyrano*)
Lewis J. Stadlen (*Candide*)

ACTRESS (MUSICAL)
Virginia Capers (*Raisin*)
Carol Channing (*Lorelei*)
Michele Lee (*Seesaw*)

FEATURED ACTOR (PLAY)

Rene Auberjonois (*The Good Doctor*)
Ed Flanders (*A Moon for the Misbegotten*)
Douglas Turner Ward (*The River Niger*)
Dick A. Williams (*What the Wine Sellers Buy*)

Like Williams Daniels of *1776*, Douglas Turner Ward refused his nomination as a featured actor, stating that his was a leading role.

Ed Flanders later won an Emmy for the TV version of *A Moon for the Misbegotten*, making him one of the few performers to win the top acting awards in theater and television for the same role.

FEATURED ACTRESS (PLAY)

Regina Baff (*Veronica's Room*)
Fionnuala Flanagan (*Ulysses in Nighttown*)
Charlotte Moore (*Chemin de Fer*)
Roxie Roker (*The River Niger*)
Frances Sternhagen (*The Good Doctor*)

FEATURED ACTOR (MUSICAL)

Mark Baker (*Candide*)
Ralph Carter (*Raisin*)
Tommy Tune (*Seesaw*)

FEATURED ACTRESS (MUSICAL)

Leigh Beery (*Cyrano*)
Maureen Brennan (*Candide*)
June Gable (*Candide*)
Ernestine Jackson (*Raisin*)
Janie Sell (*Over Here*)

OTHER AWARDS

Director (Play): Jose Quintero (*A Moon for the Misbegotten*); Director (Musical): Harold Prince (*Candide*); Score: Frederick Loewe, Alan Jay Lerner (*Gigi*); Book of a Musical: Hugh Wheeler (*Candide*); Set Design: Eugene and Franne Lee (*Candide*); Costume Design: Franne Lee (*Candide*); Lighting Design: Jules Fisher (*Ulysses in Nighttown*); Choreography: Michael Bennett (*Seesaw*)

Frederick Loewe and Alan Jay Lerner wrote the score for *Gigi* when it was made as a film in 1958. They added four new songs for this first stage version. Since it had never been performed on Broadway, the work was eligible for an Original Score award.

SPECIAL AWARDS

A Moon for the Misbegotten; *Candide*; Peter Cook and Dudley Moore; Bette Midler; Liza Minnelli; theatrical attorney John Wharton, printer Harold Friedlander, Actors' Equity, and the Theatre Development Fund (Theatre '74 Awards)

The 1973–74 ceremony could have been dubbed "The Tony Awards from Hell." The program ran nearly a full hour over its two-hour time limit and was beset with camera, sound, and blocking problems. The overtime was attributed to too many production numbers and some exceptionally long-winded winners, particularly Robert Nemiroff, producer of *Raisin*, who went on for several minutes.

There were also numerous special awards. The revivals of *A Moon for the Misbegotten* and *Candide* as well as comedy duo Peter Cook and Dudley Moore and solo performers Liza Minnelli and Bette Midler were honored. "You still dress like a stolen car," presenter Johnny Carson joked with the Divine Miss M. Four Theatre '74 presentations were also made.

Robert Preston, Cicely Tyson, and Florence Henderson hosted the program, which employed the theme of "Homecoming." The premise was that a galaxy of film and TV stars were "returning" to Broadway to present Tonys. Alan Alda, Ed Asner, Bette Davis, Cloris Leachman, Elizabeth Montgomery, Carroll O'Connor, Esther Rolle, and Suzanne Pleshette were among the award dispensers. This ploy may have dazzled viewers but it emphasized the dearth of big names on Broadway since the majority of these "homecoming" performers rarely made stage appearances. In addition to scenes from the three nominated best musicals, there were excerpts from *Lorelei* and a revival of *Good News*, and several presenters did their own specialty numbers. Beatrice Arthur warbled a tune from *A Mother's Kisses*, a musical in which she had starred that closed before reaching Broadway. Will Geer launched into a medley from the 1937 pro-labor tuner *The Cradle Will Rock*. Charles Nelson Reilly did a comic turn of songs that did *not* originate in Broadway shows in which he had played. Nancy Walker recreated a comedy sketch from *Phoenix '55*. There was enough material for several TV specials. In fact there were *two* Tony shows that year. For the first time, ABC commissioned a ninety-minute pre-Tony special which aired on two nights before the awards in the 11:30 p.m.–1 a.m. slot.

THE DRAMA DESK AWARDS

PERFORMANCES (IN ORDER OF PERCENTAGES RECEIVED)
Colleen Dewhurst (*A Moon for the Misbegotten*); Jim Dale (*Scapino*); Michael Moriarty (*Find Your Way Home*); Barbara Barrie (*The Killdeer*); Henry Fonda (*Clarence Darrow*); Jason Robards (*A Moon for the Misbegotten*); Brian Bedford (*Jumpers*); Madeline Kahn (*Boom Boom Room*); Kevin Conway (*When You Comin' Back, Red Ryder?*); Ruby Lynn Reyner (*La Bohemia*); Ed Flanders (*A Moon for the Misbegotten*); Elizabeth Sturges (*When You Comin' Back, Red Ryder?*); Seret Scott (*My Sister, My Sister*); Ian McKellen (*The Wood Demon* and *King Lear*); Kevin O'Connor (*The Contractor*); Conchata Ferrel (*The Sea Horse*); George Rose (*My Fat Friend*); Joseph Buloff (*Hard to Be a Jew*); Dick A. Williams (*What the Wine Sellers Buy*); Zero Mostel (*Ulysses in Nighttown*); Veronica Redd (*The Sirens*); Nicol Williamson (*Uncle Vanya*)

DIRECTORS (IN ORDER OF PERCENTAGES RECEIVED)
Frank Dunlop (*Scapino*); Jose Quintero (*A Moon for the Misbegotten*); Harold Prince (*Candide* and *The Visit*); Marvin Felix Camillo (*Short Eyes*)

BOOK OF A MUSICAL
Hugh Wheeler (*Candide*)

SCORE OF A MUSICAL
Al Carmines (*The Faggot*)

NEW PLAYWRIGHTS (IN ORDER OF PERCENTAGES RECEIVED)
Edward J. Moore (*The Sea Horse*); Miguel Pinero (*Short Eyes*); Mark Medoff (*When You Comin' Back, Red Ryder?*); David E. Freeman (*Creeps*); David W. Rintels (*Clarence Darrow*); Ray Aranha (*My Sister, My Sister*)

SET DESIGNERS (IN ORDER OF PERCENTAGES RECEIVED)
Franne and Eugene Lee (*Candide*); David Mitchell (*Short Eyes*); Douglas W. Schmidt (*Over Here* and *Veronica's Room*)

COSTUME DESIGNERS (IN ORDER OF PERCENTAGES RECEIVED)
Franne Lee (*Candide*); Carrie F. Robbins (*Over Here* and *The Iceman Cometh*)

CHOREOGRAPHY
Patricia Birch (*Over Here*)

THE NEW YORK DRAMA CRITICS CIRCLE AWARDS

BEST PLAY
The Contractor by David Storey

BEST AMERICAN PLAY
Short Eyes by Miguel Pinero

BEST MUSICAL
Candide by Hugh Wheeler, Leonard Bernstein, Richard Wilbur, Stephen Sondheim, and John Latouche

THE PULITZER PRIZE FOR DRAMA

No award

THE OBIE AWARDS

BEST AMERICAN PLAY
Short Eyes by Miguel Pinero

Miguel Pinero almost didn't make it to the Obies to pick up his award for *Short Eyes*, a harrowing drama of life in prison. He was out on bail, having been arrested that very morning for possession of a controlled substance.

BEST FOREIGN PLAY
The Contractor by David Storey

PLAYWRITING
Bad Habits by Terrence McNally; *When You Comin' Back, Red Ryder?* by Mark Medoff;

The Great MacDaddy by Paul Carter Harrison

DIRECTION
Marvin Felix Camillo (*Short Eyes*); Robert Drivas (*Bad Habits*); David Licht (*Hard to Be a Jew*); John Pasquin (*Moonchildren*); Harold Prince (*Candide*)

PERFORMANCES
Barbara Barrie (*The Killdeer*); Joseph Buloff (*Hard to Be a Jew*); Kevin Conway and Elizabeth Sturges (*When You Comin' Back, Red Ryder?*); Conchata Ferrell (*The Sea Horse*); Loretta Greene (*The Sirens*); Barbara Montgomery (*My Sister, My Sister*); Zipora Spaizman (*Stepenyu*)

MUSIC
Bill Elliott (*C.O.R.F.A.X.*)

DESIGN
Theoni V. Aldredge (costumes for Public Theatre productions); Holmes Easley (sets for Roundabout Theatre productions); Christopher Thomas (sets for *Lady from the Sea*)

SPECIAL CITATIONS
The Bread and Puppet Theatre; The Brooklyn Academy of Music for its British theater season; CSC Repertory Company; Robert Wilson (*The Life and Times of Josef Stalin*)

THE OUTER CRITICS CIRCLE AWARDS

Plays: *A Moon for the Misbegotten, Noel Coward in Two Keys*; Musical: *Candide*; Actor: George Rose (*My Fat Friend*); Actresses: Doris Roberts (*Bad Habits*), Janie Sell and Ann Reinking (*Over Here*); Choreography: Patricia Birch; John Gassner Playwriting Award: Mark Medoff (*When You Coming Home, Red Ryder?*); Special Award: Sammy Cahn

1974-75
THE TONY AWARDS

PLAY
Equus by Peter Shaffer
Same Time, Next Year by Bernard Slade
Short Eyes by Miguel Pinero
Sizwe Banzi Is Dead and *The Island* by Athol
    Fugard, John Kani, and Winston Ntshona
Seascape by Edward Albee
The National Health by Peter Nichols

Peter Shaffer and his twin brother Anthony are the only siblings to win best Play Tonys: Peter for *Equus* and later *Amadeus* (1980–81), Anthony for *Sleuth* (1970–71).

MUSICAL
The Lieutenant
Mack and Mabel
Shenandoah
The Wiz

ACTOR (PLAY)
Jim Dale (*Scapino*)
Peter Firth (*Equus*)
Henry Fonda (*Clarence Darrow*)
Ben Gazzara (*Hughie* and *Duet*)
John Kani and **Winston Ntshona**
    (*Sizwe Banzi Is Dead* and *The Island*)
John Wood (*Sherlock Holmes*)

John Kani and Winston Ntshona received a joint award for their roles in two plays on apartheid by the actors and South African playwright Athol Fugard. The plays had originally been presented in South Africa, followed by stagings in London, at New Haven's Long Wharf Theatre, and finally on Broadway. Because South African laws forbade Kani and Ntshona from leaving the country as actors, they were officially registered as house servants of Fugard.

ACTRESS (PLAY)
Elizabeth Ashley (*Cat on a Hot Tin Roof*)
Ellen Burstyn (*Same Time, Next Year*)
Diana Rigg (*The Misanthrope*)

Maggie Smith (*Private Lives*)
Liv Ullman (*A Doll's House*)

Ellen Burstyn had just won the Oscar for *Alice Doesn't Live Here Anymore*, making her the third actress to win both the top acting prize for film and theater in the same year. The others were Shirley Booth and Audrey Hepburn.

ACTOR (MUSICAL)
John Cullum (*Shenandoah*)
Joel Grey (*Goodtime Charley*)
Raul Julia (*Where's Charley?*)
Eddie Mekka (*The Lieutenant*)
Robert Preston (*Mack and Mabel*)

ACTRESS (MUSICAL)
Lola Falana (*Doctor Jazz*)
Angela Lansbury (*Gypsy*)
Bernadette Peters (*Mack and Mabel*)
Ann Reinking (*Goodtime Charley*)

FEATURED ACTOR (PLAY)
Larry Blyden (*Absurd Person Singular*)
Leonard Frey (*The National Health*)
Frank Langella (*Seascape*)
Philip Locke (*Sherlock Holmes*)
George Rose (*My Fat Friend*)
Dick A. Williams (*Black Picture Show*)

FEATURED ACTRESS (PLAY)
Linda Miller (*Black Picture Show*)
Rita Moreno (*The Ritz*)
Geraldine Page (*Absurd Person Singular*)
Carole Shelley (*Absurd Person Singular*)
Elizabeth Spriggs (*London Assurance*)
Frances Sternhagen (*Equus*)

Rita Moreno and George Rose complained about their classification as featured or supporting actors. Both claimed they were playing leading parts. Upon winning her category, Moreno broke into the exaggerated Hispanic accent of Googie Gomez, her character from *The Ritz*, saying, "Honey, the only thing I support is my beads." In response, a Tony Eligibility Committee was created to determine the proper categorization. But this did not solve the problem. In later years, numerous leading actors were placed in the featured or supporting division and vice versa.

FEATURED ACTOR (MUSICAL)
Tom Aldredge (*Where's Charley?*)
John Bottoms (*Dance with Me*)
Doug Henning (*The Magic Show*)
Gilbert Price (*The Night That Made America Famous*)
Ted Ross (*The Wiz*)
Richard B. Schull (*Goodtime Charley*)

FEATURED ACTRESS (MUSICAL)
Dee Dee Bridgewater (*The Wiz*)
Susan Browning (*Goodtime Charley*)
Zan Charisse (*Gypsy*)
Taina Elg (*Where's Charley*)
Kelly Garrett (*The Night That Made America Famous*)
Donna Theodore (*Shenandoah*)

OTHER AWARDS
Director (Play): John Dexter (*Equus*); Director (Musical): Geoffrey Holder (*The Wiz*); Score: Charlie Smalls (*The Wiz*); Book of a Musical: James Lee Barrett, Peter Udell, Philip Rose (*Shenandoah*); Choreography: George Faison (*The Wiz*); Set Design: Carl Toms (*Sherlock Holmes*); Costume Design: Geoffrey Holder (*The Wiz*); Lighting Designer: Neil Peter Jampolis (*Sherlock Holmes*)

SPECIAL AWARDS
Neil Simon; caricaturist Al Hirschfeld (Theatre Award '75)

In putting together the 1974–75 Tonys, producer Alexander Cohen and his writer-wife Hildy Parks had little musical material in the current season with which to work. Of the nominated musicals only *The Wiz* and *Shenandoah* were still playing. *The Lieutenant* and *Mack and Mabel* had folded. Instead of focusing on the skimpy musical present, the past was emphasized with a salute to the Winter Garden Theatre. There was no single host but a band of "strolling players" who would present awards and perform numbers from shows which had played the Winter Garden since its inception in 1911.

Larry Blyden, George S. Irving, Larry Kert, Carol Lawrence, Michele Lee, Bernadette Peters, and Bobby Van recreated moments from various

Passing Shows and *Ziegfeld Follies*, as well as from *Wonderful Town, West Side Story, Mame, Follies,* and the revival of *Gypsy* with Angela Lansbury which played the theater earlier in the season.

The presenters were stars who had trod the Winter Garden boards at some point in their careers. A few like Fred Astaire and Rosalind Russell were not even present, but participated via videotape. Those who made flesh-and-blood appearances included Buddy Ebsen, director Vincente Minnelli, Milton Berle, Carl Reiner, Carol Channing, and nonagenarian Joe Smith of the vaudeville team Smith and Dale.

The program aired on ABC from 8:30 to10:30 p.m. Local stations had scheduled programming from 10:30 to11 p.m, so there was no chance the network would allow anything like the previous year's excessive overtime. Fortunately, the program finished within the alotted two hours.

THE DRAMA DESK AWARDS

The Drama Desk changed its rules this year and switched from presenting multiple winners in its various categories to nominees and single winners.

PLAYS

Foreign Play: *Equus* by Peter Shaffer; American Play: *Same Time, Next Year* by Bernard Slade; Actor: Anthony Hopkins (*Equus*); Actress: Ellen Burstyn (*Same Time, Next Year*); Featured Actor: Frank Langella (*Seascape*); Featured Actress: Frances Sternhagen (*Equus*); Actor, special mention: Donald Sinden (*London Assurance*); Actress, special mention: Tovah Feldshuh (*Yentl the Yeshiva Boy*); Director: John Dexter (*Equus*)

MUSICALS

Musical: *The Wiz*; Actor: John Cullum (*Shenandoah*); Actress: Angela Lansbury (*Gypsy*); Featured Actor: Ted Ross (*The Wiz*); Featured Actress: Donna Theodore (*Shenandoah*); Director: Arthur Laurents (*Gypsy*); Book of a Musical: William F. Brown (*The Wiz*); Score: Charlie Smalls (*The Wiz*); Choreography: George Faison (*The Wiz*)

OTHER AWARDS

Theatrical Experience: *London Assurance*; Set Design: Carl Toms (*Sherlock Holmes*); Costume Design: Geoffrey Holder (*The Wiz*); Lighting Design: Neil Peter Jampolis (*Sherlock Holmes*)

THE NEW YORK DRAMA CRITICS CIRCLE AWARDS

BEST PLAY

Equus by Peter Shaffer

BEST AMERICAN PLAY

The Taking of Miss Janie by Ed Bullins

BEST MUSICAL

A Chorus Line by Michael Bennett, Marvin Hamlisch, Ed Kleban, James Kirkwood, and Nicholas Dante

THE PULITZER PRIZE FOR DRAMA

Seascape by Edward Albee

THE OBIE AWARDS

BEST PLAY

The First Breeze of Summer by Leslie Lee

DISTINGUISHED PLAYWRITING

Ed Bullins (*The Taking of Miss Janie*); Lanford Wilson (*The Mound Builders*); Wallace Shawn (*Our Late Night*); Sam Shepard (*Action*); Corinne Jacker (*Harry Outside*)

PERFORMANCE

Reyno and Moses Gunn (*The First Breeze of Summer*); Dick Latessa (*Philemon*); Kevin McCarthy (*Harry Outside*); Stephen D. Newman (*Polly*); Christopher Walken (*Kid Champion*); Ian Trigger (*The True History of Squire Jonathan*); Cara Duff-MacCormick (*Craig's Wife*); Priscilla Smith (*Trilogy*); Tanya Berezin (*The Mound Builders*); Tovah Feldshuh (*Yentl the Yeshiva Boy*)

DIRECTION

Lawrence Kornfield (*Listen to Me*); Marhsall W. Mason (*Battle of Angels, The Mound Builders*); Gilbert Moses (*The Taking of Miss Janie*)

SET DESIGN

Robert U. Taylor (*Polly*); John Lee Beatty (*Down*

by the River . . . , *Battle of Angels*, *The Mound Builders*)

SPECIAL CITATIONS
Andrei Serban for *Trilogy*; Royal Shakespeare Company for *Summerfolk*; Charles Ludlam for *Professor Bedlam's Punch and Judy Show*; The Henry Street Settlement; Charles Pierce; Mabou Mines

SPECIAL TWENTY-YEAR OBIES
Judith Malina and Julian Beck; Theodore Mann and Circle in the Square; Joseph Papp; Ellen Stewart; *The Fantasticks*

In an intermingling of Broadway and Off-Broadway, the twentieth annual Obies were hosted by Angela Lansbury, Sam Waterston, Melba Moore, Marilyn Sokol, and Shelley Winters, who was nominated for an Emmy that year for a guest star role on NBC's *McCloud*. She told the audience, "If I win an Emmy tonight, can I trade it for an Obie?"

THE OUTER CRITICS CIRCLE AWARDS

Play: *Equus*; Performances: Anthony Hopkins, Peter Firth (*Equus*), John Cullum, Chip Ford (*Shenandoah*), Maggie Smith (*Private Lives*), Geraldine Page (*Absurd Person Singular*); Young Players: Peter Firth (*Equus*), Tovah Feldshuh (*Rodgers and Hart, Yentl the Yeshiva Boy,* and *Dreyfus in Rehearsal*), Chip Ford (*Shenandoah*); Ensemble Playing: Ellen Burstyn, Charles Grodin (*Same Time, Next Year*); John Gassner Playwriting Award: Leslie Lee (*The First Breeze of Summer*); Special Awards: Tom Jones and Harvey Schmidt for contributions to musical theater through the Portfolio Studio, Long Wharf Theatre, and Arts Council of Great Britain

THE TONY AWARDS

PLAY
The First Breeze of Summer by Leslie Lee
Knock Knock by Jules Feiffer

Lampost Reunion by Louis LaRusso II
Travesties by Tom Stoppard

MUSICAL
Bubbling Brown Sugar
Chicago
A Chorus Line
Pacific Overtures

This was the year of *A Chorus Line*, which went on to become the longest-running show in Broadway history (until it was surpassed by *Cats* in 1997). The paean to the average Broadway show dancer swept the Tonys with nine awards. The broadcast on ABC opened with "I Hope I Get It," the first number of the show, and closed with the top-hatted, high-stepping finale "One." The musical also took seven Drama Desk Awards, the Pulitzer, and three Obies for its pre-Broadway run at the New York Shakespeare Festival. The New York Drama Critics Circle had given the show its Best Musical Award the previous year for that engagement, which began in April of 1975.

The Critics Circle choice for 1975–76 was *Pacific Overtures*. This innovative, Kabuki-inspired exploration of East-West culture clash won only two design Tonys and closed after an unprofitable run.

ACTOR (PLAY)
Moses Gunn (*The Poison Tree*)
George C. Scott (*Death of a Salesman*)
Donald Sinden (*London Assurance*)
John Wood (*Travesties*)

Although he had shunned the Oscars five years ago, nominee George C. Scott was on hand to co-host the Tonys along with his wife Trish Van Devere, Eddie Albert, Jane Fonda, Diana Rigg, and Richard Burton, who was then appearing in *Equus*.

ACTRESS (PLAY)
Tovah Feldshuh (*Yentl*)
Rosemary Harris (*The Royal Family*)
Lynn Redgrave (*Mrs. Warren's Profession*)
Irene Worth (*Sweet Bird of Youth*)

ACTOR (MUSICAL)
Mako (*South Pacific*)
Jerry Orbach (*Chicago*)

Ian Richardson (*My Fair Lady*)
George Rose (*My Fair Lady*)

In an odd quirk of classification, Ian Richardson's Henry Higgins was in competition with George Rose's Alfred P. Doolittle from the same revival of *My Fair Lady*. Both were considered leading actors by the Tony Eligibilty Committee because they were each given "star" billing above the production's title. Stanley Holloway, the original Doolittle, was nominated for a Featured Actor (Musical) Tony in 1956–57.

ACTRESS (MUSICAL)
Donna McKechnie (*A Chorus Line*)
Vivian Reed (*Bubbling Brown Sugar*)
Chita Rivera (*Chicago*)
Gwen Verdon (*Chicago*)

FEATURED ACTOR (PLAY)
Barry Bostwick (*They Knew What They Wanted*)
Gabriel Dell (*Lamppost Reunion*)
Edward Herrmann (*Mrs. Warren's Profession*)
Daniel Seltzer (*Knock Knock*)

FEATURED ACTRESS (PLAY)
Marybeth Hurt (*Trelawney of the "Wells"*)
Shirley Knight (*Kennedy's Children*)
Lois Nettleton (*They Knew What They Wanted*)
Meryl Streep (*27 Wagons Full of Cotton*)

FEATURED ACTOR (MUSICAL)
Robert LuPone (*A Chorus Line*)
Charles Repole (*Very Good Eddie*)
Isao Sato (*Pacific Overtures*)
Sammy Williams (*A Chorus Line*)

Family affair: Brother and sister Robert and Patti LuPone both received nominations.

FEATURED ACTRESS (MUSICAL)
Carole (Kelly) Bishop (*A Chorus Line*)
Priscilla Lopez (*A Chorus Line*)
Patti LuPone (*The Robber Bridegroom*)
Virginia Seidel (*Very Good Eddie*)

Carole Bishop had to change her stage name to Kelly since there already was a performer with that monicker in Actors Equity.

OTHER AWARDS
Director (Play): Ellis Rabb (*The Royal Family*); Director (Musical): Michael Bennett (*A Chorus Line*); Score: Marvin Hamlisch, Edward Kleban (*A Chorus Line*); Book of a Musical: James Kirkwood, Nicholas Dante (*A Chorus Line*); Choreography: Michael Bennett, Bob Avian (*A Chorus Line*); Set Design: Boris Aronson (*Pacific Overtures*); Costume Design: Florence Klotz (*Pacific Overtures*); Lighting Design: Tharon Musser (*A Chorus Line*)

SPECIAL AWARDS
George Abbott (Lawrence Langer Award for Lifetime Achievement in the Theatre); Richard Burton; Circle in the Square; Arena Stage, Washington, DC (Outstanding Regional Theatre); lighting technician Thomas H. Fitzgerald (posthumous); musical score preparation supervisor Mathilde Pincus

Arena Stage was the first recipient of the Outstanding Regional Theatre Award, which is based on a recommendation of the American Theatre Critics Association. The award is accompanied by a cash grant, usually presented by a corporate sponsor.

In addition to numbers from *A Chorus Line, Chicago, Pacific Overtures,* and *Bubbling Brown Sugar,* the Tonycast featured "The Ones That Got Away," a medley of songs from shows which did not win Tonys. Richard K. Schull of the *Indianapolis News* carped "some of them should have gotten away."

The League of New York Theatres and Producers in consultation with the American Theatre Wing decided on a new procedure for Tony nominations. An Eligibilty Committee of League and Wing members would decide which shows would fit into which categories. A list of all the eligible shows would then be presented to the Nominating Committee of ten critics who would make their choices by secret ballot rather than in a meeting. This would theoretically avoid electioneering and persuading. But when several worthy candidates were not nominated in later years (such as Neil Simon's *Brighton Beach Memoirs* in 1983), the system reverted back to the Nominating Committee meeting to discuss its members' choices.

THE DRAMA DESK AWARDS

PLAYS
Play: *Streamers* by David Rabe; Actor: John Wood (*Travesties*); Actress: Rosemary Harris (*The Royal Family*); Featured Actor: Judd Hirsch (*Knock Knock*); Featured Actress: Rachel Roberts (*Habeas Corpus*); Director: Ellis Rabb (*The Royal Family*)

MUSICALS
Musical: *A Chorus Line*; Actor: Ian Richardson (*My Fair Lady*); Actress (tie): Carole (Kelly) Bishop and Donna McKechnie (*A Chorus Line*); Featured Actor: George Rose (*My Fair Lady*); Featured Actress: Vivian Reed (*Bubbling Brown Sugar*); Director/Choreographer: Michael Bennett (*A Chorus Line*); Book of a Musical: James Kirkwood and Nicholas Dante (*A Chorus Line*); Score: Marvin Hamlisch and Edward Kleban (*A Chorus Line*)

OTHER AWARDS
Revival: *The Royal Family*; Unique Evening in the Theatre: *The Norman Conquests*; Set Design: Boris Aronson (*Pacific Overtures*); Costume Design: Florence Klotz (*Pacific Overtures*); Lighting Design: Jules Fisher (*Chicago*)

SPECIAL AWARDS
Playwright Horizons' new Queens Theatre in the Park; Hartman Theatre, Stamford, CT; Hudson River Museum for its exhibition of theater items

THE NEW YORK DRAMA CRITICS CIRCLE AWARDS

BEST PLAY
Travesties by Tom Stoppard

BEST AMERICAN PLAY
Streamers by David Rabe

BEST MUSICAL
Pacific Overtures by Stephen Sondheim, John Weidman, and Hugh Wheeler

THE PULITZER PRIZE FOR DRAMA

A Chorus Line by Michael Bennett, James Kirkwood, Nicholas Dante, Marvin Hamlisch, and Edward Kleban

THE OBIE AWARDS

BEST THEATRE PIECE
Rhoda in Potatoland by Richard Foreman

BEST NEW PLAYWRIGHT
David Mamet (*American Buffalo, Sexual Perversity in Chicago*)

DIRECTION
JoAnne Akalatis (*Cascando*); Marshall W. Mason (*Knock Knock, Serenading Louie*)

PERFORMANCE
Joyce Aaron (*Acrobatics*); Roberts Blossom (*Ice Age*); Robert Christian (*Blood Knot*); Crystal Field (*Day Old Bread*); June Gable (*The Comedy of Errors*); Mike Kellin (*American Buffalo*); Tony Lo Bianco (*Yanks 3 Detroit 0 Top of the Seventh*); Priscilla Lopez and Sammy Williams (*A Chorus Line*); Kate Manheim (*Rhoda in Potatoland*); T. Miratti (*The Shortchanged Review*); Pamela Payton-Wright (*Jesse and the Bandit Queen*); Priscilla Smith (*The Good Woman of Setzuan*); David Warrilow (*The Lost Ones*)

Mike Kellin, who won an Obie for the Off-Broadway production of David Mamet's *American Buffalo*, said, "Of the eleven people who saw the show, I'm very grateful six of them were *Voice* critics."

DESIGN
Santo Loquasto (sets and costumes of *The Comedy of Errors*); Donald Brooks (set of *The Tempest*)

SPECIAL CITATIONS
Michael Bennett, James Kirkwood, Nicholas Dante, Marvin Hamlisch, Edward Kleban for *A Chorus Line*; Yale Repertory Theatre production of Edward Bond's *Bingo*; Meredith Monk for *Quarry*; Morton Lichter and Gordon Rogoff for *Old Timers' Sexual Symphony*; *Chile! Chile!*; Philip Glass for the music for Mabou Mines; Neil Flanagan for distinguished contribution to Off-Broadway theater

The Obies were held at Lincoln Center, far from the usual downtown milieu. The *Voice*'s new publisher Clay Felker tried to get even ritzier by asking Elizabeth Taylor to host the ceremony (she was unavailable). The committee of Obie judges officially protested the choice of location, stating it was not in keeping with the avant-garde nature of the awards. But presenter Edward Albee said, "I wonder if we should be quite so snooty about Lincoln Center. . . . Off-Broadway is a state of mind and has nothing to do with where it's done."

THE OUTER CRITICS CIRCLE AWARDS

Performances: Eva Le Galliene (*The Royal Family*), Vanessa Redgrave (*The Lady from the Sea*), Vivian Reed (*Bubbling Brown Sugar*), Meryl Streep (Phoenix Repertory Theatre); Ensemble Performance: *The Norman Conquests*; Set Design: Holmes Easley (Roundabout Theatre Company); Costume Design: Theoni V. Aldredge; Special Awards: Circle in the Square for its twenty-fifth anniversary, Michael Bennett for the creation and direction of *A Chorus Line*; The Goodspeed Opera House; *Tuscaloosa's Calling Me*

THE TONY AWARDS

PLAY
*for colored girls who have considered suicide/when
    the rainbow is enuf* by Ntozake Shange
Otherwise Engaged by Simon Gray
The Shadow Box by Michael Cristofer
Streamers by David Rabe

Even though it played at the Off-Broadway Mitzi E. Newhouse Theatre, *Streamers*, David Rabe's Vietnam-era drama of explosive violence in an Army barracks, was in the running for a Tony. It opened at the tail end of the 1975–76 season after the Tony cut-off date, but was eligible for that year's Drama Desk Awards and won for best Play. The '76–'77 Tony for best Play, as well as the Pulitzer Prize, went to *The Shadow Box*, Michael

Cristofer's sensitive study of a group of hospice residents.

MUSICAL
Annie
Happy End
I Love My Wife
Side by Side by Sondheim

Annie and *I Love My Wife* were the only "original" musicals to be nominated. *Happy End* by Kurt Weill and Bertolt Brecht was first produced in Berlin in 1929. The current production, which had an updated book and lyrics by Michael Feingold, transferred to Broadway from the Chelsea Theatre Center. *Side by Side by Sondheim* was an imported British revue of the composer's previous songs.

As usual all four shows presented numbers at the Tonys. The extremely popular *Annie*, based on the comic strip *Little Orphan Annie*, was a shoe-in for the best Musical prize and got the most airtime with four songs. The radically adult *I Love My Wife* featured two couples sharing a bed singing about the joys of wife-swapping. After the song, the huge bed was supposed to be pulled off-stage but got stuck. Tony-winner Lenny Baker had to get out and push. The leading actor in *Happy End*, Christopher Lloyd (later to win two Emmys for his burnt-out cabbie Jim Ignatowski in *Taxi*), had broken his leg and performed on crutches.

ACTOR (PLAY)
Tom Courtenay (*Otherwise Engaged*)
Ben Gazzara (*Who's Afraid of Virginia Woolf?*)
Al Pacino (*The Basic Training of Pavlo Hummel*)
Ralph Richardson (*No Man's Land*)

ACTRESS (PLAY)
Colleen Dewhurst (*Who's Afraid
    of Virginia Woolf?*)
Julie Harris (*The Belle of Amherst*)
Liv Ullmann (*Anna Christie*)
Irene Worth (*The Cherry Orchard*)

This win made it five for Julie Harris, the most Tonys for any performer. Her previous wins: *I Am a Camera* (1951–52), *The Lark* (1955–56), *Forty Carats* (1968–69), and *The Last of Mrs. Lincoln* (1972–73).

ACTOR (MUSICAL)
Barry Bostwick (*The Robber Bridegroom*)
Robert Guillaume (*Guys and Dolls*)
Raul Julia (*Threepenny Opera*)
Reid Shelton (*Annie*)

ACTRESS (MUSICAL)
Clamma Dale (*Porgy and Bess*)
Ernestine Jackson (*Guys and Dolls*)
Dorothy Loudon (*Annie*)
Andrea McArdle (*Annie*)

FEATURED ACTOR (PLAY)
Bob Dishy (*Sly Fox*)
Joe Fields (*The Basic Training of Pavlo Hummel*)
Laurence Luckinbill (*The Shadow Box*)
Jonathan Pryce (*Comedians*)

FEATURED ACTRESS (PLAY)
Trazana Beverly (*for colored girls…*)
Patricia Elliott (*The Shadow Box*)
Rose Gregorio (*The Shadow Box*)
Mary McCarty (*Anna Christie*)

FEATURED ACTOR (MUSICAL)
Lenny Baker (*I Love My Wife*)
David Kernan (*Side by Side by Sondheim*)
Larry Marshall (*Porgy and Bess*)
Ned Sherrin (*Side by Side by Sondheim*)

FEATURED ACTRESS (MUSICAL)
Ellen Green (*Threepenny Opera*)
Delores Hall (*Your Arms Too Short to Box with God*)
Millicent Martin (*Side by Side by Sondheim*)
Julie N. McKenzie (*Side by Side by Sondheim*)

OTHER AWARDS
Revival: *Porgy and Bess*; Director (Play): Gordon Davidson (*The Shadow Box*); Director (Musical): Gene Saks (*I Love My Wife*); Score: Charles Strouse, Martin Carnin (*Annie*); Book of a Musical: Thomas Meehan (*Annie*); Choreography: Peter Gennaro (*Annie*); Set Design: David Mitchell (*Annie*); Costume Design (tie): Theoni V. Aldredge (*Annie*) and Santo Loquasto (*The Cherry Orchard*); Lighting Design: Jennifer Tipton (*The Cherry Orchard*)

The category of outstanding Revival was added this year.

SPECIAL AWARDS
Mark Taper Forum, Los Angeles, CA (Outstanding Regional Theatre); Lily Tomlin; Barry Manilow; Diana Ross; National Theatre for the Deaf; Equity Library Theatre

"Ford to New York—Drop Dead" read the headline in the *New York Daily News*. "Theatre Is Now a National Invalid," screamed a similar banner in the trade paper *Variety*. New York City was on the edge of bankruptcy and President Gerald Ford refused to bail the metropolis out. Broadway was feeling the economic impact of this crisis as well. Yet the Great White Way was still intact with enough productions to justify the annual Tony celebration.

The Tonys ceremony took survival as its theme and opened with six stars singing "I'm Still Here" from *Follies*. Stephen Sondheim wrote special lyrics to suit the occasion ("Each year they shout it/Broadway is dead/But, my dear/You're still here"). Ironically, the six hosts (Jack Albertson, Beatrice Arthur, Buddy Ebsen, Damon Evans, Jean Stapleton, and Leslie Uggams) were known mainly for their TV work and this Tony gig was the first time most of them had stepped on a Broadway stage in many years.

THE DRAMA DESK AWARDS

PLAYS
American Play: *A Texas Trilogy* by Preston Jones; Foreign Play: *Otherwise Engaged* by Simon Gray; Actor: Al Pacino (*The Basic Training of Pavlo Hummel*); Actress: Irene Worth (*The Cherry Orchard*); Featured Actor: Bob Dishy (*Sly Fox*); Featured Actress: Rosemary De Angelis (*The Transfiguration of Benno Blimpie*); Director (tie): Mike Nichols (*Comedians*) and Alan Schneider (*A Texas Trilogy*)

MUSICALS
Musical: *Annie*; Actor: Lenny Baker (*I Love My Wife*); Actress: Clamma Dale (*Porgy and Bess*); Featured Actor: The Band (*I Love My Wife*); Featured Actress: Dorothy Loudon (*Annie*);

Director, Lyrics: Martin Charnin (*Annie*); Music: Cy Coleman (*I Love My Wife*); Book: Thomas Meehan (*Annie*); Choreography: Peter Gennaro (*Annie*)

Though the Tonys and the Outer Critics Circle considered Dorothy Loudon, the deliciously evil orphanage mistress of *Annie*, a leading actress, the Drama Desk felt she was a supporting player. Conversely, Lenny Baker was a leading man to the DDs, but a featured actor to the Tonys. The Band consisted of the four musicians of *I Love My Wife* whom director Gene Saks had integrated into the action of the show.

OTHER AWARDS
Unique Theatrical Experience: John Gielgud and Ralph Richardson in *No Man's Land*; Set Design: Santo Loquasto (*American Buffalo, The Cherry Orchard*); Costume Design: Theoni V. Aldredge (*Annie*); Lighting Design: Jennifer Tipton (*The Cherry Orchard, for colored girls…*)

The Drama Desk best American Play *A Texas Trilogy* was actually three plays. Preston Jones' trio, revolving around a tiny town in the title state, played in rotating repertory. It had received raves during a run in Washington, DC, but Clive Barnes of the powerful *New York Times* dismissed it with a negative review. The three shows were too expensive to run with a mixed press and closed after a brief engagement. *Trilogy* was totally ignored by the Tonys and Jones never recovered from the disappointment, dying a few years later.

THE NEW YORK DRAMA CRITICS CIRCLE AWARDS

BEST PLAY
Otherwise Engaged by Simon Gray

BEST AMERICAN PLAY
American Buffalo by David Mamet

BEST MUSICAL
Annie by Thomas Meehan, Charles Strouse, and Martin Charnin

THE PULITZER PRIZE FOR DRAMA
The Shadow Box by Michael Cristofer

THE OBIE AWARDS

BEST NEW AMERICAN PLAY
Curse of the Starving Class by Sam Shepard.

Sam Shepard's play had not even been produced yet when it was awarded the Obie for Best New American Play. It only existed as a manuscript at that point. The seven Obie judges had split on the award with three voting for the play, two against, and two abstaining. Presenter Robert Duvall read lengthy statements for each of the factions on the Obie Committee, after which one audience member gave his own opinion: "Bullshit!" The awards were hosted by Marilyn Sokol, Paul Sorvino, and Gilda Radner who re-created her Emily Litella character from *Saturday Night Live*.

SUSTAINED ACHIEVEMENT
Joseph Chaikin

This was the first Sustained Achievement Award. The citation includes a check for $1,000 from the *Village Voice*.

DISTINGUISHED PRODUCTIONS
Playwright Eve Merriam, director Tommy Tune, costume designer Kate Carmel, and the cast of *The Club*; poet Ntozake Shange, director Oz Scott, and the cast of *for colored girls who have considered suicide/when the rainbow is enuf*; Mabou Mines (*Dressed Like an Egg*)

PLAYWRITING
David Berry (*G.R. Point*); Maria Irene Fornes (*Fefu and Her Friends*); William Hauptmann (*Domino Courts*); Albert Innaurato (*Gemini* and *The Transfiguration of Benno Blimpie*); David Rudkin (*Ashes*)

DIRECTION
Melvin Bernhardt (*Children*); Gordon Davidson (*Savages*)

PERFORMANCES
Danny Aiello, Anne DeSalvo (*Gemini*); Martin

Balsam (*Cold Storage*); Lucinda Childs (*Einstein on the Beach*); James Coco (*The Transfiguration of Benno Blimpie*); John Heard (*G.R. Point*); Jo Henderson (*Ladyhouse Blues*); William Hurt (*My Life*); Joseph Maher (*Savages*); Roberta Maxwell, Brian Murray (*Ashes*); Lola Pashalinski (*Der Ring Gott Farblonjet*); Marian Seldes (*Isadora Duncan Sleeps with the Russian Navy*); Margaret Wright (*A Manoir*)

DESIGN

Charles Ludlam (design of *Der Ring Gott Farblonjet*); Carole Oditz for costumes, Douglas Schmidt for set, and Burt Hass for lighting of *Crazy Locomotive*; Henry Millman for set and Edward M. Greenberg for lighting of *Domino Courts*

SPECIAL CITATIONS

Barbara Garson (*The Dinosaur Door*); Manhattan Theatre Club; New York Street Theatre Caravan; Theatre for the New City; Philip Glass for the music of *Einstein on the Beach*; Ping Chong (*Humboldt's Current*); the creators of *Nightclub Cantata*

THE OUTER CRITICS CIRCLE AWARDS

Broadway Musical: *for colored girls...*; Most Refreshing Musical: *Annie*; Actors: John Gielgud, Ralph Richardson (*No Man's Land*); Actress (Play): Liv Ullmann (*Anna Christie*); Actress (Musical): Dorothy Loudon (*Annie*); Directors: Andrei Serban (*The Cherry Orchard*), Gordon Davidson (*The Shadow Box*); Set Design: David Mitchell (*Annie*), Santo Loquasto (*The Cherry Orchard*); Debut of an Actress: Andrea MacArdle (*Annie*); Musical Contribution: Elizabeth Swados (*The Cherry Orchard, Nightclub Cantata,* and *Agamemnon*); John Gassner Playwriting Award: Preston Jones (*A Texas Trilogy*); Special Awards: Brooklyn Academy of Music Theatre Company for *Three Sisters* and *The New York Idea*

THE TONY AWARDS

PLAY
Chapter Two by Neil Simon
Da by Hugh Leonard
Deathtrap by Ira Levin
The Gin Game by D. L. Colburn

MUSICAL
Ain't Misbehavin'
Dancin'
On the Twentieth Century
Runaways

ACTOR (PLAY)
Hume Cronyn (*The Gin Game*)
Barnard Hughes (*Da*)
Frank Langella (*Dracula*)
Jason Robards (*A Touch of the Poet*)

ACTRESS (PLAY)
Anne Bancroft (*Golda*)
Anita Gillette (*Chapter Two*)
Estelle Parsons (*Miss Margarida's Way*)
Jessica Tandy (*The Gin Game*)

ACTOR (MUSICAL)
Eddie Bracken (*Hello, Dolly!*)
John Cullum (*On the Twentieth Century*)
Barry Nelson (*The Act*)
Gilbert Price (*Timbuktu!*)

ACTRESS (MUSICAL)
Madeline Kahn (*On the Twentieth Century*)
Eartha Kitt (*Timbuktu!*)
Liza Minnelli (*The Act*)
Frances Sternhagen (*Angel*)

Although she was nominated for best Actress (Musical), Madeline Kahn did not appear in the number from *On the Twentieth Century* at the Tonys. The actress had left the show after only three months during which she missed several performances. Kahn's understudy Judy Kaye took over, won rave reviews, became a star, and performed on the telecast.

FEATURED ACTOR (PLAY)
Morgan Freeman (*The Mighty Gents*)
Victor Garber (*Deathtrap*)
Cliff Gorman (*Chapter Two*)
Lester Rawlins (*Da*)

FEATURED ACTRESS (PLAY)
Starletta DuPois (*The Might Gents*)
Swoosie Kurtz (*Tartuffe*)
Marian Seldes (*Deathtrap*)
Ann Wedgeworth (*Chapter Two*)

FEATURED ACTOR (MUSICAL)
Steven Boockvor (*Working*)
Wayne Cilento (*Dancin'*)
Rex Everhart (*Working*)
Kevin Kline (*On the Twentieth Century*)

FEATURED ACTRESS (MUSICAL)
Nell Carter (*Ain't Misbehavin'*)
Imogene Coca (*On the Twentieth Century*)
Ann Reinking (*Dancin'*)
Charlaine Woodard (*Ain't Misbehavin'*)

OTHER AWARDS
Revival: *Dracula*; Director (Play): Melvin
Bernhardt (*Da*); Director (Musical): Richard
Maltby, Jr. (*Ain't Misbehavin'*); Score: Cy
Coleman, Betty Comden, Adolph Green (*On the
Twentieth Century*); Book of a Musical: Betty
Comden, Adolph Green (*On the Twentieth
Century*); Choreography: Bob Fosse (*Dancin'*); Set
Design: Robin Wagner (*On the Twentieth
Century*); Costume Design: Edward Gorey
(*Dracula*); Lighting Design: Jules Fisher (*Dancin'*)

Director Richard Maltby, Jr., was a little too thank-
ful in his acceptance speech. The program cut to a
commercial in the middle of it.

Elizabeth Swados became the first person to be
nominated for four Tonys in one year. She was in
the running for her score, book, direction, and
choreography of *Runaways*, a free-form musical
collage about homeless youngsters. Although she
did not collect any Tonys, Swados did cop an Obie
for the show's Off-Broadway run at the New York
Shakespeare Festival's Public Theatre.

SPECIAL AWARD
Long Wharf Theatre, New Haven, CN
(Outstanding Regional Theatre); Irving Berlin
(Lawrence Langer Award for Lifetime
Achievement); "I Love New York" Broadway Show
Tours (Theatre Award '78)

The 1977–78 Tonys almost didn't make it on the
air. After eight years, ABC decided not to renew its
contract to broadcast the awards. NBC, which had
telecast the show for 1969–70, 1968–69, and
1967–68, passed on picking them up. Fortunately,
Alexander Cohen, the producer of the Tonys, had a
relationship with the remaining network CBS. He
had produced several programs for it, including its
fiftieth-anniversary special. Cohen asked for two
and a half hours of prime time. The Big Eye executives gave him ninety minutes, claiming the potential audience was not great enough to justify more.
"We have to admit it going in," Cohen remarked
in an interview. "The Tonys are a parochial show;
it appeals to a small but select audience. . . . Before
we had two hours with a runover; this was ninety
minutes with a cut-off. After commercials we're
actually talking a seventy-two-minute show."

All of the design awards, plus the prizes for best
Score, Book of a Musical, and Revival, were presented before the telecast. The lightning-paced
show ran over the alotted hour and a half by only
seven minutes. Bonnie Franklin, then starring in
the popular sitcom *One Day at a Time*, appeared in
videotaped segments retracing her early career as a
Broadway hopeful (she had been nominated for a
Tony for her featured role in *Applause*). This tied in
with the evening's theme of "Footlights" with presenters relating their first steps in the theater.

THE DRAMA DESK AWARDS

PLAYS
Play: *Da* by Hugh Leonard; Actor: Barnard
Hughes (*Da*); Actress: Jessica Tandy (*The Gin
Game*); Featured Actor: Morgan Freeman (*The
Mighty Gents*); Featured Actress: Eileen Atkins
(*The Night of the Tribades*); Director: Melvin
Bernhardt (*Da*)

MUSICALS
Musical: *Ain't Misbehavin'*; Actor: Ken Page (*Ain't*

Misbehavin'); Actress: Nell Carter (*Ain't Misbehavin*'); Featured Actor: Kevin Kline (*On the Twentieth Century*); Featured Actress (tie): Swoosie Kurtz (*A History of the American Film*) and Bobo Lewis (*Working*); Director (tie): Peter Masterson and Tommy Tune (*The Best Little Whorehouse in Texas*) and Stephen Schwartz (*Working*); Music (tie): Cy Coleman (*On the Twentieth Century*) and Carol Hall (*The Best Little Whorehouse in Texas*); Lyrics: Carol Hall (*The Best Little Whorehouse in Texas*); Choreography: Bob Fosse (*Dancin'*)

There were no nominations for outstanding Book of a Musical.

OTHER AWARDS
Unique Theatrical Experience: Estelle Parsons (*Miss Margarida's Way*); Set Design: Robin Wagner (*On the Twentieth Century*); Costume Design: Flornece Klotz (*On the Twentieth Century*); Lighting Design: Jules Fisher (*Dancin'*)

SPECIAL AWARDS
The Off-Off-Broadway Theatre Movement

THE NEW YORK DRAMA CRITICS CIRCLE AWARDS

BEST PLAY
Da by Hugh Leonard

BEST MUSICAL
Ain't Misbehavin', revue based on the music of Fats Waller

THE PULITZER PRIZE FOR DRAMA
The Gin Game by D. L. Colburn

THE OBIE AWARDS

BEST NEW AMERICAN PLAY
The Shaggy Dog Animation by Lee Breuer

Lee Breuer set aside half of the $1,000 cash award for Best New American Play for "a revolving fund for theatre people having emergencies." Previous Obie recipient and presenter Marilyn Sokol pointed out, "I'm here to tell you that winning an Obie Award is a future guarantee of *absolutely nothing*."

Dustin Hoffman hosted the awards, which were broadcast on local public TV Channel 13.

SUSTAINED ACHIEVEMENT
Peter Schumann's Bread and Puppet Theatre

DIRECTION
Robert Allan Ackerman (*A Prayer for My Daughter*); Thomas Bullard (*Statements Made after an Arrest under the Immorality Act*); Elizabeth Swados (*Runaways*)

PERFORMANCE
Richard Bauer (*Landscape of the Body* and *The Dybbouk*); Nell Carter (*Ain't Misbehavin'*); Alma Cuervo, Swoosie Kurtz (*Uncommon Women and Others*); Kaiulani Lee (*Safe House*); Bruce Myers (*The Dybbuk*); Lee S. Wilkopf (*The Present Tense*)

DESIGN
Garland Wright, John Arnone (*K*); Robert Yudice (*Museum*)

SPECIAL CITATIONS
Ain't Misbehavin'; Eric Bentley; Joseph Dunn and Irja Koljonen (*Preface*); Jerry Mayer (*Taud Show*); Stuart Sherman; Squat

THE OUTER CRITICS CIRCLE AWARDS

Play: *Da*; Actors: Bernard Hughes (*Da*), John Wood (*Deathtrap*), Martin Balsam (*Cold Storage*); Actresses: Vicki Frederick (*Dancin'*) and Nancy Snyder (*5th of July*); Director: Melvin Bernhardt (*Da*)

THE TONY AWARDS

PLAY
Bedroom Farce by Alan Ayckbourn
The Elephant Man by Bernard Pomerance
Whose Life Is It Anyway? by Brian Clark
Wings by Arthur Kopit

It was a season of physical ailments and disabilities. *The Elephant Man*, the Tony best Play, chronicled the life of John Merrick, a victim of neurofibramotosis, a degenerating disease of the skin, bone, and nerve tissue. *Whose Life Is It Anyway?* centered on a paralyzed man fighting for his right to die, and *Wings* followed a stroke victim's journey back to life. *On Golden Pond* dealt with the tribulations of old age. In *Tribute*, Jack Lemmon was a childish press agent faced with a fatal illness. The winning musical *Sweeney Todd* wasn't much more cheerful. Its "hero" was a murderous barber [played by best Actor (Musical) winner Len Cariou] who cuts his customers' throats. Their remains are then baked into meat pies by his accomplice, the adorably amoral Mrs. Lovett [played by best Actress (Musical) winner Angela Lansbury].

MUSICAL

Ballroom
The Best Little Whorehouse in Texas
Sweeney Todd
They're Playing Our Song

Television audiences didn't hear all of the lyrics for the number from the nominated *The Best Little Whorehouse in Texas*. "The Aggie Song" was performed in the show by a winning football team which is permitted to visit the titular establishment as a reward for their victory on the gridiron. CBS "bleeped" eleven naughty double entendres. But viewers intelligent to figure out the rhymes got the message.

ACTOR (PLAY)

Philip Anglim (*The Elephant Man*)
Tom Conti (*Whose Life Is It Anyway?*)
Jack Lemmon (*Tribute*)
Alec McCowen (*St. Mark's Gospel*)

ACTRESS (PLAY) (TIE)

Jane Alexander (*The First Monday in October*)
Constance Cummings (*Wings*)
Carole Shelley (*The Elephant Man*)
Frances Sternhagen (*On Golden Pond*)

ACTOR (MUSICAL)

Len Cariou (*Sweeney Todd*)
Vincent Gardenia (*Ballroom*)

Joel Grey (*The Grand Tour*)
Robert Klein (*They're Playing Our Song*)

ACTRESS (MUSICAL)

Tovah Feldshuh (*Sarava*)
Angela Lansbury (*Sweeney Todd*)
Dorothy Loudon (*Ballroom*)
Alexis Smith (*Platinum*)

This was Lansbury's fourth Tony, tying her with Gwen Verdon for most musical performer Tonys. Lansbury's other wins were for *Mame* (1965–66), *Dear World* (1968–69), and a revival of *Gypsy* (1974–75). Lansbury holds the record for most leading Actress (Musical) Tonys since one of Verdon's wins was in the Featured Actress (Musical) category.

FEATURED ACTOR (PLAY)

Bob Balaban (*The Inspector General*)
Michael Gough (*Bedroom Farce*)
Joseph Maher (*Spokesong*)
Edward James Olmos (*Zoot Suit*)

FEATURED ACTRESS (PLAY)

Joan Hickson (*Bedroom Farce*)
Laurie Kennedy (*Man and Superman*)
Susan Littler (*Bedroom Farce*)
Mary-Joan Negro (*Wings*)

FEATURED ACTOR (MUSICAL)

Richard Cox (*Platinum*)
Henderson Forsythe (*The Best Little Whorehouse in Texas*)
Gregory Hines (*Eubie!*)
Ron Holgate (*The Grand Tour*)

FEATURED ACTRESS (MUSICAL)

Joan Ellis (*The Best Little Whorehouse in Texas*)
Carlin Glynn (*The Best Little Whorehouse in Texas*)
Millicent Martin (*King of Hearts*)
Maxine Sullivan (*My Old Friends*)

OTHER AWARDS

Director (Play): Jack Hofsiss (*The Elephant Man*); Director (Musical): Harold Prince (*Show Boat*); Score: Stephen Sondheim (*Sweeney Todd*); Book of a Musical: Hugh Wheeler (*Sweeney Todd*); Choreography: Michael Bennett, Bob Avian

(*Ballroom*); Set Design: Eugene Lee (*Sweeney Todd*); Costume Design: Franne Lee (*Sweeney Todd*); Lighting Design: Roger Morgan (*The Crucifer of Blood*)

Note: There was no outstanding Revival winner this year.

SPECIAL AWARDS

Richard Rodgers (Lawrence Langer Award for Lifetime Achievement); American Conservatory Theatre, San Francisco, CA (Outstanding Regional Theatre); Henry Fonda; Walter F. Diehl; Eugene O'Neill Memorial Theatre Center

Henry Fonda was surprised by a special Tony presented by his daughter Jane. He had been told the award was for his friend, director Josh Logan. Mindful of his duties as Tony host, he pointed to his watch during the subsequent ovation as a reminder the broadcast was only ninety minutes long. Along with co-hosts Jane Alexander and Liv Ullman, Fonda opened the show with explanations of various theatrical superstitions such as never whistling in a dressing room or mentioning *Macbeth*. All the presenters had similar anecdotes in keeping with the theme of the program writer Hildy Parks had devised, "Good Luck Tonight." After giving his prepared spiel, Jack Lemmon remarked "I don't know what that has to do with the awards, but it's what Hildy wrote."

During a tribute to Richard Rodgers, Tony producer Alexander Cohen managed to slip in a song from his own production of the composer's latest show *I Remember Mama*. The musical, based on the 1944 play, was faring poorly at the box office and failed to garner any Tony nominations. In order to gain some free TV exposure, Cohen presented a scene from *Mama* with its star Ullman, who was coincidentally co-hosting the program. The plug did not help and *Mama* closed at a loss a few months later.

THE DRAMA DESK AWARDS

PLAYS

Play: *The Elephant Man* by Bernard Pomerance; Actor: Philip Anglim (*The Elephant Man*); Actress: Constance Cummings (*Wings*); Featured Actor:

George Rose (*The Kingfisher*); Featured Actress: Pamela Reed (*Getting Out*); Director: Jack Hofsiss (*The Elephant Man*)

MUSICALS

Musical: *Sweeney Todd*; Actor: Len Cariou (*Sweeney Todd*); Actress: Angela Lansbury (*Sweeney Todd*); Featured Actor: Ken Jennings (*Sweeney Todd*); Featured Actress: Merle Louise (*Sweeney Todd*); Director: Harold Prince (*Sweeney Todd*); Music, Lyrics: Stephen Sondheim (*Sweeney Todd*); Book: Hugh Wheeler (*Sweeney Todd*); Choreography: Michael Bennett, Bob Avian (*Ballroom*)

OTHER AWARDS

Unique Theatrical Experience: *An Evening with Quentin Crisp*; Set Design (tie): John Lee Beatty (*Talley's Folly*), John Wulp (*The Crucifer of Blood*); Costume Design: Patricia Zipprodt (*King of Hearts*); Lighting Design: Roger Morgan (*The Crucifer of Blood*)

THE NEW YORK DRAMA CRITICS CIRCLE AWARDS

BEST PLAY

The Elephant Man by Bernard Pomerance

BEST MUSICAL

Sweeney Todd by Hugh Wheeler and Stephen Sondheim

THE PULITZER PRIZE FOR DRAMA

Buried Child by Sam Shepard

THE OBIE AWARDS

BEST NEW AMERICAN PLAY

Josephine by Michael McClure

SUSTAINED ACHIEVEMENT

Al Carmines

PLAYWRITING

Rosalyn Drexler (*The Writer's Opera*); Susan Miller (*Nasty Rumors* and *Final Remarks*); Richard Nelson (*Vienna Notes*); Bernard Pomerance (*The Elephant Man*); Sam Shepard (*Buried Child*)

DIRECTION

Maria Irene Fornes (*Eyes on the Harem*);
Jack Hofsiss (*The Elephant Man*)

PERFORMANCE

Mary Alice (*Nongogo* and *Julius Caesar*); Philip
Anglim (*The Elephant Man*); Joseph Buloff (*The
Price*); Constance Cummings (*Wings*); Fred
Gwynne (*Grand Magic*); Judd Hirsch (*Talley's
Folly*); Marcell Rosenblatt (*Vienna Notes*);
Elizabeth Wilson (*Taken in Marriage*)

Both *The Elephant Man* and *Wings* played Off-
Broadway before moving on Broadway. The shows
are among a handful of productions to win Tonys
and Obies in the same season.

DESIGN

Theatre X (sets and lighting of *A Fierce Longing*);
Jennifer Tipton (lighting for Public Theatre
productions)

SPECIAL CITATIONS

Gordon Chater, Richard Wherott, and Steve J.
Spears (*The Elocution of Benjamin*); JoAnne
Akalaitis, Ellen McElduff, and David Warrilow
(*Southern Exposure*); Tadeusz Kantos (*The Dead
Class*); The Negro Ensemble Company for
sustained excellence of ensemble acting; The
French Department of NYU for its Samuel
Beckett Festival

"Off-Broadway means to me, a place where they
can't fire you," commented Judd Hirsch upon
accepted his Obie. "Off-Broadway means to me,
toilets that don't flush" presenter Swoosie Kurtz
later countered. The ceremony was telecast on local
New York public TV Channel 13. In a musical
parody, Weeders, Finkle, and Fay vocalized the
thoughts of the Obie Committee: "Sometimes we
just say, Goddamnit/ Let's give another to David
Mamet."

THE OUTER CRITICS
CIRCLE AWARDS

Broadway Play: *The Elephant Man*; Broadway
Musical: *Sweeney Todd*; Performances: Tom Conti
(*Whose Life Is It Anyway?*), Carole Shelley (*The
Elephant Man*); Director: Jack Hofsiss (*The

Elephant Man); Set Design: John Wulp (*The
Crucifer of Blood*); New Talent: Philip Anglim (*The
Elephant Man*), Lucie Arnaz (*They're Playing Our
Song*), Susan Kingsley (*Getting Out*), Gregory and
Maurice Hines (*Eubie!*); John Gassner Playwriting
Award: Marsha Norman (*Getting Out*); Special
awards: Cafe La MaMa, Brandt Organization for
re-opening the Apollo and Lyric Theatres

1979-80

THE TONY AWARDS

PLAY

Bent by Martin Sherman
Children of a Lesser God by Mark Medoff
Home by Samm-Art Williams
Talley's Folly by Lanford Wilson

MUSICAL

Barnum
A Day in Hollywood/A Night in the Ukraine
Evita
Sugar Babies

ACTOR (PLAY)

Charles Brown (*Home*)
Gerald Hiken (*Strider*)
Judd Hirsch (*Talley's Folly*)
John Rubinstein (*Children of a Lesser God*)

ACTRESS (PLAY)

Blythe Danner (*Betrayal*)
Phyllis Frelich (*Children of a Lesser God*)
Maggie Smith (*Night and Day*)
Anne Twomey (*Nuts*)

Deaf actress Phyllis Frelich signed her acceptance
speech while her husband Robert Steinberg spoke
it. Frelich won for her performance as a deaf young
woman in a relationship with a hearing teacher.
Marlee Matlin would later win an Oscar for the
same role in the film version.

ACTOR (MUSICAL)

Jim Dale (*Barnum*)
Gregory Hines (*Comin' Uptown*)

Mickey Rooney (*Sugar Babies*)
Giorgio Tozzi (*The Most Happy Fella*)

ACTRESS (MUSICAL)
Christine Andreas (*Oklahoma!*)
Sandy Duncan (*Peter Pan*)
Patti LuPone (*Evita*)
Ann Miller (*Sugar Babies*)

FEATURED ACTOR (PLAY)
David Dukes (*Bent*)
George Hearn (*Watch on the Rhine*)
Earle Hyman (*The Lady from Dubuque*)

Joseph Maher (*Night and Day*)
David Rounds (*Morning's at Seven*)

FEATURED ACTRESS (PLAY)
Maureen Anderman (*The Lady from Dubuque*)
Pamela Burrell (*Strider*)
Lois de Banzie (*Morning's at Seven*)
Dinah Manoff (*I Ought to Be in Pictures*)

FEATURED ACTOR (MUSICAL)
David Garrison (*A Day in Hollywood/A Night in the Ukraine*)
Harry Groener (*Oklahoma!*)

Bob Gunton (*Evita*)
Mandy Patinkin (*Evita*)

FEATURED ACTRESS (MUSICAL)
Debbie Allen (*West Side Story*)
Glenn Close (*Barnum*)
Josie de Guzman (*West Side Story*)
Priscilla Lopez (*A Day in Hollywood/A Night in the Ukraine*)

OTHER AWARDS
Revival: *Morning's at Seven*; Director (Play): Vivian Matalon (*Morning's at Seven*); Director (Musical): Harold Prince (*Evita*); Score: Andrew Lloyd Webber, Tim Rice (*Evita*); Book of a Musical: Tim Rice (*Evita*); Choreography: Tommy Tune, Thommie Walsh (*A Day in Hollywood/A Night in the Ukraine*); Set Design (tie): John Lee Beatty (*Talley's Folly*) and David Mitchell (*Barnum*); Costume Design: Theoni V. Aldredge (*Barnum*); Lighting Design: David Hersey (*Evita*)

SPECIAL AWARDS
Helen Hayes (Lawrence Langner Award for Lifetime Achievement); Actors' Theatre of Louisville (Outstanding Regional Theatre); Goodspeed Opera House; Mary Tyler Moore (for *Whose Life Is It Anyway?*); *Variety* editor Hobe Morrison, Richard Fitzgerald of Sound Associates (Theatre Award '80)

At the top of the Tony telecast, an announcement was made that the hosts of the show would be unable to perform. After a groan from the audience, the camera panned to find Mary Tyler Moore and Jason Robards seated in the Mark Hellinger Theatre discussing the importance of understudies in stage productions. Their patter praised these valiant performers ready to go on stage at a moment's notice if the star should fall ill. Then a stagehand rushed down the aisle, whispered in both of their ears and motioned for them to follow him. The actors left their seats and then reappeared on stage as the evening's hosts.

This elaborate, rehearsed ploy was an obvious set-up to lead into the theme of the 1979–80 Tonys: understudies. Each of the presenters, including Faye Dunaway, Mia Farrow, James Earl Jones, Richard Kiley, and Nancy Marchand,

offered stories of their days subbing for a star. Eve Arden told of understudying Fannie Brice in *The Ziegfeld Follies*. She was followed by Carol Channing relating her experiences of waiting in the wings for Arden in *Let's Face It*. As time grew shorter for the ninety-minute broadcast, understudy anecdotes were cut in order to hand out the awards more quickly.

As usual, the highlights were provided by excerpted numbers from the nominated musicals. This year in addition to the four best Musical nominees, there were songs from three revivals (*Oklahoma!*, *West Side Story*, and Sandy Duncan flying through the air in *Peter Pan*). Reviews for the program were laudatory, with *The New York Times* stating, "The Tonys remain the Rolls Royce of television awards shows." The ratings were equally good with a No. 1 ranking in New York and No. 9 in the country. It was also the first time the Tonys were seen internationally, with audiences in England, Japan, the Philippines, and Australia tuning in.

The only controversy was over a special award presented to co-host Moore. The actress was not nominated for her performance in the originally male role of the paralyzed patient in *Whose Life Is It, Anyway?* A special Tony was presented to her for her "bravery" in tackling the part. The Moore award was a last-minute addition and Isabelle Stevenson, president of the American Theatre Wing, stated the Tony Rules Committee did not vote on it. There was speculation that Tony producer Alexander Cohen decided to give the citation to Moore, a highly popular television personality, in order to ensure that she would host the program and garner high ratings.

THE DRAMA DESK AWARDS

PLAYS
Play: *Children of a Lesser God* by Mark Medoff; Actor: John Rubinstein (*Children of a Lesser God*); Actress: Pat Carroll (*Gertrude Stein Gertrude Stein Gertrude Stein*); Featured Actor: David Rounds (*Morning's at Seven*); Featured Actress: Lois de Banzie (*Morning's at Seven*); Director: Vivian Matalon (*Morning's at Seven*); Music in a Play: Norman L. Berman (*Strider*)

MUSICALS

Musical: *Evita*; Actor: Jim Dale (*Barnum*); Actress: Patti LuPone (*Evita*); Featured Actor: Bob Gunton (*Evita*); Featured Actress: Debbie Allen (*West Side Story*); Director: Harold Prince (*Evita*); Music: Andrew Lloyd Webber (*Evita*); Lyrics: Tim Rice (*Evita*); Choreography: Tommy Tune (*A Day in Hollywood/A Night in the Ukraine*)

OTHER AWARDS

Set Design: John Lee Beatty (*Talley's Folly*); Costume Design: Pierre Balmain (*Happy New Year*); Lighting Design: Dennis Parichy (*Talley's Folly*); Sound Design: Norman L. Berman (*Strider*)

SPECIAL AWARDS

Nancy Marchand, Maureen O'Sullivan, Elizabeth Wilson, Teresa Wright (Ensemble Performance in *Morning's at Seven*); La MaMa Experimental Theatre Club for sponsoring New York performances by international theatre companies

THE NEW YORK DRAMA CRITICS CIRCLE AWARDS

BEST PLAY

Talley's Folly by Lanford Wilson

BEST FOREIGN PLAY

Betrayal by Harold Pinter

BEST MUSICAL

Evita by Andrew Lloyd Webber and Tim Rice

SPECIAL CITATIONS

Peter Brook's Le Centre International de Creations Theatrales for its repertory

THE PULITZER PRIZE FOR DRAMA

Talley's Folly by Lanford Wilson

THE OBIE AWARDS

The Obies celebrated their twenty-fifth anniversary. With characteristic candor, the *Village Voice* reported of its paper's own theater awards, "What is undoubtedly clear, and kind of nice in its own bumbling way, is that 24 years of practice didn't

help this year's awards be anything less than the mess we have come to know and tolerate." Christopher Durang and Alice Playten performed a ten-minute history of Off-Broadway and the Flying Karamazov Brothers did an impromptu juggling act when they won a special citation.

SUSTAINED ACHIEVEMENT

Sam Shepard

PLAYWRITING

Lee Breuer (script and direction of *A Prelude to Death in Venice*); Christopher Durang (*Sister Mary Ignatius Explains It All for You*); Romulus Linney (*Tennessee*); Roland Maldoon (script and performance of *Full Confessions of a Socialist*); Jeff Weiss [script and performance of *That's How the Rent Gets Paid (Part Three)*]

PERFORMANCE

Michael Burrell (*Hess*); Michael Cristofer (*Chincilla*); Lindsay Crouse, Michael Higgins (*Reunion*); Elizabeth Franz (*Sister Mary Ignatius Explains It All for You*); Morgan Freeman (*Mother Courage* and *Coriolanus*); John Heard (*Othello* and *Split*); Madeline Le Roux (*La Justice*); Jon Polito (Dodger Theatre and BAM Company performances); Bill Raymond (*Prelude to Death in Venice*); Dianne Wiest (*The Art of Dining*); Hattie Winston (*Mother Courage* and *The Michigan*)

DIRECTION

A. J. Antoon (*The Art of Dining*); Edward Cornell (*Johnny on the Spot*); Elizabeth Lecompte (*Point Judith*)

DESIGN

Ruth Maleczech, Julie Archer (*Vanishing Pictures*); Sally Jacobs (*The Conference of the Birds*); Beverly Emmons (distinguished lighting design); Laura Crow (costumes for *Mary Stuart*)

SPECIAL CITATIONS

The Flying Karamazov Brothers; actors of Le Centre International de Creations Theatricales for ensemble performance; Ellen Stewart and La MaMa ETC for importing foreign companies; David Jones and Richard Nelson for innovative programming at BAM Theatre Company; Ntozake Shange for her adaptation of *Mother Courage*

THE OUTER CRITICS CIRCLE AWARDS

Broadway Play: *Children of a Lesser God*; Broadway Musical: *Barnum*; Performances: Nancy Marchand, Maureen O'Sullivan, Elizabeth Wilson, Teresa Wright, Lois de Banzie (*Morning's at Seven*), Gerald Hiken (*Strider*); Direction and Choreography: Tommy Tune (*A Day in Hollywood/A Night in the Ukraine*); Auspicious Debut: Phyllis Frelich (*Children of a Lesser God*); Performance in an Off-Broadway Play: Pat Carroll (*Gertrude Stein Gertrude Stein Gertrude Stein*); Set Design: John Lee Beatty (*Tally's Folly* and *Hide and Seek*); Lyricist: Tim Rice (*Evita*); John Gassner Playwriting Award: Samm-Art Williams; Consistent Contribution to the Theatre: Curt Dempster and the Ensemble Studio Theatre; Special award: Paul Myers, head of the Billy Rose Theatre Collection of the Lincoln Center Library for the Performing Arts

THE TONY AWARDS

PLAY

A Lesson from Aloes by Athol Fugard
A Life by Hugh Leonard
Amadeus by Peter Shaffer
The Fifth of July by Lanford Wilson

MUSICAL

42nd Street
Sophisticated Ladies
Tintypes
Woman of the Year

Elizabeth Taylor, who was making her Broadway debut in a revival of Lillian Hellman's *The Little Foxes*, lost the best Actress (Play) award, but made a memorable impression at the 1980–81 Tonys. In presenting the best Musical award, the glamorous star stumbled through a list of twenty-one produc-

ers, mispronouncing and giggling as she went. The audience applauded and laughed along. David Merrick, producer of the winning show *42nd Street*, looked as if he wanted to kill Taylor for stealing his moment in the spotlight.

ACTOR (PLAY)

Tim Curry (*Amadeus*)
Roy Dotrice (*A Life*)
Ian McKellen (*Amadeus*)
Jack Weston (*The Floating Light Bulb*)

ACTRESS (PLAY)

Glenda Jackson (*Rose*)
Jane Lapotaire (*Piaf*)
Eva Le Galliene (*To Grandmother's House We Go*)
Elizabeth Taylor (*The Little Foxes*)

ACTOR (MUSICAL)

Gregory Hines (*Sophisticated Ladies*)
Kevin Kline (*The Pirates of Penzance*)
George Rose (*The Pirates of Penzance*)
Martin Vidnovic (*Brigadoon*)

ACTRESS (MUSICAL)

Lauren Bacall (*Woman of the Year*)
Meg Bussert (*Brigadoon*)
Chita Rivera (*Bring Back Birdie*)
Linda Ronstadt (*The Pirates of Penzance*)

FEATURED ACTOR (PLAY)

Tom Aldredge (*The Little Foxes*)
Brian Backer (*The Floating Light Bulb*)
Adam Redfield (*A Life*)
Shepperd Strudwick (*To Grandmother's House We Go*)

FEATURED ACTRESS (PLAY)

Swoosie Kurtz (*The Fifth of July*)
Maureen Stapleton (*The Little Foxes*)
Jessica Tandy (*Rose*)
Zoe Wanamaker (*Piaf*)

FEATURED ACTOR (MUSICAL)

Tony Azito (*The Pirates of Penzance*)
Hinton Battle (*Sophisticated Ladies*)
Lee Roy Reams (*42nd Street*)
Paxton Whitehead (*Camelot*)

FEATURED ACTRESS (MUSICAL)
Marilyn Cooper (*Woman of the Year*)
Phyllis Hyman (*Sophisticated Ladies*)
Wanda Richert (*42nd Street*)
Lynne Thigpen (*Tintypes*)

"I'm an old poker player," said best featured actress Marilyn Cooper, "and I've learned if you sit at the table long enough, eventually you'll win something." She was Tonyed for her brief role as the frumpy current wife of glamorous Lauren Bacall's ex-husband in *Woman of the Year*. Their duet of contrasting lifestyles "The Grass Is Always Greener" was a show-stopper.

OTHER AWARDS
Revival: *The Pirates of Penzance*; Director (Play): Peter Hall (*Amadeus*); Director (Musical): Wilford Leach (*The Pirates of Penzance*); Score: John Kander, Fred Ebb (*Woman of the Year*); Book of a Musical: Peter Stone (*Woman of the Year*); Choreography: Gower Champion (*42nd Street*); Set Design: John Bury (*Amadeus*); Costume Design: Willa Kim (*Sophisticated Ladies*); Lighting Design: John Bury (*Amadeus*)

Gower Champion had died just before *42nd Street* opened. David Merrick announced his passing from the stage of the theater on opening night after a smashingly successful performance. The shocking revelation catapulted the show to the front pages of newspapers and onto television news broadcasts, garnering it scads of free publicity.

SPECIAL AWARDS
Trinity Square Repertory Company, Providence, RI (Outstanding Regional Theatre); Lena Horne (*Lena Horne: The Lady and Her Music*).

"Women in the Theatre" was the theme of the 1980–81 Tonys. All of the presenters were women with the exception of Jose Ferrer, who appeared in drag reminiscent of his performance as *Charley's Aunt*. A male chorus of celebrities opened the show with a rendition of "There Is Nothing Like a Dame" from *South Pacific* while video clips of previous female Tony winners played. Co-hosts Ellen Burstyn and Richard Chamberlain introduced Helen Hayes and Patricia Neal sitting at a nightclub setting reminiscing about the first Tony

Awards and careers of women in the theater. Jane Lapotaire, nominated for her gritty portrayal of French singer Edith Piaf, performed the chanteuse's signature tune "La Vie en Rose."

Set and costume design winner John Bury apologized with "I'm sorry I'm not a woman." The best acceptance speech came from Lena Horne, honored with a special Tony for her one-woman show. "I'm just so happy I'm getting all these awards before I lose my teeth," she said.

In addition to scenes from the current nominated shows, numbers from the previous five best Musicals were done by Priscilla Lopez (*A Chorus Line*), Andrea MacArdle (*Annie*), Nell Carter (*Ain't Misbehavin'*), Angela Lansbury (*Sweeney Todd*), and Patti LuPone (*Evita*). Because the previous year's ratings were so high, the program was expanded from ninety minutes to two hours.

THE DRAMA DESK AWARDS

PLAYS
Play: *Amadeus* by Peter Shaffer; Actor: Ian McKellen (*Amadeus*); Actress: Joan Copeland (*The American Clock*); Featured Actor: Brian Backer (*The Floating Light Bulb*); Featured Actress: Swoosie Kurtz (*The Fifth of July*); Director: Peter Hall (*Amadeus*)

MUSICALS
Musical: *The Pirates of Penzance*; Actor: Kevin Kline (*The Pirates of Penzance*); Actress: Lena Horne (*Lena Horne: The Lady and Her Music*); Featured Actor: Tony Azito (*The Pirates of Penzance*); Featured Actress: Marilyn Cooper (*Woman of the Year*); Director: Wilford Leach (*The Pirates of Penzance*); Choreography: Gower Champion (*42nd Street*)

There were no nominations for Music, Lyrics, or Book of a Musical.

OTHER AWARDS
Unique Theatrical Experience: *Request Concert*; Set Design: John Lee Beatty (*The Fifth of July*); Costume Design (tie): Theoni V. Aldredge (*42nd Street*) and Patricia McGourty (*The Pirates of Penzance*); Lighting Design: Jules Fisher, Bran Ferren (*Frankenstein*)

THE NEW YORK DRAMA CRITICS CIRCLE AWARDS

BEST PLAY
A Lesson from Aloes by Athol Fugard

BEST AMERICAN PLAY
Crimes of the Heart by Beth Henley

SPECIAL CITATIONS
Lena Horne: The Lady and Her Music; The Pirates of Penzance

THE PULITZER PRIZE FOR DRAMA

Crimes of the Heart by Beth Henley

THE OBIE AWARDS

BEST NEW AMERICAN PLAY
FOB by David Henry Hwang

BEST PRODUCTION
Still Life written and directed by Emily Mann

SUSTAINED ACHIEVEMENT
Negro Ensemble Company

PLAYWRITING
Charles Fuller (*Zooman and the Sign*); Amlin Gray (*How I Got That Story*); Len Jenkin (script and direction of *Limbo Tales*)

DIRECTION
Melvin Bernhardt (*Crimes of the Heart*); Wilford Leach (*The Pirates of Penzance*); Toby Roberts (*Pericles*)

PERFORMANCE
Giancarlo Esposito (*Zooman and the Sign*); Bob Gunton (*How I Got That Story*); Mary Beth Hurt (*Crimes of the Heart*); Kevin Kline (*The Pirates of Penzance*); John Lone (*FOB* and *The Dance and the Railroad*); Mary McDonnell, Timothy Near, John Spencer (*Still Life*); William Sadler (*Limbo Tales*); Michele Shay (*Meetings*); Meryl Streep (*Alice in Concert*); Christopher Walken (*The Seagull*)

DESIGN
Bloolips (costume design of *Lust in Space*); Manuel Lutgenhorst, Douglas Ball (*Request Concert*); June Maeda (sustained excellence of set design); Dennis Parichy (sustained excellence of lighting design)

SPECIAL CITATIONS
JoAnne Akalaitis and Mabou Mines (*Dead End Kids*); Joseph Chaikin and the Winter Project (*Tourists and Refugees*); Bill Irwin for his inspired clowning; Bruce Myers (*A Dybbuk for Two People*); Repertorio Espanol

"Some actors like to work from the inside out. I like to work from the outside . . . out," commented Obie winner and co-host Kevin Kline. Sigourney Weaver shared the emcee duties.

THE OUTER CRITICS CIRCLE AWARDS

Broadway Play: *Amadeus*; Actor: Ian McKellen (*Amadeus*); Actress: Swoosie Kurtz (*The Fifth of July*); Off-Broadway Play: *March of the Falsettos*; Set Design: Robert Phillips, body of work; Lighting Design: Arden Fingerhut, body of work; Choreography: Michael Smuin, Donald MacKayle, Henry LeTang (*Sophisticated Ladies*); Revival: *The Pirates of Penzance*; John Gassner Playwriting Award: Ted Talley (*Coming Attractions*); Lucille Lortel Award for the most noteworthy new director: Geraldine Fitzgerald (*Long Day's Journey into Night* and *Mass Appeal*)

SPECIAL CITATIONS
National Critics Institute at the O'Neill Theatre Center; Most Impressive Debut: Elizabeth Taylor (*The Little Foxes*); Outstanding Debuts: Brian Backer (*The Floating Light Bulb*), Daniel Gerroll (*Knuckle* and *The Fly Boys*); Outstanding New Play: Dario Fo (*We Won't Pay! We Won't Pay!*)

Roger Rees (right) and David Threlfall (left) in the Royal Shakespeare Company's two-evening adaptation of Dickens' *The Life and Adventures of Nicholas Nickleby*, winner of the best Play Award from the Tonys and the New York Drama Critics Circle in the 1981–82 season.

THE TONY AWARDS

PLAY

Crimes of the Heart by Beth Henley
The Dresser by Ronald Harwood
The Life and Adventures of Nicholas Nickleby
   by David Edgar
'Master Harold'... and the boys by Athol Fugard

The producers of *Crimes of the Heart* attempted to have *The Life and Adventures of Nicholas Nickleby* placed in a separate category. *Crimes*, which had won the Pulitzer Prize and the New York Drama Critics Circle Award as Best American Play the year before for its Off-Broadway run at Manhattan Theatre Club, is a comedy about three Southern sisters with one set and a small cast. *Nickleby*

employed an ensemble of thirty-nine actors in over 100 roles enacting Charles Dickens' 800-page novel over the course of two evenings. The tickets were a steep $100. The *Crimes* producers felt *NN* had an unfair advantage because of its sheer size and length. The Tony administrators did not grant the request and *Nicholas* nicked *Crimes*. The Drama Desk and Outer Critics solved the problem by giving *NN* a special award.

MUSICAL

Dreamgirls
Joseph and the Amazing Technicolor Dreamcoat
Nine
Pump Boys and Dinettes

Early in the season it looked as if *Dreamgirls* had the best Musical Tony in the bag. Michael Bennett's dynamic staging of the story of a fictional black '60s' girl group not unlike the

Supremes won socko reviews and had a solid box office. The only other tuners, *Merrily We Roll Along* and *The First*, had bombed. But in the spring as the Tony cut-off date approached, three other shows popped up. *Joseph and the Amazing Technicolor Dreamcoat* and *Pump Boys and Dinettes* transferred from Off-Broadway to Broadway. *Nine*, based on Fellini's film classic *8½*, was rushed out of workshop and opened on the last possible day for Tony eligibility.

There were rumors that *Nine* defeated *Dreamgirls* because Tony voters were exacting revenge on the Shuberts, a sponsor of the latter show. The Shuberts had okayed the demolition of three theaters which they owned—the Helen Hayes, Bijou, and Morosco—to make room for the Marriott Marquis Hotel. The theater community had fought desperately to keep the theaters.

During the Tonys, presenter Milton Berle made reference to the recent destruction when an unexpected noise issued from offstage. "Are they tearing down this one, too?" the comedian quipped.

ACTOR (PLAY)
Tom Courtenay (*The Dresser*)
Milo O'Shea (*Mass Appeal*)
Christopher Plummer (*Othello*)
Roger Rees (*The Life and Adventures of Nicholas Nickleby*)

ACTRESS (PLAY)
Zoe Caldwell (*Medea*)
Katharine Hepburn (*The West Side Waltz*)
Geraldine Page (*Agnes of God*)
Amanda Plummer (*A Taste of Honey*)

ACTOR (MUSICAL)
Herschel Bernardi (*Fiddler on the Roof*)
Victor Garber (*Little Me*)
Ben Harney (*Dreamgirls*)
Raul Julia (*Nine*)

ACTRESS (MUSICAL)
Jennifer Holiday (*Dreamgirls*)
Lisa Mordente (*Marlowe*)
Mary Gordon Murray (*Little Me*)
Sheryl Lee Ralph (*Dreamgirls*)

FEATURED ACTOR (PLAY)
Richard Kavanaugh (*The Hothouse*)
Zakes Mokae (*'Master Harold'... and the Boys*)
Edward Petherbridge (*The Life and Adventures of Nicholas Nickleby*)
David Threlfall (*The Life and Adventures of Nicholas Nickleby*)

FEATURED ACTRESS (PLAY)
Judith Anderson (*Medea*)
Mia Dillon (*Crimes of the Heart*)
Mary Beth Hurt (*Crimes of the Heart*)
Amanda Plummer (*Agnes of God*)

Amanda Plummer received nominations in two categories: leading Actress (Play) for a revival of *A Taste of Honey* and Featured Actress (Play) as the demented title character in *Agnes of God*. Her father Christopher Plummer was also nominated for his Iago in an acclaimed staging of *Othello*.

FEATURED ACTOR (MUSICAL)
Obba Babatunde (*Dreamgirls*)
Cleavant Derricks (*Dreamgirls*)
David Alan Grier (*The First*)
Bill Hutton (*Joseph and the Amazing Technicolor Dreamcoat*)

FEATURED ACTRESS (MUSICAL)
Karen Akers (*Nine*)
Laurie Beechman (*Joseph and the Amazing Technicolor Dreamcoat*)
Liliane Montevecchi (*Nine*)
Anita Morris (*Nine*)

OTHER AWARDS
Revival: *Othello*; Director (Play): Trevor Nunn, John Caird (*The Life and Adventures of Nicholas Nickleby*); Director (Musical): Tommy Tune (*Nine*); Score: Maury Yeston (*Nine*); Book of a Musical: Tom Eyen (*Dreamgirls*); Chorcography: Michael Bennett, Michael Peters (*Dreamgirls*); Set Design: John Napier, Dermot Hayes (*The Life and Adventures of Nicholas Nickelby*); Costume Design: William Ivey Long (*Nine*); Lighting Design: Tharon Musser (*Dreamgirls*)

Many 1981–82 Tony winners were not even announced on the air. In order to save time, several presentations were made before the broadcast and their names were to be read as part of the program. Hal Linden was given the wrong cue cards and the awards for the design categories, as well as the best Book of a Musical, Score, Revival, and Regional Theatre went unannounced.

As a result, the Dramatists Guild, the union representing playwrights, sent an angry letter to the Tony producers stating that unless their members were guaranteed time on future shows, it would not allow material written by them to be used. That would mean no numbers from the nominated musicals. The following year, the best Score and Book of a Musical categories were restored to air-time positions.

SPECIAL AWARDS

The Guthrie Theatre, Minneapolis, MN (Outstanding Regional Theatre); The Actors' Fund of America; Warner Communications; Radio City Music Hall (Theatre Award '82).

When the Cohens began planning the 1981–82 Tonys, there were so few available musicals from which to draw numbers (only *Dreamgirls* was playing at the time) that they decided to make the show a salute to the Imperial Theatre where *Dreamgirls* was playing. This way songs from shows which had played the Imperial could be performed leading up to a big scene from the current occupant. When *Joseph, Pump Boys,* and *Nine* opened, numbers from them were added. The original choice for *Nine* was "A Phone Call from the Vatican," a solo number with Anita Morris in a flesh-colored, skin-tight suit suggestively crooning to her lover over the phone. It was judged too salacious for network television and replaced with "Be Italian."

Tony Randall played a critic guiding the audience through the decades of the Imperial's history from the '20s to the present. Numbers from shows such as *Rose Marie, Oh Kay!, Annie Get Your Gun, Oliver!, Fiddler on the Roof,* and *Pippin* were performed.

THE DRAMA DESK AWARDS

PLAYS

Play: *'Master Harold' . . . and the boys* by Athol Fugard; Actor: Christopher Plummer (*Othello*);

Actress: Zoe Caldwell (*Medea*); Featured Actor (tie): Adolph Caesar (*A Soldier's Play*) and Zeljko Ivanek (*Cloud 9*); Featured Actress: Amanda Plummer (*Agnes of God*); Director: Tommy Tune (*Cloud 9*)

MUSICALS

Musical: *Nine*; Actress: Jennifer Holiday (*Dreamgirls*); Featured Actor: Cleavant Derricks (*Dreamgirls*); Featured Actress (tie): Liliane Montevecchi and Anita Morris (both in *Nine*); Director: Tommy Tune (*Nine*); Music: Maury Yeston (*Nine*); Lyrics (tie): Maury Yeston (*Nine*) and Stephen Sondheim (*Merrily We Roll Along*)

Father and daughter Christopher and Amanda Plummer both won Drama Desk Awards. Tommy Tune added to his laurels by taking the outstanding Director Awards in both the musical and straight play categories. There were no nominations for Actor in a Musical, Book of a Musical, or Choreography.

OTHER AWARDS

Revival: *Entertaining Mr. Sloane*; Unique Theatrical Experience: John Cullum as *Whistler*; Set Design: Robin Wagner (*Dreamgirls*); Costume Design: William Ivey Long (*Nine*); Lighting Design (tie): Marcia Madeira (*Nine*) and Tharon Musser (*Dreamgirls*)

SPECIAL AWARDS

The Life and Adventures of Nicholas Nickleby; orchestrator Jonathan Tunick; The Ridiculous Theatrical Company

THE NEW YORK DRAMA CRITICS CIRCLE AWARDS

BEST PLAY

The Life and Adventures of Nicholas Nickleby by David Edgar

BEST AMERICAN PLAY

A Soldier's Play by Charles Fuller

THE PULITZER PRIZE FOR DRAMA

A Soldier's Play by Charles Fuller

THE OBIE AWARDS

BEST NEW AMERICAN PLAY (TIE)
Metamorphosis in Miniature; Mr. Dead and Mrs. Free

BEST THEATRE PIECE
Wielopole, Wielopole by Tadeusz Kantor

SUSTAINED ACHIEVEMENT
Maria Irene Fornes

PLAYWRITING
Robert Auletta (*Stops* and *Virgins*); Caryl Churchill (*Cloud 9*)

DIRECTION
Tommy Tune (*Cloud 9*)

PERFORMANCE
Kevin Bacon (*Forty Deuces* and *Poor Little Lambs*); James Barbosa (*Soon Jack November*); Ray Dooley (*Peer Gynt*); Christine Estabrook (*Pastorale*); Michael Gross (*No End of Blame*); E. Katherine Karr (*Cloud 9*); Kenneth McMillan (*Weekends Like Other People*); Kevin O'Connor (*Chucky's Hunch, Birdbath,* and *Crossing the Crab Nebula*); Carole Shelley (*Twelve Dreams*); Josef Sommer (*Lydie Breeze*); Irene Worth (*The Chalk Garden*); Lisa Banes, Brenda Currin, Elizabeth McGovern, and Beverly May (ensemble performance in *My Sister in This House*); Adolph Caesar, Larry Riley, and Denzel Washington (ensemble performance in *A Soldier's Play*)

SPECIAL CITATIONS
La MaMa for its twentieth-anniversary celebration; Harvey Fierstein for *Torch Song Trilogy*; Theatre Communications Group

Harvey Fierstein was the hit of the Obies. He won a special citation as star and author of *Torch Song Trilogy*, a three-and-a-half-hour comedy-drama of a drag queen's search for love and security. The relationship upon which the play was based had just ended with Fierstein's lover returning to his wife. "The man has his wife, but I have *this*," he cried holding aloft his Obie plaque. He began to exit, but quickly returned to say he'd just become

engaged to Tommy Tune, who was co-hosting the awards with Swoosie Kurtz. *Torch Song* won the Tony and Drama Desk Awards when it transferred to Broadway the following season.

THE OUTER CRITICS CIRCLE AWARDS

Broadway Play: *'Master Harold'...and the boys*; Broadway Musical: *Nine*; Actors: Zakes Mokae (*'Master Harold'...and the boys*), Milo O'Shea (*Mass Appeal*); Actress: Amanda Plummer (*Agnes of God* and *A Taste of Honey*); Off-Broadway Play: *A Soldier's Play*; Director: Athol Fugard (*'Master Harold'...and the boys*); Debut Performances: Matthew Broderick (*Torch Song Trilogy*), Lizbeth MacKay (*Crimes of the Heart*); Revival: *The Chalk Garden*; Book of a Musical: Paul Rudnick (*Poor Little Lambs*); John Gassner Playwriting Award: Bill C. Davis (*Mass Appeal*); Off-Off-Broadway Theatre Company: The Second Stage; Special Citation: *The Life and Adventures of Nicholas Nickleby*

THE TONY AWARDS

PLAY
Angels Fall by Lanford Wilson
'night, Mother by Marsha Norman
Plenty by David Hare
Torch Song Trilogy by Harvey Fierstein

John Glines, producer of the Best Play *Torch Song Trilogy*, shocked the Tony viewing audience when he thanked his male lover and co-producer Lawrence Lane. *Torch Song* dealt with the lives and loves of a drag queen as he searches for affection, respect, and Mister Right. Author/star Harvey Fierstein copped Tonys as best Actor (Play) and for best Play.

There was an uproar when Neil Simon's *Brighton Beach Memoirs*, considered by many reviewers to be his finest work, did not receive a best Play nomination. It had already won the New York Drama Critics Circle Award for Best Play. The show's producer Emanuel Azenberg huffed that it was a personal insult to the author since three cast members and the director Gene Saks were nominated. The Tony Administration Committee rejected the proposal of a write-in campaign for *BBM*.

As a result of this oversight, the Tony Nomination Committee would meet to discuss its choices in the future rather than voting by secret ballot as had been the custom.

MUSICAL
Blues in the Night
Cats
Merlin
My One and Only

ACTOR (PLAY)
Jeffrey DeMunn (*K2*)
Harvey Fierstein (*Torch Song Trilogy*)
Edward Herrmann (*Plenty*)
Tony LoBianco (*A View from the Bridge*)

ACTRESS (PLAY)
Kathy Bates (*'night, Mother*)
Kate Nelligan (*Plenty*)
Anne Pitoniak (*'night, Mother*)
Jessica Tandy (*Foxfire*)

ACTOR (MUSICAL)
Al Green (*Your Arms Too Short to Box with God*)
George Hearn (*A Doll's Life*)
Michael V. Smart (*Porgy and Bess*)
Tommy Tune (*My One and Only*)

Tune also won for his choreography of *My One and Only* (with Thommie Walsh). This made him the only person to win Tonys in four different categories. His other triumphs: Featured Actor (Musical) (*Seesaw*, 1973–74) and Director (Musical) (*Nine*, 1981–82).

ACTRESS (MUSICAL)
Natalia Makarova (*On Your Toes*)
Lonnette McKee (*Show Boat*)
Chita Rivera (*Merlin*)
Twiggy (*My One and Only*)

In heavily accented English, Russian ballerina Makarova gave one of the funniest acceptance speeches ever. She referred to having a pipe fall on her shoulder during out-of-town try-outs of *On Your Toes*. "God must know what he is doing," she said. "First he hit me on head. Now he give me all this excitement. I would like to thank my husband who didn't help much, but wasn't in the way."

FEATURED ACTOR (PLAY)
Matthew Broderick (*Brighton Beach Memoirs*)
Zeljko Ivanek (*Brighton Beach Memoirs*)
George N. Martin (*Plenty*)
Stephen Moore (*All's Well That Ends Well*)

FEATURED ACTRESS (PLAY)
Elizabeth Franz (*Brighton Beach Memoirs*)
Roxanne Hart (*Passion*)
Judith Ivey (*Steaming*)
Margaret Tyzack (*All's Well That Ends Well*)

FEATURED ACTOR (MUSICAL)
Charles "Honi" Coles (*My One and Only*)
Harry Groener (*Cats*)
Stephen Hanan (*Cats*)
Lara Teeter (*On Your Toes*)

FEATURED ACTRESS (MUSICAL)
Christine Andreas (*On Your Toes*)
Betty Buckley (*Cats*)
Karla Burns (*Show Boat*)
Denny Dillon (*My One and Only*)

OTHER AWARDS
Revival: *On Your Toes*; Director (Play): Gene Saks (*Brighton Beach Memoirs*); Director (Musical): Trevor Nunn (*Cats*); Score: Andrew Lloyd Webber, T. S. Eliot (*Cats*); Book of a Musical: T. S. Eliot (*Cats*); Choreography: Tommy Tune, Thommie Walsh (*My One and Only*); Set Design: Ming Cho Lee (*K2*); Costume Design: John Napier (*Cats*); Lighting Design: David Hersey (*Cats*)

T. S. Eliot's widow Valerie told the audience, "More than thirty years ago, my husband received a Tony for his *The Cocktail Party*. This award would give him special pleasure." The late poet's whimsical volume of verses *Old Possum's Book of Practical Cats* served as the basis for Andrew Lloyd Webber's megamusical. The material was declared eligible for a Tony since it had never been presented on a stage before.

SPECIAL AWARDS

Oregon Shakespeare Festival, Ashland, OR (Outstanding Regional Theatre); Theatre Collection of the Museum of the City of New York (Theatre Award '83)

The Tonys began at the Uris but ended at the Gershwin. The theater was renamed during the telecast. To celebrate, the theme of the show was the music of George and Ira Gershwin. Marvin Hamlisch, Peter Nero, Jack Lemmon, and Melissa Manchester performed Gershwin tunes at the piano while Ben Vereen, Ginger Rogers, Hal Linden, and others warbled them. Dorothy Loudon provided the comic highlight with her outrageous ad-libs on an obscure Gershwin ditty called "Vodka."

There were rumors that Richard Burton and Elizabeth Taylor, divorced but appearing together in a revival of Noel Coward's *Private Lives*, would host the ceremony. Taylor dropped out but Burton stayed on the bill to co-host with Lena Horne and Jack Lemmon.

All of the presenters were acting in Broadway shows and appeared in their costumes. Well-known stars like Diahann Carroll (in a smart tailored suit for *Agnes of God*), Donald O'Connor (in Cap'n Andy's uniform from *Show Boat*), James Coco and Colleen Dewhurst (wearing the 1930s' outfits they wore in *You Can't Take It with You*), and Mark Hamill (sporting the eighteenth-century regalia of *Amadeus*) shared the stage with such lesser-known performers as Jay Patterson (buried under his mountain-climbing paraphenalia for *K2*), Peter Michael Goetz (attired in the pajamas and bathrobe of the convalescent father of *Brighton Beach Memoirs*), and Pamela Sousa (wearing her top hat and spangled costume from the finale of *A Chorus Line*).

THE DRAMA DESK AWARDS

PLAYS

Play: *Torch Song Trilogy* by Harvey Fierstein; Actor: Harvey Fierstein (*Torch Song Trilogy*); Actress: Jessica Tandy (*Foxfire*); Featured Actor: Alan Feinstein (*A View From the Bridge*); Featured Actress: Judith Ivey (*Steaming*); Director: Trevor Nunn (*All's Well That Ends Well*)

MUSICALS

Musical: *Little Shop of Horrors*; Actress: Natalia Makarova (*On Your Toes*); Featured Actor: Charles "Honi" Coles (*My One and Only*); Featured Actress: Karla Burns (*Show Boat*); Director: George Abbott (*On Your Toes*); Music: Andrew Lloyd Webber (*Cats*); Lyrics: Howard Ashman (*Little Shop of Horrors*); Choreography: Tommy Tune, Thommie Walsh (*My One and Only*); Orchestrations (tie): Hans Spialek (*On Your Toes*) and Michael Gibson (*My One and Only*)

There were no nominations for Actor in a Musical or Book. George Abbott was not eligible for a Tony nomination because he had staged the original 1936 production of *On Your Toes*. The Drama Desk had no such stipulation and awarded Abbott the prize for best Director of a musical.

OTHER AWARDS

Revival: *On Your Toes*; Set Design: Ming Cho Lee (*K2*); Costume Design: John Napier (*Cats*); Lighting Design: David Hersey (*Cats*); Special Effects: Martin P. Robinson and Ron Taylor (as Audrey II) (*Little Shop of Horrors*)

SPECIAL AWARDS

Richard Wilbur for his English translation of *The Misanthrope*; WPA Theatre, and its artistic director Kyle Renick; critic Douglas Watt of *The Daily News*

THE NEW YORK DRAMA CRITICS CIRCLE AWARDS

BEST PLAY
Brighton Beach Memoirs by Neil Simon

BEST FOREIGN PLAY
Plenty by David Hare

BEST MUSICAL
Little Shop of Horrors by Howard Ashman and Alan Menken

SPECIAL CITATION
The Young Playwrights Festival

THE PULITZER PRIZE FOR DRAMA

'night, Mother by Marsha Norman

THE OBIE AWARDS

PLAYWRITING
Caryl Churchill (*Top Girls*); Tina Howe (distinguished playwriting); Harry Kondoleon (most promising young playwright); David Mamet (*Edmond*). Howe, Kondoleon, and Mamet shared the $1,000 prize for Best New American Play

SUSTAINED ACHIEVEMENT
Lanford Wilson; Marshall W. Mason; The Circle Repertory Company

DIRECTION
Kenneth Frankel (*Quartermaine's Terms*); Gregory Mosher (*Edmond*); Gary Sinise (*True West*); Max Stafford-Clark (*Top Girls*)

PERFORMANCE
Ernest Abuba (*Yellow Fever*); Christine Baranski (*A Midsummer Night's Dream*); Glenn Close (*The Singular Life of Albert Nobbs*); Jeff Daniels (*Johnny Got His Gun*); Ruth Maleczech (*Haff*); John Malkovich (*True West*); Donald Moffat (*Painting Churches*); Harry Wise (*The Tooth of Crime*); the cast of *Quartermaine's Terms*, the Royal Court and New York Shakespeare Festival casts of *Top Girls* (ensemble performance)

Both the original British cast of Caryl Churchill's *Top Girls*, a savage satire on the women's movement, and the Americans who replaced them won Obies for ensemble performance.

DESIGN
Heidi Landesman (*A Midsummer Night's Dream*, *Painting Churches*)

SPECIAL CITATIONS
The Big Apple Circus; Ethyl Eichelberger (*Lucrezia Borgia*); Michael Moschen, Fred Garbo, Bob Berky (*Foolsfire*); The Zagreb Theater Company for *The Liberation of Skopje*; the musical production of *The Mother of Us All*; the musical performance of *Poppie Nongena*; Dramatists Play Service for its commitment to new work;

Performing Arts Journal publications; Theatre Development Fund for its Off-Off-Broadway voucher program

In addition to winning two Tonys in 1982–83, Harvey Fierstein hosted the Obie Awards (with Julie Bovasso). At the opening of the evening, he stated in his frog-throated voice, "I just wanna say that I sat there in that audience for eleven years before I won an Obie and I just wanna ask the critics, 'Was it so terrible? Was it really that bad?'"

THE OUTER CRITICS CIRCLE AWARDS

Broadway Play: *Brighton Beach Memoirs*; Broadway Musical: *Cats*; Actor: Tony Lo Bianco (*A View from the Bridge*); Actress (tie): Anne Pitoniak and Kathy Bates (*'night, Mother*) and Jessica Tandy (*Foxfire*); Off-Broadway Play: *Extremities*; Off-Broadway Musical: *Little Shop of Horrors*; Director: Robert Allan Ackerman (*Extremities*); Set and Lighting Design: Ming Cho Lee and Allan Lee Hughes (*K2*); Debut Performances: Natalia Makarova and Lara Teeter (*On Your Toes*), Keith Carradine (*Foxfire*); Revivals: *On Your Toes, You Can't Take It with You*; Score: Alan Menken, Howard Ashman (*Little Shop of Horrors*); John Gassner Playwriting Award: William Mastrosimone (*Extremities*); Special Awards: Theatre Development, Classic Stage Company (CSC)

THE TONY AWARDS

PLAY
Glengarry Glen Ross by David Mamet
Noises Off by Michael Frayn
Play Memory by Joanna Glass
The Real Thing by Tom Stoppard

The Real Thing, Tom Stoppard's brilliantly brittle comedy-drama of the multiple loves of a playwright and his actress-wife, won five Tonys, tying with *A Man for All Seasons, Who's Afraid of Virginia Woolf?, Child's Play,* and *Amadeus* for most Tonys for a play.

The producers of two Off-Broadway shows—*And a Nightingale Sang* and *Painting Churches*—petitioned to be eligible for Tonys since they were paying their casts under a variation of the standard Broadway production contract. In recent years, shows such as *Streamers, Pump Boys and Dinettes, Grease,* and the Roundabout Theatre Company's revival of *A Taste of Honey* were in the running for Tonys despite the fact that they played in small to medium-sized houses.

But the Tony committee ruled against *Nightingale* and *Churches*. After the 1981–82 season, a new rule was introduced which stated that a show must play in a theater of at least 499 seats in order to be considered for the awards. *Nightingale* sang at Lincoln Center's 299-seat Mitzi Newhouse Theatre (where *Streamers* also played). *Churches* was ensconced at the Lambs with a seating capacity of 358. *Nightingale* was eligible for Off-Broadway's Obie Awards, but *Churches* was not since it had been honored with a playwriting Obie for author Tina Howe during its 1982–83 initial limited run at Second Stage.

MUSICAL
Baby
La Cage aux Folles
Sunday in the Park with George
The Tap Dance Kid

The main conflict of the evening was between Jerry Herman's splashy, mainstream *La Cage aux Folles* and Stephen Sondheim's more esoteric *Sunday in the Park with George*. *La Cage*, a looney comedy based on a hit foreign film about a gay couple on the French Riviera, took a total of six Tonys while *Sunday*, an impressionistic study of art and its creators, nabbed only two in the design categories. Composer Herman thanked the voters for their appreciation of "hummable" melodies in an obvious swipe at Sondheim's more sophisticated music.

ACTOR (PLAY)
Rex Harrison (*Heartbreak House*)
Jeremy Irons (*The Real Thing*)
Calvin Levels (*Open Admissions*)
Ian McKellen (*Ian McKellen Acting Shakespeare*)

Despite raves from audiences and critics alike, Dustin Hoffman was not nominated for his Willy Loman in a revival of *Death of a Salesman*. Many speculated it was because he refused to do the standard eight performances a week (he extended his limited engagement instead). Winner Jeremy Irons paid tribute to all the other fine performances that year, "both nominated and not nominated."

ACTRESS (PLAY)
Glenn Close (*The Real Thing*)
Rosemary Harris (*Heartbreak House*)
Linda Hunt (*End of the World*)
Kate Nelligan (*A Moon for the Misbegotten*)

Upon reaching the stage, a shocked Glenn Close blurted out that she had lost a bet with a friend that she wouldn't win.

ACTOR (MUSICAL)
Gene Barry (*La Cage aux Folles*)
George Hearn (*La Cage aux Folles*)
Ron Moody (*Oliver!*)
Mandy Patinkin (*Sunday in the Park with George*)

ACTRESS (MUSICAL)
Rhetta Hughes (*The Amen Corner*)
Liza Minelli (*The Rink*)
Bernadette Peters (*Sunday in the Park with George*)
Chita Rivera (*The Rink*)

After three nominations, Chita Rivera stated she was glad she finally won because she had always been in the production numbers on the Tony show, but never got to get up and make an acceptance speech. "So what was the point of buying the bottom half of the dress?" she joked.

FEATURED ACTOR (PLAY)
Philip Bosco (*Heartbreak House*)
Joe Mantegna (*Glengarry Glen Ross*)
Robert Prosky (*Glengarry Glen Ross*)
Douglas Seale (*Noises Off*)

FEATURED ACTRESS (PLAY)
Christine Baranski (*The Real Thing*)
Jo Henderson (*Play Memory*)
Dana Ivey (*Heartbreak House*)
Deborah Rush (*Noises Off*)

Along with Amanda Plummer, Dana Ivey is one of the few actresses to be nominated in two separate categories in the same year. She was up for playing the aristocratic and snobbish sister in a revival of Shaw's *Heartbreak House*, which had concluded a limited engagement, and the dual role of a nineteenth-century painter's wife and a twentieth-century minimalist composer in *Sunday in the Park with George*.

FEATURED ACTOR (MUSICAL)
Hinton Battle (*The Tap Dance Kid*)
Stephen Geoffreys (*The Human Comedy*)
Todd Graff (*Baby*)
Samuel E. Wright (*The Tap Dance Kid*)

FEATURED ACTRESS (MUSICAL)
Martine Allard (*The Tap Dance Kid*)
Liz Callaway (*Baby*)
Dana Ivey (*Sunday in the Park with George*)
Lila Kedrova (*Zorba*)

OTHER AWARDS
Revival: *Death of a Salesman*; Director (Play): Mike Nichols (*The Real Thing*); Director (Musical): Arthur Laurents (*La Cage aux Folles*); Score: Jerry Herman (*La Cage aux Folles*); Book of a Musical: Harvey Fierstein (*La Cage aux Folles*); Choreography: Danny Daniels (*The Tap Dance Kid*); Set Design: Tony Straiges (*Sunday in the Park with George*); Costume Design: Theoni V. Aldredge (*La Cage aux Folles*); Lighting Design: Richard Nelson (*Sunday in the Park with George*)

SPECIAL AWARDS
Old Globe Theatre, San Diego, CA (Outstanding Regional Theatre); *La Tragedie de Carmen*; master craftsman Peter Feller; *A Chorus Line* (special gold Tony Award for becoming the longest-running show in Broadway history); caricaturist Al Hirschfeld (Brooks Atkinson Award)

Since songwriters Stephen Sondheim, Jerry Herman, and the team of John Kander and Fred Ebb were all nominated for Tonys, the theme of the show was a salute to their past musicals. Robert Preston and Julie Andrews hosted the ceremony broadcast from the Gershwin Theatre. The set was adorned with caricatures by Al Hirschfeld, the recipient of the first (and only) Brooks Atkinson Award for distinguished achievement in the theater. The prize was discontinued after its initial presentation.

Just as she did the year before, Dorothy Loudon stole the show. This time it was with her caustic comments during the title song from Herman's *Mame*. "Jerry Herman's thinking of me for the sequel," she ad-libbed as a male chorus of stars sang her praises. The number was performed with Loudon atop a Cadillac as it was driven across the stage. "I'm keeping the car," she went on, "and the boys."

There was a slight controversy over the production of *La Tragedie de Carmen*. Initially this unique combination of opera and theater had been announced as eligible for competition with other Broadway productions. But the actors' union Equity objected. The production was under the jurisdiction of AGMA (American Guild of Musical Artists), the union which supervises opera, ballet, and concert productions. *Carmen* employed non-Equity and foreign artists. In order to avoid a fight with Equity, the Tony Administration Committee took it out of the running and gave it a special award. Coincidentally, *Carmen* was produced by Alexander Cohen, the Tonys' impresario.

THE DRAMA DESK AWARDS

PLAYS:
Play: *The Real Thing* by Tom Stoppard; Actor: Dustin Hoffman (*Death of a Salesman*); Actress: Joan Allen (*And a Nightingale Sang*); Featured Actor: John Malkovich (*Death of a Salesman*); Featured Actress: Christine Baranski (*The Real Thing*); Director: Michael Blakemore (*Noises Off*)

MUSICALS
Musical: *Sunday in the Park with George*; Actor: George Hearn (*La Cage aux Folles*); Actress: Chita Rivera (*The Rink*); Featured Actor: Martin Vidnovic (*Baby*); Featured Actress (tie): Catherine Cox (*Baby*) and Lila Kedrova (*Zorba*); Director, Book of a Musical: James Lapine (*Sunday in the Park with George*); Music: Jerry Herman (*La Cage aux Folles*); Lyrics: Stephen Sondheim (*Sunday in the Park with George*); Orchestrations: Michael Starobin (*Sunday in the Park with George*)

OTHER AWARDS

Revival: *Death of a Salesman*; One-Person Show: Ian McKellen (*Ian McKellen Acting Shakespeare*); Unique Theatrical Experience: *La Tragedie de Carmen*; Set Design: Tony Straiges (*Sunday in the Park with George*); Costume Design: Theoni V. Aldredge (*La Cage aux Folles*); Lighting Design: Richard Nelson (*Sunday in the Park with George*); Special Effects: Bran Ferren (*Sunday in the Park with George*)

There were no nominations for outstanding Choreography.

SPECIAL AWARDS

Director Alan Schneider; Michael Bennett, Joseph Papp, and The Shubert Organization for the gala 3,389th performance of *A Chorus Line*; fight choreographer B. H. Barry; the casts of *Noises Off* and *Glengarry Glen Ross* for ensemble work; Equity Library Theater; Interart Theater

THE NEW YORK DRAMA CRITICS CIRCLE AWARDS

BEST PLAY
The Real Thing by Tom Stoppard

BEST AMERICAN PLAY
Glengarry Glen Ross by David Mamet

BEST MUSICAL
Sunday in the Park with George by Stephen Sondheim and James Lapine

SPECIAL CITATION
Samuel Beckett for the body of his work

THE PULITZER PRIZE FOR DRAMA

Glengarry Glen Ross by David Mamet

THE OBIE AWARDS

BEST NEW AMERICAN PLAY
Fool for Love by Sam Shepard (playwriting and direction)

BEST MUSICAL
The Gospel at Colonus by Lee Breuer and Bob Telson

SUSTAINED ACHIEVEMENT
Music-Theatre Group

PLAYWRITING
Samuel Beckett (*Ohio Impromptu, What Where, Catastrophe, Pocket*); Maria Irene Fornes (playwriting and direction of *The Danube, Sarita,* and *Mud*); Vaclav Havel (*A Private View*); Len Jenkin (*Five of Us*); Franz Xaver Kroetz (*Through the Leaves*); Ted Tally (*Terra Nova*)

PERFORMANCE
F. Murray Abraham (*Uncle Vanya*); Kathy Whitton Baker, Ed Harris, Will Patton (*Fool for Love*); Sheila Dabney (*Sarita*); Morgan Freeman (*The Gospel at Colonus*); George Guidall (*Cinders*); Richard Jordan (*A Private View*); Ruth Maleczech, Fred Neumann (*Through the Leaves*); Stephen McHattie (*Mensch Meier*); Dianne Wiest (*Other Places* and *Serenading Louie*); Pamela Reed (sustained excellence)

DIRECTION
JoAnne Akalaitis (*Through the Leaves*); Lawrence Sacharow (*Five of Us*)

DESIGN
Adrianne Lobel (set design of *The Vampires* and *All Night Long*); Bill Stabile (set design of *Spookhouse, Damnee Hanon,* and *Sacree Sandre*); Douglas Stein (set design of *Through the Leaves*); Anne Militello (sustained excellence of lighting design)

SPECIAL CITATIONS
Percy Mtwa, Mbongen Ngema, Barney Simon (*Woza Albert*); International Theatre Institute of the U.S., Inc.; Anne and Jules Weiss "for their tireless devotion to Off and Off-Off-Broadway"; Richard Peaslee (musical score for *The Garden of Earthly Delights*)

THE OUTER CRITICS CIRCLE AWARDS

Broadway Play: *The Real Thing*; Broadway Musical:

La Cage aux Folles; Off-Broadway Play: *Painting Churches*; Revival: *Death of a Salesman*; Revue: *A…My Name Is Alice*; Actor: George Hearn (*La Cage aux Folles*); Actress: Marian Seldes (*Painting Churches*); Score (tie): Howard Marren, Susan Birkenhead (*Love*) and Gary William Friedman, Will Holt (*Taking My Turn*); Director: Michael Blakemore (*Noises Off*); Costume Design: Theoni V. Aldredge (*La Cage aux Folles*); Debut Performances: Joan Allen (*And a Nightingale Sang*), John Malkovich (*Death of a Salesman*); John Gassner Playwriting Award: Tina Howe (*Painting Churches*); Special Awards: Roundabout Theatre Company, Twiggy and Tommy Tune (*My One and Only*)

THE TONY AWARDS

PLAY

As Is by William M. Hoffman
Biloxi Blues by Neil Simon
Hurlyburly by David Rabe
Ma Rainey's Black Bottom by August Wilson

MUSICAL

Big River
Grind
Leader of the Pack
Quilters

Because of a lack of musicals, three categories were cut. There were no nominations for best Actor (Musical) and Actress (Musical) or best Choreography. Only three new musicals were still running at the time of the nominations: *Big River, Grind,* and *Leader of the Pack. Quilters, Harrigan 'n' Hart,* and *The Three Musketeers* had closed earlier in the season.

ACTOR (PLAY)

Jim Dale (*Joe Egg*)
Jonathan Hogan (*As Is*)
Derek Jacobi (*Much Ado about Nothing*)
John Lithgow (*Requiem for a Heavyweight*)

ACTRESS (PLAY)

Stockard Channing (*Joe Egg*)
Sinead Cusack (*Much Ado about Nothing*)
Rosemary Harris (*Pack of Lies*)
Glenda Jackson (*Strange Interlude*)

Zena Walker won a Tony for best Featured Actress (Play) for the same role as Stockard Channing in the original production of *Joe Egg* in 1967–68. The reason Walker was a featured actress and Channing a leading one was billing. Channing's name was above the title on the marquee and in the theater program while Walker's name was below.

FEATURED ACTOR (PLAY)

Charles S. Dutton (*Ma Rainey's Black Bottom*)
William Hurt (*Hurlyburly*)
Barry Miller (*Biloxi Blues*)
Edward Petherbridge (*Strange Interlude*)

FEATURED ACTRESS (PLAY)

Joanna Gleason (*Joe Egg*)
Judith Ivey (*Hurlyburly*)
Theresa Merritt (*Ma Rainey's Black Bottom*)
Sigourney Weaver (*Hurlyburly*)

FEATURED ACTOR (MUSICAL)

Rene Auberjonois (*Big River*)
Daniel H. Jenkins (*Big River*)
Kurt Knudson (*Take Me Along*)
Ron Richardson (*Big River*)

FEATURED ACTRESS (MUSICAL)

Evalyn Baron (*Quilters*)
Leilani Jones (*Grind*)
Mary Beth Peil (*The King and I*)
Lenka Peterson (*Quilters*)

OTHER AWARDS

Revival: *Joe Egg*; Director (Play): Gene Saks (*Biloxi Blues*); Director (Musical): Des McAnuff (*Big River*); Score: Roger Miller (*Big River*); Book of a Musical: William Hauptman (*Big River*); Set Design: Heidi Landesman (*Big River*); Costume Design: Florence Klotz (*Grind*); Lighting Design: Richard Riddell (*Big River*)

SPECIAL AWARDS

Steppenwolf Theater Company, Chicago, IL

(Outstanding Regional Theater); New York State Council on the Arts; Yul Brynner for 4,525 performances of *The King and I*; Edward Lester, founder and general manager of the Los Angeles Civic Light Opera (Lawrence Langner Award for Lifetime Achievement in the Theatre)

In order to fill the entertainment gap caused by the dearth of new musicals to showcase, the Cohens paid tribute to three composers. A group of celebrity singer-dancers ranging from Broadway vets like Chita Rivera, Lee Roy Reams, and Hinton Battle to such familiar TV stars as Susan Anton, Tom Wopat, and Dick Van Dyke performed excerpts from the works of Cy Coleman, Jule Styne, and Andrew Lloyd Webber. Not one had a new show on Broadway in 1984–85. The show concluded with a medley of songs from Webber's *Song and Dance*, Styne's *Treasure Island* and Coleman's *Thirteen Days to Broadway*, musicals the three were hoping to mount on the Main Stem by the next season. Only Webber's *Song and Dance* made it.

Behind the scenes, things were equally rocky. Relations were becoming strained between the two organizations which presented the Tonys. The League of American Theatres and Producers, which put up the greenbacks for the show, was losing $40,000–$130,000 on it every year. Much of the shortfall was due to a licensing fee the League paid to the American Theatre Wing, owners of the Tony copyright. There was grumbling among League members of pulling out of the Tonys and starting their own awards show. The Wing, meanwhile, was complaining that it was underrepresented on the Tony Adminstration Committee, which had only three Wing members.

The situation was exacerbated by Tony producer Alexander Cohen. New York Governor Mario Cuomo was scheduled to accept a special Tony on behalf of the state's Council on the Arts. He didn't show. Kitty Carlisle Hart, former actress and the head of the Council, took his place. Cohen saw the governor's no-show as a snub to the theater. During rehearsal, Cohen angrily sniped, "The governor of New York hasn't been to theater in twenty-five years and he didn't want to break his record." He resigned from the League the day after the awards ceremony. Many speculated Cohen's off-the-cuff remark upset the League, which did not

wish to alienate the Governor, a potential ally when it came to tax breaks for theater owners.

Isabelle Stevenson, the Wing's president, was also peeved about the award to the Council. The lengthy presentation of the honor took time away from the Wing's annual one-minute blurb about its activities.

THE DRAMA DESK AWARDS

PLAYS
Play: *As Is* by William Hoffman; Actor: John Lithgow (*Requiem for a Heavyweight*); Actress: Rosemary Harris (*Pack of Lies*); Featured Actor: (tie) Charles S. Dutton (*Ma Rainey's Black Bottom*) and Barry Miller (*Biloxi Blues*); Featured Actress: Judith Ivey (*Hurlyburly*); Director: John Malkovich (*Balm in Gilead*); Ensemble Acting: *Balm in Gilead*

MUSICALS
Actor: Ron Richardson (*Big River*); Featured Actor: Rene Auberjonois (*Big River*); Featured Actress: Leilani Jones (*Grind*); Music, Lyrics: Roger Miller (*Big River*); Book: Jerry Colker (*Three Guys Naked from the Waist Down*); Orchestrations: Steven Margoshes, Dan Troob (*Big River*)

Like the Tonys, the Drama Desk dropped several categories including outstanding Musical, Actress in a Musical, Director of a Musical, and Choreography.

OTHER AWARDS
Revival: *Joe Egg*; One-Person Show: Whoopi Goldberg; Unique Theatrical Experience: *The Garden of Earthly Delights*; Set Design: Heidi Landesman (*Big River*); Costume Design: Alexander Reid (*Much Ado about Nothing*); Lighting Design: Richard Riddell (*Big River*); Sound Design/Music in a Play: (tie) Nigel Hess (*Much Ado about Nothing, Cyrano de Bergerac*) and John Di Fusco (*Tracers*)

SPECIAL AWARDS
Gerard Alessandrini and *Forbidden Broadway*; cast and crew of *The Mystery of Irma Vep*; Claudette Colbert and Rex Harrison; Veterans Ensemble Theater Company (VETCO)

THE NEW YORK DRAMA CRITICS CIRCLE AWARDS

BEST PLAY
Ma Rainey's Black Bottom by August Wilson

THE PULITZER PRIZE FOR DRAMA

Sunday in the Park with George by James Lapine and Stephen Sondheim

Sunday opened too late in the 1983–84 season to be considered for that year's Pulitzer. It won the following season, becoming one of only seven musicals to be so honored. The others are *Of Thee I Sing, South Pacific, Fiorello!, How to Suceed in Business without Really Trying, A Chorus Line,* and *Rent.*

THE OBIE AWARDS

BEST NEW PLAY
The Conduct of Life by Maria Irene Fornes

SUSTAINED ACHIEVEMENT
Meredith Monk

PLAYWRITING
Christopher Durang (*The Marriage of Bette and Boo*); Rosalyn Drexler (*Transients Welcome*); William M. Hoffman (*As Is*)

DIRECTION
John Malkovich (*Balm in Gilead*); Barbara Vann (*Bound to Rise*); Jerry Zaks (*The Foreigner, The Marriage of Bette and Boo*)

PERFORMANCE
Dennis Boutsakaris (*The Nest of the Woodgrouse*); Jonathan Hadary (*As Is*); Anthony Heald (*Henry V, The Foreigner,* and *Digby*); Charles Ludlam and Everett Quinton (ensemble performance in *The Mystery of Irma Vep*); Laurie Metcalf (*Balm in Gilead*); John Turturro (*Danny and the Deep Blue Sea*); Gloria Foster, Ron Vawter (sustained excellence); the cast of *The Marriage of Bette and Boo* (ensemble performance)

DESIGN
Judy Dearing (costume design); Victor En Yu Tan (lighting design); Loren Sherman (set design)

MUSIC
Peter Gordon (*Othello*); Max Roach (*Shepardsets*)

SPECIAL CITATIONS
The Asia Society; Penn and Teller; Julie Taymor; Spalding Gray (*Swimming to Cambodia*); The Roy Hart Theater for *Pagliacci*; *An Evening with Ekkard Schall*

OBIE GRANTS
INTAR; The Production Company; The Richard Allen Center; Spiderwoman Theatre; The Split Britches Company

"This is a very tough fucking house," said Dustin Hoffman as he addressed a rowdy crowd at the thirtieth Obie Awards. "Please listen to this shit," he continued. "We're all in concert about a couple of things. The critics vote these awards and we hate their fucking guts, because they don't know as much as we know." What's important, he went on, "isn't the power the critics have in deciding these awards, but the emotional vote of your colleagues who cheer when you win."

THE OUTER CRITICS CIRCLE AWARDS

Broadway Play: *Biloxi Blues*; Broadway Musical: *Sunday in the Park with George*; Actor: Jim Dale (*Joe Egg*); Actress: Rosemary Harris (*Pack of Lies*); Off-Broadway Play: *The Foreigner*; Off-Broadway Musical: *Kuni-Leml*; Lyrics: Richard Engquist (*Kuni-Leml*); Book of a Musical: Nahma Sandrow (*Kuni-Leml*); Director: John Malkovich (*Balm in Gilead*); Set Design: Tony Straiges (*Sunday in the Park with George* and *Diamonds*); Revival: *Joe Egg*; Debut Performances: Barry Miller (*Biloxi Blues*), Whoopi Goldberg for her one-woman show; John Gassner Playwriting Award: Larry Shue (*The Foreigner*); Special Awards: *Forbidden Broadway*, Henry Hewes

THE TONY AWARDS

PLAY
Benefactors by Michael Frayn
Blood Knot by Athol Fugard
The House of Blue Leaves by John Guare
I'm Not Rappaport by Herb Gardner

"There is life after Frank Rich," joyously extolled Herb Gardner upon accepting his Tony. Rich, the critic for the powerful *New York Times*, had given Gardner's play *I'm Not Rappaport* a negative review.

Two of the four best Play nominees were actually revivals. Both *Blood Knot* and *The House of Blue Leaves* had been presented in previous productions Off-Broadway. Since the Tonys only consider Broadway shows, the two were considered eligible as new plays.

MUSICAL
Big Deal
The Mystery of Edwin Drood
Song & Dance
Tango Argentino

ACTOR (PLAY)
Hume Cronyn (*The Petition*)
Ed Harris (*Precious Sons*)
Judd Hirsch (*I'm Not Rappaport*)
Jack Lemmon (*Long Day's Journey into Night*)

ACTRESS (PLAY)
Rosemary Harris (*Hay Fever*)
Mary Beth Hurt (*Benefactors*)
Jessica Tandy (*The Petition*)
Lily Tomlin (*The Search for Signs of Intelligent Life in the Universe*)

Both Judd Hirsch and Lily Tomlin gave exceptionally long acceptance speeches. Hirsch acknowledged each of the other nominees, at length, and brought his co-star Cleavon Little to the stage. Tomlin thanked by name everyone even remotely connected with her one-woman show, including a ninety-two-year-old usher.

ACTOR (MUSICAL)
Don Correia (*Singin' in the Rain*)
Cleavant Derricks (*Big Deal*)
Maurice Hines (*Uptown . . . It's Hot!*)
George Rose (*The Mystery of Edwin Drood*)

ACTRESS (MUSICAL)
Debbie Allen (*Sweet Charity*)
Cleo Laine (*The Mystery of Edwin Drood*)
Bernadette Peters (*Song & Dance*)
Chita Rivera (*Jerry's Girls*)

FEATURED ACTOR (PLAY)
Peter Gallagher (*Long Day's Journey Into Night*)
Charles Keating (*Loot*)
Joseph Maher (*Loot*)
John Mahoney (*The House of Blue Leaves*)

FEATURED ACTRESS (PLAY)
Stockard Channing (*The House of Blue Leaves*)
Swoosie Kurtz (*The House of Blue Leaves*)
Bethel Leslie (*Long Day's Journey Into Night*)
Zoe Wanamaker (*Loot*)

FEATURED ACTOR (MUSICAL)
Christopher d'Amboise (*Song & Dance*)
John Herrera (*The Mystery of Edwin Drood*)
Howard McGillin (*The Mystery of Edwin Drood*)
Michael Rupert (*Sweet Charity*)

FEATURED ACTRESS (MUSICAL)
Patti Cohenour (*The Mystery of Edwin Drood*)
Bebe Neuwirth (*Sweet Charity*)
Jana Schneider (*The Mystery of Edwin Drood*)
Elisabeth Welch (*Jerome Kern Goes to Hollywood*)

OTHER AWARDS
Revival: *Sweet Charity*; Director (Play): Jerry Zaks (*The House of Blue Leaves*); Director (Musical): Wilford Leach (*The Mystery of Edwin Drood*); Score and Book of a Musical: Rupert Holmes (*The Mystery of Edwin Drood*); Choreography: Bob Fosse (*Big Deal*); Set Design: Tony Walton (*The House of Blue Leaves*); Costume Design: Patricia Zipprodt (*Sweet Charity*); Lighting Design: Pat Collins (*I'm Not Rappaport*)

American Repertory Theatre, Cambridge MA (Outstanding Regional Theatre)

The Tonys marked their fortieth anniversary with a huge celebration. Not only were there the usual numbers from that year's nominated musicals, but also snatches of songs from all the past Tony-winning musicals and snippets of scenes from the best plays. The tuners were represented in four separate medley segments. A highlight was provided by Chita Rivera, her leg in a cast from a recent car accident, singing "Put on a Happy Face" from *Bye, Bye, Birdie*. For the plays, an army of stars read a line or two of each of the scripts from 1946–47's production of *Cyrano de Bergerac* (actually not a best play since there was no award given that year, but Jose Ferrer had been honored for outstanding performance) to 1984–85's *Biloxi Blues*.

Kay Gardella of the *New York Daily News* declared it "The best Tony Awards show I've seen." It was also the twentieth and last Tony show for the husband and wife team of Alexander Cohen and Hildy Parks, whose contract to produce the program had expired. The rift between the League of American Theatres and Producers and the American Theatre Wing, the two organizations sponsoring the show, was mended with the Cohens left out in the cold. The producer had quit the League and attempted to persuade the Wing to present the Tonys on its own since it owned the awards. The Wing decided it could not proceed without the League's financial backing and didn't wish to incur its wrath. The powerful group of producers might forbid performers appearing in shows at League-owned theaters from participating in a non-League Tony broadcast.

As a condition of continuing the relationship, the League insisted Cohen be dropped. The Tonys got a new captain to helm the ship the following year.

THE DRAMA DESK AWARDS

PLAYS:
Play: *A Lie of the Mind* by Sam Shepard; Actor: Ed Harris (*Precious Sons*); Actress: Lily Tomlin (*The Search for Signs of Intelligent Life in the Universe*); Featured Actor: Joseph Maher (*Loot*); Featured Actress: Joanna Gleason (*Social Security* and *It's Only a Play*); Director: Jerry Zaks (*The Marriage of Bette and Boo* and *The House of Blue Leaves*)

MUSICALS
Musical: *The Mystery of Edwin Drood*; Actor: George Rose (*The Mystery of Edwin Drood*); Actress: Bernadette Peters (*Song and Dance*); Featured Actor: Michael Rupert (*Sweet Charity*); Featured Actress: Jana Schneider (*The Mystery of Edwin Drood*); Director: Wilford Leach (*The Mystery of Edwin Drood*); Music, Book, Orchestration: Rupert Holmes (*The Mystery of Edwin Drood*); Choreography: Bob Fosse (*Big Deal*)

OTHER AWARDS
Revival: *The House of Blue Leaves*; Unique Theatrical Experience: *The Search for Signs of Intelligent Life in the Universe*; One-Person/Solo Performance: Eric Bogosian (*Drinking in America*); Set Design: Tony Walton (*The House of Blue Leaves* and *Social Security*); Costume Design: Lindsay W. Davis (*The Mystery of Edwin Drood*); Lighting Design: Pat Collins (*Execution of Justice*); Special Effects: Showtech, Inc. (*Singin' in the Rain*); Sound Design/Music in a Play: Otts Muderloch (*The Search for Signs of Intelligent Life in the Universe*)

There were no nominations for outstanding Lyrics.

SPECIAL AWARDS
Agnes de Mille; Jessica Tandy and Hume Cronyn; record producer Thomas Z. Shepard; The Joyce Theatre for its American Theater Exchange program; The New Amsterdam Theater Company for its series of concert productions of American musicals; musical director Donald Pippin

THE NEW YORK DRAMA CRITICS CIRCLE AWARDS

BEST PLAY
A Lie of the Mind by Sam Shepard

BEST FOREIGN PLAY
Benefactors by Michael Frayn

The Search for Sign of Intelligent Life in the Universe by Jane Wagner starring Lily Tomlin

THE PULITZER PRIZE FOR DRAMA

No award

The Pulitzer jury recommended Robert Wilson's epic multi-media work *The Civil Wars*, but only a two-and-a-half-hour portion of it had been produced at the American Repertory Theatre in Cambridge, MA, in a limited run. The rest existed only in manuscript. Since the Pulitzer judges who made the final decision had neither seen the Cambridge production nor read Wilson's work in its entirety, they decided to give no award.

THE OBIE AWARDS

BEST NEW PLAYS
Aunt Dan and Lemon by Wallace Shawn; *Bird/Bear* by Lee Nagrin; *Drinking in America* by Eric Bogosian; *Deep Sleep* by John Jesurun; *Vienna: Lusthaus* by Martha Clarke

Wallace Shawn commented, "When I was ten years old, I had a canary that lived off Hartz Mountain birdseed—that seems important." He was referring to the *Village Voice*'s new publisher, who owned the Hartz Mountain Company. Outside the Ritz where the Obies were being presented, *Village Voice* writers mounted their own street theater. They protested their low wages, calling them "birdseed" and symbolically typed away in huge bird cages.

SUSTAINED ACHIEVEMENT
Mabou Mines

DIRECTION
Richard Foreman (*Largo Desolato*); Robert Wilson (*Hamletmachine*)

PEFORMANCE
Norma Aleandro (*About Love and Other Stories about Love*); Dylan Baker (*Not about Heroes*); Tom Cayler (*A Matter of Life and Death*); Jill Eikenberry (*Lemon Sky* and *Life Under Water*); Farley Granger, Helen Stenborg (*Talley and Son*);

Swoosie Kurtz (*The House of Blue Leaves*); Kathryn Pogson (*Aunt Dan and Lemon*); Josef Sommer (*Largo Desolato*); Elisabeth Welch (*Time to Start Living*); Elizabeth Wilson (*Anteroom*); Kevin Kline, Edward Herrmann (sustained excellence)

SPECIAL CITATIONS
Tadeusz Kantor (*Let the Artist Die*); composer Genji Ito

DESIGN
Rita Ryack (sustained excellence of costume design); Paul Gallo (sustained excellence of lighting design); Edward T. Gianfrancesco (sustained excellence of set design)

OBIE GRANTS
PS 122; Billie Holiday Theatre

THE OUTER CRITICS CIRCLE AWARDS

Broadway Play: *I'm Not Rappaport*; Broadway Musical: *The Mystery of Edwin Drood*; Off-Broadway Play: *A Lie of the Mind*; Off-Broadway Musical: *Nunsense*; Revival: *Loot*; Actor: Judd Hirsch (*I'm Not Rappaport*); Actress: Lily Tomlin (*The Search for Signs of Intelligent Life in the Universe*); Debut Performances: Anthony Rapp (*Precious Sons*), Semina de Laurentis (*Nunsense*); Off-Broadway Book and Music: Dan Goggin (*Nunsense*); Off-Broadway Lyrics: David Crane, Seth Friedman, Marta Kaufman (*Personals*); Director: John Tillinger (*Loot, The Perfect Party, and Corpse!*); Choreography: Bob Fosse (*Big Deal* and *Sweet Charity*); Set Design: Bob Shaw (*The Mystery of Edwin Drood*); Costume Design: Lindsay W. Davis (*The Mystery of Edwin Drood*); Lighting Design: Paul Gallo (*The Mystery of Edwin Drood*); John Gassner Playwriting Award: Herb Gardner (*I'm Not Rappaport*); Special Award: Elisabeth Welch (*Time to Start Living* and *Jerome Kern Goes to Hollywood*)

1986-87

THE TONY AWARDS

PLAY
Broadway Bound by Neil Simon
Coastal Disturbances by Tina Howe
Fences by August Wilson
Les Liaisons Dangereuses
    by Christopher Hampton

MUSICAL
Les Miserables
Me and My Girl
Rags
Starlight Express

It was an almost totally British year for the Tonys. English musicals swept the awards with *Les Miserables* taking eight, *Me and My Girl* three, and *Starlight Express* one. The only Yankee tuner nominated for best Musical, *Rags*, was a four-performance flop. Among the plays, *Les Liaisons Dangereuses*, an import from the Royal Shakespeare Company, received the most nonmusical nominations with seven. But American drama *Fences* won the top honors with four Tonys.

ACTOR (PLAY)
Philip Bosco (*You Never Can Tell*)
James Earl Jones (*Fences*)
Richard Kiley (*All My Sons*)
Alan Rickman (*Les Liaisons Dangereuses*)

ACTRESS (PLAY)
Lindsay Duncan (*Les Liaisons Dangereuses*)
Linda Lavin (*Broadway Bound*)
Geraldine Page (*Blithe Spirit*)
Amanda Plummer (*Pygmalion*)

ACTOR (MUSICAL)
Roderick Cook (*Oh Coward!*)
Robert Lindsay (*Me and My Girl*)
Terrence Mann (*Les Miserables*)
Colm Wilkinson (*Les Miserables*)

Lindsay and Wilkinson were also both nominated for London's Olivier Awards when their shows opened in the British capital. The results were the same there, with Lindsay triumphing.

ACTRESS (MUSICAL)
Catherine Cox (*Oh Coward!*)
Maryann Plunkett (*Me and My Girl*)
Teresa Stratas (*Rags*)

FEATURED ACTOR (PLAY)
Frankie R. Faison (*Fences*)
John Randolph (*Broadway Bound*)
Jamey Sheridan (*All My Sons*)
Courtney B. Vance (*Fences*)

FEATURED ACTRESS (PLAY)
Mary Alice (*Fences*)
Annette Bening (*Coastal Disturbances*)
Phyllis Newman (*Broadway Bound*)
Carole Shelley (*Stepping Out*)

FEATURED ACTOR (MUSICAL)
George S. Irving (*Me and My Girl*)
Timothy Jerome (*Me and My Girl*)
Michael Maguire (*Les Miserables*)
Robert Torti (*Starlight Express*)

FEATURED ACTRESS (MUSICAL)
Jane Connell (*Me and My Girl*)
Judy Kuhn (*Les Miserables*)
Frances Ruffelle (*Les Miserables*)
Jane Summerhays (*Me and My Girl*)

OTHER AWARDS
Revival: *All My Sons*; Director (Play): Lloyd Richards (*Fences*); Director (Musical): Trevor Nunn, John Caird (*Les Miserables*); Score: Claude-Michel Schonberg, Herbert Kretzmer, Alain Boublil (*Les Miserables*); Book of a Musical: Alain Boublil, Claude-Michel Schonberg (*Les Miserables*); Choreography: Gillian Gregory (*Me and My Girl*); Set Design: John Napier (*Les Miserables*); Costume Design: John Napier (*Starlight Express*); Lighting Design: David Hersey (*Les Miserables*)

John Napier took the Sore Winner Award. After winning *two* Tonys, one for the costumes of *Starlight Express* and another for the sets of *Les Miserables*, the British designer was still peeved that he hadn't been nominated for his sets for *Starlight*, a gigantic racing track for the rollerskating cast. He expressed his anger in his acceptance speech: "I just would like to have been in that room," meaning when the nominating committee passed him over. Kevin Kelly of the *Boston Globe* commented, "Leaving a trail of sour ingratitude, John Napier growled offstage like Iago plotting future revenge."

SPECIAL AWARDS

George Abbott, on the occasion of his 100th birthday; Jackie Mason for *The World According to Me*; Robert Preston (posthumous); The San Francisco Mime Troupe (Outstanding Regional Theatre)

Members of the San Francisco Mime Troupe were booed when they dedicated their award to Benjamin Linder, stating the engineer from Oregon had been killed in Nicaragua by "contras financed by America."

There was skepticism in the theater community when Don Mischer took over the Tony-producing reigns from Alexander Cohen. Cohen was a theatrical impresario while Mischer was known for his packaging of TV specials like *The Kennedy Center Honors* and *Motown 25: Yesterday, Today, Forever*. Could a TV producer with no stage credits pull off Broadway's biggest night?

The ceremony was a smash, later winning an Emmy for Outstanding Musical, Comedy or Variety Program. "The show took off from its first moment," *The New York Times* hailed. The program began with New Vaudeville clown Bill Irwin on an empty stage, demonstrating how a Broadway show is put together, leading up to the grand entrance of hostess and four-time Tony winner Angela Lansbury.

Stylish entertainment included tributes to the late Robert Preston and 100-year-old producer/ director George Abbott. There was also a surprise appearance by Beatrice Arthur to sing "Bosom Buddies" with her *Mame* co-star Lansbury. As usual, numbers from the nominated musicals were performed (including *Rags* which had closed months before). For the first time in eighteen years, scenes from the nominated plays were also presented. The only one that worked when taken out of context was a powerful moment from *Fences* with James Earl Jones and Courtney B.

Vance enacting a tense father-son confrontation. Overall, the Tonys had successfully made the transition from the Cohen era. Lansbury and Mischer returned for two more years.

THE DRAMA DESK AWARDS

PLAYS

Play: *Fences*; Actor: James Earl Jones (*Fences*); Actress: Linda Lavin (*Broadway Bound*); Featured Actor: John Randolph (*Broadway Bound*); Featured Actress: Mary Alice (*Fences*); Director: Howard Davies (*Les Liaisons Dangereuses*)

MUSICALS

Musical: *Les Miserables*; Actor: Robert Lindsay (*Me and My Girl*); Actress: Teresa Stratas (*Rags*); Featured Actor: Michael Maguire (*Les Miserbables*); Featured Actress: Jane Summerhays (*Me and My Girl*); Director: Mike Ockrent (*Me and My Girl*); Music: (tie) Noel Gay (*Me and My Girl*) and Claude-Michel Schonberg (*Les Miserables*); Book: L. Arthur Rose, Douglas Furber, Stephen Fry, Mike Ockrent (*Me and My Girl*); Orchestrations: John Cameron (*Les Miserables*); One-Person Show: *Barbara Cook: A Concert for the Theatre*

OTHER AWARDS

Set Design: John Napier (*Les Miserables, Starlight Express*); Costume Design: John Napier (*Starlight Express*); Lighting Design: Chris Parry (*Les Liaisons Dangereuses*)

SPECIAL AWARDS

Musical director Stanley Lebowsky; theatre artists Paul Davis and Frank Verlizzo; Henry Cohen, Donald Rose, and Robert Kimball for enriching our musical theater heritage by rescuing classic Broadway scores

There were no nominations for Choreography, Lyrics, or Revival.

THE NEW YORK DRAMA CRITICS CIRCLE AWARDS

BEST PLAY

Fences by August Wilson

BEST MUSICAL
Les Miserables by Claude-Michel Schonberg, Herbert Kretzmer, and Alain Boublil

THE PULITZER PRIZE FOR DRAMA

Fences by August Wilson

THE OBIE AWARDS

BEST NEW PLAYS
The Cure and *Film Is Evil, Radio Is Good*, both by Richard Foreman

PERFORMANCE
Robin Bartlett (*The Early Girl*); Rob Besserer, Anthony Holland (*The Hunger Artist*); Dana Ivey, Morgan Freeman (*Driving Miss Daisy*); Laura Hicks (*On the Verge*); John Kelly (*Pass the Blutwurst, Bitte: The Egon Schiele Story*); Christine Lahti (*Little Murders*); Gcina Mnlophe (*Born in the RSA*); Bill Raymond (*Cold Harbor*); Clarice Taylor (*Moms*); Philip Bosco, Black-Eyed Susan (sustained excellence)

DIRECTION
Carole Rothman (sustained excellence); Garland Wright (*On the Verge*)

DESIGN
Andrew Jackness (sustained excellence in set design); James F. Ingalls (sustained excellence in lighting design); Robert Israel (set and costume design of *The Hunger Artist*); Paul Gallo (lighting design of *The Hunger Artist*)

SUSTAINED ACHIEVEMENT
The Ridiculous Theatrical Company.

OBIE GRANTS
Brooklyn Arts and Cultural Association; New Theatre of Brooklyn; Irish Arts Center

SPECIAL AWARDS
Dario Fo, Franca Rame; The Non-Traditional Casting Project; La MaMa Great Jones Repertory Company for its revival of *Fragments of a Greek Tragedy*; Judith Malina for the Living Theatre Retrospectacle

Jules Feiffer prefaced his presenter duties by chastising the *Voice* critic who had negatively reviewed a revival of his play *Little Murders*. "I'm just not comfortable having my work defined by schmucks," Feiffer said. Obie hosts Christine Lahti and Morgan Freeman both won awards. "Everybody knows that the Obies are the only awards that count," commented Freeman. "The rest are just doo-doo."

THE OUTER CRITICS CIRCLE AWARDS

Broadway Play: *Fences*; Broadway Musical: *Les Miserables*; Off-Broadway Play: *The Common Pursuit*; Off-Broadway Musical: *Stardust*; Actor: James Earl Jones (*Fences*); Actress: Linda Lavin (*Broadway Bound*); Debut Performances: Colm Wilkinson and Frances Ruffelle (*Les Miserables*); Directors: Trevor Nunn, John Caird (*Les Miserables*); Set Design: John Napier (*Les Miserables*); Off-Broadway Book: Lainie Robertson (*Lady Day at Emerson's Bar and Grill*); Off-Broadway Music: Allen Toussaint (*Staggerlee*); Off-Broadway Lyrics: Barry Harmon (*Olympus on My Mind*); Revival: *All My Sons*; John Gassner Playwriting Award: August Wilson (*Fences*); Special Award; Jackie Mason's *The World According to Me*

THE TONY AWARDS

PLAY
Joe Turner's Come and Gone by August Wilson
M. Butterfly by David Henry Hwang
Speed-the-Plow by David Mamet
A Walk in the Woods by Lee Blessing

MUSICAL
Into the Woods
The Phantom of the Opera
Romance/Romance
Sarafina

The main battle of the evening was between *Phantom of the Opera*, Andrew Lloyd Webber's lush spectacle based on the horror classic, and *Into the Woods*, Stephen Sondheim's sophisticated take on fairy tales. While *Woods* took the prizes for best Book of a Musical and Score, *Phantom* swept the design awards and was named best Musical. *Woods* won the Best Musical awards from the Drama Desk and New York Critics Circle, but neither matched the box-office clout of the Tony. *Woods* had a respectable run of a year and a half, but *Phantom* is still playing to packed houses as of this writing.

ACTOR (PLAY)
Derek Jacobi (*Breaking the Code*)
John Lithgow (*M. Butterfly*)
Robert Prosky (*A Walk in the Woods*)
Ron Silver (*Speed-the-Plow*)

There were howls of protest when John Malkovich was overlooked for a best Actor (Play) nomination for *Burn This*, in which he played a passionate restauranteur.

ACTRESS (PLAY)
Joan Allen (*Burn This*)
Blythe Danner (*A Streetcar Named Desire*)
Glenda Jackson (*Macbeth*)
Frances McDormand (*A Streetcar Named Desire*)

There were so few roles for women on Broadway in 1987–88 that Frances McDormand was nominated for leading Actress (Play) for a revival of *A Streetcar Named Desire*. She played Stella, normally considered a supporting role.

ACTOR (MUSICAL)
Scott Bakula (*Romance/Romance*)
David Carroll (*Chess*)
Michael Crawford (*The Phantom of the Opera*)
Howard McGillin (*Anything Goes*)

ACTRESS (MUSICAL)
Alison Fraser (*Romance/Romance*)
Joanna Gleason (*Into the Woods*)
Judy Kuhn (*Chess*)
Patti LuPone (*Anything Goes*)

FEATURED ACTOR (PLAY)
Michael Gough (*Breaking the Code*)

Lou Liberatore (*Burn This*)
Delroy Lindo (*Joe Turner's Come and Gone*)
B. D. Wong (*M. Butterfly*)

FEATURED ACTRESS (PLAY)
Kimberleigh Aarn (*Joe Turner's Come and Gone*)
L. Scott Caldwell (*Joe Turner's Come and Gone*)
Kate Nelligan (*Serious Money*)
Kimberly Scott (*Joe Turner's Come and Gone*)

FEATURED ACTOR (MUSICAL)
Anthony Heald (*Anything Goes*)
Werner Klemperer (*Cabaret*)
Bill McCutcheon (*Anything Goes*)
Robert Westenberg (*Into the Woods*)

FEATURED ACTRESS (MUSICAL)
Judy Kaye (*The Phantom of the Opera*)
Leleti Khumalo (*Sarafina*)
Alyson Reed (*Cabaret*)
Regina Resnick (*Cabaret*)

OTHER AWARDS
Revival: *Anything Goes*; Director (Play): John Dexter (*M. Butterfly*); Director (Musical): Harold Prince (*The Phantom of the Opera*); Score: Stephen Sondheim (*Into the Woods*); Book of a Musical: James Lapine (*Into the Woods*); Choreography: Michael Smuin (*Anything Goes*); Set and Costume Design: Maria Bjornson (*The Phantom of the Opera*); Lighting Design: Andrew Bridge (*The Phantom of the Opera*)

SPECIAL AWARDS
Brooklyn Academy of Music; South Coast Repertory Theatre, Costa Mesa, CA (Outstanding Regional Theatre)

Angela Lansbury returned to host the Tonys for a second go-round. In addition to scenes from the nominated plays and musicals, there was a tribute to the late director/choreographer Michael Bennett, with numbers from *Dreamgirls* and *A Chorus Line*. A similar homage to Bob Fosse was also planned, but his ex-wife Gwen Verdon announced she was contractually obligated not to release his dances until after a PBS documentary on his life had aired.

In an example of bizarre casting, media icon Madonna, then making her Broadway debut in

Speed-the-Plow, presented the Outstanding Regional Theatre award. She complained about the microphone being too low and flubbed a few lines. "That's what I get for missing rehearsal," she admitted.

THE DRAMA DESK AWARDS

PLAYS
Play *M. Butterfly* by David Henry Hwang; Actor: Ron Silver (*Speed-the-Plow*); Actress: Stockard Channing (*Woman in Mind*); Featured Actor: B. D. Wong (*M. Butterfly*); Featured Actress: Christine Estabrook (*The Boys Next Door*); Director: John Dexter (*M. Butterfly*)

MUSICALS
Musical: *Into the Woods*; Actor: Michael Crawford (*The Phantom of the Opera*); Actress: Patti LuPone (*Anything Goes*); Featured Actor: Robert Westenberg (*Into the Woods*); Featured Actress: Joanna Gleason (*Into the Woods*); Director: Harold Prince (*The Phantom of the Opera*); Book: James Lapine (*Into the Woods*); Music: Andrew Lloyd Webber (*The Phantom of the Opera*); Lyrics: Stephen Sondheim (*Into the Woods*); Choreography: Michael Smuin (*Anything Goes*); Orchestrations: David Cullen, Andrew Lloyd Webber (*The Phantom of the Opera*)

OTHER AWARDS
Revival: *Anything Goes*; Ensemble Acting: Cast of *Oil City Symphony*; Set and Costume Design: Maria Bjornson (*The Phantom of the Opera*); Lighting Design: Andrew Bridge (*The Phantom of the Opera*)

SPECIAL AWARDS
Actors' Equity Association; The Theater on Film and Tape Collection; Yale Repertory Theatre; cabaret artist Michael Feinstein

THE NEW YORK DRAMA CRITICS CIRCLE AWARDS

BEST PLAY
Joe Turner's Come and Gone by August Wilson

BEST FOREIGN PLAY
The Road to Mecca by Athol Fugard

BEST MUSICAL
Into the Woods by James Lapine and Stephen Sondheim

THE PULITZER PRIZE FOR DRAMA

Driving Miss Daisy by Alfred Uhry

THE OBIE AWARDS

BEST NEW PLAYS
Abingdon Square by Maria Irene Fornes; *Serious Money* by Caryl Churchill

SUSTAINED ACHIEVEMENT
Richard Foreman

PERFORMANCES
Kathy Bates (*Frankie and Johnny in the Claire de Lune*); Larry Bazzell (*The Signal Season of Dummy Hoy*); Yvonne Bryceland, Amy Irving (*The Road to Mecca*); Victor Garber (*Wenceslas Square*); Erland Josephson (*The Cherry Orchard*); Gordana Rashovich (*A Shayna Maidel*); John Seitz (*Abingdon Square*); Peggy Shaw (*Dress Suits for Hire*); Tina Shepard (*The Three Lives of Lucie Charbol*); Lauren Tom (*American Notes*); George Bartenieff, Roberts Blossom (sustained excellence)

DIRECTION
Anne Bogart (*No Plays, No Poetry*); Peter Brook (*The Mahabharata*); Julie Taymor (*Juan Darien*)

DESIGN
Eva Buchmiller, Huck Snyder (sustained achievement in set design)

OBIE GRANTS
CSC Repertory; Theatre for a New Audience

SPECIAL CITATIONS
Fight choreograper B. H. Barry; Christopher Reeve for his "courageous work on behalf of Chilean artists."

THE OUTER CRITICS CIRCLE AWARDS

Broadway Play: *M. Butterfly*; Broadway Musical: *The Phantom of the Opera*; Off-Broadway Play: *Driving Miss Daisy*; Off-Broadway Musical (tie): *Oil City Symphony* and *Romance, Romance*; Actor (Play): Robert Prosky (*A Walk in the Woods*); Actress (Play): Dana Ivey (*Driving Miss Daisy* and *Wencelas Square*); Actor (Musical): Michael Crawford (*The Phantom of the Opera*); Actress (Musical): Joanna Gleason (*Into the Woods*); Debut Performances: B. D. Wong (*M. Butterfly*), Melissa Gilbert (*A Shayna Maidel*); Design of Sets, Costumes, Lighting: *The Phantom of the Opera*; Director (tie): Ron Lagomarsino (*Drivng Miss Daisy, Laughing Wild,* and *Only You*) and Jerry Zaks (*Anything Goes* and *Wencelas Square*); Off-Broadway Book, Music, and Lyrics: *Romance, Romance*; Revival: *Anything Goes*; John Gassner Playwriting Award: David Henry Hwang (*M. Butterfly*); Special Awards: Michael Feinstein, The Brooklyn Academy of Music

THE TONY AWARDS

PLAY
Largely New York by Bill Irwin
Lend Me a Tenor by Ken Ludwig
Shirley Valentine by Willy Russell
The Heidi Chronicles by Wendy Wasserstein

MUSICAL
Black and Blue
Jerome Robbins' Broadway
Starmites

There were so few new musicals during the 1988–89 season that the nominees in this category consisted of two non-Book shows (*Black and Blue*, a Parisian revue of black entertainment during the 1920s, and *Jerome Robbins' Broadway*, a retrospective of the choreographer's long career) and *Starmites*, a poorly received sci-fi comedy which was eking out a moderate run. The categories of best Book and Score of a Musical were eliminated owing to a lack of worthy candidates.

ACTOR (PLAY)
Mikhail Baryshnikov (*Metamorphosis*)
Philip Bosco (*Lend Me a Tenor*)
Victor Garber (*Lend Me a Tenor*)
Bill Irwin (*Largely New York*)

For his mime/dance entertainment *Largely New York*, New Vaudeville clown Bill Irwin became the first person since Elizabeth Swados to receive four nomination in one year: best Play (as author, although the work contained no dialogue), best Actor (Play), best Director (Play), and best Choreography.

ACTRESS (PLAY)
Joan Allen (*The Heidi Chronicles*)
Pauline Collins (*Shirley Valentine*)
Madeline Kahn (*Born Yesterday*)
Kate Nelligan (*The Spoils of War*)

ACTOR (MUSICAL)
Jason Alexander (*Jerome Robbins' Broadway*)
Gabriel Barre (*Starmites*)
Brian Lane Green (*Starmites*)
Robert La Fosse (*Jerome Robbins' Broadway*)

ACTRESS (MUSICAL)
Ruth Brown (*Black and Blue*)
Charlotte d'Amboise (*Jerome Robbins' Broadway*)
Linda Hopkins (*Black and Blue*)
Sharon McNight (*Starmites*)

FEATURED ACTOR (PLAY)
Peter Frechette (*Eastern Standard*)
Boyd Gaines (*The Heidi Chronicles*)
Eric Stoltz (*Our Town*)
Gordon Joseph Weiss (*Ghetto*)

FEATURED ACTRESS (PLAY)
Christine Baranski (*Rumors*)
Joanne Camp (*The Heidi Chronicles*)
Tovah Feldshuh (*Lend Me a Tenor*)
Penelope Ann Miller (*Our Town*)

FEATURED ACTOR (MUSICAL)
Bunny Briggs (*Black and Blue*)

Savion Glover (*Black and Blue*)
Scott Wentworth (*Welcome to the Club*)
Scott Wise (*Jerome Robbins' Broadway*)

FEATURED ACTRESS (MUSICAL)
Jane Lanier (*Jerome Robbins' Broadway*)
Faith Prince (*Jerome Robbins' Broadway*)
Debbie Shapiro (*Jerome Robbins' Broadway*)
Julie Wilson (*Legs Diamond*)

OTHER AWARDS
Revival: *Our Town*; Director (Play): Jerry Zaks
(*Lend Me a Tenor*); Director (Musical): Jerome
Robbins (*Jerome Robbins' Broadway*);
Choreography: Cholly Atkins, Henry LeTang,
Frankie Manning, and Fayard Nicholas (*Black and
Blue*); Set Design: Santo Loquasto (*Cafe Crown*);
Costume Design: Claudio Segovia and Hector
Orezzoli (*Black and Blue*); Lighting Design:
Jennifer Tipton (*Jerome Robbins' Broadway*)

SPECIAL AWARD
Hartford Stage Company, Hartford, CT
(Outstanding Regional Theatre)

Angela Lansbury was Tony mistress of ceremonies
for the third year in a row. She opened the show by
singing "Everything's Coming Up Roses" from her
Tony-winning performance in *Gypsy*. But everything was not coming up roses for Broadway.
Almost no new musicals were running on the
Main Stem and woefully few plays.

The telecast was also beset with problems. The
sound was missing from the first few seconds of
the show and the audio from a commercial covered
Lansbury's closing remarks and a reprise of
"Roses." Steve Martin brightened up the show by
mocking that year's Academy Awards with its
Snow-White-meets-Rob-Lowe opening number:
"Everybody onstage for the salute to disco by the
Mother Goose characters. Oh, I'm sorry. I thought
this was the Oscars."

THE DRAMA DESK AWARDS

PLAYS
Play: *The Heidi Chronicles* by Wendy Wasserstein;
Actor: Philip Bosco (*Lend Me a Tenor*); Actress:
Pauline Collins (*Shirley Valentine*); Featured Actor:
Peter Frechette (*Eastern Standard*); Featured
Actress: Tovah Feldshuh (*Lend Me a Tenor*);
Director: Jerry Zaks (*Lend Me a Tenor*)

MUSICALS
Musical: *Jerome Robbins' Broadway*; Actor: Jason
Alexander (*Jerome Robbins' Broadway*); Actress:
Toni DiBuono (*Forbidden Broadway*)

OTHER AWARDS
Revival: *Our Town*; Unique Theatrical Experience:
Largely New York; Set Design: Santo Loquasto
(*Cafe Crown* and *Italian-American Reconciliation*);
Costume Design: William Ivey Long (*Lend Me a
Tenor*); Lighting Design: Jennifer Tipton (*Long
Day's Journey into Night, Waiting for Godot,* and
Jerome Robbins' Broadway)

SPECIAL AWARDS
Bernard Gersten and Gregory Mosher for
revitalizing Lincoln Center; musical director John
McGlinn; Manhattan Theatre Club; musical
director Paul Gemignani; Jerome Robbins

Again because of a skimpy set of choices, numerous categories were eliminated. The Drama Desk
did not pick any nominees for Choreography,
Featured Musical Actor or Actress, Director, Book,
or Score of a Musical.

THE NEW YORK DRAMA CRITICS CIRCLE AWARDS

BEST PLAY
The Heidi Chronicles by Wendy Wasserstein

BEST FOREIGN PLAY
Aristocrats by Brian Friel

SPECIAL CITATION
Bill Irwin for *Largely New York*

THE PULITZER PRIZE FOR DRAMA

The Heidi Chronicles by Wendy Wasserstein

THE OBIE AWARDS

PERFORMANCE
Mark Blum (*Gus and Al*); Niall Buggy (*Aristocrats*); William Converse-Roberts (*Love's Labour's Lost*); Fyvush Finkel (*Cafe Crown*); Gloria Foster (*The Forbidden City*); Paul Hecht (*Enrico IV*); Nancy Marchand (*The Cocktail Hour*); Tim McDonnell (*Diary of a Madman*); Will Patton (*What Did He See?*); Lonny Price (*The Immigrant*); Everett Quinton (*A Tale of Two Cities*); Rocco Sisto (*The Winter's Tale*); Kathy Najimy and Mo Gaffney (*The Kathy and Mo Show*)

William Converse-Roberts admitted to being totally surprised at his Obie win: "I have nothing to say, I don't even know who to thank, and I was getting drunk." Fyvush Finkel pointed out the irony of an old *Village Voice* review which said he should be a waiter on Second Avenue instead of an actor. He won his Obie for playing a Second Avenue waiter. Entertainer Leo Bassi stole the show by juggling a hollow piano with his feet.

SUSTAINED ACHIEVEMENT
Irene Worth

DIRECTION
Ingmar Bergman (*Hamlet*); Peter Stein (*Falstaff*); Rene Buch (sustained excellence)

DESIGN
Donald Eastman (sustained excellence of set design); Gabriel Berry, Susan Young (sustained excellence of costume design)

SPECIAL CITATIONS
Leo Bassi (*Nero's Last Folly*); Dance Theatre Workshop; The Dramatists Guild for the Young Playwrights Festival; Janie Geiser (*Stories from Here*); Rachel Rosenthal (*Rachel's Brain*); Tamamatsu Yoshida (*The Warrior Ant*); Paul Zaloom (*The House of Horror*)

OBIE GRANTS
Cucaracha Workhouse Theater; The Living Theater; Playwrighting Workshop; INTAR Hispanic Playwrights-in-Residence Laboratory; The Frank Silvera Writers Workshop

THE OUTER CRITICS CIRCLE AWARDS

Broadway Play: *The Heidi Chronicles*; Broadway Musical: *Jerome Robbins' Broadway*; Actor (Play): Kevin Conway (*Other People's Money*); Actress (Play): Pauline Collins (*Shirley Valentine*); Actor (Musical): Jason Alexander (*Jerome Robbins' Broadway*); Actress (Musical): Ruth Brown (*Black and Blue*); Debut Performances: Peter Frechette (*Eastern Standard*), Toni DiBuono (*Forbidden Broadway*); Set, Costume, and Lighting Design: *Lend Me a Tenor*; John Gassner Playwriting Award: Jerry Sterner (*Other People's Money*); Special Awards: Mikhail Baryshnikov (*Metamorphosis*), the cast of *Lend Me a Tenor* (ensemble acting), Jewish Repertory Theatre for *Cantorial* and *Chu Chem*

THE TONY AWARDS

PLAY
Lettice & Lovage by Peter Shaffer
Prelude to a Kiss by Craig Lucas
The Grapes of Wrath by Frank Galati
The Piano Lesson by August Wilson

MUSICAL
Aspects of Love
City of Angels
Grand Hotel
Meet Me in St. Louis

ACTOR (PLAY)
Charles S. Dutton (*The Piano Lesson*)
Dustin Hoffman (*The Merchant of Venice*)
Tom Hulce (*A Few Good Men*)
Robert Morse (*Tru*)

ACTRESS (PLAY)
Geraldine James (*The Merchant of Venice*)
Mary-Louise Parker (*Prelude to a Kiss*)
Maggie Smith (*Lettice and Lovage*)
Kathleen Turner (*Cat on a Hot Tin Roof*)

Among those Maggie Smith thanked was the cat

she shared the stage with in *Lettice and Lovage*. But she cautioned that her feline co-star "had better pull itself together, because it's getting out of hand."

ACTOR (MUSICAL)
David Carroll (*Grand Hotel*)
Gregg Edelman (*City of Angels*)
Bob Gunton (*Sweeney Todd*)
James Naughton (*City of Angels*)

ACTRESS (MUSICAL)
Georgia Brown (*3 Penny Opera*)
Tyne Daly (*Gypsy*)
Beth Fowler (*Sweeney Todd*)
Liliane Montevecchi (*Grand Hotel*)

FEATURED ACTOR (PLAY)
Rocky Carroll (*The Piano Lesson*)
Charles Durning (*Cat on a Hot Tin Roof*)
Terry Kinney (*The Grapes of Wrath*)
Gary Sinise (*The Grapes of Wrath*)

Best acceptance speech: Charles Durning stated, "A lot of people think I don't deserve this. I don't deserve arthritis either, but I've got that, too."

FEATURED ACTRESS (PLAY)
Polly Holliday (*Cat on a Hot Tin Roof*)
S. Epatha Merkerson (*The Piano Lesson*)
Lois Smith (*The Grapes of Wrath*)
Margaret Tyzack (*Lettice and Lovage*)

FEATURED ACTOR (MUSICAL)
Rene Auberjonois (*City of Angels*)
Kevin Colson (*Aspects of Love*)
Jonathan Hadary (*Gypsy*)
Michael Jeter (*Grand Hotel*)

Michael Jeter stopped the show with his Charleston number from *Grand Hotel* and then stopped it again with his moving acceptance speech. He encouraged anyone listening with a drug or alcohol problem not to give up hope. "I stand before you as living proof you can stop and dreams do come true," he said on the brink of tears.

FEATURED ACTRESS (MUSICAL)
Randy Graff (*City of Angels*)
Jane Krakowski (*Grand Hotel*)

Kathleen Rowe McAllen (*Aspects of Love*)
Crista Moore (*Gypsy*)

OTHER AWARDS
Revival: *Gypsy*; Director (Play): Frank Galati (*The Grapes of Wrath*); Director (Musical): Tommy Tune (*Grand Hotel*); Score: Cy Coleman, David Zippel (*City of Angels*); Book of a Musical: Larry Gelbart (*City of Angels*); Choreography: Tommy Tune (*Grand Hotel*); Set Design: Robin Wagner (*City of Angels*); Costume Design: Santo Loquasto (*Grand Hotel*); Lighting Design: Jules Fisher (*Grand Hotel*)

SPECIAL AWARDS
Alfred Drake; Seattle Repertory Theatre (Outstanding Regional Theatre)

The main battle for theatrical prizes this season was between *City of Angels*, a jazz-filled satire on '40s' film noir, and *Grand Hotel*, Tommy Tune's high-stepping adaptation of the classic 1934 film. *Angels* was named best Musical by both the Tonys and Drama Desk Awards, while *Hotel* netted Direction and Choreography awards for Tune from the same groups.

Kathleen Turner, a nominee for best Actress (Play) for a revival of *Cat on a Hot Tin Roof*, hosted the Tony Awards ceremony. The theme for the show was "The Year of the Actor." Joseph Cates took over from the departing Don Mischer as producer, and interspersed monologues about acting from classic plays along with scenes from the nominated best plays and musicals. The result was a talk-heavy special which drew low ratings. Presenter Ron Silver provided a spark of controversy by calling for support for the endangered National Endowment for the Arts and commemorating the one-year anniversary of the Chinese government's crackdown on the student rebellion in Bejing's Tianamen Square.

August Wilson won his second Pulitzer, the Drama Desk Award, and the New York Drama Critics Circle for *The Piano Lesson*, but was snubbed by Tony voters for best Play in favor of the Chicago-based Steppenwolf Theatre Company's adaptation of *The Grapes of Wrath*. Because of its huge cast, high production cost, and lack of box-office clout, *Grapes* closed that summer despite the Tony honor.

THE DRAMA DESK AWARDS

PLAYS

Play: *The Piano Lesson* by August Wilson; Actor: Nathan Lane (*The Lisbon Traviata*); Actress: Geraldine James (*The Merchant of Venice*); Featured Actor: Charles Durning (*Cat on a Hot Tin Roof*); Featured Actress: Frances Conroy (*The Secret Rapture*); Director: Frank Galati (*The Grapes of Wrath*)

MUSICALS

Musical: *City of Angels*; Actor: James Naughton (*City of Angels*); Actress: Tyne Daly (*Gypsy*); Featured Actor: Michael Jeter (*Grand Hotel*); Featured Actress: Randy Graff (*City of Angels*); Director: Tommy Tune (*Grand Hotel*); Music: Cy Coleman (*City of Angels*); Lyrics: David Zippel (*City of Angels*); Book: Larry Gelbart (*City of Angels*); Choreography: Tommy Tune (*Grand Hotel*); Orchestration: Billy Byers (*City of Angels*)

OTHER AWARDS

Revival: *Gypsy*; One-Person Show: Robert Morse (*Tru*); Set Design: Robin Wagner (*City of Angels*); Lighting Design: Jules Fisher (*City of Angels*); Costume Design: Santo Loquasto (*Grand Hotel*)

SPECIAL AWARDS

Kevin Haney for the make-up in *Tru*; The Fund for New American Plays; Jule Styne

THE NEW YORK DRAMA CRITICS CIRCLE AWARDS

BEST PLAY

The Piano Lesson by August Wilson

BEST FOREIGN PLAY

Privates on Parade by Peter Nichols

BEST MUSICAL

City of Angels by Larry Gelbart, Cy Coleman, and David Zippel

THE PULITZER PRIZE FOR DRAMA

The Piano Lesson by August Wilson

THE OBIE AWARDS

BEST NEW AMERICAN PLAYS

Prelude to a Kiss by Craig Lucas; *Imperceptible Mutabilities in the Third Kingdom* by Suzan-Lori Parks; *Bad Penny, Crowbar,*, and *Terminal Hip* by Mac Wellman

SUSTAINED ACHEIVEMENT

ACT-UP

PERFORMANCES

Alec Baldwin (*Prelude to a Kiss*); Elzibeta Czyzewska (*Crowbar*); Karen Evans-Kandel, Ruth Maleczech, Greg Mehrten, and Isabel Monk (*Lear*); Marcia Jean Kurtz (*The Loman Family Picnic* and *When She Danced*); Stephen Mellor (*Terminal Hip*); Jean Stapleton (*Mountain Language* and *The Birthday Party*); Pamela Tyson (*Imperceptible Mutabilities in the Third Kingdom*); Courtney B. Vance (*My Children! My Africa!*); Danitra Vance (*Spunk*); Lillias White (*Romance in Hard Times*); Mary Schultz (sustained excellence)

DIRECTION

Liz Diamond (*Imperceptible Mutabilities in the Third Kingdom*); Norman Rene (*Prelude to a Kiss*); Jim Simpson (*Bad Penny*); George C. Wolfe (*Spunk*)

DESIGN

Daniel Moses Schreir (sustained excellence in sound design); George Tsypin (sustained excellence in set design)

SPECIAL CITATIONS

Eric Bogosian (*Sex, Drugs, Rock & Roll*); Dan Hurlin (*A Cool Million*); San Francisco Mime Troupe (*Seeing Double*); Joseph Papp for his couragcous stand against censorship

Magicians Penn and Teller presented the first Obie Award of the evening to Dan Hurlin for his production *A Cool Million*. Before relinquishing the framed Obie plaque, Penn and Teller had Hurlin pick a card. The card was then placed back in the deck and the deck spread out over the Obie. Penn stuck himself with a hatpin and let the blood flow over the cards and the award. He pulled out the card with the most blood. It was the one Hurlin had picked.

Among the more unusual citations were one to Joseph Papp for refusing a grant from the National Endowment for the Arts because of the Endowment's censorship of its grantees and one to the AIDS advocacy group, ACT-UP.

THE OUTER CRITICS CIRCLE AWARDS

Broadway Play: *The Grapes of Wrath*; Broadway Musical: *City of Angels*; Off-Broadway Play: *Prelude to a Kiss*; Off-Broadway Musical: *Closer Than Ever*; Actor (Play): Robert Morse (*Tru*); Actress (Play): Maggie Smith (*Lettice & Lovage*); Actor (Musical): Michael Jeter (*Grand Hotel*); Actress (Musical): Tyne Daly (*Gypsy*); Debut Performances: Rocky Carroll (*The Piano Lesson*), Megan Gallagher (*A Few Good Men*); Director: Michael Blakemore (*City of Angels* and *Lettice & Lovage*); Set, Costume, and Lighting Design: *City of Angels*; Revival (Play): *Cat on a Hot Tin Roof*; Revival (Musical): *Gypsy*; Off-Broadway Music: David Shire (*Closer Than Ever*); Off-Broadway Lyrics: Richard Maltby, Jr. (*Closer Than Ever*); Special Awards: Bill Irwin (*Largely New York*), Larry Gelbart for contributions to comedy—*Mastergate* and *City of Angels*, En Garde Arts for *Crowbar*

1990-91

THE TONY AWARDS

PLAY
Lost in Yonkers by Neil Simon
Our Country's Good by Timberlake Wertenbaker
Shadowlands by William Nicholson
Six Degrees of Separation by John Guare

While presenting the best Director (Musical) Award early in the Tony telecast, Anthony Quinn opened his envelope and read, "And the winner is *Lost in Yonkers* by Neil Simon....Oh my God! It's the wrong envelope!" When Simon was later correctly announced as the author of the Tony best Play, he saved the situation by quipping, "I was in

the men's room when Anthony Quinn was on. Did anything interesting happen?"

MUSICAL
Miss Saigon
Once on This Island
The Secret Garden
The Will Rogers Follies

ACTOR (PLAY)
Peter Frechette (*Our Country's Good*)
Nigel Hawthorne (*Shadowlands*)
Tom McGowan (*La Bete*)
Courtney B. Vance (*Six Degrees of Separation*)

ACTRESS (PLAY)
Stockard Channing (*Six Degrees of Separation*)
Julie Harris (*Lucifer's Child*)
Cherry Jones (*Our Country's Good*)
Mercedes Ruehl (*Lost in Yonkers*)

ACTOR (MUSICAL)
Keith Carradine (*The Will Rogers Follies*)
Paul Hipp (*Buddy: The Buddy Holly Story*)
Jonathan Pryce (*Miss Saigon*)
Topol (*Fiddler on the Roof*)

ACTRESS (MUSICAL)
June Angela (*Shogun*)
Dee Hoty (*The Will Rogers Follies*)
Cathy Rigby (*Peter Pan*)
Lea Salonga (*Miss Saigon*)

Controversy surrounded the Tony best Actor (Musical) and Actress (Musical). Both Jonathan Pryce and Lea Salonga had originated their roles in the London production of *Miss Saigon*, but their American transfer was met with a storm of protest. Jonathan Pryce was attacked because he was a Caucasian actor playing a Eurasian role. Filipina Lea Salonga was not an American citizen. Both were accused of taking potential jobs away from American-Asian actors. Despite these objections, producer Cameron Mackintosh brought the pair to America and both won Tonys.

FEATURED ACTOR (PLAY)
Adam Arkin (*I Hate Hamlet*)
Dylan Baker (*La Bete*)

Stephen Lang (*The Speed of Darkness*)
Kevin Spacey (*Lost in Yonkers*)

FEATURED ACTRESS (PLAY)
Amelia Campbell (*Our Country's Good*)
Kathryn Erbe (*The Speed of Darkness*)
J. Smith-Cameron (*Our Country's Good*)
Irene Worth (*Lost in Yonkers*)

FEATURED ACTOR (MUSICAL)
Bruce Adler (*Those Were the Days*)
Hinton Battle (*Miss Saigon*)
Gregg Burge (*Oh, Kay!*)
Willy Falk (*Miss Saigon*)

FEATURED ACTRESS (MUSICAL)
Daisy Eagan (*The Secret Garden*)
Alison Fraser (*The Secret Garden*)
Cady Huffman (*The Will Rogers Follies*)
La Chanze (*Once on This Island*)

At age 11, Daisy Eagan become the youngest actress to win a Tony. However, the youngest winner of either sex still remains Frankie Michaels, who won for playing *Mame*'s nephew in 1966 when he was only 10.

OTHER AWARDS
Revival: *Fiddler on the Roof*; Director (Play): Jerry Zaks (*Six Degrees of Separation*); Director (Musical): Tommy Tune (*The Will Rogers Follies*); Score: Cy Coleman, Betty Comden, Adolph Green (*The Will Rogers Follies*); Book of a Musical: Marsha Norman (*The Secret Garden*); Choreography: Tommy Tune (*The Will Rogers Follies*); Set Design: Heidi Landesman (*The Secret Garden*); Costume Design: Willa Kim (*The Will Rogers Follies*); Lighting Design: Jules Fisher (*The Will Rogers Follies*)

SPECIAL AWARDS
Father George Moore (posthumous); Yale Repertory Theater, New Haven, CT (Outstanding Regional Theatre)

Julie Andrews returned to Broadway after a thirty-year absence to host the 1990–91 Tonys. Co-host Jeremy Irons had to be shot from the waist up since he was sporting sneakers with his tuxedo. The previous year's telecast featured dramatic readings from Shakespeare and O'Neill performed by actors known mainly for their theater work. The show was a ratings failure. This year, executive producer Joseph Cates hired a slew of Hollywood stars to make up the recognition factor. Audrey Hepburn, Whoopi Goldberg, Denzel Washington, Steve Guttenberg, Shirley MacLaine, Joan Collins, and Anthony Quinn handed out the awards. Rather than excerpts from classic plays, the entertainment was purely musical. In addition to numbers from the nominated shows, old favorites were sung by hostess Andrews as well as by Topol, Robert Morse, and Michael Crawford, while from Seattle Tommy Tune and Ann Reinking performed a song from *Bye, Bye, Birdie*. The ratings were a dramatic improvement from 1989–90.

For the first time, red ribbons were worn during an awards ceremony in order to increase awareness of AIDS.

THE NEW YORK DRAMA CRITICS CIRCLE AWARDS

BEST PLAY
Six Degrees of Separation by John Guare

BEST FOREIGN PLAY
Our Country's Good by Timberlake Wertenbaker

BEST MUSICAL
The Will Rogers Follies by Peter Stone, Cy Coleman, Betty Comden, and Adolph Green

SPECIAL CITATION
Eileen Atkins for her portrayal of Virginia Woolf in *A Room of One's Own*

THE PULITZER PRIZE FOR DRAMA

Lost in Yonkers by Neil Simon

THE DRAMA DESK AWARDS

PLAYS
Play: *Lost in Yonkers* by Neil Simon; Actor: Ron Rifkin (*The Substance of Fire*); Actress: Mercedes Ruehl (*Lost in Yonkers*); Featured Actor: Kevin

Spacey (*Lost in Yonkers*); Featured Actress: Irene Worth (*Lost in Yonkers*); Director: Jerry Zaks (*Six Degrees of Separation*)

MUSICALS

Musical: *The Will Rogers Follies*; Actor: Jonathan Pryce (*Miss Saigon*); Actress: Lea Salonga (*Miss Saigon*); Featured Actor: Bruce Adler (*Those Were the Days*); Featured Actress: Karen Ziemba (*And the World Goes Round*); Director: Scott Ellis (*And the World Goes Round* and *A Little Night Music*); Music (tie): Cy Coleman (*The Will Rogers Follies*) and William Finn (*Falsettoland*); Lyrics: William Finn (*Falsettoland*); Book of a Musical: Marsha Norman (*The Secret Garden*); Choreography: Tommy Tune (*The Will Rogers Follies*); Orchestration: William Brohn (*The Secret Garden* and *Miss Saigon*); Musical Revue: *And the World Goes Round*

OTHER AWARDS

Solo/One-Person Performance: Eileen Atkins (*A Room of One's Own*); Unique Theatrical Experience: Cirque du Soleil; Revival: *A Little Night Music*; Set Design: Heidi Landesman (*The Secret Garden*); Costume Design: Patricia Zipprodt (*Shogun*); Lighting Design: David Hersey (*Miss Saigon*); Sound Design/Music in a Play: Aural Fixation (*Red Scare on Sunset*)

SPECIAL AWARDS

Brooklyn Academy of Music for bringing international productions to New York; theater artist James McMullan; New Dramatists; composer Harold Rome

THE OBIE AWARDS

BEST NEW PLAY
The Fever by Wallace Shawn

PLAYWRITING
Six Degrees of Separation by John Guare; *Sincerity Forever* by Mac Wellman

SUSTAINED ACHIEVEMENT
The Wooster Group

PERFORMANCE

Eileen Atkins (*A Room of One's Own*); Stockard Channing (*Six Degrees of Separation*); Joan Copeland (*The American Plan*); Angela Goethals (*The Good Times Are Killing Me*); Tony Goldwyn (*The Sum of Us*); Jan Leslie Harding (*Sincerity Forever*); Jodie Markell (*Machinal*); Anne Pitoniak (*Pygmalion*); John Leguizamo (*Mambo Mouth*); Michael Lombard (*What's Wrong with This Picture?*); Ron Rifkin (*The Substance of Fire*); Kathleen Widdoes (*Tower of Evil*); Bette Bourne, Precious Pearl, Peggy Shaw, Lois Weaver (ensemble of *Belle Reprieve*)

Angela Goethels became the youngest Obie winner at age 14 for *The Good Times Are Killing Me*, Linda Barry's recreation of her childhood in a racially mixed neighborhood.

DIRECTION

Michael Greif (*Machinal*); Lisa Peterson (*Light Shining in Buckinghamshire*)

DESIGN

Frances Aronson (sustained excellence of lighting design); Mark Beard (sustained excellence of set design); William Ivey Long (sustained excellence of costume design); John Gromada (sound design of *Machinal*)

SPECIAL CITATIONS

Blue Man Group; John Kelly (*Loves of a Poet*); BACA Downtown; New York Shakespeare Festival 1990–91 season; Lori E. Seid (stage management); Theatre for the New City for *Stop the War: A Festival for Peace in the Middle East*

Performance artists Blue Man Group gave their thanks in neon on mini-electric signs.

OBIE GRANTS

En Garde Arts; Hearts and Voices; Mettawee River Theater Company

THE OUTER CRITICS CIRCLE AWARDS

Broadway Play: *Lost in Yonkers*; Broadway Musical: *Miss Saigon*; Off-Broadway Play: *The Sum of Us*; Off-Broadway Musical: *Falsettoland*; Off-Broadway

Musical Revue: *And the World Goes Round*; Actor (Play): Nigel Hawthorne (*Shadowlands*); Actress (Play) Mercedes Ruehl (*Lost in Yonkers*); Actor (Musical): Jonathan Pryce (*Miss Saigon*); Actress (Musical): Lea Salonga (*Miss Saigon*); Debut Performances: Tom McGowan (*La Bete*), Jane Adams (*I Hate Hamlet*); Director: Gene Saks (*Lost in Yonkers*); Choreography: Susan Stroman (*And the World Goes Round*); Set, Costume, and Lighting Design: *The Secret Garden*; Revival: *Fiddler on the Roof*; John Gassner Playwriting Award: David Hirson (*La Bete*); Achievement Award: John Leguizamo (*Mambo Mouth*); Special Awards: Jackie Mason; cast of *And the World Goes Round* (ensemble performance); Broadway Cares

THE TONY AWARDS

PLAY
Dancing at Lughnasa by Brian Friel
Four Baboons Adoring the Sun by John Guare
Two Shakespearean Actors by Richard Nelson
Two Trains Running by August Wilson

MUSICAL
Crazy for You
Falsettos
Five Guys Named Moe
Jelly's Last Jam

ACTOR (PLAY)
Alan Alda (*Jake's Women*)
Alec Baldwin (*A Streetcar Named Desire*)
Brian Bedford (*Two Shakespearean Actors*)
Judd Hirsch (*Conversations with My Father*)

ACTRESS (PLAY)
Jane Alexander (*The Visit*)
Stockard Channing (*Four Baboons Adoring the Sun*)
Glenn Close (*Death and the Maiden*)
Judith Ivey (*Park Your Car in Harvard Yard*)

ACTOR (MUSICAL)
Harry Groener (*Crazy for You*)

Gregory Hines (*Jelly's Last Jam*)
Nathan Lane (*Guys and Dolls*)
Michael Rupert (*Falsettos*)

Overlooked: Spiro Malas in the revival of *The Most Happy Fella* was not nominated despite glowing reviews.

ACTRESS (MUSICAL)
Jodi Benson (*Crazy for You*)
Josie de Guzman (*Guys and Dolls*)
Sophie Hayden (*The Most Happy Fella*)
Faith Prince (*Guys and Dolls*)

FEATURED ACTOR (PLAY)
Roscoe Lee Browne (*Two Trains Running*)
Larry Fishburne (*Two Trains Running*)
Zeljko Ivanek (*Two Shakespearean Actors*)
Tony Shalhoub (*Conversations with My Father*)

FEATURED ACTRESS (PLAY)
Brid Brennan (*Dancing at Lughnasa*)
Rosaleen Linehan (*Dancing at Lughnasa*)
Cynthia Marsells (*Two Trains Running*)
Dearbhla Molloy (*Dancing at Lughnasa*)

FEATURED ACTOR (MUSICAL)
Bruce Adler (*Crazy for You*)
Keith David (*Jelly's Last Jam*)
Jonathan Kaplan (*Falsettos*)
Scott Waara (*The Most Happy Fella*)

FEATURED ACTRESS (MUSICAL)
Liz Larsen (*The Most Happy Fella*)
Tonya Pinkins (*Jelly's Last Jam*)
Vivian Reed (*The High Rollers Social and Pleasure Club*)
Barbara Walsh (*Falsettos*)

OTHER AWARDS
Revival: *Guys and Dolls*; Director (Play): Patrick Mason (*Dancing at Lughnasa*); Director (Musical): Jerry Zaks (*Guys and Dolls*); Score: William Finn (*Falsettos*); Book of a Musical: William Finn, James Lapine (*Falsettos*); Set Design: Tony Walton (*Guys and Dolls*); Costume Design: William Ivey Long (*Crazy for You*); Lighting Design: Jules Fisher (*Jelly's Last Jam*); Choreography: Susan Stroman (*Crazy for You*)

The Fantasticks; Goodman Theatre of Chicago (Outstanding Regional Theatre)

Revivals and stars from movies and TV dominated the 1991–92 Broadway season. New productions of *Guys and Dolls, The Most Happy Fella, A Streetcar Named Desire,* and *Private Lives* were highlights. Glenn Close, Richard Dreyfuss, Gene Hackman, Alan Alda, Joan Collins, Judd Hirsch, Jessica Lange, and Alec Baldwin took time off from the small and large screens to appear on New York stages.

Close hosted the awards ceremony and won her second Tony (for *Death and the Maiden*; her previous win was for *The Real Thing* in 1983–84). The major names made it one of the most star-studded Tony shows in years. A few ringers with only a few stage credits were tossed in as presenters. These included Danny Glover, Farrah Fawcett, and father and son Kirk and Michael Douglas.

THE DRAMA DESK AWARDS

PLAYS
New Play: *Marvin's Room* by Scott McPherson; Actor: Brian Bedford (*Two Shakespearean Actors*); Actress: Laura Esterman (*Marvin's Room*); Featured Actor: Larry Fishburne (*Two Trains Running*); Featured Actress: Christine Baranski (*Lips Together, Teeth Apart*); Director: Patrick Mason (*Dancing at Lughnasa*); Music in a Play: Jan A. P. Kaczmarek (*'Tis Pity She's a Whore*)

MUSICALS
Musical: *Crazy for You*; Actor (tie): Gregory Hines *Jelly's Last Jam*) and Nathan Lane (*Guys and Dolls*); Actress: Faith Prince (*Guys and Dolls*); Featured Actor: Scott Waara (*The Most Happy Fella*); Featured Actress: Tonya Pinks (*Jelly's Last Jam*); Director: Jerry Zaks (*Guys and Dolls*); Choreography: Susan Stroman (*Crazy for You*); Music: Erik Frandsen, Michael Garin, Robert Hipkens, Paula Lockheart (*Song of Singapore*); Lyrics: Susan Birkenhead (*Jelly's Last Jam*); Book of a Musical: George C. Wolfe (*Jelly's Last Jam*); Orchestration/Musical Adaptation: Luther Henderson (*Jelly's Last Jam*)

OTHER AWARDS
Revival: *Guys and Dolls*; Unique Theatrical Experience: *Blue Man Group*; Solo Performance: Patrick Stewart (*A Christmas Carol*); Ensemble Performance: Cast of *Dancing at Lughnasa*; Set Design: Tony Walton (*Guys and Dolls*); Costume Design: William Ivey Long (*Guys and Dolls*); Lighting Design (tie): Jules Fisher (*Jelly's Last Jam*) and Paul Gallo (*Guys and Dolls*); Sound Design: Paul Arditti (*Four Baboons Adoring the Sun*)

SPECIAL AWARDS
Andre Bishop; The Irish Repertory Theater; Broadway Cares/Equity Fights AIDS and Suzanne Ishee

THE NEW YORK DRAMA CRITICS CIRCLE AWARDS

BEST PLAY
Dancing at Lughnasa by Brian Friel

BEST AMERICAN PLAY
Two Trains Running by August Wilson

This was Wilson's fifth citation from the Drama Critics Circle, the most for any playwright. No musical was chosen because the eligible shows contained material from other sources. *Jelly's Last Jam* had music from the 1920s and 1930s by jazz great Jelly Roll Morton. *Crazy for You* was an adaptation of *Girl Crazy*, a 1930 musical with a score by George and Ira Gershwin. The two acts of *Falsettos* had been previously produced Off-Broadway in two separate productions.

THE PULITZER PRIZE FOR DRAMA

The Kentucky Cycle by Robert Schenkkan

The award was based on a production of *The Kentucky Cycle*, a six-hour saga of American history in the title state, at the Intiman Theatre in Seattle, WA. This was the first time a play won the Pulitzer without the benefit of a New York staging.

THE OBIE AWARDS

BEST NEW PLAYS
Sight Unseen by Donald Marguiles; *Sally's Rape* by Robbie McCauley; *The Baltimore Waltz* by Paula Vogel

SUSTAINED ACHIEVEMENT
Athol Fugard

SUSTAINED EXCELLENCE IN
PLAYWRITING
Neal Bell, Romulus Linney

PERFORMANCE
Dennis Boutsikaris, Deborah Hedwall (*Sight Unseen*); Laura Esterman (*Marvin's Room*); Cherry Jones (*The Baltimore Waltz*); James McDaniel (*Before It Hits Home*); S. Epatha Merkerson (*I'm Not Stupid*); Roger Rees (*The End of the Day*); Lynne Thigpen (*Boesman and Lena*); Larry Bryggman, Randy Danson, Ofelia Gonzalez, Nathan Lane (all for sustained excellence)

DIRECTION
Anne Bogart (*The Baltimore Waltz*); Mark Wing-Davey (*Mad Forest*)

DESIGN
John Arnone (sustained excellence in set design); Marina Draghici (sets and costumes for *Mad Forest*)

SPECIAL CITATIONS
Gerard Alessandrini (*Forbidden Broadway*); David Gordon (*The Mysteries* and *What's So Funny?*); New York International Festival of the Arts; The New York Shakespeare Festival production of *'Tis Pity She's a Whore*; Anna Deavere Smith (*Fires in the Mirror*); Ron Vawter (*Roy Cohn/Jack Smith*); Jeff Weiss (*Hot Keys*)

OBIE GRANTS
Downtown Art Company; Franklin Furnace; Soho Repertory Company

THE OUTER CRITICS CIRCLE AWARDS

Broadway Play: *Dancing at Lughnasa*; Broadway Musical: *Crazy for You*; Off-Broadway Play: *Marvin's Room*; Off-Broadway Musical: *Song of Singapore*; Comedy: *Catskills on Broadway*; Actor (Play): Judd Hirsch (*Conversations with My Father*); Actress (Play): Laura Esterman (*Marvin's Room*); Actor (Musical): Nathan Lane (*Guys and Dolls*);

Actress (Musical): Faith Prince (*Guys and Dolls* and *Nick & Nora*); Debut Performances: Larry Fishburne and Cynthia Martells (both in *Two Trains Running*); Director: Patrick Mason (*Dancing at Lughnasa*); Choreography: Susan Stroman (*Crazy for You*); Set, Costume, and Lighting Design: *Crazy for You*; Revival (Play): *The Visit*; Revival (Musical): *Guys and Dolls*; Off-Broadway Book, Music, and Lyrics: *Song of Singapore*; John Gassner Playwriting Award: Scott McPherson (*Marvin's Room*); Special Awards: Ellen Stewart and La MaMa Experimental Theatre Club (ETC); Tony Randall for the creation of the National Actors Theatre

1992-93

THE TONY AWARDS

PLAY
Angels in America: Millennium Approaches by Tony Kushner
The Sisters Rosensweig by Wendy Wasserstein
Someone Who'll Watch Over Me by Frank McGuinness
The Song of Jacob Zulu by Tug Yourgrau

Angels in America: Millennium Approaches, the first half of Tony Kushner's two-part epic on the U.S. reaction to the AIDS crisis, received ten Tony nominations, the highest number ever for a non-musical.

MUSICAL
Blood Brothers
The Goodbye Girl
Kiss of the Spider Woman
The Who's Tommy

ACTOR (PLAY)
K. Todd Freeman (*The Song of Jacob Zulu*)
Ron Leibman (*Angels in America*)
Liam Neeson (*Anna Christie*)
Stephen Rea (*Someone Who'll Watch Over Me*)

ACTRESS (PLAY)
Jane Alexander (*The Sisters Rosensweig*)
Madeline Kahn (*The Sisters Rosensweig*)

Lynn Redgrave (*Shakespeare for My Father*)
Natasha Richardson (*Anna Christie*)

Family category: Jane Alexander and Madeline Kahn were nominated for playing sisters, and Lynn Redgrave and Natasha Richardson became the first aunt and niece nominated in the same year.

ACTOR (MUSICAL)
Brent Carver (*Kiss of the Spider Woman*)
Tim Curry (*My Favorite Year*)
Con O'Neill (*Blood Brothers*)
Martin Short (*The Goodbye Girl*)

Double play: Brent Carver won a Tony for playing the flamboyant window-dresser Molina in the musical of *Kiss of the Spider Woman* while William Hurt won an Oscar for the same role in the movie.

ACTRESS (MUSICAL)
Ann Crumb (*Anna Karenina*)
Stephanie Lawrence (*Blood Brothers*)
Bernadette Peters (*The Goodbye Girl*)
Chita Rivera (*Kiss of the Spider Woman*)

FEATURED ACTOR (PLAY)
Robert Sean Leonard (*Candida*)
Joe Mantello (*Angels in America*)
Zakes Mokae (*The Song of Jacob Zulu*)
Stephen Spinella (*Angels in America*)

FEATURED ACTRESS (PLAY)
Kathleen Chalfant (*Angels in America*)
Marcia Gay Harden (*Angels in America*)
Anne Meara (*Anna Christie*)
Debra Monk (*Redwood Curtain*)

FEATURED ACTOR (MUSICAL)
Michael Cerveris (*The Who's Tommy*)
Anthony Crivello (*Kiss of the Spider Woman*)
Gregg Edelman (*Anna Karenina*)
Paul Kandel (*The Who's Tommy*)

FEATURED ACTRESS (MUSICAL)
Jan Graveson (*Blood Brothers*)
Lainie Kazan (*My Favorite Year*)
Andrea Martin (*My Favorite Year*)
Marcia Mitzman (*The Who's Tommy*)

Best acceptance speech: From Andrea Martin, "I'd like to thank my Armenian family for my roots and my hairdresser Gary for restoring them to their natural color."

OTHER AWARDS
Revival: *Anna Christie*; Director (Play): George C. Wolfe (*Angels in America: Millennium Approaches*); Director (Musical): Des MacAnuff (*The Who's Tommy*); Score (tie): John Kander, Fred Ebb (*Kiss of the Spider Woman*) and Pete Townshend (*The Who's Tommy*); Book of a Musical: Terrence McNally (*Kiss of the Spider Woman*); Choreography: Wayne Cilento (*The Who's Tommy*); Set Design: John Arnone (*The Who's Tommy*); Costume Design: Florence Klotz (*Kiss of the Spider Woman*); Lighting Design: Chris Parry (*The Who's Tommy*)

SPECIAL AWARDS
Oklahoma!, in recognition of its fiftieth anniversary; The International Alliance of Theatrical Stage Employee and Moving Picture Machine Operators (IATSE); Broadway Cares/Equity Fights AIDS; La Jolla Playhouse, San Diego, CA (Outstanding Regional Theatre)

Liza Minnelli hosted the Tonys telecast, which had the theme of "Celebrate 100 Years of Broadway." It could have been subtitled "Beat the Clock." New Tony producer Gary Smith was under pressure from CBS to bring the show in on time. Winners were given a strict time limit of thirty seconds for their acceptance speeches. Once the half-minute was up, the orchestra began playing "Give My Regards to Broadway" louder and louder as a not-too-subtle signal to wrap it up. Another ploy to speed up the proceedings was a superimposed list of people the honorees wished to thank. Once the winner's name was called, the "thank-you" names would appear on the bottom of the TV screen, hopefully eliminating the necessity of listing them verbally. Many grumbled at the indignity of having to race through their speeches, but the Tonys came in at only four minutes over their two-hour time period, an unheard of accomplishment for the Oscars, Emmys, or Grammys.

THE DRAMA DESK AWARDS

PLAYS

New Play: *Angels in America: Millennium Approaches* by Tony Kushner; Actor: Ron Leibman (*Angels in America*); Actress: Jane Alexander (*The Sisters Rosensweig*); Featured Actor (tie): Joe Mantello aand Stephen Spinella (both in *Angels in America*); Featured Actress: Madeline Kahn (*The Sisters Rosensweig*); Director: George C. Wolfe (*Angels in America*); Music in a Play: Ladysmith Black Mambazo (*The Song of Jacob Zulu*)

MUSICALS

Musical: *Kiss of the Spider Woman*; Actor: Brent Carver (*Kiss of the Spider Woman*); Actress: Chita Rivera (*Kiss of the Spider Woman*); Featured Actor: Mark Michael Hutchinson (*Blood Brothers*); Featured Actress: Andrea Martin (*My Favorite Year*); Director: Des MacAnuff (*The Who's Tommy*); Music: John Kander (*Kiss of the Spider Woman*); Lyrics: Joel Paley (*Ruthless!*); Choreography: Wayne Cilento (*The Who's Tommy*); Orchestration: Steve Margoshes (*The Who's Tommy*)

OTHER AWARDS

Revival: *Anna Christie*; Unique Theatrical Experience: *Fool Moon*; Solo Performance: Anna Deavere Smith (*Fires in the Mirror*); Set Design: John Arnone, Wendall K. Harrington (*The Who's Tommy*); Costume Design: Florence Klotz (*Kiss of the Spider Woman*); Lighting Design: Chris Parry (*The Who's Tommy*); Sound Design: Steve Canyon Kennedy (*The Who's Tommy*)

SPECIAL AWARDS

Early Stages; International Festival of Puppet Theatre: Puppetry at the Public; RCA Victor

THE NEW YORK DRAMA CRITICS CIRCLE AWARDS

BEST PLAY

Angels in America: Millennium Approaches by Tony Kushner

BEST FOREIGN PLAY

Someone Who'll Watch over Me by Frank McGuinness

BEST MUSICAL

Kiss of the Spider Woman by Terrence McNally, John Kander, and Fred Ebb

THE PULITZER PRIZE FOR DRAMA

Angels in America: Millennium Approaches by Tony Kushner

THE OBIE AWARDS

PLAYWRITING

The Houseguests by Harry Kondoleon; *The Destiny of Me* by Larry Kramer; *Marisol* by Jose Rivera; *Jeffrey* by Paul Rudnick

Three of the four plays honored were about AIDS. Harry Kondoleon, one of the winning playwrights, died of AIDS just a few months after the Obies.

SUSTAINED ACHIEVEMENT

JoAnne Akalaitis

Akalaitis' winning of the Sustained Achievement Obie was something of a pat on the back after she had been unceremoniously fired from her position of Artistic Director of the New York Shakespeare Festival by the Board of Directors. She was dismissed despite her status as hand-picked successor of the late Joseph Papp.

PERFORMANCE

Jane Alexander and Robert Klein (*The Sisters Rosensweig*); Frances Conroy (*The Last Yankee*); David Drake (*The Night Larry Kramer Kissed Me*); Giancarlo Esposito (*Distant Fires*); Geoffrecy C. Ewing (*The Greatest*); Hallie Foote (*The Roads to Home*); Edward Hibbert (*Jeffrey*); Bill Irwin (*Texts for Nothing*); John Cameron Mitchell (*The Destiny of Me*); Linda Stephens (*Wings*); Miriam Colon and Ellen Parker (sustained excellence)

DIRECTION

Christopher Ashley (*Jeffrey*); Michael Maggio (*Wings*); Frederick Zollo (*Aven U Boys*)

DESIGN

Loy Arcenas (sustained excellence of set design); Howard Thies (sustained excellence of lighting design)

SPECIAL CITATIONS

Cirque de Soleil; Betty Corwin of the Theatre on Film Collection of the New York Public Library; Ensemble Studio Theatre for its annual one-act marathon; International Festival of Puppet Theatre: Puppetry at the Public; Ariane Mnouchkine for *Les Atrides*; Lincoln Center Serious Fun! Festival

OBIE GRANTS

Nuyorican Poets Cafe; Pearl Theatre Company

THE OUTER CRITICS CIRCLE AWARDS

Broadway Play: *The Sisters Rosensweig*; Broadway Musical: *The Who's Tommy*; Off-Broadway Play: *Jeffrey*; Off-Broadway Musical: *Ruthless!*; Actor (Play): Robert Klein (*The Sisters Rosensweig*); Actress (Play): Madeline Kahn (*The Sisters Rosensweig*); Actor (Musical): Martin Short (*The Goodbye Girl*); Actress (Musical): Tonya Pinkins (*Jelly's Last Jam*); Debut Performances: Stephen Rea (*Someone to Watch Over Me*), Natasha Richardson (*Anna Christie*); Director (Play): Daniel Sullivan (*The Sisters Rosensweig*); Director (Musical): Des McAnuff (*The Who's Tommy*); Choreography: Hope Clarke, Gregory Hines, Ted L. Levy (*Jelly's Last Jam*); Set, Costume, and Lighting Design: *The Who's Tommy*; Revival (Play): *Anna Christie*; Revival (Musical): *Carnival*; John Gassner Playwriting Award: Paul Rudnick (*Jeffrey*); Special Achievement Awards: Julie Andrews (*Putting It Together*), David Shiner and Bill Irwin for writing and starring in *Fool Moon*, Broadway Angels Records, James H. Fleetwood Award for a promising composer to Rusty Magee for *Scapin*

1993-94

THE TONY AWARDS

PLAY

Angels in America: Perestroika by Tony Kushner
Broken Glass by Arthur Miller
The Kentucky Cycle by Robert Schenkkan
Twilight: Los Angeles, 1992 by Anna Deaveare Smith

Perestroika was the second half of *Angels in America*, Tony Kushner's epic, two-evening play about the U.S. reaction the AIDS crisis. The first part, *Millennium Approaches* won best Play the previous season, making Kushner the first dramatist to win back-to-back Tonys.

MUSICAL

Beauty and the Beast
Cyrano—The Musical
A Grand Night for Sinning
Passion •

ACTOR (PLAY)

Brian Bedford (*Timon of Athens*)
Christopher Plummer (*No Man's Land*)
Stephen Spinella (*Angels in America: Perestroika*)
Sam Waterston (*Abe Lincoln in Illinois*)

Spinella had won a Featured Actor (Play) Tony the year before for playing the same character (Prior Walter, a young man struck with AIDS and haunted by heavenly beings) in the first part of *Angels*. With this year's win, he became the first person to win two Tonys for portraying the same person.

ACTRESS (PLAY)

Nancy Marchand (*Black Comedy*)
Diana Rigg (*Medea*)
Joan Rivers (*Sally Marr...and her escorts*)
Anna Deavere Smith (*Twilight: Los Angeles, 1992*)

Diana Rigg is the third actress to be Tonyed for portraying Medea, Euripides' tragic heroine who murders her own children to revenge herself on her unfaithful husband. The others are Judith Anderson (1947–48) and Zoe Caldwell (1981–82).

ACTOR (MUSICAL)

Boyd Gaines (*She Loves Me*)
Victor Garber (*Damn Yankees*)
Terrence Mann (*Beauty and the Beast*)
Jere Shea (*Passion*)

ACTRESS (MUSICAL)

Susan Egan (*Beauty and the Beast*)
Dee Hoty (*The Best Little Whorehouse Goes Public*)
Judy Kuhn (*She Loves Me*)
Donna Murphy (*Passion*)

FEATURED ACTOR (PLAY)

Larry Bryggman (*Picnic*)
David Marshall Grant (*Angels in America: Perestroika*)
Gregory Itzin (*The Kentucky Cycle*)
Jeffrey Wright (*Angels in America: Perestroika*)

FEATURED ACTRESS (PLAY)

Jane Adams (*An Inspector Calls*)
Debra Monk (*Picnic*)
Jeanne Paulsen (*The Kentucky Cycle*)
Anne Pitoniak (*Picnic*)

FEATURED ACTOR (MUSICAL)

Tom Aldredge (*Passion*)
Gary Beach (*Beauty and the Beast*)
Jarrod Emick (*Damn Yankees*)
Jonathan Freeman (*She Loves Me*)

FEATURED ACTRESS (MUSICAL)

Marcia Lewis (*Grease*)
Sally Mayes (*She Loves Me*)
Marin Mazzie (*Passion*)
Audra Ann McDonald (*Carousel*)

OTHER AWARDS

Revival (Play): *An Inspector Calls*; Revival (Musical): *Carousel*; Director (Play): Stephen Daldry (*An Inspector Calls*); Director (Musical): Nicholas Hytner (*Carousel*); Score: Stephen Sondheim (*Passion*); Book of a Musical: James Lapine (*Passion*); Choreography: Sir Kenneth MacMillan, (*Carousel*), awarded posthumously; Set Design: Bob Crowley (*Carousel*); Costume Design: Ann Hould-Ward (*Beauty and the Beast*); Lighting Design: Rick Fisher (*An Inspector Calls*)

There were so many revivals, the category was split into two, one for straight plays and one for musical reproductions.

In a sparse year for musicals, there were few candidates for best book. Rather than nominate the universally panned *The Best Little Whorehouse Goes Public*, the Nominating Committee put up *A Grand Night for Singing*, a limited-run, plotless revue of Rodgers and Hammerstein songs. The show didn't even have a program credit for the author of the book (only a few lines to string the numbers together), so director Walter Bobbie received the nomination.

SPECIAL AWARDS

Jessica Tandy and Hume Cronyn (Lifetime Achievement); McCarter Theatre, Princeton, NJ (Regional Theatre)

The Tonys were hosted by Sir Anthony Hopkins and Amy Irving, who was not nominated for her performance in Arthur Miller's *Broken Glass*. The telecast began with a salute to the numerous musical revivals of the season. Victor Garber as Applegate, the Devil character he was playing in *Damn Yankees*, introduced numbers from new productions of such old favorites as *Carousel, She Loves Me, Grease,* and *Yankees.* Then 106-year-old George Abbott, director of the original *Yankees*, was wheeled out and officially started the show.

Glenn Close presented an award from the set of *Sunset Boulevard*, then playing in Los Angeles. In another remote transmission, the cast of Harold Prince's restaging of *Show Boat* performed "Old Man River" from Toronto. Once again, winners were given only thirty seconds to express their thanks before the orchestra starting playing to cut them off. In lieu of acceptance speeches all the design nominees gave brief videotaped presentations explaining their functions and how they contribute to a production.

The Tonys had heavy competition from the NBA basketball finals. The telecast lost the ratings match to the third playoff game between the Knicks and the Rangers.

THE DRAMA DESK AWARDS

PLAYS

Play: *Angels in America: Perestroika* by Tony Kushner; Actor: Stephen Spinella (*Angels in America: Perestroika*); Actress: Myra Carter (*Three Tall Women*); Featured Actor: Jeffrey Wright (*Angels in America: Perestroika*); Featured Actress: Jane Adams (*An Inspector Calls*); Director: Stephen Daldry (*An Inspector Calls*); Music in a Play: Stephen Warbeck (*An Inspector Calls*); Revival: *An Inspector Calls*

MUSICALS

Musical: *Passion*; Actor: Boyd Gaines (*She Loves Me*); Actress: Donna Murphy (*Passion*); Featured Actor: Jarrod Emick (*Damn Yankees*); Featured Actress: Audra Ann MacDonald (*Carousel*); Director: Nicholas Hytner (*Carousel*); Music: Stephen Sondheim (*Passion*); Lyrics: Stephen Sondheim (*Passion*); Book: James Lapine (*Passion*); Orchestration: Jonathan Tunick (*Passion*); Revival: *She Loves Me*; Choreography: Sir Kenneth MacMillan, Jane Elliott (*Carousel*); Revue: *Howard Crabtree's Whoop-De-Doo*

OTHER AWARDS

One-Person Show: Anna Deavere Smith (*Twilight: Los Angeles, 1992*); Unique Theatrical Experience: *Stomp*; Set Design: Ian MacNeil (*An Inspector Calls*); Costume Design: Howard Crabtree (*Howard Crabtree's Whoop-De-Doo*); Lighting Design: Rick Fisher (*An Inspector Calls*); Sound Design: John A. Leonard (*Medea*); Special Effects: Gregory Meeh (*An Inspector Calls*)

SPECIAL AWARDS

John Willis, editor of the *Theatre World* series; Janet Hayes Walker, artistic director of the York Theatre Company

THE NEW YORK DRAMA CRITICS CIRCLE AWARDS

BEST PLAY

Three Tall Women by Edward Albee

SPECIAL CITATION

Anna Deavere Smith for her unique contribution to the theatrical form including *Fires in the Mirror* and *Twilight: Los Angeles, 1992*

THE PULITZER PRIZE FOR DRAMA

Three Tall Women by Edward Albee

THE OBIE AWARDS

BEST NEW PLAY

Twilight: Los Angeles, 1992 by Anna Deavere Smith

SUSTAINED ACHIEVEMENT

Edward Albee

PLAYWRITING

Eric Bogosian (*Pounding Nails in the Floor with My Forehead*); Howard Korder (*The Lights*)

DIRECTION

Andre Ernotte (*Christina Alberta's Father*); David Warren (*Pterodactyls*)

PERFORMANCES

Carolee Carmello (*Hello, Again*); Myra Carter (*Three Tall Women*); Gail Grate, Michael Potts (*The America Play*); Danny Hoch (*Some People*); Judith Ivey (*The Moonshot Tape*); Peter Francis James (*The Maids*); Jefferson Mays (*Orestes*); Christopher McCann (*The Lights*); Tom Nellis (*The Medium*) Alice Playten (*First Lady Suite*); Robert Stanton (*All in the Timing*)

Sixty-four-year-old Myra Carter, who won an Obie for playing a ninety-two-year-old matriarch in *Three Tall Women*, stated, "Thank God you got me here before I died—on stage or off."

DESIGN

Kyle Chepulis (sets); Brian MacDevitt (lighting)

SPECIAL CITATIONS

Ain Gordon, David Gordon, Valda Setterfield (*The Family Business*); playwright Holly Hughes; Ricky Jay (*Ricky Jay and His 52 Assistants*); Michael John LaChiusa (*First Lady Suite, Hello Again*); John Moran and Bob McGrath (*Everyday Newt Burman, Fragments*); Tom Noonan (*Wifey*); Claudia Shear (*Blown Sideways through Life*); *Stomp*

OBIE GRANTS

The Changing Scene; HERE

THE OUTER CRITICS CIRCLE AWARDS

Broadway Play: *Angels in America, Parts I and II: Millennium Approaches* and *Perestroika*; Broadway Musical: *Kiss of the Spider Woman*; Off-Broadway Play: *Three Tall Women*; Off-Broadway Musical:

Annie Warbucks; Actor (Play): Sam Waterston (*Abe Lincoln in Illinois*); Actress (Play): Myra Carter (*Three Tall Women*); Actor (Musical): Boyd Gaines (*She Loves Me*); Actress (Musical) (tie): Audra Ann McDonald (*Carousel*) and Chita Rivera (*Kiss of the Spider Woman*); Debut Performances: Jeffrey Wright (*Angels in America*), Hynden Walch (*The Rise and Fall of Little Voice*); Director (Play): George C. Wolfe (*Angels in America* and *Twilight: Los Angeles, 1992*); Director (Musical): Scott Ellis (*She Loves Me*); Choreography: Rob Marshall (*She Loves Me* and *Damn Yankees*); Set, Costume, and Lighting Design: *Carousel*; Revival (Play): *An Inspector Calls*; Revival (Musical): *She Loves Me*; John Gassner Playwriting Award: David Ives (*All in the Timing*); Special Achievement Awards: Anna Deavere Smith, Lucille Lortel, Jane Alexander

THE TONY AWARDS

PLAY
Arcadia by Tom Stoppard
Having Our Say by Emily Mann
Indiscretions by Jean Cocteau, translated
   by Jeremy Sams
Love! Valour! Compassion! by Terrence McNally

Terrence McNally never got to thank anyone for his outstanding Play Tony. The author of *Love! Valour! Compassion!*, a touching comedy-drama of eight gay friends over three holiday weekends, was abrubtly cut off as he was starting his acceptance speech. Once again, the Tonys were tight on time and winners were only allowed thirty seconds to speak. The top play award was delivered at the end of the evening and CBS was threatening to axe the network feed at 11 p.m. promptly. *Love!* producers Lynn Meadow and Barry Grove spoke first, using up the allotted thirty seconds. McNally stepped up to the microphone and the show went to a commercial. The Dramatists Guild, the playwrights' union, filed a formal protest on McNally's behalf.

MUSICAL
Smokey Joe's Cafe
Sunset Boulevard

The 1994–95 season was a barren year for new musicals. The only eligible nominees in this category were *Smokey Joe's Cafe*, a plotless revue of rock and pop songs by Jerry Leiber and Mike Stoller, and *Sunset Boulevard*, a British import from Andrew Lloyd Webber, based on the classic 1950 film.

ACTOR (PLAY)
Brian Bedford (*The Moliere Comedies*)
Ralph Fiennes (*Hamlet*)
Roger Rees (*Indiscretions*)
Joe Sears (*A Tuna Christmas*)

Major omissions for actor in a play included highly praised performances by Nathan Lane in *Love! Valour! Compassion!* and Philip Bosco in *The Heiress*. Lane co-hosted the Tonys and mocked his nonnomination. "Not being nominated is like the Nixon stamp," he quipped. "You can lick it, but it leaves a bad taste in your mouth." The Drama Desk considered Lane a featured actor and gave him its award.

ACTRESS (PLAY)
Mary Alice (*Having Our Say*)
Eileen Atkins (*Indiscretions*)
Cherry Jones (*The Heiress*)
Helen Mirren (*A Month in the Country*)

ACTOR (MUSICAL)
Matthew Broderick (*How to Succeed in Business without Really Trying*)
Alan Campbell (*Sunset Boulevard*)
Mark Jacoby (*Show Boat*)
John McMartin (*Show Boat*)

ACTRESS (MUSICAL)
Glenn Close (*Sunset Boulevard*)
Rebecca Luker (*Show Boat*)

FEATURED ACTOR (PLAY)
Stephen Bogardus (*Love! Valour! Compassion!*)
John Glover (*Love! Valour! Compassion!*)
Anthony Heald (*Love! Valour! Compassion!*)
Jude Law (*Indiscretions*)

FEATURED ACTRESS (PLAY)
Suzanne Bertish (*The Moliere Comedies*)
Cynthia Nixon (*Indiscretions*)
Mercedes Ruehl (*The Shadow Box*)
Frances Sternhagen (*The Heiress*)

FEATURED ACTOR (MUSICAL)
Michel Bell (*Show Boat*)
Joel Blum (*Show Boat*)
Victor Trent Cook (*Smokey Joe's Cafe*)
George Hearn (*Sunset Boulevard*)

FEATURED ACTRESS (MUSICAL)
Gretha Boston (*Show Boat*)
Brenda Braxton (*Smokey Joe's Cafe*)
B. J. Crosby (*Smokey Joe's Cafe*)
DeLee Lively (*Smokey Joe's Cafe*)

OTHER AWARDS
Revival (Play): *The Heiress*; Revival (Musical): *Show Boat*; Director (Play): Gerald Guttierez (*The Heiress*): Director (Musical): Harold Prince (*Show Boat*); Score: Andrew Lloyd Webber, Don Black, Christopher Hampton (*Sunset Boulevard*); Book of a Musical: Don Black, Christopher Hampton (*Sunset Boulevard*); Choreography: Susan Stroman (*Show Boat*); Set Design: John Napier (*Sunset Boulevard*); Costume Design: Florence Klotz (*Show Boat*); Lighting Design: Andrew Bridge (*Sunset Boulevard*)

Harold Prince broke his own record with this win, making his total score of Tonys an even twenty, the most for any individual. Since *Sunset Boulevard* was the only Broadway musical of the season to boast an original score and book, it was the *de facto* winner in both categories.

SPECIAL AWARDS
Carol Channing, Harvey Sabinson (Lifetime Achievement); Goodspeed Opera House, East Haddam, CN (Outstanding Regional Theatre); National Endowment for the Arts

Broadway did not have much to offer this year. The number of shows presented during the season was an almost record low of twenty-eight. The Tonys put the best possible face on a depressing situation. Production numbers included the male cast members of *Smokey Joe's Cafe* singing "On Broadway" on the street itself and then entering the theater, and Tony winner Glenn Close demonstrating her mad passion as the former silent-screen star Norma Desmond with "Early Morning Madness" from *Sunset Boulevard*. Close co-hosted the ceremony with Gregory Hines and Nathan Lane, who stole the show with his inspired ad-libs. In one segment, he entered wearing a costume he wore from *Love! Valour! Compassion!*—high heels, an apron, sunglasses, a bonnet, and nothing else. "If I were to do a handstand now, the ratings would go through the roof," he announced.

The issue of including Off-Broadway in the Tonys was settled once and for all. The League of Off-Broadway Producers rejected a tentative move by the Tony Administration Committee to study the possibility of a special Off-Broadway Tony.

THE DRAMA DESK AWARDS

PLAYS
Play: *Love! Valour! Compassion!* by Terrence McNally; Actor: Ralph Fiennes (*Hamlet*); Actress: Cherry Jones (*The Heiress*); Featured Actor: Nathan Lane (*Love! Valour! Compassion!*); Featured Actress (tie): Tara FitzGerald (*Hamlet*) and Hallie Foote (The Horton Foote Plays); Director: Gerald Guttierez (*The Heiress*); Revival/Reinterpretation: *The Heiress*; One-Person/Solo Show: James Lescene (*Word of Mouth*); Unique Theatrical Experience: *Travels with My Aunt*

MUSICALS
Musical Presentation: *Show Boat*; Actor: Matthew Broderick (*How to Succeed . . .*); Actress: Glenn Close (*Sunset Boulevard*); Director: Harold Prince (*Show Boat*)

OTHER AWARDS
Set Design: Eugene Lee (*Show Boat*); Costume Design: Florence Klotz (*Show Boat*); Lighting Design: Richard Pilbrow (*Show Boat*)

SPECIAL AWARDS
Eileen Atkins (performance in *Indiscrections* and performance and playwriting in *Vita & Virginia*); Otis Guernsey, editor of the annual *Best Plays*

volumes; The Non-Traditional Casting Project; theater caricaturist Sam Norkin; The Barrow Group (Outstanding Off-Off-Broadway Theatre Company)

With scant offerings in the musical field, the Drama Desk eliminated several categories including Choreography, Music and Lyrics, and Featured Actor and Featured Actress in a Musical. There were so few new musicals that the categories for musical revivals and original tuners were combined into one: Musical Presentation. The winner was Harold Prince's restaging of *Show Boat*.

Gerald Guttierez, director of *The Heiress*, stopped the show by bringing his dog onstage. "I couldn't get a sitter," he explained upon accepting his award.

THE NEW YORK DRAMA CRITICS CIRCLE AWARDS

BEST PLAY
Arcadia by Tom Stoppard

BEST AMERICAN PLAY
Love! Valour! Compassion! by Terrence McNally

SPECIAL AWARD
The Signature Theatre Company

THE PULITZER PRIZE FOR DRAMA

The Young Man from Atlanta by Horton Foote

THE OBIE AWARDS

BEST NEW PLAY
The Cryptogram by David Mamet

SUSTAINED ACHIEVEMENT
Ming Cho Lee

PLAYWRITING
David Hancock (*The Convention of Cartography*); Tony Kushner (*Slavs*); Terrence McNally (*Love! Valour! Compassion!*); Susan Miller (*My Left Breast*)

DIRECTION
Robert Falls (*subUrbia*); Don Scardino (*A Cheever Evening*); Susan Shulman (*Merrily We Roll Along*)

PERFORMANCE
Joanna Adler (*The Boys in the Basement*); Eileen Atkins, Vanessa Redgrave (*Vita & Virginia*); Paul Calderon (*Blade to the Heat*); Malcolm Gets (*Merrily We Roll Along* and *Two Gentlemen of Verona*); Felicity Huffman (*The Cryptogram*); Linda Lavin (*Death-Defying Acts*); Ron Leibman (*The Merchant of Venice*); Camryn Manheim (*Missing Persons*); Kristine Nielsen (*Dog Opera*); Mary Beth Peil (*The Naked Truth, Missing Persons,* and *A Cheever Evening*); Barbara Eda-Young (*Slavs*); the cast of *Love! Valour! Compassion!* and its director Joe Mantello for ensemble performance

DESIGN
Wendall K. Harrington (sustained excellence of projection); Jennifer von Mayrhauser (sustained excellence of costume design)

SPECIAL CITATIONS
Vernel Bagneris, Morten Gunnar Larsen (*Jelly Roll*); The Five Lesbian Brothers (*The Secretaries*); The New Group (*Ecstasy*); Dael Orlandersmith (*Beauty's Daughter*); Amy and David Sedaris (*One Woman Shoe*)

OBIE GRANTS
The Archives at La MaMa; Blueprint Series at Ontologic-Hysteric Theatre; nada

The fortieth annual Obie Awards were hosted by former winner Hector Elizondo (*Steambath*, 1970–71) and Anne Meara, who was appearing Off-Broadway in her own comedy, *After-Play*. The rowdy, rambling evening was three and a quarter hours long and televised over local cable channel New York-1 News. Meara joked with her husband Jerry Stiller, who was seated in the audience, "Jerry, you've grown a beard since this thing started."

THE OUTER CRITICS CIRCLE AWARDS

Broadway Play: *Love! Valour! Compassion!*; Broadway Musical: *Sunset Boulevard*; Off-Broadway Play: *Camping with Henry and Tom*; Off-Broadway Musical: *Jelly Roll*; Actor (Play): Nathan Lane (*Love! Valour! Compassion!*); Actress (Play): Cherry Jones (*The Heiress*); Actor (Musical): Matthew

Broderick (*How to Succeed . . .*); Actress (Musical): Glenn Close (*Sunset Boulevard*); Debut Performances: Billy Crudup (*Arcadia*), Helen Mirren (*A Month in the Country*); Director (Play): Joe Mantello (*Love! Valour! Compassion!*); Director (Musical): Harold Prince (*Show Boat*); Choreography: Susan Stroman (*A Christmas Carol* and *Show Boat*); Set, Costume, and Lighting Design: *Show Boat*; Revival (Play): *The Heiress*; Revival (Musical): *Show Boat*; John Gassner Playwriting Award: Anne Meara (*After-Play*); Solo Performance: James Lescene (*Word of Mouth*); Special Achievement Awards: Jerry Lewis, The Horton Foote Plays presented by Signature Theatre Company, Encores! Concert series at City Center, cast of *Travels with My Aunt* (ensemble performance)

THE TONY AWARDS

PLAY

Buried Child by Sam Shepard
Master Class by Terrence McNally
Racing Demon by David Hare
Seven Guitars by August Wilson

Terrence McNally finally got to finish his acceptance speech. Because of time constraints, the playwright had been cut off at the previous Tonys when his *Love! Valour! Compassion!* won for Best Play. This year's win was for *Master Class*, an intense portrait of the opera diva Maria Callas. Zoe Caldwell won her fourth Tony for her performance in the lead role. McNally joined Tony Kushner (*Angels in America*) as the only two playwrights to win consecutive best Play Tonys.

MUSICAL

Bring in 'da Noise / Bring in 'da Funk
Chronicle of a Death Foretold
Rent
Swinging on a Star

Rent was the big winner at the '95–'96 Tonys, copping a total of four awards. The rock update of *La Boheme*, set in the East Village, gained tremendous

publicity when its young author Jonathan Larsen died on the night of the first preview performance at Off-Broadway's New York Theatre Workshop. Smash reviews and sell-out crowds prompted a move to Broadway's Nederlander Theatre.

But the tragic backstage story of *Rent* was upstaged when the Tony nominations were announced. *Rent* raked in ten nominations, but two other large-scale shows, *Victor/Victoria* and *Big*, were snubbed. Neither was nominated for best Musical and *V/V*'s only nod of recognition came in the form of a nomination for Julie Andrews for best Actress (Musical). Much to the consternation of Broadway insiders, two long-closed shows which had received mixed reviews, *Chronicle of a Death Foretold* and *Swinging on a Star*, filled in the slots for best Musical.

After the following Wednesday matinee performance of *V/V*, Andrews informed the audience (and the press, which had been invited) that she would stand with her "egregiously overlooked" fellow cast members and reject her nomination. The Tony Administration Committee left her name on the ballot, but the award went to Donna Murphy of *The King and I*. Andrews won and quietly accepted a Drama Desk Award and Outer Critics Circle Award.

ACTOR (PLAY)

Philip Bosco (*Moon over Buffalo*)
George Grizzard (*A Delicate Balance*)
George C. Scott (*Inherit the Wind*)
Martin Shaw (*An Ideal Husband*)

ACTRESS (PLAY)

Carol Burnett (*Moon over Buffalo*)
Zoe Caldwell (*Master Class*)
Rosemary Harris (*A Delicate Balance*)
Elaine Stritch (*A Delicate Balance*)

ACTOR (MUSICAL)

Savion Glover (*Noise/Funk*)
Nathan Lane (*A Funny Thing Happened on the Way to the Forum*)
Adam Pascal (*Rent*)
Lou Diamond Phillips (*The King and I*)

ACTRESS (MUSICAL)
Julie Andrews (*Victor/Victoria*)
Christa Moore (*Big*)
Donna Murphy (*The King and I*)
Daphne Rubin-Vega (*Rent*)

FEATURED ACTOR (PLAY)
James Gammon (*Buried Child*)
Roger Robinson (*Seven Guitars*)
Reg Rogers (*Holiday*)
Ruben Santiago-Hudson (*Seven Guitars*)

FEATURED ACTRESS (PLAY)
Viola Davis (*Seven Guitars*)
Audra MacDonald (*Master Class*)
Michele Shay (*Seven Guitars*)
Lois Smith (*Buried Child*)

FEATURED ACTOR (MUSICAL)
Wilson Jermaine Heredia (*Rent*)
Lewis J. Stadlen (*A Funny Thing…Forum*)
Brett Tabisel (*Big*)
Scott Wise (*State Fair*)

FEATURED ACTRESS (MUSICAL)
Joohee Choi (*The King and I*)
Veanne Cox (*Company*)
Ann Duquesnay (*Noise/Funk*)
Idina Menzel (*Rent*)

OTHER AWARDS
Revival (Play): *A Delicate Balance*; Revival (Musical): *The King and I*; Director (Play): Gerald Guttierez (*A Delicate Balance*); Director (Musical): George C. Wolfe (*Noise/Funk*); Score and Book of a Musical: Jonathan Larson (*Rent*); Choreography: Savion Glover (*Noise/Funk*); Set Design: Brian Thompson (*The King and I*); Costume Design: Roger Kirk (*The King and I*); Lighting Design: Jules Fisher, Peggy Eisenhauer (*Noise/Funk*)

The Nominating Committee made a special note with the best Score category. Only four songs from stage version of *State Fair* were eligible because the rest of the score had been originally written by Rodgers and Hammerstein for the 1945 screen edition. The quartet of nominated tunes were from other R&H stage shows. (In 1973–74, the songs from another movie-to-stage musical *Gigi* won the Tony for best Score, but the rules had been changed since then.)

As a publicity stunt, *State Fair* producer David Merrick sent Tony voters cotton balls to stick in their ears when the noneligible songs were sung. Merrick later launched a lawsuit against the Committee which was thrown out of court just before the awards ceremony.

SPECIAL AWARD
Alley Theatre, Houston, TX (Outstanding Regional Theatre)

"Welcome to the Tabloid Tonys," exhorted host Nathan Lane at the top of the ceremony. Indeed, there was so much gossip and controversy surrounding the event, the fact that this was the Tonys' fiftieth anniversary almost seemed like a side issue. In addition to Julie Andrews' rejection of her nomination and the omissions of *Big* and *Victor/Victoria* from the best Musical category, there was David Merrick's lawsuit against the Nominating Committee for failing to include all of Rodgers and Hammerstein's score from his production of *State Fair* and a threatened strike by the stagehands' union. Merrick's suit was thrown out of court and the strike was settled before the broadcast.

In order to include numbers from as many shows as possible, the majority of the awards were presented before the telecast and edited versions of the acceptance speeches were shown to the viewing audience. In addition to excerpts from the four best Musical candidates, there were moments from *Big*, *State Fair* and the revivals of *The King and I* and *A Funny Thing Happened on the Way to the Forum*. Andrews and the producers of *Victor/Victoria* declined to participate. With the exception of the scenes from *Rent* and *Bring in 'da Noise, Bring in 'da Funk*, the production numbers were rushed.

As for celebrating the awards' golden anniversary, there were quick clips and tributes, but the production staff did not have much to choose from. Alexander Cohen, the impresario of the Tonys from 1966–67 to 1985–86, refused to release the rights to the ceremonies he produced.

THE DRAMA DESK AWARDS

PLAYS
Play: *Master Class* by Terrence McNally; Actor: Frank Langella (*The Father*); Actress: Zoe Caldwell (*Master Class*); Featured Actor: Martin Shaw (*An Ideal Husband*); Featured Actress: Elaine Stritch (*A Delicate Balance*); Director: Gerald Guttierez (*A Delicate Balance*); Revival: *A Delicate Balance*; Solo/One-Person Show: Mary Louise Wilson (*Full Gallop*)

MUSICALS
Musical: *Rent*; Actor: Nathan Lane (*A Funny Thing...Forum*); Actress: Julie Andrews (*Victor/Victoria*); Featured Actor: Wilson Jermaine Heredia (*Rent*); Featured Actress: Rachel York (*Victor/Victoria*); Director: Christopher Renshaw (*The King and I*); Revival: *The King and I*; Choreography: Savion Glover (*Noise/Funk*); Music, Lyrics, and Book: Jonathan Larson (*Rent*); Orchestration: Steve Skinner (*Rent*)

OTHER AWARDS
Set Design (Play): Scott Bradley (*Seven Guitars*); Set Design (Musical): Brian Thomson (*The King and I*); Costume Design: Roger Kirk (*The King and I*); Lighting Design: Jules Fisher, Peggy Eisenhauer (*Noise/Funk*); Sound Design: Dan Moses Schreier (*Floyd Collins*)

SPECIAL AWARDS
George C. Scott (Lifetime Achievement in the Theatre); Signature Theatre Company; Theatreworks/USA; Repertorio Espanol

The Drama Desks were broadcast on local cable channel New York-1 News.

THE NEW YORK DRAMA CRITICS CIRCLE AWARDS

BEST PLAY
Seven Guitars by August Wilson

BEST FOREIGN PLAY
Molly Sweeney by Brian Friel

BEST MUSICAL
Rent by Jonathan Larson

SPECIAL AWARD
Encores! The Great American Musicals in Concert

THE PULITZER PRIZE FOR DRAMA
Rent by Jonathan Larson

THE OBIE AWARDS

BEST NEW PLAYS
June and Jean in Concert by Adrienne Kennedy and *Sleep Deprivation Chamber* by Adrienne and Adam Kennedy

SUSTAINED ACHIEVEMENT
Uta Hagen

DISTINGUISHED PLAYWRIGHTING
Ain Gordon (*Wally's Ghost*); Suzan-Lori Parks (*Venus*); Donald Marguiles (*The Model Apartment*); Douglas Wright (*Quills*)

DIRECTION
Ingmar Bergman (sustained excellence); Douglas Hughes (*The Grey Zone*)

PERFORMANCES
Julie Archer (design and construction) and Barbara Pollitt (performance manipulation) for the puppet Rose the Dog (*An Epidog*); Gerry Bamman (*Nixon's Nixon*); Kathleen Chalfant (sustained excellence); Lisagay Hamilton (*Valley Song*); Terri Klausner (*Bed and Sofa*); Tom McGowan (*The Food Chain*); Mark Nelson (*Picasso at the Lapin Agile*); Adina Porter (*Venus*); Marty Pottenger (*City Water Tunnel No. 3*); Virginia Rambal (*Troya de Merica* and *La Dama Duenda*); Rocco Sisto (*Quills*); Steven Skybell (*Antigone in New York*); Derek Smith (*The Green Bird*); Henry Stram (sustained excellence); James Urbaniak (*The Universe*); Mary Louise Wilson (*Full Gallop*); the entire ensemble of *Rent*

DESIGN
Jeffrey S. Koger (sustained excellence in lighting design); Neil Patel (sustained excellence in set design)

SPECIAL CITATIONS

Jonathan Larson (book and score) for *Rent*; Adam Guetell (music) and Bruce Coughlin (orchestrations) for *Floyd Collins*; Polly Pen (music in *Bed and Sofa*); Savion Glover (choreography and performance in *Noise/Funk*); Scott Elliot (direction) and the cast of *Curtains* (ensemble performance); David Van Teighem (sustained excellence of music); Repertorio Espanol's "New Voices" Program

OBIE GRANTS

New Georges; TEBA Teatro Experimental Blue Amigos

THE OUTER CRITICS CIRCLE AWARDS

Broadway Play: *Master Class*; Broadway Musical: *Victor/Victoria*; Off-Broadway Play (tie): *Molly Sweeney* and *Picasso at the Lapin Agile*; Off-Broadway Musical: *Rent*; Actor (Play): George C. Scott (*Inherit the Wind*); Actress (Play): Zoe Caldwell (*Master Class*); Actor (Musical): Nathan Lane (*A Funny Thing Happened…Forum*); Actress (Musical): Julie Andrews (*Victor/Victoria*); Debut Performances: Lou Diamond Phillips (*The King and I*), Karen Kay Cody (*Master Class*); Director (Play): Lloyd Richards (*Seven Guitars*); Director (Musical): Jerry Zaks (*A Funny Thing Happened…Forum*); Choreography: Savion Glover (*Noise/Funk*); Set, Costume, and Lighting Design: *The King and I*; Revival (Play): *Inherit the Wind*; Revival (Musical): *The King and I*; Solo Performance: Patti LuPone (*Patti LuPone on Broadway*); John Gassner Playwriting Award: Steve Martin (*Picasso at the Lapin Agile*); Special Achievement Awards: Carol Channing, Betty Corwin of the New York Public Library's Theatre on Film and Tape Archive, the cast of *Seven Guitars* (ensemble performance)

1996-97

THE TONY AWARDS

PLAY
The Last Night of Ballyhoo by Alfred Uhry
Skylight by David Hare

Stanley by Pam Gems
The Young Man from Atlanta by Horton Foote

MUSICAL
Juan Darien, A Carnival Mass
The Life
Steel Pier
Titanic

A musical about the sinking of the Titanic? Broadway insiders predicted instant disaster. Preview performances were beset with technical problems involving the complicated scenery. But when the show opened, it was not as bad as the subject matter indicated. The remaining Tony-nominated musicals of the season (*The Life*, *Steel Pier*, and the closed *Juan Darien, A Carnival Mass*) were received with mixed reviews and *Titanic* became the dark-horse winner of five awards. *The Life*, a seamy and sassy show about pimps and prostitutes in a pre-Disney Times Square, was the top choice of the Drama Desk and Outer Critics voters. A hit revival of *Chicago* toddled off with six Tonys, the most of any show this season.

ACTOR (PLAY)
Brian Bedford (*London Assurance*)
Michael Gambon (*Skylight*)
Christopher Plummer (*Barrymore*)
Anthony Sher (*Stanley*)

ACTRESS (PLAY)
Julie Harris (*The Gin Game*)
Shirley Knight (*The Young Man from Atlanta*)
Janet McTeer (*A Doll's House*)
Lia Williams (*Skylight*)

This was Julie Harris's tenth Tony nomination, adding to her record as the performer most nominated for Broadway's top award.

ACTOR (MUSICAL)
Robert Cuccioli (*Jekyll & Hyde*)
Jim Dale (*Candide*)
Daniel McDonald (*Steel Pier*)
James Naughton (*Chicago*)

ACTRESS (MUSICAL)
Pamela Isaacs (*The Life*)

Bebe Neuwirth (*Chicago*)
Tonya Pinkins (*Play On!*)
Karen Ziemba (*Steel Pier*)

FEATURED ACTOR (PLAY)
Terry Beaver (*The Last Night of Ballyhoo*)
Will Biff McGuire (*The Young Man from Atlanta*)
Brian Murray (*The Little Foxes*)
Owen Teale (*A Doll's House*)

FEATURED ACTRESS (PLAY)
Helen Carey (*London Assurance*)
Dana Ivey (*The Last Night of Ballyhoo*)
Lynne Thigpen (*An American Daughter*)
Celia Weston (*The Last Night of Ballyhoo*)

FEATURED ACTOR (MUSICAL)
Joel Blum (*Steel Pier*)
Chuck Cooper (*The Life*)
Andre De Shields (*Play On!*)
Sam Harris (*The Life*)

FEATURED ACTRESS (MUSICAL)
Marcia Lewis (*Chicago*)
Andrea Martin (*Candide*)
Debra Monk (*Steel Pier*)
Lillias White (*The Life*)

OTHER AWARDS
Revival (Play): *A Doll's House*; Revival (Musical): *Chicago*; Director (Play): Anthony Page (*A Doll's House*); Director (Musical): Walter Bobbie (*Chicago*); Score: Maury Yeston (*Titanic*); Book of a Musical: Peter Stone (*Titanic*); Choreography: Ann Reinking (*Chicago*); Set Design: Stewart Laing (*Titanic*); Costume Design: Judith Dolan (*Candide*); Lighting Design: Ken Billington (*Chicago*); Orchestration: Jonathan Tunick (*Titanic*)

The category of Orchestration was added this year.

SPECIAL AWARDS
Bernard Jacobs (Lifetime Achievement, posthumous); Berkeley Repertory Theatre, Berkeley, CA (Outstanding Regional Theatre)

It was Rosie to the rescue of the Tonys. Comedienne Rosie O'Donnell hosted the fifty-first annual awards. A tremendous fan of Broadway whose only major theater credit was a supporting role in the revival of *Grease*, O'Donnell showed her love of the stage by constantly promoting the Tonys on her hit daytime talk fest. Cast members from all the nominated productions performed on the show and drummed up viewer interest. Other O'Donnell ideas included holding the ceremony at Radio City Music Hall (a first) and making tickets available to the general public. A few theater vets grumbled at having a TV star act as emcee of Broadway's biggest night and holding the event in a non-Broadway house.

But all quibbles were swept aside when the ratings came in. The show drew a 16 share (percentage of TVs in use) and a 9.6 rating (percentage of all TV households). That was a whopping 48 percent increase from the previous year's 11 share and 6.5 rating, the lowest of any Tonycast ever.

In another innovation, the program was split between two networks. In order to accommodate musical numbers from all the nominated new shows and revivals and give the winners more than thirty seconds to express their thanks, an extra hour was donated by PBS. From 8 p.m. to 9 p.m. on participating Public Broadcasting stations, awards for design, direction, and musical score and book were presented (along with documentary segments on their contributions to their respective productions). From 9 p.m. to 11 p.m., CBS presented the bulk of the awards ceremony, the excerpted production numbers, and an opening number featuring O'Donnell singing and dancing with the casts of six hold-over Broadway hits. Not only was the split ceremony a ratings success, it also came in exactly on time—another rare Tony occurrence.

THE DRAMA DESK AWARDS

PLAYS
Play: *How I Learned to Drive* by Paula Vogel; Actor (tie): David Morse (*How I Learned to Drive*) and Christopher Plummer (*Barrymore*); Actress: Janet McTeer (*A Doll's House*); Featured Actor: Brian Murray (*The Little Foxes*); Featured Actress: Dana Ivey (*The Last Night of Ballyhoo* and *Sex and Longing*); Director: Mark Brokaw (*How I Learned*

to Drive); Revival: *A Doll's House*; Solo/One-Person Show: Fiona Shaw (*The Waste Land*)

MUSICALS

Musical: *The Life*; Actor: Robert Cuccioli (*Jekyll & Hyde*); Actress: Bebe Neuwirth (*Chicago*); Featured Actor: Joel Grey (*Chicago*); Featured Actress: Lillias White (*The Life*); Director: Walter Bobbie (*Chicago*); Revival: *Chicago*; Musical Revue: *Howard Crabtree's When Pigs Fly*; Music: Cy Coleman (*The Life*); Lyrics: Gerard Alessandrini (*Forbidden Broadway Strikes Back!*); Orchestration: Jonathan Tunick (*Titanic*); Choreography: Ann Reinking (*Chicago*)

OTHER AWARDS

Set Design (Play): David Gallo, Jan Hartley (*Bunny Bunny*); Set Design (Musical): Robin Phillips, James Noone, Christina Poddubiuk (*Jekyll & Hyde*); Costume Design: Howard Crabtree (*Howard Crabtree's When Pigs Fly*); Lighting Design: Ken Billington (*Chicago*); Sound Design: John Gromada (*The Skriker*); Unique Theatrical Experience: *The Waste Land*

SPECIAL AWARD

Moscow Theatre Sovremmenik

The Drama Desks were held in a Broadway theater (the Booth) and broadcast for the second consecutive year on New York-1 News, a local cable channel. Like the Tony ceremony, the DD show featured musical numbers from the nominated shows including selections from *Jekyll & Hyde, Violet,* and *Howard Crabtree's When Pigs Fly* which were not on the Tony telecast.

THE NEW YORK DRAMA CRITICS CIRCLE AWARDS

BEST PLAY
How I Learned to Drive by Paula Vogel

BEST FOREIGN PLAY
Skylight by David Hare

BEST MUSICAL
Violet by Jeanine Tesori and Brian Crawley

THE PULITZER PRIZE FOR DRAMA

No award

THE OBIE AWARDS

BEST PLAY
One Flea Spare by Naomi Wallace

BEST PRODUCTION
Peter and Wendy

SUSTAINED ACHIEVEMENT
Woody King, Jr.

PLAYWRITING
Eve Ensler (*The Vagina Monologues*); David Henry Hwang (*Golden Child*); Paula Vogel (*How I Learned to Drive*); Lanford Wilson (*Sympathetic Magic*)

PERFORMANCES
Andre Braugher (*Henry V*); Tsai Chin (*Golden Child*); Jennifer Dundas (*Good as New*); David Greenspan (*The Boys in the Band*); Karen Kandel (*Peter and Wendy*); Albert Macklin (*June Moon*); David Morse, Mary-Louise Parker (*How I Learned to Drive*); Sharon Scruggs (*The Trojan Women A Love Story*); Ray Anthony Thomas (*Volunteer Man*); Ching Valdes-Aran (*Flipzoids*); Joanne Camp and Arthur French (both for sustained excellence)

DIRECTION
Mark Brokaw (*How I Learned to Drive*)

DESIGN
Derek McLane (sustained excellence of set design); Shirley Prendergast (sustained excellence of lighting design); Catherine Zuber (sustained excellence of costume design)

SPECIAL CITATIONS
Roger Guenveur Smith and Mark Anthony Thompson (*A Huey P. Newton Story*); Howard Crabtree, Mark Waldrop, and Dick Gallagher for creating *Howard Crabtree's When Pigs Fly*; archivists James Hatch and Camille Billops; photographer Dona Ann McAdams; *Tap Dogs*; Jeanine Tesori (music for *Violet*)

Great Small Works; St. Paul's Community Baptist Church Drama Ministry

THE OUTER CRITICS CIRCLE AWARDS

Broadway Play: *The Last Night of Ballyhoo*; Broadway Musical: *The Life*; Off-Broadway Play: *How I Learned to Drive*; Off-Broadway Musical: *Howard Crabtree's When Pigs Fly*; Actor (Play): Christopher Plummer (*Barrymore*); Actress (Play): Janet McTeer (*A Doll's House*); Actor (Musical): Robert Cuccioli (*Jekyll & Hyde*); Actress (Musical): Bebe Neuwirth (*Chiacgo*); Featured Actor (Play): Terry Beaver (*The Last Night of Ballyhoo*); Featured Actress (Play) (three-way tie): Deborah Findlay (*Stanley*), Allison Janney (*Present Laughter*), and Celia Weston (*The Last Night of Ballyhoo*); Featured Actor (Musical): Joel Grey (*Chicago*); Featured Actress (Musical): Lillias White (*The Life*); Director (Play): John Caird (*Stanley*); Director (Musical): Walter Bobbie (*Chicago*); Revival (Play): *A Doll's House*; Revival (Musical): *Chicago*; Choreography: Ann Reinking (*Chicago*); Set Design (tie): David Gallo (*Bunny Bunny*) and Stewart Laing (*Titanic*); Costume Design: Howard Crabtree (*Howard Crabtree's When Pigs Fly*); Lighting Design (tie): Paul Gallo (*Titanic*) and Peter Kaczorowski (*Steel Pier*); Solo Performance: Felix A. Pire (*Men on the Verge of a His-panic Breakdown*)

APPENDIX:
ADDITIONAL FACTS ON WHO WON WHAT WHEN

MOST AWARDS

MOST OSCARS
Walt Disney (32)

MOST GRAMMYS
Sir Georg Solti (30)

MOST EMMYS
Dwight Hemion (16)

MOST TONYS
Harold Prince (20)

FOUR OF A KIND

The only performers to win the Oscar, Grammy, Emmy, and Tony.

HELEN HAYES
2 Oscars: Actress, *The Sin of Madelon Claudet* (1931–32); Supporting Actress, *Airport* (1970); Grammy: Spoken Word: *Great American Documents* (1976); Emmy: Actress (program unspecified) (1952); 2 Tonys: Outstanding Performance, *Happy Birthday* (1946–47), Actress in a Play, *Time Remembered* (1957–58)

RITA MORENO
Oscar: Supporting Actress, *West Side Story* (1961); Grammy: Recording for Children, *The Electric Company* (1972); 2 Emmys: Supporting Actress (Musical/Variety), *Out to Lunch* (1976–77), Actress, Single Performance in Drama or Comedy

Series, *The Rockford Files* (1977–78); Tony: Featured Actress in a Play, *The Ritz* (1974–75)

TRIPLE CROWN WINNERS

Actors who have won three of the top entertainment awards (either Oscars, Grammys, Emmys, or Tonys). Honorary or special awards are not included.

JACK ALBERTSON
Oscar: Supporting Actor, *The Subject Was Roses* (1968); 2 Emmys: Supporting Actor in Variety or Music, *Cher* (1974–75), Actor in a Comedy Series, *Chico and the Man* (1975–76); Tony: Featured Actor in a Play, *The Subject Was Roses* (1964–65)

ANNE BANCROFT
Oscar: Actress, *The Miracle Worker* (1962); Emmy: Variety or Music Program, *Annie, The Women in the Life of a Man* (1969–70); 2 Tonys: Featured Actress in a Play, *Two for the Seesaw* (1957–58), Actress in a Play, *The Miracle Worker* (1959–60)

HARRY BELAFONTE
2 Grammys: Folk Performance, "Swing Dat Hammer" (1960), Folk Performance, *An Evening with Harry Belafonte and Miriam Makeba* (1965); Emmy: Individual Performer (Variety or Music Program), *Tonight with Belafonte* (1959–60); Tony: Featured Actor in a Musical, *John Murray Anderson's Almanac* (1953–54)

INGRID BERGMAN
3 Oscars: Actress, *Gaslight* (1944), Actress, *Anastasia* (1956), Supporting Actress, *Murder on the Orient Express* (1974); 2 Emmys: Actress (Single Performance), *The Turn of the Screw* (1959–60), Actress (TV Movie or Mini-Series), *A Woman Named Golda* (1981–82) (posthumous); Tony: Outstanding Performance, *Joan of Lorraine* (1946–47)

SHIRLEY BOOTH
Oscar: Actress, *Come Back, Little Sheba* (1952); 2 Emmys: Actress in a Series, *Hazel* (1961–62 and 1962–63); 3 Tonys: Featured Actress in a Play, *Goodbye, My Fancy* (1948–49), Actress in a Play, *Come Back, Little Sheba* (1949–50), Actress in a Play, *The Time of the Cuckoo* (1952–53)

MELYVN DOUGLAS
2 Oscars: Supporting Actor, *Hud* (1963), Supporting Actor, *Being There* (1979); Emmy: Actor (Single Performance), *Do Not Go Gentle into That Good Night* (1967–68); Tony: Actor in a Play, *The Best Man* (1959–60)

HENRY FONDA
Oscar: Actor, *On Golden Pond* (1981); Grammy: Spoken Word, *Great American Documents* (1976); Tony: Outstanding Performance, *Mister Roberts* (1947–48)

LIZA MINNELLI
Oscar: Actress, *Cabaret* (1972); Emmy: Variety or Music Program: *Singer Presents Liza with a "Z"* (1972–73); 2 Tonys: Actress in a Musical, *Flora, the Red Menace* (1964–65), *The Act* (1977–78)

THOMAS MITCHELL
Oscar: Supporting Actor, *Stagecoach* (1939); Emmy: Actor (program unspecified) (1952); Tony: Actor in a Musical, *Hazel Flagg* (1952–53)

JASON ROBARDS
2 Oscars: Supporting Actor, *All the President's Men* (1976), Supporting Actor, *Julia* (1977); Emmy: Actor (TV-Movie or Mini-Series): *Inherit the Wind* (1987–88); Tony: Actor in a Play: *The Disenchanted* (1958–59)

PAUL SCOFIELD
Oscar: Actor, *A Man for All Seasons* (1966); Emmy: Actor (Single Performance): *Male of the Species* (1968–69); Tony: Actor in a Play, *A Man for All Seasons* (1961–62)

MAUREEN STAPLETON
Oscar: Supporting Actress, *Reds* (1981); Emmy: Actress (Single Performance), *Among the Paths to Eden* (1967–68); 2 Tonys: Featured Actress in a Play, *The Rose Tattoo* (1950–51), Actress in a Play, *The Gingerbread Lady* (1970–71)

BARBRA STREISAND
2 Oscars: Actress, *Funny Girl* (1968), Original Song, "Evergreen" from *A Star Is Born* (1976); 8 Grammys: Album of the Year and Female Vocalist (*The Barbra Streisand Album*) (1963), Female Vocalist ("People") (1964), Female Vocalist (*My Name Is Barbra*) (1965), Song of the Year and Female Vocalist (Pop), "Evergreen" from *A Star Is Born* (1977), Vocal Duet or Group (Pop), "Guilty" (with Barry Gibb) (1980), Female Vocalist (Pop), *The Broadway Album* (1986); 3 Emmys: Individual Achievement by an Actor or Performer, *My Name Is Barbra* (1964–65), Variety or Musical Program and Individual Performer in a Variety or Musical Program, *Barbra Streisand: The Concert* (1994–95)

JESSICA TANDY
Oscar: Actress, *Driving Miss Daisy* (1989); Emmy: Actress (TV-Movie or Mini-Series), *Foxfire* (1987–88); 3 Tonys: Outstanding Performance, *A Streetcar Named Desire* (1947–48), Actress in a Play, *The Gin Game* (1977–78), Actress in a Play, *Foxfire* (1982–83)

TWICE IN ONE YEAR

Performers who have won two major awards in one year. *Note*: Oscars are presented for work in the previous year.

Shirley Booth (Oscar and Tony, 1953)
Ellen Burstyn (Oscar and Tony, 1975)
Glenn Close (Emmy and Tony, 1995)
Audrey Hepburn (Oscar and Tony, 1954)
Frederic March (Oscar and Tony, 1947)
Michael Moriarty (Emmy and Tony, 1974)

THE ONLY PERSON TO WIN THE OSCAR, EMMY, AND TONY IN ONE YEAR

BOB FOSSE (1973)
Best Director: Oscar, *Cabaret*; Emmy, *Singer Presents Liza with a "Z"*; Tony: *Pippin*

DOUBLE-ROLLERS

Performers who have won two major awards for playing the same role in different media.

Jack Albertson (Oscar and Tony, *The Subject Was Roses*)

Anne Bancroft (Oscar and Tony, *The Miracle Worker*)

Shirley Booth (Oscar and Tony, *Come Back, Little Sheba*)

Yul Brynner (Oscar and Tony, *The King and I*)

Jose Ferrer (Oscar and Tony, *Cyrano de Bergerac*)

Ed Flanders (Emmy and Tony, *A Moon for the Misbegotten*)

Joel Grey (Oscar and Tony, *Cabaret*)

Rex Harrison (Oscar and Tony, *My Fair Lady*)

Lila Kedrova (Oscar and Tony, *Zorba the Greek* and *Zorba*, musical stage version of the film)

Mary Martin (Emmy and Tony, *Peter Pan*)

Robert Morse (Emmy and Tony, *Tru*)

Paul Scofield (Oscar and Tony, *A Man for All Seasons*)

Jessica Tandy (Emmy and Tony, *Foxfire*)

BIBLIOGRAPHY

In addition to the following books, research material was provided by the extensive clipping files of the Billy Rose Theatre Collection of the New York City Public Library at Lincoln Center.

Brown, Peter H., and Pinkston, Jim. *Oscar Dearest: Six Decades of Scandal, Politics, and Greed behind Hollywood's Academy Awards, 1927–1986.* New York: Harper and Row, 1987.

Gebert, Michael. *The Encyclopedia of Movie Awards.* New York: St. Martin's Press, 1996.

Harkness, John. *The Academy Awards Handbook.* New York: Pinnacle Books, Windsor Publishing Corporation, 1994.

Holden, Anthony. *Behind the Oscar: The Secret History of the Academy Awards.* New York: The Penguin Group, 1994.

Marsh, Dave, and Bernard, James, *The New Book of Rock Lists.* New York: A Fireside Book, Simon and Schuster, 1981, 1994.

Morrow, Lee Alan. *The Tony Award Book: Four Decades of Great American Theatre.* New York: Abbeville Press, 1987.

The New York Times Directory of the Theatre. New York: Arno Press, 1972.

O'Neill, Thomas. *The Emmys: Star Wars, Showdowns, and the Supreme Test of TV's Best.* New York: Penguin Books, 1992.

———. *The Grammys: For the Record.* New York: Penguin Books, 1993.

Phillips, Louis, and Holmes, Burnham. *The TV Almanac.* New York: Macmillan, Inc., 1994.

Schipper, Henry. *Broken Record: The Inside Story of the Grammy Awards.* New York: Birch Lane Press, 1992.

Steinberg, Cobbett. *Reel Facts: The Movie Book of Records.* New York: Vintage Books, Random House, 1978.

Walter, Clare. *The Book of Winners.* New York: Harcourt Brace Jovanovich, 1979.

Wiley, Mason, and Bona, Damien. *Inside Oscar: The Unofficial History of the Academy Awards.* New York: Ballantine Books, Random House, 1986, 1987, 1988.

INDEX

Included in this index are the recipients in the major categories of the Oscars, Grammys, Emmys, and Tonys; the Peabodys; and the Pulitzer Prize for Drama.

Abbott, George, 483
ABC, 316, 319, 346, 358, 361, 375, 396
ABC Afterschool Specials, 358, 370
ABC News Closeup/Vietnam Requiem, 399
ABC's Wide World of Sports, 340
Abe Lincoln in Illinois, 459
"Abortion Battle," 421
Abortion: Desperate Choices, 435
Abraham, F. Murray, 162
Academy Awards, inception of, 5–6
Actors' Studio, 300
Adams, Don, 342, 345, 347
Adams, Edith, 477
Adams, Jane, 580
The Adams Chronicles, 375
Adlai Stevenson Reports, 330
Adventure, 310
The Adventures of Whistling Sam, 389
The Advocates, 348
Aerosmith, 276, 285, 289
Africa, 344
"Against All Odds (Take a Look at Me Now)," 258
An Age of Kings, 327
The Ages of Man, 338
Agutter, Jenny, 357
Ain't Misbehavin', 533
Akins, Zoe, 457
The Alan Young Show, 302
Albee, Edward, 488, 500, 526, 581
Alberghetti, Anna Maria, 486
Albertson, Jack, 110, 369, 373, 494
Alcoa-Goodyear Theatre, 320
Alda, Alan, 364, 388, 397
Alda, Robert, 467
Alexander, Jane, 395, 505
Alexander, Jason, 566
Alison's House, 456
All about Eve, 55
All Creatures Great and Small, 392
Allen, Joan, 564
Allen, Rae, 511
Allen, Steve, 380
Allen, Woody, 141, 169

Alley, Kirstie, 430, 441
"Alley Cat," 212
All-4-One, 288
All in the Family, 352, 353, 355, 359
"All I Wanna Do," 287
All My Sons, 461
All Quiet on the Western Front, 8
All the King's Men, 52
All the Way Home, 485
"Always on My Mind," 252
Amadeus, 162, 542
Amanpour, Christiane, 439
Amarcord, 132
Amber Waves, 392
Ameche, Don, 165
America, 232
America, 359
The American Assassins, 370
The American Experience: The Battle over 'Citizen Kane', 451
An American in Paris, 58
American Masters: Paul Simon, 439
American Music Awards, inception of, 203, 235
American Playhouse, 428
The American Revolution '63, 333
The American Revolution: 1770-1783, A Conversation with Lord North, 354
The American Short Story, 392
American Tongues, 418
The American West: Steinbeck Country, 410
American White Paper: Organized Crime in the United States, 340
America Undercover: Drunk and Deadly, 418
Anderson, Barbara, 345
Anderson, Judith, 309, 327, 462
Anderson, Maxwell, 457
The Andersonville Trial, 351
Andrews, Julie, 98
And the Band Played On, 440
The Andy Williams Show, 331, 339, 341
Angels in America: Millenium Approaches, 576, 578
Angels in America: Perestroika, 579
Angels of Change, 439

Anhalt, Edna, 56
Anhalt, Edward, 56, 99
Animals Animals Animals, 375
Animaniacs, 439
The Anita Kerr Quartet, 217, 219
Anna Christie, 454
Annenberg, Walter, 421
Anne of Green Gables, 414
Annie, 530
Annie Hall, 140
Annie, the Women in the Life of a Man, 349
"Another Day in Paradise," 275
Anouilh, Jean, 484
Antonia's Line, 196
"Apartheid's People," 410
The Apartment, 85
Applause, 507
"Aquarius/Let the Sunshine In," 225
Arden, Eve, 306
Arkansas's Time Bomb: Teen Pregnancy, 431
Arkin, Alan, 489
Arledge, Roone, 406
Arliss, George, 8
Armed Forces Radio and Television, 431
Armistead Maupin's "Tales of the City", 443
Armstrong, Louis, 215
Arnold, Rosanne. *See* Roseanne (Arnold)
Around the World in 80 Days, 72
Arrested Development, 281
Arthur, Beatrice, 378, 420, 496
Artists' Showcase, 340
Arts in New Hamphire, 386
Ashcroft, Peggy, 163
Ashley, Elizabeth, 486
Asner, Edward, 354, 357, 369, 373, 379, 382, 390
The Assault, 169
Assignment Four, 340
Astaire, Fred, 320, 327, 382
Astaire Time, 326
Astin, Patty Duke. *See* Duke (Astin), Patty
Astor, Mary, 31
Asylum in the Streets, 403
The Atomic Bombshell, 443
Attenborough, Richard, 157
The Attic: The Hiding of Anne Frank, 421
Auberjonois, Rene, 507
The Autobiography of Miss Jane Pitman, 362
Avary, Roger, 194
Avildsen, John G., 138

Babcock, Barbara, 394
Babette's Feast, 173
Bacall, Lauren, 507, 542

Bacharach, Burt, 264
Backer, Brian, 542
Backhauling: MacNeil-Lehrer News Hour, 428
Back on the Block, 275
Bain, Barbara, 342, 345, 347
Bainter, Fay, 24
Baker, Blanche, 384
Baker, Kathy, 437, 445, 449
Baker, Lenny, 531
Baker, Marilyn, 366
Ball, Lucille, 305, 312, 342, 345
Balsam, Martin, 101, 501
Bancroft, Anne, 92, 478, 482
Baranski, Christine, 446, 552, 566
Barbarians at the Gate, 436
Barber, Red, 428
The Barbra Streisand Album, 213
Barbra Streisand: The Concert, 443, 444
Barnett, S. H., 98
Barney Miller, 386, 397
The Barry Manilow Special, 377
Barrymore, Ethel, 40
Barrymore, Lionel, 10
Barthold, Charles, 375
Bartlett, Bonnie, 413, 417
Baryshnikov on Broadway, 390, 392
Bass, Ronald, 176
Bates, Alan, 518
Bates, Kathy, 182
Battle, Hinton, 542, 553, 572
The Battle for South Africa, 386
"The Battle of the Bulge," 443
"The Battle of New Orleans," 206
The Battle of the Wetlands, 392
Bavier, Francis, 343
Baxter, Anne, 45
Baxter, Dr. Frank, 313
Baxter, Warner, 6
Bazell, Robert, 439
BBC, 308
"Beat It," 254
The Beatles, 215, 216, 295
Beatty, Warren, 153
Beck, 295
Becket, 484
Bedford, Brian, 511
The Bee Gees, 242, 244
Beery, Wallace, 11
Begley, Ed, 93, 473
Belafonte, Harry, 324, 470
Bel Geddes, Barbara, 390
Bellamy, Ralph, 478
Belle, Regina, 284

Belle Epoque, 191
The Bell Telephone Hour, 323, 334, 340
Benatar, Pat, 248, 250, 253, 256
Ben-Hur, 82
Benjamin Franklin, 366, 367
Bennett, Michael, 529
Bennett, Tony, 212, 282, 285, 289, 295, 450
Benny, Jack, 321
Benton, Robert, 147, 163
Berg, Gertrude, 302, 480
Bergen, Candice, 423, 426, 433, 441, 445
Bergen, Polly, 317
Bergman, Alan, 236
Bergman, Ingrid, 39, 73, 132, 324, 397, 461
Bergman, Marilyn, 236
Berle, Milton, 301
Bernard, James, 59
Bernstein, Leonard, 337
Bertolucci, Bernardo, 173
The Best Years of Our Lives, 44
"Bette Davis Eyes," 250
Bette Midler—Ol' Red Hair Is Back, 382
Betz, Carl, 347
Beverly, Trazana, 531
Beyond the Great Wall: Journey to the End of China, 399
Beyond the Horizon, 454
"Big, Bad John," 211
Big Blue Marble, 370
"The Big Goodbye," 418
Bigley, Isabel, 467
Big River, 555
Bill, 396
Billboard Music Awards, inception of, 203, 277
The Bill Cosby Special, 346
Bill Moyers' World of Ideas, 421
Biloxi Blues, 555
Binoche, Juliette, 199
Biography, 330
Bishop, Carole (Kelly), 528
Black and White in Color, 138
Blackmer, Sidney, 465
Black Orpheus, 83
Blake, Michael, 182
Blake, Robert, 367
Blatty, William Peter, 128
Blood and Honor: Youth under Hitler, 399
Blood, Sweat and Tears, 226
The Blue Fairy, 323
Blues Traveler, 292
Blyden, Larry, 515
Bob Hope: The First 90 Years, 437
The Bob Newhart Show, 327, 328
Bob Seger and the Silver Bullet Band, 248

Bock, Jerry, 483
The Bodyguard, 284
The Body Human: The Vital Connection, 386
Bogart, Humphrey, 58
Bolger, Ray, 464
Bolt, Robert, 104, 486
Bolton, Michael, 273, 279
Bond, Sheila, 469
Bondi, Beulah, 378
Book Beat, 346
Books of Our Time, 330
Boone, Debby, 241
Booth, Charles G., 43
Booth, Shirley, 61, 329, 332, 464, 465, 469
Boothe, Powers, 390
Borgnine, Ernest, 70
The Borrowers, 361
Borstal Boy, 507
Borzage, Frank, 4, 12
Bosco, Philip, 566
Bosley, Tom, 482
Boston, Gretha, 583
The Boston Goes to China, 389
Bostwick, Barry, 531
Both Your Houses, 457
Boulle, Pierre, 77
Box, Muriel, 45
Box, Sydney, 45
Brackett, Charles, 43, 56, 64
Brady, Alice, 20
The Brain, 406
Braingames, 410
Brando, Marlon, 66, 123, 388
Braveheart, 196
Braxton, Toni, 284, 295
Breen, Richard, 64
Brennan, Brid, 574
Brennan, Eileen, 395
Brennan, Walter, 18, 23, 28
Brian Rossi Reports, 431
Brian's Song, 354, 355
Brickman, Marshall, 141
Bricusse, Leslie, 211
The Bridge on the River Kwai, 76
"Bridge over Troubled Water," 227, 228
Bridge over Troubled Water, 227
Bridges, Beau, 432, 437
Bridgewater, Dee Dee, 525
Brigadoon, 341
Briley, John, 157
Brinkley, David, 425
Britten, Terry, 258
Broadway Melody, 6

Broderick, Matthew, 582
Broken Arrow: Can a Nuclear Weapons Accident Happen Here?, 392
Brolin, James, 350
Brooks, James L., 160
Brooks, Joe, 241
Brooks, Mel, 111
Brooks, Richard, 87
Brown, Harry, 59
Brown, Joe E., 462
Brown, Pamela, 329
Brown, Russ, 473
Brown, Ruth, 566
Brownlow, Levin, 418
Bruce Hornsby and the Range, 264
Brynner, Yul, 73, 468
Bryson, Peabo, 282, 284
Buchanan, Sidney, 32
Buddy Check 12, 443
Burghoff, Gary, 379
Buried Child, 537
Burke, Edwin, 12
Burnett, Carol, 329, 330, 333
Burns, David, 353, 479, 489
Burns, George, 135
Burnt by the Sun, 194
Burr, Raymond, 321, 327
Burrows, Abe, 488
Burstyn, Ellen, 131, 524
Burton, Richard, 484
Busfield, Timothy, 430
"Busted," 214
Butler, Frank, 40
Button Down Mind, 208
Buttons, Red, 77
Buyline: Betty Furness, 380
Bye, Bye, Birdie, 484
By the Time I Get to Phoenix, 223

Cabaret, 498
The Cable ACE Awards, inception of, 389
Caesar, Arthur, 15
Caesar, Sid, 303, 315
Caesar's Hour, 314
Cage, Nicolas, 196
Cagney, James, 33
Cagney & Lacey, 407, 411
Caine, Michael, 169
Calder-Marshall, Anna, 347
Caldwell, L. Scott, 564
Caldwell, Zoe, 496, 501, 546, 585
Call It Macaroni, 370
Cambodia: Year Ten, 425

Camera Three, 308, 380
Campbell, Glen, 222
Campion, Jane, 191
Campus Chorus and Orchestra, 302
Cannes Film Festival, inception of, 46
Can't Slow Down, 258
Capers, Virginia, 521
Capital Cities Broadcasting Corporation, 328
Capra, Frank, 15, 19, 24
Captain Kangaroo, 319, 358
Cara, Irene, 255
The Caretaker, 486
Carey, Mariah, 275
Cariou, Len, 536
Carney, Art, 131, 307, 310, 312, 404
The Carol Burnett Show, 355, 363, 367
The Carpenters, 227, 228, 230
Carroll, Diahann, 486
Carroll, Pat, 315
Carson, Johnny, 410
Carson, Robert, 21
Carter, Nell, 534
Cartoon-A-Torial, 386
Carver, Brent, 577
Carvey, Dana, 438
Casablanca, 36
Cass, Peggy, 476
Cassidy, Jack, 491
Cat on a Hot Tin Roof, 472
Cats, 549
Cavalcade, 12
Cavalcade of Books, 308
Cavett, Frank, 40, 62
CBS, 319, 323, 325, 328, 333, 361, 418, 447
CBS Children's Film Festival, 343
CBS News Sunday Morning, 389
CBS Playhouse, 343
CBS Reports, 325, 336
CBS Reports: In the Killing Fields of America, 447
CBS Reports: The Vanishing Family—Crisis in Black America, 414
Celanese Theatre, 304
The Celluloid Closet, 451
Chakiris, George, 89
The Champs, 205
"Change the World," 294
Channel One, 435
Channing, Carol, 491
Channing, Stockard, 555
Chaplin, Sydney, 476
Chapman, Tracy, 269
Chariots of Fire, 152
Charles, Ray, 208, 209

A Charlie Brown Christmas, 338
Charren, Peggy, 431
Chase, Chevy, 374
Chase, Mary, 460
Chayefsky, Paddy, 71, 121, 138
Cheers, 400, 404, 422, 429
Cher, 172
Chicago, 240
The Chieftans, 292
Child, Julia, 336
Children of a Lesser God, 538
Children's Express Newsmagazine: Campaign '88, 421
China: Beyond the Clouds, 443
China '72: A Hole in the Bamboo Curtain, 358
A Chorus Line, 527, 529
Christie, Julie, 101
A Christmas Memory, 340
Christopher, Johnny, 252
Christopher Cross, 248
Chrysler Presents the Bob Hope Christmas Special, 339
Chuck Kraemer Reporting, 439
Churchill Entertainment, Ltd., 439
"The CIA's Cocaine," 439
"Cicely," 435
Cimarron, 10
Cimino, Michael, 144
Cinema Paradiso, 180
Cirque du Soleil II: A New Experience, 432
Citizen Cohn, 435
City of Angels, 568
Civilisation, 351
The Civil War, 428
Clapton, Eric, 275, 281, 282, 295
Clark, Petula, 218
Clark, Susan, 373
Clarke, T. E. B., 62
Climate of Death, 403
Close, Glenn, 444, 552, 574, 582
Closely Watched Trains, 107
Close to Home: The Tommy Boccomino Story, 435
Close-Up, 361
CNN, 403, 418, 425, 428, 431
Coburn, Charles, 37
Coca, Imogene, 303, 308
Cocker, Joe, 253
The Cocktail Party, 465
Coco, James, 402
Coen, Ethan, 199
Coen, Joel, 199
Cohn, Marc, 278
Colbert, Claudette, 15
Colburn, D. L., 535
Cole, Natalie, 238, 279, 295

Cole, Nat "King," 207, 279, 295
Cole, Olivia, 379
Coleman, Dabney, 416
Coleman, Ronald, 47
College News Conference, 323
Collings, Pierre, 19
Collins, Pauline, 566
Collins, Phil, 259, 261
Color Adjustment, 435
Columbo, 363
Come Dance with Me, 207
Coming Out Under Fire, 447
Common Threads: Stories from the Quilt, 425
Como, Perry, 205, 310, 313, 315, 322, 375
Company, 510
Complaints of a Dutiful Daughter, 447
Concealed Enemies, 404
The Concert for Bangladesh, 231
A Connecticut Yankee in King Arthur's Court, 386
Connelly, Marc, 456
Connery, Sean, 173
Conrad, Michael, 395, 398
Conroy, Frank, 476
Constantine, Michael, 350
Conti, Tom, 536
Continental Classroom, 323
A Conversation with Jimmy Carter, 375
Conway, Tim, 360, 379, 385
Cook, Barbara, 479
Cooke, Alistaire, 358, 399
Cooper, Chuck, 589
Cooper, Gary, 31, 61
Cooper, Marilyn, 543
Coppola, Francis Ford, 119, 126, 132
Corby, Ellen, 360, 369, 374
Cornell, Katherine, 462
Corridos!: Tales of Passion and Revolution, 418
Cosby, Bill, 339, 342, 345
The Cosby Show, 407, 414
Cosmos, 392
Costa-Gravas, 157
Costigan, James, 323
Costner, Kevin, 182
Cougar, John, 253
Country Music Association Awards, inception of, 223
Coup d'Etat: The Week That Changed the World, 431
Cousteau/Amazon, 406
Craig's Wife, 455
Crawford, Broderick, 53
Crawford, Joan, 42
Crawford, Michael, 564
Crazy for You, 574
Crenna, Richard, 408

Crimes of the Heart, 544
Crisis in Central America, 410
Crisp, Donald, 31
Cristofer, Michael, 530, 532
Crivello, Anthony, 577
Cromie, Robert, 346
Cromwell, John, 468
Cronkite, Walter, 330, 392
Cronyn, Hume, 426, 433, 440, 491
Crosby, Bing, 39, 349
Crosby, Stills and Nash, 226
Cross, Christopher, 248
Crouse, Russell, 460
Crow, Sheryl, 288, 295
The Crucible, 469
Crusade in Europe, 302
Crystal, Billy, 430
Cukor, George, 98
Cullum, John, 525, 533
Culture Club, 255
Cummings, Constance, 536
Cummings, Robert, 309
Current Affairs/The Case of Dashiell Hammett, 399
Curtin, Jane, 404, 408
Curtis, Keene, 511
Curtiz, Michael, 37

Da, 533
Dale, Jim, 538
The Dale Car: A Dream or a Nightmare, 370
Dalrymple, Ian, 24
Daly, James, 339
Daly, John, 310, 316
Daly, Tyne, 401, 404, 408, 419, 449, 569
Damien, 386
Damn Yankees, 473
Damon, Cathryn, 390
Dana, Leora, 518
Dance in America, 396
Dances with Wolves, 181
Dancing at Lughnasa, 574
Dane, Clemence, 45
Dangerous Moves, 163
Daniels, William, 408, 412
Danner, Blythe, 507
The Danny Kaye Show, 333, 334
Danson, Ted, 426, 437
Dante, Nicjolas, 529
Darin, Bobby, 207
Darwell, Jane, 29
Da Silva, Howard, 384
Dave Matthews Band, 296
David Brinkley's Journal, 328

The David Frost Show, 349, 352
Davies, Valentine, 48
Davis, Ann B., 318, 322
Davis, Bette, 16, 22, 387
Davis, Geena, 176
Davis, Judy, 446
Davis, Owen, 454
Day for Night, 128
Day-Lewis, Daniel, 179
"The Days of Wine and Roses," 213
D-Day, 443
Dear America: Letters Home from Vietnam, 421
Death of a Salesman, 341, 464
Decade, 425
"Decisions," 323
de Concini, Ennio, 93
Dee, Ruby, 430
"Deep Purple," 214
The Deer Hunter, 143
The Defenders, 328, 331, 334
de Hartog, Jan, 467
de Havilland, Olivia, 44, 53
Dehn, Paul, 59
Delaney, Dana, 423, 433
A Delicate Balance, 500
Demme, Jonathan, 185
De Niro, Robert, 131, 150
Dennis, Sandy, 104, 489, 491
Dennis Miller Live, 448
Derricks, Cleavant, 546
Dersu Uzala, 135
DeShannon, Jackie, 250
The Desperate Hours, 471
"Detroit City," 214
DeVito, Danny, 395
Dewhurst, Colleen, 412, 423, 484, 521
Diagnosis: AIDS, 403
Diamond, I. A. L., 87
The Diary of Anne Frank, 473, 474
The Dick Cavett Show, 355
Dick Fleagler Commentaries, 428
The Dick Van Dyke Show, 331, 334, 337, 338
The Dinah Shore Chevy Show, 317, 319, 320
Ding Dong School, 306
Dinsdale, Shirley, 300
Dion, Celine, 282
Dire Straits, 261
The Discovery Network, 439
The Discreet Charm of the Bourgeoisie, 126
Disneyland, 308, 310
Donahue, Phil, 392
Donat, Robert, 25
The Donner Party, 435

"Don't Worry, Be Happy," 269
The Doobie Brothers, 246
The Dorothy Gordon Forum, 333
Double Fantasy, 250
Douglas, Melvyn, 95, 146, 344, 482
Douglas, Michael, 172
Douglas, Nathan E., 80
Dowd, Nancy, 144
Down at the Dunbar, 389
"Downtown," 216
Do You Remember Love?, 406, 410
Dragnet, 305
Drake, Alfred, 470
Drake, Larry, 420, 423
The Drama Desk Awards, inception of, 472, 493, 505
Dressler, Marie, 10
Dreyfuss, Richard, 140
Driftwood, Jimmy, 206
Driving Miss Daisy, 179, 565
"Dr. Suess," 351
Drug Wars: The Camarena Story, 426
Duff-MacCormick, Cara, 515
Dukakis, Olympia, 173
Duke (Astin), Patty, 93, 350, 378, 390
Dummy, 389
Dunaway, Faye, 138
Dunn, James, 43
The DuPont Show of the Week, 330
Duquesnay, Ann, 586
Durante, Jimmy, 303, 305
Durning, Charles, 569
Duvall, Robert, 159
The Dying Rooms, 447
Dylan, Bob, 246
Dysart, Richard, 433

Eagan, Daisy, 572
The Eagles, 238, 246
An Early Frost, 410
Easton, Sheena, 250
Eastwood, Clint, 188
Edgar, David, 545
Edith Ann's Christmas, 450
The Ed Sullivan Show, 311, 316, 323, 344
Edward and Mrs. Simpson, 390
Edwards, Douglas, 313
The Ed Wynn Show, 301, 302
The Effect of Gamma Rays on Man-in-the-Moon Marigolds, 513
8-1/2, 96
The Eight Decade Consortium, 396
Eleanor and Franklin, 370, 375
Eleanor and Franklin: The White House Years, 376

The Electric Grandmother, 399
The Elephant Man, 535
Eliot, T. S., 465
Elizabeth R, 355, 356
Elizabeth the Queen, 344
Elliot, Patricia, 518
Elliott Norton Reviews, 330
Emick, Jarrod, 580
The Emmy Awards, inception of, 299, 300
The Energy Crisis...An American White Paper, 361
The English Patient, 199
Epstein, Julius J., 38
Epstein, Philip G., 38
Equus, 524
ER, 443, 448
The Ernest Green Story, 439
Estabrook, Howard, 10
Etheridge, Melissa, 282, 289
The Eurythmics, 265
Evans, Maurice, 327
Evening at Pops, 351
An Evening at Tanglewood, 343
An Evening with Fred Astaire, 319, 320, 323
An Evening with John Denver, 367
"Everybody Dance Now!," 431
"Every Breath You Take," 255
Evita, 538
Ewell, Tom, 469
Expedition!, 328
Experiment in Television, 348
Exploring, 330
Eye of the Storm, 351
Eyes on the Prize: America's Civil Rights Years, 418
Eyes on the Prize II: America at the Racial Crossroads, 428
Eyewitness News, 396

Fabray, Nanette, 312, 315, 464
The Fabulous Fifties, 324, 325
Facing Reality: Politics, Drugs, and Waste, 439
Faerie Tale Theatre, 406
Faith, 269
Falk, Peter, 329, 357, 368, 373, 426
Falling into You, 294, 295
Fanny and Alexander, 160
Farnham, Joseph, 5
Farrell, Glenda, 332
Farrow, John, 74
Fat Chance, 443
"FDR," 443
Feliciano, José, 223
Female cast of *La Plume de Ma Tante*, 480
Fences, 561, 563
Ferrer, Jose, 55, 461, 467

Fiddler on the Roof, 494
Field, Sally, 146, 162, 378
Fiennes, Ralph, 582
Fierstein, Harvey, 548, 549
The 5th Dimension, 222, 226
52nd Street, 245
50 Years after the War, 447
The Final Chapter?, 410
Finch, Peter, 137
FIND Investigative Reports, 380
Fine, Holly, 428
Fine, Paul, 428
Finkel, Fyvush, 442
Fiorello!, 482, 483
The First Family, 211
"The First Time Ever I Saw Your Face," 231
Fishburne, Larry, 574
Fisher, Gail, 350
Fitzgerald, Barry, 40
Fitzgerald, Ella, 205, 207, 208, 209, 212
Flack, Roberta, 232, 234
Flanagan, Fionnula, 374
Flanders, Ed, 374, 378, 401, 522
Fleming, Victor, 26
Fletcher, Louise, 134
The Flip Wilson Show, 351, 352
Fonda, Henry, 153, 462
Fonda, Jane, 121, 144, 404
Fontaine, Joan, 31
Fontanne, Lynn, 337
Foote, Horton, 93, 160, 584
Ford, John, 16, 29, 32, 61
Forman, Milos, 135, 163
Forrest Gump, 193
Forsythe, Hendderson, 536
42nd Street, 542
Fosse, Bob, 125
Foster, Jodie, 176, 184
Foster, Lewis R., 26
The Fourposter, 467
Fourways Farm, 443
Fox, Charles, 233
Fox, Michael J., 412, 416, 419
Fox Children's Network, 439
Fraiberg, Lawrence, 410
Frank, Frederic M., 62
Frank, Gary, 379
Frank Sinatra: A Man and His Music, 338, 339
Franz, Dennis, 441, 449
Frasier, 440, 443, 444, 448
Free to Be...You and Me, 366
Frelich, Phyllis, 538
The French Connection, 121

Fricker, Brenda, 179
Friedkin, William, 121
Friel, Brian, 574
Friendly, Fred W., 328
Friendly Fire, 386, 389
"Friendly Fire," 431
Frings, Ketti, 479
Froeschel, George, 35
"From a Distance," 275
From Belfast with Love, 366
From Here to Eternity, 63
Frontline, 406
Frontline: The Choice, 421, 451
Frontline: The Gate of Heavenly Peace, 451
Frontline: Waco: The Inside Story, 447
Fuchs, Daniel, 71
The Fugitive, 338
Fulfillingness' First Finale, 236
Fuller, Charles, 547
Fuller, Penny, 398
A Funny Thing Happened on the Way to the Forum, 488
"Funny Way of Laughin'," 212
Futures, 428

Gabel, Martin, 484
Gable, Clark, 15
Gaines, Boyd, 566, 579
Galati, Frank, 568
Gale, Zona, 454
Gallagher, Helen, 468, 511
"Games People Play," 225, 226
Gandhi, 155
Garagiola, Joe, 361
Gardenia, Vincent, 427, 515
The Garden of the Finzi-Continis, 122
Gardner, Herb, 558
Garland, Judy, 210
Garner, James, 378
The Garry Moore Show, 328
Garson, Greer, 34
The Gathering, 381
Gaynor, Janet, 4
GE College Bowl, 325
Geer, Will, 369
Geldorf, Bob, 410
Gentlemen's Agreement, 47
Gentry, Bobbie, 222
George Washington, 406
Germi, Pietro, 93
Gershwin, Ira, 457
Get Out Your Handkerchiefs, 144
Get Smart, 344, 346
Getty, Estelle, 420

Getz/Gilberto, 215
Ghostley, Alice, 494
Gianetti, Alfredo, 93
Gibb, Barry, 248
Gibney, Sheridan, 19
Gibson, Mel, 196
Gibson, William, 482
Gideon's Trumpet, 392
Gielgud, John, 153, 429, 462
Gigi, 79
Gilbert, Willie, 488
Gill, David, 418
Gilroy, Frank D., 494, 495
Gimbel, Norman, 233
The Gin Game, 535
"The Girl from Ipanema," 214
"Give Me One Reason," 295
Give Me That Bigtime Religion, 403
Gladys Knight and the Pips, 234
Glaspell, Susan, 456
Glazer, Benjamin, 4, 29
Gleason, Jackie, 313, 482
Gleason, Joanna, 564
Glengarry Glen Ross, 554
Gless, Sharon, 412, 416
Glover, John, 582
Glynn, Carlin, 536
Gobel, George, 310
The Godfather, 123
The Godfather Part II, 130
Going My Way, 39
Gold, Ernest, 208
Gold, Julie, 275
Goldberg, Whoopi, 182
The Golden Girls, 411, 415
The Golden Globe Awards, inception of, 3, 39, 313
Goldman, Bo, 135, 150
Goldman, James, 111
Goldman, William, 115, 138
Goldsmith, John, 396
Gone with the Wind, 25
A Good Dissonance like a Man, 380
Gooding, Cuba, Jr., 199
Goodman, Julian, 366
Good Morning, Miss Toliver, 439
Goodrich, Frances, 473, 474
Goorjian, Michael, 441
Gordon, Irving, 278
Gordon, Ruth, 111, 388
Gordone, Charles, 509
Gorman, Cliff, 514
Gormé, Edyie, 209, 219
Gossett, Louis, Jr., 156, 378

Gough, Michael, 536
Gould, Jack, 316
Goulet, Robert, 212, 501
Gowdy, Curt, 348
Graceland, 264
"Graceland," 266
Graff, Randy, 569
Graham, Fred, 366
Grahame, Gloria, 61
Grammer, Kelsey, 441, 445
The Grammy Awards, inception of, 203
Grand Hotel, 11
The Grand Ole Opry, 403
Grant, Lee, 135, 339, 353
The Grapes of Wrath, 568
Gray, Dolores, 470
The Greatest Show on Earth, 60
Great Music from Chicago, 323
The Great Space Coaster, 403
The Great Wall of Iron, 425
The Great War and the Shaping of the 20th Century, 451
The Great White Hope, 503, 506
The Great Ziegfeld, 18
Green, Al, 288
Green, Elaine, 392
Greene, Clarence, 83
The Green Pastures, 456
Greenspan, Bud, 451
Grey, Joel, 125, 499
Griffin, Eleanore, 24
Griffith, Hugh, 82
Grimes, Tammy, 484, 507
Grizzard, George, 391, 585
Ground Zero: Victory Road, 399
Guillaume, Robert, 388, 408
Guinness, Alec, 77, 490
Gulliver's Travels, 448
Gunsmoke, 317
Guys and Dolls, 466
Gwenn, Edmund, 48
Gypsy in My Soul, 372

Hackett, Albert, 473, 474
Hackman, Gene, 121, 188
Hagen, Uta, 467, 489
Hale, Barbara, 322
Hall, Delores, 531
Hall, Joyce, 336
Hall, Juanita, 465
Hallelujah, Baby!, 500
Hallmark Hall of Fame, 418
Hamlet, 49
Hamlisch, Marvin, 236, 529

Hammerstein, Oscar, II, 465
Hampshire, Susan, 350, 353, 360
Hampton, Christopher, 176
Hank Aaron: Chasing the Dream, 447
Hanks, Tom, 190, 193
Harney, Ben, 546
Harnick, Sheldon, 483
Harper, Valerie, 354, 357, 360, 368
Harrelson, Woody, 423
Harrington, Pat, 405
Harris, Barbara, 499
Harris, Julie, 321, 329, 467, 473, 504, 518, 530
Harris, Rosemary, 373, 496
Harrison, Rex, 98, 464, 476
Harry, Jackee, 417
Hart, Moss, 457
Hartley, Mariette, 387
Hartman, Grace, 462
Hartman, Paul, 462
Harvey, 460
Hathaway, Donny, 232
Hauben, Lawrence, 135
Hawn, Goldie, 115
Hawthorne, Nigel, 571
Hayes, Helen, 11, 118, 305, 461, 478
Hayes, Joseph, 471
Hayman, Lillian, 502
Hayward, Susan, 79
The Health Quarterly: The AIDS Report Series, 435
Hearn, George, 409, 552, 583
Heartsounds, 406
Hecht, Ben, 4, 17
Heckart, Eileen, 125
Heerman, Victor, 13
Heflin, Van, 34
Heggen, Thomas, 462
The Heidi Chronicles, 566, 567
"Heil Hitler": Confessions of a Hitler Youth," 431
Heinemann, George, 355
Helgenberger, Marg, 427
Hell-Bent fer Heaven, 454
"Hello, Dolly," 214
Hello, Dolly!, 490
He Makes Me Feel Like Dancin', 403
Henley, Beth, 544
Henley, Don, 261, 273
Henley, Larry, 272
Henson, Jim, 414
Hepburn, Audrey, 64, 470
Hepburn, Katharine, 13, 106, 110, 153, 367
Herald, Heinz, 21
Herczeg, Geza, 21
Heredia, Wilson Jermaine, 586

Heritage: Civilization and the Jews, 406
The Heritage Series, 319
Herman, Jerry, 214
Herrmann, Edward, 528
Hershey, Barbara, 426
Heston, Charlton, 82
Hewitt, Don, 421
Hickson, Joan, 536
"Higher Love," 264
Hill, Arthur, 489
Hill, George Roy, 128
Hiller, Wendy, 80
Hillerman, John, 416
Hill Street Blues, 392, 396, 397, 399, 404
Hilton, James, 35
Hines, Gregory, 574
Hirsch, Judd, 394, 401, 558, 574
"Hit the Road, Jack," 211
The Hobbit, 380
Hoffman, Dustin, 146, 176, 412
Holbrook, Hal, 353, 363, 373, 496
Holden, William, 63, 363
Holgate, Ronald, 505
Holiday, Jennifer, 546
Holliday, Judy, 55, 476
Hollywood Foreign Press. *See* The Golden Globe Awards
Holm, Celeste, 48
Holm, Ian, 499
Holocaust, 382, 386
The Homecoming, 498
Home Rule Campaign, 361
Homicide: Life on the Street, 439, 447
Hoop Dreams, 447
Hootie and the Blowfish, 291, 292
Hope, Bob, 319, 344
Hopkins, Anthony, 184, 372, 394
Hopkins, Linda, 515
Horne, Lena, 250
Horner, James, 266
Hornsby, Bruce, 264
Horton, Johnny, 207
Hot Dog, 351
"Hotel California," 241
Houseman, John, 128
Houston, Whitney, 261, 267, 284, 413
Howard, Ken, 507
Howard, Sidney, 26, 455
Howard, Trevor, 331
How Come?, 366
How Do You Spell God?, 451
Howdy Doody, 300
Howe, Quincy, 313
"How Glad I Am," 216

How Green Was My Valley, 31
How to Succeed in Business without Really Trying, 486, 488
Hughes, Barnard, 384, 533
Hughes, Hatcher, 454
Hulce, Tom, 449
Hull, Josephine, 56
Hunger in America, 346
"The Hunger Inside," 443
Hunt, Linda, 160
Hunt, Helen, 449
Hunt, Martita, 464
Hunter, Holly, 190, 422, 437
Hunter, Ian McLellan, 64
Hunter, Kim, 59
Huntley, Chet, 349
The Huntley-Brinkley Report, 323, 325
Hurt, William, 165
Huston, Angelica, 166
Huston, John, 50
Huston, Walter, 50
Hutton, Timothy, 150
Hwang, David Henry, 563
Hyland, Diana, 379

I Am a Promise, 439
Ian, Janis, 238
IBM Presents Baryshnikov on Broadway, 392
"I Can't Stop Loving You," 212
Icebound, 454
Idiot's Delight, 457
"I Honestly Love You," 235
"I Left My Heart in San Francisco," 211
I'll Fly Away, 431
Ilott, Pamela, 361
I Love Lucy, 304, 306
I'm Not Rappaport, 558
The Importance of Being Earnest, 462
In Abraham's Bosom, 455
"In Celebration of US," 375
The Incident, 425
The Incredible Journey of Bill Pickney, 435
Indictment: The McMartin Trial, 443
Indochine, 188
Industry on Parade, 310
Inge, William, 89, 470
Inherit the Wind, 419
In Living Color, 426
Innervisions, 234
In Performance at Wolf Trap, 375
Intertel, 336
In the Heat of the Night, 106
In the News, 375

Investigation of a Citizen Above Suspicion, 119
Irons, Jeremy, 182, 552
Irving, George S., 518
Irving Berlin's 100th Birthday Celebration, 419
Islam in Turmoil, 421
I-TEAM: Ambulances, 403
It Happened One Night, 15
"It's Only Television," 431
"It's Too Late," 229
Ives, Burl, 80
Ivey, Judith, 555
"I Will Always Love You," 284
"I Write the Songs," 239

The Jack Benny Show, 320, 326
Jack Lemmon in 'S Wonderful, 'S Marvelous, 'S Gershwin, 355
Jackson, Glenda, 117, 128, 357
Jackson, Gordon, 374
Jackson, Michael, 255, 256, 261
Jacobi, Derek, 423, 555
Jacoby, Scott, 360
Jagged Little Pill, 291, 292
Jagger, Dean, 53
James, Mark, 252
Jannings, Emil, 4
The Japanese, 349
Japan Series, 418
Jarreau, Al, 250
JB, 480, 481
Jerome Robbins' Broadway, 566
Jeter, Michael, 434, 569
The Jewel in the Crown, 406, 408
Jhabvala, Ruth Prawer, 169, 188
Joel, Billy, 243, 245, 248
John, Elton, 265, 288
John, Tom, 340
John D. and Catherine T. MacArthur Foundation, 428
John Hammond: Frome Bessie Smith to Bruce Springsteen, 428
Johns, Glynis, 518
The Johns Hopkins Science Review, 306
Johnson, Ben, 121
Johnson, Bruce, 239
Johnson, Gerald W., 308
Jones, Cherry, 582
Jones, Henry, 478
Jones, Jack, 210, 213
Jones, James Earl, 429, 430, 504, 561
Jones, Jennifer, 36
Jones, Leilani, 555
Jones, Rickie Lee, 245
Jones, Robert C., 144

Jones, Shirley, 86
Jones, Tom, 217
Jones, Tommy Lee, 190, 401
Jordan, Neil, 188
Joseph, 444
Joshua's Confusion, 381
The Joshua Tree, 266
Journey of Hope, 183
Journey of the African-American Athlete, 451
J.T., 349
Judge Horton and the Scottsboro Boys, 375
Judy at Carnegie Hall, 210
Juilliard and Beyond, 399
Julia, Raul, 444
Julie and Carol at Carnegie Hall, 331
The Julie Andrews Hour, 359
The Julie Andrews Show, 338
Just Because: Tales of Violence, Dreams of Peace, 443
"Just the Way You Are," 243

Kahn, Madeline, 576
Kane, Carol, 397
Kani, John, 524
Kanin, Michael, 35
Karlen, John, 413
Kate and Eilish: Siamese Twins, 439
Katnilova, Maria, 494
KATU-TV, 396
Kaufman, George S., 457
Kavner, Julie, 384
Kaye, Danny, 336, 396
Kaye, Judy, 564
Kaye, Sylvia Fine, 389
Kazan, Elia, 48, 68, 461, 464
Keaton, Diane, 140
Kedrova, Lila, 98, 553
Keeshan, Bob, 386
Kelley, William, 166
Kelly, Carole. *See* Bishop, Carole (Kelly)
Kelly, George, 455
Kelly, Grace, 66
Kelly, Paul, 462
Kennedy, Arthur, 464
Kennedy, George, 107
Kennedy, Gordon, 294
The Kennedy Center Honors: A Celebration of the Performing Arts, 404, 412, 414, 440, 448
The Kentucky Cycle, 575
Kerr, John, 470
Kevin's Sentence, 447
Khouri, Callie, 185
Kids Against Child Abuse, 443
Kiley, Richard, 402, 419, 480, 496

Killian, Dr. James, 344, 370
Killing Crime: A Police Cop-Out, 399
"Killing Me Softly with His Song," 233
King, Carole, 230
The King and I, 467
"King of the Road," 217
Kingsley, Ben, 156
Kingsley, Sidney, 457
The Kingston Trio, 205
Kintner, Robert, 303
Kirkpatrick, Wayne, 294
Kirkwood, James, 529
Kismet, 470
"Kiss from a Rose," 291
Kiss Me, Kate, 464
Kiss of the Spider Woman, 576
"KKK—The Invisible Empire," 338
Kleban, Edward, 529
Klemperer, Werner, 345, 348
Kline, Kevin, 176, 534, 542
Klugman, Jack, 334, 353, 360
Knight, Gladys, 234, 265
Knight, Shirley, 528
Knight, Ted, 360, 374
Knotts, Don, 327, 329, 332, 340, 343
Koch, Howard, 38
Kolya, 199
KOMO, 451
Koppel, Ted, 406
The Koppel Report: Death of a Dictator, 428
Korman, Harvey, 357, 365
KPFR-FM, 325
Kraly, Hans, 6
Kramer vs. Kramer, 146
Kramm, Joseph, 469
Krasna, Norman, 38
"Krushchev Abroad," 323
KTLA-TV, 338, 431
KTTV-TV, 435
Kukla, Fran, and Ollie, 302
Kup's Show, 340
Kurault, Charles, 346, 370
Kurtz, Swoosie, 542, 558
Kushner, Tony, 576, 578, 579

La Cage aux Folles, 552
La Galliene, Eva, 384
Lahr, Bert, 491
LA Law, 414, 418, 422, 425, 429
Lambert, Hendricks, and Ross, 210
Lamorisse, Albert, 75
Lampert, Zohra, 369
Lancaster, Burt, 85

Landau, Martin, 193
Lane, Nathan, 585
lang, k. d., 282
Lange, Hope, 347, 350
Lange, Jessica, 156, 193
Langella, Frank, 525
Lansbury, Angela, 496, 505, 525, 536
Lapine, James, 557
Lapotaire, Jane, 542
Lardner, Ring, Jr., 35, 119
Larner, Jeremy, 126
Larroquette, John, 409, 413, 417, 420
Larry King Live Election Coverage 1992, 435
The Larry Sanders Show, 439
Larson, Jonathan, 587
Las Rosas Blancas, 370
Lassie, 313
The Last Emperor, 171
The Last Night of Ballyhoo, 588
La Strada, 75
The Last Word, 319
Late Night with David Letterman, 431
The Late Show with David Letterman, 440
Laughton, Charles, 13
Lauper, Cyndi, 259
Laurie, Piper, 416
Lavin, Linda, 561
The Law, 366
Law & Order, 450
Lawrence, Gertrude, 468
Lawrence, Vicki, 374
Lawrence of Arabia, 91
"Layla," 282
LBJ: The Early Years, 418
Leachman, Cloris, 121, 359, 365, 369, 405
Lean, David, 77, 93
Lear, Norman, 380
Learned, Michael, 360, 364, 373, 397
Lee, Peggy, 226
Leibman, Ron, 387, 576
Leigh, Vivien, 26, 59, 489
Leighton, Margaret, 354, 476, 486
Lelouch, Claude, 104
Lemmon, Jack, 70, 128
"Lenell Geter's in Jail," 403
Lennon, John, 219
Lennox, Annie, 291
Lenya, Lotte, 473
Leonard, Bill, 396
Leonard, Hugh, 533
Leonard Bernstein and the New York Philharmonic in Japan, 328
Lerner, Alan Jay, 59, 80

Les Miserables, 561
Let Freedom Ring!, 328
"Let's Twist Again," 210
Levien, Sonya, 71
Levinson, Barry, 176
Lewis, Cecil, 24
The Life and Adventures of Nicholas Nickleby, 400, 545
The Life of Emile Zola, 20
The Life of Riley, 301
The Lifers' Group—I Am My Brother's Keeper, 380
Lily: Sold Out, 394
Lily Tomlin, 363
Lincoln Center Presents Leonard Berstein and the New York Philharmonic, 323
Linden, Hal, 511
Lindsay, Howard, 460
Lindsay, Robert, 561
Lippmann, Walter, 328
Lipscomb, W. P., 24
Lisagor, Peter, 361
Lithgow, John, 449, 518
Little, Cleavon, 507
"Little Green Apples," 223
Little Moon of Alban, 320
A Little Night Music, 517
Little Rock Central High School, 389
Live Aid, 410
Live from Lincoln Center, 410
Live from the Met, 380
Lloyd, Christopher, 398, 402, 433
Lloyd, Frank, 6, 13
Lockhart, June, 462
Loden, Barbara, 491
Loesser, Frank, 488
Logan, Joshua, 462, 465
Loggins, Kenny, 245, 248
Lonesome Dove, 425
Long, Shelley, 401
Long Day's Journey into Night, 475, 477
The Long Eyes of Kit Peak, 389
Longing in Their Hearts, 288
Look Homeward, Angel, 479
Lopez, Priscilla, 540
Lord, Robert, 13
Loren, Sophia, 88
Lorne, Marion, 345
Los Angeles Film Critics Association, inception of, 3, 137
"The Lost Class of '59," 323
Lost in Yonkers, 571, 572
The Lost Weekend, 41
Loudon, Dorothy, 531
Lou Grant, 386, 389

Louis-Dreyfus, Julia, 449
The Louvre, 336
Love among the Ruins, 370
Love Is Never Silent, 411
"Love Theme from *A Star Is Born* (Evergreen)", 241
Lovett, Lyle, 288
Love! Valour! Compassion!, 582
"Love Will Keep Us Together," 237
Lowe, Chad, 438
Ludwig, William, 71
Luedtke, Kurt, 166
Lukas, Paul, 36
Lunt, Alfred, 337
LuPone, Patti, 539
Luther, 490
Lyle, Graham, 258
Lyons, Louis M., 319

MacArthur, Charles, 17
Macbeth, 325, 326
MacColl, Ewan, 231
MacDaniel, Hattie, 26
MacDonald, Audra, 586
The Machine That Changed the World, 435
"Mack the Knife," 206
MacLaine, Shirley, 159
MacLeish, Archibald, 480, 481
The MacNeil-Lehrer NewsHour: Election '88 Coverage, 421
The Macneil-Lehrer Report, 380
Mad about You, 443
Madame Rosa, 141
Magee, Patrick, 496
Magnani, Anna, 70
The Magnificent Yankee, 337
Maguire, Michael, 561
Mahaffey, Valerie, 434
Mahoney, John, 558
Make a Wish, 354
Make Room for Daddy, 306, 308
The Making of a Continent, 403
The Making of a Legend: Gone with the Wind, 421
The Making of the President, 334
"Malcolm X: Make It Plain," 443
Malden, Karl, 59, 408
Male cast of *La Plume de Ma Tante*, 480
Malkovich, John, 412
Malone, Dorothy, 74
The Mamas and the Papas," 219
Mamet, David, 554
A Man and a Woman, 104
Manchester, Melissa, 253
Mancini, Henry, 210, 213

Mandel, Johnny, 217
Mandela, 418
A Man for All Seasons, 103
Manhattan Transfer, 250, 270
Manilow, Barry, 244
Mankiewicz, Herman J., 32
Mankiewicz, Joseph L., 53, 56
Mann, Abby, 89
Mann, Barry, 266
Mann, Delbert, 71
Manoff, Dinah, 539
Man of La Mancha, 496
Mantegna, Joe, 552
The Man Who Shot the Pope: A Study in Terrorism, 399
Marat/Sade, 495
March, Frederic, 11, 44, 461, 476
Marchand, Nancy, 384, 391, 395, 398
Marco Polo, 397
Marcus Welby, MD, 349
Margolin, Stuart, 388, 391
Marguiles, Juliana, 446
Marion, Frances, 9, 12
Marsh, Jean, 368
Marshall, E. G., 329, 331
Marshman, D. M., Jr., 56
Martin, Andrea, 577
Martin, Mary, 311, 462, 465, 482
Marty, 70
Marvin, Lee, 100
Marx, Groucho, 302
Mary Alice, 438, 561
The Mary Tyler Moore Show, 367, 371, 377, 380
M*A*S*H, 363, 370
Mason, Sarah Y., 13
Master Class, 585
The Masters, 431
Matlin, Marlee, 169
Matthau, Walter, 104, 486, 494
Matthews, Dave, 296
Maverick, 320
Mayron, Melanie, 423
M. Butterfly, 563
McAndrew, William, 330
McCambridge, Mercedes, 53
McCarey, Leo, 21, 40
McCartney, Paul, 219, 236
McClanahan, Rue, 416
McClinton, Delbert, 279
McCormick, Myron, 465
McCutcheon, Bill, 564
McDonald, Audra Ann, 580
McDonald, Joseph, 303
McDonald, Michael, 245

McDormand, Frances, 199
McDowall, Roddy, 327, 482
McFerrin, Bobby, 269
McGannon, Don, 403
McGee, Frank, 338
McGoohan, Patrick, 369
McKay, Jim, 421
McKechnie, Donna, 528
McKellen, Ian, 542
McLaglen, Victor, 16
McMahon, Franklin, 375
McMahon, Frank, 507
McNally, Terrence, 582, 585
McNichol, Kristy, 379, 388
McQuarrie, Christopher, 196
McTeer, Janet, 588
M.D. International, 323
Meadows, Audrey, 310
Meat Loaf, 285
Mediterraneo, 185
Medley, Bill, 268
Medoff, Mark, 538
Meet the Press, 306, 344
Men at Work, 252
Men in White, 457
Menken, Alan, 284
Menotti, Gian Carlo, 304
Mephisto, 153
Mercer, Johnny, 213
Mercer, Marian, 505
Meredith, Burgess, 379
Merkel, Una, 473
Merman, Ethel, 467
The Merry Widow, 403
Metcalfe, Laurie, 434, 438, 442
Metropolitan Opera Association, 399
Michaels, Frankie, 496
Michell, Keith, 356
"Michelle," 219
Midler, Bette, 234, 248, 434
Midnight Cowboy, 114
Migliacci, Franco, 205
Migrant: An NBC White Paper, 351
Miles, Joanna, 365
Miles to Go Before We Sleep, 389
Milestone, Lewis, 4, 9
Milland, Ray, 41
Miller, Arthur, 461, 464, 469
Miller, Barry, 555
Miller, Jason, 517, 520
Miller, Roger, 217
Miller, Seton I., 32
Milli Vanilli, 273

Mills, John, 118
Mills, Juliet, 368
Minghella, Anthony, 199
Minnelli, Liza, 125, 494, 533
Minnelli, Vincent, 80
Minow, Newton N., 328
The Miracle of Life, 403
The Miracle Worker, 389, 482
Mirren, Helen, 448
Mission: Impossible, 341, 344
Mississippi Authority for Educational Television, 355
Miss Lulu, 454
Miss Rose White, 432
Mister Roberts, 462
Mister Rogers' Neighborhood, 346
Mitchell, Thomas, 26, 305, 469
Mobil Masterpiece Theatre, 450
Modugno, Domenico, 204
Mokae, Zakes, 546
Moment of Crisis, 435
Monk, Debra, 577
The Monkees, 341
Monroe, Bill, 358
Montalban, Ricardo, 384
Montevecchi, Liliane, 546
The Moon and Sixpence, 323
"Moon River," 210
Moon Shot, 443
Moore, Mary Tyler, 335, 339, 360, 364, 373, 438
Moore, Melba, 508
Moorehead, Agnes, 340, 343
Moreno, Rita, 89, 380, 384, 525
The More You Know, 435
Morgan, Harry, 391
Moriarty, Michael, 364, 365, 383, 521
Morissette, Alanis, 292
The Mormon Tabernacle Choir, 207
Morrison, Van, 292
Morrow, Barry, 176
Morrow, Douglas, 53
Morse, Robert, 437, 486, 568
Morton, Bruce, 375
Moscow Does Not Believe in Tears, 150
Mosel, Tad, 485
Mostel, Zero, 484, 489, 494
Mother Goose Rock 'N' Rhyme, 428
Motown Returns to the Apollo, 408
Motown 25: Yesterday, Today, Forever, 401, 403
Mount St. Helens: A Decade Later, 428
The Mouse and the Motorcycle, 414
Mr. Knozit, 343
Mr. Novak, 333
Mr. Peepers, 306

Mr. Rooney Goes to Washington, 370
Mrs. Miniver, 33
"Mr. Snow Goes to Washington," 421
"Mrs. Robinson," 223
Mr. Wizard, 308
MTV's Choose or Lose Campaign, 435
MTV Unplugged, 288, 443
MTV Video Music Awards, inception of, 260
Mudd, Roger, 389
Mulligan, Richard, 390, 423
Muni, Paul, 18, 473
The Muppets, 386, 414
The Muppet Show, 382
The Murder of Mary Phagan, 419, 421
Murphy, Anthony, 360
Murphy, Donna, 579, 586
Murphy, Rosemary, 374
Murphy Brown, 426, 431, 432
Murray, Anne, 244
Murray, Peg, 499
Murrow, Edward R., 304, 307, 308
The Music from Peter Gunn, 205
The Music Man, 478
Mutiny on the Bounty, 16
The MX Debate, 392
My Fair Lady, 97, 475
Myles, Alannah, 276
My Name Is Barbra, 337, 338
Myshkin, 361
Mysterious Cities of Clay, 386
The Mystery of Edwin Drood, 558
The Mystery of Stonehenge, 338
Mystery Science Theatre 3000, 439
My Uncle, 80
My World and Welcome to It, 349

National Association of Broadcasting, 330
National Board of Review, inception of, 3, 9
National Council of Churches, 325
The National Driver's Test, 338
National Geographic Specials, 340, 392, 414
The National Public Affairs Center for Television, 366
National Society of Film Critics, inception of, 3, 105
Natwick, Mildred, 363
Naughton, James, 569, 588
NBC, 319, 330, 354, 358, 361, 366
NBC News Special: To Be an American, 425
NBC's Saturday Night Live, 372
NBC Television Opera Theatre, 308
Neal, Patricia, 95, 461
The Necklace, 300
The Negro in Indianapolis, 349
"Nel Blu Dipinto Di Blu (Volare)," 204

Nero, Peter, 210
NET, 338, 341
NET Playhouse, 346
Neuwirth, Bebe, 427, 430, 558, 589
Neville, Aaron, 273, 275
Neway, Patricia, 482
The New Explorers, 439
Newhart, Bob, 208
Newley, Anthony, 211
Newman, Paul, 168
Newman, Phyllis, 487
Newmar, Julie, 480
"Newsnight Afghanistan," 451
Newsroom, 348
Newton-John, Olivia, 236
New York City School Corruption, 447
The New York Drama Critics Circle Awards, inception of, 457
New York Film Critics Circle, inception of, 3, 17–18
Ngor, Haing S., 162
Nicholas Nickleby, 400, 545
Nichols, Dudley, 17
Nichols, Mike, 107
Nicholson, Jack, 134, 160
Nickelodeon, 399
Nick News, 443
Nick of Time, 273
Nightline, 406
'night, Mother, 551
Night of 100 Stars, 397
The Nights of Cabiria, 77
Nilsson, Harry, 226, 232
Nine, 545
1976 Presidential Debates, 375
The 1987 Tony Awards, 416
The Nineties, 439
Nissenson, Mary, 392
Niven, David, 79
No Jacket Required, 261
Nolan, Lloyd, 311
No Place to Be Somebody, 509
Norman, Marsha, 551
Normandy: The Great Crusade, 443
North, Edmund M., 119
Northern Exposure, 431, 432
Northshield, Robert "Shad," 414
Nova, 366
Nova: Odyssey of Life, 451
Ntshona, Winston, 524
NYPD Blue, 443, 450
Nype, Russell, 467, 480

The Obie Awards, inception of, 475

O'Brien, Edmond, 67
O'Connor, Carroll, 357, 378, 382, 392, 423
O'Connor, Donald, 306
The Official Story, 166
Of Thee I Sing, 457
Oklahoma City stations, 447
Oklahoma Shame, 399
Old Age: Do Not Go Gentle, 386
The Old Maid, 457
Oliver!, 110
Olivier, Laurence, 50, 324, 359, 367, 398, 404
Olmos, Edward James, 409
Omnibus, 306, 310
O'Neal, Tatum, 128
One Flew over the Cuckoo's Nest, 134
O'Neill, Eugene, 454, 455, 475, 477
One to One: Mentoring, 451
"On Runaway Street," 421
"On the Road," 346
On the Waterfront, 66
"Operation Undersea," 308
The Opportunity Line, 343
Orbach, Jerry, 505
Orbison, Roy, 275
Ordinary People, 150
Osborne, John, 96, 490
Oscars, inception of, 5–6
O'Shea, Tessie, 492
Our Town, 458
The Outer Critics Circle Awards, inception of, 466
Out of Africa, 165
Over Easy, 386
Overture to Friendship: The Philadelphia Orchestra in China, 361

Pacino, Al, 187, 505, 530
Page, Geraldine, 165, 342, 347
The Pajama Game, 471
Palance, Jack, 185, 314
Palmer, Robert, 265, 270
Panorama, 319
Pantomime Quiz, 300
"Papa's Got a Brand New Bag," 218
Paquin, Anna, 191
Paradise Lost: The Child Murders at Robin Hood Hills, 451
Paradise Postponed, 414
Paradise Saved, 399
Parsons, Estelle, 107
Passion, 579
"Passport to Kill," 451
Paterson, Neil, 83
Patinkin, Mandy, 444, 540

Patrick, John, 470, 471
Patterson, James, 501
Patton, 117
Paul McCartney and Wings, 236
Paulsen, Albert, 336
Paxinou, Katina, 37
The Peabody Awards, inception of, 300–301
Peace...On Our Time: KMEX-TV and the Death of Reuben Salazar, 351
Pearl Harbor: Two Hours That Changed the World, 431
Pearlman, Sy, 375
The Peary Investigation, 447
Peck, Gregory, 92
Pelle the Conqueror, 177
Pensions: The Broken Promise, 358
People Century, 451
People of the Forest: The Chimps of Gombe, 431
Peploe, Mark, 173
Perelman, J. S., 74
Perlman, Rhea, 405, 409, 413, 424
The Persecution and Assassination of Jean-Paul Marat as Performed by the Inmates of the Asylum of Charenton under the Direction of the Marquis de Sade, 495
Pesci, Joe, 182
Peter Jennings Reporting: Guns, 428
Peter Jennings Reporting: Hiroshima: Why the Bomb Was Dropped, 447
Peter Pan, 311
Peter, Paul and Mary, 212, 214
Peters, Bernadette, 558
Peter the Great, 412
Petit, Tom, 349
Petty, Tom, 292
The Phantom of the Opera, 563
Philco Television Playhouse, 308
The Phil Silvers Show, 311, 314, 317
The Piano Lesson, 570
Picket Fences, 436, 440
Pickford, Mary, 6
Picnic, 470
Pierce, David Hyde, 446
Pierson, Frank, 135
Pinkins, Tonya, 574
Pinter, Harold, 498
Pinza, Ezio, 465
Pirosh, Robert, 53
Place, Mary Kay, 379
The Plane That Fell from the Sky, 403
Platoon, 168
Playhouse 90, 314, 317, 318, 320, 323
Playing for Time, 392
The Play of the Week, 323
Plowright, Joan, 484

Plummer, Amanda, 433, 546
Plummer, Christopher, 378, 521, 588
Plunkett, Maryann, 561
Poe, James, 74
The Pointer Sisters, 259
"The Poisoned Air," 341
Poitier, Sidney, 95
The Police, 250, 256
Police Accountability, 380
Police Story, 371
Police Tapes, 380
A Polish Millenium Concert, 340
Polithon '70, 351
Politics of Poison, 389
Pollack, Sydney, 166
Pomerance, Bernard, 535
"The Population Explosion," 323
Portrait of America, 403
Poston, Tom, 322
POV: Days of Waiting, 428
Power Politics in Mississippi, 375
Pressburger, Emeric, 35
Preston, Robert, 478, 498
Price, Leontyne, 402
Pride and Prejudice, 450
Prima, Louis, 205
Prime Suspect, 439
Prime Suspect 2, 437
Prime Suspect 3, 440
Prince, Faith, 574
Prince and the Revolution, 259
Prisoners of the Harvest, 399
Prisoner without a Name, Cell without a Number, 403
The Private History of a Campaign That Failed, 396
The Private Life of Plants, 447
Producers' Showcase, 311, 313
Profiles in Courage, 336
Project: China, 396
Promise, 414
The Protestant Hour, 406
Pryce, Jonathan, 531, 571
The Public Mind, 425
The Pulitzer Prize for Drama, inception of, 454
Pulitzer Prize Playhouse, 302
Puzo, Mario, 126, 132

Quayle, Anna, 489
Quayle, Anthony, 368
Quinn, Anthony, 61, 74

Rabe, David, 514
Race War in Rhodesia, 386
Radner, Gilda, 385

Raine, Norman Reilly, 21
Rainer, Luise, 18, 20
Rain Man, 176
Rains, Claude, 466
Raisin, 521
Raitt, Bonnie, 273, 279
Randall, Tony, 368
Randolph, John, 561
Raphael, Frederic, 101
Rathbone, Basil, 462
Rawlins, Lester, 534
Reading Rainbow: The Wall, 435
The Real Thing, 551
Reasoner, Harry, 340
Rebecca, 28
The Red Army, 396
Reddy, Helen, 232
Redford, Robert, 150
Redgrave, Vanessa, 141, 394
Redhead, 480
Red Skelton Show, 303
Reed, Carol, 111
Reed, Donna, 64
Rees, Roger, 546
Reflections on Elephants, 443
"Regimental Raindrops," 316
Reid, Beryl, 498
Reilly, Charles Nelson, 486
Reiner, Carl, 315, 318
Reiner, Rob, 365, 384
Reinsch, J. Leonard, 425
Reisch, Walter, 64
REM, 279
Rent, 585, 587
Requiem for a Heavyweight, 313
The Restless Earth, 358
Revere, Anne, 43, 482
Reynolds, Burt, 430
Reynolds, Frank, 348
Rice, Elmer, 456
Rice, Tim, 284
Rich, John, 354
Rich, Robert, 74
Richards, Michael, 438, 442
Richardson, Ron, 555
Richardson, Tony, 95
Richie, Lionel, 253, 261
Richlin, Maurice, 83
Rickman, Alan, 448
Rigg, Diana, 579
The Right Man, 366
Rimes, LeAnn, 295
Riskin, Robert, 15

Ritter, John, 404
Rivera, Chita, 552, 577
The River Niger, 520
A River to the Sea, 386
Road Scholar, 447
Robards, Jason, 138, 140, 419, 480
Robbins, Marty, 209
Robert Montgomery Presents, 304
Roberts, Doris, 402
Robertson, Cliff, 110, 339
Rocco, Alex, 427
Rock and Roll, 447
The Rockford Files, 381
Rock the Vote, 435
Rocky, 137
Rodgers, Richard, 465
Roe vs. Wade, 422
"The Roger Rosenblatt Essays," 406
Rogers, Fred, 435
Rogers, Ginger, 28
Rogers, Paul, 498
Rolle, Esther, 388
Romeo and Juliet on Ice, 403
Ronstadt, Linda, 240, 273, 275, 424
Room 222, 349
Rooney, Mickey, 397
Roots, 377, 380
Roots: The Next Generation, 386
"Rosanna," 251
Rose, George, 528, 558
Rose, William, 107
Roseanne (Arnold), 437
Roseanne, 435
Rosencrantz and Guildenstern Are Dead, 500
The Rose Tattoo, 466
Ross, Ted, 525
Roth, Eric, 194
Rounds, David, 539
Rouse, Russell, 83
Rowan and Martin's Laugh-In, 344, 346
Rowan and Martin's Laugh-In Special, 344
The Rowe String Quartet Plays on Your Imagination, 381
Rowlands, Gena, 416, 433
Rubin, Bruce Joel, 182
Rubinstein, John, 538
Rudd, Hughes, 375
Ruehl, Mercedes, 185, 571
Ruffelle, Frances, 561
Ruggles, Charlie, 480
Rumours, 241
"Runaway Train," 285
Rupert, Michael, 558
Rush, Geoffrey, 199

"Rush to Read," 443
Russell, Bobby, 223
Russell, Harold, 45
Russell, Rosalind, 469
Rutherford, Margaret, 95
Rwanda, 443
Ryskin, Morris, 457

Sackler, Howard, 503, 506
Sadat: Action Biography, 366
Sade, 261
Safer, Morley, 338
Saga of Western Man, 333
Sager, Carole Bayer, 264
"Sailing," 247
Saint, Eva Marie, 67, 427
St. Elsewhere, 406
Saint James, Susan, 348
St. John, Theodore, 62
Salant, Richard S., 386
Salonga, Lea, 571
Salt, Waldo, 115, 144
Sammy Davis, Jr.'s 60th Anniversary Celebration, 426
Sand, Paul, 511
Sanders, George, 55
Sanford, Isabel, 394
San Francisco, 366
San Francisco Pageant, 330
Santiago-Hudson, Ruben, 586
Sarandon, Susan, 196
Sargeant, Alvin, 141, 150
Saroyan, William, 38, 459
Saturday at the Zoo, 303
Saturday Night Fever, 243
Saturday Night Live, 428, 437
Saudek, Robert, 303
Saunders, John Monk, 10
Savalas, Telly, 364
Scacchi, Greta, 449
"Scarred for Life," 439
Schaffner, Franklin J., 118
Schary, Dore, 478
Schell, Maximilian, 88
Schenkkan, Robert, 575
Schildkraut, Joseph, 20
Schindler's List, 190
Schlesinger, John, 115
Schnee, Charles, 62
Schorr, Daniel, 435
Schulberg, Budd, 68
Schulman, Tom, 179
Schweizer, Richard, 43, 50
Scofield, Paul, 103, 347, 486

Scott, George C., 117, 353
Seal, 291
Seal, Elizabeth, 484
The Search, 310
The Search for Alexander, 399
The Search for the Nile, 358
Seascape, 526
A Season in the Sun, 418
Seaton, George, 48, 68
The Secret Life of Danny Kaye, 316
Seeds of Despair, 406
See It Now, 304, 305
Segall, Harry, 32
Seger, Bob, 248
Seinfeld, 435, 436
Seldes, Marian, 499
Sell, Janie, 522
Selleck, Tom, 404
The Selling of the Pentagon, 351
The Senator, 351
"Send in the Clowns," 237
Separate but Equal, 429
September of My Years, 217
Serling, Rod, 316
Sesame Street, 348, 425
Sevareid, Eric, 333, 343
Seven Ages in America, 435
784 Days That Changed America: From Watergate to Resignation, 399 *The Seven Lively Arts*, 317
1776, 503
72 Hours to Victory: Behind the Scenes with Bill Clinton, 435
Sewer Solvent Scandal, 443
Seymour, Jane, 420
Sgt. Pepper's Lonely Hearts Club Band, 221, 222
The Shadow Box, 530, 532
"The Shadow of Your Smile (Theme from *The Sandpiper*)," 217
Shaffer, Anthony, 510
Shaffer, Peter, 163, 524, 542
Shanley, John Patrick, 173
Shapiro, Debbie, 567
Shapiro, Stanley, 83
The Shari Lewis Show, 325
Shaw, George Bernard, 24
Shea, John, 420
Shearer, Norma, 9
Sheen, Bishop Fulton J., 305
Sheldon, Sidney, 48
Shelley, Carole, 536
Shepard, Sam, 537
Sherman, Hiram, 469, 501
Sherwood, Robert E., 45, 457, 459

Sheryl Crow, 295
She's Nobody's Baby: The History of the American Woman in the 20th Century, 396
Shoah, 418
Shogun, 392, 394
The Shop on Main Street, 101
Shore, Dinah, 310, 315, 322
The Shrike, 469
Siberia: A Day in Irkutsk, 340
The Sid Caesar, Imogene Coca, Carl Reiner, Howard Morris Special, 341
Signoret, Simone, 82, 339
Silbar, Jeff, 272
The Silence of the Lambs, 184
Silliphant, Sterling, 107
Silver, Ron, 564
Silverlake Life, 439
Silvers, Phil, 311, 467, 514
Simmons, Jean, 402
Simon, Carly, 230
Simon, Neil, 555, 571, 572
Simon, Paul, 227, 228, 238
Simon and Garfunkel, 224
The Simpsons, 450
Sims, Tommy, 294
Sinatra, Frank, 64, 207, 217, 219, 292
Sinatra: A Man and His Music, 219
Sinclair, Madge, 430
Singer Presents Burt Bacharach, 353
Singer Presents Liza with a "Z", 359
The Singing Detective, 421
60 Minutes, 351, 375
The 63rd Annual Academy Awards, 429
Skeezer, 399
Skelton, Red, 304
Skerritt, Tom, 437
The Skin of Our Teeth, 459
Sleuth, 510
"Small Happiness: Women of a Chinese Village," 418
Small Sacrifices, 425
Small World, 323
Smiley's People, 399
Smith, Alexis, 515
Smith, Harold Jacob, 80
Smith, Keely, 205
Smith, Maggie, 114, 144, 568
Smith, William, 355
Smits, Jimmy, 427
Snippets, 370
A Soldier's Play, 547
Something about Amelia, 404
"Somewhere Out There," 266
Sondergaard, Gale, 19

Sondheim, Stephen, 237, 557
Songs in the Key of Life, 239
Sorvino, Mira, 196
"Soul Cages," 279
The Sound of Music, 100, 482
South, Joe, 225, 226
South Pacific, 465
Soviets: Red Hot, 431
Spaceck, Sissy, 150
Spacey, Kevin, 196, 572
Special Bulletin, 399
A Special Gift, 389
Spielberg, Steven, 191
Spinella, Stephen, 577, 579
Spinetti, Victor, 494
Splinters, Judy, 300
Springfield, Rick, 250
Springsteen, Bruce, 259, 268, 287, 289
Spy Machines, 418
Stack, Robert, 324
Stanley, Kim, 331, 408
Stanley, Pat, 480
Stanton, Dr. Frank, 323, 325, 333, 355
Stanwyck, Barbara, 327, 339, 401
Stapleton, Jean, 353, 357, 383
Stapleton, Maureen, 153, 345, 467, 511
The Starland Vocal Band, 239
State of the Union, 460
The Statler Brothers, 218
Steenburgen, Mary, 150
Steiger, Rod, 106
Stern, Carl, 366
Sternhagen, Frances, 522, 583
The Steve Allen Show, 323
Steve and Edyie Celebrate Irving Berlin, 386
Stevens, George, 59
Stevens, Ray, 228
Stewart, Donald, 157
Stewart, Donald Ogden, 29
Stewart, James, 28
Sticks and Bones, 514
Still Crazy after All These Years, 237
Sting, 255, 267, 284
The Sting, 128
Stone, Milburn, 345
Stone, Oliver, 144, 169, 179
Stone, Peter, 98
Stoppard, Tom, 500, 527, 551
A Storm in Summer, 349
"Storm over the Supreme Court," 333
The Story of English, 414
Straight, Beatrice, 138, 469
Strange Interlude, 455

"Strangers in the Night," 218
Strauss, Peter, 387
Stravinsky's Firebird, Dance Theatre of Harlem, 399
Streep, Meryl, 147, 156, 383
A Streetcar Named Desire, 464
Street of the Flower Boxes, 361
Street Scene, 456
"Streets of Philadelphia," 287, 289
Streisand, Barbra, 110, 214, 216, 217, 241, 242, 248, 264, 446
Strip and Search, 389
Struthers, Sally, 388
Studebaker: Less Than They Promised, 403
Studio One, 303
Sturges, Preston, 29
The Subject Was Roses, 494, 495
Suddenly an Eagle, 375
Summer, Donna, 246
Sunday in the Park with George, 557
A Sunday Journal, 370
Sunday Morning: Vladimir Horowitz, 414
Sundays and Cybele, 93
Sunrise, 4
Sunrise at Campobello, 478
Sunset Boulevard, 582
Surviving Columbus, 435
Survivor, 253
Survivors of the Holocaust, 451
Sutherland, Donald, 446
Suzi's Story, 421
Sweeney Todd, 536
Sweet Nothing, 399
The Swingle Singers, 213
Swit, Loretta, 391, 398
Sybil, 375

Taishoff, Sol, 392
Talley's Folly, 541
Tally, Ted, 185
Tandy, Jessica, 179, 419, 462, 533, 549
Tapestry, 230
Taradash, Daniel, 64
Tarantino, Quentin, 194
Target Seven: Armed and Angry, 447
Tarloff, FRank, 98
A Taste of Honey, 244
"A Taste of Honey," 217
Taurog, Norman, 10
Taxi, 390, 394
Taylor, Elizabeth, 86, 103
Taylor, James, 230, 242
Taylor-Young, Leigh, 442
Teacher, Teacher, 346

The Teahouse of the August Moon, 470, 471
Teale, Owen, 589
"Tears in Heaven," 281
Terms of Endearment, 159
Terra: Our World, 392
Tesich, Steve, 147
Texaco, 399
Texaco Star Theater, 301
That Championship Season, 517, 520
"That's What Friends Are For," 264
Theater in America, 366
"Theme from *A Summer Place*," 208
"Theme from *Exodus*," 208
There Shall Be No Night, 459
They Knew What They Wanted, 455
Thigpen, Lynne, 589
A Thirst in the Garden, 375
30 Minutes, 386
thirtysomething, 419, 421
This Child Is Rated X, 354
"This Masquerade," 239
This New Frontier, 351
This Week with David Brinkley, 414
Thomas, Betty, 409
Thomas, Danny, 308
Thomas, Marlo, 412
Thomas, Richard, 360
Thompson, Emma, 187, 196
Thompson, Ernest, 153
Thompson, Sada, 382, 514
Thompson, Wayne, 252
Thornton, Billy Bob, 199
Threads of Hope, 435
Three Tall Women, 581
3-2-1 Contact Extra: I Have AIDS, A Teenager's Story, 421
Thriller, 255
Through a Glass, Darkly, 89
Tidyman, Ernest, 121
Tillstrom, Burr, 336
Time for Beany, 301, 302, 305
The Time of Your Life, 459
The Times of Harvey Milk, 410
The Tin Drum, 147
Titanic, 588
Toldy, John S., 29
Tom Brown's Schooldays, 359
Tomei, Marisa, 188
Tom Jones, 95
Tomlin, Lily, 558
The Tonight Show with Jay Leno, 444
The Tony Awards, inception of, 453, 461
Torch Song Trilogy, 548
Torn, Rip, 449

Tornado! 4:40 p.m., Xenia, Ohio, 366
To Save Our Schools, To Save Our Children, 406
Toto IV, 252
A Tour of the White House With Mrs. John F. Kennedy, 330
Towne, Robert, 132
"Town Meeting of the World," 333
The Tracey Ullman Show, 422
Tracy, Spencer, 20, 22
Travanti, Daniel J., 394, 397
The Traveling Wilburys, 273
Travesties, 527
Treasures of the British Crown, 389
Treetop House, 333
Trevor, Claire, 50, 315
Trotti, Lamar, 40
Trout, Robert, 389
Truman, 448
"Truth on Trial," 447
Truth or Consequences, 302
Tune, Tommy, 522, 549
The Tunnel, 330
Turbulent Indigo, 291
The Turned On Crisis, 354
Turner, Tina, 259, 261, 265, 270
Tut: The Boy King, 380
Twin Peaks, 428
Two Gentlemen of Verona, 514
Tyson, Cicely, 363, 364, 441
Tyzack, Margaret, 569

Uggams, Leslie, 501
Uhry, Alfred, 179, 565, 588
Ullman, Tracey, 427, 442
Umeki, Miyoshi, 77
Under the Influence, 439
"Unforgettable," 278
Unforgettable, 278
Unforgiven, 187
United Nations Day Concert with Pablo Casals, 354
The United Nations in Action, 302
United Nations Radio and Television, 316
U.S. Steel Hour, 306, 308
Universe, 392
Unknown Chaplin, 414
Unplugged, 281
Upstairs, Downstairs, 362, 367, 371, 376, 380
"Up, Up, and Away," 220, 221, 222
USA for Africa, 261
Ustinov, Peter, 86, 98, 317, 341, 350
U2, 268, 270, 282
Uytterhoeven, Pierre, 104

Vaccaro, Brenda, 365
Valentine, Karen, 350
Valentine, 389
Vance, Vivian, 307
Van Dyke, Dick, 335, 339, 484
Van Dyke and Company, 377
Van Fleet, Jo, 70, 470
Vaughn, Robert, 384
Verdon, Gwen, 470, 473, 478, 480
Vereen, Ben, 518
The Vernon Rice Awards. *See* The Drama Desk Awards
"Vets," 425
Victoria Regina, 328
Victory at Sea, 306
Vietnam: A Television History, 403
Vietnam: Ten Years After, 410
Vincent Van Gogh: A Self-Portrait, 327
VIP—Art Carney Special, 323
The Virgin Spring, 87
Visions, 375
A Visit to Washington with Mrs. Lyndon B. Johnson—On Behalf of a More Beautiful America, 338
The Voice of Firestone, 313
Voight, Jon, 144
Volver a Empezar, 157
Voodoo Lounge, 289
Vote for Me: Politics in America, 451

Waara, Scott, 574
Wagner, Lindsay, 378
Walken, Christopher, 144
Walker, Joseph A., 520
Walker, Kathryn, 373
Walker, Zena, 501
A Walk through the 20th Century with Bill Moyers, 406
The Wall, 399
Wallace, Earl W., 166
Wallace, Pamela, 166
Wallace and Gromit, 447
Wallach, Eli, 343, 467
Walston, Ray, 446, 449, 473
Walt Disney's Wonderful World of Color, 330
Walter, Jessica, 368
Walters, Barbara, 447
The Waltons, 358
War and Peace, 111
War and Remembrance, 422
Ward, David S., 128
Ward, Sela, 441
Warden, Jack, 357
Warner, David, 395
Warnes, Jennifer, 253, 268
A War of Children, 358

Warwick, Dionne, 224, 228, 245, 265
Washington, Denzel, 179
Washington, Dinah, 207
Wasserstein, Wendy, 566, 567
Watley, Jody, 267
The Wave, 396
Wayne, David, 461, 470
Wayne, John, 114
"The Way We Were," 236
WCCO-TV, 325
WCKT-TV, 325, 366, 370
WCVB, 370
WDSU-TV, 323
"We Are the World," 260, 261
Weaver, Dennis, 322
Weaver, Fritz, 507
Weaver, Sylvester, Jr., 313
Webb, James R., 96
Webb, Jimmy, 221
Webster, Paul Francis, 217
Wechsler, David, 50
Wedgeworth, Ann, 534
Weidman, Jerome, 483
Weill, Kurt, 461
Weinstock, Jack, 488
Weiss, Donna, 250
Weiss, Peter, 495
Weitz, Bruce, 405
Welland, Colin, 153
Wellman, William A., 21
Wells, George, 77
West, Claudine, 35
Westinghouse Broadcasting Company, Inc., 319
West Side Story, 88
Wettig, Patricia, 420, 426, 430
WEWS-TV, 306
"What a Fool Believes," 245
What Have We Learned, Charlie Brown?, 403
What in the World, 304
"What Is Sonata Form?," 337
"What Kind of Fool Am I," 211
"What's Love Got to Do with It?," 257, 258
What's My Line?, 305
When Hell Was in Session, 389
When It Was a Game, 431
When the Salmon Run Dry, 435
Where Have All the Flood Cars Gone?, 380
Where in the World Is Carmen Sandiego?, 435
White, Betty, 369, 374, 412
White, Lillias, 589
White, Ruth, 336
White Paper, 325
Whitfield, Lynn, 429

Whitmore, James, 462
Who Killed Lake Erie?, 348
"Who Killed Vincent Chin?," 425
"A Whole New World (Aladdin's Theme)," 284
Who's Afraid of Virginia Woolf?, 488
Whose America Is It?, 410
Whose Child Is This?, 386
"Who's Guarding the Guardians?," 451
Who's Watching the Store?, 431
WHRO-TV, 358
Why Marry?, 454
Wiest, Dianne, 169, 193
Wilder, Billy, 43, 56, 86, 87
Wilder, Thornton, 458, 459
Williams, Jesse Lynch, 454
Williams, John, 469
Williams, Paul, 241
Williams, Robin, 417, 420
Williams, Sammy, 528
Williams, Tennessee, 464, 466, 472
Willis, Bruce, 416
Willowbrook: The Last Disgrace, 358
The Will Rogers Follies, 571
Wilson, August, 561, 563, 570
Wilson, Lanford, 541
Wilson, Michael, 59
Wimperis, Arthur, 35
"Winchester Cathedral," 219
"Wind Beneath My Wings," 271, 272
Windom, William, 350
Winfrey, Oprah, 447
Wings, 4
Winningham, Mare, 391
Winters, Jonathan, 430
Winters, Marian, 468
Winters, Shelley, 82, 101, 335
Winwood, Steve, 264
Wise, Robert, 89, 101
Wise, Scott, 567
Wiseman, Frederick, 428
Wise Up!, 451
The Wiz, 524
WJAR-TV, 310
A Woman Called Golda, 396
A Woman Called Jackie, 432
The Woman Who Willed a Miracle, 403
Wonder, Stevie, 234, 236, 240, 265
Wonderful Town, 469
The Wonder Years, 419, 425
Wong, B. D., 564
Wood, John, 527
WOOD, 325
Woodard, Alfre, 405

Woods, James, 416, 422
WOOD-TV, 325
Woodward, Joanne, 77, 382, 408
World, 389
World in Crisis, 316
The World of Stuart Little, 340
Worth, Irene, 494, 527, 572
WRAL Environmental Report, 431
Wright, Jeffrey, 580
Wright, Teresa, 34
WSB, 304
WSMV, 396
WTOP-TV, 370
WTVJ-TV, 435
Wunda Wunda, 319
Wyatt, Jane, 318, 322, 324
Wyler, William, 34, 45, 83
Wyman, Jane, 50
Wynn, Ed, 301
Wynton Marsalis: Making the Music: Marsalis on Music, 447

Xerox Corporation, 338
The X-Files, 450

A Year in the Life, 415
Yesterday, Today, and Tomorrow, 99
Yordan, Philip, 68
You Are There, 316
You Can't Take It with You, 22, 457
"You Light Up My Life," 241
Young, Alan, 302
Young, Gig, 115
Young, Loretta, 47, 309, 315, 321
Young, Robert, 315, 317, 350
The Young Man from Atlanta, 584
"You Oughta Know," 292
Your Health and Your Wallet, 386
Your Hit Parade, 306, 311
Your Show of Shows, 303, 305
Youth Wants to Know, 316
"You've Got a Friend," 230
Yugoslavia: Death of a Nation, 447

Z, 115
Zaillian, Steve, 191
Zal, Roxanna, 405
Zemeckis, Robert, 194
Zerbe, Anthony, 374
Zindel, Paul, 513
Zinneman, Fred, 64, 104
Zoo Parade, 303